THE CAMBRIDGE ECONOMIC I
CHINA

China's rise as the world's second-largest economy surely is the most dramatic development in the global economy since the year 2000. Volume II, which spans China's two turbulent centuries from 1800, charts this wrenching process of an ancient empire being transformed to re-emerge as a major world power. This volume for the first time brings together the fruits of pioneering international scholarship in all dimensions of economic history to provide an authoritative and comprehensive overview of this tumultuous and dramatic transformation. In many cases, it offers a fundamental reinterpretation of major themes in Chinese economic history, such as the role of ideology, the rise of new institutions, human capital and public infrastructure, the impact of Western and Japanese imperialism, the role of external trade and investment, and the evolution of living standards in both the pre-Communist and Communist eras. The volume includes seven important chapters on the Mao and reform eras and provides a critical historical perspective linking the past with the present and future.

DEBIN MA is Professor of Economics at Hitotsubashi University, Tokyo, Japan.

RICHARD VON GLAHN is Distinguished Professor of History at the University of California, Los Angeles.

THE CAMBRIDGE ECONOMIC HISTORY OF
CHINA

Building on a wide array of recent scholarship, the two volumes of *The Cambridge Economic History of China* bring together the fruits of pioneering international studies in all dimensions of economic history, past and present. Exploring themes including political economy, agriculture, industry and trade, technology, ecological change, demography, law, urban development, standards of living, consumption, financial institutions, and national income, the two volumes together provide broad temporal coverage across all of Chinese history, including recent developments in contemporary China.

VOLUME I

To 1800

EDITED BY DEBIN MA AND RICHARD VON GLAHN

VOLUME II

1800 to the Present

EDITED BY DEBIN MA AND RICHARD VON GLAHN

THE CAMBRIDGE ECONOMIC HISTORY OF CHINA

*

VOLUME II
1800 to the Present

*

Edited by
DEBIN MA
Hitotsubashi University, Tokyo

and

RICHARD VON GLAHN
University of California, Los Angeles

CAMBRIDGE
UNIVERSITY PRESS

Shaftesbury Road, Cambridge CB2 8EA, United Kingdom

One Liberty Plaza, 20th Floor, New York, NY 10006, USA

477 Williamstown Road, Port Melbourne, VIC 3207, Australia

314–321, 3rd Floor, Plot 3, Splendor Forum, Jasola District Centre, New Delhi – 110025, India

103 Penang Road, #05-06/07, Visioncrest Commercial, Singapore 238467

Cambridge University Press is part of Cambridge University Press & Assessment, a department of the University of Cambridge.

We share the University's mission to contribute to society through the pursuit of education, learning and research at the highest international levels of excellence.

www.cambridge.org
Information on this title: www.cambridge.org/9781108442459

DOI: 10.1017/9781108348485

© Cambridge University Press & Assessment 2022

This publication is in copyright. Subject to statutory exception and to the provisions of relevant collective licensing agreements, no reproduction of any part may take place without the written permission of Cambridge University Press & Assessment.

First published 2022
First paperback edition 2025

A catalogue record for this publication is available from the British Library

Two-Volume Set ISBN   978-1-107-14606-8   Hardback
Volume I ISBN   978-1-108-42557-5   Hardback
Volume II ISBN   978-1-108-42553-7   Hardback
ISBN   978-1-108-44245-9   Paperback

Cambridge University Press & Assessment has no responsibility for the persistence or accuracy of URLs for external or third-party internet websites referred to in this publication and does not guarantee that any content on such websites is, or will remain, accurate or appropriate.

Contents

List of Figures page viii
List of Maps xi
List of Tables xii
List of Contributors to Volume II xv
Acknowledgments xvii
Note on Citations xix

Introduction to Volume II 1
DEBIN MA AND RICHARD VON GLAHN

PART I
1800–1950

1 · Ideology and the Contours of Economic Change 15
DEBIN MA

2 · Economic Transition in the Nineteenth Century 48
WILLIAM T. ROWE

3 · Agriculture 87
DEBIN MA AND KAIXIANG PENG

4 · Handicraft and Modern Industries 124
LINDA GROVE AND TŌRU KUBO

5 · The State and Enterprises in Late Qing China 167
CHI-KONG LAI

6 · State Enterprises during the First Half of the Twentieth Century 184
MORRIS L. BIAN

v

7 · Money and the Macro-economy 208
DAN LI AND HONGZHONG YAN

8 · Public Finance 244
ELISABETH KASKE AND MAY-LI LIN

9 · Financial Institutions and Financial Markets 280
BRETT SHEEHAN AND YINGUI ZHU

10 · Chinese Business Organization 324
MADELEINE ZELIN

11 · The Economic Impact of the West: A Reappraisal 354
JAMES KAI-SING KUNG

12 · Foreign Trade and Investment 414
WOLFGANG KELLER AND CAROL H. SHIUE

13 · Transport and Communication Infrastructure 457
ELISABETH KÖLL

14 · Education and Human Capital 496
PEI GAO, BAS VAN LEEUWEN, AND MEIMEI WANG

PART II
1950 TO THE PRESENT

15 · The Origin of China's Communist Institutions 531
CHENGGANG XU

16 · China's Struggle with the Soviet Growth Model, 1949–1978 565
DWIGHT H. PERKINS

17 · Living Standards in Maoist China 606
CHRIS BRAMALL

18 · The Political Economy of China's Great Leap Famine 642
JAMES KAI-SING KUNG

19 · China's External Economic Relations during the Mao Era 685
AMY KING

20 · The Chinese Economy in the Reform Era 722
BARRY NAUGHTON

21 · China's Great Boom as a Historical Process 775
LOREN BRANDT AND THOMAS G. RAWSKI

Index 829

Figures

1.1	Real index of Chinese and Japanese per capita GDP (1850 = 100)	page 19
1.2	Real value of Chinese imports and exports at 1933 constant prices (thousand yuan)	21
1.3	Western impact and Chinese response: number of newly established modern firms and banks	22
1.4	Real production and GDP indices (1912 = 100)	23
1.5	Metal currencies (silver and copper) and money supply in China, 1911–1936 (million yuan)	25
3.1	China's historical crop yield	91
3.2	Per capita output of raw grain, 1500–1950	92
3.3	Distribution of Qing crop yields based on local gazettes	94
3.4	Wage index relative to grain price in Beijing and Hebei province	96
3.5	Major disasters with a death toll above 1,000 (1840–1949)	99
3.6	Malthusian and Boserupian models	101
3.7	Percentage of idle time (left axis) and wage rates in units of copper cash (right axis)	105
3.8	Agricultural sideline production	106
3.9	Trends of agricultural commercialization	110
3.10	Diffusion of scientifically produced silkworm varieties in Japan and the lower Yangzi	116
4.1	Industrial production in mainland China, 1933	126
4.2	Imports of machinery, iron, and steel, 1886–1915	129
4.3	Silk reeling filatures	135
4.4	Silk exports by production source	139
4.5	Industrial production index, 1938–1945	154
4.6	Capital of newly built mills, classified by industry	155
4.7	Industrial production index, 1912–1949	161
7.1	The capital power of China's banking industry in 1894, 1925, and 1936	217
7.2	Banknote issuance in China from 1890 to 1936	221
7.3	The modern-oriented gross domestic fixed-capital formation in China from 1903 to 1936	236
7.4	The interbank annual interest rate in Shanghai from 1872 to 1936	237
8.1	*Lijin* revenue, 1858–1908	251
8.2	Foreign and Native Customs	253
11.1	Expansion of the treaty port system	361

11.2	Growth in the number of treaty ports and self-initiated ports	362
11.3	Geographical distribution of treaty ports and self-initiated ports	365
11.4	Foreign direct investment and debt	367
11.5	Foreign investment and foreign debt by country	368
11.6	Geographic distribution of foreign private firms	369
11.7	Foreign firms, by country of origin	370
11.8	Sectoral distribution of foreign firms	371
11.9	Domestic trade network	372
11.10	Numerical growth of foreign firms and banks	374
11.11	Geographical distribution of foreign firms and banks (1920s)	375
11.12	Rise of domestic modern firms and banks in China (total trend)	377
11.13	Geographical distribution of domestic modern firms and banks (1920s)	378
11.14	Development trend of domestic modern firms and banks	380
11.15	Development of domestic modern firms in non-port regions	381
11.16	Spatial distribution of treaty ports opened before 1865 and munition factories	382
11.17	Growth of electrical power plants in China, 1903–1931	385
11.18	Electricity generation in China, 1929	386
11.19	Adoption of the steam engine and machinery in modern Chinese firms	387
11.20	Growth of missionary activities in China	391
11.21	Missionary activities and the primary schools they founded (1922)	392
11.22	Growth of universities in China	395
11.23	Growth of universities in China, by type/funding source	395
11.24	Distribution of universities in 1937	396
11.25	Distribution of engineers in 1937	400
11.26	Number of Chinese students studying abroad and returning, a partial sample	402
11.27	Geographic distribution of constitutionalists and revolutionists (1900–1911)	407
12.1	China's foreign trade, 1865 to 1940	434
12.2	Predicted versus actual bilateral trade volume for Shanghai	438
12.3	Foreign firms in China: the case of Shanghai, 1872–1921	441
12.4	Foreign firms in China by country of origin	442
12.5	Export and import flows to and from Shanghai	443
12.6	The size of bilateral trade between regions	445
12.7	The impact of foreign influence in China: geographic effects	449
12.8	New and disappearing goods: China's exports	454
14.1	The school system before 1905	499
14.2	The civil service examination system and its associated degree titles	501
14.3	The education system after 1905	510
15.1	The institutional genes of the Chinese empire: an institutional trinity	535
15.2	The institutional genes of the imperial *junxian* system	537
15.3	The institutional trinity of the RDT/RDA system	539
15.4	Stylized governance structure of China's RDT/RDA central–local regime	540
16.1	Urban population and employment growth 1952–1990	590
17.1	Gini coefficients for rural per capita income, 1934–1978	628
17.2	Per capita rural consumption of meat and grain in Guizhou, 1938–1978	632
17.3	The urban–rural gap	637
18.1	Average GDP per capita (in constant US$), 1950–1960	655

List of Figures

19.1	Chinese total trade, 1950–2006	687
19.2	Chinese exports to and imports from the Soviet Union, 1950–1978	695
19.3	China's trade with Communist and non-Communist countries, 1950–1965	700
19.4	China's bilateral trade with leading trade partners, 1950–1978	706
19.5	China's imports of rolled steel and chemical fertilizer, 1950–1960	714
19.6	China's trade with Canada and Australia, 1955–1965	717
20.1	Consumer inflation (1979–2019)	756
20.2	Budgetary revenues and expenditures (share of GDP)	760
20.3	Industrial workers (total and state)	768

Maps

3.1	Agricultural areas of China	*page* 89
7.1	Cities with a direct money-transferring link with the major financial centers of Shanghai, Hankou, and Tianjin in 1924	218
9.1	Locations of the branches of six large remittance houses, 1870s–1880s	288
9.2	Bank offices (foreign and Chinese), 1915	289
9.3	Banks in 1947	290
9.4	Cash shops in 1947	291
9.5	Insurance company and co-operative treasury offices, 1947	293
12.1	China Maritime Customs stations and treaty ports	431
12.2	The impact of foreign influence on local capital markets	450
13.1	China's railroads, *c.* 1900	468
13.2	China's railroad network, *c.* 1935	482
18.1	Famine mortality by province, prefecture, and county, 1959–1961	651

Tables

2.1	Net flow of silver to China, 1818–1850	page 74
2.2	Silver revenue collected at Board of Revenue treasury, 1802–1850	80
3.1	Mean and distribution of agricultural yields (*shi* per *mu*) in Qing China	93
3.2	Farm size and productivity	103
3.3	Tenancy rates in the 1930s	118
3.4	Explaining interest rates across regions	121
4.1	Market share of domestic products, 1920–1936	141
4.2	Production and trade of machine-made cotton yarn and cotton pieces	143
7.1	M2/GDP in China, the UK, and the US in the late nineteenth and early twentieth centuries	239
8.1	Budget for the 26th Year of Guangxu (1900) in *kuping* taels	256
8.2	National revenue for 1911 (Ministry of Finance)	257
8.3	Revenue structure of the central government, 1913–1945	262
8.4	Income and expenditure of the Nationalist government, 1928–1937	269
8.5	Income and expenditure of the Nationalist government, 1937–1945	276
9.1	Basic functions of financial institutions in the late Qing period	282
9.2	Forms and ownership governance of financial institutions in the late Qing period	283
9.3	Estimated numbers of financial institutions in China	285
9.4	Establishment of county/city co-operative treasuries, 1937–1944	301
9.5	Growth of the capitalization of co-operatives, 1937–1945	302
9.6	Survey of rural finance in 1943	303
9.7	Survey of rural finance across China (cash lending) in 1941	305
9.8	Uses and percentage distribution for co-operative loans in Guangxi province, 1938–1941	306
9.9	The China Merchants Steam Navigation Company assets and liabilities prior to 1880	308
9.10	Loans from Shanghai's Fukang (福康) cash shop to industrial enterprises, 1899–1907	310
9.11	Index of domestic bond transactions and volume of transactions, 1926–1937	314
9.12	Stock index and volume of stock and corporate bond transactions, 1931–August 1937	315
9.13	Native provinces of bankers in 1936	318
11.1	Locations of self-initiated ports	366
11.2	Impact of foreign firms and banks on domestic modern firms and banks	379

List of Tables

11.3	Location of munition factories	383
11.4	Adoption rate of the steam engine and machinery	388
11.5	Long-term effects of treaty ports and self-initiated ports	389
11.6	Comparison of curricula in the 1900s	393
11.7	Determinants of university locations and engineers	397
11.8	Determinants of overseas studies	403
11.9	Effect of overseas studies on political participation	408
12.1	Average trade shares, 1865–1900	435
12.2	Major sources of Chinese imports, 1900–1946	436
12.3	World merchandise trade by country	436
12.4	Business investments in China by country	439
12.5	Geographical distribution of the direct business investments of four countries, 1931	440
12.6	Lower geographic barriers and welfare	446
12.7	Measuring the appearance and disappearance of goods	451
13.1	Freight turnover by modern means of transportation (in million ton-miles)	491
14.1	Estimation of the enrollment ratio of *sishu*	506
14.2	Number of post-elementary schools in China proper	508
14.3	Regulatory curriculum models for primary schools (percentage)	511
14.4	Enrollment rates per 1,000 school-age population, 1900–1950	516
14.5	Composition of persons by education level for selected counties, 1880–1920 (percentage)	517
14.6	Composition of secondary schools by type (percentage)	518
14.7	Number of engineers by birth cohort	520
14.8	Gender composition in secondary schools (1912–1946)	523
16.1	Annual plan completion record	571
16.2	Impact of the Great Leap Forward on the economy	585
16.3	Wages and the urban cost of living (1957–1964)	591
16.4	Price distortions in GDP growth estimates	597
16.5	Sources of growth (1952–1990)	598
16.6	Per capita rural economic performance	600
16.7	Urban employment and consumption estimates	601
16.8	Urban–rural per capita consumption ratio	604
17.1	Per capita net peasant income, 1954–1978	611
17.2	Alternative estimates of national per capita peasant income	612
17.3	Selected per capita urban incomes, 1943–1980	614
17.4	Trends in food consumption during the Maoist era	617
17.5	Contrasting estimates of food consumption, 1954–1978	621
17.6	Rainfall deviations in 1976–1978 and 1982–1984 from the 1951–2000 norm	623
17.7	Life expectancy and infant mortality in China, 1952–1981	625
17.8	Coefficients of variation (CVs) for provincial per capita net peasant income, 1954 and 1978	630
17.9	Per capita grain output by agricultural region, 1977	634
18.1	Weather shocks and grain output, 1953–1966	663
18.2	The effects of grain output, political rank, and CC membership on grain procurement, resale, and excess procurement, 1957–1965	672

List of Tables

19.1	Chinese export levels, 1913–2003	687
19.2	China's five largest trading partners, 1950–1952	699
20.1	Development indicators, 1978	724
20.2	Twelve key provisions of the 1993 Resolution on Creating a Market System	764

Contributors to Volume II

MORRIS L. BIAN is Professor in the Department of History at Auburn University.
CHRIS BRAMALL is Professor in the Department of Economics at SOAS University of London.
LOREN BRANDT is Noranda Chair Professor in the Department of Economics at the University of Toronto.
PEI GAO is Assistant Professor of Economics at Yale–NUS College, Singapore.
LINDA GROVE is Professor Emerita, Sophia University.
ELISABETH KASKE is Professor of Modern Chinese Society and Culture at Leipzig University.
WOLFGANG KELLER is Professor of Economics at the University of Colorado.
AMY KING is Associate Professor at the Coral Bell School of Asia Pacific Affairs, Australian National University.
ELISABETH KÖLL is Professor and William Payden Collegiate Chair in the Department of History at the University of Notre Dame.
TŌRU KUBO is Professor Emeritus at Shinshu University.
JAMES KAI-SING KUNG is Sein and Isaac Souede Professor in Economic History at the Faculty of Business and Economics, Hong Kong University.
CHI-KONG LAI is Reader in Modern Chinese History at the University of Queensland.
DAN LI is Professor of Economics at Fudan University, China.
MAY-LI LIN is an Associate Research Fellow at the Institute of Modern History, Academia Sinica.
DEBIN MA is Professor of Economics at Hitotsubashi University, Japan.
BARRY NAUGHTON is So Kwanlok Chair of Chinese International Affairs in the School of Global Policy and Strategy at the University of California at San Diego.

KAIXIANG PENG is Professor of Economics in the School of Economics and Management, Wuhan University.

DWIGHT H. PERKINS is Harold Hitchings Burbank Research Professor of Political Economy (Emeritus), Department of Economics, Harvard University.

THOMAS G. RAWSKI is Professor of Economics and History (Emeritus) at the University of Pittsburgh.

WILLIAM T. ROWE is John and Diane Cooke Professor of Chinese History at Johns Hopkins University.

BRETT SHEEHAN is Professor of History and East Asian Languages and Cultures at the University of Southern California.

CAROL H. SHIUE is Professor of Economics at the University of Colorado.

BAS VAN LEEUWEN is Senior Researcher at the International Institute of Social History, the Netherlands.

MEIMEI WANG is Assistant Researcher at the Institute of Economic Research, Chinese Academy of Social Science.

CHENGGANG XU is Honorary Professor at the Asia Global Institute, University of Hong Kong.

HONGZHONG YAN is Professor of Economics at Shanghai University of Finance and Economics.

MADELEINE ZELIN is Dean Lung Professor of Chinese Studies and Professor of History at Columbia University.

YINGUI ZHU is Professor of History (Emeritus) at Fudan University.

Acknowledgments

We are very grateful in the first place to our nearly fifty contributors, whose collective efforts and dedication made this project possible. The timely progress of this project was greatly facilitated by our ability to hold conferences to assemble the contributors to each volume, exchange ideas, and settle the division of labor among the forty chapters that ultimately were included in the published work. We are deeply indebted to the benefactors who provided financial support for the conferences. We want to thank Bas van Leeuwen for hosting the conference for the contributors to Volume II at the University of Utrecht on December 15–16, 2017, with generous financial support from the European Research Council under the European Union's Horizon 2020 Programme/ERC-StG 637695 – HinDI (as part of the Historical Dynamics of Industrialization in Northwestern Europe and China ca. 1800–2010: A Regional Interpretation project). We are thankful for organizational assistance from Robin Philips and Zipeng Zhang. The volume benefited from the participation and external discussion of Maarten Prak, Keetie Sluyterman, Jan Luiten van Zanden, and Peer Vries. Debin Ma also acknowledges some editorial-assistant support from the School of Economics of Fudan University in China.

The conference for contributors to Volume I was held on August 27–8, 2018, at the University of California, Los Angeles. We are grateful to the Chiang Ching-Kuo Foundation for International Scholarly Exchange, which provided the main financial support to underwrite the conference expenses. Additional financial support was provided by the Center for Chinese Studies and the Division of Social Sciences at UCLA, and we especially want to acknowledge the UCLA Center for Chinese Studies, its director Yunxiang Yan, and its assistant director Esther Jou for their logistical support. We also want to thank Sunkyu Lee and Kayoko Fujita for their invaluable assistance in facilitating the UCLA conference.

Lucy Rhymer at Cambridge University Press has instigated, encouraged, and guided this project at every step, and we surely would not have been able to bring it to completion without her unflagging support. We are also grateful to the sharp-eyed Emily Sharp at Cambridge University Press for all of her help in the final production of these volumes.

Note on Citations

The two volumes of the *Cambridge Economic History of China* differ in their citation of Chinese and Japanese works in the footnotes and the "Further Reading" bibliographies, reflecting differences in conventions between scholarship on premodern and modern periods.

In Volume I, book and article titles for secondary scholarship in Chinese and Japanese are given in the original language and romanization (Pinyin romanization in the case of Chinese). Names of authors are given in full (including first names).

In Volume II, Chinese and Japanese book and article titles are given in the original language and English translation without romanization. First names of authors are abbreviated.

In Volume I, footnote references to primary sources in Chinese are abbreviated as acronyms. A comprehensive list of Chinese primary sources with full bibliographic information for primary sources appears at the end of the volume.

In Volume II, full bibliographic information for references to primary sources is given in the footnote in which they are cited.

Introduction to Volume II

DEBIN MA AND RICHARD VON GLAHN

China's rise as the world's second-largest economy surely is the most dramatic development in the global economy since the year 2000. But China's prominence in the global economy is hardly new. Since 500 BCE, a burgeoning market economy and the establishment of an enduring imperial state has fostered precocious economic growth. Moreover, contrary to the view that China's economy withered under the dual constraints of Western colonialism and Chinese tradition after 1800, recent scholarship has identified the onset of modern economic growth in response to new incentive structures, investment opportunities, ideas, and technology, laying the foundation for the post-1978 economic miracle. China's combination of market-led growth under the firm hand of the state has produced a model of economic development that challenges conventional theories of capitalism and economic growth. The spectacular growth of the contemporary Chinese economy has also spurred deeper investigation into the Chinese economy – long a neglected field of study, at least in the Western academy. Scholarship on Chinese economic history has now developed to the stage where a Cambridge History devoted to the subject is appropriate and feasible. These volumes, a collaborative effort by nearly fifty scholars, bring together the fruits of pioneering Western, Japanese, and Chinese scholarship in all dimensions of economic history, past and present.

Early studies of the Chinese economy focused on China's distinctive philosophical and political traditions.[1] In his published 1911 Columbia Ph.D. thesis, *The Economic Principles of Confucius and His School*), Ch'en Huan-chang sought to introduce the basic concepts and practices of Chinese political

---

[1] For historiographic surveys of twentieth-century scholarship on Chinese economic and social history, see T. Brook, "Capitalism and the Writing of Modern History in China," in T. Brook and G. Blue (eds.), *China and Historical Capitalism: Genealogies of Sinological Knowledge* (Cambridge, Cambridge University Press, 1999), pp. 110–57; R. von Glahn, "Imagining Pre-modern China," in P.J. Smith and R. von Glahn (eds.), *The Song–Yuan–Ming Transition in Chinese History* (Cambridge, MA, Harvard University Council on East Asian Studies, 2003), pp. 35–70.

economy, highlighting the pre-eminence of the Confucian tradition.² Of course, Ch'en was writing at the moment of the dissolution of the Chinese empire and the apogee of the modern world-system defined by industrial capitalism and Western political hegemony. Already in Ch'en's book – and for long afterwards – the study of Chinese economic history was fixated on the question of the apparent lack of economic progress throughout two millennia of imperial history. Many of the answers proposed by Ch'en – Confucian disdain for moneymaking, a rigid and inert social structure, overpopulation, and isolation from the outer world – recurred in subsequent works.

The fall of the Qing empire in 1911 – and with it, the end of China's imperial past – inspired hope for China's rapid transformation into a modern, progressive nation. But the failure of Republican institutions to thrive in the wake of the empire's demise gave rise to doubts about China's ability to "learn from the West." Some intellectuals advocated wholesale repudiation of Chinese cultural traditions and embrace of Western culture as defined by cosmopolitanism, Enlightenment values, Republican government, scientific reasoning, and capitalist economic institutions. Others sought to reinvigorate China's "national essence" by reviving authentic Chinese values that had been attenuated by Western spiritual pollution and Manchu overlordship. The Japanese scholar Naitō Konan, writing in 1914, envisioned a future in which Japan supplanted China as the ascendant center of a reinvigorated "oriental culture" that would eclipse the spiritually vacuous materialism of the West. Naitō advanced the novel thesis that East Asia's "modern age" had actually begun centuries earlier, in the transition from the Tang (618–907) to Song (960–1279) dynasties. This Tang–Song transition had witnessed the triumph of autocratic monarchy over aristocratic rule and engendered a vibrant commoner culture liberated from feudal domination. But China's incipient modernity proved premature; after the Song dynasty, China's "modern age" degenerated into senility, and in contemporary times the dynamic center of oriental culture had shifted to Japan.³

The emergence of history as an academic profession in China and Japan during the 1920s was accompanied by skepticism toward received historical

---

² H.-C. Ch'en, *The Economic Principles of Confucius and His School* (New York, Columbia University Press, 1911).
³ Naitō Konan 内藤湖南, 支那論 (On China) (1914), rpt. in 内藤湖南全集 (The Complete Volumes of Naitō Konan) (Tokyo, Chikuma shobō, 1972), vol. 5, pp. 291–482; see also H. Miyakawa, "The Naitō Hypothesis and Its Effects on Japanese Studies of China," *Far Eastern Quarterly* 14.3 (1955), 533–52; S. Tanaka, *Japan's Orient: Rendering Pasts into History* (Berkeley, University of California Press, 1993).

traditions and more critical empiricism in historical methodology. But by the late 1920s historical scholarship in China became enveloped by disputes over the trajectory of Chinese history from antiquity to the present, most notably the so-called Social History Debate, which dwelled primarily on questions of feudalism and capitalism in China. Marxism and the Russian Revolution loomed large over these controversies. Left-wing scholars and writers were keen to demonstrate that China's historical experience conformed to the universal categories of historical development as defined by Western philosophers. In his *Study of China's Ancient Society* (1930), Guo Moruo was the first to apply to Chinese history the five-stage theory of human history (from primitive communism to socialism) formulated by Soviet Marxist scholars.[4] Guo argued that the onset of the Iron Age in China in the first millennium BCE inaugurated feudal relations of production that endured even under the centralized bureaucratic empires.

The anomalous character and persistence of Chinese "feudalism" – which bore little resemblance to the fragmented political order of medieval Europe – posed a vexing problem. Some historians in China sought to resolve this incongruity by espousing an economic definition of feudalism based on the antagonism between the landowning class and the peasantry, and thus postulated a feudal epoch that stretched from the ancient Zhou era throughout imperial history and continued even during the post-1911 Republican era. In Europe, Max Weber had traced the apparent stagnation of Chinese historical development to the special character of the imperial bureaucratic state, which Marxist scholars reformulated as a distinctive species of "bureaucratic feudalism." Drawing on the theories of both Marx and Weber, Karl Wittfogel, a leading figure in the Frankfurt school of Marxism, proposed that the Chinese imperial state was founded on an "Asiatic mode of production" which hindered the dynamic forces of class struggle that motivated historical change.[5] Although Soviet Marxists firmly repudiated the idea of an Asiatic mode of production, it gained considerable currency among some Chinese and many Japanese scholars in the 1930s. Characterizing China as the archetype of an "oriental society" trapped in the Asiatic mode of production provided a succinct explanation for the immobility of Chinese history, and

---

[4] Guo Moruo 郭末若, 中國古代社會研究 (A Study of Ancient Chinese Society) (Shanghai, Lianhe shudian, 1930).

[5] K.A. Wittfogel, "The Foundations and Stages of Chinese Economic History," *Zeitschrift für Sozialforschung* 4.1 (1935), 25–58; Wittfogel, "Die Theorie der orientalischen Gesellschaft," *Zeitschrift für Sozialforschung* 7.1–2 (1938), 90–122. In the postwar period Wittfogel developed a more elaborate version of this thesis. See his *Oriental Despotism: A Comparative Study of Total Power* (New Haven, Yale University Press, 1957).

for Japanese historians reinforced Japan's singular role in both "escaping from Asia" and leading it toward modernity.

To be sure, other scholars distanced themselves from these theoretical debates and focused instead on empirical study and honing analytical methods of economic history. In China, this trend coalesced around the journal *Food and Money Semi-monthly* (*Shihuo banyuekan* 食貨半月刊), inaugurated in 1934 by Tao Xisheng, which featured contributions by Tao, Ju Qingyuan, He Ziquan, Quan Hansheng, and others. The "Food and Money" group (the name derived from the title given to chapters on fiscal administration in traditional dynastic histories) sought to balance economic theories (both Marxist and non-Marxist) with empirical evidence and rigorous methodology.[6] Much of their scholarship centered on the early imperial era, especially the Tang dynasty.[7] The 1930s also witnessed a profusion of pathbreaking Japanese scholarship on Chinese economic history, likewise centered on the Tang–Song dynasties, led by Katō Shigeshi,[8] Hino Kaisaburō,[9] Sogabe Shizuo,[10] and Miyazaki Ichisada.[11] The inspiration for these studies can be traced back to Naitō's hypothesis of the Tang–Song transition as the beginning of "East Asia's modern age," as Miyazaki – Naitō's successor as professor of Chinese history at Kyoto University – entitled his influential

---

[6] For a brief introduction to the Food and Money group and its methodological approaches to economic history, see Su Yongming 苏永明, "'食货派'的经济史研究方法探讨" (An Exploration of Economic History Methodology in "Shihuo pai"), 史学史研究 (Historical Research) 2007.3, 77–83.

[7] Most notably, Ju Qingyuan 鞠清遠, 唐宋官私工業 (Government and Private Industries in Tang and Song) (Shanghai, Xin shengming shuju, 1934); Quan Hansheng 全漢昇, 中國行會制度史 (History of the Chinese Guild System) (Shanghai, Xin shengming shuju, 1935); Tao Xisheng 陶希聖 and Ju Qingyuan 鞠清遠, 唐代經濟史 (Tang Economic History) (Shanghai, Shangwu yinshuguan, 1936); Ju Qingyuan 鞠清遠, 唐代財政史 (Tang Fiscal History) (Shanghai, Shangwu yinshuguan, 1940).

[8] Katō's seminal essays on Tang–Song (and some Qing) economic history were published in a two-volume posthumous work: Katō Shigeshi 加藤繁, 支那經濟史考証 (Research on Chinese Economic History) (Tokyo, Tōyō bunko, 1952).

[9] Hino's prolific research on Tang–Song history has been reprinted in his twenty-volume collected works: Hino Kaisaburō 日野開三郎, 日野開三郎東洋史学論集 (Collected Works of Hino Kaisaburō on East Asian History) (Tokyo, San'ichi shobō, 1980–1988).

[10] Sogabe's research primarily focused on Song fiscal institutions and monetary history; see Sogabe Shizuo 曾我部静雄, 宋代財政史 (Song Fiscal History) (Tokyo, Seikatsusha, 1941); Sogabe, 中国社会経済史研究 (Research on Chinese Social and Economic History) (Tokyo, Yoshikawa kōbunkan, 1976).

[11] Miyazaki's first monograph studied the monetary history of the tenth century: Miyazaki Ichisada 宮崎市定, 五代宋初の通貨問題 (Monetary Issues in the Five Dynasties and Early Song) (Kyoto, Hoshino shoten, 1943). His body of work, which extended over the entire breadth of Chinese history, has been reprinted in his collected works, which run to twenty-four volumes: 宮崎市定全集 (Complete Works of Miyazaki Ichisada) (Tokyo, Iwanami shoten, 1991).

synthesis.¹² The priority of the Tang also can be seen in the first European-language monograph explicitly devoted to Chinese economic history, the Hungarian-born scholar Étienne Balazs's 1932 doctoral thesis for Berlin University on the economic history of the Tang dynasty.¹³ Although Balazs championed empirical research over both theoretical formulations and narrowly construed philological study, his scholarship was explicitly couched in the Weberian project of comparative study within universal categories of historical development and contributed to the conception of China as – in his words – a "permanently bureaucratic state" that obstructed the emergence of an independent merchant class and, by extension, capitalism.¹⁴

The prewar generation also pioneered the use of quantitative data for the study of Chinese economic history. Particularly noteworthy in this regard were the contributions of Quan Hansheng, the forerunner in the study of price history, international trade, and national revenue (initially focused on the Song, and later extended to the Ming–Qing periods as well), and Liang Fangzhong, who published a pathbreaking essay on Ming population, land, and taxation statistics in 1935 and a landmark study of the sixteenth-century Single-Whip tax reform in 1936.¹⁵ In addition, scholars such as Chen Hansheng and Fei Xiaotong, trained in economics and anthropology in the US and the UK respectively, published monographs on the contemporary rural economy based on extensive field research that became foundational studies.¹⁶ During the Japanese occupation

---

¹² Miyazaki Ichisada 宮崎市定, 東洋的近世 (Early Modern East Asia) (Osaka, Kyōiku taimusu sha, 1950).
¹³ Published as É. Balazs, "Beiträge zur Wirtschaftsgeschichte der T'ang-Zeit (618–906)," Mitteilungen des Seminars für Orientalische Sprachen 34 (1931), 1–92; 35 (1932), 93–165; 36 (1933), 1–62.
¹⁴ See his 1957 essay "China as a Permanently Bureaucratic Society," in É. Balazs, Chinese Civilization and Bureaucracy (New Haven, Yale University Press, 1964), pp. 13–27. For Balazs's impact on Chinese studies in France, where he spent most of his career, see H. T. Zurndorfer, "Not Bound to China: Étienne Balazs, Fernand Braudel and the Politics of the Study of Chinese History in Post-war France," Past and Present 185 (2004), 189–221.
¹⁵ Quan's studies were published in a two-volume collection, Quan Hansheng 全漢昇, 中國經濟史論叢 (Research on Chinese Economic History) (Hong Kong, Xinya shuyuan Xinya yanjiusuo, 1972), and a subsequent three-volume collection: 中國經濟史研究 (Research on Chinese Economic History) (Hong Kong, Xinya shuyuan Xinya yanjiusuo, 1976). A collection of Liang Fangzhong's writings on economic history was published as Liang Fangzhong 梁方仲, 梁方仲文集 (Collected Works of Liang Fangzhong) (Guangzhou, Zhongshan daxue chubanshe, 2004). Liang also supervised the compilation of what remains the most authoritative collection of Chinese historical statistics: Liang Fangzhong (ed.), 中国历代户口田地田赋统计 (Statistics on Chinese Population, Land, and Land Taxes) (Shanghai, Shanghai renmin chubanshe, 1980).
¹⁶ Chen H.-S., Landlord and Peasant in China: A Study of the Agrarian Crisis in South China (New York, International Publishers, 1936); Chen, Industrial Capital and Chinese Peasants (Shanghai, Kelly and Walsh, 1939); H.T. Fei, Peasant Life in China: A Field Study of Country

of China in the 1930s–1940s a legion of Japanese scholars, operating under the auspices of the Investigation Department of the South Manchuria Railway (Mantetsu Chōsabu, founded in 1907), compiled hundreds of reports on the Chinese economy that have been extensively mined by later scholars.[17] The pronounced influence of Keynesian economics among young Chinese economists also produced the first efforts to compile national income data and measure GDP in the late 1940s, efforts that would be jettisoned along with non-Marxist economics after the founding of the People's Republic of China in 1949.[18]

In the postwar era, Japanese scholarship on Chinese economic history was especially robust. The ascendancy of Marxist analysis in the Japanese academy – an explicit repudiation of the prewar imperialist project – established a new paradigm for interpreting Chinese economic history. Rejecting both the thesis of "oriental stagnation" and Naitō Konan's ideas about China's precocious modernity, economic and legal historians such as Sudō Yoshiyuki and Niida Noboru portrayed the Tang–Song transformation as the formative phase of a feudal society based on the subordination of serfs to a landlord class.[19] These servile relations were reproduced by the patriarchal social institutions of family, lineage, and guild that inhibited the emergence of the "rational" legal and economic institutions which the great German sociologists denoted by the term *Gesellschaft* (impersonal social relations). The density of patriarchal communal social relations (*Gemeinschaft*, rendered in Japanese as *kyōdōtai* 共同体) in Chinese society precluded the formation of an independent bourgeoisie and the transition to capitalism. More importantly, these studies – and a plethora of non-Marxist scholarship as well – generated a wealth of new empirical research on Chinese economic history,

---

    Life in the Yangtze Valley (London, Kegan Paul, 1939), Fei, *Earthbound China: A Study of Rural Economy in Yunnan* (Chicago, The University of Chicago Press, 1945). Foreign researchers also contributed to the compilation of social and economic statistics, most notably J.L. Buck, *Chinese Farm Economy* (Chicago, The University of Chicago Press, 1930); Buck, *Land Utilization in China* (Shanghai, Commercial Press, 1937); S.D. Gamble, *Peking: A Social Survey* (New York, George H. Doran Co., 1921).

[17] For overviews of this scholarship, see J. Young, *The Research Activities of the South Manchuria Railway Company, 1907–1945: A History and Bibliography* (New York, Columbia University Press, 1966); Matsumura Takao 松村高夫, Yanagisawa Yū 柳沢遊, and Eda Kenji 江田憲治, 満鉄の調査と研究―その「神話」と実像 (Investigation and Research on the South Manchuria Railway Company: Its "Myth" and Reality) (Tokyo, Aoki shoten, 2008).

[18] Wu Baosan 巫寶三 (ed.), 中國國民所得 (Chinese National Income) (Shanghai, Zhonghua shuju, 1947); T.-C. Liu, *China's National Income, 1931 36: An Exploratory Study* (Washington, DC, Brookings Institution, 1946).

[19] For a synopsis of the voluminous studies by Sudō and Niida (and the prodigious postwar Japanese scholarship on Tang–Song economic history generally), see the state-of-the-field essay by P. Golas: "Rural China in the Song," *Journal of Asian Studies* 39.2 (1980), 291–325.

including a growing body of work centered on the Ming–Qing period and the twentieth century.

In China, of course, orthodox Marxist historiography prevailed after 1949. However, numerous studies attesting to the vitality of the market economy in the late Ming dynasty gave rise to the idea that the "sprouts of capitalism" (*zibenzhuyi mengya* 資本主義萌芽) had begun to emerge by the late sixteenth century, if not earlier.[20] Shang Yue became the most prominent exponent of the controversial thesis that an incipient bourgeoisie had formed in the late Ming period and China thus was already beginning the transition to capitalism before it was derailed by the Manchu conquest of the Ming in 1644.[21] Japanese historians quickly joined this debate. Scholars who focused on the urban economy and merchants, such as Fu Yiling and Tanaka Masatoshi, tended to underscore the potential for indigenous capitalist transformation.[22] Historians who concentrated on relations of production in the agrarian economy and handicraft industries, such as Nishijima Sadao, were far more skeptical.[23] However, by 1960 Shang Yue's thesis on the "sprouts of capitalism" was deemed heretical within the Chinese academic establishment.

Although Shang Yue's contention that China was on the verge of a breakthrough to capitalism before the Opium War was repudiated, most scholars assented to the proposition that rising commodity production in the Ming–Qing era attested to an "advanced" form of feudalism in China, challenging the idea that the Western European historical experience exclusively defined the archetype of the feudal economy. According to this line of thought, the intrusion of foreign imperialism in the nineteenth century and China's subjugation as a "semi-colony" warped the development of Chinese capitalism, precluding the formation of an autonomous national bourgeoisie

---

[20] For a brief and regrettably tendentious introduction, see A. Feuerwerker, "From 'Feudalism' to 'Capitalism' in Recent Historical Writing from Mainland China," *Journal of Asian Studies* 18.1 (1958), 107–16.

[21] Shang Yue 尚鉞, 中國資本主義关系發生及演变的初步研究 (Preliminary Research on the Origin and Evolution of Chinese Capitalist Relations) (Beijing, Sanlian shudian, 1956).

[22] Fu Yiling 傅衣凌, 明代江南市民經济試探 (An Exploration of Jiangnan Citizens) (Shanghai, Shanghai renmin chubanshe, 1957); Tanaka Masatoshi 田中正俊, "中国歴史界における「資本主義の萌芽」研究" (Research into the "Sprouts of Capitalism" in Chinese History Studies), in Suzuki Jun 鈴木俊 and Nishijima Sadao 西島定雄 (eds.), 中国史の時代区分 (The Periodization of Chinese History) (Tokyo, Tōkyō daigaku shuppansha, 1957), pp. 219–52.

[23] Nishijima Sadao 西島定雄, "中国古代社会の構造的特質に関する問題点" (Issues Related to the Special Features of Ancient Chinese Social Structure), in Suzuki and Nishijima, 中国史の時代区分, pp. 175–208.

and instead fostering state-led "bureaucratic capitalism." Thus China remained a "semi-feudal, semi-colonial" society until the Communist Party initiated a proletarian revolution beginning in the 1930s. Notwithstanding the ideological bent of PRC scholarship in this era, a vast array of source materials, statistical series, and valuable monographic studies were published that stimulated research both within China and abroad.[24]

By contrast, in the immediate postwar era economic history was a virtually untouched subject in Western scholarship on China, which was deeply adverse to the Marxist cast of the Chinese and Japanese studies mentioned above. In an essay on the state of the field at the dawn of the 1960s, American scholar Albert Feuerwerker dourly observed that

(1) Monographic studies in Chinese rarely come up to the standards expected of European economic historians. (2) Few detailed investigations have appeared in European languages; and their quality is very uneven. (3) Perhaps both in quantity and quality the most significant body of monographic work has been done in Japan, though here too there are serious limitations growing out of the strong hold of Marxist ideology in Japanese academic circles. (4) There is, to my knowledge, no satisfactory synthetic treatment of Chinese economic history in any language to which a non-specialist might go for a substantive introduction to this subject.[25]

Feuerwerker's citations belie these grim conclusions to some extent; for example, he mentions Peng Xinwei's *Chinese Monetary History*, a magisterial survey that remains unsurpassed to this day.[26] Mention also should be made of the numerous publications during these years by Lien-sheng Yang, perhaps the first scholar to write a Ph.D. thesis at a US university (Harvard, 1946) on Chinese economic history.[27] Regrettably, the ideological struggles that convulsed China during the Cultural Revolution of the 1960s–1970s shuttered the universities, inflicted enormous personal hardship on many scholars, and effectively suspended serious scholarship.

---

[24] A. Feuerwerker, "China's Modern Economic History in Communist Chinese Historiography," *China Quarterly* 22 (1965), 31–61.
[25] A. Feuerwerker, "Materials for the Study of the Economic History of Modern China," *Journal of Economic History* 21.1 (1961), 42.
[26] Peng Xinwei 彭信威, 中國貨幣史 (Chinese Monetary History) (Shanghai, Shanghai renmin chubanshe, 1958).
[27] Yang's work includes *Money and Credit in China: A Short History* (Cambridge, MA, Harvard University Press, 1952) and *Les aspects économiques des travaux publics dans la Chine impériale: Quatre conférences* (Paris, Collège de France, 1964); and studies gathered in his essay collections *Studies in Chinese Institutional History* (Cambridge, MA, Harvard University Press, 1961) and *Excursions in Sinology* (Cambridge, MA, Harvard University Press, 1969).

In any event, the decade of the 1960s would prove to be a watershed in Western scholarship on Chinese economic history. The rise of social science research and its application to historical study provided the catalyst for a series of landmark studies that would shape Western scholarship on Chinese economic history for a generation: Ping-ti Ho's incisive dissection of historical population statistics;[28] Albert Feuerwerker's study of state-led industrialization efforts in the late nineteenth century;[29] the meticulous reconstruction of Tang fiscal administration by Denis Twitchett, which amply demonstrated the value of Japanese scholarship;[30] Robert Hartwell's provocative findings on the precocious development of the coal and iron industries in Song China;[31] the insights of economic geography applied by G. William Skinner to generate a new paradigm of market structure and marketing systems in China;[32] the application of quantitative analysis to agricultural production pioneered by Dwight Perkins;[33] Ramon Myers's revisionist analysis, drawing on quantitative data from the Mantetsu surveys, of economic performance in rural China in the Republican period;[34] Shiba Yoshinobu's empirically rich and analytically sophisticated tour de force on commerce and merchant enterprise in the Song, which became accessible to a wider audience through Mark Elvin's abbreviated translation;[35] crowned by Elvin's own theoretically innovative paradigm of the course of economic development in China across the imperial era, another work deeply informed by Japanese scholarship.[36]

[28] P.-T. Ho, *Studies on the Population of China, 1368–1953* (Cambridge, MA, Harvard University Press, 1959).

[29] A. Feuerwerker, *China's Early Industrialization: Sheng Hsuan-huai (1844–1916) and Mandarin Enterprise* (Cambridge, MA, Harvard University Press, 1958).

[30] D. Twitchett, *Financial Administration under the T'ang Dynasty* (Cambridge, Cambridge University Press, 1963)

[31] R.M. Hartwell, "A Revolution in the Chinese Iron and Coal Industries during the Northern Sung, 960–1126 AD," *Journal of Asian Studies* 21.1 (1962), 153–62; Hartwell, "Markets, Technology, and the Structure of Enterprise in the Development of the Eleventh-Century Chinese Iron and Steel Industry," *Journal of Economic History* 26.1 (1966), 29–58; Hartwell, "A Cycle of Economic Change in Imperial China: Coal and Iron in Northeast China, 750–1350," *Journal of the Economic and Social History of the Orient* 10 (1967), 102–59.

[32] G.W. Skinner, "Marketing and Social Structure in Rural China," *Journal of Asian Studies* 24.1 (1964), 3–43; 24.2 (1965), 195–228; 24.3 (1965), 363–99.

[33] D.H. Perkins, *Agricultural Development in China, 1368–1968* (Chicago, Aldine, 1969).

[34] R.H. Myers, *The Chinese Peasant Economy* (Cambridge, MA, Harvard University Press, 1970).

[35] Shiba Yoshinobu 斯波義信, 宋代商業史研究 (Tokyo, Kazama shobō, 1968), translated as *Commerce and Society in Sung China* (Ann Arbor, University of Michigan Center for Chinese Studies, 1970).

[36] M. Elvin, *The Pattern of the Chinese Past* (Stanford, Stanford University Press, 1973).

By the 1970s, then, Western scholarship on Chinese economic history had achieved a new level of maturity. The wealth of new empirical studies since then has fostered vigorous, indeed contentious, debate on issues such as the impact of Western and Japanese imperialism, the nature of the peasant economy, regional systems and market networks, and what has come to be called the "Great Divergence" debate. In particular, the past three decades have seen significant revisionist scholarship on Chinese economic performance in the tumultuous nineteenth and twentieth centuries following the intrusion of Western imperialism in the post-Opium War era. Contrary to the once dominant pessimistic interpretation of a Chinese economy withering under the dual constraints of Western colonialism and Chinese tradition, the new scholarship has identified the onset of modern economic growth in this era – at least in some crucial regions and sectors – as a powerful response to new incentive structures and investment opportunities, as well as the inflow of new ideas and technology, laying the foundation for China's economic takeoff in the post-1978 reform era. Within China, perhaps the most significant development is the publication of the three edited volumes of the *History of Chinese Capitalist Development* in 1983.[37] Under the leadership of one of the coeditors, Wu Chengming of the Chinese Academy of Social Science, these three volumes, although framed within a Marxist framework, brought together a generation of devoted senior and junior scholars to provide a comprehensive economic history of modern China from the early modern era to 1950. Wu, himself an economist who received a master's degree from Columbia University in the 1940s but was banished during China's Cultural Revolution era, emerged as an intellectual leader in economic history within China throughout the 1980s and 1990s.

Although much of the new scholarship on Chinese economic history has focused on the post-1800 period, for which quantitative data are much more abundant, there have been significant advances in the study of China's premodern economy, particularly for the ancient period. Important new data generated from archaeological research in China, ranging from textual and artifactual evidence to urban morphology and settlement studies, have yielded fresh insights into social and economic livelihood in ancient China and enable us to trace the course of economic change with much greater temporal and geographic precision. Although Western scholarship on

---

[37] Xu Dixin 許滌新 and Wu Chengming 吳承明 (eds.), 中國資本主義發展史 (Developmental History of Chinese Capitalism), 3 vols. (Beijing, Renmin chubanshe, 1985). Volume 1 was translated into English as Xu Dixin and Wu Chengming (eds.), *Chinese Capitalism, 1522–1840* (New York, St. Martin's Press, 2000).

China's premodern economic history remains modest, quantitatively speaking, compared to the prodigious output of Chinese and Japanese scholars, Western historians have done pioneering work in many aspects of the premodern economy, including environmental history; demography; legal institutions and economic organization; kinship, gender, and the household economy; political economy; and economic sociology.

These scholarly developments have coincided with the unfettering of Chinese scholarship from shopworn Marxist–Leninist ideological blinders since the early 1980s and an enormous surge in new scholarship on Chinese economic history within China. With the opening of new archives and the improvement of the academic infrastructure in China, new generations of Chinese scholars have begun to make important methodological and theoretical contributions to the study of Chinese economic history ranging from agriculture and demography to finance and law. The rapidly growing presence of Chinese scholars within the global economic history community (as seen, for example, at meetings such as the triennial World Economic History Congress) also testifies to the rising impact of Chinese economic history within the profession internationally.

A significant shift in the scholarly landscape has been the gradual rebalancing of the community working on Chinese economic history. Twenty years ago, the few scholars working on economic history were largely based outside China. The last decade has seen the steady growth of a young generation of researchers who returned to China having gained training in quantitative and economic approaches from North American and European Ph.D. programs. In conjunction with the rising stock of foreign-trained Ph.D.s in economic history, universities in China and Hong Kong now produce a steady stream of Ph.D.s trained in quantitative economic history, many of whom are making careers in China. The sheer quantity of the new scholarship on Chinese economic history since the 1970s defies adequate summary in this brief essay, but it will be cited copiously throughout these volumes. In addition, synthetic surveys of Chinese economic history have now begun to appear.[38] Along with these surveys are two commissioned special journal issues devoted entirely to Chinese economic history.[39]

---

[38] L. Brandt, D. Ma, and T.G. Rawski, "From Divergence to Convergence: Reevaluating the History behind China's Economic Boom," *Journal of Economic Literature* 52.1 (2014), 45–123; R. von Glahn, *The Economic History of China from Antiquity to the Nineteenth Century* (Cambridge, Cambridge University Press, 2016); Okamoto Takashi 岡本隆司 (ed.), 中国経済史 (Economic History of China) (Nagoya, Nagoya daigaku shuppankai, 2013).

[39] D. Ma (ed.), *Money, Finance and Commerce in Chinese History*, special issue of *Frontier of Economics in China* 13.3 (2018); K.J. Mitchener and D. Ma (eds.), *A New Economic History of China*, special issue of *Explorations in Economic History* 63 (2017).

The Cambridge Economic History of China is divided chronologically into two volumes, with the first volume devoted to the period before 1800 and the second volume to the period from 1800 to the present. Each volume is further subdivided into two broad chronological sections, but within these divisions the chapters are organized topically rather than chronologically. Part I of Volume I (in six chapters) covers the period from 1000 BCE to 1000 CE, with Part II (in twelve chapters) devoted to the period from 1000 to 1800. The unequal portions assigned to the pre-1000 and 1000–1800 periods reflect differences in the depth and breadth of the scholarship at this point in time. The usual periodization of Chinese history posits a sharp break between the middle imperial period of 750–1500 (often subsumed under the Tang–Song transition rubric discussed above) and the 1500–1800 era (whether this period should be defined as China's "early modern" era remains controversial). The scholarship usually reflects this divide as well. However, given the topical structure of the volume, we believe that the 1000–1800 period should be treated as an integral whole.

Volume II similarly is divided into two broad chronological parts that are subdivided into thematic chapters. Part I covers the period from 1800 to 1950, encompassing the last century of the Qing dynasty and the Republican era (1911–1949), in fourteen chapters. Part II, in seven chapters, examines the dramatic transformations of the Chinese economy since the founding of the People's Republic of China in 1949.

As the first attempt in the Cambridge History series to focus on Chinese economic history, our two volumes will remedy a large lacuna in the discipline of economic history and respond to the increasing demand from both specialists and the general public for a comprehensive introduction to the subject. These volumes will provide an authoritative survey incorporating up-to-date research at the frontiers of knowledge, including quantitative data that are accessible to a general economic history audience, as well as addressing some of the most important current debates in Chinese and global economic history. We also hope that these volumes will serve both as a standard reference and as a resource for teaching.

PART I
★
1800–1950

I

Ideology and the Contours of Economic Change

DEBIN MA

When visited by the British trade mission led by Lord George Macartney, who aimed to show off the best of Western trade and technology, the Qianlong Emperor of Qing China was known to have famously replied in 1792, "Our Celestial Empire possesses all things in prolific abundance and lacks no product within its borders. There is therefore no need to import the manufactures of outside barbarians in exchange for our own produce."[1] Qianlong's statement came at the height of Qing's glory, overseeing a remarkable tripling of population and a doubling of territory between the fifteenth and eighteenth centuries. No single political entity at the time achieved such size in both geography and population with such stability and cohesion.

The Qing's self-conceit was shattered only five decades after Qianlong's statement by China's humiliating military defeat to the much smaller polity of Britain in the infamous 1842 Opium War, which in turn reduced the mighty Qing to semicolonial status through the treaty port system. The mid-nineteenth-century confrontation symbolizes the clash between a highly centralized singular Chinese empire and a fragmented and competitive European state system empowered by centuries of waves of commercial, financial, political, technological, and scientific revolutions. More importantly, during the tumultuous century after China's forced opening in the mid-nineteenth century, the mixed Chinese record, especially in relation to neighboring Japan, raises the more pertinent question of why it took so long for China to industrialize after the Industrial Revolution had been well underway elsewhere.

With China's unprecedented economic growth during the last four decades and her emergence as the world's second-largest economy, the tide

---

I want to thank Joel Mokyr, Kaixiang Peng, Jared Rubin, and Rui Wang for comments and encouragement. But my special gratitutde goes to Thomas Rawski, who provided meticulous comments and feedback that greatly improved the chapter. I remain responsible for all errors.
[1] Quote from https://en.wikipedia.org/wiki/Macartney_Embassy, accessed August 14, 2016.

has turned with the myth of the once mighty Qing making a curious comeback in the increasingly popular claim that current Chinese economic success marked only a triumphant return to China's eighteenth-century glory. The claim is as misleading as a misconstrued conflation of total GDP with per capita GDP. In per capita terms, eighteenth-century China probably remained a poor agrarian economy, which could still be the largest economy in the world thanks to her sheer population size and because per capita income differences in the preindustrial world were relatively small before the onset and spread of the Industrial Revolution. It might have been the largest but not the leading economy, with limited impact in external trade and investment globally.[2]

Writing before the onset of China's current boom, earlier generations of scholars had to explain China's historical economic stagnation, often due to the prevalence of nepotism, corruption, and other elements of Chinese social structure and behavior that prevented a dynamic response of the sort attained during Japan's Meiji era (1868–1912). But China's recent reversal of fortune seems to have generated a tide of scholarship that now advances the opposite view, attributing recent Asian prosperity to the same "cultural values" formerly thought to have obstructed economic dynamism, and arguing that there were no fundamental shortfalls in China's political, legal, or other institutional traditions. Pomeranz's influential book on *The Great Divergence* (2000) further argues that Britain's head start in industrialization arose from its domestic supplies of cheap coal and because its colonies provided superior access to land-intensive goods rather than from any advantage linked to political, legal, or other institutional factors.[3]

For the 1850–1949 period under study, this chapter emphasizes the fact that, ultimately, industrial revolution in modern East Asia started with borrowed institutions and ideology. This takes us back to the much older conceptual framework of modernization known as "Western impact and Chinese response" in the Chinese or East Asian context. In particular, this chapter reasserts the peculiar and unusual importance of the external or Western

---

[2] It is true that there was substantial trade in the export of Chinese silks and tea and an inflow of Latin American silver ingots and coin as well as New World crops such as maize and potatoes.

[3] L. Brandt, D. Ma, and T. Rawski, "From Divergence to Convergence: Re-evaluating the History behind China's Economic Boom," *Journal of Economic Literature*, 52.1 (2014), 45–123; K. Pomeranz, *The Great Divergence: China, Europe, and the Making of the Modern World Economy* (Princeton, NJ, Princeton University Press, 2000).

influence on a large country like China. Developing a new conceptual framework, I argue that given the dual monopoly of ideology and power under the Qing, political and economic changes often had to be initiated from outside the empire. Openness and external influence could act as a constraint in a polity lacking internal checks and balances. The external represents a new source of alternative power that breaches the monopoly of power and ideology. However, how much the external could exert an impact depends on how much it elicits formal institutional and ideological change in the domestic context.

In this regard, I show that rather than resource endowments such as coal, or even the discovery of New World resources, what impeded China's progress in the globalized world is what some historians of China have called the scarcity of "intellectual resources" 思想资源, or what sometimes is referred to as ideology.[4] However, the scarcity of intellectual resources in mid-nineteenth-century Qing China is of a particular sort, that of confronting the rapidly advancing West transformed by the Industrial Revolution. This Chinese scarcity could have been overcome through massive borrowing, learning, and importing of Western ideology and institutions, which is partly what Meiji Japan succeeded in doing. These intellectual resources allowed the late industrializer to construct an entirely different set of political governance, economic systems, and social organization.[5]

I argue that both the capacity and the willingness to borrow and learn themselves are endogenous to China's pre-existing political institutions and geopolitical position in East Asia. In this regard, China's highly centralized and absolutist political regimes and traditional dominance in a China-centered world order have led not only to a closure of mind to new

---

[4] These ideological or intellectual resources represent our ways of understanding, interpreting, and theorizing about the world we live in and the ways we interpret the past, construct the present, and imagine the future. They both support and constrain our institutions, policies, and day-to-day decisions. See Wang Fansen 王汎森, "戊戌前后思想资源的变化：以日本因素为例" (Changes in Intellectual Resources before and after the Hundred Days Reform), 二十一世纪 (Twenty-First Century) 45 (February 1998), 47–54.

[5] See Wang Fansen 王汎森, 权力的毛细血管作用，清代的思想、学术与心态 (The Penetrating Role of Power, Ideas, Academics, and Moods in Qing) (Beijing, Beijing daxue chubanshe, 2015). Jin Guantao 金观涛 and Liu Qingfeng 刘青峰, 兴盛与危机，论中国社会的超稳定结构 (The Cycle of Growth and Decline: On the Ultrastable Structure of Chinese Society) (Beijing, Falu chubanshe, 2011). Jin Guantao 金观涛 and Liu Qingfeng 刘青峰, 开放中的变迁，再论中国社会超稳定结构 (The Transformation of Chinese Society (1840–1956): The Fate of Its Ultrastable Structure in Modern Times) (Beijing, Falu chubanshe, 2011). Ge Zhaoguang 葛兆光, "十八世纪中国的盛世危机" (Crisis in China's Glorious Eighteenth Century), February 19, 2019, www.ftchinese.com/author/%E8%91%9B%E5%85%86%E5%85%89.

intellectual resources, but also to failure to recognize or perceive impending crisis and threats. So the process of change is not automatic, requiring complicated and sometimes risky feedback processes between social and political experiments, institutions, and ideology. This chapter links this complicated process of Western impact and Chinese response by connecting the changing incentives to economic agents on the ground with the shifting ideologies of elites at the top. It matches the contours of economic change with the specific timing of intellectual and ideological transformations during this period and embed our narrative in two specific cases of commercial and financial development. The first section lays out the quantitative profile of Chinese economic change from 1850 to 1950. The second section turns to historiography and builds a new analytical framework linking ideology with economic changes. The third section examines the three phases of economic change based on the new analytical framework.

The Chinese Economy, 1842–1949: Stagnation or Takeoff?

Stagnation or Takeoff?

Our analysis of the Chinese economic record starts with the aggregate economic indicator of GDP. However, despite a new wave of historical GDP research, estimates before the 1930s still need to be treated with caution and used with hesitation given the controversies on long-term statistics as basic as population and agricultural acreage.[6] Nonetheless, few would disagree that China of the nineteenth and twentieth centuries is a traditional agrarian economy with a 60 to 70 percent share of GDP in the agriculture sector.

---

[6] See S. Broadberry, H. Guan, and D.D. Li, "China, Europe, and the Great Divergence: A Study in Historical National Accounting, 980–1850," *Journal of Economic History* 78 (2018), 955–1000. Y. Ma and H. de Jong, "Unfolding the Turbulent Century: A Reconstruction of China's Historical National Accounts, 1840–1912," *Review of Income and Wealth* 65.1 (2019), 75–9. X. Yi, Z. Shi, B. van Leeuwen, Y. Ni, Z. Zhang, and Y. Ma, "Chinese National Income, ca. 1661–1933," *Australian Economic History Review* 57.3 (November 2017), 368–93. A Maddison, *Chinese Economic Performance in the Long Run*, 2nd ed, rev. and updated (Paris, Development Centre of the Organization for Economic Co-operation and Development, 2007). For problems with data, see discussion in D. Ma, "Economic Growth in the Lower Yangzi Region of China in 1911–1937: A Quantitative and Historical Perspective," *Journal of Economic History* 68.2 (2008), 385–92. T.G. Rawski, *Economic Growth in Prewar China* (Berkeley, University of California Press, 1989).

Figure 1.1 plots China's real per capita GDP index against that of Japan. The figure reveals the sluggish performance of Qing and Republican China relative to Japan's transformation. Although the indexing of the level of the per capita GDP of the two economies in 1850 both at 100 seems arbitrary at first sight, it actually turns out to be consistent with a comprehensive study based on the reconstruction of the 1930s benchmark purchasing-power parity estimates which places the Japanese per capita GDP level at about three times that of China during the 1930s, a ratio that broadly matches that in Figure 1.1.[7] Projecting this 1930s three-to-one ratio back to 1850 with the trend of growth rates of these two countries leads to a comparable level of per capita GDP for the two countries around the mid-nineteenth century in Figure 1.1. Hence our implicit estimate of a common starting point for these two countries in 1850 presumes that the divergence between Japan and China only started only after their being forced open by Western imperialist forces rather than before. This contradicts the recent claim of the so-called "Little Divergence" within Asia before the mid-nineteenth century.[8]

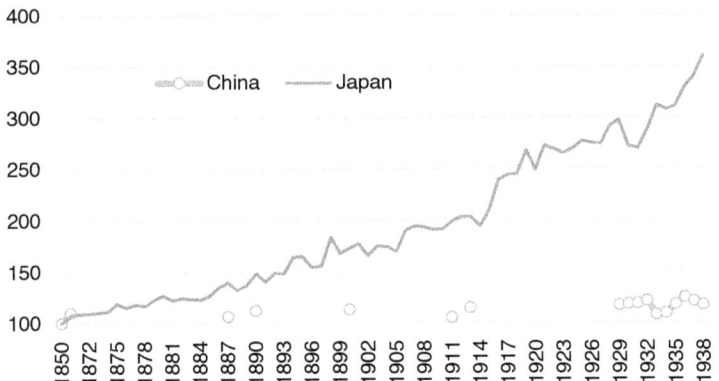

Figure 1.1 Real index of Chinese and Japanese per capita GDP (1850 = 100)
Sources: Maddison Project database, at www.rug.nl/ggdc/historicaldevelopment/maddison/releases/maddison-project-database-2018?lang=en, but database reindexed at 100 in 1850

[7] K. Fukao, D. Ma, and T. Yuan, "Real GDP in Pre-war East Asia: A 1934–36 Benchmark Purchasing Power Parity Comparison with the U.S.," *Review of Income and Wealth* 53.3 (2007), 503–37.

[8] According to a recent estimate by J.-P. Bassino, S. Broadberry, K. Fukao, B. Gupta, and M. Takashima, "Japan and the Great Divergence, 730–1874," *Explorations in Economic History* 72 (April 2019), 1–22, Japanese per capita GDP in 1990 dollars stood at 904 against China's 600 in 1850. This led to the claim of the "Little Divergence'" within East Asia before it was opened to Western colonialism. This would be inconsistent with the estimated series in Figure 1.1 which used growth rates data back-projected from the 1930s.

But was the Chinese economy as stagnant as revealed in Figure 1.1, and specifically, how well did aggregate GDP statistics capture the overall pattern of economic change during this era? Thomas Rawski noted the jarring mismatch between the rapid pace of growth in modern sectors such as trade, modern industry, banking, and monetary aggregates and the relatively stagnant GDP profile in Figure 1.1. The reason behind this mismatch is that the share of modern sectors is a tiny part of GDP dwarfed by the traditional agriculture and handicrafts sectors. For example, modern factory production – which recorded 8 percent annual growth between 1912 and 1936 – was only 3.4 percent of the total GDP even in the 1930s.[9] The attempts by Rawski to raise the agricultural growth rate in order to make a case for overall economic growth between 1912 and 1936 were – as he himself admitted – based on strong assumptions. In another attempt at reconciliation, Ma derived regional GDP estimates and argued that increased per capita output and structural changes of the sort associated with Simon Kuznets's concept of modern economic growth only occurred in two major regions of the lower Yangzi and the Northeast (Manchuria), where foreign investment and institutions were quite important.[10] In this chapter, rather than attempt to reconcile the aggregate with the sectoral statistics, I intend to reconstruct a new narrative as revealed by the statistics to capture the timing and multifaceted nature of economic change in modern China.

External Trade, Industry, Infrastructure, and Capital Accumulation

We first start out with one of the most reliable and continuous economics statistics for the entire 1865–1949 period – the import and export data as recorded by China Maritime Customs.[11] In contrast to aggregate GDP statistics, Figure 1.2 reveals a remarkable expansion of China's international trade, with real Chinese imports and exports increasing eight- to tenfold between 1867 and 1932. However, external trade did not take off right away after China's forced opening in the mid-nineteenth century. While the increase in external trade was continuous, there was clearly an acceleration from the 1880s and 1890s onward, raising the Chinese share in world trade to a peak of more than 2 percent of global trade flows in the late 1920s, a ratio that was not regained until the 1990s. So the dream of China as a huge market for British manufacture – "every

---

[9] Ma, "Economic Growth," 364. [10] Ma, "Economic Growth."
[11] See below in this chapter and the chapters by Shiue and Keller, Kaske and Lin in this volume on the organization and data of the Maritime Customs system.

Ideology and the Contours of Economic Change

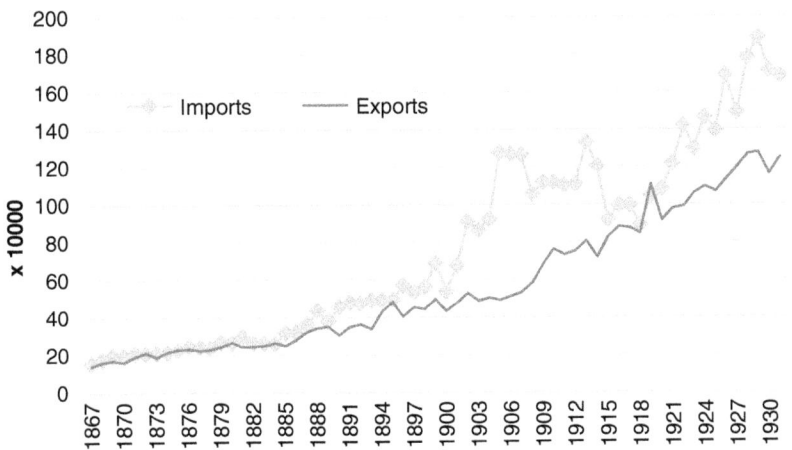

Figure 1.2 Real value of Chinese imports and exports at 1933 constant prices (thousand yuan)
Source: Minami Ryoshin 南亮進 and Makino Fumio 牧野文夫 (eds.), アジア長期経済統計 3 中国 (Long-Term Asian Statistics, vol. 3, China) (Tokyo, Tōyō Keizai Shinpōsha, 2014), Table 6.1.9

Chinaman wears a cotton cloth of the Lancashire factories" – barely came to fruition until three decades after Britain's forced imposition of free trade.

It turns out that the 1880–1890 turning point in Chinese foreign trade was not entirely coincidental. In the absence of comprehensive economic statistics for the entire period, we can gauge economic activities from the meticulous firm and banks data compiled by a generation of scholars, which culminated in the works of Du Xuncheng.[12] Figure 1.3 plots the number of newly established Chinese and Western firms and banking institutions from the 1840s. Du classfied his firms as the so-called nationalist capitalist enterprises, which are basically Chinese modern firms connected with the use of Western technology and production methods. Not surprisingly, following the signing of the Nanjing Treaty in 1842, Western firms and banks took the lead in establishing trade and financial enterprises in the designated treaty port areas, with a steady pace of growth marked by a small uptick from the 1890s for Western firms. While Western firms and banks were leading the way, Chinese follow-up or catch-up in terms of the number of firms remained modest until the 1890s, when an outburst of growth completely overtook Western establishments. The peak of the establishment of modern Chinese

---

[12] I want to thank James Kung for alerting me to the use of this set of data for this purpose.

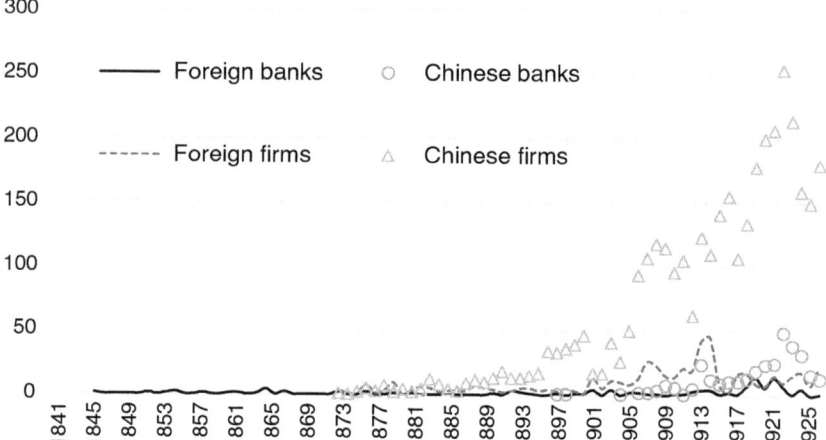

Figure 1.3 Western impact and Chinese response: number of newly established modern firms and banks
Sources: Du Xuncheng 杜询诚, 民族资本主义与旧中国政府, 1840–1937 (Chinese Capitalism and the Old Chinese Government, 1840–1937) (Shanghai, Shanghai shehui kexueyuan chubanshe, 1991). Huang Guangyu 黄光域, 外国在华工商企业辞典 (Dictionary for Foreign Industrial and Business Enterprises in China) (Sichuan, Sichuan renmin chubanshe, 1995)

banks occurred during the 1910s and 1920s as modern banks were only permitted around the turn of the century following Qing legislation.

Although a very problematic measure of actual economic activities, the number of firms and banks turned out to capture quite accurately both the timing and the turning point of Chinese industrialization. Calculations from the data compiled by Du Xuncheng showed that the nominal annual industrial investment by Chinese nationals in the 1914–1925 period was eleven times that of the 1840–1911 period.[13] Similarly, Rawski's figure for "modern-oriented" fixed investment (calculated from consumption of cement, steel, and machinery) grew at an average annual rate of 8.1 percent between 1903 and 1936, outpacing Japanese gross domestic fixed capital formation in mining, manufacturing, construction, and facilitating industries, which advanced at an annual rate of 5.0 percent. Likewise, between 1902 and 1931, inflows of foreign direct investment also grew at annual rates of 8.3 percent, 5 percent, and 4.3 percent for

---

[13] Du used 1911 as the cutoff period; the contrast of industrial expansion versus stagnation would be even sharper if the cutoff period was the mid-1890s. Throughout this period, the Chinese monetary standard was silver-based with moderate inflation. See Ma, "Economic Growth."

Ideology and the Contours of Economic Change

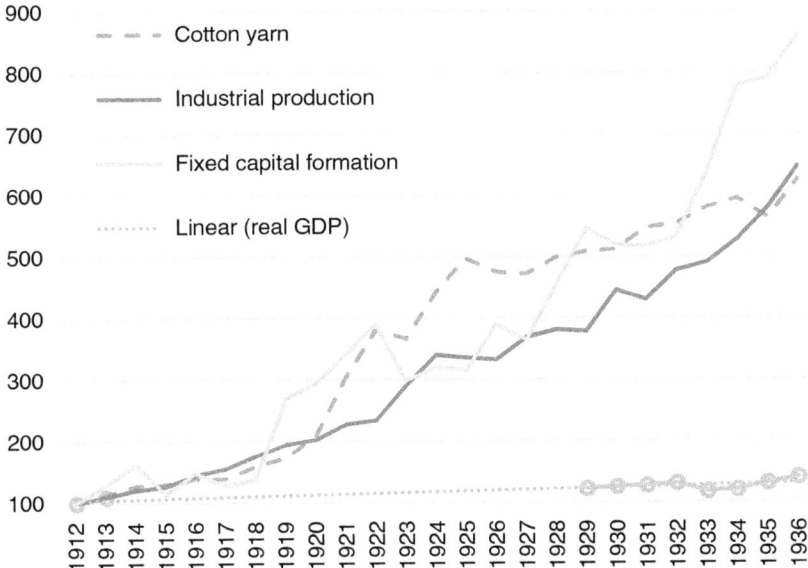

Figure 1.4 Real production and GDP indices (1912 = 100)
Sources: Minami and Makino, アジア長期経済統計, Tables 4.D.1 for cotton yarn and 4.2.1 for industrial production. T.G. Rawski, *Economic Growth in Prewar China* (Berkeley, University of California Press, 1989), Table 5.2, p. 245, for fixed capital formation

Shanghai, Manchuria, and the rest of China respectively.[14] Transport development measured by China's railway track length increased sharply from a mere 364 kilometers in 1894 to over 21,000 by 1937.[15]

Figure 1.4 plots the real production indices of machine-produced cotton yarn, modern industrial production, and capital stock. They grew by between six- and eightfold between 1912 and 1936 against a largely stagnant real GDP for the same period. These statistics were consistent with the historical narrative. Beginning at the very end of the nineteenth century, activity in mining and manufacturing accelerated sharply from its small initial base. Factory production, initially focused on textiles, food processing, and other consumer products, concentrated in two regions: the lower Yangzi area, where both foreign and Chinese entrepreneurs pursued factory expansion in and around Shanghai, and China's northeast or Manchurian region, where Japanese initiatives predominated. By

---

[14] See L. Brandt, D. Ma, and T.G. Rawski, "From Divergence to Convergence: Reevaluating the History behind China's Economic Boom," *Journal of Economic Literature* 52.1 (2014), 45–123.
[15] See Elisabeth Köll's chapter in this volume for railways and telegraph lines.

23

1935, Chinese factories, including some owned by British or Japanese firms, produced 8 percent of the world's cotton yarn (more than Germany, France, or Italy) and 2.8 percent of global cotton piece goods production. Despite the importance of foreign investment in Shanghai and especially in Manchuria, Chinese-owned companies produced 73 percent of China's 1933 factory output. Growing production of light consumer and industrial goods, combined with the accumulation of experience in operating and repairing modern machinery, generated backward linkages that spurred new private initiatives in machinery, chemicals, cement, mining, electricity, and metallurgy.[16]

A Financial Revolution

The spectacular growth of Chinese banks from the 1900s, as revealed in Figure 1.3, was the outcome of a remarkable triumph of a free-banking version of the silver standard championed by largely privately held Chinese banks, foreign financial institutions, and traditional money shops. Figure 1.5 shows that while total specie, as measured by silver bullion, dollars, and copper cash, barely registered any increase during 1911–1936, total money supply (M1), which includes specie, increased at an annual rate of 5 percent between 1911–1916 and 1931–1936. This is only possible because the bank notes and deposit components of M1 surged at a remarkable annual rate of 9.5 percent during the same period. As a result, the estimated share of notes and deposits in M1 money supply rose from between 22.3 and 34.6 percent in 1910 to a minimum of 40.4 percent in 1925 and 83.2 percent in 1936, with the turning point marked by an uptick in M1 around 1917–1918.[17] Overall, Chinese banks – mostly modern but also including native banks – accounted for the lion's share of the growth in this period. The ratio of deposits held by Chinese modern banks relative to foreign banks increased from about two in the 1910s to about four in 1930–1935. The same ratio for banknotes held by Chinese over foreign banks increased from 1.5 to about three for the same period. Remarkably, price levels remained stable, whereas total money supply nearly tripled between the 1910s and 1930s, while annual GDP growth registered no more than 2 percent during the same period, indicating a heightened degree of monetization and financial deepening. These growth rates translate into what Ma observed as nothing short of a financial revolution, as demonstrated in Figure 1.5.[18]

---

[16] See Rawski, *Economic Growth in Prewar China*, Chapter 2.
[17] Rawski, *Economic Growth in Prewar China*, p. 157.
[18] See D. Ma, "The Rise of a Financial Revolution in Republican China in 1900–1937: A Survey and New Interpretation," *Australian Economic History Review* 59.3 (November

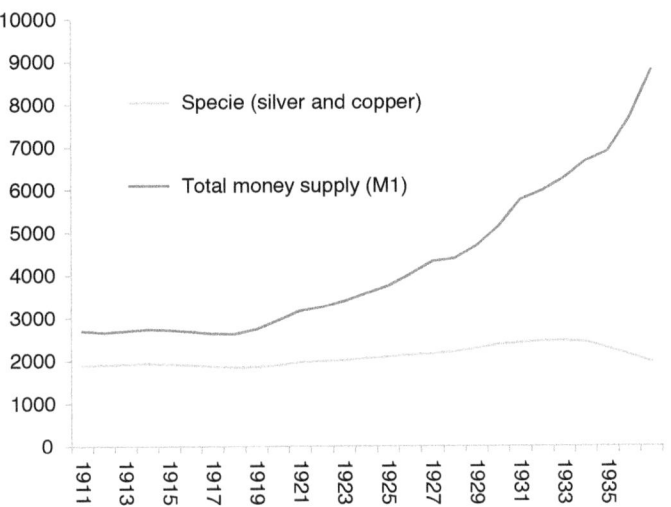

Figure 1.5 Metal currencies (silver and copper) and money supply in China, 1911–1936 (million yuan)
Source: D. Ma, "The Rise of a Financial Revolution in Republican China in 1900–1937: A Survey and New Interpretation," *Australian Economic History Review* 59.3 (2019), 242–62

Nonetheless, the fact that most of the transformations we have described so far were connected with China's modern and foreign sectors has led to the rise of what many called a dualistic economy characterized by a sharp divide between the small pockets of modern cities or treaty ports and the vast rural hinterland, a phenomenon famously described by R.H. Tawney as "small islands of privilege at the seaports and on the great rivers … a modern fringe … stitched along the hem of the ancient garment."[19] Rhodes Murphey went further, to describe the impact of treaty ports on China as being like "a fly (who) could ultimately irritate its host enough to provoke a violent counterreaction, but not to change the elephant's basic nature."[20]

However, as I will argue below, because of political-economy and institutional spillover, the impact of the external and modern sector cannot be captured by quantitative effects alone. To understand this peculiar pattern of economic change, namely an economic takeoff around the end of the nineteenth century after a hiatus of four decades after being opened to

---

2019), 242–62. See the chapter by Li and Yan in this volume for a longer period of money supply.
[19] R.H. Tawney, *Land and Labour in China* (London, Allen and Unwin, 1932), p. 13.
[20] Cited in E. Motono, *Conflict and Cooperation in Sino-British Business, 1860–1911: The Impact of the Pro-British Commercial Network in Shanghai* (New York, St. Martin's Press, 2000), p. 166.

Western imperialism, I turn to a review of historiography and build a new conceptual framework to link intellectual evolution with economic cycles.

Paradigms and Frameworks

Western Impact and Chinese Response: A Re-assessment of Historiography

Among the most important modernization paradigms that explains the modern Chinese development is the so-called Western-impact-and-Chinese-response framework championed by the sinologist John Fairbank. Writing in 1954, Teng and Fairbank remarked,

> Since China is the largest unitary mass of humanity, with the oldest continuous history, its overrunning by the West in the past century was bound to create a continuing and violent intellectual revolution ... Throughout this century of the "unequal treaties," the ancient society of China was brought into closer and closer contact with the then dominant and expanding society of Western Europe and America. This Western contact, lent impetus by the industrial revolution, had the most disastrous effect upon the old Chinese society. In every sphere of social activity the old order was challenged, attacked, undermined, or overwhelmed by a complex series of processes – political, economic, social, ideological, cultural – which were set in motion within China as a result of this penetration of an alien and more powerful society. The massive structure of traditional China was torn apart ... The old order was changed within the space of three generations.[21]

To some degree, for China, as for many other non-Western countries, modernization is nearly equivalent to westernization, and in this regard the Chinese record is a partial failure in comparison with Japan, the only non-Western country to succeed at that time. However, this Fairbankian impact-and-response framework itself was challenged by Fairbank's own student, Paul Cohen. In his widely acclaimed book *Discovering History in China*, Cohen argues that the impact-and-response framework may inadvertently lead to an amplification or simplification of the Western influence in China, neglecting the role of Chinese agency and China's internal dynamics. Indeed, as Cohen argued, much of the so-called Chinese response to or embrace of the West may well be superficial, and reflect more the domestic dynamics. There were also regional and temporal variations of the Western influence, which could

---

[21] Written by Ssu-yu Teng and John K. Fairbank, cited in P. Cohen, *Discovering History in China: American Historical Writing on the Recent Chinese Past* (New York, Columbia University Press, 1984), pp. 9–10.

be highly visible or even predominant among certain social groups and the treaty port zones, or more specifically in what Cohen referred as the Hong Kong–Shanghai corridor, but largely absent from the vast hinterland. In short, Cohen calls for the discipline of sinology to return to China and to viewing China on her own terms.[22]

Cohen's approach of "discovering history in China" offers a powerful corrective to what some would see as the Eurocentric tinge in the Fairbank framework and a possible inspiration to the recent California school's emphasis on China's own superior indigenous initial conditions in living standards, commercial and contractual traditions, and human capital before the mid-nineteenth-century onset of Western imperialism in China. Most interestingly, the lower Yangzi region, which the California school championed as having comparable living standards and developments to England or the Netherlands during the eighteenth century, also hosted the treaty port of Shanghai, which was to become the leading financial and industrial city of the nineteenth–twentieth centuries. In this regard, the Shanghai "economic miracle" of the twentieth century can be viewed as as much an import from the West as attributable to its own superior native roots.[23]

This overseas intellectual inward turn towards a China "on her own" forms an interesting contrast to Chinese historiography within mainland China, which at least from the 1950s had long built a dogmatic version of the Marxist narrative that posits a unilinear, universal – ironically highly Eurocentric – version of the law of societal evolution, progressing from the lowest stage of slavery in ancient times, to feudalism, capitalism, socialism, and communism. In this historiography, with the nineteenth- and twentieth-century Chinese economy and society characterized as semicolonial and semifeudal, the encroachment of Western imperialism – although a national humiliation – represents progress, or an assault on a backward "feudalist" Qing China by a more advanced and productive capitalist system.[24] In this regard, the paradigms of modernization and Marxism converge.

Very curiously, one offshoot of this mainland Marxist historiography is a lively debate on the so-called "Sprouts of Capitalism," inspired by Mao Zedong's claim in 1939: "The development of China's commodity economy within her feudal society has spawned the sprouts of capitalism. Even without the influence of Western capitalism, China will gradually develop into a capitalist

---

[22] Cohen, *Discovering History in China*.
[23] See Ma, "The Rise of a Financial Revolution," for the Shanghai miracle.
[24] Xu Dixin 许涤新 and Wu Chengming 吴承明, 中国资本主义发展史，第一卷 中国资本主义的萌芽 (A History of Capitalist Development in China, Vol. 1, Sprouts of Chinese Capitalism) (Beijing, Renmin chubanshe, 1993).

society on its own."²⁵ Generations of Chinese scholarship labored to discover those so-called traces or "sprouts" of capitalist production relations in traditional Chinese agriculture, handicrafts, and commerce. Despite coming from different or opposite ideological and institutional backgrounds, this emphasis on indigenous sources of Chinese development saw an interesting confluence with the California school. Alternatively put, just as China might have progressed "naturally" to capitalism without the onslaught of Western imperialism, the Industrial Revolution might have equally eluded the West or England had they not stumbled up coal deposits or the discovery of the New World.

The idea that eighteenth-century China might already have been on the cusp of, or a natural progression toward, modern capitalism or industrial revolution does not sit well with the lackluster Chinese aggregate economic record of the nineteenth to twentieth centuries, as partly revealed in Figure 1.1. While it is beyond the scope of this chapter to evaluate the entire literature on pre-nineteenth-century China's initial conditions, I argue that our interpretation of the patterns of economic change or the lack thereof in modern China needs to be placed in the context of a rapidly industrializing West and Japan and needs to be sought in the scarcity of intellectual resources rather than of natural resources. Below we turn to our framework on the importance of intellectual resources.

Ideology and Economic Changes: A New Framework

Although they were an ethnic minority from China's seminomadic northeastern frontier, the ascendancy of Manchu rule under the Qing actually marked the culmination of a millennia-long evolution and maturing of a highly centralized, unitary Chinese political regime governed by an absolutist emperor at the top of the power pyramid. Aided by a formal bureaucracy recruited through a highly structured nationwide (national–metropolitan–provincial) civil service examination rooted in Confucian classics, imperial China could implement a system of direct administrative rule (*junxian* 郡县) with mostly educated officials assigned to directly govern over a thousand counties nationwide over her vast territories on a two- to five-year rotating basis. Hence the combination of direct administrative rule with the legitimacy of imperial personnel appointment became a potent instrument of political control and rule that no or few other traditional regimes had mastered.²⁶ In this regard,

---

²⁵ Xu and Wu, 中国资本主义发展史, p. 4.
²⁶ Two caveats were important to this system. First, however much impersonality and neutrality characterized China's imperial regime, they were frequently compromised by the emperor's personal rule, and his personal entourage of eunuchs, consort, and other inner court staff. Second, the highly centralized personnel appointment coexisted with

Chinese rulers managed to break free from the constraints of feudal and local autonomous institutions that had characterized Europe, and possibly much of the rest of the world for that matter. Beyond the borders of empire, where they could not implement direct rule, the Qing, like previous dynasties, constructed a China-centered international order through the so-called tributary-states trade system. This system engulfed neighboring small states or territories in East and Southeast Asia as near protectorates that would pose no major military or political threat. Hence absolutism Chinese-style curtailed interstate competition and weakened independent vested interests, civil society, and autonomous political and social groups, all to serve the purpose of minimizing any potential threat to the throne from below.[27]

In this system, imperial or political legitimacy hinged on the state's capacity to suppress internal dissent and external challenge. Although military superiority or repressive capacity remained paramount to political legitimacy, they were insufficient by themselves and were only resorted to under extreme cases of threat. Hence crucial to this legitimacy is the development of a consistent ruling ideology or belief system that would be – in our case – Confucianism or neo-Confucianism that rationalized Chinese-style absolutist imperial rule. To establish the monopoly of this ideology over the interpretation of political and social events, systematic control and manipulation of information or alternative ideologies were essential to the system as characterized by the widespread incidence of literary inquisitions and intellectual persecutions.[28] Although this system was effective in perpetuating imperial rule and the status quo, it stifled the possibilities of endogenous development of ideological and institutional transformation from within and from below, leading to what Jin Guangtao and Liu Qingfeng termed the super-stable structure of the Chinese empire before the mid-nineteenth century.[29] Changes or even revolutions could happen in this system. But without corresponding intellectual development in new political and institutional ideologies, this just meant that violent revolution or dynastic overthrow (as happened

---

a very decentralized delegation of economic resources at the local level. See D. Ma, "Political Institutions and Long-Run Economic Trajectory: Some Lessons from Two Millennia of Chinese Civilization," in M. Aoki, T. Kuran, and G. Roland (eds.), *Institutions and Comparative Economic Development* (Basingstoke, Palgrave Macmillan, 2012), pp. 78–98.

[27] See Ma, "Political Institutions and Long-Run Economic Trajectory"; Ma and Rubin, "The Paradox of Power."

[28] Wang Fansen 权力, Jin Guantao 金观涛, and Liu Qingfeng 刘青峰, 兴盛与危机，论中国社会的超稳定结构 (The Cycle of Growth and Decline: On the Ultrastable Structure of Chinese Society) (Beijing, Falu chubanshe, 2011). Ge Zhaoguang, "十八世纪中国的盛世危机."

[29] Jin and Liu, 兴盛.

very often in Chinese history) were part of dynastic changes that harbored no fundamental institutional change.

The link between the stagnation of ideology and the limits to institutional change is echoed by another intellectual historian. Wang Fansen contends that the contours of China's traditional intellectual resource endowments define the boundaries of political and social changes and the horizon over which Chinese intellectuals could hover for solutions. The most outstanding examples are the late Ming–early Qing Confucian scholars such as Huang Zhongxi 黃宗羲 and Gu Yanwu 顾炎武, who were resurrected in the late nineteenth century as China's enlightened sages for their penetrating insights and attacks on the ills of the Ming's absolutist and repressive regime. However, when it came to proposals for reform, the seventeenth-century Huang and Gu could only conceive of a passionate call to return to Chinese antiquity and the classics. These attitudes are, as Wang argues, typical of Chinese elite intellectuals of the time in general.[30]

By the mid-nineteenth century, however, the resources of a vast and unexplored intellectual horizon had opened up, but they were from an alien Western tradition, written in Western languages that few, if any, Chinese intellectuals mastered or even heard of at the time. But it was not merely the scarcity of foreign-language talents or the suitability of Western ideology to Chinese reality that posed the problem. Rather it was something far more basic and fundamental: the willingness and capacity to recognize, first, cognitive dissonance within China's existing system, and, following that, the need for a paradigmatic change. As eloquently stated by historian of thought Ge Zhaoguang, it was precisely the glory of Qing's so-called triumphant eighteenth century that sowed the seeds of her failed response to Western challenge in the mid-nineteenth century. The Qing rulers' success in the control of a vastly expanding and diverse empire increasingly through repression of intellectual dissent and unity of ideology left her with a unique sense of grandeur and confidence that meant she could only treat the outside world with nothing but sheer ignorance and arrogance. In that regard, Qianlong's reply to Lord Macartney in 1792 is quite gracious by that account. This is echoed by Wang Fansen: until a major political and social-economic crisis could be keenly perceived, the Chinese intellectual soil – thoroughly soaked in the deep cultural self-confidence of the traditional literati – was simply not fertile enough for the transplant of new intellectual resources.[31]

---

[30] Wang, 戊戌. [31] Ge, 十八世纪; Wang, 戊戌.

In comparison, Tokugawa Japan's relatively decentralized feudal system, peripheral geopolitical position in the China-centered world order, and long tradition of absorbing foreign (mainly Chinese) culture and ideologies engendered a different cultural attitude towards Western impact and ideology during the mid-nineteenth century. For example, catalytic events such as the 1842 Sino-British Opium War did not propel immediate institutional or political changes in Qing China, but did send a powerful warning of the impending Western threat to the elites of neighboring Tokugawa Japan. Indeed, China's defeat in the 1840s and subsequent failures may have so alarmed Tokugawa Japan that in a couple of decades that it turned China from once being a model to be admired to being a lesson to be avoided.[32]

But effecting paradigmatic changes carries risks and uncertainties as they upset the traditional ideological equilibrium. They are more likely to take place through other successful examples or the arrival of new ideas or paradigms that provide a new and consistent framework to explain the cognitive dissonance. In this regard, China's defeat in the 1894–1896 Sino-Japanese War provoked greater reaction for Chinese reform than the initial Western imperialism. The Meiji success with Western models as a newly westernizing Asian nation in response to the same Western challenge that Qing China had faced now began to stir up cognitive dissonance in the giant neighboring Qing.

In this sense, institutional change requires time, experiments (or sometimes historical accidents), and a feedback loop between events, experiments, and ideas. We arrive at a model explaining why reform had the twists and turns with their particular temporal and regional patterns as described above in this chapter. Our framework is consistent with some of the theoretical and historical works of Timur Kuran, Joel Mokyr, Murat Iyigun, and Jared Rubin, which emphasizes the importance of ideas and the multiple equilibria of divergent paradigms, as well as cumulative progress, or sudden surges forward or sliding backward. Our emphasis on ideology and ideological change pushes us beyond just the paradigm of institutions as emphasized by the advocates of institutionalism.[33]

---

[32] Wang, 戊戌.
[33] For models of ideology and ideological change, see M. Iyigun and J. Rubin, "The Ideological Roots of Institutional Change" (2017 working paper). T. Kuran, *Private Truths, Public Lies: The Social Consequences of Preference Falsification* (Cambridge, MA, Harvard University Press, 1997). For the importance of ideas and feedback loops, see J. Mokyr, *The Gifts of Athena: Historical Origins of the Knowledge Economy* (Princeton, NJ, Princeton University Press, 2002). For an overwhelming emphasis on the role of institutions, see D. Acemoglu, S. Johnson, and J. Robinson, "Institutions as the Fundamental Cause of Long-Run Economic Growth," in P. Aghion and S. Durlauf (eds.), *Handbook of Economic Growth* (Amsterdam, Elsevier, 2005), pp. 385–472.

Western Impact and Chinese Response Again

Within our new framework, we return to the paradigm of Western impact and Chinese response with an important twist: the impact of the West is critically important, but only to a degree and in the manner in which the Chinese (or Japanese) manage to respond. We emphasize the role of Chinese agency in utilizing, adapting, and eventually redesigning new rules and institutions to propel economic change.

In the nineteenth and twentieth centuries, Western imperialism did not fully subjugate China, but manifested itself through the acquisition of trading rights, leased territories, and treaty ports, as well as extraterritoriality and spheres of interest. In the early twentieth century, when central control was weakened, Western treaty ports expanded rapidly at the expense of Chinese sovereignty. The expansion of these privileges and extraterritorialities in an era of political chaos and national disintegration turned out to be a blessing in disguise for two reasons.

First, some of these "privileges" happened to coincide with necessary conditions for growth, namely the maintenance of peace and public order, the security of property rights and contract enforcement, freedom from arbitrary taxation or official exaction, and the right to transparent rules and predictable jurisprudence. Second and more importantly, as shown later, foreign "privileges" in the treaty ports were often taken advantage of by Chinese businesses and residents.

Here, we examine the evolution of two key consequences of Western intervention. First is Shanghai, China's largest treaty port, particularly its International Settlement, which resulted from a merger of all Western (and later Japanese but excepting the French) concessions operating with a governance structure akin to a European type of self-governing incorporated urban community. Shanghai's foreign residents organized a Municipal Council with members elected by an association of taxpaying Western, later Japanese and eventually (in 1928) Chinese, residents. The council operated according to the rule of law vested in its own mini-constitution, levying taxes and fees; running its own prison, police, and volunteer army; and providing public goods such as roads, utilities, and port facilities. The power and territory of the International Settlement greatly expanded in the wake of the 1911 Qing collapse, with full territorial jurisdiction over all its residents, including the Chinese.[34]

The second key institution – China Maritime Customs – had similar origins and a similar trajectory. The low fixed tariffs imposed by Western powers were initially collected by Chinese customs officials, but increasingly overseen by foreign consuls who set up the China Maritime Customs in Shanghai in 1854. Although nominally an imperial Chinese organization, the Customs gained autonomy with Britons dominating its senior staff. Its staff gradually came to include large numbers of Westerners and later Japanese, with the promotion of Chinese nationals into senior positions only starting in 1929.[35] With over 20,000 staff in forty main customs houses across China, the Customs rapidly emerged as China's most stable and efficient centralized hierarchic bureaucracy even as China herself descended into political disintegration. Following the Qing collapse in 1911, the Maritime Customs effectively took over the collection of the Customs charges and the distribution of the net revenue.

The insertion of these colonial institutions unintentionally ruptured China's long-standing imperial monopoly of power. The resulting gaps in imperial control created room for newly emergent Chinese business interests, many with deep links to foreign businesses, to create new networks of power and wealth that intensified growing pressure for formal political and institutional changes, especially following China's defeat in the 1894–1896 Sino-Japanese War. However, the institutional changes arising from Western influence could only have nationwide effects after they had triggered intellectual and political responses from Chinese elites, which is where we turn to now.

Liang Qichao 梁启超, China's foremost intellectual and reformer of the era, succinctly summarized the Chinese response. Writing in 1923, Liang surmised that changes or reforms would have never got off the ground until the Chinese were willing to recognize and acknowledge that there were problems to begin with. This partly began during the period from 1842 to 1894 when the Qing saw firsthand the power of Western military equipment used to suppress the Taiping Rebellion (1851–1864). This opened the door to the introduction of Western (particularly military) technology and machines, or, in Liang's phrase, material things (*qiwu* 器物).

---

[34] See Ma, "Economic Growth"; Ma, "The Rise of a Financial Revolution"; I. Jackson, *Shaping Modern Shanghai: Colonialism in China's Global City* (Cambridge, Cambridge University Press, 2018).

[35] H. van der Ven, *Breaking with the Past: The Maritime Customs Service and the Global Origins of Modernity in China* (New York, Columbia University Press, 2014).

China's 1894–1896 naval defeat by Japan shattered her confidence in her own systems, terminated this initial stage, and inaugurated a second stage of introducing new "institutions" – (*zhidu* 制度). This process, which continued for two decades until roughly 1917–1918, brought the comprehensive importation of Western-style government and law, along with modern corporate enterprises and financial institutions. The third stage followed the recognition that institutional transfers could not succeed without understanding and absorbing their underlying cultural and ideological foundations as reform demands changes in both spirit and form. The result was the New Culture movement, which brought the massive introduction of Western culture and ideology (*wenhua* 文化), even leading to the radical abrogation of Confucian ideology.[36]

Building on the insights of Liang, Yang Nianqun added a geographic dimension to Liang's temporal stages of reform, matching each of these three reform sequences with distinctive regional political elites and with Ming–Qing schools of Confucianism, centered in the provinces of Hunan, Guangdong, and Jiangsu–Zhejiang, corresponding to China's middle Yangzi, Lingnan, and lower Yangzi macro-regions respectively.[37] Yang's regional study drew inspiration from Paul Cohen's early work on late Qing reform, which emphasized the regional dimension of Western influence and highlighted the major cultural divide separating China's littoral and hinterland. More importantly, both Liang and Yang point to China's own intellectual endeavor in absorbing Western impact, as Cohen would put it, on her own terms. These intellectual and ideological responses by the intellectual and political elites paralleled practical efforts on the part of new economic actors and networks who took advantage of Western privileges to push the boundaries beyond the traditional structure.

Patterns of Economic Change: From Machines to Institutions to Ideology

The Age of "Machines"

The mid-nineteenth century, marked by the encroachment of Western imperialism on Chinese shores, started off disastrously for the Qing dynasty.

---

[36] Liang Qichao 梁启超, "五十年中国进化概论" (A Summary of Fifty Years of Chinese Evolution), in 饮冰室文集点校第五集 (Selected Articles of the Yinbinshe Collection, Vol. 5) (Kunming, Yunnan Jiaoyu chubanshe), pp. 3247–52.

[37] Yang Nianqun 杨念群, 儒学地域化的近代形态：三大知识群体互动的比较研究 (The Modern Form of Regional Schools of Confucius: A Comparative Research into the Interaction of Three Intellectual Groups) (Beijing, Sanlian chubanshe, 1997).

Qing's defeats in the Opium War (1842) and other military battles, and even the devastating Taiping Rebellion, which saw a calamitous cumulative loss of 60 million to 80 million lives, did not shake the elites' faith in traditional ideology and institutions.[38] Political elites from China's agrarian mid-Yangzi heartland of Hunan and Anhui, such as Zeng Guofan 曾国藩 and Li Hongzhang 李鸿章, rose to national prominence following their success in mobilizing fiscal and military resources from their home provinces to eventually suppress the Taipings. Closely aligned with the official ruling ideology, the Tongzhi Restoration (1861–1875) – which Mary Wright famously called the last stand of Chinese conservatism – engineered a remarkable economic recovery through the revitalization of traditional institutions: the reinstatement of Confucian orthodoxy, the restoration of the national civil service examination (largely interrupted during the Taiping Rebellion), and temporary exemption from land taxes to lure cultivators to resettle war-torn agricultural regions.[39]

As a natural extension of the Tongzhi Restoration, the Self-Strengthening movement (1860–1894) initiated programs that aimed to expand Chinese military strength by developing a small number of Western-style, capital-intensive enterprises financed or sponsored by the state and directed by prestigious officials or merchants with official connections. Although these enterprises, which included arsenals, factories, and shipyards, were fraught with inefficiency and corruption, they did record modest achievements. (See the chapter by Chi-kong Lai in this volume.)

Nonetheless, the overall ideological orientation during this period remained backward-looking. In contrast to the concurrent Meiji reform in Japan, there were no reforms that touched the fundamentals of the traditional regime: there was no introduction of a modern constitution or commercial law and no reform in the currency system, modern banks and modern infrastructure such as railroads were expressly prohibited, and steamships were limited to the Yangzi and other major rivers. Nonetheless, the ground on which the traditional structure had rested were shifting with the insertion of Western imperialism.

Foreign Trade in the Age of Machines

Although the treaty port system accelerated the arrival of new technologies and institutions, industrialization lagged far behind the opportunities opened

---

[38] For the controversies among Qing officials' interpretation of the Opium War defeat, see Mao Haijian 茂海建, 天朝的崩溃鸦片战争再研究 (The Fall of the Celestial Empire: A Re-examination of the Opium War) (Beijing, Sanlian shudian, 2013).

[39] M. Wright, *The Last Stand of Chinese Conservatism: The T'ung-Chih Restoration, 1862–1874* (Stanford, CA, Stanford University Press, 1962).

up by the inflow of trade and technology. Attempts by Chinese and European entrepreneurs to take advantage of opportunities linked to new technologies and trade arrangements reveal the presence of powerful obstacles to innovation within China's late Qing economy. These are most clearly visible in the obstacles confronting private efforts to introduce new technologies and business structures.[40]

These obstacles existed precisely because the legality of traditional Chinese commercial and business activities rested on patronage rather than universal property rights. Often commercial guilds and organizations acquired monopoly privileges in exchange for paying a fixed tax quota to the government, and hence some form of shelter from arbitrary exactions. This institutional arrangement, according to Eiichi Motono, formed the structural foundation of traditional Chinese merchant groups and networks under official patronage.[41]

However, the Western presence established a new source of power and authority in China. The "unequal treaties" granted every foreigner the right to trade and own property in the treaty ports, most importantly subject to Western legal systems. The imposition of "free trade" and extraterritorial privileges turned out to have unintended consequences. The treaty port system imposed by Western "free-trade" imperialism set Chinese trade tariffs at a modest 3 or 5 percent during this period. To shelter their trade from the arbitrary native transit taxes known as lijin 釐金, the Westerners insisted on a flat transit tax when their goods moved through China's interior. These transit levies were assessed and, after 1911, collected by the foreign-controlled China Maritime Customs.[42]

Chinese merchants soon found opportunities to benefit from these "Western" privileges through false registration of their produce as destined for export (rather than domestic use), outfitting their ships (or junks) with Western flags, and investing their capital in foreign-owned businesses or simply registering their businesses as owned by foreign nominees.[43] More critically, what Motono referred to as English-speaking Chinese merchants began to develop their own commercial networks outside the traditional commercial groups, who had relied on the payment of native transit taxes as

---

[40] See Brandt, Ma, and Rawski, "From Divergence to Convergence."
[41] Motono, *Conflict and Cooperation*. Also see the chapter by Chi-kong Lai in this volume.
[42] See the chapter by Kaske and Lin in this volume.
[43] See Motono, *Conflict and Cooperation*.

a means to acquire monopoly privileges. Motono identified the late 1880s – a timing that corresponds well with the first surge of Chinese firms, as revealed in Figure 1.2 – as the key turning point when traditional Chinese commercial organization began to crumble.[44] Motono argues convincingly that these merchant–official nexuses forged through tax-farming arrangements formed the structural foundation of traditional Chinese merchant groups and networks. The Western presence, although small in relation to China's national economy, constituted a new source of power and authority in China that drew away Chinese merchants towards new commercial groups formed outside the tax-farming-based system. This eroded the imperial system's long-standing monopoly over political power, just like "a great dike may be breached by tiny termites."[45] He sees the transit pass system as a vehicle for eroding the authority of mercantile guilds, fracturing traditional group solidarity among members of particular trades, and enhancing the property rights and security available to Chinese businesses.

By co-operating with, utilizing, or embracing Western extraterritorial privileges, mostly in the treaty ports, these forces formed pressure points that eroded the power base of traditional vested interests. Or, as more effectively put by Motono, it was the Chinese themselves who promoted a Western impact on China.[46] But being confined largely within the treaty port zones and the Western sphere of influence, this "Western impact" generated a "dual-track" system which often placed Chinese business interests in an unfavorable position. They caused backlashes and pushbacks and stirred up calls for formal political and institutional changes within China to level the playing field.

These trickles and leakages turned into torrents following China's defeat in the Sino-Japanese War of 1894–1895 and the signing of the Treaty of Shimonoseki, which granted foreigners the right to establish factories in the treaty ports. Previously, foreigners only had the "privileges" to engage in trade and finance, but not manufacture. This new arrangement imposed by the Treaty of Shimonoseki opened the floodgates of foreign direct investment and pushed the Qing to accept and grant much broader property rights and protection to all Chinese, not just in business but also in manufacturing. This forms the essence of the 1903–1911 late Qing legal reform in commercial law and the promotion of chambers of commerce.

---

[44] See Motono, *Conflict and Cooperation*, pp. 166–70.
[45] See Motono, *Conflict and Cooperation*, p. 169.
[46] Motono, *Conflict and Cooperation*, p. 167.

The Age of Institutions and China's Turning Point

China's defeat in the Sino-Japanese War of 1894–1896 by Japan, a nation long regarded as a student rather than an equal, inflicted a profound mental shock on Chinese elites and the public at large. It marked the end of the Self-Strengthening movement and led to a sudden surge of interest in the Japanese experience. Huang Zunxian 黄遵宪, the Qing ambassador to and keen observer of Meiji Japan, wrote a landmark study of Japan's transformation in 1887. Despite being delivered to Zeng Guofan and Li Hongzhong and circulated privately, Huang's work drew little attention even when it was printed in 1895. But China's stunning defeat in 1896 turned this book into an instant best seller, as lamented by one gentry that had we all paid attention to Huang's book earlier, China would have been spared over 200 million silver taels of war reparations – something equivalent to five times the Qing state's annual peacetime revenue – extracted by Japan following her 1896 military victory.[47]

Intellectual historian Ge Zhaoguang marks 1896 as China's key intellectual turning point. He shows that during the 300 years before 1894, Japan translated 129 Chinese works while the Chinese translation of Japanese works amounted to a mere twelve. This trend reversed in the decade after 1896 with 958 Chinese translations of Japanese works but only sixteen translations in the other linguistic direction.[48] Indeed, when Japan became the first Asian society to translate Western materials, the shared vocabulary of Chinese characters quickly installed Japan as the natural intermediary in transmitting Western culture to China, especially because of the inflow of massive numbers of Chinese students and the outflow of Japanese advisers and teachers to China.[49]

China's naval defeat directly triggered the Hundred Days reform in 1898 backed by the young Guangxu Emperor (r. 1875–1908). Although centered in Hunan – the heartland of Self-Strengthening bureaucrats – the reform's intellectual leaders came from Guangdong-based elites, such as Huang Zungxian, Kang Youwei 康有为, and Liang Qichao, who had prior exposure to Western influence. Although the reform was quickly crushed by conservatives surrounding the emperor's aunt, Dowager Empress Cixi, the agenda of the failed Hundred Days reform formed the core of the Qing constitutional movement of 1903–1911, modeled directly on Japan's Meiji reforms.

[47] Jin and Liu, 开放中的变迁, p. 66. [48] Ge, 中国思想史, p. 478.
[49] M. Jansen, "Japan and the Chinese Revolution of 1911," in J.K. Fairbank and K.C. Liu (eds.), *The Cambridge History of China*, vol. 11, *Late Ch'ing, 1800–1911*, part 2 (Cambridge, Cambridge University Press, 1980). Wang, 戊戌.

Beyond military victories, Meiji Japan offered a remarkable example of a nation with similar (or humbler) cultural heritage which had, however, managed to implement a comprehensive and thorough reform agenda when confronted with a common Western threat. Through the successful adoption of the gold standard in 1897 and the recovery of extraterritoriality in 1899, Japan's westernizing reform introduced Western institutions but actually kept Western capital and influence at bay.[50]

China's new reform effort, heavily influenced by Meiji, was comprehensive and ambitious. It aimed to prepare China for a constitutional monarchy by drafting a formal constitution that would establish national, provincial, and local parliaments. Military modernization was high on the reform agenda. Administrative reforms sought to modernize public finance and adopt a national budget. The reform initiative gave birth to new Ministries of Education, Trade, and Agriculture and encouraged the founding of local chambers of commerce. Policy initiatives aimed at currency reform, the establishment of modern banks, and the expansion of railroads and other public infrastructure. The abolition of the millennia-old civil service examination in 1905 opened the door to a modern school system, giving birth to what are today China's best-known universities.

Although the resulting political decentralization may have inadvertently hastened the Qing collapse, the rise of the new republic opened the door to a massive Chinese experimentation with new ideologies and institutions from the West. This indeed began China's age of modernity, a genuine experiment with constitutionalism, the rise of regional cosmopolitanism, and the introduction of modern company law and of such new business techniques as double-entry bookkeeping.[51]

Growing local autonomy fostered by political decentralization encouraged the growth and maturing of civil society and, more importantly, boosted political and ideological competition across different provinces and towns as well as treaty ports. The comprehensive data presented in Chapter 11 of this volume by James Kai-sing Kung show the turn-of-the-century breakpoint in education, missionaries, and numbers of treaty ports, which partly became the institutional foundation underpinning the rise of modern industry, banking, public finance, and monetary regime as discussed above in this chapter.

---

[50] Y. Yoda, *The Foundations of Japan's Modernization: A Comparison with China's Path towards Modernization* (trans. Kurt W. Radtke) (Leiden, Brill, 1996).
[51] F. Dikötter, *The Age of Openness: China before Mao* (Hong Kong, Hong Kong University Press, 2010).

The Rise of Financial Revolution in the Age of Institutions

The temporal retreat of central imperial power opened new possibilities for the rise of a quasi-political structure that rested on the institutional nexus of Western treaty ports (most notably Shanghai) and the Maritime Customs service.[52] Both these institutions were intimately connected with Western institutions or Western imperialism in China, which initially only served to protect the limited Western or foreign business interests in the context of extraterritorial privileges. However, in the wake of 1903 constitutional reform and the Qing's collapse in 1911, this mechanism began to be transferred to China domestically.

The financial revolution that emerged during the politically chaotic 1910s and 1920s illustrates the interplay between Western impact and Chinese response. Shanghai's free-trade extraterritorial status had long attracted what later became some of the world's premier Western banking institutions, such as the Hong Kong and Shanghai Banking Corporation (HSBC) and Chartered Bank. But modern Chinese banks, which only started near the end of the nineteenth century, also found their homes there.[53] Even traditional family-owned native banks increasingly chose to locate inside the Western-controlled Settlement. The relocation of the Shanghai Native Bankers' Association from the Chinese part of the city to within the Settlement in 1917 and the founding of an association of modern Chinese banks in 1918 marked the rise of Shanghai's Chinese banking community as the leading force in China's macro-economic, monetary, and financial regulation within a largely self-regulated free banking framework.

Initially, when the Chinese government borrowed from the foreign market, its obligation to repay could be partly enforced through the coercive power of Western gunboats and through the important intermediary institution of the China Maritime Customs, as the agency was relatively insulated from the threat of the Chinese imperial government. When, in 1911, the Maritime Customs directly took over the collection and remittance of the Customs revenue, it opened an account with HSBC, which eventually became the custodian bank of that portion of Customs revenue pledged as security for the service of the government's foreign debt.[54]

---

[52] Ma, "The Rise of a Financial Revolution."
[53] In particular, the jurisdictional autonomy of the Settlement which sheltered the Bank of China's Shanghai branch from the Beijing government's ruinous fiscal demand in 1916 highlights the value of the independence of the Settlement. See the chapter by Li and Yan in this volume.
[54] Ma, "The Rise of a Financial Revolution."

Ideology and the Contours of Economic Change

This institutional mechanism for external borrowing was soon transferred to become the cornerstone for a domestic market for Chinese government bonds through the intermediary of large Chinese public banks. China's domestic public debt originated in 1914 with the new Republican government in Beijing setting up an independent committee composed of Chinese and Western bankers and Maritime Customs officials. This mechanism ensured that tax revenue earmarked for debt repayment was remitted to a special revenue account set up in the Western banks and later in Chinese banks headquartered in Shanghai's International Settlement. Maritime Customs revenue formed the most secure form of central revenue for a weakened Beijing government and therefore the most reliable collateral for servicing the government's foreign debt. With government bonds serving as part of reserves for banknotes, modern banks injected new sources of money into the macro-economy. The new viability of domestic public debt spawned a vibrant secondary market in the 1920s and 1930s.

This key nexus offered an unusual but credible commitment for the security of bondholders' property rights and the repayment of government obligations, which laid the institutional foundation for a financial revolution. In a sharp departure from the traditional political regime that left credibility at the mercy or benevolence of a strong and stable state, management of the state's obligations to bondholders now rested with an institutional mechanism that had grown autonomous from the center. It was that particular mechanism that allowed Chinese bankers and bondholders to place some constraint on the power of the government with regard to public finance, and by doing so it enabled the Chinese government to tap into the private wealth of Chinese citizens for borrowing without coercion.

The Age of Culture and China's Fateful Ideological Turn

In 1923, barely four years after the May 4th mass movement in 1919 kicked off China's new age of cultural movement, Liang Qichao wrote with exuberance that Chinese understanding of Western ideology and culture had gradually but irreversibly progressed since the days of Self-Strengthening. It was only in 1876 that a remark by Guo Songtao 郭嵩焘, China's ambassador to Britain, that the new Western "barbarians" confronting China then – unlike previous Asian threats – also had 2,000 years of civilization, caused a huge uproar and was roundly condemned as near blasphemy. Under Self-Strengthening, despite the recognition of Western military and technological superiority, Western knowledge came to China only in drips through a limited number of indirect translations of Western works commissioned at various governmental arsenals.

This changed rapidly following China's military loss to Japan. Liang quipped that the first generation of advocates of Western learning were great classic Confucian scholars – himself included – who knew nothing of any Western languages. The same was true of the next generation of advocates of Western learning, most of whom were Chinese students returned from study in Japan. By the 1920s, however, a third generation of young scholars, many returning from studies in Europe and North America, finally took over the baton of Western learning and in certain cases carried it to the extreme, such that, as Liang claimed, Karl Marx was now vying for equal status with Confucius.

Liang's exuberant banter about China's intellectual transformation could not conceal the complex and wrenching emotions incurred in the struggle to introduce an alien culture and ideology to China as well as Japan. Indeed, in both countries the first step to legitimizing the pursuit of Western learning started with a step backward: going back to the Chinese classics.

Meiji Japan, for example, called upon the orthodox Zhuxi 朱熹 neo-Confucian principles to legitimize the ouster of the Tokugawa shogunate and the reinstatement of the Meiji imperium under a centralized bureaucratic system. In similar fashion, the rediscovery of China's long-marginalized anti-mainstream Wang Yangming 王阳明 school of Ming dynasty Confucianism inspired generations of revolutionaries in Meiji Japan, China, and East Asia in general. The most striking or audacious was Kang Youwei's so-called rediscovery and restoration of "authentic" Confucian classics, which he claimed had been distorted and contaminated during the Han dynasty. These "genuine" – most likely fictitious – classics, Kang claimed, already contained the seeds of ideas that would support and legitimize the Chinese reform agenda in the 1890s.[55]

But by the 1920s, China's intellectual mainstream had moved far beyond this phase of atavistic nostalgia. Indeed, after the 1911 Qing collapse, the new Republican era saw no equivalent of the Ming loyalists like Gu Yanwu and Huang Zhongxi who had refused to serve the new Qing ruler despite their unrelenting assault on the ills of Ming absolutism. Similarly, there were few who retained the faith in Qing orthodoxy that leaders like Zeng Guofan and Li Hongzhang once had just a few decades earlier. China's Republican era

---

[55] Yan Shaodang 严绍璗, 日本中国学史 (Sinology in Japan) (Beijing, Xueshu chubanshe, 2009), pp. 98–134.

ushered in a new generation that embraced Western learning and ideology with few nostalgic backward glances. But China's intellectual turn toward the West soon developed in unexpected directions.

Political reality following the Qing's collapse in 1911 revealed harsh and dark sides marked by the rise of warlordism, factionalism, civil and military strife, and fiscal bankruptcy, leading to a rising sense of national disintegration and international humiliation. As initial euphoria turned to despair, the Beijing government largely abandoned parliamentary experiments in 1923 soon after Liang enthusiastically wrote about the extent and durability of cultural change. Ravaged by World War I, Western imperialism and liberal ideology went into retreat and the world saw a turn from "Woodrow Wilson towards Vladimir Lenin."[56] Liang's suggestion that Marx might rival the standing of Confucius in the eyes of Chinese elites suddenly acquired ominous weight as the rise of a domestic Communist movement and the Guomindang's engagement first with the Soviet Union and then with Nazi Germany marked an increasing turn toward authoritarianism.

The founding of a national capital in Nanjing returned China's political center to the heart of its wealthiest region of the lower Yangzi, which had long been distrusted by the Qing court and suspected of anti-Manchu sentiments. But by the 1920s, the lower Yangzi had developed new elites associated with the Shanghai-based treaty port system, symbolized by the powerful Song family, which hailed originally from Guangdong but were educated in Christian mission schools and American colleges. Another was the Nationalist leader Chiang Kai-shek, who married one of the glamorous Song sisters. Chiang, a Ningpo native with strong connections to Shanghai's financial elites and underworld leaders, graduated from a military academy in Japan, where he developed a lifelong admiration for Wang Yangming. Although Chiang promoted modern innovations, he was raised on the traditional Confucian classics and became a faithful admirer of Zeng Guofan, the Taiping nemesis and upright architect of the Self-Strengthening movement. Under Chiang, the Nanjing regime was increasingly authoritarian but charged with a full ten-year national modernization agenda until it was interrupted by the 1937 Japanese invasion.

---

[56] Luo Zhitian 罗志田, "'六个月乐观'的幻灭：五四前夕士人心态与政治" (The Disillusion of "Six Months of Optimism": The Mood and Politics of Intellectuals on the Eve of the May Fourth Movement), 历史研究 (Historical Research) 4 (2006), 105–91.

The End of the Financial Revolution or Coming Full Circle?

The unexpected cultural turn may have turned China's modernization path to her own authoritarian or absolutist roots. The paradox of this combination came into full view in the continuing phase of financial revolution in the Nanjing era. In its earlier days, the newly established Nanjing-based Nationalist government in 1927, especially under the new pro-business finance minister Song Ziwen 宋子文 – the American-educated brother of the powerful Song sisters – respected the institutional mechanism for public debt set up under the previous Beiyang regime. It succeeded in taking over the core institutional element of financial revolution through the establishment of an independent Sinking Fund Commission headed by representatives of the Shanghai banking community and government officials. They constituted a powerful independent check on the government's promise to repay.

The domestic debt issued in 1927–1931 nearly doubled the total for the entire Beiyang era from 1912 to 1926. The ratio of domestic to foreign public debt, which had stood at one to seven during the Beiyang era, rose sharply to six to four during the decade following the 1927 creation of the Nanjing government. In this way, the nascent Nanjing government created favorable conditions for diffusing the fruits of financial revolution in the form of new monetary and financial institutions and instruments unimaginable within the treaty port framework. An important consequence of the banks' increased holding of securitized government bonds was the rapid increase in the banks' capacity to expand their issue of bank notes as China's banking regulations allowed modern banks to use securities – mostly government bonds – to serve as 40 percent of the reserves needed to issue notes. This serves as the critical anchor for China's financial revolution as it expanded the balance sheet of private banks and enhanced the rise of credible banknote issues, as illustrated in Figure 1.5.[57]

However, once the Nanjing regime consolidated its power, its leaders moved to re-establish a more authoritarian system that would rein in the treaty port autonomy, particularly in Shanghai, China's commercial, financial, and industrial capital. The nationalization of major Chinese banks and the establishment of a fiat currency in 1935 and 1936 respectively – without, however, the simultaneous establishment of an internal form of checks and balances and along with the waning of Western imperialism and its

---

[57] See Ma, "The Rise of a Financial Revolution"; also see the chapter by Li and Yan in this volume.

associated fiscal–financial nexus – set the stage for the rise of hyperinflation in the 1940s.[58] The resurgence of a fiat-money-based hyperinflation in the 1940s marked another coming full circle to the eras of China's historical hyperinflation in the Song and Yuan dynasties whose issuance of paper money exploded under wartime pressures.

Japan's full-scale invasion in 1937 and China's drive for resource mobilization pushed toward the rise of a wartime command economy.[59] The ascendancy of Communist rule and ideology followed decades of gradual but increasing radicalization of the modernization ideology. When the Communists took power, they were armed with another ideology borrowed from the Soviet Union: Marxism or Communism then established as the new ruling orthodoxy grafted onto China's authoritarian or totalitarian roots.[60] Indeed, China's new Communist leader, Mao Zedong, who spent his formative years in his revolution-enlightened native Hunan, became a modernizer, but remained a great admirer of China's historic founders of often brutal absolutist dynasties, Qin Shihuang 秦始皇 and Zhu Yuanzhang 朱元璋. Mao drew as much inspiration from Chinese classics as from Marxist theory. Most ironically, just as Confucianism was extended or rediscovered to legitimize westernization and modernization in the early twentieth century, so Communism, the most radical ideological import from the West, was now deployed to legitimize a newly invigorated and technologically enhanced version of Chinese absolutism.

Conclusion

This chapter has built explicit links between intellectual and ideological cycles and phases of economic change in China. By incorporating ideology into the narrative of modern China's economic history, it has emphasized the importance of the Western impact within a framework that also assigns a central role to the Chinese response to and adaptation of Western ideology and practice. This new narrative adds missing elements to the Great Divergence debate, which has considered initial conditions mainly in the form of institutional structures and natural-resource endowments. By highlighting the importance of intellectual resources, this approach exposes the limitations of the Great Divergence thesis, which has tended to project late development

---

[58] See Ma, "The Rise of a Financial Revolution"; also see the chapters by Li and Yan and by Kaske and Lin in this volume.
[59] See the chapter by Bian in this volume.   [60] See the chapter by Xu in this volume.

experience onto historical initial conditions or institutions and to ignore the dependence or reliance of East Asian industrialization on borrowed institutions and ideology. It is the greatest irony that both the Marxist discussion of the sprouts of capitalism and the Great Divergence inquiry into why China failed to generate an early industrial revolution are founded on the implicit assumption of a unilinear or Eurocentric version of historical evolution or inevitability (of industrial revolution).

The problem of ideas looms particularly large in China's historical context of absolutist institutions. In the absence or weakness of a domestic "voice," the "exit" option often remained the sole constraint to the centralized monopoly of power in imperial China. In this regard, leakages in the form of physical capital or intellectual resources from this monopoly rule carried particular weight and significance. Utilization and absorption of these leakages proceeded on two levels – in a bottom-up process whereby rational economic agents took advantage of Western extraterritorial privileges and among upper-echelon political and intellectual elites who eventually modified ideology to legitimatize modernization policy at the national and political level. It was only when these two levels connected or met that China saw the largest of transformations.

This process worked not only in the nineteenth and twentieth centuries, but also in the post-1978 reform era. There, ideology in the top echelon and experiments at the bottom often interacted with tension.[61] Ultimately, it was a rapid convergence of ideology to meet the global standards and rules after China joined the WTO in 2001 that saw China's most phenomenal transformation. The regime at the center was more willing to compromise rather than exercise arbitrary and unchecked power. However, three decades of unprecedented growth led to a resurgence in confidence, in particular in China's own ideology and historical legacy. But if such resurging confidence, as the eighteenth-century Qing once had, leads to a revival of Qing-style closure to information flow and restriction of independent thinking, will all the reforms and revolutions be another repeat of history? Let us hope not.

Further Reading

Brandt, L., D. Ma, and T. Rawski, "From Divergence to Convergence: Re-evaluating the History behind China's Economic Boom," *Journal of Economic Literature* 52.1 (2014), 45–123.

Cohen, P., *Discovering History in China: American Historical Writing on the Recent Chinese Past* (New York, Columbia University Press, 1984).

---

[61] See the chapters by Naughton and by Brandt and Rawski in this volume for the reform period.

Fukao, K., D. Ma, and T. Yuan, "Real GDP in Pre-war East Asia: A 1934–36 Benchmark Purchasing Power Parity Comparison with the U.S.," *Review of Income and Wealth* 53.3 (2007), 503–37.

Ge Zhaoguang 葛兆光中国思想史第二卷七世纪至十九世纪中国的知识，思想与信仰 (History of Chinese Thought, Vol. 3, Chinese Knowledge, Thought, and Beliefs between the Seventh and Nineteenth Centuries) (Shanghai, Fudan daxue chubanshe, 2001).

Ge Zhaoguang "葛兆光十八世纪中国的盛世危机" (Crisis in China's Glorious Eighteenth Century), Feb. 19, 2019, www.ftchinese.com/author/%E8%91%9B%E5%85%86%E5%85%89.

Jin Guantao 金观涛, and Liu Qingfeng 刘青峰, 兴盛与危机，论中国社会的超稳定结构 (The Cycle of Growth and Decline: On the Ultrastable Structure of Chinese Society) (Beijing, Falu chubanshe, 2011).

Jin Guantao 金观涛 and Liu Qingfeng 刘青峰, 开放中的变迁，再论中国社会超稳定结构 (The Transformation of Chinese Society (1840–1956): The Fate of Its Ultrastable Structure in Modern Times) (Beijing, Falu chubanshe, 2011).

Liang Qichao 梁启超, "梁启超五十年中国进化概论" (A Summary of Fifty Years of Chinese Evolution), in 饮冰室文集点校第五集 (Selected Articles of the Yinbinshe Collection, Vol. 5) (Kunming, Yunnan Jiaoyu chubanshe, 1923), pp. 3247–52.

Ma, D., "Economic Growth in the Lower Yangzi Region of China in 1911–1937: A Quantitative and Historical Perspective," *Journal of Economic History*, 68.2 (2008), 385–92.

Ma, D., "The Rise of a Financial Revolution in Republican China in 1900–1937: A Survey and New Interpretation," *Australian Economic History Review* 59.3 (2019), 242–62.

Ma, D., and J. Rubin, "The Paradox of Power: Principal–Agent Problems and Administrative Capacity in Imperial China (and Other Absolutist Regimes)," *Journal of Comparative Economics* 47.2 (2019), 277–94.

Maddison, A., *Chinese Economic Performance in the Long Run*, 2nd ed., rev. and updated (Paris, Development Centre of the Organisation for Economic Co-operation and Development, 2007).

Mokyr, J., *The Gifts of Athena: Historical Origins of the Knowledge Economy* (Princeton, NJ: Princeton University Press, 2002).

Motono, E., *Conflict and Cooperation in Sino-British Business, 1860–1911: The Impact of the Pro-British Commercial Network in Shanghai* (New York, St. Martin's Press, 2000).

Rawski, T.G., *Economic Growth in Prewar China* (Berkeley, University of California Press, 1989).

Xu, Dixin 许涤新 and Wu Chengming 吴承明,中国资本主义发展史，第一卷 中国资本主义的萌芽 (A History of Capitalist Development in China, Vol. 1, Sprouts of Chinese Capitalism) (Beijing, Renmin chubanshe, 1993).

Wang Fansen 王汎森, "戊戌前后思想资源的变化：以日本因素为例" (Changes in Intellectual Resources before and after the Hundred Days Reform), 二十一世纪 (Twenty-First Century) 45 (February 1998), 47–54.

Wang Fansen 王汎森, 权力的毛细血管作用，清代的思想、学术与心态 (The Penetrating Role of Power, Ideas, Academics, and Moods in Qing) (Beijing, Beijing daxue chubanshe, 2015).

Yan Shaodang 严绍璗, 日本中国学史 (Sinology in Japan) (Beijing, Xueshu chubanshe, 2009).

2

Economic Transition in the Nineteenth Century

WILLIAM T. ROWE

The Great Qing Empire (1644–1912) was the most populous political entity that had yet existed on the landmass that we now refer to as "China," and its economy was possibly one of the most developed. But by the first several decades of the nineteenth century, the Jiaqing and early Daoguang reigns, there had emerged a general consensus among elites both in and out of government that the empire was facing a multifaceted and potentially catastrophic crisis of the economy, polity, and society. By this point the Qing had already begun to be significantly incorporated into the early modern world economy, although it had not yet experienced, as it very shortly would, military conflict with the West and the invasion by Western agents of economic and cultural change that would follow in its wake.

Articulating a Chinese establishment view of Qing economic history, the senior historian Dai Yi invoked the image of a "camel's hump" (*tuofeng* 驼峰): recovery from devastation in the late sixteenth century and the seventeenth, a period of great prosperity during the Yongzheng and Qianlong reigns (1723–1795), and finally a period of collapse into poverty and semicolonialism. Dai stressed the Opium War (1837–1842) as a benchmark in this downward spiral, leaving more or less unanswered the question of what happened during the early decades of the nineteenth century.[1]

Persons in the mid-Qing would not have found Dai's analogy entirely improbable. In a poem of 1758, the Qianlong Emperor first articulated the formula *chiying baotai* 持盈保泰, or "hold onto the surplus and preserve the abundance." This would become a theme in his pronouncements over the several decades to follow. He invoked this notion, not coincidentally, in

---

I wish to thank Debin Ma, Thomas Rawski, and Joshua Rowe for helpful comments on an earlier draft of this chapter.

[1] Dai Yi 戴逸, "在清代經濟宏觀趨勢與總體評價學術研討會上的發言" (Speech to the Conference on Macro-economic Trends and Overall Appraisal of the Qing Dynasty), 清史研究 (Studies in Qing History) 2008.3, 14.

the process of the conquest and incorporation of Xinjiang, probably his greatest military adventure, and it reflected the emperor's pride that he had expanded imperial territory to a greater degree than had any of his pre-Qing or Qing predecessors. At the same time, he had overseen a seemingly unprecedentedly flourishing economy and the fiscal security of the imperial state.

His formula, however, also expressed a new and gnawing anxiety that this pinnacle of achievement would face constant pressures of erosion. This mounting imperial fear, it has been argued, lay behind the increasingly authoritarian and repressive policies of the later Qianlong reign, up to and including the regime of the arriviste strongman Heshen. Nor did this mounting fear end with the passing of Qianlong and his henchman in 1799. A parallel trope of late Qianlong rhetoric, *shoucheng* 守成 (preserve the achievements of Qing imperial forebears), was inherited by the succeeding Jiaqing Emperor, and routinely invoked, first specifically to dismantle Heshen's apparatus of personal corruption, and thereafter to legitimate a range of policies to combat decay of the fragile "complete prosperity" (*quansheng* 全盛) of the empire at its mid-eighteenth-century peak.[2] This anxiety about decline – political, economic, civilizational – was by no means confined to the court. As Susan Mann Jones and Phillip A. Kuhn wrote, in the classic English-language study of this era, "The widespread feeling that 1775–80 was a turning point in [Qing] history – a turning downward – pervades the political and social commentaries written by officials and scholars of the early nineteenth century."[3]

Gao Wangling has argued convincingly that the prosperous age of the eighteenth century was in no small measure the result of insightful government policies favorable to economic development.[4] By contrast, such matters as the Jiaqing Emperor's seemingly weak-kneed failure to thoroughly purge officialdom of the corrupt underlings installed by Heshen, and the Daoguang Emperor's arbitrary and unsteady pursuit of the Opium War, have contributed to the conventional view of the early nineteenth century as an era of

---

[2] Gao Xiang 高翔, "從持盈保泰到高壓統治：論乾隆中期政治轉變" (From "Preserve the Abundance" to Repressive Governance: Political Transformation in the Mid-Qianlong Reign), 清史研究 (Studies in Qing History) 1991.3, 8–13; Guan Wenfa 關文發, 嘉慶帝 (The Jiaqing Emperor) (Changqun, Jilin wenshi chubanshe, 1993), pp. 59–114.

[3] S.M. Jones and P.A. Kuhn, "Dynastic Decline and the Roots of Rebellion," in J. K. Fairbank (ed.), *The Cambridge History of China*, vol. 10, *Late Ch'ing, 1800–1911*, part 1 (New York, Cambridge University Press, 1978), p. 161.

[4] Gao Wangling 高王凌, 十八世紀中國的經濟發展和政府政策 (Government Policy and Eighteenth-Century Chinese Economic Development) (Beijing, Zhongguo shehui kexue chubanshe, 1995).

weak governance. Recent scholarship, however, emphasizing such factors as campaigns for court and official frugality, rehabilitation of upright ministers cashiered under Heshen, regularization of the practices of such institutions as the Grand Council and the Imperial Household Department, a somewhat relaxed tolerance for literati dissent, and an advertised willingness to listen and respond to popular grievances, has contributed to a more favorable assessment of the Jiaqing court, at least, and a new credence assigned to the genuineness of a purported "Jiaqing restoration" (*xianyu weixin* 咸與維新).[5]

Ecological Decay

A substantial body of research has concurred in the view that the Qing empire – including most regions of its Chinese-dominated core (*neidi* 內地) – suffered acute ecological deterioration in the half-century straddling the assumption of power by the Jiaqing Emperor. Floods and droughts increased in frequency and severity, harvests were less abundant, rural refugees were more ubiquitous, and the need for relief distribution became more urgent. Short-term climate change may have been one factor. Studying Lingnan (southeast China), for example, Robert Marks has found that the annual average temperature fell by one degree centigrade over the course of the early nineteenth century: declining in the 1810s, stabilizing in the 1820s, falling again over the 1830s, and "bottoming out" in the 1840s. Frosts were first reported in late 1808, with a virtually unprecedented two to three inches of snowfall in 1809. This sudden wave of cooling "shocked harvest yields," leading to continuing regional dearth over the decades to follow.[6]

But although natural causes played some part in ecological decay, the major factor was clearly human activity, both negligent and aggressive. In 1801, the Hai river basin of Zhili province experienced one of its greatest floods in recorded history, affecting 122 counties and creating hundreds of thousands of refugees. Between 1801 and 1802, the price of staple grain in the area nearly tripled, and many farmers were forced to sell off their land at greatly depressed prices. In 1813–1814, the same region experienced a major

---

[5] See, for example, Zhang Yufen 張玉芬, "論嘉慶初年的咸與維新" (On the "Comprehensive Reform" of the Early Jiaqing Reign), 清史研究 (Studies in Qing History) 1992.4, 49–54; and D. McMahon, "Dynastic Decline, Heshen, and the Ideology of the Xianyu Reforms," *Tsing Hua Journal of Chinese Studies*, new series 38.2 (June 2008), 231–55; W. Wang, *White Lotus Rebels and South China Pirates: Crisis and Reform in the Qing Empire* (Cambridge, MA, Harvard University Press, 2014).

[6] R.B. Marks, *Tigers, Rice, Silk, and Silt: Environment and Economy in Late Imperial South China* (Cambridge, Cambridge University Press, 1998), pp. 217–18.

drought-induced famine, with rainfall reported at only slightly more than half of that in normal years; again, grain prices more than doubled, and thousands of farmers abandoned their land to become refugees. Another major flood came in 1822–1823. Thereafter, throughout the Daoguang reign, flood disasters in the Hai river basin became a virtually annual event.

The principal reason for the flooding was the progressive silting of the Hai and its tributaries. As Lillian Li concludes, although silting of the Hai had become an increasing problem since the Liao dynasty (947–1125), disastrous consequences had really only become evident in the mid-Qing. Li identifies a "reign cycle" of government attention to dredging the river system, with lax maintenance in the latter years of each Qing ruler contributing to catastrophic flooding and hence heightened responsiveness at the outset of the succeeding reign. In terms of both maintenance and relief delivery, however, she also notes greater diligence and effectiveness in the Jiaqing versus the Daoguang reign, leading her to identify the Daoguang era as the "turning point" in the Hai system's ecological decline.[7]

But if the problem in the Hai river basin was primarily that of state neglect, an equally great – perhaps yet greater – problem was uncontrolled (mostly private) reclamation of agricultural land. As the Qing court became increasingly cognizant of its growing population and the need to assure a steady food supply, in the late Kangxi reign it began to encourage massive development of new arable. This went well beyond the resettlement of Sichuan and other regions that had been devastated during the dynastic transition, to include the "opening" (*kaiken* 开垦) of highlands, marshes, riverbanks, lakeshores, seacoasts, and virtually every scrap of historically unfarmed land both in the interior and on the frontiers. Sometimes government "encouragement of agriculture" (*quannong* 劝农) got a bit out of hand, as in the Yongzhang reign, when false reporting of reclaimed land and the forced introduction of agriculture to unsustainable farmland demanded retrenchment in subsequent years. But overall the process of land development continued through the end of the eighteenth century and into the nineteenth.[8]

The region in which the unintended effects of excess reclamation were revealed most clearly, and with greatest human and economic consequence,

---

[7] L.M. Li, *Fighting Famine in North China: State, Market, and Environmental Decline, 1690s–1990s* (Stanford: Stanford University Press, 2007), pp. 31, 250–66.

[8] The classic work is Peng Yuxin 彭雨新, 清代土地開墾史 (A History of Land Development in the Qing Period) (Beijing, Nongye chubanshe, 1990). On the Yongzheng campaigns, see W.T. Rowe, *Saving the World: Chen Hongmou and Elite Consciousness in Eighteenth-Century China* (Stanford: Stanford University Press, 2001), pp. 56–68.

was the middle Yangzi, especially that sector of Hubei province's central plain lying like a slice of pie between the valleys of the Yangzi and Han rivers northwest of its apex at the river confluence of Wuhan. This region is laced with small tributaries and constitutes, in Pierre-Étienne Will's apt term, a vast "interior delta."[9] Extending this region a little more broadly, we might include also the area of Hunan's Dongting lake and Xiang river valley to the south, and the Han river highlands to the northwest, all of which participate in a coherent and interdependent ecological system.

This entire, highly productive, region existed throughout the early and mid-Qing in what Will describes as a "fragile equilibrium" of land and water. Spring floodwaters descended on the region from the mountains of the west and northwest, eventually to be led to the sea via the lower Yangzi river. The relatively lesser capacity of the lower Yangzi outlet, however, dictated that these waters be held for a period of time in the great floodwater receptacles of the middle Yangzi lakes, rivers, and floodplains. Initially this abundance of water was a great asset to the region, allowing the absorbtion of rapidly growing population into subsistence agriculture, and also entrepreneurial investment in polder lands for commercial rice production for downriver export to the markets of the lower Yangzi throughout the "prosperous age" of the eighteenth century. Already by that time, however, perceptive officials such as Hunan governors Yang Xifu in the 1740s and Chen Hongmou in the 1750s had begun to be concerned about the problem of constricting the region's natural capacity to contain seasonal floodwaters, and the threat this posed to the entire region's hydraulic security. They consequently began to promulgate restrictions on unchecked lakeshore and riverbank encroachment, but the pressures of both population growth and market opportunity rendered these proscriptions largely ineffective.[10]

Compounding this tension was the ever more intensive settlement of highlands, most dramatically along the Han river in northwest Hubei and adjacent areas of Sichuan and Shaanxi. Large swaths of mountainside that had effectively been virgin forest under the Ming had been legally opened to farming, initially during the sixteenth century and then with ever greater intensity during the eighteenth.[11] This process was catalyzed in part by the

---

[9] P.-É. Will, "Un cycle hydraulique en Chine: La province du Hubei du XVIe au XIXe siècles," *Bulletin de l'École Française d'Extreme Orient* 68 (1980), 261–87. See especially the map on p. 287.

[10] P.C. Perdue, *Exhausting the Earth: State and Peasant in Hunan, 1500–1850* (Cambridge, MA, Harvard University Press, 1987), pp. 192–3, 221, 228.

[11] E.S. Rawski, "Agricultural Development in the Han River Highlands," *Ch'ing-shih wen-t'i* 3.4 (1975), 63–4.

dissemination to the area of highland-adaptable New World crops, especially maize and sweet potatoes, but indigenous crops, including staples such as beans and commercial products such as tung, also played a role in highland reclamation. Perhaps the majority of this extensive agriculture up through the eighteenth century was slash-and-burn shifting cultivation, practiced by a group that came to be known throughout central and south China as *pengmin* 棚民 ("shed people"), an emerging legal category of households with an incipient ethnic identity. In the Han valley, as in highland areas of Jiangxi, Jiangnan, Lingnan, and elsewhere, shed people carved out their own ecological and occupational niche. They coexisted tenuously with economically favored residents of the plains and river valleys, providing the latter with charcoal and other specialty products but competing often violently over land, water, educational opportunities, and other scarce resources.[12] Beginning in the third quarter of the eighteenth century, Qing officials launched periodic drives to "register" this population, which meant effectively curbing their transience and settling them on the land.[13] This policy was abetted considerably by terracing of the highlands for wet-rice cultivation in the decades before and after 1800.[14] By this time localities in the Han river valley had also developed a wide range of specialized exports, including pears, walnuts, chestnuts, melons, bark paper, fungus, gypsum, saltpeter, and badger and fox furs.[15]

Both shifting and sedentary agriculture in the highlands contributed to the region's ecological deterioration. In the highlands themselves, soil fertility declined in successive harvests after initial clearance, even as the areas were asked to absorb continuing waves of immigration and were characterized by the same deeply exploitative forms of land tenure (multiple lords to a field, indentured permanent tenancy, heavy up-front rent deposits) that characterized most areas newly developed for agriculture during the Qing's "prosperous age." According to the classic study by Suzuki Chusei, these conditions,

---

[12] S. Averill, "The Shed People and the Opening of the Yangzi Highlands," *Modern China* 9.1 (January 1983), 84–126; A. Osborne, "The Local Politics of Land Reclamation in the Lower Yangzi Highlands," *Late Imperial China* 15.1 (June 1994), 1–46; S.-T. Leong, *Migration and Ethnicity in Chinese History: Hakkas, Pengmin, and Their Neighbors* (Stanford, Stanford University Press, 1997).
[13] Liu Min 劉敏, "論清代棚民的戶籍問題" (The Problem of Registering the Shed People in the Qing), 中國社會經濟史研究 (Studies in Chinese Socio-economic History) 1983.1, 17–29.
[14] Rawski, "Agricultural Development in the Han River Highlands," 65–6.
[15] T.-J. Liu, *Trade on the Han River and Its Impact on Economic Development, c. 1800–1911* (Nankang, Institute of Economics, 1980), pp. 7–10.

compounded by fiscal oppression, were major contributors to the outbreak of the White Lotus rebellion in this area in the 1790s.[16]

It was not only highlands and marshes that were enclosed for rice production. Large stretches of the Jianghan plain had originally been cordoned off for horse pasture by the Qing conquerers, under the control of the banner garrison at Jingzhou. Between the late seventeenth and the late nineteenth centuries, most of this land had been progressively ceded to Han farmers for the construction of polders, with the horse population declining from over 13,000 to a mere 2,000. The encroachment onto this potential floodplain was a major contributor to the increasingly serious flooding of the Jianghan "interior delta" after the late eighteenth century.[17]

In the broader middle Yangzi region, declining water retention in deforested highlands and accelerating river and lake silting from hillside topsoil runoff simply aggravated critical problems of hydraulic management. The precarious condition of the entire region was suggested as early as 1763, when Hunan governor Chen Hongmou ordered the demolition of the illegal Yanglinzhai dike in Xiangyin county, which resulted in the unanticipated collapse of four other major dikes protecting Yanglinzhai, and the dislocation of scores of households.[18] But it was the 1788 bursting of the Wancheng dike, on the Yangzi in western Hubei, that incontestably revealed to all the calamitous state of the interior delta, leaving the major prefectural seat of Jingzhou under three meters of water and the downstream Wuhan conurbation itself disastrously flooded. Less devastating floods followed on a nearly annual basis. When the noted hydraulic expert Wang Zhiyi was posted to the Huguang governor-generalship in 1807, he conducted a thorough analysis of the region, deducing that the entire area bounded by the Yangzi and the Han had been reduced to a basin, more often inundated than arable. He undertook vast and costly repair works, which had a positive impact on the hydraulic security of the region for the remainder of the Jiaqing reign. But the entire Yangzi–Han–Xiang area began again to suffer major flooding with the accession of the Daoguang Emperor in 1820. Particularly devastating instances of these nearly annual

---

[16] Suzuki Chusei 鈴木中正, 清朝中時研究 (A Study of the Mid-Qing Period) (Toyohashi, Aichi University Research Institute on International Problems, 1952).
[17] Y. Gao, "The Retreat of the Horses: The Manchus, Land Reclamation, and Local Ecology in the Jianghan Plain (ca. 1700s–1850s)," in Liu (ed.), *Environmental History in East Asia: Interdisciplinary Perspectives* (London, Routledge, 2014), pp. 100–25.
[18] Perdue, *Exhausting the Earth*, p. 228.

events occurred in 1831 and in the closing years of Daoguang's troubled reign in 1848–1849.[19]

The most alarming and symbolic evidence of ecological decay in the mid-Qing involved the progressive deterioration and eventual abandonment by the administration of the Grand Canal, an ancient semi-natural, semi-manmade waterway dating back in part to the reign of the first emperor, Qin Shihuang.[20] In the Ming and Qing the principal governmental use of the Canal was for the annual northern shipment of central China rice, the so-called "Grain Tribute," relied upon (in the Qing) to feed the large populations of bannermen in the capital and along the northern frontiers. The viability of these shipments required scrupulous dredging not only of the canal bed itself, but also of the Yellow River and other north China waterways that flowed into the canal. When this was not faithfully done, as was the case in the late eighteenth and early nineteenth centuries, the canal silted up and northbound rice shipments were endangered and reduced. This problem had been increasingly evident during the Jiaqing reign, prompting reform proposals of various kinds, including the replacement of the grain tribute system as a whole by a new structure of agricultural colonies (*tuntian*) that would ideally serve to make bannerman populations self-sufficient in grain.[21]

Anxiety suddenly intensified into genuine panic in 1803, when the rupture of the Hengjialou dike in Henan spilled large quantities of silt-laden water into the canal. Northbound grain tribute boats were halted at Zhangqiu, Shandong, by the silt buildup, and many failed altogether to make it through. The Jiaqing Emperor opened the "pathways of words" (*yanlu*), calling upon officials to submit suggestions on how to rehabilitate the canal and the tribute

---

[19] Will, "Un cycle hydraulique en Chine," pp. 282–5. See also T.-J. Liu, "Dike Construction in Ching-chou," *Papers on China* 23 (1970), 1–28; and W.T. Rowe, *Hankow: Conflict and Community in a Chinese City, 1796–1895* (Stanford, Stanford University Press, 1989), pp. 147–8.

[20] Hoshi Ayao 星斌夫, 大運河：中國の 漕運 (The Grand Canal: Grain Tribute in China) (Tokyo: Kondō shuppansha, 1971); H.C. Hinton, *The Grain Tribute System of China, 1845–1911* (Cambridge, MA, Harvard East Asia Series, 1956); J.K. Leonard, *Controlling from Afar: The Daoguang Emperor's Management of the Grand Canal Crisis, 1824–1826* (Ann Arbor, Center for Chinese Studies, 1996); Jones and Kuhn, "Dynastic Decline and the Roots of Rebellion," 119–28; Zhang Yan 張岩, "包世臣與近代前夜的 '海運南漕' 改革" (Bao Shichen and Seaborne Grain Tribute Reform), 近代史研究 (Studies in Modern History) 2000.1, 129–53; Ni Yuping 倪玉平, "道光六年糟糧海運的幾個問題" (Some Problems Regarding the Sea Transport of Grain Tribute in 1825), 清史研究 (Studies in Qing History) 2002.3, 70–5.

[21] C. He and Y. Wei, eds., 皇朝經世文編 (Collected Writings on Statecraft from the Present Dynasty), *juan* 47, 48. See also W.T. Rowe, *Speaking of Profit: Bao Shichen and Reform in Nineteenth-Century China* (Cambridge, MA, Harvard University Asia Center, 2018), Chapter 4.

system. Among the responses was the first call for abandoning the Grand Canal altogether, in favor of coastal shipping of tribute grain from Shanghai to the north. No major action was taken, however, and throughout the remainder of Jiaqing's reign grain tribute problems visibly worsened.

The succeeding Daoguang Emperor, a committed ditherer on most issues, was forced into decisive action when the Gaojiayan dike at Qingjiang in northern Jiangsu ruptured in 1824, allowing only very few grain tribute boats to get through to the capital. The emperor convened an emergency conference of high officials, but their deliberations were inconclusive and their suggestions timid. One man, however, Board of Revenue president Yinghe (1771–1839), presented a bold plan to shift the following year's shipment from the canal to the coastal route, adding that the shipment should be conducted not by government personnel but instead by commercial contractors. With the posting to Jiangsu of a new corps of crisis managers, including provincial governor Tao Zhu, provincial treasurer He Changling, and both men's activist adviser Wei Yuan, Yinghe's plan was in fact implemented for the 1825 shipment.

Inasmuch as that year's tribute grain shipment was successfully completed, by sea, the project might be considered a success, and Wei Yuan in particular lauded it as a revolutionary and long-overdue innovation.[22] But the success was a qualified one. There were significant unanticipated cost overruns.[23] There were incidences of violent unrest by laid-off canal workers that continued to escalate in intensity and notoriety over the following quarter-century.[24] And although Yinghe had specified that the sea route was to be a temporary measure only, with the cost savings applied largely to the repair of the Grand Canal, in fact those repairs were never effectively carried out, and use of the canal for tribute shipments was gradually abandoned altogether.[25] Indeed, grain tribute receipts by the capital region continued to steadily decline over the remainder of the Daoguang reign until, with the interruption of shipments in kind by the Taiping wars, most of the impositions were commuted to cash in 1857–1858.[26]

---

[22] He and Wei, 皇朝經世文編, *juan* 48:70–1.
[23] Ni Yuping 倪玉平, 清朝嘉道財政與社會 (Government Finance and Society in the Qing Jiaqing and Daoguang Reigns) (Beijing, Commercial Press, 2013), pp. 244–76.
[24] Hoshi, 大運河, pp. 233–6.
[25] Hinton, *The Grain Tribute System*, p. 28; Jones and Kuhn, "Dynastic Decline and the Roots of Rebellion," 122.
[26] Xia Nai 夏鼐, "太平天國前後長江各省之田賦問題" (Problems of Land Tax Collection in the Yangzi Provinces before and after the Taiping Rebellion), 清華學報 (Tsinghua University Studies) 10.2 (April 1935), 419–25; W.T. Rowe, "Hu Lin-i's Reform of the Grain Tribute System in Hupeh, 1855–58," *Ch'ing-shih wen-t'i* 4.10 (December 1983), 33–86.

Mid-Qing impact on the natural environment worked in other ways as well. Meng Zhang has recently shown that demand for timber in the building construction boom of eighteenth-century Jiangnan spawned a long-distance trade in timber from a progressively widening range of upriver provinces, including Jiangxi, Hubei, Hunan, Sichuan, and Guizhou. She argues, however, that wholesale deforestation of these regions was ameliorated by self-imposed controls on harvesting and efforts at replanting on the part of commercial interests concerned about the lucrative trade's long-term sustainabililty.[27]

Similar restraint was not apparent in other newly booming trades. As the prosperous age progressed, heightened demand for luxury goods spurred "resource rushes" in both frontier and overseas production areas, along with the development of new trade networks involving merchants and carriers of all backgrounds, including Europeans and Americans. Sable pelts from Siberia (via Kiakhta); sea otter furs from Hokkaido, Siberia, and North America (via Canton); steppe mushrooms from Mongolia; pearls from Jilin; jade from Xinjiang and Burma; ginseng from Manchuria; mother-of-pearl from Sulu; sandalwood from Timor; birds' nests from Borneo; sea cucumbers from Southeast Asia, Australia, and Fiji; and many other goods flowed into the empire. Demand was spurred initially by the court, but progressively spread to wider circles of wealthy consumers. By the early 1800s, most of these trades had entered a phase of rapid decline: Jilin, for example, produced 2,890 pearls in 1795 but only 895 in 1815, while 17,446 sea otter pelts entered Canton in 1806, as compared to a mere 329 in 1831. Various factors played a role in these declines, but the most ubiquitous feature was the exhaustion of resource supply due to overexploitation. In other words, the mid-Qing's very prosperity contributed directly to environmental decay and commercial contraction as the eighteenth century gave way to the nineteenth.[28]

Demographic Crisis?

Contributing substantially to ecological deterioration and in turn aggravated by it was the mid-Qing's growing population pressure. All parties at the time, and virtually all scholars since, have recognized the immense increase in the

---

[27] Meng Zhang, *Timber and Forestry in Qing China: Sustaining the Market* (Seattle: University of Washington Press, 2021).

[28] J. Schlesinger, *A World Trimmed with Fur: Wild Things, Pristine Places, and the Natural Fringes of Qing Rule* (Stanford: Stanford University Press, 2017), pp. 50–4, 73, 133.

empire's population, and have attributed this in part to prolonged experience of peace and stable governance. But had this growth reached a stage of profound crisis by the turn of the nineteenth century and the accession of the Jiaqing Emperor? Put another way, had the Qing empire, with its expanding borders but deteriorating ecology, reached or perhaps begun to exceed its maximum carrying capacity for human beings by this time? This question has provoked spirited disagreement, down to the present day.

If not the first to sound the alarm, at least the most frequently cited, was the Changzhou scholar Hong Liangji (1746–1809). In an essay of 1793 – five years before Thomas Malthus, at the other end of the Eurasian continent, published his yet more famous *Essay on the Principle of Population* – Hong argued that "today's population is five times as large as that of thirty years ago, ten times as large as that of sixty years ago, and not less than twenty times as large as that of one hundred years ago." By contrast, during that same span the amount of available farmland "has only doubled, or, at the most, increased three to five times." What could be done about this? Government could encourage agricultural improvement and the reclamation of new arable, lower agrarian taxes, maintain granary stocks, and distribute famine relief; Hong acknowledged that the Qing had done most of these things relatively well, but this was not enough. Under these conditions, Heaven will necessarily intervene to reduce the population via "flood, drought, and plague," but that too will likely be insufficient to resolve the problem of food supply. This was a catastrophically bleak portrayal of the unforeseen negative consequences of generations of apparent prosperity.[29]

Among modern scholars, Hong found his greatest support in the work of the demographic historian Ping-ti Ho. Though hardly accepting Hong's wild speculations about the pace of Qing population growth, Ho's more careful research did show the population more than doubling (from around 150 million to more than 300 million) over the course of the eighteenth century. And, while not necessarily accepting Hong's dire predictions of demographic crisis, Ho did conclude that in the Qing "the optimum condition (the point at which 'a population produces maximum economic welfare') at the technological level of the time, was reached between 1750 and 1775." Barring the introduction of new technology, and especially given continuing rapid population growth, as it entered the nineteenth century

---

[29] L. Hong, "Yiyan," in Hong, *Juanshi geji* (trans. K.-C. Liu), in W.T. de Bary and R. Lufrano (eds.), *Sources of Chinese Tradition*, vol. 2, 2nd ed. (New York, Columbia University Press, 2000), pp. 174–6.

the Qing's relationship between population and land was doomed to become increasingly adverse.[30] Relying largely on Ho's population figures but adding his own calculations of cultivated acreage (expanding nearly threefold between 1400 and 1770) and grain yields per acre (increasing by nearly 50 percent over this same period), the agricultural economist Dwight Perkins helped explain how the Qing had avoided a demographic crisis during the "prosperous age," but left unchallenged Ho's conclusion of a dramatically worsening man–land ratio as extensive growth approached its limits in the nineteenth century.[31]

Ho wrote in the late 1950s and Perkins in the late 1960s, and since that time there has been a largely positive reappraisal of the performance of the empire's early modern economy. If the *locus classicus* for those who see a crisis of provisioning emerging around 1800 is Hong Liangji, revisionists might find their inspiration in Hong Liangji's younger contemporary Bao Shichen (1775–1855). Bao, to my knowledge, never quoted Hong directly, though they traveled in the same scholarly circles in Changzhou and shared some of the same patronage networks, but he seems clearly to be referring to him when he derides "petty Confucians" (*xiaoru* 小儒) for making dire predictions without the benefit of either detailed field observation or mathematical precision, both of which he claims to provide. Bao emphatically denied that continuing population growth was a liability, arguing that there was more than ample space in the existing agrarian regime for further extensive and (especially) intensive growth, when directed by scholars, officials, and landowners who knew what they were doing. More people simply meant more workers, and more productive workers at that.[32]

Bao Shichen's most influential modern heir is unquestionably the prolific economic historian Li Bozhong. Focusing narrowly on the empire's most developed economic region, Jiangnan, Li argues that early and mid-Qing population growth is somewhat overstated. By his calculations, between 1680 and 1850 Jiangnan's population rose from around 20 million to something over 36 million. This seemingly impressive growth, however, was merely half of the growth rate registered by the empire as a whole, and in fact some 20 percent slower than the growth rate of Jiangnan itself over the centuries of Ming stability. This relatively modest growth continued into the early nineteenth century: whereas the empire's total population grew 39 percent over the years from 1789 to 1838, that of Jiangsu rose only 32 percent and of

[30] P.-T. Ho, *Studies in the Population of China, 1368–1953* (Cambridge, MA, Harvard University Press, 1959), pp. 270, 277–8.
[31] D. Perkins, *Agricultural Development in China, 1368–1968* (Chicago, Aldine, 1969), pp. 16–17.
[32] Rowe, *Speaking of Profit*, Chapter 3.

Zhejiang only 31 percent, and in the core Jiangnan prefecture of Jiaxing growth was only 21 percent. Li attributes this restrained growth to self-conscious "modern birth control techniques," including infanticide, late marriage, abortion, and abstinence.[33]

Li concedes that by the late eighteenth century the introduction of new arable had been pretty much exhausted in Jiangnan, but, guided in part by the writings of Bao, he argues that greater productivity was being achieved as late as the Taiping wars of the 1850s. The adoption of double-cropping rice and winter dry-field crops increased productivity of the land, while the development of off-farm employment, notably in the textile trades and especially of female workers, enhanced labor productivity. More controversially, Li argues that the shrinking size of family farms to an "optimal" size actually aided production by encouraging more efficient intensified labor use. He concludes, "There was a shortage, not a surplus, of labor even in mid-Qing Jiangnan."[34]

Ho Ping-ti's former student James Lee has developed a model of Qing population behavior that incorporates elements both of his mentor's arguments and of those of Li Bozhong. Contra Malthus, who depicted China as an egregious example of blind human reproduction, Lee stresses the continuing availability in the Chinese demographic repertoire of both "preventive" and "positive" checks on population growth, including infanticide; these checks were applied by households with varying rigor, depending on their perception of food supply and economic opportunity. In the early and mid-Qing "prosperous age" these checks were relaxed, and population grew relatively rapidly. Agreeing with Li Bozhong that Jiangnan probably experienced less dramatic growth than other areas, Lee extends this to argue that the form of "modern population growth" in the Qing empire was nearly the opposite of that at the other end of the Eurasian continent: whereas in Europe this growth was evidenced most in already densely populated areas, in China the major loci of growth were peripheral areas of pioneering settlement, such as the southwest and internal highlands. In the early nineteenth century these areas "filled up," resulting in decreased immigration, increased application of preventive and positive checks, and a slowing of empire-wide population growth. (In one local population he has studied in detail, Lee finds male

---

[33] Li Bozhong 李伯重, "控制增長以保福容福榕: 清代前中期江南的人口行為" (Restricting Growth in Order to Preserve Wealth: Population Behavior in Early and Mid-Qing Jiangnan), 新史學 (New Historiography) 5.3, 1994.9, 25–71.

[34] B. Li, *Agricultural Development in Jiangnan, 1620–1850* (New York, St. Martin's Press, 1998), p. 147.

population growth of 1.2 percent per year for 1774 to 1804, slowing to 0.2 percent per year from 1805 to 1873.) This suggests significant demographic pressure, but hardly the Malthusian crisis predicted by Hong Liangji.[35]

Other scholarship has argued that the Qing dealt relatively successfully with population pressure by restructuring or intensifying production. Focusing on state policy, Gao Wangling points out that the throne was alert to a looming population crisis already by the early eighteenth century, and had responded with a multifaceted program not only of intensive and extensive agricultural improvement, but also of deliberate economic diversification, through its nurturance of nonagricultural sectors such as handicrafts and mining. (By implication, if there was a downturn in the economy after the Qianlong reign, in Gao's logic this would have been the result not of factors of resources or labor, but rather of the progressive failure of official initiative and morale.)[36]

Most recently, Richard von Glahn has martialed wage and price data to argue – as Bao Shichen would have predicted – that more intensive and efficient allocation of labor allowed the Qing to avert the worst effects of population pressure. Prior to the Taiping catastrophe, for example, there was no telltale spike in male mortality. Von Glahn finds a secular rise in the price of grain over the course of the eighteenth century, but this was accompanied by comparable rises in the price of cotton, silk, and other consumer goods, leading him to conclude that the inflation was due not to "the stress of overpopulation" but instead to a "substantial growth of the total money supply."[37] Into the nineteenth century, he again finds no evident long-term correlation of prices and wages with population growth. After a spike in the 1810s, grain prices indeed trended downward over the 1820s and 1830s, while real wages (measured in grain) remained fairly static throughout the entire 1800–1850 period. In sum, "The evidence does not suggest that China had reached the point of a Malthusian demographic crisis" any time prior to the mid-century rebellions.[38]

---

[35] J. Lee and C. Campbell, *Fate and Fortune in Rural China: Social Organization and Population Behavior in Liaoning, 1774–1873* (Cambridge, Cambridge University Press, 1997); J. Lee and F. Wang, *One Quarter of Humanity: Malthusian Mythology and Chinese Realities* (Cambridge, MA, Harvard University Press, 1999).

[36] Gao Wangling 高王凌, "關於康乾盛世的幾個問題" (Some Problems Concerning the Prosperous Age from Kangxi to Qianlong), 清史研究通訊 (Bulletin of Qing Historical Studies) 1990.4, 21–6.

[37] R. von Glahn, *The Economic History of China: From Antiquity to the Nineteenth Century* (Cambridge, Cambridge University Press, 2016), pp. 329–30.

[38] Von Glahn, *The Economic History of China*, 363–4.

The issue of population pressure is also reflected in what has become a contentious debate on standards of living. Raised most provocatively by Kenneth Pomeranz in his study of the "Great Divergence" in economic development at opposite ends of the Eurasian continent, the argument that wealthier areas of Qing China in the eighteenth century enjoyed living standards at least on a par with those in more favored areas of Europe seems to have originated in the work of the Chinese scholar Fang Xing. In a pioneering 1996 article, Fang calculated the percentages that early Qing peasant households in Jiangnan spent on food, shelter, clothing, and fuel. On the basis of his estimate that such households spent only 55 percent of their annual budget on grain and 76 percent on food overall, he concluded that most lived in relative "comfort" (wenbaoxing 温饱型), comparing well to other rural areas not only in China but also elsewhere in the world.[39] Commenting on Fang's conclusion, Pomeranz pointed out that contemporaneous English peasant households spent roughly the same portion of their budget on food, but added that Fang "almost certainly undercounts non-grain consumption" on items like family rituals, jewelry, and entertainment, suggesting that food expenditures in Jiangnan were considerably lower than those in England.[40] He argues as well that consumption of "everyday luxuries" such as tea and sugar was higher in eighteenth-century Jiangnan than in England. In my view we can discount tea, a domestic product in China and a costly import in England, but sugar makes a potentially useful surrogate for discretionary spending. Pomeranz finds that Chinese sugar consumption as late as 1800, while lower than that in England (the world leader), remained notably higher than that in continental Europe.[41] In terms of nutrition, Pomeranz estimates the Qing empire-wide average calorie consumption during the eighteenth century to be 2,651 per day, a figure which "compares well" with that of Britain, and was "quite far above" estimates for Europe as a whole.[42] Life expectancies in the Qing empire, though there was substantial diversity by region, were overall "quite comparable" to those in England.[43] On the basis of Fang's, Pomeranz's, and independent calculations, the most recent scholarship tends to concur that standards of living in the more developed areas of the Qing during the "prosperous age" were higher than

---

[39] Fang Xing 方行, "清代江南農民的消費" (Peasant Expenditures in Qing Jiangnan), 中國經濟史研究 (Studies in Chinese Economic History) 1996.3, 93–4.
[40] K. Pomeranz, *The Great Divergence: China, Europe, and the Making of the Modern World Economy* (Princeton, Princeton University Press, 2000), p. 137.
[41] Pomeranz, *The Great Divergence*, pp. 118–23. [42] Pomeranz, *The Great Divergence*, p. 39.
[43] Pomeranz, *The Great Divergence*, pp. 36–7.

they had ever been, higher than those in the West, and "unsurpassed by any other contemporary society."[44]

If this consensus view holds true, what happened to standards of living as the prosperous age faded into the age of crisis in the late eighteenth and early nineteenth centuries? In Jiangnan, population grew steadily and rapidly, from 172 million in 1750 to 254 million a hundred years later, when the Taiping wars precipitated a sudden and dramatic decline (to 105 million in 1880). Beginning in the early nineteenth century, this growth was accompanied not by further expansion in cultivated acreage, but rather by a modest decline.[45] Combined with partible inheritance and relatively free alienability of land, the result was considerable shrinkage of the average family farm size, estimated by Li Bozhong as nine *mu* in the mid-nineteenth century, down from fifteen *mu* two centuries earlier.[46]

The Jiaqing reign also witnessed a sudden spike in rice prices. Data collected by Yeh-chien Wang for Wuchang prefecture (Hubei), a modestly prosperous area of central China, show rice prices holding remarkably stable at fifty-three grams of silver per hectal from 1769 through 1790; by 1801 they had soared to 89.6 grams of silver, remaining in that range through the late 1830s.[47] Annual data collected by Tanaka Issei for Xiaoshan county (Zhejiang) indicate some radical short-term vacillations, but basically echo the Wuchang pattern: a price of 2.3 taels per *shi* in 1781, remaining relatively stable for a decade (2.2 taels in 1791), then leaping to 2.85 taels in 1800.[48] A similar *fin de siècle* spike occurred throughout the empire. Kishimoto Mio reports an aggregate empire-wide rice price of 1.75 taels per *shi* in 1760, inflating to 2.2 taels in 1800.[49] And rice prices directly mattered to life experiences. As in other preindustrial economies, they had nearly immediate consequences for fertility and mortality rates; in the Qing, "As prices rose, so did female infanticide, resulting in lower recorded female births."[50]

---

[44] Huang Jingbin 黃敬斌, 民生與家計：清初至民國時期江南居民的消費 (Popular Livelihoods and Household Budgets: Jiangnan Residents' Expenditures from Early Qing to the Republican Era) (Shanghai, Fudan University Press, 2009), p. 330; von Glahn, *The Economic History of China*, p. 350.
[45] Huang, 民生與家計, pp. 14–15.   [46] Li, *Agricultural Development*, p. 138.
[47] Yeh-chien Wang, "Spatial and Temporal Patterns of Grain Prices in China, 1740–1910," unpublished paper.
[48] Tanaka's data cited in Sui-wai Cheung, *The Price of Rice: Market Integration in Eighteenth-Century China* (Bellingham, WA, Center for East Asian Studies, 2008), p. 153.
[49] Kishimoto Mio 岸木美緒, "清朝中期經濟政策の基調" (Preliminary Investigation of Mid-Qing Economic Policy), *Chikaki ni arite* 11 (1987), 18.
[50] Lee and Wang, *One Quarter of Humanity*, p. 111.

What were the implications for household consumption patterns? In his pioneering study, Fang Xing found that while the share of overall food expenditures within household budgets rose from 76 percent in the early Qing to 83 percent around 1880, expenditures on non-grain foodstuffs comprised a much greater percentage of this over time, rising from 21 percent to 29 percent; Fang interprets this as evidence of rising, not falling, rural standards of living in Jiangnan well into the late nineteenth century.[51]

A more detailed analysis has been undertaken by Huang Jingbin. Huang asks whether the passage from the mid-eighteenth to the mid-nineteenth century in Jiangnan indeed saw the progressive immiseration of rural households. He notes that literati writings from throughout the era consistently complain about peasant "extravagance" (shechi 奢侈), but observes that this complaint almost always was directed at ritual and festival spending, not at daily consumption patterns. In terms of the latter, Huang calculates that household consumption of staples such as grain and salt remained relatively constant over the course of this period (12.5 dan for grain, 37.5 catties for salt), while consumption of all other foodstuffs (vegetables, meat, eggs, oil, sugar, wine) declined by an average of 20 percent. Consumption of sugar, for example, declined from 27.5 to 20 catties per year. As percentages of household expenditure, grain rose from 39.7 percent in the mid-eighteenth century to 45 percent in the mid-nineteenth, while expenses on other foodstuffs fell, from 11.2 percent to 9.5 percent, and those on clothing, medical care, and education (everything, that is, other than housing rent, which rose from 3.8 percent to 5.8 percent) shrank as well. There was, then, Huang concedes, a fall-off in standards of living, but not so great as to qualify as immiseration, or to negate Fang Xing's conclusion that Jiangnan rural households remained relatively "comfortable."[52] He adds, provocatively, that after the 1850s the combination of population decline due to the Taiping war and regional development of foreign trade brought surviving Jiangnan households a half-century of renewed prosperity comparable to or greater than that of the eighteenth century.[53]

We have less information on living standards in regions outside the disproportionately prosperous Jiangnan. Based on wage data for nonfarm workers in Beijing, Debin Ma and his colleagues argue that real income in fact declined steadily over the late eighteenth and early nineteenth centuries,

---

[51] Fang, "清代江南農民的消費", 97. Pomeranz, The Great Divergence, p. 247, reports Fang's findings on this score with some skepticism.
[52] Huang, 民生與家計, pp. 103, 307–8, 325–31.
[53] Huang, 民生與家計, p. 327.

bottomng out below subsistence level in the 1830–1860 period.⁵⁴ Another recent study by Wu Xiaozhen looks at the area in and around Hengzhou prefecture in southern Hunan. This was long a region of middling economic security, but during the late eighteenth and early nineteenth centuries the region's exports of both rice and tea expanded dramatically, in what appears a clear pattern of economic development. This was accompanied, however, by the first systematic cultivation of maize, sweet potatoes, and other New World crops, which, though highly unfavored by local tastes, displaced rice as the chief dietary staple. Wu argues that this must be interpreted as a clear decline in living standards, ironically accompanying and in some measure due to economic growth.⁵⁵

Scattered evidence points to demographic consequences of a presumed decline in living standards in the Jiaqing and Daoguang reigns. Studying lineage genealogies from Tongcheng, a prosperous county in the periphery of the lower Yangzi region, Ted Telford has found male life expectancy at birth to have declined from 39.6 in the mid-eighteenth century to 34.9 in the early nineteenth.⁵⁶ In a local banner population in Liaoning, James Lee and Cameron Campbell found the male population growing 0.2 percent per year over the 1805–1873 period, a dramatic decline from the average of 1.2 percent per year in the preceding 1774–1804 era, the result primarily of lowered birth rates, resulting from rigorous exercise of birth control by people observing a significant decline in life opportunites.⁵⁷ This decline in birth rates was undoubtedly even more pronounced among women, leading to an increasingly skewed sex ratio, and – in a culture in which marriage and reproduction were a moral imperative – a growing incidence of bachelorhood. In his Tongcheng sample, for example, Telford found that the share of unmarried males among those born in the last quarter of the eighteenth century was 31.6 percent, a number which rose to 38.6 percent for those born in the first two decades of the nineteenth century, 46.4 percent for those born in the 1820s and 1830s, and 52 percent for those born in the 1840s.⁵⁸ Similarly, in their Liaoning sample, Lee and Campbell found

---

⁵⁴ R.C. Allen, J.-P. Bassino, D. Ma, C. Moll-Murata, and J.L. van Zanden, "Wages, Prices, and Living Standards in China, 1738–1925, in Comparison with Europe, Japan, and India," *Economic History Review* 64 (2011), Figs. 5, 6.
⁵⁵ Wu Xiaozhen 吳小珍, "糧食生產供求變動與地方的經濟：以湘南為中心" (Shifts in Food Supply and Qing Local Economies: The Case of Southern Hunan), 清史研究 (Studies in Qing History) 2012.3, 45–57.
⁵⁶ T.A. Telford, "Patching the Holes in Chinese Genealogies: Mortality in the Lineage Population of Tongcheng County, 1300–1800," *Late Imperial China* 11.2 (December 1990), 133.
⁵⁷ Lee and Campbell, *Fate and Fortune in Rural China*, p. 47.
⁵⁸ T.A. Telford, "Family and State in Qing China: Marriage in the Tongcheng Lineages, 1650–1880," in Institute of Modern History (ed.), *Family Process and Political Process in Modern Chinese History* (Taipei, Academia Sinica, 1992), pp. 921–42.

a declining marriage rate among males of sixteen to thirty-five *sui* from eighty-eight per thousand in the pre-1805 period to seventy-five per thousand after that year.[59] Matthew Sommer has documented in dramatic detail some of the consequences of this skewed sex ratio and distorted marriage market, including changing cultural norms that effectively sanctioned such heterodox practices as polyandry, wife pimping, and wife selling.[60]

Economic Slowdown?

If the early nineteenth century was "a watershed that marked the beginning of a prolonged period of intensified Malthusian pressure,"[61] and China's ratio of population to cultivated land was increasingly adverse, was the overall economy assisting by providing nonfarm employment opportunities for surplus agricultural labor?

In a masterful article, the economic historian Peng Zeyi traced the impressive development of the Qing economy in the first half of the dynasty, but then characterized the half-century from 1784 to 1839 as one of "stagnation" or even "contraction."[62] In Peng's calculations, cultivated acreage empire-wide shrank 1.6 percent over the thirty years between 1784 and 1813, even while population continued to grow rapidly. State-owned manufacturing enterprises declined. Annual capital budgets (*yongyin* 用银) of the porcelain factories at Jingdezhen fell from 8,000 taels in 1740, to 7,000 taels in 1799, to a mere 2,500 taels in 1812. Official textile mills in Nanjing and elsewhere, and the government mints at Beijing, also experienced significant slowdowns. Much of the contraction of state-owned enterprises, of course, represented loss of market share to the private sector, but Peng points out that private enterprises likewise declined during this era. The salt industry of Sichuan shrank dramatically from 1780 to 1820, and the copper and other mines of the southwest saw their production fall roughly 1 percent per year between 1783 and 1797. Urban handicrafts, being more dispersed, are harder to measure, but Peng saw contraction there as well. In what might be his most debatable argument, he sampled some seventy-nine artisan and merchant guilds from fifteen major commercial cities (including Hankou, Suzhou, Chongqing,

---

[59] Lee and Campbell, *Fate and Fortune in Rural China*, p. 48.
[60] M.H. Sommer, *Polyandry and Wife Selling in Qing Dynasty China* (Berkeley, University of California Press, 2015). The reference to Bao Shichen is on pp. 337–8.
[61] Lee and Campbell, *Fate and Fortune in Rural China*, p. 44.
[62] Peng Zeyi 彭澤益, "清代前期手工業的發展" (The Development of Handicrafts in the Early Qing), 中國史研究 (Studies in Chinese History) 1981.1, 43–60.

Changsha, and Foshan), and found their dates of formal organization to overwhelmingly concentrate in this era (four in 1671–1715, sixteen in 1716–1785, and fifty-nine in 1786–1839). Whereas others might see this as evidence of commercial efflorescence, Peng holds a negative view of guilds as exclusionary defensive organizations, and hence finds support in this for his contention that interregional commerce was also under severe pressure during the turn-of-the-century decades. In this era, he concludes, "The independent development of [urban] commercial capital proceeded in inverse proportion to the development of the overall economy."[63]

Is Peng correct in his view of this era as one of generalized economic contraction? Let us consider one facet of the economy which might plausibly be seen as a proxy for the overall economy, and historically the early modern Chinese economy's driving sector: the rice trade down the Yangzi from Wuhan to Nanjing and Suzhou. There is an active historiography on this question. Few dispute the baseline figure provided by Han-sheng Chuan and Richard Kraus of between 8 million and 15 million *dan* of rice following this route in the 1730s.[64] A recent, careful study of grain prices throughout rice consumption areas of south China suggests that as late as 1795 market price cointegration (suggestive of arbitrage via vigorous inter-market exchange) remained somewhat higher than that in Western Europe and only very slightly behind that of England.[65]

The question is what happened after that, and why. Based on stele records of the Hunan provincial club in Nanjing, Nakamura Jihei concluded that the downriver rice trade had decreased considerably by 1800.[66] Studying a prefectural gazetteer of Yongzhou, Hunan, Kitamura Hironao found that rice exports to the lower Yangzi from the single rice-producing county of Qiyang, amounting to over 100,000 *dan* annually around 1800, had ceased altogether by the time of the gazetteer's publication in the 1830s; Kitamura thus argued for a sudden cessation of the Yangzi rice trade as a whole at the end of the Qianlong reign.[67] Chuan and Kraus themselves were less categorical, though they too observed a major shrinkage of the trade. Disputing

---

[63] Peng, "清代前期手工業的發展," 52.
[64] Han-sheng Chuan and R.A. Kraus, *Mid-Qing Rice Markets and Trade: An Essay in Price History* (Cambridge, MA, Harvard University East Asian Monographs, 1975), p. 77.
[65] C.H. Shiue and W. Keller, "Markets in China and Europe on the Eve of the Industrial Revolution," *American Economic Review* 97.4 (September 2007), 1189–1216.
[66] Nakamura Jihei 中村治兵衞, "清代湖廣米流通の一面" (One Aspect of the Huguang Rice Trade in the Qing Era), 社會經濟史學 (Studies in Socio-economic History) 18.3 (1952), 53–65.
[67] Kitamura Hironao 北村敬直, "清代の商品市場について" (On Mid-Qing Commodity Markets), 經濟學雜誌 (Journal of Economics) 28.3-4 (1953), 5, 8.

Dwight Perkins's claim that the downriver rice trade had *totally* disappeared by c. 1930, they instead argued for a long-term decline to some 2.7 million *dan* in the early twentieth century, roughly one quarter of the volume at the trade's eighteenth-century peak.[68] A recent study by Sui-wai Cheung finds two boom periods of downriver rice shipments in 1724–1727 and 1732–1755, with a subsequent modest revival in 1777–1786. Though reports in 1788 indicate that middle Yangzi rice was "unmarketable" in Jiangnan at that time, the trade actually revived once more in 1795 and remained active at least through the remainder of the Jiaqing reign, though the trend thereafter was downward.[69] Surveying this historiography, Richard von Glahn concludes that the overall evidence "points to a decline in the scale of interregional trade in grain beginning in the 1790s."[70]

Why these vicissitudes in the trade, and what does the decline signify? Cheung argues that the key factor at all times was demand in the lower Yangzi for rice from upriver regions – its oscillation between rice deficit and rice surplus. Although agriculture in Jiangnan was increasingly commercialized, and its population heavily engaged in handicrafts and other non-grain-producing work, Cheung follows Li Bozhong in seeing the region as by no means "overpopulated," and in normal years self-sufficient in grain. Thus what lay behind the occasional spikes in downriver rice imports in both the eighteenth and the nineteenth centuries was weather-induced short-term harvest shortfalls.[71] Chuan and Kraus, by contrast, look for answers in the exporting rather than the importing region.[72] They reason that the decline in the middle to lower Yangzi rice trade logically reflected either a decline in central China's interregional commerce overall, or else a substitution of other commodities for rice; they indicate doubt that the latter was the case, but, as we shall see in a minute, I think they may be wrong. A secular decline in the downriver rice trade, moreover, might reflect a general decommercialization of middle Yangzi (and upper Yangzi) agriculture – an option I believe to be patently not the case. Alternatively, it might reflect a diversion of commercialized rice to local consumption on the part of the production regions' own increasingly non-grain-producing urban and rural populations. As indicated by the growing incidence of collective protests in extraction centers of Hunan, against the rising local rice prices resulting from extra-regional

---

[68] Chuan and Kraus, *Mid-Qing Rice Markets*, p. 77.
[69] Cheung, *The Price of Rice*, pp. 97–102.   [70] Von Glahn, *Economic History of China*, p. 331.
[71] Cheung, *The Price of Rice*, pp. 113, 135–6.
[72] Chuan and Kraus, *Mid-Qing Rice Markets*, p. 78.

exports – an early example being that in Xiangtan in 1819 – this is much more likely to have been the case.⁷³

What does this say about the state of long-distance domestic commerce overall, as the Qing entered the nineteenth century? By most accounts, it was flourishing. Wu Chengming conservatively estimates the overall value of traded commodities in the empire around 1840 to be some 387,624,000 taels of silver, among which roughly 163 million was in rice, 107 million in cotton and cotton cloth, 59 million in salt, 32 million in tea, and 27 million in silk and silk cloth. With the possible exception of rice, these levels were all at the highest they had ever been.⁷⁴ A classic study by Peng Yuxin showed the interregional trade passing through the central China entrepôt of Hankou in the nineteenth century to link all provinces of the empire, comprise scores of commodities, and reach annual values of hundreds of millions of taels.⁷⁵

Let us look briefly at the regional economy I know best, that of the middle Yangzi. This was the region that would have been most seriously impacted by a decline in the downriver rice trade. But at least two commodities advanced to offset any such losses in regional exports: tea and cotton. Three middle Yangzi counties – Hunan's Anhua and Linxiang and Hubei's Puqi – generally produced more than half of the region's tea output, but almost all parts of the region adopted some tea production as market conditions warranted. At least by the Ming era, teas from these counties circulated within the region itself, but due to their perceived inferiority to products of other regions they did not enjoy much of a domestic interregional market. The foreign market was a different story. It was middle Yangzi tea that had supplied the famous tea-for-horse exchange with the Mongols during the Ming and early Qing, shipped up the Han river and overland to the great border market of Zhangjiakou. With the Kangxi Emperor's privatization of this trade in the 1710s it increased dramatically. Exports to Asiatic Russia had also followed this route since the twelfth century, after 1727 exchanged at the treaty market of Kiakhta. But the growing population of Siberia brought an

---

⁷³ P.C. Perdue, "Insiders and Outsiders: The Xiangtan Riot of 1819 and Collective Action in Hunan," *Modern China* 12.2 (April 1986), 166–201. See also Shigeta Atsushi 重田德, "清朝における 湖南米市場の一考察" (Hunan Rice Markets in the Qing Dynasty), 東洋文化研究所紀要 (Memoirs of the Institute of Oriental Culture) 10 (1956), 427–98; and R.B. Wong, "Grain Riots in the Qing Dynasty," *Journal of Asian Studies* 41.4 (August 1982), 767–88.

⁷⁴ Wu Chengming 吳承明, "論清代前期我國國內市場" (The Domestic Market in the Early Qing), 歷史研究 (Historical Studies) 1983.1, 99.

⁷⁵ Peng Yuxin 彭雨新, "抗日戰爭前漢口的洋行和買辦" (Foreign Firms and Compradores at Hankou Prior to the Sino-Japanese War), 理論戰線 (Theoretical Front) 1959.2, 22–9.

estimated sixfold increase in the trade's volume during the early nineteenth century.[76]

The early development of Qing tea exports to Britain in the eighteenth century left the middle Yangzi largely unaffected, since the inferior product could little compete with the better teas of coastal areas. This changed dramatically, however, with the abolition of the Canton monopoly in 1842. The removal of legal restraints on the trade brought a sudden increase in demand, causing the price of Fujian and Zhejiang teas to skyrocket, and offering European buyers reason to seek out new and cheaper sources of supply. The middle Yangzi in the 1840s thus underwent a virtual invasion by Cantonese and other commercial entrepreneurs, proselytizing a shift to tea cultivation. Fanning out from the established tea districts, these merchants persuaded growers in a widening circle of production areas to convert from other crops to tea, or, where green tea was already grown, to red tea for the European market. At first most of this product went south to Guangzhou, then gradually shifted to Shanghai, and, with the opening of the middle Yangzi itself to foreign trade in 1861, to Hankou. Tea thus became the region's chief foreign export, and likely for a period its most important commercial crop. In Anhua county, by the 1860s, it constituted the major source of livelihood for an estimated 90 percent of the population.[77]

After tea came cotton. In arguing for the rapid relative decline of China's economy in the late eighteenth and early nineteenth centuries, Kenneth Pomeranz argues that empire-wide cotton cultivation and processing increased only very slightly, if at all, in the century following 1750. In the lower Yangzi, there was probably a slight decline, and in north China the drop-off was "considerable." This leaves the middle Yangzi provinces, which, in Pomeranz's words, while they "did increase their cotton cultivation after 1750 ... never became very large producers."[78] On this point he is simply wrong.

Cotton had been cultivated extensively in northern portions of the middle Yangzi since the sixteenth century, with the region's output ranking only behind that of the lower Yangzi. While much of this crop went for household consumption, by the eighteenth century the majority was taken by handicraft weavers producing for the market, and the concentration of such activity in

---

[76] M.I. Sladkovsii, *Economic Relations between Russia and China* (Jerusalem, 1966), p. 71.
[77] Shigeta Atsushi 重田德, "清末における 湖南茶的新展開" (The New Development of Hunan Tea Production in the Late Qing), in Shigeta, 清代社會經濟史研究 (Studies in Qing Socio-economic History) (Tokyo, Iwanami Shoten, 1975), pp. 207–38.
[78] Pomeranz, *The Great Divergence*, pp. 139–41.

centers such as Wuhan and Changde led to the rise of a brisk intra-regional trade. By the nineteenth century, a considerable portion of middle Yangzi cotton also found its way into the interregional trade, especially to Sichuan, which took hundreds of thousands of bales per year.[79]

The middle Yangzi, notably the Hubei county of Xianning, by the late Ming had also acquired an empire-wide reputation for its cotton cloth. By the eighteenth century, cotton textiles spun and woven by urban, rural, and especially suburban households were sent to many parts of the empire. The areas around Wuhan, Changde, Yiyang, and especially Shashi and Jingzhou prefecture in western Hubei were major suppliers to this intra-regional trade, though production was also dispersed well beyond these centers. Shashi, with its "Thirteen Guilds" management combine, comprising merchant groups from throughout the empire, was described by early Western reporters as the greatest weaving center in all of China. Much of the product went upriver, to Sichuan, Yunnan, and Guizhou, and downriver to Jiangxi.[80]

In sum, if the rice trade downriver on the lower Yangzi declined in the early nineteenth century, as most scholars now agree, and even if trade on that artery declined as a whole (domestic customs revenues at Suzhou are reported to have dropped from 583,000 taels in 1791 to 391,000 taels forty years later[81]), this does not necessarily indicate a contraction of the overall Qing commercial economy as the empire entered the nineteenth century. What it more likely indicates, as G. William Skinner has argued, is that there was a diversification of commodities and trade routes as the Qing economy fleshed out beyond one or two staples.[82]

Maritime Trade

China's maritime trade grew steadily over the course of the "prosperous age," and continued to do so throughout the period under discussion here. Following the Kangxi Emperor's lifting of the "sea ban" (*haijin* 海禁) and establishment of the Maritime Customs (*haiguan* 海关) in 1683–1684, except for a brief hiatus under the "second sea ban" of 1716–1728, the Qing administration generally encouraged the development of East Asian intra-regional

---

[79] A. Feuerwerker, "Handicraft and Manufactured Cotton Textiles in China, 1871–1930," *Journal of Economic History* 30.2 (1970), 340.
[80] Wu, "論清代前期我國國內市場," 104–6; Lyon Chamber of Commerce, *La mission lyonnaise d'exploration commerciale en Chine 1895–97* (Lyon, A. Rey, 1898), pp. 2.280–1.
[81] Von Glahn, *Economic History of China*, p. 371, citing figures from Wu Chengming.
[82] G.W. Skinner, "Regional Urbanization in Nineteenth-Century China," in Skinner (ed.), *The City in Late Imperial China* (Stanford, Stanford University Press, 1977), p. 713 note.

maritime trade throughout this era. Qing trade with Southeast Asia continued to expand at least through the 1840s, with dozens of ports, large and small, along the southeast coast hosting customs office branches and participating in that trade.[83] Despite the Tokugawa shogunate's imposition of restrictions on the export of monetary metals to China in 1685, trade with Japan remained active as well. In the single year 1830, some 222 oceangoing ships called at Shanghai, Ningbo, and Suzhou, having stopped previously at various ports in Southeast Asia and Japan.[84]

The largest single import commodity within this regional trading network was rice from Siam. Whereas under the Ming Siamese exports to China comprised primarily luxury goods such as fine timber, with the lifting of the sea ban rice – a staple – became the backbone of the trade. Imports of rice into Guangdong and other grain-deficient southeastern provinces were repeatedly encouraged by Qing regional officials whenever shortages became acute, throughout the late eighteenth and early nineteenth centuries. During the heyday of the trade in 1809–1833, rice was Siam's largest export, and the Qing empire its largest customer. With Qing imperial policy toward Chinese merchants personally going abroad gradually easing over the eighteenth century, it was those merchants who dominated the trade; Viraphol reports that during the first few decades of the nineteenth century, Chinese vessels carried around eighty-five tons of rice into the empire per year, nearly three times the volume of their closest competitor, the British. But the number of European ships plying the China coast was growing rapidly. In 1837, over 200 Western ships called at Guangzhou, nearly twenty times the number that had called there a century earlier, in 1732.[85]

It was, of course, the Sino-British trade that came to dominate this exchange, growing progressively over the late eighteenth century. This growth accelerated with the end of the European wars in 1815, again with the introduction of the steamship into East Asian waters in 1830, and yet again with the abolition of the East India Company's monopoly in 1834. The driving force behind this expansion was the British demand for Chinese tea. Tea exports from the Qing to England rose from virtually nil in the final years of the sea ban, to 15 million pounds in 1785, and double this amount around 1830.

---

[83] Huang Guosheng 黃國盛, 鴉片戰爭前的東南四省海關 (Maritime Customs in China's Four Southeastern Provinces Prior to the Opium War) (Fuzhou, Fujian renmin chubanshe, 2000), pp. 178–9.
[84] G. Zhao, *The Qing Opening to the Ocean: Chinese Maritime Policies, 1684–1757* (Honolulu, University of Hawaii Press, 2013), pp. 135–6, 171–2.
[85] S. Viraphol, *Tribute and Profit: Sino-Siamese Trade, 1652–1853* (Cambridge, MA, Harvard University Press, 1977), pp. 109–20, 180.

Total Sino-British trade – imports and exports – grew in value from 23 million dollars in 1817 to nearly 37 milliion in 1833. The imports to China included various luxury goods (pepper, ivory, shark fins, etc.) as well as the trade's staple, South Asian raw cotton, which was overtaken by opium in 1823. Qing imports of this last item grew ninefold between the turn of the century and the outbreak of the Opium War.[86]

If there was, as some have suggested, a contraction of Qing interregional domestic trade at the same time that the foreign maritime trade continued its rapid growth, is the story of the early nineteenth century one of transition from a balanced redistributive economy to an extraction economy in service to an external metropolis? The best data we have suggest that this was hardly the case. According to figures generated by Wu Chengming, as late as 1840 Qing maritime exports of tea (some 605,000 *dan*) remained less than a third of tea produced for the domestic market (more than 2,000,000 *dan*), while raw cotton imports remained less than a quarter of that grown and marketed domestically.[87] The Qing empire's economy was simply too large and its markets too developed to be reduced to dependency.

The Daoguang Depression

The reign of the Daoguang Emperor (1821–1850), and especially the quarter-century following 1825 or 1826, have become familiar to historians as the era of the "Daoguang depression" (*Daoguang xiaotiao* 道光蕭條). In some recent Chinese scholarship, indeed, this phenomenon is paired with the so-called "Kangxi depression" of the decades around 1700, essentially bookending the intervening "prosperous age" of the eighteenth century, and signifying the completion of an economic cycle.[88]

While there is much debate about the nature and causes of the depression, there is general agreement regarding three major trends. First is the deflation of commodity prices (in silver). We generally accept that prices underwent a prolonged benign inflation over the century following the Kangxi Emperor's declared opening of the Qing to foreign trade in 1682, followed by perhaps forty years (1780–1820) during which the price rise continued at a markedly slower pace. Then, in Yeh-chien Wang's words, "The second quarter ... of the nineteenth century was generally a period of severe

---

[86] M. Greenberg, *British Trade and the Opening of China, 1800–42* (Cambridge, Cambridge University Press, 1951), pp. 3, 76–89, 103, 217, 221.
[87] Wu, "論清代前期我國國內市場," 99.
[88] Ni, 清朝嘉道財政與社會, p. 1.

deflation. The movement of prices lost its vigor at the beginning of the century and remained virtually at a standstill for more than a decade; then it took a sharp turn downward until 1850." Wang very ambitiously constructs a price index of all commodities throughout the empire. Setting the year 1682 as 100, he finds a steady rise to 300 in 1815, followed by a dramatic decline to 150 by 1850.[89]

Second, scholars agree that during this same period there was a sudden shift in the Qing's balance of silver flows, from large annual inflows to massive outflows. Table 2.1, originally by Richard von Glahn, offers the following table of this dramatic turnaround:[90]

A study by Yu Jieqiong found a net inflow of 74.7 million silver dollars over the years from 1801 to 1826, compared to a net outflow of 133.7 million in 1827–1849.[91]

The third component of the Daoguang depression about which scholars agree is that silver became much more expensive in terms of copper (*yingui qianjian* 银贵钱贱). The Qing inherited from its predecessor a bimetallic currency system, based on uncoined silver specie, the unit of account for which was the "tael" (*liang* 两), and statutory coin (*zhiqian* 制钱) made of copper alloy, the unit of the latter being the "cash" (*wen* 文). Whereas a string of 1,000 copper cash (*chuan* 串) carried a par value of one silver tael, the disastrous experiences of the late Ming had convinced the Qing that efforts to maintain a 1,000:1 exchange rate by administrative fiat were counterproductive. Instead, it settled for the goal of

Table 2.1 Net flow of silver to China, 1818–1850

1818–1820	+ 9.89 million pesos
1821–1825	+ 21,01 million pesos
1826–1830	– 12.96 million pesos
1831–1835	– 19.81 million pesos
1836–1840	– 29.49 million pesos
1840–1845	– 51.33 million pesos
1846–1850	– 30.59 million pesos

[89] Yeh-chien Wang, "The Secular Trend of Prices during the Ch'ing Period (1644–1911)," *Journal of the Institute of Chinese Studies of the Chinese University of Hong Kong* (1972), 361. See also R.H. Myers, *The Chinese Economy: Past and Present* (Belmont, CA, Wadsworth, 1980), pp. 71–4.
[90] Von Glahn, *Economic History of China*, p. 367. The "peso" is the Spanish Carolus peso, known after 1800 in China as the "yuan."
[91] Cited in Wang, "The Secular Trend of Prices," 365.

maintaining "stability" in the money market, over both time and space. In this effort it enjoyed only mixed success. In the late seventeenth century, copper–silver exchange rates of well over 1,000:1 were not at all unusual, but, from the beginning of the eighteenth century, copper coin became increasingly "expensive," and rates of 700:1 or 800:1 were the norm.[92]

In the Daoguang reign this trend was dramatically reversed. Local situations varied considerably, of course, but we might consider as representative the series of exchange rates discovered for Shaanxi province by Hans Ulrich Vogel. For the entire eighteenth century, Vogel tells us, the exchange rate in Shaanxi remained well below 1,000:1, but in the Daoguang reign the value of copper cash in terms of silver taels rapidly declined: 1,370:1 in 1831, 1,480:1 in 1842, and as high as 1,800:1 in 1846.[93] This increasingly skewed exchange rate also implies that commodity prices in silver were ever more divorced from prices in copper. Following a price series for some dozen retail items in a store in Ningjin county, Zhili, Yeh-chien Wang shows prices in copper cash remaining relatively stable over the first half of the nineteenth century, even as prices of the same items in silver fell by more than half between 1815 and 1849.[94]

These, then, are the areas of general agreement. The relationship among these trends, and patterns of causation, have occasioned spirited debate, both at the time and today. It was very likely none other than Bao Shichen who, in 1820, first tied the silver shortage directly to the opium trade.[95] Bao calculated that in contemporary Suzhou, opium users spent altogether between 3 million and 4 million taels per year on their habit, and on this basis estimated an empire-wide annual outlay of no less than 100 million taels. Unsurprisingly, since opium was nearly wholly a foreign import, some 80 million taels of silver per year were exported to pay for the drug. Bao did not identify this specifically as a net unfavorable balance of trade, but this was done at least as early as 1833 in a memorial of censor Sun

---

[92] The classic work is Peng Xinwei 彭信威, 中國貨幣史 (Chinese Monetary History) (Shanghai, Renmin chubanshe, 1965; first published 1954). See also Chen Zhaonan 陳昭南, 雍正乾隆年間的銀錢比價變動 (Changing Relative Prices of Silver and Copper in the Yongzheng and Qianlong Reigns) (Taipei, Zhongguo xueshu ju, 1966); Kuroda Akinobu 黑田明伸, "清代銀錢二貨制的構造とその崩壊" (The Structure and Collapse of Silver–Copper Bimetallism in the Qing), 社會經濟史學 (Studies in Socio-economic History) 57.2 (1992), 93–125; R. von Glahn, *Fountain of Fortune: Money and Monetary Policy in China, 1000–1700* (Berkeley, University of California Press, 1996); W.T. Rowe, "Provincial Monetary Practice in Eighteenth-Century China," in C. Moll-Murata, J. Song, and H.U. Vogel (eds.), *Chinese Handicraft Regulations of the Eighteenth Century* (Munich, Iudicium, 2005), pp. 347–71.
[93] H.U. Vogel, "Chinese Central Monetary Policy, 1644–1800," *Late Imperial China* 8.2 (1987), 27.
[94] Wang, "The Secular Trend of Prices," 355.   [95] Rowe, *Speaking of Profit*, pp. 151–5.

Lanzhi.[96] Bao argued that exports of silver for opium caused a severe shortage of capital in domestic markets, but again did not refer to the problem of bimetallic exchange rates. Nevertheless, he argued that the problems caused by opium imports, economic and otherwise, were so severe that it was worth the risk of war to close them down altogether.

In a powerful article of 1983, Peng Zeyi greatly elaborated on Bao Shichen's analysis, sharing with him the identification of opium imports as the principal cause of the Daoguang depression. Peng noted that the outflow of silver in the four years between 1843 and 1846 alone equaled close to 10 percent of the total amount of silver in circulation in the Qing domestic economy. This prompted hoarding behavior, decreasing investment in agricultural and handicraft production, especially in the empire's most developed areas – Jiangnan, Hunan, and Sichuan. A crisis of credit in the commercial economy threated the acceptability of widely circulated banknotes. Prices paid to producers fell – by as much as 50 percent for commercial rice producers. Tax burdens on cultivators (normally assessed in silver and collected in the depreciated copper coin) rose,[97] as did rents charged by taxpaying landlords, and many farmers lost land title and leaseholds. Resistance movements became more frequent and severe. The first sign of relief came in the 1850s, when increased tea and silk exports helped correct the balance of trade and the Qing's hemorrhage of silver slowed.[98]

More recent scholarship, however, has called into question the role of opium in precipitating the Daoguang depression. He Liping, for example, calculates that the total outflow of silver due to opium imports over the entire depression era lay between 3.6 percent and 6.7 percent of the empire's total silver supply. While this was not insignificant, to be sure, He argues that it was not sufficient in itself to cause either the skewed monetary exchange rate or the commodity price deflation that characterized the period.[99]

---

[96] Wang Hongbin 王宏斌, "林則徐關於銀貴錢賤的認識與困惑" (Lin Zexu on the Problem of Expensive Silver and Cheap Copper Coin), 史學月刊 (History Monthly) 2006.9, 35–41.

[97] Yeh-chien Wang found conversion rates used in land tax collection to have risen from 880:1 in Jianding in 1759 to 1,360:1 in Xiaoshan in 1800, and to 2,600:1 in Ningbo in 1852. Y.-C. Wang, *Land Taxation in Imperial China, 1750–1911* (Cambridge, MA, Harvard University Press, 1973), p. 61.

[98] Peng Zeyi 彭澤益, "鴉片戰後十年間銀貴錢賤波動下中國經濟與階級關係" (The Impact of Expensive Silver and Cheap Copper Coins on the Chinese Economy and Class Relations in the Post-Opium War Decade), in Peng Zeyi, 十九世紀後半期的中國財政與經濟 (Government Finance and the Economy in Late Nineteenth-Century China) (Beijing, Renmin chubanshe, 1983), pp. 24–71.

[99] He Liping 賀力平, "鴉片貿易與白銀外流關係之再檢討" (A Re-examination of the Relationship between the Opium Trade and Silver Outflow), 社會科學戰線 (Social Science Front) 2007.1, 63–80.

Man-houng Lin argues that the annual outflow of silver in the years from 1808 to 1856 averaged roughly 8 million taels, an amount equivalent to one-quarter of the Qing's annual land tax revenue and 6 percent of the government's annual revenues as a whole. She argues, like He Liping, that this amount, though large, was not large enough to constitute the determining factor in the depression. She agrees that a silver shortage was largely to blame, but rather a short-term "global silver shortage" brought about by declining production at the source, the New World mines.[100] Richard von Glahn agrees with Lin that opium was not the major problem, but disagrees on the causal role of global silver supplies. Instead, he finds the roots of the depression in the overall contraction of the *domestic* economy. He cites as an indicator of this the slowdown in domestic interregional trade (a factor about which, as noted above, I am not necessarily in agreement), and points out that, unlike the domestic trade, the empire's foreign trade – its silk and tea exports – continued to grow steadily throughout the depression era. The outflow of silver, then, was for von Glahn "a consequence, not a cause, of an economic decline that traced back to the final decades of the eighteenth century."[101]

Government Finance

Nothing more clearly reveals the economic tribulations of the Jiaqing and Daoguang reigns than the vicissitudes of government finance. As Gao Xiang has pointed out, when the Qianlong Emperor boasted that he had presided over a "prosperous age," it was less the condition of the overall economy than that of the central government treasury to which he was referring. Although there were several stores of wealth at the court's disposal, both the most important and the readiest measure of the Qing's fiscal health was the silver accounts of the Board of Revenue treasury (*hubu yinku* 户部银库). By this measure, the Qianlong Emperor's boast was hardly an idle one. Standing at 33,950,000 taels at the outset of his reign in 1736, treasury reserves had risen by about 25 percent through the late 1750s, when the imperial adventures in what became Xinjiang essentially ate up this surplus. On the rise again after 1760, due in large measure to active campaigns for sales of gentry degrees and

---

[100] M.-H. Lin, *China Upside Down: Currency, Society, and Ideologies, 1808–1856* (Cambridge, MA, Harvard University Asia Series, 2006), pp. 22, 133.
[101] Von Glahn, *Economic History of China*, p. 374. See also R. von Glahn, "Foreign Silver Coins in the Market Culture of Nineteenth-Century China," *International Journal of Asian Studies* 4.1 (2007), 61–2.

official ranks (*juanna* 捐納), treasury reserves grew substantially over the following three decades, reaching an all-time high of 83,408,014 taels in 1778. Corruption and waste in the final years of Qianlong's reign reduced this surplus somewhat, but in the final year of Gaozong's formal reign, 1795, the level of reserves remained at a quite comfortable 69,391,990 taels.[102] Over the first decade of the Jiaqing reign, according to the standard account, the treasury surplus was effectively "wiped out."[103] This is an exaggeration, to be sure, but there is little question that the severe depletion of treasury funds in this era was real, and legitimate reason to view this as a turning point in the long-term decline of Qing fiscal capacity.

Treasury reserves underwent a sudden dramatic decline during the final years of the retired emperor's life and his successor's first years on the throne. Reserves were 19,185,592 taels in 1798, less than a third of what they had been three years before, and less than a quarter of their level of a decade earlier.[104] By 1801, they were 16,930,000 taels – less than they had been at any time since the late seventeenth century. But this would also prove to be a low point for the Jiaqing reign. Over the first decade of the nineteenth century, treasury reserves gradually recovered to the 30-million-tael range, and they remained relatively stable over the 1810s, 1820s, and 1830s. Beginning in 1840, at the height of the Opium War, they plummeted again, reaching a new low of 9,933,790 taels in 1843.[105]

The decline in treasury reserves in the Jiaqing and Daoguang reigns reflected a highly unsteady balance of current accounts, and a reluctant abrogation of the long-standing Qing policy of *liangru weichu* 量入為出 – "calculate expenditures on the basis of revenues." The treasury enjoyed a surplus of revenues over expenditures of nearly 12 million taels as late as 1791, but in the first year of Jiaqing's nominal rule in 1796 this had turned around to a deficit of nearly 13 million, and the following year it peaked at negative 28,807,266. In 1798 the annual deficit declined to around 9 million, reflecting a sudden rise in revenues of between 6 million and 16 million. With some occasional ventures into positive territory, annual deficits continued at

---

[102] Gao, "從持盈保泰到高壓統治," 9; Ni, 清朝嘉道財政與社會, pp. 83–4.
[103] Jones and Kuhn, "Dynastic Decline and the Roots of Rebellion," 144.
[104] Peng, "鴉片戰後十年間銀貴錢賤波動下中國經濟與階級關係," 51; Ni, 清朝嘉道財政與社會, p. 169.
[105] Shi Zhihong 史志宏, 清代戶部銀庫收支和庫存統計 (Statistics on Income, Outlays, and Current Balances in the Board of Revenue Treasury during the Qing Era) (Fuzhou, Fujian renmin chubanshe, 2009), p. 104. See also E. Kaske, "Fund-Raising Wars: Office Selling and Interprovincial Finance in Nineteenth-Century China," *Harvard Journal of Asiatic Studies* 71.1 (June 2011), 91; and Ni, 清朝嘉道財政與社會, pp. 169–70.

levels between 1 million and 5 million until the death of the Daoguang Emperor at mid-century.[106]

What so rapidly tipped the balance between income and expenditure was the enormous cost of suppressing the White Lotus Rebellion, coinciding with the first ten years of the Jiaqing Emperor's reign. Military expenses had always comprised the largest share of central government expenditures; Wei Yuan estimated them at an average of 17 million taels per year during the Qianlong reign (far greater than the next largest budgetary items: *yanglian* 养廉 pay supplements to civil and military officials, at 4.3 million, and Yellow River maintenance costs, at 3.8 million).[107] But the cost of suppression of the White Lotus was out of all proportion to this – due in no small part to real and fraudulent payments for civilian militiamen to fight for the Qing cause.[108] The sudden rise in negative balance of accounts in 1797 was due to a dramatic jump in annual treasury expenditures, from 18 million to 35 million taels, mostly spent on the war. The total cost of defeating the rebellion has been estimated at between 120 and 200 million taels, several times the reserves of the treasury in even its best years.[109]

Turning to the revenue side, Yeh-chien Wang long ago established that there was a substantial growth in total central government revenues over the second half of the Qing era, from an annual income of just under 74 million taels in 1753 to 292 million in 1908. Most of this came from new exploitation of commercial taxation, which rose tenfold over the later Qing, from accounting for 26.5 percent of total revenues to 64.9 percent. But though the land tax (*diding* 地丁) thus comprised an ever smaller percentage of revenues, it too rose in absolute terms, nearly tripling from 37,817,000 in 1753 to 103,400,000 in 1908.[110]

Wang's long-term figures, however, mask the fact that for most of the Jiaqing and Daoguang reigns – before the landmark shift to reliance on commercial taxes in the 1850s – government revenues were in decline. There were wide fluctuations from year to year, but the trend of decline is suggested by the figures in Table 2.2 for revenue collected in silver at the Board of Revenue treasury:[111]

---

[106] Ni, 清朝嘉道財政與社會, pp. 165–8, 380.
[107] Ni, 清朝嘉道財政與社會, p. 79.
[108] Y.C. Dai, "Civilians Go into Battle: Hired Militias in the White Lotus War, 1796–1805," *Asia Major*, third series 22.2 (2009), 145–78.
[109] Jones and Kuhn, "Dynastic Decline and the Roots of Rebellion," 144; Dai, "Civilians Go into Battle," 163; Kaske, "Fund-Raising Wars," 91.
[110] Wang, *Land Taxation*, 72.
[111] Shi, 清代戶部銀庫收支和庫存統計, pp. 197–8, 227–8; Ni, 清朝嘉道財政與社會, pp. 166–7.

Table 2.2 Silver revenue collected at Board of Revenue treasury, 1802–1850

1802	11,496,754 taels
1811	9,448,666 taels
1821	7, 630,389 taels
1831	7,010,524 taels
1841	6,796,038 taels
1850	7,748, 585 taels

Within this total revenue, the land tax, the single largest component, continued to increase modestly at least until the 1810s, and remained relatively stable for several years thereafter. At least by the 1840s, however, most provinces began to report massive shortfalls in land tax and grain tribute collections relative to assessments. One of the most egregious was Hubei, which in 1842 actually collected only 528,486 taels – merely 46 percent of its assessment – and by 1850 only 334,179. Similar shortfalls occurred in the grain tribute, the government's second-largest contributor to total revenue in these years. Official response in both cases was reform, not by increasingly effective collection, but by lowering assessments.[112]

The third-largest contributor to Qing central revenues was the salt administration, which in the mid-eighteenth century yielded just under 9 million taels, amounting to some 11.8 percent of central government revenue.[113] Salt, however, was among the first revenue sources to exhibit marked decline: Peng Zeyi calculates a shrinkage of salt revenues by 13.3 percent over the years from 1753 to 1812, even while land tax revenues increased by 10.9 percent and total revenues by 6.3 percent.[114] The basic problem was smuggling of "private salt," which had already become noticeable at the height of the prosperous age, and which significantly worsened into the early nineteenth century.

Most observers agreed that smuggling was a direct result of the inefficient structure of the existing salt administration. The empire was divided into several large salt districts for salt production and distribution. Within each district, a limited number of enfeoffed "official-merchants" held franchises to

---

[112] Xia, "太平天國前後長江各省之田賦問題," 420.   [113] Wang, *Land Taxation*, p. 72.
[114] Peng, "鴉片戰後十年間銀貴錢賤波動下中國經濟與階級關係," 51.

purchase from the producers and distribute very large annual quotas of salt, via specified routes and to specified local markets. Successive price markups along the way made the eventual price to consumers in many cases unaffordably high. But there were alternative sources of salt: that privately produced outside the state system, that illegally brought into one salt district from a competing neighboring district, and, not least, that carried over quota by government merchants themselves. All of these increasingly undersold the legal "government salt," and reduced the revenue that salt produced.

In 1832–1833 Liang-Jiang governor-general Tao Zhu undertook a fundamental reform of operations in the Liang-Huai salt district, of which he was collaterally commissioner. Liang-Huai was the most lucrative of the several geographic districts into which the imperial salt administration was divided. It was tasked with distributing the rich product of the salt fields in the Yangzhou hinterlands throughout two subdistricts: Huainan, encompassing portions of northern Jiangsu and most of Jiangxi, Hubei, and Hunan, and Huaibei, covering most of Anhui and Henan. Tao's reform lifted most of the restrictions on salt distribution in Huaibei: (1) transport and sales were no longer restricted to the 200-odd enfranchised merchants, but declared open to any enterprising merchant whose integrity and financial soundness could be ascertained, (2) to facilitate entry into the trade of these often smaller merchants, units of salt for sale were drastically reduced in size to more manageable job lots, which might be carried alongside commodities other than salt; and (3) routes and marketplaces within districts were no longer for the most part prescribed, and state-mandated brokers and other middlemen were eliminated. Most contemporaries agreed that Tao's reforms were an unmitigated success, and they were soon imitated in some of the empire's other salt districts.[115] By 1908, central salt revenues amounted to roughly 45 milllion taels, nearly five times what they had been in the mid-eighteenth century.[116] This was celebrated by contemporaries as evidence that fiscal and economic reform could indeed be achieved, even in this age of manifest crisis.

---

[115] Saeki Tomi 佐佰富, "清代道光朝における 淮南鹽政的改革" (The Reform of the Huainan Salt Administration during the Qing Daoguang Reign), in Saeki, 中國史研究 (Studies in Chinese History) (Kyoto, Tōyōshi kenkyūkai, 1969), 2.621–66; Saeki, 清代鹽政の研究 (A Study of the Qing Salt Administration) (Kyoto, Tōyōshi kenkyūkai, 1956); T.A. Metzger, "T'ao Chu's Reform of the Huaipei Salt Monopoly (1831–1833)," *Papers on China* 16 (1962), 1–39; Ni, 清朝嘉道財政與社會, pp. 276–311; Rowe, *Speaking of Profit*, Chapter 5. For follow-up reforms affecting the Huainan portion of the Liang-Huai district, see W.T. Rowe, *Hankow: Commerce and Society in a Chinese City, 1796–1889* (Stanford: Stanford University Press, 1984).

[116] Wang, *Land Taxation*, p. 72.

In the shorter term, faced with growing imbalances between revenues and expenditures, the Jiaqing court and its successors increasingly relied upon improvised and irregular generators of income. Notable among these were campaigns to solicit "contributions," in exchange for granting of gentry degrees or brevet (less often substantive) official rank. Sales of degrees and ranks (*juanna*) had been utilized in the prosperous age itself to finance such things as the Yongzheng Emperor's massive buildup of reserves in the ever-normal granary (*changping cang* 常平倉) system, and Qianlong's prosecution of the Jinchuan campaigns. But in the Jiaqing reign they became critical to the regime's very survival. The 1798 Sichuan and Hubei Reconstuction Campaign (*Chuan Chu shanhou juanshu* 川楚善後捐輸), enacted to finance the protracted White Lotus war, attracted nearly 11 million purchasers and netted 30 million taels, in Elisabeth Kaske's words "the highest sum ever reached in a single contribution campaign." In Zhejiang province alone it brought in just under 2 million taels, or approximately 90 percent of the province's annual land tax quota. Such ad hoc revenue-raising mechanisms, along with proliferating non-statutory surtaxes, would become increasingly central to government finance over the remainder of the nineteenth century.[117]

What Happened in the Early Nineteenth Century?

Economic historians have been fairly unanimous in identifying the years around 1800 as a turning point in Chinese economic history. Writing in the *Cambridge History of China* in 2002, for example, Ramon Myers and Yeh-chien Wang argued that it was then that "negative externalities," such as environmental decay, joined with "market failure," monetary deflation, rising unemployment, a growing tax burden, a cooling climate, and rising social tensions to turn what had been until recently a prosperous economy into a desperately struggling one.[118] More recently, Richard von Glahn has likewise pinpointed the year 1800 as marking the transition from an early modern era of economic "maturation" to one of wrenching "restructuring." Though skeptical about the claim of an impending Malthusian trap, he is inclined to

---

[117] Kaske, "Fund-Raising Wars," 91; L. Zhang, "Legacy of Success: Office Purchase and State–Elite Relations in Qing China," *Harvard Journal of Asiatic Studies* 73.2 (2013), 260, 270; Xu Daling 許大齡, 清代捐納制度 (The System of Sales of Degrees and Ranks in the Qing Period) (Taipei, Wenhai chubanshe, 1977).

[118] R.H. Myers and Y.-C. Wang, "Economic Developments, 1644–1800," in W.J. Peterson (ed.), *The Cambridge History of China*, vol. 9, part 1, *The Ch'ing Empire to 1800* (New York, Cambridge University Press, 2002), pp. 564, 640–1.

accept arguments for a declining per capita GDP, and emphatic that this era witnessed the onset of a general "economic depression," marked by "static or declining real prices and wages," lasting at least through the great rebellions of the mid-nineteenth century.[119]

Kenneth Pomeranz has famously sought to place China's economic experience of this period in comparative perspective, identifying it as that of a "Great Divergence" from both the Western experience and its own presumed path of development. Pomeranz argued eloquently that the Qing during the "prosperous age" enjoyed standards of living comparable or even superior to those of Europe, and that there seemed little in Chinese economic thought and institutions that would forecast a future markedly worse than that of Europe. And yet that is precisely what happened. The reason, of course, was industrialization in Europe and its absence in China, a divergence Pomeranz attributes not to pathology but to "conjunctures," the essentially serendipitous convenient availability of fossil fuel deposits in Europe and the exploitation of the New World (using unfree African labor) to remove the "land constraint" that typically inhibited industrialization in the Qing and elsewhere.

On the basis of what we have seen above, I am inclined to agree with the general thrust of Pomeranz's arguments (though not, for the most part, his identification of the specific reasons for Qing divergence). Certainly, we can all agree that the Qing did not undergo anything like industrialization before this was introduced from outside. But if the Jiaqing and Daoguang reigns did not see anything as revolutionary as industrialization, they did witness a continued incremental development of the proto-industrial economy that had been emerging at least since the sixteenth century: agricultural commercialization and diversification, niche-seeking product specialization, exploitation of new markets, forging of highly sophisticated distribution networks, and proliferation of handicraft manufacture. All of this required a substantial level of innovative entrepreneurship, which early modern China was hardly lacking.

An outstanding but not unique example was the capital-intensive salt industry of Furong, Sichuan. Building upon the highly sophisticated capital mobilization instruments of the lineage trust (*tang* 堂) and the highly refined regime of property rights and written contracts in late imperial business culture, Furong merchants created and re-created partnerships of great scale and achieved considerable vertical integration of fuel supply, salt

---

[119] Von Glahn, *Economic History of China*, Chapter 9.

extraction and refinement operations, and long-distance marketing. The real takeoff of Furong's salt industry came only in the 1850s, when Sichuan salt captured much of the middle Yangzi market away from the rebel-plagued Liang-Huai saltyards at Yangzhou. But Furong was able to do this so adroitly because the organizational and technological structure had already been built up, largely in the Jiaqing and Daoguang reigns.[120]

In this chapter we have concentrated on just a few prominent features relevant to the Jiaqing and early Daoguang economy. Ecological deterioration was widespread, severe, and largely man-made, a direct consequence of developmental choices made during the "prosperous age." Its first critical manifestations appeared in this era, but worsened thereafter. None of the ecological cataclysms of the Jiaqing and Daoguang reigns remotely approached in severity those of the century to follow – the north China famines of 1876–1879 and 1928–1930, and the great Yangzi flood of 1931 – in each of which millions of persons lost their lives. This was in part because the chief state bulwark against massive dearth, the granary system, continued to function tolerably well in the early nineteenth century, forfeiting its utility altogether only during the civil wars of the 1850s.[121]

On the question of demographic crisis, we would come down somewhere between the pessimism of Hong Liangji and the optimism of Bao Shichen: while there might not have been a looming Malthusian crisis, and there was still room for per acre and even perhaps per capita productivity rises, it does seem likely that continued population growth had some, if selective, negative impact on standards of living.

There was a notable slowdown in the Qing economy beginning in the late eighteenth century, but this was somewhat selective. If intra-regional trade in grain on the Yangzi declined a little, this was almost certainly offset by corresponding growth of other trade routes and commodities. Any overall decline in long-distance domestic trade was offset by the rise in overseas trade – not merely with the West but with Nanyang and other intra-Asian trade partners.[122] The development of new markets brought with it, as in the middle Yangzi region, not devolution into dependent monoculture but rather a vigorous diversification of product base. Neither did the Qing

---

[120] M. Zelin, *The Merchants of Zigong: Industrial Entrepreneurship in Early Modern China* (New York, Columbia University Press, 2005).
[121] P.-É. Will and R.B. Wong, with J. Lee, *Nourish the People: The State Civilian Granary System in China, 1650–1850* (Ann Arbor, Center for Chinese Studies, 1991), p. 75.
[122] See, for example, figures on domestic versus maritime customs revenues in von Glahn, *Economic History of China*, p. 370.

economy as a whole devolve into dependency on a foreign metropolis, notwithstanding the steady growth in volume of maritime trade. After c. 1825, economic "depression" certainly occurred, marked by the shortage of silver, the skewing of bimetallic exchange rates, and the deflation of commodity prices (especially those paid to farmers), but the more fundamental causes of the depression remain under debate; by the 1840s, and the opening of new ports for foreign trade, the effects of this depression seemed to be easing.

A severe fiscal crisis around the turn of the nineteenth century was only gradually, and probably never completely, relieved. The short-term answers included stopgap measures such as sales of offices and contribution drives, and significant but piecemeal reforms such as those undertaken in the grain tribute and salt administrations during the Daoguang reign. The long-term solution was a wholesale fiscal restructuring, shifting the basis of state finances from agriculture to commerce, but this only began to be enacted in the 1850s, under the pressure of the Taiping wars. One is tempted to agree with Ni Yuping's conclusion that the late Qing state – far from achieving a condition of lasting "sustainability" – never fully recovered the degree of initiative, energy, fiscal sufficiency, and economic policy competence that it sacrificed in the last decades of the eighteenth century.[123] The mid-Qing state was far from perfectly clear-sighted – its lapses in vision in large measure led to the negative consequences of the post-"prosperous age" – and the Jiaqing and Daoguang administrations did have their own moments of decisive action. But clearly *one* of the factors that underlay the Great Divergence was the declining leadership of the imperial state.

Further Reading

Chuan, H.-S., and R.A. Kraus, *Mid-Qing Rice Markets and Trade: An Essay in Price History* (Cambridge, MA, Harvard University East Asian Monographs, 1975).

Gao Wangling 高王凌, 十八世紀中國的經濟發展和政府政策 (Government Policy and Eighteenth-Century Chinese Economic Development) (Beijing, Zhongguo shehui kexue chubanshe, 1995).

Huang Guosheng 黃國盛, 鴉片戰爭前的東南四省海關 (Maritime Customs in China's Four Southeastern Provinces Prior to the Opium War) (Fuzhou, Fujian renmin chubanshe, 2000).

---

[123] Ni, 清朝嘉道財政與社會, p. 377. See also the chapter by Elisabeth Kaske in the present volume.

Huang Jingbin 黃敬斌, 民生與家計：清初至民國時期江南居民的消費 (Popular Livelihoods and Household Budgets: Jiangnan Residents' Expenditures from Early Qing to the Republican Era) (Shanghai, Fudan University Press, 2009).

Jones, S.M., and P.A. Kuhn, "Dynastic Decline and the Roots of Rebellion," in J.K. Fairbank (ed.), *The Cambridge History of China*, vol. 10, *Late Ch'ing, 1800–1911*, part 1 (New York, Cambridge University Press, 1978).

Kuroda Akinobu 黑田明伸, "清代銀錢二貨制的構造 とその 崩壞" (The Structure and Collapse of Silver–Copper Bimetallism in the Qing), 社會經濟史學 (Studies in Socio-economic History) 57.2 (1992), 93–125.

Lee, J., and F. Wang, *One Quarter of Humanity: Malthusian Mythology and Chinese Realities* (Cambridge, MA, Harvard University Press, 1999).

Li, Bozhong, *Agricultural Development in Jiangnan, 1620–1850* (New York, St. Martin's Press, 1998).

Ni Yuping 倪玉平, 清朝嘉道財政與社會 (Government Finance and Society in the Qing Jiaqing and Daoguang Reigns) (Beijing, Commercial Press, 2013).

Peng Zeyi 彭澤益, "清代前期手工業的發展" (The Development of Handicrafts in the Early Qing), 中國史研究 (Studies in Chinese History) 1981.1 43–60.

Perdue, P., *Exhausting the Earth: State and Peasant in Hunan, 1500–1850* (Cambridge, MA, Harvard University Press, 1987).

Pomeranz, K., *The Great Divergence: China, Europe, and the Making of the Modern World Economy* (Princeton, Princeton University Press, 2000).

Rowe, W.T., *Speaking of Profit: Bao Shichen and Reform in Nineteenth-Century China* (Cambridge, MA, Harvard University Asia Center, 2018).

Saeki Tomi 佐佰富, 代鹽政の研究 (A Study of the Qing Salt Administration) (Kyoto, Tōyōshi kenkyūkai, 1956).

Suzuki Chusei, 鈴木中正, 清朝中時研究 (A Study of the Mid-Qing Period) (Toyohashi, Aichi University Research Institute on International Problems, 1952).

Von Glahn, R., *The Economic History of China: From Antiquity to the Nineteenth Century* (Cambridge, Cambridge University Press, 2016).

Wu Chengming 吳承明, "論清代前期我國國內市場" (The Domestic Market in the Early Qing), 歷史研究 (Historical Studies) 1983.1, 96–106.

3

Agriculture

DEBIN MA AND KAIXIANG PENG

For over two millennia, China has sustained the largest single human society on the planet through the development of one of the most sophisticated agrarian systems in history. Even until quite recently, agriculture occupied a central place in the Chinese economy, commanding a dominant 60 to 70 percent of the total economy. Agricultural institutions define the Chinese economic system and agricultural production drove long-run economic change or growth in China. Agriculture was at the center of the Great Divergence debate. Agricultural harvest successes or failures sometimes spelled the rise and fall of dynasties throughout history. Moving to the modern era, Chinese agriculture became the scapegoat for China's modernization failure and was regarded as the incubator for Communist revolution. However, given its overriding importance, research on modern Chinese agriculture has been surprisingly understudied for the last few decades.

This chapter provides a selective survey of some of the key themes in modern Chinese agriculture during the nineteenth and twentieth centuries. It provides a critical survey on the general trends in agricultural output during this period and existing interpretations. The deteriorating land–labor ratio over time has easily given rise to a Malthusian type of interpretation of Chinese agriculture in the form of the so-called "high-level equilibrium trap" hypothesis proposed by Mark Elvin and later the "involution" thesis according to Philip Huang. Both posit a largely pessimistic vision of a long-run decline in agricultural productivity and output per capita in the face of resource constraints and overpopulation over time. However, the more optimistic vision, as recently championed by the California school, posits that Chinese agricultural expansion achieved efficiency from gains in the use of better fertilizers, rationalization of resource use, agricultural

We wish to thank Matthew Noellert and Thomas Rawski for very useful comments.

intensification, and cash crop cultivation. This technical bias induced by the lower Yangzi's relative factor endowment, combined with the expansion in regional trade and geographic division of labor, constituted what they viewed as Smithian growth.[1] Our survey goes on to reconstruct a model that reconciles these relatively pessimistic and optimistic assessments of the Chinese mode of agricultural production. Based on that, it argues that traditional Chinese institutions have shown remarkable resilience to adapt to the introduction of new crops, heightened commercialization, and technological and organizational innovation.

Long-Run Trends in Agricultural Output

Labor-intensive cultivation has been a long-standing feature of Chinese and East Asian agriculture for millennia, marked by small-scale family farms, very high labor input, and land productivity. China's first large-scale survey, by the team led by John Lossing Buck of Nanjing University in the 1920s and 1930s, revealed a mean farm size of a mere 3.76 acres compared with 14.28, 63.18, and 156.85 acres for the Netherlands, the UK, and the US respectively. Farm sizes in China's northern wheat region were slightly larger than in the southern rice region, standing at 5.63 and 3.14 acres respectively.[2] John Buck's study also mapped out the main crop mix across China's twenty-two provinces in the 1930s, as shown in Map 3.1.

The most typical form of this labor-intensive cultivation (精耕细作) is the highly developed rice culture in the lower Yangzi region, where the so-called "ten *mu* per family" (one *mu* = 0.16 acre) came into firm shape at the beginning of the nineteenth century.[3] Intensive agriculture has given rise to very high land productivity, probably matching some of the highest in the most advanced agricultural regions employing modern technology even in the early twentieth

---

[1] The articles of debate can be found in the May 2002 (61.2) issue of the *Journal of Asian Studies*. For the earlier debate between Philip Huang, Thomas Rawski, and Ramon Meyers around the 1990s on whether or not there were improvements in agricultural productivity and living standards in Chinese agriculture for the early twentieth century, see Chapter 6 of P. Richardson, *Economic Change in China, c. 1800–1950* (Cambridge, Cambridge University Press, 1990).

[2] J.L. Buck, *Land Utilization in China* (Nanking, University of Nanking Press, 1937), p. 268. For per capita acreage between the eighteenth and early twentieth centuries, see Shi Zhihong, 史志宏, 清代农业的发展和不发展 (1661–1911 年) (Development or Non-development of Qing Agriculture: 1611–1911) (Beijing, Shehui kexue wenxian chubanshe, 2017), pp. 141–3.

[3] Li Bozhong 李伯重, 多视角看江南经济史 (1250–1850) (An Economic History of Jiangnan in Multiple Perspectives (1250–1850)) (Beijing, Sanlian shudian, 2003), pp. 241–88.

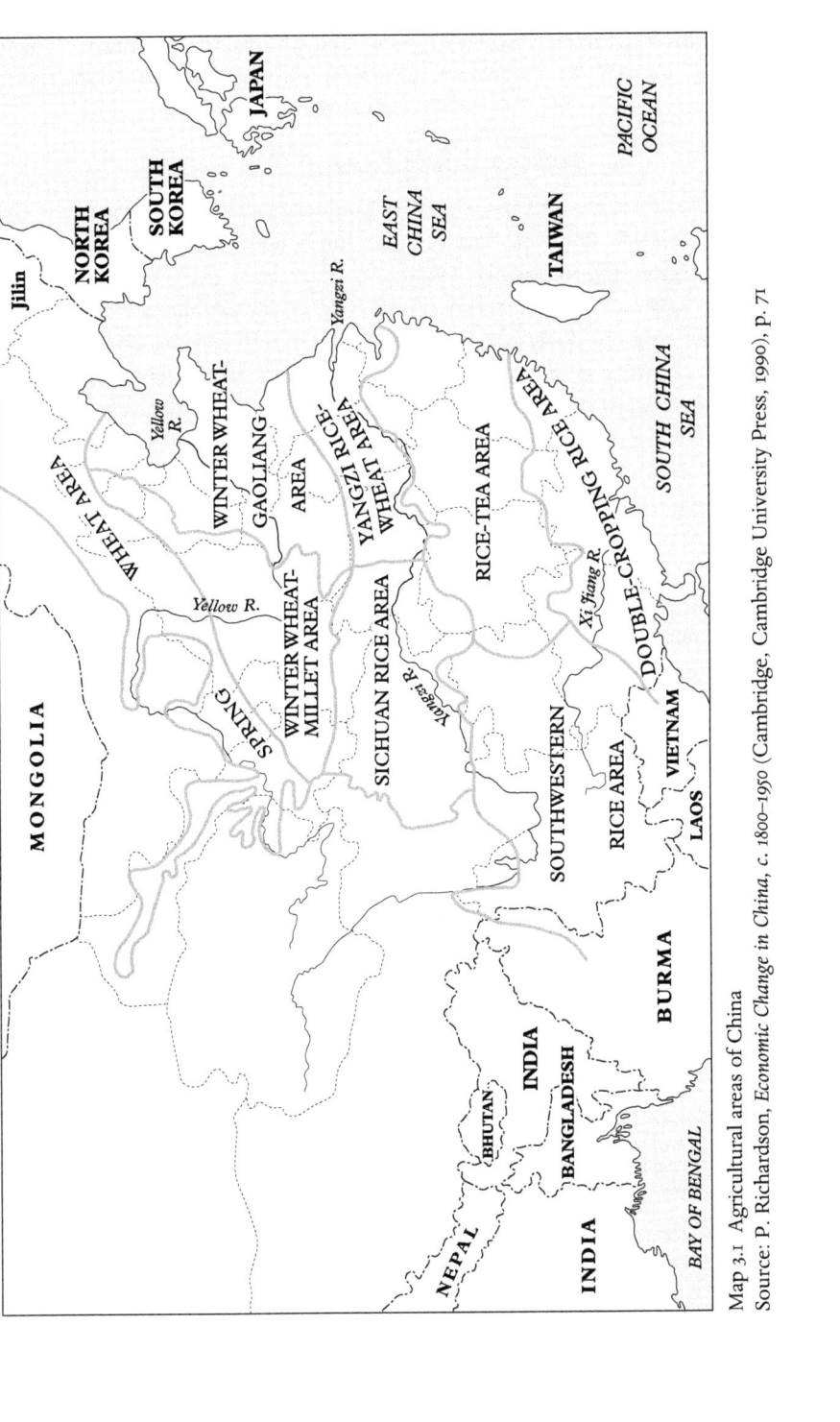

Map 3.1 Agricultural areas of China
Source: P. Richardson, *Economic Change in China, c. 1800–1950* (Cambridge, Cambridge University Press, 1990), p. 71

century. However, labor productivity would be far lower in that regard.[4] Here, we turn to examine long-term agricultural output trends under China's land cultivation system for the nineteenth and twentieth centuries.

Long-Term Agricultural Decline: Fact or Fiction?

Figure 3.1 shows an upward trend in long-term crop yields between the sixteenth century and the turn of the nineteenth century, both in the Jiangnan region and nationally. However, after about 1800, all series except Perkins's (1969) show a sharp downturn. Indeed, the estimates by Wu (1985, 1998) show that the decline in crop yield for the few decades after the mid-eighteenth century actually wiped out all the gains accumulated during the previous centuries. Figure 3.2 shows this decline in yields that accounted for a corresponding decline in various per capita grain output estimates from the early nineteenth century, and ultimately per capita GDP estimates in the face of rising population.[5] Again, with the exception of Perkins's estimates, these declines continued after the mid-nineteenth century even when there occurred catastrophic population loss during the 1860s Taiping Rebellion and the gradual modernization of Chinese agriculture from the late nineteenth century.

How well do these estimates of declining land yields and per capita grain output stand scrutiny? One thing to bear in mind is that the crop yield data for the 1930s and 1950s derived from large-scale or nationwide statistical surveys are of much better quality than estimates for earlier periods. Therefore it is striking to see that all these studies cited above, except Perkins (1969),[6] show crop yield and per capita grain output estimates for the peak period of the Qing much higher than for the 1930s and 1950s, leading to a possible suspicion of sample selection bias in terms of crop yield data for the pre-1930s period. As we will show later, 1930s levels of per capita grain output were high even compared with the Communist period or the early reform era of the 1980s. It is also possible that the peak value for grain output per capita for Qing China has been overestimated, and that its actual decline during and after the nineteenth century was more gradual and slower than estimated by Shi and Guo.

---

[4] See J.L. Buck, *Land Utilization in China* (Nanking, University of Nanking, 1937), p. 226; D.H. Perkins, *Agricultural Development in China, 1368–1968* (Chicago, Aldine Publishing, 1969), Chapter 2. Also see R.C. Allen, "Agricultural Productivity and Rural Incomes in England and the Yangtze Delta, c. 1620–c. 1820," *Economic History Review* 62.3 (August 2009), pp. 525–50.

[5] For long-term GDP estimates, see S. Broadberry, H. Guan, and D.D. Li, "China, Europe and the Great Divergence: A Study in Historical National Accounting, 980–1850," *Journal of Economic History* 78.4 (2018), 955–1000.

[6] These in-text citations are given in full in Figure 3.1.

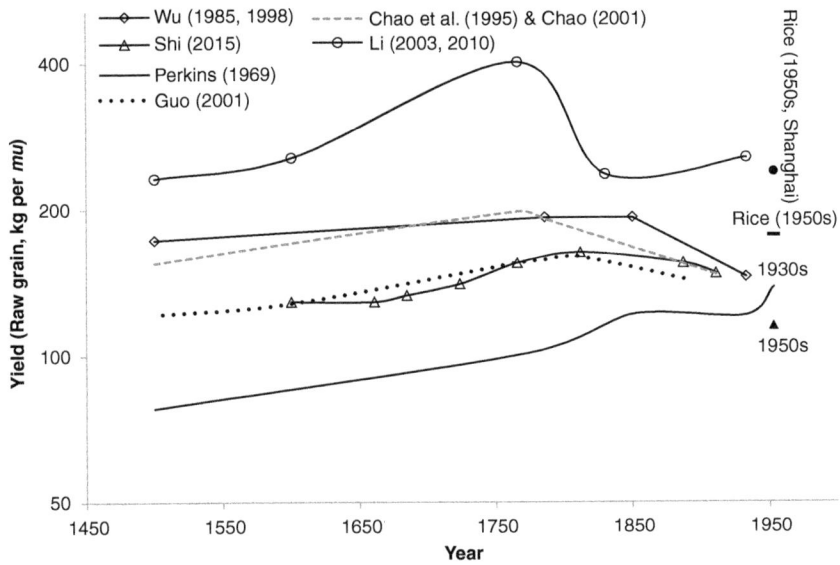

Figure 3.1 China's historical crop yield
Notes: (1) Except for rice yield in the 1950s, crop yield per *mu* in this figure refers to yield averaged by agricultural acreage, while sown acreage, equal to multiplying agricultural acreage by the multiple-crop index, is more used in China's current statistics.
(2) Li's (2003; 2010) figures are for the Yangzi delta only, while all other series are national estimations.
(3) Chao et al. (1995) estimates average land yield from 1750 to 1900, and Chao (2001) estimates land yield during the Song dynasty and links it to 1750.
(4) For comparison, estimations based on statistical surveys in the 1930s and 1950s are labeled specifically. Yield in the 1950s is the average of yields from 1952 to 1957, and the estimation method is described in Peng (2015).
Sources: D.H. Perkins, *Agricultural Development in China, 1368–1968* (Chicago, Aldine Publishing, 1969); Wu Hui 吴慧, 中国历代粮食亩产研究 (Study of Grain Yield per *Mu* in Chinese History) (Beijing, Zhongguo nongye chubanshe, 1985); Wu Hui, "历史上粮食商品率商品量测估—以宋明清为例" (Estimates of Ratio and Quantity of Food Commercialization: Song, Ming, and Qing Case Study), 中国经济史研究 (Research in Chinese Economic History) 1998.4, 16–36; Kang Chao 赵冈 et al., 清代粮食亩产量研究 (Study of Grain Yield per *Mu* in the Qing Dynasty) (Beijing, Zhongguo nongye chubanshe, 1995); Kang Chao, 农业经济史论集：产权、人口与农业生产 (Collection of Papers on Agricultural Economic History: Property Rights, Population, and Production) (Beijing, Zhongguo nongye chubanshe, 2001), p. 173; Guo Songyi 郭松义, "明清时期的粮食生产与农民生活水平" (Food Production and Living Standard of Peasants in the Ming and Qing Dynasties), 中国社会科学院历史研究所学刊 (Journal of the CASS Institute of History) 2001.1, 373–96; Li Bozhong 李伯重, 多视角看江南经济史 (1250–1850) (An Economic History of Jiangnan in Multiple Perspectives (1250–1850)) (Beijing, Sanlian shudian, 2003), pp. 83, 128, 326–7; Li Bozhong, 中国的早期近代经济—1820年代华亭–娄县地区 GDP 研究 (An Early Modern Economy in China: A Study of the GDP of Huating–Lou Area, 1823–1829) (Beijing, Zhonghua shuju, 2010), pp. 395–8; Shi Zhihong 史志宏, "清代农业生产指标的估计" (Estimates of Indicators of Agricultural Production in the Qing Dynasty), 中国经济史研究 (Research in Chinese Economic History) 2015.3, 5–30; Z. Shi, *Agricultural Development in Qing China: A Quantitative Study, 1661–1911* (Leiden, Brill, 2017); Peng Kaixiang 彭凯翔, "人口增长下的粮食生产与经济发展—由史志宏研究员的清代农业产出测算谈起" (Grain Production and Development under the Growth of Population: A Discussion from Shi Zhihong's Estimation of Agriculture Production in the Qing Dynasty) 中国经济史研究 (Research in Chinese Economic History) 7 (2015), 38–49

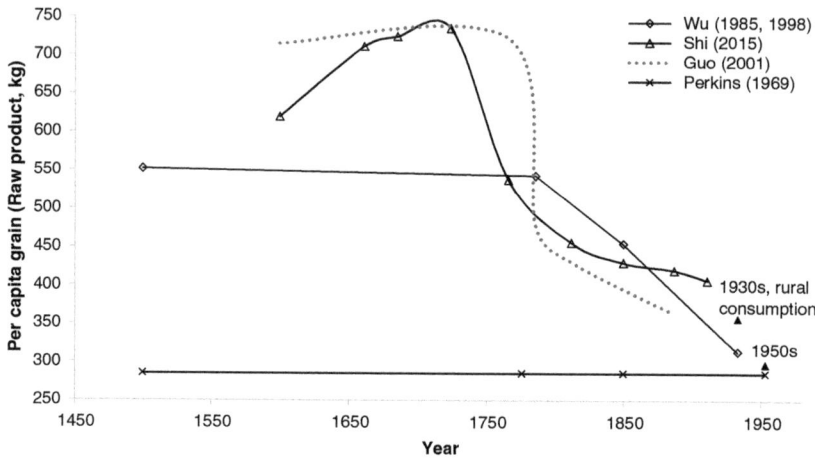

Figure 3.2 Per capita output of raw grain, 1500–1950
Notes: for the discussion of 1930s rural grain consumption, see later section on consistency checks. Sources for other estimates are the same as for Figure 3.1.

Take the example of the estimates by Chao et al. (1995), which provides the most systematic evidence of this decline based on the Qing primary sources. Chao et al. calculated a long-term annual decrease of 0.2 percent between 1750 and 1900, as shown in Figure 3.1. Their nationwide average yield between 1750 and 1900 of 2.3 *dan* (about 177 kilograms) per *mu* is slightly lower than the land-tax-based yield estimate made by Wu (1985; 1998) but somewhat higher than that made by Shi Zhihong for the first half of the nineteenth century. But Chao et al.'s estimate of land yield was derived by doubling the rental share rate recorded from the land tax account book by assuming a constant 50/50 share of rent, a practice also followed by Wu (1985; 1998), Shi (2017), Guo (2001), and others. This reliance on land rent data, due to their abundance and low variation in land rent, is understandable, but the assumption of a constant ratio of land rent to yield is highly problematic for the entire period of study. Indeed, given the increasing trend of urban-based landlords, who were becoming increasingly detached from their land, and the increasing switch from sharecropping to fixed land rents, tenants' control over their land strengthened over time with landlords' share of the output possibly going down and correspondingly reducing their investment in land improvement.[7] Hence the assumption of a constant ratio could lead to a downward bias in crop yield.

[7] Gao Wangling 高王凌, "关于近代粮食亩产量的估算问题—清代粮食亩产量研究>读后" (On the Estimation of Modern Grain Yield per *Mu*: Review of Study on Grain

Table 3.1 Mean and distribution of agricultural yields (*shi* per *mu*) in Qing China

Region	Period	obs	mean	median	sd	min	max
Northern China	1644–1795 (early Qing)	264	0.71	0.55	0.62	0.02	3.40
Northern China	1796–1850 (mid-Qing)	56	0.70	0.58	0.65	0.06	3.25
Northern China	1851–1911 (late Qing)	137	0.64	0.50	0.57	0.06	4.00
Southern China	1644–1795 (early Qing)	801	2.72	2.38	1.62	0.26	18.00
Southern China	1796–1850 (mid-Qing)	555	3.00	2.65	1.70	0.40	13.66
Southern China	1851–1911 (late Qing)	473	3.03	2.67	1.65	0.38	12.50

Note. According to Shi, *Agricultural Development in Qing China*, northern China includes 东北 the Northeast, 甘肃 Gansu, 河南 Henan, 山东 Shandong, 山西 Shanxi, 陕西 Shaanxi, and 直隶 Zhili. Southern China includes 安徽 Anhui, 福建 Fujian, 广东 Guangdong, 广西 Guangxi, 贵州 Guizhou, 湖北 Hubei, 湖南 Hunan, 江苏 Jiangsu, 江西 Jiangxi, 四川 Sichuan, 云南 Yunnan, and 浙江 Zhejiang.

Here we will conduct some cross-checks and tests by looking at nearly 3,000 cases of yield data collected from local gazettes by Shi.[8] One advantage of these yield data is that they are mostly for "public land" (*gongtian* 公田), with much simpler and more stable rental contractual relationships than those used in land rent account books. These records also include data from places like Huizhou, where the rental record books and land transaction books showed a declining yield in late Qing given by other studies. Table 3.1 shows that the mean and distribution of land yields across the three different periods of Qing are quite close. Actually, land yields in mid- and late Qing were slightly higher in southern China. The standard deviation of land yields in northern China shrank because of the increase in sample size. As shown later, the New World crops, which diffused rapidly in the late Qing, were not recorded, so the actual distribution of land yields in late Qing could tilt more towards the right. All in all, these micro-level data do not support declining land yields in mid- and late Qing.[9]

Yield per *Mu* in the Qing Dynasty"), 中国经济史研究 (Research in Chinese Economic History) 2000.2, 156–60.

[8] Shi Zhihong, *Agricultural Development in Qing China: A Quantitative Study, 1661–1911* (Leiden, Brill, 2017).

[9] To justify their findings, Chao et al., Wu, and others have listed factors such as soil degradation, climate change, and environmental damage caused by the introduction of maize into China. Kang Chao 赵冈 et al., 清代粮食亩产量研究 (Study of Grain Yield per *Mu* in the Qing Dynasty) (Beijing, Zhongguo nongye chubanshe, 1995); Wu Hui 吴慧, 中国历代粮食亩产研究 (Study of Grain Yield per *Mu* in Chinese History) (Beijing, Zhongguo nongye chubanshe, 1985). For a different interpretation

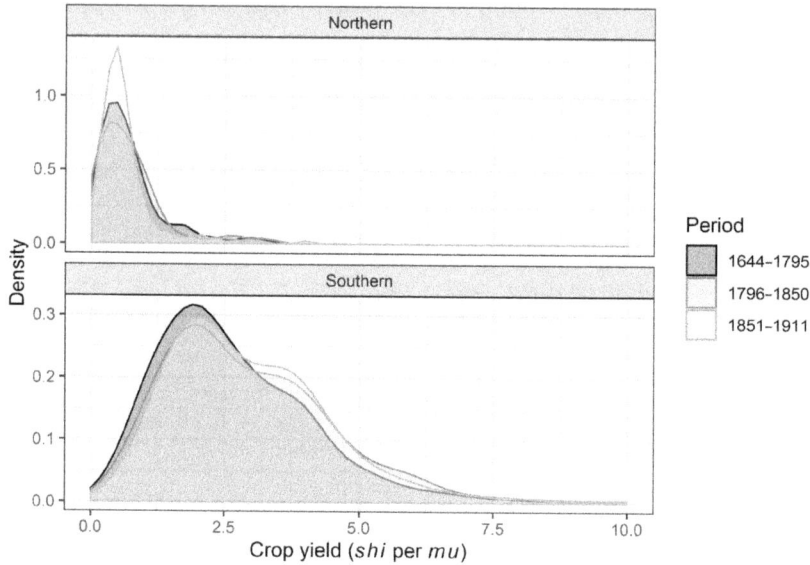

Figure 3.3 Distribution of Qing crop yields based on local gazettes
Source: Shi, *Agricultural Development in Qing China*.

Consistency Checks from the Consumption and Demand Side

We now turn to some cross-checks from consumption and market prices. For example, Wu himself estimates that historically (mostly in the Ming and Qing eras) the farming and non-farming population consumed, on average, 17.5 kilograms and 16.4 kilograms of processed rice per person per month, respectively. With about 70 percent of the total population engaged in farming, this amounts to an aggregated average consumption per capita of 17.2 kilograms per month (0.575 kilogram per day for thirty days per month), or 206.5 kilograms per year. Adding non-staple foods, seeds, fodder, etc., which, as Wu suggests, constituted a 30 percent share of total grain output, we can derive a per capita grain consumption of 295 kilograms per year.[10] This level is consistent with the 307 kilograms of processed grain consumption per capita for rural households for the 1930s, but higher than the national average in the 1950s,

---

on the environmental damage caused by the introduction of maize into China, see Wang Baoning 王保宁 and Zhu Guangyong 朱光涌, "从抵制到接受: 清代浙江的玉米种植" (From Resistance to Acceptance: Maize in Zhejiang Province in the Qing Dynasty)", 中国历史地理论丛 (Journal of Chinese Historical Geography), 2019.1, 108–17. We will examine environmental issues below.

[10] Wu, 中国历代粮食亩产研究, 64–8.

which was about 297 kilograms of raw grain or 208 kilograms of processed grain.[11] Note that the 1930s level of per capita grain consumption, based on a large-scale survey, is not exceeded until the late 1980s. Furthermore, the reported per capita consumption for meat and eggs was sixteen kilograms per year in the 1930s, similar to the average consumption level in 1978. Similar studies also show that daily calorie and protein intake reached about 3,000 to 4,000 calories and 100 grams during the 1930s.[12] All these consumption-side estimates match the 1930s per capita grain output levels better than they do those from before the nineteenth century, as shown in Figure 3.2.

If there was a drastic decline in per capita grain output and consumption in the late nineteenth century, there would have also been a corresponding decline in real wages as well as large shifts in relative prices between wages (prices of labor-intensive goods) and grain prices. However, based on the limited regional wages and prices, we do not observe such a decline for the set of relative prices. Figure 3.4 presents a set of wages for agricultural, handicraft and industrial laborers in Beijing and other regions relative to grain price. Although scattered and somewhat volatile, none of them show a persistent downward trend. Data elsewhere on relative prices also reveal that rural and urban wages kept pace with other items of daily living such as cotton cloth, fuel, vegetables, meat, and housing.[13]

---

[11] Peng, "人口增长下的粮食生产与经济发展."

[12] Data for the PRC period come from 中国农业统计资料汇编 1949–2004 (Statistics on Chinese Agriculture, 1949–2004) (Beijing, Zhongguo tongji chubanshe, 2005). Data for the 1930s come from 农情报告 1937–38 (Crop Reporting in China, 1937–38) (Nanjing, National Agricultural Research Bureau, Ministry of Industry); Qiao Qiming 乔启明, 中国农村社会经济学 (Social Economics in Rural China) (Shanghai, Shangwu Yinshuguan, 1945), pp. 410–18.

[13] R.C. Allen, C. Moll-Murata, D. Ma, and J. van Zanden, "Wages, Prices, and Living Standards in China 1738–1925: In Comparison with Europe, Japan, and India," *Economic History Review* 64.S1 (2011), 8–38. Peng Kaixiang 彭凯翔, 清代以来的粮价: 历史学的解释与再解释 (Rice Prices since the Qing Dynasty: A Historical Interpretation and Reinterpretation) (Shanghai, Shanghai renmin chubanshe, 2006), pp. 32–41. Peng Kaixiang 彭凯翔, 从交易到市场—传统中国民间经济脉络试探 (From Dealings to the Market: A Discussion of the Private Economy of Traditional China) (Hangzhou, Zhejiang daxue chubanshe, 2015), pp. 90–101, 302–12. Zhang Li 张丽, 非平衡化与不平衡: 从无锡近代农村经济发展看中国近代农村经济的转型 (Unbalanced and Imbalance: The Transformation of China's Modern Rural Economy from the Perspective of Wuxi's Modern Rural Economic Development) (Beijing, Zhonghua Shuju, 2010), pp. 16–18, 327–45. T.G. Rawski, *Economic Growth in Prewar China* (Berkeley, University of California Press, 1989). L. Brandt, *Commercialization and Agricultural Development: Central and Eastern China, 1870–1937* (Cambridge, Cambridge University Press, 1989).

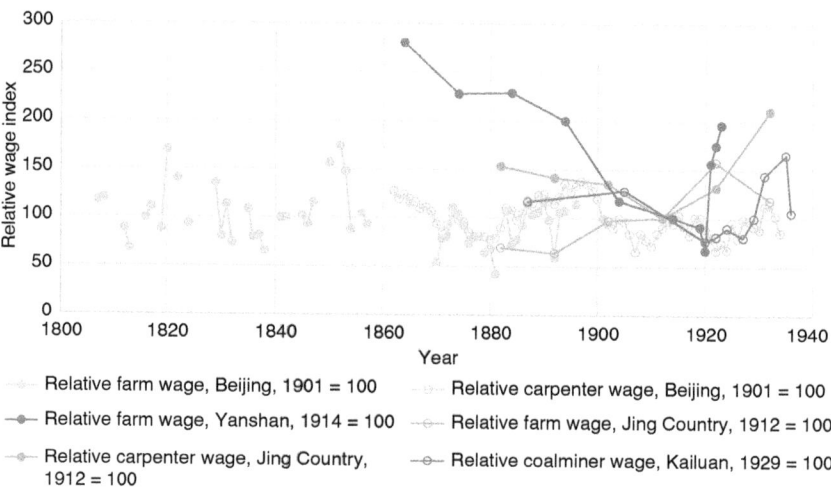

Figure 3.4 Wage index relative to grain price in Beijing and Hebei province
Notes: Most data are indexed with different base years. Kailuan prices are for flour and other series are for wheat.
Sources: Beijing: Peng Kaixiang 彭凯翔, 从交易到市场—传统中国民间经济脉络试探 (From Dealings to the Market: A Discussion of the Private Economy of Traditional China) (Hangzhou, Zhejiang daxue chubanshe, 2015), pp. 95–7, 304–5.
Jing county: 景县志 (Jing County Annals) (1932), 中国地方志集成·河北府县志辑 Collection of Chinese Local Chronicles, Hebei Section, 50 (Shanghai, Shanghai shudian chubanshe, 2006), vol. 6, pp. 4–6. See Peng, 从交易到市场, pp. 84–5, 194–5, for details about silver–copper exchange in conversion.
Yanshan: John Lossing Buck 卜凯, 河北盐山县一百五十农家之经济及社会调查 (Economic and Social Survey of 150 Farmers in Yanshan County, Hebei Province) (Nanjing, Jinling daxue nonglinke, 1929), pp. 160–1.
Kailuan: Nankai daxue jingji yanjiusuo jingjishi yanjiushi 南开大学经济研究所经济史研究室, 旧中国开滦煤矿的工资制度和包工制度 (Wage System and Labor Contract System of Kailuan Coal Mine before the PRC) (Tianjin, Tianjin renmin chubanshe, 1983), p. 123. The series is based on real wages of coal miners.

In short, the case for a Malthusian trap or decline for Chinese agriculture in the nineteenth and twentieth centuries seems far from being established based on existing studies of land yield and per capita grain output. While this chapter does not reconstruct new estimates, it may be fair to say that while Perkins (1969) might have given a "subsistence-level" estimate for per capita output, other scholars' estimates have probably reflected the productive capacity of China's arable land. The two groups capture the lower and the upper bounds of grain output respectively.

Agriculture

Explaining Per Capita Output Stability

If our survey here casts doubt on a long-term decline, how do we explain the relative stability throughout this period, and how did Chinese agriculture keep pace with population increase given the land constraints of the nineteenth and twentieth centuries? Per capita grain output is derived from multiplying yield by total acreage divided by total population. As is well known, historical data on population and acreage are heavily contested. Although it may be difficult to ever arrive at precise historical estimates, there may well be various mitigating factors to population and acreage data that prevented a Malthusian fall in per capita grain output.

On total land acreage, Ho observes that the arable land was substantially underreported in official historical documents.[14] For this reason, Shi uses the modern-era land data published in 1952 by the National Bureau of Statistics of China as a reference point to go back and re-estimate aggregate arable land areas for the Qing and modern periods.[15] He concludes that there were probably 1.2 billion *mu*, or 50 percent, more arable land than was officially recorded in the late Daoguang reign (1821–1850), and that agricultural acreage increased from 0.83 billion *mu* to 1.46 billion between early seventeenth-century Ming and the late nineteenth century, an increase of 76 percent.[16] Shi goes further to say that as the 1952 land data were underassessed as well, his estimates for the Qing period should be on the conservative side.[17]

Shi argues that by the mid-Qing, cultivation peaked and reached its saturation point in inland core agricultural regions. The pace of increase slackened between the early nineteenth century and 1911 in China proper, but growth in southwestern China remained at a high level. Moreover, the opening of new frontiers in northeastern China, Mongolia, and Xinjiang raised the total acreage by another 0.3 billion *mu*.[18] It is likely that agricultural acreage

---

[14] Ping-ti Ho 何炳棣, 中国古今土地数字的考释与评价 (Interpretation and Evaluation of Ancient and Modern Land Figures in China) (Beijing, Zhongguo shehui kexue chubanshe, 1988).
[15] Shi, *Agricultural Development in Qing China*.
[16] Shi, 清代农业的发展和不发展, pp. 130–5.
[17] In fact, until the late twentieth century, a general practice was to state "1 billion *mu*" to describe the aggregate arable land amount of China. But, systematic census and satellite-based assessment put the actual total above 2 billion *mu*, catching everyone by surprise.
[18] Cao estimated that the total population increased from 383 million to 436 million during 1820–1911, with population in northeast China rising from 2.49 million to 18 million, which is about 30 percent of the total population increase. See Cao Shuji 曹树基, 中国人口史 (Population History of China), vol. 5, 清时期 (Qing Dynasty) (Shanghai, Fudan daxue chubanshe, 2001); updated estimations can be found in Chapter 8 by Cao Shuji in our volume I.

increases largely slowed or stagnated in the early twentieth century given the civil strife and natural disasters.[19] As Xin finds, there were substantial uncultivated areas around the Three Gorges on the Yangzi river even by the time of the late nineteenth century. Cultivatable land was not totally exhausted until the 1930s.[20] There is also the possibility of exploration of hilly or marginal land, more efficient utilization of agricultural land, innovation in agricultural technology and crop varieties, and so on, a point we will elaborate on later.[21]

The second factor is obviously population. The eighteenth-century population explosion inevitably led to a dramatic decline in the land–labor ratio in agriculture and a potential food crisis. However, the nineteenth century saw a dramatic downturn in the fourteen-year-long Taiping Rebellion (1851–1865) that led to a population loss of 70 million, mostly in China's most densely settled and developed area of the lower and middle Yangzi. This was followed by another population loss exceeding 10 million in the Muslim rebellion in northwestern China (1862–1873).[22] Whether or not these disasters can be characterized as Malthusian is another question, but they certainly leveled the population to that of the early nineteenth century and temporarily relieved land constraints.

Another notable cause of population loss is natural disaster. Figure 3.4 shows that the period under study had one of the highest frequencies of natural disasters documented in recent studies. Although the increasing frequency of disaster may well be due to better records during this period, it may also be closer to reality. The most prominent "Ding-wu Disaster" (丁戊奇荒) of 1876–1879 and 1928–1930 led to population losses, respectively, of as much as 20 million and 10 million in northern China and nationwide. Figure 3.5 shows that among all the natural disasters, drought and flood were more frequent and caused possibly more human loss compared with others such as pests, earthquakes, typhoons, or the cold. It is important to note that apart from these large-scale disasters, most disasters are fairly localized and of limited duration. Hence their damage may be limited. We have evidence from Huizhou land rental data showing that most disasters in the second half of the nineteenth century remained

---

[19] Yan Zhongping 严中平 et al., 中国近代经济史统计资料选辑 (A Selection of Statistical Data of the Modern Economic History of China) (Beijing, Zhongguo shehui kexue wenxian chubanshe, 2012), p. 238.
[20] Xin Deyong 辛德勇, 历史的空间与空间的历史 (The Space of History and the History of Space) (Beijing, Beijing shifan daxue chubanshe, 2005), pp. 36–7.
[21] Han Maoli 韩茂莉, 中国历史农业地理 (Historical Agricultural Geography of China) (Beijing, Beijing daxue chubanshe, 2012), pp. 5–10; J.L. Buck (ed.), *Land Utilization in China: Statistics* (Nanjing, Jinling daxue chubanshe, 1937), pp. 40–4.
[22] Cao, 中国人口史, vol. 5, 清时期, pp. 455–689.

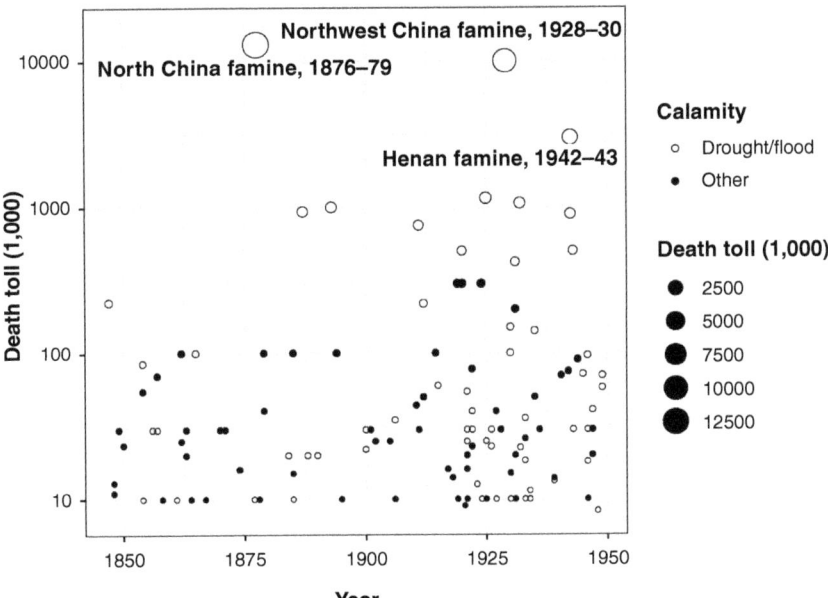

Figure 3.5 Major disasters with a death toll above 1,000 (1840–1949)
Source: Xia Mingfang 夏明方, 民国时期自然灾害与乡村社会 (Natural Disasters and Rural Society during the Republic of China) (Beijing, Zhonghua shuju, 2000), pp. 395–403.

localized.[23] Also, by the early twentieth century, as Hou Yangfang shows, public health, railroads, and, to a lesser extent, the rise of relief organizations provided much more effective relief efforts and possibly prevented much larger population loss compared with earlier periods.[24]

Models of Chinese Agriculture: High-Level Equilibrium Trap, Involution, or Industrious Revolution?

What are the micro-factors in terms of the choice of technology, combination of factor use, and household production and management decisions that underlie

---

[23] See Jiang Taixin 江太新 and Su Jinyu 苏金玉, "论清代徽州地区的亩产" (On the Yield per *Mu* of the Huizhou Area in the Qing Dynasty), 中国经济史研究 (Research in Chinese Economic History) 3 (1993), 36–61. It provides rent collection records of forty-seven pieces of land from 1883 to 1908 to show the effect of disasters. However, correlation between most of the forty-seven areas was very weak, which shows that the effect of disasters was localized even within one region.

[24] Hou Yangfang 侯杨方, 中国人口史 (Population History of China) (1910–1953), vol. 6 (Shanghai, Fudan daxue chubanshe, 2001), pp. 587–610.

the long-run macro trends of Chinese agricultural output and productivity? The deteriorating land–labor ratio over time easily gave rise to a Malthusian-type interpretation of Chinese agriculture in the form of the hypothesis of the so-called "high-level equilibrium trap" proposed by Mark Elvin and later the "involution" thesis according to Philip Huang. Both posit a largely pessimistic vision of a long-run decline in agricultural productivity and output per capita in the face of resource constraints and overpopulation over time. However, the more optimistic vision recently championed by the California school posits that Chinese agricultural expansion, particularly in the highly developed lower Yangzi area, proceeded in a different technological and institutional trajectory from the well-known British or Western European model. In agriculture, efficiency came from gains in the use of better fertilizers, the rationalization of resource use, agricultural intensification, and cash crop cultivation. This technical bias, induced by the lower Yangzi's relative factor endowment, and combined with the expansion of regional trade and the geographic division of labor, constituted what has been viewed as Smithian growth. To a certain degree, the California school thesis is a variation of the Boserupian classification (according to Ester Boserup) of long-term economic growth which viewed resource constraints more optimistically as a stimulus to technical change and intensification.[25] Here, by expanding and developing an analytical framework originally derived from Mark Elvin and Philip Huang, but more rigorously formulated by Kang Chao, we show that a more rigorous Boserupian framework of innovation can reconcile the two opposing sides of the debates and reveal the resilience of Chinese agriculture beyond the Malthusian trap.

From a Malthusian to a Boserupian Framework

In Figure 3.6(a), we show a production function where total output (TP) reaches the highest average output (AP) at point A given the fixed land constraint. In a Malthusian model, whenever AP exceeds average subsistence cost (indicated by the forty-five-degree line), it will induce a population rise to

---

[25] It is regrettable that the recent heated debate between the "involutionists" and the California school has taken few cues from the extensive induced-innovation literature. The induced-innovation theory, a more rigorous formulation of the Boserupian thesis, was statistically tested in seminal works by Hayami Yujiro and Vernon Ruttan in the 1980s to explain the successful economic growth of modern Japan under severe factor-endowment constraints. It clearly revealed the insufficiency of the simplistic Malthusian framework, which ignored the potentials of factor-biased technological progress, factor substitution, and the expansion of trade based on comparative advantage that would prevent the fall in marginal productivity of labor and release the factor endowment constraints. See Y. Hayami and V. Ruttan, *Agricultural Development: An International Perspective* (Baltimore, Johns Hopkins University Press, 1985).

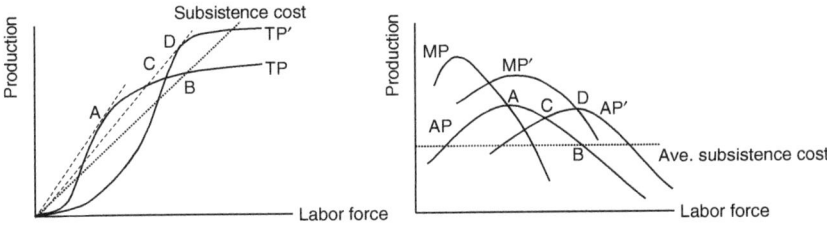

Figure 3.6 Malthusian and Boserupian models

eat up the surplus, leading to new equilibrium AP at point B, a point that approximates the so-called high-level equilibrium trap condition. As mentioned by Kang Chao, given inequality, the actual Malthusian equilibrium point tilts towards the left of B.

In the case of modern agricultural improvement, the Malthusian trap or equilibrium is relieved through technical innovation of the labor-saving and (land) resource-using type (as in the case of the British or American type of agriculture, which uses inanimate power sources and mechanization). This can be indicated by a general upward shift of the production function that raises both marginal product (MP) and AP over time. Clearly, Chinese or East Asian agriculture under severe land constraint did not take that direction. Instead, we can show a Boserupian type of innovation in the adoption of labor-using technology and institutions that shift TP to TP' in Figure 3.6(a). In the Boserupian model, when population reaches point C, people can opt out of a new production function in the form of TP'. TP' is not a general upward shift of production function or an increase in total factor productivity across the board, but it does increase total output and absorb more labor with the much larger population size.[26] By moving AP from A to D, the Boserupian innovation temporarily releases the system from the Malthusian threat through a combination of intensive cultivation and a greater degree of the division of labor and commercialization in response to rising population density.

In Figure 3.6(b), we illustrate the changes using marginal and average product curves. The shift from TP to TP' leads to a shift towards AP' and MP'. If the Boserupian innovation is continuous, it could lead to multiple or constant shifts of TP to TP', which can trace out a more general production function that is the envelope of TP and TP'. This envelope expands the production frontier and

---

[26] See K. Chao, *Man and Land in Chinese History: An Economic Analysis* (Stanford, Stanford University Press, 1986), pp. 20–2.

improves efficiency even though AP' at point D may be lower than AP at point A (although this is theoretically ambiguous). As you can see, AP' and MP' at point D represent a drastic improvement over AP and MP had TP not shifted to TP', which represents the dire scenario of the Malthusian trap or involution under a much larger population size and a deteriorating land–labor ratio.

The Boserupian innovation leading to the movement from MP to MP' is realized through several channels: the greater application of irrigation, fertilizer, and intensive cultivation, which raised land productivity of a single crop; the intensification of multi-cropping and crop rotation; the introduction of more labor-intensive, profitable cash crops; and finally the shift to agricultural and handicraft sideline production which relies less on the use of land. This is sometimes alternatively called Smithian growth.

By the nineteenth century, the potential for raising land yield on a single crop was largely exhausted within China's long-established traditional agricultural regions. Although there are slight differences in the application of draft animals and fertilizer, various studies show that yield based on single cropping shows small variation with farm size by the 1930s.[27] Based on the study by John Buck, Table 3.2b shows that smaller farm size tended to have a slightly higher double-cropping index and higher yield, but the difference is not overwhelming. On the other hand, the increasing share in the cultivation of cash crops such as peanuts, tobacco, and American cotton due to heightened commercialization, as shown later, could generate higher revenue, flatten the marginal revenue, or push it further outward.

We can see in Table 3.2 that average labor productivity seems to be rising with farm size. In other studies in northern China and the lower Yangzi, we also see labor productivity and net income increase with farm size before it reaches a certain scale. These all seem to indicate that the impact of technological adjustment in the labor-intensive direction is limited, and support the involution thesis proposed by Philip Huang.[28] However, this argument needs to be qualified on several theoretical and empirical grounds. First, the efficiency argument based on average product rather than marginal product

---

[27] These new findings based on the micro-level data used by John Buck can be seen in H. Hoken and Q. Su, "An Analysis on the Inverse Relationship between Yield and Farm Size in Rural China in the 1930s," in H. Hu, F. Zhong, and C.G. Turvey (eds.), *Chinese Agriculture in the 1930s: Investigations into John Lossing Buck's Rediscovered "Land Utilization in China" Microdata*, https://doi.org/10.1007/978-3-030-12688-9.

[28] P. Huang, *The Peasant Economy and Social Change in North China* (Stanford, Stanford University Press, 1985). Cao Xingsui 曹幸穗, 旧中国苏南农家经济研究 (Study of the Economy of Farmers in Southern Jiangsu before the PRC) (Beijing, Zhongyang bianyi chubanshe, 1996), pp. 86–130.

Table 3.2 Farm size and productivity

	Small farms	Medium farms	Medium-large farms	Large farms	Very large farms
Average farm area in acres	1.43	2.84	4.92	7.17	13.02
Crop acres per man-equivalent	1.5	2.1	2.6	3.2	4
Index of double cropping	153	151	149	147	143
Index of crop yield	100	99	100	98	100
Composite land yield index*	129.74	101.43	95.51	91.11	82.21
Man-equivalent per farm	1.2	1.7	2.3	2.8	3.7
Production of grain equivalent in kilograms per man-equivalent	828	1168	1448	1679	2073
Percentage of net income from other than farm sources	21	14	11	10	9
Number of idle months per able-bodied man	1.6	1.7	1.8	1.8	1.8

Notes: Except for the composite land yield index, all other data are from John Lossing Buck, *Land Utilization in China: Statistics* (Nanking, University of Nanking, 1937), pp. 267–88, 295. The composite land yield index was compiled by Hao Hu and Minjie Yu, who recalculated it with slightly different criteria based on the Buck data. See Hao Hu and Minjie Yu, "The Relationship between Farm Size and Land Productivity in Early Twentieth-Century China," in Hao Hu, Funing Zhong, and Calum G. Turvey (eds.), *Chinese Agriculture in the 1930s: Investigations into John Lossing Buck's Rediscovered "Land Utilization in China" Microdata*, https://doi.org/10.1007/978-3-030-12688-9.

may exaggerate the role of farm size given that large farm size could also be associated with other larger fixed investment or outlays. In fact, with an active market in land and labor (including short-term labor), higher labor productivity in large farms may be attributable to greater management skills, better access to capital, other productive inputs, and, most importantly, the hiring of laborers from outside the farm. Larger farms may also benefit from lower transaction costs in marketing and other activities and higher potential for crop diversification than smaller farms. All these are more likely to push small-scale farmers into sideline production or off-farm work (particularly in areas where farms are located near urban areas or newly industrialized areas). This is also revealed by the higher percentage of income derived from other farm sources from smaller farmers in Table 3.2.[29]

---

[29] D. Benjamin and L. Brandt, "Markets, Discrimination, and the Economic Contribution of Women in China: Historical Evidence," *Economic Development and Cultural Change* 44.1 (October 1995), 63–104.

Agricultural Sideline Production

We now turn to examine the issue of agricultural sideline production, a longstanding feature of the Chinese agrarian system which combines main agricultural production with household subsidiary and handicraft activities. The increasing role of household subsidiary and handicraft production has long been held to be the cornerstone of the "involution" thesis that posits overpopulation pushing agricultural households increasingly into lower-productivity activities and ultimately into poverty. However, a critical problem with this argument is that it may overlook the important fact that subsidiary or sideline production may be closely related to high agricultural seasonality due to China's monsoon climate.[30] Handicraft industries such as cotton spinning or weaving, developed since China's Ming and Qing periods, require little capital and are easily tailored to household production by women and children during the agricultural slack season. Hence the argument for involution based simply on lower or diminishing returns to labor in cotton cultivation or textile handicrafts relative to grain or staple production is insufficient. While more systematic evidence is needed, we illustrate the impact of agricultural seasonality by showing the striking inverse relationship between daily agricultural wages and the percentage of idle time throughout a year in northern China in Figure 3.7.

We now develop a new theoretical framework to interpret the impact of seasonality. Figure 3.8 shows that in the absence of cash crop cultivation or handicrafts, the marginal revenue of labor is MR_1 during the agricultural season but drops drastically to MR_2. The total number of work days will be determined by the intersection of marginal cost (MC) of labor and MR_2. Now we introduce cash crops or sideline activities such as cotton cultivation. Given that returns on cotton cultivation were lower than on grain cultivation, as indicated in the literature, marginal returns on combined grain and sideline activities would be MR_2 and MR_2', which are both lower than MR_1 and MR_1' respectively. However, the total income based on MR_2 and MR_2' may not necessarily be lower than that from MR_1 and MR_1' for two reasons. First, the total number of workdays has now been extended in the scenario of combined agricultural and sideline activities. Second, MR_2', which takes account of the introduction of sideline activities, is higher than MR_1' during the agricultural slack season.

---

[30] For an extended interpretation of this issue, see Lu Feng 卢锋, "我国传统农业生产结构特征" (Structural Characteristics of Traditional Agricultural Production in China), in 半周期改革现象：我国粮棉流通改革和食物安全研究 (The Phenomenon of Semi-cycle Reform: A Study of Grain and Cotton Circulation Reform and Food Safety in China) (Beijing, Beijing daxue chubanshe, 2004), pp. 437–44.

Agriculture

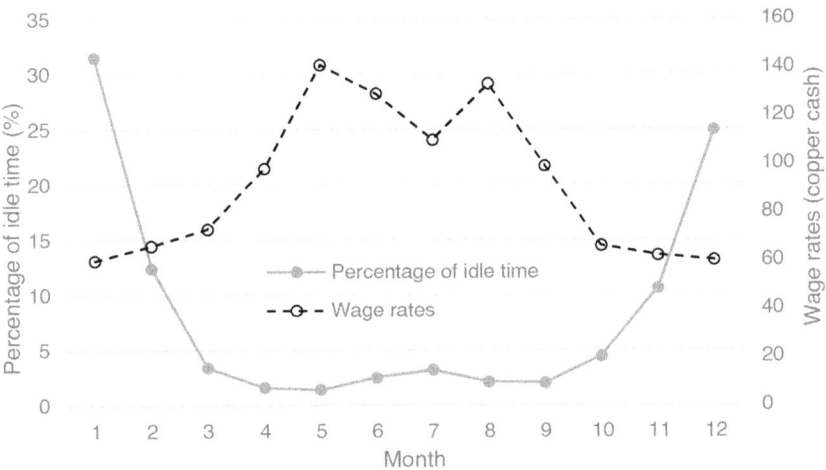

Figure 3.7 Percentage of idle time (left axis) and wage rates in units of copper cash (right axis)
Source notes: percentage of idle time of farmers from Buck, *Land Utilization in China*, p. 296; wage rates (1807–1858) from Sydney Gamble, "Daily Wages of Unskilled Chinese Laborers 1807–1902," *Far Eastern Quarterly* 3.1 (November 1943), 41–73

Moreover, if the desire to keep small farms as families' livelihood reduces the marginal disutility of work, this will push MC towards MC′, further extending workdays annually.[31]

We can now see the insufficiency of the involution argument of Philip Huang which hinges on the simple fact that both MR_1' and MR_2' are lower than MR_1, but ignores the fact that MR_1 is only applicable during the agricultural harvest season. The new system of mixed cultivation and sideline production extends the number of workdays and at the same time raises the marginal returns during the agricultural slack season. Over time, this combined effect may increasingly dominate the income from pure agricultural work given that increasing commercialization, improving transport, and rising prices for cash crops raise the returns on handicraft and sideline production. Rather than immiseration or exploitation, as the "involution" thesis may imply, total annual household income may increase.[32] All of these go to show that so-called "hidden employment" or "surplus labor" was far

---

[31] However, data do not seem to support this hypothesis, as Table 3.2 reveals that the number of idle months varies little with farm size. Data show only that among the very small farms – the bottom 1 percent of farms – the number of idle months reaches as high as 2.3. Buck, *Land Utilization in China*, p. 307.

[32] There is no definitive resolution on the empirical evidence supporting either side of the debate. See Li Bozhong 李伯重, 江南农业的发展 1620–1850 (Agricultural Development in Jiangnan, 1620–1850) (Shanghai, Shanghai guji chubanshe, 2007);

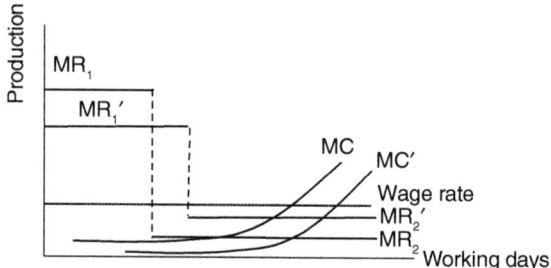

Figure 3.8 Agricultural sideline production

less severe and has been increasingly resolved through the combined agro-handicraft eco-system in China. It is ironic that from a comparative perspective what is classified here as "involution" or the "high-level equilibrium trap" in the Chinese context bears a striking resemblance to what other scholars describe as "industrious revolution" for preindustrial Europe and Japan.[33]

One revealing "natural experiment" on the importance of sideline activity can be seen in the case of the Kaixian Gong village 开弦弓村, known as Jiang village, in the lower Yangzi area known once for its highly developed silk production. In 1956, in an attempt to modernize, radical governmental policies largely eliminated its sideline production and shifted labor and land to grain production. With massive investment in irrigation and fertilizer, along with enhanced multi-cropping, land productivity and total agricultural output increased by nearly 60 percent in 1956 compared with 1936. However, it turned out that this just barely made up for the value of sideline production that had been sacrificed in the process. The value of sideline production, which had once accounted for 45 percent of total income in 1936, was reduced

---

P. Huang, *The Peasant Family and Rural Development in the Yangzi Delta, 1350–1988* (Stanford, Stanford University Press, 1990); K. Pomeranz, *The Great Divergence: China, Europe, and the Making of the Modern World Economy* (Princeton, Princeton University Press, 2000). Also see the chapter by Kenneth Pomeranz in Volume I of *The Cambridge Economic History of China*.

[33] For "industrious revolution," see J. de Vries, *The Industrious Revolution: Consumer Behavior and the Household Economy, 1650 to the Present* (Cambridge, Cambridge University Press, 2008); A. Hayami, *Japan's Industrious Revolution: Economic and Social Transformations in the Early Modern Period* (Tokyo, Springer, 2015). For seasonality and sideline occupation in the US, England, and Japan, see K.L. Sokoloff and D. Dollar, "Agricultural Seasonality and the Organization of Manufacturing in Early Industrial Economies: The Contrast between England and the United States," *Journal of Economic History* 57.2 (1997), 288–321; O. Saito and M. Takashima, "Estimating the Shares of Secondary- and Tertiary-Sector Outputs in the Age of Early Modern Growth: The Case of Japan, 1600–1874," *European Review of Economic History* 20.3 (2016), 368–86.

to only 20 percent (despite the much higher price of agricultural sideline goods in 1956).[34]

What this Communist era "natural experiment" reveals is the resilience of traditional Chinese rural household production to deal with the seasonality problem. Labor reallocation across seasonal cycles, coupled with a very active labor market, particularly for short-term hire, promoted commercialization and industrialization. Indeed, given the relatively high labor return during the agricultural harvest season, incentives to migrate to urban centers for full-time nonagricultural work may be dampened. As shown in Figure 3.8, if urban wage rates are still below MR_I or $MR_I{'}$, rural laborers may not find it attractive enough to move to full-time occupations in the city. This explains the viability of rural-based industry even in the face of rapid industrialization.[35] Overlooking or grossly misunderstanding this important mechanism in the Chinese agricultural–industrial ecosystem led to disastrous outcomes in the Communist era's collectivization movement. Indeed, the revival of rural-based industrialization, such as the township and village enterprise, provided the engine of Chinese economic growth during the reform era of the 1980s and 1990s.[36]

New Elements in Chinese Agriculture

In comparison with the sweeping transformations in modern industry, finance, and other sectors, changes in the agricultural sector remained far more limited. However, some changes did happen in both crops and the spatial structure of cultivation. The opening of treaty ports, the rise of agricultural exports more closely linked to international markets, and the shift of grain tribute from the Grand Canal to the sea route from the mid-nineteenth century, along with the construction of railroads from the twentieth century, are among the main factors effecting change. Institutional and political changes also led to agricultural improvement, investment in technological innovation, and organizational changes, particularly in marketing,

---

[34] Fei Xiaotong 费孝通, 江村经济—中国农民的生活 (Economy in Jiang Village: Peasant Life in China) (Shanghai, Shangwu yinshuguan, 2001), pp. 258–69.
[35] Xiao Bucai 萧步才, "江苏省江阴县手工织布业调查资料: 上" (Investigation Data of Handwoven Cloth in Jiangyin, Jiangsu Province: 1)", 学术月刊 (Academic Monthly) 1958.1, 87–9.
[36] See Chapter 18 on the Great Leap Famine by James Kung below for the disasters of agricultural collectivization. For the importance of 1980s rural industrialization, see the chapter by Barry Naughton and also B. Li, *Agricultural Development in Jiangnan, 1620–1850* (Basingstoke, Macmillan, 1998).

processing, and the production of agricultural commodities for export and industrial production.

Acceleration in the Diffusion of New Crops

One of the longest-lasting transformations in Chinese agriculture from the sixteenth century onward is the introduction and diffusion of New World crops such as maize and sweet potatoes. While their introduction fundamentally changed the structure of grain consumption in China, the nationwide diffusion of these crops achieved consequential proportions and nationwide significance only by the late nineteenth and early twentieth centuries. Even in the eighteenth century, despite governmental encouragement, most crops were diffused through the migration of people. By the nineteenth century, maize and sweet potatoes were largely restricted to the southern regions where they initially came in, with maize concentrated in the high plateau of the southwest and sweet potatoes in the hills of the southeast.[37] But by the 1910s, things had fundamentally changed as both crops, which had few demands regarding irrigation and temperature, expanded throughout the whole of northern China, with the cold-resistant corn spreading further into northeast China and Inner Mongolia following the new wave of Chinese migration. By that point, with northern China rising to become the center of cultivation, the share of these crops in total output only trailed rice and wheat at the national level. While the share of maize and sweet potatoes was only about 2 percent in the early nineteenth century, it reached 5 percent and 10 percent in 1914 and 1930 respectively (converted using a 4:1 ratio between sweet potatoes and raw grain).[38]

It turns out that the process of diffusion of New World crops is far more complicated and multifaceted. Often the diffusion started with migration, which itself is driven by population increase.[39] Then, once brought to wider areas of China, these New World crops would take time to take root and

---

[37] Cao Shuji 曹树基, "清代玉米番薯分布的地理特征" (Geographical Characteristics of the Distribution of Corn and Sweet Potato in the Qing Dynasty)", 历史地理研究 (Historical Geography Study) 1990.2, 287–303.

[38] Li Xinsheng 李昕升 and Wang Siming 王思明, "清至民国美洲作物生产指标估计" (An Estimate of the Production of New World Crops in China from the Qing Dynasty to the Republican Era), 清史研究 (Qing History Journal) 2017.3, 126–39.

[39] This contradicts a recent study that argues that the introduction and diffusion of New World crops accounted for the population explosion during the eighteenth and early nineteenth centuries. See S. Chen and J. Kung, "Of Maize and Men: The Effect of a New World Crop on Population and Economic Growth in China," *Journal of Economic Growth* 21.1 (2016), 71–99.

thrive after local adaptation and competition with existing indigenous crops.⁴⁰ This process reinforced an interactive rather than a one-way causal relationship between the diffusion of New World crops and population expansion. Indeed, crop diffusion often followed rather than preceded (or caused) population expansion. This explains why the spread of New World crops continued and even accelerated nationwide after population pressure in China significantly decreased due to the massive population loss and the opening of China's northeastern frontier after the mid-nineteenth century. Migration, warfare, and new transport infrastructure all enhanced the movement of population and reinforced the diffusion of crops.

Besides corn and sweet potatoes, the diffusion of other New World Crops such as Irish potatoes also accelerated during this period. Although introduced to China relatively late as they appeared in only scattered records in the eighteenth century, the importance of Irish potatoes in China varies greatly by location.⁴¹ As a highly cold-resistant crop, Irish potatoes reached much higher-elevation plateaus than can be reached by maize and sweet potatoes and opened up new frontiers of cultivation on China's barren northwestern frontier. In the 1930s, Irish potatoes had a share in total staples consumption ranging from 10 to 20 percent among rural households in Shanxi, Suiyuan, Chahar, Qinghai, Gansu, Ningxia, and other northwestern provinces.⁴² For these provinces, the importance of Irish potatoes as a staple food exceeded that of maize and sweet potatoes. Other notable crops, such as peppers, tomatoes, pumpkins, apples, and other foreign vegetables, as well as American types of peanuts for oil production, also came into significance after the nineteenth century.

Agricultural Commercialization

Another important driving force behind agricultural development during this period is the heightened degree of commercialization. The broad quantitative profile is captured by the well-known comprehensive study of Wu Chengming and Xu Dixin. Figure 3.9 shows that both the absolute values and the shares of almost all crops produced for the market rose between 1840 and 1920 (in 1894

---

⁴⁰ Han, 中国历史农业地理, pp. 529–56. Wang Baoning "王保宁, 花生与番薯：民国年间山东低山丘陵区的耕作制度" (Peanuts and Sweet Potatoes: The Farming System in the Low Hill Area of Shandong in the Republic of China), 中国农史 (Agricultural History of China) 2012.3, 54–68.
⁴¹ Ping-ti Ho 何炳棣, 美洲作物的引进、传播及其对中国粮食生产的影响 (Introduction and Dissemination of American Crops and Their Impact on China's Grain Production, 11), 世界农业 (World Agriculture), 1979.6, 25–31. Han, 中国历史农业地理, pp. 661–4.
⁴² 农情报告, 1937–1938.

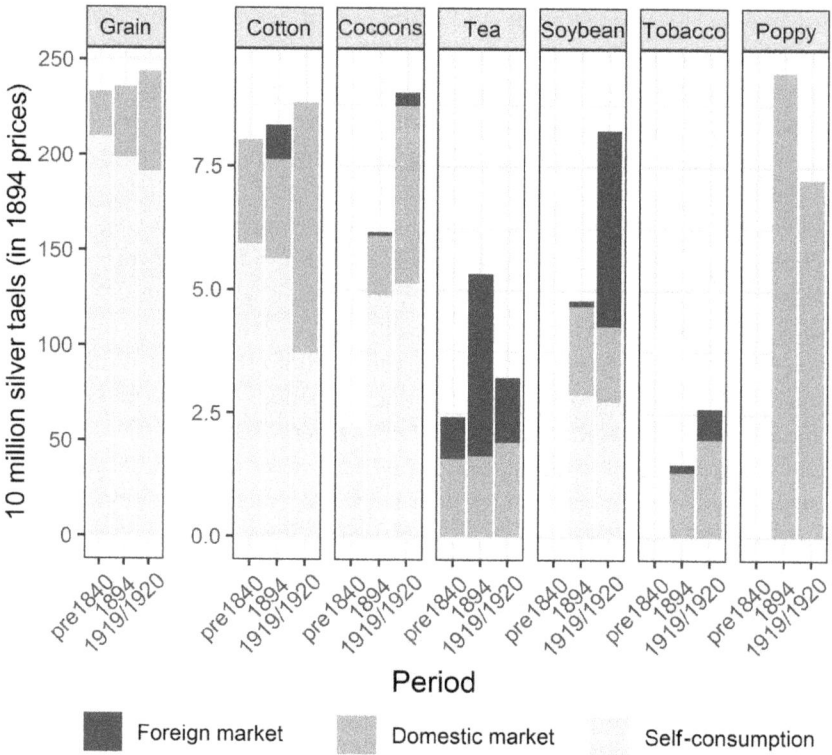

Figure 3.9 Trends of agricultural commercialization
Source: Xu Dixin 许涤新 and Wu Chengming 吴承明, 中国资本主义发展史 (History of Capitalist Development in China) (Beijing, Renmin chubanshe, 1990), vol. 2, pp. 279–304, 966–95

constant prices). The figure also reveals different patterns, with cocoons produced for domestic reeling production and cotton increasingly sold to mechanized manufacturers. But both silk and cotton in the end were becoming more commercialized. On the other hand, tea and soybeans increased their share of commercialization by being directly sold to the international market. Meanwhile, self-consumption and the domestic market remained predominant for grain.[43]

There is variation in the performance of agricultural commodities under enhanced commercialization and international trade. Chinese tea, which

---

[43] Another estimate by Shi Zhihong also shows that the share of cash or economic crops slowly increased between the eighteenth and early twentieth centuries, and that it had reached 20 percent by the nineteenth century. See Shi, 清代农业的发展和不发展, p. 127.

used to be dominant in the global market, faced severe competition from India and Japan and began to decline from the end of the nineteenth century, and only attained half its previous level by the 1930s, leading to a corresponding reduction in tea production and tea cultivation acreage.[44] The result for cotton production was mixed, with the share sold to modern spinning factories increasing but the share for home production decreasing. Meanwhile, cocoon production kept up with the increased demand for raw-silk exports and domestic demand until the Great Depression and the rise of artificial silk in the 1940s.[45]

Increased commercialization led to the rise of new cash commodities, most notably soybeans and bristles from northeastern China; hides, leather, wool, and eggs from the middle and western parts of China; and wood oil from southern China. Using the comparative advantage of low labor cost, eastern coastal provinces began to turn out miscellaneous textiles, such as trimmings, straw cloth, and straw braid.[46] Clearly commercialization brought rural households genuine economic benefits, and in some cases even wealth.[47] They also introduced market risk and in some cases global risk, as marked by the 1930s Great Depression.[48] The most extreme case is the cultivation and commercialization of opium, a product over which China once lost a war with Britain in the 1840s. Ironically, through domestic cultivation and import substitution, Chinese opium finally drove out foreign opium and became the number one cash crop by the late nineteenth century (see Figure 3.9). Obviously, opium generated huge profits for cultivators as well as warlords, and in many cases led to serious social and economic problems.

---

[44] Xu Daofu 许道夫, 中国近代农业生产及贸易统计资料 (Statistics on Agricultural Production and Trade in Modern China) (Shanghai, Shanghai renmin chubanshe, 1983), p. 257.

[45] Zhang, 非平衡化与不平衡, pp. 29–35.

[46] See Wang Jingyu 汪敬虞, 中国近代经济史 1895–1927 (China's Modern Economic History 1895–1927) (Beijing, Renmin chubanshe, 2012), pp. 879–970; Xu, 中国近代农业生产及贸易统计资料, pp. 160–336.

[47] See R.H. Myers, *The Chinese Peasant Economy: Agricultural Development in Hopei and Shantung, 1890–1949* (Cambridge, MA, Harvard University Press, 1970); Brandt, *Commercialization and Agricultural Development*; Rawski, *Economic Growth in Prewar China*; David Faure, *The Rural Economy of Pre-Liberation China: Trade Expansion and Peasant Livelihood in Jiangsu and Guangdong, 1870–1937* (Oxford, Oxford University Press, 1989).

[48] Xia Mingfang 夏明方, 民国时期自然灾害与乡村社会 (Natural Disasters and Rural Society during the Republic of China) (Beijing, Zhonghua shuju, 2000), pp. 171–9.

Agricultural Improvement and Modernization

Although Chinese agriculture remained largely traditional, technological and organizational modernization did proceed prominently in several key agricultural crops or commodities often connected with international factors and in some cases under the direct sponsorship and management of industrial enterprises. A more significant development is the gradual establishment of national infrastructure to support agriculture. Although long an agrarian state where agriculture is at the center of economic activity, traditional imperial China had little formal infrastructure to support agriculture. Agricultural administration was loosely attached to the board of finance and construction. The late Qing reform (1903–1911) set up a special agricultural department (农务司) under the New Ministry of Agriculture, Industry, and Commerce to implement agricultural improvement and policies such as organizing and managing newly established agricultural schools and experiments. The local level also saw the official establishment and sponsorship of schools, experimental stations, and publications for research and education. The founding of the new Nationalist government heralded a new level of agricultural-improvement policies and infrastructure, as seen in the establishment of a national-level research institute, the National Agricultural Research Bureau (中央农业实验所), along with prominent private institutions such as the well-known Nanjing University Agricultural Department. China now had a truly national-level agricultural survey, research, and improvement infrastructure and policies.[49]

The best-known case of agricultural improvement through multinational corporations is tobacco cultivation. Although introduced to China from the New World during the sixteenth century and widely diffused by the end of the Qing, domestically grown tobacco leaves were not suited to the modern production of cigarettes. In the early twentieth century, the giant British American Tobacco Company began to introduce American tobacco. However, unlike the spontaneous introduction of centuries earlier, the British American Tobacco Company sent a team of experts to survey nearly 100 counties in fourteen provinces in order to determine the most suitable location of cultivation before 1914. Once they had started, the company aggressively adopted such measures and policies as distributing free seeds,

---

[49] A case in point is the compilation of agricultural manuals, which go back two millennia in China. With intense interest in sericultural improvement, the publication of new sericulture manuals from the end of the nineteenth century reached more than 140 types, which exceeded the total of the past millennia. Hua Degong 华德公, 中国蚕桑书录 (Bibliography of Chinese Sericulture Books) (Beijing, Nongye chubanshe, 1990).

demonstrating new ways of planting, designing tobacco drying rooms, and adopting a high-price repurchase program. These aggressive direct purchase and distribution programs outcompeted and supplanted traditional distribution networks, such as guilds. Given the taxation revenue from tobacco cultivation, the local government was also taking a more proactive attitude.[50] This "corporate" type of agricultural sponsorship achieved great success, later imitated by large Chinese tobacco companies such as the Nanyang Brothers. Through successful import substitution, Chinese-produced tobacco rapidly expanded, taking a large share of the domestic market and even gaining a share of the international market, leading to the rise of specialized areas of tobacco cultivation in China.[51]

The introduction of American cotton followed a very different pattern as the huge size of the domestic cotton market and production made it impossible for any single firm or corporation to take on the task. The main improvement needed was that Chinese short-staple cotton was unsuitable for machine spinning. Here the government stepped in first through the initiative of the Hu-Guang governor Zhang Zhidong and other local officials, later joined by the newly founded Ministry of Agriculture, Industry, and Commerce to distribute the seeds of American cotton in the late Qing. By the Republican period, the initiative had been taken up by both the central and local governments, by cotton manufacturing associations, and by individual enterprises. More importantly, efforts had broadened to include such activities as the establishment of experimental farms, developing improved seed varieties, organizing associations, and conducting scientific research, sometimes in collaboration with the newly risen universities. Although overall achievements were limited due to a host of technical and environmental factors and the share of long-staple cotton remained relatively low, the cultivation of American cotton did expand rapidly. Statistics for 1934 show that American cotton took a 50 percent share of the total cultivated acreage of cotton and 52 percent of total cotton production.[52]

---

[50] Li Gengwu 李耕五, 许昌烤烟发展史话 (History of the Development of Tobacco in Xuchang) (Xuchang, Xuchang kaoyan fazhan shihua bianji weiyuanhui, 1992), pp. 18–25.

[51] S. Cochran, *Big Business in China: Sino-Foreign Rivalry in the Cigarette Industry, 1890–1930* (Cambridge, MA, Harvard University Press, 1980); Zhang Youyi 章有义, 中国近代农业史资料 (Historical Data of Modern Chinese Agriculture), vol. 2 (Beijing, Shenghuo dushu xinzhi sanlian shudian, 1957), pp. 225–6.

[52] See Yan Zhongping 严中平, 中国棉纺织史稿 (History of Chinese Cotton Textiles) (Beijing, Kexue chubanshe, 1955), pp. 323–40; Kang Chao 赵冈 and Jessica C.Y. Chao 陈钟毅, 中国棉纺织史 (The Development of Cotton Textile Production in China) (Beijing, Zhongguo nongye chubanshe, 1997), pp. 40–3; Shen sung-chiao 沈松侨, "經濟

The diffusion pattern of sugar beet falls between those of American tobacco and cotton. Originally sugar was only produced from sugarcane grown in southern China. In 1906, the governor-general of Fengtian, Zhao Erxun, set up experimental farms to introduce sugar beet following the advice of Japanese experts and later the continued efforts of the Japanese Southern Manchurian Company. Upon success, the Southern Manchurian Company set up a sugar manufacturing company to advance seeds, loans, and fertilizer to farmers with guaranteed purchase of the autumn harvest. This model was followed by Chinese manufacturers, such as the Jinan Puyi sugar factory in Shandong province. Like American tobacco, this corporate plus rural-household model led to the rise of concentrated production areas of sugar beet.[53]

One of the most fascinating developments was in sericulture, which produces cocoons for the reeling of raw silk for both export and the domestic market. Unlike Chinese tea exports, Chinese raw-silk exports remained competitive until about the 1910s; from then on Japanese silk began to take over and was dominant by the 1920s and 1930s. Japanese success was built on nearly five decades of sericultural improvement and research in the breeding of better silkworm varieties. Its major breakthrough came in the discovery and development of the so-called first generation (F1) hybrid variety based on the systematic application of Mendelian genetic principles. In just a decade, diffusion of the F1 variety rose to nearly 100 percent between 1913 and 1920. The Japanese success was founded on a combination of university-based research, conglomerate enterprise promotion of better varieties, and distribution arrangements with sericultural farmers.

The Japanese success awoke the world's long-time leader based in the lower Yangzi. After the founding of the new Nationalist government in Nanjing, Jiangsu province, in 1927, the Chinese silk reeling center migrated from Shanghai to the city of Wuxi in Jiangsu province. Under the leadership of a giant silk reeling conglomerate, the Yongtai Company, there were efforts to push for sericultural improvement and technological diffusion in the 1930s. With government support and through the establishment of silkworm rearing co-operatives, cocoons were sold directly to reeling factories. In 1932, the

作物與近代河南農村經濟 (1906–1937)—以棉花與菸草為中心" (Cash Crops and the Modern Rural Economy of Henan Province, 1906–1937: Focusing on Cotton and Tobacco), 近代中国农村经济史论文集 (Collection of Papers on the Rural Economic History of Modern China) (Taipei, Zhongyang yanjiuyuan jindaishi yanjiusuo, 1989), pp. 347–9.
[53] Han, 中国历史农业地理, p. 743. Zhang, 中国近代农业史资料, vol. 2, pp. 161, 171.

Yongtai Reeling Company began to set up long-term exclusive contracts with farmers or co-operatives in the lower Yangzi, a system very similar to the subcontractual direct-purchase system pioneered by large silk reelers in Japan. Starting in 1932, the provincial governments of both Jiangsu and Zhejiang began to take a direct role in promoting sericultural improvement and technological diffusion by designating model districts across the region, and set up a national-level sericultural research and improvement organization.

The outcome was a 1930s lower Yangzi catch-up with Japan that was nothing short of remarkable. Figure 3.10 plots the lower Yangzi diffusion curve for the scientifically improved variety, mostly of the F1 types. For Jiangsu province, the share of scientifically produced silkworm eggs increased from 5 percent to almost 100 percent within only five to seven years. Diffusion lagged somewhat in Zhejiang, but the overall rate of diffusion in the lower Yangzi in the 1930s was comparable to the Japanese diffusion of the F1 hybrids in the 1910s and 1920s.[54]

In comparison with this remarkable, though limited, success, agricultural development in terms of mechanization remained low, except in northeastern China, which had farms relatively larger in size. By 1949, there were only 401 tractors. Mechanized water pumps gained some ground in the highly commercialized lower Yangzi. In Wuxi, the acreage irrigated by mechanized water pumps reached more than 60 percent. However, less than 1 percent of the acreage was irrigated mechanically in the entirety of Jiangsu and Zhejiang provinces combined.[55] This is understandable given the very labor-intensive nature of Chinese agriculture; modernization went more in the direction of biological or chemical improvement rather than in the mechanical direction.[56]

Land Institutions, Distribution, and Rural Credit

Land Institutions

Despite the nominal claim that all land belongs to the emperor, imperial China was under a more or less de facto regime of private property rights with a vibrant

---

[54] D. Ma, "Why Japan, Not China, Was the First to Develop in East Asia: Lessons from Sericulture 1850–1937," *Economic Development and Cultural Change* 52.2 (January 2004), 369–94. Wang Xiang 王翔, 中国近代手工业史稿 (History of the Modern Chinese Handicraft Industry) (Shanghai, Shanghai renmin chubanshe, 2012), p. 380.

[55] Wang Fangzhong 王方中, "旧中国农业中使用机器的若干情况" (Some Information about the Use of Machinery in Agriculture in Traditional China), 中国近代经济史论文选 (Essays on the Modern Economic History of China), vol. 2 (Shanghai, Shanghai renmin chubanshe, 1985), pp. 843–6.

[56] See Hayami and Ruttan, *Agricultural Development*; Ma, "Why Japan, Not China."

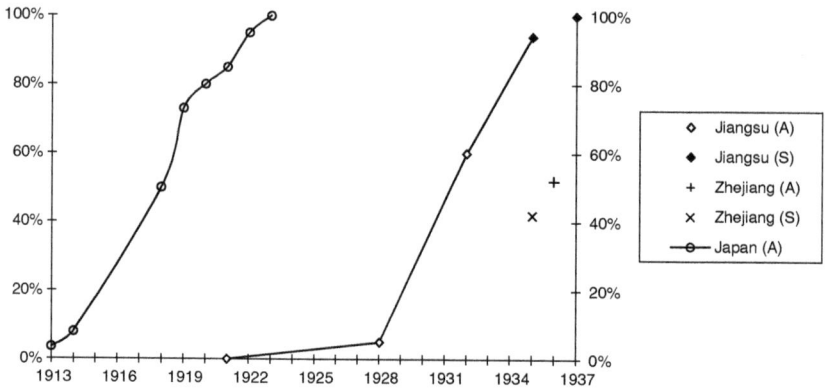

Figure 3.10 Diffusion of scientifically produced silkworm varieties in Japan and the lower Yangzi. A = autumn crop; S = summer crop
Source: D. Ma, "Why Japan, Not China, Was the First to Develop in East Asia: Lessons from Sericulture 1850–1937," *Economic Development and Cultural Change* 52.2 (January 2004), 369–94

land market regulated by local customs and rules. Because of the multiple claims to a single piece of property, land rights took on many different forms or layers in commercial transactions.[57] These multiple and sometimes vaguely defined land rights systems have been viewed as the cause of agricultural stagnation in traditional China. One of the most cited cases is the pervasive tenancy system, particularly sharecropping – often viewed as inefficient, reducing the incentives of cultivators. Such a view has been well challenged both theoretically and on empirical grounds. Theoretical work based on risk diversification and monitoring costs reveals the rationality of sharecropping not just in China but around the world.[58] Indeed, the Chinese case reveals precisely that it was the most developed regions, such as the lower Yangzi, that also had the most-developed tenancy system. Furthermore, from the nineteenth century onward, the importance of sharecropping declined drastically relative to the fixed rent system.

[57] For a nuanced discussion of Chinese traditional land rights, see the chapter by Kishimoto Mio in Volume I. For a more recent contribution see Long Denggao 龙登高, 中国传统地权制度及其变迁 (The Evolution of Traditional Institutions of Land Property Rights in China) (Beijing, Zhongguo shehui kexue chubanshe, 2018); Cao Shuji 曹树基 and Liu Shigu 刘诗古, 传统中国地权结构及其演变 (The Structure and Evolution of Traditional Land Property Rights in China) (Shanghai, Shanghai jiaotong daxue chubanshe, 2014).

[58] S.N.S. Cheung, *The Theory of Share Tenancy, with Special Application to Asian Agriculture and the First Phase of Taiwan Land Reform* (Chicago, The University of Chicago Press, 1969); A. Braverman and J. Stiglitz, "Sharecropping and the Interlinking of Agrarian Markets," *American Economic Review* 72.4 (1982), 695–715; K. Otsuka, H. Chuma, and Y. Hayami, "Land and Labor Contracts in Agrarian Economies: Theories and Facts," *Journal of Economic Literature*, 30.4 (1992), 1965–2018.

Indeed, there is a large literature that argues that Chinese tenants often had far stronger tenancy rights, as indicated by the widespread existence of perpetual tenancy or soil rights. These rights were relatively secure and could even be transacted or used as collateral in the market, as regulated by well-developed customs and rules. These greatly resolved the incentive problems and reduced the transaction costs associated with the tenancy system.[59] Table 3.3 reveals that areas in central and southern China that had a much higher rate of tenancy were among the most productive and commercialized regions in China, possibly with stronger and more sophisticated traditions of customary law and enforcement mechanisms.[60]

There is a fundamental problem of land property rights regulated by customs rather than by formal rules, courts, and legal procedures. Although county magistrates and imperial government did conduct the equivalent of civil or commercial litigation, its aim focused heavily on social and political stability rather than legal justice.[61] Clearly, customary rules carry strong elements of moral economy. The most important example is the practice of *zhaojia* 找价, a custom that allows the seller of the land to reclaim additional compensation from the buyer after the purchase has been finalized, especially when the land value increases subsequent to the transaction. These claims could occur on a regular basis many years after the purchase. While there is no denying that this understandably leads to disputes, opportunistic behavior, and uncertainty over investment and property, various new archives from after the nineteenth century show that the *zhaojia* practice become regularized through customs and evolved into a more predictable system of installment payments by the buyer.[62]

All in all, new studies increasingly recognize the rationality and efficiency attained by what had long been thought "backward" traditional practices in a society without strong formal legal rules and enforcement.[63] While there is some validity in the claim that the Chinese legal institutions and practice might have led to divergence in long-term agricultural trajectories between China and England,[64] it is difficult to argue the case for general institutional

---

[59] Cao and Liu, 传统中国地权结构及其演变, pp. 18–34, 63–99.
[60] Z. Chen, K. Peng, and W. Yuan, "Usury, Market Power and Poverty Traps: A Study of Rural Credit in 1930s' China," *Frontiers of Economics in China* 3 (2018), 369–96.
[61] D. Ma, "Law and Economy in Traditional China: A 'Legal Origin' Perspective on the Great Divergence," in Ma, *Law and Long-Term Economic Change: A Eurasian Perspective* (Stanford, Stanford University Press, 2011).
[62] Peng, 从交易到市场, p. 227–9.
[63] Long, 中国传统地权制度及其变迁; Cao and Liu, 传统中国地权结构及其演变.
[64] T. Zhang, *The Laws and Economics of Confucianism: Kinship and Property in Preindustrial China and England* (Cambridge, Cambridge University Press, 2017).

Table 3.3 Tenancy rates in the 1930s

Province	Share of rental land in total cultivated acreage (1934)	Share of tenants and part-tenants in total farm households	
		NARB (1931–1934)	Buck (1929–1933)
South			
Jiangsu	42.33	59.60	62.15
Zhejiang	51.31	77.80	65.46
Anhui	52.64	65.00	62.12
Jiangxi	45.10	72.80	71.07
Hubei	27.89	69.00	60.31
Hunan	47.80	73.40	60.70
Fujian	39.33	73.20	74.30
Guangdong	76.95	81.00	81.55
Guangxi	21.20	67.00	50.35
Sichuan	--	75.40	55.07
Yunnan	--	63.80	46.67
Guizhou	--	64.20	55.22
North			
Hebei	12.89	32.60	19.26
Shandong	12.63	30.80	21.79
Henan	27.27	44.00	31.10
Shanxi	--	38.20	34.55
Shaanxi	16.64	46.80	30.65
Chahar	10.20	61.80	--
Suiyuan	8.75	45.60	8.45
Gansu	--	41.20	36.54
Ningxia	--	39.00	3.00
Qinghai	--	41.00	53.73
Liaoning	--	--	64.10
Average	30.73	54.25	50.80

Notes. The ratio of rented crop land comes from Guomin zhengfu zhujichu tongjiju 国民政府主计处统计局, 中国土地问题之统计分析 (Statistical Analysis of Land Problems in China) (Nanjing, Zhengzhong shuju, 1946), p. 63. The percentages for farmers who were tenants or part-owners are taken from two sources. "NARB" cites 农情报告汇编 (Crop Reporting in China, 1934) (Nanjing, National Agricultural Research Bureau, Ministry of Industry, 1936), p. 62. "Buck" cites the averages of farm and agricultural surveys in Buck, *Land Utilization in China*, pp. 57–9.

failure in the traditional property rights regime as far as short-term efficiency is concerned. Indeed, the explosive growth and recovery in agricultural output in the early 1980s following the adoption of the so-called

Agricultural Household Responsibility and the resolution of the collective commune reveals again the resilience of traditional Chinese agrarian land institutions.

Distribution and Credit

One of the long-standing debates around Chinese agriculture is the question of distribution and exploitation. The thesis mostly advanced by the Marxist framework advocated that the prevalence of small-scale farming and vulnerability to risk exposes peasants to land deprivation and exploitation through usury. The actual empirical evidence of any of these is unclear. An important study by Loren Brandt and Barbara Sands on land and income distribution in early twentieth-century China does not reveal very high inequality in land distribution. Their calculations give a Gini coefficient for land distribution of 0.55–0.6, which is high but not extreme. But their income Gini for rural households stood at 0.4–0.45. Using village-level data, they reveal that the discrepancy between income and land distribution was derived from two major sources. First is that factor markets in land and labor have served to equalize returns on agricultural production through the renting of surplus land and the hiring of surplus labor. Second, with commercialization, a third of net village income was actually derived from nonagricultural labor, sometimes from out-migrants working in newly arisen industrial centers.[65] Their studies of moderate inequality in Chinese rural areas have been confirmed by a host of new studies.[66] Indeed, according to Kang Chao's study based on much more scattered and controversial evidence, there was no long-term increase in land inequality in the millennium between the Song and Republican China.[67]

Turning to the question of usury, new studies reveal that the story is far from a simple case of exploitation by the rich and powerful with monopoly power. Surveys show that in the 1930s most regions in rural China had an annual interest rate in the range of 30 percent. Interest rates were far higher in the more impoverished regions than in highly commercialized areas. But this had less to do with exploitation and monopoly power than with higher transaction costs incurred in the size of loans often in relatively more

---

[65] L. Brandt and B. Sands, "Beyond Malthus and Ricardo: Economic Growth, Land Concentration, and Income Distribution in Early Twentieth-Century Rural China," *Journal of Economic History* 50.4 (1990), 807–27.

[66] Guan Yongqiang 近代中国的收入分配：一个定量的研究 (Income Distribution in Modern China: A Quantitative Study) (Beijing, Renmin chubanshe, 2012), Chapter 3.

[67] Chao Gang 赵冈, 中国传统农村的地权分配 (Land Distribution in Traditional Rural China) (Beijing, Xinxing chubanshe, 2006).

impoverished areas.[68] This is even true of relatively low-risk loans with land collateral. What is more accurate is that it reflected a general phenomenon of relative capital scarcity in the Chinese economy. It was overall capital constraint that clearly acted against capital accumulation in Chinese agriculture and tilted it further in the direction of labor-intensivity.

In Table 3.4 we reproduce a recent study that uses the county data from the survey conducted by the Department of Agricultural Economics at the University of Nanking under the supervision of Buck from 1929 to 1933 to test different hypotheses. The interest rate is regressed to the wealth-inequality or Gini coefficient; the percentage of creditors from the "exploiting class" (*class*); the percentage of owner-farmers (*ownerp*); proxies of per capita income, including the crop output per capita (*GrainPC*) and daily wage (*Wage*); and proxies of market and monetization development level, including the level of waterage in local agricultural trade (*waterage*) and the proportion of rent payment in money (*mrent*). We also control for the total percentage of lending by formal financial institutions (*finst*) and per capita acreage of arable land (*land*).

Regression results show that the Gini coefficient has no robust positive effect on the interest rate, while the coefficient *class* alone is insignificant. The percentage of owner-farmers, *ownerp*, is significantly positive at the 5 percent level; that is, a higher percentage of farmers tilling their own land means higher interest rates, rejecting the hypothesis of class exploitation and supporting the other hypotheses that tenancy reflects more efficient and functioning markets and better-developed institutions for the rural credit market. Meanwhile, the income effect of *GrainPC* and *Wage*, and the effect of the monetization development level represented by *mrent*, are negative, as expected, and significant at the 5 percent level.

Conclusion

Ultimately, agricultural modernization and rising agricultural productivity will lead to a shrinking of the agricultural sector and a shift of resources to other sectors. Until about three decades ago, Chinese agriculture and agricultural population weighed heavily on the Chinese economy and were at the center of debate about long-term economic growth or stagnation. Much

---

[68] Chen, Peng, and Yuan, "Usury, Market Power and Poverty Traps." Peng Kaixiang 彭凯翔, Chen Zhiwu 陈志武, and Yuan Weipeng 袁为鹏, "近代中国农村借贷市场的机制" (Mechanisms of Rural Credit Markets in Modern China), 经济研究 (Economic Research Journal), 2008.5, 147–59.

Table 3.4 Explaining interest rates across regions

Variable	(1) Ordinary least squares	(2) Two-stage least squares
Gini	20.283**	−26.979
	(10.019)	(33.071)
class	0.050	0.051
	(0.044)	(0.065)
finst	−0.173*	0.182
	(0.097)	(0.246)
ownerp	0.058**	0.133**
	(0.028)	(0.067)
GrainPC	−0.330***	−0.356***
	(0.083)	(0.110)
land	2.040**	1.895
	(0.882)	(1.289)
Wage	−11.250**	−12.234**
	(4.783)	(5.743)
mrent	−0.060**	−0.116***
	(0.025)	(0.036)
waterage	−3.725*	−3.441
	(1.999)	(2.443)
C	35.090***	36.870***
	(5.738)	(11.506)
adj. R^2	0.450	0.247
Obs.	118	118

Notes. dependent variable: average interest rate; *Gini*: Gini coefficient; *class*: weight of exploiting class in credit; *ownerp*: percentage of owner-farmers; *finst*: weight of financial institutions in credit; *Wage*: daily wage; *GrainPC*: crop output per capita; *land*: per capita arable land; *waterage*: waterage in local agricultural trade; *mrent*: proportion of rent payment in money. Asterisks ***, **, * represent significance levels of 1 percent, 5 percent, and 10 percent respectively. For more details, see Zhiwu Chen, Kaixiang Peng, and Weipeng Yuan, "Usury, Market Power and Poverty Traps: A Study of Rural Credit in 1930s' China," *Frontiers of Economics in China* 3 (2018), 369–96.

more research needs to be done. This survey, though highly selective, does not support the case of a rapid or general decline in overall agricultural performance or per capita grain output during the period under study. It also shows that while Chinese agriculture remained largely traditional, there were important and significant new developments towards modernization.

Most importantly, despite being saddled with too many ideological labels and conceptual frameworks, both the technology and the institutions of Chinese agriculture displayed remarkable resilience, not only in sustaining the livelihood of a quarter of the world's population, but also in adapting to new modernization challenges. Hence it is time to recognize and understand the logic of Chinese agriculture on her own terms through the changing times, and a thorough understanding of it will be critical to the success of any genuine reform.

Further Reading

Brandt, L., and B. Sands, "Beyond Malthus and Ricardo: Economic Growth, Land Concentration, and Income Distribution in Early Twentieth-Century China," *Journal of Economic History* 50 (December 1990), pp. 807–27.

Buck, J.L., *Land Utilization in China: Statistics* (Nanking, University of Nanking, 1937).

Cao Shuji 曹树基 and Liu Shigu 刘诗古, 传统中国地权结构及其演变 (The Structure and Evolution of Traditional Land Property Rights in China) (Shanghai, Shanghai jiaotong daxue chubanshe, 2014).

Cao Xingsui 曹幸穗 and Wang Siming 王思明 (eds.), 中国农业通史: 近代卷 (General History of Chinese Agriculture: Modern Times) (Beijing, Zhongguo nongye chubanshe, 2020).

Chao, K., *Man and Land in Chinese History: An Economic Analysis* (Stanford, Stanford University Press, 1986).

Chen, Z., K. Peng, and W. Yuan, "Usury, Market Power and Poverty Traps: A Study of Rural Credit in 1930s' China," *Frontiers of Economics in China* 3 (2018), 369–96.

Han Maoli 韩茂莉, 中国历史农业地理 (Beijing, Beijing daxue chubanshe, 2012).

Huang, P., *The Peasant Economy and Social Change in North China* (Stanford: Stanford University Press, 1985).

Li, B., *Agricultural Development in Jiangnan, 1620–1850* (Basingstoke, Macmillan, 1998).

Li Bozhong 李伯重, 中国的早期近代经济—1820 年代华亭 – 娄县地区 GDP 研究 (Beijing, Zhonghua shuju, 2010).

Min Zongdian 闵宗殿 (ed.), 中国农业通史: 明清卷 (General History of Chinese Agriculture: Ming and Qing Dynasties) (Beijing, Zhongguo nongye chubanshe, 2020).

Ma, D., "Why Japan, Not China, Was the First to Develop in East Asia: Lessons from Sericulture 1850–1937," *Economic Development and Cultural Change* 52.2 (January 2004), 369–94.

Peng Kaixiang 彭凯翔, 清代以来的粮价: 历史学的解释与再解释 (The Rice Price since the Qing Dynasty: A Historical Interpretation and Reinterpretation) (Shanghai, Shanghai renmin chubanshe, 2006), pp. 32–41.

Peng Kaixiang 彭凯翔, "人口增长下的粮食生产与经济发展—由史志宏研究员的清代农业产出测算谈起" (Grain Production and Development under the Growth of Population: A Discussion from Shi Zhihong's Estimation about Agricultural Production in the Qing Dynasty), 中国经济史研究 (Research in Chinese Economic History) 7 (2015), 38–49.

Perkins, D.H., *Agricultural Development in China, 1368–1968* (Chicago, Aldine Publishing, 1969).

Richardson, P., *Economic Change in China, c. 1800–1950* (Cambridge, Cambridge University Press, 1990).

Shi, Z., *Agricultural Development in Qing China: A Quantitative Study, 1661–1911* (Leiden, Brill, 2018).

4
Handicraft and Modern Industries

LINDA GROVE AND TŌRU KUBO

Industrialization in China has followed complicated paths over the last century and a half. China, like Russia, Germany, and Japan, followed in the footsteps of the pioneering industrial nations. For the first pioneering generation, industrialization developed indigenously, building on preindustrial handicraft traditions, inventing new technologies using water and steam power, and creating new corporate management systems. The new technologies of steamships, railroads, the telegraph, and the telephone transformed transportation and communication networks. Private entrepreneurs played central roles in the development of the new industrial systems, aided by protective tariffs and other state measures designed to promote industrial and commercial development.

For the second generation of industrializing nations, there was no need to invent technologies since they could be purchased and transplanted. In China, as in Japan and other later developing countries, the state took the lead in pushing for change, formulating industrialization policies and providing investment funds for new industries. The early push for industrialization came during a period of political crises. The late imperial Chinese state suffered repeated shocks, beginning with the loss of the Opium War and the subsequent forced opening of Chinese territory to foreign trade, followed by the fourteen-year struggle against the Taiping and other rebellious groups that resulted in the deaths of a reported 20 million people and widespread destruction in the Yangzi valley, China's most developed region. It is not surprising that early industrialization efforts focused on military technology. As Chinese industry developed in the late nineteenth and early twentieth centuries, industrialization moved beyond military defense to light industry. Factories were established to process goods for export and produce goods to substitute for imports that had flooded the markets following the opening of the treaty ports. By the 1920s and 1930s, there were large and small factories not only in the treaty port cities, but in many smaller cities and towns. Some produced for export markets, others for domestic consumption.

Some early Chinese industrial enterprises match conventional images of modern industry – large-scale enterprises in purpose-built factory buildings with mechanized production processes, staffed by disciplined workers, and following Western corporate models. But alongside those modern factories, we find many other industrial and semi-industrial forms that mixed the use of mechanical and human power, relied on skills learned through training in traditional modes of production, located production in small workshops and homes, and drew on indigenous commercial networks and business practices. Minami and Makino's compilation of long-term Asian statistics, which provides the best estimate of the balance between modern industry and handicraft production in important industries, shows that in 1933 over 90 percent of output in the food, beverages and tobacco sector was produced by handicraft means, over 60 percent of textile goods, apparel and leather came from handicraft, and 53.9 percent of goods in the chemical, metal, and machinery sector also came from handicraft workshops (Figure 4.1).[1]

China's industrialization experience followed multiple paths. The first path was a government-led path based on imported technology and investment of relatively large supplies of capital to create modern factories, most commonly in heavy industry. A second path, developed by indigenous Chinese capital, was modeled on Western enterprise, but was based on intensive use of labor in light industrial production. A third path, also created by indigenous Chinese capital, grew out of handicraft traditions and combined human labor and mechanized or semi-mechanized production processes to produce light industrial goods.

This chapter examines the "new" – i.e. the modern industrial and semi-industrial systems that developed in the late nineteenth and the twentieth centuries – but also what happened to the "old"; that is, the systems that linked agricultural production with handicraft processing to provide food, clothing, and other goods consumed by China's vast rural and urban populations. We will look at China's largest traditional handicraft industries, silk and cotton, which were transformed beginning in the late nineteenth century. The first of these, silk, was directly linked to an explosion in the export trade while the second, cotton, is an example of the transformations involved in import-substitution industrialization. We will add to the consideration of these two well-studied examples brief consideration of industries that produced soap, matches,

---

[1] Minami Ryoshin 南亮進 and Makino Fumio 牧野文夫 (eds.), アジア長期経済統計 3 中国 (Long-Term Asian Statistics, vol. 3, China) (Tokyo, Tōyō Keizai Shinpōsha, 2014), p. 111.

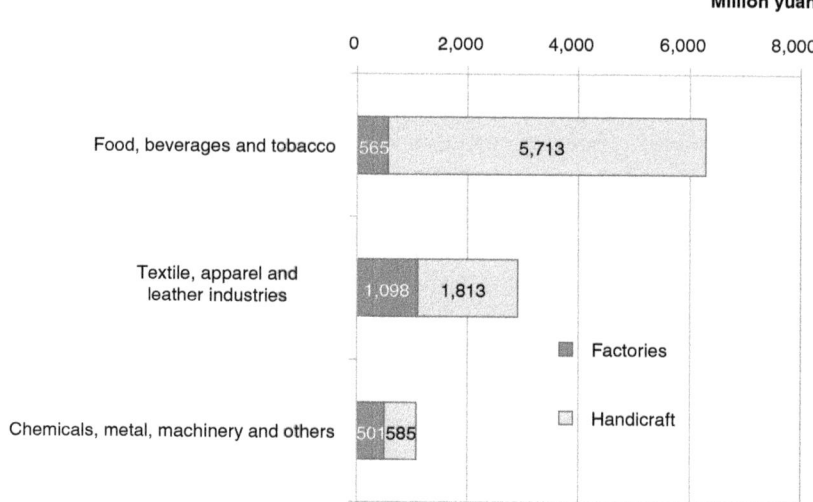

Figure 4.1 Industrial production in mainland China, 1933
Source: Minami Ryoshin 南亮進 and Makino Fumio 牧野文夫 (eds.), アジア長期経済統計 3 中国 (Long-Term Asian Statistics, vol. 3, China) (Tokyo, Tōyō Keizai Shinpōsha, 2014), p. 111

cosmetics, and other new products that entered the Chinese market in the twentieth century. For a detailed analysis of the role of the state in building heavy industries, including mining and shipping, and the creation of an ideology supporting the development state, readers should refer to Chapter 6 by Morris L. Bian in this volume.

Foreign models, as well as foreign investment, played major roles in China's industrialization. The foreign models came from the pioneering industrialized states of Britain and the United States, but also – and most importantly – from one of the first successful late-developing states, Japan. Shortly after the end of the Sino-Japanese War, Sino-Japanese relations took a positive turn: thousands of Chinese students were sent to Japan to study in universities and technical and vocational schools, and hundreds of Japanese scholars, teachers, and technicians were invited to work in China as advisers to national and provincial government-sponsored projects.[2] In later years,

---

[2] D. Reynolds, China 1898–1912: The Xinzheng Revolution and Japan (Cambridge, MA, Council on East Asian Relations, Harvard, 1993); Jiang Pei 江沛, 留日学生、东游官绅与直隶省的近代进程 1900–1928 (Overseas Students and Official Missions and Modern Development in Zhili Province, 1900–1928), 史学月刊 5 (2005), 56–66; Ōsato Hiroaki 大里浩秋 and Son An Suk 孫安石 (eds.), 中国人日本留学史研究の現段階 (The Current State of Research on the History of Chinese Students in Japan) (Tokyo, Ochanomizu shobō, 2009).

Japanese companies became major foreign investors in Chinese light industry, and during the war years took over Chinese firms in the occupied areas of China. The legacy of Japanese involvement in light industry and in the development of heavy industry in Manchuria during the colonial period helped to create a base for the rapid development of Chinese manufacturing after 1949.

While foreign models and technology are an important part of the story of Chinese industrialization, the largest role was played by the thousands of Chinese entrepreneurs who established factories and workshops throughout the nation. For a long period after 1950, these entrepreneurs received little attention; however, since the launching of the reform policies in the early 1980s, there has been renewed interest in the contributions of China's early entrepreneurs to modern economic development.

The final section of this chapter will look at the wartime and postwar reorganization of Chinese industry that laid the base for the nationalization of industry in the early 1950s and offer an evaluation of modern industrial growth and its impact on the development of the Chinese economy in the first half of the twentieth century.

Industrialization from Abroad

Modern mechanized industry was introduced to China in the mid-nineteenth century. China's experience differed from that of the early-industrializing nations, including Britain and the United States, where industrialization began with light industry, primarily textiles. One of the distinctive characteristics of the Chinese case – a characteristic it shares with Japan and some other late-developing countries – is that mechanization was first introduced in defense-related industries, including munitions and shipbuilding. The first mechanized factories were transplants from the West, importing machinery, raw materials, and Western engineers who supervised production. By the early twentieth century, China began to import machinery from Japan, and Chinese engineers who had studied in Europe, the United States, and Japan began to replace foreign engineers, assuming leadership roles in modern enterprises.

In the 1860s the Qing government, involved in a long internal war to suppress the Taiping Rebellion, decided to create a modern defense industry to ensure that in the future China could provision its military and build modern ships to control shipping in its own waters. The government established three state-owned enterprises, the Jiangnan Arsenal in Shanghai (1865), the Mawei Shipbuilding Yard in Fuzhou (1866), and the Tianjin Arsenal (1867). The Jiangnan Arsenal was the most successful of these enterprises: by the early 1890s the Jiangnan Arsenal had 662 machines and employed 2,913 workers and had developed into a major shipbuilding company that is still active in the twenty-first century.[3] The Mawei Shipbuilding Yard and the Tianjin Arsenal had less happy fates. The Mawei Shipbuilding Yard was partially destroyed during the 1884 Sino-French war, and the Tianjin Arsenal was destroyed by the troops of the Eight-Power Allied Expedition Force that occupied north China during the Boxer Rebellion.

Ship repair and servicing facilities established by foreign companies in the treaty ports after the 1840s were a second source of the modern defense industries. Foreign companies established docking facilities in Hong Kong, Guangzhou, Shanghai, and other port cities to repair and service commercial ships; some of those establishments later developed shipbuilding capacity. For example, two companies established in Shanghai, the Boyd Company (1862) and S.C. Farnham (1863), by the 1880s had the capacity to construct 2,000-ton ships. Each of the firms had divisions for forging parts and other metalwork and employed several hundred Chinese workers.[4]

These factories used imported machinery and imported raw materials, and Western engineers provided technical direction. Maritime Customs statistics show a steady increase in machinery imports and raw materials for the factories after 1880, when such goods were first included in the statistical records (Figure 4.2). Scrap metal occupied a large share of the imports, including scrap metal from European factories, as well as used horseshoes from the cities of Glasgow and London.[5]

Technology Transfer

Acquiring technology from overseas was the first step in building a modern industrial base. However, for sustained growth the receiving country needed to develop capacity to educate engineers and skilled workers to take over management of the transplanted factories. In the late nineteenth century, there was only limited progress in China in transferring technological knowledge and skills. In

---

[3] Shanghai Shehui Kexueyuan Jingji Yanjiusu 上海社会科学院经济研究所 (ed.), 江南造船厂厂史 (A Factory History of the Jiangnan Shipbuilding Company) (Shanghai, Shanghai Shehui kexueyuan chubanshe, 1983).
[4] Sun Yutang 孙毓棠 (ed.), 中国近代工业史资料 (Materials on the History of Chinese Modern Industry), 2 vols., part 1 (Beijing, Kexue chubanshe, 1957).
[5] China Imperial Maritime Customs, *Returns of Trade and Trade Reports for the Year of 1891* (Shanghai, 1892).

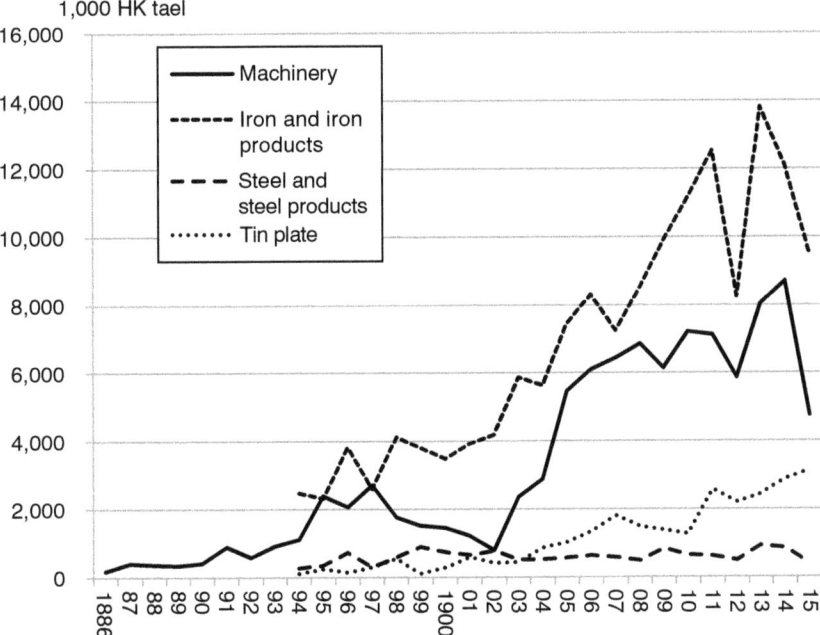

Figure 4.2 Imports of machinery, iron, and steel, 1886–1915
Source: China Imperial Maritime Customs, *Returns of Trade and Trade Reports*, 1887–1910, 1911–1915

the early factories, including both defense-related and light-industrial operations, foreign engineers supervised work. The Qing government was aware of the problem and launched a major project to develop human capital by sending Chinese students to study in Europe and America; however, only about 4–5 percent of the first generation of returnees took positions in manufacturing.[6] Overall, Chinese modern manufacturing in the late nineteenth century was almost completely dependent on European and American machinery and engineering skills.

While the formal government programs had little impact on developing higher-level engineering skills, the state-run defense factories did serve as incubators for building a cadre of skilled workers who played a major role in the development of the Chinese machine-making industry. Workers who had mastered skills through employment in the defense factories were

---

[6] Xu Dingxin 徐鼎新, 中国近代企业的科技力量与科技效应 (Impact and Scientific-Technical Levels in China's Modern Enterprises) (Shanghai, Shanghai Shehui kexue chubanshe, 1995).

responsible for the establishment of most of the early twentieth-century machine workshops and factories.

Some of the earliest examples of this spin-off phenomenon are Chinese-owned machine-making enterprises, including Da Long in Shanghai and the machine-making workshops of Tianjin's Santiaoshi district.[7] Da Long began repairing ships and later began to make parts for modern textile enterprises; the Tianjin machine shops produced parts for modern industry as well as iron gear looms for rural industrial districts. In the mid-Yangzi city of Hanyang, the Zhou Heng Shun machine-making factory, which developed out of a handicraft metalworking shop, grew into a mechanized factory that could produce steam engines and pumps for mining operations.[8]

Late Qing Technical Education Efforts

Following China's defeat in the Sino-Japanese War (1894–1895), ever-broadening groups came to share a sense of crisis about the survival of China. Zheng Guanying's popular book *Warnings to a Prosperous Age* raised the specter of a "commercial war" with the West, inspiring efforts to "save the country through enterprise." During the first decade of the twentieth century, the national government and some provincial governments established training schools for technicians and scholarship programs to send talented students overseas. Sheng Xuanhuai, one of the leading officials promoting modern industry, played a central role in developing engineering education, establishing the Beiyang Xuetang (forerunner of Tianjin University) in 1895 and the Nanyang Gongxue (forerunner of Shanghai Jiaotong University) in 1896.

Technical training entered a new stage under the New Government policies, instituted by Yuan Shikai after he was appointed governor-general of Zhili province in the wake of the Boxer Rebellion. Yuan's industrial promotion policies were based on practices of Meiji Japan. He hired Japanese advisers and recruited Japanese teachers to staff the Zhili

---

[7] Shanghai shi Gongshang Xingzheng Guanliju 上海市工商行政管理局 (eds.), 上海民族橡胶工业 (Shanghai National-Capital Rubber Industry) (Beijing, Zhonghua shuju, 1979); Shanghai Shehui Kexueyuan Jingji Yanjiusuo 上海社会科学院经济研究所 (ed.), 大隆机器厂的产生、发展和改造 (The Birth, Development, and Reform of the Dalong Machine Making Company) (Shanghai, Shanghai renmin chubanshe, 1980); Nankai daxue lishixi 南开大学历史系 (ed.), 天津三条石早期工业资料调查 (A Survey of Materials on Early Industry in Tianjin's Santiaoshi), unpublished manuscript, 1958; Gail Hershatter, "Flying Hammers, Walking Chisels: The Workers of Santiaoshi," *Modern China* 9 (October 1983), 387–419.

[8] Yan Peng 严鹏, 战略性工业化的曲折展开: 中国机器工业的演化 1900–1957 (The Torturous Development of Strategic Industrialization: The Evolution of China's Machine-Making Industry, 1900–1957) (Shanghai, Shanghai renmin chubanshe, 2015), pp. 39–40.

Gongyiju, which promoted light industries. The Zhili Gongyiju established a training school, a demonstration factory, and a product exhibition hall. Six hundred student apprentices studied weaving, dyeing, textile design, soap-making, carpentry, ceramics, matches, and drafting. Some of the students were sent to Japan to study at technical schools, and some served apprenticeships in Japanese factories.[9]

The Role of Japanese Technology Transfer

While earlier studies have focused on technology transfer from Britain, Europe, and the United States, Japanese technology also played a significant role in Chinese industrial development, particularly in the silk and cotton industries. Many of the leaders of the postwar textile industry in China, including Zhu Xianfang, head of the Nantong Textile Institute, and Zhang Fangzuo, head of the Textile Research Institute, had studied in Japan.

From the 1920s on, Japanese textile technology came to be used widely in China, with the introduction of the Minorikawa multi-thread reeling machine and the Toyoda automatic loom. Japanese technology also had a major impact on the handicraft weaving industry, with the import and spread of the iron gear loom. The iron gear or treadle loom, invented in Japan in the late 1880s and introduced to China by the Zhili Gongyiju, functioned like a power loom, but with "power" supplied by the weaver pumping the treadles. The loom had been used in rural workshops in Japan that did not have access to electricity and came to be widely used in weaving workshops all over China into the 1950s.[10] Japanese technology played a role in the development of other light industries, including matches and rubber shoes; overseas Chinese entrepreneurs from Japan included the founders of the Nanyang Brothers Tobacco Company, the chief rival of the British American Tobacco Company.[11]

A third major transfer from Japan in the 1920s and 1930s was on-the-job training (OJT) regimes for technicians and skilled workers, which spread from the Japanese-owned cotton mills in China to their Chinese-owned

---

[9] L. Grove, "Technology Transfer, Imitation and Local Production: The Soap Industry in Early Twentieth Century Tianjin," in K. Furuta and L. Grove, *Imitation, Counterfeiting and the Quality of Goods in Modern Asian History* (Singapore, Springer, 2017), pp. 161–82; D. Reynolds and C. Reynolds, *East Meets West: Chinese Discover the Modern World in Japan, 1854–1898* (Ann Arbor, Association for Asian Studies, 2014).

[10] L. Grove, *A Chinese Economic Revolution: Rural Entrepreneurship in the Twentieth Century* (Lanham, Rowman & Littlefield Publishers Inc., 2006).

[11] S. Cochran, *Big Business in China: Sino-Foreign Rivalry in the Cigarette Industry, 1890–1930* (Cambridge, MA, Harvard University Press, 1980).

rivals.¹² In the case of the silk industry, there had been little technological innovation following the introduction of European technology in the late nineteenth century; this began to change in the early twentieth century, when silk filatures started to provide training for their workers.

Privately Funded Technology Education

Technical education was not exclusively the work of public institutions. Entrepreneurs also sponsored specialized training schools. In 1912 the well-known textile entrepreneur Zhang Jian set up a Textile Training Institute in Nantong, the home base of his Da Sheng cotton mills, and by the latter half of the 1930s two-thirds of the textile engineers working in Chinese mills were graduates of his school.¹³

Export-Oriented Industrialization

The second path to industrialization was modeled on Western experience in producing light industrial goods, with factories combining imported machinery with intensive labor. Sugihara Kaoru has argued that this labor-intensive industrialization model was characteristic of industrial production in both China and Japan.¹⁴ Private capital played the central role in light industrialization. We have divided our consideration into two parts, first looking at export-oriented production, which developed relatively early, and then considering industries which supplied substitutes for imports in domestic markets.

Export-oriented production was not a new phenomenon in the nineteenth century. Chinese craftsmen had engaged in export-oriented production for centuries. Chinese ceramics are found in archaeological sites throughout Southeast Asia and the Middle East, and reports of Chinese silk can be found in Roman records. In more recent centuries, eighteenth-century craftsmen produced a variety of goods for export. Among the goods in the Canton trade were Chinese specialties, including silk, tea, and ceramics, but also made-to-order furniture; ceramic dinner and tea sets with company coats of arms; genre paintings; glass paintings, including reproductions of Peale's

---

¹² Tomizawa Yoshia 富澤芳亜, 近代中国の工業教育と紡績技術者養成 (Technical Education in Modern China and the Development of Textile Engineers), 経済史研究 20 (2017), 47–96.
¹³ Xu, 中国近代企业的科技力量与科技效应, 6.
¹⁴ K. Sugihara, "Labour-Intensive Industrialization in Global History: An Interpretation of East Asian Experiences," in G. Austin and K. Sugihara (eds.), *Labour-Intensive Industrialization in Global History* (London and New York, Routledge, 2013), pp. 20–64.

famous portrait of George Washington; and much else. What was new in the late nineteenth century was the use of machines, imported from the West, that changed manufacturing processes.

In this section on export-oriented industries, we will first review the introduction of new technologies and their impact on the silk industry and then briefly consider other export-oriented industries, including those that processed agricultural raw materials, as well as the development of new export industries that drew on the abundant supply of rural surplus labor, organized in new ways and serving new markets.

The Movement for Modern Filatures

The Chinese began producing and trading silk fabrics several thousand years ago, and silk was already an important product in the Canton export trade before the opening of the treaty ports in the mid-nineteenth century. The Yangzi delta area had developed as the center of Chinese silk production during the Song and Yuan dynasties. During the Ming dynasty, silk production flourished in areas around Lake Tai, and by the sixteenth and seventeenth centuries, Huzhou prefecture, south of the lake, had established a reputation for its high-quality Tsatlee silk. After the opening of the treaty ports, demand for Chinese raw silk exploded and silk became the most important commodity in China's export trade. A silkworm epidemic in Europe contributed to rising demand, but equally important was a more than fivefold increase in the per capita consumption of silk goods in the United States, Great Britain, Germany, and France.[15]

The boom in the market for Chinese raw silk did not last. In China raw silk was produced in rural households using handicraft methods, and the quality of the silk varied depending on the skills of individual producers. At the height of the boom even inferior raw silk could be sold for a good price, but the mixing of good and inferior qualities damaged the reputation of Chinese silk.[16] As questions were raised about quality, the price of raw silk traded in Shanghai fell: the average price in 1874–1883 was 30 percent lower than ten years earlier.[17]

---

[15] G. Federico, *An Economic History of the Silk Industry* (Cambridge, Cambridge University Press, 1997).
[16] L. Li, *China's Silk Trade: Traditional Industry in the Modern World, 1842–1937* (Cambridge, Council on East Asian Studies, 1981).
[17] Suzuki Tomoo 鈴木智夫, 洋務運動の研究 (Research on the Self-Strengthening Movement) (Tokyo, Kyūko Shoin, 1992), p. 322.

Falling silk prices were the impetus for foreign trading firms to introduce mechanized silk filatures to improve the quality of silk. The American trading firm Russell & Co. set up the first modern silk filature in 1878 and a leading Chinese silk merchant, Huang Zongxian, established a filature in 1880. By the early twentieth century, 80 to 90 percent of the output of the mechanized silk filatures was destined for the export market.[18]

Although the factories referred to above are usually cited as the first modern silk filatures, there had been efforts to set up mechanized filatures twenty years earlier. The British trading firm Jardine, Matheson had supported the establishment of a mechanized filature in Shanghai in 1861. However, difficulties in obtaining cocoons, together with a shortage of skilled labor, made the factory financially unstable, and it closed in 1869.[19]

Other efforts to set up mechanized filatures in the 1870s also ran into problems: local merchants and members of the elite who were worried that mechanized filatures would destroy the existing handicraft industry, impoverishing thousands of rural producers, organized protests. As a result, when mechanized filatures were established in the early 1880s, the Shanghai intendant ordered the factories to close. Representatives of foreign governments entered the dispute, eventually reaching an agreement with the Liangjiang governor-general that allowed the mechanized filatures to operate; however, the factories were assessed a new tax and limits were placed on the number of factories.[20]

At about the same time that these struggles were taking place in the Shanghai region, an overseas Chinese merchant from Vietnam, Chen Qiyuan, set up a mechanized filature in Nanhai county, Guangdong; other merchants in the region soon followed his example. Chen's factory used treadle-style reeling equipment rather than steam-powered machines. Chen's efforts, like the early efforts to establish modern filatures in Shanghai, met with protests. As the number of silk reeling workshops increased, there was a shortage of cocoons, and traditional silk-goods merchants began to protest; in 1881 protesters attacked the factory. Worried about social stability, the local government ordered the factories to temporarily close.

---

[18] Xu Xinwu 徐新吾, 中国近代缫丝工业史 (A History of Chinese Raw Silk Manufacture) (Shanghai, Shanghai renmin chubanshe, 1990).
[19] Kubo Tōru 久保亨, Kajima Jun 加島潤, and Kigoshi Yoshinori 木越義則, 統計でみる中国近現代経済史 (Economic History of Modern China: Based on Statistical Data) (Tokyo, Tōkyō daigaku shuppankai, 2016), p. 33.
[20] Suzuki, 洋務運動の研究, pp. 324–8.

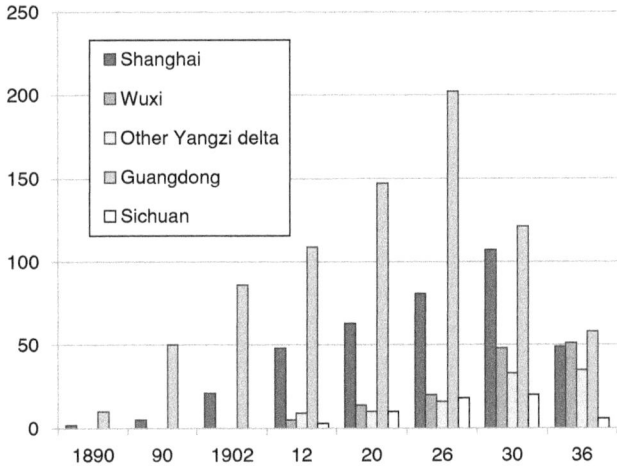

Figure 4.3 Silk reeling filatures
Source: Kubo Tōru 久保亨, Kajima Jun 加島潤 and Kigoshi Yoshinori 木越義則 (eds.), 統計でみる中国近現代経済史 (Economic History of Modern China: Based on Statistical Data) (Tokyo, Tōkyō daigaku shuppankai, 2016), p. 36

While some have argued that the opposition to the introduction of modern silk filatures reflected the conservative nature of Chinese society, we should not overemphasize the protests, since from the 1890s to the 1920s modern silk filatures were established in many parts of the country, with large concentrations in Wuxi in Jiangsu province and in Sichuan province, as well as in Shanghai and Guangdong. The number of mechanized filatures grew from eighty-seven in 1894 to 115 in 1902, 171 in 1910, and 274 in 1918 (Figure 4.3).[21] Patterns of production varied from region to region. Soda has argued that three factors contributed to the success of the Shanghai modern filatures: first, a steady supply of women workers from northern Jiangsu province; second, the establishment of a system of cocoon brokers which stabilized the market for raw materials; and third, the establishment of a system of rental factories, which reduced start-up costs.[22] In Wuxi, which was a relative newcomer to sericulture, there was no local tradition of silk hand-reeling; rural producers specialized in raising silkworms and selling the cocoons to modern filatures.[23] In Shunde there were various styles of

[21] Xu, 中国近代缫丝, 142.
[22] Soda Saburo 曽田三郎, 中国近代製糸業史の研究 (Research on China's Modern Silk Industry) (Tokyo, Kyūko Shoin, 1994).
[23] L.S. Bell, *One Industry, Two Chinas: Silk Filatures and Peasant-Family Production in Wuxi, 1865–1937* (Stanford, Stanford University Press, 1999).

management; at the peak, some 150,000 women worked in filatures, and the area became well known for its independent women workers who refused to marry.[24]

In the mid-nineteenth century, the advent of silkworm disease in Europe presented new market opportunities, but Japan also rose as a strong competitor, soon surpassing China as an exporter of raw silk.[25] To understand the competition, we need to consider the technologies in different production centers. Shanghai's mechanized filatures used Italian technology that separated the boiling and reeling processes, directly reeling the silk. While this method was not as efficient as other reeling technologies, it produced the high-quality raw silk that was in great demand in the French textile center of Lyon for the production of luxury fabrics. In contrast, Japanese filatures used "Suwa-style" equipment in which the boiling of cocoons and reeling were completed in one process. The Suwa-style process produced a consistent quality of medium-grade raw silk at a low cost; such raw silk was in high demand in the United States, where it was well adapted as weft for power-loom weaving.[26] The differential in production costs gave Japan an advantage, and the gap in exports between Japan and China steadily increased. As for the raw silk produced in Guangdong, most was of lower quality and was sold in the domestic market or exported to the United States.

One of the keys to Japanese success was a government-sponsored effort to improve sericulture techniques, including the establishment of special schools to train instructors in improved techniques. By the late 1890s local gentry and county magistrates in the silk regions of Jiangnan also began to set up schools, the most successful of which were the Hangzhou School for Sericulture and the Hushuguan Sericulture School for Girls; many of the graduates of these schools were sent to Japan for further studies, including Fei Dasheng, who was the elder sister of the anthropologist Fei Xiaotong and played a central role in modernizing the Wuxi silk industry.[27]

With the beginning of the Depression in 1929, demand for luxury products like silk sharply declined, and the Chinese silk industry suffered a major blow. This downturn coincided with the growing popularity of rayon, which served as a cheap substitute for silk. As the recovery from the Depression began, there was a shift in the location of the Chinese mechanized silk

---

[24] Lü Xuehai 吕学海, 顺德丝业调查报告 (Research Report on the Shunde Silk Industry), manuscript copy, Nankai University Library, 1938.
[25] D. Ma, "The Modern Silk Road: The Global Raw-Silk Market, 1850–1930," *Journal of Economic History* 56.2 (1996), 330–55.
[26] S. Soda, 中国近代製糸業.   [27] Bell, *One Industry*.

industry. Jiangnan production shifted from Shanghai, where capital shortage had resulted in instability, to Wuxi, which was closer to the cocoon-producing regions.[28] The shift to Wuxi was related to the development, with provincial government encouragement, of infrastructure to support sericulture, including sericulture schools, agricultural extension, and mandatory use of inspected silkworm eggs. Reforms of the silk industry were promoted by the Wuxi Cocoon Merchant Guild, whose members included most of the larger silk firms.

Scholars have offered different explanations for what was once viewed as Japan's success and China's failure in the global silk markets of the 1920s and 1930s. Some praised Japan's initiatives at quality control and lamented China's failure to adopt similar policies until later in the 1930s; others argued that the commercial systems involved in Chinese cocoon supply jacked up prices and reduced profits; while others put the blame on the slow response of the Chinese state.[29] Debin Ma, focusing on the period up to 1900, argued that technological adaptation was more successful in Japan and Guangdong than in the Yangzi delta region and that development of short-term capital markets was equally important.[30]

A careful look at the records shows that Chinese silk exports continued to rise throughout the 1920s and that the number of silk filatures continued to increase. So rather than Japanese success and Chinese failure, we might see Japan as very successful, and China also as successful, but to a lesser degree. The major differences were directly related to the markets each country targeted: Japan focused on the booming market for middle-quality silk in the US, while China targeted the European market for high-quality silk, which stagnated in the 1920s. Moreover, in the 1930s the silk industries of both countries entered a new stage of growth. One sign of this was an effort by China's largest silk company, Yong Tai, to directly enter the New York silk market.[31] Another sign of China's relative success was the response of

---

[28] Okumura Satoshi 奥村哲, 中国の資本主義と社会主義：近現代史像の再構成 (Capitalism and Socialism in China: Reformulating Images of Modern and Contemporary History) (Tokyo, Sakurai shoten, 2004).

[29] Li, *Chinese Silk Industry*; R. Eng, *Economic Imperialism in China: Silk Production and Exports* (Berkeley, University of California Press, 1986); Federico, *Economic History*. K. Furuta, "Peasant, Market Town, and Handicraft Technology," in A. Hayami and Y. Tsubouchi (eds.), *Economic and Demographic Development in Rice Producing Societies: Some Aspects of East Asian Economic History, 1500–1900* (Proceedings of the 10th International Economic History Congress, Leuven, 1989).

[30] D. Ma, "Between Cottage and Factory: The Evolution of Chinese and Japanese Silk-Reeling Industries in the Latter Half of the Nineteenth Century," *Journal of the Asia Pacific Economy* 10.2 (2005), 195–213.

[31] Okumura, 中国の資本主義.

Japanese silk companies to challenges from their Chinese rivals: in the early war years, Japanese silk companies lobbied occupation authorities to limit production in China's modern silk factories.

Mechanized Silk Filatures and the Handicraft Silk Industry

The silk complex – the raising of silkworms, reeling raw silk, and silk weaving – was for centuries one of China's major handicraft industries. Rural households cultivated mulberry trees, raised silkworms, and used hand machines to reel the raw silk. Some households also wove silk fabrics, while others sold raw silk to merchants who sold it or put it out to weavers working under their direction. The development of mechanized silk filatures pulled apart the silk complex, creating two separate and distinct markets: the first market was for raw silk processed in mechanized filatures, and was, at least at first, primarily for the export market. The other market was for raw silk produced in rural homes or semi-industrial handicraft workshops using hand- or foot-powered reeling equipment; this market came to primarily serve domestic customers. From the 1870s to 1929 we see a slow, but steady, increase in China's production of raw silk, and a slow, but steady, move from home processing toward processing of cocoons in modern filatures or in small workshops using hand- or foot-powered machines (Figure 4.4). The percentage of silk processed in mechanized filatures advanced from 13.1 percent in 1881–1885, to 25 percent by the first decade of the twentieth century, to 60 percent in 1936.[32] For producers of raw silk, the changes came over a long period of time, and as late as the mid-1930s, 40 percent of China's raw silk was still produced by handicraft methods. When Lü Xuehai investigated the Shunde silk industry in Guangdong in 1937, he found that households involved in sericulture moved back and forth between selling cocoons to filatures and processing by hand at home, adjusting their activities to market prices.

New Export-Oriented Handicraft Industries

Silk was the most important semi-processed export commodity in China in the late nineteenth and early twentieth centuries. However, following the opening of the treaty ports, foreign merchants identified other potential export opportunities: some linked farmers to foreign markets, and others made use of the large supply of underemployed female labor in the countryside. An example of the first was the export of dried-egg products. The egg

---

[32] Wang Xiang 王翔, 中国近代手工业史稿 (A History of China's Modern Handicraft Industry) (Shanghai, Shanghai renmin chubanshe, 2012), p. 295.

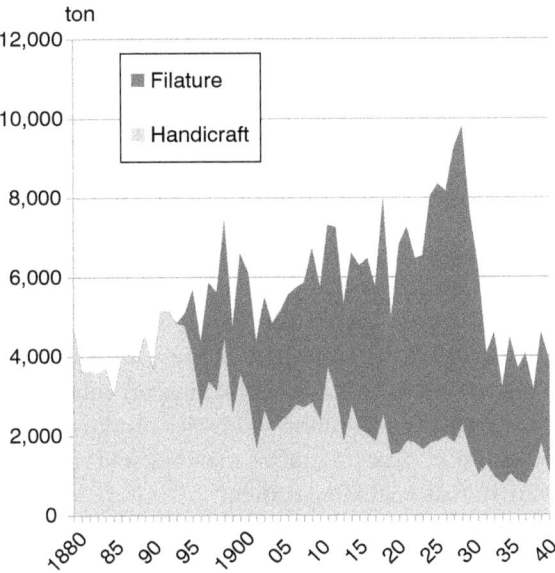

Figure 4.4 Silk exports by production source
Source: L. Hsiao, *China's Foreign Trade Statistics, 1864–1949* (Cambridge, MA, Harvard University Press, 1974), pp. 33, 36 for filature, pp. 31, 32, 34, 35 for handicraft

export business, which was started by a German merchant in Hankou in 1887, flourished during the First World War when European demand for egg products soared.[33] Hairnets, straw hats, and embroidery are other examples of new export items that made use of rural labor. Many of these new rural handicrafts were introduced by Western missionaries, who sought ways to provide remunerative labor for the rural poor. In some cases, the new processing industries used local raw materials, for example the straw used for weaving braid for hats, but in other cases the raw materials were imported. When missionaries first promoted hairnet weaving as a rural industry, human hair was imported from Europe. Later, Chinese hairnet producers switched to use Chinese hair. In the case of the lace and embroidery industries, the designs came from overseas, with rural women working in their homes under putting-out arrangements.[34]

---

[33] Yoshida Tateichiro 吉田建一郎, "戦間期中国における鶏卵: 鶏卵加工品輸出と養鶏業" (The Chinese Poultry Industry and Export of Egg Yolk and Processed Egg Products during the Interwar Years), 東洋学報 (Journal of East Asia) 86.4 (2005), 503–34.
[34] S. Mann, "Women's Work in the Ningbo Area, 1900–1936," in T. Rawski and L. Li (eds.), *Chinese History in Economic Perspective* (Berkeley, University of California Press, 1992),

By the 1930s lists of Chinese exports came to include products of modern factories as well. Japanese-owned cotton mills in China began to pioneer markets in Southeast Asia, and in 1935 a Chinese Industrial Goods Export Association was established to promote the export of manufactured goods.[35]

Import-Substitution Industrialization

When nineteenth-century British traders lobbied their government to force open Chinese markets, the motivation was access to one of the world's largest markets. However, the market never reached the levels foreign manufacturers envisioned, in large part because of the strong push-back from Chinese entrepreneurs, who developed import-substitution industries. The largest of the import-substitution industries produced consumer goods like cotton textiles, flour, cigarettes, beer, matches, and rubber shoes, as well as construction materials, including cement.

Many of the products manufactured in China's factories and workshops were new "exotic products"; first introduced from the West, consumption spread out from the treaty port cities into smaller towns in the interior.[36] Some of the new products replaced existing Chinese consumer items: for example, Western-style candles used for lighting quickly replaced traditional Chinese candles, just as modern laundry and toilet soaps replaced indigenous cleansing agents. While some of the products – for example cotton yarn and cement – were produced in modern factories using imported technology, others were produced in small factories and workshops, using a mixture of handicraft and mechanized production processes. In the early years, treaty restrictions limited the use of protective tariffs and Chinese manufacturers struggled against cheap imports. After China regained tariff autonomy in 1930, domestic producers were protected by higher tariffs and came to dominate the domestic market for many consumer goods, as seen in Table 4.1.

Production processes and product chains in China's modern consumer-goods industries linked modern factories with rural handicrafts. The

---

pp. 243–70; Peng Zeyi 彭泽益 (ed.), 中国近代手工业史资料 (Materials on the Chinese Modern Handicraft Industry) (Beijing, Sanlian shudian, 1962).

[35] Kubo Tōru 久保亨, 戦間期中国〈自立への模索〉：関税通貨政策と経済発展 (China's Quest for Sovereignty in the Interwar Period: Tariff Policy and Economic Development) (Tokyo, Tōkyō daigaku shuppankai, 1999).

[36] F. Dikötter, *Exotic Commodities: Modern Objects and Everyday Life in China* (New York, Columbia University Press, 2007).

Table 4.1 Market share of domestic products, 1920–1936 (%)

	Cotton yarn	Cotton pieces	Cement
1920	68.9	19.4	59.9
1930	102.3	55.3	84.6
1936	102.3	86.5	92.0

Source: Kubo, Kajima, and Kigoshi, 統計でみる, pp. 23, 24, 52

best-known example of this phenomenon was use of cotton yarn from urban spinning mills as raw material in rural weaving.

The handicraft cotton industry was one of the first of China's traditional industries to feel the impact of the opening of foreign trade in the mid-nineteenth century. British manufacturers had hoped to find a large market in China for cotton piece goods, but soon discovered that while there was a large market for machine yarn, it was more difficult to sell cotton fabrics. Machine yarns made steady inroads in the Chinese market, and by the end of the nineteenth century, imports supplied about 40 percent of the total Chinese consumption of yarn.

Seeing the high demand for machine yarns, European and American trading firms were inspired to establish spinning mills in China. In the 1860s and 1870s two British trading firms in Shanghai drafted a plan to set up a modern spinning and weaving mill to produce fabrics in imitation of Chinese "native cloth."[37] Chinese cotton fabric merchants, who controlled the trade in native cloth, opposed the plan. The Qing government, concerned about the fate of rural weaving households whose livelihood depended on income from weaving and worried about allowing foreigners to establish factories within its territory, blocked the plan.

Following the failure of the foreign investors to receive approval for a modern cotton mill, a consortium of Chinese merchants, including the Guangdong comprador Zheng Guanying (1842–1922), gained support from the leading official Li Hongzhang (1823–1901) for a similar plan. The company, based on a collaboration between private capital and the state, was established with the explicit purpose of providing substitutes for imports to improve China's unfavorable balance of trade. At that time, cotton cloth accounted for 30 percent of China's total imports.

---

[37] Suzuki, 洋務運動, 328–9.

It was not long before more cotton mills were established in Shanghai. The Treaty of Shimonoseki, ending the Sino-Japanese War, for the first time explicitly allowed foreign capital to establish factories in China, and this shift touched off a factory-founding rush, first by European and American investors, and then by Chinese entrepreneurs.[38]

Production in cotton spinning mills grew rapidly in the 1910s and the 1920s, and in cotton weaving mills in the 1920s and 1930s: by the 1930s, both sectors were supplying most of the domestic demand (Table 4.2). Japanese-owned and Chinese-owned firms played the central roles in this rapid expansion, while many of the early European and American firms failed. Among the European and American firms, the only successful venture was the Ewo (Yi He) spinning mill founded by Jardine, Matheson, the leading British trading company.

What accounted for the Western investors' bad track record? Nakai has argued that many of the foreign firms invested very little of their own capital, leaving them dependent on Chinese merchants for the supply of raw cotton and the sale of finished goods, resulting in high capital and distribution costs. Beginning in the 1910s, some of the firms declared bankruptcy and others sold out to Japanese or Chinese buyers.

A second question is related to the strong role of Japanese capital in the Chinese cotton industry. What inspired Japanese investment and why was it so successful? As background, we should note that Japanese cotton companies had been important players in the Chinese market from the late nineteenth century. As the Japanese cotton industry developed in the 1880s and 1890s, production capacity exceeded demand in the Japanese domestic market. Firms had to export if they wanted to continue to grow, and Japanese firms had built up capital holdings, so they had money to invest. At the same time, stricter enforcement of the 5 percent import tariff rate was making it more difficult for Japanese goods to compete in the Chinese market. This combination of factors led Japanese cotton firms to invest in China. The Japanese investments were made with adequate capital backing, overcoming the problems that had faced Western firms.[39]

Let us now turn to the fate of the Chinese-owned cotton mills. How were they able to survive in a situation where their capital and technological resources

---

[38] Kubo, Kajima, and Kigoshi, 統計でみる中国近現代経済史, p. 25; Nakai Hideki 中井英基, 張謇と中国近代企業 (Zhang Jian and the Modern Chinese Enterprise) (Sapporo, Hokkaidō daiguku toshokankokai, 1996).

[39] Takamura Naosuke 高村直助, 近代日本綿業と中国 (The Modern Japanese Cotton Industry and China) (Tokyo, Tōkyō daiguku shuppankai, 1982).

Table 4.2 Production and trade of machine-made cotton yarn and cotton pieces

Year	Production of cotton yarn (10,000 tonnes)	Import of cotton yarn (10,000 tonnes)	Production of cotton pieces (million m²)	Import of cotton pieces (million m²)	Export of cotton pieces (million m²)
1880	—	0.9	—	451.6	—
1890	0.4	6.5	5.2	518.2	—
1900	6.1	9.0	42.3	531.6	—
1910	8.6	13.8	50.5	566.5	—
1920	16.8	8.0	160.4	670.5	2.2
1930	44.0	1.0	565.3	500.7	43.9
1936	39.7	0.5	1,203.1	196.5	8.1
1950	43.7	—	2,520.0	—	27.7

Source: Kubo, Kajima, and Kigoshi, 統計でみる, pp. 19–20

were less than those of their Japanese rivals? The rivalry between Japanese and Chinese firms played out in different ways in different parts of the country. In northern China (Tianjin and Qingdao), where Japanese military and political influence was particularly strong, Japanese firms held the leading position. In Shanghai, competition was even; sometimes Japanese firms moved ahead, and sometimes Chinese firms seemed to be in a more favorable position. Chinese firms dominated in the rest of the country. Mori has noted that Japanese and Chinese firms targeted different markets, with Chinese spinning firms producing lower-count yarns, while Japanese firms specialized in higher-count yarns.[40] This division was not absolute and was reversed in some cases. When we look at profitability, we can see that the profits of some Chinese-owned mills – for example Yong An and Shen Xin in Shanghai, Hua Xin in Ji Xian (Henan), and Jin Hua in Yuci (Shanxi) – equaled those of the Japanese-owned mills. The Chinese-owned mills in Shanghai benefited from superior management, good engineers, and access to relatively cheap imported cotton. The Chinese-owned firms in the interior of north China and in the Zhejiang–Jiangsu region were close to cotton-growing regions which supplied cheaper cotton; located in areas where rural weaving was highly developed, there was a ready market for their output.[41]

---

[40] Mori Tokihiko 森時彦, 中国近代綿業史の研究 (A Study of the History of the Modern Chinese Cotton Industry) (Kyoto, Kyōto daigaku shuppankai, 2001).
[41] Kubo Tōru 久保亨, 戦間期中国の綿業と企業経営 (Cotton Industry and Management in Wartime China) (Tokyo, Kyūko Shoin, 2005); Juanjuan Peng, *The Yudahua Business Group in China's Early Industrializaton* (Lanham, Lexington Books, 2020).

The domestic cotton industry benefited from favorable conditions between 1910 and 1930. During World War I, imports sharply declined, creating what Marie-Claire Bergère described as the "golden age of Chinese capital." Other factors that have been cited as contributing to the growth of the cotton industry include government policies to protect native industries, developments in the Chinese machine-making industry, and co-operative efforts by government and nongovernment groups to promote a shift to longer-staple American cotton which was more suitable for machine spinning.[42]

Modern Cotton Mills and Competition with Handicraft

One of the central debates in Chinese economic history has been the question of what happened to traditional hand-loom weaving when faced with competition from modern machine production. The traditional system of cloth production was embedded in the rural household economy, which linked agricultural production of fiber with hand spinning and weaving. In China the spinning and weaving parts of this production nexus were usually joined together. While some households sold homespun yarn in the periodic markets in Jiangnan, the trade was limited, and merchants were only able to gain control over the production process through putting-out arrangements after machine yarns became available.[43]

Access to machine yarn produced change in two directions: first, cotton weaving spread to regions of the country which did not grow cotton and had previously imported finished fabrics from the Jiangnan region. Second, handloom weavers in many of the older cotton-producing regions began to substitute machine-spun yarn for homespun.[44] The spread of the use of machine-spun yarns was uneven, progressing rapidly in some regions, much more slowly in others. By the early 1920s hand spinning had virtually disappeared in the old cotton centers, and by 1936 roughly 75 percent of the yarn consumed in China came from modern spinning mills. A study of Jiangsu province by Ma Junya and Tim Wright provides a detailed examination of regional differences. They argue that weaving declined in the

---

[42] M.-C. Bergère, *The Golden Age of the Chinese Bourgeoisie* (Cambridge, Cambridge University Press, 1989). Kubo, 戦間期中国〈自立〉.

[43] Nishijima Sadao 西嶋定生, "The Formation of the Early Chinese Cotton Industry," translated in L. Grove and C. Daniels (eds.), *State and Society in China* (Tokyo, University of Tokyo Press, 1984), pp. 17–77.

[44] L. Grove, "Rural Manufacture in China's Cotton Industry, 1890–1990," in D. Farnie and D. Jeremy (eds.), *The Fibre That Changed the World: The Cotton Industry in International Perspective, 1600–1990s* (Oxford, Oxford University Press, 2004), pp. 431–59.

Songjiang–Taicang region, which had been China's leading cotton-weaving center since the sixteenth century. In the Songjiang–Taicang region, labor moved from the countryside into Shanghai. At the same time, handicraft weaving using machine yarn flourished in regions just north of the Yangzi river, while in the far north of the province, rural households that had abandoned weaving before machine yarn became available devoted themselves to farming.[45]

To understand what happened to hand weaving we need to briefly explore changes in technology. In 1840 home weavers used various types of wooden looms that produced "native cloth," a narrow, relatively thick fabric made with low-count cotton yarn. This competed in the market with much wider "foreign cloth" that was machine woven using higher-count yarns. By the late nineteenth century, hand weavers were beginning to use the "flying shuttle," which produced wider fabrics and doubled output per day. The next step was the introduction of the iron gear loom, which again doubled the daily volume of cloth in comparison with a wooden loom with a flying shuttle.

These improvements in technology led to the establishment of new industrial districts that produced large volumes of cloth, competing with imported goods and the output of mechanized weaving factories. The best known of these districts were in north China – Gaoyang and Baodi in Hebei province and Wei Xian in Shandong. They represented a new mode of production that combined weaving on the iron gear loom with finishing and dyeing in workshops and factories that used imported chemical dyes and mechanized finishing equipment. The flexibility of the technology allowed for production of a wide variety of stripes, checks, and patterned fabrics. Wholesale merchants in the industrial districts managed production as well as sales through their nationwide networks of sales branches that closely linked production to market demand.[46] By the 1920s and 1930s, the iron gear loom had spread from north China to small workshops and factories in the Jiangnan region. Xu Xinwu estimated that by 1930 there were 1,500 small weaving factories in the Shanghai region alone, producing 3 million bolts of cloth a year.[47]

---

[45] J. Ma and T. Wright, "Industrialization and Handicraft Cloth: The Jiangsu Peasant Economy in the Late Nineteenth and Early Twentieth Centuries," *Modern Asian Studies* 44.6 (October 2010), 1337–72.
[46] Grove, *Economic Revolution*.
[47] Xu Xinwu 徐新吾 (ed.), 江南土布史 (A History of Native Cloth in Jiangnan) (Shanghai, Shanghai Shehui kexue chubanshe, 1992).

The small weaving factories that flourished in the years before the war are prime examples of what Peng Nansheng has termed semi-industrialization, a style of operation that combined features of handicraft and modern industry: work was done in workshop or factory settings, used a mixture of machine and human labor, and had close links to the market.[48] Semi-industrial workshops and small factories were located in small towns or villages. For weavers employed in the workshops and factories, farming became a sideline activity, with weaving providing the main source of income. Technologies were mixed: for example, on the eve of the anti-Japanese War there were 8,000 looms in operation in Jiangsu's Changshu county, including eighty-four Toyoda power looms, 300 iron gear looms that had been motorized, 2,000 iron gear looms powered by treadles, and 4,000 to 5,000 flying-shuttle looms.[49]

Merchant capital played a central role in organizing the weaving industry, linking producers with markets. The production style was sharply distinguished from that of the modern mechanized factories that produced large volumes of standard products, which were sold through independent trading firms. Small-scale producers kept a sharp eye on the market, producing a changing array of goods, adjusting production to market demand. The development of modern infrastructure in the twentieth century – telegraphy for communicating with distant branch offices, the postal service, motorized vehicles and trains for dispatching goods – facilitated the new styles of operation.

Other New Import-Substitution Industries

As new consumer products were introduced from overseas, Chinese entrepreneurs studied production and sales techniques and set up firms to manufacture substitutes. The list of such industries and products is long; here we will look at the production of matches and soap as two examples of light industry that developed to serve domestic markets. In both cases, technology transfer from Japan played a crucial role. Soap and matches were introduced to the Chinese market by Western firms in the treaty ports. Both products had also been introduced to the Japanese market in the nineteenth century, and by the 1870s Japanese firms were producing domestic substitutes; by the early twentieth century, Japanese producers began to market their products

---

[48] Peng Nansheng 彭南生, 半工业化: 近代中国乡村手工业的发展与社会变迁 (Semi-industrialization: The Development of Rural Handicraft Industry in Modern China and Social Change) (Beijing, Zhonghua shuju, 2007).
[49] Xu, 江南土布.

in China and other parts of Asia. This process of imitation was repeated in China, but rather than learning from the Western originators of the products, Chinese entrepreneurs turned to Japanese imitators for models and technical advice.[50]

Our first example is the production of matches. Matches were invented in Europe in the early nineteenth century and entered the Chinese market in the 1860s. It was not long before Chinese entrepreneurs began to make imitations, and by the late 1920s, 180 workshops and factories were producing matches for Chinese consumers. By the 1930s there were match factories in almost every province of China: some were small workshops that used hand labor; others were modern factories with specialized equipment for both production and packaging. It was quite common for factories to combine the use of mechanized production with hand labor by women and children to produce and pack the matchboxes.[51]

Matches are a good example of a new "exotic" product that quickly spread among Chinese consumers to become an essential part of daily life; they are also a good example of the market-oriented pattern of production of light-industrial goods and of Japanese influence on the development of a Chinese industry. The first Chinese-owned factory was established by a returnee student from Japan, and through the early 1920s many of the Chinese factories employed Japanese technicians who supervised production and trained Chinese staff.[52] Most match factories, including the smallest operators with only a few employees, employed sales personnel who managed marketing, directly linking production with sales.[53]

Soap, like matches, was first introduced to the Chinese market through the treaty ports in the nineteenth century, and use spread quickly, pushed by early twentieth-century campaigns for a more hygienic lifestyle which was promoted as one of the central features of modernity. The first Chinese-owned soap factory was established in Tianjin in 1903 by a patriotic businessman who was an early promoter of the "national products" movement, which urged Chinese to produce and consume Chinese-made products. The Tianjin Soap Company was a spin-off based on technology introduced

---

[50] Furuta and Grove, *Imitation, Counterfeiting and the Quality of Goods in Modern Asian History*.
[51] Liu Dajun 刘大钧, 中国工业调查报告 (Report on a Survey of Chinese Industry) (1937; reprint by Fujian Jiaoyu chubanshe, 2010).
[52] K.Y. Chan, "Playing with 'Alien Fire' (*Yanghuo*): Matches in Late Nineteenth- and Early Twentieth-Century China," in Furuta and Grove, *Imitation, Counterfeiting and the Quality of Goods in Modern Asian History*, pp. 203–23.
[53] Liu, 中国工业.

from Japan by the Zhili Gongyiju. The company employed a graduate of the Tokyo Higher Industrial School as its chief engineer and used Japanese and German machinery. The company quickly became the model for other aspiring entrepreneurs. By the 1930s there were at least thirty-five soap factories in the city of Tianjin, serving the north China market.[54]

Soap factories were developed independently in other cities, most of which followed the same "spin-off" pattern of development. The technology in use in the soap industry, like that in match production, was relatively easy to master; factories used a mixture of methods and levels of mechanization, and in most factories at least some of the processes – most commonly packaging – was done by hand.

Both in the West and in Japan some firms successfully created dominant brands that sold in national and international markets; well-known foreign brands like Leverhulme's Sunlight, Unilever's Lux, and Kao from Japan's largest soap manufacturer, were aggressively advertised in Chinese periodicals in the 1920s and 1930s. In contrast, none of the Chinese-owned soap or match companies in the pre-World War II era were able to create national brands, leaving space in the market for dozens of competitors, each selling in local or regional markets.

The small workshops and factories in the match and soap industries are representative of small-scale production in light industry in the prewar period. These enterprises shared certain common characteristics which can be seen in contemporary small-scale industry in China in the post-1980 reform era. In terms of scale, firms were small and organized following the principles of traditional Chinese business partnerships. Production processes combined the use of machines with human labor. Products were produced in small lots, and a single firm often produced small lots of different variations of the same generic product. Production was closely linked to assessments of market demand, and producers had their own sales staff which managed liaison with wholesale and retail customers. Technologies were simple and flexible, allowing for quick adjustment of product characteristics to meet market demand.

Company Founders and Management Styles

Most of the first generation of industrial entrepreneurs were merchants with experience in foreign trade, including some who had worked for foreign

---

[54] L. Grove, "Technology Transfer, Imitation and Local Production: The Soap Industry in Early Twentieth-Century Tianjin," in Furuta and Grove, *Imitation, Counterfeiting and the Quality of Goods in Modern Asian History*, pp. 161–82.

companies.⁵⁵ Zheng Guanying, who played a central role in the establishment of the first modern cotton mill, was a well-known comprador merchant and public intellectual, and Liu Hongsheng, who established the Da Zhonghua Match Company and the Shanghai Cement Company, got his start as an agent selling coal from the British Kailuan Mines. Overseas Chinese entrepreneurs also made major contributions to China's industrialization. Guo Le, the head of Yong An, China's second-largest cotton spinning and weaving corporation, came from an Overseas Chinese family from Australia; the brothers Jian Zhaonan and Jian Yujie, who founded the largest Chinese-owned tobacco company, the Nanyang Brothers Tobacco Company, and Yu Zhiqing, founder of the largest rubber company, were Overseas Chinese from Japan; Chen Qiyuan, who established the first mechanized silk filature in Guangdong, was from a family that had business enterprises in Vietnam and had worked in Vietnam for almost twenty years. Most of the men who founded the mechanized silk filatures in Shanghai, and later in Wuxi, also began as merchants, as did Yan Yutang, the first manager of the Da Long Machine Workshop, who began his career working for one of the foreign-capital ship repair companies.

The Rong brothers, founders of the Mao Xin and Fu Xin flour mills, as well as China's largest textile conglomerate, Shen Xin, were unusual in that they got their start as managers of a native bank (*qianzhuang*). Another group of entrepreneurs began from official backgrounds. Zhang Jian, the Nantong entrepreneur who founded the Da Sheng cotton mill; Xie Nanming, who established the Yong Tai filature in Wuxi; and Zhou Xuexi, founder of the Qi Xin Cement Company in Tangshan, all belong to this category. However, there were only a few entrepreneurs who began their careers as bureaucrats, and most of the investors in their companies were merchants. Overall, merchants played the central role in the rush to found modern industries in the late nineteenth and early twentieth centuries.

There was a distinct shift in the kinds of men who came to head Chinese industrial companies in the 1920s and 1930s. The new generation of enterprise leaders were men who had graduated from universities with degrees in engineering or business management. Our list of such industrial leaders includes many with overseas degrees. Among the industrial leaders were graduates from Japanese institutions, including the Tokyo Higher School of Technology, Kyoto University, and the Kiryu Higher School of Technology; from MIT and the University of Illinois in the United States; from the Berlin

---

⁵⁵ Kubo, 戦間期中国の綿業, 235–58.

Technical University in Germany; and from the Jiangnan Arsenal School in China. Among the foreign-university graduates we can identify several who were the sons of first-generation entrepreneurs, sent by their fathers to acquire technological or business skills.

Just as the second-generation managers tended to have professional skills, management styles also changed: many of the founders organized their firms following the partnership forms (*hegu* 合股) that were common in Chinese commerce.[56] As firms grew larger, there was a tendency to move toward a Western-style limited-liability corporate form; however, there is no question that the principles of traditional partnership forms continued to have a major impact on Chinese business management. This was particularly true in the early years when Western-style business firms were rare, and investors were worried about the risks; moreover, alternative investment opportunities, including moneylending, offered much higher interest rates.[57] As a result, firms like the Shen Xin cotton spinning and weaving company began operations with much borrowed capital. To recruit investors, some firms, including the Shanghai Merchant Steamship Company and Da Sheng, guaranteed investors a fixed rate of return (*guanli* 官利), which they began to pay even before the enterprise began operations.[58]

As we move from the 1920s to the 1930s, leading industrial firms began to find ways around this problem. For example, the Yong An textile company, strongly committed to the benefits of the limited-liability form of organization, found ways to limit the level of guaranteed return. Thus, by the 1930s, firms that had begun as partnerships expanded their operations, increased capital, and reorganized as limited-liability companies. There were, of course, firms that failed: for example, despite the expansion of its scale of operations, Shen Xin hesitated and by the mid-1930s had piled up huge debts. Nevertheless, the overall trend was for a shift from the traditional partnership form to the limited-liability company.

Our explanation of business practices among industrial firms would not be complete without some reference to the question of family involvement in management. Just as family management plays a major role in the twenty-first century in many Chinese firms in Taiwan and Southeast Asia, so families

---

[56] Negishi Tadashi 根岸佶, 商事に関する慣行調査報告書：合股の研究 (A Report on the Study of Commercial Customs: A Study of Chinese-Style Business Partnerships) (Tokyo, Tōa Kenkyūsho, 1943).
[57] Zhu Yingui 朱荫贵, 引进与变革：近代中国企业官利制度分析 (Introduction and Change: An Analysis of the System of "Guaranteed Interest" in Modern Chinese Enterprises), 近代史研究 4 (2001), 145–67.
[58] Zhu, 引进与变革, Introduction; Nakai, 張謇と中国近代企業.

were at the core of some of China's most successful 1930s firms. Firms in which the family was a central organizing principle included the cotton textile firms of the Rong and Guo families, the silk firms of the Xie family, and the Nanyang brothers' tobacco company. Keeping management within a family was an effective way to guarantee a family's control. However, when we compare the Chinese family firm to family firms in Japan, we also note some significant differences. First, the man taking control of a company in the second generation was not always the eldest son. While this practice reflected China's system of equal inheritance among sons, in contrast to Japan's stress on the rights of the eldest son, it also gave the Chinese-style family firm flexibility in choosing appropriate successors.

Entrepreneurs in Small-Scale Firms

Entrepreneurial practices among small-scale, semi-industrial firms also experienced major change in the early twentieth century. Most of the early proprietors of semi-industrial firms were merchants who moved from trading into control over production, primarily through putting-out systems. Partnerships, which were usually drawn up for limited periods of time, were the most common form of organization. The capital demands of semi-industrial firms were much lower than those of modern industrial enterprises, and since most of the investment was in circulating capital used to buy raw materials, it was possible to form partnerships for two to three years. At the end of the contract, partners decided whether to continue the arrangement or to seek new business partners.

Many of the managers of modern industrial firms got a start through working for foreign firms in the treaty ports. The entrepreneurs of semi-industrial firms were more likely to have started as commercial apprentices before breaking off to set up their own independent firms. In the Gaoyang industrial district another source of entrepreneurial talent was men with technical skills, gained through study at modern vocational schools in China and Japan.

We know much less about entrepreneurship in semi-industrial firms than we do about the capitalist entrepreneurs who created large industrial firms. Thanks to the survival of company archives, business historians have been able to analyze the management practices of large modern firms.[59] Accounts of small-scale firms, on the other hand, depend on oral history and the

---

[59] E. Köll, *From Cotton Mill to Business Empire: The Emergence of Regional Enterprises in Modern China* (Cambridge, MA, Harvard University Press, 2003).

recollections of former employees, and provide less information on the day-to-day operations of enterprises.

After 1950, large firms were taken over by the state and became the basis of state-owned enterprises. In some cases, their former owners and managers were kept on as technical advisers. Small factories were also taken over by the state in the 1950s. In industrial districts like Gaoyang and Weifang, the small firms were mechanized, and technically skilled former owners were kept on as managers while many of the men who had worked in the wholesale trade were absorbed into state-owned marketing companies. In the early 1980s, when the reform policies allowed private enterprise to flourish, the sons and grandsons of former entrepreneurs were among the first to set up factories and trading companies.[60]

Industry during the War Years

Beginning during the war years there was a major shift in investment from light industry to heavy and chemical industries. This shift was evident in areas under the national government, as well as in Japanese-occupied areas. During the war years, China was split between five different administrative zones: (1) areas under the control of the national government with its wartime capital in Chongqing; (2) Manchukuo, which was set up as a puppet state under Japan in 1932; (3) Japanese-occupied north China under a puppet provisional government of the Republic of China (after 1940 under the North China Political Affairs Commission); (4) central and south China under the reformed government of the Republic of China; and (5) Communist-controlled anti-Japanese base areas in the northwest and behind the Japanese military lines in rural areas of northwest, north, central, and south China.

In the 1920s and 1930s, the national government had worked hard to build infrastructure that integrated the various regions of the country. The division during the war years brought great economic losses, not only through loss of plants and equipment, but also through the cutting of production chains that linked the regions of China. During the war years, administrators in each of the zones drafted industrial policies which they implemented with varying degrees of success. These state-led development initiatives in each of the

---

[60] D. Wank, *Commodifying Communism: Business, Trust and Politics in a Chinese City* (Cambridge, Cambridge University Press, 1999); Grove, *Economic Revolution*.

zones shaped investment decisions and laid a base for the reorganization of industry in the late 1940s and early 1950s.

Wartime Developments in Areas under the National Government

As tensions with Japan rose in the early 1930s, the national government began planning for war, creating a National Defense Planning Commission in 1932, known after 1935 as the National Resources Commission. The commission brought together China's leading economists, scientists, and engineers to draw up plans for a "national defense economy" to meet the Japanese military challenge. Overall strategy called for a retreat to the interior, transfer of existing industrial resources from the coastal regions, and creation of new defense-related industries under a system of state capitalism.[61]

The wartime national government retreated to a region where modern industry was poorly developed. In a 1933 national survey of factories registered under the factory law, the provinces of Sichuan, Hunan, Guangxi, and Shaanxi, which were under national government control during the war years, had only 2.6 percent of the total of 2,435 factories, accounting for 3.1 percent of total invested capital and 2.2 percent of workers. During the war the government invested in defense-related industries, including power generation, mining, chemical industries, fuel refining, and munitions. At the same time, it strove to provide a minimal level of consumer goods to a population that had been swollen by an influx of refugees from Japanese-occupied areas. Much of the investment in light industry was left to private investors, and by the 1940s the government sought to strengthen its control over private industry.

As we can see from Figure 4.5, the index numbers for industrial production in national government-controlled Sichuan and Yunnan provinces rose steadily from 1938 to 1942, followed by a sudden decline beginning in 1943. The early war years saw much new investment, as well as the transfer of factory equipment from Japanese-occupied areas. Private investors also created some new factories. However, as the war progressed, Japanese blockades made it more difficult to acquire the necessary machinery and raw materials, and some factories were forced to reduce or suspend production.

Production in national government-controlled areas made up 8 percent of the national total of mining and industry in 1938–1940, rising to about 10 percent

[61] W. Kirby, "The Chinese War Economy," in J. Hsiung and S. Levine (eds.), *China's Bitter Victory: War with Japan 1937–1945* (Armonk and London, M.E. Sharpe, Inc., 1992), pp. 185–212.

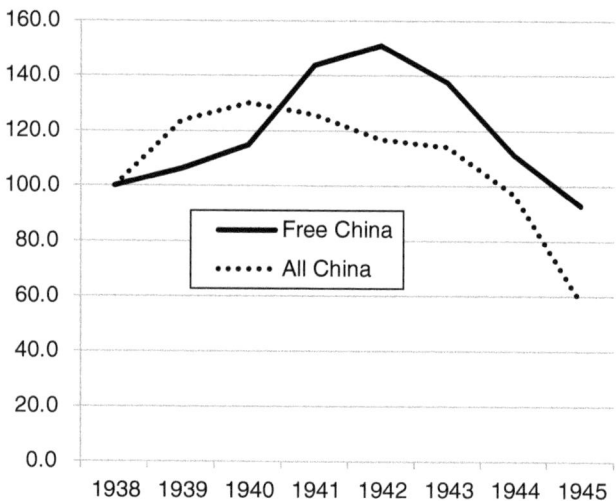

Figure 4.5 Industrial production index, 1938–1945
Source: Kubo Tōru 久保亨, 20 世紀中国経済史論 (Economic history of Twentieth-Century China) (Tokyo, Kyūko Shoin, 2020), p. 135

during the 1941–1944 period. Thus, while the 10 percent figure for 1941–1944 may still seem to be very small, it represented more than double the prewar level.

When we look at the figures by sector (Figure 4.6) we see an increase in the number of firms in defense-related sectors, including metallurgy, machine making, electronics, and chemicals. Taking into consideration the munitions industry, which was not included in the statistical calculations, we estimate that two-thirds of the new factories were in heavy industries.[62] Moreover, since capital investment in chemical and heavy industries tends to be much higher than investment in other lines of production, this may lead to an overestimate of the weight of heavy industry in total productive capacity.

The earliest new factories in the interior were established in 1938, with most of the investment coming from private capital. Between 1939 and 1941, new state-owned firms took the lead: some were under the National Resources Commission, and others were established by provincial governments. After 1942, new investment was largely from private investors. A comparison of the total invested capital with records from before the war shows that state investment represented about 20 percent of total capital investment in 1936, but was up to 40 percent in 1944. These figures also exclude the munitions industry.

---

[62] We should note that light-industrial matches and soap were included in the chemical industry.

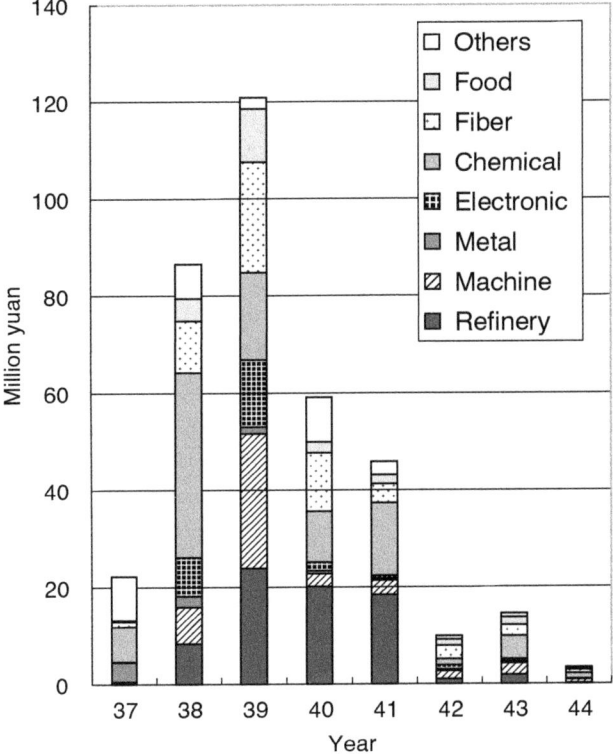

Figure 4.6 Capital of newly built mills, classified by industry
Source: Kubo, 20 世紀中国経済史, p. 138

Developing industry in the interior under wartime conditions was not easy. Difficulties in acquiring raw materials and fuel were a major block to sustained development. This was particularly a problem for privately owned light industry, especially after 1942. In the case of the cotton industry, transportation costs rose, and there was a shortage of electricity and machine parts, as well as a shortage of skilled labor. After 1943 there was a sharp drop in the supply of raw cotton, which led to a dramatic decline in the production of cotton yarn. Peasants, unhappy with the government's low procurement price for raw cotton, sometimes sold cotton to mills in Japanese-occupied areas. As the controls stiffened, textile entrepreneurs lost the will to go on.[63]

[63] Kubo Tōru 久保亨, 20 世紀中国経済史論 (Economic History of Twentieth-Century China) (Tokyo, Kyūko Shoin, 2020), p. 166.

Wartime Developments in Japanese-Occupied Areas

Japanese occupation forces strove to build economic systems to sustain the war effort in China, as well as to contribute to the economic development of the Japanese empire. Economic planning began in Manchukuo in 1932 and continued in north and central China after those areas were occupied by the Japanese Army. Comprehensive plans were drawn up independently for each occupied area, laying out investment strategies that highlighted the contributions each of the areas was expected to make to the development of the Japanese empire.

Manchukuo

Japanese planners targeted Manchukuo for heavy industrial development, including development of iron and steel, as well as expansion of mining of coal, magnesium, and other metals. In August 1936, as efforts were being made to prepare for war, the Army Ministry issued guidelines for development, and the Kantō Army, the military unit responsible for control of Manchukuo, together with the South Manchurian Railway Company, a statutory company that had been created to manage railroads and economic development in the region, drew up a five-year plan for industrial development. The plan called for what can be characterized as slow, steady development.

When war broke out in the summer of 1937, Japanese authorities in the home islands pushed the Manchukuo puppet government to speed up the plan. Investment in the mining sector doubled, and in the following years there was increased pressure to develop natural resources. Production targets steadily rose, even though there was little evidence that the original lower targets were attainable. As the war in China expanded and war conditions at home worsened, it became more difficult to gain foreign exchange, shipping capacity declined, and it was increasingly difficult to obtain from Japan or from Germany the construction materials that were needed to implement the policies. Few of the targets stipulated in the plans were met.

The plans for Manchukuo had put little stress on developing light industries, and by the end of the war the region was left with a distorted economic structure, including bloated steel and mining sectors. Production of steel and sulfur continued to rise, reaching a peak in 1943. We can get some idea of the scope of the development by looking at the facilities that remained after Japan's defeat: the steel industry had an annual capacity of 2.5 million tons, and electric generation capacity (primarily hydropower) was 1.7 million kilowatts. There were three main hydropower plants, and transmission lines linked the power plants to the cities of Anshan and Dalian.[64]

North China

Economic planning in the occupied regions of north China began in November 1938 with the establishment of the North China Development Company, a national policy company. Half of the initial capital of 350 million yen was contributed by the Japanese government, with the remaining investment coming from private companies. A series of subsidiary companies were established to oversee development of railroads, power generation, and telephone and telegraph networks. Development plans envisioned complementary relations between the region and the Japanese home economy, with north China supplying raw materials as well as agricultural products, primarily cotton, for Japanese industry. Seventy percent of the investment of the North China Development Company was put into infrastructure, including railroads and expansion of ports to improve shipment of natural resources. With the support of the state sector, private firms also flocked to north China. A new steelworks was established at Shijingshan (the forerunner of post-1949 Capitol Steel), and major Japanese makers like the Toyota automobile company and the precision machine company Koito Seisakujo, along with other heavy industrial firms, built facilities in occupied north China.

However, not everything went according to plan. In the early stages of the war, Japanese policy was focused on exploiting resources to supply the Japanese economy, a policy that weakened the economy of north China. In response to the shortages of goods and rising inflation, in the early summer of 1940 the Japanese government revised occupation policies, drafting a new five-year development plan which put more stress on assuring adequate supplies of goods for the north China population. However, with the beginning of the Pacific war, there were new calls for goods to supply the Japanese home economy, and pressure on north Chinese resources increased. This exploitation of resources exhausted north China's economy, and shipments of goods to Japan met only 60 to 70 percent of targets.[65]

Overall, the Japanese plans for economic construction in north China ended in failure. However, some of the investments did create facilities that remained after the war. For example, the newly constructed steel plants

---

[64] Yamamoto Yuzo 山本有造, 「満洲国」経済史研究 (An Economic History of "Manchuria") (Nagoya, Nagoya daigaku shuppankai, 2003).
[65] Nakamura Takafusa 中村隆英, 戦時日本の華北経済支配 (Japan's Control of the Wartime North China Economy) (Tokyo, Yamakawa shuppansha, 1983).

reached a production capacity of 756,000 tons, and an electric power grid was constructed in Hebei and Shandong Provinces.[66]

Central China

Japanese government planning for the areas under the provisional government of the Republic of China followed the same organizational strategy as that for the occupied areas of north China. A national policy company, the Central China Promotion Company, was given responsibility for supervision of railroads, electric power, mining, industry, and fisheries. Subsidiaries under this company stressed heavy industry, including the mining of iron ore and coal, maintenance of the railroads, and economic recovery in Shanghai and other cities.[67]

The central China region, including Shanghai and the Yangzi valley, had been the center of light-industrial development in the first three decades of the twentieth century, and Japanese plans called for the exploitation and development of the existing light-industrial base. As we have seen earlier, silk and cotton were the most important light industries in the central China region.

Silk Filatures

Reforms in the silk industry were still in progress at the beginning of the war. After Japanese forces occupied the silk-producing regions of Zhejiang and Jiangsu, the Central China Cocoon and Silk Company (Kachū Sanshi Kabushiki Kaisha) took control of the silk trade. Despite the efforts of the new state policy company, the silk industry went into a sudden and sharp decline. The major problem was a shortage of cocoons, brought on by shifts in the agricultural economy. Rising demand for cotton and wheat drove up prices, and land that had been devoted to cultivating mulberry trees to feed silkworms was converted into cotton and wheat fields. With the start of the Pacific war, the global market was basically closed, and the Central China Cocoon and Silk Company piled up debts and was shut down in 1943. Meanwhile, the national government supported investment in the Sichuan silk industry, building an infrastructure base that would

---

[66] Ju Zhifen 居之芬 and Zhang Limin 张利民 (eds.), 日本在华北经济统制掠夺史 (History of Japanese Plunder and Economic Control in North China) (Tianjin, Tianjin Guji chubanshe, 1997).

[67] Hara Akira 原朗, 「大東亜共栄圏」の経済的実態 (Economic Realities of the "Greater East Asia Co-prosperity Sphere"), 土地制度史学 18.3 (1976), 1–28.

support development of Sichuan as a silk production center in the postwar years.⁶⁸

Cotton Spinning and Weaving

The cotton industry fared somewhat better than the silk industry during the war years. Some of the Chinese owners of cotton mills followed the national government to the wartime capital in Chongqing, moving equipment from their coastal plants into the interior. While Chinese industry in the coastal provinces suffered losses, the great exception to that story of wartime loss was the success of Japanese-owned cotton mills during the early war years. Wartime shortages led to a sharp rise in prices and to higher profits. Japanese cotton firms, which were already well established in the lower Yangzi region, increased capacity when the Japanese military turned operation of confiscated Chinese-owned mills over to Japanese firms.⁶⁹ Chinese-owned mills located in the concession areas of Shanghai, which remained outside the control of the Japanese military until the start of the Pacific war, also reaped high profits, and some Chinese firms continued operations by dividing and transferring their machinery to rural locations in the Jiangnan region.⁷⁰ Textile entrepreneurs who had followed the national government to its wartime capital also earned high profits during the war years, benefiting from the inflation in prices for consumer goods.

Wartime Developments in the Anti-Japanese Base Areas

The anti-Japanese base areas under Communist Party control in northwest China and behind the Japanese lines in north and central China had been established in remote areas with no modern industrial base. During the war years, efforts were made to mobilize handicraft producers to provide basic commodities for the war effort. Small factories and workshops, using traditional technology, produced munitions for the resistance forces, and women throughout the border areas were mobilized to spin and weave to produce uniforms for the army and clothing for the civilian population. The co-operative forms developed in the base areas

---

⁶⁸ Kubo, Kajima, and Kigoshi, 統計でみる中国近現代経済史, p. 38.
⁶⁹ Takamura, 近代日本綿業と中国.
⁷⁰ Wang Zijian 王子建, "'孤岛'时期的民族棉纺织工业" (National-Capital Cotton Industry during Shanghai's "Isolated Island" Period), in 中国近代经济史研究资料 (Materials on Modern Chinese Economic History), vol. 10 (Shanghai, Shanghai shehui kexue chubanshe, 1990); Kubo, 20 世紀中国経済史論, pp. 467–9.

served as a model in the early 1950s for the reorganization of rural handicraft industries.

Postwar Reorganization of Chinese Industry

At the end of the war the national government faced the formidable task of reintegrating the economy and reviving industrial production against a background of continued political turmoil. The uneasy wartime alliance with the Communist Party quickly unraveled, and civil war began in the summer of 1946. In the northeast (Manchuria), Soviet armies launched an invasion less than a week before the end of the war and occupied most of the major cities of the region

As we can see from the industrial production index (Figure 4.7), industrial production had begun to recover in the first months after the end of the war, only to plunge beginning in 1947. To understand why this happened, we need to consider the unintended consequences of trade and financial policies. While the war had been long and exhausting, physical destruction of industrial facilities in most parts of China was relatively limited. Both in the areas under the national government and in the Japanese-occupied areas of the country, wartime investment in heavy industrial facilities had increased capacity in mining, iron and steel production, and hydroelectric power generation. Light industries, on the other hand, had suffered losses, and factories that were still in operation were running below capacity, largely because they could not acquire raw materials. Production of cotton goods and raw silk, the former for domestic consumption and the latter for export trade, required the restoration of commodity chains that linked agriculture to industry.

During the war years, the Republic of China had joined the American-led alliance of free economies under the Bretton Woods agreement, and postwar trade and monetary policies followed the alliance's guidelines – including a system of fixed exchange rates, convertibility of currency, and support for free trade. China seemed to be in an advantageous position to move from a wartime economy to a peacetime economy. First, the government had built up significant foreign-currency reserves during the war years: these funds had been accumulated from wartime aid and profits on controlled trade and are estimated at US$800 million to US$900 million. Added to this were the assets that were seized from the Japanese at the end of the war. The government thought it had adequate funds, and in February 1946 announced that it was freeing the foreign-currency market and opening up free trade.

Figure 4.7 Industrial production index, 1912–1949
Source: Kubo, 20 世紀中国経済史, 90–1

The open-market plans ended in disaster. The foreign-exchange rate was set at a higher rate than current market exchange values, and the favorable exchange rates led to a huge inflow of imports from the United States. Government planners had anticipated an influx of producer goods to aid the recovery of domestic manufacturing, but the influx of consumer goods acted as a drag on the recovery of domestic producers. By June of 1947, domestic manufacturing stood at only 35.1 percent of the highest prewar level.

On the other hand, the exchange rate for export exchange had been set at a high rate, and it served as a brake on exports, which went into sharp decline. This imbalance produced a huge trade deficit, resulting in a reduction of US$115 million in foreign-currency reserves within less than six months. There was no question that the plans to open the market had been introduced at too rapid a pace.[71]

In August 1946, a delegation of Shanghai economic leaders demanded a fundamental reconsideration of economic policies. They argued that the

---

[71] Kubo Tōru 久保亨, "対外経済政策の理念と決定過程" (Principles behind the Decision-Making Process Related to Trade-Related Economic Policies), in Himeta Mitsuyoshi 姫田光義, 戦後中国国民政府史の研究, 1945–1949 (Study of the History of the Chinese National Government in the Postwar Period, 1945–1949) (Tokyo, Chūō daigaku shuppanbu, 2001), pp. 235–61.

Sino-American trade agreement of November 1946, which had promoted freer trade, had speeded up the inflow of American goods. Even though the treaty terms were in theory equal, given the great gap in economic strength between the US and China there was little question that the benefits of reducing Chinese regulations were going to American capital. Opposition from Chinese economic leaders led to a growing national consensus and the national government was forced to abandon its economic liberalization policies. On February 16, 1947, the government announced emergency regulations that banned the sale of foreign exchange and reinstituted rationing for daily necessities.

Meanwhile, plans to take over Japanese assets in the former occupied areas were running into difficulties. Reintegration of the regional economies was a major stumbling block. During the war years there were four separate currency regimes: the northeast (Manchukuo) ran on Japanese yen; north China ran on *lianyinquan* 聯銀券; central China ran on *choubeiquan* 儲備券; and areas under the control of the national government, as well as the Communist anti-Japanese base areas, ran on the national government's *fabi* 法币. One of the first steps to achieve reintegration of the economy was reintegration of the currencies. Conversion rates between the puppet currencies and the *fabi* were all set at disadvantageous rates for those in the former occupied areas, leading to an overvalued *fabi*. Conversion thus produced inflation in the coastal cities. At the same time, the rates facilitated the flow of high-quality goods produced in the coastal regions into the interior at low prices, which had a negative impact on manufacturers in the interior. As funds flowed from the interior into the coastal regions, the interior regions of China suffered from a shortage of capital and fell into depression.

In the coastal regions, there were clashes over who should reap the benefits of the assets seized from Japanese entities in the formerly occupied areas, and efforts to adjudicate the matter ran into great difficulties. In the north China region individual factories, power plants, and mines were taken over by different organizations, breaking the integration that had been created under the Japanese occupation. And in the Soviet-occupied northeast, many industrial assets were dismantled and shipped to the Soviet Union.

Failure of the economic liberalization policy and the difficulties of taking over Japanese assets created financial problems for the postwar government. Delays in the recovery of both production and circulation of goods led to shortages in the markets and rising prices. Despite rising inflation, the government continued to pile up large deficits as it struggled to acquire goods to support the civil war, adding to inflationary pressure.

Although the national government had won victory in its war with Japan, the Chinese economy failed to recover. The failure of the postwar liberalization policy and the unrealistic plans for integrating formerly occupied and unoccupied regions resulted in rising inflation and the inability of the government to control the economy, dealing a death blow to economic integration efforts.

Organizational Legacies

Organizations created in the postwar period to deal with assets confiscated from Japanese owners smoothed the way for nationalization of industry in the post-1949 period. We can see this by looking at what happened in the cotton industry. After the war, Japanese-owned assets were seized by the national government. The government established a state company, the Chinese Textile Construction Company (Zhongguo Fangzhi Jianshe Gongsi 中国纺织建设公司) to operate the mills for three years, after which they were to be sold to private investors.[72] The national government collapsed before the sale to private investors could be carried out, and the government of the People's Republic of China took over the company, which became the core of a new state corporation to control the cotton industry. Similar companies were established for other major industries, creating the base for consolidation of industrial production under a series of state-owned companies. Through the process of socialist transformation in the early 1950s, factories that were still in private hands were converted to public ownership and put under state-owned industrial groups.

Much of Chinese industrial production in the early 1950s came from what we have referred to as semi-industrial firms, which mixed machine production and handicraft methods. State policies in the early 1950s for the socialization of handicraft industries drew on the practices of handicraft co-operatives developed in the anti-Japanese base areas during the war years. Individual handicraft workers were organized into co-operatives, which operated under the supervision of state bodies that controlled the supply of raw materials and sale of finished products. Over the years, some of the co-operatives developed into factories, and the most successful of the factories were taken over by the state and turned into state-owned enterprises. Others continued as

---

[72] Kubo, Kajima, and Kigoshi, 統計でみる中国近現代経済史, p. 29.

small-scale operations controlled by rural communes, providing low-cost goods for local consumption.

Concluding Remarks

In the late 1980s, when Thomas Rawski outlined his approach in *Economic Growth in Prewar China*, he summarized his argument in four key concepts: "domestic, private, civilian, and competitive."[73] Arguing against Marxist-influenced interpretations that stressed the impact of foreign imperialism, state control, and the exploitative nature of elite manipulation of markets, Rawski chose those four concepts to argue that key players in the prewar modern Chinese economy were private firms, primarily owned by Chinese capital, and that state investment, planning, and control played a relatively minor role. Furthermore, he argued that Chinese markets were highly competitive, and that the Chinese economy was characterized by significant growth in both the agriculture and industrial sectors. Our understanding of the prewar economy is in basic agreement with Rawski's view, although we have a more expansive understanding of modern industrialization. We have argued for multiple paths to industrialization: a state-centered path, a path centered on private capital, and a semi-industrial path. Our analysis of the two basic types of private capital development – export-oriented industrialization and import-substitution industrialization – fits very well with Rawski's understanding of prewar growth. Our third path – semi-industrial development – adds an additional dimension by including in the industrial sector the thousands of small semi-industrial firms that mixed mechanized production with hand labor. As we, and others, have argued, production by semi-industrial firms was strongly market-dependent, making full use of the new forms of transportation (railroads and scheduled bus services) and communications (telephone, telegraph, and the postal network) to link rural and small-town production units to regional and national markets. We see in this third path to industrialization organizational forms and production processes that share many similarities with the hundreds of thousands of small private firms created in China after the launching of the economic reforms in the early 1980s. In many cases, contemporary twenty-first-century firms have been

---

[73] T. Rawski, *Economic Growth in Prewar China* (Berkeley and Los Angeles, University of California Press, 1989), p. 3.

created in regions that were the sites of semi-industrial development in the prewar period and build on the entrepreneurial practices of earlier times.

Wartime developments serve as a bridge to the postwar period and early 1950s. The Japanese occupation of China and the eight-year-long war led to heavy loss of human life and property. The war years also saw a major restructuring of the Chinese economy in Japanese-occupied areas, as well as in areas under the national government and in Communist base areas. We have stressed several common themes that characterized development in all the areas. First, state planning played a central role in the wartime economy in each of the areas, and there was a shift from a dominance of privately owned industry to a greater role for state planning and investment in infrastructure, mining, and industrial enterprises. Second, to meet wartime needs, investment in each of the areas concentrated on sectors that could contribute to the war effort.

In the confusion of the postwar era and the difficulties resulting from the overly hasty introduction of freer trade and capital markets, the economy went into severe decline. It is thus difficult to measure the impact of wartime investment in the various regions of occupied and unoccupied China on industrial output. However, as our argument for the wartime period suggests, there was significant investment in infrastructure, including mining and power generation, in both occupied and unoccupied China, and that investment, together with the organizational changes, created a base for development of the state-centered economy in the 1950s.

Further Reading

Cochran, S., *Big Business in China: Sino-Foreign Rivalry in the Cigarette Industry, 1890–1930* (Cambridge, MA, Harvard University Press, 1980).

Cochran, S., and A. Hsieh, *The Lius of Shanghai* (Cambridge, MA, Harvard University Press, 2013).

Faure, D., *China and Capitalism: A History of Business Enterprise in Modern China* (Hong Kong, Hong Kong University Press, 2006).

Furuta, K., and L. Grove (eds.), *Imitation, Counterfeiting and the Quality of Goods in Modern Asian History* (Singapore, Springer, 2017).

Grove, L., *A Chinese Economic Revolution: Rural Entrepreneurship in the Twentieth Century* (Lanham, Rowman & Littlefield Publishers, Inc., 2006).

Kirby, W., "The Chinese War Economy," in J.C. Hsiung and S.I. Levine (eds.), *China's Bitter Victory: War with Japan 1937–1945* (Armonk and London, M.E. Sharpe, Inc., 1992), pp. 185–212.

Köll, E., *From Cotton Mill to Business Empire: The Emergence of Regional Empires in Modern China* (Cambridge, MA, Harvard University Asia Center, 2003).

Kubo, T., "Changing Patterns of Industrialization and Emerging States in Twentieth Century China," in K. Otsuka and K. Sugihara (eds.), *Paths to the Emerging State in Asia and Africa* (Singapore, Springer, 2019), pp. 20–64.

Kubo Tōru 久保亨, 20 世紀中国経済史論 (Economic History of Twentieth-Century China) (Tokyo, Kyūko Shoin, 2020).

Kubo Tōru 久保亨, Kajima Jun 加島潤, and Kigoshi Yoshinori 木越義則 (eds.), 統計でみる中国近現代経済史 (Economic History of Modern China: Based on Statistical Data) (Tokyo, Tōkyō daigaku shuppankai, 2016).

Peng Nansheng 彭南生, 半工业化：近代中国乡村手工业的发展与社会变迁 (Semi-industrialization: The Development of Rural Handicraft in Modern China and Social Change) (Beijing, Zhonghua shuju, 2007).

Peng Zeyi 彭泽益 (ed.), 中国近代手工业史资料 (Materials on the History of the Chinese Modern Handicraft Industry), 4 vols. (Beijing, Sanlian shudian, 1957).

Rawski, T., *Economic Growth in Prewar China* (Berkeley, University of California Press, 1989).

Sheehan, B., *Industrial Eden: A Chinese Capitalist Vision* (Cambridge, MA, Harvard University Press, 2015).

Sugihara, K., "Labour-Intensive Industrialization in Global History: An Interpretation of East Asian Experiences," in G. Austin and K. Sugihara (eds.), *Labour-Intensive Industrialization in Global History* (London and New York, Routledge, 2013), pp. 20–64.

Sun Yutang 孫毓棠 (ed.), 中国近代工业史资料 (Materials on the History of Chinese Modern Industry), 4 vols. (Beijing, Kexue chubanshe, 1957).

Wang Xiang 王翔, 中国近代手工业史 (A History of China's Modern Handicraft Industry) (Shanghai, Shanghai renmin chubanshe, 2012).

Xu Dingxin 徐鼎新, 中国近代企业的科技力量与科技効応 (Technical Strength and Technical Productivity of Modern Chinese Enterprises) (Shanghai, Shanghai kexue xueyuan chubanshe, 1995).

Xu, Xinwu, "The Struggle of the Handicraft Cotton Industry against Machine Textiles in China," *Modern China* 14.1 (1988), 31–49.

Xu Xinwu 徐新吾, 中国近代缫丝工业史 (A History of the Modern Chinese Silk Industry) (Shanghai, Shanghai renmin chubanshe, 1990).

5
The State and Enterprises in Late Qing China

CHI-KONG LAI

This chapter focuses on the so-called Self-Strengthening era during the second half of the nineteenth century when the Qing empire was expanding state involvement in industry and technology from its traditional ideology. The origin and motivation of state involvement in the private market during this era is different from that in the early twentieth century, during which China began to take lessons from Meiji Japan and the ideology of modernization (see Bian's chapter in this volume). There were some elements of continuity here – in remnants of "Self-Strengthening" through the state efforts both to build up modern enterprises and develop science and technology. This chapter explains the impact of the state sector's emergence that was manifested in the development and expansion of state arsenals and modern enterprises.

There is already a considerable literature, to which Chinese, Japanese, and Western scholars have contributed, on the role of the state in the development of Chinese enterprises in the late nineteenth century, among which the studies by Albert Feuerwerker, Kwang-Ching Liu, Wellington K.K. Chan, Yen-p'ing Hao, Chi-kong Lai, Xia Dongyuan 夏东元, Zhang Guohui 张国辉, and Long Denggao 龙登高 are a few of the most important.[1] Elisabeth

---

[1] See, for example, A. Feuerwerker, *China's Early Industrialization: Sheng Hsuan-huai (1844–1916) and Mandarin Enterprise* (Cambridge, MA, Harvard University Press, 1958); K.-C. Liu, *Anglo-American Steamship Rivalry in China* (Cambridge, MA, Harvard University Press, 1962); Liu, "Steamship Enterprise in Nineteenth-Century China," *Journal of Asian Studies* 18.4 (November 1959), 435–55; W.K.K. Chan, *Merchants, Mandarins and Modern Enterprise in Late Ch'ing China* (Cambridge, MA, Harvard University Press, 1977); Y.-P. Hao, *The Comprador in Nineteenth Century China: Bridge between East and West* (Cambridge, MA, Harvard University Press, 1970); Hao, *The Commercial Revolution in Nineteenth Century China: The Rise of Sino-Western Mercantile Capitalism* (Berkeley, University of California Press, 1986); C.-K. Lai, "'The Qing State and Modern Enterprise: The China Merchants' Company, 1872–1902," in J.K. Leonard and J.R. Watt (eds.), *To Achieve Security and Wealth: The Qing Imperial State and the Economy, 1644–1911* (Ithaca, NY, The Cornell East Asia Series, 1993), pp. 139–56; Zhang Guohui 张国辉, 洋务运动与中国

Köll and Anne Reinhardt clearly show how the government utilized the building of the railway and the shipping companies to expand its political power and agenda.[2]

The Origin of Self-Strengthening Ideologies and Policies

This section will illustrate the links between state policy and enterprises in the cultural, institutional, and economic contexts of late Qing China. The tradition of state involvement in large-scale enterprises can be traced back to three government-regulated enterprises in the late Ming and mid-Qing periods: the special role of the Jiangsu and Zhejiang seagoing junks in the transport of tribute grain; state monopolies in salt, tea, and ginseng; and the mining industries.

The key to government-sponsored enterprises was the concept of zhaoshang 招商 – recruiting investors and managers. Under the system of zhaoshang, officials tapped private wealth to meet the state's needs. In return for the chance to obtain a profit, investors had to meet the obligations placed upon them by officials. China has had a long tradition of using the method of "recruiting merchants" in government-sponsored projects. A major example in Chinese economic thought was Liu Yan's 刘晏 (718–80) policy in the mid-Tang period. Liu Yen advanced the zhaoshang concept of recruiting merchants to undertake government-regulated enterprises, such as the salt trade, the grain transport service, and the granary system.[3] Later, this legacy of zhaoshang became one of the most effective means of government intervention in the private economy. Such zhaoshang terminology appeared more and more frequently as the years went by. The phrase zhaoshangju 招商局 was

---

近代企业 (The Self-Strengthening Movement and China's Modern Enterprise) (Beijing, Zhongguo shehui kexue chubanshe, 1979); Long Denggao 龙登高, Chang Xu 常旭, and Xiong Jinwu 熊金武, 国之润，自疏浚始：天津航道局120年发展史 (One Hundred Years of Development: The Tianjin Waterway Bureau) (Beijing, Qinghua daxue chubanshe, 2017). Long, Chang, and Xiong's book critically evaluates the quality of state building in the modern enterprise's role in conservancy operations.

[2] See E. Köll, *Railroads and the Transformation of China* (Cambridge, MA, Harvard University Press, 2019). Anne Reinhardt also compares China with India in the steamship navigation business. She also illustrates how the coming of Western steamships impacted the state in the development of China's shipping network in late Qing China. See her *Navigating Semi-colonialism: Shipping, Sovereignty, and Nation-Building in China, 1860–1937* (Cambridge, MA, Harvard University Press, 2018).

[3] See K.-C. Liu, "Statecraft and the Rise of Enterprise: The Late Ch'ing Perspective," in *The Second Conference on Modern Chinese Economic History* (Taipei, The Institute of Economics, Academia Sinica, 1989), p. 8.

used in the salt trade and other enterprises before 1865,[4] seven years before the establishment of the China Merchants Steam Navigation Company (CMSNC) under the so-called Self-Strengthening movement. Did the policy change over time? Many Chinese officials not only studied the classics, but also cited them as metaphors to justify their policies.

Most of the Confucian officials who endorsed ritual and ethics believed that wealth should be shared by the public.[5] The Chinese state's legitimacy was also usually achieved through policies for "benefiting the people." The rhetoric of *jun* 均 (equitability) and *gong* 公 (publicness)[6] was dominant in Confucian discourse.[7] The ideal of equal allotment of land can be traced back to the so-called "well-field system" in China's fabled antiquity.[8] Conceptually, this notion of civic betterment may be viewed as a type of public moral discourse. This public moral discourse focused on three sets of preferences or priorities: (1) public good over private interest, (2) the fundamental over the secondary (*benmo* 本末), and (3) "state intervention" over "laissez-faire" economic policy.

Another way of approaching the political economy of China during the mid-nineteenth century is to look at the statecraft debate about the state in relation to the market. The main debate centered on the issue of whether the government should interfere with the market and, if so, in what way. In the Chinese tradition, there were at least two contending views of the relationship between the state and the market: "state intervention" as formulated in

---

[4] See Li Hongzhang 李鴻章, 未刊朋僚信稿 (Unpublished Letters to His Friends and Colleagues) (Shanghai Library), Li Letters 6:29.

[5] For Chinese economic thought, see D. Faure, "The Introduction of Economics in China, 1850–2010," in V. Goossaert, J. Kiely, and J. Lagerwey (eds.), *Modern Chinese Religion II, 1850–2015*, vol. 1 (Leiden, Brill, 2016), pp. 65–88. Also see Faure, *China and Capitalism: A History of Business Enterprise in Modern China* (Hong Kong, Hong Kong University Press, 2006); Kwang-ching Liu, "Introduction: Orthodoxy in Chinese Society," in Liu (ed.), *Orthodoxy in Late Imperial China* (Berkeley, University of California Press, 1990), pp. 8–12.

[6] On the Chinese concept of "public" (*gong*), see J. Fewsmith, *Party, State, and Local Elites in Republican China: Merchant Organizations and Politics in Shanghai, 1890–1930* (Honolulu, University of Hawaii Press, 1985), pp. 18–20; W.T. Rowe, "The Public Sphere in Modern China," *Modern China* 16.3 (July 1990), 309–29; and M.B. Rankin, "The Origins of a Chinese Public Sphere: Local Elites and Community Affairs in the Late Imperial Period," *Études chinoises* 9.2 (Autumn 1990), 13–60.

[7] According to Lien-sheng Yang, "Chinese economic history is full of terms using the character chun [*jun*]." See L.-S. Yang, "Economic Aspects of Public Works in Imperial China," in Yang, *Excursions in Sinology* (Cambridge, MA, Harvard University Press, 1969), p. 232.

[8] See D.C. Lau, trans., *Mencius* (Hong Kong, The Chinese University Press, 1984), pp. 96–101.

the doctrine of Legalism,[9] on the one hand, and the "laissez-faire" principle, on the other.

From the above discussion of public moral discourse in Chinese economic thought, we can understand that most Chinese officials tended to favor state control in the economic sphere. There were two main reasons. The first was the official belief in the "public good," which is best represented in the texts of the Confucian classics and other writings of ancient thinkers. The second was the rhetoric of *benmo*, which disparaged both the merchant's status and mercantile activity in premodern China.

But in reality, the Chinese state alone did not have sufficient resources to regulate the market bureaucratically. In this institutional context, how did a centralized, premodern political system such as the Chinese bureaucracy administer markets? The Qing state was using more remunerative methods to recruit private merchants in the later period.[10] This perspective on the state's positive role in the economy can also be documented by brief reference to the seagoing junk business. Beginning in the early 1800s, ideas about statecraft were reformulated by scholars – the most influential of whom was Wei Yuan 魏源 (1794–1857), an adviser to key government officials – in response to the problems of the mid-Qing period, for example the need for reform in the salt monopoly, the control of river flows, and the transport of tribute grain.

Chinese state officials could manipulate symbolic capital, such as official titles, as an inducement for merchant participation. Officials were trying to appeal to "norms" associated with high status and prestige. Remunerative methods imply profit or (and) monetary rewards. In the case studies above, the Qing state also used material rewards to recruit other types of merchants. This combination of both normative and remunerative strategies was one of the more successful aspects of mid-Qing state policy in the economy.

This mid-Qing legacy of *zhaoshang* was the key to governmental enterprises in late Qing China. When late Qing officials undertook to promote modern enterprises in China, the first company was in fact popularly called the Bureau to Recruit Investors and Managers (*zhaoshangju*). Later, this legacy became one of the most effective means of government intervention in the economy. During the mid-nineteenth century, the Qing state, in

---

[9] The concept of state intervention is Legalist economic doctrine. To a Legalist, material welfare far exceeds any virtues; only material welfare can centralize both the government and the economy into a strong state, powerful enough to survive in the "modern world." See A. Waley, *Three Ways of Thought in Ancient China* (Stanford, Stanford University Press, 1982), p. 159.

[10] See V.J. Symons, *Ch'ing Ginseng Management: Ch'ing Monopolies in Microcosm* (Tempe, Center for Asian Studies, 1981), p. 44.

response to the economic and commercial penetration of foreign powers, played an active role in many new business and industrial ventures, particularly those with security implications.[11]

The Beginning of Self-Strengthening and the Arsenal Industry

The 1861 *coup d'état* to replace the eight powerful ministers, planned by Prince Gong (also known as Yixin 弈訢, 1833–98) and the Empress Dowager Cixi 慈禧 (1835–1908), resulted in greater flexibility in government policy during the Tongzhi 同治 (1862–74) reign and the early years of the Guangxu 光绪 (1875–1908) period.[12] After various turbulent events, such as the Taiping Rebellion (1850–64), a number of senior ministers and provincial leaders, including Wen Xiang 文祥 (1818–76), Zeng Guofan 曾國藩 (1811–72), Li Hongzhang 李鴻章 (1823–1901), Zuo Zongtang 左宗棠 (1812–85), and Ding Richang 丁日昌 (1823–1882) were advocates of Self-Strengthening reforms to safeguard China from the peril of Western incursions. These reformist officials built arsenals and organized state-sponsored enterprises for the steamship carrying trade, coal and iron mining, textile manufacturing, telegraphs, banking, and the railway service. They may be regarded as advocates for China's early industrial modernization.[13]

Before China's state involvement in industry and commerce, the first priority was national defense against the rising threat of Western imperialism.[14] The greatest concern for the Qing state was the development of China's industrial and technological capabilities for the improvement of military forces.[15] In the 1860s and 1870s, China accelerated its pace in naval construction; officials thus advocated domestic manufacturing of weapons,

---

[11] For an overview of the evolution of state control economy in modern China, see Du Xuncheng 杜恂诚, Yan Guohai 严国海, and Sun Lin 孙林, 中国近代国有经济思想,制度与演变 (The Institution and Evolution of State-Owned Economy and Thought in Modern China) (Shanghai, Shanghai renmin chubanshe, 2007).

[12] See M.C. Wright, *The Last Stand of Chinese Conservatism: The T'ung-Chih Restoration, 1862–1874* (Stanford, Stanford University Press, 1957), pp. 16–17. Also see T.-Y. Kuo and K.-C. Liu, "Self-Strengthening: The Pursuit of Western Technology," in J.K. Fairbank (ed.), *The Cambridge History of China*, vol. 10, *Late Ch'ing, 1800–1911*, part 1 (Cambridge, Cambridge University Press, 1978), pp. 491–3.

[13] For an overview of the PRC scholarship in the 1980s, see J. Chen, "Recent Chinese Historiography on the Western Affairs Movement (the Yangwu yundong, ca. 1860–1895)," *Late Imperial China*, June 1986, 112–27.

[14] Xia Dongyuan 夏东元, 洋务运动史 (The History of the Self-Strengthening Movement) (Shanghai, Huadong shifan daxue chubanshe, 2010), pp. 67–8.

[15] Li Hongzhang and other officials believed that the Qing lost wars because Western armies used more advanced weapons while the Qing army was still using swords.

especially the building of steamships, for coastal defence.[16] During this period, Qing officials established some arsenals, such as the Anqing Arsenal (1861),[17] the Jinling Machine Manufacturing Arsenal (1865), and the Tianjin Machine Manufacturing Bureau (1867).[18] But the most significant was the Jiangnan Arsenal, constructed in Shanghai, which contributed mightily to China's industrial and military modernization, developing vital fields of the economy for the benefit of the state's military endeavors. It became the leading ordnance enterprise in the Far East.[19] In the period from 1868 to 1876, the arsenal produced eleven ships which were deemed to be higher in quality than those produced in the Yokosuka Dockyard in Japan.[20]

The Foochow Naval Shipyard (Fuzhou Shipping Bureau, also known as Mawei Shipping Bureau), managed by Shen Baozhen 沈葆楨 for much of its existence and founded by Zuo Zongtang in 1866, was intended as a multi-role facility.[21] Financing a modern defense enterprise required much greater governmental intervention than did traditional enterprises. However, the Qing government, whose revenue represented no more than 3 percent of the country's gross national product, was an "unbelievably weak instrument" for playing this role alone.[22]

Like the arsenal at Jiangnan, the Fuzhou shipyard's production declined after 1874 with financial and administrative problems taking their toll on the availability of funds and expertise.[23] The period from 1874 to 1897 saw a more focused approach to the training of engineers and officers to manage and maintain the fleets as well as to gain knowledge on the latest developments in

---

[16] D. Pong, *Shen Pao-Chen and China's Modernization in the Nineteenth Century* (New York, Cambridge University Press, 1994), p. 312.
[17] D. Wright, "Careers in Western Science in Nineteenth-Century China: Xu Shou and Xu Jianyin," *Journal of the Royal Asiatic Society* 5.1 (1995), 49–90.
[18] Xia, 洋务运动史, pp.119, 124–5, 127–30.
[19] T. Kennedy, *The Arms of Kiangnan: Modernization in the Chinese Ordnance Industry, 1860–1895* (Boulder, CO, Westview Press, 1978), pp. 146, 150–60; B.A. Elman, "Naval Warfare and the Refraction of China's Self-Strengthening Reforms into Scientific and Technological Failure, 1865–1895," *Modern Asian Studies* 38.2 (2004), 292; K. Biggerstaff, *The Earliest Modern Government Schools in China* (Ithaca, NY, Cornell University Press, 1961), pp. 165–6.
[20] Meng Yue, "Hybrid Science versus Modernity: The Practice of the Jiangnan Arsenal, 1864–1897," *East Asian Science, Technology, and Medicine* 16 (1999), 16–17; Pong, *Shen Pao-Chen and China's Modernization in the Nineteenth Century*, p. 224; Biggerstaff, *Government Schools*, pp. 246–7.
[21] H.-C. Wang, "Transferring Western Technology into China: 1840s–1880s," D.Phil. thesis, Oxford University (2007).
[22] Pong, *Shen Pao-Chen and China's Modernization in the Nineteenth Century*, p. 199. See Kaske and Lin's chapter in this volume.
[23] Biggerstaff, *Government Schools*, pp. 214–19.

mining, metallurgy, and weaponry.[24] Students were sent to Britain, France, and Germany to study Western science and technology so that they could establish a generation of engineers skilled in modern warfare and equipment design. Nevertheless, military modernization during the Self-Strengthening movement forced the development of other modern industries, e.g. communications and textiles.

Officials and Business Enterprise in the Self-Strengthening Era

Beyond the arsenal, the concept of fighting or competing for *liquan* 利权 (economic profits and sovereign rights) against Western imperial business intrusion was beginning to take hold.[25] "Merchant thinkers" and officials such as Zheng Guanying 郑官应 (1842–1922), Ma Jianzhong 马建忠 (1845–1900), Guo Songtao 郭嵩焘 (1818–91), and others elaborated on the importance of the development of "self-interest" discourse for encouraging merchants' motivation to invest in modern enterprises. On the governmental side, powerful local officials sponsored new industries and made sure that these efforts would advance the consolidation of their political status and the expansion of their spheres of influence. These officials assumed successive new roles: first supervisors, then managers, then investors, and finally, for some, official-entrepreneurs. In assuming these new roles, official promoters raised new ideas about *liquan* and its connection to the role of merchants in the state efforts to build up modern enterprises.

Past research on the modern enterprise in the Self-Strengthening movement mainly focused on organizational structure, the scope of influence and the reasons for failure, and its role in the emergence of the bureaucratic and national capitalists.[26] Below, I will explore the influence of the relationship between political and commercial relations on the establishment, development, and survival of these enterprises by comparing the growth experiences of the enterprises founded by Li Hongzhang, Zhang Zhidong 张之洞 (1837–1909), and Yuan Shikai 袁世凯 (1859–1916) in the last fifty years of the Qing dynasty. It helps illuminate the role played by government control in the development of enterprises under conditions in which owner-managers themselves were lacking legal protection.

---

[24] Elman, "Naval Warfare," 300.
[25] See S. Halsey, *Quest for Power: European Imperialism and the Making of Chinese Statecraft* (Cambridge, MA, Harvard University Press, 2015), pp. 5–11.
[26] Feuerwerker, *China's Early Industrialization.*

Li Hongzhang was a major figure in the push for the Qing regime's modernization effort. In the 1870s he began a twenty-five-year term as governor-general of the capital province, Zhili, during which time he initiated projects in commerce and industry. He served as a grand secretary and superintendent of trade for the northern ports and thus was responsible for supervising trade with the West out of treaty ports north of the Yangtze river. During this long tenure, Li involved himself in several major modernizing projects: an arsenal at Tianjin, a commercial steamship line, a coal mine, a railroad, a telegraph line, a cotton mill, and a modern mint. Thus Li Hongzhang played a double role as grand secretary and superintendent of trade – a national-level appointment – and also a provincial-level role in establishing his enterprises. Thus he was able to encourage and promote modern enterprises simply through policies at the national level. It is also worth mentioning that governors or governors-general could establish enterprises outside their provinces, so that the enterprises were, in a sense, national enterprises even though they were established by provincial-level officials. Li was able to contribute to the modernization of China's economy by utilizing the role of the state and in building modern enterprise through corporations in four major westernized industries: the shipping industry, the telegraph industry, mining (coal, steel, lead, copper, etc.), and textiles.

Under the system of so-called *guandu shangban* 官督商办 (official supervision with merchant management), industries were joint official–merchant undertakings.[27] This system was designed to tap into the accumulated funds of Chinese merchants from foreign trade and ancillary services in the treaty ports. Under this system, Li Hongzhang required merchants to invest their own capital and to run modern enterprises at their own risk and under government supervision. For example, officials such as Sheng Xuanhuai 盛宣怀 supervised while comprador Tong Kingsing 唐景星 managed some of the state's modern enterprises. Their supervisory and managerial skills led to discontent as financial losses and abuse of power occurred. But even though Li's power was not enough to protect his enterprises from the influence of other segments of the bureaucracy, he did try to protect merchant managers from bureaucratic interference.

The China Merchants Steam Navigation Company was the first example of this kind of enterprise. At that time, navigation transport was controlled by foreign companies, which enabled foreigners to earn huge profits. The

---

[27] Feuerwerker, *China's Early Industrialization*, p. 11.

introduction of Chinese navigation would attract Chinese merchants to use their own national steamships and thus boost other Chinese business.

Li oversaw the founding of the China Merchants Steam Navigation Company (CMSNC) in 1872. This groundbreaking project was to be owned and primarily financed by merchants, thus shifting the risk of the success of the endeavor over to private investors. In the first several years the endeavor proved successful, becoming bigger than any of the Western steamship companies. In 1877 the CMSNC became the first Chinese national enterprise to acquire a foreign company. By 1877, the company owned twenty-nine steamships. The ships were not only useful for commercial use; they carried food relief during the famine in north China in 1876 and carried troops to where they were needed at various times.[28] The company also invested in different business sectors.

The CMSNC was a unique, hybrid experiment, undertaken by Qing officials and Chinese merchants to counter the inroads of Western steam shipping in China's coastal trade. Its purpose was to "recover China's economic rights [*liquan*]." The CMSNC was China's first joint-stock company (*gongsi* 公司), and its use of this organizational structure marked a new departure in Chinese business practice. Yet government–merchant co-operation in the creation and development of this enterprise followed earlier, well-established patterns of Qing government co-operation with private merchant groups to achieve mutually advantageous goals. In such cases, the government recruited private human, organizational, and material resources to launch various kinds of joint ventures that used different approaches to "government supervision and merchant operation" (*guandu shangban*). From 1872 to 1884, the CMSNC struggled to weld together old patterns of government–business co-operation with its new joint-stock structure during a period of challenging and rapidly changing political and economic conditions. In the end, the company failed. But the experiment

---

[28] See C.K. Lai, "Li Hung-chang and Modern Enterprise: The China Merchants' Company, 1872–1885," in S.C. Chu and K.-C. Liu, *Li Hung-chang and China's Early Modernization* (Armonk, M.E. Sharpe, 1994), pp. 227, 222. Also see Chi-kong Lai 黎志刚, "轮船招商局国有问题, 1878–1881," *Bulletin of the Institutute of Modern History, Academia Sinica* 17 (1988), 15–40; Chi-kong Lai, "轮船招商局经营管理问题, 1872–1901" (Problems in the Management of the China Merchants' Company), *Bulletin of the Institutute of Modern History, Academia Sinica* 19 (1990), 67–105. Most recently, Reinhardt, *Navigating Semi-colonialism*, Chapters 2–3, explains the steamship business by discussing three major shipping companies between 1860 and 1882. The China Navigation Company and the Indo-China Steam Navigation Company were controlled by British companies. On the other hand, the China Merchants Steam Navigation Company, which was sponsored by the Qing government, became the largest shipping firm.

showed that, from 1872 to 1884, when the operational management of the company was left in the hands of merchants and simultaneously received government support in the form of annual subsidies (assigned as the official carrier of state goods on designated routes and other temporary financial assistance), and the exclusive right to carry the grain tribute rice to the capital (with the imported British vessel *Eaton*; then later *Yongqing*, *Fuxing*, and *Liyun*), it succeeded. However, the corruption of the era, including nepotism and embezzlement, resulted in the loss of funds to other ventures which collapsed in the turmoil of the 1880s. When government involvement in the actual management of the firm increased from 1885 to 1911, the CMSNC failed.

The China Merchants Company was established as an effort to compete profitably with foreign shipping. Profits were returned to investors, but ultimately failed to reclaim the domestic shipping industry.[29] Under the supervision of governor-general Li Hongzhang (later Yuan Shikai, then the minister of posts and communication), new regulations came out in 1909, and semiofficial status was only modified rather than ended by the government's acceptance of the new corporate structure. In September 1909, the company held the first shareholder meeting in Shanghai and the first board of directors was formed. It was registered with the Ministry of Agriculture, Industry, and Commerce as a private mercantile enterprise in 1911.[30] In 1912 a decision was made in an extraordinary shareholder meeting, agreeing to lend the company's assets to the new government of Sun Yat-sen for a mortgage loan.

With the early success of the CMSNC project, it became a model for the founding of similar commercial ventures such as the Hubei Coal Mining Company in 1875, the Kaiping Mining Company in 1877, the Shanghai Cotton Textile Mill in 1878, and the Imperial Telegraph Administration in December 1881.[31]

In 1877, Li Hongzhang founded the Kaiping Mining Company, which is considered the most triumphant enterprise supported by the Qing state because there was also a collaboration with the commercial sector to allow private investors to fund the mine.[32] Li drew on his successful experience in forming the China Merchants Shipping Company, and he appointed Tong

[29] Xia, 洋务运动史, pp. 192, 195–6.
[30] Chu and Liu, *Li Hung-chang and China's Early Modernization*, p. 167.
[31] Lai, "Li Hung-chang and Modern Enterprise," 218.
[32] See T. Wright, *Coal Mining in China's Economy and Society 1895–1937* (Cambridge, Cambridge University Press, 1984); E.C. Carlson, *Origins and Early Development of the Kaiping Enterprise: The Kaiping Mines, 1877–1912* (Cambridge, MA, Harvard University Asia Center, Harvard University, 1971), pp. 1–23; Q. Liu, "Yan Fu and Kaiping Mines:

Kingsing to supervise the mines. As an excellent comprador businessman, Tong was familiar with market conditions and the management practices of new enterprises.[33] And more importantly, his arrival attracted much merchant investment in the new mining business. Tong Kingsing was a professional manager, trusted by Li. With his prestige in the business world, the Kaiping Mining Company managed to raise 7,000 of the 8,000 shares planned in its first year of operation.[34] With the "introduction" of Sheng Xuanhuai and Li Hongzhang's "sponsorship," Tong was able to successfully take charge of the Kaiping Mining Company. Li Hongzhang maintained a "confident" attitude towards his managers, did not interfere too much in the management and operation of enterprises, and generously provided help and political protection when enterprises faced difficulties in funding and public opinion.[35]

During this period, various operations were established, including (not a complete list) the Zichuan Lead Mine (1875), the Lanzhou Weaving Bureau (1877), the Jingmen Coal Mine (1879), the Imperial Telegraph Administration (1881), the Pingquan Copper Mine (1881), the Mohe Gold Mine (1889), the Shanghai Cotton Cloth Mill (1890), the Hanyang Ironworks (1890), and the Imperial Bank of China (1896).

This modern-enterprise model in late Qing was not a fully "westernized" management model and the start-up scale of investment in most of these enterprises in the 1895–1913 period was limited.[36] With government supervision of funds, investment in these modern enterprises came with significant financial risks as cases of mismanagement, financial misconduct, financial discrepancies, and corruption occurred. As a result, merchants became discouraged and increasingly cautious of becoming involved in state-supervised modern enterprises.

The Meaning of Economic Liberalism in Early Modern China," in G. Campagnolo (ed.), *Liberalism and Chinese Economic Development: Perspectives from Europe and Asia* (New York, Routledge, 2016), pp. 49–62. For Chinese scholarship, see Yun Yan 云妍, 近代开滦煤矿研究 (A Study of the Kailuan Coal Mines in Chinese Modern Times) (Beijing, Renmin chubanshe, 2015).

[33] Tang Tingshu 唐廷枢, "请开采开平煤铁并兴办铁路禀" (Self-Strengthening Movement VII) (Shanghai, Shanghai Renmin Publishing, 2000), pp. 119–24.

[34] F. Zhao, "Kailuan Coal Mines: The Best Coal Mine Was Robbed by Japan," *Yingcai* 10 (2012), n.p.

[35] W.K.K. Chan, "Government, Merchants and Industry to 1911," in J.K. Fairbank and K.-C. Liu (eds.), *The Cambridge History of China*, vol. 11, *Late Ch'ing, 1800–1911*, part 2 (Cambridge, Cambridge University Press, 1980), p. 436.

[36] Sun Yutang 孫毓棠, 中国近代工業史資料 (Information on the Modern Industrial History of China), first series, 1840–1895, vol. 2 (Beijing, Kexue chubanshe, 1957), pp. 1166–9; A. Feurwerker, "Economic Trends in the Late Ch'ing Empire, 1870–1911," in Fairbank and Liu, *The Cambridge History of China*, vol. 2, p. 37.

Zhang Zhidong became the governor of Shanxi in 1882; governor-general of Guangdong and Guangxi from 1884 to 1889; governor-general of Jiangsu, Anhui, and Jiangxi in the lower Yangzi region during the First Sino-Japanese War; a long-serving governor-general of Hubei and Hunan from 1889 to 1907; and a grand councillor after 1907.[37] He was the most influential reformer after Li Hongzhang. To escape the vicious cycle of officially supervised modern enterprises, Zhang Zhidong pursued the new scheme of *guanshang heban* 官商合辦. Merchant–state official joint management was introduced not only to improve merchant–state relations but also to allow for a different business environment after a series of setbacks. This scheme offered merchant partnerships to those who invested in the Hubei Cotton Cloth Mill, and they were assured of annual dividends; it also allowed for a more balanced relationship between the officials and the merchants. These partnerships with merchants did not change this trend of increasing bureaucratic involvement.

As early as 1881, Zhang was at great pains to duplicate the Tianjin model (pioneered by Li Hongzhang) in Shanxi. When Zhang Zhidong established his enterprises, he took a different approach from Li Hongzhang. He didn't trust businessmen who knew the economy. From 1888 to 1906, in the management of several factories, including the Hubei Cotton Cloth Mill, regardless of the proportion of merchant investment, Zhang insisted on appointing his own managers to manage the enterprise. These policies greatly hurt the enthusiasm of businessmen for investing in his business.

Steel- and ironworks were the key industries of Zhang's Self-Strengthening industrial policy. The Hanyeping company was not the first industrial plant established in China,[38] but it was officially established under Zhang Zhidong. Quan Hansheng's history of the Hanyeping Company is the classic on this topic. He explores the running of the Hanyeping Company in three phases: *guanban* 官辦 (government-run), *guandu shangban* (official supervision and merchant management), and *shangban* 商辦 (merchant management).[39]

---

[37] See Li Xizhu 李細珠, 张之洞与清末新政研究 (The Study of Zhang Zhidong and Late Qing Reform) (Beijing, Zhongguo shehui kexue chubanshe, 2015); Feng Tianyu 冯天瑜 and Chen Feng 陈锋 (eds.), 张之洞与中国近代化 (Zhang Zhidong and China's Modernization) (Beijing, Shehui kexue chubanshe, 2010). For English-language scholarship on Zhang Zhidong, see, for example, W. Ayers, *Chang Chih-tung and Educational Reform in China* (Cambridge, MA, Harvard University Press, 1971); and D.H. Bays, *China Enters the Twentieth Century: Chang Chih-tung and the Issues of a New Age, 1895–1909* (Ann Arbor, The University of Michigan Press, 1978).

[38] The first industrial plant was built in Guizhou in 1889 due to misperceptions that the area was rich in raw materials and in order to counter foreign imports.

[39] Quan Hansheng 全汉昇, 汉冶萍公司史略 (A Brief History of the Hanyeping Iron and Coal Mining and Smelting Company, 1890–1926) (Hong Kong, The Chinese University of Hong Kong Press, 1972). Also see Zhang Houquan 张后铨, 汉冶萍公司史 (A

When Zhang Zhidong founded the Hanyang Ironworks, he was supported by the central government. Zhang lacked relevant knowledge of production technology and scientific business management concepts. As a result, mistakes were made in fuel, machinery, and equipment, and in the selection of the site of the steel plant, leading to losses. When losses occurred, Zhang Zhidong pinned his hopes on the Qing government at first. However, due to defeat in the Sino-Japanese War of 1894–1895, the Qing government was unable to support his enterprises and he had to invite businessmen to undertake them. The government became the creditor of Hanyang Ironworks. After the failure of the *guanban* Hanyang Ironworks, Sheng Xuanhuai took over, which also marked the beginning of the *guandu shangban* stage of the Hanyeping Company.

A shortage of funds in the course of private-enterprise operations was likely to cause bankruptcy, but this was not a difficult problem for these *guandu shangban* enterprises – they pulled money from other companies to fill the gap. In 1904, Sheng Xuanhuai drew more than a million taels from the China Merchants to add to the Hanyang Ironworks.[40] In 1908, he drew more than 40,000 taels of share capital from the Hua Sheng Spinning and Weaving Mill to add to the Hanyeping Coal and Iron Co.[41] But such adjustments could also pose a hazard to the company being drawn from. Zhang Zhidong drew on the profits and capital of the Hubei Cotton Cloth Mill to support his other enterprises, resulting in stagnation in its development.[42]

After Sheng Xuanhuai took over the Hanyang Ironworks, the first thing to be solved was the problem of raising capital. His solution was to raise funds through a public offering, recruit private shareholders, and hope to obtain the support of private capital.

During the period of *guandu shangban*, the output and turnover of the company increased significantly and achieved gratifying results. However, Sheng Xuanhuai used the *guandu shangban* model to supervise the business and did not recognize the rights of investors. On the surface, ownership was subordinate to the government, but in fact it was controlled by Sheng. This

History of the Hanyeping Corporation) (Beijing, Shehui kexue wenxian, 2014); Dai Lu 代鲁, 汉冶萍公司史研究 (A Study of the History of the Hanyeping Corporation) (Wuhan, Wuhan daxue chubanshe, 2013). Also see T. Kennedy, "Chang Chih-tung and the Struggle for Strategic Industrialization: The Establishment of the Hanyang Arsenal, 1884–1895," *Harvard Journal of Asiatic Studies* 33 (1973), 154–82.

[40] Chan, "Government, Merchants and Industry to 1911," p. 429.
[41] Tianjin archives collection, Interest-Bearing Roll of Deposits in the Shanghai Textile Mill and Hanyeping Coal and Iron Co., New Stock Volume.
[42] Chan, "Government, Merchants and Industry to 1911," p. 429.

was a serious violation of the original intention of private investors to pursue profits, not to mention promote the growth of new enterprises. This mode greatly limited and fettered the collection of private funds, which was very unfavorable to the capital accumulation of the Hanyeping Company. After 1908, Sheng Xuanhuai put forward the idea of *shangban* or merchant management. The Hanyeping Company emerged as the result of a merger between the Hanyang Ironworks, the Daye Iron Mine (大冶鐵礦), and the Pingxiang Coal Mine.

The merger was an attempt to regain investor confidence and secure funding to maintain the daily operations of the company which were essential in the production of top-quality steel. The merger allowed companies to purchase shares, giving Hanyeping greater business opportunities with investors' money, e.g. to repay outstanding debts, reinvest in existing machinery, and obtain extended loans. Past problems of poor credibility, such as excessive borrowing and high debt accumulation, were enough to drive away existing and/or potential investors.

In the industrial development of modern China, the combination of bureaucrats (*guan*) and merchants (*shang*) promoted the emergence of industrial development. However, in order to continue national industrial development, it was necessary for *guan* and *shang* to go their separate ways and reduce the interference of state power in the industrial process. Despite this company's failure in some respects, it became a crucial part of the Qing government's industrial promotion efforts, bringing China one step further along the road to industrialization.

Railway development undertaken by late Qing officials like Zhang Zhidong signaled a major advance in Chinese transport capabilities, as shown in Elisabeth Köll's recent book focusing on the Jin-Pu Railway. Many years later, Li Hongzhang, along with Zhang Zhidong and Liu Mingchuan, advocated for railways to be put in place. The development of the railways took the form of partnerships with the foreign powers. The government signed agreements with the British and the Germans to build important lines to connect the coast to cities like Beijing. By using the concessions, the government did not have to invest the whole of the capital for this state building project. The Jin-Pu Railway was roughly concentrated around the northeastern part of China, connecting Beijing and Shanghai, as well as connecting with the countryside. However, as most countries had significant railway networks by the 1900s, China was lagging behind.[43]

---

[43] Köll, *Railroads and the Transformation of China*, pp. 19–50.

As governor of Shandong (1899–1901), as governor-general of the capital province, Zhili (1901–7), and later as grand councillor (1908) and prime minister, Yuan Shikai enacted broad effective reforms in areas such as currency, banking, agriculture, industrial development, policing, education, and others.[44] Yuan Shikai did contribute positively to China through reforms and enterprise policies. Yuan's official, Zhou Xuexi, offered companies political protection. The creation and development of the Qi Xin Cement C.o 启新洋灰公司 was like that of the Kaiping Mining Company, but depended even more on the support of official funds. At the beginning of the development of the Qi Xin Cement Co., one million silver dollars in start-up funds was needed, and Zhou Xuexi received the strong support of Yuan Shikai because of their affinity. This million dollars was all supported by a Tianjin Official Silver bank loan at Yuan Shikai's behest, and the loan period was for ten years with annual interest of 5 percent. Yuan Shikai was involved in the first attempt to introduce business regularization by initiating the Company Law in 1904 under the Qing government.[45] As David Faure argues, the introduction of company law was a game changer as it provided some legal protection for private business.[46]

Conclusion

The relationship between "officials" and "businessmen" was quite special in the "Self-Strengthening" enterprises, which perhaps marked the first time in the recent history of China that the administration had publicly supported businesspeople in establishing and developing large modern enterprises related to the state. In the absence of a strong private sector, the rise of modern industry during the late Qing was mainly a governmental effort, which yielded uncertain benefits. Thus modern-type enterprises were started

---

[44] E. Yong, *The Presidency of Yuan Shih-k'ai: Liberalism and Dictatorship in Early Republican China* (Ann Arbor, University of Michigan Press, 1977), pp. 54–5. Also see S.R. MacKinnon, *Power and Politics in Late Imperial China: Yuan Shi-kai in Beijing and Tianjin, 1901–1908* (Berkeley, University of California Press, 1980); J. Ch'en, *Yuan Shih-K'ai*, 2nd ed. (Stanford, Stanford University Press, 1972).

[45] W.C. Kirby, "China Unincorporated: Company Law and Business Enterprise in Twentieth-Century China," *Journal of Asian Studies* 54.1 (February 1995), 43.

[46] D. Faure, *China and Capitalism: A History of Business Enterprise in Modern China* (Hong Kong, Hong Kong University Press, 2006), pp. 45–64. Also see Zhang Zhongmin 张忠民, 艰难的变迁:近代中国公司制度研究 (The Difficulty of Change: A Study of the Institution of the Modern Corporation in Modern China (Shanghai, Shanghai shehui kexue chubanshe, 2002); Gao Xinwei 高新伟, 中国近代公司治理 (1872–1949) (Corporate Governance in Modern China (1872–1949) (Beijing, Shehui kexue wenxian chubanshe, 2009).

in the late Qing with state encouragement, but failed to develop into a genuine "industrial revolution."

The Qing court does deserve credit for supporting massive infrastructure projects that led to the expansion of shipping companies, as well as the extension of telegraph networks and railway lines. This infrastructure improved commercial transactions in late Qing and later Republican China. The absence of, for example, commercial and private property laws led the private sector to rely too heavily on official protection. The partnership also sometimes resulted in the incompetent interference of officials, and permitted corruption by entrepreneurs. Hence the introduction of a nationwide Company Law (1904) to protect industrialized corporations marked the beginning of a new phase as the Chinese state adapted its relationship with private business to modernize the economy.[47] In the end, the law still did not provide sufficient protection for private property rights as nationalization of private businesses still occurred on a regular basis.

Further Reading

Bickers, R., and L. Jackson (eds.), *Treaty Ports in Modern China: Law, Land and Power* (London, Routledge, 2016).

Chan, W.K.K., *Merchants, Mandarins and Modern Enterprise in Late Ch'ing China* (Cambridge, MA, Harvard University Press, 1977).

Chen, J., "Recent Chinese Historiography on the Western Affairs Movement (the Yangwu yundong, ca. 1860–1895)," *Late Imperial China*, June 1986, 112–27.

Chu, S.C., and K.-C. Liu (eds.), *Li Hung-chang and China's Early Modernization* (Armonk, M.E. Sharpe, 1994).

Faure, D., *China and Capitalism: A History of Business Enterprise in Modern China* (Hong Kong, Hong Kong University Press, 2006).

Feng, Tianyu 冯天瑜 and Chen Feng 陈锋 (eds.), 张之洞与中国近代化 (Zhang Zhidong and China's Modernization) (Beijing, Shehui kexue chubanshe, 2010).

Feuerwerker, A., *China's Early Industrialization: Shen Hsuan-huai (1844–1916) and Mandarin Enterprise* (Cambridge, MA, Harvard University Press, 1958).

Halsey, S.R., *Quest for Power: European Imperialism and the Making of Chinese Statecraft* (Cambridge, MA, Harvard University Press, 2015).

Hao, Y., *The Commercial Revolution in Nineteen-Century China: The Rise of Sino-Western Mercantile Capitalism* (Berkeley, University of California Press, 1986).

Kirby, W.C., "China Unincorporated: Company Law and Business Enterprise in Twentieth-Century China," *Journal of Asian Studies* 54.1 (February 1995), 43–63.

Leonard, J.K., and J.R. Watt (eds.), *To Achieve Security and Wealth: The Qing Imperial State and the Economy, 1644–1911* (Ithaca, NY, Cornell University Press, 1992).

---

[47] Kirby, "China Unincorporated," 43.

Li, Xizhu 李细珠, 张之洞与清末新政研究 (The Study of Zhang Zhidong and Late Qing Reform) (Beijing, Zhongguo shehui kexue chubanshe, 2015).

Pong, D., *Shen Pao-chen and China's Modernization in the Nineteenth Century* (New York, Cambridge University Press, 1994).

Quan, Hansheng 全汉昇, 汉冶萍公司史略 (A Brief History of the Hanyeping Iron and Coal Mining and Smelting Company, 1890–1926) (Hong Kong, The Chinese University of Hong Kong Press, 1972).

Reinhardt, A., *Navigating Semi-colonialism: Shipping, Sovereignty, and Nation-Building in China, 1860–1937* (Cambridge, MA, Harvard University Press, 2018).

Xia Dongyuan 夏东元, 洋务运动史 (The History of the Self-Strengthening Movement) (Shanghai, Huadong shifan daxue chubabshe, 2010).

Zhang Guohui 张国辉, 洋务运动与中国近代企业 (The Self-Strengthening Movement and China's Modern Enterprise) (Beijing, Zhongguo shehui kehui chubanshe, 1979).

Zhang Zhongmin 张忠民, 艰难的变迁:近代中国公司制度研究 (The Difficulty of Change: The Study of the Institution of the Modern Corporation in Modern China (Shanghai, Shanghai Shehui kexue chubanshe, 2002).

6

State Enterprises during the First Half of the Twentieth Century

MORRIS L. BIAN

The first half of the twentieth century witnessed the rise of the state sector of the Chinese economy. The rise of the state sector manifested in the development and expansion of central state enterprises and regional state enterprises and resulted from the ideology and policy of the developmental state.[1] This chapter traces the emergence and evolution of the ideology and policy of the developmental state, describes the development and expansion of central state enterprises and regional state enterprises, and addresses the issue of change and continuity across the 1949 divide.

Creating the Ideology and Policy of the Developmental State

During the first half of the twentieth century, the Nationalist elite developed an ideology of the developmental state. In its final form, the ideology of the developmental state consists of an emphasis on state-owned enterprise,

---

[1] The concept of the "developmental state" was used first by Chalmers Johnson in his study of Japanese industrial policy. According to Johnson, the Japanese developmental state is characterized by the existence of an elite bureaucracy with sufficient scope to take the initiative and operate effectively, the existence of a pilot organization to lead economic development, and the perfection of market-conforming methods of state intervention in the economy. Taking as their point of departure Johnson's account of the Japanese developmental state, recently a number of scholars have examined the theory and practice of the developmental state in the context of East Asia. The concept of the developmental state has also been fruitfully appropriated by scholars of Republican China. See C. Johnson, *MITI and the Japanese Miracle: The Growth of Industrial Policy, 1925–1975* (Stanford, CA, Stanford University Press, 1982); Meredith Woo-Cumings (ed.), *The Developmental State* (Ithaca, NY, Cornell University Press, 1999); V. Chibber, "Building a Developmental State: The Korean Case Reconsidered," *Politics & Society* 27.3 (September 1999), 309–46; W.C. Kirby, "Engineering China: Birth of the Developmental State, 1928–1937," in Wen-hsin Yeh (ed.), *Becoming Chinese: Passages to Modernity and Beyond* (Berkeley, University of California Press, 2000), pp. 137–60; J.B. Knight, "China as a Developmental State," *World Economy* 37.10 (October 2014), 1335–47.

a stress on heavy industry, a focus on national defense, and a determination to create a planned socialist economic system. Although this ideology took its final form during the Second Sino-Japanese War (1937–1945), core elements of this ideology can be traced to the writings of Sun Yat-sen, the founding father of the Chinese republic. As early as 1912, Sun stated that all major industries in China should be owned by the state. Sun Yat-sen's *International Development of China* also laid the foundation for the Nationalist conception of heavy industry, discussing the development of key and basic industries.[2] Finally, the idea of economic planning came from Sun Yat-sen as well. According to Sun, China must develop a comprehensive plan to take advantage of the opportunity of the post-World War I period and to make use of new capital and experienced personnel of the belligerent nations to develop large-scale industries.[3] In his 1924 lectures on the Three Doctrines of the People, Sun continued to emphasize state-owned industries.

It should be pointed out that Sun Yat-sen was not alone in emphasizing state ownership; leading members of the Beijing government such as Zhou Xuexi and Zhang Jian also advocated state ownership and management of key industries.[4] As a result, despite the enactment of laws and the creation of regulations promoting the development of private enterprise, those very laws and regulations also stipulated state ownership and management of key industries such as salt and kerosene as well as telecommunications.

During the 1920s, the Nationalist Party incorporated many of Sun's views into its platform, including those on the scope and function of state-owned and private enterprise. Thus the 1924 *Manifesto of the First Nationalist Party Congress* provided that enterprises that were monopolistic in nature and the development of which lay beyond private means ought to be undertaken and managed by the state.[5] After the success of the Nationalist Revolution, the party's leadership accepted Sun's vision of economic development and made it part of the dominant ideology of the Chinese state. During the late 1930s

---

[2] Sun Yat-sen 孙中山, 建国方略 (Strategy for China Reconstruction) (Shanghai, Shangwu yinshu guan, 1927). The second part – *Material Reconstruction* – was translated into English in 1921 and published in 1922 as *International Development of China* by G. P. Putnam's Sons, 2nd ed. (New York and London, The Knickerbocker Press, 1929).
[3] Sun Yat-sen, *Fundamentals of National Reconstruction* (Taipei, Sino-American Publishing Co. Ltd, 1953), p. 189.
[4] Wu Qian 武乾, "北洋政府时期的经济法与经济体制的二元化" (Economic Law and the Development of Two Orientations of the Economic System), 法商研究 (Study of Law and Commerce) 1 (2003), 126–32.
[5] Xiao Jizong 萧继宗 (ed.), 中国国民党宣言集 (Collection of Manifestos of the Chinese Nationalist Party), vol. 69 (Taipei, Zhongguo Guomindang zhongyang weiyuanhui dangshi weiyuanhui, 1976), p. 91.

and the 1940s, in response to the crisis and war, leading figures of the Nationalist government, such as Weng Wenhao, elaborated on Sun Yat-sen's views. Weng Wenhao was the most important economic figure in the Nationalist government (outside the financial sector), serving, for example, as head of the Ministry of Economic Affairs from 1938 to 1946. In a 1938 report, Weng divided state-owned enterprise into four broad categories: national defense, basic manufacturing industries, important mineral products, and power. Weng declared emphatically that these enterprises aimed to increase the productive capacity of the nation; they were not designed to compete for profit with the people.[6] By 1942, however, Weng's position had shifted to emphasize state-owned enterprise even more. In that year, Weng argued that, first, China must industrialize. Second, China must focus on heavy industry in order to bring industrialization to fruition. Finally, the government must rely on state-owned enterprise to lay the foundation for China's heavy industrial development.[7] Less than a year later, Weng offered a more concrete definition of the scope of state-owned and private enterprise. In principle, basic industries should be owned and managed by the state. In contrast to the large scope of state-owned enterprise in these industries, light industries should in principle be owned and managed by private enterprise.[8]

As was the case with the emphasis on state-owned enterprise and heavy industry, the focus on national defense was also the outcome of an evolution of several decades. Fundamentally, it was the increasing Japanese threat to China's national security after the mid-1930s and the crisis triggered by the war that caused the Nationalists to underline the importance of national defense. The focus on national defense did not find explicit expression in Sun Yat-sen's Three Doctrines of the People. The first indication of a major shift from the preoccupation with people's livelihood to a focus on national defense was the four-year plan of national reconstruction adopted by the Fourth Nationalist Party Congress in response to the Japanese invasion of Manchuria in November 1931. With national survival at stake, the plan focused on national defense, used a hypothetical enemy as the target of

---

6 "经济部近时工作纪要" (Work Summary by the Ministry of Economic Affairs), 新经济 (The New Economy) 1.2 (December 1, 1938), 58–62.
7 Weng Wenhao 翁文灏, 国营重工业的意义与任事同人的责任 (The Meaning of State-Owned Heavy Industry and the Responsibility of Fellow Comrades), 资源委员会公报 (Bulletin of the National Resources Commission) 3.2 (August 16, 1942), 75–80.
8 Weng Wenhao 翁文灏, "中国经济建设概论" (Survey of Chinese Economic Reconstruction), in Weng Wenhao, 中国经济建设论丛 (Collection of Essays on Chinese Economic Reconstruction) (National Resources Commission, 1943), pp. 81–2.

reconstruction, and defined the scope of reconstruction according to necessity and viability.⁹

As war approached, the Fifth Nationalist Central Executive Committee in February 1937 declared that Chinese economic reconstruction had two objectives: to meet the needs of national defense and to improve people's welfare. The first objective was designed to bring to fruition the Doctrine of Nationalism; the second objective was meant to implement the Doctrine of People's Livelihood.¹⁰ Subsequently, the crisis prompted by the war greatly strengthened this national-defense orientation. In a 1938 essay, Qian Changchao, deputy director of the National Resources Commission, stated that all economic reconstruction should focus on national defense, and China must take immediate steps to create a center for national defense in the interior.¹¹ Weng Wenhao shared Qian's belief in the primary importance of national defense. In a 1942 speech, Weng described how the Soviet Union and Germany had undertaken large-scale heavy industrial reconstruction by using five-year and four-year plans, and he pointed out that both the Soviet Union and Germany believed that economic reconstruction was the only solution to national rejuvenation. As long as economic reconstruction was designed to increase national strength, it was appropriate for the whole nation to work hard and endure hardships.¹²

Another integral part of the Nationalist ideology of economic development was the determination to create a planned socialist economic system. Should the government follow the earlier policy of the first industrialized nations by keeping its hands off economic activities, or was the goal of a modern industrial nation to be achieved through economic planning and eventually through a planned socialist economic system? The Nationalist elite clearly chose the latter path. After the Sino-Japanese War erupted, the Provisional Nationalist Party Congress, meeting in April 1938, adopted a Program for the War of Resistance and Nation Building, declaring that

---

⁹ 国家建设初期方案案 (Resolution on National Reconstruction in the Near Future), November 21, 1931, in 中华民国史档案资料汇编 (Collection of Archival Materials in the History of Republican China), part 5, vol. 1, zhengzhi, no. 2, p. 337.
¹⁰ 中国经济建设方案 (Resolution on Chinese Economic Reconstruction), February 19, 1937, in 中华民国史档案资料汇编, part 5, vol. 1, zhengzhi, no. 2, pp. 618–25.
¹¹ Qian Changchao 钱昌照, "两年半创办重工业之经过与感想" (The Experience of and Reflection on Creating Heavy Industry for the Past Two and a Half Years), 中国第二历史档案馆档案 (Second Historical Archives, China), 28.2, 939. See also 新经济 (New Economy) 2.1 (June 16, 1939), 2–6.
¹² Weng Wenhao 翁文灏, "国防经济建设之要义" (The Meaning of Economic Reconstruction for National Defense), July 25, 1941, reprinted in 资源委员会公报 1.2 (August 16, 1941), 69–72.

China must create a planned economic system, encourage domestic and foreign investment, and expand wartime production.[13] Writing in 1941, Weng Wenhao distinguished among the planned economic system of the Soviet Union; the economic systems completely controlled by the governments of Germany, Italy, and Japan; and the partially controlled economic systems in Great Britain and the United States. Although Weng recognized merits in all three types of economic system, he believed that none of them was entirely consistent with China's needs. Consequently, Weng proposed that China eclectically adopt elements from all three of these systems. As he put it, China ought to create a planned and controlled economic system, under which the government should take major responsibility by making national defense its top priority, by promoting state-owned enterprise, and by controlling private enterprise.[14]

In short, the Nationalist ideology of economic development resulted in part from Sun Yat-sen's legacy, but, more importantly, also from the increasing Japanese threat to China's national security and the wartime crisis. The Nationalist elite collectively developed an ideology of economic development based on state-owned enterprise, heavy industry, national defense, and the determination to create a planned socialist economic system. Ultimately, this ideology led directly to the development and expansion of central and regional state enterprise.

Developing and Expanding Central State Enterprises in Heavy Industry

After establishing a functional central government in 1928, the Nationalist regime began creating the institutional framework for economic planning and the development and expansion of central state enterprises. The government created a National Reconstruction Commission in 1929 and a National Economic Commission in 1931. During this period, the government drew up at least four major economic plans. The 1932 National Defense Planning Commission was the first institutional embodiment of the new defense orientation. Chiang Kai-shek was president of this commission and the Military Affairs Commission to which it reported, but Weng Wenhao was

---

[13] 中国国民党抗战建国纲领 (Program for the War of Resistance and Nation Building), April 1, 1938, in 中华民国史档案资料汇编, part 5, vol. 2, zhengzhi, no. 1, 386–9.
[14] Weng Wenhao 翁文灏, "经建方向与共同责任" (The Direction of Economic Reconstruction and Our Shared Responsibility), 中国第二历史档案馆档案 (Second Historical Archives, China), 28.2, 314. See also 新经济 6.7 (January 1, 1942), 136–9.

secretary-general, and Qian Changzhao deputy secretary-general. The commission was staffed by technocrats and had well over 100 members by 1934.[15] In April 1935, the commission was renamed the National Resources Commission, which marked an important change in purpose and direction. During the next three years the National Resources Commission, under the same leadership, changed its orientation from resource investigation and planning to heavy industrial reconstruction. In effect, the organization was transformed from Chiang Kai-shek's brain trust to an organization in charge of industrial development. Under the Three-Year Plan for Heavy Industrial Reconstruction completed in 1936, heavy industry received the lion's share of investment capital. Geographically, most planned factories were to be built in interior provinces such as Hunan and Jiangxi for fear of further Japanese aggression.[16] Twenty-one out of thirty planned factories and mines were under construction by the time the Sino-Japanese War broke out in July 1937.

The outbreak of war and the relocation of the Nationalist government to Chongqing led to further changes in the National Resources Commission's organization and activities. In March 1938 the Nationalist government placed the commission under the jurisdiction of the newly created Ministry of Economic Affairs, with Weng Wenhao as minister. Although Weng Wenhao and Qian Changzhao continued to lead the organization, their official titles were changed from secretary-general and deputy secretary-general to director and deputy director respectively. The commission's function was redefined to include the creation and management of state-owned industries and state-owned enterprises.[17]

The eruption of war caused serious disruptions in the implementation of the three-year reconstruction plan and forced some of the half-finished factories to relocate to the interior. Despite the disruptions and forced relocation, the National Resources Commission continued to rely on the mechanism of planning for heavy industrial reconstruction. If anything, wartime military and economic mobilization added a greater sense of urgency for planned and co-ordinated development. Thus, after relocating

---

[15] 国防设计委员会人事文件 (Personnel Documents of the National Defense Planning Commission), 1934, 中国第二历史档案馆档案 (Second Historical Archives, China), 47, 115.
[16] Qian Changzhao 钱昌照, "两年半创办重工业之经过与感想," 中国第二历史档案馆档案 (Second Historical Archives, China), 28.2, 939. See also 新经济 2.1 (June 16, 1939), 2–6.
[17] 经济部资源委员会组织条例 (Organizational Regulations of the National Resources Commission), August 1, 1938, in 资源委员会月刊 (National Resources Commission monthly) 1.1 (April 1939), 63–4.

and constructing factories in the interior between late 1938 and early 1939, the commission developed a new Three-Year Reconstruction Plan for Heavy Industry. The plan called for the establishment of new factories or the expansion of existing ones in the metallurgical industry, the chemical industry, the liquid-fuel industry, the machine industry, transportation and communication equipment, and the leather and rubber industries.[18] Although precise figures of total government spending are unavailable, documents that are available indicate that the government appropriated ¥329.97 million (¥28.21 million in 1936 constant price) for heavy industrial reconstruction during the three-year period.[19]

In early 1941, the National Resources Commission drafted another comprehensive economic plan, the Outline of a Three-Year Plan for National Defense Industries. The Eighth Plenary Session of the Fifth Central Executive Committee of the Nationalist Party adopted it in April 1941. According to this plan, between 1942 and 1944 the National Resources Commission would establish new factories or expand existing ones in the metallurgical, machine, electrical, chemical, food, and energy industries. The total initial capital needed was estimated at ¥816.69 million and $25.56 million, in addition to ¥259.74 million in liquid assets.[20]

Where did the National Resources Commission receive the investment capital from? How did it finance heavy industrial projects? Archival documents indicate that the commission received investment capital from three sources: annual budget appropriation from the state treasury, short-term loans and investment from state-run banks, and profits from the export of mineral resources. Annual budget appropriations from the state treasury constituted the major source of investment capital. Among these, the single most important source of investment was an annual budget appropriation from the state treasury. Archival sources indicate that, after experiencing a steady rise from 1936 to 1941, the value of annual state appropriations suffered a steep decline from 1942 to 1945. The share of the National Resources Commission in the state budget showed

---

[18] 西南各省三年国防建设计划 (Three-Year Reconstruction Plan for National Defense in Southwestern Provinces), 1939, 中国第二历史档案馆档案 (Second Historical Archives, China), 28.2, 37.
[19] Ziyuan weiyuanhui 资源委员会 (ed.), 复员以来资源委员会述要 (A Survey of the Achievements of the National Resources Commission since 1945) (Nanjing, National Resources Commission, 1948), pp. 38–9.
[20] 国防工业战时三年计划纲要 (Outline of the Three-Year Plan for National Defense Industries), 中华民国史档案资料汇编, part 5, vol. 2, caizheng jingji, no. 6, 120–8.

a similar trend: after reaching a high of 2.8 percent in 1940, it declined rapidly.[21]

Once the appropriations from the national budget were made available, the National Resources Commission distributed them among heavy industries, such as energy, coal, petroleum, metal, iron and steel, machines, electrical, and chemical. The commission's own statistics reveal that between 1936 and 1945 the commission received ¥119.21 billion in investment capital (¥71.78 million in 1936 constant price). Among the nine industries, the energy industry received ¥50.73 billion, which accounted for 42.56 percent of the commission's investment capital. The industry that received the second-largest share was the petroleum industry (15.83 percent), with a total of ¥18.87 billion.[22]

The allocation of investment capital made it possible for the National Resources Commission to establish or take over roughly 130 heavy industrial enterprises and organizations between 1936 and July 1945: nine in metallurgy, seven in machines, five in electrical equipment, thirty-seven in chemicals, thirty-eight in mining, twenty-seven in energy, and seven service organizations. Among them, the commission wholly owned and managed seventy-five enterprises and organizations, partially owned and managed thirty-seven enterprises and organizations, and invested in eighteen enterprises and organizations. In addition, the majority were established between 1938 and 1942. Among those enterprises and organizations whose dates of establishment are available, four were established in 1936, three in 1937, eleven in 1938, nineteen in 1939, fifteen in 1940, twenty-four in 1941, sixteen in 1942, nine in 1943, ten in 1944, and one in early 1945.[23] After the war ended, the commission expanded its operations as it took over or confiscated enterprises controlled or managed by the Japanese and their Chinese collaborators. By 1949, the commission had 30,000 staff members and more than 600,000 workers. After 1949, some commission personnel followed the Nationalist regime to Taiwan, but many stayed in mainland China and joined the Communist government, including key commission leaders Weng Wenhao and Qian Changzhao. Virtually all commission enterprises and corporations remained state-owned enterprises or were reorganized as state-owned enterprises after the Communist takeover.

---

[21] Ziyuan weiyuanhui, 复员以来资源委员会述要 (1948), pp. 38–9.
[22] Ziyuan weiyuanhui, 复员以来资源委员会述要 (1948), p. 40.
[23] This calculation is based on "资源委员会经办事业一览表" (Tabulation of Enterprises and Organizations of the National Resources Commission), 资源委员会公报 9.2 (August 16, 1945), 43–51.

Developing and Expanding Regional State Enterprises

Regional state enterprises emerged in China toward the last decades of the nineteenth century. Until the early 1930s, however, most of these enterprises were individual entities with little connection or co-ordination between them. Many were enterprises in the ordnance industry. The creation of a national government in Nanjing in 1927, the diffusion of Sun Yat-sen's Three Doctrines of the People in various provinces, the national effort to make plans for economic reconstruction, Japanese occupation of Manchuria in 1931 and the threat it imposed to national security, and the perceived need for Self-Strengthening by provincial authorities, all contributed to new efforts to develop regional state enterprise in the early 1930s. In Shanxi province, for instance, provincial authorities began to prepare for the establishment of what would become the Northwestern Industrial Corporation in 1932. Then, during the late 1930s and early 1940s, large enterprise corporations consisting of numerous enterprises developed in sixteen provinces. Although the enterprises under these corporations varied significantly in terms of the cause of their establishment, source of investment, authority and management structure, mode of operation, and scale and scope, they were all regional state enterprises in terms of ownership, sources of investment, and stated objectives. Below I examine regional state enterprises in Guangdong, Shanxi, and Guizhou provinces, focusing on developments during the 1930s and early 1940s.

Regional State Enterprises in Guangdong Province

In Guangdong, regional state enterprises date from Xicun Cement Plant, which the governor of Guangdong established in 1906. The plant failed to succeed even after its conversion to a private enterprise in 1921.[24] After the establishment of a national government in Nanjing in 1927, and echoing national effort toward economic reconstruction, the Department of Reconstruction in Guangdong drafted in 1929 a Program of Material Reconstruction for Guangdong, which included a plan to build a new cement factory at Xicun in Guangzhou. More plans for Guangdong province and for

---

[24] Zhang Xaohui 张晓辉, 民国时期广东社会经济史 (A Social and Economic History of Guangdong Province during the Republic Period) (Guangzhou, Guangdong renmin chubanshe, 2005), pp. 180–1; Wu Zhengliang 卢征良 and Ke Weiming 柯伟明, "20 世纪 30 年代广东省营企业统制经营问题研究 – – 以广东士敏土厂为中心" (A Study of Controlled Business Operation in Guangdong Province during the 1930s with a Focus on the Guangdong Cement Plant), 民国档案 (Republic Archives) 1 (2017), 96–103.

Guangzhou municipality were made during the next two years. By the summer of 1932, Chen Jitang, governor of Guangdong province, had combined existing plans and programs into what became known as the Three-Year Administrative Plan for Guangdong Province.²⁵ Among other things, the plan envisioned the establishment of twenty-four regional state enterprises with an initial capitalization of ¥97 million. In the end, the plan's implementation resulted in the establishment of only six regional state enterprises: the Guangdong Cement Plant, two sugar refineries, the Guangdong Chemical Plant, the Guangdong Textile Plant, and the Guangdong Chemical Fertilizer Plant.²⁶ In 1936, these seven factories were capitalized at ¥6.5 million with a total of 3,860 employees.

After the Japanese occupation of Guangzhou in 1938, there was an increasing paucity of military and civilian goods, as well as rising inflation. In response, in February 1940 the provincial government created the Guangdong Wartime Trade Administration for distributing goods and administering wartime trade. The Guangdong Wartime Trade Administration succeeded in what it did and made a profit the year it was created. In June of 1941, the national government promulgated Regulations Concerning Wartime Supervision and Management of Regional Trade, which provided that provincial governments establish a corporation in accordance with regulations concerning special limited-liability corporations. Following this mandate, the provincial government reorganized the Guangdong Wartime Trade Administration into the Guangdong Enterprise Corporation (GDEC), which became operational on January 1, 1942.²⁷

Unlike its predecessor, the GDEC's business was not confined to trade; it encompassed agriculture, industry, mining, trade, and transportation, for the GDEC was designed to "promote economic reconstruction of Guangdong

---

²⁵ Lian Haowu 连浩鎏, "陈济棠据粤的由来与'广东省三年施政计划'的缘起" (How Chen Jitang Took Over Guangdong Province and the Origins of the Three-Year Administrative Plan for Guangdong Province), in 广东党史资料 (Material for Studying the History of the Chinese Communist Party in Guangdong Province) 35 (2001), 378–420; A. H.Y. Lin, "Building and Funding a Warlord Regime: The Experience of Chen Jitang in Guangdong, 1929–1936," *Modern China* 28.2 (April 2002), 177–212; Xiao Zili 肖自力, 陈济棠 (Chen Jitang) (Guangzhou, Guangdong renmin chubanshe, 2002), pp. 304–5.
²⁶ Lian Haowu 连浩鎏, "陈济棠主粤时期 (1929–1936年) 广州地区的工业发展及其启示" (Industrial Development and Its Implications When Guangdong Province Was under Chen Jitang's Control, 1926–1936), 中国社会经济史研究 (Studies in Chinese Social and Economic History) 1 (2004), 90–9.
²⁷ Ge Hongbo 葛洪波, "广东实业有限公司经营管理研究" (A Study of the Operation and Management of Guangdong Industrial Limited Liability Corporation), unpublished master's thesis, Jinan University, 2001, 7.

province."²⁸ Initially, the GDEC made the development of agriculture its top priority because of Guangdong's traditional lack of grain supply and the worsening situation of grain supply after war had erupted. Still, the GDEC began making preparations to build factories soon after its establishment. By the end of 1942, the GDEC had established a total of eight plants in machinery, communications equipment, pharmaceutical products, chemical products, construction material, sugar products, and chemical fertilizers (the factories were the Yuecang Machine Works, the Yuehua Electrical Works, the Yuede Pharmaceutical Factory, the Yueli Fertilizer Plant, the Yuexin Construction Material Plant, the Yuebei Chemical Plant, and the Yuexing Sugar Refinery).²⁹ These plants were capitalized at ¥50 million at the end of 1944.³⁰ The GDEC also developed eight farms during the same period. Unfortunately, Japanese occupation of northern Guangdong led to the confiscation and destruction of the buildings and equipment of these factories.³¹

After the Japanese surrender in August 1945, the Guangdong provincial authorities took over the plants run by the Japanese and their Chinese collaborators and placed them under the supervision and management of the Guangdong Industrial Corporation (GDIC).³² In November 1945, the provincial government made the GDIC the leading organ for developing the Guangdong economy by placing under its jurisdiction all factories and farms as well as marketing and transportation operations that aimed to increase production and improve people's welfare.³³ As of July 1948, the GDIC had a total of eight plants under its jurisdiction. They were the Xicun Cement Plant, the Shunde Sugar Refinery, the Guangzhou Textile Plant, the Guangzhou Second Textile Plant, the Xicun Brewery, the Guangzhou Ice Plant, the Meilu Jute Plant, and the Guangzhou Machine

---

²⁸ 广东企业公司章程 (Bylaws of Guangdong Enterprise Corporation), 1941, 广东省档案馆档案, 19/1/13.
²⁹ 广东企业公司三十一年度业务报告 (Report by Guangdong Enterprise Corporation on Its 1942 Business Operation), 广东省档案馆档案, 19/1/46.
³⁰ Ge, 广东实业有限公司经营管理研究, 9.
³¹ Huang Juyan 黄菊艳, 抗战时期广东经济损失研究 (A Study of Economic Damage Done to Guangdong Province during the Sino-Japanese War) (Guangzhou, Guangdong renmin chubanshe, 2005), pp. 132–3, 141–2.
³² The Guangdong Enterprise Corporation (GDEC) was renamed the Guangdong Industrial Corporation (GDIC) on 1 September 1943. See 广东实业公司业务报告, 1945 年 9 月至 1946 年 7 月 (Report by Guangdong Industrial Corporation on Its Business Operations from September 1945 to July 1946), 广东省档案馆档案, 19/1/64.
³³ 广东省政府工作报告 (Work Report of Guangdong Provincial Government for January through June 1946), p. 176, 广东省档案馆档案, zhengzhi/204. See also internal correspondence of the Guangdong Industrial Corporation dated December 4, 1945, 广东省档案馆档案, 19/1/370.

Works.³⁴ By early 1949, the number of GDIC factories had increased to ten.³⁵ Even though the number of enterprises was incredibly small, these factories had some of the best machinery and equipment of any Chinese enterprise, for most of their machinery and equipment had been imported from advanced industrial countries such as Denmark, Britain, and the United States.³⁶

In terms of source of investment, the sole and exclusive investor in the GDEC (GDIC after September 1, 1943) was the Guangdong provincial government. Correspondingly the provincial government appointed individuals to serve as the corporation's general manager and associate managers. At the same time, the provincial government appointed three superintendents to supervise the corporation's management and operation. Finally, the provincial government created a board of directors for the corporation, which consisted of the corporation's general manager and high-ranking officials of the provincial government, such as the head of the Department of Reconstruction and the Department of Finance. The superintendents and the board of directors did not meet separately, however; they held joint meetings. According to the corporation's bylaws, the board of directors ought to have met once a month. In reality, however, the board of directors only met nine times during the war.³⁷

In terms of corporate structure, the corporation created departments of general affairs, planning, operation, and transportation at the time of its establishment. Each department was subdivided into sections. In addition, the corporation had an audit office, a secretary, an engineer, and a special commissioner. In September 1943, the corporation abolished the Department of Operation and reorganized the Department of Planning into the Department of Production and the secretary into a secretariat. Another major reorganization took place in July 1946 when the board of superintendents and directors approved new Regulations on the Organizational Establishment of the Guangdong Industrial Liability Corporation, which stipulated the creation, under the corporation's general manager, of divisions of general affairs, production, business operation, and transportation; offices

---

³⁴ 广东实业公司沿革及业务状况 (The Evolution and Business Operations of Guangdong Industrial Corporation), July 1948, 广东省档案馆档案, 19/1/358.
³⁵ 广东实业公司概要 (Introduction to Guangdong Industrial Corporation), February 1949, 广东省档案馆档案, 19/1/56.
³⁶ Ge, 广东实业有限公司经营管理研究, 13.
³⁷ Ge, 广东实业有限公司经营管理研究, 22–3.

of central accounting and inspection; and a secretariat.[38] Further reorganization took place in early 1947.[39]

Regional State Enterprises in Shanxi Province

In Shanxi province, the first regional state enterprise emerged in the 1880s, but most of these enterprises had failed by the end of the first decade of the twentieth century.[40] The first major effort to develop modern industries began after Yan Xishan became governor of Shanxi province in 1917.[41] Between 1917 and 1930, the Shanxi provincial government established more than twenty regional state enterprises.[42] Although Yan Xishan was defeated by Chiang Kai-shek during the Central Plains War of 1930, he was appointed by Chiang as Shanxi's pacification commissioner after the Manchurian Incident in 1931. Yan Xishan was determined to consolidate his power and contribute to national rejuvenation by developing the Shanxi economy. In April 1932 Yan Xishan created a Planning Commission of Shanxi Province, with himself as commissioner, and began making a ten-year reconstruction plan for Shanxi province. Among other things, the Ten-Year Shanxi Reconstruction Plan called for "an increase in people's production and the development of public enterprise."[43]

Although this document served as a blueprint for Shanxi's development, planning for the Northwestern Industrial Corporation (NIC) – the government entity in charge of developing Shanxi's industrial economy through the creation of regional state enterprises – had started at the beginning of 1932, several months before Yan Xishan created the Planning Commission of Shanxi Province. Still, not until August 1933 was the NIC formally established.[44] Yan Xishan exercised direct control of the NIC in his capacity

---

[38] 广东实业有限公司组织规程 (Regulations on the Organizational Establishment of Guandgong Industrial Corporation), 广东省档案馆档案, 6/2/1592.
[39] 广东实业公司业务报告, 1946 年 10 月至 1947 年 4 月 (Report by Guangdong Industrial Corporation on Its Business Operations from October 1946 to April 1947), 广东省档案馆档案, 19/1/48.
[40] Jing Zhankui 景占魁 and Kong Fanzhu 孔繁珠, 阎锡山官僚资本研究 (A Study of Bureaucratic Capitalism under Yan Xishan) (Taiyuan, Shanxi jingji chubanshe, 1993), pp. 40–1.
[41] On how the Beijing government appointed Yan Xishan Shanxi governor, see Jing Zhankui 景占魁, 阎锡山传 (A Biography of Yan Xishan) (Beijing, Zhongguo shehui chubanshe, 2008), pp. 70–5.
[42] Jing and Kong, 阎锡山官僚资本研究, pp. 69–72.
[43] Jing Zhankui 景占魁, 阎锡山与西北实业公司 (Yan Xishan and Northwestern Industrial Corporation) (Taiyuan, Shanxi jingji chubanshe, 1991), pp. 41–4.
[44] Lian Feng 连峰, "山西地方工业化的初步尝试—以西北实业公司为例" (Early Efforts toward Industrialization in Shanxi Province: A Case Study of the

as company president.[45] According to NIC bylaws promulgated in August 1935, the NIC was "designed to promote industrial development in the northwest." The bylaws stipulated a governance structure that consisted of a central administration; an office of managers; a factory administration in charge of all eleven plants; departments of mining, technology, and research; and sections of general affairs, accounting, operation, and evaluation/review.[46] In 1936, the NIC underwent a major reorganization. The central administration and factory administration were abolished and replaced by company headquarters. Under the company headquarters were four division-level units: divisions of work affairs, operation, general affairs, and accounting. Each division was subdivided into several departments.[47]

The NIC expanded rapidly between 1933 and 1937. By the time the Sino-Japanese War broke out, the NIC had thirty-three enterprises with a total of 20,648 employees. Twenty-three of them were capitalized at ¥20.514 million. After the Japanese occupation of Taiyuan in November 1937, the Japanese military confiscated much of the NIC's machinery and equipment and shipped them to Japan and other parts of occupied China in support of the Japanese war effort.[48] The NIC managed to ship a small portion of the NIC's machinery and equipment into Sichuan before Taiyuan fell. In the summer of 1939, the NIC reinvented itself as the New Northwestern Industrial Corporation in Yichuan, Sichuan province, with Yan Xishan as company president and Peng Shihong as general manager. Given its drastic reduction of business operations, the New Northwestern Industrial Corporation had only three division-level units: divisions of work affairs, general affairs, and accounting. The earlier division of operation was now a department under the division of general affairs. The period of the Sino-Japanese War was not the best years for the NIC: it had only nine plants as of August 1945, with 3,486 employees.[49]

Despite wartime setbacks, the war's conclusion brought about the NIC's revival and expansion (the NIC began using its old name immediately after the war). The NIC not only took over a total of twenty-eight of its former

---

Northwestern Industrial Corporation), unpublished master's thesis, Shanxi University, 2012, 20.

[45] Jing, 阎锡山与西北实业公司, pp. 55–6.
[46] 西北实业公司章程 (Bylaws of the Northwestern Industrial Corporation), in Jing, 阎锡山与西北实业公司, pp. 59–62.
[47] Jing, 阎锡山与西北实业公司, p. 80.
[48] Jing, 阎锡山与西北实业公司, p. 218.
[49] Jing, 阎锡山与西北实业公司, pp. 221–2.

enterprises; it also confiscated more than a dozen private enterprises and made them part of the NIC.[50] At about the same time, the number of NIC employees increased from 14,060 in 1946 to 23,421 toward the end of 1947.[51] Due in part to the expansion of its scale and scope, the NIC revised its governance structure in early 1946 to consist of company headquarters, a secretariat, and six division-level units: divisions of industry, mining, power, operations, general affairs, and accounting, with each division subdivided into several departments.[52] The case of Shanxi reveals that a pattern of development relying on regional state enterprises had taken shape before the Communist takeover of China.

Regional State Enterprises in Guizhou Province

Unlike the early establishment of the NIC in Shanxi province, the Guizhou Enterprise Corporation (GZEC) in Guizhou province came into existence in 1939. The GZEC's establishment was a direct response to the sustained systemic crisis triggered by the outbreak of the Sino-Japanese War in the context of increasing penetration of central authority into Guizhou province. Politically, Guizhou remained under warlord control until 1935, when the Nationalist government reorganized the Guizhou provincial army and appointed Wu Zhongxin provincial governor. Economically, modern industry was virtually nonexistent in Guizhou province as late as the late 1930s. After the Sino-Japanese War erupted, the Nationalist government relocated to Chongqing in Sichuan province. Many factories, organizations, and universities also relocated to southwestern provinces, including Guizhou province. According to a Ministry of Economic Affairs official in charge of factory relocation, 452 private firms had relocated to southwestern provinces by 1942. As a result, southwestern provinces acquired a strategic position they had never occupied before the war.

In December 1937, the Nationalist government appointed Wu Dingchang (1884–1950) governor of Guizhou province. As a young man, Wu studied in Japan's Tokyo Business College before the 1911 Revolution. During the two decades from 1911 to 1931, he was actively involved in politics and business, occupying various positions such as deputy head of the Ministry of Finance (1918) and general manager of the Salt Commercial Bank (1925). He was a founding member of the National Defense Planning Commission. He

---

[50] Jing, 阎锡山与西北实业公司, p. 271–6.
[51] Jing, 阎锡山与西北实业公司, p. 290.
[52] Jing, 阎锡山与西北实业公司, pp. 280–1.

became head of the Ministry of Industries in 1935. He served in that position until his appointment as governor of Guizhou province two years later.[53]

Wu Dingchang arrived in Guiyang toward the end of December 1937. Within a year, Wu had initiated efforts to create a Guizhou enterprise corporation. According to a resolution adopted by the Commission of Guizhou Provincial Government in March 1939,

> Guizhou province has become an important base area and a center of transportation in the interior. We must exploit Guizhou resources in order to effectively contribute to the mission of war of resistance and nation building . . . However, we cannot fulfill such a heavy responsibility without creating new organizations, centralizing human and financial resources, and making long-term comprehensive plans.[54]

For the next two months, a preparatory committee drafted corporate bylaws, identified sources of investment, and determined the scope of business operations. The GZEC became operational on June 1, 1939.

Throughout the 1930s and 1940s, the GZEC relied heavily on the central government and state-run financial institutions for investment capital due to Guizhou's economic underdevelopment. On average, central government subsidies accounted for 58 percent of total Guizhou provincial revenue each year from the 1936 to the 1940 fiscal year.[55] Statistics compiled by Guizhou provincial government revealed a similar situation: on average, central government subsidies accounted for 58 percent of total Guizhou provincial revenue each year from the 1938 to the 1941 fiscal year.[56] To realize its objective of exploiting Guizhou resources and developing Guizhou industries, the GZEC had to rely on the central government and state-run financial institutions for investment capital.

At the time of its founding, the GZEC was capitalized at ¥6 million, and much of that came from provincial and central governments and state-run banks. The Guizhou provincial government invested ¥1.23 million (20.5 percent). The Ministry of Economic Affairs provided ¥1.25 million (20.83 percent). The Bank of China, the Bank of Communications, and the Farmers' Bank of China between them contributed ¥3.50 million (58.33 percent).

---

[53] Zhuang Kuming 莊焜明, "吴鼎昌与抗战时期贵州经济建设 (一九三八至一九四四)" (Wu Dingchang and Guizhou Economic Reconstruction during the Sino-Japanese War, 1938–1944), 近代中国 (Modern China) 133 (1999), 117–39.
[54] 贵州省档案馆档案, M1/374, March 1939.
[55] Ding Daojian 丁道谦, 贵州地方财政概况 (A Survey of Guizhou Financial Conditions) (Guiyang, Guizhou minyi yuekanshe, 1949), p. 23.
[56] Wu Dingchang 吴鼎昌, 黔政五年 (Administrative Experience in Guizhou over the Past Five Years) (Guiyang, Guizhou sheng zhengfu bianyin, 1943), p. 4.

Private individuals subscribed ¥20,000 (0.34 percent). Despite the relatively large initial capitalization, the expansion of business activities, inflation pressure, and the lack of working capital prompted the GZEC to increase its capital to ¥10 million in June 1940, to ¥20 million in May 1942, to ¥30 million in February 1943, and to ¥50 million in August 1947.[57] The lion's share of investment capital continued to come from provincial and central governments and state-run banks after each capital infusion. At the same time, given its stated objective of exploiting Guizhou resources and developing Guizhou industries, the GZEC made the development of industrial and mining enterprises its top investment priority.

As someone who had discussed economic issues and engaged in business activities for more than twenty years, Wu Dingchang was determined to avoid the pitfalls of state-owned enterprises by requiring the GZEC to create a corporate structure. In a May 1939 speech, Wu stated that the provincial government could adopt one of two forms for organizing planned economic activities: joint government–merchant management or joint management by the central government and the provincial government. After considerable deliberations, the provincial government adopted the form of joint government–merchant management because Wu and others believed that business growth required continuity that the formal administrative bureaucracy could not provide.[58] As Wu explained, it would take a long time before the planned enterprises could generate returns. Given frequent personnel transfers within government administration, however, it was difficult to ensure personnel continuity and policy consistency. What they needed was a business organization that was impervious to frequent changes of government personnel to assure continuity of business operations. The GZEC was meant to be such an organization.

Following Wu Dingchang's plan, the GZEC was entrusted with the responsibility of exploiting Guizhou's resources and developing Guizhou's industry, with state-run banks and Guizhou provincial government providing most of the investment capital. On the other hand, following the provisions of the 1929 Company Law, the GZEC created a corporate structure that consisted of a shareholder meeting, a board of directors, a standing board of directors, a team of managers, and divisions and departments under the general manager. One could argue that the GZEC developed multiple

---

[57] 贵州省档案馆档案, MG41/36, November 1949.
[58] Wu Dingchang 吴鼎昌, 花溪闲笔 (Reminiscences of My Time in Charge of Guizhou Provincial Administration, 1938–1940) (Guiyang, Guizhou ribaoshe, 1940), pp. 2, 24–5.

identities: it was a regional state enterprise in terms of ownership and source of investment. It possessed the core characteristics of a modern Western shareholding company because of its corporate structure. And it was a holding company or investment management company seen from the perspective of capital organization and mode of operation.

Following such a development strategy, the GZEC divided enterprises associated with it into "wholly owned," "partially owned," and "sponsored" enterprises. Wholly owned enterprises were enterprises in which the corporation held all equity as well as appointing key management personnel. Partially owned enterprises were enterprises in which the corporation held more than 50 percent of all equity. By contrast, sponsored enterprises referred to enterprises in which the corporation held less than 50 percent of all equity. As a result, the corporation did not exercise control over sponsored enterprises; instead, it enjoyed rights and privileges similar to those of other shareholders of the sponsored enterprises.[59]

The GZEC had thirteen units at the time of its establishment in 1939. The number of units increased to twenty-two in 1940, twenty-four in 1941, and twenty-eight in 1942. The number of units began to decrease after 1942, to twenty-six in 1943, twenty in 1944, eighteen in 1945, and sixteen in 1946. After 1946, however, the downward trend was reversed: the number of units increased to seventeen in 1948 and twenty in 1949.[60]

The GZEC sustained a loss of ¥25,252 in 1939 (¥8,417 in 1936 constant price).[61] However, the corporation earned a profit every year for the next six years, reaping the largest amount of annual profit in 1941: ¥692,393 in 1940 (¥86,549 in 1936 constant price); ¥2,525,854 in 1941 (¥120,278 in 1936 constant price); ¥3,239,772 in 1942 (¥50,621 in 1936 constant price); ¥4,639,973 in 1943 (¥18,634 in 1936 constant price); ¥7,844,044 in 1944 (¥10,147 in 1936 constant price); ¥9,439,609 in 1945 (¥3,680 in 1936 constant price).[62] As late as 1947, in part because of the effect of inflation, the corporation made a profit of ¥2,310,542,515 (¥23,376 in 1936 constant price).[63]

[59] He Jiwu 何辑五, 十年来贵州经济建设 (Guizhou Economic Reconstruction for the Last Decade) (Nanjing, Nanjing yinshuguan, 1947), pp. 60–1.
[60] 贵州省档案馆档案, MG41/36, November 1949; MG 41/16, 1942; 贵州企业季刊 (Guizhou Enterprise Quarterly) 1.2 (February 1943), 90–106; 重庆市档案馆档案, 0101/4112, June 1943; 0101/1308, 1944; 0101/1452, June 1948.
[61] 贵州省档案馆档案, MG 41/16, 1942.
[62] 贵州省档案馆档案, MG 41/16, 1942; MG 41/23, 1942; 重庆市档案馆档案, 0101/4112, 1943.
[63] Guizhousheng danganguan 贵州省档案馆 (ed.), 贵州企业股份有限公司 (Archival Materials of the Guizhou Enterprise Limited Liability Corporation) (Guiyang, Guizhou renmin chubanshe, 2003), pp. 503–29.

After the Communist takeover of Guiyang, the Chinese Communist Party (CCP) dismantled the GZEC's corporate structure and replaced it with a bureaucratic structure. It also removed retained staff from positions of authority and imposed control over them. Still, Guizhou's regional state enterprises continued to expand as regional state enterprises under CCP authority and control. While the CCP dismantled the enterprises' corporate structure and created a bureaucratic structure, it was less successful in destroying the connective tissues that sustained, bound, and gave shape and support to Guizhou's regional state enterprises. Contrary to conventional wisdom, the sovietization of Chinese enterprise management was not a sudden process; rather, the national campaign to transplant the Soviet model during the 1950s represented the culmination of efforts that had begun two decades earlier. And, despite its efforts to implement Soviet-style economic accounting by discrediting Western-inspired practices, the CCP continued to rely on an indigenized Western accounting system as late as the mid-1950s. Finally, the CCP inherited and expanded the institutions of social services and welfare that had developed during the Sino-Japanese War. In short, the changes in Guizhou's regional economic institutions after 1949 were simultaneously revolutionary and evolutionary.[64] In a paper presented at the Joint Conference of the Association for Asian Studies and the International Convention of Asian Scholars held in Honolulu, Hawaii in 2011, I described the changes in Guizhou's regional economic institutions after 1949 as "transforlutionary" in light of the fact that these changes were characterized by both transformation and evolution.[65]

The Significance of Public Enterprise in Overall Industrial Development

How significant was the expansion of central and regional state enterprises in China's overall industrial development? To address this question, I turn now to a comparison between public and private enterprise in heavy industries.[66]

---

[64] M.L. Bian, "Redefining the Chinese Revolution: The Transformation and Evolution of Guizhou's Regional State Enterprises, 1937–1957," *Modern China* 41.3 (May 2015), 313–50.

[65] As I explained elsewhere, no word in the English language is capable of capturing the sense of transformative and evolutionary change that occurs simultaneously. We can denote this type of change by coining a new word – transforlution – that combines the meaning of transformation and evolution. This type of change is transforlutionary by definition. See M.L. Bian, "Interpreting Enterprise, State, and Society: A Critical Review of the Literature in Modern Chinese Business History, 1978–2008," *Frontiers of History in China* 6.3 (September 2011), 423–62.

[66] Public enterprise included both central state enterprises and regional state enterprises.

State Enterprises during the First Half of the Twentieth Century

I will first discuss the structure of Chinese industry and the position of heavy industry within that structure before the Sino-Japanese War. I will then compare public enterprise with private enterprise in heavy industry during the war.

In the spring of 1933, the National Defense Planning Commission launched a survey of Chinese industry as part of its mission of resource investigation. Between April 1933 and October 1934, a group of researchers from the China Economic Statistics Institute inspected firms in fourteen provinces and more than 120 municipalities and counties. The statistics they gathered were then compiled and published by the National Resources Commission in early 1937 as a *Report on the Conditions of Chinese Industry*. The report did not cover Gansu, Xinjiang, Yunnan, Guizhou, Ningxia, and Qinghai provinces; nor did it include Manchuria, which was under Japanese occupation. Moreover, the report excluded government arsenals and firms that did not use mechanized power and employed fewer than thirty workers.[67] Still, the *Report on the Conditions of Chinese Industry* was the most comprehensive industrial census for prewar China.

The census takers found that China had 2,435 factories under Chinese ownership, which had a capital of ¥406,872,634 and employed 435,257 workers.[68] At the time of the census, the Chinese economy was predominantly private, and the role of the state sector, though increasing over time, remained small. Within what was essentially a market-oriented private economy, light industry dominated. Food/beverage/tobacco and textile products made up more than 70 percent of the total output of China's manufacturing industry in 1933, whereas basic metals (iron and steel) and other metal products such as machinery accounted for less than 9 percent.[69]

Contemporary statistics from the Ministry of Industries also show the dominant position that light industry occupied in the overall structure of Chinese industry. Available sources reveal that, between 1932 and 1937, the number of registered factories reached 3,885, with a capital of ¥377,848,000 and employing 457,143 workers. As far as the proportions between heavy and light industry are concerned, light industry (such as the food processing, textiles, and chemical industries) accounted for 3,305 factories or 85.1 percent of the total, ¥308,643,000 in capital or 81.68 percent, and 432,049 workers or

---

[67] Liu Dajun 刘大钧 (ed.), 中国工业调查报告 (Report on the Conditions of Chinese Industry) (Shanghai, Jingji tongji yanjiu suo, 1937), vol. 1, pp. 1–5.
[68] Liu, 中国工业调查报告, vol. 2, pp. 33–64.
[69] T.G. Rawski, *Economic Growth in Prewar China* (Berkeley, University of California Press, 1989), pp. 3, 85, 360–1.

94.5 percent. In sharp contrast, heavy industry (such as the hydroelectric generating, metallurgical, machine, electrical, and ordnance industries) accounted for only 580 factories or 14.83 percent of the total, ¥69,205,000 in capital or 18.32 percent, and 25,094 workers or 5.49 percent.[70]

Within the industrial structure dominated by light industry, the proportion of public enterprise was even smaller than that of private enterprise. The *Report on the Conditions of Chinese Industry* notes that out of the 2,435 factories surveyed, only sixty-six were public enterprises, and most of them were in the hands of provincial authorities.[71] Data compiled in 1935 by the Ministry of Industries reveal an even clearer picture of the share of public enterprise. The data show a total of seventy-two public enterprises in China, with ¥30,297,726 in capital, 40,669 workers, 38,779 horsepower, and ¥74,828,733 in value of output. Among them, fifty-one were in either heavy industry or the transportation industry. These fifty-one enterprises had ¥18,075,979 in capital, 26,966 workers, 33,169 horsepower, and ¥61,870,831 in value of output. What is more, of all the public enterprises, only seventeen were in heavy industry proper (the metallurgical, metals, machine, and energy industries), with ¥12,320,992 in capital, 8,258 workers, 23,376 horsepower, and ¥53,365,723 in value of output.[72] The data show that during the mid-1930s, public enterprises in heavy industry made up only 2.9 percent of all factories, 17.8 percent of all capital, and 32.9 percent of all workers.[73]

The decade between 1935 and 1945 witnessed a fundamental change in the existing position of public and private enterprise. According to a statistical survey conducted by the Bureau of Statistics of the Ministry of Economic Affairs, the relative position of public and private enterprise had changed radically by 1942. The result is more revealing when we compare the average capital, number of workers, and power equipment in public and private enterprise in heavy industry. By 1942 public enterprise had clearly overtaken private enterprise in the amount of capital, number

---

[70] Weng Wenhao 翁文灏, "中国工商经济的回顾与前瞻" (The Retrospect and Prospect of Chinese Industrial and Commercial Economy), 资源委员会公报 5.2 (August 16, 1943), pp. 59–68; Huang Bingwei 黄秉维, "五十年来之中国工矿业" (Chinese Industry and Mining in the Last Fifty Years), in Zhongguo tongshang yinhang 中国通商银行 (ed.), 五十年来之中国经济 (The Chinese Economy in the Last Fifty Years, 1896–1947) (Shanghai, Zhongguo tongshang yinhang bian, 1947), reprint (Taipei, Wenhai chubanshe, n.d.), p. 173.

[71] Liu, 中国工业调查报告, vol. 2, pp. 33–64.

[72] Guomin zhengfu zhujichu tongjiju 国民政府主计处统计局 (ed.), 中华民国统计提要 (Statistical Abstract of Republican China) (Chongqing, Guomin zhengfu zhujichu tongjiju, 1940), Table 50, p. 85.

[73] Weng, 中国工商经济的回顾与前瞻, pp. 59–68; Huang, 五十年来之中国工矿业, p. 173; 中华民国统计提要, p. 85.

of workers, and power equipment. On average the amount of capital of a public enterprise was eighteen times that of a private enterprise, the number of workers 3.7 times that of a private enterprise, and the power equipment 2.2 times that of a private enterprise.[74] It is estimated that by 1942, the National Resources Commission already had under its control ¥8 billion, which constituted roughly 40 percent of the modern industrial capital in China's interior.[75]

Statistics on the increase in output of major products in heavy industry provide further evidence of the dominant position that public enterprise achieved during the Sino-Japanese War. The output of public enterprise in some industries was very small one year after the war began, yet by the time the war ended their share of total output had increased dramatically. For instance, in 1938 the share of output of the state-owned iron and steel industries was only 5.8 percent and 20 percent respectively. By the end of 1945, however, their share of output had increased to 64.8 percent and 96.4 percent respectively. Moreover, the manufacturing of many heavy industrial products was from the very beginning a monopoly of state-owned industries. Finally, the average figures of public enterprise's share of product show a steady increase during the eight-year period: 55.6 percent in 1938, 61.9 percent in 1939, 62.7 percent in 1940, 65.5 percent in 1941, 70.5 percent in 1942, 75.5 percent in 1943, 77.9 percent in 1944, and 79.9 percent in 1945.[76]

To summarize, all the evidence points to a significant expansion of state-owned heavy industry during the war. One could even argue that public enterprise's share of product in heavy industry, as well as light industry, expanded significantly during the war. After analyzing the output statistics of seventeen major heavy and light industrial products, Xu Dixin and Wu Chengming concluded that public enterprise's share of product was 21.2 percent in 1938. By 1944, however, public enterprise's share of product had reached 53.7 percent.[77] In other words, public enterprise had clearly achieved

---

[74] Guomin zhengfu jingjibu tongjiju 国民政府经济部统计局 (ed.), 后方工业概况统计 (A Statistical Survey of Chinese Industry) (Chongqing, Guomin zhengfu jingjibu tongjiju, 1943), p. 11.
[75] Wu Taichang 吴太昌 et al., 中国国家资本的历史分析 (A Historical Analysis of China's State Capital) (Beijing, Zhongguo shehui kexue chubanshe, 2012), p. 232.
[76] Wu Taichang 吴太昌, "抗战时期国民党国家资本在工矿业的垄断地位及其与民营资本比较" (The Monopolistic Position of the Nationalist State Capital in Industry and Mining and Its Comparison with Private Capital during the Sino-Japanese War), 中国经济史研究 (Studies in Chinese Economic History) 3 (September 1987), 133–50.
[77] The seventeen products used in their estimates are coal, pig iron, steel, nonferrous metals, petroleum, electricity, alcohol, gas substitutes, acid, alkali, cement, machinery and electrical products, cotton yarn, cotton cloth, flour, matches, and paper. See Xu Dixin 许涤新 and Wu Chengming 吴承明 (eds.), 新民主主义革命时期的中国

a dominant position by the end of the Sino-Japanese War.[78] After 1949, public enterprises – central state enterprises and regional state enterprises – would serve as the foundation for the CCP effort to bring about China's industrialization and modernization for the rest of the twentieth century.[79]

Further Reading

Bian Linan 卞历南, 制度变迁的逻辑：现代中国国营企业制度之形成 (The Dynamics of Institutional Change: The Making of the State Enterprise System in Modern China) (Hangzhou, Zhejiang daxue chubanshe, 2011).

Bian Linan 卞历南, 西方学界最近 40 年对中国企业史研究的述评 (A Critical Examination of Western Studies of Chinese Business and Economic History, 1978–2018) 经济社会史评论 (Social & Economic History Review) 16.4 (November 2018), 104–24.

Bian, M.L., "Explaining the Dynamics of Change: Transformation and Evolution of China's Public Economy through War, Revolution, and Peace, 1928–2008," in B. Naughton and K.S. Tsai (eds.), *State Capitalism, Institutional Adaptation and the Chinese Miracle* (Cambridge, Cambridge University Press, 2015), pp. 201–22.

Bian, M.L., *The Making of the State Enterprise System in Modern China: The Dynamics of Institutional Change* (Cambridge, MA, Harvard University Press, 2005).

Bian, M.L., "Redefining the Chinese Revolution: The Transformation and Evolution of Guizhou's Regional State Enterprises, 1937–1957," *Modern China* 41 (May 2015), 313–50.

Bian, M.L., "The Sino-Japanese War and the Formation of the State Enterprise System in China: A Case Study of the Dadukou Iron and Steel Works, 1938–1945," *Enterprise & Society* 3.1 (March 2002), 80–123.

Kirby, W.C., "Engineering China: Birth of the Developmental State, 1928–1937," in W.-H. Yeh (ed.), *Becoming Chinese: Passages to Modernity and Beyond* (Berkeley, University of California Press, 2000), pp. 137–60.

Wu Taichang 吴太昌, 抗战时期国民党国家资本在工矿业的垄断地位及其与民营资本比较 (The Monopolistic Position of Nationalist State Capital in Industry and Mining and Its Comparison with Private Capital during the Sino-Japanese War), 中国经济史研究 (Studies in Chinese Economic History) 3 (September 1987), 133–50.

资本主义 (Chinese Capitalism during the Period of New Democratic Revolution, 1921–1949) (Beijing, Renmin chubanshe, 1993), pp. 521, 541–5.

[78] M.L. Bian, *The Making of the State Enterprise System in Modern China: The Dynamics of Institutional Change* (Cambridge, MA, Harvard University Press, 2005), p. 75; Zhang Zhongmin 张忠民 and Zhu Ting 朱婷, 南京国民政府时期的国有企业 (A Study of State-Owned Enterprises in Republican China, 1927–1949) (Shanghai, Shanghai caijing daxue chubanshe, 2007), p. 167.

[79] M.L. Bian, "Explaining the Dynamics of Change: Transformation and Evolution of China's Public Economy through War, Revolution, and Peace, 1928–2008," in B. Naughton and K.S. Tsai (eds.), *State Capitalism, Institutional Adaptation and the Chinese Miracle* (Cambridge, Cambridge University Press, 2015), pp. 201–22; Bian, "Transforlution and Hybridization: Reinterpreting Changes in China's Public Economy, 1918–2018," unpublished book manuscript.

Wu Taichang et al. 吴太昌等人合著, 中国国家资本的历史分析 (A Historical Analysis of China's State Capital) (Beijing, Zhongguo shehui kexue chubanshe, 2012).

Xu, Dixin 许涤新 and Wu Chengming 吴承明 (eds.), 新民主主义革命时期的中国资本主义 (Chinese Capitalism during the Period of New Democratic Revolution, 1921–1949) (Beijing, Renmin chubanshe, 1993).

Xue Yi 薛毅, 国民政府资源委员会研究 (A Study of the National Resources Commission) (Beijing, Shehui kexue wenxian chubanshe, 2005).

Zhang Shouguang 张守广, 大变局: 抗战时期的后方企业 (Great Change: A Study of Business Enterprises in China's Interior during the Sino-Japanese War) (Nanjing, Jiangsu renmin chubanshe, 2008).

Zhang Shouguang 张守广, 抗战大后方工业研究 (A Study of Industry in China's Interior during the Sino-Japanese War) (Chongqing, Chongqing chubanshe, 2012).

Zhang Zhongmin 张忠民 and Zhu Ting, 南京国民政府时期的国有企业 (A Study of State-Owned Enterprises in Republican China, 1927–1949) (Shanghai, Shanghai caijing daxue chubanshe, 2007).

Zhao Xingsheng 赵兴盛, 传统经验与现代理想: 南京国民政府时期的国营工业研究 (A Study of State-Owned Industries in Republican China) (Jinan, Qilu shushe, 2004).

7
Money and the Macro-economy

DAN LI AND HONGZHONG YAN

Introduction

An understanding of how the money market developed is vital because money serves as the blood of an economy. From 1800 to 1937, the Chinese money market transitioned from a highly fragmented bimetallic system to a gradually integrated silver yuan system in tandem with a silver-backed fiduciary paper-money system until a fiat money system was established. As a consequence, the economy became increasingly monetized as the growth rate of the money supply gradually surpassed the overall economic growth rate without evident inflation pressure on general price trends. This development resulted both from the efforts of governments and private institutions in response to various types of shock separately and from the outcomes of competition and co-operation between the two stakeholders over time.

During the mid-Ming dynasty (1364–1644), a "parallel bimetallism" monetary standard consisting of silver and copper was established in China. Unlike the bimetallic system consisting of gold and silver in the history of many European countries – in which the two precious metals were usually minted with rates regulated by states or by the market – silver and copper in China complemented (rather than substituted) each other. In China, (unminted) silver bullion served as the major medium of exchange in wholesale commerce, long-distance trade, and tax payment, while copper cash (*zhiqian* 制钱)[1] served as a currency in petty exchange. High transaction costs led to this functional exclusiveness of silver and copper in the market: in retail, the cost of assessing silver bullion probably easily surpassed the value of petty exchange; likewise, low-valued copper cash was too expensive and weighty

---

We are grateful to the editor, Debin Ma, for his insightful comments and suggestions for improving this chapter.

[1] Copper cash were moulded as a circle with a square hole in the center, through which a string could go to tie them together.

to be used for wholesale and/or long-distance trade. Hence, to serve different market levels and purposes, people had to exchange copper cash for silver bullion or vice versa at an exchange rate that fluctuated according to relative changes in the supply and demand of the two commodity monies.

The Qing government (1644–1912) managed the supply of copper cash but left the monetization of silver entirely in the hands of private institutions. China did not have many silver lodes, and foreign silver had been flowing into China since the sixteenth century through international trade in the private sector. Soon the business sector welcomed silver bullion as a high-denomination means of payment, and the government further accommodated and promoted the silverization of the economy by accepting silver for taxes and distributing it for expenditures. Hence silver weight (tael or *yinliang* 银两)[2] evolved into one of the most important units of account until 1933, when the Republican government abolished it. However, there were no unified silver bullion standards or tael units because they varied across different locations.[3]

Overall, the Chinese bimetallic monetary system was split into manifold regional currencies, which hindered interregional trade and hence slowed economic development. The journey towards an integrated money market began with the import of Spanish pesos (along with silver bullion), namely Spanish silver coins minted in Mexico. By the early 1800s, Spanish pesos had become so widely circulated that they became a new de facto monetary standard, expressed in Chinese as yuan,[4] and gradually complemented or replaced silver bullion as a means of payment in commerce. Inspired by the success of foreign silver coins, the Qing government started to mint silver coins in its late years to compete with foreign coins. The official silver coins minted by the Beiyang government finally gained a foothold in the money market during the warlord era (1912–1927) with help from the private financial sector, which tirelessly promoted the circulation of official silver coins.[5]

---

[2] In Chinese, it is called the *liang* 两, which was about thirty-eight grams of silver in the Qing dynasty.
[3] H.B. Morse, *The Trade and Administration of the Chinese Empire* (London, Longmans, Green, and Co., 1908), pp. 145–7. As observed by Morse, in many cases, the weight "tael" even had several standards in one locality.
[4] R. von Glahn, "Foreign Silver Coins in the Market Culture of Nineteenth-Century China," *International Journal of Asian Studies* 4.1 (2007), 51–78.
[5] "Beiyang government" refers to the Republican government with a capital in Beijing from 1912 to 1927. The Warlord Era in China featured a nominal central government in Beijing. There were approximately 1,300 warlords, who controlled provinces, counties, or only several districts, depending on their power. Scholars have not reached a consensus on the exact dates of the Warlord Era.

Despite the turmoil in our study period, including numerous riots, civil wars, foreign invasions, regime shifts, natural disasters, and other chaos, the Chinese pace towards money market integration due to the spread of official silver coin was unstoppable. A key contributor to (and benefactor of) this process was the banking sector. The banking sector adopted the silver yuan (or dollar, yinyuan 银元) as the most important unit of account for business. Both foreign and domestic banks competed to issue banknotes convertible with silver yuan under a free banking system; hence the money supply – mainly the banknote supply – increased. Moreover, the domestic banks aggressively branched across the nation, which made interregional money transfer, exchange, and remittance – mainly denominated in silver yuan – more affordable for businesses. Therefore a nationwide and integrated money market came into being. In 1935, China went off silver and adopted a fiat money standard.

As money market integration continued, there was an obvious power shift in money supply from the private financial sector to the government. However, this progress was far from linear, with both progress and twists resulting from co-operation and competition between the government and the private sector in the face of constraints and shocks. Examples of the interplay between the two vividly show how the government gradually took control of the monetary sector at the expense of private institutions, which eventually lost ground.

An increasingly unified and expanding money market benefited economic growth in prewar China from at least four perspectives. First, it largely reduced transaction costs, which facilitated the commercialization of the Chinese economy, and trade led to specialization; second, it mobilized the very scarce savings of an underdeveloped country to support the development of a modern industrial sector, which was small but sowed the seeds for Chinese industrialization until the Second Sino-Japanese War in 1937; third, the expansion and integration of the money market gradually lowered the interest rate, which facilitated more investment and capital formation for economic growth; finally, the increasing supply of paper money alleviated monetary shocks caused by the changing market conditions of the monetary metal silver, which was a commodity to the rest of the world, and stabilized economic development.

The Chinese experience in the money market from 1800 to 1937 is of particular interest because it provides a typical case of how a traditional fragmented bimetallic money market transitioned to a modern centralized fiat money system. This process includes how the money market was affected by China's participation in the world trade network, how modern monetary and financial technologies spread in a large but underdeveloped economy, how local private institutions took opportunities to improve business practice and develop a modern banking industry from scratch, and how various governments managed the monetary system in the face of a series of internal and external challenges. This chapter will outline not only the development process but also how a better monetary system works well for economic development.

Three Media of Exchange

This section presents the main nature and characteristics of the major Chinese currencies of copper, silver, and paper money and summarizes the evolution and changing importance of the three media of exchange from 1800 to 1937.

Copper

The Qing court actively controlled the supply of copper cash. Its system for minting copper cash consisted of two central minting bureaus – the Bao Quan Mint (宝泉局) and the Bao Yuan Mint (宝元局) affiliated with the Ministry of Revenue (hubu 户部) and the Board of Work (gongbu 工部) respectively – and approximately eighteen local mints in the early nineteenth century.[6] The smallest cash was called one wen (文) and weighed approximately five grams.[7] Usually, the larger the denomination was, the heavier the cash. A string could go through the square hole in the cash and so they could be tied together. One thousand wen could be tied together in what was called one guan (贯)[8] and exchanged for approximately one silver tael around the year 1800.[9]

Copper cash might have varied in pattern but they were always inscribed with the denomination, the imperial reign name at the time of production, and the mint of origin. Coins minted by a local government were confined to

---

[6] The number of local mints could vary over time. Usually there was one mint in each province.
[7] The weight of one wen varied slightly over time too. For details, please see Peng Xinwei 彭信威, 中国货币史 (The Monetary History of China) (Shanghai, Shanghai People's Publishing House, 1987; first published 1954), pp. 557–74.
[8] It could also be called one diao 吊 or chuan 串.
[9] See Table 4 in Hongzhong Yan, "Economic Growth and Fluctuation in the Early Qing Dynasty: From the Perspective of Monetary Circulation," Frontiers of History in China 4.2 (2009), 221–64. The conversion rate fluctuated over time.

circulation in the province of their origin and were rarely taken outside provincial borders. The cash produced by the two central minting bureaus achieved relatively wide circulation since the government distributed them, together with silver ingots, to cover fiscal expenditures on troops, public projects, construction, and other items in minute detail. The total output of cash in 1865 was approximately 2.46 million *guan*, 55 percent of which were produced by the two central mints.[10] Counterfeiting was illegal and subject to severe punishment (e.g. beheading). Nonetheless, when severe debasement occurred, the counterfeited copper cash flooded in, which drove the seigniorage revenue for the government down to a negligible level. It was private competition that effectively constrained the extent of the government's power to debase copper cash for a prolonged period.[11]

In 1900, Guangdong province first imported machines to make copper coins (*tongyuan* 铜元): unlike copper cash, copper coins had no square hole in the center. Machine-made copper coins looked more delicate than cash, were difficult to counterfeit, and gained popularity in the market. Many other provinces joined Guangdong in producing machine-made coins. Approximately 97 to 98 percent of the machine-made coins in circulation were inscribed with a domination value – "1 cash is equivalent to 10 wen." Although it was possible for machine-made coins to be more standardized, there were numerous types of coin circulating in the market, varying across regional and even local markets.[12] Overall, the market in copper currency was fragmented despite being under government control and regardless of what production technology was adopted.

The importance of copper currency (cash and coins together) in the total money supply declined over time: during the 1800s–1850s, the share of copper currency in the total money supply was approximately 25 percent,[13] declining to merely 3–4 percent in the 1930s.[14] On the one hand, this was due to the increase in the supply of paper money over time (to be described later), which significantly enlarged the monetary base; on the other hand, since 1914 the Beiyang government started to mint silver coins, and, in addition to the one-yuan coin,[15] it minted silver coins with denominations of fifty cents, twenty

---

[10] E. Kann, *The Currencies of China* (Beijing, Commerce Publishing House, 1926), p. 411.
[11] S. Qian and L. Wu, "Who Defended Monetary Stability in a Specie Regime? Evidence from the Chinese History," *Frontiers of Economics in China* 13.3 (2018), 397–435.
[12] Peng, *Monetary History*, pp. 569–73.   [13] Yan, "Economic Growth," 221–64.
[14] T.G. Rawski, *Economic Growth in Prewar China* (Berkeley, University of California Press, 1989), Table c16, p. 394.
[15] The one-yuan official silver coin was nicknamed "Yuan's Big Head" because the image of the head of President Yuan Shikai was inscribed on it.

cents and ten cents. As the official silver coins gained popularity across the nation (see below), silver dimes and cents even eroded the realm of copper currency as small change.

Silver

Although the Qing court left the supply of silver to the market, it promoted the use of silver as a medium of exchange through taxation and fiscal expenditure. Except for some tribute grain being paid in kind, all other taxes, including land tax, salt tax, tariffs, and customs duties, were paid in silver. For government expenditures, silver, together with rice and copper cash, was used to pay the salaries of government officials, soldiers, workers hired for public projects, stipends for royal family members, government and military expenditures, royal expenses, and so on. Despite the ratio of the components of silver, rice, and copper cash varying for different purposes and over time, silver was no doubt the most important means of payment.[16] On the eve of the first Opium War (1840–1842), 74 percent of total fiscal revenues worth 65.8 million silver taels was paid in silver, and 84 percent of the total fiscal expenditure of 46 million taels was paid out in silver.[17] Fiscal silverization helped make silver, despite its not being under government control, the most influential means of payment and unit of account. Fiscal silverization accompanied the silverization of economic activities overall. Up until the 1840s–1850s, 75 percent of the total money supply of 436 million silver taels was silver, and the rest was copper cash.[18]

However, instead of forming a unified monetary standard, the silver system became divided into manifold regional currencies: the types and qualities of silver varied across the nation. Hence the value of a "tael" in one place differed from that in other places, and numerous exchange rates among "taels" in different places were needed for interregional trade. Native financial institutions emerged, first mainly to assess the quality of silver bullion by putting a stamp on it and to exchange "taels" across localities. Later, they extended their business scope to taking deposits, making loans, remitting and transferring money across the nation, and extending credit by issuing paper monetary instruments mainly backed by silver. The most

---

[16] Yan, "Economic Growth," 221–64.
[17] Revenue and expenditure in rice were 80 million and 34.6 million *dan* (a unit of rice of approximately fifty kilograms) respectively. The rice price was estimated at 2.16 taels per *dan*. Peng, *Monetary History*, p. 851. See also Tang Xianglong 汤象龙, 中国近代财政经济史论文选 (Selected Papers on Modern Chinese Financial and Economic History) (Sichuan, Southwestern University of Finance and Economics Press, 1987), pp. 204, 221.
[18] Yan, "Economic Growth," 221–64.

important native financial institutions in the early nineteenth century were called *qianzhuang* 钱庄, known as "native banks," which differed from the Western-style modern banks that emerged in China later.

In addition to silver bullion, Spanish pesos, namely Spanish silver coins (*yinyuan*) minted in Mexico, flooded into China and achieved popularity in southern coastal provinces. These silver coins formed a satisfactory medium of exchange and enjoyed a premium generally more than 30 to 40 percent over their intrinsic value.[19] By the 1820s, Chinese merchants were occasionally found to export silver bullion in exchange for foreign silver coins to make a profit out of this premium.[20] In the 1850s, the *lijin* 釐金 duty, an internal transit duty on commodities, emerged and was collected in silver coins instead of bullion, which was different from other government taxes.[21] Consequently, the transit duties officially promoted the usage and spread of coins in commercial activities at the time.

Inspired by the success of foreign silver coins, the Guangdong government started to mint silver coins in 1889. However, the silver coins minted by the provincial government did not have the prestige of Spanish pesos: not because they contained less silver but because they were easier to counterfeit than Spanish pesos. Chinese craftsmen could easily produce coins identical to government-minted coins with less silver content, but they failed to mimic the fine details of the pattern and the Spanish letters inscribed on the foreign coins. The debased counterfeited coins drove the full-bodied official coins out of circulation. In the end, the status of foreign silver coins in the Chinese market remained unshaken until the early twentieth century.

In 1914, the Beiyang government started to mint silver coins, which circulated together with foreign silver coins in the market. Surprisingly, official coins gradually gained a foothold in the market, despite it being a highly fragmented era politically – the warlord era. Official coins became the most popular currency in the market: in 1924, approximately 960 million silver yuan circulated in China, and less than 4 percent of them were foreign coins.[22] This success was partially due to good timing: the foreign silver coins minted after Spanish American independence lost their universal standard and thus became less appealing to Chinese merchants, and the import of

---

[19] For details, see Morse, *Trade and Administration*, pp. 163–5.
[20] Von Glahn, "Foreign Silver Coins," 51–78.
[21] See Kaske and Lin's chapter in this volume for details.
[22] See the survey conducted by the Domestic Exchange Office of the Shanghai Commercial and Savings Bank 上海商业储蓄银行国内汇兑处, 国内商业汇兑要览 (An Overview of Domestic Commercial Exchange) (Shanghai, Shanghai Commercial and Savings Bank, 1925).

foreign coins dropped.[23] Moreover, after Mexico left the silver standard in 1903, it almost stopped minting silver coins. The shortfalls in foreign coins were readily filled by high-quality and standardized official coins, which were produced by machines at the time and were more resistant to counterfeiting.

Paper Money

Although China pioneered the large-scale circulation of paper money as early as the Northern Song dynasty (960–1127), its modern vintage started in 1845 following the entry of foreign banks,[24] which began to issue banknotes circulating in treaty ports and some foreign spheres of influence. These notes were backed either by silver – namely banknote holders could exchange notes for silver ingots in taels or coins in yuan in the issuing bank – or by foreign paper money, such as Hong Kong dollars,[25] Russian roubles, or Japanese yen. The Commercial Bank of China, the first modern Chinese bank, established in 1896, also rushed to issue banknotes two years later. More newly established domestic modern banks entered the arena of paper money issuance.

It was not until the waning years of the Qing dynasty that the court realized that it was necessary to consolidate the right to issue paper money in the hands of the government and established a government bank – the Bank of the Great Qing[26] – in 1905, on which was bestowed the right to represent the government to issue paper money and manage the national treasury. Another government bank, the Bank of Communications, was set up in 1907. However, there was no law stipulating that only government banks had the right to issue paper money until two laws were issued in 1909 and 1910.[27] These laws clearly stated that only the Bank of the Great Qing, as the central bank, could issue paper money, and other banks or financial institutions should stop banknote issuance immediately. However, these laws were no longer enforced following the collapse of the Qing dynasty in

---

[23] A. Irigoin, "The End of a Silver Era: The Consequences of the Breakdown of the Spanish Peso Standard in China and the United States, 1780s–1850s," *Journal of World History* 20.2 (2009), 207–44.

[24] The introduction of modern banking to China was led by a British bank – the Oriental Bank, which was a British–Indian joint venture established in Bombay in 1842. It set up a branch in Hong Kong and an agency in Guangdong in 1845 and expanded to Shanghai in 1848.

[25] Hong Kong was a British colony at the time.

[26] This was the predecessor of the Bank of China.

[27] One was the Provisional Regulations on Paper Money in 1909, and the other was the Rules of the General Bank in 1910.

1911. Despite this, as we will see in the following section, paper money was to take off in the next two decades under a largely free banking system.

Money, Financial Institutions, and the State

This section describes the money market transition from highly fragmented to unified by focusing on the roles played by two institutions: financial institutions, especially the domestic modern banking industry, and various governments during the period of study.

The Role of Financial Institutions in the Money Market

The evolution of the Chinese monetary system can only be understood as part of a remarkable transformation of China's financial system during this period.[28] Figure 7.1 provides us with a glimpse of this extraordinary transformation. It shows the capital power of three categories of financial intermediaries: native financial institutions, domestic modern banks, and foreign banks in 1894, 1925, and 1936. The total capital power of financial intermediaries quadrupled from merely 863 million yuan in 1894 to 3,557 million in 1925 and increased by another 2.5 times to 8,925 million in 1936.[29] Among these three types, modern domestic banks performed strikingly well. In 1894, there was no modern Chinese bank. In 1925, modern domestic banks had already taken the largest share, at 40.5 percent, of the total capital power in the banking industry, and they grew to take the lion's share at 77.7 percent in 1936.

In addition to the dramatic growth in the capital power of domestic modern banks, the banking network expanded rapidly: after the establishment of the first domestic modern bank in 1896, the number of modern banks grew to 164, with 1,627 branches in over 500 localities throughout China in

---

[28] See Sheehan and Zhu's chapter in this volume for a comprehensive survey of China's banking sector.

[29] We use the nominal value rather than the real value because a consistent price index series for the whole period from 1894 to 1936 is not available. However, we believe that price changes did not change the magnitude of the banking expansion observed here to a significant extent. For instance, according to the wholesale price indices constructed by Yuru Wang 王玉茹, "城市批发物价变动与近代中国经济增长" (Urban Wholesale Price Change and Economic Growth in Modern China), *Journal of Shanxi University*, Philosophy and Social Science Edition 5 (2006), 29–36, given the base year of 1930 = 100, the corresponding indices for 1925 and 1936 are 92.88 and 94.78 respectively. The price index for 1894 is not available. According to the same estimation, the wholesale price index increased by 40 percent from 1912 to 1925. If we assume a similar magnitude of price change for the 1894–1912 period, the total price change from 1894 to 1925 is slightly more than 100 percent. Thus, even after accounting for this magnitude of price change, the real increase in the banking capital from 1894 to 1925 was still fast.

Money and the Macro-economy

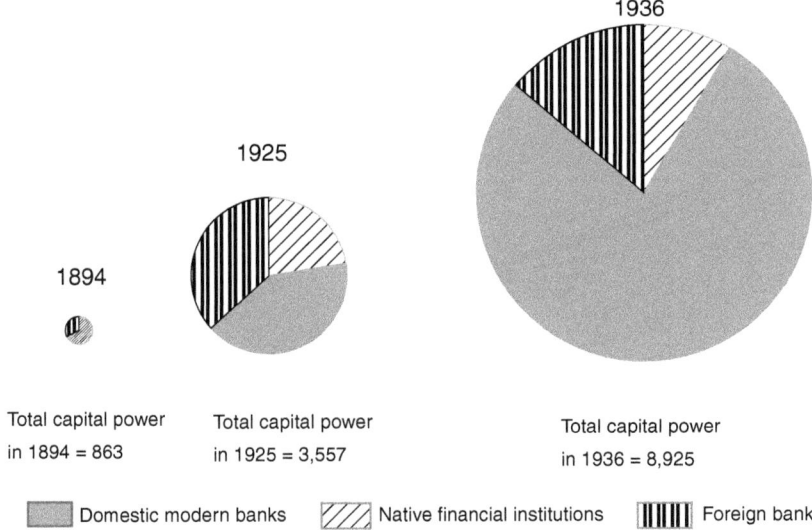

Figure 7.1 The capital power of China's banking industry in 1894, 1925, and 1936 (million silver yuan)
Note. Native financial institutions in 1894 consisted of *piaohao* and *qianzhuang*. In 1894, *piaohao* took a 32.5 percent share of the total capital power, only slightly less than *qianzhuang*'s 35 percent share. However, *piaohao* totally disappeared after the Qing dynasty collapsed, since it relied on official patronage for transferring government funds across the nation and failed to adapt to the new political and economic environment. Therefore the category native financial institutions in 1925 and 1936 only refers to *qianzhuang*, also called native banks.
Source: data are from Table 8.1 in L. Cheng, *Banking in Modern China: Entrepreneurs, Professional Managers, and the Development of Chinese Banks, 1897–1937* (Cambridge, Cambridge University Press, 2003), p. 241. The capital power defined there consisted of capital and other funding in 1894 (p. 19) and of capital, notes, and deposits in 1925 and 1936 (pp. 34, 241)

1936.[30] As early as the 1920s, three cities – Shanghai in the south, Tianjin in the north, and Hankou in the center – emerged as financial centers connecting regional markets. Map 7.1 shows the locations of 104 cities in nineteen provinces surveyed by the Shanghai Commercial Savings Bank in 1924, and lines indicate that there existed channels for one city to transfer funds directly to another city. It was evident that Shanghai was already the national financial center, to which the majority of the cities had a direct financial link, while Tianjin and Hankou served as regional financial centers. A city

---

[30] Research Division of the Bank of China 中国银行经济研究室, 全国银行年鉴 (Bank Statistical Yearbook) (Shanghai, 1937), pp. 26–32.

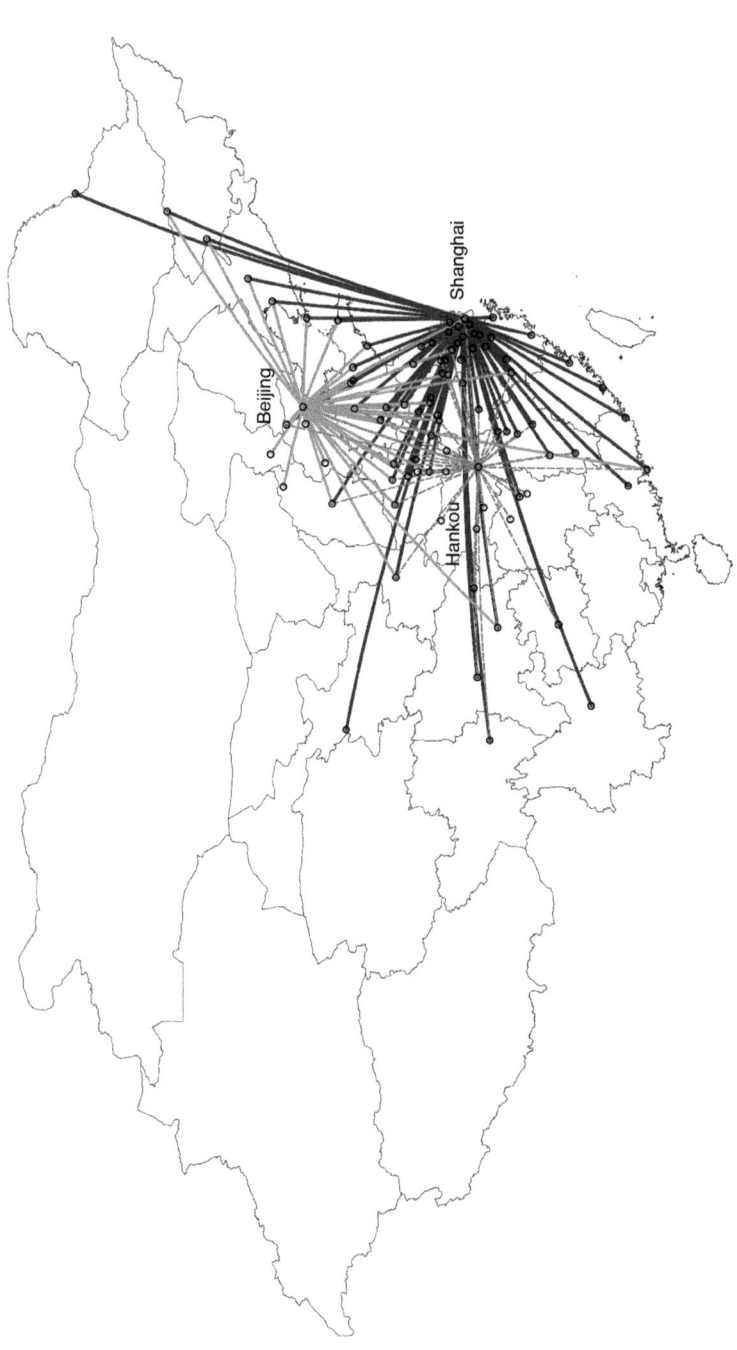

Map 7.1 Cities with a direct money-transferring link with the major financial centers of Shanghai, Hankou, and Tianjin in 1924
Source: the Domestic Exchange Office in the Shanghai Commercial Savings Bank conducted a survey of financial markets in 104 cities in 1924 and published the results in 国内商业汇兑要览 (An Overview of Domestic Commercial Exchange) (Shanghai, Shanghai Commercial and Savings Bank, 1925). This map was constructed by the authors according to information on whether a city could transfer funds to the three major financial centers directly or not

without direct access to one of the major cities could always transfer funds to the regional center and from there to another major city or its intended destination. This resembles a hub-and-spoke system in air transportation, and enabled money to flow freely across the whole nation.

The rapid growth of China's financial institutions and intermediation led to China's monetary transformation in the rise of first the official silver coins, then paper money. Many native banks in Shanghai united to promote the circulation of official coins by gradually phasing out the tael–yuan exchange rate quotations for foreign coins and published quotations for official coins only from June 11, 1919.[31] This gesture established the predominant status of official coins in the national market, since Shanghai was the national financial center.[32] The domestic modern banks also tried hard to promote the usage of official coins. For them, one standardized yuan system was far better than the complicated and fragmented tael system, which was simply out of their control due to lack of human capital in assessing silver bullion and exchanging different silver bullion across localities or with coins. The complication of the tael system made the rapid branching of a modern bank almost impossible and simply did not fit the structure and procedure of a modern bank.[33] Hence the promotion of official silver coins well suited the developmental goal of domestic modern banks.

The silver yuan, as a unit of account, further spread across the nation along with the expanding business scope of banking. In addition to taking deposits and making loans, the business scope of banking extended to issuing commercial papers and banknotes, transferring bills, discounting and rediscounting bills, and so on, which were all mainly denominated in yuan. As the domestic banking sector grew stronger and more mature, the yuan replaced the tael as the major medium of exchange, and silver coins spread extensively in local markets, even in remote rural areas. According to the survey mentioned above, in the early 1920s

---

[31] The daily tael–yuan exchange rate quotations in Shanghai can be found in People's Bank of China, Shanghai Branch 中国人民银行上海分行, 上海钱庄史料汇编 (The Archival Materials of Shanghai Native Banks) (Shanghai, Xinhua Bookstore Press, 1961), pp. 610–27. The quotation of the exchange rate started from January 1865 for the exchange rate of Mexican silver tael for Mexican silver coins until June 11, 1919. Afterwards, the quotations were for taels–official silver coins.

[32] As shown in D. Ma and L. Zhao, "A Silver Transformation: Chinese Monetary Integration in Times of Political Disintegration, 1898–1933," *Economic History Review*, 2020, 513–39, there was a clear trend of increasing monetary integration based on the empirical analysis of monthly and daily prices of silver yuan in Shanghai, Tianjin, and eighteen other cities in northern and central China from 1898 to 1933.

[33] It is true that some native banks failed due to business lost in assessing bullion and exchanging taels. However, many native banks successfully shifted their business to lending, and some even remodeled to become modern banks. This type of structural shift in the banking industry was productive.

official silver coins became the most widely circulated currency in most of the 104 places surveyed, including remote areas such as Guiyang in Guizhou province and San Yuan in Shanxi province.[34]

The Role of the State in the Money Market

The ascendency of official silver coins prepared the Chinese market for the rise of a single silver yuan standard, which was delinked from the silver tael.[35] As early as 1917, the business world started to discuss the feasibility of abandoning the tael and adopting the yuan as the only silver standard.[36] However, due to the lack of a powerful central government and the deficiency of official coins at the time, this proposal from the business world was temporarily neglected until March 10, 1933, when the Nationalist government (hereafter the Government[37]) was able to respond to appeals from the business world and issued the Decree to Abolish the Tael and Adopt the Yuan to stipulate that the yuan was the only unit of account for transactions and contracts. Those who possessed silver bullion could either turn silver bullion in to the central mint to mint coins or exchange it for coins at the Central Bank, the Bank of China (BoC), and the Bank of Communications (BoCom) at an exchange rate of 0.715 tael to the yuan. A unified money market with a single yuan standard had finally arrived in China.

Despite the official silver coins achieving great success during the warlord era, as described above, the Beiyang government could not control the paper money supply, which became an increasingly important component of the total money supply. The two government banks (BoC and BoCom), together with domestic and foreign modern banks and native banks, competed to issue banknotes under the free banking system. Moreover, the two government banks became increasingly independent: the BoC became more of a private bank than a government bank as the private share increased from 50 percent in 1915[38] to 80 percent in 1928,[39]

---

[34] Both provinces were economically underdeveloped and located in inland China.

[35] D. Ma, "Chinese Money and Monetary System, 1800–2000, Overview," in G. Caprio (ed.), *Handbook of Key Global Financial Markets, Institutions, and Infrastructure*, vol. 1 (Oxford, Elsevier, 2013), pp. 57–64.

[36] See articles on the monetary situation in China published by the *Bankers' Weekly* before 1921 and collected in Xu Cangshui 徐沧水 (ed.), 中国今日之货币问题 (Monetary Issues in Today's China) (Shanghai, Bankers' Weekly Press, 1921).

[37] After 1927, the capital moved to Nanjing when the Nationalist Party took power.

[38] The Revised Rules of the Bank of China, passed by the Senate on September 30, 1915. See Bank of China 中国银行总行 and Second Historical Archives of China 中国第二历史档案馆, 中国银行史资料汇编上编, 1912–1949 (Compilation of the Archives of the Bank of China, 1912–1949) (Beijing, The Archive Press, 1991), p. 115.

[39] The Rules of the Bank of China, enacted by the Republican government on December 26, 1928. Bank of China and Second Historical Archives of China, 中国银行史资料汇编上编, p. 124.

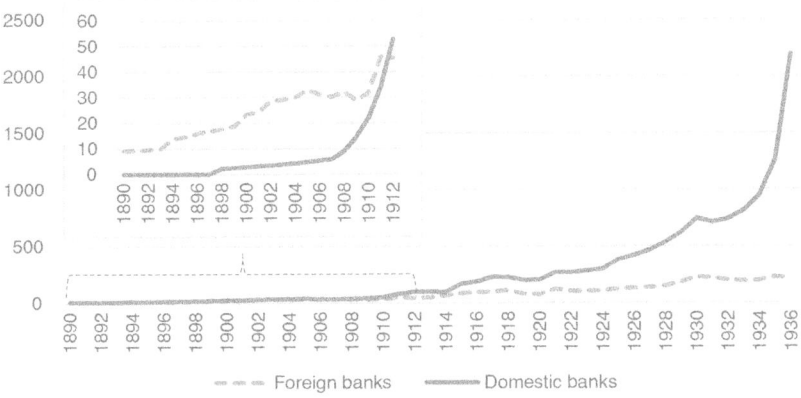

Figure 7.2 Banknote issuance in China from 1890 to 1936 (million silver yuan)
Sources: data on banknote issuance for both foreign and domestic banks from 1912 to 1936 are from T. Rawski, *Economic Growth in Prewar China* (Berkeley, University of California Press, 1989), p. 380, Table c9. We extend Rawski's note issuance for foreign banks to 1890 based on the same source – Xian Ke 献可, 近百年来帝国主义在华银行发行纸币概况 (Issue of Paper Currency by Imperialist Banks in China during the Past Century) (Shanghai, Shanghai People's Publishing House, 1958). Domestic modern banks started to issue banknotes in 1898. Issuance by domestic banks from 1898 to 1911 is based on Commercial Bank of China 中国通商银行, 五十年来之中国经济—中国通商银行创立五十周年纪念册 (Fifty Years of the Chinese Economy: The Commemorative Book of the 50th Anniversary of the Establishment of the Commercial Bank of China) (Shanghai, Commercial Bank of China, 1947), pp. 4–5. This book records the volume of banknotes issued by domestic modern banks in 1898, 1904, and 1912. We fill in missing values by linear interpolation between the values for these three years

and the bank occasionally refused to obey government orders; the BoCom followed suit and became more privatized as well.[40] It was the Beiyang government's partial loss of control over these government banks that made them behave like commercial banks and seek to build a good reputation in the banknote market. Figure 7.2 shows the volumes of circulating banknotes issued by domestic and foreign banks from 1890 to 1936. It was during the warlord era that the banknotes issued by domestic banks began to outnumber those issued by foreign banks, which indicates that people came to trust domestic banknotes. Moreover, the gap was enlarging over time: the volume of foreign banknotes was

---

[40] For the BoCom, the government share dropped from 40 percent in 1914 to 20 percent in 1928. See Bank of Communications 交通银行总行 and Second Historical Archives of China 中国第二历史档案馆, 交通银行史料第一卷 1907–1949 (Archives of the Bank of Communications, vol. 1, 1907–1949) (Shanghai, China Financial Publishing House, 1995), pp. 19, 23.

212.7 million, only approximately 10 percent of the volume of domestic banknotes in 1936. Among all the domestic banknotes, usually more than 65 percent were issued by the two government banks in the 1910s and 1920s.[41]

The credibility of domestic banknotes was built on the fact that these banknotes were convertible with silver coins since, by law, the notes were backed by 60 percent silver and 40 percent securities, mainly consisting of government bonds. After the Nationalist Party took power and established the capital in Nanjing in 1927, in 1928 the two government banks moved their headquarters from Beijing to Shanghai, which was nearer to the new capital city, following the government order. A natural concern was whether the Government would intervene in the operations of the government banks, which would probably threaten the convertibility of their banknotes.

The BoC responded quickly. In March 1928, it founded an eleven-member committee of public representatives to monitor the reserves for banknote issuance to assure the public of the convertibility of its banknotes. The committee consisted of two members from each of three organizations, namely the Shanghai General Chamber of Commerce, the Shanghai Bankers' Association, and the Shanghai Native Bankers' Association; two representatives from any other financial institution that used its banknotes; and three members from the Board of Directors and Supervisors of the BoC.[42] These people were all reputable businessmen and bankers whose business would be severely affected if the BoC's banknotes became inconvertible. They hired an auditing house to check the bank's silver reserves against its notes on a monthly basis and published the auditing results in the *Shanghai Newspaper* (*Shenbao*, 申报) after each examination. This practice assured the public about the convertibility of the BoC's banknotes. Soon, this practice was followed by other note-issuing banks, including the BoCom and even the Central Bank, newly established in 1928.

The Government started to consolidate monetary power and aimed to establish a unified money market. The Government achieved its goal by "walking on two legs": on one leg, it gradually encroached on the private share of the banking sector until almost the whole sector was nationalized; on the other leg, it took control of the money supply step by step until a fiat money system was established with the Central Bank as the sole issuer of paper money.

The Government gained control of the banking sector in three ways. First, it issued significantly more government bonds than its predecessors had: 2,325 million silver yuan worth of bonds in less than ten years, compared to

---

[41] Rawski, *Economic Growth*, Table c2, p. 371.
[42] *Bankers' Weekly* 银行周报, 1917–1950, Shanghai Bankers' Association, April 3, 1928.

only 630 million issued by its predecessors in Beijing in more than fifteen years.[43] The domestic modern banks in Shanghai became the largest bondholder: approximately one-third to two-thirds of all extant bonds were in their hands.[44] The banks held government bonds both for investment and as reserves for banknote issuance. A by-product of the bond policy was that the banking industry was closely tied to the government.[45] Second, the Central Bank was established in 1928. This fully government-owned bank was initially small in capital, with only 20 million yuan paid in government bonds. Despite its small capital power compared with that of the other two government banks, the Central Bank was granted four important monopoly rights: banknote issuance, official coin mintage, state treasury management, and the underwriting of treasury bonds. It soon gained importance in the banking sector. Finally, the government took the bold step of nationalizing the banking sector in 1935. In March 1935, the government suddenly nationalized the BoC and the BoCom – the two government banks all but dominated by private shareholders – by injecting government bonds as capital. Then, within less than half a year, other major private banks were nationalized.[46] The government share in the banking industry increased from less than 12 percent in 1934 to 72.8 percent in 1936.[47]

Simultaneously, the Government adopted monetary policies towards establishing a fiat money system that was fully government-controlled. After abolishing the tael and establishing the yuan as the only unit of account and medium of exchange in 1933, the Government significantly empowered its position in the money supply since it controlled the official coin mintage and partially controlled the supply of paper money pegged to and convertible with silver coins through government banks. Two years later, the Government implemented another monetary reform: it left the silver standard and adopted a fiat money system. Before this reform, there was a free banking system in which the Central Bank,

---

[43] See C.-Y. Ho and D. Li, "Reputation Building of a Nascent Government in Debt Finance: Lessons from the Bond Market in China, 1912–1937," working paper (2018), Fudan University.
[44] See Wu Chengxi 吴承禧, 中国的银行 (The Chinese Banks) (Shanghai, The Commercial Press, 1934), pp. 68–73; Zhang Naiqi 章乃器, 中国货币金融问题 (Monetary and Financial Issues in China) (Shanghai, Shenghuo shudian, 1936), pp. 68–9; K.N. Chang, "Toward Modernization of China's Currency and Banking, 1927–1937," in P.K.T. Sih (ed), *The Strenuous Decade: China's Nation-Building Efforts, 1927–1937* (New York, St. John's University Press, 1970), p. 147; P.M. Coble, *The Shanghai Capitalists and the Nationalist Government, 1927–1937* (Cambridge, MA, Harvard University Council on East Asian Studies, 1986), pp. 74–5.
[45] Coble, *Shanghai Capitalists*, p. 77.
[46] Including the Commercial Bank of China, the Ningbo Commercial and Savings Bank, and the National Industrial Bank of China.
[47] Research Division of the Bank of China, *Statistical Yearbook*, pp. A55, B11, B16.

three government banks,[48] and private banks all could issue banknotes. After the reform, all private banks were forbidden to issue paper money, and the government banks increased the paper money supply. As shown in Figure 7.2, the banknotes issued by domestic banks increased dramatically from 747.7 million yuan in 1934 to 1,976.7 million yuan in 1936, in which the notes issued by the Central Bank increased by four times, the notes issued by the BoC increased by 1.8 times, and the notes issued by the BoCom increased by 2.7 times. In 1942, paper money issuance was further consolidated solely in the hands of the Central Bank.[49]

Competition and Co-operation between the Government and the Private Financial Sector in the Money Market

Many phenomena in the money market during our period of study were consequences of co-operation and/or competition between the government and the private financial sector when facing constraints, internal turmoil, external invasions, and many other shocks. Competition from the private sector disciplined the government and prevented it from overusing its power over the money supply, and co-operation helped the government expand its monetary power and achieve its goal of building a unified and growing money market. Although an increasingly powerful authoritarian regime could achieve the success of unifying the money market, it could also weaken the private sector and block or even stop further development in the money and financial markets. This section illustrates how the interplays between the two parties contributed to the evolution (and sometimes regression) of the money market by presenting one case from each of three different eras: the late Qing dynasty, the warlord era, and the Nationalist prewar era.

No Debasement Please!

To address the fiscal crisis caused by the Taiping Rebellion in 1850–1860, the Qing ruler, the Xianfeng Emperor, decided to generate government revenue by debasing copper cash and issuing paper notes. The government first started to issue a "big coin" equivalent to ten wen in 1853. For instance, a copper cash with a stamped value equivalent to ten wen might only contain

---

[48] First, only the two government banks, the BoC and BoCom, could issue banknotes. Later, the Bank of Farmers was added.
[49] See Hong Jiaguan 洪葭管, 中央银行史料 1928.11–1949.05 (The Archival Materials of the Central Bank of China: 1928.11–1949.05) (Beijing, China Finance Publishing House, 2005), pp. 1–14, for a brief history of the Central Bank of China.

copper content equal to two original one-wen coins. The government later issued several more types of larger cash equivalent to 20, 50, 100, 500, and even 1,000 wen, but with certainly far less copper content, as indicated by their nominal value. Simultaneously, the government cast iron cash with the same stamped value as that of copper cash (another form of debasement) and issued paper notes. The government pushed these new currencies through the market with the coercive power of the state, e.g. by distributing them as part of the salary of government officials and soldiers.

The private sector responded to these monetary policies promptly. On the one hand, "big cash" made counterfeiting so profitable that people were willing to risk their lives to melt down the original one-wen cash to produce big cash. Soon the number of counterfeited big cash equal to 500 or 1,000 wen surpassed the number of official big cash. Similarly, counterfeiting paper notes was probably easier, and some counterfeits were even made by greedy government officials. The government itself became a victim of these counterfeit currencies since governmental agencies occasionally received them as payment. In the end, some governmental agencies refused "big cash" and paper notes as payment, which openly denied the legitimacy of these currencies.

On the other hand, businessmen priced their products differently according to what currency a shopper used. If a shopper used the original one-wen copper cash, the price of the goods remained more or less the same as before the rebellion. If a shopper used big cash, the price would increase dramatically until big cash was traded at a value close to that of its intrinsic copper content. If a shopper used paper notes or iron cash, shop owners might refuse to sell products to him or her. In an extreme case, on January 11 (according to the lunar calendar) of the seventh year of the Xianfeng reign,[50] more than half of the rice shops and grocery stores in Beijing shut down to protest that they did not want the big iron cash equivalent to ten wen as payment. The high prices due to the usage of big cash made soldiers and other governmental staff, who received big cash as their salary, barely able to make ends meet, and the government had to give them a salary raise. This further encroached on the already limited seigniorage revenue of minting debased coins, which were mainly circulated in Beijing and its surrounding areas.[51]

---

[50] According to the Western calendar, it was February 4, 1857. It was during the Chinese Spring Festival.
[51] For a more detailed description of the case, please see Peng, *Monetary History*, pp. 616–20.

Counterfeiting and the resistance to big cash and paper notes from the private sector forced the Qing court to stop the practice less than four years after it had started. It was exactly the competition and resistance from the private sector that prohibited the government from massive debasement. Interestingly, for a one-wen copper cash, the size, design, and weight might vary across dynasties, across different emperor reigns within one dynasty, and sometimes across different periods within one emperor's reign, but the copper content of a one-wen cash never deviated far from one *qian* 钱.[52] Therefore the circulating copper cash at a given time could consist of cash from previous dynasties, cash minted during the current dynasty, foreign copper cash, counterfeit cash, and private cash. As long as these cash contained copper content close to one *qian* and were traditionally accepted by the local market, they all functioned well as small change. Ironically, competition from the private sector helped the government maintain a fairly good standard in the supply of official copper cash,[53] which solved the "big problem of small change" in China.[54]

Bank Reputation or Government Reputation

Although Yuan Shikai's attempt to restore the monarchy failed in March 1916,[55] the damage to the government's fiscal status was evident. The headquarters of the two government banks – the BoC and the BoCom – located in Beijing were pressured to lend enormously to the government. Consequently, the Beijing branches increased the issuance of banknotes without an appropriate amount of silver reserve. These banknotes were called the Beijing currency (*jingchao* 京钞) because they were issued by Beijing branches and circulated mainly in Beijing and its immediate environs. Rumors about Beijing currency becoming inconvertible with silver coins brewed soon after Yuan's failure to restore the monarchy, and bank runs were imminent. On May 12, Yuan Shikai ordered the two banks to stop cashing their banknotes. The Beijing currency soon became irredeemable, and its market price in terms of silver yuan dropped to approximately 60 percent of face value.[56] Even governmental agencies, such as railway

---

[52] One *qian* is 3.75 grams. [53] Qian and Wu, "Monetary Stability," 397–435.
[54] Ma, "Monetary System," pp. 57–64.
[55] Yuan Shikai, the president of the nascent Republican government from 1912, proclaimed himself the new emperor, the Hongxian Emperor, on January 1, 1916. Due to widespread opposition and revolts by both his former supporters and regional governors, he stepped down from the throne on March 22 and acted as the president again until his death on June 6 in the same year.
[56] *Bankers' Weekly*, May 4, 1918.

companies, the Maritime Customs, post offices, and tax agencies, refused the banknotes issued by these two government banks, regardless of which branch issued the banknotes. The panic soon spread to banknotes issued by other banks. The specter of a serious financial crisis was haunting China.

At this critical moment, the managers of the BoC's Shanghai branch heroically stood up to resist the government order and insisted on the convertibility of banknotes issued by the Shanghai branch.[57] This branch issued more than half of the total banknotes issued by the whole bank. The remaining convertibility of the Shanghai banknotes of the BoC not only helped prevent the spread of financial crisis across the nation but also established a sterling reputation for the branch's banknotes.

The BoC did not leave the inconvertible Beijing currency unattended: the BoC and the BoCom urged the government to repay their loans so that they could use the advance to buy back the inconvertible Beijing currency. In 1918, the government agreed to issue two bonds to pay back bank loans: one was a seven-year, 6 percent short-term bond with a volume of 48 million backed by Maritime Customs revenue; the other was a seven-year, 6 percent long-term bond with a volume of 45 million backed by unspecified government revenue and lijin 厘金. All Beijing currency holders could exchange their paper money at face value with a composition of half of each bond. Thus a 100-yuan banknote could be exchanged for fifty yuan of the short-term bond and fifty yuan of the long-term bond.[58] Another bond, the Financial Reorganization Short-Term, was issued in 1920 with a total amount of 60 million backed by Maritime Customs revenue to swap for the remaining Beijing currency.[59] All the inconvertible Beijing currency was finally redeemed by government bonds.

As both the BoC and the BoCom acted more like private banks due to the declining governmental share, they started to resist loaning to the government and its officials. For instance, after two crises on the convertibility of BoCom banknotes due to government default on loans to the bank in 1916 and 1921, the bank set up a new board of directors in June 1921 to reform the bank. One important direction for the reform was to promulgate the rules for

---

[57] See D. Ma, "Financial Revolution in Republican China during 1900–1937: A Survey and New Interpretation," *Australian Economic History Review*, 2019, 242–62, on how the Shanghai branch of the BoC successfully resisted the order from Beijing and kept the convertibility of its banknotes.

[58] Shanghai Commercial and Savings Bank 上海商业储蓄银行, 内国公债要览 (An Overview of Domestic Bonds) (Shanghai, Shanghai Commercial and Savings Bank, 1931), pp. 1–6.

[59] Qian Jiaju 千家驹, 旧中国公债史资料, 1894–1949 (Archival Sources on Domestic Government Bonds in China, 1894–1949) (Beijing, Zhonghua Book Company, 1984), pp. 61–3.

lending, including no more loans to any government agencies from then on and no loans to government officials unless proper collateral was provided.[60]

Behind these two government banks stood their private shareholders – private banks. Almost all major private banks held shares in either the BoC or the BoCom or both.[61] These private banks pushed the government banks to act like real commercial banks while enjoying privileges granted by the government. These private shareholders helped the government banks maintain a good reputation and win trust among the people in the warlord era when the central government was weak. The sterling reputation enabled these banks to attract ever-increasing deposits and simultaneously to lend out more, issue more banknotes, and underwrite dramatically swelling government bonds after the Nationalist Party seized power in 1927. However, the fruit of this good reputation was harvested by the Government, which gradually increased its influence over the two banks and finally nationalized them in 1935.

Fragile Co-operation between Private Bankers and the Nationalist Government

One striking feature of the financial market in prewar China was that the secondary market for government bonds thrived in terms of its increasing size and liquidity from 1927 to 1931 – the nascent years of the Nationalist government.[62] This is a puzzle given that the Nationalist government was new and authoritarian, without any investor-friendly institutions in place. Moreover, it faced numerous internal and external military threats, which added significant risks to holding its bonds. Ho and Li point out that the government tried hard to build its reputation by settling its predecessors' debts and consistently servicing the debts, which successfully distinguished it from its predecessors and helped win trust among individual investors.[63] However,

---

[60] Bank of Communications and Secondary Historical Archives of China, *The Bank of Communications*, p. 9.
[61] For details on the shareholders of the two government banks, please see Bank of China and Secondary Historical Archives of China, *The Bank of China*, pp. 88–94, for the BoC; and Bank of Communications and Secondary Historical Archives of China, *The Bank of Communications*, vol. 1, pp. 25–32, for the BoCom.
[62] Over the fifteen years of the Beiyang government in Beijing, it issued thirty-five bonds worth a total of 643 million silver yuan, among which six bonds could be floated on the secondary market. In contrast, throughout the four years from 1927 to 1931, the nationalist government issued twenty-six bonds, with the amount of the bonds reaching 1,069 million, which exceeded the total amount of bonds issued in the Beiyang era by 66 percent. Moreover, given the significant amount of bonds issued, more than 70 percent could be floated on the secondary market. Ho and Li, "Reputation Building."
[63] Ho and Li, "Reputation Building."

building the government's reputation would not have been successful without help from private bankers. Nonetheless, co-operation became fragile when the government deviated from its goal of maintaining its reputation due to other urgent needs. The rise and fall of the Sinking Fund Commission for the Shanghai Maritime Customs 2.5 Percent Surtax Treasury Note (hereafter the Commission) is a typical example to illustrate this relationship between the two.

After the Nationalist government issued its first bond in Shanghai – the Shanghai Maritime Customs 2.5 Percent Surtax Treasury Note of 30 million silver yuan – the Commission was set up to handle the sinking fund and bond repayments. The Commission consisted of fourteen members, among whom three were officials from the central government and the rest mainly local bankers and/or businessmen.[64] However, the government seemed rarely involved: first, no government officials were included in the five members of the standing committee,[65] which represented the Commission in handling all related businesses; second, the three officials were always absent from Commission meetings;[66] finally, the government refused to cover operating costs for the Commission despite its being nominally under the Bureau of Domestic Bonds – a government organ – hence the Commission had to raise funds to cover operating costs by itself.[67]

Domestic modern banks in Shanghai held the largest number of government bonds, ensuring that bond credibility was aligned with the Commission's interests. The specified portion of customs revenue earmarked for paying the note was handed to the Commission directly from the Maritime Customs.[68] The Commission publicized the information on the

---

[64] Among the remaining eleven members, two were from the Shanghai local government and were important local businessmen, and the rest were all from the local financial industry and various chambers of commerce.

[65] The five members were Li Fusun, Xie Taofu, Lin Kanghou, Xu Jingren, and Wu Linshu. The first four were bankers, and the last was in the textile industry. Li Fusun was the chairman of the Shanghai Bankers' Association.

[66] See the meeting minutes of the Commission of the Second Historical Archives of China 中国第二历史档案馆，中华民国史档案资料汇编第五辑第一编 (Collection of Archives and Documents of the Republic of China, vol 5.1, Public Finance and Economics) (Nanjing, Jiangsu Ancient Books Publishing House, 1991), pp. 471–519.

[67] The committee raised funds for covering operating costs by depositing some sinking funds in non-designated private banks and native banks to earn higher interest, and sometimes even making loans. See Shijuan Song 宋时娟, "江海关二五附税国库券基金保管委员会研究" (Research on the Sinking Fund Commission for Shanghai Maritime Customs 2.5% Surtax Treasury Note), unpublished master's thesis, Fudan University, 2000.

[68] Unlike Francis Aglen, the inspector-general of the Customs from 1911 to 1927 who controlled the sinking funds and influenced or even decided on the debt reimbursement, Frederick Maze, the inspector of the Shanghai Maritime Customs and later the

revenue of the sinking fund and bond repayments monthly in newspapers. It hired a local accounting firm to audit the fund quarterly, and similarly the auditing results also appeared in newspapers.[69] The transparency of the sinking fund increased the Commission's accountability. The Commission achieved unprecedented success, as the 2.5 Percent Surtax Treasury Note was duly serviced and fully reimbursed right on schedule in 1929.

Nonetheless, clashes between the government and the Commission emerged. One dispute rested on their different standpoints: the government desperately needed to raise funds by floating debts with less concern about debt service, while the Commission stood up for the bondholders' sake to ensure that bonds be duly serviced. According to its name, the Commission was supposed to be responsible only for ensuring the repayment of the note, and it was supposed to be disbanded after the note was fully reimbursed. However, the Commission took over management of the sinking funds of another twenty bonds (and notes), sometimes voluntarily, sometimes reluctantly or under government pressure. For instance, because a newly issued bond without secure collateral would undercut the credibility not only of the new bond itself but also of extant bonds as a whole, the Commission requested that the government consult it before issuing any new bonds. However, the government did not always do so, and intended to manage the sinking funds of the new bonds by itself, but failed to find a market. Therefore the Commission was requested by the government (sometimes together with institutional bondholders) to take over the management of the new bonds, and it had no choice but to try hard to secure the collateral.[70] Even though the Commission took on more responsibility, transparency remained, and the repayments of the bonds in its custody were usually well carried out.[71] Li Fusun, the head of the Commission, stated proudly, "A bond without its sinking fund managed by our commission cannot win the trust of society."[72]

Another dispute regarded the Commission's right to designate banks for depositing the sinking funds. To attract more investment in government

new general inspector, was not included in the commission at this time due to the rise of nationalism.

[69] See *Shanghai Newspaper* 申报, various issues, 1921–1942, for the information.

[70] For instance, the commission secured the amount of revenue earmarked for bond repayment from the Excise Duty Bureau and the Internal Transaction Tax Bureau. In addition, tobacco firms directly bought certificates of tobacco tax payment from the commission, and the proceeds were used as collateral for bonds.

[71] For some bonds, including the Tianjin Maritime Customs 2.5% Surtax Treasury Note in 1928, the 20th-Year Jiang-Zhe Silk Industry Bond in 1931 and the Hebei Hai River Project Short-Term Bond in 1929, the respective sinking-fund commissions were established following an institutional arrangement similar to the commission.

[72] See the meeting minutes of the twentieth meeting of the Commission on April 17, 1929. See Second Historical Archives of China, *Documents & Archives*, pp. 489–91.

bonds from various banks, the Commission deposited funds not only in large banks but also in various small or native banks according to whether the bank purchased bonds up to a certain threshold. Small banks could use bonds and silver at a ratio of four to six to exchange for banknotes from large banks,[73] and they could receive coupon payments of the bonds. This arrangement did not take up their scarce funds. The additional benefit of receiving deposits from the Commission provided them more incentive to buy bonds. However, when the Central Bank was established in November 1928, the Department of Finance required the Maritime Customs to send the sinking fund for domestic bonds to the Central Bank (*Shanghai Newspaper*, November 15, 1928) without consulting the Commission. Obviously, this encroached on the Commission's rights. The Commission negotiated with the government for several rounds, and a compromise was finally reached: the Central Bank took 40 percent of the sinking funds as deposits, and the Commission took the remaining 60 percent.[74]

One last noticeable clash occurred concerning the bond repayments. The government wanted to stop debt services temporarily after the Japanese occupied Manchuria in September 1931 and bombed Shanghai in January 1932, which reduced the financial resources pledged for debt repayments.[75] The Commission protested against this proposal. The two parties negotiated for many rounds. Given that there was obviously not enough funding for debt repayments, both sides yielded: the Commission accepted the bond reorganization scheme of reducing the yearly amount of principal service by half and hence extending the remaining maturity two times longer; in return, the government promised that it would not issue bonds for the next four years.[76] This deed saved the government from fiscal crisis in 1932, and it revealed that the Commission was not as hardline as it claimed to be.

---

[73] The amount of banknotes that could be exchanged for bonds was based on the bonds' market value, not face value.
[74] Song, "Sinking Fund Commission," p. 23.
[75] The cession of Manchuria to Japan led to an estimated annual loss of 70 million silver yuan in customs revenue and transaction tax revenue – approximately one-tenth of the government revenue from these two tax items, which served as the major funding source for bond repayment. The amount of loss arising from the Shanghai incident was estimated at 1.56 billion yuan. More than 16,000 civilians were killed or missing, one-fourth of Shanghai's factories were destroyed and many were damaged, and 80 percent of industrial workers became unemployed. *Shanghai Newspaper*, March 20, 1932.
[76] For the detailed negotiations between the bankers and the government during this bond reorganization, see Coble, *Shanghai Capitalists*, pp. 102–9.

Soon after the 1932 bond reorganization, the Commission was restructured to be the Sinking Fund Commission for National Bonds – a name that had been rejected by Li Fusun in the early years but was accepted at this time. In addition to the name, more government officials were added to the new Commission. The government's promise not to issue new bonds in the following four years turned out to be empty: it resumed issuing bonds within the year to keep itself financially afloat. In total, another thirteen bonds were issued in the 1932–1935 period, only two of which could be floated on the secondary market.[77] The new Commission had little voice to protest the government's blatant violation of the 1932 deed. In 1936, the government conducted another bond reorganization without any legitimate pretext and totally bypassed the new Commission.[78] Together with the bank coups in 1935, the private financial sector was emasculated by the ever more powerful Nationalist government.

Money Market Integration and Its Impact on the Economy

How monetary and financial development may benefit the economy has been discussed both theoretically and empirically in an excellent review article by Levine.[79] Although it is impossible for us to pin down to what extent money and financial market development contributed to GDP growth in China during the period of our study, their positive effects were certain: money market integration and financial developments facilitated trade, channeled financial resources for modern industry, reduced interest rates, and stabilized the economy.

Since the silver tael had never reached the same standard across localities, silver in one locality was treated as merchandise in distant places and was "bartered" for other merchandise. This type of costly barter exchange, in addition to high transportation costs and other market frictions, prevented a trading network from coming into being in premodern China – a large, populous, and diverse country where trade should have benefited the economy enormously if it could have developed. Perkins notes that for almost

---

[77] Ho and Li, "Reputation Building."
[78] For detailed information on the 1932 and 1936 bond consolidations, see Li Dan 李丹, 历史"大数据": 民国证券市场之量化研究 ("Big Data" in History: The Development of Security and Bond Markets in Republican China) (Beijing, Peking University Press, 2016), pp. 199–207.
[79] R. Levine, "Finance and Growth: Theory and Evidence," *Handbook of Economic Growth* 1 (2005), 865–934.

1,000 years before 1900, the share of total agricultural output dedicated to long-distance trade remained steady at a level of no more than 7 to 8 percent in China.[80]

As the silver yuan gradually replaced the silver tael to become the most widely accepted unit of account, these easily recognizable silver coins significantly reduced transaction costs and hence promoted trade. In the 1920s, the total volume of interprovincial long-distance trade had increased to more than three times what it had been in the late nineteenth century.[81] Rawski also finds that the domestic inter-port trade (inbound and outbound) increased by 6.3 times from 1891 to 1931 based on the data compiled by the Maritime Customs.[82] Certainly this dramatic expansion in domestic long-distance trade was caused not solely by money market integration but also by other factors, such as transportation development, the rise of modern industry, and integration into global markets.[83] However, the effect of money market integration on trade is not negligible: transaction costs probably not only fall once when the economy moves to money, but may continue to fall through financial innovation, which continuously stimulates trade. More trade leads to greater specialization, which drives productivity growth. These productivity gains feed back into financial market development. As the virtuous circle continues, the economy grows, and GDP per capita increases.[84]

One example of how money market integration affected the economic landscape at the time through its impact on trade is the formation of treaty port–hinterland economic zones. Wu identifies six treaty port–hinterland economic zones in the 1920s.[85] These economic zones had treaty ports as hubs with vast hinterlands attached through trade. Increasingly more land gradually transformed to producing agricultural goods for trade rather than

---

[80] D.H. Perkins, *Agricultural Development in China, 1368–1968* (Edinburgh, Edinburgh University Press, 1969), pp. 145–73.
[81] Perkins, *Agricultural Development in China*, pp. 145–73.
[82] Rawski, *Economic Growth*, p. 193,
[83] International trade grew by almost ten times in value from 1891 to 1931. Rawski, *Economic Growth*, Table 4.2, p. 193.
[84] Levine, "Finance and Growth," pp. 865–934.
[85] The Shenyang–Dalian-centered zone in northeast China, the Beijing–Tianjin-centered zone in north China, the Qingdao–Jinan-centered zone in Shandong and its surrounding areas, the Shanghai-centered zone in the Yangzi delta, the Xiamen–Fuzhou-centered zone in Fujian and its surrounding areas, and the Hong Kong–Guangzhou-centered zone in south China. See Wu Songdi 吴松弟, "中国近代经济地理格局形成的机制与表现" (The Formation of Economic Geography in Modern China: Mechanism and Pattern), *Journal of Historical Science* 8 (2009), 65–72. Wu Songdi 吴松弟, 中国近代经济地理：绪论和全国概况第一卷 (Economic Geography in Modern China: Introduction and Overview, vol. 1) (Shanghai, East China Normal University Press, 2015).

for self-sufficiency, and production in the hinterlands became pegged to market conditions in their hub cities. For instance, in the 1920s, the Shenyang–Dalian-centered economic zone in northeast China produced 60 to 70 percent of the world output of soybean, 90 percent of which was exported abroad.[86] Shenyang and Dalian became the world trading center for soybean, and vast areas of the hinterland were devoted to producing this economic agricultural product.

These economic zones could not have come into being without money market integration. In the absence of the gradual circulation of standardized official silver coins in villages and the expansion of the financial network as documented above in this chapter, it would have been highly costly for millions of peddlers, vendors, and traders to come to villages to buy agricultural goods to be sold in cities and the international market. Only when a standardized medium of exchange – silver coins – became widely acceptable did transaction costs decline, which attracted more people into the trading business. Financial development further facilitated trading, for instance by providing credit, transferring bills, and exchanging international currencies. Trade linked villages to cities and induced specialization; hence an economic circle emerged. When the money market developed more as regional financial centers emerged, trade expanded, and an economic zone appeared.

In addition to facilitating trade, monetary and financial developments may change people's incentives to save and invest. In the case of China's underdeveloped economy during the period of our study,[87] it was crucial for economic development to pool the very limited savings together and lend them out to ease the external financing constraints that impede modern industrial development. In traditional China, hoarding was a common practice that allowed rich families to save because depositing silver tael in native financial institutions would have incurred a high assessment cost, which

---

[86] Hu Xuemei 胡雪梅, "东北大豆出口贸易与近代中国东北开发, 1860–1931" (Soybean Exports in Northeast China and the Development of Northeast China in Modern Times, 1860–1931), *Northern Cultural Relics* 3 (2002), 93–9.

[87] It is true that China was a poor country at the time. However, this does not imply that the people had no extra wealth to save. Wang cites Zhang Zongli's estimation that the gentry class (approximately 2 percent of the overall population) at the end of the nineteenth century earned an income sixteen times that of an average family. The compradors in the five treaty ports, although numbering no more than several hundred in each port, earned approximately 530 million silver taels (approximately 741 million silver yuan) from 1842 to 1894 – twice the national tax revenue. Additionally, the total savings deposited in foreign banks in Shanghai in prewar China amounted to between 400 million and 500 million yuan. See Wang Yejian 王业键, 中国近代货币与银行的演进, 1644–1937 (The Evolution of Money and Banking in Modern China, 1644–1937) (Beijing, Institute of Economics, Academia Sinica, 1981).

impeded these institutions from taking small deposits from the general public. For instance, native banks were only willing to take deposits larger than a certain threshold, which varied from bank to bank, from cofounders and a few wealthy friends and relatives.[88] Occasionally, a large amount of silver bullion was deposited by a wealthy family in a financial institution – not for interest revenue but for safety purposes. Sometimes, depositors even had to pay a fee for depositing silver bullion in a native bank. Moreover, it was not relatively much safer to deposit money in native banks than it was to hoard since native banks were vulnerable to shocks due to their small scale and limited capital. Hence the total savings in financial institutions in historical China could be small.

Depositing money in financial institutions gradually became an option for rich families, and even the general public, to restore the value of their wealth when the money market evolved and the banking sector expanded. On the fund supply side, when the money market was transitioning from a highly fragmented silver tael system to an integrated silver yuan system in tandem with a silver-backed fiduciary paper money system, financial institutions became more willing to take deposits from a broader social base, since taking standardized coins or paper money as deposits was much less costly than taking silver bullion. Moreover, households, especially urban residents, could easily access banking services due to the rapid branching of domestic modern banks across the nation, and depositing money in large nationwide banks, such as the BoC and the BoCom, was much safer than putting money in small native banks. Consequently, bank savings increased dramatically: national deposits increased by almost eight times in less than three decades from 1910 to 1936, and reached a staggering amount of 5.9575 billion silver yuan in 1936, approximately 54 percent of the total money supply (M2) in the year.[89]

On the demand side, capital could flow more freely and at less cost across county, city, and provincial borders since the standardized money was universally accepted and the banking network was extensive. The transaction costs and information asymmetry involved in the capital flow across localities caused by the fragmented silver tael system were eliminated. Capital would flow to places where it was in high demand and most efficiently used, such as cities with firms clustered in modern industries. The modern industry was no doubt the largest beneficiary of the capital flow. As the most efficient and fastest-growing sector, the modern sector absorbed capital and became the main driver of productivity

---

[88] The People's Bank of China, Shanghai Branch, 上海钱庄史料汇编, p. 10.
[89] Rawski, *Economic Growth*, Table c16, p. 394.

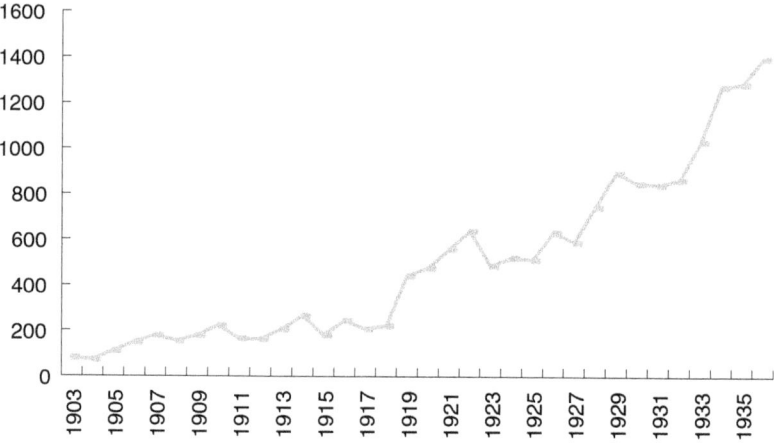

Figure 7.3 The modern-oriented gross domestic fixed-capital formation in China from 1903 to 1936 (measured in 1933 million silver yuan)
Note. The modern-oriented gross domestic fixed-capital formation was constructed as a measure for the apparent consumption of cement, iron and steel products, and machinery. For details, please see Rawski, *Economic Growth*, pp. 242–8.
Source: Rawski, *Economic Growth*, p. 245, Table 5.2

growth in China. Figure 7.3 shows the fixed-capital formation in the modern-oriented sector growing from 223 million in 1910 to 1,398 million in 1936, measured by 1933 silver yuan, an increase of more than six times (less than the growth rate of approximately eight times in overall deposits during the same period).

As more investment went to the modern sector, its output value grew handsomely: in the thirty-three years from 1887 to 1920, the proportion of output value of modern industries in the total output value increased from zero to 6.4 percent. In the following sixteen years, the proportion skyrocketed to 13.6 percent in 1936, with total industrial output reaching 3.9 trillion silver yuan, and the annual growth rate was as high as 7.2 percent.[90] Yan further shows that the correlation coefficients among M2 money supply, modern fixed-capital formation, and gross modern industrial output all exceeded 0.96 from 1912 to 1936.[91]

Money market integration and financial developments boosted both fund supply and demand, which left the direction of change in interest rate ambiguous. Despite there being no reliable nationwide interest rate for

[90] Yan Hongzhong 燕红忠, "货币供给量、货币结构与中国经济趋势, 1650–1936" (Money Supply, Monetary Structure, and Economic Development Trends in China, 1650–1936), *Journal of Financial Research* 7 (2011), 57–69.
[91] Yan, "货币供给量."

China in the period under study, the interest rate in Shanghai was readily available and of good quality. This interest rate could be regarded as the basic rate of the Chinese capital market at the time.[92] Figure 7.4 shows the yearly interbank loan interest rate – an interest rate on loans stipulated by the Association of Native Banks in Shanghai, by which modern banks also abided – from 1872 to 1936. Despite the fluctuation of the interest rate over time, the declining trend was obvious. Moreover, this declining trend occurred not in a peaceful period but in an era full of political chaos, numerous external invasions, countless civil wars, and many other natural as well as man-made disasters, which all would have probably put upward pressure on interest rates due to the high uncertainty. Simultaneously, the various governments also borrowed from the financial market significantly, either as bank loans or as government bonds, which increased fund demand and therefore put upward pressure on interest rates. Despite all these negative odds, the interest rate continued to drop, which implies that the increase in fund supply continuously exceeded the increase in fund demand over the period under study. As Wang points out,[93] the key for industrialization in prewar China did not depend on whether or not China had enough savings, but on how efficiently the surplus could be channeled to investment in the modern sector.

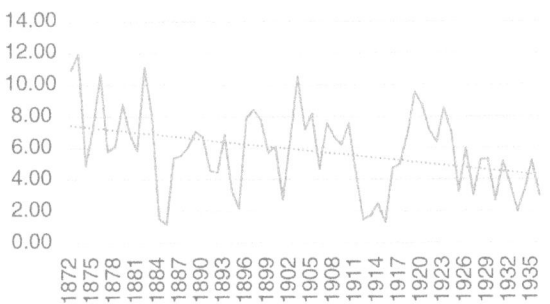

Figure 7.4 The interbank annual interest rate in Shanghai from 1872 to 1936
Source: the annual interest rate is calculated as the average monthly interest rates provided in People's Bank of China, Shanghai Branch 中国人民银行上海分行, 上海钱庄史料汇编 (Archival Materials of Shanghai Native Banks) (Shanghai, Xinhua Bookstore Press, 1961), pp. 630–42

[92] Yan, "货币供给量." [93] Wang, *Money and Banking*, p. 86.

Given that the majority of modern banks and firms were located in treaty ports and/or in concession areas in a treaty port, these modern institutions were better shielded from the aforementioned chaos.[94] Banks in relatively safe places, especially Shanghai, attracted funds from all over China. Modern firms clustered in these places due to the availability of capital supply and security, which were crucial for modern firms to emerge and thrive. The declining interest rate further eased the external financing constraints that impede firm expansion in modern industry. Moreover, the trade boom and industrialization process facilitated the urbanization process: compared with 1900–1910, in 1938, the number of cities with a population of more than 100,000 had increased by more than 70 percent.[95]

Last, the transition from a mainly silver money system to a fiat money system helped shield the Chinese economy from the monetary shocks caused by the changing market conditions of silver, which was a commodity to the rest of the world, and stabilized the economy. This impact can be well illustrated by the experience of the Chinese economy around the Great Depression.[96] When the world silver price increased from 1931, caused by the great powers consecutively abandoning the gold standard, and skyrocketed after the American Silver Purchase Act in 1934, China suffered a massive silver outflow, and deflation kicked in while the rest of world was recovering from the Depression. Only after the Nationalist government implemented currency reform in November 1935 and moved from silver to a fiat money system did the three government banks increase note issues,[97] and the deflationary spiral then stopped and was reversed. By mid-1937, the general price level had returned to the 1931 average.[98]

The Chinese money market obviously became deeper due to money market integration and financial market developments. As shown in Table 7.1, from 1887 to 1920, the M2 supply in China grew by 82.52 percent, which was exceeded by the GDP growth rate of 88.82 percent. This indicates

---

[94] See Ma, "Financial Revolution," for detailed description on the role of concession areas in fostering the development of the financial industry at the time.

[95] See Perkins, *Agricultural Development*, pp. 171, 388–95, Appendix, Table 5.1.

[96] For a detailed description and analyses of various industries and economy as a whole in China during the Great Depression, see T. Shiroyama, *China during the Great Depression: Market, State, and the World Economy, 1929–1937* (Cambridge, MA, Harvard University Council on East Asian Studies, 2008).

[97] For a detailed description of the currency reform, see A.N. Young, *China's Nation-Building Effort, 1927–1937* (New York, Hoover Press, 1971), pp. 216–39.

[98] Young, *China's Nation-Building Effort*, p. 109

Table 7.1 M2/GDP in China, the UK, and the US in the late nineteenth and early twentieth centuries (million US$)

China		1887	1920	1936
	M2	635	1,159	2,908
	GDP	4,346	8,206	8,865
	M2/GDP (%)	14.62	14.13	32.8
UK		1880	1913	1929
	M2	3,486	6,960	15,696
	GDP	11,310	22,860	24,762
	M2/GDP (%)	30.82	30.45	63.39
US		1880	1913	1929
	M2	2,030	15,730	46,600
	GDP	18,765	53,942	90,308
	M2/GDP (%)	10.82	29.16	51.6

Notes: M2 and GDP in China are measured at the current value in 1936 with the exchange rate of yuan to US$ at 0.303. M2 and GDP in the UK and the US are measured at the current value of 1929 with the exchange rate of sterling to US$ at 6.

Sources: this table is adjusted by the authors based on Yan Hongzhong 燕红忠, 中国的货币金融体系, *1600–1949* (The Monetary and Financial System in China, 1600–1949) (Beijing, China Renmin University Press, 2012), pp. 305–6, Table 13–1. Yan cites the money supply in China from Peng Xinwei 彭信威, 中國貨幣史 (Chinese Monetary History) (Shanghai, Shanghai renmin chubanshe, 1958), pp. 888–9 for 1887; and from Rawski, *Economic Growth*, p. 394, Table c16, for 1920 and 1936 (he uses the series with the larger estimators, namely series B in the table); GDP in China for 1887 from Liu Foding 刘佛丁, Wang Yuru 王玉茹, and Yu Jianwei 于建玮, 近代中国的经济发展 (Economic Development in Modern China) (Jinan, Shandong People's Press, 1997), p. 95; and from Wu Chengming 吴承明, 中国的现代化：市场与社会 (Chinese Modernization: Market and Society) (Beijing, Joint Publishing, 2001), pp. 109–10 for 1920 and 1936; and the money supply and GDP in the UK and the US from Milton Friedman and Anna J. Schwartz, *Monetary Trends in the United States and the United Kingdom: Their Relations to Income, Prices, and Interest Rates* (Chicago, University of Chicago Press, 1983), pp. 144–61

that the money supply in China only matched economic expansion, which left the M2/GDP ratio stable at approximately 14 percent. The financial deepening sped up afterwards as the money supply grew more than 150 percent, while GDP grew by merely 8 percent from 1920 to 1936. Hence the depth of the money market measured by M2/GDP more than doubled, from

14.13 percent in 1920 to 32.8 percent in 1936. This dramatic monetization was unprecedented in Chinese monetary history. However, we should not overestimate this achievement, as both the UK and the US experienced dramatic monetization in the earlier 1913–1929 period similar to that in China during 1920–1936. Moreover, compared with the money market in the UK and the US, the Chinese money market was very shallow, as the M2/GDP ratio in China in 1936 was approximately half of that in the UK and two-thirds of that in the US in 1929. Hence there would still probably have been plenty of room for money and financial markets to continue to play a more active role in facilitating economic development in China if progress had not been halted by the Second Sino-Japanese War.

Conclusions

The period from 1800 to 1937 witnessed China's journey towards a unified money market. It started from the market response to and the government's accommodation of the influx of foreign silver. The two types of foreign silver – bullion and coins – coexisted and competed in the money market, and silver coins ultimately became the dominating currency due to their convenience. Consequently, the yuan, as the unit of account for foreign silver coins, became the most important unit of account, based on which an integrated money market began to come into being. The Beiyang government started to mint official silver coins in the early 1910s, and with help from the private financial sector, especially the expanding domestic modern banking sector, official coins gradually outpaced foreign silver coins and became the dominant medium of exchange in the very complex and fragmented money market in China. In 1933, the silver yuan officially became the only unit of account, and hence a unified silver yuan standard was established. The supply of both silver coins and banknotes exchangeable with coins was largely under government control. As China went off silver two years later, a fiat money system fully under government control was founded. As the money market evolved, it facilitated banking expansion, trade, industrialization, and economic stabilization, which promoted economic growth.

The money market integration under study here was an outcome of both a bottom-up evolution from the private sector and a top-down reform from the government. The demand for a standard medium of exchange from the goods market together with the tireless promotion of silver yuan from an ever-expanding financial industry formed the major market force pushing China towards a unified money market. However, the journey did not progress linearly over time but sped up when a powerful central government with modern monetary knowledge took power.[99] The decisive actions taken by the Nationalist government were crucial steps towards monetary unification. The bottom-up force and the top-down reform could be complementary, as the government responded to the market's demand, and the private sector helped the government expand its monetary power. However, the two forces could also be confrontational, as the government gained more power in a unified money market and the private sector lost its ground in banknote issuance. Even worse, the private financial sector was emasculated by the ever more powerful Nationalist government.

This chapter has provided only a very brief summary of the evolution of the money market in historical China. Studies of historical money market development in China are much less common than those of the US, Britain, France, and other European countries.[100] However, there are still many important questions and puzzles that remain to be answered: for instance, why did China, as a centralized country unlike disintegrated Europe, fail to create a unified money market much earlier in history? Why did China, as a country where

---

[99] The success achieved by the Nationalist government in such a short period can be attributed to two factors. One is that the money and financial markets had become integrated through the expanding modern banking network, where large government banks, such as the BoC and BoCom, dominated the network before 1927. Hence the government could easily affect the national money market insofar as it could influence and/or control these major banks. The other is that there was a group of financial experts in the Nationalist government, for instance Song Ziwen and Kong Xiangxi, the ministers of finance consecutively from 1928 to 1937, who knew how to build a modern unified money market. They knew that the key to maintaining an active bond market was to keep a good reputation (see Ho and Li, "Reputation Building"); they knew the importance of having a central bank; they sought advice, consultancy, and assistance from foreign experts, including Arthur Young, Oliver C. Lockhart, F.B. Lynch, Frederick W. Leith-Ross and many others (see Young, *Nation Building*) when they encountered difficulties in economy and finance.

[100] A few exceptions include Kann, *The Currencies of China*, R. von Glahn, *Fountain of Fortune: Money and Monetary Policy in China, 1000–1700* (Berkeley, University of California Press, 1996); and von Glahn, "Foreign Silver Coins," 51–78; Ma, "Monetary System," pp. 57–64; Ma, "Financial Revolution"; Ma and Zhao, "Silver Transformation," in English; in Chinese see Peng, *Monetary History*; Wang, *Money and Banking*; Wu Jingping 吴景平, 上海金融业与国民政府关系研究, 1927–1937 (Research on the Relationship between the Shanghai Financial Industry and the Nationalist Government, 1927–1937) (Shanghai, Shanghai University of Finance and Economics Press, 2002); Yan Hongzhong 燕红忠, 中国的货币金融体系, 1600–1949 (The Monetary and Financial System in China, 1600–1949) (Beijing, China Renmin University Press, 2012); Zhang, 中国货币金融问题 and others on the prewar China.

the earliest fiat money appeared in human history, as early as the Northern Song dynasty (960–1279), only establish a fiat money system by 1935? Why did China lag far behind Europe and the US in financial development in modern history? More research on this topic is desired to shed light on these questions and to offer a better understanding of contemporary Chinese money and financial markets due to path dependence.

Further Reading

Chang, K.-N., "Toward Modernization of China's Currency and Banking, 1927–1937," in P. K.T. Sih (ed.), *The Strenuous Decade: China's Nation-Building Efforts, 1927–1937* (New York, St. John's University Press 1970), pp. 129–65.

Cheng, L., *Banking in Modern China: Entrepreneurs, Professional Managers, and the Development of Chinese Banks, 1897–1937* (Cambridge, Cambridge University Press, 2003).

Coble, P.M., *The Shanghai Capitalists and the Nationalist Government, 1927–1937* (Cambridge, Harvard University Council on East Asian Studies, 1986).

Irigoin, A., "The End of a Silver Era: The Consequences of the Breakdown of the Spanish Peso Standard in China and the United States, 1780s–1850s," *Journal of World History* 20.2 (2009), 207–44.

Ma, D., "Chinese Money and Monetary System, 1800–2000, Overview," in G. Caprio et al. (eds.), *Handbook of Key Global Financial Markets, Institutions, and Infrastructure*, vol. 1 (Oxford, Elsevier, 2012), pp. 57–64.

Ma, D., "Financial Revolution in Republican China during 1900–1937: A Survey and New Interpretation," *Australian Economic History Review*, 2019, 242–62.

Peng Xinwei 彭信威, 中国货币史 (Chinese Monetary History) (Shanghai, Shanghai People's Publishing House, 1987; first published 1954).

Von Glahn, R., "Foreign Silver Coins in the Market Culture of Nineteenth-Century China," *International Journal of Asian Studies* 4.1 (2007), 51–78.

Von Glahn, R., *Fountain of Fortune: Money and Monetary Policy in China, 1000–1700* (Berkeley, University of California Press, 1996).

Wang Yejian 王业键, 中国近代货币与银行的演进, 1644–1937 (The Evolution of Money and Banking in Modern China, 1644–1937) (Beijing, Institute of Economics, Academia Sinica, 1981).

Wu Chengxi 吴承禧, 中国的银行 (The Chinese Banks) (Shanghai, The Commercial Press, 1934).

Wu Jingping 吴景平, 上海金融业与国民政府关系研究, 1927–1937 (Research on the Relationship between the Shanghai Financial Industry and the Nationalist Government, 1927–1937) (Shanghai, Shanghai University of Finance and Economics Press, 2002).

Xu Cangshui 徐沧水 (ed.), 中国今日之货币问题 (Monetary Issues in Today's China) (Shanghai, Bankers' Weekly Press, 1921).

Yan, Hongzhong, "Economic Growth and Fluctuation in the Early Qing Dynasty: From the Perspective of Monetary Circulation," *Frontiers of History in China* 4.2 (2009), 221–64.

Yan Hongzhong 燕红忠, "货币供给量、货币结构与中国经济趋势, 1650–1936" (Money Supply, Monetary Structure and Economic Development Trend in China, 1650–1936), *Journal of Financial Research* 7 (2011), 57–69.

Yan Hongzhong 燕红忠, 中国的货币金融体系, 1600–1949 (The Monetary and Financial System in China, 1600–1949) (Beijing, China Renmin University Press, 2012).

Zhang Naiqi 章乃器, 中国货币金融问题 (The Monetary and Financial Issue in China) (Shanghai, Shenghuo shudian, 1936).

8

Public Finance

ELISABETH KASKE AND MAY-LI LIN

At the turn of the nineteenth century, the Qing dynasty entered a phase of social and economic decline. By 1850, mounting crises had exploded in a devastating series of rebellions (best known for the Taiping Rebellion, 1850–1864). By 1880, up to a quarter of the population had perished, although the numbers are debated. The civil wars revealed the bankruptcy of the dogma of fixed tax quotas that had governed China's fiscal thought since the Ming dynasty (see the chapter by von Glahn and Lamouroux in Volume 1). New commercial taxes, most prominently foreign customs and *lijin* 釐金 (literally "one-thousandth") trade tariffs, soon exceeded agricultural taxes and increased state revenue.[1] Fiscal recovery was short-lived, however, as the double defeat in the First Sino-Japanese War (1894–1895) and the Boxer Rebellion (1900–1901) once again threw Qing finances into turmoil. Servicing the war loans and indemnities while simultaneously promoting costly "New Policy" *(xinzheng* 新政) reforms (1901–1911), the imperial government gradually lost control of the provinces and was unable to check the nationalist awakening of its citizenry. This led to the 1911 Revolution and, eventually, national disintegration during the warlord era. In 1928, the Nationalist Party partly reunified the country and dedicated itself to fiscal consolidation and state developmentalism, despite persistent warlordism and a fledgling communist insurgency. However, the short era of growth known as the "Nanjing decade" was again interrupted after 1937 by the Japanese invasion, which placed the wealthiest revenue-generating regions outside the control of the Nationalist government, and the ensuing civil war with the

---

E. Kaske whishes to thank Ziyan Zhu, Gus Chan, and Rewert Hoffer for pre-screening some of the literature and help with final editing.

[1] Zhou Yumin 周育民, 晚清財政與社會變遷 (Late Qing Fiscal Policies and Social Change) (Shanghai, Shanghai renmin chubanshe, 2000), pp. 238–9; Yeh-chien Wang, *Land Taxation in Imperial China, 1750–1911* (Cambridge, MA, Harvard University Press, 1973), p. 80.

rising Communist Party. The history of institutional change in modern China has to be understood as a response to these historical crises and turning points.

The central conflict of the era was the ability of the center to obtain revenue from the provinces. Under the Qing dynastic system, the center controlled the revenues extracted at the local level through distributional authority rather than direct institutional intervention, but this authority gradually eroded after the mid-nineteenth-century rebellions. Beijing's control of provincial revenues was all but lost after 1916, and only incompletely restored after 1928 by the Nanjing government through military force, nimble bank finance, and revenue-sharing negotiations. The history of a decentralized fiscal system cast a long shadow, leaving the center increasingly dependent on revenues from foreign trade, salt, and the fledgling modern industries of a few coastal provinces. The Japanese occupation cut off the Nationalist government from these sources of revenue and forced it to build up its own revenue-extracting capacities on the ground, but the fruits of these efforts would be reaped by the Communist regime after 1950.

Given the limitations of space and available literature, this chapter focuses on revenue and cannot exhaustively explore expenditures or the relationship between public finance and the wider economy. Assessments of the share of government expenditure in the economy depend on the underlying estimates of national income. Extrapolating from Liu and Yeh's computation of China's GDP for 1933, Wang Yeh-chien has estimated that the share of government revenue and expenditure in GDP remained roughly the same until 1908, about 2.4 percent, even as nominal revenue grew eightfold and real tax revenue tripled between 1861 and 1911, with most of the growth happening after 1895.[2] Between 1908 and 1933, total central and local government expenditure grew slightly faster than GDP, from 2.4 percent to about 4 percent.[3] By 1933, the central government alone consumed about 2.3 percent of GDP, or 2 percent if only non-borrowed revenue is considered. The deficit

---

[2] T. Liu, K.C. Yeh, and T. Chong, *The Economy of the Chinese Mainland: National Income and Economic Development, 1933–1959* (Princeton, NJ, Princeton University Press, 1963), pp. 94, 375–9; Wang, *Land Taxation in Imperial China*, p. 133. For a higher estimate based on a lower assessment of "national income," see A. Feuerwerker, "The State and the Economy in Late Imperial China," *Theory and Society* 13.3 (May 1, 1984), 300.

[3] Y. Xu, Z. Shi, B. van Leeuwen, Y. Ni, Z. Zhang, and Y. Ma, "Chinese National Income, ca. 1661–1933," *Australian Economic History Review* 57.3 (November 2017), 368–93. For a higher estimate see Kubo Tōru 久保亨, "財政史" (Fiscal History), in Kubo Tōru 久保亨 (ed.) 中国経済史入門 (An Introduction to China's Economic History) (Tokyo: Tōkyō daigaku shuppankai, 2012), p. 129.

was 12.3 percent.[4] While this is a far cry from that of Britain, the most developed fiscal state at the time, it may be roughly compared to that of the US before the New Deal, which served as a policy model for Nationalist fiscal planners. In the same year, the non-borrowed revenues of the US federal government were 3.4 percent of GDP, but since the US had a larger deficit during the Great Depression, spending was at 7.9 percent.[5] Despite fiscal modernization, the extractive capacities of the Chinese government remained limited throughout our period.

The Crisis and Restoration of Qing Fiscal Governance, 1800–1894

The White Lotus Rebellion (1796–1804) was a turning point for the Qing. Its suppression lasted for eight years and consumed the total government revenue of almost two years (up to 120 million taels). While statutory revenue had been frozen at the quotas of 1766 due to a hardening dogma of "benevolent" governance, the war demonstrated that it was easier to fix revenues than to control expenditures. Since the Qing paid for wars from accumulated treasure, the silver reserves of both Beijing and the provinces declined drastically, never to fully recover.[6]

The court responded to the crisis with an austerity program starting from the imperial house itself. The grand imperial tours and building projects of the previous century stopped. This restored legitimacy, but could neither improve the deteriorating economic and social conditions of a growing population nor stop the increasing opium imports from (and silver drain to) an expanding British Empire. Recurring floods and the collapse of the Yellow River–Grand Canal system in 1823 aggravated the fiscal crisis. The restoration of the tribute grain shipments to Beijing along the Grand Canal came at huge expense (the less costly option of shipping by sea was tried briefly but soon given up).[7] With an increase of the land tax (nominally

---

[4] Jiang Liangqin 姜良芹, 南京國民政府內債問題研究:以內債政策及運作績效為中心 (A Study of Domestic Debt under the Nanjing Nationalist Government: Domestic Loan Policy and Performance) (Nanjing, Nanjing daxue chubanshe, 2003), p. 314.
[5] Table 1.2 – Summary of Receipts, Outlays, and Surpluses or Deficits (–) as Percentages of GDP: 1930–2025, Historical Tables, Office of Management and Budget, The White House, www.whitehouse.gov/omb/historical-tables.
[6] Y. Dai, *The White Lotus War: Rebellion and Suppression in Late Imperial China* (Seattle, WA, University of Washington Press, 2019); Z. Shi, *Central Government Silver Treasury: Revenue, Expenditure and Inventory Statistics, ca. 1667–1899* (Leiden, Brill, 2016).
[7] J.K. Leonard, *Controlling from Afar: The Daoguang Emperor's Management of the Grand Canal Crisis, 1824–1826* (Michigan, University of Michigan Press, 1996).

73 percent of total revenue) ruled out by the emperors' claim to benevolence, public debt was also not an option, as the fixed-quota tax system and the high interest rates would have made future repayments impracticable. The only legitimate measure available to finance the growing deficit was to cut spending by withholding the "silver to nourish integrity" emoluments received by officials and to expand "contributions," i.e. exactions from holders of imperial privileges like officials or salt merchants as well as the sale of rank and office.[8] Government-licensed salt syndicates became a particular target of exactions. Unlike the land tax, salt tax arrears were almost never forgiven, and the statutory salt tax quota (nominally 8.6 percent of revenue in 1766) was only one-quarter to half of what was actually collected.[9] As contributions piled up, while the high salt price, a looming currency crisis, and rampant smuggling depressed sales, tax debts ballooned in the 1820s, and the salt tax all but collapsed.[10]

By the time of the First Opium War (1839–1842), which firmly established British military dominance in Chinese waters, the imperial treasury was bankrupt. The burden of the war of about 52 million taels (including indemnities), almost a year of statutory revenue, was borne by the provinces.[11] The war and another breach of the Yellow River dikes in 1842 deepened the recession which already plagued the economy due to the silver crisis. The calamity soon erupted into a series of rebellions, of which the Taiping Rebellion was only the most infamous. The total direct costs of these wars from 1851 to 1874 have been estimated at around 800 million to 850 million taels, about twelve times the annual statutory revenue of the empire.[12] These estimates do not account for the loss of human life or the destruction of productive capacity and ecology. As the dynasty could no longer invest in

---

[8] E. Kaske, "Austerity in Times of War: Government Finance in Early Nineteenth-Century China," *Financial History Review* 25.1 (April 2018), 71–96.

[9] Saeki Tomi 佐伯富, 清代鹽政の研究 (A Study of the Qing Salt Administration) (Tokyo: Tōyōshi kenkyūkai, 1956), p. 223; Ni Yuping 倪玉平, 博弈與均衡：清代兩淮鹽政改革 (Games and Equilibrium: The Reforms of the Liang Huai Salt Administration during the Qing Dynasty) (Fujian, Fujian renmin chubanshe, 2006), pp. 62–70.

[10] Chen Feng 陳鋒, 清代鹽政與鹽稅 (Salt Administration and Salt Tax during the Qing Dynasty) (Wuhan, Wuhan daxue chubanshe, 2013), pp. 258, 264; T. Metzger, "The Organizational Capabilities of the Ch'ing State in the Field of Commerce: The Liang-Huai Salt Monopoly, 1740–1840," in W.E. Willmott (ed.), *Economic Organization in Chinese Society* (Stanford, CA: Stanford University Press, 1972), p. 18.

[11] Mao Haijian 茅海建, "鴉片戰爭清朝軍費考" (The Military Expenses of the Qing Empire during the Opium War), *Jindaishi yanjiu* 6 (1996), 34–80; Zhou, 晚清財政與社會變遷, pp. 79–80.

[12] Zhou, 晚清財政與社會變遷, pp. 153; Zhou Zhichu 周志初, 晚清財政经济研究 (Late Qing Government Finance and Economy) (Jinan, Qi Lu shushe, 2002), p. 205.

maintaining the dikes, the Yellow River changed course in 1855, thus rendering the Grand Canal largely defunct.[13]

The wars produced a new generation of provincial leaders, who had raised militias to fight the rebellions. The system of governance they aimed to restore, hand in hand with the imperial government, professed to be a slightly modified version of the prewar economic and fiscal regime.[14] However, the balance between the center and the provinces changed forever, materialized in new institutional settings. For one thing, in the chaos of the rebellions, new military institutions – army secretariats, paymaster and reconstruction bureaus – took over civil roles in resettling deserted land, rebuilding destroyed cities, and repairing irrigation infrastructure.[15] They became the core of a growing permanent provincial administration staffed with "deputies" (*weiyuan* 委員) who stood outside the statutory bureaucracy but, unlike the latter, had more clearly defined jurisdictions and fixed monthly salaries (*xinshui* 薪水).[16] Second, the war also gave rise to new internal transit duties, known as *lijin*, which paid for the institutional expansion, as well as a foreign-managed customs administration in charge of the treaty port trade that had been opened up by the two Opium Wars.

The growth of commercial taxation and the rise of foreign debt is the important and often-told story of late Qing fiscal reforms. Before the 1850s, only one customs system existed, with thirty-four tollhouses along the seaboard, major trade routes, and the northern frontiers.[17] By the 1860s, three types of revenue were collected from moving trade, each with its own tariff schedule and collection agencies: Native Customs (*changguan* 常關), the Maritime Customs Service (*haiguan* 海關, hereafter MCS), and the *lijin* duties. By 1893, according to an estimate by British consul Jamieson, total revenue had increased to 89 million taels and the share of the land tax fallen to

---

[13] I. Amelung, *Der Gelbe Fluß in Shandong (1851–1911): Überschwemmungskatastrophen und ihre Bewältigung im China der späten Qing-Zeit* (Wiesbaden, Harrassowitz, 2000).

[14] M.C. Wright, *The Last Stand of Chinese Conservatism: The T'ung-Chih Restoration, 1862–1874* (New York, Atheneum, 1969).

[15] C. Wooldridge, *City of Virtues: Nanjing in an Age of Utopian Visions* (Seattle, University of Washington Press, 2015), pp. 117–49; E. Schluessel, "Water, Justice, and Local Government in Turn-of-the-Century Xinjiang," *Journal of the Economic and Social History of the Orient* 62.4 (May 16, 2019), 599–625.

[16] Xiao Zongzhi 肖宗志, 候補文官群體與晚清政治 (Expectant Officials and Politics in Late Qing China) (Chengdu, Bashu shushe, 2007); Guan Xiaohong 关晓红, 从幕府到职官：清季外官制的转型与困扰 (From Private Secretary to Official: The Transformation and Predicament of the Provincial Bureaucracy in Late Qing China) (Beijing, Sanlian shudian, 2014).

[17] H.J. van de Ven, *Breaking with the Past: The Maritime Customs Service and the Global Origins of Modernity in China* (New York, Columbia University Press, 2014), pp. 54–60.

36 percent. Over 40 percent came from customs and *lijin* duties; 15 percent from salt.[18] The relative shift from agricultural to commercial taxes has been lauded as a sign of modernization and state strengthening, but it also led to a shift in the balance of power between the central government and the provinces. From this perspective, not the more famous MCS but the *lijin* collectorates were the more revolutionary institutions, because they carved out an independent fiscal space for the provinces.[19]

Lijin duties emerged in the early 1850s out of a flurry of imposts on trade, commodities, and property levied by the army headquarters during the chaos of the civil wars. Most were abolished after the wars, especially levies on land, but provincial leaders defended and eventually salvaged the trade duties – in exchange for a sharing deal with the central government.[20] The term *lijin* was used to refer to at least three types of duty that were accounted separately, namely stationary excises and transit duties on general merchandise ("commodities *lijin*"), inland duties on foreign and native opium after its legalization in 1858 ("opium *lijin*"), and, finally, extra levies on salt in addition to the regular salt tax ("salt *lijin*"). The transit duties on commodities usually stand as synecdoche for all *lijin* duties until their abolition in 1931. In general, duties for a large variety of commodities had to be paid at least twice – at the place of origin and the place of sale – within each province. In reality, toll stations along the road could be more frequent, to say nothing of crossing provincial boundaries. Tax rates, names, and modes of collection differed widely. Further duties were levied from the producers (mostly tea and silk) and as a sales tax (*luodishui* 落地稅).[21]

The *lijin* duties were reviled by Chinese and Western merchants alike, because they imposed a regressive tax burden on the people and made exports more expensive.[22] However, as an institution they also introduced important innovations. First, although some of the stationary excises were

---

[18] G. Jamieson, *The Revenue and Expenditure of the Chinese Empire* (Shanghai, Shanghai Mercury, 1897), pp. 21–2.
[19] Iwai Shigeki 岩井茂樹, 中国近世財政史の研究 (A Study of the Fiscal History of Modern China) (Kyoto: Kyōto daigaku gakujutsu shuppankai, 2004), Chapter 4; Shi Zhihong 史志宏 and Xu Yi 徐毅, 晚清財政: 1851–1894 (Late Qing Fiscal Policy: 1851–1894) (Shanghai, Shanghai caijing daxue chubanshe, 2008), pp. 239–40, 249–50.
[20] E.G. Beal, *The Origin of Likin, 1835–1864* (Cambridge, MA, Harvard University Press, 1958), pp. 121–4; Xu Yi 徐毅, 江蘇匣金制度研究: 1853–1911 年 (A Study of the Lijin in Jiangsu, 1853–1911) (Shanghai, Shanghai caijing daxue chubanshe, 2009). On land see Shi and Xu, 晚清財政: 1851–1894, p. 95.
[21] Luo Yudong 羅玉東, 中國釐金史 (The History of Lijin in China) (Shanghai, Shangwu Yinshuguan, 1936), pp. 55–61; Jamieson, *The Revenue and Expenditure of the Chinese Empire*, pp. 16–18, 33–8.
[22] Luo, 中國釐金史, p. 135.

self-declared (*renjuan* 認捐) by guilds or handled by tax farmers, most transit duties were levied by salaried staff of new provincial bureaus. Unlike regular bureaucrats, tax collectors served under the direct control of the governor and fulfilled specialized tasks, unencumbered by multiple administrative duties. This improved efficiency and monitoring. Second, unlike other taxes the *lijin* duties were assessed and collected in coin instead of silver. This was not only an advantage at the time of their invention when silver was expensive; it also reduced opportunities for collectors to profit from arbitrage to the disadvantage of taxpayers. The *lijin* bureaus were among the first government institutions to regularly report currency exchange rates.[23]

Most importantly, the *lijin* duties became the main source of provincial revenue. The central government only partially succeeded in bringing *lijin* revenue under control. Even though the provinces reported *lijin* income from 1869, they soon settled on a fixed quota of less than 15 million taels for the commodities *lijin* alone (Figure 8.2), whereas the real revenue was closer to 21 million taels (the balance became known as *waixiao* 外銷, meaning outside the auditing of the Board of Revenue).[24] *Lijin* on native opium was never reported, and on foreign opium only reluctantly (see below). As the rebellions blurred the boundaries of government-controlled salt markets, salt *lijin* duties (both stationary and transit) became another source of *waixiao* income for some provinces. Most famously, Sichuan's cheaper salt, manufactured from brine wells, broke the monopoly of expensive Southern Huai sea salt and flooded Hubei and Hunan, whose provincial coffers also benefited from *lijin* on the salt imports. The once powerful Southern Huai salt division appealed to the court in Beijing, but failed to restore complete market dominance. Sichuan in turn reformed its salt administration and greatly increased its salt tax revenue.[25] Growing revenues allowed the provinces to expand their bureaucracies, enlarge their footprint in society, and finance modernization projects. This marked an end to the state of minimal government that had

---

[23] W. He, *Paths toward the Modern Fiscal State: England, Japan, and China* (Cambridge, MA, Harvard University Press, 2013), pp. 164–9. For less optimistic assessments, see Luo, 中國釐金史, pp. 125–7; Zhou, 晚清財政经济研究, pp. 78–9, 85; Zhou, 晚清財政與社會變遷, pp. 260–1.

[24] Luo, 中國釐金史, pp. 119–20; He, *Paths towards the Modern Fiscal State*, pp. 169–72; Zhou, 晚清財政與社會變遷, pp. 344, 352–8.

[25] Ni, 博弈與均衡, pp. 134–42; Chen, 清代鹽政與鹽稅, pp. 143–54; Zhou, 晚清財政與社會變遷, pp. 297–301; M. Zelin, *The Merchants of Zigong: Industrial Entrepreneurship in Early Modern China* (New York, Columbia University Press, 2005), pp. 81–4, 98–9, 152–8; S.A.M. Adshead, *Province and Politics in Late Imperial China: Viceregal Government in Szechwan, 1898–1911* (London, Curzon Press, 1984), pp. 37–42.

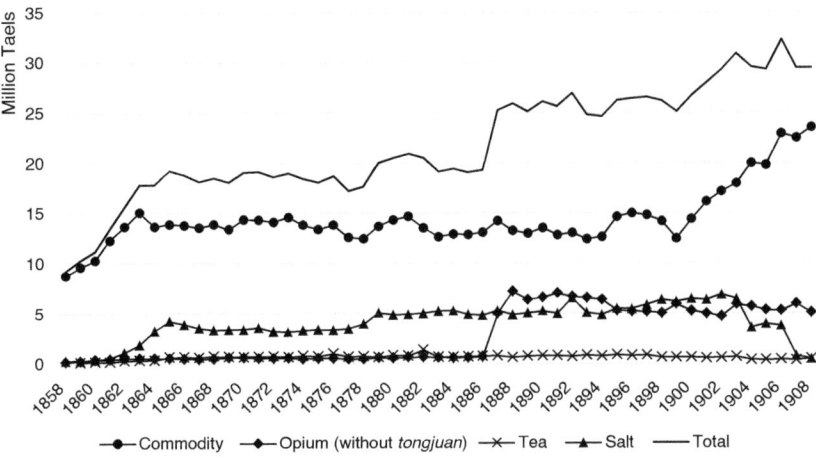

Figure 8.1 *Lijin* revenue, 1858–1908
Source: Zhou Yumin 周育民, "晚清厘金歷年全國總收入的再估計" (A Recalculation of the Total Annual *Lijin* Revenue during the Late Qing), *Qingshi Yanjiu* 3 (2011), 1–24

characterized the Qing ideal.[26] The potential of the *lijin* duties to finance provincial fiscal autonomy would also make them a favorite target of abolition for all centralizing movements in the twentieth century.

The rise of autonomous provincial finances has been interpreted as a sign of a devolution of power. However, as Hon-wai Ho has argued, the growth of regionalism was not a zero-sum game, as long as total revenues were growing and the center continued to negotiate sharing arrangements.[27] Marianne Bastid speaks of a "deconcentration" of an already decentralized fiscal system.[28] It is true that the growing influence of provincial governors forced Beijing to negotiate, sometimes tenaciously, to restore and maintain the traditional remittances to the capital (*jingxiang* 京餉) or poorer provinces

---

[26] Iwai, 中国近世財政史の研究, pp. 128–37; Yang Mei 楊梅, 晚清中央與地方財政關係研究：以厘金為中心 (A Study of the Central and Local Fiscal Relationship in Late Qing China: With a Focus on *Lijin*) (Beijing, Zhishi chanquan chubanshe) pp. 84–94; Shi and Xu, 晚清財政：1851–1894, pp. 260–1.

[27] S. Spector and F.H. Michael, "Regionalism in Nineteenth-Century China," in S. Spector, *Li Hung-Chang and the Huai Army: A Study in Nineteenth-Century Chinese Regionalism* (Seattle, University of Washington Press, 1964), pp. 23–43; Ho Hon-wai 何漢威, "從清末剛毅、鐵良南巡看中央和地方的財政關係" (Late Ch'ing Center–Province Fiscal Relations as Seen in the Imperial Missions of Kang-i and T'ieh-liang in 1899 and 1904), *Bulletin of the Institute of History and Philology, Academia Sinica* 68 (March 1997), 55–115.

[28] M. Bastid, "The Structure of the Financial Institutions of the State in the Late Qing," in S.R. Schram (ed.), *The Scope of State Power in China* (Hong Kong, Chinese University of Hong Kong, 1985), pp. 51–79.

(*xiexiang* 協餉), and that the provincial auditing reports (*zouxiao* 奏銷) were more fiction than real. The Board of Revenue never gained complete knowledge of provincial finances despite a cautious attempt at accounting reform in 1884. Nonetheless, Beijing's revenues continued to improve, at least until the Sino-Japanese War, as the center managed to mobilize an increasing share of both old and new provincial revenues. In addition to a fixed quota of 8 million (later 10 million) taels of traditional *jingxiang* remittances for the maintenance of the capital, the provinces were also allotted payments to so-called "dedicated funds" (*zhuanxiang jingfei* 專項經費). These included defense-related funds (for the capital, the northeastern border and the modern navy), augmentations of the metropolitan salaries, subsidies for the imperial household, and allocations for new government expenditures (the Foreign Legations Fund established in 1876 and the Railway Fund established in 1889). According to Zhou Yumin, total assignment orders to the central government in 1898 amounted to 22 million taels, about a quarter of revenues, even as not all of it actually arrived. Much of these funds came from "provincial" *lijin* revenues.[29]

Customs revenue, on the other hand, was considered central government revenue, but frequently also financed projects in the provinces, especially those related to defense and military industrialization. The newer of the two customs services, the MCS, goes back to 1854 when foreign merchants in Shanghai, opened as a treaty port by the Nanjing Treaty of 1842, came to self-organize their duty payments to the customs tollhouse during a local rebellion. The model was regularized and extended to the other treaty ports (increased from five to sixteen) after 1861. From 1864, Inspector General Robert Hart resided in Beijing. Each treaty port was furnished with a commissioner and a staff of mostly foreign career bureaucrats. Notwithstanding its foreignness and "semi-colonial" characteristics, the MCS was not yet the *imperium in imperio* that would mark the Beiyang and warlord periods after the 1911 Revolution.[30] The foreign customs commissioners in the treaty ports served as middlemen between the foreign merchants, their consuls, and the Chinese customs superintendents, a "frontier regime," in the words of Van de Ven.[31] However, under the Qing the funds were still stored in traditional Chinese customs banks, albeit under separate accounts, and controlled by superintendents embedded in the usual bureaucratic hierarchies.

---

[29] Zhou, 晚清財政與社會變遷, pp. 242–4, 370–1. Cf. Iwai, 中国近世財政史の研究, p. 90.
[30] Cf. Dai Yifeng 戴一峰, 近代中國海關與中國財政 (The Maritime Customs and Fiscal Policies in Modern China) (Xiamen, Xiamen daxue chubanshe, 1993), pp. 28–36.
[31] Van de Ven, *Breaking with the Past*, p. 65.

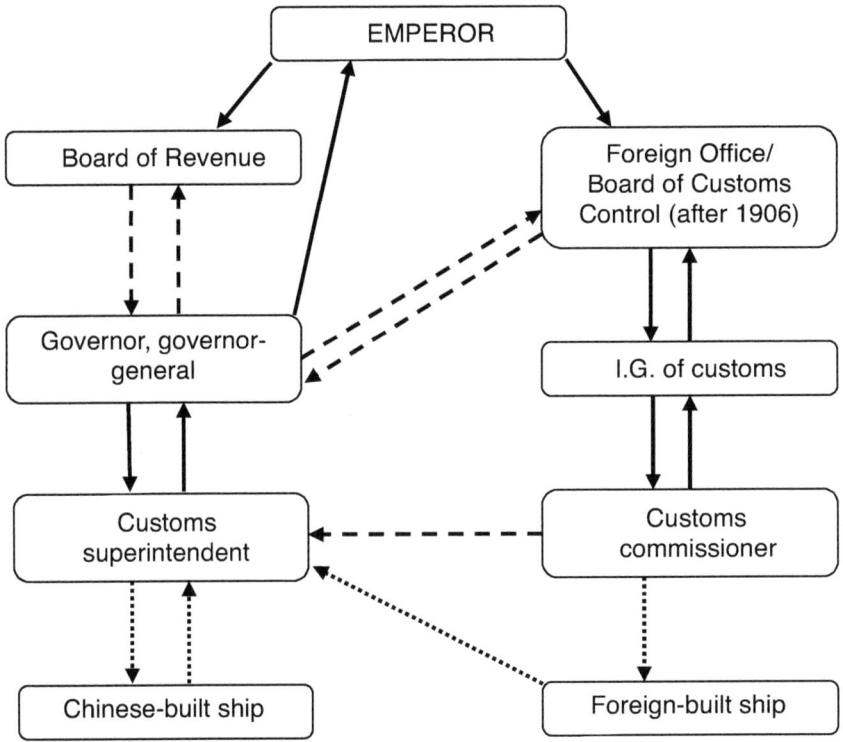

Figure 8.2 Foreign and Native Customs
Source: Ren Zhiyong 任智勇, 晚清海關再研究：以二元體制為中心 (A New Study of the Late Qing Maritime Customs: With a Focus on the Dual System) (Beijing, Zhongguo renmin daxue chubanshe, 2012), p. 88. Dotted line: tax assessment (down) and tax payment (up); solid line: hierarchical relationship, report (up), order (down); dashed line: equal relationship

Because Maritime Customs funds were treated as an extension of the Native Customs system, they were at the disposal of the imperial government and served as a counterbalance to the greater independence of the provinces. The insertion of a foreign institution changed information flows more than revenue flows: the Native Customs continued to operate according to the quota system, with extra-quota income spent locally or ending in the pockets of the collectors. In contrast, fixed quotas were abandoned for the "foreign tax" (*yangshui* 洋稅), and the expansion of revenue, tightly controlled by modern statistical methods, was allowed to follow the growth (and occasionally contraction) of trade. Foreign supervision of the Maritime Customs revenue thus performed an important function of checking the acquisitive habits of the Chinese tax collectors and solving the information asymmetry between the imperial center and regional fiscal extraction.[32]

The fact that the revenue under MCS supervision was subject to statistics rather than fixed quotas, and thus protected from revenue leakage, made it an ideal security for China's indemnities and foreign loans. One of the service's first tasks after its regularization in 1861 had been to oversee the collection of revenue to pay the indemnities for the Second Opium War. In 1867, when Zuo Zongtang borrowed the first out of six war loans totaling 15.95 million taels to recover the northwestern provinces and Xinjiang from Muslim rebels, the Zongli Yamen (Foreign Office) and Inspector General of Customs Robert Hart devised a formal process that required imperial endorsement for all foreign loans secured with customs revenue, which thus became a sovereign debt. This strengthened the position of the central government, as governors could no longer borrow without central approval.[33] However, the close association of the central government with customs revenue and foreign loans created a trajectory of deepening dependence well into the 1930s.

By 1894, the Qing had largely recovered from the civil wars. The land tax had been restored to its prewar quotas, and the central government had a reasonably firm grip (by Qing standards) on provincial resources, was almost debt-free, and, officially at least, had no deficits. Steven Halsey has argued that Qing China had emerged as a military–fiscal state able to mobilize indirect taxes for national defense. Compared to Brewer's ideal-type British fiscal–military state a century earlier, the transformation of the Chinese state was far from complete. It lacked not only tools of sustainable public deficit finance but also a professional tax administration in the Weberian sense, with the exception of the foreign-staffed MCS, which in 1893 contributed about 25 percent to the total budget. Strictly speaking, the central government did not even have the power of the purse as the decentralized fiscal system delegated revenue extraction to the provinces.[34]

---

[32] Jamieson, *The Revenue and Expenditure of the Chinese Empire*, pp. 3, 6, 18–20; Dai, 近代中國海關與中國財政, pp. 94–7; Ren, 晚清海關再研究, pp. 133–5.

[33] Ma Jinhua 馬金華, 外債與晚清政局 (Foreign Loans and Late Qing Politics) (Beijing, Shehui kexue wenxian chubanshe, 2011), p. 73; Hamashita Takeshi 濱下武志, 中国近代経済研究：清末海関財政と開港場市場圏 (Economic History of Modern China: Maritime Customs Finance and Open Port Market Zones in Late Qing China) (Tokyo: Institute of Oriental Culture, Tokyo University, 1989), pp. 71–2; Z. Ren, 晚清海關再研究, pp. 117–35.

[34] S.R. Halsey, *Quest for Power: European Imperialism and the Making of Chinese Statecraft* (Cambridge, MA, Harvard University Press, 2015), pp. 81–112; J. Brewer, *The Sinews of Power: War, Money, and the English State, 1688–1783* (Cambridge, MA, Harvard University Press, 1990), pp. xiii, 75; He, *Paths toward the Modern Fiscal State*.

It is, therefore, useful to follow Ja Ian Chong's suggestion to distinguish authority from capacity.[35] The imperial government in Beijing had authority, through the power to appoint officials and as the symbolic center of the empire. But it had the capacity neither to actually know the full extent of provincial finances nor to force the governors to follow orders. The erosion of the dynasty's authority began when the indemnities of two military defeats forced the center to encroach upon provincial fiscal interests and unhinged the balance that had emerged from the dual system of trade taxation.

The Success and Failure of Qing Centralization, 1895–1911

The defeats in 1895 and 1900 pushed the Qing back into a fiscal predicament. The war loans and indemnities of the Sino-Japanese War left the empire with annual debt payments of roughly 24 million taels out of a total revenue of 89 million. The Boxer indemnities six years later brought annual payments to 42 million taels.[36] The crisis generated some appreciation for Western ideas of governance. In 1894 and 1898, the Board of Revenue experimented with domestic bonds, but the bonds were soon converted into old-style contributions to be repaid with rank and office instead of principal and interest. The name "trust bonds" (*zhaoxin gupiao* 昭信股票) did as much to destroy trust in the government as their failure itself.[37] On the eve of the Boxer Rebellion, the board for the first time produced a rudimentary budget which anticipated future revenue and differentiated between central and provincial finances. The budget revealed substantial growth during the postwar years but also a large deficit (see Table 8.1), even though these numbers do not include the shares allocated to the provinces to repay the various war loans.[38] In response to the deficit, the throne sent an imperial commissary to the provinces;

---

[35] J.I. Chong, "Breaking Up Is Hard to Do: Foreign Intervention and the Limiting of Fragmentation in the Late Qing and Early Republic, 1893–1922," *Twentieth-Century China* 35.1 (November 2009), 75–98.

[36] Liang Qichao 梁啟超, 中國國債史 (A History of Chinese National Debts), in Liang, 飲冰室合集 (Collected Works from the Ice Drinker Studio), vol. 6 (ed. Lin Zhijun 林志鈞) (Beijing, Zhonghua shuju, 1989), pp. 5967–8.

[37] Li Wenjie 李文杰, "息借商款與晚清財政" (The "Xijie Shangkuan" Bond and Late Qing Fiscal Policies), *Lishi Yangjiu* 1 (2018), 68–86; Iwo Amelung 阿梅龍, "國債概念的接受與中國早期發行之公債" (The Concept of Government Debt and the Earliest Public Debt in China), in I. Amelung 阿梅龍, 真實與建構: 中國近代史及科技史新探 (Truth and Construct: New Explorations on the History of Science in Modern China) (Beijing, Shehui kexue wenxian chubanshe, 2019), pp. 274–90.

[38] Peng Yuxin 彭雨新, "清末中央與各省財政關係" (Central and Provincial Fiscal Relationships in the Late Qing), *Shehui kexue zazhi* (Peking) 1 (1937), 83–110.

Table 8.1 Budget for the 26th Year of Guangxu (1900) in *kuping* taels

	Revenue	Expenditure	Balance
Central government	18,764,600	23,036,200	−4,271,600
Provinces	79,500,000	92,000,000	−12,500,000
Total	98,264,600	115,036,200	−16,771,600

Source: Luo Yudong 羅玉東, "光緒朝補救財政之方策" (Strategies to Salvage Government Finance in the Guangxu Period), *Zhongguo Jindai Jingjishi Yanjiu Jikan* 中國近代經濟史研究集刊 1.2 (May 1933), 216

however, the goal was not to reform provincial institutions but to negotiate higher remittance quotas to Beijing.[39]

More ambitious New Policy reforms began in the provinces after the Boxer Rebellion, where they drove up the costs of government. Left alone to carry the double burden of the indemnities and the costly modernization of schooling and policing, the provinces broke all traditional limitations on raising taxes and invented countless "miscellaneous imposts," including surcharges on old taxes and new excises. Provincial governments imported machines to mint silver and copper coins, established banks, and issued paper money or government bonds (see the chapter by Li and Yan in this volume).[40] They also began a gradual process of intra-provincial centralization by reorganizing their diverse and poorly co-ordinated fiscal bureaus into a hierarchical structure.[41]

Fiscal reorganization at the center did not start before a government reform commission traveled to Japan, Europe, and the USA in 1905–1906. On September 1, 1906, an imperial edict announced the plan to institute a constitutional monarchy. The Board of Revenue changed its name to Ministry of Finance (*duzhibu* 度支部) – literally "ministry in control of expenditure," symbolizing the departure from the traditional focus on fixed-quota

---

[39] Ho, "從清末剛毅"; Liu Zenghe 劉增合, "財" 與 "政"：清季財政改制研究 ("Finance" and "Politics": A Study of Late Qing Fiscal Reforms) (Beijing, Sanlian shudian, 2014), pp. 83–6.
[40] Wang Shu-hwai 王樹槐, 庚子賠款 (The Boxer Indemnities) (Taipei, Institute of Modern History, Academia Sinica, 1974), Chapter 2; Hamashita, *Economic History of Modern China*, pp. 58–64, 166–70; Ho Hon-wai 何漢威, "從銀賤錢荒到銅元泛濫：清末新貨幣的發行及其影響" (From Silver Glut and Coin Shortage to Surplus of Copper Coins: The Issuance of New Currencies during the Late Qing Period and Its Effects), *Bulletin of the Institute of History and Philology, Academia Sinica* 62.3 (1993), 389–494; Pan Guoqi 潘國旗, 近代中國國內公債研究 (1840–1926) (A Study of Public Bonds in Modern China (1840–1926)) (Beijing, Jingji kexue chubanshe, 2007).
[41] Liu, "財"與"政", pp. 352–66.

Table 8.2 National revenue for 1911 (Ministry of Finance)

Source	In *kuping* taels	Percentage of total
Land tax	48,101,346	16.2
Public enterprises	46,600,899	15.7
Salt tax	46,312,355	15.6
Lijin duties	43,187,907	14.5
Miscellaneous incomes	35,244,750	11.9
Maritime Customs	35,139,918	11.8
Miscellaneous taxes	26,163,842	8.8
Native Customs	6,999,370	2.4
Contributions	5,652,333	1.9
Domestic debt	3,560,000	1.2
Total national revenue	296,962,720	

Source: H. Ho, "A Final Attempt at Financial Centralisation in the Late Qing Period, 1909–11," *Papers on Far Eastern History* 32 (September 1985), 53

revenues – and converted its subdivisions from mixed territorial-cum-functional into modern functional departments. In 1907, a statistical department was added. The nine-year schedule for constitutional preparation promulgated in 1908 stipulated the clearing (*qingli* 清理) of provincial finances in 1909–1910.[42] The ministry dispatched fiscal supervisors (*jianliguan* 監理官) to establish a hierarchical chain of command between the ministry and the provincial treasurers, with the goal of limiting the autonomy of the governors. While this was not entirely successful, the investigation managed to uncover local fees and extra-account (*waixiao*) revenues and forced the provinces to accelerate the centralization of their fiscal bureaucracies. In 1910, the provinces submitted their reports to the Ministry of Finance, which published the first national budget for 1911 (Table 8.2).[43]

The budget revealed a national revenue of almost 297 million taels, four times the statutory revenue of 71 million taels at the beginning of the nineteenth century. The importance of foreign customs revenue had been eclipsed by salt taxes and income from public enterprises (industries, telegraphs, mines, mints, etc.). There still was a deficit of 42 million taels which

---

[42] R.S. Horowitz, "Breaking the Bonds of Precedent: The 1905–6 Government Reform Commission and the Remaking of the Qing Central State," *Modern Asian Studies* 37.4 (October 2003), 775–97; N. Meienberger, *The Emergence of Constitutional Government in China (1905–1908)* (Bern: Peter Lang, 1980), pp. 42–5; M.E. Cameron, *The Reform Movement in China, 1898–1912* (New York, AMS Press, 1974), pp. 103–4; Chen Feng 陳鋒 and Cai Guobin 蔡國斌, 清代財政史 (A Fiscal History of the Qing Dynasty) (Changsha, Hunan renmin chubanshe, 2013), pp. 171–6.
[43] Liu, "財" 與 "政", pp. 142–98, 373–8; see also Zhou, 晚清財政與社會變遷, pp. 428–9.

the National Assembly – newly convened in 1910 as a consultative organ to the government – converted (on paper at least) into a surplus mainly by cutting the budgets of the Ministries of War and of Post and Communications. But the major unresolved question in the budget was the division between the central, provincial, and local revenues. The debate over how to share tax revenues had been going on in the provinces since 1906. Many favored the Japanese model, which distinguished between "national" (*guojia* 國家) and "regional/local" (*difang* 地方) taxes, but no agreement was reached as to how to fit the province into this dichotomy. The budget subsumed all revenues under central control, making them "national taxes," and kept 62 percent of expenditures at the disposal of the Beijing ministries, the army, and the court; only 21 percent went to the provinces for their expenses (not counting the 37 million taels that were added to the total budget as expenditures of local governments). This in fact eliminated the provinces as autonomous fiscal agents. In reality, the Beijing government did not have the effective power to control the provincial budgets.[44] Before a similar budget for 1912 could pass the Assembly in the fall of 1911, the revolution upended the dynasty.[45]

By the summer of 1911, the Qing still appeared relatively successful. The provinces had substantially increased their extractive capacities, while the center seemed to have more knowledge and receive a larger share of the fiscal bounty. What went wrong? Arguably, the seeds for the secession of the provinces and the collapse of the Qing dynasty were sown early on in the division between *lijin* and customs duties and the dependence of the central government on the foreign-managed MCS. The conflict of interests between the center and the provinces was exacerbated by the war indemnities, which eroded the authority of the imperial government faster than it was able to increase its capacity to rule.

The relationship between the MCS and the Qing government grew closer after 1867, when all customs-secured loans required central government sanction. In the same year, the responsibilities of the MCS were expanded to include the collection of duties from all steamships, Chinese or foreign-owned, while non-treaty ports were closed to steamship traffic. By legalizing the practice of *lijin* evasion by Chinese merchants using foreign-flagged steamships, this provision increased the share of revenue that the central government could control through the MCS. The Chefoo Convention of 1876

---

[44] Ho, "A Final Attempt at Financial Centralisation in the Late Qing Period, 1909–11," p. 38; Liu, "財" 與 "政", pp. 226–30, 296–347. The remaining 17 percent went on servicing debt.
[45] "前清宣統四年全國歲入歲出總預算" (Annual Revenues and Expenditures for 1912), *Yinhang Zhoubao* 銀行週報 (Bank Weekly) 26.27–8 (1942), 24–8.

(ratified only in 1887) not only opened additional treaty ports to expand steamer shipping, but also brought the *lijin* on foreign opium under the MCS,[46] thus depriving the provinces of more extra-account revenue (see Figure 8.2).

The indemnities for the Sino-Japanese War and the Boxer Rebellion forced the Qing government to bring more of the provincial revenues under central control, without benefiting from these revenues to enhance its own capacity to govern. Only the former involved a formal loan issued as bearer bonds in the markets. The Treaty of Shimonoseki required China to pay 200 million taels in indemnities and 30 million for Japan's withdrawal from Weihaiwei within seven years at 5 percent interest. In order to facilitate interest-free early repayment within three years, the Qing government borrowed three gold loans each of £16 million (in 1895, 1896, and 1898) from Russo-French and Anglo-German banking consortia at interest rates between 4 and 5 percent payable within thirty-six to forty-five years (the last instalment would be paid in 1943). Borrowing bought time but increased effective costs due to loan discounts and exchange rate losses (known as *bangkui* 镑亏, "sterling loss"). Worse were the political costs, since the lending powers seized concessions and leases for themselves.[47]

The indemnities expanded the authority of the MCS, which evolved into "a debt-collection agency for foreign financial interests," and thus "a typical 'informal empire' institution," in Van de Ven's words.[48] The contract for the second Anglo-German loan stipulated that the MCS should take over the revenue of seven *lijin* collectorates as security.[49] While Inspector General Robert Hart refused to take out new loans to pay the Boxer indemnities, his MCS took charge of the revenues of the Native Customs stations located within fifty *li* (roughly eighteen miles) of the treaty ports.[50] Provincial resistance to the loss of vital revenues destabilized the already vulnerable revenue-sharing system.

---

[46] A. Reinhardt, "Treaty Ports as Shipping Infrastructure," in R.A. Bickers and I. Jackson (eds.), *Treaty Ports in Modern China: Law, Land and Power* (London, Routledge, 2016), pp. 104–5.

[47] Liang, 中國國債史, pp. 5943–54. See also A.G. Coons, *The Foreign Public Debt of China* (Philadelphia, University of Pennsylvania Press, 1930), p. 12; Pan, 近代中國內公債研究, pp. 85–91.

[48] Van de Ven, *Breaking with the Past*, pp. 9, 134.

[49] F.H.H. King, C.E. King, and D.J.S. King, *The Hongkong Bank between the Wars and the Bank Interned, 1919–1945*, vol. 2 (Cambridge, Cambridge University Press, 1988), pp. 287–8; Van de Ven, *Breaking with the Past*, p. 142; Hamashita, *Economic History of Modern China*, p. 53.

[50] R. Hart, "Memorandum Concerning the Indemnity to Be Paid by China, 25th March 1901," in Maritime Customs (ed.), *Documents Illustrative of the Origin, Development, and Activities of the Chinese Customs Service*, vol. I: *Despatches, Letters, Memoranda, etc. 1842–1901* (Shanghai, Statistical Department of the I.G. of Customs, 1938), pp. 604–10; Liang, 中國國債史, pp. 5967–8; W. Tsai, "The Inspector General's

The Boxer indemnities were crucial in changing the balance between the center and the provinces. During the Rebellion, the southeastern governors had maintained neutrality while foreign powers invaded the capital. They saw the indemnities as a responsibility of the central government and mostly refused to mobilize more *lijin* duties for their repayment. Instead, almost a third came from salt price surcharges (*yanjin jiajia* 鹽斤加價), i.e. a surtax on the fixed sales price of salt in the monopoly trade, and one-fifth from surcharges on the land tax, both revenues of the central government. A further fifth came from new excises and imposts, which became a pretext also to greatly expand provincial and local levies. The Boxer indemnities thus opened the floodgates for the chaotic proliferations of taxes and surcharges that would form the basis of warlord finance in Republican China and make fiscal standardization difficult (see below).[51]

Loath to lose the mainstay of their fiscal independence, the provinces also resisted the Mackay Treaty of 1902, which replaced multiple *lijin* toll stations with a single excise of 7.5 percent *ad valorem* in exchange for the powers' consent to raise customs tariffs from 7.5 to 12.5 percent. Only seven provinces, mostly poorer ones with little *lijin* revenue to lose, implemented the provincial "consolidated tax" (*tongjuan* 統捐 or *tongshui* 統稅).[52] As a result, the treaty was never ratified. The "consolidated tax" was more successful as a replacement for the opium *lijin*, but it was soon obliterated by the political will to abolish the vice of opium. The imposts offered by Beijing to make up the loss, another salt price surcharge and a newly created stamp duty (*yinhuashui* 印花稅), covered less than 20 percent of the estimated 28 million taels in lost revenue, while further alienating the provinces.[53]

The straw that broke the camel's back was the imperial government's belated attempt to nationalize railway development (see the chapter by Köll in this volume). Absent guidance from Beijing, provincial leaders had been at

---

Last Prize: The Chinese Native Customs Service, 1901–31," *Journal of Imperial and Commonwealth History* 36.2 (June 2008), 243–58.

[51] Chong, "Breaking Up Is Hard to Do," 75–98; Hamashita, *Economic History of Modern China*, pp. 52–3, 85–7; Wang, 庚子賠款, Table 26, p. 151; Zhou, 晚清財政與社會變遷, pp. 368–70.

[52] Luo, 中國釐金史, pp. 137, 53–4; Yang, 晚清中央與地方財政關係研究, pp. 67, 72, 241–4; Zhou, 晚清財政與社會變遷, pp. 365–6; D. Wang, *China's Unequal Treaties: Narrating National History* (Lanham, Lexington Books, 2005), pp. 19–22.

[53] Liu Zenghe 劉增合, 鴉片稅收與清末新政 (Opium Tax Revenue and Late Qing New Policy Reforms) (Beijing, Sanlian shudian, 2005), pp. 142–7, 181–264; Ho Hon-wai 何漢威, "清季國產鴉片的統捐與統稅" (The Consolidated Tax on Native Opium during the Qing Period), in 薪火集：傳統與近代變遷中的中國經濟 (Passing on the Torch: China's Economy from Tradition to Modern Transformation) (Taipei, Daoxiang chubanshe, 2001), p. 586 and *passim*.

the helm of railway nationalism in China since the 1890s. The redemption of the American concession for the Canton–Hankou railway and the favorable loan terms for the Tianjin–Pukou railway (the "Pukou terms") became landmark cases towards railway sovereignty. Many provinces made plans for railway construction and mobilized patriotic sentiment to raise native funds. By 1911, however, the Ministry of Communication decided to nationalize these regional lines with the help of a loan from a four-power banking consortium (Germany, Britain, France, the USA) secured by *lijin* and salt revenues of Hubei and Hunan (hence "Huguang loan"). The move met fierce resistance, which became a major trigger of the 1911 Revolution.[54]

Beijing Finance under Warlord Regimes, 1912–1926

That the newly founded Republic of China eventually ended up in the hands of provincial warlords shows that fiscal–military integration had been more successful on the provincial than on the national level. This made it difficult for any new national regime to establish a secure fiscal basis. During the four decades following the revolution, no regime was able to hold all of China's territory. Any contender for central government was forced to renegotiate the allocation of revenues from more or less independent regional powers. During the Beiyang and warlord eras (1912–1927), budgetary imagination and fiscal reality diverged widely. The land tax, though still in the budget, hardly ever arrived in Beijing and was formally yielded to the provinces by the Nationalists in 1927 (see below). Foreign-managed customs and salt tax administrations secured the most reliable revenue sources for the center. Thanks to securities provided by these institutions, domestic debt flourished despite political instability, and borrowing (including foreign loans) maintained a level of over 20 percent of revenue until the Sino-Japanese War (Table 8.3).

Since, during the revolution, most provinces had cut their remittances, the ability to borrow became vital for the young republic. After Yuan Shikai replaced revolutionary leader Sun Yat-sen as provisional president in March 1912 and moved the capital from Nanjing to Beijing, his government instantly began negotiations with the Huguang loan banks and in April 1913 signed a £25 million reorganization loan agreement with a regrouped five-power consortium. More than two-thirds of the loan sum was retained for debt service, reparations to foreigners harmed during the unrest, and the

---

[54] E. Köll, *Railroads and the Transformation of China* (Cambridge, MA, Harvard University Press, 2019); E. Kaske, "Taxation, Trust, and Government Debt: State–Elite Relations in Sichuan, 1850–1911," *Modern China* 45.3 (May 1, 2019), 239–94.

Table 8.3 Revenue structure of the central government, 1913–1945 (%)

	Customs	Salt taxes	Agricultural taxes	Taxes on industry and commerce	Government enterprises	Debt
1913–1919	15.1	17.2	17.7	7.6	–	20.6
1928–1932	44.8	18.5	–	9.0	0.6	20.2
1933–1937	31.2	16.6	–	11.6	3.7	23.6
1938–1945	3.1	3.0	3.6	2.6	3.7	78.5

Source: Kubo Tōru 久保亨, Kajima Jun 加島潤, and Kigoshi Yoshinori 木越義則 (eds.), 統計でみる中国近現代経済史 (Chinese Modern and Contemporary Economic History as Seen in Statistics) (Tokyo, Tōkyō daigaku shuppankai, 2016), p. 162

reform of the salt tax administration which served as security.[55] The loan was contentious from the beginning. Opposition by the Nationalist Party contributed to a breakup of the volatile coalition and the "second revolution." It has also been seen as symbolic of China's loss of sovereignty. In fact, Yuan's negotiators were quite successful in minimizing foreign political influence while turning foreign support and diplomatic recognition to the advantage of his government.[56]

As part of the loan terms, Yuan established a Sino-Foreign Salt Inspectorate with foreign deputies at the chief and district inspectorates as well as audit offices. Reforms under the British chief inspector, Sir Richard Morris Dane, moved tax collection to the site of production, created a professional corps of administrators, improved tax assessment, lowered collection costs, and centralized tax receipts and statistics. This brought a greater share of salt revenues under the control of the central government, making the salt tax into the largest revenue stream of the government in Beijing ahead of customs duties. Similarly to the Maritime Customs Service, the Sino-Foreign Salt Inspectorate managed to insulate itself from the political chaos of the early Republican era and survived as

---

[55] Jia Shiyi 賈士毅, "五十年來中國之財政" (The Fiscal Policy of China during the Last Fifty Years), in Liang Qichao 梁啟超 (ed.), 晚清五十年來之中國 (China during the Fifty Years since the Late Qing) (Hong Kong, Longmen shudian, 1922), pp. 107–27.
[56] Lin May-li 林美莉, "善後大借款析論：民國財政的奠基與民族主義的激盪" (An Analysis of the Reorganization Loan: Fiscal Foundation of the Republic of China and Catalyst of Nationalism), in Wang Jianlang 王建朗 and Huang Ko-wu 黃克武 (eds.), 兩岸新編中國近代史 (New Studies on the History of Modern China from Both Sides of the Taiwan Strait) (Beijing, Shehui kexue wenxian chubanshe, 2016), pp. 597–626.

an institution, even as revenues were frequently seized by warlord regimes after 1917.[57]

The importance of the MCS as revenue agency for the central government increased after the revolution, not least because it shook off the control of the Chinese superintendent.[58] In 1913, Yuan established a National Loans Bureau with Inspector General Francis Aglen as vice chair, expanding the activities of the MCS from securing foreign debt to supporting a market for domestic bonds. The successful floating of domestic debt was an important novelty of the Republican era, especially for the central government. Shortly before the revolution, the Qing had issued "Patriotic Bonds" (*aiguo gongzhai* 愛國公債) and included some 3.5 million taels of public debt as a legitimate revenue in the budget of 1911 (see Table 8.3). With the debacle of the 1898 "trust bonds" still in everyone's memory, subscriptions to the bonds were almost exclusively involuntary payments by government officials and Manchu nobles. Nonetheless, Yuan Shikai's government assumed responsibility for their repayment, and issued a number of new public bonds. The fact that the MCS stepped in to provide security greatly enhanced their popularity.[59]

Yuan Shikai's regime was reasonably effective in restoring fiscal authority. The government produced a modern budget. Customs and salt surplus (*guanyu* 關餘 and *yanyu* 鹽餘), i.e. the income from customs and salt taxes after servicing China's foreign debt, provided a moderately stable income. Government bonds were oversubscribed. Silver coins bearing President Yuan's image were hugely popular and facilitated monetary integration.[60] Beijing also managed to persuade the provinces to provide fiscal information and remit revenue quotas. While the postrevolutionary coalition government had adopted Sun Yat-sen's idea of "distributed powers" (*junquan* 均權) and divided all tax revenues into "national" and "regional/local" taxes,

---

[57] S.A.M. Adshead, *Modernization of the Chinese Salt Administration, 1900–1920* (Cambridge, MA, Harvard University Press, 1970); J.C. Strauss, *Strong Institutions in Weak Polities: State Building in Republican China, 1927–1940* (Oxford and New York, Clarendon Press, 1998), Chapter 3.

[58] D. Ma, "The Rise of a Financial Revolution in Republican China in 1900–1937: An Institutional Narrative," *Australian Economic History Review* 59.3 (November 2019), 242–62.

[59] Pan, 近代中國國內公債研究, p. 115; Zhang Guisu 張桂素 (ed.), "宣統年間發行愛國公債史料" (Histortial Material on Issuing the "Patriotic Government Bonds" during the Xuantong Reign), *Lishi dang'an* 4 (1997), pp. 67–76; Van de Ven, *Breaking with the Past*, Chapter 5.

[60] A. Kuroda, "The Collapse of the Chinese Imperial Monetary System," in K. Sugihara (ed.), *Japan, China, and the Growth of the Asian International Economy, 1850–1949* (Oxford, Oxford University Press, 2005), pp. 103–26.

Yuan's increasingly authoritarian regime turned to centralization. Beijing directly appointed the heads of the provincial finance departments, restored the Qing remittance system from general tax revenue, and additionally designated five exclusive imposts for the central government (*zhongyang zhuankuan* 中央專款), namely the tobacco and liquor tax, the stamp duty, the contract enforcement fee, the tobacco and liquor license fee, and the brokerage fee.[61] In 1914, Yuan's Ministry of Finance made another attempt to abolish the *lijin* transit duties, which had been designated "national" tax in 1912. In order to signal to the international community China's willingness to ratify the Mackay Treaty, Jiangsu became a test case to replace its multiple *lijin* stations with a single excise of 7.5 percent levied at the place of production (*chuchang shui* 出廠稅) and sale (*xiaochang shui* 銷場稅). Other provinces followed reluctantly, but readjusted their tax assessment and used tax farming in order to offset the steep fall in revenue seen in Jiangsu. In February 1916, the Ministry of Finance ordered all provinces to replace *lijin* with the consolidated tax (*tongjuan*).[62]

These advances were upended by Yuan Shikai's ill-fated self-coronation and soon by his death in 1916. The provinces seceded, and regional warlords became largely independent rulers of their territories. They not only stopped remittances of tax revenues, but also seized large parts of the salt tax, especially after 1920. Several salt-secured loans, including the Huguang loan of 1911, went into default. The reorganization loan remained secure, because it had been placed under Customs security in 1917, when the German and Austro-Hungarian shares of the Boxer indemnities were canceled. The drying up of sources for foreign debt during World War I strengthened demand for domestic debt. As the chapter by Sheehan and Zhu in this volume shows, the relationship between the government and the banking sector grew much closer after the war, and the stock exchanges emerging after 1918 increasingly relied on government bonds. In 1921, the MCS helped Finance Minister Zhou Ziqi to design the Consolidated Debt Service, which combined the customs-secured bonds with unsecured bonds, including the Late Qing Patriotic Bond, and brought them under the combined security of the Customs, the Salt Tax Administration, and the alcohol and tobacco monopolies. The insulation of the service from onslaughts by the changing Beijing governments made the consolidated bonds very secure and greatly

---

[61] Jiao Jianhua 焦建華, 中華民國財政史 (A Fiscal History of the Republic of China) (Changsha, Hubei renmin chubanshe, 2015), pp. 141–2.
[62] Lin May-li 林美莉, 西洋稅制在近代中國的發展 (The Development of Western Taxation Methods in China) (Taipei, Academia Sinica, 2005), pp. 98–103.

enlarged the capital reserves of China's banks.[63] This only deepened the dependence of whoever controlled the central government on the MCS, even though very little of the customs revenue was directly available. Between 1897 and 1910, the Qing government had used 30 to 40 percent of the annual customs revenue for military expenditures, and 20 to 30 percent for indemnities and foreign loans.[64] The Beiyang government already used three-quarters of customs revenue for debt service. Only 2 percent was remitted to the government as Customs surplus and became a target of competition by various regimes.[65] From 1912 to 1928, the leadership of the Ministry of Finance changed thirty-two times (although several ministers served more than once), with tenures from less than a month to one year. Often, the main qualification for the job was the ability to borrow. The only budget drafted after 1915 was that of 1919 when an attempt was made to appease the warring factions, but it remained little more than fiction. By 1922, state bankruptcy was imminent.[66]

Following two civil wars between the Zhili and Fengtian cliques, a semblance of order returned to Beijing in 1924 with the installation of Duan Qirui as provisional executive of government. Duan established a Financial Rehabilitation Committee which soon undertook the third attempt to abolish the *lijin* transit duties. The committee created formal bodies on the national and provincial level to investigate the myriad of transit duties and stationary excises summarized under the term *lijin*. The plan was to abolish the former within two years and expand business and consumption taxes in compensation. The move was predicated on a renewed push for higher customs tariffs. As one of the victorious countries of World War I, Chinese representatives had demanded full tariff autonomy and an immediate rise of import tariffs to 12.5 percent during the Paris Peace Conference of 1919 and the Washington Naval Conference of 1921. In October 1925, the Beiyang government assembled representatives of twelve nations in Beijing at a Special Tariff Conference which estimated the lost *lijin* revenue at

---

[63] Van de Ven, *Breaking with the Past*, pp. 183–5; A. Feuerwerker, "The Foreign Presence in China," in J.K. Fairbank (ed.), *The Cambridge History of China*, vol. 12, *Republican China 1912–1949*, part 1 (Cambridge, Cambridge University Press, 1983), p. 192; A.N. Young, *China's Nation-Building Effort, 1927–1937: The Financial and Economic Record* (Stanford, CA, Hoover Institution Press, 1971), pp. 21, 115–18.

[64] Tang Xianglong 湯象龍, 中國近代海關稅收和分配統計 (1861–1910) (Statistics of Customs Revenues and Their Distribution in Modern China (1861–1910)) (Beijing, Zhonghua shuju, 1992), pp. 27, 34.

[65] Zhang Xianwen 張憲文 (ed.), 中華民國史 (A History of the Republic of China) (Nanjing, Nanjing daxue chubanshe, 2005), vol. 2, p. 128.

[66] Jia, "五十年來中國之財政", 127; Jiao, 中華民國財政史, pp. 143–50.

C$70 million and proposed to replace this income with a customs surtax of 2.5 percent. Even though no formal agreement was reached until the collapse of Duan's regime in April 1926, the new Beijing government in February 1927 one-sidedly implemented the 2.5 percent customs surtax on imports, estimating potential revenue of C$40 million. By this time the Nationalist Party had just began its Northern Expedition and denied all legitimacy to the negotiations.[67]

Ja Ian Chong has argued that foreign intervention was largely responsible for the persistence of the Beijing government during the period of fragmentation and warlordism. Instead of settling in their respective territorial footholds, various warlord factions continued to compete for control over Beijing, because this could gain them diplomatic recognition and political legitimacy, as well as access to customs and salt tax surpluses and foreign loans, especially those secured by assets like railroads under the Ministry of Communications.[68] According to Ma Jinhua's calculation, various Beiyang regimes borrowed 633 loans from abroad with a total loan sum of C$1.556 billion. The reorganization loan of 1913 comprised only 16 percent of the total.[69] Dependence on foreign loans was a double-edged sword. Weak fiscal governance at the center and lack of authority to persuade regional regimes to remit tax revenues forced each new regime to make an effort to secure the loans of its predecessor and gain new loans from abroad. Given the rise of public opinion and nationalism as a social force since the early 1900s, regional powers could use this dependence on foreign loans to delegitimize the central government. This happened, for example, with the reorganization loan of 1913, which was used by Sun Yat-sen to mobilize against Yuan Shikai's government, and with the Nishihara loans to Duan Qirui's regime in 1916–1917, which became one of the triggers of the May Fourth Movement in 1919 after the case was leaked to the public.

---

[67] Lin, 西洋税制, pp. 114–19; Kubo Tōru 久保亨, 戦間期中国自立への模索: 関税通貨政策と経済発展 (China's Quest for Sovereignty in the Inter-war Period: Tariff Policy and Economic Development) (Tokyo: Tōkyō daigaku shuppankai, 1999), p. 23; Van de Ven, Breaking with the Past, pp. 202–4, 208–9. The Nationalists introduced a similar customs surtax, called "inland tax" (neidishui 內地稅), but such surtaxes soon became obsolete when full tariff autonomy was achieved. See below.

[68] Chong, "Breaking Up Is Hard to Do," 89–90.

[69] Ma Jinhua 馬金華, 中國外債史 (A History of Foreign Loans in China) (Beijing, Zhongguo caizheng jingji chubanshe, 2005), pp. 109, 194, 235–7.

Nation-Building during the Nanjing Decade, 1927–1938

Nationalism and careful financial planning were crucial for the success of Chiang Kai-shek's Northern Expedition. The Central Finance Conference in Nanjing in June 1927 solicited the support of the leaders of the modern financial and industrial sectors based in Shanghai (known as the Jiangsu–Zhejiang group), as well as the provincial leaders of Jiangsu, Zhejiang, Anhui, Fujian, Guangdong, and Guangxi. In December 1928, a new government was formed in Nanjing. The new Finance Ministry proved more stable than its predecessor. Two of the ministers – the American-trained economists Song Ziwen (T.V. Soong) and Kong Xiangxi (H.H. Kung) – had long tenures and considerable political influence. Their American training and collaboration with foreign experts like the Kemmerer commission and the League of Nations shaped their fundamentally modern outlook. This was reflected in more ambitious fiscal policies that not only aimed at fiscal survival but also conceived the developmental state.[70] Even though the Nationalists never regained full control over the provinces and some regions remained out of their reach altogether, the Nanjing government ameliorated center–province fiscal relationships by convening several national finance conferences (1927, 1928, 1934, 1941) to renegotiate revenue-sharing arrangements.

Overall, the Nationalist Party's nation-building process was successful. Continued reliance on Sino-foreign co-operation in the customs and salt administrations aside, the Nationalists were committed to modernizing their tax structure and cutting their dependence on foreign loans. They finally managed to abolish the *lijin* duties and replace them with a nationwide consolidated tax levied on modern machine-produced products, which became the third pillar of non-borrowed revenue of the central government (see Table 8.4). They introduced modern direct taxes like income, estate, and business taxes. They successfully utilized national banks to consolidate China's foreign and domestic debt, stabilize government revenue by bond purchases, and establish a fiat currency to insulate China's economy from the effects of international silver price fluctuations during the Great Depression. The most momentous change, however, was the central government's decision to relinquish control of the land tax, which for millennia had been

---

[70] W.C. Kirby, "Engineering China: Birth of the Developmental State, 1928–1937," in K. Pomeranz (ed.), *The Pacific in the Age of Early Industrialization* (Burlington, VT, Ashgate, 2009), pp. 215–38; P.B. Trescott, "Western Economic Advisers in China, 1900–1949," *Research in the History of Economic Thought and Methodology* 28.1 (2010), 1–37.

the mainstay of China's government revenue. This focused Nationalist tax policies on a more modern, urban-focused tax structure, but would become a strategic vulnerability once Japan occupied the eastern seaboard.

The reassignment of the land tax was part of a new division between national and provincial taxes decided at the 1927 Central Finance Conference. The list of national taxes, i.e. the revenue of the national government, now included the salt tax, foreign and native customs duties, and tobacco and alcohol excises, as well as special taxes on cigarettes and kerosene, the mining tax, stamp duty, and the *lijin* transit duties until their abolition. Among taxes designated provincial revenue, commercial excises and levies had traditionally belonged to the provinces. However, it was an unusual step for the central government to officially surrender the land tax to the provinces, and thereby give up fiscal control over agricultural production that made up 65 percent of GNP. Scholars have argued that the move only recognized the political realities established under the various Beiyang regimes and aimed at winning the support of the regional powers.[71] However, the actual fiscal policies of the Nanjing government were staunchly centralist. The economist Li Quanshi has explained the contradiction with the legacy of Sun Yat-sen's National Development Plan and the constitution of the Nationalist Party, which both conceived the relationship between center and provinces as one of "distributed powers." The central government should only be charged with affairs of national relevance, while the provinces were ultimately responsible for local self-government and the provision of public goods. The handling of the land tax by the Nationalist government enjoyed wide support among contemporaries.[72]

However, ceding the land tax to the provinces also made it difficult to alleviate the heavy burden of the farmers caused by tax practices inherited from the warlord regimes. In the dual land tax system established during the late Qing New Policy reforms, both local and national surtaxes (*fujiashui* 附加稅) were added to the traditional base tax quota (*zhengshui* 正稅). Even though the Beiyang government had tried to limit the total sum of surtaxes to

---

[71] J.K. Fairbank 費正清, 劍橋中華民國史 (Cambridge History of the Republic of China), trans. Zhang Jiangang 章建剛, vol. 1 (Shanghai, Renmin chubanshe, 1992), pp. 115–17; Iwai, 中国近世財政史の研究, pp. 381–2.

[72] Li Quanshi 李權時, "國地財政劃分近況" (The Current Situation of the Fiscal Division between Central and Local Governments), *Xintuo Jikan* 1.4 (1936), 1–20; Zhang Lianhong 張連紅, 整合與互動：民國時期中央與地方財政關係研究 (Integration and Interactions: A Study of the Fiscal Relationship between Central and Local Government in Republican China) (Nanjing, Nanjing shifan daxue chubanshe, 1999), pp. 169–70.

Table 8.4 Income and expenditure of the Nationalist government, 1928–1937. Unit: C$ million (1929–1935 silver yuan, 1936–1937 *fabi* 法币)

Item	1928.7–1929.6	1929.7–1930.6	1930.7–1931.6	1931.7–1932.6	1932.7–1933.6	1933.7–1934.6	1934.7–1935.6	1935.7–1936.6	1936.7–1937.6
Balance									
Revenue (excl. debt)	333	438	498	553	559	622	745	817	870
Expenditure	413	539	714	683	645	769	941	1073	1167
Deficit	80	101	216	130	86	147	196	256	297
Deficit finance									
Bonds, treasury notes	69	91	193	125	26	80	164	148	223
Bank loans, advances	32	10	125	5	86	91	36	128	113
Foreign debt (cotton–wheat loan)						8	25		
Tax revenue									
Customs	179	276	313	370	326	352	353	272	379
Salt tax	30	122	150	144	158	177	167	184	197
Consolidated tax	30	41	53	89	80	106	105	135	158
Total	323	462	535	616	587	660	649	624	769

Source: Ma Jinhua 馬金華, 中國外債史 (A History of Foreign Loans in China) (Beijing, Zhongguo caizheng jingji chubanshe, 2005), p. 305

20 percent of the base tax, these regulations were largely ignored. Provinces, counties, and even villages took an "entrepreneurial stance" towards taxation and added dozens of surtaxes. Even though each was levied at an incrementally small amount earmarked for specific expenditures, such as education, river conservancy, military, police, or famine relief, they could add up to as high as twenty to thirty times the base tax quota.[73] One way to reduce the tax burden was to improve the financial situation of the counties. At the Second National Finance Conference in 1934, the Ministry of Finance asked the provinces to drastically reduce the surtaxes in exchange for returning the licensing fees for tobacco and alcohol producers to provincial control and sharing 40 percent of the stamp duty (10 percent for the provincial government, 30 percent for the county).[74] The ministry also urged local governments to expedite a land survey in order to collect a land value tax on urban property and make rural land tax rates more equitable. Since a land survey would have required considerable mobilization of resources, few communities complied, and the outbreak of the Second Sino-Japanese War further stalled progress.

The successful abolition of the *lijin* duties after various failed attempts since 1902 has been celebrated as a major achievement of Nationalist fiscal policies. The Nationalists' approach – first proposed in 1926 – radically differed from their predecessors' in that they decoupled the *lijin* abolition from the international customs tariff negotiations. Two taxes were designated to replace the *lijin*, the consolidated tax for the central government and the business tax (*yingyeshui* 營業稅) for the provinces. The First National Finance Conference convened in Shanghai in July 1928 ratified the plan. With the new year of 1931, the *lijin* finally ceased to exist.[75] The consolidated tax (*tongshui*) expanded the intra-provincial *tongjuan* of the late Qing and Beiyang regimes to a national scale. Chinese products were taxed at the place of

---

[73] Zhu Xie 朱偰, "中國田賦問題參考資料：中國附加稅之沿革" (References for the Land Tax Problem in China: The Evolution of Surtaxes in China), *Guoli Zhongyang Daxue Shehui Kexue Congkan* 1.1 (1934), 1–19; Patricia Thornton, "Beneath the Banyan Tree: Popular Views of Taxation and the State during the Republican and Reform Eras," *Twentieth-Century China* 25.1 (November 1999), 6–7; Zhang, 整合與互動, pp. 117–18.

[74] Second Historical Archives (ed.), 中華民國工商稅收史料選編 (Selected Archives on Industrial and Commercial Taxes in Republican China) (Nanjing, Nanjing daxue chubanshe, 1996), vol. 1, p. 1168; "財政部河北印花菸酒局特刊" (Special Issue of the Stamp, Tobacco and Alcohol Bureau of the Hebei Fiscal Bureau) (1935), in Chen Zhanqi 陳湛綺 (ed.), 國家圖書館藏民國稅收稅務檔案史料匯編 (Archival Materials concerning Tax Revenue and Taxation Stored in the Collection of the National Library) (Beijing, Quanguo tushuguan wenxian suowei fuzhi zhongin, 2008), p. 523.

[75] Lin, 西洋稅制, pp. 128–31.

production (producers for export could file a tax return); imports at the place of sale. The first such new-style consolidated tax had been the cigarette tax started in 1918 in five southeastern provinces. After 1931, this tax was expanded to cotton, matches, cement, and machine-milled wheat flour and became known as the "five-product consolidated tax." By 1936, the Ministry of Finance had expanded the tax to almost all Chinese provinces; enlarged the range of products to cured tobacco leaves, foreign liquors, beer, and pure alcohol; and unified administration under a central Tax Office (shuiwushu 稅務署). In this year, the consolidated tax yielded C$161.580 billion in revenue, about 60 percent of the lijin transit taxes prior to their abolition, and contributed 22.11 percent of the national taxes which constituted the backbone of Nationalist revenue.[76]

Customs and salt taxes continued to be the most important revenue sources for the central government, contributing 44.43 percent and 29.81 percent respectively in 1936. As the powers gradually agreed to full tariff autonomy, the import tariffs were raised in four steps – in 1928, 1930, 1933, and 1934 – to 20 percent. In 1930, the MCS began to assess tariff rates in the virtual customs gold unit instead of silver (Haiguan tael) to prevent a steep fall in customs revenue due to the falling silver price during the Great Depression. Beginning in January 1931, customs revenues were stored in the Bank of China, Bank of Communications, and Central Bank, before being remitted to the Hong Kong and Shanghai Bank for the repayment of the loans or indemnities. In this way, the Chinese government gradually regained full control of its customs revenues.[77] The salt tax was restored to the central government at the level of 60 percent by 1929 and almost completely by 1936. During the Northern Expedition, the Nationalists had briefly abolished the Sino-Foreign Salt Inspectorate as they rallied against the unequal treaties. However, Finance Minister Song Ziwen quickly restored the service after 1928 under the control of the ministry and absolved of the responsibility to guarantee and repay foreign debt. Salt tax revenue was directly remitted to

---

[76] Lin, 西洋稅制, pp. 142–4; Guojia Shuiwu Zongju 國家稅務總局 (ed.), 中華民國工商稅收史：貨物稅卷 (A History of Commercial and Industrial Taxation in Republican China: Commodity Taxes) (Beijing, Zhongguo caizheng jingji chubanshe, 2001), pp. 166–7.

[77] Young, China's Nation-Building Effort, p. 48; Hamashita, Economic History of Modern China, pp. 83–4; Dan Guanchu 單冠初, "南京國民政府收復關稅自主權的歷程" (The History of Reclaiming Tariff Autonomy under the Nanjing Nationalist Government), Ph.D. thesis, Fudan University, 2003; Caizhengbu Guanshui Zongju 財政部關稅總局 (ed.), 中華民國海關簡史 (A Short History of the Maritime Customs Service during the Republican Period) (Taipei, Caizhengbu guanshui zongju, 1995), pp. 22–6.

the Bank of China or the Central Bank and managed by the Ministry of Finance. Even as the new Salt Law promulgated in May 1931 failed to abolish the monopoly of the salt trade syndicates inherited from the Qing, successive reforms managed to rationalize and increase tax rates and improve revenue.[78]

Enhanced control over customs and salt revenues helped to restore China's credit by settling the sovereign loan defaults (among them the Tianjin–Pukou loan in 1936 and the Huguang loan in 1937). However, the Nationalist regime did not rely on foreign debt as much as its predecessors had. By 1928, China's credit in the international bond markets was shattered and the costs of borrowing from abroad were rising under the condition of falling silver prices. This may have been an advantage, given the thorny political questions raised by foreign debt. As a result, domestic debt became much more important. Finance Minister Song Ziwen inherited C$1.347 billion in government bonds. During his tenure from May 1927 to November 1933, his ministry issued twenty-seven bonds with a total value of C$1.03 million. Between 1927 and 1937 there was an estimated total of C$4.503 billion in domestic debt, as against C$876 million in foreign debt. These bonds were managed by Chinese banks mostly located in Shanghai and seen as evidence that the Jiangsu- and Zhejiang-dominated banking syndicates supported Chiang Kai-shek's regime, even though they were often coerced. In contrast to the Beiyang regime, the Nationalist government spent most of its borrowed revenue (40 percent of domestic debt and 75.65 percent of foreign debt) on productive purposes like railways, telegraphy, electricity, aviation, and river conservancy.[79]

Wartime Finance, 1937–1949

The Japanese invasion of 1937 was a severe blow to the Nationalist government, whose main sources of income – customs, salt, and

---

[78] Yeh Mei-chu 葉美珠, "國民政府鹽務稽核所的興革試析, 1928–1936" (The 1928–1936 Reforms of the Inspectorate of Salt Revenue under the National Government of China: A Preliminary Study), *Bulletin of Academia Historica* 49 (September 2016), 1–32; Strauss, *Strong Institutions in Weak Polities*, Chapter 3; Guojia Shuiwu Zongju 國家稅務總局 (ed.), 中華民國工商稅收史：鹽稅卷 (A History of Commercial and Industrial Taxation in Republican China: Salt Tax) (Beijing, Zhongguo caizheng jingji chubanshe, 1999), pp. 82–6; Young, *China's Nation-Building Effort*, pp. 54–63.

[79] Sun Di 孫迪, 民國時期經濟建設公債研究 (1927–1937) (A Study of Public Bonds for Economic Development during the Republic of China (1927–1937)) (Shanghai, Shanghai shehui kexueyuan chubanshe, 2015), pp. 211, 222; Jiang, 南京國民政府內債問題研究, pp. 85–7; Young, *China's Nation-Building Effort*, pp. 97–142; P.M. Coble, *The Shanghai Capitalists and the Nationalist Government, 1927–1937* (Cambridge, MA, Harvard University, 1986), pp. 29–40.

consolidated tax – drew heavily from the provinces now under Japanese occupation. In 1928, there were forty regular Maritime Customs stations and sixteen Native Customs stations under the fifty-*li* rule (see above). By 1937, there were still thirty-six stations, but by 1942 fully half of them had fallen under Japanese control. Left without its traditional revenue, the MCS collected an interport duty, which was extended from steamships to all modes of transport in 1937, and from 1942 a highly unpopular wartime consumption tax (abolished in 1945). Under these pressures, the service unraveled.[80] The Sino-Foreign Salt Inspectorate also disintegrated after the most important salt-producing regions were lost to Japanese occupation. In January 1939, China stopped servicing all foreign debt secured by customs and salt revenues. In the rural and impoverished hinterland the costs of providing salt for the alimentation of the populace often exceeded income. From May 1942 to January 1945, the government implemented a sales monopoly (*zhuanmai* 專賣) and increased the tax rates several times. However, under the impact of rampant inflation the share of the salt tax in total revenue declined.[81]

The war provided the Nationalist government in its Chongqing exile with both the need and the legitimacy to regain control of provincial revenues and private incomes to extract revenue from the economically backward hinterland. The Third National Finance Conference in June 1941 effectively eliminated the fiscal autonomy of the provinces. The land tax was converted from a monetary tax to collection in kind under the management of the central government. Two-thirds of the collected grain was designated for the army; the rest was reserved for the salaries of civil bureaucrats or to be sold cheaply to stabilize market prices.[82] Critics have argued that this new tax regime increased the burden of the peasants and contributed to the defeat of the

---

[80] Jin Baoguang 金葆光 (ed.), 海關權與民國前途 (Customs Sovereignty and the Future of the Republic of China) (Shanghai, Commercial Press, 1928), pp. 84–7; Sun Baogen 孫寶根, 抗戰時期國民政府關稅政策研究 (1937–1945) (A Study of the Customs Policy of the Nationalist Government during the Sino-Japanese War (1937–1945)) (Beijing, Zhongguo shehui kexue chubanshe, 2014), pp. 6, 66; F. Boecking, "Unmaking the Chinese Nationalist State: Administrative Reform among Fiscal Collapse, 1937–1945," *Modern Asian Studies* 45 (March 2011), 277–301.

[81] Guojia Shuiwu Zongju, 中華民國工商稅收史, pp. 301–3; Dong Zhenping 董振平, 抗戰時期國民政府鹽務政策研究 (A Study of the Salt Policy of the Nationalist Government during the Anti-Japanese War) (Jinan, Qi Lu shushe, 2004), pp. 62–70.

[82] Chen Yousan 陳友三 and Chen Side 陳思德, 田賦徵實制度 (The System of Levying the Land Tax in Kind) (Chongqing, Zhengzhong shuji, 1945), p. 3; Jiang Yongjing 蔣永敬, "孔祥熙與戰時財政—法幣政策與田賦徵實" (H.H. Kung and Wartime Finance: Currency Policy and Levying the Land Tax in Kind), in Chin Hsiao-yi 秦孝儀 (ed.), 抗戰建國史料: 田賦徵實 (Materials of the Anti-Japanese War: Levying the Land Tax in Grain) (Taipei, Zhongguo Guomindang dangshi weiyuanhui, 1989), vol. 4, pp. 365–7.

Nationalists by the Communists in 1949. However, the Communist Party in 1950 not only copied the land tax collection in kind from the Nationalists but also relentlessly increased the degree of extraction, leading to violent uprisings.[83] For Chiang Kai-shek and other leaders of the Nationalist Party the recentralization of the land tax was not simply a wartime expedient but constituted a "correction" of what they considered an aberration from the traditional fiscal ideal of the land tax as the "orthodox tribute" (*zhenggong* 正貢) that tied the people to the state.[84] Chiang's state authoritarianism was diametrically opposed to the political philosophy that had supported the separation of central and local finances, but it was smoothly inherited by the Communist Party.

For the consolidated tax, the Nationalist government increased the tax rates and broadened the range of taxable commodities to include, newly, beverages and sugar products. However, some areas haphazardly implemented government monopolies on sugar, matches, or tobacco products, leading to confusion about whether the consolidated tax or the monopoly applied. Cash-strapped local governments frequently ignored the one-tax rule and erected new tax stations resembling the old *lijin* system. The share of the consolidated tax in the total tax revenue of the government increased during the war, but this was mainly due to the sharp drop in customs and salt revenues during wartime, and in general non-borrowed income was dwarfed by inflation and debt. After the end of the war, the consolidated tax was again expanded and, together with taxes on tobacco and alcohol, as well as mining, given a systematic legal basis under the new name of "commodities taxes" (*huowushui* 貨物稅).[85]

The Nationalists' commitment to modernizing the tax structure is best represented by the expansion of direct taxes. The stamp duty and business tax had been shared with provincial and local governments as a replacement for lost *lijin* revenues in 1931. The Sino-Japanese War afforded the Nationalists an opportunity to bring these taxes back under central control (in 1940 and 1941) and add modern income and estate taxes. Income and estate taxes had been

---

[83] Gao Wangling 高王凌, 中國農民反行為研究 (1950–1980) (A Study of the Counter-actions of Chinese Peasants (1950–1980)) (Hong Kong, Chinese University of Hong Kong, 2013), pp. 297–304.
[84] Lu Fang-sang 呂芳上 (ed.), 蔣中正先生年譜長編 (Chronological Biography of Chiang Kai-shek) (Taipei, Guoshi Guan, 2014), vol. 6, p. 572.
[85] Guojia Shuiwu Zongju, 中華民國工商稅收史, pp. 181–98, 204–5; Hou Kunhong 侯坤宏, 抗戰時期的中央財政與地方財政 (Central and Local Fiscal Policies during the Anti-Japanese War) (Taipei, Guoshi Guan, 2000), pp. 104–7; Zhang Sheng 張生, 南京國民政府的稅收 (1927–1937) (The Tax Revenue of Nanjing Nationalist Government (1927–1937)) (Nanjing, Nanjing chubanshe, 2001), p. 4.

discussed since Yuan Shikai's regime, but their implementation was hampered by an insufficient legal infrastructure and resistance from the elites. Under the Nanjing government, collection of the income tax started only in October 1936, when patriotic sentiment could be mobilized for its support in the face of an impending Japanese invasion. The war period also brought a temporary "wartime profit tax," which extracted heavy fines from profits in industry and commerce that were deemed excessive. This can be seen as a special kind of income tax. The levying of the estate tax only began in July 1940. After dismal results in the beginning, the Ministry of Finance achieved more success by incentivizing people to report tax evasion. Between 1940 and 1944, direct taxes made up 20 to 30 percent of non-borrowed revenue, but their share of total revenue was low, peaking in 1943 at 6.54 percent. While the actual contribution of these new tax categories to government revenue was limited, the Nationalist government repeatedly stressed their importance for the process of fiscal modernization. Under the call for national resistance, the government was able to use tax reform to integrate the scattered individuals of the country under its political rule and thus create a modern fiscal state. Most importantly, direct taxes equally applied to both Chinese nationals and foreign nationals living in China, and compliance by foreigners increased as China joined the allied forces and the limitations of China's fiscal sovereignty were gradually removed.[86]

Although the Nationalist government managed to centralize and even modernize its tax system and grow its revenue, the gap between noninflationary cash receipts and huge expenditures kept growing under the conditions of the war. Collection of taxes in kind, including the land tax and also the business tax, somewhat reduced inflationary pressures, but debt still made up between 70 and 90 percent of government revenue during the war (Table 8.5).

As traditional means of deriving both non-borrowed and borrowed income failed, most of this debt was in fact an expansion of the money supply. It is true that China during the war borrowed huge sums from the Soviet Union, the US, and Britain. Wu Chengming has estimated that China's total foreign debt between 1865 and 1948 was equivalent to US$2.5 billion, two-thirds of which occurred after the outbreak of the Second Sino-Japanese War.[87] However, in the absence of collateral from tax revenues, these loans largely shifted to barter arrangements. To take only the US as an example, the

---

[86] Lin, 西洋稅制, pp. 55–7, 209–13, 221–4, 260–4, 296–302, 339.
[87] Wu Chengming 吳承明, 中國資本主義與國內市場 (Chinese Capitalism and the National Market) (Beijing, Zhongguo shehui kexue chubanshe, 1985), p. 47.

Table 8.5 Income and expenditure of the Nationalist government, 1937–1945. Unit: C$ million (*fabi*)

	1937.7–1938.6	1938.7–1938.12	1939	1940	1941	1942	1943	1944	1945
Balance									
Revenue (excl. debt)	815	315	740	1,325	1,310	5,630	20,403	38,503	1,241,389
Expenditure	2,091	1,169	2,797	5,288	10,003	24,511	58,816	171,689	2,348,085
Deficit	1,276	854	2,057	3,963	8,693	18,881	38,413	133,186	1,106,696
Deficit finance									
Public debt	256	18	25	8	127	363	3,880	1,989	62,820
Bank advances	1,195	854	2,310	3,834	9,443	20,081	40,857	140,090	1,042,257
Tax revenue									
Indirect taxes	427	200	451	190	500	1,165	4,299	20,932	79,234
Direct taxes	24	11	32	76	166	1,641	7,870	10,215	20,740
Monopolies	—	—	—	—	—	1,357	3,157	3,504	2,270
Total tax revenues	451	211	483	266	666	4,163	15,326	34,651	102,253

Source: Ma, 中國外債史, p. 330

four loans borrowed before Pearl Harbor, totaling US$117 million, were earmarked to purchase military equipment in the US and repaid by deliveries of wood oil, tin, tungsten, and other metals. During the Pacific War, the USA provided US$1.5 billion in aid, the majority through the lend–lease program. But while these loans were vital during the war, they were no solution to fiscal crisis.[88]

In the face of escalating military expenses, the government had tried to fall back on domestic debt and issued seven bonds with a total nominal value of C$2.757 billion between August 1937 and June 1939, but subscription was muted, and most of the bonds were absorbed by four government banks, the Central Bank, the Bank of China, the Bank of Communications, and the Farmers' Bank of China (the "big four").[89] From 1937 to 1945, the huge payment deficit of the government was almost completely made up by these so-called "bank advances" (*yinhang diankuan* 銀行墊款). In reality, the advances meant a huge increase of money supply in the fiat currency *fabi* 法幣 ("legal tender") which, once it entered the market, caused runaway inflation.[90] During the civil war from 1945 to 1949, the central government took control of commodity taxes and direct taxes and restored customs and salt revenues, but income still proved insufficient, even more so as the government had declared a tax holiday on the land tax to celebrate victory. In July 1946, the tax holiday was hastily rescinded and collection in kind restarted. But deficits were still over 60 percent and could only be covered by inflation. Loss of control over finances was the main reason for the failure of the Nationalist government.[91]

---

[88] Ma, 外債與晚清政局, pp. 13–17; Lin May-li 林美莉, "戰時旳財政經濟" (Wartime Finance and Economy), in Lu Fang-sang 呂芳上 (ed.), 中國抗日戰爭史新編 (戰時社會) (A New History of the Anti-Japanese War (Wartime Society)) vol. 4 (Taipei, Guoshi Guan, 2015), pp. 151–6.

[89] Zhongguo lianhe zhunbei yinhang 中國聯合準備銀行 (ed.), 中國內外債詳編 (Internal and External Debts of China) (Beijing, June 1940), in Chen Zhanqi 陳湛綺 (ed.), 民國時期中國內外債史料詳編 (Comprehensive Anthology Concerning Internal and External Debts in the Republic of China) (Beijing, Quanguo tushuguan wenxian suowei fuzhi zhongxin, 2010), p. 258.

[90] K. Chang, *The Inflationary Spiral: The Experience of China, 1939–1950* (Cambridge, MA, MIT Technology Press, 1958); A.N. Young, *China's Wartime Finance and Inflation, 1937–1945* (Cambridge, MA, Harvard University Press, 1965); Dai Jianbing 戴建兵, 金錢與戰爭：抗戰時期的貨幣 (Money and War: Currency during the Anti-Japanese War) (Guilin, Guangxi shifan daxue chubanshe, 1995); Lin May-li 林美莉, 抗戰時期的貨幣戰爭 (The Currency War in Wartime China, 1937–1945) (Taipei, Institute of History, Taiwan Normal University, 1996).

[91] Lin, "戰時旳財政經濟"; Jiao, 中華民國財政史, pp. 1044–63.

Conclusion

Overall, we can observe three major tendencies in fiscal development during the period from 1800 to 1950. First, the capacity of the state to tax its subjects increased after 1850, and the footprint of government in society grew in proportion. Following the civil wars of the mid-nineteenth century, the Qing gradually abandoned the traditional political ideal of measuring expenditure on the basis of fixed revenue (*liang ru wei chu* 量入為出) and was forced to seek new revenues to cover expenditures (*liang chu wei ru* 量出為入). It is true that the increase of foreign trade and the establishment of the Maritime Customs Service was an important factor that moved China into fiscal modernization. However, we should not overlook responses by Chinese governments to political crises as modernizing forces in the fiscal structure, from the *lijin* duties, which emerged as a response to the Taiping Rebellion, to income taxes rolled out during the Second Sino-Japanese War. *Lijin* duties opened the way for taxes on the consumption of commodities. Income taxes expanded taxation to the incomes of industrialists, merchants, and individuals. Their importance consisted in shifting the tax system away from its traditional focus on agriculture.

Second, the capacity to tax grew unevenly between the central government and the provinces. Provincial capacity building was way ahead of the central government well into the 1930s. While the fiscal autonomy of the provinces was growing gradually due to *lijin* duties since the 1850s and the uncontrolled growth of miscellaneous excises and surtaxes after 1895, the central government continued to rely on revenue-sharing negotiations with the provinces to obtain income. To a large degree, especially during the late Qing and the Beiyang era, the central government also utilized foreign loans and "informal empire institutions" like the Maritime Customs or the Sino-Foreign Salt Inspectorate as leverage against provincial interests. At worst, the government had to fall back entirely on customs and salt funds left after servicing those loans.

Third, what triggered fundamental reform was not fiscal crisis alone but the arrival of Western ideas and know-how. Conventions and vested interests posed formidable obstacles to the acceptance of Western fiscal technologies throughout the nineteenth century, but they were firmly established by 1908. By the 1930s, Chinese fiscal policies were based on cutting-edge economic theories. The Nationalist government had all the trappings of a modern fiscal state and skillfully used domestic borrowing and monetary policy for economic stabilization and development. However, its capacity to tax did not grow in sync with its fiscal know-how. The Nationalist model of revenue sharing limited the central government to "modernized" taxes like customs, salt tax, and the so-called "consolidated taxes" on certain machine-produced goods, while unreformed rural taxes like the land tax, which represented 65 percent of the economy, were left to the provinces. Despite ten years of modernization promoted by the Nanjing regime, China remained starkly divided into the modern cities that served as the connection point between China and the global economy and the autonomously self-reproducing village society inland. This created a strategic vulnerability when the Japanese occupation after 1937 cut the government off from the main sources of its modernized tax revenue. The war forced the regime to focus its attention back on the important land tax while continuing its modernizing zeal by experimenting with new income and estate taxes. As Iwai Shigeki has argued, the war taught the regime that warlord-like adaptability to living off the land was necessary to survive. This village hinterland provided the foundation for an eight-year struggle against Japanese occupation, but also for the insurmountable Communist insurrection.[92]

Further Reading

Boecking, F., *No Great Wall: Trade, Tariffs and Nationalism in Republican China, 1927–1945* (Cambridge, MA, Harvard University Asia Center, 2017).

Chong, J.I., "Breaking Up Is Hard to Do: Foreign Intervention and the Limiting of Fragmentation in the Late Qing and Early Republic, 1893–1922," *Twentieth-Century China* 35.1 (November 2009), 75–98.

He, W. *Paths toward the Modern Fiscal State: England, Japan, and China* (Cambridge, MA, Harvard University Press, 2013).

Iwai Shigeki 岩井茂樹, 中国近世財政史の研究 (A Study of the Fiscal System in Late Imperial China) (Kyoto, Kyōto daigaku gakujutsu shuppankai, 2004).

Kaske, E., "Austerity in Times of War: Government Finance in Early Nineteenth-Century China," *Financial History Review* 25.1 (April 2018), 71–96.

Lin May-li 林美莉, 西洋稅制在近代中國的發展 (The Development of Western Taxation Methods in China) (Taipei, Academia Sinica, 2005).

Van de Ven, H.J., *Breaking with the Past: The Maritime Customs Service and the Global Origins of Modernity in China* (New York, Columbia University Press, 2014).

Zanasi, M. *Saving the Nation: Economic Modernity in Republican China* (Chicago, The University of Chicago Press, 2010).

Zhou Yumin 周育民, 晚清財政與社會變遷 (Fiscal Policies and Social Change during the Late Qing) (Shanghai, Shanghai renmin chubanshe, 2000).

---

[92] Iwai, 中国近世財政史の研究, pp. 515–16.

9
Financial Institutions and Financial Markets

BRETT SHEEHAN AND YINGUI ZHU

Many studies of the history of Chinese finance lack systematic empirical investigation, are limited to the period before the outbreak of war in 1937, or focus on Shanghai, skewing our understanding of the full scope of Chinese finance in this period. This chapter draws heavily on new work, as well as on the empirical work of the two authors, though many areas for further research remain.

Finance and Institutional Development

By the mid-nineteenth century, a variety of financial institutions served China, including rotating credit societies, pawnshops, cash shops, and remittance houses. Available evidence indicates great variation in practice both across and within regions. In rotating credit societies (*qianhui* 錢會/*lunhui* 輪會) members made contributions on a fixed schedule, and collected funds would be distributed by rotation or sometimes by drawing lots or by auction.[1] Pawnshops (*diandang* 典當/*dangpu* 當鋪/*xiangya* 餉押/*xiang'an* 餉按/*ya* 押) loaned money based on possessions which borrowers left at the shop as collateral.[2] Those institutions specializing in exchanging money, commercial transactions, commercial deposits, or commercial lending were

---

[1] K.S. Tsai, "Banquet Banking: Gender and Rotating Credit Associations in South China," *China Quarterly* 161 (March 2000), 143–6; Yu Jiang 俞江, "清中期至民國的徽州錢會" (Rotating Credit Societies in Huizhou from the Mid-Qing to the Republican Periods) 安徽大學學報 (Journal of Anhui University) 4 (2017), 1–22.

[2] Chang Mengju 常夢渠 and Qian Chuntao 錢椿濤 (eds.), 近代中國典當業 (Pawn Shops in Modern China) (Beijing, Zhongguo Wenshi chubanshe, 1995); Liu Qiugen 劉秋根, 中國典當制度史 (An Institutional History of Chinese Pawnshops) (Shanghai, Guji chubanshe, 1995); T.S. Whelan, *The Pawnshop in China*, based on Yang Chao-yü, 中國典當業 (The Chinese Pawnbroking Industry), with a historical introduction and critical annotations (Ann Arbor, Center for Chinese Studies, The University of Michigan, 1979). On types of articles pawned in the late Qing period and terms of loans in Shanghai in the 1930s, see Liu, 中國典當制度史, pp. 150, 184–6.

called *qianpu* 錢鋪, *qiandian* 錢店, *qianzhuang* 錢莊, or *yinhao* 銀號, with many other regional variations.³ Here they will be called "cash shops," a literal translation close to most of the Chinese versions which is preferable to the colonial and unhelpful "native bank" used by most English-language authors. Remittance houses, a term with resonance to their origins as trading houses, specialized in long-distance remittance and were often called *piaohao* 票號.⁴

The second half of the nineteenth century witnessed the appearance of a new kind of financial institution when foreign banks (*yinhang* 銀行) began offering financial services in China. Chinese subsequently began forming institutions based on these foreign models, adopting the same term. *Yinhang* are often called "modern banks" in the literature, but "modern" also has colonial overtones of superiority, so *yinhang* will be referred to simply as "banks."⁵

China's rotating credit societies, pawnshops, cash shops, remittance houses, and banks were not as functionally distinct as the different terms suggest. Nonetheless, Table 9.1 presents a rough schematic of the types and functions of financial institutions in China by the late Qing period.

Organizational form and managerial governance varied considerably as well, but a few generalizations can be made (Table 9.2). Rotating credit societies grew out of local social and family networks and had membership rather than ownership. Pawnshops, money exchange shops, and cash shops tended to have only one office and were formed as sole proprietorships, family-owned firms, or partnerships.⁶ It was not unusual for investors to own shares in multiple shops, and these often shared similar names, making them a "family" (*lianhao*

---

³ Hong Xiaguan 洪葭管 (ed.), 中國金融史 (*A History of Chinese Finance*) (Chengdu, Xinan Caijing daxue chubanshe, 1993), p. 81. On the importance of monetary exchange, see Zhongguo renmin yinhang zonghang jinrong yanjiusuo jinrong yangjiushi 中國人民銀行總行金融研究所金融研究室 (Finance Research Department of Finance Research Institute of the People's Bank of China), 近代中國的金融市場 (*Modern China's Financial Markets*) (Beijing, Zhongguo Jinrong chubanshe, 1989), pp. 10–11; and B. Sheehan, "Unorganized Crime: Forgers, Soldiers, and Shopkeepers in Beijing, 1927, 1928," in B.K.L. So and M. Zelin (eds.), *New Narratives of Urban Space in Republican Chinese Cities: Emerging Social, Legal, and Governance Orders* (Leiden and Boston, Brill, 2013), p. 103.
⁴ Zhang Guohui 張國輝, 中國金融通史 (*A General History of Chinese Finance*), vol. 2, (1840–1911) 清鴉片戰爭時期至清末時期 (From the Opium War to the End of the Qing Dynasty (1840–1911)) (Beijing, Zhongguo Jinrong chubanshe, 2003), p. 180.
⁵ Zhang, 中國金融通史, Chapters 1, 4, 6, 7, esp. p. 15 on the terminology of cash shops; Hong, 中國金融史, Chapter 3; L. Cheng, *Banking in Modern China* (Cambridge, Cambridge University Press, 2003), pp. 10–11, omits foreign banks as a category, but otherwise follows convention; Z. Ji, *A History of Modern Shanghai Banking: The Rise and Decline of China's Finance Capitalism* (Armonk, NY and London, M.E. Sharpe, 2003), p. xxi, combines *piaohao* and "native banks," but otherwise follows convention.
⁶ Ma Min 馬敏 and Zhu Ying 朱英, 中國經濟通史 (*A General Economic History of China*), vol. 8, part 2 (Changsha, Hunan renmin chubanshe, 2002), p. 550.

Table 9.1 Basic functions of financial institutions in the late Qing period

	Retail services primarily to ordinary individuals		Services to ordinary individuals and/or the wealthy, businesses, and government			Services primarily to the wealthy, businesses, or government		
	Rotating credit societies	Pawnshops	Pawnshops	Cash shops specializing in exchange	Businesses providing monetary exchange as a sideline	Cash shops	Remittance houses	Banks (foreign and Chinese)
Take deposits	X		X	X	X	X	X	X
Make loans	X	X	X	X		X	X	X
Exchange money		X	X	X	X	X	X	X
Issue drafts on goods transactions				X	X	X	X	X
Issue paper money exchangeable to silver or copper		X		X		X	X	X
Purchase gold, silver, or copper as investments		X		X		X	X	X
Remit money across long distances						X	X	X

Table 9.2 Forms and ownership governance of financial institutions in the late Qing period

	Ownership			Branching		
	Individual or partners	Family	Joint-stock corp.	Single office	Groups linked by common owners	Branches
Rotating credit societies	N/A	N/A	N/A	N/A	N/A	N/A
Pawnshops	X	X		X	Sometimes	Occasionally
Cash shops	X	X		X	Sometimes	Occasionally
Remittance houses		X			Sometimes	X
Banks			X			X

聯號) of related financial institutions.[7] Remittance houses were usually controlled by one family, though they took investments from minority shareholders, and, as with cash shops, some families invested in more than one remittance house, making a "family" of related institutions. With expansive branch networks, remittance houses tended to be larger than cash shops. Foreign and Chinese banks were usually limited-liability corporations with numerous shareholders, large size, and substantial branch networks. Most foreign banks were branches of banks with head offices in their home countries, though a few "foreign" banks existed only in China and were referred to as "foreign" only because of the status of their owners and clientele.

The literature on Chinese financial history remains split about indigenous Chinese financial institutions. Many scholars have indicted them as feudal, poorly managed, part of a perceived weakness of the late Qing political economy, or tools in the control of foreign imperialists.[8] Some scholars, however, look to these institutions, especially remittance houses, as evidence that Chinese capitalism was not inferior to that of the West.[9]

---

[7] A. McElderry, *Shanghai Old-Style Banks (Ch'ien-chuang) 1800–1935* (Ann Arbor, Center for Chinese Studies, the University of Michigan, 1976), pp. 51–2.
[8] For examples, see Tong Yuansong 童元松, "晚清錢莊動蕩衰弱的原因初探" (The Decline of Cash Shops in the Turmoil of the Late Qing), 黑龍江史志 (Heilongjiang History) 11 (2008), 16–17; Zhang, 中國金融通史, p. 7; Ma and Zhu, 中國經濟通史, p. 567; and McElderry, *Shanghai Old-Style Banks*, pp. 21–2.
[9] L. Wang, "Introduction," in Wang, *Chinese Hinterland Capitalism and Shanxi Piaohao: Banking, State, and Family, 1720–1910* (New York, Routledge, 2021)., forthcoming, provides an excellent review and critique of these arguments in relation to remittance houses.

Important new studies paint a more complex picture. Relations between foreign banks and cash shops were interdependent, and Chinese businesspeople were adept at using foreign-bank funding for their own purposes and profits.[10] Individual cash shops remained relatively small with little capital. Rather than a weakness, as pointed out by some critics, this practice could function as a method of risk management. For example, one Shanghai financier invested in partnership in seven cash shops, and after they all failed in a financial crisis, continued to invest in several more cash shops with other partners.[11] By keeping capital in his own hands, instead of the firms', he managed his risk, and could even continue to invest after a crisis.

Estimates for numbers of financial institutions are shown in Table 9.3. The precipitous decline in numbers of pawnshops over the nineteenth century has been attributed to the chaos of the civil wars in the mid-nineteenth century and to taxation, as well as to competition from cash shops, remittance houses, and banks.[12] Both cash shops and remittance houses grew in relation to the circulation of goods during a long period of increasing commercialization over the course of the Qing dynasty.[13] The first business devoted to remittances probably appeared in the 1820s.[14] Merchants in Shanxi province were well positioned to capitalize on the expanding trade with Russia, and they came to dominate the remittance-house sector.[15] Both remittance houses and cash shops grew as trade with the West expanded again after about 1870. In addition, remittance houses became involved in providing services to the Qing state, which contributed to their growth. They peaked in number in about 1883. Six remittance houses with the most extensive branch networks, and best-surviving historical records, had a total of ninety-two branches in the 1870s and the 1880s.[16] The remaining twenty-two remittance houses were smaller, so perhaps at their peak the remittance houses as a group had 200 or 300 branches. The first foreign banks

---

[10] S. Nishimura, "The Foreign and Native Banks in China: Chop Loans in Shanghai and Hankow before 1914," *Modern Asian Studies* 39.1 (2005), 109–32; G. Moazzin, *Networks of Capital: German Bankers and the Financial Internationalisation of China (1885–1919)*, Ph.D. thesis, University of Cambridge, 2017, Chapter 2.

[11] Moazzin, *Networks of Capital*, Chapter 2.

[12] Liu, 中國典當制度史, p. 259; Du Xuncheng 杜恂誠, 中國金融通史 (A General History of Chinese Finance), vol. 3, 北洋政府時期 (Beiyang Government Period) (Beijing, Zhongguo Jinrong chubanshe, 1996), p. 295; Chang and Qian, 近代中國典當業, p. 28; Whelan, *The Pawnshop in China*, pp. 6–12.

[13] Zhang, 中國金融通史, pp. 3, 19, 29; Nishimura, "The Foreign and Native Banks in China," 110; Du, 中國金融通史, p. 233.

[14] Zhang, 中國金融通史, pp. 37–9. [15] Wang, "Introduction."

[16] Huang Jianhui 黃鑒暉 et al. (eds.), 山西票號史料, 增訂本 (Historical Materials on Shanxi Remittance Houses), expanded ed. (Taiyuan, Shanxi Jingji chubanshe, 2002), pp. 213, 215–16, 1279.

Table 9.3 Estimated numbers of financial institutions in China

Type	Beginning of nineteenth century	End of nineteenth/beginning of twentieth century	1930s on the eve of World War II	1947
Rotating credit societies	Unknown	Unknown	Unknown	Unknown
Pawnshops	21,000	4,000?	3,386	Unknown
Cash shops	Unknown	4,000?	4,000?	966 firms with 1,076 offices
Remittance houses	None	28 firms with perhaps 200 or 300 offices	Few or none	None in their earlier form
Banks	None	34 firms (12 foreign) with 111 offices (43 foreign)	193 firms (39 foreign) with 1,738 offices (146 foreign)	622 firms (16 foreign) with 4,217 offices (40 foreign)
Rural co-operative treasuries	None	None	Unknown	335 offices (1947 publication); 479 (1944 per Table 9.5)
Trust companies			Unknown	21 firms with 27 offices
Insurance companies			Unknown	129 firms with 378 additional offices

Sources: Liu Qiugen 劉秋根, 中國典當制度史 (An Institutional History of Chinese Pawnshops) (Shanghai, Guji chubanshe, 1995), p. 259; Chang Mengju 常夢渠 and Qian Chuntao 錢椿濤 (eds.), 近代中國典當業 (Pawnshops in Modern China) (Beijing, Zhongguo Wenshi chubanshe, 1995), p. 28; Du Xuncheng 杜恂誠, 中國金融通史 (A General History of Chinese Finance). vol 3, 北洋政府時期 (Beiyang Government Period) (Beijing, Zhongguo Jinrong chubanshe, 1996), pp. 233, 295; Huang Jianhui 黃鑑暉, et al. (eds.), 山西票號史料, 增訂本 (Historical Materials on Shanxi Remittance Houses, expanded edn) (Taiyuan, Shanxi Jingji chubanshe, 2002), pp. 213, 215–16, 1279; *Zhongguo Yinhang (Taiwan) Jingji Yanjiu Shi* 中國銀行 (台灣) 經濟研究室, 全國銀行年鑑, 民國 26 年 (All China Bank Annual, 1937) (Taipei, Wenhua chubanshe, 1987, reprint of 1937 ed.), vol. 1, 81r–23 (original pagination S53–S65); Zhongyang Yinhang Jihe Chu 中央銀行稽核處 (Central Bank of China Auditing Department), 全國金融機構一覽 (Chinese Financial Institutions at a Glance) (n.l., Liulian yinshua gongsi, 1947); Jiang Jianqing 姜建清 and Jiang Lichang 蔣立場, 近代中國外商銀行史 (A History of Foreign Banks in Modern China) (Beijing, Zhongxin chubanshe, 2016), pp. 98–102, 164–5

arrived in Hong Kong and the treaty ports in the 1840s, but foreign banking did not really take off until the 1860s with the need for the Qing state to turn to foreign financing, and then especially after the 1870s with the rise in foreign trade after the conclusion of China's mid-nineteenth-century civil wars.[17] Chinese began founding banks based on these foreign models in the very late nineteenth century, but real growth in the Chinese sector did not come until the interwar period in the late 1910s and the 1920s.[18] Subsequently, remittance houses and cash shops both declined in total number while banks saw dramatic expansion.[19]

The numbers of banks and bank offices do not tell the whole story of the rise of Chinese, banking, however, because the size of many of these banks dwarfed that of pawnshops, cash shops, and even remittance houses. Cheng Linsun estimates that by 1936 Chinese banks held about 81 percent of the capital power in the Chinese financial market, with foreign banks holding 11 percent and cash shops 9 percent.[20] These numbers do not consider pawnshops or rotating credit societies, and likely understate cash shop strength because cash shops kept their affairs as secret as possible. Nonetheless, the dominance of Chinese banks by the 1930s was undeniable. Interestingly, China had a small number of very large banks and a large number of very small banks, a fact that still begs full explanation.[21]

In the early twentieth century, many new kinds of financial institution appeared in China. "Lottery"-type savings societies, savings associations, savings departments of banks, a postal savings bank, and savings departments at retail establishments like department stores all aimed at attracting small deposits from ordinary individuals who had previously been excluded by many of the institutions of the financial industry.[22] In the 1940s, rural

---

[17] On the rise of foreign banking in this period, see Jiang Jianqing 姜建清 and Jiang Lichang 蔣立場, 近代中國外商銀行史 (A History of Foreign Banks in Modern China) (Beijing, Zhongxin chubanshe, 2016), Chapter 3.

[18] Zhang Jia'ao 張嘉璈, 各省金融概略 (Summary of Financial Matters in China's Provinces) (n.p., 1915).

[19] Zhongguo Yinhang (Taiwan) Jingji Yanjiu Shi 中國銀行 (台灣) 經濟研究室, 全國銀行年鑑, 民國 26 年 (All China Bank Annual, 1937) (Taipei, Wenhua chubanshe, 1987, reprint of 1937 ed.), vol. 1, 811–23 (original pagination S53–S65). My figures, which are based on a page-by-page compilation of the volume, differ slightly from the summation in the book's Appendix 2, which only specified 3,077 offices. Jiang and Jiang, 近代中國外商銀行史, pp. 98–102, 164–5; Zhongyang Yinhang Jihe Chu 中央銀行稽核處 (Central Bank of China Auditing Department), 全國金融機構一覽 (Chinese Financial Institutions at a Glance) (n.l., Liulian yinshua gongsi, 1947), Appendix 2.

[20] Cheng, Banking in Modern China, p. 78.

[21] B. Sheehan, "Myth and Reality in Chinese Financial Cliques in 1936," Enterprise and Society 6.3 (September 2005), 458.

[22] On the savings industry, see B. Sheehan, "The Modernity of Savings," in M.Y. Dong and J. Goldstein (eds.), Everyday Modernity in China (Seattle, University of Washington Press, 2006), pp. 121–55.

co-operative treasuries were formed to provide credit to farmers. In addition, a number of other kinds of financial institution came into existence, such as insurance companies, trust banks, investment companies, and stock exchanges.[23]

Finance and Geography

Map 9.1 shows the branch networks of six important remittance houses in the 1870s and 1880s. In general, branches were located along major transportation routes such as the upper, middle, and lower Yangzi river; along the Grand Canal through north China; and into northern border regions toward Mongolia (Zhang Jiakou) and up the Gansu corridor toward Russia (Qin'an, Lanzhou, Liangzhou). In addition, there were clusters of branches in tea-producing regions in Jiangxi and Hunan, and in the ports, which acted as centers of trade with the West, such as Guangzhou, Fuzhou, and Shanghai.[24] We have no comparable record of pawnshop or cash shop locations in the nineteenth century, but there is reason to believe they were widely dispersed.

A 1915 survey showed a different pattern for banks which were located in east coast cities, including newly prominent treaty ports, such as Yantai, Qingdao, and Yingkou (Map 9.2).

The rise of banking and the introduction of new kinds of financial institution in the decades after 1915 changed China's financial geography again. Map 9.3 shows how extensive bank networks had become by 1947 on the eve of the Communist revolution.[25] Bank offices were densely packed throughout "China Proper" (south of the Great Wall, east of the Tibetan plateau, east of the deserts). Bank offices now followed many established transportation routes where remittance houses previously held sway, including the Gansu corridor toward Central Asia, but extended much further, and also tracked important new transportation routes, including the path of the South Manchurian Railway in the northeast. In 1947, bank geography also showed the impact of political events and structures. The large number of banks in

---

[23] Zhongyang Yinhang Jihe Chu, 全國金融機構一覽, Appendix 2.
[24] Remittance house location data for Map 9.1 from Huang, 山西票號史料, pp. 212–16. All of the maps in this chapter were created using the China Historical GIS (CHGIS) of the Harvard-Yenching Institute. More information is available at www.fas.harvard.edu/~chgis.
[25] Bank office location data for Map 9.4 from Zhongyang Yinhang Jihe Chu, 全國金融機構一覽. There were sixty-nine bank offices for which we could not match place names in the CHGIS, but these were less than 2 percent of the total offices.

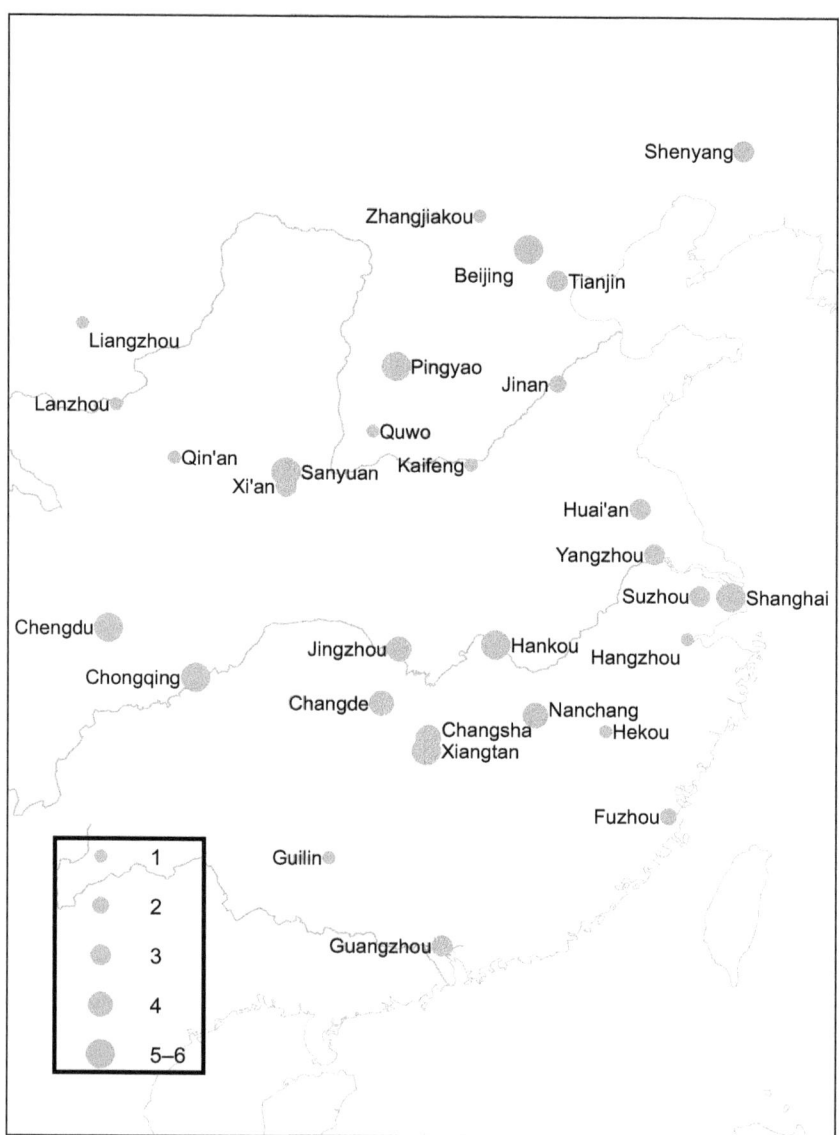

Map 9.1 Locations of the branches of six large remittance houses, 1870s–1880s

the southwest, especially in Sichuan province, shows the impact of World War II when the province hosted the Nationalist regime's wartime capital. Shanxi province, under the quasi-independent rule of Yan Xishan, had very few banks, almost all of which were concentrated in the capital, Taiyuan. The

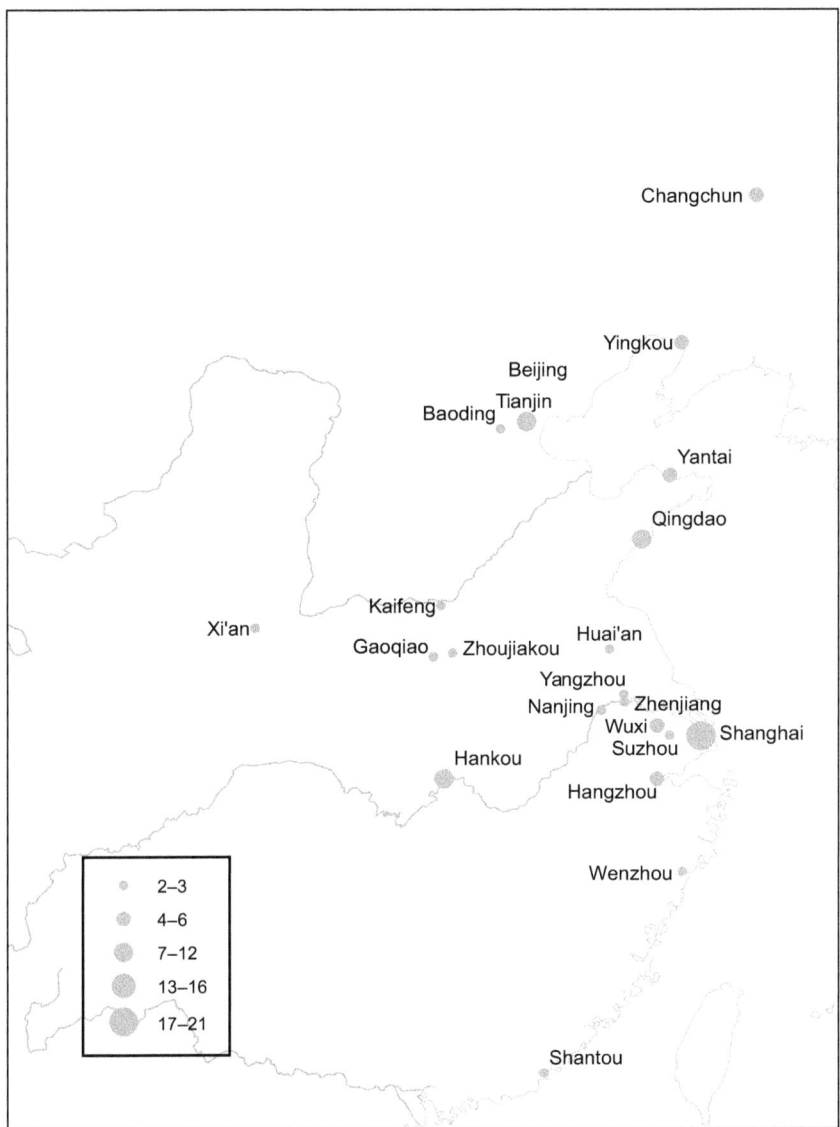

Map 9.2 Bank offices (foreign and Chinese), 1915

surprisingly large number of banks on China's western periphery in Gansu and Xinjiang were almost all branches of the state-run provincial banks of those provinces.

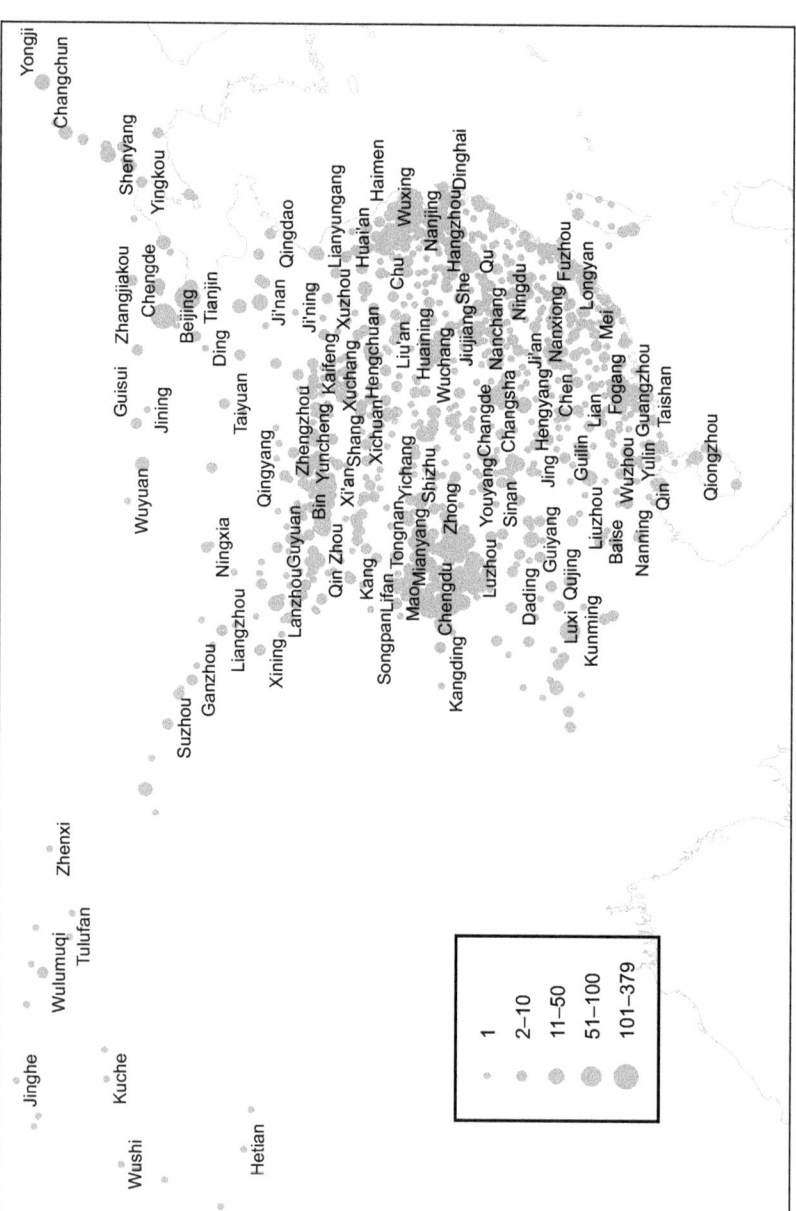

Map 9.3 Banks in 1947

Financial Institutions and Financial Markets

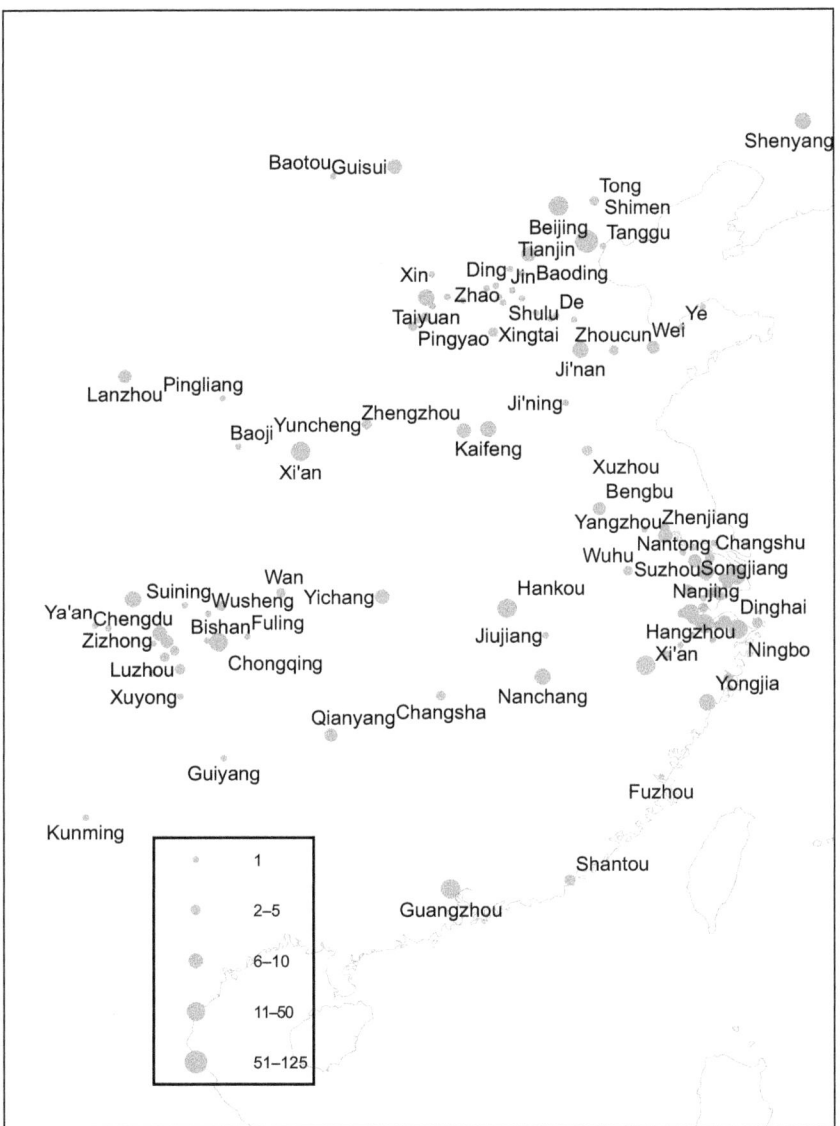

Map 9.4 Cash shops in 1947

Map 9.4 shows both the contraction and the stubborn persistence of cash shops in the face of the dominance of banks. In 1947, cash shops not only existed in hinterland areas such as Shanxi where they outnumbered bank offices, but also continued to thrive on the north China plain, in Sichuan province, and in the lower Yangzi region, all areas of banking strength. Even banking centers like Shanghai, Tianjin, and Guangzhou hosted large numbers of cash shops. The substantial number of cash shops, like the large number of small banks, which coexisted with China's small number of behemoth state and private banks remains an area requiring further research.[26]

Map 9.5 shows the financial geography of two new kinds of financial institution that appeared in the twentieth century: rural co-operative treasuries and insurance companies.[27] The former were almost exclusively rural (a few were located in provincial capitals and other administrative centers) while the latter clustered in China's largest cities. This split shows a growing rural–urban divide in specific kinds of new financial institution at the same time as bank networks worked toward greater national integration. As bank offices grew in cities and on the coast, state-sponsored financial institutions like rural co-operative treasuries and provincial banks extended tendrils into the countryside, keeping the urban–rural divide from being complete.

Maps 9.1 and 9.2 show that China had no single dominant financial center in the nineteenth century, but instead had a dispersed, multi-nodal pattern of financial centers ranging from the capital, Beijing; to Pingyao in Shanxi province, home to many remittance houses; provincial capitals; important transportation hubs on rivers, the Grand Canal, or overland trade routes; and treaty ports such as Shanghai, Fuzhou, and Tianjin.

The pattern of dispersed, multi-nodal financial centers persisted well into the twentieth century. Du Xuncheng argues for two major centers, Beijing and Shanghai, by the 1910s and 1920s, based in part on the growth of the state banks, but the evidence for this is not so clear.[28] In terms of bank headquarters, Tianjin rivaled Beijing, for example. More importantly, the locations of headquarters did not correspond exactly with financial strength, as shown by statistics from the Bank of China, the largest bank in China, often accounting for as much as a quarter of total bank assets. The Bank of China published statistics based on the twenty regions into which the bank divided its branch

---

[26] Cash shop location data for Map 9.5 from Zhongyang Yinhang Jihe Chu, 全國金融機構一覽. There were four cash shops for which we could not match place names in the CHGIS, but these were less than 1 percent of the total offices.
[27] Insurance company offices and rural co-operative treasury location data for Map 9.6 from Zhongyang Yinhang Jihe Chu, 全國金融機構一覽. There were twelve rural co-operative treasury locations for which we could not match place names in the CHGIS, but these were less than 3 percent of the total offices.
[28] Du, 中國金融通史, pp. 5–6.

Financial Institutions and Financial Markets

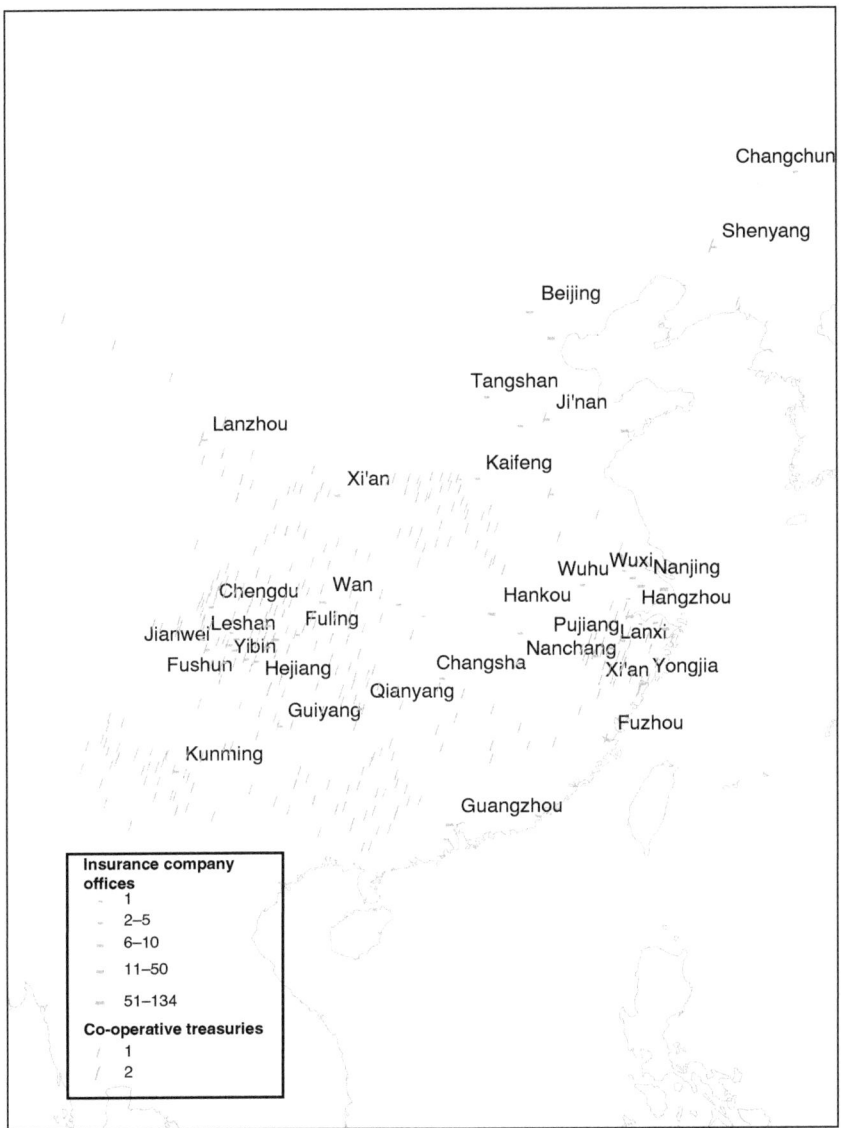

Map 9.5 Insurance company and co-operative treasury offices, 1947

network for the three years from 1919 to 1921. The relative financial strength of those regions can be seen by looking at total currency issue plus deposits, total remittances in and out, and annual profit. Although Shanghai and Beijing did indeed rank first in size (currency plus deposits), Shanghai, in particular, lagged in remittances, ranked only eleventh among twenty. Less important regions like Ningbo, Zhejiang province, and Changchun each had surprisingly high amounts of inflow and outflow, showing the importance of these places as financial centers as well. In addition, even by size, no one region had more than 20 percent of currency issue and deposits.[29]

Subsequently, Beijing's importance faded after the Nationalists moved the capital to Nanjing in 1928, and Tianjin, second only to Shanghai in the numbers of Chinese bank headquarters, diminished after Japanese aggression in north China catalyzed a number of banks to move to Shanghai for greater safety. Thus Shanghai became China's domestic pre-eminent financial center only under the Nationalist regime in the 1930s, and even then, the country's vast area supported a large number of secondary and tertiary centers.[30]

As for international urban systems, at least through the 1920s, Chinese banks generally lacked well-developed international branches, knowledge, and operations.[31] Nonetheless, because of the presence of foreign banks, by one scholar's estimate, the colony of Hong Kong and the treaty ports of Shanghai and Tianjin were three of the ten top international banking centers in the world in 1905.[32] This was part of a trend in the early twentieth century which saw the emergence of a number of new regional and local centers.[33]

Financial Institutions and the State

Over the century from 1850 to 1950 the Chinese state became more involved in the finance sector when state finances became intertwined with services

---

[29] Zhongguo yinhang zonghang 中國銀行總行 and Zhongguo di'er lishi dang'an guan 中國第二歷史檔案館 (eds.), 中國銀行行史資料彙編上編 (1912–1949) (Historical Materials on the History of the Bank of China, Set 1 (1912–1949)) (Beijing, Dang'an chubanshe, 1991), vol. 3, pp. 1851–1902.

[30] Wu Jingping 吳景平, "近代上海金融中心地位與南京國民政府之關係" (The Status of Modern Shanghai as a Financial Center and Its Relations to the Nationalist Government in Nanjing) 史林 (Historical Review) 2 (2002), 92; B. Sheehan, "Urban Identity and Urban Networks in Cosmopolitan Cities: Banks and Bankers in Tianjin, 1900–1937," in J. Esherick (ed.), *Remaking the Chinese City: Modernity and National Identity, 1900–1950* (Honolulu, University of Hawaii Press, 2000), pp. 51–3; Jiaotong yinhang zonghang 交通銀行總行 and Zhongguo di'er lishi dang'an guan 中國第二歷史檔案館 (eds.), 交通銀行史料 (Historical Materials on the Bank of Communications) (Beijing, Zhongguo Jinrong chubanshe, 1995), vol. 1, pp. 95–7.

[31] Jiang and Jiang, 近代中國外商銀行史, p. 307.

[32] H.C. Reed, *The Preeminence of International Financial Centers* (New York, Praeger, 1981), p. 131.

[33] S. Nishimura, T. Suzuki, and R. Michie, "Introduction," in Nishimura, Suzuki, and Michie (eds.), *The Origins of International Banking in Asia: The Nineteenth and Twentieth Centuries* (Oxford, Oxford University Press, 2012), p. 7.

from financial institutions in the last half of the nineteenth century, when various state organs began founding banks at the end of the nineteenth century, and when the state moved to high levels of government sponsorship and control of some financial institutions in the 1930s and 1940s.[34]

Over the course of the seventeenth and eighteenth centuries, many statutes and edicts recognized and regulated the functions of pawnshops and cash shops on matters such as the amount of interest that could be charged, the issuance of paper money backed by copper or silver, and the need for guarantors to support liabilities.[35] In the eighteenth century it became common for government officials to invest public funds with pawnshops in order to earn interest.[36] In the early nineteenth century, individuals who purchased honorary titles from the Qing state often submitted those funds to Beijing through remittance houses.[37]

Nonetheless, as the rise of remittance banks in the nineteenth century made the transfer of funds cheaper and safer than ever before, officials at the Qing court still insisted on the transfer of tax revenues by government shipment of silver under state supervision and control. As late as 1848, an official in Zhejiang province and his superior were both cashiered because the former sent funds to Beijing by remittance rather than the expensive and potentially dangerous shipment of silver ingots overland.[38]

The mid-century rebellions made physical transfer even more difficult, and in 1862 the Qing court finally gave tacit approval to sending money through remittance houses.[39] This ad hoc approval ushered in a new era in relations between the state and the finance sector, and simultaneously led to some of the dramatic growth for the remittance houses recounted above. From 1863 to 1893, there were at least 3,000 instances of tax remittance via private remittance houses for amounts totaling as much as 5.2 million taels per year. Remittance houses also loaned money to local and provincial officials to help them meet their tax quotas. For three decades, Qing fiscal

---

[34] These milestones differ from standard timelines based on the beginning and ending of political regimes. See Sun Jianhua 孫建華, "晚清金融創新與發展的階段性特徵及其變遷" (Characteristics and Evolution of the Periods of Development of Chinese Finance in the Late Qing Period) 學理論 33 (2010), 141–2.
[35] Yan Hongzhong 燕红忠, 晋商与现代经济 (Shanxi Merchants and the Modern Economy) (Beijing, Jingji kexue chubanshe, 2012), pp. 192–4. Yan sees this as a relaxation of government regulation because of the legal recognition given to financial institutions, but the nature of these laws made many functions subject to regulation.
[36] Whelan, *The Pawnshop in China*, p. 10.
[37] Zhang Guohui 張國輝, 晚清錢莊和票號研究 (Qianzhuang and Piaohao in the Late Qing Period) (Beijing, Zhonghua shuju, 1989), p. 37.
[38] Wang, *Hinterland Capitalism*, Chapter 3. [39] Wang, *Hinterland Capitalism*, Chapter 3.

operations and remittance houses were intertwined, although, as Luman Wang argues, this interdependence was decentralized, ad hoc, wracked by scandal, rife with bribery, limited by the local supplies of silver at the disposal of the remittance houses, and constantly under pressure from officials at court who had deep suspicions of private financial institutions.[40] Suspicions, however, ran deep on both sides, as the Qing state frequently asked the remittance houses to make large "donations" to the state to help with fiscal difficulties throughout the 1880s.[41]

Equally complex were relations between the Qing state and foreign financial institutions, as the former borrowed large amounts of money from the latter. From 1877 to 1895, the Hong Kong and Shanghai Banking Corporation (HSBC) alone extended loans of over £12 million to the Qing court and various provincial governments.[42] In addition, a variety of foreign bank consortia negotiated more or less successfully to lend money to the Qing government and its successors.[43] Foreign banks also financed the huge indemnities paid after defeat in war to Japan in 1895 and after the Boxer Uprising in 1900.[44]

By then, however, the ongoing political and fiscal crisis sent the Qing government into high gear of institutional reform, which included founding a number of government-sponsored banks. In 1897 the official Sheng Xuanhuai established a bank in Shanghai modeled on the foreign HSBC.[45] Many provinces founded their own official banks, as did the Qing Board of Revenue and the Communications Ministry.[46] Often authorized to remit government revenues, these new government banks posed an existential threat to the remittance houses.[47] In the end, the remittance houses did not survive as an active group of financial institutions much beyond the fall of the Qing dynasty in 1911.

In January 1908, the newly formed Ministry of Finance promulgated regulations which categorized all domestic financial institutions, including

---

[40] Wang, *Hinterland Capitalism*, Chapter 3; see also Zhou Yumin 周育民, 晚清財政與社會變遷 (Government Finance and Social Change in the Late Qing Period) (Shanghai, Shanghai renmin chubanshe, 2000), pp. 277–82.
[41] Wang, *Hinterland Capitalism*, Chapter 4.
[42] F.H.H. King, *The History of the Hongkong and Shanghai Banking Corporation*, vol. 1, *The Hongkong Bank in Late Imperial China 1864–1902: On an Even Keel* (Cambridge, Cambridge University Press, 1988), pp. 548–9.
[43] Du, 中國金融通史, p. 40.
[44] W. He, *Paths toward the Modern Fiscal State: England, Japan, and China* (Cambridge, MA, Harvard University Press, 2013), p. 177.
[45] He, *Paths toward the Modern Fiscal State*, p. 175; Wang, *Hinterland Capitalism*, Chapter 4.
[46] Wang, *Hinterland Capitalism*, Chapter 4. [47] Wang, *Hinterland Capitalism*, Chapter 4.

remittance firms, money shops, and banks, as "ordinary banks" (*putong yinhang* 普通銀行).[48] In spite of this law, finance professionals and the general public alike continued to distinguish among remittance houses, cash shops, and banks.

The close and complex involvement of the state with financial institutions continued after the fall of the Qing dynasty in 1911. Most importantly, the Bank of China and the Bank of Communications functioned for much of the next four decades as appendages of the central state, often lending money directly to the government or underwriting the issuance of public debt.[49] Control of the two banks became a common issue of dispute between various political factions and private investors in the banks.[50] At the local level, provincial and other local government banks continued into the republic, but often with disastrous results as they were used to finance the activities of the various warlords and political factions vying for power in Republican China.[51] Not all of the state banks were completely subservient to government will. The Bank of China, in particular, had moments of quasi-independence from the state.[52] Nonetheless the general trend was for government control and regulation of the financial system, and this became particularly apparent with the rise of the Nationalist regime after 1927.

As one of its first acts, the new Nationalist regime created its own central bank while also increasing the percentage of government ownership in the Bank of China and the Bank of Communications, China's two largest banks.[53] The state created a Financial Supervision Bureau in 1927 to oversee and inspect financial institutions; then, in 1931, the regime issued a series of laws to regulate China's financial sector. Its new banking law repeated many of the provisions of both the late Qing law referred to above and a 1924 law issued during the warlord period. This new banking law, like those earlier laws, specified that all institutions which took deposits, made loans, or remitted

---

[48] Wang, *Hinterland Capitalism*, Chapter 4.
[49] G. Mickey, "Safeguarding National Credibility: Founding the Bank of China in 1911," *Twentieth Century China* 37.2 (2012), 139–60; Du 中國金融通史, pp. 97–100.
[50] Du, 中國金融通史, pp. 107–35.
[51] Du, 中國金融通史, pp. 222–31; Brett Sheehan, *Trust in Troubled Times: Money, Banking, and State–Society Relations in Republican China* (Cambridge, MA, Harvard University Press, 2001), Chapter 4.
[52] Du, 中國金融通史, pp. 96, 104–6, 128–9. On the limits of independence during this period, see Sheehan, *Trust in Troubled Times*, p. 145 and Chapters 3, 4.
[53] P.M. Coble, *The Shanghai Capitalists and the Nationalist Government, 1927–1937* (Cambridge, MA, Harvard Council on East Asian Studies, 1986); Sheehan, *Trust in Troubled Times*, Chapters 5, 6; Hong Xiaguan 洪葭管, 中國金融通史 (A General History of Chinese Finance), vol. 4, 國民政府時期 1927–1949 (The Nationalist Period (1927–1949)) (Beijing, Zhongguo jinrong chubanshe, 2008), pp. 48–9; Sheehan, *Trust in Troubled Times*, pp. 129–31, 145.

money were banks (*yinhang*). Thus, in law, there were no differences between cash shops and banks, though in practice most cash shops failed to meet the capital requirements of the new law, refused to publish their financial statements, and continued using one or another of the local variations for "cash shop" in their names through the 1940s.[54]

In 1935, against the backdrop of the American Silver Purchase Act, which created a major crisis for China's continued use of the silver standard, the Nationalist regime took undisputed control of the Bank of China and the Bank of Communications.[55] For the rest of the Republican period, a large sector of state-controlled banks coexisted with a smaller sector of private banks. In 1936, for example, the assets of the four banks controlled directly by the central state – the Central Bank, the Bank of China, the Bank of Communications, and the Farmers' Bank of China – stood at 59 percent of the total assets of Chinese banks. The Bank of China alone held a whopping 25 percent of total bank assets. Eleven provincial and municipal government banks held another 11 percent of bank assets, and the remaining 30 percent of bank assets was divided among 139 private banks.[56]

Bank offices in areas controlled by the Communist regime often served as government organs, but tended to be very small and will not be discussed at length here.[57] The Japanese invasion in 1937 reshaped relations between the financial sector and the state. The Japanese occupation regime set up its own reserve banks and took over the "enemy" foreign-bank offices in the occupied areas.[58] In turn, the Nationalist regime reorganized its central state financial institutions on a wartime footing.[59] After the Japanese surrender, one or another of the Nationalists' centrally controlled financial institutions took over nine banks and a dozen other financial institutions run by the Japanese or their allies.[60]

Finance and Agriculture

China's smallholder agriculture required small amounts of highly dispersed financing with variation based on locality and season. Much of our

---

[54] Sheehan, *Trust in Troubled Times*, pp. 147–8.
[55] Coble, *The Shanghai Capitalists*, pp. 172–92; and Sheehan, *Trust in Troubled Times*, 166.
[56] Zhongguo Yinhang (Taiwan), 全國銀行年鑑, vol. 1, pp. 811–23 (original pagination S53–S65).
[57] For a fuller account of finance in the Communist areas, see Jiang Hongye 姜宏業, 中國金融通史 (A General History of Chinese Finance), vol. 5, 新民主主義革命根據地時期 (The Period of New Democracy and the Revolutionary Base Areas) (Beijing, Zhongguo Jinrong chubanshe, 2008).
[58] Sheehan, *Trust in Troubled Times*, p. 175; Du, 中國金融通史, pp. 345–6, 361–3, 367–70.
[59] Hong, 中國金融通史, p. 385.   [60] Hong, 中國金融通史, p. 477.

knowledge of rural finance comes from surveys made in the 1930s and 1940s, and it is unknown how much these surveys reflect long-term practice.

Prior to the 1930s, rural finance relied on personal loans between people and on pawnshops.[61] Even in the 1930s, when banks had exploded on the scene, total bank loans to rural China were less than 2 million yuan in 1933, about 10 million-plus yuan in 1934, and about 14 million yuan in 1935. As for cash shop lending in rural China, "although exact figures are not known, it is reasonable to think that it was not significant." In contrast, in 1937, 3,386 pawnshops had made loans to peasants, totaling 14,931,500 yuan.[62] Interest rates charged by pawnshops varied greatly by locality. One survey in 1931 noted that "more than half the pawnshops in urban and rural areas charged two to three percent [monthly] interest."[63] Most loans were for less than one year.

Rural finance changed dramatically in the 1930s and 1940s when the Nationalist government became a significant provider of rural capital through specialized banks, such as the Farmers' Bank of China, and through the promotion of rural co-operatives. In September 1941 the Nationalist government expanded the Farmers' Bank of China's scope of operations, and increased its capital to 20 million yuan. In September of 1942 "capital was raised again from twenty million to sixty million yuan."[64] At the same time, the government began heavily promoting the formation of co-operatives and co-operative treasuries. Rural co-operatives in China date back to the reform movements of the 1910s.[65] As a result of the war, they became the central

---

[61] Mi Gonggan 宓公幹, 典當論 (On Pawnshops) (Shanghai, Shangwu Yinshu Guan, 1936); Qu Yanbin 曲彥斌, 中國典當史 (A History of Chinese Pawnshops) (Shenyang, Shenyang chubanshe, 2007); Huang Jianhui 黃鑒暉, 中國典當業史 (A History of China's Pawnshop Industry) (Taiyuan, Shanxi Jingji chubanshe, 2006); Liu, 中國典當制度史; Yang Zhaoyu 楊肇遇, 中國典當業 (China's Pawnshop Industry) (Shanghai, Shangwu Yinshu Guan, 1933).

[62] Qian Chengxu 錢承緒 (ed.), 中國金融之組織 – 戰前與戰後 (Chinese Finance before and after the War) (Shanghai, Zhongguo Jingji Yanjiu Hui, 1941), pp. 95–6.

[63] Mi, 典當論, pp. 192–3.

[64] Yao Gongzhen 姚公振, 中國農業金融史 (A History of Chinese Rural Finance) (Shanghai, Zhongguo wenhua fuwushe, 1947), pp. 320–1.

[65] For documents about rural loans and the activities of rural co-operatives, see Lu Guoxiang 陸國香, 湖南農村借貸之研究 (Research on Rural Loans in Hunan) (n.l., Guomin zhengfu shiye bu maoyi ju, 1935); Wang Zhixin 王志莘 and Wu Jingfu 吳敬敷, 農業金融經營論 (On Rural Credit Management) (Shanghai, Shangwu Yinshu Guan, 1936); Yao, 中國農業金融史; Li Jinzheng 李金錚, 民國鄉村借貸關係研究 (Research on the Relationship between Lending and Borrowing in the Countryside in the Republican Period) (Beijing, Renmin chubanshe, 2003); Gong Guan 龔關, 國民政府與中國農村金融制度的演變 (Development of the System of Chinese Rural Finance during the Nationalist Period) (Tianjin, Nankai daxue chubanshe, 2016).

link in the Nationalist government's attempts to solve the problem of military and civilian food supply. The number of co-operatives increased fourfold and of co-operative members tenfold between 1936 and 1945, to 172,053 and 17.2 million respectively.[66] At the same time, rural co-operative treasuries – the organizations that took on the major role in providing rural credit as part of the co-operative system – grew quickly as well. Table 9.4 shows a high tide of co-operative treasuries founded between 1938 and 1940. Sichuan province, the location of the Nationalists' wartime capital, started early and had the most, a little more than a quarter of the total. During the wartime period, most were county- or city-level co-operative treasuries with minimum capital of 100,000 yuan. Below the level of cities and counties, there were county treasury representative offices, co-operative trust associations, and united co-operatives (*dailichu* 代理處, *xinyong hezuoshe* 信用合作社, *lianheshe* 聯合社).[67]

Capital invested in co-operative treasuries increased as well, as shown in Table 9.5. From 1937 to 1941, total capital invested in co-operatives grew from 5.3 million to about 48.3 million yuan, a nearly tenfold increase in four years.

Although co-operatives raised capital by themselves, much more capital came from external sources. On the one hand, government organs subscribed to purchase shares.[68] For example, from January to November 1941, the four central government banks purchased shares in 317 rural co-operative treasuries, totaling 59,304,493 yuan.[69] On the other hand, capital remained only a small percentage of loans made, amounting to 19 percent or less from 1937 to 1941, and a peak of 59 percent at the end of 1945 – indicating other external sources of funding.

Table 9.6 shows the impact of rural co-operative treasuries on changing the supply of rural capital in 684 counties in fifteen provinces. The percentage of rural households borrowing money increased steadily. By 1943, 61 percent, or well over half, of all rural households needed credit. Individuals provided 43 percent of total rural credit in 1938. Subsequently, credit from individuals began to decline as credit from co-operatives increased. By 1942 the co-operative organizations together, directly and indirectly, accounted for 40 percent of rural credit. Banks also grew as a source of rural credit, reaching 22 percent in 1943. By then, that previous mainstay of rural credit, the pawnshop, only provided 7 percent, and cash shops only 2 percent.

In spite of the growth of financial institutions, much rural credit still remained personal. According to one survey in 1941, rich peasants were the

---

[66] Zhongguo Hezuo Shiye Xiehui 中國合作事業協會, 抗戰以來之合作運動 (The Co-operative Movement since the Beginning of the Anti-Japanese War) (1948), pp. 13–14.
[67] Yao, 中國農業金融史, p. 273. [68] Yao, 中國農業金融史, pp. 272–3.
[69] For all the figures cited here, see Yao, 中國農業金融史, pp. 320–1.

Table 9.4 Establishment of county/city co-operative treasuries, 1937–1944

Province	1937	1938	1939	1940	1941	1942	1943	1944	Unknown	Total	Note
Sichuan	5	57	17	33	5	1		1	2	121	
Xikang			7	1	2					10	
Guizhou		15	26	12		1				54	
Yunnan			1	8	1	25	2			37	Also 1 county-level preparation office
Guangxi		16	13	13	16	2	3	2	2	65	12 treasuries had ceased operation
Hubei		1	9				2			12	
Hunan	6	6	5	9	1		1		1	29	
Jiangxi	2	1				1			5	9	2 treasuries had ceased operation
Zhejiang		17	2	10	7	1	2			39	Also 1 county-level preparation office
Fujian				3	2					5	
Henan			9	18	21	6				54	
Shaanxi		1	6	8		4	1			20	
Gansu (worker co-operative)				19	2					19	
Total	13	112	95	136	57	41	11	1	10	474	

Note in original table: besides those listed here, there were two treasuries in Shandong, one in Hebei, and two in Anhui for a total of 493 (including those that had ceased operations).

Source: Zhongguo Hezuo Shiye Xiehui 中國合作事業協會 (China Co-operative Enterprises Association), 抗戰以來之合作運動 (The Co-operative Movement in the Period since the Start of the Anti-Japanese War) (Nanjing, Zhongguo hezuo shiye xiehui, 1948), pp. 45–6

Table 9.5 Growth of the capitalization of co-operatives, 1937–1945 (yuan)

Year	Capital investment	Average share value	Average co-operative member shareholding	Balance of loans made	Capital as % of loans
1937	5,309,079	115.3	2.5	27,055,948	19
1938	7,994,055	122.8	2.6	61,948,345	13
1939	12,611,944	137.9	2.9	112,611,898	11
1940	25,513,370	191.1	3.5	155,578,662	16
1941	48,301,078	310.3	5.2	249,878,770	19
1942	93,291,530	513.1	9.2	387,694,457	24
1943	326,485,306	1,957.0	23.7	802,376,044	41
1944	707,380,719	4,120.3	44.7	1,187,853,797	59
1945	1,461,082,953	8,492.2	84.8	2,482,932,926	59

Source: Zhongguo hesuo shiye xiehui, 抗戰以來之合作運動, p. 34

largest individual providers of rural credit, accounting for more than 45 percent in both 1940 and 1941. Landlords were the next-largest source of loans, with 30 percent, followed by merchants with 25 percent. As for lending terms, the most common lending was based on collateral. Among the fifteen provinces in the survey, more than 50 percent of loans in most places were based on collateral, and in some places the proportion was as high as 70 percent. We can conclude that without friends and family, other social connections, or assets to pledge as collateral, the chances of being able to borrow were extremely small. Interest rates were also very high, rarely less than 2.8 percent a month and sometimes as high as 3.4 percent.[70]

Table 9.7 shows the interest rates on and length of loans in rural finance from 1940 and 1941. Interest rates on loans – based on credit, guarantee, or collateral – are similar to the rates on individual loans noted above. Loans from co-operatives had lower rates, with a weighted average of 1.2 percent in both 1940 and 1941. Interest rates on loans from co-operatives were even lower than from the rotating credit societies founded among the people themselves.

Continued differences in interest rates probably arose either from the limited coverage of co-operatives; from the fact that control of

---

[70] "Nonglin bu Zhongyang Nongye Shiyansuo Nongye Jingjixi Diaocha" 農林部中央農業試驗所農業經濟系調查 (Investigation of the Agricultural Economics Department of the Agricultural Institute of the Ministry of Agriculture and Forestry), Archives of the Ministry of Agriculture and Forestry, Institute of Modern History, Academia Sinica, Taiwan, 20-07: 55-2. Note: The original chart was named "Survey of rural finance across China (continued), Table 1 cash loans (continued)."

Table 9.6 Survey of rural finance in 1943 (according to lending institution, weighted average)

Province	No. of counties reporting	% of rural households borrowing money	Lending institution (%)						State organs (co-operative treasuries)	Individuals
			Banks	Cash shops	Pawn-shops	Shops	Co-operatives			
1938	681	51	8	3	13	14	17		2	43
1939	673	55	8	2	11	13	23		2	41
1940	621	50	10	2	9	13	26		2	38
1941	693	51	17	2	9	11	30		4	27
1942	716	55	19	2	8	10	34		6	21
1943	684	61	22	2	7	8	32		5	24
1943 detail by province										
Zhejiang	23	56	33	8	3	6	8		20	22
Jiangxi	43	56	16		6	8	24		2	44
Hubei	18	57	30				31		4	35
Hunan	49	64	24		1	6	35		2	32
Sichuan	121	54	22	3	9	4	31		8	23
Henan	50	76	28	3	6	10	35		3	15
Shaanxi	62	62	30	2	4	9	30		1	24
Gansu	43	64	30	1	7	8	41		1	12
Qinghai	5	56	6		12	23	12		18	29
Fujian	46	58	15		9	15	44			17

Table 9.6 (cont.)

Province	No. of counties reporting	% of rural households borrowing money	Lending institution (%)						
			Banks	Cash shops	Pawn-shops	Shops	Co-operatives	State organs (co-operative treasuries)	Individuals
Guangdong	42	63	34	5	7	13	13		28
Guangxi	72	59	15	2	11	6	36	10	20
Yunnan	49	64	15		8	8	31	6	32
Guizhou	54	50	7		5	5	42	9	32
Ningxia	7	58	12		4	16	28		40

Note from original table: (1) co-operatives borrowed money indirectly and loaned money directly; (2) "state organs" are co-operative treasuries

Source: 農林部中央農業實驗所農業經濟系調查 (Survey by the Agricultural Economics Section of the Agriculture Laboratory of the Agriculture and Forestry Department), Archive held at Zhongyang Yanjiu Yuan Jindai Lishi Yanjiusuo 中央研究院近代歷史研究所 (Academia Sinica, Modern History Institute), 20-07, Zonghao 宗號 55-2

Table 9.7 Survey of rural finance across China (cash lending) in 1941

	Lending interest rate (monthly %)					Lending term (percentage distribution)				
Province	Credit	Guarantee	Collateral	Lending societies	Co-operatives	1–3 months	4–6 months	7–9 months	10–12 months	13 months or more
Ningxia	3.0	3.0	3.2		1.0	33	33		34	
Qinghai	2.5	2.7	2.7	2.0			10	10	52	28
Gansu	1.6	2.2	2.4	2.3	1.2	13	20	2	59	6
Shaanxi	1.8	2.1	2.5	2.1	1.3	26	33	1	39	1
Henan	2.1	2.4	2.5	2.2	1.3	16	26	1	57	
Hubei	1.7	2.0	2.5	2.0	0.9	7	19		69	5
Sichuan	1.9	2.2	2.2	1.9	1.3	12	20	1	63	4
Yunnan	2.1	2.5	2.5	1.8	1.2	10	20	2	57	11
Guizhou	1.5	1.9	2.3	2.2	1.2	8	10		71	11
Hunan	1.5	1.9	2.0	2.0	1.1	10	14	5	66	5
Jiangxi	1.5	1.5	1.7	1.6	1.1	1	21	1	74	3
Zhejiang	1.3	1.2	1.3	1.4	1.1	12	32		50	6
Fujian	1.4	1.5	1.7	1.5	1.0	2	18	2	72	6
Guangdong	1.9	1.7	1.9	1.9	1.0	4	28		51	17
Guangxi	1.7	1.8	2.1	2.1	1.2	3	28	1	60	8
Weighted average	1.8	2.1	2.2	2.0	1.2	11	23	1	59	6
1940	1.9	2.1	2.1	1.9	1.2	5	16	8	65	6

Source: 農林部中央農業實驗所農業經濟系調查

co-operatives often lay with specific individuals and co-operatives could not necessarily become conduits for credit to the general populace; or from problems inherent in the co-operatives themselves, such as the complexity of procedures, limits on available funds, and so on.

Rural credit went to a variety of purposes. According to a 1941 survey by the Chinese Economic Yearbook, in the four counties of Haining, Jiaxing, Pinghu, and Haiyan, of peasants who borrowed money from pawnshops, "55 percent did so for direct support of production." Although this statistic cannot necessarily represent all of China, "it is believable that more than one-third" of China's rural pawnshop loans "was used for production."[71] The figures in Table 9.8 showing statistics from Guangxi province from 1938 to 1941 allow us to see the uses of rural loans in one Nationalist-controlled area during the war. The bulk of rural loans for all four years went either to production (plowing cattle, fertilizer, and seeds) or consumption (grain), but the latter steadily decreased.

Table 9.8 Uses and percentage distribution for co-operative loans in Guangxi province, 1938–1941

	1938	1939	1940	1941
Plowing cattle	17.63	19.00	23.27	29.34
Fertilizer	21.70	22.45	21.69	16.61
Seeds	9.78	10.49	6.60	5.89
Grain	33.03	24.73	18.83	15.78
Tools	3.41	2.40	2.72	2.14
Wages	4.10	4.70	4.16	5.67
Loan repayment	0.66	1.19	4.13	8.51
Water improvements	1.60	4.19	3.76	4.41
Sideline production			6.23	6.54
Living needs				0.35
Raising animals	5.66	5.97	3.51	
Other	2.43	4.88	5.10	4.76

Source: "廣西經濟建設統計提要" (Outline of Guangxi Economic Development Statistics), February 1943, archive held at Zhongyang Yanjiu Yuan Jindai Lishi Yanjiusuo 中央研究院近代歷史研究所 (Academia Sinica, Modern History Institute), 20-07 Zong Hao 宗號 55-3

[71] Qian, 中國金融之組織 – 戰前與戰後, pp. 95–6.

From existing research there is no evidence of reports of severe problems in agriculture or the supply of grain in Nationalist areas. There certainly were multiple factors involved, but rural finance, especially the development of co-operatives and their work making rural loans for production and cultivation, undoubtedly played an active role which changed the long-existing conditions of rural finance.

Finance and Business, Commerce, and Industry

There is evidence to indicate that a significant amount of early industrial capital came from financial institutions such as pawnshops, remittance houses, and especially cash shops, as seen in case studies of two of the most important early industrial firms.[72]

The statistics in Table 9.9 show that the China Merchants Steam Navigation Company (China's first mechanized transport firm, hereafter China Merchants) received a substantial portion of its financing from cash shops: 470,000 taels (calculated together with loans from individuals), 610,000 taels (calculated alone), and 590,000 taels (calculated with individuals) in 1876 to 1877. As one company manager noted, "When operating cash was short, [we] frequently got accommodation from Shanghai's cash shops."[73] The Qing official Li Hongzhang noted, "The firm has had difficulty raising capital, so it must temporarily borrow from cash shops."[74] The China Merchants executive Xu Run 徐潤 stated, "For ten years running at year end the company owed more than a million taels to cash shops and individuals drawn from the merchant-gentry class."[75] From these sources, it is clear that financing from cash shops for China Merchants was extremely important, if not decisive, in the company's early years.

Likewise, development of the Hanyeping (漢冶萍) Company (the largest mining and steel company during this period of China's history) coal mine at Ping county almost entirely relied on cash shops. The Ping county coal mine opened in 1898 and during its first years of operation, all funds to meet

---

[72] See Wang Yejian 王業鍵, 中國近代貨幣與銀行的演進 1644–1937 (The Development of Money and Banks in Modern China 1644–1937) (Taipei, Zhongyang Yanjiuyuan Jingji Yanjiusuo, 1981).

[73] "Zhaoshangju Disanjie Zhanglue" 招商局第三屆賬略 (Third Accounting Report of the China Merchants Steam Navigation Company), in Li Yadong 李亞東 (ed.), 招商局創辦之初 (1873–1880) (The Early Years of the Founding of the China Merchants Steam Navigation Company) (Beijing, Zhongguo Shuhui kexue chubanshe, 2010), pp. 98.

[74] Li, 招商局創辦之初, p. 54.

[75] Xu Run 徐潤, 徐愚齋自敘年譜 (Self-Recorded Annals of Xu of the Modest Studio) (Taipei, Taiwan Shangwu Yinshuguan, 1981), p. 177.

Table 9.9 The China Merchants Steam Navigation Company assets and liabilities prior to 1880 (taels)

Year	Capital	Loans from government	Loans from cash shops	Loans from individuals	Deposits from Renhe Insurance (Renhe Baoxian 仁和保險)
1873–1874	476,000	123,023			
1874–1875	602,400	136,957	475,354 (cash shops and individuals together)		
1875–1876	685,100	353,499	613,228	238,328	200,000
1876–1877	730,200	1,866,979	593,449	87,884	350,000
1877–1878	751,000	1,928,868	1,472,404 (cash shops and individuals together)		418,430
1878–1879	800,600	1,928,868	624,088 (cash shops and individuals together)		582,632
1879–1880	830,300	1,903,868	533,029 (cash shops and individuals together)		619,848

Source: Tang Tingshu 唐廷樞 and Xu Run 徐潤, "招商局第一至第七屆賬略" (The China Merchants Steam Navigation Company Accounting Periods One through Seven), in Li Yadong 李亞東 (ed.), 招商局創辦之初 (1873–1880) (The Early Years of the Founding of the China Merchants Steam Navigation Company (1873–1880)) (Beijing, Zhongguo Shuhui kexue chubanshe, 2010), pp. 39–174.

expenses "were borrowed from cash shops ... Invested capital came only after 1899, and then only in small amounts to pay back loans, but not enough to satisfy needs."[76] In January 1905, the Ping county coal mine borrowed 416,000 taels from cash shops.[77] Besides the coal mine, the Hanyeping company itself had large loans from cash shops. In August 1917, Hanyeping borrowing from more than thirty cash shops in Hankou reached more than 350,000 taels, in addition to loans from Shanghai cash shops.[78] At this time it was common for a given large firm to have loans from dozens of cash shops. A given cash shop could also have loans to many firms. Table 9.10 shows loans made to industry by the notorious Fukang, which became closely intertwined with a variety of government projects and eventually crashed spectacularly.

For some firms, reliance on cash shops came because they were excluded from funding at the new state banks founded in the late Qing period. One cotton mill executive noted, "we could not even get in the door of a state bank. Our relations were primarily with cash shops."[79] Another businessperson stated, "banks did not have relations with business and industry, which completely relied on cash shops."[80] Spoken by individuals in Hubei province

---

[76] Zhang Zanchen 張贊宸, "奏報萍鄉煤礦歷年辦法及礦內已成工程" (Memorial and Report on the Management of the Coal Mine at Pingxiang and Engineering in Progress in the Mine), in Hubeisheng Dang'anguan 湖北省檔案館 (ed.), 漢冶萍公司檔案史料選編 (Selected Archival Documents on the Hanyeping Company), vol. 1 (Beijing, Zhongguo shehui kexue chubanshe, 1994), p. 205. As of January 1905, capital shares in the Pingxiang Coal Mine were one million kuping taels (p. 204). On Hanyeping, see Zhang Zhidong 張之洞, "鐵廠招商承辦議定章程折" (Memorial on the Regulations Decided for Merchant Capital for an Iron Factory), in Yuan Shuyi 苑書義 (ed.), 張之洞全集 (Collected Works of Zhang Zhidong) (Shijiazhuang, Hebei renmin chubanshe, 1988), pp. 1167.

[77] Zhang Zancheng 張贊宸, "奏報萍鄉煤礦歷年辦法及礦內已成工程" (Memorial and Report on the Pingxiang Coal Mine Methods over the Years and Construction Already Completed within the Mine), in Hubei Sheng Dang'an Guan 湖北省檔案館 (Hubei Provincial Archive) (ed.), 漢冶萍公司檔案史料選邊 (Collection of Historical Materials on the Hanyeping Company), vol. 1 (Beijing, Zhongguo shehui kexue chubanshe, 1994), p. 205.

[78] Hubeisheng Dang'anguan 湖北省檔案館 (ed.), 漢冶萍公司檔案史料選編 (Selected Archival Documents on the Hanyeping Company), vol. 2 (Beijing, Zhongguo shehui kexue chubanshe, 1994), p. 727.

[79] Zhang Songqiao, "1959 年張松樵回憶錄未刊稿" (unpublished 1959 memoir), in Yudahua fangzhi ziben jituan shiliao bianjizu bian 裕大華紡織資本集團史料編輯組 (ed.), 裕大華紡織資本集團史料 (Historical Materials on the Yudahua Textile Group) (Wuhan, Hubei renmin chubanshe, 1984), p. 61.

[80] "錢遠聲、王仰蘇訪問記錄" (Record of the Interview of Qian Yuansheng and Wang Yangsu), in Zhongguo renmin yinhang Shanghai fenhang 中國人民銀行上海分行 (ed.), 上海錢莊史料 (Historical Materials on Shanghai Qianzhuang) (Shanghai, Shanghai renmin chubanshe, 1960), p. 170.

Table 9.10 Loans from Shanghai's Fukang (福康) cash shop to industrial enterprises, 1899–1907 (taels)

Year	Enterprise	Loan amount	Year	Enterprise	Loan amount
1899	Textile Bureau (紡織局)	20,246 (credit)	1904	Lunhua Silk Factory (綸華絲廠)	5,720 (credit)
1899	Ruilun Silk Factory (瑞綸絲廠)	5,112 (credit)	1904	Hengchang Silk Factory (恆昌絲廠)	44,000 (collateral)
1900	Hengchang Silk Factory (恆昌絲廠)	80,000 (credit)	1905	Hengchang Silk Factory (恆昌絲廠)	33,233 (collateral)
1902	Xiechang Match Factory (燮昌火柴廠)	5,000 (credit)	1906	Youxin Cotton Mill (又新紗廠)	10,317 (credit)
1902	Ruishun Silk Factory (瑞順絲廠)	65,000 (collateral)	1906	Hanyeping (漢冶萍局)	10,200 (credit)
1902	Fengji Oil Factory (豐記油廠)	22,259 (collateral)	1906	Youxin Cotton Mill (又新紗廠)	20,000 (collateral)
1902	Textile Bureau (紡織局)	20,000 (collateral)	1907	Gong Yi Cotton Mill (公益紗廠)	20,279 (credit)
1903	Lunhua Silk Factory (綸華絲廠)	10,315 (credit)	1907	Hanyeping (漢冶萍局)	20,267 (credit)
1903	Ruilun Silk Factory (瑞綸絲廠)	100,000 (collateral)	1907	Youxin Cotton Mill (又新紗廠)	10,337 (credit)
1903	Baochang Silk Factory (寶昌絲廠)	40,000 (collateral)	1907	Qixin Cement Company (啟新洋灰公司)	10,244 (credit)
1904	Ruishun Silk Factory (瑞順絲廠)	45,000 (credit)	1907	Huaxing Flour Company (華興麵粉公司)	10,184 (credit)

The original source divided loans into mining, credit loans, and collateral loans, but they have all been combined here, but with notes to distinguish loans made on credit versus collateral. Some enterprises received two loans in a year, hence credit loans and collateral loans.
Source: Zhongguo Renmin Yinhang Shanghai Fenhang 中國人民銀行上海分行 (ed.), 上海錢莊史料 (Historical Materials on Shanghai Qianzhuang) (Shanghai, Shanghai renmin chubanshe, 1960), pp. 784–5

and Shanghai respectively, these words show the functions of cash shops in supporting the development of business and industry.

The importance of cash shops for modern industry and business continued well into the Republican period. For example, in 1931 the Rong Family Company purchased the Shanghai Housheng (厚生) Cotton Mill for 3.4 million taels. Housheng was operating at a loss and could not repay money owed to the Dunyu (敦裕) cash shop. Rong Zongjing purchased it for the amount owed to the cash shops plus a little more for Housheng's owners. Rong borrowed the money against collateral from some cash shops. As a result, "Rong did not spend any money, but simply transferred balances among accounts at cash shops."[81]

During and after World War I the size and breadth of bank lending to industry increased noticeably.[82] For example, in 1919 the Kincheng (Jincheng) Banking Corporation's loans to industry and railroads reached a total of 2.81 million yuan. By 1923, they had grown to 7.59 million yuan, and by 1927 again to 15.32 million yuan.[83] The Shanghai Commercial and Savings Bank's loans to industry and business totaled more than 3.6 million yuan by the end of 1926, and "stood at 19.9 percent of all loans made."[84]

An even clearer change, however, came in the ten years from 1927 to 1937. As of 1930, fifteen important banks in Shanghai had loaned a total of 91.49 million yuan to industry and mining. By 1933, that figure had grown to 163.38 million, and by 1936 it had increased again to 291.25 million, increasing 2.18 times in seven years.[85] A survey made at the time examined the capital structures of 100 enterprises between 1932 and 1939 which had total financing of 262.2 million yuan. Of this amount, 114.9 million yuan, or 43.8 percent, was borrowed from banks (mostly) and a few cash shops.[86] The Kincheng Bank's loans to industry and mining usually made up more than 20 percent of its lending. The Shanghai Commercial and Savings Bank's share was more than 30 percent. The National

---

[81] Shanghai shekeyuan jingjisuo 上海社科院經濟所 (ed.), 榮家企業史料 (Historical Materials on the Rong Family Enterprises), vol. 1 (Shanghai, Shanghai renmin chubanshe, 1980), p. 253.
[82] See Li Yixiang 李一翔, 近代中國銀行與企業的關係 1897–1945 (Relations between Banks and Enterprises in Modern China, 1897–1945) (Taipei, Dongda Tushu Gongsi, 1997), Chapter 1.
[83] 金城銀行史料 (Historical Materials on the Jincheng [Kincheng] Bank) (Shanghai, Shanghai renmin chubanshe, 1983), p. 14.
[84] 上海商業儲蓄銀行史料 (Historical Materials on the Shanghai Commercial and Savings Bank) (Shanghai, Shanghai renmin chubanshe, 1990), p. 161.
[85] Li, 近代中國銀行與企業的關係, p. 65, Table 13.
[86] Chen Zhen 陳真 (ed.), 中國近代工業史資料 (Historical Materials on the History of Chinese Industry), vol. 4 (Beijing, Sanlian shudian, 1961), p. 67, Table 9.

Commercial Bank had the highest ratio with about 50 percent of its loans normally made to business and industry.[87] State banks like the Bank of China and the Bank of Communications also saw a dramatic increase in loans to business and industry in the 1930s. The Bank of China loaned 30 million to 50 million yuan to business and industry every year, reaching a total of 80.22 million yuan in loans to industry and 400 million to commercial enterprises at the end of 1936.[88] The Bank of Communications, "at the end of 1936 had loaned 69.22 million yuan to business and industry combined. This was an increase of 35.55 million over the previous year and a tenfold increase over 1932."[89]

The rise of banking also changed the basis of credit with a multiplication of types of collateral lending in contrast to credit loans, which were simply based on the creditworthiness of individuals. Although pawnshops had long made collateral loans in China, cash shops relied more on credit loans.[90] In contrast, banks often relied on collateral, and even built large warehouses to keep track of assets pledged to support transactions. Numerous banks also established investigation offices in major cities such as Shanghai, Tianjin, and Hankou to investigate the creditworthiness of borrowers so they could lend on personal credit or make overdrafts when appropriate.[91]

Finance and Capital Markets

The roles in capital markets of cash shops and banks have been discussed above, so here we will examine the role and status of stock markets in modern Chinese finance.[92] In the years before and after 1880, almost forty firms raised

[87] Li, 近代中國銀行與企業的關係, p. 67, Table 14.
[88] Zhongguo yinhang hangshi bianjiweiyuanhui 中國銀行行史編輯委員會 (ed.), 中國銀行行史, 1912–1949 (History of the Bank of China, 1912–1949) (Beijing, Zhongguo Jinrong chubanshe, 1995), p. 255.
[89] Jiaotong yinhang zonghang 交通銀行總行 and Zhongguo di'er lishi dang'an guan 中國第二歷史檔案館, 交通銀行史料, vol. 1, p. 289.
[90] Zhongguo renmin yinhang Shanghai fenhang, 上海錢莊史料, p. 215.
[91] Yang Yinpu 楊蔭溥, 中國金融研究 (Research on Chinese Finance) (Shanghai, Shangwu yinshuguan, 1936), p. 159.
[92] On stockmarkets, see Liu Zhiying 劉志英, 近代中國華商證券市場研究 (Research on Chinese Stock Markets in Modern China) (Beijing, Zhongguo shehui kexue chubanshe, 2011); and Liu Zhiying 劉志英, 近代上海華商證券市場研究 (Research on Chinese Stock Markets in Modern Shanghai) (Shanghai, Xuelin chubanshe, 2004); Zhu Yingui 朱蔭貴, 近代中國: 金融與證券研究 (Modern China: Research on Finance and Stock Markets) (Shanghai, Shanghai renmin chubanshe, 2012), Zhu Yingui 朱蔭貴, "近代上海證券市場上股票買賣的三次高潮" (Three High Tides of Buying and Selling on Shanghai Stock Markets), 中國經濟史研究 (Research on Chinese Economic History) 3 (1998), 58–70, Zhu Yingui 朱蔭貴, "抗戰時期的上海華商證券市場" (Stock Markets in Shanghai during the Anti-Japanese War), 社會科學 (Social Science) 2 (2005), 88–97; and Zhu Yingui 朱蔭貴, "試論近代中國證券市場的特點" (Characteristics of Stock

approximately 10 million taels in capital through issuing shares on China's capital market. The time of this surge gave birth to a private exchange firm buying and selling shares of different companies on behalf of clients.[93] In 1891 foreign residents of Shanghai organized a stock exchange for trading foreign stocks and bonds. Only in 1914, however, did the new Republican government in Beijing formally promulgate its "stock market law." Then it took until 1918 for the Beijing Stock Exchange, the Shanghai Stock and Commodities Exchange, and the Shanghai Stock Exchange to receive permission to open.

The opening of these three exchanges one after the other marked a new era in the market for stocks in China. All the way up to the outbreak of full-scale war with Japan in 1937, however, these stock markets focused on the buying and selling of government bonds. When the Beiyang government (1912–1937) issued bonds domestically, they were usually underwritten by banks and then circulated to society on the stock market. The Beijing Stock Exchange's request for permission to operate from the Department of Agriculture and Commerce said that "the buying and selling of public bonds and securities is gradually increasing, but there is no central place to evaluate [them], so prices go up and down without standards."[94] Thus it is clear that the reason for the founding of the Beijing Stock Exchange was to solve problems in the circulation of securities, especially government bonds. "From 1912 to 1926, the Beiyang government issued 27 different domestic bonds for a total of 876,792,228 yuan."[95] As a result, "the time when the government's issue of bonds and treasury notes was at its most excessive and chaotic was also the time when the Beijing Stock Exchange flourished and prospered most."[96] During the period of rule by the Nanjing Nationalist government from 1927 to 1937, the Nationalist government continued to issue large amounts of domestic bonds, totaling more than 3.6 billion yuan.[97] In the securities market, "98 percent of the transactions were government bonds, so sometimes stock exchanges were called government bond exchanges."[98]

Markets in Modern China: A Preliminary Assessment), 經濟研究 (Economic Research) 3 (2008), 150–60; and Zhang Zhongmin 張忠民, "抗戰時期上海的產業證券與新興企業集團 – 以新亞集團為例" (Shanghai Industrial Securities and New-Style Enterprise Groups during the Anti-Japanese War: The Case of the Xinya Group), 上海經濟研究 (Research on the Shanghai Economy) 3 (2002), 72–9.

[93] Zhu, 近代上海.
[94] "北京籌設證券交易所" (Beijing Plans Stock Exchange), 銀行週報 (Bankers' Weekly) 2.11 (March 26, 1918).
[95] See Qian Jiaju 千家駒 (ed.), 舊中國公債史資料 (Documents on the History of Public Debt in Old China) (Beijing, Caizheng Jingji chubanshe, 1955), pp. 10–11.
[96] Zhongguo renmin yinhang zonghang, 近代中國的金融市場, p. 166.
[97] Qian, 舊中國公債史資料, pp. 19, 23.
[98] Zhu Sihuang 朱斯煌 (ed.), 民國經濟史 (Economic History of the Republican Period), photocopied ed. (Taipei, Xuehai chubanshe, 1970), pp. 143, 152.

Table 9.11 comes from a Japanese survey made at the time. Table 9.12 comes from statistics kept by Chinese sources. The figures in these tables show that the government bond price index reached its lowest point in 1932 at about the time of the Japanese invasion of Manchuria and the attack on Shanghai by Japanese forces. The fundamental reason for the dip, however, grew from the Nationalist government's desire to extend the period over which the principal would be repaid and to reduce interest, policies which caused trust in the bonds to drop precipitously. After reorganization of government debt, however, there was recovery and stability by 1934. In 1935

Table 9.11 Index of domestic bond transactions and volume of transactions, 1926–1937 (thousands of yuan)

Year	Bond index	Transaction volume	Commodity securities transaction volume
1926		450,738	
1927		238,169	
1928		370,487	
1929		1,320,555	97,703
1930		2,341,820	90,615
1931	85.62	3,362,540	555,022
1932	60.68	901,710	303,939
1934	78.48	3,182,685	230,090
1935	97.94	4,773,410	
1936	98.25	4,909,980	
Jan. 1937	93.94	146,365	
Feb. 1937	94.91	118,360	
March 1937	97.28	197,600	
April 1937	102.12	296,035	
May 1937	103.02	231,325	
June 1937	110.35	485,815	
July 1937	106.91	604,260	
Aug. 1937	101.73	328,201	

Notes. (1) The volume of securities traded refers to the volume on the Shanghai Chinese Stock Exchange. The volume of commodities securities traded refers to transactions on the Shanghai Commodities Exchange. Figures for transactions in 1934 are for the period after the merger of the two exchanges, and are for the fiscal, not calendar, year. They represent transactions for January–May 1933. (2) Bond index uses July 1931 = 100. (3) The bond index for 1931 is the average for the second half of the year. (4) The bond index for 1932 is the average of January and April–December.
Source: Zhong Zhina Zhenxing Zhushi Huishe Diaochake 中支那振興株式會社調査課 (ed.), "振興調查資料第二十八號" (Zhenxing Survey Number Twenty-Eight), in 上海華商證券業概況 (Shanghai's Chinese Stock Exchanges) (1941), pp. 12–13

Table 9.12 Stock index and volume of stock and corporate bond transactions, 1931–August 1937

Year	Stock index	Stock transaction volume (shares)	Corporate bond transaction volume (thousands of yuan)
1931	99.76	7,269	
1932	80.28	4,338	20,299
1933	71.36	8,534	51,422
1934	65.29	18,453	44,059
1935	57.11	898	12,437
1936	57.66	9,685	16,413
Jan. 1937	48.30	3,135	1,068
Feb. 1937	46.72	3,684	1,956
March 1937	48.50	4,271	965
April 1937	48.60	3,692	1,045
May 1937	47.10	1,229	1,493
June 1937	46.67	1,389	2,235
July 1937	46.22	542	2,167
Aug. 1937	44.33	177	181

Notes: (1) Stock Index July 1931 = 100. (2) Figures for 1931 are for the second half of the year. (3) The stock index for 1931 is the average of January and April–December.
Source: Zhongguo Jingji Tongji Yanjiusuo 中國經濟統計研究所 (ed.), 經濟統計月志 (Economic Statistics Monthly) 4.10 (October 1937), 20, Table 5, and 22, Table 8

the index reached a new high, and it grew steadily through March of 1937, breaking previous records. The stock share price index did exactly the opposite. After 1931 it continuously decreased, reaching a low in 1936, then it continued to drop in 1937. The difference in the directions of the two indices reflects the dynamism of the government bond market and a slump in the stock market. Looking at the volume of transactions, the volume of government bond trading grew rapidly after weathering the drop in 1932. It exceeded 4.7 billion yuan in 1935, 4.9 billion yuan in 1936, and 2.4 billion yuan for the first eight months of 1937. The volume of stock trades varied greatly over time. At the peak in 1934, 18,453,000 shares were traded, but in 1935 the volume was only 898,000 shares for the whole year. In addition, the volume of corporate bonds was minimal. At its greatest, the volume was a little more than 50 million yuan a year; at its least, just over 10 million yuan. The volume of corporate bonds trades also generally declined over the course of the period.

Beginning in 1935, the Shanghai Stock Exchange started a market in the shares of the finance industry and businesses, but the securities market "became monopolized by government debt. The cold shoulder given to stock shares was completely the opposite to that of public bonds."[99] The economist Zhang Naiqi said that Shanghai had a "Chinese Stock Exchange, and it was for the purchase and sale of government bonds – it was a public debt market and not a market in the securities of productive businesses."[100]

Finance and Society

Financial institutions were recognizable icons of town and city life in China. In the early to mid-nineteenth century, pawnshops often dominated local skylines in villages and cities. One foreign observer noted during a tour of rural southern China that in each village there "stands one conspicuous great solid square structure of granite, lined with brick, about four stories high ... [it is] the village pawnshop." The same observer continued, in the large city of Guangzhou, "there are upwards of a hundred first class pawn-towers, besides a multitude of the second and third class."[101] Cash shops and remittance houses tended to keep lower profiles, though they were often grouped together along particular streets or in particular neighborhoods.[102] As banks grew in the twentieth century, they built large and imposing buildings, often in the foreign concessions, which provided physical manifestations of their strength and influence. The buildings along the Shanghai Bund are probably the best-known example, but other financial centers like Tianjin had similar streets.[103]

Financial institutions and financiers loomed large in the cultural imagination as well, though their symbolism varied significantly depending on the point of view. The *Dream of the Red Chamber*, the Qing period's most famous novel, mentions pawnshops more than thirty times in episodes ranging from the pathos of a poor relative of the Jia family who suffers from the cold because she pawned her winter clothes to one somewhat tainted source of the Xue family's fabulous wealth.[104] As banks came to dominate the Chinese

[99] Wu Yitang 吳毅堂 (ed.), 中國股票年鑑 (China Stock Share Annual) (n.l., Zhongguo gupiao nianjian she, 1947), p. 3.
[100] Zhang Naiqi 章乃器, "中國貨幣金融問題" (The Problem of China's Money and Finance), in Zhang Lifan 章立凡 (ed.), 章乃器文集 (Collected Works of Zhang Naiqi) (Beijing, Huafu chubanshe, 1997), p. 425.
[101] C.F. Gordon Cummings, quoted in Whelan, *The Pawnshop in China*, p. 19.
[102] Shen Danian 沈大年 et al. (eds.), 天津金融簡史 (A Brief History of Tianjin Finance) (Tianjin, Nankai daxue chubanshe, 1988), pp. 10–11; McElderry, *Shanghai Old-Style Banks*, pp. 42–3.
[103] Sheehan, *Trust in Troubled Times*, 104–5.
[104] Cao Xueqin, *The Story of the Stone*, trans. D. Hawkes (New York, Penguin Books, 1982), vol. 3, *The Warning Voice*, Chapter 57, pp. 88–115, and vol. 4, *The Debt of Tears*, Chapter 85, p. 133.

financial scene, banks and bankers became recognizable icons of cities. In Cao Yu's 1936 play *Sunrise*, the banker Pan Yueting joined other unsavory urban archetypes such as the gangster, the society matron, the gigolo, and the obsequious student.[105] Bankers were not always perceived negatively. Wen-hsin Yeh has shown how bankers and bank compounds became a model of professionalism and modernity.[106]

Turning to the relationship between finance and personal networks, the role of native place stands out. For the nineteenth century, most remittance bankers came from Shanxi province and cash shops were often divided into groups or *bang* 幫 based on the native place of the individuals owning or running those firms. In Shanghai many cash shop owners and managers came from Ningbo and Shaoxing in Zhejiang province. In Tianjin there was a dominant local group of cash shops owned and managed by Tianjin natives along with others run by sojourners from a number of other parts of China.[107] Native place played an important role in networks of bankers as well, and much of the literature in both English and Chinese focuses on the importance of elite bankers from Jiangsu and Zhejiang provinces, often referred to as the Jiangsu–Zhejiang clique.[108] Table 9.13 shows the native places of 3,278 bankers who held positions as middle managers, upper managers, and directors of Chinese banks according to a banking directory from 1936.[109] Unfortunately, the native place of almost a third of the bankers in the volume is not stated, thus conclusions can only be preliminary. Zhejiang and Jiangsu natives did, indeed, have a large presence in the ranks of these bankers, but so did natives of a number of other provinces, including Hebei, Sichuan, Guangdong,

---

[105] Sheehan, "Urban Identity," pp. 47–8.
[106] W.-H. Yeh, "Corporate Space, Communal Time: Everyday Life in Shanghai's Bank of China," *American Historical Review* 100.1 (1995), 97–122.
[107] McElderry, *Shanghai Old-Style Banks*, pp. 52–3; Shen, 天津金融簡史, pp. 10–11.
[108] S.M. Jones, "The Ningpo Pang [Ningbo Bang] and Financial Power at Shanghai," in M. Elvin and G.W. Skinner (eds.), *The Chinese City between Two Worlds* (Stanford, CA, Stanford University Press, 1974), p. 73; Yao Huiyuan 姚會元, 江浙金融財團研究 (Research on the Zhejiang–Jiangsu Financial Clique) (Beijing, Zhongguo Caizheng Jingji chubanshe, 1998), pp. 7–8; M.-C. Bergère, "The Shanghai Bankers Association, 1915–1927: Modernization and the Institutionalization of Local Solidarities," in F. Wakeman Jr. and W.-H. Yeh (eds.), *Shanghai Sojourners* (Berkeley, Institute of East Asian Studies, Center for Chinese Studies, 1992), pp. 15–34; A. McElderry, "Confucian Capitalism? Corporate Values in Republican Banking," *Modern China* 12 (July 1986), 401–16; McElderry, "Robber Barons or National Capitalists: Shanghai Bankers in Republican China," *Republican China* 11 (November 1985), 52–67; Cheng, *Banking in Modern China*, pp. 46–52.
[109] Zhongyang yinhang jihe chu 中央銀行稽核處 (Central Bank of China Auditing Department), 全國金融機構一覽 (Chinese Financial Institutions at a Glance) (n.l., Liulian yinshua gongsi, 1947).

Table 9.13 Native provinces of bankers in 1936

Unknown	1,115	34.0%
Zhejiang	729	22.2%
Jiangsu	616	18.8%
Hebei	173	5.3%
Sichuan	159	4.9%
Guangdong	109	3.3%
Anhui	86	2.6%
Shandong	78	2.4%
Hunan	42	1.3%
Fujian	32	1.0%
Hubei	32	1.0%
Shanxi	32	1.0%
Liaoning	24	0.7%
Jiangxi	21	0.6%
Yunnan	7	0.2%
Henan	6	0.2%
Shaanxi	6	0.2%
Guizhou	4	0.1%
Jilin	2	0.1%
Guangxi	1	0.0%
Total	3,274	

Source: Zhongyang Yinhang Jingji Yanjiu Chu 中央銀行經濟研究處 (Research Office of the Central Bank of China), 全國銀行人事一覽 (Chinese Banking Personnel at a Glance) (Shanghai, 1936)

Anhui, and Shandong. It is also possible that inclusion of the armies of lower-level bank employees such as tellers and clerks would provide a different distribution.

Common province alone tells us little about the way networks actually functioned. For example, the density of interlocking directorship ties among members of boards of directors of Chinese banks in 1936 was no greater for bankers from the same province than it was for the population as a whole. Density increased "among bankers from adjacent counties or among important, or elite, bankers who each held seats on many different banks. The former suggests local kinds of connections such as dialect, early schooling or family [while the latter suggests] shared professional interest."[110] Politics also affected personal networks of bankers because of the close connection between banking and the state in China.[111] Thus generalizations about native place and networks of bankers need to be supplanted by solid empirical evidence and much work remains to be done.

Financial trade associations were fixtures in national and local power structures. Some had long histories that date back to the late seventeenth or the eighteenth century.[112] These organizations also reflected the fragmented nature of the finance industry. Shanghai had two cash shop associations, one for shops in the Chinese city and one for those in the foreign concessions.[113] In a similar vein, Tianjin's cash shop guild excluded firms owned by nonnatives of the city until after 1930.[114] When banks appeared on the scene in the late nineteenth and early twentieth centuries, bankers, too, formed associations in cities and towns around China, though foreign and Chinese bankers formed separate associations. Sometimes these associations came together in larger umbrella organizations, but the norm was to associate by type, location, and, often, native place of ownership.[115] These professional associations co-ordinated operational relations between financial institutions, such as the clearing of drafts drawn on each other, and provided a platform to deal with a variety of government relations ranging from negotiating the amounts of government demands for loans to protesting the wording of regulatory laws.[116] Financial trade associations also played a role in responding to the financial crises which periodically erupted, though not always with success.[117]

---

[110] Sheehan, "Myth and Reality," 470–3.
[111] Sheehan, "Urban Identity," pp. 54, 56; B. Sheehan, "Warlords, Cadres and Bankers: Private Commercial Banking in the Republican and Post-Mao Periods," *Journal of Asian Business* 14.1 (1998), 16.
[112] Ou Jiluan 歐季鸞, 廣州之銀業 (Guangzhou's Cash Shop Industry) (Guangzhou, Jingji zhi diaocha chu, 1932), p. 1; Hong Xiaguan 洪葭管, "略論山西票號, 上海錢莊的性質和歷史地位" (A Brief Discussion of the Nature and Historical Status of Shanxi Remittance Banks and Shanghai *qianzhuang*), *Jindaishi yanjiu* 2 (1983), 259; Chang and Qian, 近代中國典當業, p. 139.
[113] Jiang and Jiang, 近代中國外商銀行史, p. 308; Bergère, "Shanghai Banker's Association"; Cheng, *Banking in Modern China*, pp. 192–5; Sheehan, *Trust in Troubled Times*, p. 81; McElderry, *Shanghai Old-Style Banks*, pp. 42–3.
[114] McElderry, *Shanghai Old-Style Banks*, pp. 52–3; Shen, 天津金融簡史, pp. 10–11.
[115] Jiang and Jiang, 近代中國外商銀行史, p. 309.
[116] See, for example, B. Sheehan, "Urban Identity," p. 60; and Sheehan, *Trust in Troubled Times*, Chapter 4; Ye Shichang 葉世昌, "銀行公會, 錢業公會抵制 1931年 '銀行法'" (Resistance to the 1931 "Banking Law" by the Bankers' Association and Cash Shop Guilds), 中國金融史集刊 (Journal of Chinese Financial History) 2 (2007), 94–105.
[117] Sheehan, *Trust in Troubled Times*.

Pawnshops were by far the most likely institutions to provide credit to ordinary individuals. A 1932 survey in Guangxi province showed "35 percent of transactions less than one yuan, 40 percent one to three yuan, 15 percent three to five yuan, 7 plus percent five to ten yuan, and 2 plus percent ten to thirty yuan. Transactions of more than 30 yuan were very rare."[118] City residents often used pawnshops for daily needs, as with Nanjing rickshaw drivers surveyed in the fall of 1932. Among the 1,350 rickshaw drivers surveyed, "547, or about 40 percent, had debts." Besides those who borrowed from family and friends, 220 owed money to pawnshops.[119] A 1933 survey of 311 worker households in Guangzhou showed that "151 had borrowed money, and 176 had used pawnshops... Of worker households which use pawnshops 92.61 percent do so to satisfy daily needs and only 7.39 percent did so for other purposes."[120] One scholar from the Republican period believed, "The pawnshop industry worked out of the spotlight, but effectively acted as the financial fulcrum for ordinary people."[121]

In the early twentieth century, ordinary people, especially urban residents, began to have access to financial institutions as places to deposit money as well. Banks began offering special departments and programs to attract small depositors and lottery-type savings societies which drew account numbers at random for special rewards sprang up to compete with them.[122] The government-run postal savings bank extended retail banking services to many small cities across China. In addition, many kinds of business in China had long taken deposits, and by the late 1920s and early 1930s some of these began competing with banks for savings from small depositors, much to the dismay of China's bankers. In a letter to the Shanghai Bankers' Association dated 20 March 1930, the Shanghai Commercial and Savings Bank complained that firms "take advantage of newspaper advertising to unhesitatingly tempt customers with high interest rates to draw [funds] from all directions."[123] Many of these firms were retail businesses with large existing customer bases

[118] Guanxi tongji ju 廣西統計局 (ed.), 廣西年鑑 (Guangxi Annual) (1936), p. 635.
[119] Qian, 中國金融之組織 – 戰前與戰後, p. 95.
[120] Qian, 中國金融之組織 – 戰前與戰後, p. 95.
[121] Ou Jilan 歐季鸞, 廣東典當業 (Guangdong's Pawnshops) (Guangzhou, Zhongshan daxue jingji diaocha chu, 1934), p. 125.
[122] Sheehan, "The Modernity of Savings," pp. 121–55.
[123] "上海商業儲蓄銀行致上海銀行公會函" (Shanghai Commercial and Savings Bank to Shanghai Bankers' Association), Archives of the Shanghai Bankers' Association, S173-1-203, 20–1; Liu Qiugen 劉秋根, 明清高利貸資本 (High Interest Loans Capital in the Ming and Qing Dynasties) (Beijing, Shehui Kexue Wenxian chubanshe, 2000), pp. 138–9; Wang Zhixin 王志莘, 中國之儲蓄銀行史 (A History of China's Savings Banks) (Shanghai, Xinhua Xintuo Chuxu Yinghang, 1934), p. 319.

such as the Sincere, Yong'an, Xinxin, and Zhongyuan department stores.[124] Others developed savings departments separately from their main line of business. For example, the Rong family, which by 1928 had twelve flour mills and six cotton mills, also founded a specialized savings office estimated to save "200,000–300,000 yuan every year" over the interest charged by financial institutions.[125]

Conclusion

Over the century roughly from 1850 to 1950, Chinese financial institutions and markets witnessed a number of developments. There was remarkable growth in the number and size of financial institutions, especially banks, and a multiplication of kinds of financial institution, as banks based on Western models, retail savings societies, savings banks, trust banks, stock markets, rural co-operatives, rural co-operative treasuries, and insurance companies joined the cash shops, remittance houses, pawnshops, and informal rotating credit societies which dominated China's financial world for much of the nineteenth century, and in some cases even into the twentieth. The financial sector, especially banks, was highly involved with the state and ties to the state increased over time. By the 1930s and 1940s, the vast majority of financial assets were in large, state-controlled banks. As a corollary of the increasing state role in finance, credit from financial institutions in rural China shifted from reliance on pawnshops to rural co-operatives, though the latter reached only a small number of rural households. Financial institutions such as cash shops, remittance houses, and banks worked actively in the business-to-business sector and even became involved to some extent in financing early attempts at industrialization. In contrast, stock markets focused on trading government bonds and had less to do with commerce or industry. China's financial geography changed as financial institutions became more numerous, larger, more broadly situated across the peripheral regions of China, and more densely packed in urban and commercial centers. Although China remained a place with multiple financial centers, by the 1930s Shanghai had emerged as the pre-eminent financial city of China. Financial institutions and the people who ran them played important roles in society as institutions and as symbols. Native place played an important role in

---

[124] Wang Zhixin, 中國之儲蓄銀行史, p. 319.
[125] Shanghai shekeyuan jingjisuo, 榮家企業史料, p. 276; 茂新福新申新總公司三十周年紀念冊 (Thirtieth Anniversary Memorial Volume of the Maoxin, Fuxin, Shenxin Company) (January 1929), Appendix, "勸告同仁儲蓄宣言" (Savings Announcement).

networks of financial professionals, but that role needs to be understood in relation to other important political and institutional elements. Finally, the growth of new institutions such as rural co-operative treasuries and deposit services for ordinary individuals made the financial sector more and more enmeshed in the lives of ordinary individuals, though unevenly so.

In the end, although financial professionals and government regulators made very conscious attempts to "modernize," "standardize," "centralize," and "professionalize" finance, Chinese financial institutions as a whole remained highly decentralized, unevenly distributed across space, and hugely varied in form and function. Even as the growth of a vibrant banking sector linked many parts of China, a rift widened between kinds of financial institution in urban and rural China. Financial institutions and markets, and the financiers who ran them, remained generally fragmented, with periodic moments of greater or lesser connection subject to the vagaries of economic trends and political events.

Further Reading

Chang Mengju 常夢渠 and Qian Chuntao 錢椿濤 (eds.), 近代中國典當業 (Pawnshops in Modern China) (Beijing, Zhongguo Wenshi chubanshe, 1995).

Cheng, L. *Banking in Modern China* (Cambridge, Cambridge University Press, 2003).

Du Xuncheng 杜恂誠, 中國金融通史 (A General History of Chinese Finance), vol 3, 北洋政府時期 (Beiyang Government Period) (Beijing, Zhongguo Jinrong chubanshe, 1996).

Gong Guan 龔關, 國民政府與中國農村金融制度的演變 (Development of the System of Chinese Rural Finance during the Nationalist Period) (Tianjin, Nankai daxue chubanshe, 2016).

He, W., *Paths toward the Modern Fiscal State: England, Japan, and China* (Cambridge, MA, Harvard University Press, 2013).

Hong Xiaguan 洪葭管 (ed.), 中國金融史 (A History of Chinese Finance) (Chengdu, Xinan Caijing daxue chubanshe, 1993).

Huang Jianhui 黃鑒暉, 中國典當業史 (A History of China's Pawnshop Industry) (Taiyuan, Shanxi Jingji chubanshe, 2006).

Jiang Hongye 姜宏業, 中國金融通史 (A General History of Chinese Finance), vol. 5, 新民主主義革命根據地時期 (The Period of New Democracy and the Revolutionary Base Areas) (Beijing, Zhongguo Jinrong chubanshe, 2008).

Jiang Jianqing 姜建清 and Jiang Lichang 蔣立場, 近代中國外商銀行史 (A History of Foreign Banks in Modern China) (Beijing, Zhongxin chubanshe, 2016).

Li Jinzheng 李金錚, 民國鄉村借貸關係研究 (Research on the Relationship between Lending and Borrowing in the Countryside in the Republican Period) (Beijing, Renmin chubanshe, 2003).

Li Yixiang 李一翔, 近代中國銀行與企業的關係 1897–1945 (Relations between Banks and Enterprises in Modern China, 1897–1945) (Taipei, Dongda tushu gongsi, 1997).
Liu Qiugen 劉秋根, 中國典當制度史 (An Institutional History of Chinese Pawnshops) (Shanghai, Guji chubanshe, 1995).
Liu Zhiying 劉志英, 近代上海華商證券市場研究 (Research on Chinese Stock Markets in Modern Shanghai) (Shanghai, Xuelin chubanshe, 2004).
Liu Zhiying 劉志英, 近代中國華商證券市場研究 (Research on Chinese Stock Markets in Modern China) (Beijing, Zhongguo shehui kexue chubanshe, 2011)
Qu Yanbin 曲彥斌, 中國典當史 (A History of Chinese Pawnshops) (Shenyang, Shenyang chubanshe, 2007).
Sheehan, B., "The Modernity of Savings," in M.Y. Dong and J. Goldstein (eds.), *Everyday Modernity in China* (Seattle, University of Washington Press, 2006), pp. 121–55
Sheehan, B., "Myth and Reality in Chinese Financial Cliques in 1936," *Enterprise and Society* 6.3 (September 2005), 452–91.
Sheehan, B., *Trust in Troubled Times: Money, Banking, and State–Society Relations in Republican China* (Cambridge, MA, Harvard University Press, 2001).
Sheehan, B., "Urban Identity and Urban Networks in Cosmopolitan Cities: Banks and Bankers in Tianjin, 1919–1937," in J. Esherick (ed.), *Remaking the Chinese City: Modernity and National Identity, 1900–1950* (Honolulu, University of Hawaii Press, 2000), 47–64.
Wang Yejian 王業鍵, 中國近代貨幣與銀行的演進 1644–1937 (The Development of Money and Banks in Modern China 1644–1937) (Taipei, Zhongyang Yanjiuyuan Jingji Yanjiusuo, 1981).
Wu Jingping 吳景平, "近代上海金融中心地位與南京國民政府之關係" (The Status of Modern Shanghai as a Financial Center and Its Relations to the Nationalist Government in Nanjing), 史林 (Historical Review) 2 (2002), 90–121.
Yan Hongzhong 燕红忠, 晋商与现代经济 (Shanxi Merchants and the Modern Economy) (Beijing, Jingji kexue chubanshe, 2012).
Yao Gongzhen 姚公振, 中國農業金融史 (Agricultural Finance History of China) (Shanghai, Zhongguo wenhua fuwushe, 1947).
Yeh, W., "Corporate Space, Communal Time: Everyday Life in Shanghai's Bank of China," *American Historical Review* 100.1 (1995), 97–122.
Zhang Guohui 張國輝, 中國金融通史 (A General History of Chinese Finance), vol. 2, (1840–1911) 清鴉片戰爭時期至清末時期 (From the Opium War to the End of the Qing Dynasty (1840–1911)) (Beijing, Zhongguo Jinrong chubanshe, 2003).
Zhang Guohui 張國輝, 晚清錢莊和票號研究 (Qianzhuang and Piaohao in the Late Qing Period) (Beijing, Zhonghua shuju, 1989).
Zhu Yingui 朱蔭貴, "抗戰時期的上海華商證券市場" (Stock Markets in Shanghai during the Anti-Japanese War), 社會科學 (Social Science) 2 (2005), 88–97.
Zhu Yingui 朱蔭貴, "試論近代中國證券市場的特點" (Characteristics of Stock Markets in Modern China: A Preliminary Assessment), 經濟研究 (Economic Research) 3 (2008), 150–60.
Zhu Yingui 朱蔭貴, "近代上海證券市場上股票買賣的三次高潮" (Three High Tides of Buying and Selling on Shanghai Stock Markets), 中國經濟史研究 (Research on Chinese Economic History) 3 (1998), 58–70.
Zhu Yingui 朱蔭貴, 近代中國: 金融與證券研究 (Modern China: Research on Finance and Stock Markets) (Shanghai, Shanghai renmin chubanshe, 2012).

10

Chinese Business Organization

MADELEINE ZELIN

In this chapter we will examine how key institutions were mobilized to shape China's early modern business practices under weak state engagement with the economy, and a growing foreign presence. Business practices in the late imperial period rested on four pillars, each a fundamental part of the institutional framework that structured social and economic life. The first, family, provided templates for the utilization of capital and labor and the mobilization of trust, tools that proved as useful for China's late imperial commercial economy as for the early modern economy of industrial enterprise and global engagement. The second might be termed the system of private ordering that served generations of Chinese merchants and others in combining capital and establishing the terms of economic interaction, often through written contracts whose provisions established highly flexible forms of partnership that continued to form the basis of most Chinese business until the early PRC. The third, native place, in significant ways mirrored the intangible assets provided by ties of kinship, offering a predetermined basis for co-operation, nurturing and protecting group interests and skills and, like the fourth, grounding these intangibles in very tangible organizations catering to inhabitants of a particular city, region, or province. The fourth pillar, the guild, drew on many of the practices associated with the other three. The guild, however, played a special role in the ordering of Chinese manufacturing and trade, translating China's complex and unregulated currency system for its merchant constituency, and mediating both the legal and the fiscal relationships between merchants and an often weak and poorly informed state.

These four pillars were by no means unique to China. Nor was the preference shown by many Chinese multi-owner firms for partnerships and family firms,[1] although the utility of these firms in addressing specific challenges facing Chinese enterprise helps explain the particular organizational forms that emerged during the late imperial period and persisted into the republic. At the same time we will eschew explanations based on "culture." While individual actors may have understood their behavior to have reflected cultural commitments, here we will focus on the enactment of those commitments in the choices made and the strategies deployed to manage the challenges of China's particular business environments. Inasmuch as these four pillars retained their influence well into the twentieth century, the last section of this chapter will address some of the ways in which the pressures of foreign contact and global economic interaction affected long-established modes of business organization in China. New technologies, foreign business models, borrowed legal frameworks, and the end of imperial rule could not but have had an impact on business organization. However, the lesson of recent scholarship on early twentieth-century Chinese business has been that their impact was far more diverse and uneven than we might have anticipated based on standard theories of the firm and that many of the key elements of business practice that emerged over the length of the last dynasty continued to serve businesspeople and the entities they created long after emperors were but a distant memory.

Family

Family as the node of economic activity is a universal phenomenon and family firms have continued to play a significant role, numerically, if not in terms of total capitalization, in most parts of the world.[2] While scholars no longer consider the "family firm" to have uniquely Chinese salience, characteristics of Chinese family organization played a significant role in the structuring of Chinese business in the early modern period. As a biological and social construct, the Chinese family provided intersecting bases for trust and the pooling of resources. Patriarchal authority and generational hierarchy, key Confucian expressions of a well-ordered society, were baked into

---

[1] For example, T.W. Guinnane and J. Schneebacher, *Capital Structure and the Choice of Enterprise Form: Theory and History*, Economic Growth Center Discussion Paper No. 1061 (New Haven, Yale University, 2018), p. 2, demonstrate that as late as 1890 three-quarters of all firms were ordinary partnerships in France, Germany, and Spain, despite the availability for some time of general incorporation.

[2] A. Colli and M.B. Rose, "Family Business in Comparative Perspective," in F. Amatori and G. Jones (eds.), *Business History around the World* (Cambridge, Cambridge University Press, 2003), pp. 339–52.

both the imperial code and social practice. Among their key manifestations was the joint household, whose common property was managed by the patriarch, and only passed on to the next generation in the act of household division, a predominately male affair that could occur during the lifetime of the patriarch but ideally took place after his death. Household division itself was conceived of as an egalitarian process in which each son received an equal share of the estate. Partible succession created a shared stake in the common property, while deferred division could supply a common pool of resources available for profitable deployment.[3] If culture played a role in encouraging co-operation toward growth of the estate, it did so by sustaining the belief that each male household member was linked through time and placed on earth to bring honor to the ancestors and to lay the groundwork for the success of future generations.

How did these distinctive features of the joint household, its commonly held property and the moral vision that encased it, shape Chinese business organization? Much has been made of the family as a basis for trust, and indeed in China, as elsewhere, the face-to-face bonds of familiarity and mutual dependence of family contributed to the willingness of people to lend money, broker deals, and join in business endeavors. However, it was in its ability to exercise authority over its members and to lay claim to common resources that the family and its joint household economy most influenced the evolution of Chinese business organization. The case of the Guo Family Shop, a late Qing business of no particular distinction, illustrates this point. The shop was founded in the late Qing by a member of the Guo family of Shangyu county, Zhejiang. The founder, who had three sons who most likely worked alongside their father, operated the shop as a single proprietorship until his death, when the joint household of which he was the head underwent division. We do not know what other assets comprised the Guo estate, but as a result of a dispute with creditors that emerged following the death of the elder brother, we know that the three brothers emerged from the process of division as equal partners in what was now a single-surname partnership. While the brothers still referred to their business simply as the Guo Family Shop, our use of the term "partnership" underscores a change in the relationship among stakeholders. When the family branch headed by the youngest brother wished to leave the business, the two remaining branches had to buy

---

[3] For a more detailed examination of the process and implications of household division see D. Wakefield, *Fenjia: Household Division and Inheritance in Qing and Republican China* (Honolulu, University of Hawaii Press, 1998). The distribution to adopted sons and sons of concubines, as well as the portion to which daughters were entitled, varied over time.

him out, leaving, as recorded in court documents, the representatives of the senior branch (a widow and her adopted son) and the middle branch each partners with a 50 percent stake in the shop. The litigation that has left a record of this firm took place at a moment when the law affecting business was being moved from the realm of custom to that of code, a process that, we will see, took decades and never fully escaped the ambiguities created by the legacy of the joint household. However, throughout the case, the identity of the firm as a partnership was never in doubt.[4]

The process by which household division created single-surname partnerships is often missing from our discussion of Chinese business, but it is a key to understanding the organization and longevity of so-called family businesses. While many firms did not survive household division, their assets (and their debts) being distributed among the founder's heirs, many of the most successful firms in the late imperial period were founded by one household head and thrived for long periods as single-surname partnerships. Because they began as closely held businesses we often do not know much about their organization until they were embroiled in lawsuits, or changes in their ownership or management structure brought them to public attention in the last years of the Qing dynasty. Ruifuxiang, wholesalers and retailers of native cloth, was founded in the seventeenth century by the Meng family of Shandong, and although it encountered difficult times in the eighteenth century, it was still a family partnership when its business once again took off in the 1870s.[5] In 1669 Yue Xianyang founded Tongrentang as a purveyor of Chinese medicine. His son opened a shop in the Qianmen commercial district of Beijing, and by 1723 the shop, still under exclusive Yue ownership, became purveyors of medicines to the imperial court. In 1753 a fire destroyed the shop and the family was forced to sell shares to outside investors in order to reopen. In the 1880s a concerted effort to buy out nonfamily shareholders restored the business to the Yues, who re-created the ideal of the family firm by employing only family members.[6] A similar story could be told about another famous Beijing medicine shop. Founded in the early Ming dynasty by Yue Fengyi, Wangquantang remained solely in Yue hands until the 1740s, when debt forced them to enter into a shareholding partnership with a family

---

[4] M.B. Young, "Law and Modern State-Building in Early Republican China: The Supreme Court of Peking (1911–1926)," unpublished Ph.D. thesis, Harvard University, 2004, p. 174.
[5] W.K.K. Chan, "The Organizational Structure of the Traditional Chinese Firm and Its Modern Reform," *Business History Review* 56.2 (1982), 222–3.
[6] S. Cochran, *Chinese Medicine Men: Consumer Culture in China and Southeast Asia* (Cambridge, MA, Harvard University Press, 2006), pp. 18–23.

named Suo.[7] Similar stories can be told about salt merchants from Tianjin, long-distance merchant families from Huizhou and Shanxi, and the large-scale salt manufacturers and wholesalers of Zigong, Sichuan.

Whether they remained solely family-owned, were forced by circumstances to bring in outside partners, constituted themselves from the start as shareholding partners among kin,[8] or invested jointly with other families,[9] family-owned businesses relied on a number of organizational devices that emerged out of the joint household and continued to contribute significantly to the more complex business practices of the late Qing and the twentieth century.

Two of the most important of these devices were the lineage trust and the lineage accounting office. To understand the lineage trust let us return to the joint household and the practice of family division. The process by which the assets of a household were passed on to its coparceners in late imperial China required their fragmentation as each son received an equal share of the estate. Even for those with middling resources this contravened the need to devote a portion of the estate to ritual expenses incurred in honoring their ancestors. By the Song dynasty (960–1279), households with sufficient means were encouraged to create endowments to which were contributed land and other income-producing assets that were protected from family division and could grow in value, and whose management and the purposes to which the income was put created a focus of solidarity for the descendants of its founders. The status of these trusts, most commonly called *tang* 堂, was reinforced by custom, contract, and individual lineage regulations until 1756,

---

[7] Liu Yongcheng 刘永成 and He Zhiqing 赫治清, "万全堂的由来与发展" (The Origin and Development of Wanquantang), 中国社会经济史研究 (Research on the Economic and Social History of China) 1 (1983), 8.

[8] For example, two branches of the Zhao family began a business which in 1838 was expanded to included four branches, each contributing cash for a total of 12,000 taels. Two shops sold oil, salt, and grain in the Qianmen commercial district of Beijing. In this case the investment was passive, with management left to others while profits and losses were shared in proportion to each branch's investment. Yang Guozhen 杨国桢, 明清以来商人'合本'经营的契约形式," (The Contractual Form of Merchant "Joint Shares" Business since Ming and Qing," 中国社会经济史研究 (Research on Economic and Social History of China) 3 (1987), 4.

[9] For example, during the mid-nineteenth century, Du Baotian, Yuan Tinglu, and Yuan Baozhai opened the Zhengxunxiang as a partnership that appears to have operated a workshop producing writing paper. When Yuan Baozhai died his four shares were sold to Zhang Xiangzhi's Tongtaihang, a medicinal herb shop that may have simply viewed the shares as an income-producing asset. Xie Jing 谢晶, "设有法律的秩序: 晚清巴县工商业合伙研究" (Order in the Absence of Law: Research on Partnership in Handicraft and Commerce in late Qing Baxian), unpublished MA thesis, Central Nationalities University, 2012, p. 21.

when they were also protected from intra-familial predation in the Qing Code.[10] For Chinese business they became a unique mechanism through which to effect some of the benefits of incorporation.[11]

The salt manufacturers of Zigong, Sichuan provide some of the best data on the way in which lineage trusts functioned as business entities. The men who began investing in drilling deep brine wells and moved from evaporating salt using coal-fired furnaces to developing China's first industrial natural gas wells did not start out as well-capitalized business entrepreneurs.[12] Most were farmers and small merchants, some of their families had produced degree holders, and many dabbled in well drilling in a region of southern Sichuan dotted with salt derricks and abandoned wells. The Wangs, who emerged as one of the most successful of China's salt producers and wholesalers, were typical in their use of the institutions of the joint household economy. By the nineteenth century they had already established a modest trust to support an ancestral hall and ritual activities. However, it was the success in the development of salt wells and evaporation furnaces that led the head of the senior branch of the Wang lineage, Wang Langyun, to create a trust that would be central to the family's economic juggernaut. Twenty operating wells and 600 *mu* of agricultural land were set aside as an initial endowment, income-producing resources that would not only support elderly lineage members, maintain ancestral graves, memorialize chaste widows, pay for ancestral rites, and contribute to the education of lineage males.[13] Its real significance

---

[10] Yunsheng Xue 薛允升 and Jingjia Huang 黃靜嘉, 讀例存疑重刊本 (Doubtful Points on Reading the Substatutes) (Taipei, Chengwen chubanshe, 1970), pp. 626–7; M. Zelin, "The Firm in Early Modern China," *Journal of Economic Behavior & Organization* 71.3 (2009), 626–7.

[11] A similar logic facilitated the creation of shareholding associations devoted to sustaining temples and various ritual activities, allowing non-kin to create partnerships in land, irrigation works and other revenue-generating assets. Shares in such trusts could form a component of joint household property. For examples of such associations see Li Li 李力, "清代民间契约中关于'伙'的观念和习惯" (The Concept and Common Practice of "Huo" in Qing Civil Contracts), 法学家 (Legal Profession) 6 (2003), 41–2. Cohen has argued that by the end of the last dynasty about a third of the "best wet rice land" in Minong county, Taiwan was owned by associations "mainly dedicated to the worship of gods or ancestors." M. Cohen, "Writs of Passage in Late Imperial China," in M. Zelin, J.K. Ocko, and R. Gardella (eds.), *Contract and Property in Early Modern China* (Stanford: Stanford University Press, 2004), p. 43.

[12] For a detailed analysis of the Zigong salt manufacturers, their technological and business contributions, and the impact of China's changing political landscape on their business fortunes, see M. Zelin, *The Merchants of Zigong: Industrial Entrepreneurship in Early Modern China* (New York, Columbia University Press, 2005).

[13] M. Zelin, "The Rise and Fall of the Furong Saltyard Elite: Merchant Dominance in Late Qing China," in J. Esherick and M.B. Rankin (eds.), *Chinese Local Elites and Patterns of Dominance* (Berkeley, University of California Press, 1990), pp. 94–6.

was as a mechanism to keep intact the wealth produced by the lineage businesses and to manage reinvestment in those businesses while satisfying the desire for benefit by the large numbers of lineage members who would ultimately be only passive beneficiaries. In its founding regulations, after accounting for the above-mentioned non-business expenses, it was stipulated that half the income of the trust would be reinvested in the trust itself and half would be allocated to constituent lineage branches to develop their own business and landed assets.

Over time, the management of individual business entities within the trust would change. In particular, like many late nineteenth-century Chinese firms, we see in the Wang lineage trust a shift to non-kin professionals in key management positions. The lineage trust as a corporate entity not only managed wholly owned lineage properties. In the late nineteenth century and the twentieth it increasingly became an investor in shares in business ventures with other households and lineage trusts. Indeed, in this respect, long before the introduction of a formal company law in China, the lineage trust could be seen as having a form of legal personhood. However, the legacy of the joint household remained. Most importantly, overall managerial authority continued to be vested in the senior male member of the senior lineage branch.[14] And the kinship requirement for participation in profit-sharing remained inviolate.[15]

How did entrepreneurial lineage trusts manage increasingly complex assets while continuing to maintain their commitments to coparceners whose numbers increased with each new birth? Not surprisingly, lineage trusts, like most Chinese businesses for which we have data, maintained a central accounts office (zhangfang 账房). Accounts offices differed in the functions they performed, the degree to which they exercised hierarchical coordination over all business assets, and the extent to which they employed

---

[14] While the patriarchal principle does not seem to have been questioned in earlier years, during the 1920s it became a source of intense competition as the lineage trust suffered from mounting debt and political pressures. For an account that clearly favors the opposition, see Benqing Chen 陈本清, "渝沙债团与王三畏堂债务始末" (The Yusha Debt Group and the Whole Story of the Debts of the Wang Sanwei Tang), 自贡文史资料选集 (Zigong Selected Historical Archives) 22 (1992), 1–10.

[15] Unlike other forms of partnership, which distributed profit and loss according to one's contribution to the firm, a subject addressed below, one's share in the profits of this and other lineage-trust-based businesses depended on one's position within a lineage branch, the number of claimants in that branch, and the generational depth of the lineage itself. For an example of a New Territories lineage trust whose shareholders now span the globe, see J.L. Watson, "Presidential Address: Virtual Kinship, Real Estate, and Diaspora Formation: The Man Lineage Revisited," *Journal of Asian Studies* 63.4 (2004), 893–910.

non-kin specialists to carry out their work. However, most served as both a business office and the main site for the administration of lineage affairs, under the unified authority of the lineage head. Few lineage trusts with significant business activities have left detailed records of their operations but their traces abound in the genealogies of notable local families. At one extreme, for example, were the locally powerful Wen lineage of Guisheng county in Jiangxi, who owned thirteen mountains whose tenants either mined coal or harvested timber. Rents collected by the lineage maintained an ancestral hall and supported lineage members with monthly allowances.[16] No elaborate internal business organization was necessary to enable this lineage to generate sufficient wealth to allow lineage members to obtain official degrees and lineage leaders to participate in regional politics.

At the other extreme were the large lineage-based salt manufacturers of Zigong, Sichuan. They too deployed the institution of the lineage trust as a mechanism to manage diverse assets as well as the ritual and philanthropic concerns of increasingly wealthy single-surname partnerships. At the height of the salt boom in the mid-nineteenth century, the wealthiest of the salt entrepreneurs refined the use of the trust. While maintaining their founding trust, the Hu Yuanhe tang, in 1867 the Hus established a separate trust, the Shenyi tang, devoted exclusively to the salt business. The main office (*zongguifang* 总柜房) of the Shenyi tang was usually headed by a family member whose title was general director (*zongzhanggui* 总账柜). Under him were five departments: (1) an accounts office (*guifang* 柜房) run by a chief accountant (*zongzhang* 总账) and two assistants (*bangzhang* 帮账) in charge of the overall productivity of the lineage's wells and furnaces; (2) a procurement department (*huowugu* 货物股) in charge of purchasing all supplies needed for the daily operation of the wells and furnaces; (3) an external affairs department (*jiaojigu* 交际股) in charge of buying brine for the lineage's furnaces and selling salt at lineage-owned retail shops; (4) a department of agricultural estates (*nongzhuanggu* 农庄股) in charge of collecting rents and selling grain; and (5) a cash department (*xianjingu* 现金股) in charge of daily cash expenditures and silver–copper exchange transactions.[17] Despite its focus on the family's salt business it remained an appendage of the main lineage trust, along with separate offices devoted to lineage schools, its

---

[16] J. Hornibrook, "Local Elites and Mechanized Mining in China: The Case of the Wen Lineage in Pingxiang County, Jiangxi," *Modern China* 27.2 (2001), 202–28.

[17] Shaoquan Hu 胡少权, "贡井胡元和的兴起与衰落" (The Rise and Fall of Gongjing Hu Yuanhe), 自贡文史资料选集 (Selected Historical Archives of Zigong) 12 (1981), 55–6.

agricultural estate, and a wide array of family employees. In the early twentieth century, when the three branches that had comprised the original Hu Yuanhe trust decided to divide their assets and establish separate ancestral trusts, the Shenyi tang was maintained intact but its constituent businesses were turned over to outsiders to run.[18]

Other salt producers developed somewhat different models based on the lineage trust. For example, the Li Siyou tang maintained overall supervision of its business and family interests through its main lineage trust. However, separate managerial hierarchies were established for each business division – furnaces, pipes, brine wells, and wholesale distribution.[19] Each operated as a separate management unit reporting to the main accounts office of the lineage trust and its general manager, who by the end of the century was no longer a family member. At the beginning of each year representatives of the four branches of the lineage met at the general accounts office to hear reports on the state of the constituent firms, review their accounts and discuss strategy for the coming year. In some respects the annual meeting of the four branches at the lineage headquarters resembled a typical board of directors meeting in which shareholders had the opportunity to examine the work of their hired managers and assess the health of the business. However, we are reminded of the thin line between lineage and business by the fact that each branch was allocated a fixed allowance for family and ritual expenses each year, with a warning that at no other time were they to withdraw money from the business treasury.[20]

Private Ordering

As we saw above, when kinship combined with the institutions of the joint household, individual households did not partake of the benefits of income-producing assets as shareholders. Their interest in the income produced could not be augmented or sold. And the manner in which they enjoyed the benefit of that income might shift depending on whether division was based on total number of lineage males or on division among branches regardless of each branch's male population. However, both individual joint households and lineage trusts also engaged in business as participants

---

[18] Hu, "贡井胡元和," 70.
[19] Zilin Li 李子琳, "自流井李四友堂由发轫到衰亡" (The Rise and Fall of Ziliujing Li Siyou Tang), 四川文史资料选集 (Selected Historical Archives of Sichuan) 4 (1962–1963), 150–1.
[20] Li, "自流井李四友堂由发轫到衰亡."

in shareholding partnerships with kin and non-kin alike.²¹ Chinese shareholding practices drew on three of the pillars noted at the beginning of this chapter. While kinship could create natural partnerships, it also facilitated formal shareholding arrangements. Whereas earlier examples may exist, at least by the sixteenth century we have contracts memorializing the creation of long-term, jointly owned and jointly managed property in support of purposes other than the ritual functions of the ancestral line, or that brought together investors whose association did not arise primarily out of kinship.

Such partnerships took many forms. Drawn up in 1568 in Qimen county, Anhui, one such document states that its signatories are engaged in joint management of timber resources. While the surviving document is in the form of an oath signed by three branches of the Li lineage pledging not to cut down trees or steal timber for personal use and establishing fines to be imposed on those who do, the forested mountain is clearly thought of as more than a simple lineage endowment. The warning is addressed to "households with shares and households that do not have shares" and the mountain itself is referred to as a "jointly owned mountain."²² A 1432 contract from Xiuning county, Anhui is even more explicit in its description of a partnership in mountain resources. In this case three men of different surnames established joint ownership of a mountain, allocating six shares to Xie Dexiang, and one share each to Wu Yanduan and to Li Zhongjie and his unnamed brother.²³ Cohen describes an innovative family division in Minong county, Taiwan, whereby instead of distribution of patrilineal resources and the establishment of new household properties by each of three brothers of the Liu family, the property accumulated by their father was kept intact and each brother was assigned a number of shares in a jointly owned sugar plantation. Farmed by a tenant, the brothers then received a portion of the rent according to their shares.²⁴ Allee points to similar partnerships among entrepreneurial tea producers in late Qing Taiwan. In

---

²¹ For a detailed discussion of the roots of Chinese shareholding practices, see M. Zelin, "A Deep History of Chinese Shareholding," *Law and History Review* 37.2 (May 2019), 325–51.
²² Zhang Chuanxi 张传玺 (ed.), 中國歷代契約會編考釋 (Compilation and Interpretation of Chinese Historical Contracts), 2 vols. (Beijing, Beijing daxue chubanshe, 1995), pp. 1078–9. A similar document in the unpublished collection of Huizhou contracts compiled by the late Tian Tao memorialized a dispute over the exploitation of forest land for firewood and resulted in the division of a jointly owned mountain into a mountain in which owners had specified shares. Tian Tao collection, Ming Wanli 14, Wang Hongqing et al., Qingjie Hemo contract (not published).
²³ Zhang, 中國歷代契約會編考釋, pp. 1089–90.
²⁴ Cohen, "Writs of Passage in Late Imperial China," 82.

one case land was first purchased from the original aboriginal owners, and then a partnership consisting of six shares was created, in which he estimates approximately half of the shares were sold to non-kin.[25]

While kinship and/or propinquity/native-place relationships facilitated the creation of trust that enabled these partnerships to be formed, China's strong tradition of contractually based private ordering served as the scaffolding upon which a robust shareholding tradition was built. Indeed, it is through the rich collections of business contracts collected by Chinese scholars and preserved in Chinese legal archives that we know much of what we know about the organization of Chinese business.

Contracts memorialized the establishment or dissolution of a partnership and the sale or transfer of shares, and were intended to serve as actionable proof of the intent of investors. Partnership contracts followed patterns that can be traced to an even deeper history of land sale and lease contracts going back to the early years of the Chinese state. Models were recorded in encyclopedias and merchant guidebooks,[26] and by the nineteenth century merchants seem to have deliberately emulated elements of the organizational models of prominent merchant communities, in particular the far-flung traders from the western province of Shanxi. While varying in their details, most founding contracts named the investors and their respective contributions in cash and kind and the number of shares to which each was entitled. Common also was the stipulation of a timetable for the settling of accounts, at which the firm's ledgers would be inspected and dividends determined and distributed. By the nineteenth century, it was common for founding documents to clearly state that profits and losses were allocated according to the number of one's shares or the proportion of total capital one had invested. Some founding documents indicate that a manager, who may or may not have been an investor, was engaged and named at the time the partnership was formed.[27]

Before we look at specific contracts and what they can tell us about business organization in the late imperial period it is worth noting what the contract culture of China bequeathed to all Chinese shareholding partnerships. First, while the imperial code and state policy were concerned with the

---

[25] M.A. Allee, "The Status of Contracts in Nineteenth-Century Chinese Courts," in Zelin, Ocko, and Gardella, *Contract and Property*, pp. 162–3.
[26] R.J. Lufrano, *Honorable Merchants Commerce and Self-Cultivation in Late Imperial China* (Honolulu, University of Hawaii Press, 1997).
[27] We see both of these stipulations in a model contract in the 1895 compilation *Shuji Bianmeng* translated in R. Gardella, "Contracting Business Partnerships," in Zelin, Ocko, and Gardella, *Contract and Property*, p. 332.

maintenance of patriarchal authority, status, and generational hierarchy within households, they made almost no effort to regulate economic relationships that fell outside the joint-household framework.[28] This meant that contracts in China were in a real sense the record of the will of the parties who wrote them and were primary evidence in litigation over real and business property and obligations.[29] Unless otherwise stipulated in the agreement creating a shareholding partnership, shares could be freely bought and sold.[30] At the same time, the absence in China of a law requiring the dissolution of partnerships upon the death or withdrawal of a shareholder meant that Chinese businesses could survive numerous shifts in the composition of ownership. Indeed, a subset of partnership contracts could be categorized as share reorganization contracts as new partners were brought in and old ones left.[31] These two characteristics of shareholding practice help explain the longevity of some of the family firms we have already examined, particularly as they took on outside partners in times of financial stress, and in some cases, like the Yues of the Tongren tang medicine firm, consolidated family ownership when business turned around in the nineteenth century. The flexibility afforded by shareholding in the absence of legal regulation may have combined with the underdevelopment of formal credit institutions in encouraging firms like the Tongren tang to rely on equity expansion when in need of infusions of capital.

What can surviving partnership contracts tell us about the organization of business in the late imperial period? First, we can see that investment took many forms and had an impact on the relative rights and obligations of partners. Particularly in industries that relied on natural resources, including

---

[28] The state did attempt to regulate the freely contracted relationships that fell within the kinship rubric, with varying success, as Sommer and Ransmeier show in their respective work on polyandry and the sale of wives and on the transactional family and the market in people in Qing and Republican China. M. Sommer, *Sex, Law, and Society in Late Imperial China* (Stanford, CA, Stanford University Press, 2000); Sommer, *Polyandry and Wife-Selling in Qing Dynasty China: Survival Strategies and Judicial Interventions* (Oakland, University of California Press, 2015); J. Ransmeier, *Sold People: Traffickers and Family Life in North China* (Cambridge, MA, Harvard University Press, 2017).

[29] For a discussion of contract in the establishment of property rights during the last imperial dynasty, see M. Zelin, "A Critique of Rights of Property in Pre-war China," in Zelin, Ocko and Gardella, *Contract and Property*, pp. 17–36.

[30] Some contracts stipulated a right of first refusal for fellow shareholders. See, for example, K.M. Bun, "Custom, Code and Legal Practice, the Contracts of Changlu Salt Merchants in Late Imperial China," in Zelin, Ocko, and Gardella, *Contract and Property*, p. 279.

[31] Share reorganization could take many forms, ranging from simple transfer to the complex reallocation of profit and losses found in Zigong *shangxiajie* agreements. Zelin, *Merchants of Zigong*, pp. 42–8.

land, it was common to find businesses established between owners of underexploited real property and entrepreneurs eager to develop mining and commercial agriculture. This contract from the Mentou gou coalmines outside Beijing was concluded in 1655 but already has many of the characteristics of such businesses:[32]

> The writers of this contract to form a partnership to open a pit are Wang Conglian and others [these would include the signatories and the landowners listed below]. In previous years we opened the Daxing pit at Jingming si. Now are going to reopen the pit, but we are short of capital. We have come to an agreement with the middleman Zhang Yingji to contact the Sun and Ma families to put up money and enter into partnership. The pit will be divided into forty-five shares. The owner of the land [on which the pit is located], Ming Xiangxing, will receive five shares. The Zhang and the Wang families will receive twenty-four shares. The Sun and Ma families will receive sixteen shares. When the pit begins to produces coal, we will first deduct and pay the new costs of production and deduct the Wangs' old costs of production in the amount of 10,300 cash. Once [production costs are] deducted and paid, if there are profits they will be divided equally [according to shares?]. This is everyone's wish and there are no regrets. Fearing that in the future there will be no evidence, we are writing this contract and two copies will be kept as proof.
>
> Dated Tongzhi 12, 8, 3 [followed by signatures of the parties and a middleman]

In an earlier partnership the Wangs and the Zhangs had put up capital and joined forces with landowners sitting on potentially rich coal reserves to excavate a mine. While they were possibly neighbors, they give no indication of kinship. It is likely that the two households financing the excavation ran out of money before they were able to start production and, with the help of someone who had connections to people with liquid assets, they sought to dig further. We do not know what the contribution of each party was, but shares were most likely allocated on the basis of relative cash contributions.

Although we lack some information, this and other early coal mining partnerships were important precursors to more complex business arrangements in extractive industry. At Baxian, Sichuan, where coal lay close to the surface and the costs of production were low, coal mining partnerships often consisted of no more than a few local men who leased a potential mine from

---

[32] Zhiping Chen 陈支平 and Zengrong Lu 卢增荣, "从契约文书看清代工商业合股委托经营方式的转变" (The Transformation in Qing Joint-Stock Trust Management as Viewed from Contracts), 中国社会经济史研究 (Research on Chinese Social and Economic History) 2 (2000), 29–30.

a neighborhood farmer.³³ We find similar arrangements among parties in the timber industry. Indeed, Meng Zhang has shown that indigenous Miao people participated in the commercial timber industry in southeastern Guizhou by emulating landowner–planter share contracts used by Chinese to develop timber plantations.³⁴ At its most sophisticated, the combination of landowner shares and investor shares is found in the Zigong salt industry, where the development of what became one of late imperial China's most capital-intensive industries began when entrepreneurial middlemen joined forces with local landowners and both local and extraprovincial investors to exploit southern Sichuan's rich brine deposits. Here the crucial role of the middleman in bringing together investors and landowners, and in supervising the initial drilling of the brine well, led to the granting of partnership shares to the middleman as well as to the contributors of factors of production. At Zigong we can see the gradual shift in importance of land versus capital reflected in the structure of shareholding. Initially many investor partnerships in effect rented potential well sites from landowners who hedged their bets by retaining the ability to return their land to farming. By the mid-nineteenth century, landlords had in effect relinquished control and received a decreasing share in the well being drilled on their land as capital expenditure on drilling deep wells increased.³⁵

The granting of shares in the partnership to non-investors is seen as one of the most important contributions of the Shanxi merchants mentioned above, whose businesses ranged from wholesale distribution of salt and other commodities, to retail marketing, to the creation of some of China's earliest banks for long-distance remittance of funds. "Body shares" addressed both the problem of short-term working capital discussed below and principal–agent problems of particular interest to merchants with business branches in distant markets. Silver shares (*yingu* 银股) went to the investors whose capital created the firm. Body shares (*shengu* 身股) were granted to those hired staff, branch managers, and even clerks who rose to the top of their ranks. The shift from salaried employee to equity stakeholder was seen as

---

³³ For example, Yang Yingquan and Yao Chengxiu rented a piece of land from the Jinyun temple and sublet part of it to a man named Zhang, who mined it with one hired laborer. Baxian Archives, 6.3.16552
³⁴ M. Zhang, "Financing Plantation Forestry in Southwest China: Securitization of Timberlands and Shareholding Practices, 1700–1900," AAS New Frontiers in Asian Economic History Workshop, East Lansing, Michigan, May 11–15, 2017, 10–14.
³⁵ For a detailed discussion of the allocation of shares among landowners, middleman developers, and owners of capital and other critical inputs in Zigong well partnerships, see Zelin, *The Merchants of Zigong*, pp. 24–49.

a way to ensure honesty and loyalty and continued hard work. Every three years the accounts of the firm were settled and all holders of body shares, including staff, received a portion of the profits commensurate with their shares.[36] Chinese scholars have noted that over time the number of body shares could exceed the number of investor or silver shares. However, there are no studies of the impact this may have had on the viability of the firm. The practice of issuing body shares continued into the mid-twentieth century, as noted in accounts of Shanxi merchants in Manchuria written in the 1940s.[37] In their study of the Rishengchang, one of the early Shanxi remittance banks, Randal Morck and Fan Yang argue that managers who were granted body shares received dividends, but unlike equity shareholders they had no claim to the equity of the firm, nor could their shares be inherited. However, their kin did receive a death benefit of sorts, in the form of term-limited dividend-generating death shares (gugu).[38]

The practice of ensuring the loyalty of managers by giving them a share in the firm can be seen elsewhere as well. For example, in 1878 Qu Fulu and Li Yingzhou wrote an agreement stating that they had purchased a fully equipped rice mill for 1,700 taels.[39] Together the partners would hold ten shares. Qu Fulu would get 6.5 shares for an investment of 1,105 taels. Li Yingzhou would get 3.5 shares for an investment of 595 taels. Two additional shares were established for a total of twelve. One was designated the property in perpetuity of the mill's manager, Jiang Rongzhuang. The other was to be assigned to the God of Wealth,[40] a rather recent object of merchant devotion and mercantile virtues.

The assignment of a share to the God of Wealth reminds us of another problem addressed in shareholding partnerships, that of short-term finance and working capital. There is a mistaken notion that the absence of modern

[36] Xu Ke 徐珂, Qingbai Leichao 清稗类钞, 17 ce, Nongshanglei, 70–1, cited in Jianhui Huang 黄鉴晖 and Zhongguo Renmin Yinhang Shanxisheng Fenhang 中国人民银行山西省分行 (eds.), 山西票号史料 (Historical Archives of Shanxi Piaohao) (Taiyuan, Shanxi Jingji chubanshe, 2002), p. 582.
[37] Wu Xiyong 吴希庸, "近代东北移民史略" (A Brief History of Migrants to the Northeast in Modern China), 东北季刊 (Northeast Quarterly) 38 (1941), 219–342. I want to thank Martin Fromm for bringing this to my attention.
[38] R. Morck and F. Yang, "The Rise and Fall of the Rishengchang Bank Model: Limiting Shareholder Influence to Attract Capital," in J.G.S. Koppell (ed.), *The Origins of Shareholder Advocacy* (New York, Palgrave Macmillan, 2011), pp. 195–8. Unfortunately, the one example they provide is from the 1940s so we do not know whether the practice of issuing death shares was the result of foreign influences.
[39] Li, "清代民间契约中关于'伙'的观念和习惯," 43.
[40] R. von Glahn, "The Enchantment of Wealth: The God Wutong in the Social History of Jiangnan," *Harvard Journal of Asiatic Studies* 51.2 (1991), 651–714.

banks slowed Chinese industrialization by depriving businessmen of long-term finance. Banks were not an important source of long-term venture capital in the early modern West any more than they were in China. While China's so-called native banks (*qianzhuang* 钱庄) played a vital role in clearing commercial accounts and both native banks and remittance banks issued commercial paper, Chinese business partnerships had to find other ways to provide liquidity to pay wages, purchase supplies, and market goods. In the founding document of the rice mill above, it is likely that the one share of profits set aside for the God of Wealth was really meant to be a form of retained earnings for just such a purpose. Replacing wages with dividends for senior staff also served this purpose.

We have other evidence that manufacturing firms did try to anticipate ongoing expenses and working capital. Some, such as those formed to mill sugar in nineteenth-century Taiwan, appear to have anticipated annual infusions of working capital from shareholders who expected their advances to be more than offset by profits at the end of the milling season.[41] Once again, shareholding practices mitigated the need for short-term credit. At Shanxi firms, partners were sometimes called upon to contribute *fuben* 副本, a form of deposit that remained in the firm, accrued interest, and could be used if needs arose, but was not treated as equity investment and did not earn dividends.[42] One of the jobs of the middleman/manager at the brine wells in Zigong was to ensure that equity partners made periodic payments to cover the cost of drilling and that no profits were divided from the sale of brine before a well was fully operational.[43] On the other hand, not all businesses were able to solve the problem of working capital. Robert Eng describes late nineteenth- and early twentieth-century silk manufacturers who formed partnerships to build filatures. Upon completion and finding themselves lacking working capital, they often leased the factories to other partnerships who actually produced yarn.[44] Eng attributes this practice to weaknesses in capital markets but acknowledges that particular characteristics of the silk

---

[41] C.M. Isett, "Sugar Manufacture and the Agrarian Economy of Nineteenth-Century Taiwan," *Modern China* 21.2 (1995), 244.
[42] Zhongmin Zhang 张忠民, 艰难的变迁，近代中国公司制度研究 (A Difficult Transition: A Study of the Chinese Company) (Shanghai, Shanghai Academy of Social Sciences Press, 2001), pp. 28–30.
[43] Zelin, *Merchants of Zigong*, pp. 39–42.
[44] R.Y. Eng, "Chinese Entrepreneurs, the Government, and the Foreign Sector: The Canton and Shanghai Silk-Reeling Enterprises, 1861–1932," *Modern Asian Studies* 18.3 (1984), 360–1.

market also contributed to partnerships treating filatures more as real estate than as integrated manufacturing firms.

While our discussion of partnerships gives the impression of a business world of active investor managers, late imperial Chinese were also well acquainted with the roles of passive investors. On the one hand, foreign observers and Chinese surveys of local customs point to the propensity of people with small amounts of capital to invest as dormant partners, with limited or no liability for debt. In a debate over Chinese notions of liability, George Jamieson, a late nineteenth-century observer of Chinese business practices based in China, noted that China had the equivalent of the dormant partnership in which some partners did not play an active role in the firm and were not liable for its debts.[45] On the other hand, we have seen that as long as the Chinese household was by law and custom a joint economy, any individual investor named on a partnership agreement really represented a group of closely related kin. What we have not foregrounded is that a large number of investors in Chinese business were and would continue to be shareholders in other businesses as well as the larger corporate bodies represented by lineage trusts.[46] Cross investment was also characteristic of so-called liaison stores (lianhao 联号) in which investors and managers of one store invested with those of other stores to establish new stores, often diversifying their core business and providing a hedge against business failure.[47] The world of Chinese business was thus one in which tangled webs of lineage trusts and multi-member households, as well as individual businesses, invested in other businesses, local and sometimes distant, in related and at times in very different trades. Diversified portfolios were important hedges against loss, and cross investment, even in the late imperial period, provided an important mechanism for horizontal and vertical integration.

Native-place affiliations and guilds facilitated the business development described above. Regional merchant groupings could be based on common origins in a county, town, province, or region. Among the most successful

---

[45] "Chinese Partnership: Liability of the Individual Members," *Journal of the North China Branch of the Royal Asiatic Society* 21.2 (1887), 48.
[46] Elisabeth Köll notes that most of the shareholders in Dasheng Cotton Mill were other businesses or lineage trusts. E. Köll, *From Cotton Mill to Business Empire: The Emergence of Regional Enterprises in Modern China* (Cambridge, MA, Harvard University Asia Center, 2003), p. 128–9. A variation on cross investment has been identified in the liaison firms
[47] M.-H. Lin, "Interpretive Trends in Taiwan's Scholarship on Chinese Business History, 1600 to the Present," *Chinese Studies in History* 31.3–4 (1998), 70–1. Most research on *lianhao* has focused on Manchuria.

merchants of the late imperial period were long-distance traders from the northwest provinces of Shanxi and Shaanxi and from Huizhou in Anhui province, both groups benefiting from the opportunities presented by the government system of licensing the long-distance trade in salt. Other regional merchant groups are better known for their role in the expansion of China's maritime trade, particularly those based in Fujian and Guangdong. According to Cheong, most of the prominent Guangdong merchants who comprised the so-called Cohong that enjoyed a government monopoly in the Canton trade with Western merchants traced their origins to Fujian and Zhejiang and "went to their previous contacts in the producing regions to obtain their export goods, finished the silks in their own Hongs, and used the same network for the redistribution of imports."[48] To these long-distance merchants could be added smaller but no less significant groups, such as the Ningbo merchants who, like many of their counterparts from other provinces, engaged in long-distance trade in foodstuffs, grain, and other staples, as well as playing a critical role in the development of commercial banking in southern China.

Not surprisingly, native place affinities became an important source of trust and facilitated the kind of investment and cross investment mentioned above. During the last dynasty a critical mass of fellow countrymen in a distant market eased relations with local officials. There is also evidence that the ability to deposit cash in the shops of fellow countrymen in distant markets anticipated the development of remittance banking and the use of new instruments of exchange.[49] Native-place ties also served as a conduit for the exchange of market information and the spread of organization strategies. At a more local level, well into the twentieth century, propinquity also served as a lubricant for entrepreneurs seeking investors in new business ventures. Men like Chen Qiyuan utilized local ties to obtain credit and labor to start one of China's first steam silk filatures in his native Nanhai county, Guangdong.[50] Sun Yingde, a blacksmith from the Canton region working around the Shanghai docks, joined forces with a relative to repair steamships, eventually building a machine and machine tools factory that employed

---

[48] W.E. Cheong, *The Hong Merchants of Canton: Chinese Merchants in Sino-Western Trade* (London, Curzon Press, 1996), p. 376.

[49] S. Guo, "The Shanxi Merchants in Beijing in the Qing Dynasty: An Analysis Based on 136 Samples of Merchants and Their Activities," *Frontiers in History in China* 4.2 (2009), 167–9.

[50] D. Ma, "Between Cottage and Factory: The Evolution of Chinese and Japanese Silk-Reeling Industries in the Latter Half of the Nineteenth Century," *Journal of the Asia Pacific Economy* 10.2 (2005), 203–5.

some 200 men.⁵¹ Indeed, investors in some of China's most famous industrial conglomerates, such as Zhang Jian (Dasheng Cotton Mill) and Fan Xudong (Jiuda Salt Refinery), discussed below, were friends, family, and local acquaintances.

Guilds served a different purpose. Although they sometimes originated as native-place associations established to serve the needs of officials, scholars, and long-distance merchant sojourners in far-flung parts of the empire, by the end of the Qing many guilds had become specialized agencies joining members of particular trades. Guilds expedited the system of private ordering discussed above by authorizing and promulgating "customs of the trade" and enforcing business standards among their member firms. Their ability to play this role depended not only on the growing wealth and influence of more prosperous merchant communities. The state itself came to rely on guilds to collect taxes, to regulate the value of the tael in market transactions, and to mediate merchant disputes. These roles would continue to be of importance into the twentieth century.⁵²

A New Deal for Business?

Beginning in the sixteenth century, Chinese merchants had increasing opportunities to interact with Western counterparts, who brought with them Western modes of business organization. These early contacts do not appear to have upended prevailing practices on either side. While Western participants in the Canton trade benefited from the development of the *commenda*, similar modes of investment in long-distance trade had existed in China as early as the Song dynasty, and Chinese familiarity with them encouraged some Chinese to invest in Western trading ventures.⁵³

With the end of the Opium War in the early 1840s and the loosening of restrictions on foreign trade at Chinese ports, opportunities to engage with foreign businessmen expanded. Foreigners took up residence in increasing

---

⁵¹ W.K.K. Chan. "Sources of Capital for Modern Industrial Enterprises in Late Ch'ing China," in R.A. Brown (ed.), *Chinese Business Enterprise: Critical Perspectives on Business and Management* (London and New York, Routledge 1996), p. 51.

⁵² K.-C. Liu, "Chinese Merchant Guilds: An Historical Inquiry," *Pacific Historical Review* 57.1 (1988), 15–18.

⁵³ R. Harris, "The Institutional Dynamics of Early Modern Eurasian Trade: The Commenda and the Corporation," *Journal of Economic Behavior & Organization* 71.3 (2009), 612. For a detailed discussion of the business interactions of Chinese and Western Traders in the Canton region, see P.A. van Dyke, *The Canton Trade: Life and Enterprise on the China Coast, 1700–1845* (Hong Kong and London, Hong Kong University Press, 2005).

numbers as ports opened to international trade by treaty and Chinese continued to invest in foreign ventures. David Faure cites a Chinese study that claims that as much as 70 percent of investment in Western shipping in China may have been financed by Chinese, while Hao Yen-ping argues for a 50 percent position for Chinese capital in Western insurance ventures in China.[54] At the same time, Chinese merchants began to participate in foreign business as so-called compradors. These Chinese agents of foreign firms acted both as liaisons with Chinese business and primary producers, and as entrepreneurs in their own right, constituting a key component of the investors in Chinese efforts to develop modern industry, commerce, and transportation. However, until the 1860s these contacts did not suggest a template for a dramatic reimagining of Chinese business organization.

Two simultaneous events changed the meaning that Western business organization would have for China. One was the end of the Taiping Rebellion in 1864. While Chinese officials had the opportunity to observe British steamships and armaments during the Opium War it was not until the Taiping Rebellion that the confluence of enhanced authority on the part of powerful provincial officials and the opportunity for Chinese forces to use foreign ordnance created the impetus for large-scale, albeit regionally based, programs directed at Chinese military modernization. These efforts, known collectively as the Self-Strengthening movement, began with Chinese investment in China's first modern arsenals and shipyards and soon stimulated efforts to produce steamships for civilian use as well as a variety of manufactured products.

The legacy of the Self-Strengthening movement is credited with some of China's earliest forays into military modernization, the development of mechanized mines, steam transportation, and the industrial production of textiles and other consumer goods. Its contributions to business organization were fleeting, but hold some lessons for the relationship between business practices before and after the intensification of China's economic engagement with the West. Most important were the aforementioned efforts by provincial officials, in particular men like Li Hongzhang, who, as organizer of the regional Huai Army, was instrumental in defeating the Taiping rebels. Following the war Li Hongzhang was rewarded with the civilian post of governor of Jiangsu and later governor-general of Hunan and Hubei. These posts, when combined with the political and fiscal authority he had accrued during the war, allowed him and other governors

---

[54] D. Faure, *China and Capitalism: A History of Business Enterprise in Modern China* (Hong Kong, Hong Kong University Press, 2006), p. 51; Y.-P. Hao, *The Comprador in Nineteenth Century China: Bridge between East and West* (Cambridge, MA, Harvard University Asia Center, 1970), pp. 252–3.

with similar histories to take a leading role in introducing modern technology and production methods in both the civilian and military spheres.

Most of the modern industrial projects founded during the 1860s, shipyards and arsenals, were government-funded and government-managed.[55] By the 1870s the focus of provincial development efforts shifted away from defense. One "innovation" emerging from the new focus on mining, shipping, textiles, and consumer goods was the government-supervised–merchant-managed or *guandu shangban* 官督商办 enterprise. The *guandu shangban* enterprises of the 1870s and 1880s were envisioned as joint-stock companies. Merchants (and others) were offered the opportunity to buy shares in return for dividends, often set at a fixed rate as an inducement to investors.[56] Sale of shares, even to parties without strong personal ties, as a mode of finance and distribution of profits and losses was not new. However, *guandu shangban* enterprises pioneered the public offering, including their publication in the growing number of newspapers that emerged in China in the 1870s and 1880s. The model for investment prospectuses (*zhaogu zhangcheng* 招股章程) may have been that of the China Merchants Steam Navigation Company. However, hundreds of these solicitations could be found in newspapers like *Shenbao* by the early 1780s.[57] As Wellington Chan has noted, the term *guandu shangban* had a precedent in the organization of the salt gabelle, and the employment of hired managers was common in Chinese partnerships and even family businesses.[58] Businesses patronized by Li Hongzhang, such as the China Merchants Steam Navigation Company, the Kaiping Mining Company, and the Shanghai Cotton Cloth Mill, all had merchant managers, often former compradors in Western firms. These managers operated with relative independence from their official patrons and their shareholders were largely passive recipients of dividends, playing little role in oversight over their investments. Managerial practices that included the movement of funds between enterprises sponsored by a particular official patron, as well as more questionable expenditure of firm funds for personal use, had an impact on the

---

[55] See Chapters 5 and 6 of this volume.
[56] Guaranteed rates of dividend payments, often around 8 percent of investment, blurred the line between loans and equity investment, as did the term applied to these dividends, "official interest" (*guanli* 官利). Government involvement in these businesses could provide tangible benefits, as in the promise to ship government tribute tax rice exclusively on ships of the China Merchants Steam Navigation Company. S. R. Halsey, "Sovereignty, Self-Strengthening, and Steamships in Late Imperial China," *Journal of Asian History* 48.1 (2014), 81–111.
[57] See, for example, the *zhaogu zhangcheng* calling for investors in the Pingquan Mining Bureau published in *Shenbao* 申报, 6th month, 11th day, 1882.
[58] W.K.K. Chan, *Merchants, Mandarins, and Modern Enterprise in Late Ch'ing China* (Cambridge, MA, Harvard University East Asian Research Center, 1977), pp. 70–1.

performance of *guandu shangban* enterprises and the willingness of merchants to invest in their shares.[59] Some of these practices, particularly cross subsidization of firms connected through a family interest or a particular entrepreneur, however, were part of the managerial repertoire of traditional Chinese business overall and, as we will see, would continue into the twentieth century.

Another impetus toward change was the British adoption of the Joint-Stock Companies Act in 1856 and the extension of most of its provisions to Hong Kong in the Company Ordinance of 1865. By requiring accounting transparency, annual shareholders' meetings, and other shareholder protections, the new British laws (and similar laws emerging out of other European countries doing business in China) could have addressed some of the problems that emerged under *guandu shangban* and later under more clearly private entities. For British subjects doing business with subjects of the Qing empire, the most important issue raised by these new laws concerned limited liability and the handling of company liquidation, inasmuch as China did not have a similar law and foreign courts had no jurisdiction over Chinese investors in the European and American companies.[60] The absence of a company law in China was a major factor leading to British pressure for Chinese legal reform. However, even before the promulgation of a company law, Chinese private businesses began to partake of what they perceived as useful elements of the Western business form. Often these adaptations were superficial. For example, during the Self-Strengthening period businesses established under government auspices had adopted the term *ju* 局, or bureau, symbolic of their ties to the state bureaucracy and older corporate forms, while most private businesses continued to use terms like *hang* 行 or *hao* 号 as suffixes to business names. By the 1870s, the term *gongsi* 公司 or "company" had come to signify a new understanding of the private business firm and in 1875 the emperor himself abandoned the term *ju* in favor of *gongsi* in his call for officials to encourage the development of business.[61]

---

[59] Chan, *Merchants, Mandarins, and Modern Enterprise*, pp. 72–5, attributes the corruption associated with these firms largely to the influence of Sheng Xuanhuai, an official who took over supervision of Li Hongzhang's business initiatives in the 1880s. See also A. Feuerwerker, *China's Early Industrialization: Sheng Hsuan-Huai (1844–1916) and Mandarin Enterprise* (Cambridge, MA, Harvard University Press, 1958).

[60] E. Motono, *Conflict and Cooperation in Sino-British Business, 1860–1911: The Impact of the Pro-British Commercial Network in Shanghai* (New York and London, St. Martin's Press, 2000), pp. 66–72.

[61] Liufang Fang 方流芳, "公司词义考：解读语词的制度信息" (The Etymology of *Gongsi*: Institutional Information from the Reading of Words), *Sino-Foreign Legal Studies* 3 (2000), 277–99. Fang argues that the term *gongsi* originally was understood to apply only to the British East India Company.

A formal market in Chinese shares did not emerge until after the fall of the Qing dynasty.[62] However, Chinese businessmen were quick to imitate the foreign use of advertisements for public share offerings. Founded by foreigners in 1861, *Shanghai xinbao*, the first Chinese-language commercial journal, was devoted almost entirely to advertisements for shares. By the 1870s Chinese entrepreneurs were soliciting investors by publishing prospectuses in major newspapers like the Chinese-language newspaper *Shenbao*. These investment prospectuses (*zhaogu zhangcheng*) give us a glimpse of some of the organizational aspirations of firms as they sought to create an impersonal market for shares.

A prospectus soliciting investment in the Hangzhou Electric Light Company appeared in 1897 in the *Jicheng bao*.[63] As a wholly private public utility that requested and received a monopoly to establish electric lighting in that city it was under somewhat greater official scrutiny than would be other kinds of endeavor. But its organizational provisions reflect the prevailing practices of businesses reaching out to stranger-investors in the late nineteenth century.

The Hangzhou Electric Light Company sought investors with the goal of raising approximately 150,000 taels to buy equipment for the manufacture of electric lamps and cable and to operate coal yards and warehouses. Among the organizational commitments made in the prospectus was the selection of a ten-man board of general directors from among those holding the largest number of shares and election from their ranks of one general manager and one assistant manager. The managers would meet and deliberate with the directors on important matters, requiring six out of the ten directors' approval for major decisions. Income and expenditure were to be handled exclusively by the company accounts officer, who would compile a summary accounting each month, quarterly closings, and an annual general settlement of accounts. After the payment of the shareholders' guaranteed dividend (*guanli*), salaries and wages, and other expenses, any surplus would be set in a reserve fund and would go to providing bonuses for the founders as well as additional dividends for shareholders.

Unlike traditional shareholding firms in which proof of investment was based on holding a copy of the founding contract, the Electric Light Company would follow the Western practice of issuing share certificates.

---

[62] W.A. Thomas, *Western Capitalism in China: A History of the Shanghai Stock Exchange* (Aldershot and Burlington, VT, Ashgate, 2001), pp. 245–7.
[63] "杭州電燈公司招股章程" (The Hangzhou Electric Light Company Share-Offering Articles of Association), *Jichengbao* 8.12 (1897), 25–29.

But like traditional firms, if a shareholder wished to sell his shares, he would have to offer them first to the existing shareholders. If there were no takers he could offer his shares to outsiders, informing the company so that the names of shareholders would remain up to date. Finally, as a confirmation of the role that personal relationships of family or native place traditionally played in hiring, the prospectus assured investors that no one would be hired as a sinecure, that all persons recommended to work for the company would be vetted by the company managers, and that all personnel with responsibility for finances or materials would be required to have a guarantor. In the event that the managers recommended expansion of the business they would be required to call a meeting of all shareholders, providing notice a month in advance by placing an announcement in *Shenbao* and other newspapers.

The Hangzhou Electric Light Company was typical of firms founded in the last years of the nineteenth century to introduce new and often expensive technologies in the area of mechanized production and transportation. Their large capital requirements differentiated them from earlier shareholding partnerships. But their business models would not have seemed alien to the merchants they sought to attract to their shareholder registers. These firms were founded before the Qing dynasty provided a legal basis for incorporation. Promulgated in 1904, China's first company law (*Gongsi lü*) acknowledged the juridical status and new names for existing business forms, such as the single proprietorship, the simple partnership, and the unlimited company, and for the first time provided the option for Chinese firms to register as limited companies.[64] While fairly rudimentary, the new law introduced ideas that in various combinations would be taken up by twentieth-century business founders, including limited liability, the rights and obligations of shareholders, the establishment of formal boards of directors, and rules to encourage financial transparency, such as the requirement that all firms engage auditors independent from management. The new law also memorialized practices that existed under the regime of private ordering, such as the freedom to buy and sell shares unless otherwise stipulated in the founding document, issuing shares as bonuses, and the ability of a company to assess shareholders for additional funds.

What impact did the company law have on the organization of business? Some scholars have argued that the impact was negligible, as evidenced by the small number of firms that registered as limited-liability joint-stock

---

[64] Shanghai Municipal Archives (ed.), 旧中国的股份制 (1868–1949) (The Joint-Stock System in Old China) (Shanghai, Zhongguo dangan chubanshe, 1996), pp. 11–24.

companies.⁶⁵ On the other hand, many businesses borrowed from the repertoire of organizational provisions found in this and subsequent company laws without registering with the government. The absence in China of legal restrictions on the longevity of firms that were not incorporated made limited liability one of the few benefits available only through registration as a corporation under the new law. By the early twentieth century, registered and unregistered firms were including in their founding documents stipulations on the conduct of shareholder meetings, the formation of boards of directors, the duties of managers, and so on, and using mechanisms such as partnership contracts and ledgers to regulate shareholder rights and keep track of the transfer of shares.⁶⁶ At the same time, Chinese businesses in the early twentieth century remained hybrid institutions, each making use in its own way of earlier and more recently introduced managerial and organizational techniques.

Business Organization in Flux

The early twentieth century was a period of experimentation, especially for those firms engaging in the production and sale of new kinds of products, making use of new technologies, and expanding their reach into new markets. In some instances, family investment and control were central to the business model and remained at its core despite expansion in both the scope of business and its geographical location. The Meng family continued to run its Ruifuxiang as a closely held family firm, working through "a personalized network of trusted subordinates and a formal structure of meetings and reports."⁶⁷ By the twentieth century it had expanded from retail and wholesale trade in native cloth to opening stores in several cities in eastern China. It expanded its product line into imported fabrics, cosmetics, and luxury goods, and opened pawnshops, Chinese medicine shops, and shops specializing in handicraft weaving. According to Wellington Chan, each kind of firm was part of its own managerial hierarchy and accounting structure. However, all

---

⁶⁵ An early article that set the terms for this discussion is W.C. Kirby, "China Unincorporated: Company Law and Business Enterprise in Twentieth-Century China," *Journal of Asian Studies* 54.1 (1995), 43–63. Kirby says only 227 companies had registered as limited-liability companies by 1908 and only twenty-two of these were the kind of large company the law was meant to enable.

⁶⁶ Li, "清代民间契约中关于'伙'的观念和习惯," 42. Suzhou Archives, 乙 14-002-0059-020, provides an example of a small shareholding partnership engaged in a dispute over shares in which the company shareholder ledger was brought as evidence in court.

⁶⁷ Chan, "The Organizational Structure of the Traditional Chinese Firm," 222–5.

business accounts were handled through the same accounts office that dealt with the Meng lineage estate.[68] Family control persisted even in firms that registered as limited-liability companies. The Nanyang Brothers Tobacco Company was founded as a family firm by Jian Zhaonan and his uncle, Jian Kongzhao, in the last years of the Qing and took advantage of the new company law to incorporate in the 1910s. In the 1920s it expanded its holdings to include newspapers, an insurance company, and a remittance firm while retaining a majority of shares in the name of family members.[69] By the 1920s the Jians had joined other family firms that had been using professional managers since the late Qing, but tensions between the board of directors and the family reflect a familiar reluctance to relinquish family operational control.

Whether dominated by a single family or a single entrepreneur, investment and management of many firms during this early period of industrial development reflected what we might call relationship capitalism.[70] The Rong family of Wuxi are known for their development of modern flour and cotton mills. By the early 1920s these mills were clustered into three managerially independent groups, the Maoxin and Fuxin flour mills and the Shengxin Cotton mills. While the Rongs had varying numbers of shares in each mill, other shareholders, both individuals and lineage trusts, held shares in more than one mill, creating interlocking ownership structures that encouraged some co-operation, for example in the sharing of brand names and in negotiating loans. A central office in the combined names of the three groups performed some co-ordinating functions, including purchasing. And individual mills kept deposits in the central office in part for this purpose. While the nature of the relationship among the mills is often difficult to discern, the importance of that relationship, bound by the Rong connections, facilitated cross-subsidization within the group in the development of new mills and temporarily aided mills in need of cash.[71]

---

[68] Chan, "The Organizational Structure of the Traditional Chinese Firm," 222–5.

[69] D. Faure, "The Control of Equity in Chinese Firms within the Modern Sector from the Late Qing to the Early Republic," in R.A. Brown (ed.), *Chinese Business Enterprise in Asia* (London, Routledge, 1995), pp. 68–72. Faure relates a similar story of family ownership and control at the Guo's Wing On department stores, the Hengfeng Spinning Mill, and the Yans' Dalong Machine works, which, despite its growing size and diversification into the production of diesel engines and spinning and weaving machines, as well as the operation of textile mills, remained a closely held family firm.

[70] I use the term "relationship capitalism" because "network capitalism" implies more formal ties among participants than appears to have been the case in China during the early twentieth century.

[71] This section relies on a new interpretation of the Rong enterprises in K.Y. Chan, "Making Sense of the 'Business Group' in Modern China: The Rong Brothers Businesses, 1901–37," *Australian Economic History Review* 51.3 (2011), 219–44.

Individual entrepreneurs with social and political capital appear as central in the development of many of China's pioneering modern businesses, dating back to the projects sponsored by powerful official patrons during the Self-Strengthening period. Fan Xudong, considered the founder of China's modern chemicals industry, benefited from investment from one of China's leading statesmen, Liang Qichao, who brought along family and friends as shareholders in Fan's modern Jiuda Salt Refinery. When Fan sought to expand into the production of soda ash in the late 1910s, his position as founder facilitated his reliance on capital and other resources from Jiuda to build Yongli Soda Ash. These included loans and direct investment from Jiuda, as well as shared land, dockyards, and senior management.[72]

Zhang Jian, one of the new group of literati businessmen of the late nineteenth century, began his entrepreneurial career by promoting mechanized cotton yarn production. Unable to raise sufficient capital from private investors, he accepted a donation of machinery from the governor-general of Liangjiang and established his Dasheng Number One Cotton Mill as a state–private joint enterprise (*guanshang heban* 官商合办). Unlike earlier state–private ventures, Zhang was able to retain managerial control and by the turn of the century had infused his business with additional private investment, particularly from local cloth merchants in the vicinity of the mill in Nantong, Jiangsu. Zhang Jian followed the cotton mill by founding flour and oil mills, shipping lines, land reclamation companies, a publishing house, and a distillery.[73]

Although Zhang Jian and his family never had a majority of shares in the businesses he established, Zhang relied on family members for their day-to-day management. Overall co-ordination and control were exercised through Zhang's personal Shanghai-based accounts office, which managed accounts of affiliated companies as well, acted as their paymaster and broker, and handled their diverse financial transactions. This office both functioned as the business office for what Köll calls Zhang's "conglomerate" and was the office that handled all of Zhang and his family's personal accounts. This allowed the movement of money between accounts, shifting money from one business to another and between Zhang's own accounts and those of his companies. The central accounts office, while it did not co-ordinate the business activities of

---

[72] M.B. Kwan, *Beyond Market and Hierarchy: Patriotic Capitalism and the Jiuda Salt Refinery, 1914–1953* (New York, Palgrave Macmillan, 2014), pp. 27–30, 73–4. Kwan notes that by providing loan guarantees from Jiuda, Yongli was also able to get interest free and below-market-rate loans from the main bank with which Jiuda was associated.

[73] Köll, *From Cotton Mill to Business Empire*, pp. 64–8.

each unit, also allowed a degree of vertical integration, something we see in the Zigong saltyards as well, where brine from one family's wells might move through that same family's pipes, to be evaporated at the family's furnaces and sold by its wholesalers, all of which were managed as separate vertical business lines.[74]

While the backgrounds of the most notable entrepreneurs of this period differed, the use of the central account office as a co-ordination mechanism was a central feature of early twentieth-century Chinese business. Liu Hongsheng began his career as comprador for the London-registered Chinese Engineering and Mining Company. Liu formed partnerships on his own with other coal distributors, investing in mining and wharfs and eventually diversifying into matches, coal briquettes, textiles, banking, and real estate. While he was never able to bring his business interests together under a single management structure, they were nevertheless linked horizontally through Liu and his personal account office.[75] Following the privatization of the Hubei Textile Bureau founded by Governor-General Zhang Zhidong, its branch factories established independent management structures, each handling its own accounts. However, with the demise of the dynasty a new management agreement was made with Xu Rongting and his Chuxing Company, under whose central account office certain co-ordinating functions, including shareholder relations and dealings with foreign machine parts suppliers, were managed. Xu's success attracting investors for these factories as private enterprises was assisted by his close relationship with the erstwhile president of the Chinese republic, Li Yuanhong.

Conclusion

How should we understand the continuation of key organizational characteristics of Chinese businesses as China entered a period of legal reform accompanied by rapidly changing politics, technology, and international relations? Of course things did not stay the same. The businesses we have foregrounded in the post-imperial period were increasingly large in scale and scope, with a central focus on manufacturing. Single proprietorship and partnerships continued to dominate the business landscape in China as in the West, but it is in this modern sector that we see Chinese entrepreneurs grappling with new business opportunities in

---

[74] Zelin, *Merchants of Zigong*, pp. 133–44.
[75] K.Y. Chan, *Business Expansion and Structural Change in Pre-war China: Liu Hongsheng and His Enterprises, 1920–1937* (Hong Kong, Hong Kong University Press, 2006), pp. 27–46.

a context that was nothing if not unstable. When China finally opened its first stock exchange in 1920, it was dominated by government and military bonds and closed with the Japanese occupation, having been plagued by speculation for the span of its short history.[76] Passage of a company law in 1904 and its revision in 1914 introduced new standards of business practice that were not always enforced by changing governments and a weak modern judiciary. In many trades guilds retained power by setting silver exchange rates in a state that did not establish a fiat currency until the 1930s and in which courts of law relied on chambers of commerce and their member guilds to assist in the adjudication of complex commercial cases. These are just a few of the constraints that confronted modern firms.

It is therefore not simply a matter of cultural preference that many of the institutions that served late imperial businesspeople found new life in the ways we have noted above. Family, friends, and influence networks continued to encourage co-operation and co-investment. Lineage trusts, with their claims to collective assets and longevity, continued to be major investors in modern firms, and the lineage accounts office served as a model for the central accounts office and its tools for flexible co-ordination, including the movement of funds between related but not necessarily co-invested businesses. And the diversified portfolio, as a technique for spreading risk and influence, continued to play a major role in the business strategies of what has come to be seen as the model of the modern Chinese conglomerate.

Further Reading

"The Canton Trade: Life and Enterprise on the China Coast, 1700–1845," at www.jstor.org/stable/j.ctt1xwbc2, accessed September 14, 2020.

Chan, K.Y., *Business Expansion and Structural Change in Pre-war China: Liu Hongsheng and His Enterprises, 1920–1937* (Hong Kong, Hong Kong University Press, 2006).

Chan, K.Y., "Making Sense of the 'Business Group' in Modern China: The Rong Brothers Businesses, 1901–37," *Australian Economic History Review* 51.3 (2011), 219–44.

Chan, W.K.K., "The Organizational Structure of the Traditional Chinese Firm and Its Modern Reform," *Business History Review* 56.2 (1982), 218–35.

Cheong, W.E., *The Hong Merchants of Canton: Chinese Merchants in Sino-Western Trade* (Richmond, Curzon, 1997).

Cochran, S., *Big Business in China: Sino-Foreign Rivalry in the Cigarette Industry, 1890–1930* (Cambridge, MA, Harvard University Press, 1980).

Cochran, S., *Encountering Chinese Networks: Western, Japanese, and Chinese Corporations in China, 1880–1937* (Berkeley, University of California Press, 2000).

---

[76] E. Hertz, "The Shanghai Stock Market, an Institutional Overview," in Brown, *Chinese Business Enterprise*, p. 117.

Fang, L., "Chinese Partnership," *Law and Contemporary Problems* 52.3 (1989), 43–68.
Faure, D., "The Control of Equity in Chinese Firms within the Modern Sector from the Late Qing to the Early Republic," in R.A. Brown (ed.), *Chinese Business Enterprise in Asia* (London, Routledge, 1995), 60–79.
Feuerwerker, A., *China's Early Industrialization: Sheng Hsuan-Huai (1844–1916) and Mandarin Enterprise* (Cambridge, MA, Harvard University Press, 1958).
Gardella, R., "Contracting Business Partnerships in Late Qing and Republican China: Paradigms and Patterns," in M. Zelin, J.K. Ocko, and R. Gardella (eds.), *Contract and Property in Early Modern China* (Stanford, Stanford University Press, 2004), pp. 327–47.
Kim, K., *Borderland Capitalism: Turkestan Produce, Qing Silver, and the Birth of an Eastern Market* (Stanford, Stanford University Press, 2016).
Kirby, W.C., "China Unincorporated: Company Law and Business Enterprise in Twentieth-Century China," *Journal of Asian Studies* 54.1 (1995), 43–63.
Köll, E., *From Cotton Mill to Business Empire: The Emergence of Regional Enterprises in Modern China* (Cambridge, MA, Harvard University Asia Center, 2003).
Kwan, M.B., "Managing Market, Hierarchy, and Network: The Jiuda Salt Industries, Ltd., 1917–1937," *Enterprise & Society* 6.3 (2005), 395–418.
Lai, C.-K., "The Qing State and Merchant Enterprise: The China Merchants' Company, 1872–1902," in J.K. Leonard, J.R. Watt, and Cornell University (eds.), *To Achieve Security and Wealth: The Qing Imperial State and the Economy, 1644–1911* (Ithaca, NY, East Asia Program, Cornell University, 1992), p. 146.
Liu, K.-C., "Financing a Steam-Navigation Company in China, 1861–62," *Business History Review* 28.2 (1954), 154–81.
Lufrano, R.J., *Honorable Merchants: Commerce and Self-Cultivation in Late Imperial China* (Honolulu, University of Hawaii Press, 1997).
Moll-Murata, C., "Chinese Guilds from the Seventeenth to the Twentieth Centuries: An Overview," *International Review of Social History* 53, Supplement S16 (2008), 213–47.
Motono, E., *Conflict and Cooperation in Sino-British Business, 1860–1911: The Impact of the Pro-British Commercial Network in Shanghai* (New York and London, St. Martin's Press, 2000).
Pomeranz, K., "'Traditional' Chinese Business Forms Revisited: Family, Firm, and Financing in the History of the Yutang Company of Jining, 1779–1956," *Late Imperial China* 18.1 (December 22, 1997), 1–38.
Qiao, Zhijian, "The Rise of Shanxi Merchants: Empire, Institutions, and Social Change in Qing China, 1688–1850," Ph.D. thesis, Stanford University, 2017.
Qiu Pengsheng 邱澎生, "由公产到法人–清代苏州，上海商人团体的制度变化" (From "Common Property" to Corporation: The Institutional Changes of the Merchant Associations of Suzhou and Shanghai in Late Qing), 法制史研究 (Research on Legal History) 10 (2006), 117–40.
Rowe, W.T., *Hankow, Commerce and Society in a Chinese City, 1796–1889* (Stanford, CA, Stanford University Press, 1984).
Ruskola, T., "Conceptualizing Corporations and Kinship: Comparative Law and Development Theory in a Chinese Perspective," *Stanford Law Review* 52.6 (2000), 1599–1729.
Zelin, M., *The Merchants of Zigong: Industrial Entrepreneurship in Early Modern China* (New York, Columbia University Press, 2005).

11

The Economic Impact of the West
A Reappraisal

JAMES KAI-SING KUNG

Introduction

For the Chinese, the nineteenth century was a period of waking up and realizing why the Middle Kingdom had fallen behind the West in economic growth.[1] Not only had this large and once prosperous country fallen behind economically (with its apparent failure to industrialize), it also fell prey during the two Opium Wars to the same country that first embarked upon the Industrial Revolution – Britain. Consequently, a long period of autarky came to an end.[2] While initially China was forced to open up only several "treaty ports" for trade and commerce, eventually the entire country was subjected to the influences of the West, and in spheres that went far beyond trade and commerce to also include industry, education, and even politics.[3] By assembling data from a variety of previously untapped historical sources,

---

I thank the editor, Debin Ma, Ghassan Moazzin, Dwight Perkins, and Thomas Rawski for useful suggestions on an earlier draft. I am most grateful to Ting Chen for compiling the various data sources, and to Bin Huang and Yan Zhou for excellent research assistance. Generous financial assistance from Sein and Isaac Souede is gratefully acknowledged.

[1] For two millennia, China regarded itself as the Middle Kingdom, the most civilized state under heaven, around which it developed a hierarchical system, the tributary system, in dealing with international relations. Specifically, China was at the center of the system, and surrounded by tributary states in Asia (e.g. Korea, Vietnam, Burma). These peripheral states were required to honor China by sending tribute periodically, and their kings were expected to adopt the Chinese culture. J.K. Fairbank, *The Chinese World Order: Traditional China's Foreign Relations*, vol. 32 (Cambridge, MA, Harvard University Press, 1968).

[2] To restrict the spread of Christianity, Qing China had implemented a closed-door policy since around the early eighteenth century (c. 1721), following an ongoing dispute that started as early as in 1645 between Roman Catholic missionaries and the Qing emperors concerning whether Chinese ritual practices of honoring family ancestors and other deities were compatible with Catholic beliefs.

[3] Many Chinese historians thus see this period as marking the beginning of a century of humiliation – a "dark and shameful period" in China's history.

this chapter attempts to analyze the Western influences that shaped the economic trajectories of late imperial China.

Clearly, for a topic as broad as the economic impact of the West, it is impossible to encompass every single aspect in which China had been affected in the process. Our choice of which aspects to examine, therefore, is unavoidably subjective and selective to some extent. Nonetheless, our choice is not arbitrary, but premised importantly on the key changes that occurred in the economy, society, and polity of late imperial China.

To a large extent, this chapter was inspired by Robert Dernberger's important question regarding the role of the foreigner in China's economic development[4] – a question prompted by the forced opening up of China by the Western powers (including Japan) on the one hand, and its failure to industrialize even after foreign firms and banks had entered the local market via the treaty ports on the other. In the absence of relevant systematic data, the mere juxtaposition of these two historical events unwittingly led to a largely negative assessment of the effects of treaty ports on China's economic development. For example, Dernberger laments an "overwhelming acceptance of a single major theme" among "leading Western-trained anthropologists, sociologists, and economists," that the treaty ports had destroyed "the economic and social fabric of China's countryside."[5] And while some speak favorably of the effects of trade and resource transfers as they occurred in the treaty ports, they see such benefits as necessarily confined within the treaty ports; there were virtually no "trickle-down" effects on the vast hinterland. China remained essentially a "dual" economy consisting of a small "modern" sector and a sizeable "traditional" sector, the totality of which resembles the stylized economy described by Lewis's "two-sector" model.[6]

---

[4] R.F. Dernberger, "The Role of the Foreigner in China's Economic Development, 1840–1949," in D.H. Perkins (ed.), *China's Modern Economy in Historical Perspective* (Stanford, Stanford University Press, 1975), pp. 19–47.

[5] Dernberger, "The Role of the Foreigner in China's Economic Development," p. 22. Dernberger was referring to Chen Han-seng, H.D. Fong, Fei Hsiao-tung, Franklin Ho, and so forth. Philip Huang's account of how China's indigenous weaving cottage industry was devastated by the Japanese iron gearwheel, which was a thousand times more productive, represents a prominent case in point. P.C.C. Huang, *The Peasant Economy and Social Change in North China* (Stanford, Stanford University Press, 1985).

[6] W.A. Lewis, "Economic Development with Unlimited Supplies of Labor," *Manchester School* 22.2 (1954), 139–91. Also see, for example, C.-M. Hou, *Foreign Investment and Economic Development in China, 1840–1937* (Cambridge, MA, Harvard University Press, 1965); R. Murphey, *The Treaty Ports and China's Modernization: What Went Wrong?* (Ann Arbor, University of Michigan Center for Chinese Studies, 1970).

Of course not everyone sees the foreigner as the culprit in China's lack of economic development in the late Qing period and beyond. An ailing government, inadequate savings for capital formation, technical backwardness, and perhaps also the unique characteristics of the Chinese family and the social institutions in which it was embedded were all considered "indigenous obstacles" hindering development.[7] Indeed, it is from this point of view that Dernberger credits the foreigner with catalyzing the modernization of the Chinese economy. Specifically, he views trade, technology transfer, and foreign direct investment (FDI) as the foreigner's "largest contribution to China's economic development."[8]

A thorough, unbiased analysis and thus conclusive assessment is hard to reach, however, in the absence of systematic data. To address the kind of questions raised by economic historians and other social scientists nearly half a century ago, we make use of newly assembled data to examine the role played by FDI and foreign debt (FD) in treaty port development (a classic question posed earlier), and the extent to which markets had developed or integrated in facilitating the distribution of goods for import and export (i.e. whether or not treaty port development produced "spillover effects"). We find that between the two, FDI outsized FD by a wide margin, and that of all the countries involved, Japan invested the most, followed by the United Kingdom.[9] To identify more precisely the sectoral and geographic

---

[7] A. Feuerwerker, *China's Early Industrialization: Sheng Hsuan-huai (1844–1916) and Mandarin Enterprise* (Cambridge, MA, Harvard University Press, 1958); M.J. Levy, "Contrasting Factors in the Modernization of China and Japan," *Economic Development and Cultural Change* 2 (1953), 161–97; D.H. Perkins, "Government as an Obstacle to Industrialization: The Case of Nineteenth-Century China," *Journal of Economic History* 17.4 (1967), 478–92. Regardless of whether the foreigner was a culprit, Cohen criticizes this paradigm pioneered by John K. Fairbank and others that views Qing China as playing a merely passive role in response to its contact with the West, to the extent that it was incapable of change without Western interference. P. Cohen, *Discovering History in China: American Historical Writing on the Recent Chinese Past* (New York, Columbia University Press, 1984).

[8] Dernberger, "The Role of the Foreigner in China's Economic Development," p. 46. While certain sectors of the population or economy may have been "impoverished," it was not due to foreign penetration; rather, the peasant economy had been struggling with growing land shortages amid continuing population growth, not to mention the competition it faced from China's own modernization efforts. Using the textile and food processing sectors as examples, Dernberger argues (at pp. 36–7) that "the major damage done to the handicraft industries was due largely to the Chinese response to the challenge of modernization and not to the competition of the foreigner," and that "the foreign goods were of a different type and were sold in a different segment of the market from those issuing from the traditional handicraft sector." Evidence on these claims, however, remains scant.

[9] Wu Chengming 吳承明, 帝国主义在旧中国的投资 (Investment in Old China by Imperialists) (Beijing, Renmin chubanshe, 1955). Xu Dixin 許滌新 and Wu Chengming

distributions of foreign investments, we exploit a unique data set compiled by Chang,[10] who documents the number of foreign firms and banks entering China for the 1841–1916 period. We find that the food and beverage and machinery sectors outsized each of the other sectors established by foreigners, with Britain and Japan having established the largest cumulative number of firms. Insofar as the development of markets was concerned, our analysis finds that the twelve earliest treaty ports covered the majority of the trading networks, with Shanghai and Nanjing having much bigger rippling effects than those established later.

Our goal, however, is to provide a fresh perspective from which to understand the role of treaty ports in spurring the development of modern institutions – both business and financial – in the final chapter of the imperial Chinese economy. An important economic influence of the West is that, under the rubric of the "Self-Strengthening movement," it effectively elicited a concerted response from the political elites (with the likes of Zeng Guofan 曾國藩 and Li Hongzhang 李鴻章, and later Zhang Zhidong 張之洞) to develop the country's industrial and military capabilities. This is reflected in the establishment of wide-ranging enterprises from steamships and engines to arsenal, naval, and military academies, and a host of industrial concerns such as coal mines, cotton mills, and iron and steel complexes to serve these enterprises, as well as basic infrastructure such as railways and the telegraph to facilitate development.[11] While these concerted efforts represented mostly state endeavors or specifically those of the regional political elites,[12] the industrialization effort that grew out of the "Self-Strengthening movement" undoubtedly created a qualitatively new social and political atmosphere in China's continuing efforts toward modernization within the institutional context of the treaty ports and the so-called "self-initiated ports" (zikai shangbu 自開商埠, hereafter SIPs) – the latter established for the dual purposes of avoiding granting further "concessions" or specifically a range of extraterritorial rights to the Western powers, and competing with the treaty ports that were dominated (at least initially) by foreigners.

吳承明, 中國資本主義發展史 (A History of Capitalist Development in China), vol 3 (Beijing, Renmin chubanshe, 1993).

[10] Y. Chang 張玉法, "清末民初的外資工業" (Foreign Industries in Late Qing and Early Republican China), Bulletin of the Institute of Modern History, Academia Sinica, 1987, 129–249.

[11] For example, see T.Y. Kuo and K.C. Liu, "Self-Strengthening: The Pursuit of Western Technology," in J.K. Fairbank (ed.), The Cambridge History of China, vol. 10, Late Ch'ing, 1800–1911, part 1 (Cambridge, Cambridge University Press, 1978), pp. 491–542; J.D. Spence, The Search for Modern China (New York, W.W. Norton & Company, 1990).

[12] Feuerwerker, China's Early Industrialization.

To fully appreciate the influence of the foreign firms and banks introduced into China (all of which had their operations set up in treaty ports), we perform a multivariate analysis and confirm that a good majority of the modern domestic firms and banks had chosen to set up operations in close proximity to their foreign counterparts *inside* the treaty ports, suggesting the possible existence of a "demonstration effect." Moreover, this effect is further confirmed by the finding that, of those which had chosen to locate outside the treaty ports, the vast majority were located in the SIPs. The fact that only a handful of modern Chinese banks were located in cities with no special administrative status suggests that businesses paid a "premium" for setting up shop in the treaty ports and to a lesser extent the SIPs.

But treaty ports may have produced positive, dynamic effects that went beyond the private firms' choice of locations. A recent study has documented a strong positive correlation between greater military investment during the Self-Strengthening movement and greater output in civilian industrial sectors in the 1930s through input–output linkages.[13] On this basis we conduct a multivariate analysis, and find that the earlier treaty ports, particularly the first five established in the 1840s, are strongly correlated with the locations of munition factories, confirming the existence of a dynamic effect of the ports.

Another hallmark of modern economic development pertains to technological adoption. For instance, in order for modern industrial firms to use the steam engine, electricity was essential. We find that private electricity plants, while small in scale, had unwittingly sprung up all over China. While these small private power plants appeared in every nook and cranny of the country, they were especially concentrated in south and south-central China – regions where public efforts were visibly lacking. On the whole, the wide geographic availability of electrical power supply was an important precondition for the increased adoption of the steam engine among firms in both types of port cities from 1880 onwards. A similar growth trend was observed among firms adopting machinery.

Treaty ports and SIPs served as the engines of growth historically, but how lasting are their impacts? To find out, and following Jia,[14] we compare the treaty ports and SIPs with the non-port cities, and find that both types of historical ports outperform their non-port counterparts in terms of GDP, per capita GDP, fiscal income, and manufacturing output of 2010, suggesting that

---

[13] S. Bo, C. Liu, and Z. Yan, "Military Investment, Industrial Linkage, and the Rise of Cluters: Evidence from China," Working Paper, Jinan University, 2020.

[14] R. Jia, "The Legacies of Forced Freedom: China's Treaty Ports," *Review of Economics and Statistics* 96.4 (2014), 596–608.

they might have had a long-term effect on economic development. A potentially fruitful topic of future research concerns the possible channels through which their effects persist over time.

Another angle from which to assess the contributions of treaty ports to economic development is to examine the extent to which human capital or education developed in that context vis-à-vis the non-port environment. We begin with the role of the missionaries. By introducing an entirely new curriculum that incorporated not only the modern sciences of mathematics and physics but also such social science subjects as geography, the missionaries gradually but surely overhauled the Chinese educational system underpinned by the Confucian classics. In an attempt to replace the civil service examination system and modernize the education system, the Qing government established a set of "new schools" ranging from primary to middle schools and equipped with a largely modern curriculum close on the heels of the missionary endeavors. Complementing this effort, the Qing government further decreed that at least one modern university be established in every single provincial capital alongside the private and missionary universities. Our analysis finds that both treaty ports and SIPs are correlated with the establishment of universities in general, and of universities with an engineering school in particular. We give special emphasis to engineering schools as they provided the specific human capital required by many industrial firms established back then. Not surprisingly, there were more engineers in the treaty ports and SIPs, who presumably were employed by the modern industrial firms located therein.

It is certainly no exaggeration to suggest that, by making a last-ditch effort, Qing China had made major strides on the economic front in its last fifty years or so of imperial rule, to the extent that the empire could have been successfully transformed down the road had it not been brought down abruptly by the 1911 Xinhai Revolution 辛亥革命. Perhaps this reflects how history is made. While the political elites (the Constitutionalists) had mustered the will and energy to strengthen a significantly weakened China, for instance by spearheading the development of modern firms and banks and establishing a national assembly, by adopting a modern education system based on the corpus of knowledge allegedly "useful" for modernization, and by sending students overseas to acquire new knowledge deemed useful for reforming China, the revolutionaries saw the Manchu empire as incapable of creating a new and stronger China. With Western ideas and political ideologies infiltrating China rapidly via the media (newspapers) and the universities, among other channels, it was the overseas students – especially those who studied in Japan and were supposed to return to help build a new China – who were most inclined to join the revolutionary organizations, whose alliance eventually succeeded in overthrowing the Qing government. The rest, as they say, is history.

The remainder of this chapter is organized as follows. In the next section, we first provide a brief introduction to the treaty ports and SIPs. This is followed immediately by an examination of their impact in terms of FDI and FD, market integration, "demonstration effects" for the domestic modern firms and banks, and technology adoption. Without claiming causality and identifying the specific channels, we also make an attempt to assess their effects over the long run. We then examine the development of human capital or education in the treaty ports vis-à-vis the non-port cities, by emphasizing the initial role of the missionaries in introducing to the Chinese a brand new curriculum based on Western education, and the birth of the modern university and specifically the training of engineers amid China's nascent industrialization. Finally, we examine the growing popularity of studying in Japan after China's defeat in the Sino-Japanese War, and how that may have made possible the 1911 Xinhai Revolution. The chapter ends with a few brief concluding remarks.

Treaty Ports

Treaty ports were ports conceded by the Qing government after its defeat by Great Britain during the First Opium War in 1840. A treaty (the Treaty of Nanking of 1842) was signed, according to which five ports located on the south and southeast coast of China – Shanghai, Guangzhou (previously Canton), Fuzhou (Foochow), Xiamen (Amoy), and Ningbo (Ningpo) – were forced to open up to the West for international trade (panel A of Figure 11.1).

In the treaty ports, Great Britain successfully negotiated a set of privileges beyond the restricted rights of the previous "Canton system," whereby foreigners were allowed to conduct business with the Chinese only in the port city of Canton and only via the institutional arrangement known as the "Thirteen Hongs."[15] The treaty now allowed the foreigners to reside and

---

[15] For example, see J.K. Fairbank (ed.), *The Cambridge History of China*, vol. 11, *Late Ch'ing 1800–1911*, part 2 (Cambridge, Cambridge University Press, 1980). Essentially the "Thirteen Hongs" monopolized trading with the foreigners; in other words, anyone who wished to trade with China could only do so via the "hongs."

The Economic Impact of the West

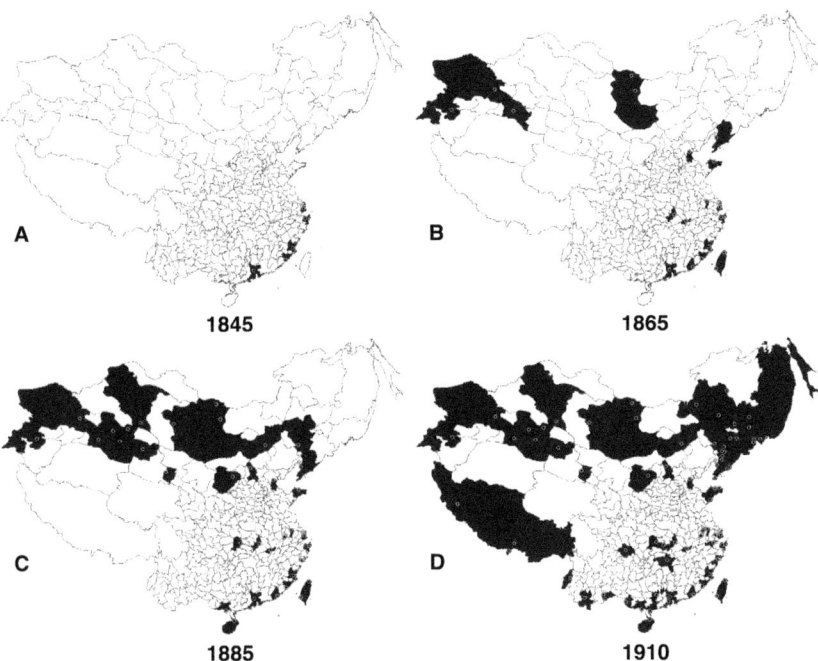

Figure 11.1 Expansion of the treaty port system (indicated by the prefectures in which they were located)
Source: Zhang Hongxiang 張洪祥, 近代中國通商口岸與租界 (Treaty Ports and Concessions in Chinese History) (Tianjin, Tianjin renmin chubanshe, 1993)

conduct business in the port cities, to spread Christianity, and even to lease land in perpetuity in the so-called "concessions" or *zujie* 租界. Moreover, the extraterritorial privileges conferred upon the foreigners allowed them essentially diplomatic immunity as they were exempted from Chinese jurisprudence but instead abided by the legal system of their mother country.[16]

But it was the Second Opium War of 1856 that culminated in the further expansion of these ports from a handful to approximately forty between 1860 and 1894, after China was forced to sign two additional treaties (the Treaty of Tientsin (now Tianjin)) and the Treaty of Peking (now Beijing)) upon its defeat – treaties that essentially reaffirmed and expanded the initial privileges conferred in 1842. As Figure 11.1 shows, China was forced to open up eleven

[16] For example, see J.K. Fairbank, *Trade and Diplomacy on the China Coast: The Opening of the Treaty Ports, 1842–1854* (Cambridge, MA: Harvard University Press, 1953).

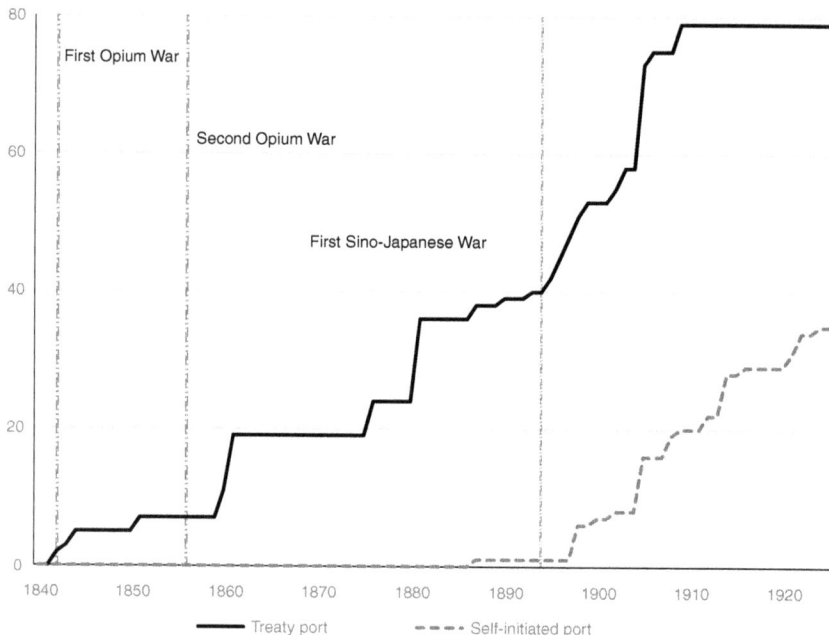

Figure 11.2 Growth in the number of treaty ports and self-initiated ports
Source: Chang Yufa 張玉法, 近代中國工業發展史, 1860–1916 (A History of Modern Chinese Industrial Development: 1860–1916) (Taipei, Gui guan tu shu you xian gong si, 1992)

more ports, this time along the coast and in particular along the Yangzi river – the country's main navigable river, and also up in the far north (panel B). With the passage of time, more ports were added, especially in both the northeast and the northwest (panel C).

The subsequent treaties did not merely expand the number of ports in which foreigners could conduct trade and business in China. These new treaties gave foreigners access also to the non-treaty ports, namely the inland regions, as explorers, businessmen, and missionaries, among other roles.[17]

Finally, after half a century of development, treaty ports were further expanded with the signing of the Treaty of Shimonoseki in 1895, after China was defeated by the Japanese in the First Sino-Japanese War a year earlier. It was during the 1895–1910 period that the number of treaty ports peaked, reaching a total of seventy-seven, excluding Taiwan and Hong Kong, which

[17] Spence, The Search for Modern China.

were colonies of Japan and the UK respectively. In particular, more ports had now been added in both the northeast and the southwest alongside further expansion elsewhere, enlarging the ports' trading networks with those of the hinterland (see panel D in Figure 11.1). Figure 11.2 shows the expansion of treaty ports over time.

"Self-Initiated Ports" (SIPs)

Existing literature has focused almost exclusively on the role of the treaty ports, while neglecting that played by the "self-initiated ports," which essentially represented a concerted response by the Chinese to the escalating demand made by the foreign powers to open up more ports for trade and business after China's defeat in the Sino-Japanese War.[18] What the Chinese feared was not treaty ports per se, which they recognized had attracted trade and other investment opportunities. Rather, they were concerned that some of the treaty ports might end up becoming "concessions" to the foreign powers, as in the case of Shanghai, which would necessitate their conceding the associated fiscal (taxes), judicial, and policing rights – the so-called "extraterritoriality," all of which contravened the Qing legal code and administrative practices.[19] While the humiliation that resulted from granting extraterritoriality to the foreign powers had led to a new sense of national indignation and heightened concerns about sovereignty, the awareness that treaty ports might bring trade and investment benefits led the Qing government to willingly open up more ports, but on their own terms.

To convince the foreign powers that their business interests would not be compromised in the SIPs, they were guaranteed the same freedom to trade and invest in these ports, which were now overseen by the provincial governor or *xunfu* 巡撫. More importantly, the Chinese promised to set up a new legal system that would better protect foreign business interests, and to invest in public infrastructure and employ measures to strengthen public health. Unlike in the concessions, however, the Chinese government would maintain the rights to collect taxes, adjudicate disputes, and provide public

---

[18] For an in-depth discussion of the self-initiated ports, see Zhang Hongxiang 張洪祥, 近代中國通商口岸與租界 (Treaty Ports and Concessions in Chinese History) (Tianjin, Tianjin renmin chubanshe, 1993); Zhang Jianqiu 張建俅, 清末自開商埠之研究 (1898–1911) (Research on the Self-Initiated Ports of the Late Qing (1898–1911)) (Taipei, Huamulan wenhua chubanshe, 2009).

[19] For example, Zou Rong 鄒容 – a revolutionary – was pursued by the Qing government for his inflammatory writings against the Manchu regime. By living in the foreign concession of Shanghai, he was spared arrest and possibly execution, as the foreign authorities steadfastly refused to hand him over to the Qing administration. See Spence, *The Search for Modern China*.

security – the set of rights that collectively define sovereignty. And instead of perpetuity, land rights would only be extended to foreigners for a maximum of sixty years – a measure presumably designed to retain sovereign rights.

Altogether thirty-five SIPs were established, and about half (seventeen) were explicitly established for the purpose of avoiding the need to give concessions to the foreign powers. For instance, the "Ningbo model"[20] – a prefecture located in southeast China and which is in close proximity to Shanghai – was proposed by Zhang Zhidong, the governor-general of the provinces of Jiangsu and Jiangxi after easing Emperor Guangxu's concern about the appropriateness of setting up SIPs. Yuezhou prefecture in Hunan province is another example of one of the earlier SIPs. Additionally, as soon as the Qing government became convinced that the proactive establishment of SIPs could in fact help preserve its power, another eighteen of these zones were further established as "trade hubs" in direct competition with the treaty ports. A related strategic concern was that, in anticipating the construction of the railway, the Qing government feared that failure to establish a SIP in each of these "economic zones" might run the risk of losing their control rights to the foreigners. Figure 11.2 shows the development of SIPs in the context of the overall development of treaty ports. Although both types of ports had experienced sharp growth since 1895, it is clear that the SIPs were essentially a product of the Treaty of Shimonoseki.

An interesting question arises in regard to the *locational* choice of the two types of ports. Were the SIPs set up strategically to capture the benefits of trade? If so, were they chosen in close geographic proximity to the treaty ports? Figure 11.3 shows that by and large the SIPs were established near the treaty ports. It would appear that their specific locations were so chosen as to maximize the prospects of trade. To address this issue more systematically we perform a simple multivariate analysis. As reported in Table 11.1, we find that treaty ports and SIPs are indeed significantly correlated, regardless of whether we are using locations of the treaty ports – defined by the prefecture in which a port was located (column 1), or distance to the treaty ports as the pertinent measure (columns 3–4). Additionally, Table 11.1 also reveals that the SIPs were located close to the railway line, lending weight to the claim that

---

[20] While Ningbo was one of the five earliest treaty ports, the Taiping Rebellion significantly weakened the foreigners' dominance there. This unwittingly enabled the Chinese to regain much of the de facto control rights in Ningbo, despite its treaty port status. Inspired by the Ningbo experience, Zhang Zhidong thus proposed to Emperor Guangxu that China should establish more ports to capture the benefits of trade, but retain more control over fiscal and other property rights in the newly established ports.

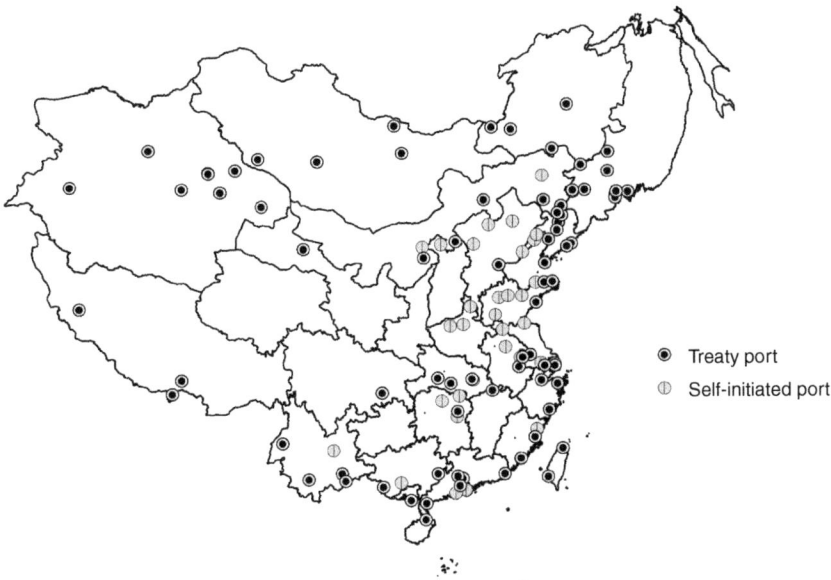

Figure 11.3 Geographical distribution of treaty ports and self-initiated ports
Source: Chang, 近代中國工業發展史

they were initiated because the Chinese did not want to see cities with easy access to the railway line falling into the hands of foreign powers (columns 2–4).[21]

The Impact of Treaty Ports

Foreign Direct Investment and Foreign Debt

Conventionally, treaty ports were viewed either as a carrier of technology via trade and investments,[22] or as a destructive force capable of impoverishing certain sectors of the population and economy, particularly the

---

[21] In Table 11.1 we also compare several key features of the two types of port cities, ranging from geographic characteristics (e.g. distance to major navigable river and to coast) to population density and growth rate in various periods where such data are available (1776, 1820, and 1851), but we fail to find any significant statistical difference. Thus we do not report their results separately.
[22] See Hou, *Foreign Investment and Economic Development in China*; Murphey, *The Treaty Ports and China's Modernization*; Dernberger, "The Role of the Foreigner in China's Economic Development."

Table 11.1 Locations of self-initiated ports

	(1)	(2)	(3)	(4)
		Self-initiated ports		
Treaty ports	1.409***	0.913**		
	(0.411)	(0.455)		
Railway		0.599***	0.652***	0.631***
		(0.107)	(0.105)	(0.133)
Distance to treaty port				
0 kilometer			1.897***	1.691**
			(0.643)	(0.739)
1–50 kilometers			1.739**	1.442*
			(0.718)	(0.800)
50–100 kilometers			2.183***	2.089***
			(0.734)	(0.765)
100–200 kilometers			1.417*	1.378*
			(0.747)	(0.822)
Distance to main river (log)				−0.056
				(0.040)
Distance to coast (log)				−0.047
				(0.049)
Distance to provincial capital (log)				0.001
				(0.042)
Observations	377	377	377	367
Robust standard error	Yes	Yes	Yes	Yes

Note. These are logistic regressions. Robust standard errors in parentheses, $^{*}p < 0.1$, $^{**}p < 0.05$, $^{***}p < 0.01$.

countryside.[23] Despite the fact that treaty ports had existed for a long time (since the 1840s), systematic data on FDI and FD are available only for a much later period (c. 1902–1936).[24] Figure 11.4, which shows these trends, reveals that FDI always exceeded FD, and with a widening trend since around the late 1910s, whereas FD (which did not include government bonds) remained basically stable during the entire period in which such information is available. Figure 11.5 further decomposes the sources of FDI and FD by host

---

[23] See H.D. Fong, *Rural Industries in China* (Shanghai, China Institute of Pacific Relations, 1933); H. Chen, *Landlord and Peasant in China: A Study of the Agrarian Crisis in South China* (New York, International Publishers, 1936); H.-T. Fei, *Peasant Life in China: A Field Study of Country Life in the Yangtze Valley* (London, Routledge & Keegan Paul, 1939); A. Feuerwerker, *The Chinese Economy, 1912–1949*, No. 1 (Ann Arbor, University of Michigan, Center for Chinese Studies, 1968).

[24] The data for 1902, 1930, and 1935 are extracted from Wu, 帝国主义, pp. 52–3; and the rest re-estimated by Xu and Wu, 中國資本主義發展史.

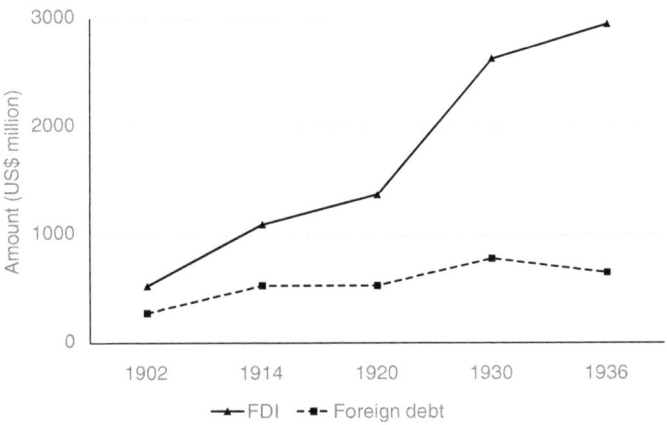

Figure 11.4 Foreign direct investment and debt
Source: Xu Dixin 許滌新 and Wu Chengming 吳承明 (eds.), 中國資本主義發展史 (Developmental History of Chinese Capitalism), 3 vols. (Beijing, Renmin chubanshe, 1985)

country. Among the six countries with major investment/debt relations with China, Japan ranked first, with disproportionate growth in FDI in the 1930s, followed by the United Kingdom. FDI for the remaining four countries, namely the United States, France, Germany, and Russia, was much smaller in magnitude.[25]

While these data are informative, a major limitation is that they are reticent on both geographic and sectoral distributions, although intuition would suggest that the bulk of these investments and debts had likely flowed into the Japanese and British spheres of the treaty ports and to a lesser extent the SIPs. To find out more about their geographic and sectoral distributions we turn to a data set compiled by Chang on the number of foreign industrial firms entering China and their initial registered capital,[26] and the nature of their business. Figure 11.6 shows the geographic distribution of these foreign private firms, whereas Figure 11.7 breaks down their investment by country of origin. Consistent with the initial observation that Japan was the largest source of FDI, these firms were indeed mostly located in the northeastern part of China – a territory where Japan had a distinct "sphere of influence," followed by the southern coast, presumably representing Britain's economic interest. Figure 11.7 confirms that Japan and Britain were indeed the biggest

---

[25] That Japan was the most enthusiastic investor in China might be seen as a harbinger of Japanese military aggression later on.
[26] Chang, "清末民初的外資工業." There were many missing values, however.

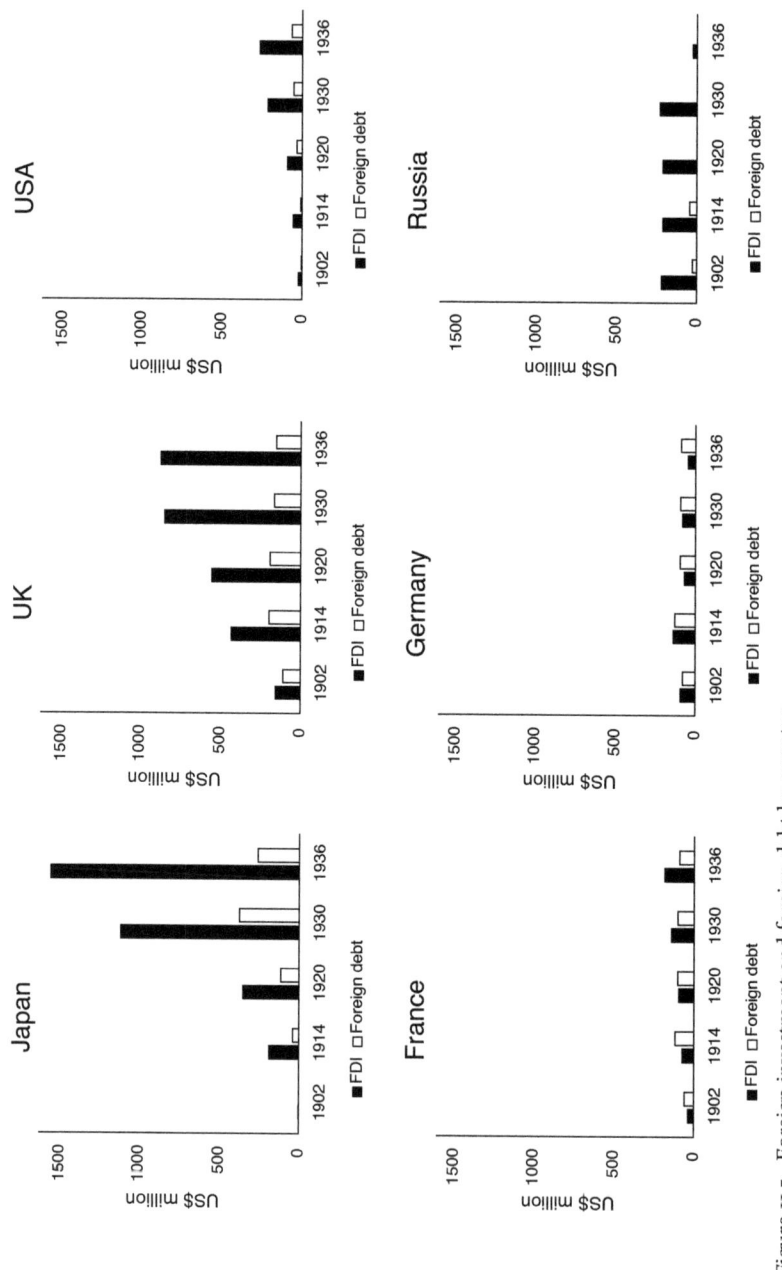

Figure 11.5 Foreign investment and foreign debt by country
Source: Xu and Wu, 中國資本主義發展史

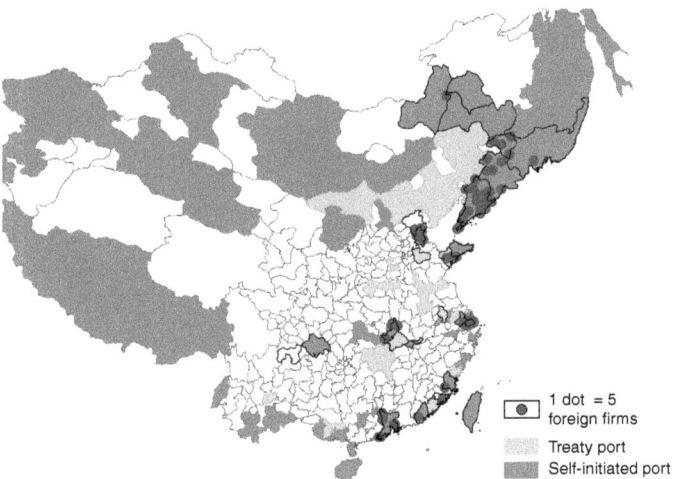

Figure 11.6 Geographic distribution of foreign private firms
Source: Chang, 近代中國工業發展史

foreign investors in China. What Figure 11.7 also tells us is that, while Japan's foreign investments in China remained low for the first fifty years or so before surging after 1900 and surpassing those of Britain by around the mid-1910s, Britain's rise as a major foreign investor in China followed a smoother gradual trend for more than half a century.[27]

Chang's data also enable us to identify the sectors in which these foreigners were investing.[28] Figure 11.8 shows their distribution based on our own classification. With the exception of ten firms which we find difficult to classify,[29] we sort the remaining 485 foreign firms that entered China between 1841 and 1916 into twelve sectors. As shown, the largest sector was food and beverages, which included tobacco, alcohol, tea, sugar, salt, soda, flour, and oil processing, followed (by a wide margin) by machinery, which included shipping, motor vehicles, electrical appliances (both manufacturing and

---

[27] Though referring to a much later period (c. 1936), Duus finds that the great majority of cotton mills in China were owned by the Japanese, accounting for 40 percent and 57 percent of all of China's machine-spun yarn and machine-woven cloth respectively. P. Duus, "Zaikabo: Japanese Cotton Mills in China," in P. Duus, R. Myers, and M. Peattie (eds.), *The Japanese Informal Empire, 1895–1937* (Princeton, Princeton University Press, 1989), pp. 129–249.
[28] Chang, "清末民初的外資工業."
[29] For example, a couple of these firms were engaged in the production of musical instruments, whereas several others were canneries.

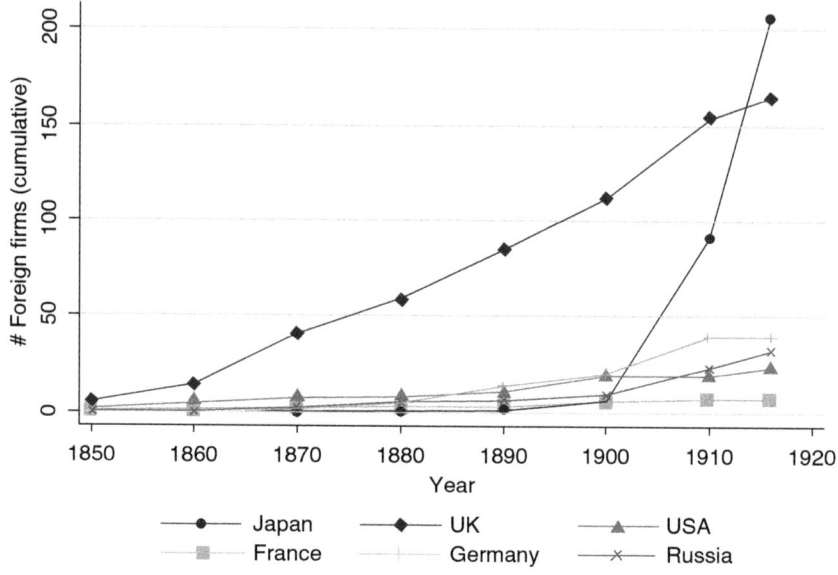

Figure 11.7 Foreign firms, by country of origin
Source: Chang, 清末民初的外資工業

maintenance), and others. The next three largest sectors were utilities (primarily electricity, water, and gas), textiles and silk, and chemicals (dyes, matches and kerosene, paint, cosmetics, soap, rubber, tires, and so forth). Virtually all of these sectors were related to consumption (with shipping perhaps the only exception), suggesting that the foreign firms were likely capitalizing on the changing consumption habits and possibly rising standard of living of the Chinese people.

Treaty Ports and Market Integration

A particular perspective from which to assess the effects of treaty ports is to examine the extent to which they helped develop or integrate markets, such as by sourcing goods from all over China for export, and, conversely, importing and disseminating goods from abroad. By making use of a survey conducted in the mid-1930s by the postal office (Chunghwa Post), which contains information on the geographic distribution of goods shipped from virtually all the counties in China via both types of ports, we are able to document not only trade flows but also their corresponding value. We begin with panel A of Figure 11.9, which shows the already wide geographic

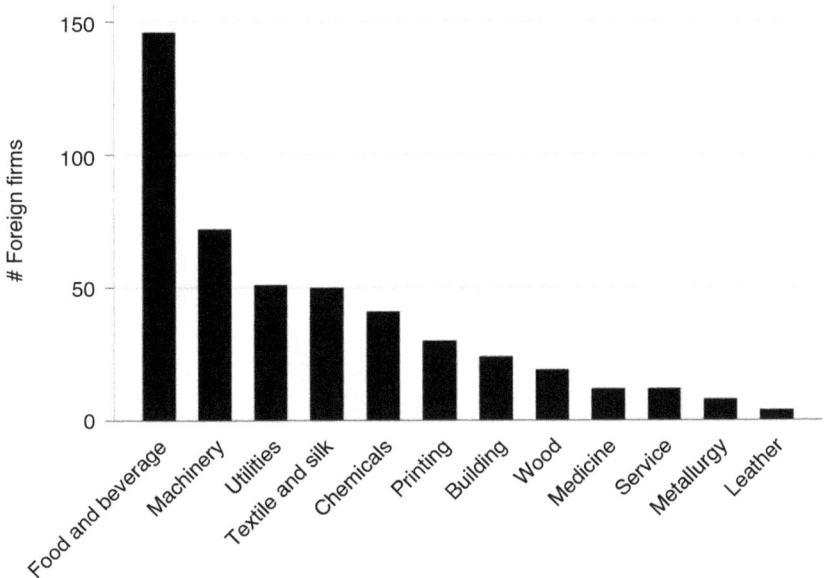

Figure 11.8 Sectoral distribution of foreign firms
Source: Chang, 清末民初的外資工業

coverage of trade after the signing of the Treaty of Nanking of 1842. In particular, the twelve earliest treaty ports were the ones where the majority of trading networks were established.[30] In terms of trade volume, Shanghai and Nanjing had an approximately 27 percent larger value of shipments than those ports founded later, and double the value of shipments of the SIPs. But huge discrepancies also existed among these earlier treaty ports. Shanghai, for example, was nearly three times the size of Guangzhou and Fuzhou and nine times that of Xiamen. Their differences notwithstanding, by 1935 nearly everywhere in China sold produce to these dozen treaty ports. In panel B, more trading networks were established after the signing of the subsequent two treaties (Treaty of Tientsin in 1858 and Treaty of Peking in 1861). In panels C and D, we connect the flow of goods to those treaty ports opened later and the SIPs, which when compared with the earlier ports had a very limited scope

---

[30] These twelve ports were Shanghai, Xiamen, Ningbo, Guangzhou, and Fuzhou under the Treaty of Nanking of 1842; Jiujiang, Nanjing, Shantou, Yantai, Yingkou, and Zhenjiang under the Treaty of Tientsin of 1860; and Tientsin under the Treaty of Peking of 1861.

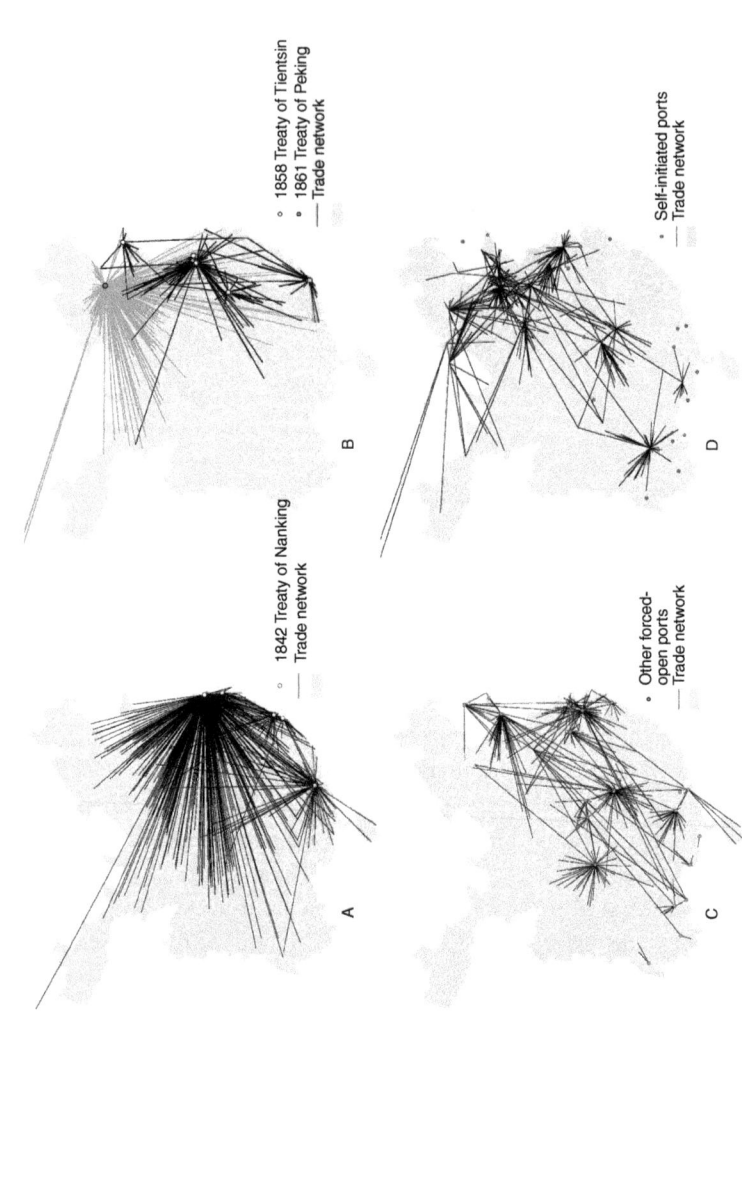

Figure 11.9 Domestic trade network
Source: Chunghwa Post survey (1935)

Treaty Ports and Modernization

The role of treaty ports in facilitating modern economic growth is a question that had to wait until the early 1990s for a systematic answer, after historian Du Xuncheng (1991) assembled a list of newly established industrial firms and banks for the 1840–1927 period.[31] As suggested by the title of his book, 民族資本主義與舊中國政府 (National Capitalism and the Old Chinese Government), the kinds of firms enumerated therein were all established by the Chinese, and the majority of them were either state-owned (*guanban* 官辦) or privately owned, with the rest being privately funded but managed by government officials (*guandu shangban* 官督商辦).[32] In this context we use the number of modern firms and the number of modern financial institutions (or simply banks) enumerated in Du's book as the two indicators of modern economic growth. Our first step is to examine the role of treaty ports in attracting these foreign institutions, before examining the "demonstration effect," if any, that they may have had on their domestic counterparts. Upon establishing these lines of evidence, we then examine the locational choice of the domestic firms and banks, i.e. whether they set up operations in the treaty ports, the SIPs, or the non-port cities. Basically, we would expect all foreign firms and banks to establish their operations in the treaty ports, and a substantial proportion of the domestic firms and banks to do so in both treaty ports and SIPs. Last but not least we examine the issue of technology adoption; specifically, we are interested in finding out the extent to which domestic firms adopted the Industrial Revolution technology of the steam engine and/or electricity.

Figure 11.10 first shows the growth trend of foreign firms and banks. Whereas foreign firms grew more linearly in the earlier period (between 1840 and 1890), foreign banks experienced two spikes of growth – one

---

[31] To be sure, Feuerwerker has also estimated that at least 549 Chinese-owned modern mining and manufacturing enterprises had been established by 1913, a mere two years after the fall of the Qing dynasty. Du's number, however, is in the thousands. Feuerwerker, *The Chinese Economy, 1912–1949*; Du Xuncheng 杜恂誠, 民族資本主義與舊中國政府, 1840–1937 (Chinese Capitalism and the Old Chinese Government, 1840–1937) (Shanghai, Shanghai shehui kexueyuan chubanshe, 1991).

[32] Chang also enumerates firms for the 1841–1916 period, but he classifies them according to whether they were foreign (1987) or domestic (1989). Chang, *Foreign Industries in Late Qing and Early Republican China*; Chang Yufa 張玉法, "清末民初的民營工業" (Domestic Private Industries in Late Qing and Early Republican China), *Bulletin of the Institute of Modern History, Academia Sinica*, 1989.

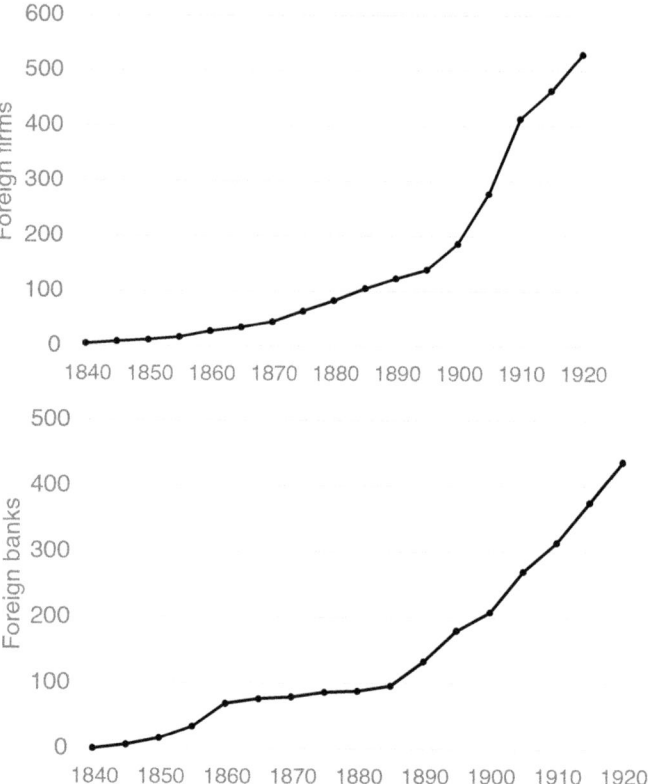

Figure 11.10 Numerical growth of foreign firms and banks
Source: Huang Guangyu 黃光域, 外國在華工商企業辭典 (Dictionary for Foreign Industrial and Business Enterprises in China) (Chengdu, Sichuan renmin chubanshe, 1995), for foreign firms; *Yearbook of National Banks* (1934) for foreign banks

between 1840 and 1890 and the other between 1900 and 1920. In Figure 11.11 we superimpose the locations of the foreign firms and banks on those of the treaty ports. We find the two to be highly correlated spatially, which is as expected given that it would be highly unlikely for foreign institutions to be established in cities outside the treaty ports where the foreigners would be distinctly less protected.

We then examine the development of domestic firms and banks based on Du's data.[33] As Figure 11.12 shows, the latter experienced rapid growth only

[33] Du, 民族資本主義與舊中國政府.

The Economic Impact of the West

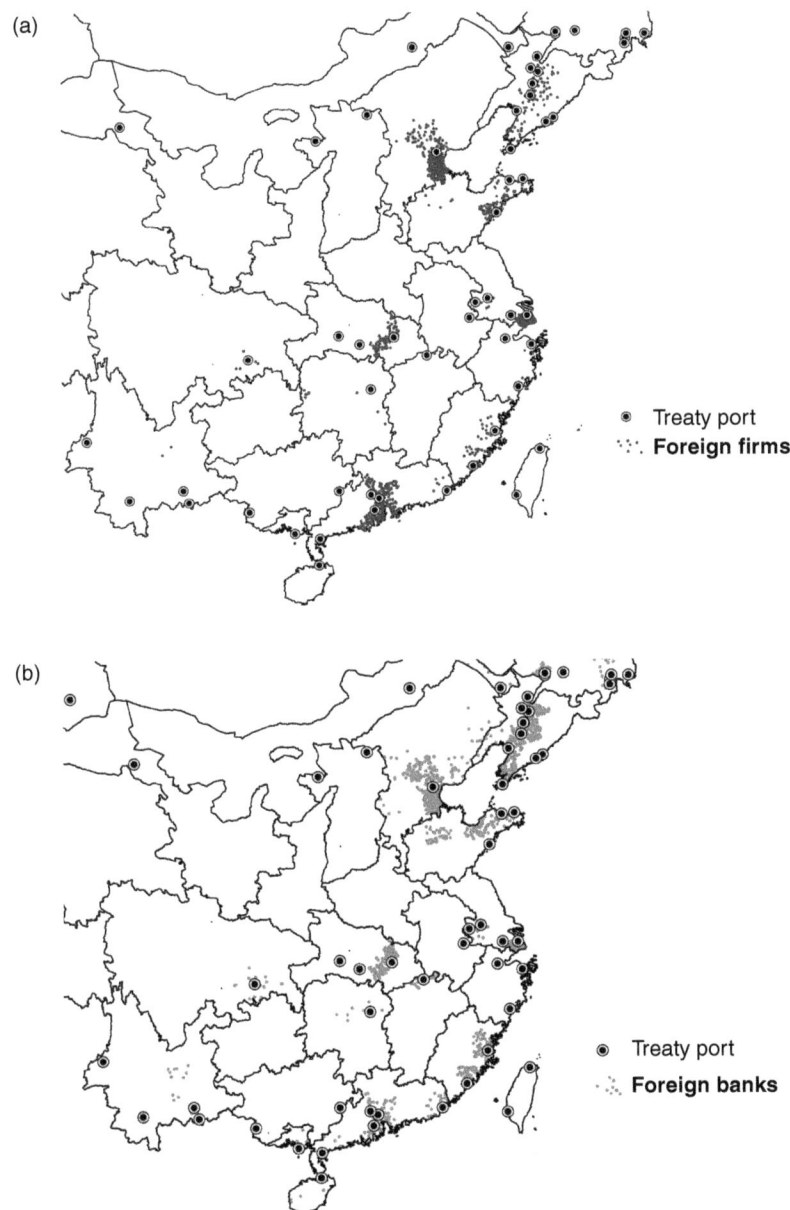

Figure 11.11 Geographical distribution of foreign firms and banks (1920s)
Data Source: Huang, 外國在華工商企業辭典, for foreign firms; *Yearbook of National Banks* (1934) for foreign banks

after the 1900s, presumably after the Treaty of Shimonoseki, as earlier alluded. Figure 11.13, which geo-codes the locations of the domestic institutions, shows that they are in strikingly close proximity to where the SIPs were established, suggesting that the foreign firms and banks might have produced a "demonstration effect" on the domestic institutions. To test this conjecture, we perform a multivariate analysis. Regardless of whether we are using treaty ports to proxy for "Western" economic impact (e.g. columns 1 and 3 of Table 11.2) or more specifically using the actual number of foreign firms and banks (columns 2 and 4) as predictors, the relationship between these measures and the number of domestic firms and banks is statistically significant, suggesting that foreign firms and banks likely had a "demonstration effect" on the domestic institutions.[34] Using only the treaty ports sample for the test similarly confirms this salient finding (columns 5 and 6).

Another angle from which to examine the role of the treaty ports and SIPs is to ask where the modern Chinese firms and banks chose to set up their operations.[35] Did they, for instance, also choose to operate in the treaty ports for possible agglomeration and other benefits conferred by their foreign counterparts, or did they opt for the SIPs or even the non-port cities, to avoid fierce competition? Figure 11.14 provides some clues to this important strategic question. More firms had chosen to operate within the treaty ports than in the SIPs or the non-ports, a trend that became more pronounced after 1890 (panel A).[36] This difference is even sharper for the banks, especially after 1910 (panel B). Only a handful of banks had chosen to establish themselves in cities with no special administrative status. The distinctly greater preference on the part of the domestic banks to operate in the treaty ports may underscore their reliance on the legal and accounting systems, which are essential for the proper functioning of the modern financial system.

---

[34] The idea of a "demonstration effect" hinges on whether there were factors other than foreign firms and banks affecting the rise of the domestic institutions. If there were, and we are unable to identify them, we would have overestimated the effect of the foreign institutions.

[35] Firms are considered modern provided that (a) their operations were powered by the steam engine or electricity, (b) they were relatively large, (c) they had a registered capital of at least 10,000 silver *yuan* or approximately 1,094 pounds sterling, (d) they employed at least thirty workers, (e) they produced an annual output of at least 50,000 silver *yuan* in value, and (f) they adopted modern (hierarchical) management practices. Similarly, the modern Chinese banks are not *qianzhuang* or native banks. Chang, "清末民初的民營工業."

[36] For example, for the 1916–1920 period, a treaty port prefecture attracted an average of fifteen modern domestic firms, whereas an SIP prefecture attracted six and a non-port prefecture three.

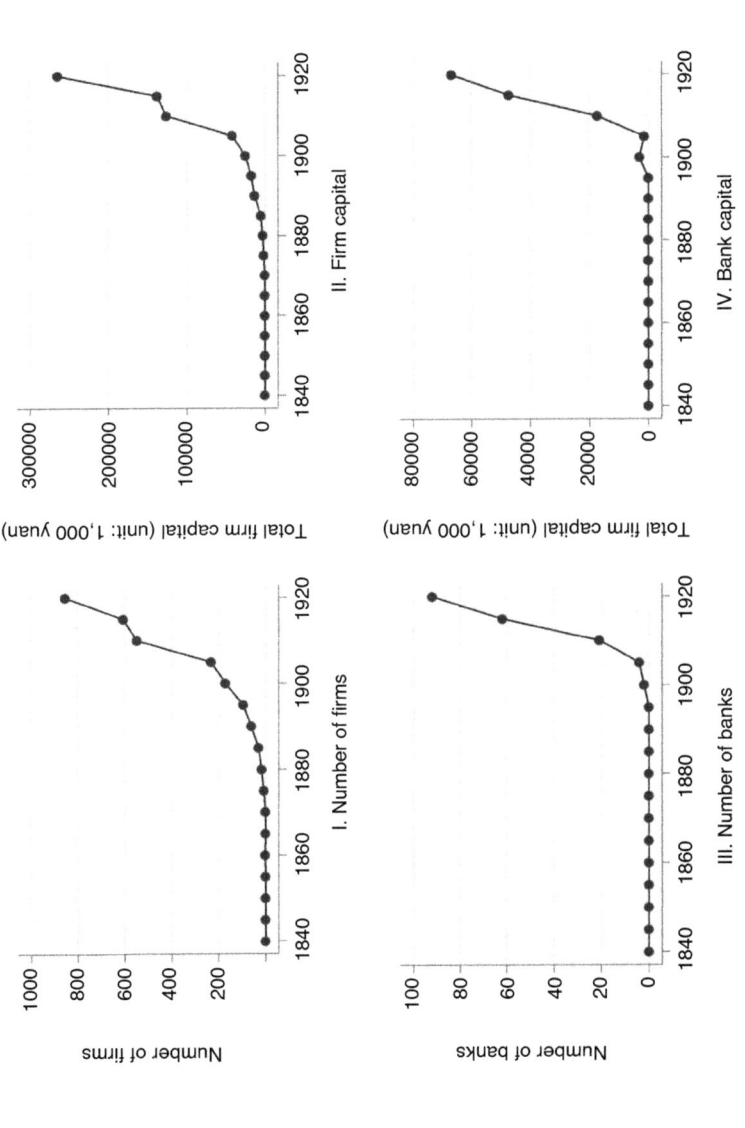

Figure 11.12 Rise of domestic modern firms and banks in China (total trend)
Source: Du, 民族資本主義与旧中国政府

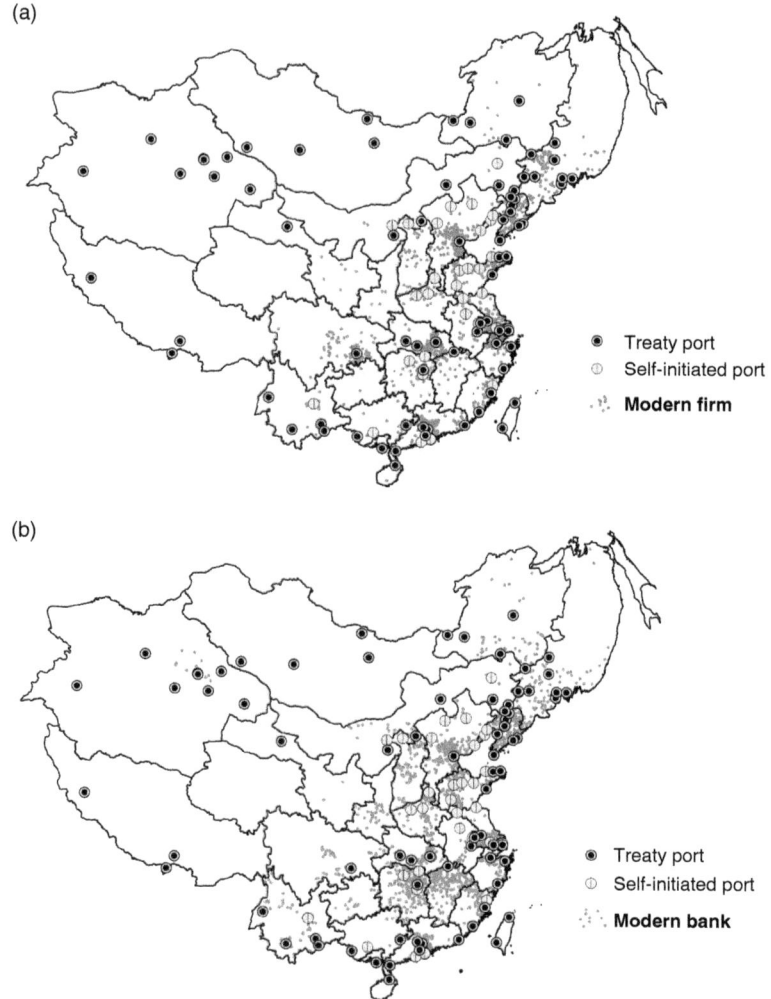

Figure 11.13 Geographical distribution of domestic modern firms and banks (1920s)
Source: Du, 民族資本主義与旧中国政府

Even though some modern Chinese firms and banks chose not to operate in either the treaty ports or the SIPs, they could still have been connected to these ports. We plot the locations of modern firms outside the treaty ports and SIPs according to the distance to their nearest treaty port and SIP (Figure 11.15). As can be seen, a good proportion of these institutions were actually located in close proximity to either a treaty port or a SIP, despite not being right in these ports.

Table 11.2 Impact of foreign firms and banks on domestic modern firms and banks

	Full sample				Treaty ports sample			
	Domestic firms (log)	Domestic banks (log)	Domestic firms (log)	Domestic banks (log)	Domestic firms (log)	Domestic banks (log)
Treaty ports	0.378***	0.176*	0.105***	0.083**		
	(0.090)	(0.090)	(0.032)	(0.034)		
Foreign firms (log)		0.748***			0.667***	
		(0.068)			(0.112)	
Foreign banks (log)				0.181***		0.105***
				(0.057)		(0.039)
Prefecture fixed effects	Yes	Yes	Yes	Yes	Yes	Yes
Year fixed effects	Yes	Yes	Yes	Yes	Yes	Yes
Provincial specific time trend	Yes	Yes	Yes	Yes	Yes	Yes
Observations	6786	6786	6786	6786	936	936
Adjusted R^2	0.478	0.603	0.200	0.208	0.760	0.324

Note. Standard errors in parentheses, $^*p < 0.1$, $^{**}p < 0.05$, $^{***}p < 0.01$

The extent to which treaty ports affected the locational choice of private firms and banks can be further illustrated by the extent to which they affected the locational choice of the munition factories established during the Self-Strengthening movement (c. 1868–1890). Bo, Liu, and Zhou find that some of these factories were located in or near the ports,[37] as Figure 11.16 shows, presumably to facilitate the import of raw materials and machinery from abroad. To confirm this, we regress the locations of munition factories first on the five earliest treaty ports selected after the Treaty of Nanking (c. 1842), then on the next nine agreed in the Treaties of Tientsin and Peking after China lost to Britain again in the Second Opium War and added during 1860–1864. Reported in columns 1 and 5 of Table 11.3, we find that the earliest treaty ports can indeed significantly account for the locational choice of the munition factories after controlling for a number of geographic variables.

---

[37] Bo, Liu, and Yan, "Military Investment, Industrial Linkage, and the Rise of Clusters."

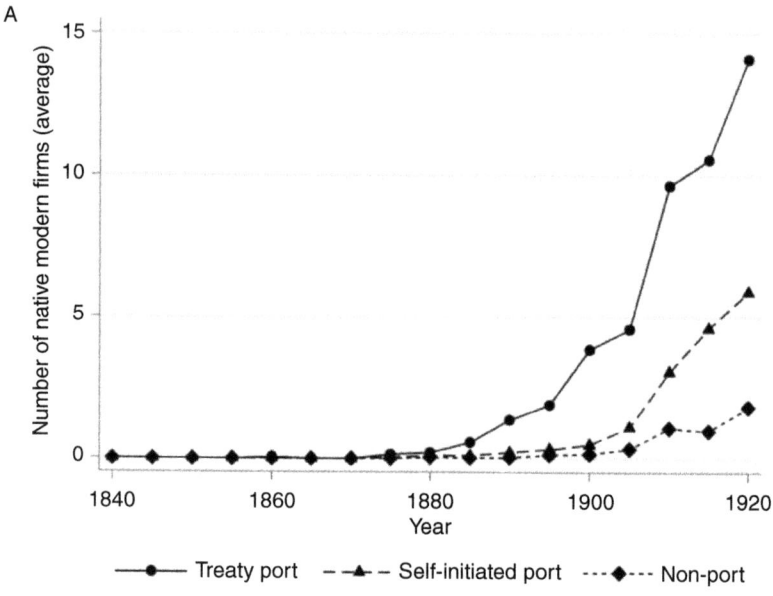
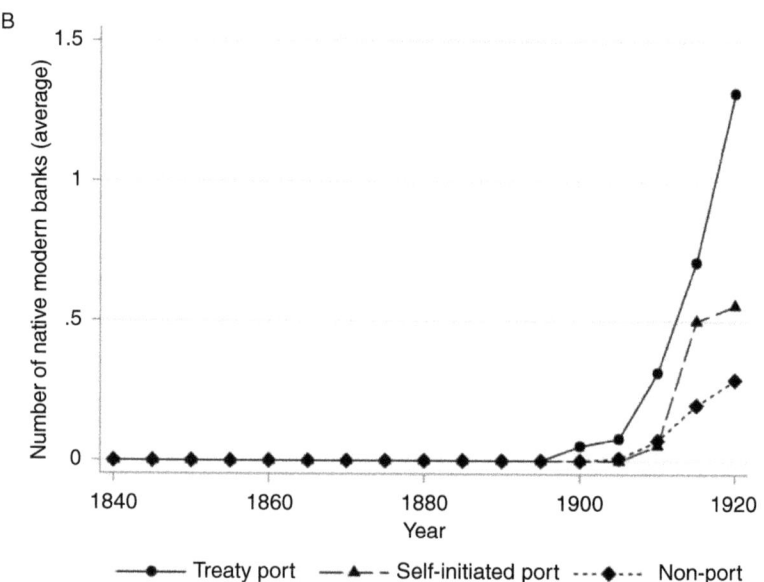

Figure 11.14 Development trend of domestic modern firms and banks
Source: Du, 民族資本主義與舊中國政府

The Economic Impact of the West

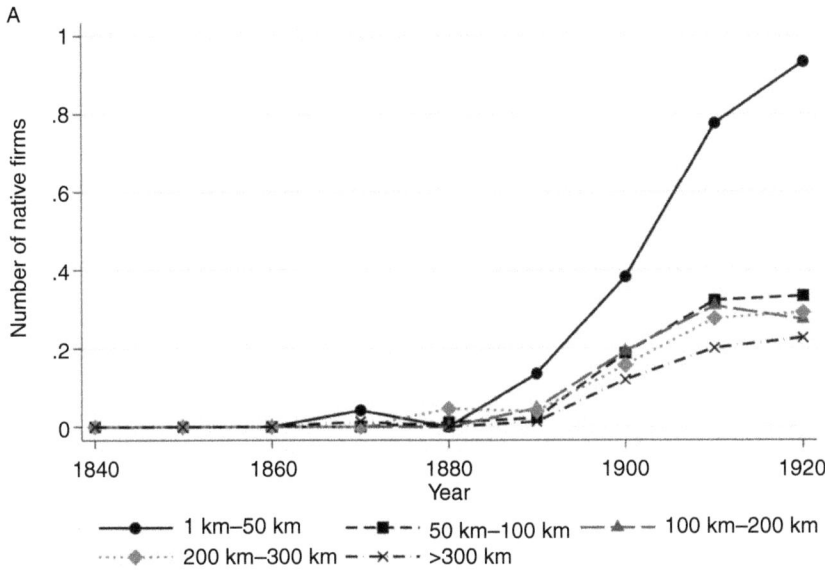

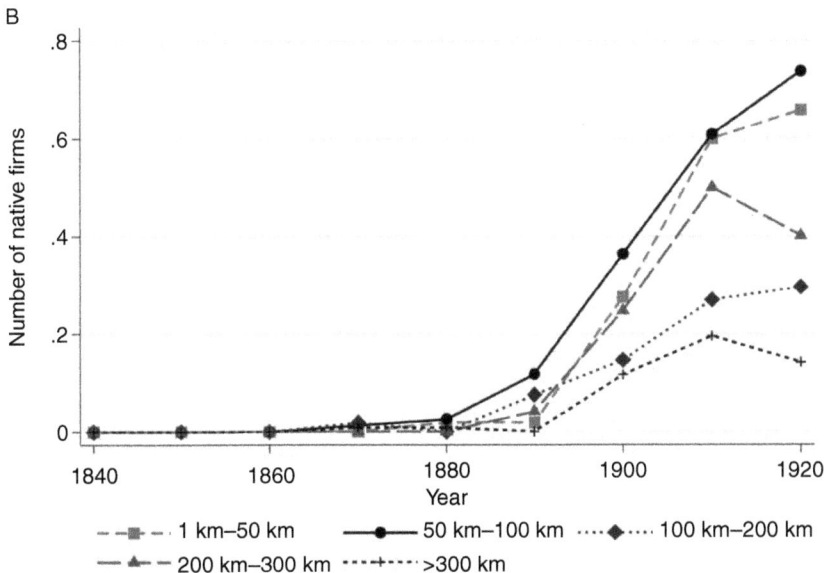

Figure 11.15 Development of domestic modern firms in non-port regions
Note. In panel A, distance indicates a prefecture's distance to the nearest treaty port. Likewise, in panel B, distance indicates a prefecture's distance to the nearest self-initiated port.
Source: Du, 民族資本主義與舊中國政府

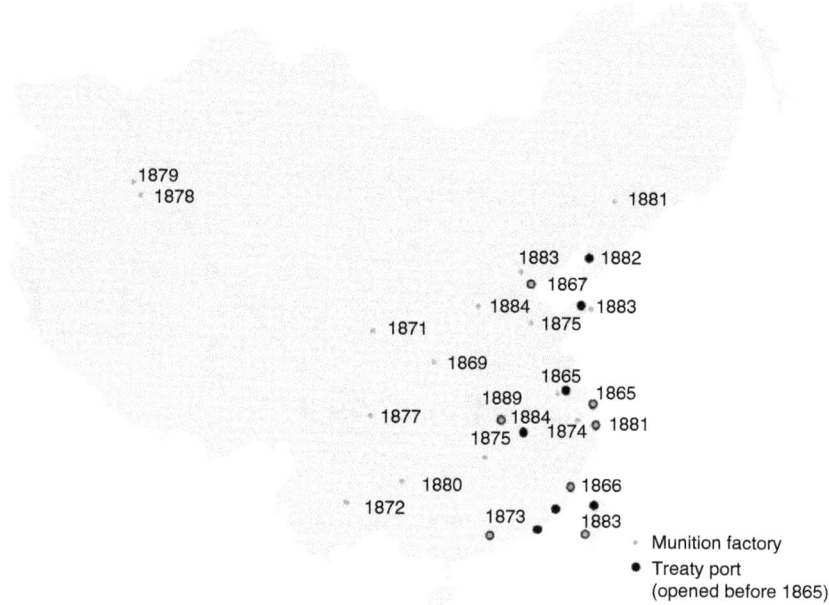

Figure 11.16 Spatial distribution of treaty ports opened before 1865 and munition factories
Source: Chang, 清末民初的外資工業; Fan Baichuan 樊百川, 清季的洋務新政 (The Qing Westernization Movement) (Shanghai, Shanghai shudian chubanshe, 2003)

Last but not least, we examine the issue of technology adoption, for the simple reason that the modernity of firms also depends crucially on whether they adopted an Industrial Revolution technology – most notably the steam engine and (subsequently) electricity. Figure 11.17 shows the overall growth trend of the capacity of China's power plants (1903–1931), with 1920 representing a year of rapid growth. Figure 11.18 maps the geographic distribution of China's earlier electrical plants in 1929, including those constructed by foreigners. An interesting feature of the development of electric power plants in that period is that the government only played a small part; in fact most of these plants were built through private endeavors. While most of the private electrical plants tended to be smaller in scale (in terms of generation capacity), they were built all over China. In particular, many were located in south and south-central China – locations where government efforts were visibly lacking.[38] Similar to the government-funded plants, the bulk of the foreign-built power generators

---

[38] These regions may have become more decentralized economically after the Taiping Rebellion, when a province like Hunan (in south-central China) had built up its own strong army with its tax income.

Table 11.3 Location of munition factories

	Munition factories
Treaty ports (first 5)	4.066***
	(1.145)
Distance to treaty port (first 5)	
0 kilometer	3.920***	2.568*	1.353
	(1.152)	(1.333)	(1.562)
1–200 kilometers	−0.557	−1.659	−3.743**
	(1.059)	(1.223)	(1.619)
200–400 kilometers	−0.384	−0.951	−0.726
	(0.775)	(0.741)	(0.924)
400–600 kilometers	−0.834	−1.441	−2.260*
	(1.054)	(1.288)	(1.373)
Treaty ports (first 14)				3.785***
				(0.662)
Distance to treaty port (first 14)	
0 kilometer					3.556***	3.825***	2.871**
					(0.718)	(1.119)	(1.168)
1–200 kilometers					0.200	0.368	−1.285
					(0.650)	(0.817)	(1.268)
200–400 kilometers					−0.736	−0.627	−1.281*
					(0.818)	(0.876)	(0.768)
400–600 kilometers					−1.146	−1.074	−1.579
					(1.085)	(1.097)	(1.076)

Table 11.3 (cont.)

	Munition factories				
Distance to coast (log)	−0.423* (0.221)	−0.782** (0.370)			0.080 (0.238)	−0.285 (0.368)
Distance to main river (log)		−0.173 (0.194)				−0.033 (0.194)
Distance to provincial capital (log)		−0.868*** (0.184)				0.837*** (0.170)
Observations	301	301	301	301	301	301
Robust standard error	Yes	Yes	Yes	Yes	Yes	Yes

Note. These are logistic regressions. Robust standard errors in parentheses, * p < 0.1, ** p < 0.05, *** p < 0.01.

The Economic Impact of the West

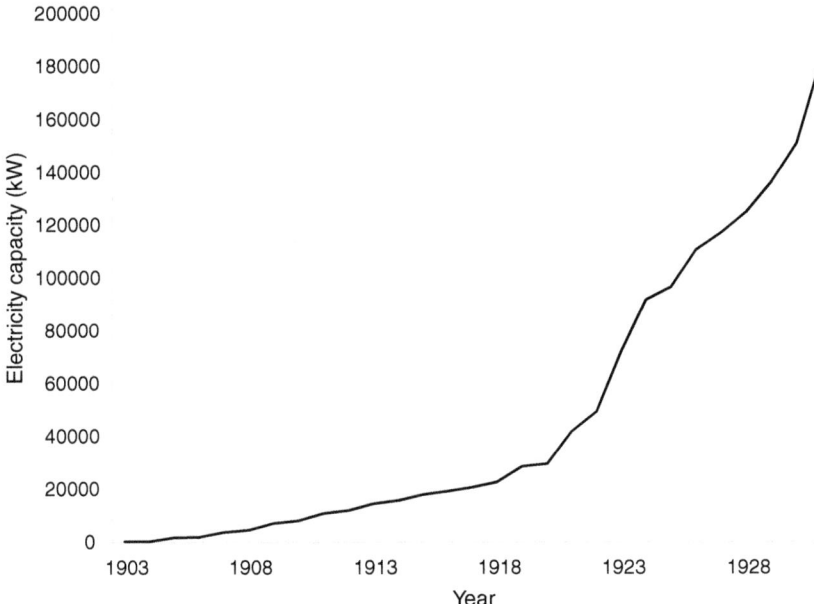

Figure 11.17 Growth of electrical power plants in China, 1903–1931
Source: *Shun pao* yearbook (1936)

were concentrated in north and northeastern China, where private interests, albeit small, were also well represented. Judging from the geographical coverage of the private electrical plants, it is by no means an exaggeration to suggest that private interests played a uniquely important role in spearheading the development of modern industrial firms in China.

As elsewhere, electrification came much later than the steam engine, and China was no exception in that regard.[39] Before the advent of electricity, firms in China were considered to be "modern" if they used machinery without necessarily powering it by steam; prominent examples included cotton gins in the textile industry, silk filatures, and bean cake fertilizer plants, according to a survey of so-called modern firms established between 1841 and 1916 by Chang.[40] This may explain why, when comparing the two panels of Figure 11.19, which plots the average number of firms adopting the

---

[39] Even in Japan, where industrialization occurred much earlier, many factories in the nine dominant industrial sectors still used the internal combustion engine in non-powered factories as late as the 1940s, according to R. Minami, "Mechanical Power in the Industrialization of Japan," *Journal of Economic History* 37.4 (1977), 935–58.

[40] Chang Yufa 張玉法, 近代中國工業發展史, 1860–1916 (A History of Modern Chinese Industrial Development, 1860–1916) (Taipei, Gui guan tu shu you xian gong si, 1992).

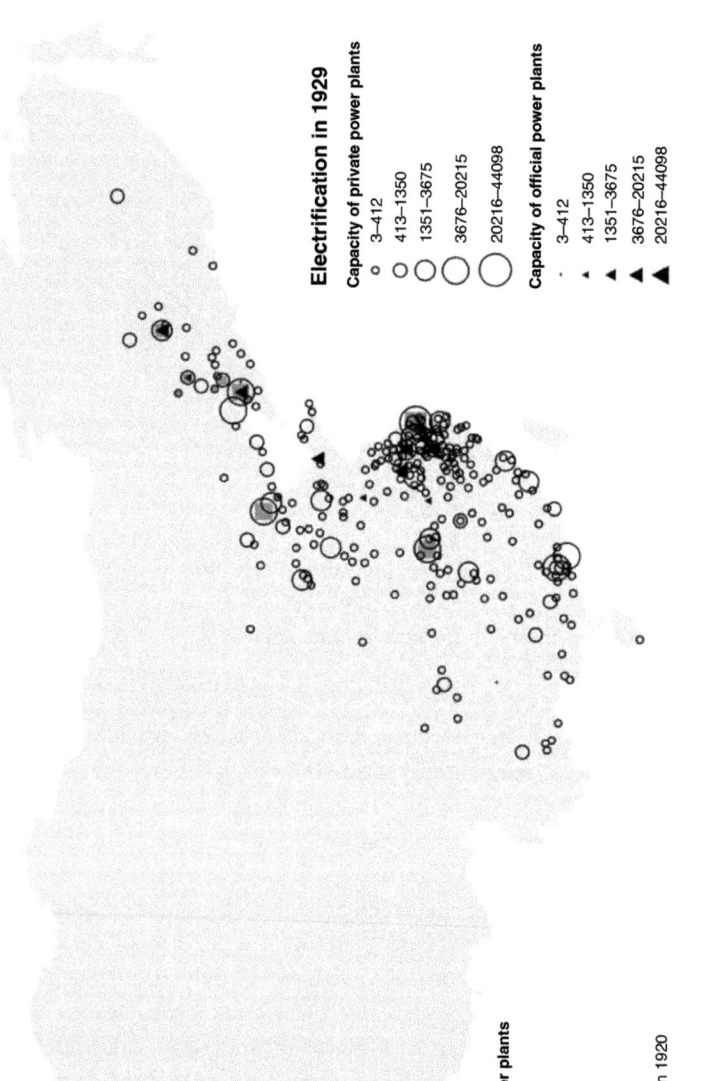

Figure 11.18 Electricity generation in China, 1929
Source: *Shun pao* yearbook (1936)

The Economic Impact of the West

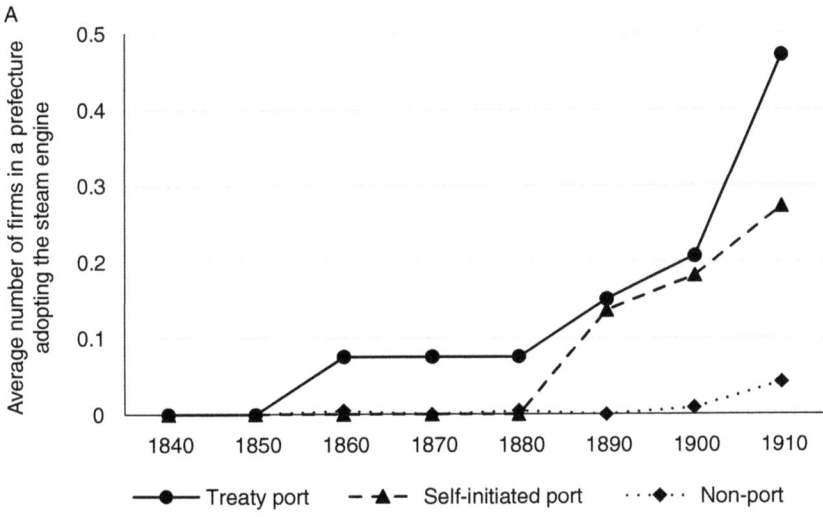

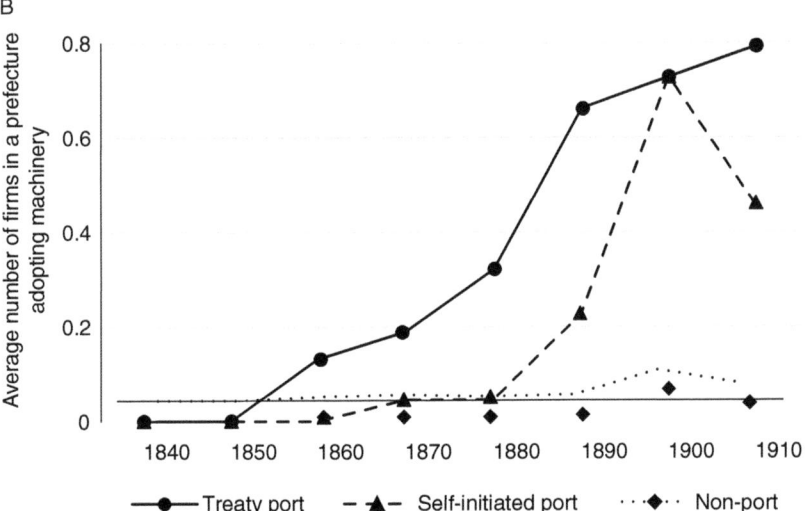

Figure 11.19 Adoption of the steam engine and machinery in modern Chinese firms
Source: Chang, 清末民初的外資工業

steam engine (panel A) and machinery (panel B) over time, more firms adopted machines than adopted the steam engine, and the trend toward mechanization started much earlier (from around 1850) than that toward the steam engine (panel A) – whose wider adoption had to wait until the 1880s

Table 11.4 Adoption rate of the steam engine and machinery

	Steam engine			Machinery		
	Treaty port	Self-initiated port	Non-port	Treaty port	Self-initiated port	Non-port
Adoption rate	6.8%	7.6%	6.4%	17.9%	15.6%	16.1%

Source: Chang, 清末民初的外資工業

(panel B).[41] In terms of the geography of adoption, both machinery and steam engines were more widely adopted by firms located in the treaty ports than in the SIPs and non-port cities.[42] However, if we consider the *percentage* rather than the number of firms adopting the two new technologies, it was actually similar across the three types of cities (Table 11.4).

The "Persistent" Effects of Treaty Ports

Using population and GDP growth as gauges in her study of the long-run growth effect of China's treaty ports, Jia finds that while treaty ports had no discernible effect on development during the communist period, prefectures in which treaty ports had been formerly established systematically experienced faster economic development in the wake of China's "open-door" policy in the 1980s.[43] To confirm this, we use four economic indicators in contemporary times (c. 2010) – GDP, GDP per capita, a prefecture's fiscal income, and industrial output – to compare the performance of treaty ports and SIPs with that of prefectures without any historical port status. We find that both types of ports perform significantly better today regardless of whether we control for a gamut of geographic factors that are likely correlated with economic performance (Table 11.5). For example, in column 1, both treaty ports and SIPs have higher GDP today than non-ports; controlling for various geographic factors only reduces their magnitude but not level of significance (column 2). The larger magnitude of treaty ports implies that

---

[41] The later adoption of the steam engine can be accounted for by the fact that the first steam engine in China was built by Xu Shou 徐壽 in 1862 based on technology brought back from Europe, after which it took another decade or so before steam power began to be adopted on a wider scale.

[42] In the case of the steam engine, while firms in the SIPs had mostly caught up by 1890, this lasted for a mere ten years before the gap widened again. The same trend applies to foreign firms. By the same token, with the exception of a brief interlude (c. 1900), more firms in the treaty ports embraced mechanization than did firms in SIPs or non-port cities.

[43] Jia, "The Legacies of Forced Freedom."

Table 11.5 Long-term effects of treaty ports and self-initiated ports

	GDP (log)	Fiscal income (log)		Industrial output (log)		GDP per capita (log)	
Treaty ports	0.780***	1.008***	0.730***	0.796***	0.609***	0.486***	0.417***
	(0.158)	(0.185)	(0.142)	(0.206)	(0.146)	(0.094)	(0.089)
Self-initiated ports	0.580***	0.712***	0.362**	0.697***	0.282*	0.292***	0.211**
	(0.143)	(0.174)	(0.153)	(0.196)	(0.155)	(0.095)	(0.098)
Population (log)		0.761***	0.693***		0.718***		
		(0.059)	(0.088)		(0.090)		
Geographic controls	Yes	Yes	Yes	Yes	Yes	Yes	Yes
Observations	287	250	250	287	250	286	250
Adjusted R^2	0.148	0.598	0.491	0.093	0.454	0.116	0.147
Robust standard error	Yes	Yes	Yes	Yes	Yes	Yes	Yes

Notes. Standard errors in parentheses, * $p < 0.1$, ** $p < 0.05$, *** $p < 0.01$. Geographic controls include longitude, latitude, distance to main river, and distance to coast.

they have a larger effect than the SIPs. The long-run effects of these two types of ports are consistently the same for fiscal income (columns 3 and 4), industrial output (columns 5 and 6), and GDP per capita (columns 7 and 8).

Treaty Ports and Human Capital Development

We have shown that treaty ports are highly correlated with economic development in both the short and the long run. In this section, we document the relationship between treaty ports and human capital development via the channel of education.

The Role of Missionaries

Joseph Needham once remarked that the traditional Chinese education underpinned by Confucianism (the lynchpin of the civil service examination) provided a set of skills and knowledge not conducive to economic development,[44] a remark strongly hinting at China's failure to industrialize at a time when Western Europe succeeded. Beginning with Simon Kuznets and subsequently reiterated by Joel Mokyr,[45] economists have adopted the term "useful knowledge" to emphasize that some types of knowledge are more useful than others in stimulating economic development. In the Chinese context, the opening up of the country as a consequence of the two Opium Wars brought back the Western missionaries (along with the merchants and the diplomats), whose interests lay not merely in converting China to Christianity but more so in introducing to the Chinese a brand new system of values and knowledge fundamentally different from what the Chinese had held dear for millennia.[46] For instance, the missionaries had translated and published many Western texts in a variety of disciplines ranging from the pure sciences and medicine to the social sciences, erected schools that adopted a curriculum fundamentally different from that of the Confucian classics-based civil service examination, and put up hospitals practicing Western medicine. As Jonathan Spence observes, "Through their texts, their presses, their schools, and their hospitals, the effort of the missionaries affected Chinese thought and practice. The strength of that

---

[44] J. Needham, *The Great Titration* (Toronto, University of Toronto Press, 1969).
[45] S. Kuznets, *Economic Growth and Structure* (New York, W.W. Norton, 1965). Joel Mokyr, *The Gifts of Athena: Historical Origins of the Knowledge Economy* (Princeton, Princeton University Press, 2002).
[46] Y. Bai and J.K.S. Kung, "Diffusing Useful Knowledge While Spreading God's Message: Protestantism and Economic Prosperity in China, 1840–1920," *Journal of the European Economic Association* 13.4 (2015), 669–98.

influence is impossible to calculate, but the missionaries did offer the Chinese a new range of options, a new way of looking at the world."[47]

Christianity returned to China after more than a century since it was banned by the Kangxi Emperor in 1721. Initially, missionary activities were permitted only in the treaty ports after China's defeat in the First Opium War and with the signing of the Treaty of Nanking in 1842. It was only after China's second defeat in 1856 and the signing of the Treaty of Tientsin that missionaries were allowed to enter the inland regions. A nationwide survey of missionary activities conducted by Milton Stauffer in 1922 confirmed that the Protestant missionaries began to cover China far and wide only after the 1860s (Figure 11.20).[48] By the early 1920s, Stauffer's survey revealed that more than 94 percent of Chinese counties had records of a missionary presence. More specifically, 84 percent of these counties kept records of the Protestant communicants, with 78 percent having established Protestant congregations or evangelistic centers.

Where they had penetrated, the Protestant missionaries did far more than disseminate the Christian texts. Believing that China was backward and needed

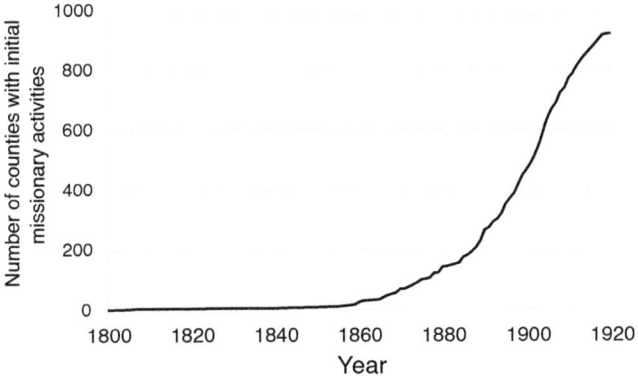

Figure 11.20 Growth of missionary activities in China
Source: M.T. Stauffer, *The Christian Occupation of China: A General Survey of the Numerical Strength and Geographical Distribution of the Christian Forces in China* (Shanghai, China Continuation Committee, 1922)

---

[47] Spence, *The Search for Modern China*, p. 208.
[48] Stauffer does not include data on the number of Catholic communicants, however. Using the number of Catholic stations to proxy for the influence of Catholic missionaries on economic prosperity (measured by the degree of urbanization), Bai and Kung find no significant association between the two. M.T. Stauffer, *The Christian Occupation of China: A General Survey of the Numerical Strength and Geographical Distribution of the Christian Forces in China* (Shanghai, China Continuation Committee, 1922); Bai and Kung, "Diffusing Useful Knowledge While Spreading God's Message."

Western culture to help it develop, the missionaries built a large number of schools – mostly primary but also some secondary ones. Figure 11.21 reveals the close correlation between their presence and the density of primary schools they erected – be that on the coastal seaboard in the east and southeast or up in the north.[49] By introducing for the first time a thoroughly Western-based curriculum with subjects ranging from those in the pure sciences such as mathematics to the social sciences and humanities, such as geography and history, the missionary primary schools had an enormous influence on the government schools at all levels in terms of curriculum. Table 11.6 reveals the differences in the curriculum between the missionary schools (c. 1876) and the "new schools" (c. 1904) set up everywhere in the country by the Chinese

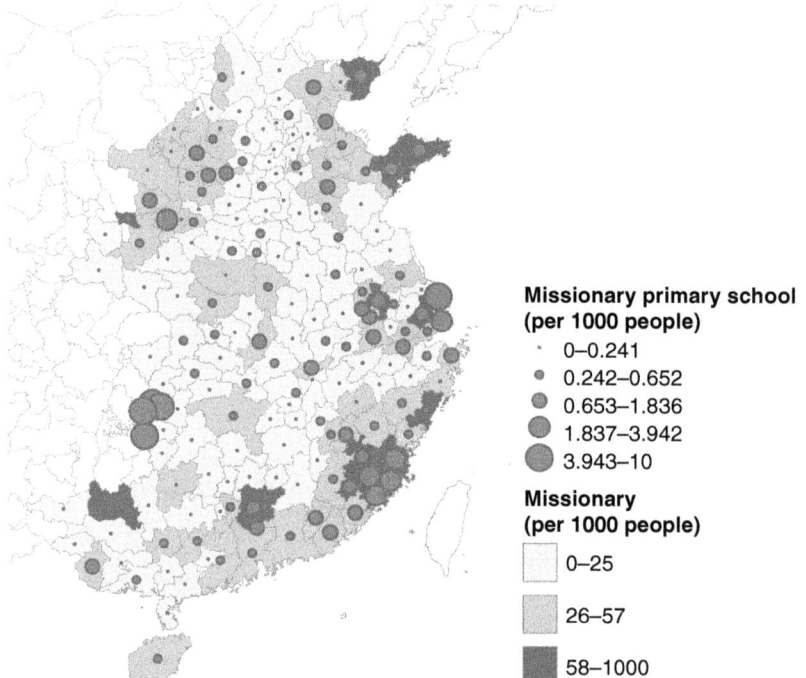

Figure 11.21 Missionary activities and the primary schools they founded (1922)
Source: Stauffer, *The Christian Occupation of China*

---

[49] The western region seems to represent an exception, where there were disproportionately more primary schools than there was missionary presence.

Table 11.6 Comparison of curricula in the 1900s

Curriculum	Missionary (since 1876)	New school curriculum (1904)
Bible	Yes	
Ideology and classics		Yes
Chinese classics	Yes	Yes
Chinese characters	Yes	Yes
History	Yes	Yes
Geography	Yes	Yes
Mathematics	Yes	Yes
Physical education	Yes	
Physics	Yes	Yes
Music		Yes
Painting and mapping	Yes	Yes

Source: Gu Changsheng 顧長聲, 傳教士與近代中國 (Missionary and Modern China) (Shanghai, Shanghai renmin chubanshe, 2004); Qiu Xiuxiang 邱秀香, 清末新式教育的理想與現實 (The Ideality and Reality of New Education in Late Qing: An Exploration of the Rise of New Primary Schools) (Department of History, National Chengchi University, 2000)

government.[50] The two types of schools adopted similar curricula, except that Bible study in the curriculum of the missionary schools was replaced by the compulsory subject of ideology and classics aimed at indoctrinating the students to obey authority, particularly the emperor (as such, the subject was still premised on the Confucian classics). A great majority of the subjects in the curriculum of the new schools were novel to the Chinese.

Bai and Kung make use of Stauffer's data to examine whether Protestantism helped promote economic prosperity by means of Max Weber's "Protestant ethic" (of working hard and saving for future investments).[51] Using a cross-sectional measure of urbanization rates in the early 1920s and a panel of data on the growth of modern firms for the 1895–1930 period as proxies for economic prosperity, they find that prefectures with more Protestant communicants were more urbanized in the early 1920s and their modern firms exhibited more robust growth during the period in question. However, they find that what was

[50] To be sure there were fewer secondary schools than primary schools (Qing Government First Education Census, 1907). Moreover, their distribution also appeared to be more skewed. Geographically the secondary schools were concentrated disproportionately on the southeast coastal seaboard, the south coast, along the Yangzi river, and in the northeast (where junior primary schools abound).

[51] Bai and Kung, "Diffusing Useful Knowledge While Spreading God's Message."

effectively promoting economic prosperity back then was not a cultural ethic but rather education and health care, as the Protestant missionaries had erected schools (both primary and middle) and hospitals in prefectures where they were stationed. In particular, by providing useful knowledge more effectively, prefectures with more middle schools and hospitals were poised to grow distinctly faster.

Modern Universities

Not only had the opening up of China radically changed the fundamentals of basic education (up to senior middle school), but it also paved the way for the modern university. Immediately after 1860 (shortly after the Second Opium War treaty was signed), a handful of military and language colleges were established by the Qing government with the overriding aim of teaching new military technologies and foreign languages.[52] The number increased sharply after 1905 upon the abolition of the civil service examination (Figure 11.22). Still more universities were established in the Republican period. By 1937, more than 200 modern colleges and universities had been established. As Figure 11.23 shows, most universities in China were founded by the Chinese government. While private universities also grew rapidly at the turn of the century and accounted for more than a third (36 percent) of all universities present by the 1930s, and with missionary universities also experiencing stable growth, in the Chinese context public universities still accounted for approximately half of all universities in China.[53]

We can see from Figure 11.24 that nearly all provincial capitals (the small dots) had at least one university as per government mandate. It is also worth noting that, with the exception of the southwest and to a lesser extent the southeast, a great majority of the universities were also located in or around the treaty ports and SIPs. This is not hard to understand. To the extent that the treaty ports spearheaded the development of the local economy by virtue of accommodating more foreign firms and banks, they increased the demand for upper-tail human capital, which in the context of a modern economy would be engineers, accountants, and lawyers.[54] This surge in demand for

---

[52] In our classification that follows we do not consider them as universities.
[53] The earliest universities in China – those established before 1900 such as Saint Johns and Dongwu – were invariably founded by the missionaries.
[54] For the importance of upper-tail human capital in the French Industrial Revolution, for example, see M. Squicciarini and N. Voigtlander, "Human Capital and Industrialization: Evidence from the Age of Enlightenment," *Quarterly Journal of Economics* 130.4 (2015), 1825–83.

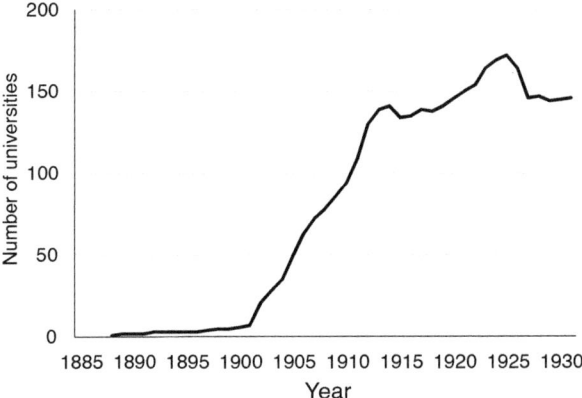

Figure 11.22 Growth of universities in China
Source: *Second China Education Yearbook* (1948)

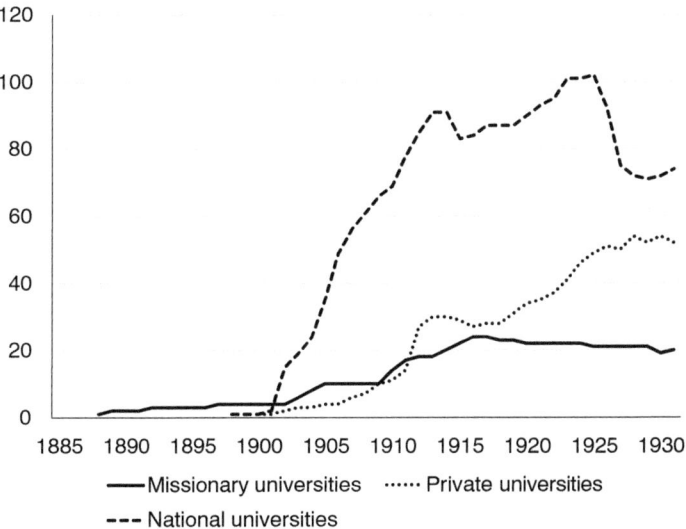

Figure 11.23 Growth of universities in China, by type/funding source
Source: *Second China Education Yearbook* (1948)

new forms of human capital would in turn stimulate the demand for universities, especially those associated with private initiatives.

To put the development of human capital in the treaty ports in context, we conducted a multivariate analysis and report the results in Table 11.7. In

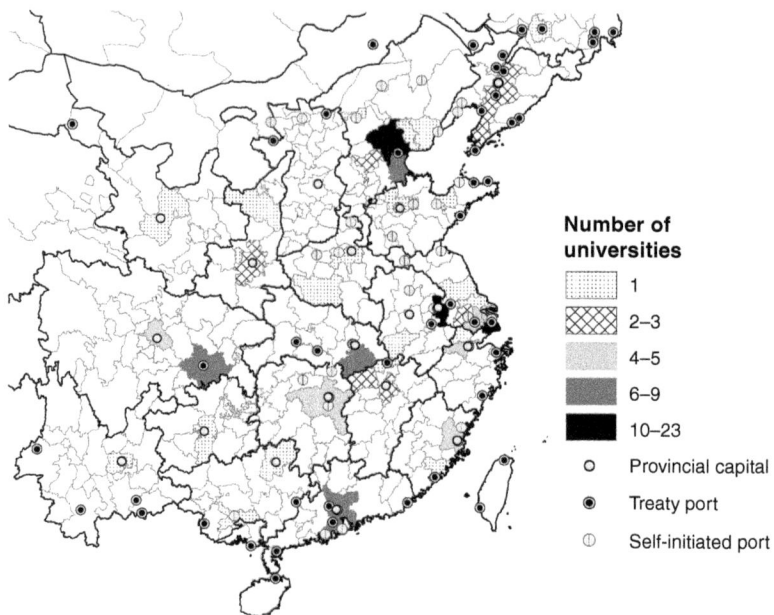

Figure 11.24 Distribution of universities in 1937
Source: *Second China Education Yearbook* (1948)

column 1, we find that both treaty ports and SIPs are significantly correlated with the development of universities at respectively a 1 percent and a 5 percent level of statistical significance; the magnitude is larger for treaty ports than for SIPs. In other words, higher education in twentieth-century China was better developed in the treaty ports than in the SIPs, which is hardly surprising. In column 2 we replace the two kinds of ports by both foreign and domestic firms and banks, and find that only foreign firms and domestic banks are significantly correlated with the development of universities (the former at the 10 percent level and the latter at the 5 percent level of conventional statistical significance). In columns 3 and 4 we divide the universities into those with an engineering school and those without, assuming that engineers are more important for the growth of industrial firms.[55] Once again, both treaty ports and SIPs are significantly correlated with universities with an engineering school, as are foreign firms (whose level

---

[55] For the importance of engineering for economic growth, see F. Caicedo and W. Maloney, "Engineering Growth: Innovative Capacity and Development in the Americas," CESifo Working Paper Series 6339, CESifo Group Munich, 2017.

Table 11.7 Determinants of university locations and engineers

	Universities		Universities with an engineering school		Universities without an engineering school		Engineers		
	(1)	(2)	(3)	(4)	(5)	(6)	(7)	(8)	(9)
Treaty ports	0.391*** (0.072)		0.113*** (0.039)		0.217*** (0.065)		1.096*** (0.170)		
Self-initiated ports	0.179** (0.082)		0.108** (0.046)		0.133* (0.075)		0.911*** (0.195)		
University with engineering school (log)									0.600** (0.298)
University without engineering school (log)									0.066 (0.200)
Foreign firms (log)		0.186* (0.097)		0.100** (0.044)		0.073* (0.038)		0.297*** (0.104)	0.151 (0.109)
Domestic firms (log)		0.047 (0.037)		−0.007 (0.020)		0.020 (0.022)		0.716*** (0.058)	0.647*** (0.057)
Foreign banks (log)		−0.001 (0.190)		0.058 (0.079)		0.177** (0.072)		−0.155 (0.195)	−0.291 (0.194)
Domestic banks (log)		0.183** (0.072)		0.075 (0.055)		0.242*** (0.042)		−0.124 (0.114)	0.184 (0.123)
Jinshi density (log)	0.174** (0.084)	0.097 (0.067)	0.004 (0.046)	−0.050 (0.038)	0.192** (0.076)	0.073 (0.057)	0.346* (0.198)	0.120 (0.154)	0.072 (0.154)

Table 11.7 (cont.)

	Universities		Universities with an engineering school		Universities without an engineering school		Engineers		
	(1)	(2)	(3)	(4)	(5)	(6)	(7)	(8)	(9)
Shengyuan quota density (log)	−0.008	0.058	0.009	0.044	−0.092	0.002	0.028	0.090	0.113
	(0.100)	(0.060)	(0.055)	(0.036)	(0.091)	(0.067)	(0.208)	(0.183)	(0.180)
Provincial capital	1.066***	0.833***	0.402***	0.337***	0.747***	0.508***	1.885***	1.201***	0.770***
	(0.092)	(0.168)	(0.051)	(0.110)	(0.084)	(0.067)	(0.218)	(0.181)	(0.209)
Population density (log)	0.014	0.002	−0.005	−0.009	−0.006	−0.011	0.125	−0.018	0.009
	(0.034)	(0.020)	(0.019)	(0.013)	(0.031)	(0.023)	(0.078)	(0.064)	(0.062)
Provincial fixed effects	Yes	Yes	Yes	Yes	Yes	Yes	Yes	Yes	Yes
Observations	255	255	255	255	255	255	255	255	255
Adjusted R^2	0.610	0.721	0.352	0.567	0.461	0.701	0.602	0.769	0.777

Note. Standard errors in parentheses, * $p < 0.1$, ** $p < 0.05$, *** $p < 0.01$

of statistical significance has now increased from 10 percent to 5 percent). In columns 5 and 6 we change the dependent variable to "universities without an engineering school." While similar results are found using treaty ports and SIPs as the explanatory variables, this time not only are the foreign firms significantly correlated with this dependent variable, but so too are the banks – both foreign and domestic (which enjoy the highest level of conventional statistical significance (1 percent)). This result is highly intuitive, as banks are likely to exhibit a stronger demand for such specialists as accountants, lawyers, and bankers than for engineers.

We then examine the geographic distribution of the engineers' workplace and the kind of institutions with the strongest demand for their expertise. We report the results in columns 7 through 9. Foremost is that a good majority of the engineers worked in the treaty ports and SIPs (column 7); the larger coefficient of treaty ports suggests that they provided more employment opportunities for the engineers, again an unsurprising result (see also Figure 11.25 for their geographic distribution).

We also find that the only demand for engineering expertise came from firms – both foreign and domestic (column 8); the larger coefficient on the domestic firms suggests that they had a greater demand for engineers. The greater demand from domestic firms is further confirmed in column 9, after controlling for the type of universities, i.e. whether a university had an engineering school. Consistent with intuition, banks did not require the service of engineers.

Finally, given that provinces were decreed to set up universities in their capital city, this variable is significant throughout the regressions, as can be visualized also in Figure 11.24. While significantly correlated with the establishment of universities, *jinshi* 進士 density – which measures the number of *jinshi* scholars in the Ming–Qing period produced by each prefecture normalized by its population – fails to account for the presence of those universities with an engineering school (compare, for example, columns 1 and 3). Moreover, once we control for the presence of firms, *jinshi* density becomes insignificant (columns 2 and 4). *Shengyuan* 生員 quota, which has been used as a proxy for social mobility and as a corollary for political stability,[56] has no explanatory power for the founding of universities. The same applies to population density.

---

[56] Y. Bai and R. Jia, "Elite Recruitment and Political Stability: The Impact of the Abolition of China's Civil Service Exam System," *Econometrica* 84.2 (2016), 677–733.

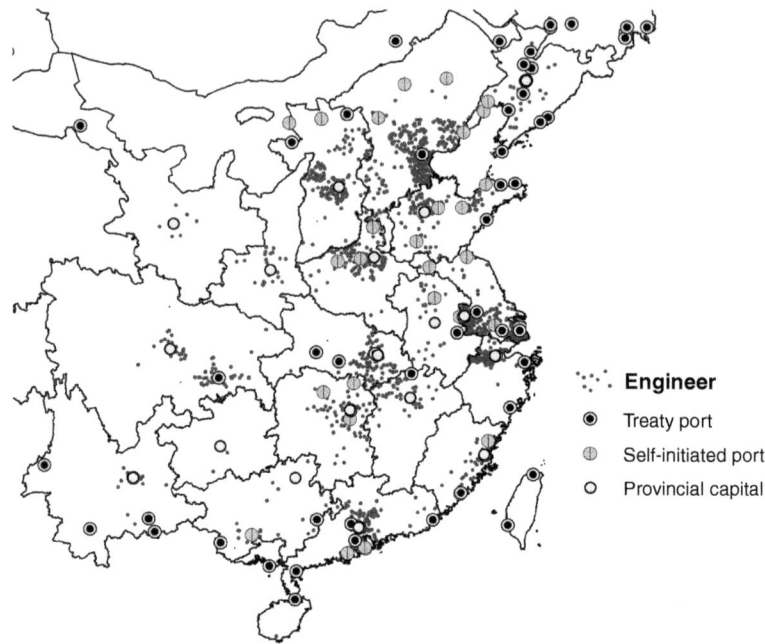

Figure 11.25 Distribution of engineers in 1937
Resouce Committee 资源委员会 (ed.), 中国工程人名录 (A Directory of Chinese Engineers) (Changsha, Commercial Press, 1941)

Beyond the Treaty Ports: Overseas Studies and Political Change

The treaty ports brought not just economic change but also social and political change, some of which was drastic beyond all expectations. The Xinhai Revolution of 1911, for example, represents an extreme case in point, whose unexpected occurrence brought an end to millennia-long imperial China.

Ever since China first opened up to the West, Western knowledge and ideas (including ideologies) spread like wildfire through the media, the translation of books, and, as mentioned earlier, the adoption of a Western-style education. Of the many new ideas disseminated in China, the call for political reforms was high on the agenda, chiefly because China had fully revealed its weaknesses in military and technological capabilities – weaknesses that many saw as deeply rooted in its backwardness in different arenas vis-à-vis the Western powers.

Although one could learn about the West via the universities, newspapers, and translated texts, a better way to acquire new corpuses of knowledge firsthand and to gain educational qualifications was to study overseas, as the political elite Zhang Zhidong strongly advocated.[57] While the Qing government had already begun sending students to study science and engineering in the United States as early as the 1870s, and later on to Europe to study military technology, the scale was modest – only 100 or so students in total in either case. The third and also by far the biggest wave of studying abroad did not happen until after 1895, when China had been defeated in the First Sino-Japanese War a year earlier. Since then, cumulatively tens of thousands of students went to study in Japan, a trend that accelerated in 1905, when China's millennia-long civil service examination was eventually abolished. Figure 11.26, which is plotted based on part of Zhou's data on overseas study,[58] shows the number of students who studied overseas and returned to China upon completing their studies.[59] The nearly identical patterns of the two curves suggest that the majority of students who studied overseas did return to China.

As we shall see later, the 1911 Revolution was engineered by what may categorically be known as the Revolutionaries or the Revolutionary Alliance, many of whom had studied in Japan. For this reason, it is important to understand why Japan became the most popular destination among Chinese students. But before doing so, we would like to examine why it became popular to study abroad in the first place. In the light of the importance of Western influence, we propose several factors that we consider were

---

[57] As the governor-general of the provinces of Hunan and Hubei, Zhang remarked that "to study in the West for one year is better than reading Western books for five years ... to study in a Western school for one year is better than to study for three in the Chinese schools." Cited in M. Jansen, "Japan and the Chinese Revolution of 1911," in J.K. Fairbank and K.-C. Liu (eds.), *The Cambridge History of China*, vol. 11, *Late Ch'ing, 1800–1911*, part 2 (Cambridge, Cambridge University Press, 1980), p. 349.

[58] Zhou Mian 周棉, 中國留學生大辭典 (Chinese Overseas Student Dictionary) (Nanjing, Nanjing University Press, 1999).

[59] There are altogether some 3,000 or more students in the overall sample of Zhou, 中國留學生大辭典, but only 600 up until 1911. See Sanetō Keisha, 中国人日本留学史 (A History of Chinese Students in Japan) (Tokyo, Kuroshio shuppan, 1970); and Li Xisuo 李喜所, 近代中国的留学生 (Foreign-Trained Students in the History of Modern China) (Beijing, Renmin chubanshe, 1987) for the estimates, which are cited in D. Reynolds, *China, 1898–1912: The Xinzheng Revolution and Japan* (Cambridge, MA, Harvard University Press, 1993), p. 41, according to whom "(t)he flow of Chinese students to Japan was the most dramatic single development in relations between China and Japan after 1898."

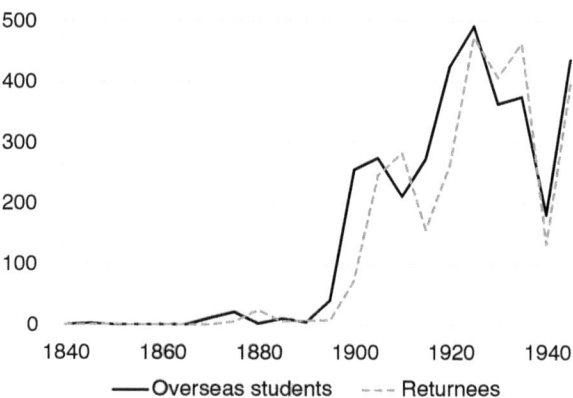

Figure 11.26 Number of Chinese students studying abroad and returning, a partial sample
Source: Mian Zhou 周棉, 中國留學生大辭典 (Chinese Overseas Student Dictionary) (Nanjing, Nanjing University Press, 1999)

likely highly correlated with this particular outcome. These factors include treaty ports and, to a lesser extent, the SIPs for their disproportionately greater exposure to Western culture and thoughts, and more specifically foreign firms and banks and (to a lesser extent) modern Chinese firms and banks; an edifice of modern education ranging from primary and secondary schools to the universities; missionary presence, and so forth. The results are reported in Table 11.8.

We can see from column 1 that treaty ports (but not SIPs) are significantly correlated with overseas studies, suggesting that exposure – including its duration – to Western culture, ideas, and so forth may have increased one's proclivity towards studying overseas. So too does missionary presence; individuals living in prefectures where the missionaries had set up operations for longer were also more likely to study overseas. The same applies to the densely populated prefectures and the provincial capitals, for the reason that news and information about the West were likely more rapidly and thoroughly diffused. An interesting variable in this connection is *jinshi* density, which is strongly correlated with studying overseas. This may suggest that individuals coming from places with a strong tradition of civil service examination success were perhaps more inclined to acquire new knowledge and/or seek modern qualifications by studying abroad.

In column 2 we replace the two treaty port variables with the firm and bank variables (one foreign and the other domestic), and find that only *firms*

Table 11.8 Determinants of overseas studies

	Studying overseas			
	(1)	(2)	(3)	(4)
Treaty ports	0.329**		0.229*	0.291*
	(0.139)		(0.135)	(0.148)
Self-initiated ports	0.098		0.039	0.075
	(0.150)		(0.145)	(0.157)
Domestic firms (log)		0.118**		
		(0.055)		
Domestic banks (log)		0.047		
		(0.109)		
Foreign firms (log)		0.169*		
		(0.099)		
Foreign banks (log)		0.062		
		(0.217)		
Modern universities (log)			0.381***	0.346***
			(0.135)	(0.123)
Primary schools (log)			0.184***	0.171***
			(0.054)	(0.052)
Secondary schools (log)			0.168*	0.102
			(0.101)	(0.107)
Duration of missionary presence	0.105***	0.072*		0.090*
	(0.036)	(0.038)		(0.045)
Railway	0.198	−0.042	0.0110	0.041
	(0.159)	(0.168)	(0.167)	(0.147)
Population density (log)	0.184***	0.155**	0.120*	0.121**
	(0.065)	(0.065)	(0.064)	(0.050)
Jinshi density (log)	0.767***	0.705***	0.650***	0.645***
	(0.151)	(0.150)	(0.147)	(0.191)
Shengyuan quota density (log)	−0.403	−0.340	−0.565	−0.560
	(0.833)	(0.819)	(0.804)	(0.822)
Provincial capital	0.538***	0.367**	−0.010	−0.030
	(0.172)	(0.182)	(0.229)	(0.332)
Provincial fixed effects	Yes	Yes	Yes	Yes
Observations	239	239	239	239
Adjusted R^2	0.538	0.559	0.570	0.576

Note. Standard errors in parentheses, $^*p < 0.1$, $^{**}p < 0.05$, $^{***}p < 0.01$

are significantly correlated with studying abroad. The other variables that are significant in column 1 continue to be significant in column 2, although except for *jinshi* density their levels of statistical significance are all reduced. We then control for the possible influence of modern education in column 3, and find that all the three measures – primary, secondary, and university – are significantly correlated with studying overseas, with university and primary education being much more significant than secondary schools. Of the three, universities are the most important (the coefficient is more than twice that of the primary schools). In column 3, provincial capital is no longer significant, suggesting that its previous significance was likely due to the omission of the universities. Likewise, treaty ports have also become less significant, suggesting that a large part of their influence on studying abroad is likely coming from modern education, in particular the universities. Finally, in column 4, we put the missionary variable back in the regression, and find that secondary schools have now become insignificant, but primary schools and universities continue to correlate significantly with studying abroad. Summing up, modern education, missionary presence, and a strong tradition of human capital and other unobserved aspects of treaty ports can importantly explain the decision to study overseas. These interesting correlates notwithstanding, we need to be cognizant of the fact that more than half of the overseas students were sponsored by the government at various levels.

So the questions that need addressing at this point are: (1) why Japan, (2) who went overseas and what levels of education and subjects of study did they pursue, and (3) why did the Japanese experience turn them against China?

Japan was favored for a variety of reasons. Given the similar challenges confronting China and Japan, the Japanese experience demonstrated the possibility of transforming an imperial/feudal regime into a constitutional monarchy without necessarily overthrowing the former – a reform deemed desirable by the Manchu regime.[60] Success in this matter also won Japan an alliance with Britain. But Japan was also favored after it convincingly defeated the Russians – a much more sizeable country – in the Russo-Japanese War, an outcome hinting at the importance of having a superior political system. Third, the geographic proximity of Japan easily made it a far more convincing case than either the United States or Europe insofar as the costs of travel and tuition were concerned, regardless of who bore the costs.[61] Finally, by that time, the Japanese had already translated most of the Western works deemed essential to the Chinese.[62]

---

[60] To learn from a number of more advanced countries about how constitutional governance was run, in 1905 the Qing government dispatched five ministers to as many as thirteen countries, including Japan, the United States, Britain, France, Germany, and Russia, although it turned out that the regime favored Japan.
[61] These costs were estimated at about a fifth of those of studying either in the United States or in Europe by Zhang Zhidong.
[62] See Jansen, "Japan and the Chinese Revolution of 1911"; Reynolds, *China, 1898–1912*.

While the earlier batch of students were largely sponsored by the government at various levels, with the abolition of the traditional civil service examination in 1905 an increasing proportion would have to become self-sponsored as many must have felt uncertain about their career prospects and hence the need to upgrade their qualifications.[63] Still others might have gone in the hope of acquiring knowledge that might contribute to a stronger China.

The level of studies pursued by the self-sponsored students also varied; the great majority of them (75 percent) attended senior secondary schools, specialized or professional schools, and even short cram courses that lasted for three to nine months and in some cases up to twelve months (*sokuseihan* 促成班). These programs allegedly catered to the Chinese students' educational needs. Another 15 percent were enrolled in unspecified preparatory programs, presumably involving intense training in the Japanese language. In terms of disciplines, the vast majority of self-sponsored students were enrolled in the liberal arts and teacher training (arts, business, and social sciences),[64] and only those who were sponsored by the government specialized in military studies.[65] Less than 10 percent were enrolled in schools equivalent in status to universities approved by the Japanese government; these students studied a variety of subjects ranging from science, engineering, and medicine to law, business, and agriculture.

The next question is why the Japanese experience turned the overseas students against China. Essentially, in Meiji Japan a number of Western ideas about government were no longer foreign to the overseas Chinese students, who now could freely discuss the possibilities of future government without being held back by traditions. Furthermore, with the positive examples of a rising Japan and the negative daily experiences of both condescension and discrimination fueling their sense of nationalism, these students now perceived a modernized Japan as a benchmark against which to critically evaluate the weaknesses of the Qing government. While some (the constitutionalists) might wish to follow in the footsteps of the Meiji reformers by establishing a parliament (which eventually failed),[66] others (the

---

[63] Many indeed had gone to Japan for short courses or "cram programs," or in the words of Reynolds, *China, 1898–1912*, p. 61, "quick certification for choice jobs back home."
[64] Waseda University, for example, was famous for its teacher-training program. Reynolds, *China, 1898–1912*, p. 61.
[65] Sanetō, *Chugokujin Nihon Ryugakushi*.
[66] By drawing upon the expertise of a great many political elites and literati with the likes of Zhang Jian 张謇 and Liang Qichao 梁啟超, the constitutionalists petitioned thrice for the establishment of a national assembly after establishing the provincial assemblies,

revolutionists) remained agnostic that the Manchu would be capable of continuing their rule of a strengthened China – especially after witnessing its failure to fend off the imperial Western powers that were encroaching upon China's own economic interest. These two major political powers changed China's destiny fundamentally. Between the two, the revolutionists were the ones whose goal was to establish a Republican government via revolution. To this end, a good number of revolutionary groups were established, most notably the Revive China Society (*Xinzhonghui* 興中會, founded in 1894), the Restoration Society (*Guangfuhui* 光復會, founded in 1904), and the Chinese Revolutionary Alliance (*Zhongguo tongmenghui* 中國同盟會, founded in 1905 by Sun Yat-sen 孫中山). Figure 11.27 shows the geographic distribution of these two political organizations. While they did overlap in some regions (most notably the lower Yangzi delta region, for instance), they also occupied different parts of the country. For instance, there were more revolutionists in the south-central part of China, which is where the revolution was initially staged.[67]

Shortly after staging a revolutionary uprising in the south-central city of Wuchang (Hubei province) on October 10, 1911, many revolts and uprisings ensued, resulting in as many as fourteen provinces announcing independence from the Qing state, and the subsequent announcement of the founding of the Republic of China in January 1912.

What precisely is the connection between studying in Japan and the 1911 Revolution that overthrew the Qing dynasty? Owing to data limitations, we can only address this question indirectly by examining how studying in Japan might have borne upon the returnees' choice of political organization and membership, with implications for revolutionary outcome based on the analysis conducted in Table 11.9.[68] Specifically, the dependent variable is membership of a political organization – constitutionalist versus revolutionist, whereas the independent variable is the subjects in which they majored while in Japan.[69] Before doing so, however, we want to identify the general outcome of studying overseas first. As

but failed. J. Esherick, "Reconsidering 1911: Lessons of a Sudden Revolution," *Journal of Modern Chinese History* 6.1 (2012), 1–14.

[67] What we are not establishing are the causal links between where the revolutionists were located and the occurrence of the revolutions, which would require additional work coding the geography of conflict and social networks among the leading revolutionaries.

[68] As with Table 11.8 we rely on the data provided by Zhou, 中國留學生大辭典, on the 600 or so students (out of a total of a few thousands that studied abroad) for the analysis.

[69] Ideally, we should also include a measure of whether one was sponsored by the government or not, as that may affect a student's political outlook and thus choice of political organization, as well as choice of major. Unfortunately, such information is not available from Zhou, 中國留學生大辭典.

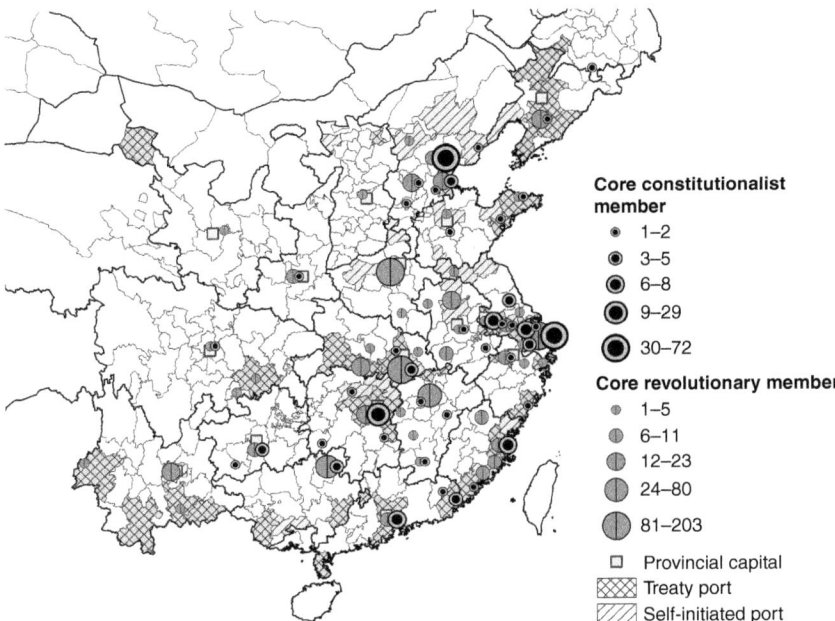

Figure 11.27 Geographic distribution of constitutionalists and revolutionists (1900–1911) Source: Chang Yufa 張玉法, 清季的立憲團體 (The Constitutionalists in the Late Qing) (Taipei, Institute of Modern History, Academia Sinica, 1971); Chang Yufa 張玉法, "清季的革命團體" (The Revolutionists in the Late Qing), *Bulletin of the Institute of Modern History, Academia Sinica*, 1975

shown in columns 1 and 6, studying overseas is insignificantly correlated with the choice of joining the constitutionalists but positively and significantly correlated with the decision to join the revolutionists.

We then examine the specific outcome of studying in Japan, by interacting the overseas studies variable with Japan (columns 2 and 7). While column 2 shows that studying overseas is now significantly correlated with joining the constitutionalists, its coefficient is negative, suggesting that these students were perhaps not as politically oriented – perhaps due to the nature of their professional training in subjects like science and engineering. Conversely, those studying in Japan were significantly more likely to join a political party – be it the constitutionalists (column 2) or the revolutionists (column 7) – the much larger coefficient in column 7 suggests that these students were distinctly more likely to join the revolutionists.

Table 11.9 Effect of overseas studies on political participation

	Constitutionalist organizations					Revolutionist organizations				
	(1)	(2)	(3)	(4)	(5)	(6)	(7)	(8)	(9)	(10)
Studying overseas	−0.0001	−0.0142**	−0.0140*	−0.0058	−0.0174	0.2130***	0.0021	−0.0260	0.0034	−0.0330
	(0.0039)	(0.0067)	(0.0078)	(0.0079)	(0.0116)	(0.0198)	(0.0325)	(0.0328)	(0.0394)	(0.0409)
Studying overseas*Japan		0.0175**	0.0177*	0.0143*	0.0178*		0.2630***	0.2370***	0.2140***	0.2230***
		(0.0087)	(0.0092)	(0.0083)	(0.0102)		(0.0390)	(0.0401)	(0.0432)	(0.0442)
Studying overseas*Military			−0.0006	−0.0062	0.0031			0.1060***	0.0990***	0.1190***
			(0.0123)	(0.0112)	(0.0106)			(0.0357)	(0.0361)	(0.0364)
Studying overseas*Graduate				−0.0167**	−0.0021				−0.0873	−0.0852
				(0.0071)	(0.0099)				(0.0531)	(0.0529)
Age					−0.0038					0.0459***
					(0.0023)					(0.0032)
Age²					0.0001**					−0.0002***
					(0.0000)					(0.0001)
Studying overseas*female					−0.0055					0.0839
					(0.0059)					(0.0852)
Studying overseas*jinshi					0.2170**					−0.1290
					(0.0980)					(0.1420)
Studying overseas*juren					0.1040					0.0982
					(0.0636)					(0.0993)
Studying overseas*xiucai					0.0242					0.0191
					(0.0277)					(0.0555)

Individual fixed effects	Yes	Yes	Yes	Yes	Yes	Yes	Yes	Yes
Year fixed effects	Yes	Yes	Yes	Yes	Yes	Yes	Yes	Yes
Clustered at individual level	Yes	Yes	Yes	Yes	Yes	Yes	Yes	Yes
Prefecture specific time trend	Yes	Yes	Yes	Yes	Yes	Yes	Yes	Yes
Observations	13777	13777	13777	13777	13777	13777	13777	13777
Number of people	599	599	599	599	599	599	599	599
Adjusted R^2	0.490	0.491	0.491	0.450	0.484	0.584	0.595	0.597	0.598	0.659

Note. Standard errors in parentheses, $^*\ p < 0.1$, $^{**}\ p < 0.05$, $^{***}\ p < 0.01$. In this analysis, a dummy indicating whether a student joined a constitutionalist/revolutionist organization is used as the dependent variable.

Next we consider the effect of major (field of specialization) on the choice of political organization. We find that those who specialized in military studies were significantly and positively correlated with joining the revolutionists (column 8), but insignificantly correlated with joining the constitutionalists (column 3). Given that after 1902 the Qing government strictly prohibited all self-sponsored students from enrolling in just about any military program, those specializing in military studies were almost certain to be government officials who were expected to take up a military appointment upon completing their training in Japan but instead rebelled against the government. The finding intriguingly reflects the possible irony that these Qing officials may have defected from the Manchu regime soon after acquiring more military knowledge. In fact, officers of the New Army were heavily recruited by the revolutionists.

What was the effect of graduate education on political participation? Columns 4 and 9 were designed to examine this question. A graduate education significantly dissuaded the students from joining the constitutionalists (column 4), whereas its effect on joining the revolutionists is insignificant (column 9). These findings are consistent with the economic intuition that political participation comes at a higher opportunity cost for the more educated.[70] Finally, in columns 5 and 10 we add other control variables that may also bear upon the choice of political organization. These include overseas students' age, gender, and whether they had achieved a traditional qualification, with *jinshi* 進士 (national civil service examination) being the highest level of achievement, followed by *juren* 舉人 (provincial civil service examination) and *xiucai* 秀才 (county/prefectural civil service examination). Given that all the variables of interest are included in columns 5 and 10, they are de facto the full model and as such represent a summary finding. First of all, column 5 shows that studying overseas in general is still significantly and negatively correlated with joining the constitutionalists, but studying in Japan is not, albeit with a marginal significance (10 percent). In contrast, of those who chose the revolutionary path, studying in Japan in general and majoring in military studies in particular were significant correlates, which is consistent with the historical narrative that the New Army, many of whose officers were trained in Japan, played a pivotal role in the revolution by virtue of their access to weaponry (column 10). In terms of individual characteristics, not surprisingly our findings suggest that those who were older tended to join the

---

[70] See, for example, F. Campante and D. Chor, "Schooling, Political Participation, and the Economy," *Review of Economics and Statistics* 94.4 (2012), 841–59.

constitutionalists (column 5), whereas younger individuals often chose to follow the path of the revolutionists (column 10). Perhaps there were not many females involved, but gender has no effect for either type of organization. Interestingly, those who had already achieved a *jinshi* or *juren* qualification prior to studying in Japan were more inclined to join the political organization established to preserve the status quo (i.e. the constitutionalists), whereas the same qualifications are insignificantly correlated with the revolutionists (compare columns 5 and 10). Considering that those who had achieved a *jinshi* or *juren* had invested tremendous human capital under the old elite system, their preference to preserve the status quo was thus easy to understand.

Conclusions

The nineteenth century is of unique importance to late imperial China. After experiencing nearly two centuries of peace and economic prosperity, the Qing tasted military defeat repeatedly within a short span of just two decades at the hands of Great Britain – a country the size of a single Chinese province but otherwise a military and industrial powerhouse. This series of defeats sparked a new era for imperial China, one that was short-lived because the vastly complicated development of events in the latter half of the nineteenth century only culminated in the unwitting demise of the last imperial dynasty. For some time now, economic historians have vehemently debated the implications of the economic impact of the West, except that the lack of data has precluded a serious analysis. Against this background, we compiled a data set from a variety of data sources, the purpose of which was to provide a preliminary assessment of the Western impact on the Chinese economy in the last episode of the imperial dynasty. Others before us have analyzed the possible impact of the treaty ports established by the foreign powers, but here we used the micro-level data of foreign firms and banks as a unique starting point and analyzed their impact on the growth of domestic firms and banks, and confirmed their positive influence. In doing so we go beyond the "blackbox" approach of analyzing the treaty ports, which were likely to encompass more than just the economic institutions of firms and banks. At the very least we hope to have introduced a fresh approach to analyzing the economic impact of the West.

Indeed, in addition to confirming a demonstration and persistent effect of the foreign modern institutions (both firms and banks) on China's own in both the short and the long run, evidence further suggests that human capital also developed more rapidly in the treaty ports. Not only had the missionaries played a significant role in erecting schools at virtually all levels, but they also brought with them a new curriculum to China. Importantly, it was also a time when the modern university came of age in China. And while all provincial capitals had by imperial decree established one or more universities, their numbers were distinctly higher in the treaty ports and SIPs, testifying to their economic importance. Specifically, both foreign and domestic firms are significantly associated with the presence of engineers – a specific form of human capital essential to industrialization.

In spite of these positive developments on the economic front, and partly because it was weak to begin with, the Qing government could not survive the havoc wreaked by those who went to study in Japan and came back with the idea of using revolution as a platform for effectuating political change. Inspired by the Western ideas disseminated through the modern education system, the missionary presence, and the newspapers, those who went to Japan for a brief stint might just have come to the realization that Qing China had become both too stubborn and too feeble a regime for saving. Hence, while it was Britain and Europe more generally that planted the seeds of economic change in China by exposing it to the West, Japan arguably served as the last straw on the camel's back in bringing an end to imperial China. Of course, as history unfolds, the end of the Qing only marked the beginning of what promised to be another politically tumultuous episode for the country, but that goes beyond our present scope.

Further Reading

Bai, Y., and J.K-S. Kung, Diffusing Useful Knowledge While Spreading God's Message: Protestantism and Economic Prosperity in China, 1840–1920, *Journal of the European Economic Association* 13.4 (2015), 669–98.

Chang, Yufa 張玉法, "清末民初的外資工業" (Foreign Industries in Late Qing and Early Republican China) *Bulletin of the Institute of Modern History, Academia Sinica* 1987, 129–249.

Chang, Yufa 張玉法, 近代中國工業發展史, 1860–1916 (A History of Modern Chinese Industrial Development, 1860–1916) (Taipei, Gui guan tu shu you xian gong si, 1992).

Dernberger, R.F., "The Role of the Foreigner in China's Economic Development, 1840–1949," in D.H. Perkins (ed.), *China's Modern Economy in Historical Perspective* (Stanford, Stanford University Press, 1975), pp. 19–47.

Du Xuncheng 杜恂誠, 民族資本主義與舊中國政府, 1840–1937 (Chinese Capitalism and the Old Chinese Government, 1840–1937) (Shanghai, Shanghai shehui kexueyuan chubanshe, 1991).

Esherick, J., "Reconsidering 1911: Lessons of a Sudden Revolution," *Journal of Modern Chinese History* 6.1 (2012), 1–14.
Feuerwerker, A., "The Foreign Presence in China," in J.K. Fairbank (ed.), *The Cambridge History of China*, vol. 12, *Republican China, 1912–1949*, part 1 (Cambridge, Cambridge University Press, 1983), pp. 128–207.
Jansen, M., "Japan and the Chinese Revolution of 1911," in J.K. Fairbank and K.C. Liu (eds.), *The Cambridge History of China*, vol. 11, *Late Ch'ing, 1800–1911*, part 2 (Cambridge, Cambridge University Press, 1980), pp. 339–74.
Jia, R., "The Legacies of Forced Freedom: China's Treaty Ports," *Review of Economics and Statistics* 96.4 (2014), 596–608.
Perkins, D.H., "Government as an Obstacle to Industrialization: The Case of Nineteenth-Century China," *Journal of Economic History* 17.4 (1967), 478–92.
Reynolds, D., *China, 1898–1912: The Xinzheng Revolution and Japan* (Cambridge, MA, Harvard University Press, 1993).
Shen Diancheng 沈殿成, 中國人留學日本百年史 (A History of a Hundred Years of Chinese Studying in Japan) (Liaoning, Liaoning jiaoyu chubanshe, 1997).
Zhang Hongxiang 張洪祥, 近代中國通商口岸與租界 (Treaty Ports and Concessions in Chinese History) (Tianjin, Tianjin renmin chubanshe, 1993).
Zhang Pengyuan 張朋园, 中国民主政治的困境, 1909–1949 (The Predicament of Democracy in China, 1909–1949) (Changchun, Jilin chu ban ji tuan you xian ze ren gong si, 2008).
Zhang Jianqiu 張建俅, 清末自開商埠之研究 (1898–1911) (Research on the Self-Initiated Ports of the Late Qing) (Taipei, Huamulan wenhua chubanshe, 2009).

12

Foreign Trade and Investment

WOLFGANG KELLER AND CAROL H. SHIUE

Introduction

By the mid-eighteenth century, the Qing dynasty (1644–1911) was the dominant power within Asia. Its political system and institutions of state building were founded on structures inherited from previous Chinese dynasties as well as on the social and cultural codes of interaction among polities across Central Eurasia, East Asia, and Southeast Asia. Foreign trade between China and other countries within and outside Asia was a calculated matter of political strategy and economic gain. In the decades leading up to the First Opium War of 1839 to 1842, China's stance with respect to the Sino-Western trade became increasingly at odds with British ambitions in Asia. The growing tensions stemmed from abiding differences in the political economy of not just two nations, but two empires. The overseas influence of the British Empire took on a forceful new impetus with the British Industrial Revolution, and, over the nineteenth century, technological improvements in transport continued to power Western expansion in global trade.

The Opium War of 1839 to 1842 was the turning point after which foreign, and particularly Western, nations took greater control over not only China's international trade policy, but also important legal and economic institutions. After 1842, Chinese ports that had previously been closed to Western traders were forced open to trade and investment. In these so-called "treaty ports," tariffs on foreign imports into China were fixed at a low rate. Beyond trade, consular offices and foreign courts were established in China, and foreign nationals were exempt from the jurisdiction of Chinese law. The implications

---

Kyle Butts, Jacob Howard, Peiyuan Li, William Ridley, and Javier Andres Santiago provided excellent research assistance. Support from the National Science Foundation (Grants SES 0453040 and SES 1124426) is gratefully acknowledged.

of the semicolonial treaty port system for China's long-run development have been the subject of perennial interest.[1]

What has been less emphasized in the literature is that what we know about China's foreign trade increased dramatically during this period. Before the 1800s, the quality of archival data on the quantities, prices, and types of goods in China's foreign trade, although substantial, is on the whole variable. After the mid-nineteenth century, there was a sea change in what was systematically recorded about China's imports and exports. The reason was not China's new interest in foreign trade, nor improved statistical capacity due to a rising level of development, but Western interests in China.

This chapter discusses China's openness to foreign influence from 1800 to 1950 from the point of view of new sources of information on foreign trade and investment that became available because of Western influence in China. In particular, the China Maritime Customs (CMC) service was instrumental in helping to revolutionize the system of foreign-trade statistics in China. The records are the result of a complex yet consistent set of rules, and are of high quality.[2] Notably, the CMC data give more detail than is found even in

---

[1] The impact of the treaty port system includes questions related to technology transfer, legal institutions, state building, nation building, foreign policy, society and community, and other topics. A number of historical overviews have been written by nineteenth-century observers. W.F. Mayers, N.B. Dennys, and C. King, *The Treaty Ports of China and Japan: A Complete Guide to the Open Ports of Those Countries, Together with Peking, Yedo, Hongkong and Macao* (London, Trübner, 1867) is a compilation by British consular officers about treaty ports and companies in China and Japan. Another comprehensive treatment by a customs official in China is H.B. Morse, *The International Relations of the Chinese Empire*, vol. I (London, Longmans, Green, and Company, 1910). See also C.S. See, *The Foreign Trade of China* (New York, Columbia University Press, 1919); Jiang Tingfu 蔣廷黻, 中國近代史 (Modern Chinese History) (Shanghai, Shanghai guji chubanshe, 2001; first published Changsha, Shangwu, 1938); M. Greenberg, *British Trade and the Opening of China 1800–1842* (Cambridge, Cambridge University Press, 1951); A. Feuerwerker, *The Foreign Establishment in China in the Early Twentieth Century* (Ann Arbor, University of Michigan, 1976); Feuerwerker, "Economic Trends in the Late Ch'ing Empire, 1870–1911," in J.K. Fairbank and K.C. Liu (eds.), *The Cambridge History of China*, vol. 11, *Late Ch'ing, 1800–1911*, part 2 (Cambridge, Cambridge University Press, 1980), pp. 1–69, for additional analysis. Recent historical treatments of the era can be found in J.M. Downs, *The Golden Ghetto: The American Commercial Community at Canton and the Shaping of American China Policy, 1784–1844* (Hong Kong, Hong Kong University Press, 2014); R. Bickers, and I. Jackson (eds.), *Treaty Ports in Modern China: Law, Land, and Power* (London, Routledge, 2016); A. Reinhardt, *Navigating Semi-colonialism: Shipping, Sovereignty, and Nation-Building in China, 1860–1937* (Cambridge, MA, Harvard University Press, 2018).

[2] R. Murphey, *The Outsiders: The Western Experience in India and China* (Ann Arbor, University of Michigan Press, 1977), pp. 213–14, stated, "the recorded figures probably inflated the real import and export of goods by close to 100 percent," erroneously concluding that the data were unreliable due to double counting of what was traded. In actuality, a high degree of internal consistency and accuracy allows us to reconstruct real imports and exports at the port level.

modern-day international trade data as they capture re-exports, allowing gross trade to be distinguished from net trade flows.[3]

In order to understand the opening of China in the nineteenth century, the next section, "China's Foreign Trade before 1839 and the Opium Wars," discusses the historical background of trade before 1840, and the motivations and attitudes towards trade at the time. In the section headed "China's Foreign Trade during the Treaty Port Era (1842–1943)," we consider the history of the CMC and the development of the organization during the treaty port era (1842–1943). Drawing on recent work and original quantitative research, we summarize recent findings based on the CMC data, especially with respect to China's foreign trade at the aggregate level and its composition by foreign country.[4]

Beyond the resource gains that arise from commodity trade, trade also affects development by transferring knowledge with respect to new products, institutional environments, and different legal systems.[5] The section titled "Foreign Direct Investment in China" briefly outlines the evolution of foreign-owned firms in China and aggregate levels of foreign direct investment, both of which became more systematically recorded during this period.

Since foreign trade often requires shipments from points of local production to ports of export, a high degree of domestic market integration between regions where goods are produced and the ports where the goods are ultimately destined for export would have been important for the flow of exports. Domestic markets in eighteenth-century China were populated by many buyers and sellers and were relatively efficient. But how did foreign

---

[3] See W. Keller, B. Li, and C.H. Shiue, "Shanghai's Trade, China's Growth: Continuity, Recovery, and Change since the Opium War," *IMF Economic Review* 2 (2013), 336–78, data appendix, for a discussion of data quality of the CMC trade data.

[4] In particular, see W. Keller, B. Li, and C.H. Shiue, "China's Foreign Trade: Perspectives from the Past 150 Years," *World Economy* 6 (2011), 853–92; W. Keller, B. Li, and C.H. Shiue, "The Evolution of Domestic Trade Flows When Foreign Trade Is Liberalized: Evidence from the Chinese Maritime Customs Service," in M. Aoki, T. Kuran, and G. Roland (eds.), *Institutions and Comparative Economic Development* (New York, Palgrave Macmillan, 2012); Keller, Li, and Shiue, "Shanghai's Trade, China's Growth"; W. Keller, J.A. Santiago, and C.H. Shiue, "China's Domestic Trade during the Treaty-Port Era," *Explorations in Economic History* 1 (2017), 26–43; and W. Keller, and C.H. Shiue, "Capital Markets and Colonial Institutions in China," presentation at NBER Summer Institute, July 2020 (Cambridge, MA).

[5] See W. Keller, M. Lampe, and C.H. Shiue, "International Transactions: Real Trade and Factor Flows," in S. Broadberry and K. Fukao (eds.), *Cambridge Economic History of the Modern World*, vol. 1, *1700 to 1870* (Cambridge, Cambridge University Press, 2021), pp. 412–37, for a survey on real trade and factor flows in the eighteenth and nineteenth centuries from the viewpoint of global trade.

trade affect the domestic economy? The section titled "Quantifying Foreign Influence in China during the Treaty Port Era" quantifies the effect of foreign trade in China from two key perspectives: the size and distribution of its welfare effects and the geographic scope of foreign influence on domestic capital markets.

Finally, in the section titled "The Granular View: Chinese Commodity-Level Trade," we show how commodity-level trade statistics can be used to obtain a more granular view of trade, and in particular of the role of the extensive margin; that is, goods that newly enter foreign trade. As there were important revisions to the manner in which China's foreign-trade data were collected throughout the period, we discuss new methodologies that can be implemented to address changes in the definition of new goods. A number of broader lessons are discussed in the concluding section.

China's Foreign Trade before 1839 and the Opium Wars

To understand foreign trade in China prior to the Opium Wars, it is essential to consider the motivations and preoccupations of Chinese and Western traders and their respective governments in the period leading up to the nineteenth century.[6] Moreover, China didn't have one foreign policy, but multiple policies that depended on the region in question. In addition, these policies changed over time.

Whether over land or sea, China's borders were always porous to foreign traders. Early on, in the Western Han (206 BCE–9 CE), China's push into Central Asia was instrumental in supporting the caravan trade on the famous Silk Road. In the Tang–Song transition (755–1127) the Yangzi river valley

---

[6] Secondary accounts on the nature of the conflicts of the Opium Wars: A. Waley, *The Opium War through Chinese Eyes* (Palo Alto, Stanford University Press, 1963); H. Chang, *Commissioner Lin and the Opium War* (Cambridge, MA, Harvard University Press, 1964); I.C.Y. Hsü, *The Rise of Modern China* (Oxford, Oxford University Press, 1970); J. Beeching, *The Chinese Opium Wars* (New York, Harcourt Brace Jovanovich, 1975); Su Zhiliang 苏智良, 中国毒品史 (A History of Drugs in China) (Shanghai, Shanghai renmin chubanshe, 1997); R. Wakeman, *Strangers at the Gate: Social Disorder in South China, 1839–1861* (Berkeley, University of California Press, 1997); P.W. Fay, *The Opium War, 1840–1842: Barbarians in the Celestial Empire* (Chapel Hill, University of North Carolina Press, 1998); T. Brook and B.T. Wakabayashi (eds.), *Opium Regimes: China, Britain, and Japan, 1839–1952* (Berkeley, University of California Press, 2000); J. Spence, "Opium," in Spence, *Chinese Roundabout* (New York, Norton, 1992), pp. 228–58; J.G. Lutz, *Opening China: Karl F.A. Gützlaff and Sino-Western Relations, 1827–1852* (Grand Rapids and Cambridge, William B. Eerdmans Publishing, 2008); J. Lovell, *The Opium War: Drugs, Dreams and the Making of Modern China* (New York, Abrams Press, 2015).

emerged at the center of China's economy, and with it more urbanization and expanded domestic markets.[7] Significantly, China's cross-border commodity exchange permanently shifted away from the Silk Road, and towards maritime trade. By the turn of the tenth century, Chinese merchants were conducting trade over long distances with numerous foreign countries, from Arabia and Persia to Java, Brunei, India, Japan, the Korean peninsula, and the Philippine archipelago.[8] Intra-Asian maritime trade was active especially in the South China Sea. Over approximately 900–1300, triggered by the outward-looking policies of the Song and Yuan, an increase in maritime trade occurred based on the export of pepper, safflower, and spices from Southeast Asia to China, in exchange for ceramics and metals.[9] Over Central Eurasia, nomadic Kazakhs and Mongolian tribes traded horses and furs in exchange for Chinese tea, cloth and silks, and grain.[10]

Even as private, merchant-organized foreign trade routes were established, from the point of view of the state, foreign trade was tied to foreign diplomacy. The diplomatic terms were formalized in the framework of the tribute system (chaogong tizhi 朝貢體制). Notably, the tributary system encompassed different regional interests. Prior to the Opium Wars, the Qing state organized the management of foreign relations into separate offices: the Court of Colonial Affairs (lifanyuan 理藩院), which dealt with Inner Asian regions, including Mongolia, Russia, and Tibet; and the Board of Rites (libu 禮部), which handled court religious ceremonies but also the relations with sinified tributaries. The tributaries retained their own sovereignty, but their rulers accepted the emperor of China as the nominal political and cultural hegemon, and they were rewarded for their

---

[7] H. Miyakawa, "The Naitō Hypothesis and Its Effects on Japanese Studies of China," *Far Eastern Quarterly* 4 (1955), 533–52; see also chapter in R. von Glahn, *The Economic History of China: From Antiquity to the Nineteenth Century* (Cambridge, Cambridge University Press, 2016), pp. 208–17.

[8] B.K.L. So and J. Su, *Prosperity, Region, and Institutions in Maritime China: The South Fukien Pattern* (Cambridge, MA, Harvard University Asia Center, 2000), p. 35.

[9] See G. Wade, "An Early Age of Commerce in Southeast Asia, 900–1300 CE," *Journal of Southeast Asian Studies* 2 (2009), 221–65; A. Reid, "'An Age of Commerce' in Southeast Asian History," *Modern Asian Studies* 1 (1990), 1–30; and Reid, "The Seventeenth-Century Crisis in Southeast Asia," *Modern Asian Studies* 4 (1990), 639–59. Reid, "The Seventeenth-Century Crisis," argues that these trades continued until the mid-seventeenth century, when the expansion of the Dutch East India Company into the region effectively ended the maritime trade boom.

[10] See P.C. Perdue, *China Marches West: The Qing Conquest of Central Eurasia* (Cambridge, MA, Harvard University Press, 2005), pp. 400–2, 575, for accounts related to the private trade and co-operative official exchange of Central Eurasia.

loyalty.[11] The Qing also recognized arms-length relationships with non-tributary states, depending on the circumstances.[12]

Tributary trade – in which states ritually presented China with gifts, and often received gifts of even greater value in return – was used to maintain and to expand relationships with neighboring polities.[13] According to Fairbank and Fairbank and Têng, the tribute system governed the entire foreign-relations world order of China's empire up to the nineteenth century, and this narrow mind-set precluded the possibility of free trade and nation-state diplomacy based on terms of mutual equality.[14]

Recent research by numerous scholars has re-examined these interpretations in major ways. In particular, the importance of tributary trade has been shown to have weakened significantly over time, even if the tributary *system* as such provided a way for China to promote diplomatic relations. The Ming emperors were the last to prohibit maritime trade in favor of tributary trade, and even they didn't succeed fully in enforcing the ban. Moreover, compared to Ming emperors, Qing rulers were generally more relaxed about market-based exchange. Although Qing emperors also used maritime trade bans (*haijin* 海禁), the most stringent of the bans were imposed for political ends rather than in pursuit of any autarkic ideals. Between 1656 and 1684, the Qing imposed a maritime ban in order to subdue the Zheng empire – a powerful merchant organization that was loyal to the former rulers of the Ming

---

[11] Korea, for example, was considered a loyal tributary state, and thus Ming troops were sent in the 1590s to help Korea fight off the Japanese. Other close tributaries included Vietnam, Siam, Laos, Burma, Cambodia, Liuqiu (Rykukyu), Luzon and Java, and the Central Asian peoples such as the Kazakhs, Kirghiz, and Badakhshanis. In 1754, Qianlong refers to Java as "already within the compass of Our enlightened government." M. Elliot, *Qianlong: Son of Heaven, Man of the World* (New York, Pearson, 2009), p. 126.

[12] For example, the Portuguese did not accept the emperor of China as the nominal authority but were, nonetheless, allowed to settle in Macau, establishing a private trade center there in the mid-sixteenth century.

[13] Stability on the frontiers in Central Asia could have meant a net gain from the perspective of China's rulers if that reduced the chance of military encounters; see Perdue, *China Marches West*, pp. 402–3.

[14] J.K. Fairbank, "Tributary Trade and China's Relations with the West," *Far Eastern Quarterly* 1.2 (1942), 129–49; Fairbank, *Trade and Diplomacy on the China Coast: The Opening of the Treaty Ports, 1842–1854* (Cambridge, MA, Harvard University Press, 1969); J.K. Fairbank, and S.Y. Têng, "On the Ch'ing Tributary System," *Harvard Journal of Asiatic Studies* 2 (1941), p. 140, citing Jiang Tingfu: in the 11th and 12th centuries, "the neo-Confucian philosophy worked, which began to dominate China, worked out a dogma in regard to international relations, to hold sway in China right to the middle of the nineteenth century ... That dogma asserts that national security could only be found in isolation and stipulates that whoever wished to enter into relations with China must do so as China's vassal, acknowledging the supremacy of the Chinese emperor and obeying his commands, thus ruling out all possibility of international intercourse on terms of equality."

dynasty.[15] Immediately after the Zheng empire was vanquished in 1684, the Qing Kangxi Emperor opened all coastal ports to private trade and established customs stations to collect taxes.[16]

Because of the precedents set up during Kangxi's reign (1661–1722), which moved the Qing further away from the traditional tributary system, private trade frequently overshadowed the importance of tributary trade.[17] The Sino-Western trade, which first emerged out of a demand for Chinese luxury goods – tea, silk, porcelain, furniture, art, and lacquers – continued to operate over the eighteenth century. In addition to maritime exchange among traders in the South China Sea, Chinese merchants sailed to Nagasaki regularly to trade with Japanese merchants and entrepreneurs, and private Japanese traders plied the Chinese coastal trade.[18] Moreover, maritime exchange among Asian traders in the South China Sea may have extended beyond trade to organized private enterprises.[19]

Evidence of the pervasiveness of these global trading networks can be seen in the movement of precious metals as silver from overseas surged into China in exchange for Chinese goods.[20] In the seventeenth century, China imported around 115 tons of silver annually, approximately half of which came from mines in Japan, and the other half from the Americas.[21] Whether this extensive global trade was the cause or the outcome of the divergence in living

---

[15] In 1661, Zheng Chenggong (also known by Koxinga), successfully laid siege to the Dutch fort, Zeelandia, located in Taiwan, and, in open defiance of the Qing, established a separate state named Ming Eastern Capital *(dongdu Mingjing* 東都明京*)*. The Zheng family was one of the most successful merchant organizations of the period, with annual profits from maritime trade at least one-third that of the Dutch VOC; see Appendix 3 in X. Hang, *Conflict and Commerce in Maritime East Asia: The Zheng Family and the Shaping of the Modern World, c. 1620–1720* (Cambridge, Cambridge University Press, 2015).

[16] W. Rowe, *China's Last Empire: The Great Qing* (Cambridge, MA, The Belknap Press of Harvard University Press, 2009), pp. 136.

[17] Rowe, *China's Last Empire*, p. 136, concludes that tributary trade was "nil"; whereas T. Hamashita, *China, East Asia, and the Global Economy: Regional and Historical Perspectives* (London and New York, Routledge, 2008), Chapter 2, depicts tributary trade as being intertwined with commercial trade.

[18] Since the 1970s, historians have challenged the "national seclusion" view of Japan, documenting the continuous arrival of foreign trading vessels in Japan from the seventeenth through the nineteenth centuries. See Figure 1.2 in H. Peng, *Trade Relations between Qing China and Tokugawa Japan, 1685–1859* (Singapore, Springer, 2019); Hamashita, *China, East Asia, and the Global Economy*, presents a regional maritime history based on networks of trade that cut across national borders

[19] Hamashita, *China, East Asia, and the Global Economy*, Chapters 3–6.

[20] See Hamashita, *China, East Asia, and the Global Economy*, Chapter 4. G. Zhao, *The Qing Opening to the Ocean: Chinese Maritime Policies, 1684–1757* (Honolulu, University of Hawaii Press, 2013), synthesizes additional evidence on China's role in early globalization.

[21] See von Glahn, *The Economic History of China*, p. 309; R. von Glahn, "Foreign Silver Coins in the Market Culture of Nineteenth Century China," *International Journal of*

standards between China and Europe in the twentieth century has been the subject of long-standing debates.[22] What seems clear, however, is that accumulating qualitative and quantitative evidence largely overturns the perspectives of an earlier literature that tended to paint China as a closed and isolationist state before Western nations "opened" its markets.

Furthermore, not only does the recent evidence on international silver flows point to considerable foreign-trade activity, but it also appears that the Qing, and the earlier Ming state, paid attention to the advantages of empire building.[23] The Qianlong Emperor (1711–1799) achieved successes on this front. At its maximal geographical extent, the total territories of the Qing dynasty were about double the extent governed by the Ming. Around the year 1780, the Qing state was the second-largest Chinese empire, surpassed only by the Mongol Empire of Kublai Khan. Neither could it be claimed that the Chinese state had no challengers, as there were numerous and near-continuous conflicts both from within and against nearby states.[24] Instead, the Qing state had no challengers of equal stature in Asia because it had successfully eliminated the threats from neighboring regions, as well as the domestic rebellions from within. The military campaigns by the Qing state over Central Asia, for example, nearly obliterated the Dzungar

---

Asian Studies 1 (2007), 51–78, documents that foreign coins could be found circulating alongside domestic currencies, or as the dominating means of payment.

[22] Offering a contrasting point of view to Wallerstein's treatment of Asia as a semi-peripheral area relative to the European core before the mid-nineteenth century, A. G. Frank, *ReOrient: Global Economy in the Asian Age* (Berkeley, University of California Press, 1998), argues that a global economy in 1400–1900 centered on Asia. E. Jones, *The European Miracle: Environments, Economies and Geopolitics in the History of Europe and Asia* (Cambridge, Cambridge University Press, 2003); and K. Pomeranz, *The Great Divergence: China, Europe, and the Making of the Modern World Economy* (Princeton, Princeton University Press, 2000), offer competing explanations and points of emphasis, with the latter arguing that it was the relaxing of ecological constraints in Europe brought about by access to New World resources that laid the foundations for the Great Divergence between China and Europe. Also see R. Findlay and K. O'Rourke, *Power and Plenty: Trade, War, and the World Economy in the Second Millennium* (Princeton, Princeton University Press, 2007), who focus on the role of empire and the global connections established through trade.

[23] G. Wade, "The Zheng He Voyages: A Reassessment," *Journal of the Malaysian Branch of the Royal Asiatic Society* 1 (2005), 37–58, links the Zheng He voyages to aggressive attempts to dominate trade routes in the Middle East and East Asia, and suggests that the voyages constitute maritime proto-colonialism.

[24] Referencing what he felt to be his top ten military achievements during his reign, Qianlong wrote, "The ten instances of military merit include the two pacifications of the Dzungars, the quelling of the Muslim tribes, the two annihilations of the Jinchuan [rebels], the restoring of peace to Taiwan, and the subjugations of Burma and Vietnam; adding the recent twin capitulations of the Gurkhas makes ten in all. Why is there any need to include those three trivial rebellions in the inner provinces?" Elliot, *Qianlong*, p. 89.

(Zunghar) population of 600,000.[25] A combination of diplomacy and military aggression had thus made it possible for the Qing to achieve a high level of political, economic, and civilizational hegemony.

The stance of the Qing emperors towards the Sino-Western trade was not inconsistent with their overall strategy of statecraft. Within China, three key ports directed the trade coming from the West: Macau, Canton (now Guangzhou), and Hong Kong. Starting from the year 1684, and for more than 150 years after, the Qing managed Sino-Western trade through a merchant guild, or "Cohong" (公行). These merchants were appointed by the state to manage the European trade. The official superintendent of maritime customs, known as the "hoppo," collected duties on foreign trade through the Cohong merchants. These revenues were sent directly to the imperial household. After 1757, and until 1842, all Western trade had to be conducted from Canton. The Canton system allowed British, Dutch, French, Austrian, Swedish, Spanish, American, and other traders to carry out trades with a member of the Hong merchants. In practice, this meant that traders were required to live in special quarters, in buildings called "factories." The factories were located outside the city along Canton Harbor and included space for warehouses and offices.

Although Qing emperors personally gained revenues from the Sino-Western trade, they did not seek to expand trade or diplomatic relations beyond the Canton system. This may seem irrational, but it might be remembered that the early and mid-Qing rulers incorporated foreign trade as a lever of power within a very different set of institutional constraints. Both national security interests and economic gain entered into Qing calculations of how to handle Western traders. Rulers were concerned about the encroachment of foreigners and their activities on domestic interests and attempted to impose regulations. Thus, appointed Cohong merchants were responsible not only for the payment of transit dues of foreign traders, but also for the good behavior of foreign crews, in addition to managing the actual trade. Furthermore, Qing regulations limited foreign merchants' personal or diplomatic channels of communication with Qing government officials. Outside the four-month trading season, foreigners had to relocate away from Canton and to Macau.

From the British trader's perspective, the Canton system was unsatisfactory. Western traders who came to China often represented companies or syndicates that were funded by wealthy landowners and entrepreneurs in an industrializing Europe, or from the United States. They wanted more interaction and more

---

[25] About 90 percent of the Dzungars were killed, died, or were taken captive; Elliot, *Qianlong*, pp. 94. Qianlong targeted young and strong men for massacre in order to destroy the Dzungars as a people; Perdue, *China Marches West*, p. 283.

representation of their interests in China. These organizations were in some cases powerful enough to influence government politics at home.[26] One prominent example of the close connection between merchants' interests and their political activity is the British East India Company (BEIC), which operated from 1600 until 1834. The BEIC was a trading monopoly that competed with the nationally chartered Dutch East India Company (Vereenigde Oost-Indische Compagnie, VOC) in Asia. The expansion of foreign trade into Asia was a central aim of the British government and the BEIC.

An incident that compellingly illustrates the different motivations of Britain and China was Lord Macartney's mission to China. In 1792, Macartney was commissioned by Henry Dundas (who was president of the board of the BEIC, and a member of Britain's Home Ministry) to speak to the Qing court on behalf of British interests. Specifically, Macartney was instructed to relay to China's emperor "the mutual benefit to be derived from trade between the two Nations."[27] He was also to bring some products in order to "excite at Peking a taste for many articles of English workmanship hitherto unknown there ... [and] turn the balance of the China trade considerably in favour of Great Britain."[28] As imported opium was already a growing point of discord, Macartney was also instructed that should the subject of opium come up, and "if it should be made a positive requisition or any article of any proposed commercial treaty, that none of that drug should be sent by us to China, you must accede to it, rather than risk any essential benefit by contending for a liberty in this respect."[29]

On September 14, 1793, Macartney arrived in the court of Qianlong, who was over eighty years old at the time, with numerous gifts, most of which were European luxury items, such as German planetariums and clocks by Vulliamy. From Qianlong's written reply to King George III, we know that Macartney successfully transmitted to the Qing court Britain's requests,

---

[26] R. Brenner, *Merchants and Revolution: Commercial Change, Political Conflict, and London's Overseas Traders, 1550–1653* (Princeton, Princeton University Press, 2003), examines the relationship between English commerce and the political activities of overseas traders in the seventeenth century.

[27] J. Chen, P. Cheng, M. Lestz, and J. Spence, *The Search for Modern China: A Documentary Collection*, 3rd ed. (New York, W.W. Norton & Company, 2013), "Lord Macartney's Commission from Henry Dundas, 1792," p. 80.

[28] As quoted from H.B. Morse, *The Chronicles of the East India Company: Trading to China 1635–1834*, 5 vols. (Oxford, The Clarendon Press, 1926–1929), vol. 2, p. 215, as cited in M. Berg, "Britain, Industry and Perceptions of China: Matthew Boulton, 'Useful Knowledge' and the Macartney Embassy to China," *Journal of Global History* 2 (2006), 269–88.

[29] Chen et al., *The Search for Modern China*, "Lord Macartney's Commission from Henry Dundas, 1792," p. 81.

which Qianlong understood well. They were: (1) to have more ports in China to be open for purposes of trade, (2) to be able to establish a repository at the capital in Beijing, (3) to have an island where merchants can reside and goods can be warehoused, (4) to be able to have a place inside the city of Canton where foreign merchants may reside, (5) to have reduced duties on merchandise, (6) to have reduced tariffs on ships, and (7) to gain the full liberty to disseminate European religions to Chinese subjects.[30] Judging from the tone of Qianlong's long reply to Macartney's entreaties, he did not view Britain as more than a presumptuous faraway state that had overstepped proper boundaries of civilized relations.

A common interpretation of Qianlong's dismissal of Macartney's requests is that it encapsulates "the Chinese policy of superior indifference to Western things."[31] Yet a closer reading of the events suggests that, far from being indifferent, Qianlong was an astute collector of foreign objects, as he already possessed in his residence exactly the kinds of mechanical devices that Macartney had brought with him on his journey to China.[32] Apparently, unbeknown to Macartney, similar objects had arrived in China through existing channels of the Canton trade. Macartney later wrote in his journal that on his tour of Qianlong's pavilion, he saw

> stupendous vases of jasper and agate; with the finest porcelain and japan,[33] and with every kind of European toys and sing-songs; with spheres, orreries, clocks and musical automatons of such exquisite workmanship, and in such profusion, that our presents must shrink from the comparison and hide their diminished heads.[34]

The Macartney mission did not fundamentally alter the way Sino-Western trade was conducted. Corporate interests in China had neither the explicit military backing of the state, nor, for the most part, the means to wage war against the state. Instead, Chinese merchants typically tried to acquire official or semiofficial roles within the state. Thus, many well-off merchants in China sought to gain greater influence in the government by purchasing degrees or

---

[30] Chen et al., *The Search for Modern China*, pp. 90–3.
[31] D.S. Landes, "Why Europe and the West? Why Not China?", *Journal of Economic Perspectives* 2 (2006), 18.
[32] "On the court's side, questions concerning Macartney's pronouncements about the British gifts still lingered. As if to address this issue directly, the embassy was taken to buildings filled with intricate European clocks and mechanical devices ... The point being made that the things Macartney had brought were in no way unique to his king's domain." From J.L. Hevia, *Cherishing Men from Afar: Qing Guest Ritual and the Macartney Embassy of 1793* (Durham, NC, Duke University Press, 1995), p. 179.
[33] Objects made with a dark lacquer.
[34] Cited in Hevia, *Cherishing Men from Afar*, p. 176. See also Berg, *Britain, Industry and Perceptions of China*, pp. 269–88.

investing in the education of their sons so that someone in the clan could gain the ear of an official, or, better, be anointed into officialdom themselves.[35]

British and other Western traders felt slighted as they sought to engage China in the new diplomatic language of equal nation-states and negotiated benefits, while Qing emperors still considered the arrival of Western traders on China's shores to be nothing more significant than the understandable desire of foreigners to partake of the benefits of China's civilization and the blessings of the emperor. British, American, and European merchants chafed under the restrictions of Qing policies, but not so much as to be willing to give up their share of the profits from the Canton trade.

The differences in the political economy in the two empires, and how each conceptualized domestic and foreign relations, seem to be especially striking in the years leading up to the Opium War.[36] Because of the successful spread of the British Industrial Revolution, our modern system of foreign trade and diplomacy aligns with that of the European system, but it might be remembered that Europe had itself only not that long ago – sometime between the Treaty of Westphalia (1646–1648), the revolutionary decade of 1789 to 1799 in France, and the Congress of Vienna (1814–1815) – settled on the nation-state framework as a formal system of international relations among sovereign states.[37] Before that, customs, personal relationships, and family alliances through marriage tended to play a larger role in foreign diplomatic negotiations in Europe too.

From the start of the Sino-Western trade, European traders sought access to Chinese markets not only to buy Chinese goods, but also to sell their own wares in what they imagined to be an immense market. The problem, however, was not simply market access, but a lack of products that ordinary consumers in China could afford. As late as the 1830s, traders of one of the

---

[35] These official positions were frequently the most rewarding from a socioeconomic point of view; see C.H. Shiue, "Human Capital and Fertility in Chinese Clans," *Journal of Economic Growth* 4 (2017), 351–96.

[36] The similarities and differences in the economy and political system of China and Europe are further analyzed in detail in R.B. Wong, *China Transformed: Historical Change and the Limits of European Experience* (Ithaca, NY, Cornell University Press, 1997); Pomeranz, *The Great Divergence*; and R.B. Wong and J. Rosenthal, *Before and beyond Divergence: The Politics of Economic Change in China and Europe* (Cambridge, MA, Harvard University Press, 2011). On the influence of cultural change in China and Europe, see J. Mokyr, *A Culture of Growth: The Origins of the Modern Economy* (Princeton, Princeton University Press, 2016), pp. 287–320.

[37] For contrasts of Europe's "Westphalian system" with East Asia's formal hierarchy in international relations, see D. Kang, *East Asia before the West: Five Centuries of Trade and Tribute* (New York, Columbia University Press, 2010); and Hamashita, *China, East Asia, and the Global Economy*.

dominating trading houses at the time – Jardine, Matheson & Co. – reported that the Chinese native *nankeen* cotton cloth (named for Nanjing) was superior in quality and cost compared to Manchester cotton goods.[38] Thus, even though cotton was one of the core industries that was revolutionized by the British Industrial Revolution, it would still be some time before machine-produced textiles could compete with the low costs of labor production in China. By contrast, as industrialization spread from Britain to Northwest Europe and its offshoots, wealthier classes in urban centers may have been better able to afford foreign imports and Chinese luxury goods.[39] Not only did tea drinking become fashionable, but consumers were fascinated with chinoiserie and other Chinese decorative goods. Chinese craftsmen and manufacturers, for their part, also eagerly created custom-designed products for foreign markets.

The good that tipped the trade balance was opium.[40] In 1773, 140,000 pounds of opium were imported into China from India; by the early 1820s, imports had grown tenfold.[41] Opium was illegal and yet openly smuggled, bought, and sold on the watch of Qing merchants and officials alike. In the 1830s, 20 to 30 percent of government officials consumed opium, and the Daoguang Emperor (r. 1820–1850) was himself an addict.[42] At first considered a foreign luxury good and a symbol of privilege and hospitality, opium became widely used throughout Chinese society. Early debates in the Qing court about the appropriate response to opium imports considered the pros and cons of legalization and taxation of the drug, as opposed to strict prohibition.[43] Eventually, opium imports became a scapegoat for the failures

---

[38] Greenberg, *British Trade and the Opening of China*, p. 2.
[39] Average wages of urban residents in major cities of Western Europe like London were likely trending higher than those of their counterparts in Beijing or even Suzhou. R. Allen, J.P. Bassino, D. Ma, C. Moll-Murata, and J.L. van Zanden, "Wages, Prices, and Living Standards in China, 1738–1925: In Comparison with Europe, Japan, and India," *Asia in the Great Divergence*, special issue of *Economic History Review* 64.S1 (2011), 3–38. Additional research is needed before we can be sure, but to the extent that average wages are correlated with incomes of the wealthier classes within each region, the trends may be similar.
[40] For perspectives on the history of the consumption of opium, see F. Dikötter, L. Laamann, and Z. Xun, "Narcotic Culture: A Social History of Drug Consumption in China," *British Journal of Criminology* 2 (2002), 317–36; also see Su, 中国毒品史.
[41] Spence, *Chinese Roundabout*, pp. 233–5.
[42] P.C. Perdue, "The First Opium War: The Anglo-Chinese War of 1839–1842," *MIT Visualizing Cultures*, 2011, https://visualizingcultures.mit.edu/opium_wars_01/ow1_essay01.html.
[43] See the arguments from proponents of legalization and taxation, as well as prohibition, in J. Slade, *Narrative of the Late Proceedings and Events in China* ([Canton], Canton Register Press, 1839), pp. 1–140.

of the government, social unrest, and the economic decline that characterized the last third of the Qing Dynasty.[44]

In 1839, Qing commissioner Lin Zexu was sent by the Daoguang Emperor to end the opium problem through prohibition. Lin took the moral high ground on the matter of opium, eventually destroying a large cargo of opium when his entreaties to cease the opium trade were ignored.[45] In response, British traders declared property damage and quickly resorted to military action. It was the new technology of the steam engine outfitted on British boats, however, that determined the outcome of the Opium Wars. Finally, European grievances about the restrictive conditions of the Canton system could be forcefully expressed in the form of the steamships that could deftly steer into the shallow harbor waters of Canton. British military forces took Canton, moved up the coast and along the Yangzi river, captured Shanghai, and eventually reached the Grand Canal, in effect threatening Peking itself.[46]

China quickly surrendered, agreeing to sign the Treaty of Nanking (Nanjing) (1842), which stipulated that an indemnity had to be paid as compensation to Britain; in addition, Hong Kong was ceded to Britain. Beyond the initial four treaty ports (Xiamen, Fuzhou, Ningbo, and Shanghai), additional ports were later opened to foreign trade. Trade duties were limited to 5 percent *ad valorem* or less on all goods. Moreover, foreign nationals were given the right to reside and own property in designated treaty ports. In addition, foreigners in China would be subject to the legal jurisdiction of their own country rather than to Chinese laws.

The issue of the legality of opium in China was hardly worth even a mention in the Treaty of Nanking. Indeed, the *coup d'état* was not about making the opium trade legal in China. The real prize was about market access and the entry of foreign businesses into China's economy. This

---

[44] More recently, Z. Wang, *Never Forget National Humiliation: Historical Memory in Chinese Politics and Foreign Relations* (New York, Columbia University Press, 2012), pp. 96–8, argues that after 1991, historical revisionism shifted from class struggle to struggle with outside forces.

[45] Lin's communication to Charles Elliot, the British superintendent of trade, in March of 1839: "While our Celestial Court has in humble submission to it ten thousand (i.e. all) regions, and the heaven-like goodness of the great Emperor overshadows all, the nation aforesaid (Britain) and the Americans have, by their trade at Canton during many years, enjoyed, of all those in subjection, the largest measure of favors," "but that they have brought opium – that pervading poison – to this land: thus profiting themselves by the injury of others." Great Britain Foreign Office, *Correspondence Relating to China: Presented to Both Houses of Parliament, by Command of Her Majesty* (London, T.R. Harrison, 1840), pp. 268–9.

[46] Romanization of names of locations and treaty ports in this chapter will follow that used by the CMC in the nineteenth and twentieth centuries. Pinyin will be used in other cases.

sentiment was voiced by the British plenipotentiary, Sir Henry Pottinger, who announced after Britain's victory over China in the First Opium War (1840–1842) that China's potential for trade was so vast "that all the mills of Lancashire could not make stocking stuff sufficient for one of its provinces."[47] His overly ambitious forecast was slow to come to fruition, however.

Initially, the Qing court did not see the Treaty of Nanking as the resolution of a grand showdown, but rather as a small concession made in order to smooth over a conflict that could eventually be redressed in China's favor. For Britain, however, signed treaties between nations, compelled or not, were all that mattered in the new era defined by contractual agreements between nation-states. In 1844, the United States and France concluded similar treaties with China, the Treaty of Wanghia and the Treaty of Whampoa respectively. China's reluctance to enforce the terms of the earlier treaties led to the Second Opium War (1856–1860), and further treaty ratifications and most-favored-nation clauses that allowed all foreign powers operating in China to seek the same concessions. The various treaties thus gradually opened China to international markets and ushered in an age of ever-increasing commerce with the rest of the world until 1949, when Mao Zedong came to power.

China's Foreign Trade during the Treaty Port Era (1842–1943)

The Treaty of Nanking (1842) put into motion a significant transformation of China's trade environment. It was followed by the Treaty of Tientsin (Tianjin) (1858), which opened yet more treaty ports, and it also laid the foundation for foreign-trade policies in China in essential ways. The most important of the clauses of the Treaty of Tientsin established a system under which trade duties would be collected under a consistent system across treaty ports. In principle, this implied that foreign goods would be taxed only once upon entry into China and thereafter be exempt from further duties even if the goods were transported further inland. Among other rights granted to foreign traders and residents, foreign vessels were permitted on the Yangzi river and foreign merchants could also employ Chinese ships to carry their goods. The British were officially permitted, in 1848, to establish a foreign settlement in Shanghai. During the treaty port era, foreigners came to have

---

[47] China Maritime Customs (CMC), *Decennial Reports, Fifth Issue (1922–1931)*, vol. 1 (Shanghai, Statistical Department of the Inspectorate General of Customs, 2001), p. 39.

a much more active role in the wider economy than in earlier times, which included the ownership of hundreds of firms and businesses, including banks and shipyards.

The China Maritime Customs and Its Records

While the Treaty of Nanking did away with several existing elements of China's foreign-trade system, the Chinese customs authority initially retained its oversight of the processing of foreign trade. However, the erosion of the central government's authority after the Opium War and the government's lasting preoccupation with the suppression of domestic uprisings (in particular the Taiping Rebellion of 1844 to 1860) meant that foreign-trade revenue collection fell primarily into the hands of provincial and local authorities. These local officials were ill-equipped to handle the larger volume of trade coming in, and foreign trade was not subject to a consistent set of rules. Rather, the payment of trade taxes was a matter of bargaining power, and the system was rife with corruption.[48]

The China Maritime Customs (CMC) was founded in 1854 by the foreign consuls in Shanghai to collect maritime-trade taxes that had been going unpaid due to the inability of Chinese officials to collect them during the Taiping Rebellion. Although the CMC was nominally under the jurisdiction of China's Foreign Office (the zongli yamen 總理衙門), which was newly established in 1861, in practice it operated under the management of foreign powers. In the beginning, its staff were mostly British. Later, nationals from other Western countries joined. The top CMC position and director of its operations was the inspector general, who worked side by side with his Chinese counterpart, called the superintendent of customs, who oversaw the collection of trade taxes from the so-called native trade; that is, from Chinese-owned junks.

Early opposition to the CMC arose largely from foreign consuls who feared that the CMC would usurp some of their powers. Foreign merchants were also initially opposed to the CMC because now they had to deal with customs formalities that before had been left in their entirety to Chinese middlemen and clerks. Within only a couple of years, however, foreign traders and entrepreneurs had come to prefer the consistent and predictable

---

[48] Tax collection was poor even in major ports such as Shanghai. The British consul of Shanghai estimated in one year that the loss of tariff revenue in Shanghai was at least 25 percent, and complained that "two or three sleepy menials at $5 or $6 a month" were the sole means existing for the collection of duty, with which he was bound by the Treaty of Nanking to co-operate. CMC, *Decennial Reports, Fifth Issue*, vol. 1, p. 81.

customs treatment by the new CMC system, and over time foreign merchants were generally in favor of the foreign inspectorship system – this smoothed the frictions between consuls and CMC officials.

Although the Chinese central government resented the loss of sovereignty that came with the Treaty of Nanking and customs operations by the CMC, the introduction of the CMC also substantially increased the net tariff revenues it received.[49] Local Chinese government officials likely experienced a net decline in benefits as the CMC reduced their ability to withhold revenues from the central government and strike deals for personal enrichment. Moreover, smugglers, pirates, and adventurers saw their prospects of gain diminished with the arrival of the CMC, especially because over time the CMC extended its responsibilities to include antismuggling operations. Later, the CMC also expanded its involvement into postal administration, coastal policing, harbor and waterway management, and weather reporting.

From the point of view of the treaty powers, the establishment of the CMC not only broadened their political influence in China but also ensured that China would have the means to pay the indemnities imposed on it after the First and Second Opium Wars. The information generated by this system was so credible that China was able to put the tariff revenue down as collateral against which it could borrow from abroad at relatively low rates of interest. A further motive, arguably the most important, was that the treaty powers wanted to support the expansion of commercial exchange between China and their own economies, which necessitated a more open and consistent Chinese system.

The CMC's jurisdiction extended to "foreign-type" vessels, in particular steamships, whether owned by foreigners or by Chinese, and to junks chartered by foreigners. In addition to calculating tax revenues that were due, the CMC was responsible for the examination of cargo, the prevention of smuggling, and the assessment of treaty tariffs on exports, imports, and coastal trade. The nominal tariff was fixed to yield a rate of approximately 5 percent *ad valorem*; however, over time the effective rate was often lower, around 3 percent or less, due to price increases.

The number of treaty ports and customs houses expanded until there were over forty by the year 1907. Map 12.1 displays the locations of CMC stations

---

[49] Robert Hart, the inspector general of the CMC from 1863 to 1911 and one of the most influential individuals in the history of the service, estimated that under the native customs system the costs of tariff collection were larger than the customs system's revenues, while under the CMC at Shanghai these costs were only around 2 percent of the revenues; CMC, *Decennial Reports, Fifth Issue*, vol. 1, p. 81.

Foreign Trade and Investment

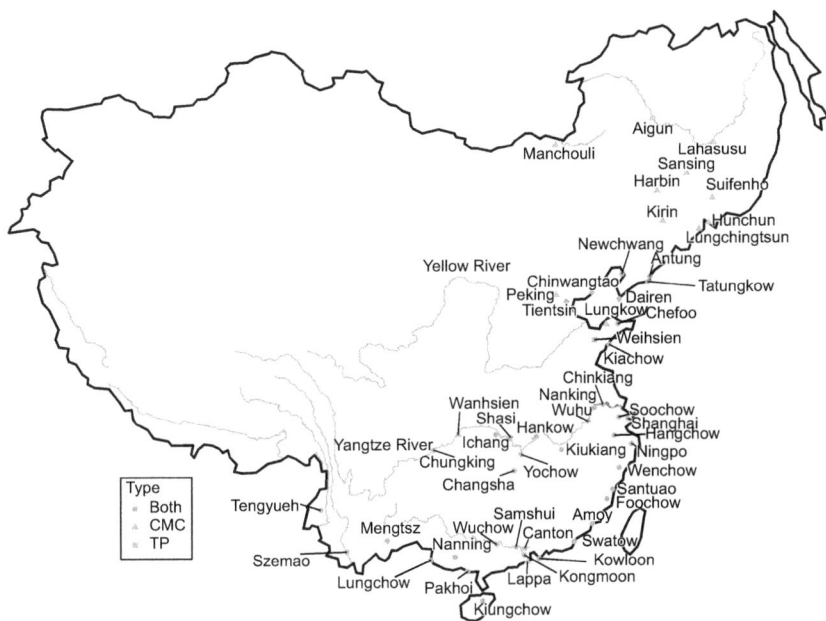

Map 12.1 China Maritime Customs stations and treaty ports
Source: CMC customs stations given in T. Lyons, *China Maritime Customs and China's Trade Statistics, 1859–1948* (Trumansburg, NY, Willow Creek Press, 1973); and treaty ports (TP) with entries in the *Returns of Trade* of 1910

that were established over the organization's existence.[50] The CMC did not establish customs stations in all ports, but focused on the ports that were important for foreign trade. Generally, the more important ports were opened relatively early, which means that even in the 1860s the CMC covered 80 to 90 percent of all foreign trade. With the opening of the CMC customs station in Kowloon (which was located opposite Hong Kong Island and was thus important for the trade with Hong Kong) in the year 1886, virtually all of China's foreign trade was covered.

The CMC's statistical records on trade are contained primarily in the *Returns of Trade*, with additional statistics and more descriptive accounts available in the *Trade Reports* and *Special Collections*. From the start of the CMC in 1859 to its end in 1948, records on trade were entered at least at annual intervals. There is some daily information (e.g. for Shanghai) during

---

[50] The map gives the list of treaty ports in the CMC *Returns of Trade* of 1910. There were ninety-two treaty ports by 1917, but many were self-initiated ports.

some periods. Previous studies have given overviews of the institutional features of the CMC organization and have provided broad outlines of some of the contents of the CMC trade data.[51]

One of the most notable aspects of the CMC's trade records is that they capture trade flows that are difficult or impossible to obtain even in modern-day advanced economies. Most data on international trade consider the country as the unit of observation. By contrast, the CMC recorded information not only by country, but by port. That is, the focus of observation is not country-to-country trade, but rather country-to-port-of-entry trade, where the port is treated independently as if it were a country. In this case, the port is the customs area. This allows for analyses that consider international trade flows at the intra-national level because the data effectively integrate domestic trade with international trade. This unique perspective on the movement of goods had much to do with the political circumstances at the time, when the treaty ports of China were treated as enclaves over which certain foreign countries had trading rights.

In order to assess trade duties in this elaborate system, the CMC's staff recorded the quantity and value of the goods carried. For example, in 1881, one can find over twenty different categories of cotton goods being imported (from velvets and velveteens to Turkey red cloths), at least ten different varieties of woolen goods, and some seventy different sundries that included window glass, alpaca umbrellas, needles, and dried clams. From 1875 until around 1933, values were reported in terms of silver, also known as the Customs tael (or *haiguan liang* 海關兩). Rates of exchange between the Customs tael and the local currency existed for each port and were also reported by the CMC.[52]

Some qualifications should be noted. First, the CMC improved its record keeping over time, so that it was not until 1867 that relatively uniform methods of accounting were put in place. Second, the statistics do not refer

---

[51] Lyons, *China Maritime Customs and China's Trade Statistics, 1859–1948*, outlines the contents of the CMC data and also paints a detailed portrait of the tea trade at several Chinese ports. On the institutional history of the CMC, see L. Hsiao, *China's Foreign Trade Statistics* (Cambridge, MA, Harvard University Press, 1974); H. van de Ven, "Globalizing Chinese History," *History Compass* 1 (2004), 1–5; D. Brunero, *Britain's Imperial Cornerstone: The Chinese Maritime Customs Service, 1854–1949* (New York, Routledge Curzon, 2004); and R. Bickers, "Revisiting the Chinese Maritime Customs Service, 1854–1950," *Journal of Imperial and Commonwealth History* 2 (2008), 221–6; R. Nield, *China's Foreign Places: The Foreign Presence in China in the Treaty Port Era, 1840–1943* (Hong Kong, Hong Kong University Press, 2015).

[52] Between 1875 and 1933, there were more variations in currency units for value – these included the Spanish dollar, the British pound, local currency, gold units, the gold dollar, and the Chinese dollar.

to the entirety of China's trade, but only to the trade through treaty ports, and of this trade, only that part that was carried on foreign vessels or on Chinese ships of the foreign type (that is, steamers). At the same time, the foreign-flag vessels included not only ships, but also those transports traveling overland to Russia. Further, from the year 1901 on, the CMC also took over the operation of Native Customs stations within twenty-five kilometers of open ports and began to collect data on trade going through these stations as well. The records on flows of those Chinese-produced goods were published in separate tables.

The trade statistics are broadly consistent, both internally with other numbers reported by the CMC and externally with foreign-partner trade records where the data are considered to be of high quality. With the decline of "junk" shipping, the coverage of foreign trade in the CMC data by the year 1904 was essentially 100 percent. At the same time, the CMC data collection system underwent a number of changes, in part due to changing international practice, and in part due to structural economic changes. This is to be expected over a long period of close to 100 years – 1859 to 1948. We will return to this below in our discussion of China's commodity-level trade.

China's Overall Foreign Trade

In this section, we summarize China's overall foreign trade. This provides a benchmark for the more disaggregated analysis below. All data are taken from the annual CMC reports. Figure 12.1 shows the evolution of China's aggregate foreign commodity trade. It is clear from the figure that the expansion in China's trade remained relatively stagnant from 1865 to 1885. However, overall trade growth averaged 3.5 percent per year for imports and 2.7 percent for exports over the 1865–1900 period.

Two things are apparent. First, for the period shown, China was more likely to have a trade deficit than a trade surplus in its commodity trade, the difference to be covered by bullion or international debt. Second, the volume of China's overall foreign trade was relatively stable before the year 1885. Afterwards, the evolution of China's trade was reasonably well characterized by a linear growth trend of about 5 percent per year.

Country Composition

Turning to the composition of China's foreign trade across countries, we analyze the nineteenth and twentieth centuries separately because several major changes took place over this period. Table 12.1 shows China's main trade partners in both imports and exports between the years 1865 and 1900.

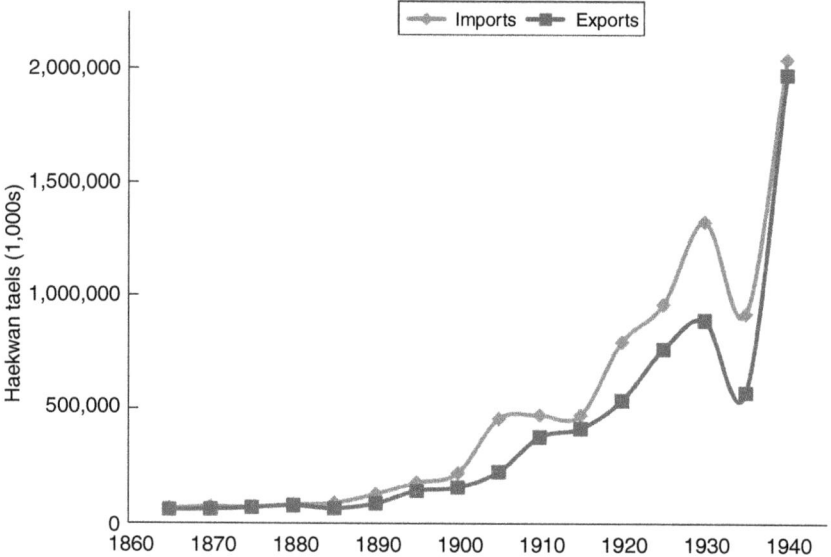

Figure 12.1 China's foreign trade, 1865 to 1940
Notes. Reported are nominal values of Customs taels, the currency adopted by the CMC. No adjustments have been made for territorial changes, for example Manchuria, which became a client state of Japan in 1931. Shown in the graph are total imports; a fraction between 1 and 5 percent of these were re-exported from China to other countries

The role of Hong Kong in intermediating China's trade through re-exports (entrepôt trade) is well known. Only a small fraction of China's imports from Hong Kong are produced in Hong Kong, and analogously, only a small part of Chinese exports to Hong Kong are consumed in Hong Kong. Table 12.1 quantifies this for the nineteenth century, with around 40 percent of China's imports originating in Hong Kong, and nearly 30 percent of its exports destined for Hong Kong. Because the ultimate origin and destination of China's trade via Hong Kong is not known for all years, the following analysis nets out trade through Hong Kong.[53]

Table 12.2 presents the breakdown of China's imports for 1900 to 1946, showing that with the turn of the century a number of additional countries became important in China's trade. During the first half of the twentieth century, Japan was the most important source of Chinese imports, followed by the United States, while Great Britain had fallen to third place. Beyond the

---

[53] A quantitative analysis of Hong Kong's role as entrepôt is in Keller, Li, and Shiue, "China's Foreign Trade," 853–92.

Table 12.1 Average trade shares, 1865–1900

Imports	%	Exports	%
Great Britain	24.82	Hong Kong	26.94
Hong Kong	41.36	Great Britain	31.65
British India	18.23	Continental Europe	11.86
Japan	5.80	United States	11.07
United States	2.65	Russia	5.82
Continental Europe	2.31	Japan	4.93
Other countries	4.84	Other countries	7.73

level of overall trade, the types of goods imported from these countries differed, with Great Britain and the United States exporting relatively more machinery and other producer goods than Japan to China. Significant amounts of imports originated from nearby sources such as the Dutch East Indies, French Indochina, Singapore, and Australia. Among the continental European countries, the relatively early industrializers, such as Germany and Belgium, were more important than countries that industrialized later, such as Italy. Overall, while the relative importance of trade with the British Empire had diminished, the evolution of China's trade patterns transitioned smoothly along the foundations laid during the nineteenth century.

It is useful to examine China's share of world trade in comparison with other countries. While statistics on China's trade were meticulously recorded by the CMC, it was only at the beginning of the twentieth century that trade statistics for many other countries in the world became available. These figures are given in Table 12.3.[54]

China accounted for about 2 percent of world trade from 1913 to 1938, with a peak in the 1920s. As we will see below, it took a large part of the twentieth century before it was able to capture a similar share of world trade. The value of China's foreign trade corresponds to about three-quarters of that of Japan and around two-thirds of that of British India. Unsurprisingly, China's foreign trade during this period fell far short of that of industrialized countries such as Great Britain, the United States, and Germany.

---

[54] For countries other than China, see League of Nations, *Statistical Yearbook of the League of Nations* (Geneva, League of Nations, 1940).

Table 12.2 Major sources of Chinese imports, 1900–1946

Country	%
Japan	24.51
United States	22.05
Great Britain	17.02
British India	9.65
Germany	4.19
Java (Dutch East Indies)	2.91
French Indochina	2.39
Russia (Soviet Union)	2.10
Belgium–Luxembourg	1.85
Singapore	1.56
Australia	1.25
Other countries	10.53

Note. Figures represent each country's share of total imports directly into China net of imports from Hong Kong.

Table 12.3 World merchandise trade by country

	Year				
Country	1913	1925	1930	1938	Mean
China	1.88	2.30	1.83	1.98	2.00
Great Britain	15.24	14.90	13.44	13.90	14.37
United States	11.15	14.31	12.61	10.70	12.19
Japan	1.79	3.07	2.62	3.20	2.67
British India	3.60	3.59	2.87	2.50	3.14
Germany	13.12	8.00	9.65	9.20	9.99

Notes. Figures for China are from the CMC reports, various volumes. Numbers in the table measure exports plus imports as a percentage share of the world total.

The Volume of Trade

This section considers the volume of foreign trade of China. For concreteness, we focus on the most important port of China during this period, which was Shanghai.[55] We employ the so-called gravity equation of trade to examine Shanghai's bilateral trade with foreign countries. Generally, this is

[55] See Keller, Li, and Shiue, "Shanghai's Trade, China's Growth," 336–78, for additional analysis.

because the gravity equation is highly successful in explaining bilateral trade, and it has been established that many trade theories imply a version of the gravity equation.[56] It is also of interest to see whether Shanghai's bilateral trade volumes during the treaty port era were unusual. The fact that trade treaties were imposed upon China may give rise to doubts as to whether a model of trade based on voluntary exchange can fit the data. For example, if there were forced trade for certain bilateral partners, then this could violate the gravity model if the trades were imposed in a way that ran counter to the economic basis of trade. What we demonstrate is that in the case of China's opening, the gravity model still applies, suggesting that natural trade flows resulted when ports were opened, with implications of gains from trade to China and foreign partners.

The gravity equation of trade is, in its simplest form, given by

$$TRADE_{ij} = \frac{GDP_i^\alpha GDP_j^\beta}{DIST_{ij}^\gamma} \quad (1)$$

where i and j are two trading economies. TRADE is either exports or imports, GDP is gross domestic product, and DIST is shipping distance. The idea is that bilateral commercial interaction is increasing in the size of each economy (the GDPs) and declining as trade barriers increase (distance would be one example of a trade barrier). In its log-linearized regression form, the equation is

$$\ln TRADE_{ij} = \alpha \ln GDP_i + \beta \ln GDP_j + \gamma \ln DIST + X'_{ij}\delta + \epsilon ij, \quad (2)$$

where X refers to a set of control variables, and ϵ is a regression error. We expect $\alpha, \beta > 0$ and $\gamma < 0$. The usual signs of the estimated coefficients are $\hat{\alpha} > 0$ and $\hat{\beta} > 0$ because bilateral transactions increase in the size of the trade partners, and $\hat{\gamma} < 0$ because greater distance implies more resistance to trade due to higher transport costs and other impediments. The term X includes time-fixed effects in some specifications.

The following countries and regions are included in the analysis: continental Europe, Egypt, Hong Kong, Japan, the Philippines, Singapore, Thailand, and the United States.[57] Among these, Hong Kong and Singapore were entrepôts, and to control for this we include an indicator variable. GDP for Shanghai is proxied by population. Using data for the years 1869 to 1904,

---

[56] An overview is presented in J. Anderson, "The Gravity Model," *Annual Review of Economics* 3 (2011), 133–60.
[57] Results for foreign GDP and distance are similar when we include the United Kingdom.

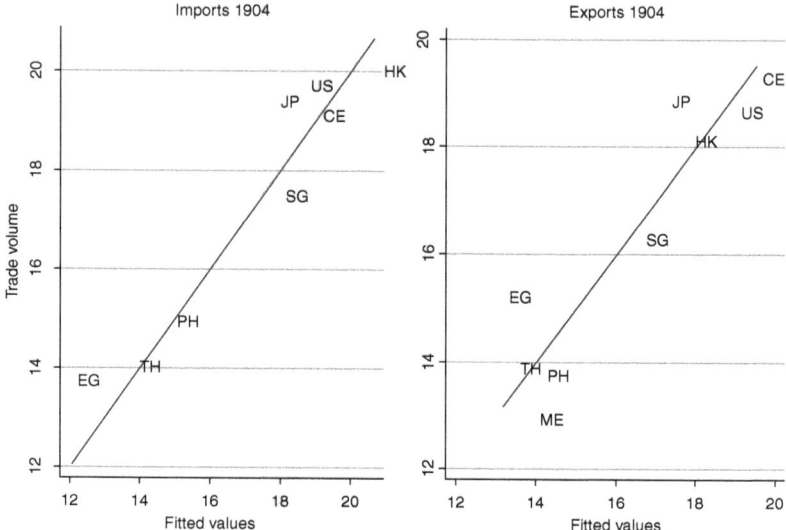

EG: Egypt; TH: Thailand; PH: Philippines; SG: Singapore; HK: Hong Kong; JP: Japan; US: USA; CE: Continental Europe; ME: Mexico

Figure 12.2 Predicted versus actual bilateral trade volume for Shanghai
Notes. On the horizontal axis is the predicted value of trade using values of the independent variables in the year 1904 and the gravity equation coefficients of Table 12.4. On the vertical axis the actual value of trade for the same years is given. Trade data from *Decennial Reports, First Issue (1882–1891), Second Issue (1892–1901), Third Issue (1902–1911), Fourth Issue (1912–1921),* and *Fifth Issue (1922–1931)* (Shanghai, Statistical Department of the Inspectorate General of Customs, 2001); and *Shanghai Statistical Yearbooks,* various volumes

we estimate a positive coefficient on foreign GDP and a negative coefficient on distance. Furthermore, the coefficients are not far from plus one (GDP) and minus one (distance).[58]

The fit of the gravity equation can be assessed by comparing actual with predicted trade for a particular year. The results for 1904 are reported in Figure 12.2. The diagonal in each of the graphs of Figure 12.2 denotes the forty-five-degree line, where the prediction is equal to actual trade. We see that bilateral trade during the treaty port era indeed follows the gravity equation. The gravity equation in trade is typically derived for models of market economies based on voluntary exchange; the results indicate that it also explains trade volumes at a time when colonial trade and regular trade are intertwined.[59]

---

[58] This is in line with other findings by K. Head and T. Mayer, "Gravity Equations: Workhorse, Toolkit, and Cookbook," in G. Gopinath, E. Helpman, and K. Rogoff (eds.), *Handbook of International Economics,* vol. 4 (Amsterdam, Elsevier, 2014), pp. 131–95.
[59] See Keller, Li, and Shiue, "Shanghai's Trade, China's Growth," 336–78, for further analysis.

Foreign Direct Investment in China

With the arrival of foreign traders, consulates, firms, and residents, Chinese treaty ports were exposed to aspects of British and Western technologies in mechanization, transportation, and steam power, and other innovations in financial institutions and banking. Two channels through which major transfers of technology can take place between countries are capital flows, first through foreign investments, and second through foreign firms and residents. There is abundant evidence both for direct capital flows and for the possibility of knowledge and technological know-how to have diffused from Western countries to China.[60]

Capital Flows

In this and the following subsection, we highlight the fact that capital flows increased during the nineteenth and early twentieth centuries. Remer shows that foreign direct investment (FDI) grew considerably over time, even after adjusting for inflation. As shown in Table 12.4, in 1902, business investments totaled around US$503.2 million and this grew to US$1,048.5 million in 1914 and US$2,474.5 million in 1931. The primary investors were Britain, who invested around 30 to 40 percent in each year, and Japan, who became a large investor by 1931 with 36.9 percent of investment. Russia, on the other hand, was a large investor in 1902 with 43.7 percent of the investment, but was down to only 11.1 percent by 1931. To put the total FDI numbers in context, Remer notes comparable estimates for India in 1933, with between

Table 12.4 Business investments in China by country

	1902		1914		1913	
	US$ million	% of total	US$ million	% of total	US$ million	% of total
Britain	150	29.8	400	36.9	963.4	38.9
Japan	1	0.2	210	19.4	912.8	36.9
Russia	220.1	43.7	236.5	21.8	273.2	11.1
US	17.5	3.5	42	3.9	155.1	6.3
France	29.6	5.9	60	5.5	95	3.9
Germany	85	16.9	136	12.5	75	3
Total	503.2	100	1,084.50	100	2,474.50	100

Source: C.F. Remer, *Foreign Investment in China* (New York, Macmillan Company, 1933), Table 13

---

[60] See also data tabulated in Kung's chapter in this volume.

Table 12.5 Geographical distribution of the direct business investments of four countries, 1931

	Direct business investments (US$ million)					
	Great Britain	Japan	Russia	USA	Total	% of total
Shanghai	737.4	215		97.5	1,049.90	46.4
Manchuria		550.2	261.8		812	36
Rest of China (incl. Hong Kong)	226	108.9	11.4	52.7	399	17.6
Total business investments	963.4	874.1	273.2	150.2	2,260.90	100

Source: Remer, *Foreign Investment in China*, Table 11

US$2,000 million and US$3,500 million in total FDI. Similar to the trade flows, FDI activity was concentrated at Shanghai (and to a lesser extent Manchuria). In 1931, as seen in Table 12.5, 46.4 percent of the business FDI was based in Shanghai.

Foreign Firms and Residents

Foreign direct investment can be seen as not just a transfer of capital, but also a transfer of technological know-how. Furthermore, foreign-owned companies and individuals can be sources of spillovers to the local economy. Generally, it is challenging to find quantitative evidence of technological know-how transfers in historical contexts, but CMC statistics can provide useful information for China, as summarized in the following.

Figure 12.3 details foreign presence over time for some of the largest treaty powers, as measured by the number of foreign firms. Great Britain's position as the premier colonial power of the day is evident from the hundreds of firms and thousands of residents present in China over the fifty years portrayed. Other powers saw their presence grow over time, though the number of German firms and residents declined noticeably following the country's defeat in World War I.

Initially, much of the foreign-owned activity was linked to trade, such as retail and wholesale operations, banking to finance the trade, insurance to cover trade risk, shipyards to repair ships, and railroads to provide land-based transportation. From there it spread into other sectors of the economy. Manufacturing and mining became important especially after the Treaty of

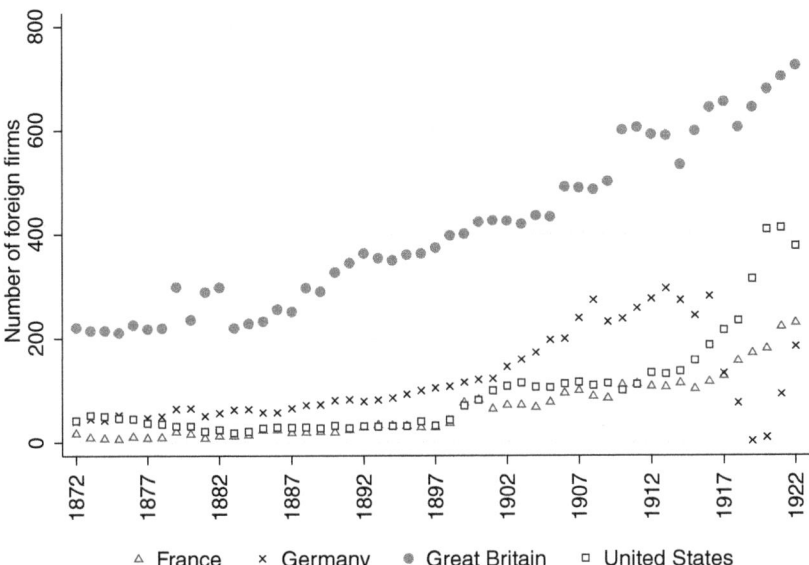

Figure 12.3 Foreign firms in China: the case of Shanghai, 1872–1921
Notes. Shown are shares of firms by foreign country
Source: *Decennial Reports*, various volumes

Shimonoseki (1895) established the legal right of foreigners to set up manufacturing firms in China.[61]

As the most important destination for FDI, Shanghai's situation merits closer examination. During the treaty port era, the number of foreign firms in Shanghai was 152 for the year 1872 and 1,741 in the year 1921, implying an annual growth rate of about 5 percent. These firms originated primarily from Japan and Britain, with concerns from these countries accounting for 35 and 30 percent respectively (Figure 12.4). The largest five sources accounted for 87 percent of all FDI into Shanghai.

There was much heterogeneity in the nature and scope of foreign firms operating in China.[62] They included large firms such as the British Jardine, Matheson & Co. trading firm. From its head office in Hong Kong and with branches in every major port, it not only controlled its trade operations, but also

---

[61] Historical treatments of the role of foreign investment in the period can be found in C.M. Hous, *Foreign Investment and Economic Development in China 1840–1937* (Cambridge, MA, Harvard University Press, 1965), Chapter 3; and Feuerwerker, *The Foreign Establishment in China*, Chapter 5.
[62] See Feuerwerker, *The Foreign Establishment in China*, pp. 80–1.

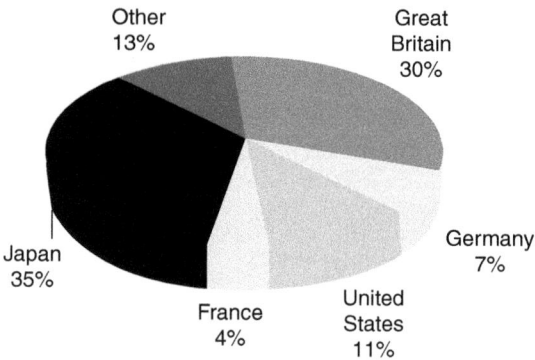

Figure 12.4 Foreign firms in China by country of origin

managed other activities such as the operation of the forty-one Yangzi steamers of its affiliate, the Indo-China Steam Navigation Company, the large Shanghai and Hongkew Wharf Company, the Ewo Cotton Mill, and a silk filature in Shanghai. At the other end of the spectrum was the modest retail store Schlachterei W. Fütterer, which was the butcher for Shanghai's German community.

Quantifying Foreign Influence in China during the Treaty Port Era

Integrated Statistics on Foreign and Domestic Trade

When a country shifts to opening its economy to more foreign trade, this also affects commerce in the country's interior. In the case of China during this period this can be traced out because every port was treated as its own customs area. Figure 12.5 illustrates the nature of the information contained in the CMC reports. Figure 12.5 shows the trade flows to and from Shanghai, for example, that were reported by the CMC. These flows are decomposed and labeled from one to nine. The first breakdown is by type of good; flows 1 to 4 concern goods that are produced abroad (foreign goods, abbreviated F), while flows 5 to 9 show trade in goods that are produced in China (Chinese-produced goods, abbreviated D). Flow 1 gives the imports of goods from Japan into Shanghai. Other imports of foreign goods into Shanghai consist of those coming from other Chinese treaty ports; in the figure, flow 4 represents the foreign goods reaching Shanghai via Xiamen. Once imported into Shanghai, these foreign goods may be re-exported. The CMC data allow us to distinguish between re-exports of foreign goods to foreign countries (flow 2) and those to other treaty ports within China (flow 3).

The statistics on re-exports of foreign goods provide key information on the extent to which foreign imports diffused throughout the country, something that has important welfare implications in the case of a large country such as China. They also offer a direct measure of the consumption of foreign goods in the treaty ports, as within-port foreign-goods consumption may be obtained by subtracting re-exports from foreign imports. Separately from foreign-goods trade, the CMC data also report trade in Chinese-produced goods. Flow 5, for example, shows Chinese-produced goods that are exported from Shanghai to foreign countries. These exports are direct exports in the sense that the goods are produced in the greater Shanghai area. The direct exports are to be distinguished from other Chinese-produced goods that are exported abroad from Shanghai but were produced elsewhere in China (flow 6). Both direct exports and re-exports capture major aspects of the evolution of an economy. In particular, the size of direct exports demonstrates the change in the production possibility of the local economy, while the extent of re-exports sheds light on the development (and trade integration) of the hinterland as well as the capacities of the entrepôts (in this case, Shanghai).

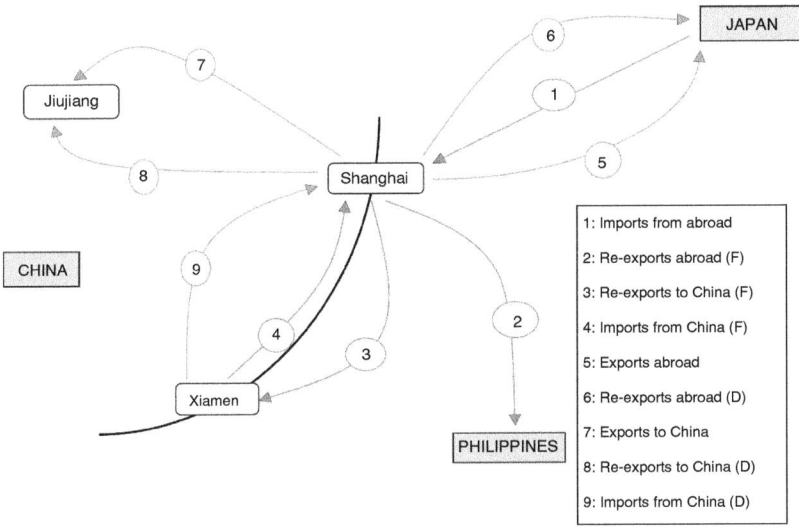

Figure 12.5 Export and import flows to and from Shanghai

Flow 7 represents Shanghai-produced goods that are exported to other parts of China, whereas flow 8 gives the export of Chinese-produced goods that flow from one region of China to another through Shanghai. The information on domestic exports of Chinese-produced goods at the port level is thus comparable to the information on foreign exports. Finally, flow 9 shows Shanghai's imports of Chinese goods that were produced elsewhere in China.

Welfare Effects from Foreign Influence: China's Domestic Trade

This section quantifies the size and distribution of welfare effects from new technology due to foreign influence in terms of China's domestic trade using a well-known trade model (that of Eaton and Kortum).[63] The model captures the Ricardian determinants of comparative advantage and differences in relative productivities across goods, and relates them to the geography separating the trading partners.

First, there is the technology of each trading partner, which determines the cost at which a good can be produced in different regions, and therefore determines which region has the lowest factory-gate production costs. Second, there is the size of trade barriers between regions; for example, trade barriers between regions i and j determine the trade-cost-inclusive price in region j of a good that is produced in region i. Because trade costs increase with geographic distance between regions, geography is the second key force in the model. Using historical data on prices, trade flows of domestically produced goods, and input uses, we can calibrate and solve the model in the context of China in the treaty port era.

Figure 12.6 shows the volumes of aggregate bilateral trade, with the thickness of each line proportional to the size of the flow. The maximum distance between any two regions in our bilateral pairs is about 2,700 kilometers. Exports are shown in the same shade as the region's label and are offset towards the center of the figure. We see that Hankow exports a large amount of its production to Shanghai, for example, while Tientsin's imports from Hankow are smaller than Tientsin's imports from Shanghai. Importantly, the trade volumes shown in Figure 12.6 are for locally produced goods.

---

[63] This section is based on Keller, Santiago, and Shiue, "China's Domestic Trade," 26–43. See also J. Eaton and S. Kortum, "Technology, Geography, and Trade," *Econometrica* 70.5 (2002), 1741–79.

Foreign Trade and Investment

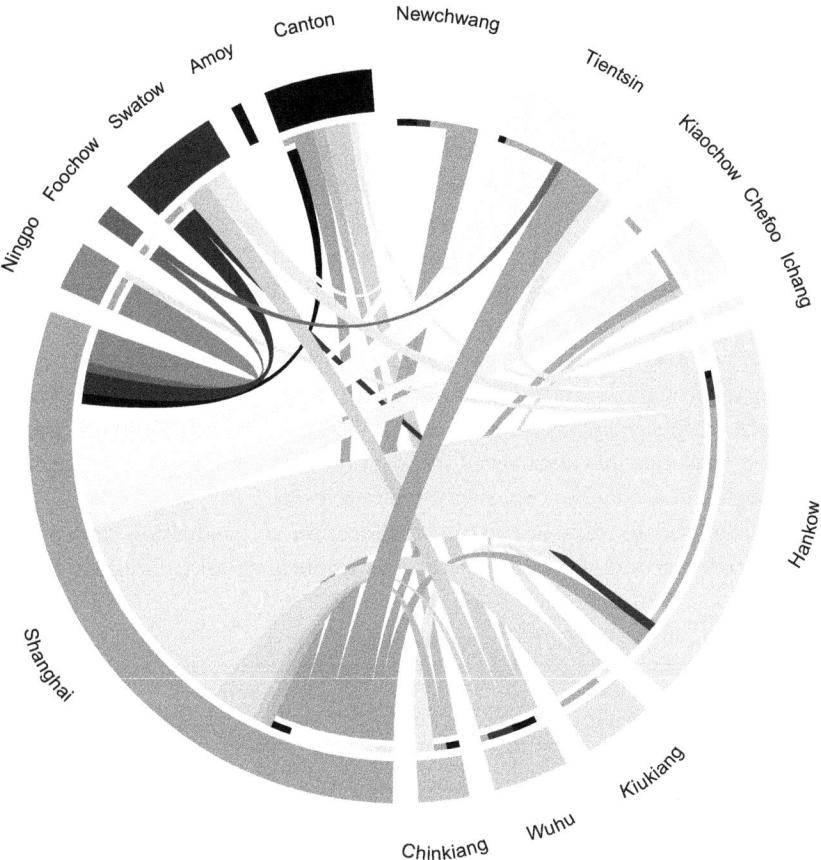

Figure 12.6 The size of bilateral trade between regions
Source: calculated from CMC trade data

Commodity-level trade data are employed to estimate a key model parameter governing the strength of comparative advantage. Employing twenty-six homogeneous commodities that are traded between virtually all fifteen regions – including coal, matches, and cotton yarn – price differences across ports are used to pin down this parameter. The commodity-level trade data are also employed to estimate trade costs between any two regions, because arbitrage ensures that the price difference for a given good between two regions is an upper bound on the trade costs between these two regions.[64]

---

[64] See Keller, Santiago, and Shiue, "China's Domestic Trade," 26–43, for information on other, related, data.

With key parameters and the model in hand, one can perform interesting counterfactual experiments. One is to increase the parameter capturing port productivity by 20 percent. This magnitude is reasonable given that customs operation by the CMC brought with it a wide range of improvements, such as dredging of the harbor, the construction of new lighthouses, increased protection from pirates, and the customs process itself. Increasing the productivity of Shanghai by this amount while leaving all other parameters unchanged raises GDP (our measure of welfare) in Shanghai by 1.5 percent, and general equilibrium effects lead to an increase of GDP by about a quarter of 1 percent on average in the other regions.

Table 12.6 presents the results of reductions in trade costs, as would have happened through the introduction of foreign steamship technology. Trade increases by 13 percent as a result of the lower trade costs. Welfare gains, however, are unevenly distributed across ports, and some regions, in particular Shanghai and Ningbo, experience welfare losses.

The intuition for this lies in the reallocation of production and trade. Lower trade barriers diminish the relative importance of technology-based

Table 12.6 Lower geographic barriers and welfare

	Trade barriers ↓50% % change relative to baseline		
	Welfare	Prices	Wages
Amoy	2.58	−7.15	−2.07
Chefoo	0.17	4.25	9.36
Chinkiang	0.75	−2.90	−3.53
Foochow	2.15	0.05	4.02
Canton	1.67	−0.03	3.24
Hankow	2.01	10.23	10.30
Ichang	8.90	−26.89	−24.80
Kiaochow	1.95	−6.13	−2.79
Kiukiang	3.51	−8.00	−2.26
Newchwang	4.22	−3.48	9.96
Ningbo	−31.41	15.12	−32.25
Swatow	0.27	3.22	14.44
Tientsin	3.43	4.25	8.95
Wuhu	2.38	−4.59	1.77
Shanghai	−17.29	23.73	−7.76
% change in overall trade 13.14			

Note. Table shows results of lowering geographic barriers by 50 percent relative to baseline trade costs.

advantages. Notice that the four regions with the lowest welfare gains are Shanghai, Ningbo, Chefoo, and Swatow. They turn out to be also the four regions with the highest level of labor-cost-adjusted technology. For such regions, lower trade barriers mean that they might no longer be the low-cost source of supply in a region because with lower trade costs that region now imports from elsewhere. As a result, welfare in the high-technology regions might fall.

Further, Shanghai and Ningbo are relatively centrally located in China, which means that before the reduction of trade barriers these regions had a sizable advantage based on low transport costs compared to other regions. In contrast, Chefoo and Swatow are located in geographically more remote parts of China. They lose some markets as a result of the lower trade barriers at the same time as they maintain their hold on others precisely because of their geographic location. As a consequence, Chefoo and Swatow lose less than Shanghai and Ningbo.

The Geographic Scope of Foreign Influence

The previous analysis has assessed the welfare effects of foreign trade and technology for China through the lens of a specific trade model. The impact of foreign influence in China can also be studied using a less structural but regression-based approach. Specifically, foreign influence in China originated from the foreign places, often treaty ports, in which the foreigners with their firms, families, and institutions were located. While treaty ports never accounted for more than 10 percent of China's output, foreign influence in the treaty ports might have generated spillovers for neighboring areas and China's hinterland.[65] Moreover, this literature emphasizes the role of institutions for the impact of foreign countries in China.[66]

---

[65] See B.K.L. So, H. Yip, T. Shiroyama, and K. Matsubara, "Modern China's Treaty Port Economy in Institutional Perspective," presented at the All-University of California Group in Economic History, February 2011 (Berkeley, CA).

[66] D. Ma, "The Rise of Modern Shanghai, 1900–1936: An Institutional Perspective," in B.K. L. So and R.H. Myers (eds.), *The Treaty Port Economy in Modern China: Empirical Studies of Institutional Change and Economic Performance* (Berkeley, University of California Institute of East Asian Studies, 2011), pp. 33–46, discusses the expansion of Western institutions in Shanghai in the early twentieth century; T. Shiroyama, "The Shanghai Real Estate Market and Capital Investment, 1860–1936," in So and Myers, *The Treaty Port Economy in Modern China*, pp. 47–74, deals with institutional changes in real estate markets that promoted economic change; and K. Chan, "The Rice and Wheat Flour Market Economies in the Lower Yangzi, 1900–1936," in So and Myers, *The Treaty Port Economy in Modern China*, pp. 75–95, shows how the expansion of vertical integration in grain markets was directly related to the presence of foreign technologies and economic activity in treaty ports.

Connecting the anecdotal and case study evidence, Keller and Shiue estimate the impact of foreign institutions on the level of interest rates in China's regional capital markets during the nineteenth century. Using variation on the location of opening treaty ports, customs stations, and foreign consulates, which supported trade by enforcing law courts in China, they show that foreign institutions had a positive impact by substantially lowering regional interest rates relative to areas without foreign influence.[67]

Their work also quantifies the scope of foreign influence by estimating the size of geographic spillovers of the foreign impact. Figure 12.7 shows that a foreign consulate located up to 200 kilometers from the center of the region leads to a lower interest rate by about 1.3 percentage points, and a similar effect comes from an open treaty port within 200 kilometers. The results point to a relatively strong impact through foreign consular courts, with their foreign legal practices due to extraterritoriality, because consulates generated significant spillovers for up to 400 kilometers (in contrast to treaty ports).

The implications for the geographic scope of foreign influence can be seen by plotting the predicted effects from the regression on a map of China (see Figure 12.8). While the analysis confirms that foreign influence in China was strongest where foreigners had their strongest presence, Figure 12.8 also indicates that by the 1890s, the geographic scope of foreign influence may have been felt in the majority of China's areas.

The Granular View: Chinese Commodity-Level Trade

Quantifying New and Disappearing Goods in China's Trade

New goods in trade matter for several reasons. For one, in the absence of comprehensive information on supply, exports of a new good are proof of a certain level of production capability. The arrival of new goods also provides evidence on the level of specialization in production. On the demand side, new goods reflect changes in consumption patterns, and they are indicative of changes in income because demand is non-homothetic (e.g.

---

[67] Chinese capital markets are compared with British markets for the 1770–1860 period in W. Keller, C.H. Shiue, and X. Wang, "Capital Market Development in China and Britain, 18th and 19th Century: Evidence from Grain Prices," *American Economic Journal: Applied Economics* 13.3 (2021), 31–64; see also W. Keller, C.H. Shiue, and X. Wang, "Capital Markets and Grain Prices: Assessing the Storage Cost Approach," *Cliometrica* 14 (2020), 367–96, for more on the estimation of comparable interest rates.

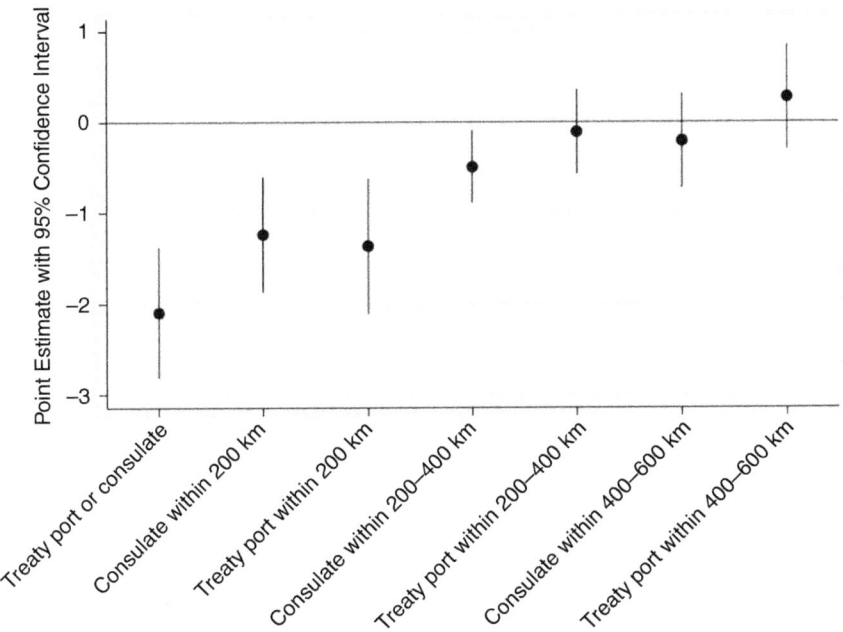

Figure 12.7 The impact of foreign influence in China: geographic effects
Source: W. Keller and C.H. Shiue, "Capital Markets and Colonial Institutions in China," presentation at NBER Summer Institute, July 2020 (Cambridge, MA)

the share spent on luxury goods increases with income). New goods can also be an important source of utility (welfare) gains.[68]

The importance of new goods and of disappearing goods between two years s and t, with s being earlier, can be quantified by considering the set of goods that is available in year s, the set of goods available in year t, and the set of goods that is available in *both* years s and t. Clearly, the set of goods available in *both* years will typically be smaller than the set of goods that is available in a *single* year.[69] Now consider the value of goods available both in years s and t evaluated at prices of year s, relative to the value of goods of year s at prices of year s; call this expression λ_s. Because both of these bundles are evaluated in year-s prices but the first set is (weakly) smaller than the second, λ_s must be smaller than or equal to one ($\lambda_s \leq 1$). Also, let the value of goods

---

[68] See R. Feenstra, "New Product Varieties and the Measurement of International Prices," *American Economic Review* 1 (1994), 157–77, for more analysis.
[69] The former will be smaller than the set of goods available in at least one of the years, except when the sets of goods in s and t are the same.

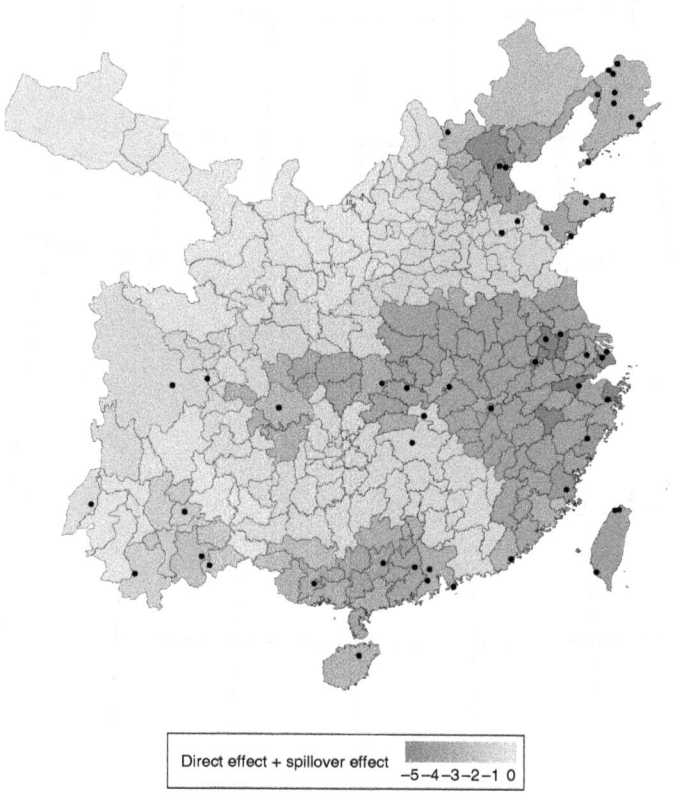

Map 12.2 The impact of foreign influence on local capital markets
Note. Figure gives predicted effects for the year 1890 of analysis underlying Figure 12.7; treaty ports shown

available both in years s and t be evaluated at prices of year t, relative to the value of goods of year t at prices of year t, be denoted by λ_t. For analogous reasons, also λ_t must be smaller than or equal to one ($\lambda_t \leq 1$).

Table 12.7 shows what the values of λ_t and λ_s tell us about the importance of new and disappearing goods. To begin with, $\lambda_t = 1$ indicates that all goods that are available in year t were also available in s (no new goods). In contrast, $\lambda_t < 1$ indicates that some of the goods available in year t were not available in year s. That is, some new goods appeared by year t. The case $\lambda_s = 1$ indicates that all the goods that were available in year s are also available in year t (none of the goods disappeared). Finally, $\lambda_s < 1$ indicates that some of the goods available in year s were not available in year t (some goods disappeared by period t). Thus, for any earlier year s and later year t, λ_t provides information about new goods while λ_s tells us about disappearing goods.[70]

To implement this in our case, ideally one would like to have the value of trade on every item in every year – at the most disaggregated, eight-digit level – that was ever exported in *any* year during the period from 1867 to 1930. Because the information collected by the CMC covers virtually the universe of China's foreign trade it is well suited for an extensive-margin analysis. At the same time, the CMC reports China's universe of exports with a classification that has a varying degree of disaggregation and is changing over time. In essence, in the early years China's exports are relatively low and only a few relatively aggregate categories are distinguished, while in the final years of the sample period exports are higher and many more goods are reported at a relatively disaggregated level. The category that ensures that CMC statistics cover the universe of exports in every year is called "Sundries, unenumerated," which is listed in every year. The Sundries category is not further defined but it includes all other goods that do not fit into any of the other categories defined in the CMC statistics in a particular year.

Our approach for studying the extensive margin of trade is based on the fact that the CMC produced a major update of its goods classification only every couple of years.[71] In a year when there is a major increase in terms of reported product groups, one typically observes a substantial decline in Sundries exports. This is indicative of the fact that before this year, the newly reported product groups were part of the Sundries category. To fix

Table 12.7 Measuring the appearance and disappearance of goods

	$\lambda_s = 1$	$\lambda_s < 1$
$\lambda_t = 1$	• Same goods in both years	• Some goods disappear between years s and t between years s and t • No new goods by years t
$\lambda_t < 1$	• No goods disappear between s and t years • New goods by year t	• Some goods disappear between years s and t • New goods by year t

[70] For values of λ_s and λ_t below 1, it is important to keep in mind that these expressions reflect the value, not the product count, of disappearing and new goods respectively.
[71] To identify these years we employ a threshold value for the change in Sundries exports from one year to the next; different threshold values are employed to ensure the robustness of the analysis.

ideas, beginning in the year 1896, CMC statistics report the value of "Cattle, Sheep, Goats, and Pigs" as its own export category. Presumably, this is due to the fact that there was a sizable and sustained export of these animals, but it would be erroneous to conclude that China did not export *any* cattle, sheep, goats, or pigs before the year 1896 – export of such livestock is not a "new-good" export of China in the year 1896. Rather, prior to that year, the value of the exports of such livestock was recorded as part of the Sundries category. Further, starting in the year 1910, CMC statistics report export values for "Cattle," "Sheep," "Goats," and "Pigs" separately.

An extreme approach to the new-goods margin is to assume that there are not any new goods, only redefinitions of previously traded goods. In the example, this means that, given that we observe positive exports of "Cattle," "Sheep," "Goats," and "Pigs" separately in the year 1930, we assume that all of these items were also exported already in the year 1867. Our way of implementing this approach to estimate disaggregated export values for 1867 (and any later year) is to use the 1910 export values of "Cattle," "Sheep," "Goats," and "Pigs" to allocate the given export values of the single category "Cattle, Sheep, Goats, and Pigs" during 1896 and 1909 between the four different types of livestock. To obtain values for earlier years we use the fact that livestock exports before 1896 are part of Sundries, which implies that livestock exports in 1895 are equal to the change in Sundries exports between 1895 and 1896.[72] We arrive at disaggregated export values for the year 1867 (and any later year) by using the change in Sundries exports between 1895 and 1867 together with the disaggregated livestock shares that are available for the years 1910 to 1930.

While this approach is conceptually straightforward, λ_t is equal to one for every year t; that is, there are no new goods by assumption. To allow for the possibility of new goods, we define a baseline threshold value of exports for the new good relative to the change in Sundries exports category. Thus, for example, if the exports of "Cattle" in 1895 that we estimate based on the change in Sundries exports from 1895 to 1896 are below this threshold, we take "Cattle" to be a newly exported item in the year 1896. We vary this baseline threshold to ensure the robustness of our analysis.

---

[72] In practice, "Cattle," "Sheep," "Goats," and "Pigs" exports are not the only new categories that are introduced in the year 1896. We account for that by assuming that the sum of all new category exports in a year, when there are major changes, is equal to the change in Sundries trade.

Mapping China's Trade to the First International Trade Classification

The League of Nations' minimum list of commodities (MLC, 1935) emerged as the first way of recording international trade data in a consistent way from the 1931 League of Nations' tariff nomenclature. The MLC is the precursor of the modern-day standard international trade classification (SITC). At the time of the MLC's creation China's government stated that it was not prepared to compile statistics based on the MLC classifications. However, to be able to consistently track China's international trade over time and for making international comparisons, we have matched CMC information on Chinese exports of the years 1867 to 1930 to the MLC classification.

We create a match to the MLC classification by assigning each CMC export to an MLC commodity number with up to eight digits for every year from 1867 to 1930. For example, our version of the MLC classification contains in its Chapter 8 the item "Beans and Peas," classified with item number 0803 (Item 03 in Chapter 08). This item is further disaggregated into other items, such as "Beans" (080301) or "Peas" (080302). The item "Beans" contains an even finer classification with different varieties of beans such as "Beans, Black" (08030101) or "Beans, Green" (08030103), among others.

This detailed mapping of China's commodity-level trade enables us to consistently track the evolution of China's exports starting in a period for which, to date, there is little systematic information. It is also instrumental in studying the changing commodity structure in China's trade, in particular the emergence of new goods, to which we turn now.

The Importance of New and Disappearing Goods

The sixty-four years of data, from 1867 to 1930, provide an excellent setting to explore the introduction of new goods and the disappearance of existing goods. We construct a 64 × 64 matrix of λ_s for each s and t pair, which is shown in Figure 12.8.

For any pair of different years ($s < t$), λ_t is shown in position (t, s) to the right of the diagonal in Figure 12.8, and λ_s in position (s, t) to the left of the diagonal in Figure 12.8. In particular, in our baseline approach the (1930, 1867) element is equal to 0.334. This indicates that the 1930 value of the goods available in both 1867 and 1930 represents about one-third of the 1930 value of all the goods available in the year 1930. Thus many new goods appeared between 1867 and 1930, or at least the new goods had relatively high value compared to the old

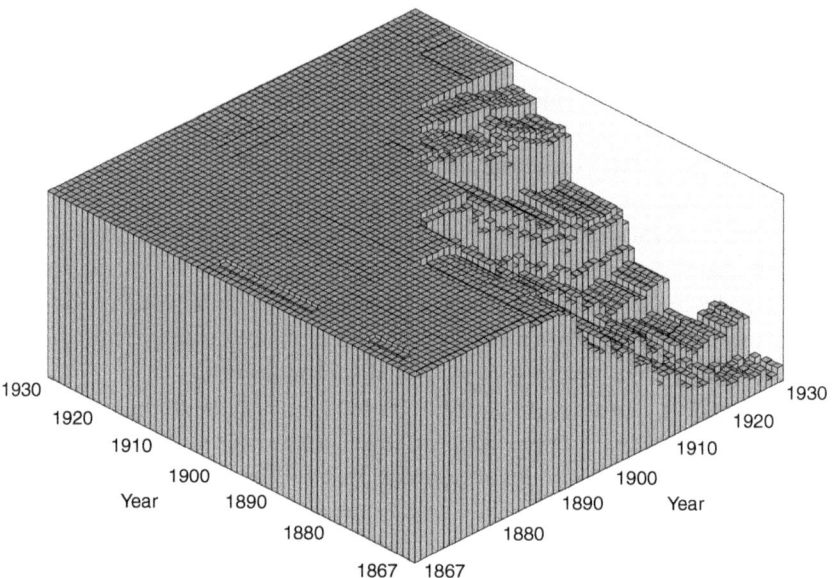

Figure 12.8 New and disappearing goods: China's exports
Source: authors' computations based on trade statistics in China Maritime Customs Service, *Returns of Trade and Trade Reports* (various years) (Shanghai, Statistical Department of the Inspectorate General of Customs, 2001)

(1867) goods. This indicates that there was a substantial change in the composition of the goods exported from China over this period. Furthermore, the (1867, 1930) element in this matrix is equal to 0.999. Thus the 1867 value of the goods available in both 1867 and 1930 represents almost 100 percent of the 1867 value of all the goods available in that year. It means that either only a few goods disappeared between 1867 and 1930, or those goods that disappeared had a relatively low value. This indicates that the appearance of new goods (or their value) tends to be more important than the disappearance of old goods in China in the nineteenth and early twentieth centuries.

The work on mapping the commodity-level trade of China over time is still in progress, yet the above analysis has shown that investigations of various margins of trade are feasible with historical trade data for China. The new goods that enter foreign trade are likely to generate implications for welfare; they are likely to impact domestic markets and domestic firms by changing the conditions for innovation and competition. The fact that the CMC collected detailed statistics on commodity-level trade means that we will ultimately be able to produce a complete picture of the historical evolution of China's comparative advantage and trade, which is rarely available in the case of other countries.

Conclusions

Today, China is one of the largest traders in the world. Unlike the emperors of the past, China is actively engaged in and pursuing the gains from openness, be that commodity trade or foreign direct investment. Nevertheless, China's prominence in global trade today can be linked to its historical past. From the seventeenth to eighteenth centuries, China's foreign trade and foreign diplomacy were an inherent part of the socioeconomic and political context of Asia. The empire had emerged as a dominant power in the region through a wide combination of strategies that included tributary trade, colonialism, economic investment, and military conquest. Compared to the Ming state, the Qing state had a relatively laissez-faire stance towards the activities of merchants in domestic markets and within the sphere of intra-Asian foreign trade. Nevertheless, Qing emperors reserved the right to regulate trade, and in particular the Sino-Western trade. For over a century, China was able to enforce its foreign policy on Western traders. In 1839, a combination of conflicts over market access, opium imports, and foreign diplomacy resulted in the Opium Wars. Over the nineteenth century, China was forced to sign a series of treaties with foreign powers that legally entitled Western nations and Japan to establish numerous ports of trade, customs stations, consular cities, and other types of port cities within China.

The treaty port system originated in the effort to open up China's markets to Western traders, and subsequent institutions that arrived in China sought to support that trade. Apart from the China Maritime Customs Service, pervasive legal institutions – in the form of consular offices and formal courts – were also established to support foreign trade. From the mid-nineteenth century until the departure of the China Maritime Customs Service in the twentieth century, the quantity and quality of data that were collected on Chinese international and domestic trade increased dramatically. This chapter has documented the trends and highlighted a few methodologies that can be used to allow researchers to gain a window into the economy of China during this time. These data can be used to investigate numerous additional questions about international and domestic trade, as well as the impact of foreign trade on the welfare of China. In addition, as the data are particularly detailed with respect to port-level information, it is exceptionally valuable for understanding the conceptual relationships between international trade and regional (domestic) trade more generally when a country changes its trading regime.

We find that already by the 1890s foreign influence in China was strongest where foreigners had their strongest presence, and spillover effects may have resulted in the majority of China's areas being affected. While we have yet to reach a complete understanding of the global effects of foreign trade and factor flows in the past two centuries, beyond the direct impact of trade and specialization, the most important effects during the treaty port era are likely related to interactions with foreign institutions and technology transfer. Investigations of the various margins of trade on welfare, innovation, and competition are promising areas of further research. More generally, it will open new ground with respect to our understanding of China's history of development as it relates to the legacy of the treaty port era.

Further Reading

China Maritime Customs (CMC), *Decennial Reports, First Issue (1882–1891), Second Issue (1892–1901), Third Issue (1902–1911), Fourth Issue (1912–1921) and Fifth Issue (1922–1931)* (Shanghai, Statistical Department of the Inspectorate General of Customs, 2001).

Great Britain Foreign Office, *Correspondence Relating to China: Presented to Both Houses of Parliament, by Command of Her Majesty* (London, T.R. Harrison, 1840).

Hamashita, T., *China, East Asia, and the Global Economy: Regional and Historical Perspectives* (Hoboken, Routledge, 2008).

Keller, W., M. Lampe, and C.H. Shiue, "International Transactions: Real Trade and Factor Flows," in S. Broadberry and K. Fukao (eds.), *Cambridge Economic History of the Modern World*, vol. 1, *1700 to 1870* (Cambridge, Cambridge University Press, 2021), pp. 412–37.

Keller, W., B. Li, and C.H. Shiue, "China's Foreign Trade: Perspectives from the Past 150 Years," *World Economy* 6 (2011), 853–92.

Keller, W., B. Li, and C.H. Shiue, "The Evolution of Domestic Trade Flows When Foreign Trade Is Liberalized: Evidence from the Chinese Maritime Customs Service," in M. Aoki, T. Kuran, and G. Roland (eds.), *Institutions and Comparative Economic Development* (Basingstoke, Palgrave Macmillan, 2012), pp. 152–72.

Keller, W., B. Li, and C.H. Shiue, "Shanghai's Trade, China's Growth: Continuity, Recovery, and Change since the Opium War," *IMF Economic Review* 2 (2013), 336–78.

Keller, W., J.A. Santiago, and C.H. Shiue, "China's Domestic Trade during the Treaty-Port Era," *Explorations in Economic History* 1 (2017), 26–43.

Keller, W., and C.H. Shiue, "Capital Markets and Colonial Institutions in China," presentation at NBER Summer Institute, July 2020 (Cambridge, MA).

Keller, W., C.H. Shiue, and X. Wang, "Capital Market Development in China and Britain, 18th and 19th Century: Evidence from Grain Prices," *American Economic Journal: Applied Economics* 13.3 (2021), 31–64.

Morse, H.B., *The Chronicles of the East India Company: Trading to China 1635–1834*, 5 vols. (Oxford, The Clarendon Press, 1926–1929).

Morse, H.B., *The International Relations of the Chinese Empire*, 3 vols. (London, Longmans, Green, and Company, 1910–1918).

13

Transport and Communication Infrastructure

ELISABETH KÖLL

Modern means of transportation and communication along water, rails, and roads had a profound impact on the economic and social development of China from the mid-nineteenth century onward. After the arrival of the steamship in the 1840s and the telegraph in the early 1860s, railroad construction began to emerge slowly at the close of the century, followed by bus and motor traffic bringing about macadamized city streets and highway expansion, with a modest level of air traffic taking off in the 1930s. This chapter addresses the structural changes in transportation and communication that characterized the transition from the last decades of the Qing empire (1644–1911) through the Republican period (1911–1949) to the early years of the People's Republic of China (PRC).

The focus on modern, mechanized infrastructure such as railroads or steamships should not be interpreted as disregard of traditional transportation methods via junk boats, wheelbarrows, or animal-drawn carts which continued to offer important transportation services, especially in rural China, well into the twentieth century. By contrast, this chapter elucidates the high level of complementarity between traditional and modern transportation methods from the late nineteenth century onward and emphasizes the pragmatic embrace of technological changes in transportation among all socioeconomic levels of Chinese society. The chapter also pays more attention to railroads than to other transportation methods due to the rail network's continuing geographical expansion and close affiliation with government agendas under different regimes beyond the 1949 revolution. Most national histories of railroads in Britain, the United States, India, and Japan explore their development in the context of technological innovation and the Industrial Revolution, the rise of capitalism, and the emergence of the modern nation-state.[1] As China's political economy was characterized by government patronage and the absence of capitalism and large-scale industrial investment before 1949, the introduction of modern transportation infrastructure particularly benefited growth in the commercial agriculture sector while it played a much lesser role in expanding industrial production.

Considering China's large territorial expanse, regional socioeconomic diversity, and decentralized, often volatile, political landscape prior to the founding of the PRC, it should not come as a surprise that the introduction of modern transportation infrastructure did not lead to a nationwide pattern of economic and market integration but intensified regional economic integration instead. For example, during the Republic, passenger rail transportation overwhelmingly consisted of passengers of modest means who traveled by third or fourth class and generated the bulk of revenue for Chinese railroad companies. Another important feature of the passenger market was that the majority of the traveling public used the network primarily for short distances. As a result, the passenger business reinforced the regionalizing effects of the freight traffic, with its powerful stationmasters and line-based logistics companies. As this chapter will demonstrate, freight and passenger services thus contributed to the regional rather than the nationwide orientation of transportation infrastructure in China before 1949.

In a broader historical perspective, this chapter tries to outline the evolution of China's transportation network, the competing business interests among different transportation technologies and companies, and the economic goals and regulations reflecting different local, regional, and central government agendas – patterns that still inform infrastructure development in contemporary China. In many ways, the development of modern transportation infrastructure allows us to examine the competitive roles of the state at various administrative levels and of private actors in the historical process of moving people, goods, and ideas across China, as well as the continuities and changes they imposed on Chinese economy and society.

---

[1] R. Fogel, *Railroads and American Economic Growth: Essays in Econometric History* (Baltimore, Johns Hopkins University Press, 1964); H.J. Habakkuk, *American and British Technology in the Nineteenth Century* (Cambridge, Cambridge University Press, 1962); J.F. Stover, *Iron Road to the West: American Railroads in the 1850s* (New York, Columbia University Press, 1978); P. O'Brien, *The New Economic History of the Railways* (New York, St. Martin's Press, 1977); T.R. Gourvish, *Railways and the British Economy, 1830–1914* (London, Macmillan, 1980); J. Metzer, *Some Economic Aspects of Railroad Development in Tsarist Russia* (New York, Arno Press, 1977); S.J. Ericson, *The Sound of the Whistle: Railroads and the State in Meiji Japan* (Cambridge, MA, Harvard Council on East Asian Studies, 1996); I.J. Kerr (ed.), *Railways in Modern India* (New Delhi: Oxford University Press, 2001).

Beginnings: Postal and Telegraph Communication

Before steamships and railroads made their appearance in China, long-distance communication in the nineteenth century was conducted within a postal system (*yizhan* 驿站) that exclusively served the needs of the Qing imperial government. Private citizens had to rely on commercial letter agencies for sending correspondence across the country, whereas informal messengers such as travelers or muleteers took on the function of postal delivery in less accessible regions in the interior or rural areas. Any service had to cope with vast distances within the empire as well as the lack of good roads, many of them made of pounded earth, which turned into mud during rain and were not conducive to heavy traffic. By comparison, water transportation along canals and rivers was more convenient and faster, especially with the arrival of steamships on inland waterways in the second half of the nineteenth century. For example, letter agencies used steamboats to transfer large mailbags whose content was sorted and delivered by carriers from local agencies when the steamships reached the port. Some of the postal transmission of urgent Chinese government documents was taken over by telegraph offices as the *yizhan* system gradually deteriorated during the last decades of the Qing dynasty due to the neglect of maintenance of roads and equipment.[2]

In 1861 Sir Robert Hart, director of the Chinese Maritime Customs Service, submitted a number of proposals to the Qing court for the organization of a modern postal system, pointing out the potential benefits for the government in the form of increased trade and tax revenue. However, against the background of various domestic crises and fear of increasing foreign intervention, the Qing government was not yet ready to undertake this modernization project. A mix of mounted and foot courier services, government dispatch bureaus, commercial letter agencies, foreign postal agencies servicing Westerners in the treaty ports, and the Customs Post as part of the Maritime Customs Service offered their services until a Chinese postal system was founded in 1896.[3]

As a new postal system, the Imperial Post Office (*youzhengju* 邮政局) was established via extension of the Customs Post into the interior with the goal of eventually covering the whole empire, managed by Hart under the supervision of the Qing government. Due to the connection with the

---

[2] Y.-W. Cheng, *Postal Communication in China and Its Modernization, 1860–1896* (Cambridge, MA, Harvard University East Asian Research Center, 1970), pp. 3–5, 44, 82–3.

[3] Cheng, *Postal Communication*, pp. 5–6; W. Tsai, "Breaking the Ice: The Establishment of Overland Winter Postal Routes in the Late Qing China," *Modern Asian Studies* 47.6 (2013), 1749–81.

customs service, itself modeled on the British civil service system, the Chinese post office system was modeled on the British Post Office with appropriate modifications. Despite slow beginnings, China already had more than a thousand post offices by 1903. After the founding of the Republic in 1911, the Chinese Post Office became independent of the customs service. Like many other new administrative institutions evolving in the new Republic, the post office became part of the government's institution-building process in terms of structuring its organization and hierarchies, defining responsibilities, and prescribing regulations. In 1921, comprehensive regulations for the postal administration were publicized by the government, and in 1935 the Ministry of Communications and Transportation introduced the legal framework of the postal service with the announcement of a Postal Law (youzhengfa 郵政法). Apart from its domestic postal and financial services, the Post Office also provided an important link to transnational Chinese communities through its overseas remittance network which maintained operation through crises and war until 1949.[4]

An important step towards modern communication involved the introduction of the telegraph into China, especially as a requirement for the construction and operation of railroads. The Great Northern Telegraph Company, a Danish business controlled by a majority of British shareholders, laid the underwater telegraph lines from Europe via Russia to Shanghai in 1870. Three foreign submarine cable companies, Great Northern Telegraph, British-owned Eastern Extension Telegraph, and Commercial Pacific Cable, an American firm, were in competition with each other and instrumental in connecting China with other parts of Asia: by 1871 submarine cables already connected Shanghai with Nagasaki. Recent research has focused on the intersection between technology and politics and explored the tensions and multilayered conflicts among different political interest groups impacting the transfer of cable technology and its commercial use in a semicolonial context.[5]

---

[4] Cheng, *Postal Communication*, pp. 104–5; Qiu Runxi 仇潤喜 and Li Guangyu 李光焴 (eds.), 天津郵政史料 (Historical Materials on the Tianjin Postal Administration), vol. 1 (Beijing, Beijing hangkong xueyuan chubanshe, 1988), pp. 341–55; L.J. Harris, "The Post Office and State Formation in Modern China, 1896–1949," Ph.D. thesis, University of Illinois at Urbana–Champaign, 2012.

[5] E. Baark, *Lightning Wires: The Telegraph and China's Technological Modernization, 1860–1890* (Westport, CT, Greenwood Press, 1997), pp. 56–9; S. Wei, "Circuits of Power: China's Quest for Cable Telegraph Rights 1912–1945," *Journal of Chinese History* 3 (2019), 116–18; A. Feuerwerker, *China's Early Industrialization: Sheng Hsuan-huai (1844–1916) and Mandarin Enterprise* (Cambridge, MA, Harvard University Press, 1958).

However, despite their near monopoly position in control over submarine cables linking China to the world, Western companies did not own a significant number of lines on land, which came to stay firmly in Chinese hands. In December 1881, a telegraph line between Tianjin and Shanghai was opened to traffic. The line's main office in Tianjin came under the control of Sheng Xuanhuai as the officially appointed manager of the new Imperial Telegraph Administration (*dianbao zongju* 电报总局) established in 1882, with a branch office in Shanghai supervised by the official Zheng Guanying, the city's circuit attendant. After the telegraph central office moved from Tianjin to Shanghai in 1884, it became the core of China's telegraph network, which played an important role in facilitating future railroad development. Eventually the Imperial Telegraph Administration became the Telegraph Bureau under the control of the Ministry of Posts and Communications in 1907.[6]

China's Imperial Telegraph Administration was structured according to the concept of government supervision and merchant management (*guandu shangban* 官督商办), with the goal of revitalizing China's statecraft, institutions, and economy like many new official–private ventures founded during China's Self-Strengthening movement in the 1880s. According to the 1882 regulations drawn up by Sheng Xuanhuai, "The first purpose of telegraph lines constructed in China is to transmit military messages; in addition they serve the convenience of the merchants and populace." However, despite the central government's politically driven agenda, most telegraph lines were in fact built and maintained by provincial governments. The Qing government thus passed on the costs for constructing and maintaining the telegraph system to the private investors while also demanding special rates and preferential treatment for its telegrams.[7]

Although the telegraph played a significant role in the communication sector's development, the fact that the Imperial Telegraph Administration operated like a government monopoly without serious business competition presented a problem. Past interpretations by historians like Albert Feuerwerker have argued that the Telegraph Administration suffered from administrative mismanagement, unfamiliarity with telegraphic affairs,

---

[6] Baark, *Lightning Wires*, p. 166; Feuerwerker, *China's Early Industrialization*, pp. 189–210; Xiong Yuezhi 熊月之, 上海通史 (A Comprehensive History of Shanghai), vol. 4 (Shanghai, Shanghai renmin chubanshe, 1999), pp. 332–3.

[7] Feuerwerker, *China's Early Industrialization*, pp. 189–210, esp. p. 193; W. Yoon, "Dashed Expectations: Limitations of the Telegraphic Service in the Late Qing," *Modern Asian Studies* 49.3 (2015), 834.

excessive bureaucratic interference, and corruption. Recent research by Wook Yoon has added valuable operational context from the consumers' perspective by demonstrating how various technical problems and misguided pricing strategies presented a major obstacle to turning the telegraph into a popular method of communication for the general population. Providing maintenance of the telegraph lines with line guards on patrol and constant repairs due to theft or weather damage were expensive yet necessary to guarantee the delivery of telegrams on time. As a result, the combination of negligent staff at work and disrepair created constant delays of telegram delivery. At the same time, the government considered a potential solution via the construction of submarine cables too much of an expense, and radiotelegraphy was only introduced in the early 1900s for naval military purposes.[8]

Similar to the evolving telegraph network in Japan, in the beginning China's telegraph communication was intended for the use of the government and military authorities, but not for private residents. To complicate matters for potential users of the telegraph service, no standardized system of phoneticization or romanization was available at the time when telegraphy started to take off in China in the 1880s, thus making the process of sending a telegram slower and more expensive than in other language environments. Nonofficial users of the service were also charged high fees for the transmission of telegrams while in the West technological improvements made telegram service increasingly less expensive in the late nineteenth century. Only after nationalization and the merging of provincial telegraph administrations with the Telegraph Bureau in 1911 did pricing become fairer for all customers and network maintenance improve.[9]

Despite these considerable obstacles, the advantage of telegraphy as a communication technology spread quite quickly in the early twentieth century when phone and telegraph communication began to assist Chinese commercial ventures, businesses, and affluent urban residents. Before 1900, especially foreign-trade businesses operating from the treaty ports benefited from the telegraph system, which allowed for more efficient communications with their agents in the field. Chinese businessmen made use of the telegraph for commercial purposes, such as gaining up-to-date information

[8] Feuerwerker, *China's Early Industrialization*, pp. 205–6; Yoon, "Dashed Expectations," 841–3.
[9] K. Yasar, *Electrified Voices: How the Telephone, Phonograph, and Radio Shaped Modern Japan, 1868–1945* (New York, Columbia University Press, 2018), p. 38; Yoon, "Dashed Expectations," 835, 854.

on local and regional prices for agricultural commodities. However, whereas scholars have argued in the case of Japan that "the telegraph was put to work in the consolidation of the nation-state and the projection of Japanese imperial power,"[10] it is much harder to make a similar case for China. As recent historical studies have shown, the telegraph as information technology complicated China's connections in global politics during the late Qing because it contributed to a certain, limited degree of internal political integration and simultaneously to destabilization due to increased military mobility.[11] In terms of advancing China's economic growth, the expansion and use of the telegraph contributed to the proliferation of financial and commercial centers such as Shanghai while also linking these centers more efficiently to the rural and urban marketplaces in the interior provinces and regions.[12]

After the founding of the Republic in 1911, the Ministry of Communications did not pay much attention to the telegraph administration due to its limited revenue contribution and a new focus on railroad development. According to contractual agreements with foreign companies, the Telegraph Bureau received only 13.5 percent of the telegraph tariff for outgoing cables. Even when the ministry received a substantial loan from the three investing foreign companies in 1911, secured by China's future telegraph revenue until 1930, only 10 percent of the loan was used to improve the national telegraph network. Reflecting the ministry's new political and economic priorities, the rest was channeled into subsidizing the railroad sector.[13] After the Nationalist Party (Guomindang) came to power under Chiang Kai-shek in 1928, the strongly desired reclamation of cable rights failed because the government was unable to pay back the loans it had contracted earlier with the foreign companies, and any existing wireless services were too unreliable to replace the cable services at the time. Only in 1933, after the Guomindang government was able to clear its debt with the foreign investors, were new contracts with license agreements issued to the foreign companies. The outbreak of the Second Sino-Japanese War in 1937 brought new challenges to the telegraph system. Control over

---

[10] Yasar, *Electrified Voices*, p. 40.
[11] R. Thompson, "The Wire: Progress, Paradox and Disaster in the Strategic Network of China, 1881–1901," *Frontiers of History in China* 10.3 (2015), 395–427; S. Halsey, *Quest for Power: European Imperialism and the Making of Chinese Statecraft* (Cambridge, MA, Harvard University Press, 2015).
[12] Zhang Zhongli 張仲禮 (ed.), 東南沿海城市與中國近代化 (Eastern and Southern Coastal Cities and China's Modernization) (Shanghai, Shanghai renmin chubanshe, 1996), pp. 472–3.
[13] Wei, "Circuits of Power," 119–21. Banks tied to the Communications clique also received subsidies from the loan.

information became a strategic goal of the Japanese occupation, with censors posted in foreign cable companies to monitor telegrams to foreign destinations. In 1942 Japan took control of all three major cable companies in China and transferred many of their cables to South Asia to assist the Japanese war effort in the Pacific theatre.[14]

Steamships and Railroads in a Semicolonial Context

Steamships as new transportation infrastructure started to expand their network along China's coast and rivers in the early 1860s. As a result of the 1842 Treaty of Nanking (Nanjing) concluding the First Opium War (1839–1842), steamships sailing under foreign flags were permitted to participate in China's coastal trade and began to serve not only the purpose of import and export trade but also the needs of Chinese merchants in domestic trade. The opening of treaty ports after the First and Second Opium Wars provided the foreign steamships with an expanding network of wharves, repair stations, warehouses, and company offices along China's coast and the Yangzi river. Chinese traders and merchants valued the steam-powered speed of freight transportation, armed protection of their freight in case of piracy, and availability of cargo insurance, which Chinese junk transportation did not offer at the time. Domestic junk boats continued their trade on canals and smaller rivers, while foreign steamships began to dominate the Yangzi river trade from the 1860s onward. The trade became so profitable for Europeans that they specifically brought ships to the China coast to participate in the "coasting trade" which was embraced by Chinese merchants. According to agreements by treaty port commissioners, the foreign steamships paid Maritime Customs duties irrespective of who owned the cargo of the ship.[15]

The Treaty of Tientsin (Tianjin), concluding the Second Opium War (1856–1860), evolved into an effort to negotiate issues related to the Qing empire's sovereignty in terms of foreign shipping and trade in China. The 1861 regulations recognized officially the coasting trade and stipulated rules for collecting custom fees. The Yangzi river was also declared open to foreign shipping and trade, but the treaty ensured that foreign shipping companies were not able to sail and do business beyond the scope of the treaty ports along the Yangzi river. Similar in function to emerging major rail hubs, treaty

---

[14] Wei, "Circuits of Power," 127–33.
[15] A. Reinhardt, *Navigating Semi-colonialism: Shipping, Sovereignty, and Nation-Building in China, 1860–1937* (Cambridge, MA, Harvard University Asia Center, 2018), pp. 23–5; Halsey, *Quest for Power*, pp. 187–9.

ports now became hubs for foreign and domestic shipping businesses generating forward and backward economic linkages. According to Anne Reinhardt's multifaceted study of Yangzi river shipping, the expansion of the steam network benefited foreign shippers, especially British and American, but not necessarily foreign traders doing business in China's domestic market. Foreign merchants were losing business to their Chinese competitors, who, due to a combination of steam transportation, better local market information, and lower overhead costs, were able to sell goods at lower prices.[16]

The founding of the China Merchants Steamship Navigation Company (CMSNC) in 1872 signaled the beginning of government efforts to insert itself into the shipping business in order to secure the empire's economic and political interests, in particular to ensure that inland water routes would not be completely in the hands of foreign shipping companies. The CMSNC was able to maintain a de facto government monopoly in Chinese steam navigation and transportation in the treaty port network until 1911 because the Qing government allowed private Chinese merchants to set up steamship companies only in the late 1890s. These companies did not enjoy the government patronage and business advantages extended to the CMSNC, but official encouragement at least fostered the development of small shipping firms in Chinese ownership which became a vital part of the shipping traffic on China's inland waterways.[17]

With the cost advantage of water over land transportation, sailboat traffic did not decline due to the increased steamboat traffic. In fact, throughout the Republican period unmechanized boat traffic increased even at major ports where steamships and motorboats offered their services. As Thomas Rawski has argued, before World War II "the history of water carriage is one of growth rather than displacement, with the use of inherited modes expanding along with the rise of new technology."[18] According to his estimate of limited available data, the number of motorized vessels increased steadily from just twenty-seven in 1885 to 517 in 1900, 1,559 in 1915, 2,734 in 1924, and 3,895 in 1935, and in those years the amount of tonnage transported increased accordingly.[19] In contrast to the railroads, which suffered serious track and

---

[16] Reinhardt, *Navigating Semi-colonialism*, pp. 26–7.
[17] Reinhardt, *Navigating Semi-colonialism*, pp. 54–5.
[18] T.G. Rawski, *Economic Growth in Prewar China* (Berkeley, University of California Press, 1989), p. 189.
[19] Rawski, *Economic Growth*, p. 190, Table 4.1. The number of vessels in 1935 excludes Manchuria.

equipment damage due to reckless warlord activities in the 1910s and early 1920s, as well as during Chiang Kai-shek's Northern Expedition in 1926–1927, commercial shipping only stagnated when some ships were taken over for military purposes, but quickly recovered afterwards. Especially the number of smaller vessels with a tonnage of less than 100 tons increased in the prewar period, reflecting the trend of more mechanized vessels serving smaller ports in interior provinces.[20]

The semicolonial origins of China's railroads bore both similarities and differences to railroad construction in other parts of the world in the late nineteenth and early twentieth centuries. Railroad construction in India began in the 1850s under the British, and European contractors built railroads under semicolonial conditions in the independent countries of Latin America, Southern Europe, and the Middle East. China, however, was host to more than half a dozen imperial powers competing to dominate the construction of this new infrastructure. The fragmentation of China's own central political authority since the mid-nineteenth-century Taiping Rebellion (1850–1864) further complicated the situation as it allowed for rivalries among powerful provincial leaders and the European powers. In short, the founding era of Chinese railroads was dominated by intra-imperial rivalry at the Qing court, provincial officials in disputes with local authorities and court factions, and tensions and misunderstandings among the colonial powers and their Chinese hosts.[21]

Foreign companies had long been eager to lay tracks in China, but official opposition kept them at bay for much of the late nineteenth century. In 1863, twenty-seven foreign firms petitioned Li Hongzhang, then acting governor of Jiangsu province, for the right to build a line between the administrative town of Suzhou and Shanghai, the major trading port in the lower Yangzi region, but Li denied the petition and even refused to forward it to the emperor. Nothing happened until 1875, when the British trading firm of Jardine, Matheson, without officially clearing it with the authorities in advance, constructed a ten-mile track between Shanghai and Wusong. As the British company's prospectus optimistically stated, "The disposition of the local authorities is favourable to the scheme, and there is good reason to believe that no objection

---

[20] Rawski, *Economic Growth*, p. 191; E. Köll, *Railroads and the Transformation of China* (Cambridge, MA, Harvard University Press, 2019), pp. 69–71.
[21] P.A. Kuhn, "The Taiping Rebellion," in J.K. Fairbank (ed.), *The Cambridge History of China*, vol. 10, *Late Ch'ing, 1800–1911*, part 1 (Cambridge, Cambridge University Press, 1978), pp. 264–350; Halsey, *Quest for Power*.

will be offered to it at Peking."[22] Due to the narrow gauge the required rolling stock was relatively inexpensive, and the company hoped to benefit from the already considerable traffic between Shanghai and the Wusong port. In addition, the consortium also envisioned a successful construction as an opportunity to showcase the many advantages of railroads and their future potential for China's extensive inland trade.[23] The train ran for more than a year, but in 1877 the Chinese government ultimately purchased and demolished the line, fearing that foreigners would take control of this means of transportation for imperialist military purposes. The railroad was later moved to Taiwan, but officials there were never able to operate it due to a lack of funds.[24]

Whereas only 195 miles of track had been built in China proper by 1894, the First Sino-Japanese War altered the political calculus in favor of railroad development. China's loss to Japan in 1895 not only triggered efforts to promote indigenous industrialization but also provided a new impetus to railroad construction by weakening the government's bargaining position vis-à-vis foreign companies that were seeking a foothold in China. Industrial development suddenly became a priority for the government in order to compete with Japan and other nations on equal commercial terms. Officials-turned-entrepreneurs like Zhang Jian (1853–1926) became advocates of railroads, characterizing them as the "root of industry," resulting in commercial and military prosperity and, by extension, social harmony.[25]

The construction of the trunk line from Tianjin to Pukou, connecting the capital with Nanjing and by extension Shanghai, grew from this political moment and exemplifies the complex process of negotiations within multinational rail syndicates and with the Chinese government. After the creation of a German sphere of interest (centered at the treaty port of Qingdao) in Shandong province in the late nineteenth century, Germany and Great Britain obtained a joint concession to construct a railroad line between the city of Tianjin and the northern bank of the Yangzi river in 1898 (see Map 13.1). The plan was to establish a transportation and communication artery linking Tianjin, in the north of China and easily accessible from

---

[22] "Provisional Prospectus, Woosung Road Company, Limited," Morrison Pamphlets P-III-b, no. 854, Toyo Bunko Library, n.d., n.p. The railroad's gauge was two feet six inches.
[23] "Provisional Prospectus."
[24] H.-C. Wang, "Merchants, Mandarins, and the Railway: Institutional Failure and the Wusong Railway, 1874–1877," *International Journal of Asian Studies* 12.1 (January 2015), 50.
[25] E. Köll, *From Cotton Mill to Business Empire: The Emergence of Regional Enterprises in Modern China* (Cambridge, MA, Harvard University Asia Center, 2003), pp. 31–51.

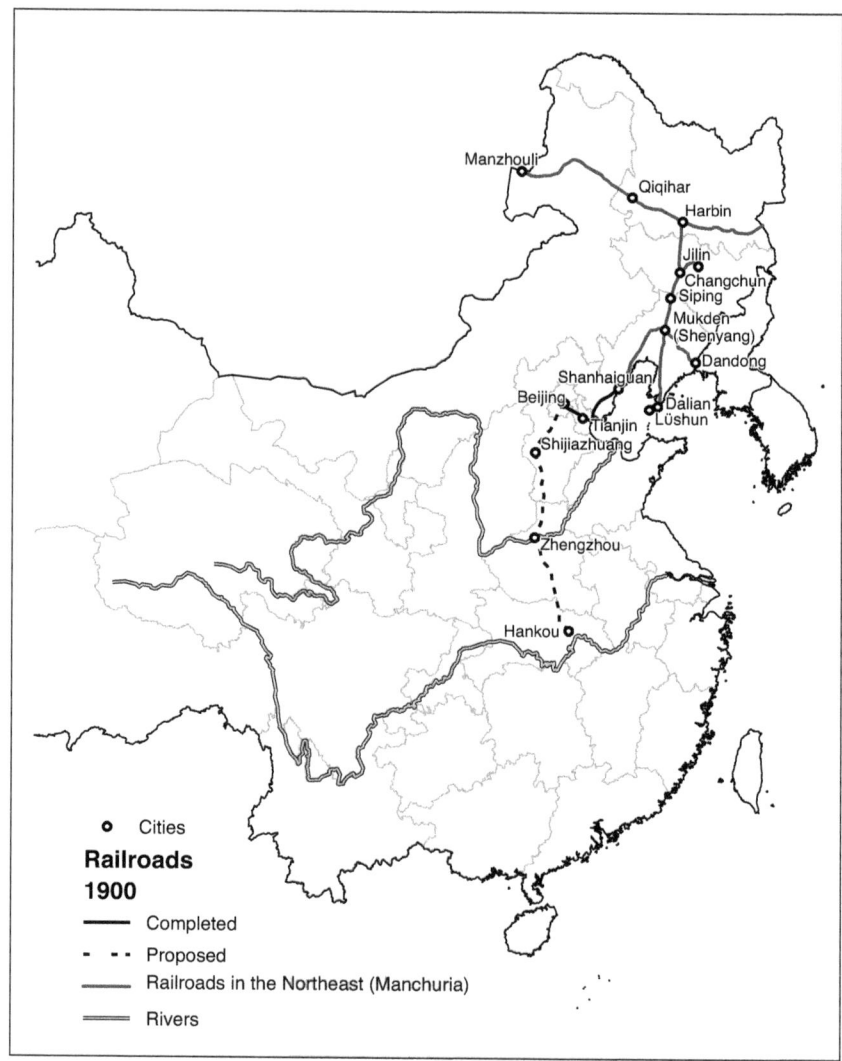

Map 13.1 China's railroads, c. 1900
Map © Elisabeth Köll (cartographic design by Matthew Sisk)

Beijing, to Nanjing in the south via Pukou, a location for crossing the Yangzi river. The British pledged to build and operate the part of the line within Jiangsu province, the southern section, and the Germans would be in charge of the line passing through Shandong and Zhili provinces in the northern section. In 1899 a British–German syndicate signed an agreement with the

Chinese government to build the railroad.[26] It took several years to negotiate the methods of financial control, construction, equipment, and operation of the line. Although the Boxer Uprising in 1900 delayed the project, construction of the line proceeded relatively swiftly, and both sections were completed and connected in 1912.[27]

Similar to early industrial enterprises and other railroad lines in China, financing the Tianjin–Pukou Railroad proved to be extremely difficult.[28] As in the case of British India, local owners of capital initially made the rational choice to invest in more familiar ventures, thus preferring investments in land resources and real estate over more risky railroad investments.[29] It was not until 1905, toward the end of the Qing dynasty, that domestic investment in industry slowly increased in a changing business environment that saw the introduction of limited liability in China's first Company Law, chambers of commerce, and the first modernization efforts in the banking sector. In 1908 the financial terms for the Tianjin–Pukou railroad were finally agreed upon: the first loan arrangement of the so-called Imperial Chinese Government 5 Percent Tientsin–Pukow Railway Loan consisted of a bond issue of £5 million on London's financial market, issued in two installments, with 65 percent German capital and 35 percent British capital.[30]

Although the loan was oversubscribed in Europe several times (£1.89 million was raised by the Deutsch-Asiatische Bank in Germany for the 401 miles of the German section and £1.1 million was raised in London for the 235 miles of the British section), the market issue also attracted some private Chinese investors and the provincial governments of Zhili, Shandong, Jiangsu, and Anhui, which together invested £260,000.[31] Interest was to be paid from the profits of the railroad, and the loan was guaranteed by the

---

[26] Mi Rucheng 密汝成 (ed.), 中華民國鐵路史資料, 1912–1949 (Materials on the Railroad History of Republican China, 1912–1949) (Beijing, Zhongguo shehui wenxian chubanshe, 2002).

[27] Lin Cheng, *The Chinese Railways: A Historical Survey* (Shanghai, China United Press, 1935); Jin Jiafeng 金家鳳, 中國交通之發展及其趨向 (Developments and Trends in China's Transportation) (Nanjing, Zhongzhong shuju, 1937).

[28] Lü Weijun 呂偉俊 et al., 山東區域現代化研究: 1840–1949 (Research on the Regional Modernization of Shandong: 1840–1949) (Jinan, Qilu shushe, 2002), pp. 54–9.

[29] I.J. Kerr, *Engines of Change: The Railroads That Made India* (Westport, CT, Praeger, 2007), p. 24.

[30] Cheng, *Chinese Railways*, p. 82; P.H.B. Kent, *Railway Enterprise in China: An Account of Its Origin and Development* (London, E. Arnold, 1907), pp. 152–3; R.W. Huenemann, *The Dragon and the Iron Horse: The Economics of Railroads in China* (Cambridge, MA, Harvard University Press, 1984), p. 120. Huenemann quotes a 5.85 percent true interest rate on the 1908 loan.

[31] E.-H. Lee, *China's Quest for Railway Autonomy 1904–1911* (Singapore, Singapore University Press, 1977), Table 4; (Santo tetsudo kaisha 山東鐵道會社), 山東鐵道ニ關スル調査

central government and secured by the income from the *lijin* 厘金 (commercial transit tax) and internal provincial revenue from the four provinces through which the line ran. In contrast to previous foreign-loan arrangements, the Tianjin–Pukou Railroad itself was not mortgaged as collateral. These new financial arrangements became known as Pukow Terms in loan negotiations between different investor groups. For the first time, construction of a line was undertaken by foreign partners, but overall managerial control lay in the hands of the Chinese government, at least on paper.[32]

However, while foreigners eagerly subscribed to Chinese railroad bond issues on overseas markets, the handling of domestic subscriptions turned into a political issue and in the case of Sichuan province led to serious political protests that eventually became part of the 1911 revolutionary movement. As Elisabeth Kaske has argued, "the crisis of 1911 in Sichuan was caused by a very peculiar system of tax appropriation for the Railway Company that became known as 'rent shares' (租股 *zugu*) and made rural landowners into shareholders." Whereas most other provinces tried (rather unsuccessfully) to raise funds for local railroad ventures through commercial taxes or by approaching urban commercial elites, Sichuan's method of raising funds through the rent share tax was successful, but also meant that rural elites through their investment became drawn into the political disputes between provincial and national interests.[33] When the central government announced the nationalization of all the trunk lines, including the planned Sichuan–Hankou railroad in May of 1911, the landowner–shareholders protested against the government's plan to offer them national bonds as compensation and challenged the provincial authorities. As Kaske shows, the issue of railroad finance through local investors became an issue of "political participation for the rural elites" which could not be solved during the last months of the Qing, nor during the Republic, so that plans for building the Sichuan railroad never materialized in pre-1949 China.[34]

報告: 附錄津浦鐵道借款契約 (Research Report on the Shandong Railway Company: Appendix with the JinPu Railway Loan Agreement) (Dairen, Manshu Nichinichi Shinbunsha, Taishō 4 [1915]); Ghassan Moazzin, "Networks of Capital: German Bankers and the Financial Internationalisation of China (1885–1919)," Ph.D. thesis, Cambridge University, 2017.

[32] (Santo tetsudo kaisha 山東鐵道會社), 山東鐵道ニ關スル調査報告, appendix on Pukou terms in 1915. On the use of *lijin* in government finance, see the chapter by Elisabeth Kaske and May-li Lin in this volume.

[33] E. Kaske, "Sichuan as a Pivot: Provincial Politics and Gentry Power in Late Qing Railway Projects in Southwestern China," in U. Theobald and Cao Jin (eds.), *Southwest China in a Regional and Global Perspective (c. 1600–1911)* (Leiden and Boston, Brill, 2018), p. 383.

[34] Kaske, "Sichuan as a Pivot," pp. 402–4, esp. p. 402.

While these events were going on in China's interior provinces, the emerging railroad network in Manchuria and the activities of the South Manchurian Railway (SMR) began to assume an important role in the historical and political trajectory of Sino-Japanese relations in the early twentieth century. Railroad development in China's northeastern region of Manchuria took place in the context of foreign imperialism, often also characterized as railroad imperialism. Russia started the construction of the old Chinese Eastern Railway between Manchouli and Suifenhe which was completed in 1901, adding a southern section leading to Port Arthur (Lüshun) near Dalian two years later. After their victory over Russia in the 1904–1905 war, the Japanese obtained the right to occupy the Guandong territory on the southern tip of the Liaodong peninsula and exert control over the line from Port Arthur to Changchun under the new name of the South Manchurian Railway. In order to administer the railroad and the track right of way, the SMR Company was founded in 1906 and came to act as both a business enterprise and an agency for the interests of the Japanese government.[35]

The SMR became the economic and political backbone of Japan's imperialistic ambitions in Manchuria. Japanese funding led to increased railroad construction in Manchuria throughout the 1920s with a new branch line eventually linking Manchuria with Korea. Some Chinese financing found its way into railroad construction at the end of the decade but did not create any real competition for Japanese-led rail construction. During the so-called Mukden Incident of September 1931, the Japanese militarist government staged a pretext to send in troops and take control of Manchuria with the formal creation of the puppet state of Manchukuo in the following spring.

Interruptions and Consolidation during the Early Republic

The founding of the Republic in 1911 triggered the move to nationalize China's railroads, but the process was slow and incomplete due to the financial and managerial contractual arrangements with foreign syndicate partners. Over time, improved business legislation, government policies regarding railroad

---

[35] B.A. Elleman and S. Kotkin (eds.), *Manchurian Railways and the Opening of China: An International History* (Armonk, NY and London, M.E. Sharpe, 2010). On railroad imperialism, see B.A. Elleman, E. Köll, and Y.T. Matsusaka, "Introduction," in Elleman and Kotkin, *Manchurian Railways and the Opening of China*, pp. 3–9; Xie Xueshi 解學詩 and Matsumura Takao 宋村高夫, 滿鉄與中國勞工 (The South Manchurian Railway and Chinese Labor) (Beijing, Shehui kexue wenxian chubanshe, 2003).

transportation, and access to financial markets increased indigenous Chinese investment during the following two decades, whereas foreign investment, except for that from Japan, began to decline due to World War I and China's fragmented internal political situation. Between 1895 and 1914, a total of 3,325 miles of new track were laid in China proper, and by the mid-1930s the total mileage supervised by the Ministry of Railways had grown to about 8,200 miles.[36]

It is important to note that the term "nationalization" did not imply a sudden, radical transfer of ownership and managerial control by the Chinese government, expropriating all foreign rail investment. For example, in 1922 about 25 percent of Chinese railroad lines were still owned and operated by foreigners and another 25 percent was under foreign influence due to continuing loan agreements.[37] From the Chinese government's perspective, the transition toward nationalization was meant to establish the political and economic independence of a strategic sector and to secure national interests against foreign control. However, at the company level the transition toward nationalization was a slow and complicated process, producing hybrid structures that only nominally were fully fledged Chinese rail companies.[38] In financial terms, the Chinese government continued to service the foreign loans of the former joint syndicates, and it even raised new bond issues on the public markets of London and New York. In managerial terms, foreigners still held many senior positions in Chinese railroad companies until the late 1920s, whether they were fully government-owned or under Chinese managerial control, due to contractual commitments tied to the loan contracts and the lack of an open labor market for both Chinese engineers and highly skilled workers.[39]

However, in the midst of the frequent administrative reorganization during the early Republican period, the most important bureaucratic structure, which has become the hallmark of China's railroad system, emerged: the Railroad Management Bureau (*tielu guanliju* 铁路管理局), commonly referred to as the Railroad Bureau (*tieluju* 铁路局). Structurally, railroad bureaus grew out of the lines' former head offices, but during the post-1911 transition they came under the direct jurisdiction of the Ministry for

---

[36] Cheng, *Chinese Railways*, pp. 63–5.
[37] "Railroad Finances," *Journal of the Association of Chinese and American Engineers* 3.5 (June 1922), 22–3.
[38] I use the term "railroad companies" to refer to the post-1911 nationalized railroads as enterprises managed and owned by the government.
[39] Köll, *Railroads and the Transformation of China*, pp. 82–4.

Communication and Transportation. It is important to note that the Railroad Bureau structure has survived with great resilience into the twenty-first century and still functions as a blueprint for China's current rail administration under the same name as it did some 100 years ago.[40]

The regional Railroad Bureau structure emerging as a formalized system encouraged a considerable degree of autonomy during the institution-building process of the railroad sector in the early Republic. However, this system developed in the context of the line-specific financial arrangements and the physical damage to tracks and rolling stock due to warlord battles at a time when no operational synergies existed for either the larger region or the nation as such. It is misleading to discuss a connecting rail "network" in the early days of the Republic even though there were a considerable number of individual lines. The first through-transport on the five largest railroads in eastern and central China became possible in April 1914, but many other lines were not connected until much later. By the early 1920s the sixteen railroad bureaus covered the existing network of major lines, with headquarters in eleven cities throughout the country. In sum, regional political fragmentation and severely limited network connectivity engendered a regionally divided railroad system, thereby exacerbating political efforts to centralize rail organization and administration.[41]

Freight Transportation and Economic Impact

Many historical debates about the socioeconomic effects of railroads involve the issue of their potential contribution to growth through so-called backward linkages – increased demand for labor, coal, steel, or financial services – and forward linkages in the form of the economic effects due to lower transportation costs for agriculture and industry. Macroeconomic studies by Ernest Liang and Thomas Rawski have made convincing arguments that cities and villages along certain railroad lines profited from the increased transportation and communication options that stimulated the

---

[40] Shandong sheng defang shizhi biancuan weiyuanhui, 山東省地方史志編纂委員會, 山東省志: 鐵路志 (Gazetteer of Shandong Province: Railroad Gazetteer) (Jinan, Shandong renmin chubanshe, 1993), pp. 547–56. Detailed information on each of China's current railroad bureaus is available through the official railroad web portal at www.tielu.cn, accessed September 13, 2020.

[41] Köll, *Railroads and the Transformation of China*, pp. 59–60; Yang Yonggang 楊勇剛, 中國近代鐵路史 (A History of Railroads in Modern China) (Shanghai, Shanghai shudian chubanshe, 1997), p. 154; Wang Xiaohua 王曉華 and Li Zhancai 李佔才, 艱難延神的民國鐵路 (The Difficult Expansion of Railroads during the Republic) (Zhengzhou, Henan renmin chubanshe, 1993), pp. 76–7.

commercialization of agriculture during the Republican period. According to such interpretations, lower transaction costs resulted in higher incomes for farmers, facilitated the integration of their products into the national market system, and even linked some of them to international markets. The interplay of specific local and regional economic conditions, however, limited the stimulation and created pockets of economic development rather than a national trend of economic growth tied to rail infrastructure during the Republican period.[42]

Although railroads attracted a considerable number of passengers when lines or sections of lines opened, long-distance freight transport usually generated more revenue, especially in the case of major trunk lines such as the Tianjin–Pukou and Beijing–Hankou railroads. Although we have only fragmentary information on the volume and revenue from freight generated by each individual railroad line in the 1910s, data collected by the Commission for the Unification of Chinese Railway Statistics and Accounts, under the aegis of the Ministry of Communications and Transportation, provide helpful insights into the capacity and economic viability of freight transportation at the time.[43]

Statistics published as official records beginning in 1915 indicate the predominance of freight transportation to generate revenue for the major trunk lines across the north China plain and the interior. In the case of the Beijing–Hankou and the Qingdao–Jinan lines, freight transportation constituted two-thirds of their revenue. As for the Tianjin–Pukou line, 46 percent of its transportation revenue came from goods and 39 percent from passengers in 1915. This ratio remained fairly stable until after the Guomindang took over the government in Nanjing in 1927, when tourist services and passenger express trains led to increased passenger revenue. As for product types, for

---

[42] A. Fishlow, *American Railroads and the Transformation of the Ante-bellum Economy* (Cambridge, MA, Harvard University Press, 1965); Fishlow, "Internal Transportation in the Nineteenth and Early Twentieth Centuries," in S.L. Engerman and R.E. Gallman (eds.), *The Cambridge Economic History of the United States*, vol. 2 (Cambridge, Cambridge University Press, 2008), pp. 543–642; D. Bogart and L. Chaudhary, "Engines of Growth: The Productivity Advance of Indian Railways, 1874–1912," *Journal of Economic History* 73.2 (June 2013), 339–70; E.P. Liang, *China, Railways and Agricultural Development, 1875–1935* (Chicago, The University of Chicago Press, 1982); Rawski, *Economic Growth*.

[43] Ministry of Communications (subsequently Ministry of Railways), 中國鐵路統計 (*Statistics of Government Railways*) (Beijing [subsequently Nanjing], Tiedaobu tongjichu, 1915–1936). Because of the impact of the civil war on railroad operations, reports were published with long delays. The volume with 1925 data was published in 1929, and the volume with 1928 data appeared in 1933. From 1926 onward each volume contained English and Chinese versions. Beginning in 1930, the name of the series changed slightly to 中華國有鐵路會計統計匯編 (*Statistics of Chinese National Railways*).

many years the Tianjin–Pukou railroad was the most agricultural-commodities-oriented trunk line, with the Shanghai–Nanjing line as the extension to the Yangzi delta and the port of Shanghai. Mineral freight (especially coal) accounted for an even larger proportion of the revenue in the 1930s. By 1935, freight accounted for 51 percent of the total revenue generated by the national railroad system. Agricultural products and manufactured goods were also the largest categories of freight in waterborne transportation. As Thomas Rawski has demonstrated, unmechanized junk traffic did not decline but expanded due to increased mechanized and motorized boat traffic.[44]

Shorter railroad lines with continuing competition from water-based transportation, such as the Shanghai–Nanjing and Shanghai–Hangzhou–Ningbo Railroads, derived most of their revenue from passenger transportation. These lines began as and remained primarily passenger lines; agricultural products and manufactured goods presented a relatively small proportion of the freight. For example, freight revenue in 1910 amounted to little more than 16 percent of the passenger revenue for the Shanghai–Nanjing Railroad.[45]

Chinese railroads most notably offered rapid transportation of bulk agricultural commodities to new markets beyond the local and even the regional economies. Freight statistics reveal the content and direction of commodity flows. The combination of line location, complementary infrastructure, pre-existing agricultural patterns, and linkages to commercial hubs and ports conditioned the economic function of each railroad. Peanuts, tobacco, cotton, and silk were among the agricultural commodities that experienced increased demand and supply because of railroad transportation. Silk producers were early adopters of rail transportation to carry their goods to markets, especially along the Shanghai–Nanjing line, the conduit to the silk factories in the Yangzi delta's treaty ports and the hinterland. The producers of silkworm cocoons valued the speedy delivery of their precious, time-sensitive cargo to the spinning factories in Shanghai.[46]

---

[44] Ministry of Communications, 中國鐵路統計, various years; Rawski, *Economic Growth*, pp. 202–8.
[45] Ministry of Communications, 中國鐵路統計, various years.
[46] "In Praise of the Peanut," *North-China Herald*, January 13, 1911, 85; "Taianfu [Shantung]," *North-China Herald*, May 20, 1911, 484; Amano Motonosuke 天野元之助, 山東省經濟調査 (Economic Survey of Shandong Province), vol. 3, 山東農業經濟論 (Report on Shandong's Agricultural Economy) (Dalian: Minami Manshu tetsudo kabushiki kaisha, 1936), p. 125; "The Cocoon Season," *North-China Herald*, June 24, 1910, 761.

Railroads also proved to be crucial for the business in sheep, goat, and pig intestines. Tianjin became China's leading collecting and exporting center for intestines, which were transported by the Zhengding–Taiyuan and Long–Hai railroads from the interior Sha'anxi, Henan, and Shanxi provinces. Because the preserved intestines needed to retain some moisture during transit, these commodities benefited from speedy rail transport. Once they reached Tianjin, merchants specializing in intestines further processed and repacked the consignment and shipped it to foreign markets, with the United States as the largest consumer of Chinese animal intestines in the early twentieth century.[47]

The Beijing–Hankou line presents an example of a railroad achieving high revenue through the freight transport of mineral and agricultural products. Output from the coal mines close to the station of Zhoukoudian in the form of big and small coal blocks and hard coal dust was transported by rail to markets in Beijing, Tianjin, and Dingzhou. Fifteen other mineral products from lime to iron sand complemented a list of twenty-six agricultural commodities ranging from wheat and beans, collected near the northern end of the line, to rice, other grains, and cotton, moved from the regions of the southern end of the line. Foodstuffs ranging from oil, peaches, and water melons to eggs and yams, plus medicinal drugs, tobacco, tea, hides, wool, and animal bones, as well as fertilizers and different types of wood, were transported every year, plus a variety of handicraft manufactured goods ranging from cotton cloth to paper and earthenware. As the author of a 1929 review article noted, in order to increase the crops of the farming regions along the Beijing–Hankou line, the building of various branch railroads to the main line would be a foremost concern "so that the transportation of goods from the place of production to the place of consumption may become easier and speedier."[48]

For personal consumption, railroads transported larger volumes of basic goods, such as milled flour, salt, sugar, kerosene, matches, cigarettes, and fertilizer to the predominantly rural populations along the lines. Foreign imports carried by rail included cotton goods and Japanese sewing cotton (thread), Indian and Japanese cotton yarn, Japanese matches, and dried and salted fish, as well as American kerosene. Railroads also imported more luxurious items, such as dresses, furniture, foreign candles, glassware,

[47] "Intestines for Foreign Markets," *Chinese Economic Journal* 5.53 (1929), 811–16.
[48] K. Loh, "Products along the Peiping–Hankow Railway," *Chinese Economic Journal* 5.44 (1929), 328.

porcelain, and tea leaves in smaller quantities to meet the needs and tastes of a small affluent population of consumers.[49]

The economic potential of railroads to stimulate production and trade in agricultural commodities was recognized by Chinese farmers and actively promoted by companies whose business was based on the processing of raw agricultural products. For example, the British American Tobacco Company (BAT) introduced and promoted cultivation of American tobacco seed along the railroad lines in Shandong province. Under the direction of its capable Chinese agent, a former employee of the Jiaozhou–Jinan railroad, BAT built facilities for curing tobacco leaf and imported machinery of the highest technological standards at six railroad stations. To encourage tobacco growing during the early 1910s, BAT extended lucrative offers to farmers, ranging from free tobacco seed to loans of specialized equipment, credit access, and on-the-spot cash payments for entire crops. As Sherman Cochran has shown, these arrangements were so successful for BAT, expanding Shandong tobacco acreage from thirty-nine acres in 1913 to 23,000 acres in 1920, that the company saw no necessity to continue the policies afterwards.[50]

Coping with freight and its seasonal demands added to the existing operational and managerial rolling-stock difficulties experienced by almost all Chinese railroads. As foreign railroad-accounting advisers to the Chinese government pointed out, contrary to the custom in the United States, freight cars were not assigned by a central distribution office in the line's management but rather by the many dozens of individual stationmasters. The assignment of freight cars based on local needs and particularistic interests without sufficient attention to planning for seasonal demands for special shipments became a negative aspect of this highly localized, stationmaster-centric organizational model. In addition to bribery and the chronic shortage of wagons for goods, the lack of efficient connections between lines became yet another material constraint on freight traffic that contributed to a predominantly local orientation.[51]

---

[49] "Trade in South China: The Crisis during 1920," *North-China Herald*, July 30, 1921, 354; Qingdao shi gangwuju 青島市港務局 (ed.), 中華民國 20 年港務統計年報 (Yearbook of the Port Statistics for the 20th Year of the Republic [1931]) (Qingdao, 1931), pp. 286–9.

[50] S. Cochran, *Encountering Chinese Networks: Western, Japanese, and Chinese Corporations in China, 1880–1937* (Berkeley, University of California Press, 2000), pp. 64–5; Liang, *China, Railways*, pp. 116–17.

[51] J.F. Baker, "Comparison of Chinese and American Railway Practices," in J.H. Arnold, *Commercial Handbook of China* (Washington, DC, Government Printing Office, 1926), pp. 127–8.

In this context railroad companies indirectly initiated the evolution of an entire new group of logistics enterprises, the so-called transportation companies (*yunzhuan gongsi* 运转公司). These logistics companies played an important role as partners in transshipping regional goods and fulfilling business functions that railroad companies were unable to manage on their own, such as freight insurance and guaranteed deliveries. Transportation companies quickly emerged to fill this niche, and by the mid-1910s this logistical practice was relatively standardized. In the case of the Tianjin–Pukou railroad, the transportation companies negotiated special agreements whereby the line gave them exclusive lower rates on freight in return for shouldering the burden of liability. The registration of transportation companies with the Tianjin–Pukou Railroad Bureau and the rail administration required the disclosure of company information similar to the registration of businesses required by the 1904 Company Law. Specifically, the transportation companies had to be Chinese-owned. That Chinese transportation companies in their agreements with individual railroad lines held a de facto monopoly over rail shipping business drew criticism, especially from envious foreign competitors.[52]

One problem every railroad line had to face was the *ad valorem* transit tax or *lijin*, which had been collected for goods since the late nineteenth century, most commonly at 2 percent, along the transit routes and sometimes also as a production tax, similar to a sales tax, at the point of origin or at the final destination. In the early years of railroad construction, the *lijin* was often blamed for the relatively low utilization of railroads for freight transport because merchants favored transport by other means to avoid the taxation. The general manager of the Shanghai–Nanjing line complained in 1910 that railroads lost out on business because merchants using the line had to pay the "legitimate" *lijin* at the full amount, but only paid 30 percent of the authorized figure when sending their goods by water. Naturally, railroads tended to lose business to rival boat traffic.[53]

In light of high shipping costs, including taxation, smuggling activities along the railroad lines increased. Smuggling activities were not only actions

---

[52] Köll, *Railroads and the Transformation of China*, pp. 101–11; letter, Dechamfils to Sir John Jordan, January 17, 1919, Foreign Office archives, FO 228/2803, British National Archives.
[53] A. Feuerwerker, "Economic Trends, 1912–1949," in J.K. Fairbank (ed.), *The Cambridge History of China*, vol. 12, *Republican China 1912–1949*, part 1 (Cambridge, Cambridge University Press, 1983), pp. 61–2; "The Shanghai–Nanking Railway," *North-China Herald*, January 14, 1910, 67. Rawski also cites similar incidents in *Economic Growth*, pp. 232–3.

orchestrated to transport "illegal goods," but one of the foremost methods of tax avoidance integrated into the operational structure of the railroad lines and their workforce. For example, railroad workers carried goods on their own in order to avoid the taxes and freight charges.[54] The government supported efforts to reduce the extraneous costs on merchants shipping goods via rail by convening the Peking Railroad Conference "to restore the sadly abused but very great earning power of the Chinese Railways" a few months before the Nationalists came to power in 1928. This move reflected the railroad administration's desire to restore state control over freight traffic and its revenue but also to run the railroad lines more like for-profit business entities in order "to bring back that public confidence and economy of management which the Government Railways used to enjoy only a few years ago both at home and abroad."[55]

In the case of Manchuria, railroads provided access to the interior for commercial farming, mining, and metallurgy enterprises. Throughout the 1930s the combination of railroads, intensive mining, and ironworks turned Manchuria into China's center for heavy industry, with a continued legacy in the post-1949 period. According to propagandist Japanese sources, the heavy-handed economic influence of Japan resulted in astonishing growth rates in Manchuria: between 1908 and 1930, railroad construction rose by 84 percent and soybean cultivation by 290 percent, with high growth rates in bean-cake production and coal output from the Fushun mines and an overall increase in foreign trade of 510 percent. In 1934, the Soviet Union succumbed to Japanese pressure and sold the northern half of the Chinese Eastern Railway up to the Soviet border to Japan. As a result, by 1935 all railroads in Manchuria came under the unified management of the SMR, which operated the government lines and SMR railroads as well as most bus lines and river transportation. In 1936, just a year before Japan's invasion of China, the rail network in Manchuria comprised 5,530 miles.[56]

---

[54] "Opium on Railways," *North-China Herald*, January 11, 1919, 70. For a comprehensive treatment of smuggling, see P. Thai, *China's War on Smuggling: Law, Economic Life, and the Making of the Modern State, 1842–1965* (New York, Columbia University Press, 2018).
[55] "The Peking Railway Conference: List of Reforms Necessary for Efficiency," *North-China Herald*, August 13, 1927, 272.
[56] *Economic Conditions in Manchoukuo* (Manchuria Daily News, 1940), pp. 3-4, 8; Minami Manshū Tetsudō Kabushiki Kaisha 南滿洲鐵道株式會社, 南滿洲鐵道株式會社十年史 (A Ten Years' History of the South Manchurian Railway Company) (Dalian, Minami Manshū Tetsudō Kabushiki Kaisha, 1919); Department of Foreign Affairs, Manchoukuo Government, *General Survey of Conditions in Manchoukuo* (Hsinking, 1936), pp. 47–9.

With its territorial expansion and socioeconomic control backed by Japan's imperialist agenda, the SMR increasingly grew into a bureaucratic and strategic enterprise that pursued reorganization with the aim of rationalizing its railroad management and creating economic efficiencies. For example, motor roads were considered important for the defense and industrial development of Japanese interests and thus their management was transferred to the SMR by the Manchukuo government. An employees' consumption guild was established in 1919 to provide SMR employees with access to daily necessities at special prices. Despite Japan's tight control over its political and economic interests, the majority of Japanese merchants operated their businesses directly from within the Guandong leased territory and the heavily protected SMR rail corridor. Issues connected to personal safety, a volatile currency situation, and relatively high operating expenses made it preferable for Japanese merchants to stay inside the SMR zone. British, American, and other foreign businesses were able to monopolize the petroleum, tobacco, and sugar markets in Manchuria.[57] However, even Chinese merchants were attracted by the safety of the SMR zone and endured the presence of Japanese security forces, however heavy-handed. For example, in 1920 103,000 Chinese lived and worked in the SMR zone together with 72,000 Japanese.[58]

As with rail lines in other parts of China, the logistics infrastructure accompanying the tracks became equally important to sustaining the economic impact of the rail network. In the case of the SMR, a complex system of warehouses for soybeans, beancake, and soybean oil supported the boom in commercial agriculture of soy and its by-products by securing efficient onward transport of the commodities. In twelve major cities the SMR also opened and managed bonded warehouses which allowed shippers to avoid the inconvenience of clearing customs with their freight in the port cities before international export.[59]

Passenger Transportation and Mobility

The significance of rail travel in Republican China lies less in the size, scope, and nature of the business than in the ways it contributed to the transformation of individual practices and social interactions in the public space

[57] Department of Foreign Affairs, Manchoukuo Government, *General Survey*, p. 52.
[58] *Economic Conditions in Manchoukuo*, p. 56; A. Kinnosuke, *Manchuria: A Survey* (New York, R.M. McBride & Co., 1925), p. 86.
[59] *Economic Conditions in Manchoukuo*, pp. 59–61.

associated with the railroad. Passenger services on railroads involved a new and decidedly modern mode of engaging with the social world, one that promoted values and behavior radically different from those cultivated by the traditional social order. This is not to say that the railroads dramatically changed Chinese mobility. For one thing, Chinese had long made use of water transport along canals, rivers, and coastal routes as well as of road transport on foot, horses, bullock carts, and other vehicles. The high cost of rail travel relative to purchasing power, the short average length of a rail journey, and the relatively small proportion of the population riding the rails suggest that the advent of railroads did not significantly shift existing mobility paradigms and practices. Following the pattern set by freight transport, railroads assumed a new and significant socioeconomic role for passengers via their integration into the already existing or the newly evolving networks of transportation (see Map 13.2).[60]

Passenger ticket sales were an important source of revenue for all the nation's railroad lines. In each year between 1915 and 1935, passenger traffic accounted for 32 to 41 percent of revenue for all Chinese government railroads. Although major trunk lines such as the Beijing–Hankou and the Beijing–Mukden lines derived most of their revenue from freight transportation, they still transported a considerable number of passengers. For example, 70 percent of the revenue of the Beijing–Hankou line in 1935 came from freight; yet in the same year the railroad also transported a total of more than 3.4 million passengers.[61]

For some lines, passenger traffic was the major source of revenue. Short lines in the Yangzi and Pearl river deltas – the Canton–Kowloon, Shanghai–Nanjing, and Shanghai–Hangzhou–Ningbo lines – connected passengers from the densely populated hinterland to the commercial centers of Hong Kong or Shanghai. In 1918, the Shanghai–Nanjing Railroad derived 71 percent of its revenue from passenger traffic; this figure decreased slightly to 64 percent in 1923, rose to 72 percent in 1930, and then declined to 66 percent in 1935, the last year of available data. The Shanghai–Hangzhou–Ningbo Railroad followed a similar pattern, with approximately 65 percent of its revenue originating from passenger traffic; passenger-related revenue on the Canton–Kowloon line remained almost constant at 85 percent throughout the 1920s and 1930s.[62]

[60] Köll, *Railroads and the Transformation of China*, pp. 131–40.
[61] Figures extrapolated from Ministry of Communications, 中國鐵路統計, various years.
[62] Figures extrapolated from Ministry of Communications, 中國鐵路統計, various years.

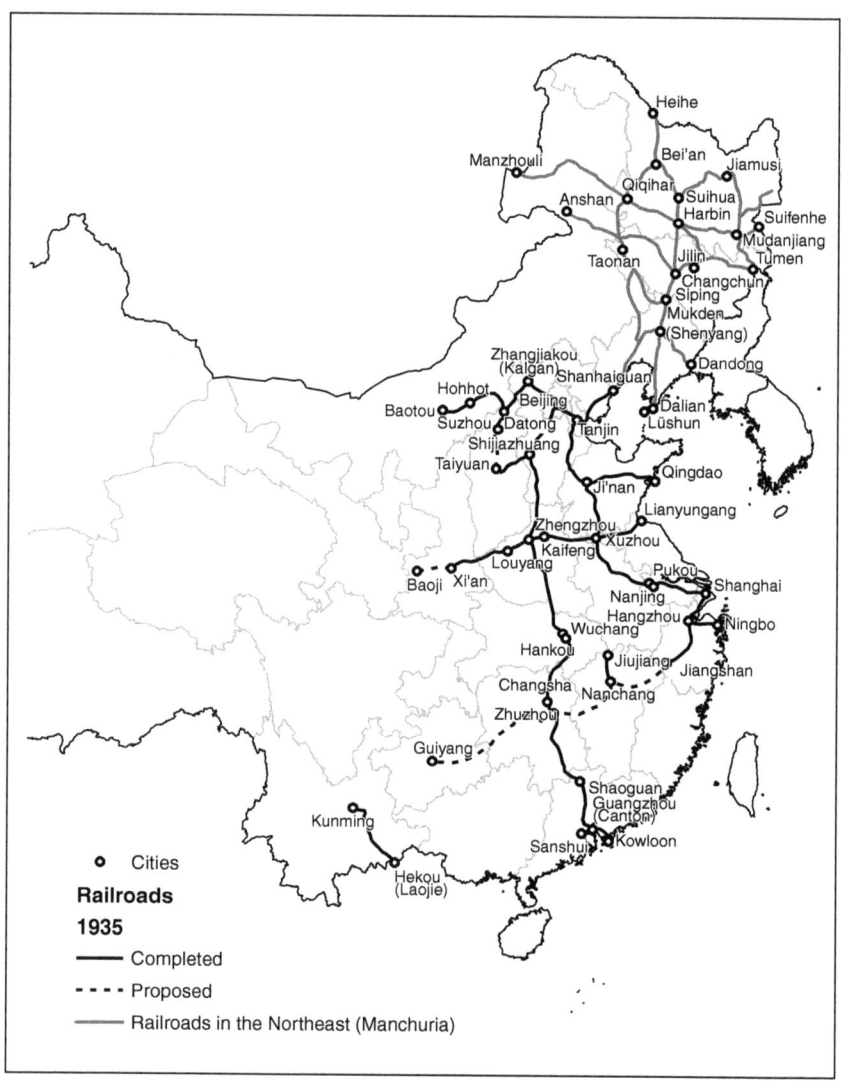

Map 13.2 China's railroad network, c. 1935
Map © Elisabeth Köll (cartographic design by Matthew Sisk)

System-wide, passenger traffic underwent a substantial and steady increase in volume on all national lines during the Republican era, although it fluctuated considerably from year to year in response to adverse economic conditions and political upheavals. According to data extrapolated from the annual statistics collected by the Ministry of Communications, a total of

12.6 million passenger journeys were taken on Chinese national railroads in 1915, the first year of recorded data. This number quickly doubled to 24.6 million in 1918 and then rose to almost 40 million in 1923. During the crucial civil war years from 1926 to 1928, the statistics include information only on revenue figures, not on the volume of passengers. This hiatus might be explained by the fact that during those years railroad companies were forced to transport military personnel and soldiers without compensation. With the consolidation of political control under the Nanjing government after 1927, passenger travel quickly recovered. In 1932, there were 34 million passenger journeys in total, and this number increased to almost 44 million in 1935, just before the 1937 Japanese invasion and occupation interrupted the railroad system as well as data collection for several years.[63]

Although revenue from passenger transportation on most lines, especially the major trunk lines, was secondary to revenue from freight, its distribution among the different categories of passengers is quite surprising. Annual statistics indicate that ticket sales for third- and fourth-class services were by far the most important revenue stream for the passenger business of the railroad companies. This pattern applied to traffic on all long-distance trunk lines, including the Tianjin–Pukou and Beijing–Hankou railroads. Fourth-class travel was no longer offered after 1932, with the exception of two short lines connecting Shanghai with the capital in Nanjing and Hangzhou on the West Lake, and Jinan with Qingdao. In these cases, fourth-class travel was the preferred choice for regional commuters. With the move of the capital from Beijing to Nanjing after 1927, the number of first-class tickets increased as government officials and businessmen began commuting back and forth between the two hubs. Even so, first-class travel was never financially or numerically significant. The statistics make it clear that a long train journey from terminal to terminal was a first-class affair for only a limited number of passengers who had disposable income, and it never became a major revenue source for the Chinese railroads.[64]

If we consider transportation companies as forward linkages resulting from the freight business created by Chinese railroads, the establishment of new steam-powered launch companies represented forward linkages resulting from the need for additional passenger transportation services. For example, soon after completion of the Shanghai–Hangzhou railroad a new launch company named Dexin formed a business co-operation with the line

[63] Figures extrapolated from Ministry of Communications, 中國鐵路統計, various years. Passenger journey data were based on tickets sold and included repeat journeys.
[64] Figures extrapolated from Ministry of Communications, 中國鐵路統計, various years.

to facilitate passenger transport. According to their agreement, both companies sold through-tickets for journeys that combined launch and rail travel from Suzhou to Hangzhou, including free through-baggage service. The Dexin launch took passengers on the six-and-a-half-hour boat trip via the Grand Canal from Suzhou to Jiaxing, where they could catch the fast train from Shanghai at 3 p.m. and arrive two hours later in Hangzhou. Commercial launch services also ferried railroad passengers across major rivers lacking bridges.[65]

Launch services to railroad terminals could be such a lucrative business that it led occasionally to price wars between competing launch companies. After the southern section of the Canton–Hankou railroad reached the North river (Beijiang) in 1911, passengers continued their trip via steam launches to Yingde and from there via a "shallow-draught stern-wheeler" to Shaozhou, thus reducing the travel time from fourteen days to only two days. Two rival companies competed for passengers between Yingde and the railroad head in Guangzhou, leading to a price war and even a fist fight between the two launch crews.[66]

Sometimes steam launches and railroads were competitive rather than complementary means of transportation. In Shanghai, for example, the Shanghai–Hangzhou Railroad attracted disapproval in 1911 for locating its terminal too far from the center of trade and the Huangpu river. As a result, the steam launch companies retained their edge and, on the basis of their low prices, were still a competitor to the railroad line in 1918. Throughout the 1910s and the 1920s new launches and ferry services in their function as complementary transportation businesses brought passengers to railroad stations along sparse trunk line systems, often far from final passenger and freight destinations.[67]

Motor Roads and Aviation

Modern roads and highways became a lynchpin in China's infrastructure development during the Republican period. Serious construction began in the early years of the Republic when foreign-trained engineers advising the

---

[65] "Soochow: A New Line to Hangchow," *North-China Herald*, June 10, 1910, 618.
[66] "Shiuchow [Kwangtung]: Railway Matters," *North-China Herald*, May 20, 1911, 483–4.
[67] "The Provincial Railways: Hangchow," *North-China Herald*, September 9, 1911, 660; "The Trade of Shanghai," *North-China Herald*, August 31, 1918, 532–4; "Soochow: A New Line to Hangchow"; "The Trade of Shanghai," *North-China Herald*, August 31, 1918, 532–4.

Beijing Ministry of Communications lobbied for modern feeder roads as a necessity for new railroads in operation to generate positive returns. Although a presidential mandate with regulations for new road construction was announced in 1919, it did not result in a concerted government effort of creating a national highway system. Instead, Chinese and international welfare organizations and provincial interests became the driving force behind modern road construction.

In the treaty ports, public-works departments of the foreign concessions undertook the construction of new, modern roads in the city. In the countryside, some road-building programs were carried out in the context of the 1920 famine to provide stricken areas with an economic stimulus through employment options. For example, the government announced that it would employ about a million famine victims in north China for the construction of roads between Beijing and Shandong, Henan, and Zhili provinces at an estimated cost of 200,000 dollars, with funds raised by additional salt and stamp taxes and increased postal and telegraphic charges.[68] Between 1923 and 1928, the China International Famine Relief Commission became strongly involved in road-building programs, funding the construction of dykes and roads. In addition, some provinces, with encouragement from the central government, started independent road construction programs under the supervision of Chinese engineers.[69]

Similar to the push for administrative reorganization of the rail network, modern road construction gained serious attention as a project of national economic and political importance once the Nationalist government under Chiang Kai-shek took control in 1928. In the following year, the National Highway Planning Commission, initiated and supervised by the new Ministry of Railways, began its work and drew up projection and construction plans as well as regulations for the raising of funds through appropriations from government revenue and proceeds from bond issues and special road debentures. The regulations also specified the conscription of private labor for national highway construction, which put a considerable burden on the male population between the ages of eighteen and fifty residing in the rural areas touched by the proposed highways. Most of the modern road construction did not involve macadam or gravel but consisted of simple earth construction. Railroad dump cars and steam rollers were the only industrial

---

[68] "Road Making for Victims," "New Railways for Famine Relief," and "The Great Famine in China: Cheap Transport of Grain," *North-China Herald*, October 2, 1920, p. 22.

[69] V. Smith with A. Chuh, *Motor Roads in China* (Washington, DC, United States Government Printing Office, 1931), pp. 7–9.

equipment, although most of the time iron hand rollers filled with cement and pulled by workers were the more common construction tools.[70]

Figures for the expansion of road mileage during the Republican period vary, but according to a reliable source from 1931, China had about 40,000 miles of roads suitable for motor traffic at the time, including caravan routes in Manchuria and Mongolia.[71] Passenger cars amounted only to a small number, with about 40,000 motor vehicles in all of China in the early 1930s and one-third of the vehicles operating in Shanghai's foreign concession. As main users of these newly built roads, the increasing importance of bus lines as infrastructure connecting rail stations and river docks with rural and urban locations became evident. According to annual reports published by the Ministry of Railways, by the early 1930s each major railroad was served by a number of bus lines serving stations with a specific local and regional coverage, with fixed schedules and ticket prices. The demand for bus transportation of passengers and their goods in commercially vibrant market areas along railroads such as the Shanghai–Hangzhou–Ningbo line was so high that private motor trucks supplemented the bus system and, under the eyes of the local authorities, offered freight transport to individual destinations for hire.[72]

As in the case of logistics companies serving the railroads, provincial governments often preferred to operate or grant franchises to private bus companies for the exclusive use of certain roads, with the result that government officials and bus lines became the main users. However, these franchise arrangements often suffered from the problem that provincial road authorities considered the bus service a government monopoly and thus favored government bus lines over private companies. Even if private lines came to a franchise agreement with a provincial government, the conditions were often extremely harsh, including the requirement that private bus lines had to maintain and repair the roads on which they operated. Similar to the relationship between railroad bureaus and private logistics companies, the heavy-handed approach of the government authorities vis-à-vis private companies was clearly weighted in favor

---

[70] Smith and Chuh, *Motor Roads*, pp. 11, 13–14, 21–3.
[71] Smith and Chuh, *Motor Roads*, p. 21. Thomas Rawski provides a fairly similar figure of 41,000 miles for 1931 in *Economic Growth*, p. 214, Table 4.8.
[72] Tiedaobu nianjian bianzuan weiyuanhui 鐵道部年鑑編纂委員會, 鐵道年鑑 (Railroad Annual Statistics) (Nanjing, Tiedaobu tiedao nianjian bianzuan weiyuanhui, 1933–1936), vol. 3, 1936, pp. 1737–1750, 1744. Around 1930, Shanghai had 8,533 passenger cars, 174 buses, 1,731 trucks, and 852 motorcycles. Smith and Chuh, *Motor Roads*, p. 81.

of government control and did not exactly encourage private business competition.[73]

Compared to rail and shipping infrastructure, the development of civil aviation in China before the beginning of the Japanese occupation in 1937 was modest, with only thirty airplanes covering air routes of about 8,600 miles linking major cities, especially in the eastern and southern part of China. Recruiting and training of Chinese pilots in sufficient numbers was a considerable challenge for the airline companies in the early 1930s, and airlines had to readjust passenger and freight charges in order to make air transport a viable transportation option, even for well-off customers. Similar to railroads and shipping, commercial aviation included foreign joint ventures in the beginning. In 1929 the China National Aviation Corporation (CNAC) was founded as a Sino-American joint enterprise for passenger and mail services in China. After reorganization, 55 percent of the capitalization was subscribed by the Chinese government and 45 percent by the American partner. The board consisted of nine directors, with five members appointed by the Ministry of Communications and four by the American shareholders. In the early 1930s three routes connecting Shanghai to Beijing, Chengdu, and Guangzhou were the major flights, and a daily service from Shanghai to Beijing was started in 1934.[74]

Passenger numbers started out small but increased relatively quickly, although on a small scale. CNAC planes carried a total of 220 passengers in 1929, rising to 12,800 passengers in 1937. Despite the outbreak of the war, passenger and mail transportation continued, albeit within different territorial boundaries. When Chiang Kai-shek's government moved to Chongqing as the capital of Free China in 1938, the flight network shifted its boundaries and began to concentrate on connecting major cities in China's southwest, southeast, and northwest, which were still in unoccupied territory and accessible by air. As statistics show, throughout the war years CNAC had rising passenger numbers, especially once government officials and refugees moved to Chongqing.[75]

The Central Air Transport Corporation (CATC) was another case of Sino-foreign collaboration. Originally founded in 1931 as the Eurasia Aviation Corporation with the Ministry of Communications and the German

---

[73] Smith and Chuh, *Motor Roads*, pp. 23–4, 113.
[74] Chinese Ministry of Information (comp.), *China Handbook, 1937–1945* (New York, The Macmillan Company, 1945), pp. 233–6.
[75] Chinese Ministry of Information, *China Handbook*, pp. 233–6; China Handbook Editorial Board (comp.), *China Handbook, 1950* (New York, Rockport Press, 1950), pp. 626–32.

Lufthansa company as partners, the enterprise became wholly Chinese-owned after China cut its relations with Germany as a member of the war's Axis powers in 1941. As a government line, CATC had a much smaller footprint, with a small number of planes, passengers, and limited service routes focusing on Chongqing and Kunming as wartime capitals in Free China.[76]

Postwar Reconstruction and Rail Expansion

In the decade following World War II, the world's railroad networks fell on either side of a distinct and growing gulf. Railroads were a mature or even declining technology in nations with democratic political systems and relatively free market economies. Western Europe did not see significant additions to track mileage after the war. The US rail network actually shrank by an average of 600 miles per year between 1945 and 1954. In contrast, railroads flourished in countries under Communist leadership. The USSR added an average of 534 miles per year in the decade after World War II, and post-revolutionary Cuba boasted more railroad track per square mile in the 1960s than any other country in the world. Throughout the Cold War era, railroads thrived in socialist states with centralized economic planning. After the founding of the People's Republic of China on October 1, 1949, the administrative organization and management of the railroad system were integrated into a core part of the new government's political and economic agendas. As physical entities and means of transportation, all existing railroad lines became part of the People's Railroad (*renmin tielu* 人民鐵路) system.[77]

At the end of the Japanese occupation and World War II in China, about 14,500 miles of the rail network were serviceable, but tracks, rolling stock, and maintenance facilities had suffered considerable damage. The damage due to civil war fighting led to a further deterioration of the network so that by early 1948 only about 5,000 miles of track were operational. Especially in the south of China, the rail network was damaged or destroyed. On the whole, the lines within the rail network of Manchuria suffered less damage than the majority of the railroads in China proper, partly because there the fighting between Japanese and Russians and between Chinese Communists and Nationalists

---

[76] Chinese Ministry of Information, *China Handbook*, pp. 236–8; Chia-hua Chu, *The Ministry of Communications in 1934* (Shanghai, China United Press, 1935), pp. 14–15.
[77] J.N. Westwood, "Soviet Railway Development," *Soviet Studies* 11.1 (July 1959), 33; Ivan Wiesel, "Cuban Economy after the Revolution," *Acta Oeconomica* 3.2 (1968), 203–20.

was "more highly localized than elsewhere." Thus Manchuria's network of standard-gauge railroads became operational long before the remaining lines recovered their service.[78]

In China's First Five-Year Plan (1953–1957) railroads were designated to support the country's industrial development. Whereas the expansion and renewal of the railroad network was not an explicit focus, the plan projected 2,500 miles of new railroad tracks as well as rail reconstruction work, including modifying some single-track lines to become double-track. By the end of the First Five-Year Plan, total operating mileage had increased by approximately 2,400 miles, of which 500 miles consisted of new double- or multitrack sections. Electrification of the Chinese rail system did not take place until 1962, with a meager sixty miles of electrified lines. This situation did not improve significantly until the beginning of the economic reforms in 1978.[79]

Executing huge, ambitious rail construction projects in remote areas of the country required a large, disciplined, and dedicated workforce willing to operate under often inhospitable and even dangerous conditions. Throughout the 1950s the railroad system had become home for PLA members demobilized after World War II and the Korean War. To expedite strategic rail infrastructure projects, in 1953 the Central Army Committee decided to establish the Railroad Army Corps (tiedaobing 铁道兵) as a centralized military vanguard for constructing new railroad lines in south, central, and western China. The organizational origins of the tiedaobing can be found in the "railroad columns" (tiedao zongdui 铁道总队) of soldiers. The PLA mobilized these soldiers to repair sections of damaged railroad tracks in the northeast that were of strategic importance to the advance of the Communist troops in 1948. Renamed the Railroad Corps (tiedao bingtuan 铁道兵团) after the end of the civil war in 1949, they continued to repair and construct railroads until they were officially integrated into the PLA as Chinese People's Liberation Army railroad soldiers (Zhongguo renmin jiefangjun tiedaobing 中國人民解放軍鐵道兵). By combining centrally directed construction and a military presence, this strategic approach enabled the

---

[78] N.S. Ginsburg, "China's Railroad Network," *Geographical Review* 41.3 (July 1951), 470–4, esp. 470. On wartime damage during the Japanese occupation, see Shanghai shi dang'anguan 上海市檔案館 (ed.), 日本在華中經濟掠奪史料, 1937–1945 (Historical Materials on Japan's Economic Plunder of Central China, 1937–1945) (Shanghai, Shanghai shudian chubanshe, 2005).

[79] Zhongguo tiedao xuehui 中國鐵道學會, 中國鐵路, 1949–2001 (Chinese Railroads, 1949–2001) (Beijing, Zhongguo tiedao chubanshe, 2003), p. 32. Total operating mileage was 13,160 miles by late 1949, 14,200 miles in 1952, and 16,600 miles in 1957. Total mileage of double- and multitrack sections amounted to 540 miles in 1949, 880 miles in 1952, and 1,400 miles in 1957.

building of ambitious railroad projects in difficult terrain, such as the 1,200-mile-long line from Lanzhou to Urumqi, built between 1952 and 1962, and the 705-mile-long Chengdu–Kunming Railroad completed in 1970.[80]

Economic reconstruction and the government's plan to introduce industrialization as rapidly as possible presented major challenges but also great opportunities for China's railroads. On the one hand, much hard manual work was required to repair the war-damaged network because of scarce machinery and little modern technical and managerial expertise. The assistance of Soviet experts helped improve the productivity of logistics operations and efficiency in equipment maintenance, but the departure of the Soviets did not lead to a decline in the rail sector. On the other hand, the desire of the Party and the government to compensate for the lack of appropriate capital investment by focusing on the mass mobilization of workers and any available resources meant that new railroad construction was undertaken.[81]

In the 1950s railroad expansion served the goals of the First Five-Year Plan to accelerate industrialization and was aligned with PRC interests regarding national defense. The "outsourcing" of railroad construction to the PLA in many ways was a brilliant move because it allowed a riskier approach to the construction of new lines, while also providing the benefits of the disciplined work ethic of railroad soldiers and the mobility of the military. At the same time, the experiences of former *tiedaobing* on construction sites also demonstrated that certain issues related to railroad construction, such as negotiating land acquisitions, hiring local labor, and interacting with the local population, were not fundamentally different from the practices employed during the Republican period. Railroad soldiers brought economic and social change to the local communities indirectly via rail construction, but they also came to be seen as state protectors and mediators, without their own entrenched interests in railroad development.[82]

Reconstruction in the 1950s also reframed the identity of railroads as administrative and managerial institutions and aligned them with the new socialist vision of the Chinese state. Values such as discipline, managerial efficiency, punctuality, and so forth, which during the Republican period were interpreted as virtues of Western modernity and technological

---

[80] Gao Guangwen 高光文, 鐵道兵 (Railroad Army Corps) (Beijing, Zhongguo qingnian chubanshe, 1972), p. 29; Chen Yuanmou 陳遠謀, 昨日鐵道兵 (Yesterday's Railroad Soldiers) (Beijing, Zhongguo shuji chubanshe, 1994).
[81] See D. Kaple, "Agents of Change: Soviet Advisers and High Stalinist Management in China, 1949–1960," *Journal of Cold War Studies* 18.1 (Winter 2016), 11.
[82] Köll, *Railroads and the Transformation of China*, pp. 240–7.

progress, were now reinterpreted as values representing the goals of revolutionary socialism. This reinterpretation and transfer of values from Western to socialist modernity conformed with the economic goals established in the First Five-Year Plan, but also helped create an identity for railroad workers based on expertise, skills, and professional dedication to their work.[83]

The years after the founding of the PRC were characterized by a relatively quick recovery of China's rail network. Between 1949 and the Great Leap Forward campaign in 1957, freight transport rose almost five times and passenger transport three times. In terms of different infrastructure methods in China's circular flow of passengers and freight during the 1950s, the numbers indicate the trend of a continuing focus on rail transportation with an increasing expansion of the road system. As Table 13.1 indicates, although railroad freight turnover increased rapidly in the 1950s, the ton-miles carried by modern water transport increased even more dramatically. Due to Cold War military activities in the Taiwan Strait, inland water transportation developed much more rapidly than coastal shipping.

As a general trend, water navigation was clearly more important than road transportation in terms of total freight transportation, while railroads continued to carry the lion's share of China's freight across the nation. The figures for passenger transportation during the 1950s were not that different: in 1952, 81 percent of passengers traveled by rail, 9 percent in motor vehicles, just under 10 percent on waterways, and only 0.1 percent by air. By the end of the First Five-Year-Plan in 1957, motor transportation for passengers had

Table 13.1 Freight turnover by modern means of transportation (in million ton-miles)[84]

Year	Railroads	Motor vehicles	Ships and barges	Total
Pre-1949 peak	25,103	286	7,972	33,361
1949	11,433	155	2,678	14,266
1950	24,488	236	1,802	26,526
1952	37,382	478	6,593	44,453
1954	57,937	1,205	11,582	70,724
1955	60,987	1,566	15,186	77,739
1956	74,906	2,169	17,529	94,664
1957	83,630	2,448	21,369	107,447

[83] Köll, *Railroads and the Transformation of China*, pp. 247–52.
[84] V.D. Lippitt, "Development of Transportation in Communist China," *China Quarterly* 27 (July–September 1966), 101–19, table adapted from Table 5, p. 113.

increased to 18 percent, with railroads at 73 percent, whereas water and air transport maintained almost the same percentages as in 1952.[85]

Whereas China's progress in the expansion of rail infrastructure was considerable, road construction continued to lag behind those efforts for a long time. By 1956, China had just about 38,000 miles of all-weather roads and 56,000 miles of fair-weather roads. As one observer estimated that year,

> about one quarter of the rural population at the time is not within a day's walk of any road ... The communications suffice to link villages to their market towns, but, except for the big rivers and the railways, transportation costs over long distances are very high and discourage much movement of grain and other heavy products.[86]

It would take China just another fifty years to overcome the problem and emerge as a global leader in the construction of modern highways, bridges, and road infrastructure in and outside China at the beginning of the twenty-first century.

Conclusion

For a long time, historians have looked at China's modern transportation and communication networks emerging in the nineteenth century as a "problem," lagging behind Western countries in scale and speed due to the impact of Western imperialism and semicolonialism. However, recent studies by historians have revisited the constraints of semicolonialism in the context of Chinese statecraft during the late Qing from a new perspective. For example, Stephen Halsey argues that the CMSNC became "an effective tool for mercantilist statecraft" which provided a business model for the shipping industry by integrating logistics, insurance, and sales into its business portfolio. China's emerging railroad network of the late nineteenth and early twentieth centuries presents another example of a positive development where Chinese railroad companies as state-directed enterprises broke the Western dominance in syndicates and slowly emerged as a technology with important economic and social impact. Anne Reinhardt has shown how

---

[85] Miao Qiulin 苗秋林 (ed.), 中國鐵路運輸 (China's Rail Transportation) (Beijing, Zhongguo tiedao chubanshe, 1994), p. 43, Tables 2-2-1, 2-2-2.
[86] Report from February 16, 1956, No. 63/"S," "Road Communications in China," 1372/1/56, Foreign Office files FO 371/120962, British National Archives. See also C. Meysken, *Mao's Third Front: The Militarization of Cold War China* (Cambridge, Cambridge University Press, 2020).

important the enactment of Chinese sovereignty was for the steam transport network and Chinese shipping businesses.

Whether in the telegraph, shipping, or railroad sector, government-sponsored companies enabled China's integration into the global communications network. Especially for the pre-1949 period the question of sovereignty played an important role in the negotiations between the Chinese state, its officials, and foreign political and business interests which often, expressing Chinese concerns, centered on the question of total control over the infrastructure ventures. As we have seen, the nationalization process and changes after the 1911 Revolution gave the Chinese state ultimate authority while still honoring the financial obligations and managerial concessions without breach of contract.[87]

Lack of funding for rail construction through share capital, bond issues, and bank loans characterized China's government responses throughout the 1880s and 1890s, slowing down the planning, construction, and operation of railroads. Although Sun Yat-sen envisioned the establishment of shipbuilding yards in his 1921 program as part of his industrial development scheme for the Chinese nation, cheap labor and materials did not translate into the robust rise of a Chinese shipbuilding industry. Along similar lines, Sun's plea for the establishment of locomotive and railroad equipment factories was based on his expectation that foreign capital and expertise would help initiate these industries.[88]

By comparison, Meiji Japan provides a good example of a national railroad initiative where capital in the form of private investment was scarce, but where the government became instrumental in raising funds through government deposits in banks to enable the pooling of private capital. To that end the Meiji government introduced a National Banking Act and promoted the establishment of a modern banking sector. In contrast to China's government response to lacking private investment, the Japanese government encouraged bank shareholders to fund rail construction with the promise of government subsidies for the project. As a result, these bank shareholders began to purchase the shares of the Nippon Railway, Japan's first privately held joint-stock company, which resulted in the building of 1,300 miles of railroad in Japan through private investment as early as 1892.[89] In this context,

---

[87] Halsey, *China's Quest*, pp. 211, 236; Reinhardt, *Navigating Semi-colonialism*, p. 296; Köll, *Railroads and the Transformation of China*, p. 296.
[88] Sun Yat-sen, *The International Development of China* (Shanghai, Commercial Press, 1920), pp. 194–5.
[89] S. Ericson, *The Sound of the Whistle: Railroads and the State in Meiji Japan* (Cambridge, MA, Harvard East Asian Monographs, 1996), p. 51.

it is fair to argue that the late and slow trajectory of the rail sector in China was at least partly due to the lack of sufficient institutional reforms that could have brought about modern banks and legal changes for incorporated joint-stock companies to motivate investors. However, it is also clear that the late and initially slow trajectory of railroad development was not due to the new technology itself or its perception and reception by the Chinese public.[90]

The history of China's infrastructure development is as much a global story as it is a Chinese story. This chapter has shown how China adopted telegraphs, postal systems, railroads, steamships, and so on from the West as technological and infrastructural concepts while retaining Chinese agency as operators, managers, builders, and consumers of their services. From a global perspective, much of China's transportation and communication network was financed and built under semicolonial conditions; and even after nationalization, Western advisers and a mix of European and North American methods shaped the emergence of Chinese railroad and shipping management, training, and administration. Especially in the rail sector, China remained dependent on rolling stock and equipment imports from Great Britain and the United States until the end of World War II. From 1949 to the political rift in 1961, engines, rail equipment, and technical advisers mostly hailed from the Soviet Union. China's rail development today, especially its high-speed sector, still depends on technology imports, keeping alive political debates about indigenous innovation and perceived dependency on foreign technology.[91] However, at the beginning of the twenty-first century, China's infrastructure development has reached a new phase as the government is engaged in the "One Belt, One Road" initiative, with the aim of placing China at the center of economic globalization through infrastructure expansion in and outside China. Railroads and highways, as part of a newly envisioned Silk Road, will complement shipping along the Maritime Silk Road in the quest to connect China with markets, products, and people on a truly global scale.

Further Reading

Baark, E., *Lightning Wires: The Telegraph and China's Technological Modernization, 1860–1890* (Westport, CT, Greenwood Press, 1997).

---

[90] See also H.-C. Wang, "Institutional Failure." Wang convincingly argues for institutional failure as the main reason for the Wusong railroad's lack of success.

[91] N. Ahrens, "Innovation and the Invisible Hand: China, Indigenous Innovation, and the Role of Government Procurement," *Carnegie Papers*, Asia Program, no. 114, July 2010 (Washington, DC, Carnegie Endowment for International Peace, 2010).

Chang Rui-te 張瑞德, 中國近代鐵路事業管理的研究, 1876–1937 (Railroads in Modern China: Political Aspects of Railroad Administration, 1876–1937) (Taipei, Institute of Modern History, Academia Sinica, 1991).

Chang Rui-te 張瑞德, 平漢鐵路與華北的經濟發展, 1905–1937 (The Peking–Hankow Railroad and Economic Development in North China, 1905–1937) (Taipei, Institute of Modern History, Academia Sinica, 1987).

Ding Xiangyong 丁賢勇, 新式交通與社會變遷：與民國浙江為中心 (New Communications and Social Transformation: Focusing on Zhejiang Province during the Republican Period) (Beijing, Zhongguo shehui kexue chubanshe, 2007).

Duus, P., R.H. Myers, and M.R. Peattie (eds.), *The Japanese Informal Empire in China, 1895–1937* (Princeton, NJ, Princeton University Press, 1989).

Faure, D., *China and Capitalism: A History of Modern Business Enterprise in China* (Hong Kong, Hong Kong University Press, 2006).

Feuerwerker, A., *China's Early Industrialization: Sheng Hsuan-huai (1844–1916) and Mandarin Enterprise* (Cambridge, MA, Harvard University Press, 1958).

Halsey, S.R., *Quest for Power: European Imperialism and the Making of Chinese Statecraft* (Cambridge, MA, Harvard University Press, 2015).

Huenemann, R.W., *The Dragon and the Iron Horse: The Economics of Railroads in China* (Cambridge, MA, Harvard University Press, 1984).

Kaske, E., "Sichuan as a Pivot: Provincial Politics and Gentry Power in Late Qing Railway Projects in Southwestern China," in U. Theobald and C. Jin (eds.), *Southwest China in a Regional and Global Perspective (c. 1600–1911)* (Leiden and Boston, Brill, 2018), pp. 379–423.

Köll, E., *Railroads and the Transformation of China* (Cambridge, MA, Harvard University Press, 2019).

Leung, C.-K., *China, Railway Patterns and National Goals* (Chicago, The University of Chicago Press, 1980).

Liang, E.P., *China, Railways and Agricultural Development, 1875–1935* (Chicago, The University of Chicago Press, 1982).

Moazzin, G., "Sino-Foreign Business Networks: Foreign and Chinese Banks in the Chinese Banking Sector, 1890–1911," *Modern Asian Studies* 54.3 (May 2020), 970–1004.

Rawski, T.G., *Economic Growth in Prewar China* (Berkeley, University of California Press, 1989).

Reinhardt, A., *Navigating Semi-colonialism: Shipping, Sovereignty, and Nation-Building in China, 1860–1937* (Cambridge, MA, Harvard University Asia Center, 2018).

Shen Zhihua 沈志華, 蘇聯專家在中國, 1948–1960 (Soviet Experts in China, 1948–1960) (Beijing, Xinhua chubanshe, 2009).

Smith, V., with A. Chuh, *Motor Roads in China* (Washington, DC, United States Government Printing Office, 1931).

Thai, P., *China's War on Smuggling: Law, Economic Life, and the Making of the Modern State, 1842–1965* (New York, Columbia University Press, 2018).

Zhuang Weimin 庄維民, 近代山東市場經濟的變遷 (The Transformation of the Market Economy in Modern Shandong) (Beijing, Zhonghua shuju, 2000).

14

Education and Human Capital

PEI GAO, BAS VAN LEEUWEN, AND MEIMEI WANG

Introduction

China has the largest education system in the world today. It educated more than 260 million people and employed 15 million teachers in 2015.[1] Besides its social impact, educational development has often been argued to be one of the primary reasons behind China's stunning economic growth after the economic reform implemented in 1978. It is therefore of paramount importance to understand how education evolved in Chinese history.

Throughout the very long educational history of China, the period that is studied in this volume (1800–1949) is particularly important as the education system underwent extraordinary changes and unprecedented expansion. For over 1,300 years, the traditional Confucian teaching system had played an essential role in shaping China's social and political structure, economic development, and cultural norms. From the late nineteenth century onwards, a series of transformations occurred to shift this long-lasting traditional system to a modern education system that was approximating a Western model. This new system helped to educate millions of students, formed modern human capital, cultivated new intellectual elites, and encouraged modern economic growth in China.

Despite its importance, there is very limited empirical evidence on the measurement of education levels as well as the related concept of human capital formation over the period studied in this volume. Some studies show that the high demand for education generated by the civil service examination system may arguably have led to relatively high levels of

---

The research leading to these results received funding from NYU-Shanghai and the European Research Council under the European Union's Horizon 2020 Programme (ERC-StG 637695 – HinDI) as part of the Historical Dynamics of Industrialization in Northwestern Europe and China c. 1800–2010: A Regional Interpretation project.

[1] Y. Pan, S. Vayssettes, and E. Fordham, *Education in China: A Snapshot* (Paris, Organisation for Economic Co-Operation and Development, 2016).

human capital.² However, based on the limited statistics on China, a considerable lead in mean education levels appears to have been in existence in the West even before the nineteenth century.³ This debate in the literature continues as a result of the paucity of data for China. Unfortunately, reliable estimates of educational attainment prior to 1949, such as literacy rates, enrollment ratios, and average years of schooling, are still wanting.

This chapter surveys some major changes in the way in which people acquired education in China from *c*. 1800 to 1949 and tries to provide a general picture of the trajectory of the expansion of education based on various sources. Human capital can be created through both formal education and training of other kinds, such as apprenticeships. Although we occasionally touch upon the latter, the main focus of this chapter is on the human capital acquired through the formal education system. This chapter is organized as follows. We will first detail the traditional Confucian teaching system, then introduce the newly created modern education system that was built after the turn of the twentieth century. The drastic educational expansion and modernization also profoundly impacted China in various social and economic areas, such as female education and the economic structure, which will be discussed in the final two sections.

The Traditional Education System before 1905

Before it came to an end in 1905, the traditional Confucian teaching system directly shaped China's social and political structure, economic development, and culture. One distinguishing characteristic of this system was that its foremost purpose was to select state officials and social elites from the best candidates via a series of competitive examinations.⁴ This means that

---

[2] J. Baten, D. Ma, S. Morgan, and Q. Wang, "Evolution of Living Standards and Human Capital in China in the 18th–20th Centuries: Evidence from Real Wages, Age-Heaping, and Anthropometrics," *Explorations in Economic History* 47.3 (2010), 347–59; E. Rawski, *Education and Popular Literacy in Ch'ing China* (Ann Arbor, University of Michigan Press, 1979).

[3] D. Cressy, "Levels of Illiteracy in England, 1530–1730," *Historical Journal* 20 (1977), 1–23; P. Gao, "Risen from the Chaos: The Emergence of Modern Education in China," in D. Mitch and G. Cappelli (eds.), *Globalization and the Rise of Mass Education* (Cham, Palgrave Macmillan, 2019), pp. 279–309; D. Mitch, "Education and Skill of the British Labour Force," in R. Floud and P. Johnson (eds.), *The Cambridge Economic History of Modern Britain*, vol. 1 (Cambridge, Cambridge University Press, 2004), pp. 332–56.

[4] The imperial civil service examination system was implemented as early as the Tang dynasty (618–896) and continued for more than 1,000 years until its abolition in 1905. This system served to recruit state bureaucrats and elites from the top national talents.

education had been the path to upward social mobility as such success in education could bring exceptionally high social and economic returns.[5] In this section, we briefly introduce the traditional system before 1905 first, and then survey the quantitative evidence on educational outcomes.

The Acquisition of Education

The way in which people acquired education changed significantly over the course of the period studied. In nineteenth-century China, education was conducted through educational institutions that are not very familiar to twenty-first-century readers. Under this system the educational structure was vaguely defined, with no clear regulation on schooling levels, division of grades, and the length of schooling.[6] As shown in Figure 14.1, many types of educational institutions with overlapping functions coexisted. This system can be roughly divided into two levels based on different functions. The elementary education was intended to provide basic schooling to the masses, while the main function of high-level education was to train examinees to prepare for the civil service examinations.

Elementary-Level Education

Unlike most modern societies, the Qing government supported high-level education more than elementary-level education.[7] The state only financed the civil service examination together with a large number of government schools to further train established scholars; in contrast, the responsibility to provide basic education was mainly taken by private households and local communities. The most common educational institutions where primary-school-age children went to acquire basic literacy and numeracy were collectively called sishu 私塾.[8] Sishu literally means private schools, which were often single-teacher operations run

---

[5] The successful candidates would be selected as state bureaucrats and social elites, and they could also enjoy various privileges, including exemption from corporal punishment and corvée (labour service), reduced tax payments, the right to wear a scholar's robe, and so on. Apart from official economic returns, some studies also show that Chinese bureaucrats incurred extremely high private gains from corruption of all sorts, sometimes amounting to fourteen to twenty-two times their official salary. See, for example, C. Chang, *The Income of the Chinese Gentry* (Seattle, University of Washington Press, 1962), pp. 32–43. S. Ni and P.H. Van, "High Corruption Income in Ming and Qing China," *Journal of Development Economics* 81.2 (2006), 316–36.

[6] B.A. Elman, *A Cultural History of Civil Examinations in Late Imperial China* (Berkeley, University of California Press, 2000).

[7] Rawski, *Education and Popular Literacy*, p. 24.

[8] There were many different types of *sishu*. A more detailed elaboration of this is outside the scope of the present study. But, very generally, they were family *sishu*, lineage or village *sishu*, and purely private *sishu*. Rawski, *Education and Popular Literacy*, pp. 44–53.

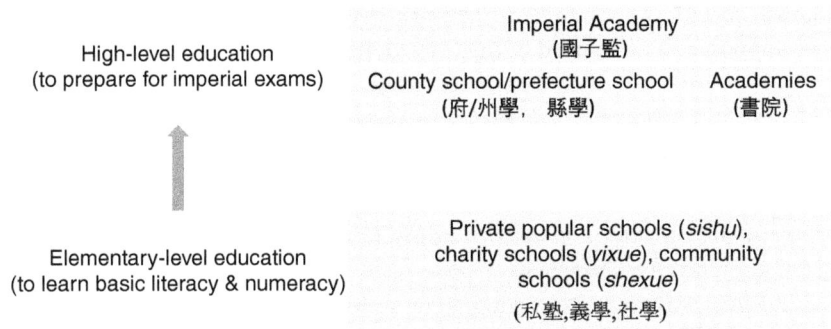

Figure 14.1 The school system before 1905

for profit, while some also received financial support from wealthy local families. Public effort was not entirely absent in elementary-level education,[9] and there were two types of public schools: *yixue* 義學 (charity schools)[10] and *shexue* 社學 (community schools).[11] However, the number of these schools was very small. According to Rawski, over the Qing dynasty only about 13,400 out of 40 million school-aged boys enrolled in these publicly provided elementary schools.[12]

Without a clearly defined educational structure, there was no explicit regulation on the length of schooling at every level. Chang notes that boys started their study at quite a young age, ranging from five to seven years old, and on average it took about three to four years to learn the basics of literacy.[13] The curriculum focused mainly on literacy and numeracy. Commonly used textbooks were the Confucian classic texts that were considered suitable for teaching young children.[14] Apart from classic texts, practical knowledge was often incorporated in the material. For instance, simple accounting practice and contract writing were also found to be

---

[9] Similar common schools with one teacher and all the students in one class were also widely found in eighteenth-century Europe and the US.
[10] *Yixue* were established mainly by local communities to provide education for the children from poor families.
[11] *Shexue* were public primary schools set up by local governments mainly in rural areas; after the 1750s they were gradually shut down.
[12] Rawski, *Education and Popular Literacy*. Also see, for example, Ma Yong 馬鏞, 中國教育制度通史 (A General History of Chinese Education), 5 vols. (Jinan, Shandong Education Press, 2000).
[13] C. Chang, *Chinese Gentry: Studies on Their Role in Nineteenth-Century Chinese Society* (Seattle, University of Washington Press, 1955).
[14] *Sanzijing* 三字經, *baijiaxing* 百家姓, *qianziwen* 千字文, and *qianjiashi* 千家詩 were traditional textbooks for enlightened education.

popular teaching content.¹⁵ Sometimes even astronomy, geography, and agronomy were introduced in the classrooms.

High-Level Education

The post-elementary education had only one purpose – training established scholars for the imperial civil service examinations, therefore advanced educational institutions, in various forms, functioned as training and examination centers. As shown in Figure 14.2, the examination system had a pyramidal structure consisting of a series of tests administered at the county, provincial, and central levels. The academic degrees associated with each level of the examination formed a "ladder of success" in Chinese society.

Different from the fact that private schools dominated elementary-level education, the imperial government played an essential role in high-level education by directly financing the examinations and setting up many government schools. Students usually started their studies for the examination in privately run senior *sishu* where classic canons and articles were taught.¹⁶ Once the examinees passed the highest level of the entry examination, the licensing examination (*yuankao* 院考),¹⁷ they obtained the degree of *shengyuan* 生員 and were entitled to attend the publicly provided county or prefectural school (*fuxue* 府學, *zhouxue* 州學, *xianxue* 縣學) to pursue their studies.¹⁸ The most outstanding students could be further selected into the Imperial Academy (*guozijian* 國子監) in Beijing.¹⁹ Apart from these

---

¹⁵ Li Bozhong 李伯重, "19 世紀初期華婁地區的教育產業" (Educational Institutions of the Hualou Area in the Early Nineteenth Century), *Studies in Qing History* 2 (2006), 60–74.
¹⁶ Rawski, *Education and Popular Literacy*, pp. 31.
¹⁷ The primary entry examination was presided over by the magistrate of the county, followed by an examination presided over by the head of the prefectural government. If successful, the student could attend the prefectural exam (*yuankao*), also called "licensing exam" in some studies. The prefectural exam was presided over by the highest educational officer of the province.
¹⁸ Prefectural schools (府學) were built in prefectural seats and county schools (縣學) in county seats. These schools were publicly funded and managed directly by the government. They not only provided training to students; more importantly they were official examination centers. Their main function was to hold regular mock examinations and register further preselection examinations (*keshi* 科試) for each student. Only those who passed the preselection examination were qualified to take the next-level exam – the provincial level.
¹⁹ The Imperial Academy was established in Beijing by the central government. As the model of teaching for other local official schools, its students had privileges such as more funding and better teachers. The emperor himself sometimes even gave irregular lectures there.

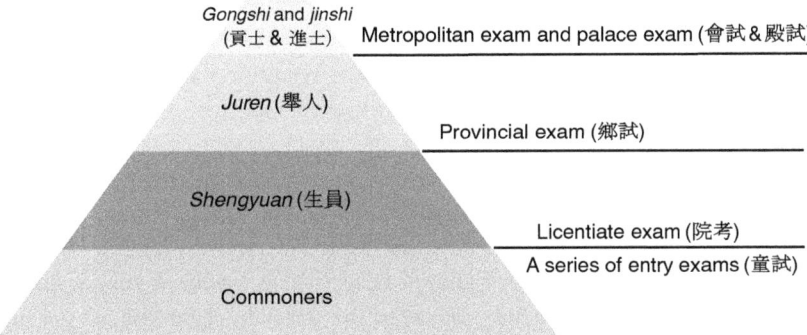

Figure 14.2 The civil service examination system and its associated degree titles
Notes. The lowest academic degree was shengyuan 生員, which was awarded to examinees who had passed the licentiate examination. Becoming shengyuan guaranteed a place in a county or prefectural school that was provided by the state for examinees to further their study. Only qualified candidates in those government schools were entitled to participate in the next-level examination – the provincial examination, and those who passed could obtain the degree title juren 舉人. The metropolitan examination was held in the capital, Beijing, and juren who passed this level of examination were called gongshi 貢士. The final test was the palace examination, and the successful candidate could obtain the highest degree – jinshi 進士.

government schools, examinees could also attend private academies (shuyuan 書院) for more training.[20] These academies were privately funded but endorsed by the state. As private educational institutions, they were more tolerant in term of admission standard. Some academies only accepted high-degree holders, while others also allowed examinees with weaker academic backgrounds to attend.[21]

The curriculum for this stage of schooling focused entirely on the Confucian classics. Ancient canons and classic articles were used as textbooks to extend the training in writing and critical thinking. The curriculum experienced slight changes over time, but throughout the Qing period it had three main parts: (1) reading classical texts,[22] (2) memorizing a shared

---

[20] Private academies served multiple functions. First, they were libraries where Confucian classics were kept for examinees to read. They were also centers of scholarly discussion and research for established scholars.
[21] Some academies admitted tongsheng (童生) who had only passed some low-level examinations but obtained no official degree title yet, while others only accepted degree holders, including shengyuan (生員) and juren (舉人).
[22] Students refined their linguistic skills by reading classical articles and anthologies written in traditional script.

canon,[23] and (3) the ability to write elegant essays, known as eight-legged essays.[24] The strikingly narrow-focused curriculum has been criticized by both reformers at the time and contemporary scholars. The educational content was too distant from both modern scientific inquiry and practical economics,[25] which could discourage young talents from pursuing a wider spectrum of knowledge and set back the development of technology and modern science in China.[26]

In theory, the civil service examination was open to all males; however, only a small proportion of people would choose to pursue high-level education because the preparation for the examinations was time-consuming. In addition, the length of study required to pass the examinations varied significantly among individuals and was difficult to predict.[27] On average, the basic learning to read the classic canons, poems, and articles took approximately six or seven years, and several more years were needed to study eight-legged-essay writing. Most of the lower-degree holders (*shengyuan*) enrolled in government schools at the age of twenty. Given that boys often started elementary schooling at the ages of five to seven, it took about fifteen years to obtain the lowest degree. Most of the top-degree holders (*jinshi*) completed the final palace examination in their late thirties.[28] That is why even with high monetary return and social privilege attached to the degrees, post-elementary education remained less attractive to people with humble backgrounds. For instance, Wang studied 1,000 lower-degree holders (*shengyuan*) in Zhili province and found that more than 50 percent of them came from high-income families with members among the landholding

---

[23] The compulsory readings were ancient Confucian canons, i.e. the Four Books, the Five Classics and classic annotations of these canons by scholars. The Four Books and Five Classics are the authoritative books of Confucianism in China. The Four Books are the Analects 論語, the *Mencius* 孟子, the *Great Learning* 大學, and *The Doctrine of the Mean* 中庸. The Five Classics are the *Classic of Poetry* 詩經, the *Book of Documents* 尚書, the *Book of Rites* 禮記, the *Book of Changes* 易經, and the *Spring and Autumn Annals* 春秋.
[24] Elman, *A Cultural History*, pp. 46–93.   [25] Elman, *A Cultural History*, pp. 53–64.
[26] See, for example, G. Clark and R.C. Feenstra, *Technology in the Great Divergence: Globalization in Historical Perspective* (Chicago, The University of Chicago Press, 2003), pp. 277–322; J. Mokyr, *The Gifts of Athena: Historical Origins of the Knowledge Economy* (Princeton, Princeton University Press, 2002); D.S.Landes, "Why Europe and the West? Why Not China?", *Journal of Economic Perspectives* 20 (2006), 3–22; J.Y. Lin, "The Needham Puzzle: Why the Industrial Revolution Did Not Originate in China," *Economic Development and Cultural Change* 43.2 (1995), 269–92; D. Cantoni and N. Yuchtman, "The Political Economy of Educational Content and Development: Lessons from History," *Journal of Development Economics* 104 (2013), 233–44.
[27] See, for example, Elman, *A Cultural History*; Y. Xu, P. Földvári and B. van Leeuwen, "Human Capital in Qing China: Economic Determinism or a History of Failed Opportunities?", MPRA Paper 43525, University Library of Munich, Germany (2013).
[28] Chang, *Chinese Gentry*.

gentry, merchants, or officials. A similar composition can also be observed when looking at the top-degree holders (*jinshi*).[29] Consistently using personal information about 4,035 *juren*, Kung and Jiang also found that only 20.27 percent of their fathers were commoners who held no degree titles.[30]

Apprenticeship

Formal schooling is only one part of education. Vocational training that provides job-specific skills also generates human capital. Similar to Europe before the Industrial Revolution, vocational education in China for many professions, especially in handicraft and service industries, was conducted through apprenticeship.[31] The learning was usually arranged in a format where each student worked under the supervision of a master craftsman. However, as handicraft, trade, and service sectors only occupied a small share in the whole economy before the twentieth century,[32] apprentices were unlikely to consist of more than 4 percent of the labour force. Prior to 1900, only a very small number of children had the opportunity to be an apprentice.[33]

Unlike what we see in medieval Europe, where the relationship between apprentices and their master was based on formal contracts,[34] apprenticeships were not strictly regulated in China and the training content was not standardized even within the same industry. Guilds indeed attempted to provide more regulations on apprenticeship from the nineteenth century onwards, but the recruitment standards, apprenticeship lengths, and the cap on the number of apprentices under one master all varied widely across

---

[29] Wang Yaosheng 王躍生, "清代生監的人數計量及其社會構成" (The Calculation and the Social Composition of *Shengyuan* and *Jiansheng* in Qing China), *Nankai Journal* 1 (1989), 40–7.

[30] Q. Jiang and J.K.S. Kung, "Social Mobility in Late Imperial China: Reconsidering the 'Ladder of Success' Hypothesis," *Modern China*, 2020, https://doi.org/10.1177/0097700420914529.

[31] Li Quanshi 李權時, 商業教育 (Commercial Education) (Shanghai, Zhonghua Book Company, 1933).

[32] Y. Xu, Z. Shi, B. van Leeuwen, Y. Ni, Z. Zhang, and Y. Ma, "Chinese National Income, ca. 1661–1933," *Australian Economic History Review* 57.3 (2017), 368–93; Y. Guo, Z. Zhang, B. van Leeuwen, and Y. Xu, "A View of the Occupational Structure in Imperial and Republican China (1640–1952)," *Australian Economic History Review* 59.2 (2019), 134–58.

[33] This situation only changed after the expansion of state-owned craft workshops (*gongyiju* 工艺局) in the 1900s.

[34] Zhao Xueyao 趙學瑤, Yu Ping 於萍, and Lin Ruoxin 林若鑫, "中西方傳統學徒制比較研究" (A Comparative Study of Traditional Apprenticeship in China and Western Countries), *Vocational and Technical Education* 37.34 (2016), 35–40.

professions.³⁵ The age of admission for apprentices was quite flexible and children could start their training at any age between twelve and eighteen.³⁶ There was no admission requirement on educational background for craftwork apprentices, and the selection standards placed more emphasis on candidates' characteristics, such as diligence and honesty. In contrast, industries like the mercantile trade, publishing, and banking adhered to very specific standards when recruiting their apprentices. For instance, old-style Chinese banks set explicit rules that only candidates with at least eight years of *sishu* education were considered eligible.³⁷ The length of training also varied greatly, from two or three years to five to seven years (the most common duration was approximately three years).³⁸ For example, the first-year training in commerce was devoted to routine services in order to develop trainees' basic work ethics and social skills. In the second year, training shifted towards professional skills such as accounting, letter writing, and business etiquette. In the third year, professional training, including negotiating skills, was deepened.³⁹

Measuring the Expansion of Education

Existing literature remains inconclusive on the level of human capital in China throughout the nineteenth and early twentieth centuries, because

---

³⁵ Regarding regulations on the number of apprentices, the figure varies across industries. For instance, in Changsha city, each workshop producing galvanized iron was allowed to admit only one apprentice; while two or three apprentices per filature were allowed for the silk industry, and five apprentices for each pawnshop. Zhong Li 李忠 and Xiaoning Wang 王筱宁, "社會教育在底層民眾實現社會流動中扮演的角色—以清末民國時期的學徒教育為例" (The Role of Public Education on Upward Social Mobility of Commoners: Taking Apprenticeship in Late Qing and Republican China as an Example), *Social Sciences in Nanjing* 4 (2008), 107–14. See also Qi Xia 漆俠, 宋代經濟史 (Economic History of the Song Dynasty) (Shanghai, Shanghai renmin chubanshe, 1987).

³⁶ Peng Zeyi 彭澤益, 中國工商行會史料集 (Collection of Historical Archives of the Chinese Guilds of Industry and Commerce), vol. 1 (Beijing, Zhonghua shuju, 1995).

³⁷ With the modernization of the education system, in 1904 this requirement was changed to the possession of a senior primary-school diploma. In 1922 it changed to the possession of a junior secondary-school diploma. See Qiu Zhenkang 裘振康, "紹興錢莊培植學生的一些情況" (The Situation of Student Cultivation in the Old-Style Chinese Bank of Shaoxing), in *Literature and Historical Archives of Shaoxing*, 9 vols. (Shaoxing, Shaoxingshi Wenshi Ziliao Weiyuanhui, 1990), pp. 106–9.

³⁸ Early in the twentieth century, John Stewart Burgess investigated sixteen craft guilds in Beijing. He found that three industries set the apprenticeship to last for three years, ten industries called for three years and three months and in the three other industries the duration was four, six, or seven years. See J.S. Burgess, *The Guilds of Peking* (New York, Columbia University Press, 1928).

³⁹ Luo Lun 罗伦 and Fan Jinmin 范金民, "清抄本生意世事初階述略" (An Introduction to *Shengyi Shishi Chujie*), *The Documantat* 2 (1990), 233–9.

direct evidence utilizing systematic data on schooling level is scarce. Without more empirical studies directly measuring educational outcomes in China during the period studied, the debate will continue.

Literacy Rate

The literacy rate is one of the most easily quantifiable indicators to measure education and human capital. Perkins estimates that in the 1880s less than 50 percent of males above school age could be regarded as literate on the basis of Maritime Customs reports.[40] Similarly, Rawski argues that basic education had already diffused nationwide, resulting in a respectably high literacy rate in nineteenth-century China. She points out that, even though the variation across regions could be remarkably wide, a rough guess at the literacy rate during the late Qing might be 30 to 45 percent for males and 2 to 10 percent for females.[41] Consistent with these estimates, other researchers also document that written communications of all kinds were widely used in hiring labor, renting property, and spreading news even in remote rural communities, which indicates a society with relatively high literacy rates.[42] If such evidence is valid, nineteenth-century China should have a similar rate of literacy to that in late Tokugawa Japan, where the rate for men was at 40 to 50 percent, and for women at 13 to 17 percent.[43] However, compared to Europe and North America, which were leaders in terms of the public provision of education at all levels, the literacy rate in China lagged far behind. Before 1900, about 80 percent of Americans could be regarded as receiving some level of education;[44] and this figure was 88 percent in Germany, 77 percent in the UK, and 70 percent in France.[45]

Elementary-Level Schooling

Data on school enrollments in China over our period of study are very limited, especially for elementary-level education. As discussed previously,

---

[40] D.H. Perkins, *China's Modern Economy in Historical Perspective* (Cambridge, MA, Harvard University Press, 1975), p. 4.
[41] Rawski, *Education and Popular Literacy*, pp. 8–23.
[42] M. Zelin, "Merchant Dispute Mediation in Twentieth-Century Zigong, Sichuan," in K. Bernhardt and P.C.C. Huang (eds.), *Civil Law in Qing and Republican China* (Stanford, CA, Stanford University Press, 1994), pp. 249–86.
[43] K. Ohkawa and H. Rosovsky, *Japanese Economic Growth: Trend Acceleration in the Twentieth Century* (Stanford, CA, Stanford University Press, 1973), p. 8.
[44] S.E. Black and K.L. Sokoloff, "Long-Term Trends in Schooling: The Rise and Decline of Public Education in the United States," in E. Hanushek and F. Welch (eds.), *Handbook of the Economics of Education* 1 (San Diego, CA, North-Holland, 2006), pp. 69–105.
[45] A. Green, *The Rise of Education Systems in England, France and the USA* (London, Macmillan, 1990).

Table 14.1 Estimation of the enrollment ratio of *sishu*

Year	Province	County	School-age population (7–12)	Sishu		Enrollment ratio (%)
				School	Enrollment	
1911	Zhejiang	Zhuji	47,684	790	10,981	23.0
1909		Daishan	7,967	100	1,390	17.5
1909		Fenghua	34,103	399	5,920	17.4
1907		Putuo	8,264	80	1,112	13.5
1911	Hebei	Funing	29,142	227	3,155	10.8
1911		Zhaoxian	15,109	200	2,780	18.4
1911		Wangdu	7,709	71	987	12.1
1910	Anhui	Lingbi	30,869	191	2,727	8.8
1911	Fujian	Jianyang	15,955	200	1,000	6.3
1904	Shandong	Jimo	35,624	241	4,653	13.1

Source: X. Hu, 清末中國民眾私塾就學率的考察 (A Study of Private-School Enrollment Ratios at the End of the Qing Dynasty) *Lifelong Education and Libraries* 9 (2009), 29–36

most primary-school-age children attended *sishu* that were not public educational institutions, therefore their information was never included in the official statistics. Table 14.1 presents some scattered county-level statistics, indicating that basic education already had a wide coverage in nineteenth-century China, with an average enrollment rate of approximately 14 percent. This number matches some historical anecdotal evidence that almost all villages had at least one or two *sishu* to train their children in basic literacy and numeracy.[46] But regional variation could be remarkably wide. Looking at rich southern counties in the nineteenth century, most of the students in the elementary-level schools were commoners, which implies that the elementary-level education spread widely to all social groups in the highly commercialized and prosperous Yangzi delta. In contrast, in the rural counties of Yunnan and Jiangxi, 80 to 90 percent of the population were reported as never receiving any level of education in the 1900s.[47]

---

[46] China proper has about 1,660 counties and about 9,000 villages. Traditional private popular schools penetrated into each village, so that there were probably more than 10,000 *sishu* across China.

[47] Yin Mengxia 殷梦霞 and Tian Qi 田奇, 民國人口資料彙編 (Historical Data of Population and Household Registers in the Republic of China) (Beijing, Guojia Tushuguan chubanshe, 2009).

High-Level Schooling

Unlike the absence of *sishu* in official records, data on high-level education are more abundant because the state directly managed these government schools. In Table 14.2 we present the regional distribution of the two types of high-level educational institutes, county or prefectural schools and private academies. As shown in Table 14.2, high-level education institutions also spread nationwide. Among the 1,660 counties in China proper,[48] about 88.5 percent set up at least one government school (county or prefectural schools) to train established scholars to prepare for the civil service examinations. Private academies present a slightly different pattern. Regional disparity was higher, with 20 percent of counties having no academy, 45 percent having fewer than three and 10 percent having more than ten.

It is impossible to estimate the enrollment ratio for high-level education, but the number of examinees who participated in the civil service examination system offers a crude way to gain some insights on this question. There was a long-standing quota system to regulate the number of examinees who were allowed to enroll in county or prefectural schools.[49] The original quotas, assigned to counties, ranged from zero to twenty.[50] Wealthier and strategically more important counties were granted higher quotas. Before the Taiping Rebellion (1851), 23,852 examinees passed the licentiate examination each time. According to Chang, the success rate was only about 1 or 2 percent,[51]

---

[48] The central plain of China includes eighteen provinces but about 80 percent of the population. It is a term often used to express a distinction between the core and frontier regions of China.

[49] There were two kinds of quota. One was assigned directly to each county and the other was a prefectural-level quota that was comparatively small. The figures presented in Table 14.2 are the sum of all county-level quota within a given prefecture plus the prefectural-level quota.

[50] The Imperially Established Institutes and Laws of the Great Qing Dynasty (大清會典) carefully documented the quota system across counties throughout the Qing period. Whereas the quota system remained stable between 1644 and 1851, because of the outbreak of the Taiping Rebellion (1850–1864) the Qing government increased the quotas for many regions in order to strengthen its alliances among the local gentry against rebel forces. After the war, the revised quota assigned in 1873 persisted until the abolition of the exam system. See, for example, Chang, *Chinese Gentry*, pp. 83–92; P. Ho, *The Ladder of Success in Imperial China: Aspects of Social Mobility, 1368–1911* (New York, Columbia University Press, 1962).

[51] Wang has different estimates than Chang. He argues that in the areas with large numbers of applicants the success ratio could be even lower than 1 percent, but in the areas with relatively few applicants, the ratio was 3 to 4 percent. See, for example, Chang, *Chinese Gentry*; Wang Ligang 王立剛, "清代童試錄取率研究" (A Study of the Admission Rate to the Preliminary Stage of the Imperial Examinations), *Tribune of Social Sciences* 3 (2014), 67–76.

Table 14.2 Number of post-elementary schools in China proper

Province	Government school				Private academy
	Prefectural school	County school	Quotas for students		
			Early Qing	Late Qing	
Anhui	12	58	1,279	1,604	312
Fujian	12	60	1,111	1,426	366
Gansu	13	69	925	931	66
Guangdong	12	89	1,359	1,768	531
Guangxi	12	66	1,024	1,122	188
Guizhou	11	71	766	767	158
Henan	13	105	1,667	1,902	404
Hubei	10	68	1,117	1,543	234
Hunan	13	71	1,262	1,675	489
Jiangsu	11	69	1,404	764	301
Jiangxi	14	79	1,360	2,130	957
Shaanxi	12	89	1,147	1,254	156
Shandong	12	107	1,870	1,993	311
Shanxi	20	101	1,528	1,612	181
Sichuan	16	150	1,486	2,017	609
Yunnan	21	80	1,369	1,372	301
Zhejiang	11	78	1,803	2,177	698
Zhili	17	133	2,711	2,751	284

Note. "China proper" is a term used to express a distinction between the core and the frontier regions of China. More explicitly, China proper covers eighteen provinces: Anhui, Fujian, Gansu, Henan, Hubei, Hunan, Jiangsu, Jiangxi, Guangdong, Guangxi, Guizhou, Shaanxi, Shandong, Shanxi, Sichuan, Yunnan, Zhejiang, and Zhili. It accommodated more than 80 percent of the population (measured by late Qing population data).
Sources: 康熙朝大清會典 (Collected Statutes of the Great Qing Dynasty); 欽定學政全書 (The Encyclopaedia of Educational Affairs); Ji Xiaofeng 季嘯風, 中國書院辭典 (Dictionary of Academies in China) (Hangzhou, Zhejiang Jiaoyu chuban jituan, 1996)

which means the total number of candidates who participated in the licensing examination could be as large as 1.2 million. Given that the population was around 400 million, this crude estimate suggests that China indeed had a "bottom-heavy" talent pool with a large number of males at least receiving six to ten years of education.[52]

---

[52] Many candidates would take the exam multiple times before they successfully obtained a pass, therefore there was a high repeating ratio among these 1.19 million candidates.

The Modern Education System after 1905

From the late nineteenth century onwards, China's defeat in a series of wars against the West and Meiji Japan led to an increasing awareness of the importance of Western technology in Chinese society.[53] As a way to achieve national salvation, a number of Western-influenced reforms, touching on different aspects of society, were implemented over the course of our period of study. This modernization movement included a call to remodel the traditional Confucian education system. This section introduces the new education system first, and then surveys evidence measuring the educational outcomes of early twentieth-century China.

The New Education System

Education reforms began with cautious steps in the late nineteenth century when a small number of foreign-language schools, military schools, and modern teacher-training schools were built. The real milestone occurred in 1905 when a memorandum was unexpectedly issued to abolish the civil service examination system at all levels and a new education system was officially implemented nationwide approximating a Western model.[54]

The Formal Education System

Compared to the traditional Confucian teaching system, the new education system had several distinguishing features. First, as shown in Figure 14.3, the newly implemented system had a clearly defined educational structure with explicit regulations on schooling levels, the division of grades, and the length of schooling.[55] The first schooling-level structure was a 9–4–6 division: primary school for nine years, secondary school for four years, and tertiary school for six years, which was modeled after the Japanese arrangement. In addition,

---

[53] For instance, there were the two Opium Wars, the First Sino-Japanese war, the Sino-French War, and the occupation of Beijing by eight nations after the Boxer Rebellion.

[54] The education models developed in Europe, the US, and Japan from the early nineteenth century onwards are different in many ways, but fundamentally they are similar and have several core characteristics: they are universal, mandatory, secular, and academic. This education model is widely considered to be an institutionalized model of national development around the globe. See Green, *The Rise of Education Systems*, p. 297.

[55] The structure was altered several times in the following decades, and Japanese influence weakened as Western influence became more prominent. In 1912, the division became 7–4–4. On October 26, 1921, the education system was changed again to follow the American style, which favored a 6–6–4 division.

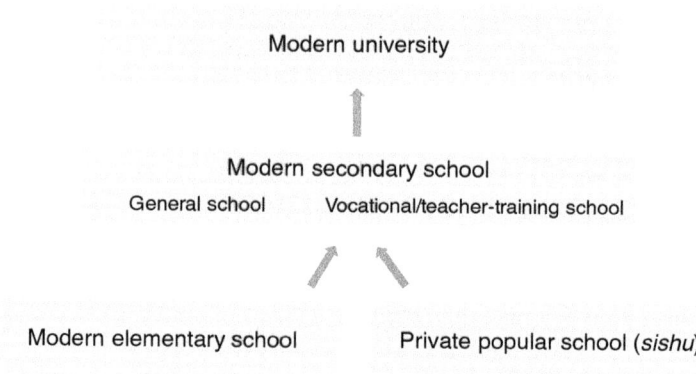

Figure 14.3 The education system after 1905

a tripartite system was introduced, with parallel tracks for general, vocational, and teacher-training schools above the secondary education level. General schools emphasized academic learning, vocational and technical schools provided job-specific skills for a wide arrange of trades and professions, and teacher-training schools were intended to churn out a large number of eligible teachers for this rapidly expanding education system. Throughout the period under study, general education remained the dominant form of schooling.

Second, unlike the Confucian teaching system under which elementary-level schools were mainly provided by private households and local communities, for the first time greater public effort went into primary education.[56] Public funding was more supportive towards primary education while the private sector was allowed to play a greater role in high-level education. The proportion of public primary schools (excluding *sishu*) rose from 75 percent in the 1910s to 95 percent in the 1940s, indicating the state's strong attempt to make at least primary education become available to the masses.[57]

The most far-reaching change occurred in educational content. The Confucian teaching system only provided incentive for young talents to study Confucian classics, which was believed to have prevented the rise of modern science and technology in China. When the imperial government abolished the examination in 1905, classical Chinese lost its appeal and modern subjects were incorporated into the new curriculum. For public

---

[56] Universal access to education that is at least partly provided by the state first emerged in Europe and North America from the early nineteenth century onwards, while China's attempt to publicly provide mass education to its children started relatively late.
[57] Gao, *Risen from the Chaos*, p. 286.

schools, the state drafted clear regulatory curriculum models for each level of schooling, and the teaching content emphasized new academic learning, technological know-how, and new ideological campaigns. As an example, Table 14.3 presents changes in regulatory models for primary school curriculums by the Ministry of Education from 1904 to 1948, and a similar pattern can be observed in the curriculum models for secondary schools. The major change was a substantial decline in the weight given to the Chinese classics; at the same time new Western subjects, including arithmetic, physics, and geography, together with new moral doctrines, e.g. nationalism and the "Three Principles of the People,"[58] were introduced to the masses and spread through the expanding education system. The improvement in curriculum was not confined to newly established public schools. To ensure that all types of schools conformed to similar teaching standards, government also urged still-existing *sishu* to reform their teaching content.

However, we would also like to stress that the real improvements were less than one might have expected. The changes in curriculum bore at best a limited resemblance to the road map provided by the state. For instance, the government placed explicit eligibility requirements on teachers' education backgrounds as it was essential to appoint teachers who had the

Table 14.3 Regulatory curriculum models for primary schools (percentage)

Course		1904	1912	1922	1936	1948
Chinese and Confucian classics		35	20	20	17.5	15
Arithmetic		10	15	17.5	15	12.5
English		10	15	17.5	15	15
Art and physical education		10	10	10	15	10
Manual work		5	15	10	15	15
Social science	History	20	15	15	10	15
	Geography					
Natural science	Physics	10	10	10	12.5	17.5
	Chemistry					

Note. Since 1912, the Confucian classics ceased to form an independent course in schools; what remain are some selections in the textbooks of Chinese courses
Source: Shu Xincheng 舒新城, 近代中國教育史料 (A Summary of Historical Materials of the New Education in China) (Shanghai, Zhonghua shuju, 1928), p. 79

[58] This was a political philosophy developed by Sun Yat-sen. The Three Principles comprised nationalism, democracy, and the livelihood of the people.

academic competence to deliver the right training to students;[59] however, such rules were never implemented in practice. Roughly 80 percent of primary-school teachers still failed to meet the standard set by the Ministry of Education until the 1940s;[60] and about 65 percent of *sishu* in 1935 continued to teach the old Confucian content without remodeling their curriculum.[61] Similarly, the quality of high-level education also failed to meet standards. A survey of the China Vocational Education Association reports that a large share of their graduates was far from proficient in their command of professional knowledge and skills.[62]

Apart from insufficient numbers of eligible teachers and a shortage of funding, the implementation of the new system also encountered strong resistance from local people. To a great extent, the general public showed little interest in or understanding of this new education system, especially during the early stages of its development. In fact, this highly Western-influenced system was widely considered to be a severe threat to the enduring cultural and social norms of local society. The Republican government initiated a national program known as the "Temple Destruction Movement," which encouraged local governments to seize the assets of Buddhist and Daoist temples in order to support the expansion of modern education.[63] Such destruction of establishments symbolic of traditional culture led to widespread resistance. The central government indeed exerted various efforts and tried to smooth the transformation and gain more support from the general population. For instance, graduates under the new system were allowed to have degree titles equivalent to those under the traditional system.[64] In the same vein, the admission requirements for modern

---

[59] For teaching posts in primary schools, only graduates of teacher-training schools (equivalent to secondary school) were eligible; and for a secondary-school post, a degree from an advanced teacher-training school (equivalent to a university) was required.

[60] Chen Dongyuan 陳東原 (ed.), 第二次中國教育年鑑 (The Second Education Yearbook) (Shanghai, Shangwu Yinshuguan, 1948).

[61] Wu Jiping 吳寄萍, 改良私塾 (Improved *Sishu*) (Shanghai, Zhonghua shuju, 1939).

[62] Wang Ji 王婕, 民國時期大學生就業研究 1912–1937 (Research on the Employment of Tertiary-Education Students in Republican China 1912–1937) (Zhengzhou, Zhengzhou University, 2012).

[63] P.R. Katz, *Religion in China and Its Modern Fate* (Waltham, MA, Brandeis University Press, 2014).

[64] All students who had at least obtained a senior primary-school diploma could be awarded such traditional scholarly titles as *jinshi*, *juren*, and *gongsheng*, and various official ranks. For example, after finishing a minimum of three years of study in a college with at least medium grades in the graduation examinations, graduates could be awarded the academic title of *juren*, and they were eligible for official posts equal to assistant magistrate. Alternatively, they could be employed by industrial and commercial companies, or start their own.

secondary schools were tolerant and open to students from *sishu* that had reformed their teaching content.

Apprentices in a Time of Change

The rise of formal vocational education presented strong competition to the traditional apprenticeship. These two educational tracks provided similar on-the-job training with different advantages. Formal vocational education was geared towards modern industries and offered students formal educational credentials, while apprenticeships had deeper roots in traditional professions, such as handicrafts, which continued to dominate in industry and accounted for a large part of the economy.[65] From 1900 onwards, a series of new polices were issued to regulate apprenticeship, including training quality and the rights of apprentices.[66] In the meantime, the imperial government also established a large number of state-owned handicraft workshops.[67] Between 1902 and 1911, 757 such agencies were set up in twenty-two provinces, and each workshop could hire dozens to hundreds of apprentices.[68] The enrollment scale was further expanded after 1911. A survey conducted in 1913 shows that 63.7 percent of workshop owners in the machinery industry in Shanghai started their career as apprentices.[69] Even though we cannot pin down accurately the number of apprentices participating in these training programs, it is clear that apprenticeship continued to play a crucial role in the training of skilled workers in early twentieth-century China.

---

[65] For instance, 72 percent of the output value of manufacturing industry was contributed by handicraft industries in 1933. See Wu Baosan 巫寶三, 中國國民所得 1933 (Chinese National Income in 1933) (Beijing, Shangwu Yinshuguan, 2011).

[66] In 1929, the Factory Law (*gongchangfa* 工廠法) issued by the national government in Nanjing stipulated that factory owners had a duty to educate their apprentices, and in 1932 the Revised Factory Law (*xiuzheng gongchangfa* 修正工廠法) gave further protection to apprentices' right to education by basically setting the final level attained during apprenticeship equal to that of senior primary school. See Peng Nansheng 彭南生, 行會制度的近代命運 (The Fate of the Guild System in Modern Times) (Beijing, Renmin chubanshe, 2003).

[67] These agencies include *Gongyiju* 工藝局, *Gongyi Chuanxisuo* 工藝傳習所, or *Quangongchang* 勸工場.

[68] Chen Shaowen 陳紹聞 and Guo Xianglin 郭庠林, 中國近代經濟簡史 (A Brief Economic History of Modern China) (Shanghai, Shanghai renmin chubanshe, 1983).

[69] Peng Zeyi 彭澤益 (ed.), 中国近代手工业史资料 1840–1949 (Historical Achievements of the Handicraft Industry in Modern China 1840–1949) (Shanghai, Sanlian chubanshe, 1957).

Missionary Education

One important event that laid the foundation for China's modern education system was the appearance of mission schools. The presence of Christian missionaries expanded significantly with the opening up of China following its defeat in the Opium War (1842), and one important missionary activity was the founding of schools. Not only did the number of mission schools expand quickly; they also functioned as a role model of Western educational practice for Chinese schools. For instance, they influenced their Chinese counterparts by introducing a qualitatively new curriculum of subjects. By 1920, missionaries had established lower primary schools in 719 counties and higher primary schools in 314 counties, which enrolled 122,089 and 30,067 students respectively. While enrollment figures for high schools are not available, a survey conducted in the 1920s reveals that there were 254 secondary schools spread across 9 percent of sampled counties.[70] For tertiary education, from the late nineteenth century, a number of Christian colleges were also built. With only three domestic state-managed universities existing at that time,[71] Christian colleges not only presented a model of tertiary education to their Chinese counterparts but also, by educating a large number of professionals and intellectual elites, had a long-lasting social, economic, and political influence in twentieth-century China.

Measuring Educational Expansion

Studies on literacy rates suggest a rapid expansion of basic education over the early twentieth century. Ch'ien finds that the literacy rate was about 70 percent in the 1920s, which is a substantial jump compared to the level in the late nineteenth century.[72] Gamble and Burgess show that 84 percent of residents in Beijing were literate.[73] In urban Canton, the literacy rate was also believed to be as high as 80 to 90 percent in the 1930s.[74] However, contradictory

---

[70] M.T. Stauffer, *Christian Occupation of China: A General Survey of the Numerical Strength and Geographical Distribution of the Christian Forces in China* (Shanghai, China Continuation Committee, 1922); Y. Bai and J.K.S. Kung, "Diffusing Knowledge While Spreading God's Message: Protestantism and Economic Prosperity in China, 1840–1920," *Journal of the European Economic Association* 13.4 (2015), 669–98.

[71] E. Widmer and D.H. Bays, *China's Christian Colleges: Cross-cultural Connections, 1900–1950* (Stanford, CA, Stanford University Press, 2009).

[72] T.S. Ch'ien, *The Government and Politics of China, 1912–1949* (Stanford, CA, Stanford University Press, 1950). pp. 13.

[73] S.D. Gamble and J.S. Burgess, *Peking: A Social Survey* (New York, George H. Doran, 1921), p. 507.

[74] J.L. Buck, *Land Utilization in China: A Study of 16,786 Farms in 168 Localities, and 32,256 Farm Families in Twenty-Two Provinces in China, 1929–1933* (Chicago, The University of Chicago Press, 1937).

evidence can also be found in the existing literature. For instance, in Ting county of Zhili province, only 20 percent of the population over six years old in the 1930s could be considered literate.[75]

Systematic enrollment data are available for modern education institutions from the early twentieth century onwards, and we present enrollment rates per 1,000 school-aged children in China for schooling at all levels in Table 14.4. Before discussing the figures, it is important to stress that Table 14.4 only includes modern public schools that were financed at least in part by public funding due to the absence of *sishu* in official statistics. To facilitate international comparison, a broader school-age band (five to fourteen) is adopted for primary schooling, twelve to seventeen for secondary schooling (twelve to fourteen for lower secondary schools and fifteen to seventeen for higher secondary schools), and seventeen to twenty-two for higher education.[76]

Looking at primary education first, enrollment ratios rose from 1.2 percent in the early twentieth century to 12 percent in the 1930s, which is a similar level to that of India (11.3 percent) but much lower than that of Japan (60.9 percent).[77] The substantial rise in primary schooling was interrupted by the Japanese invasion between 1937 and 1945, which was then followed by a four-year civil war. The enrollment ratio dropped sharply in wartime and recovered slowly, and the prewar level was only reattained after 1947. Even though official records exclude *sishu*, selective regional evidence indicates that they remained very popular through the first half of the twentieth century. In 1924, the China Education Department reported that the number of students attending *sishu* should be at least the same as the number of students in formal primary schools. Similarly, approximately 20,000 students were enrolled in 1,000 traditional popular schools in Canton city, a figure higher than the number of students in formal primary schools.[78] In 1930, Zhili province reported enrollment ratios for both traditional and modern primary schools, which also presents the same pattern of these two types of elementary-level schools being substitutes. In 1935, a nationwide report records that traditional popular schools accommodated 1,752,014 students while

---

[75] S.D. Gamble and T. Hsien, *A North China Rural Community* (New York, Institute of Pacific Relations, 1954), p. 185.
[76] P.H. Lindert, *Growing Public*, vol. 1,*The Story: Social Spending and Economic Growth since the Eighteenth Century* (Cambridge, Cambridge University Press, 2004); C.D. Goldin and L.F. Katz, *The Race between Education and Technology* (Cambridge, MA, Harvard University Press, 2009)
[77] Lindert, *Growing Public*, vol. 1, pp. 91–03.
[78] Tao Zhixing 陶知行 (ed.), 中國教育統計概覽 (A Summary of Chinese Education Statistics) (Shanghai, Zhonghua Jiaoyu Gaijinshe, 1923), p. 6.

Table 14.4 Enrollment rates per 1,000 school-age population, 1900–1950

	China		
Year	Primary	Secondary	Tertiary
1907	12	0.7	0.07
1916	47	1.7	0.07
1922	72	2	0.05
1933	119	7.5	0.05
1949	214	20.7	0.21

Year	India		
1900	47	21.2	0.9
1910	65	35.1	1.3
1920	80	42.1	2.6
1930	113	65.7	3.1
1950		166.1	10.8

Year	Japan		
1900	507	50	5.7
1910	599	132.4	10.7
1920	602	310.7	15.9
1930	609	505.4	29.8
1950		695.1	46.5

Year	United States		
1900	939	106	
1910	975	145	
1920	924		
1930	921	511	
1950	978	745	

Sources: for China, the enrollment data come from *Yearbooks on Education* in corresponding years, and population and age structure are from Hou Yangfang 侯楊方,中國人口史：民國時期 (Population History of China: Republic of China Period) (Shanghai, Fudan daxue chubanshe, 2001); for the United States, India, and Japan the data come from P. H. Lindert, *Growing Public*, vol. 2, *The Story: Social Spending and Economic Growth since the Eighteenth Century* (Cambridge, Cambridge University Press, 2004).

the number of students enrolled in modern primary schools was 15,110,119.[79] In short, *sishu* remained popular and functioned as a substitute for formal primary

[79] Wu, 改良私塾.

Table 14.5 Composition of persons by education level for selected counties, 1880–1920 (percentage)

Province	County	Year	No education	Primary schools Sishu	Primary schools Modern	Secondary schools	Higher education
Fujian	Fuqing	1880	90	10	0	0	0
		1900	83	12	5	0	0
		1920	82	9	9	1	0
Sichuan	Chongqing	1880	78	22	0	0	0
		1900	76	24	0	0	0
		1920	69	27	2	1	1
Zhili	Beijing	1880	89	11	0	0	0
		1900	87	11	2	0	0
		1920	86	10	4	1	0

Sources: Cao Ning 曹寧, 民國人口戶籍史料續編 (Population Sequel Collection in the Period of the Republic of China) (Beijing, Guojia Tushuguan chubanshe, 2013); Second Suburban Bureau of Beiping Bureau of Public Security 北平市警察局郊二區分局, 1946 年 11 月戶口調查表西店和西洼村 (Household Survey Table of Xidian and Xiwa villages, November 1946); Second Suburban Bureau of Beiping Bureau of Public Security 北平市人民政府公安局人民政府公安局郊二分局, 戶口調查表 (Household Survey Table), 1949-4-18; First Suburban Bureau of Beiping Bureau of Public Security 北平市警察局郊一區分局, 民國 37 年戶口調查表 (Household Survey Table, 1948)

schools until the 1940s. Hence, if we include these informal schools, China's educational outcome should not be as low as suggested by the official statistics shown in Table 14.4 (also Table 14.5).

The progress of secondary education must be based on a large pool of primary schools, which means that the early twentieth century in China does not appear to be a time of rapid expansion. As shown in Table 14.4, in 1907 only about one in every 1,000 school-age children (i.e. 0.1 percent) attended secondary school, and this figure was far lower than the level of India (2 percent) and Japan (13.9 percent). Secondary-schooling expansion accelerated only after the 1920s. This may be attributed to the separation of lower secondary school from higher secondary school in 1922.[80] A similar pattern

[80] Issuing lower secondary-school diplomas to students who finished three years of secondary schooling partially accounted for the significant decline in the number of dropouts. See Zhu Youhuan 朱有瓛, 中國近代學制史料第三輯下 (Historical

Table 14.6 Composition of secondary schools by type (percentage)

Year	General	Teacher-training	Vocational
1912	60.1	30.4	9.5
1916	67.8	20.6	8.7
1922	49.9	35.1	16.8
1930	62.6	28.3	9.1
1937	65.4	19.2	15.4
1941	73.3	14.5	12.2
1945	73.5	15.2	11.4

Source: Chen Dongyuan 陳東原 (ed.), 第二次中國教育年鑑 (The Secondary Education Yearbook) (Shanghai, Shangwu Yinshuguan, 1948), p. 1428

can be seen when looking at tertiary education,[81] the scale of which remained minimal throughout the period of study, with enrollment ratios below 0.1 percent before the 1940s. To put these figures into perspective, the enrollment ratio was 4.05 percent in Japan at this time, and in India 0.48 percent (i.e. more than four times the level for China).[82] The regional variation was significantly wide, though, with 60 percent of universities being concentrated in metropolises like Beijing and Shanghai.

Apart from general education, vocational and teacher-training education also expanded quickly under the new system. As shown in Table 14.6, general schools still dominated in secondary education, while about 30 to 40 percent of students chose vocational and teacher-training tracks. The total number of students in vocational schools in 1912 was around 32,000; this figure rose to 50,000 in the mid-1930s. One thing worth stressing is that teacher-training schools were particularly important, especially in the early stages, because training eligible teachers was crucial for the new education system. Furthermore, these teacher-training schools also played an essential role in female education, since teaching was regarded as one of the few acceptable career options for females.

Materials of the Modern Educational System in China), vol. 3, part 2 (Shanghai, Huadong Shifan daxue chubanshe, 1992).

[81] Tertiary education includes universities (four-year program) and colleges (usually institutions that offered a two-year program).

[82] One thing worth stressing is that the Japanese invasion did not greatly impact tertiary education. Most of the universities, located in big cities, were able to take advantage of the relative safety of the international settlements and French concessions in these cities. Meanwhile, the universities located in occupied China did not cease to operate; they merely fled south and continued to function throughout the war.

Education and Socioeconomic Changes

As discussed, the education system in China underwent unprecedented expansion and modernization between 1800 and 1950, which affected the society profoundly in various ways. In this section, we briefly discuss three of the main socioeconomic changes, namely economic modernization, female education, and the rise of new intellectual elites.

Educational Development and Economic Modernization

There is a growing body of work that studies the association between the introduction of Western-influenced new institutions and economic development in China in the late nineteenth and early twentieth centuries.[83] However, empirical studies directly examining the economic and social impact of this educational movement remain limited.[84] Did the rise of modern education contribute to the development of modern industry and economic growth in China? How did the new education system affect social mobility?

Some studies specifically look at the impact of the abolishment of the civil service examination. The civil service examination system did not incentivize young talents to study practical knowledge, which was an institutional obstacle to the rise of modern technology. The rapid expansion of modern schools with a modern curriculum could cultivate new intellectual elites and form professional human capital for various modern industries in China. Such changes could greatly promote modernization and industrialization in late nineteenth- and twentieth-century China. For instance, as presented in Table 14.7, the number of engineers in China expanded rapidly after the birth cohorts of the 1890s. Bai also finds that misallocation of talents largely existed under the civil service examination system, therefore regions with better talent pools established significantly more modern firms after the abolishment of the old examination system.[85]

---

[83] See D. Ma, "Why Japan, Not China, Was the First to Develop in East Asia: Lessons from Sericulture, 1850–1937," *Economic Development and Cultural Change* 52.2 (2004), 369–94; D. Ma, "Economic Growth in the Lower Yangzi Region of China in 1911–1937: A Quantitative and Historical Analysis," *Journal of Economic History* 68.2 (2008), 355–92; R. Jia, "The Legacies of Forced Freedom: China's Treaty Ports," *Review of Economics and Statistics* 96.4 (2014), 596–608.

[84] There are no census or individual-level survey data that include questions about both income and education for this period.

[85] Y. Bai, "Farewell to Confucianism: The Modernizing Effect of Dismantling China's Imperial Examination System," *Journal of Development Economics* 141 (2019), 102382.

Table 14.7 Number of engineers by birth cohort

Birth cohort	1870s	1880s	1890s	1900s	1910s
Number of engineers	10	270	1,206	2,503	3,640

Source: Design Board of National Defense 國防設計委員會, 中國工程名人錄 (Who's Who of Chinese Engineers) (Chongqing, Shangwu Yinshuguan, 1941)

Conversely, the rise of modern industries and commerce further stimulated the demand for modern education from the late nineteenth century onwards. New talents were in short supply especially in those emerging sectors, such as the railroad, the telegraph, steamships, the mining industry, law, and modern manufacturing. Utilizing a railroad company's employee records, Yuchtman finds that the wage premium of modern education was higher than that of traditional education, indicating that the number of newly educated elites did not meet market demand.[86] Another example is that the Tianjin Technology and Business University reported that their graduates, especially those that majored in engineering and business, had very bright career prospects in the 1930s. Graduates with business majors mainly landed good posts in the modern banking industry and the public sector, while engineering graduates had even more diverse career choices, ranging from construction to rail transport, water conservancy, civil engineering, and municipal administration.[87]

However, we cannot be overly optimistic about the extent of modern education's contribution to economic development. First, as shown in Table 14.4, only a very selective group of people received post-elementary education. Liang et al. analyzed the family background of 110,000 university students during the 1906–1952 period and found that more than 60 percent of them had parents with high-income occupations and came from large cities.[88] Another problem lies in the pronounced mismatch between students' choice of major and the labour market's needs. The rapid expansion of high-level education did not meet the substantial rising demand for modern human

---

[86] N. Yuchtman, "Teaching to the Tests: An Economic Analysis of Traditional and Modern Education in Late Imperial and Republican China," *Explorations in Economic History*, 63 (2017), 70–90.

[87] Chen Yanzhong 陳炎仲, "工學院之過去未來" (The Past and the Future of Tianjin Technology and Business University), *Gongshang Xuesheng* 1.4 (1937), 6.

[88] Liang Chen 梁晨, Dong Hao 董浩, Ren Yunzhu 任韻竹, and Li Zhongqing 李中清, "江山代有才人出—中國教育精英的來源與轉變 1865–2014" (Social Transformation and Elitist Education: Changes in the Social and Geographical Origins of China's Educated Elites 1865–2014), *Sociological Research* 3 (2017), 48–70.

capital in China partly because science and engineering remained unpopular among students. In the 1930s, over 70 percent of university graduates chose to major in the arts and social science, even though these majors did not guarantee bright career prospects.[89] As Zhu Jiaye, the minister of education in Republican China, once pointed out, unemployment was widespread among university graduates. On the contrary, experts with specialized skills or professional knowledge, especially in the sciences and engineering, were in short supply.[90] According to an official report of Shanxi province, the total number of graduates from colleges and universities was 8,905 in the three decades after 1905, and about half of them (4,700) were out of work.[91] As a response, the central government even began to issue regulations to restrict the number of students majoring in the arts from 1934, with the effect that the share of students choosing science subjects rose to 59.4 percent in 1939. Furthermore, the efficiency of the labor market at the time was also questionable since a large proportion of students never had the opportunity to apply the knowledge and skills that they had obtained in their own jobs. For example, the National Federation of Education in 1917 reported that some graduates trained in textile schools ended up as teachers in primary schools and those that attended agricultural schools worked as general administrative assistants.[92]

Rising Gender Equality

Besides economic modernization, another social improvement under the modern education system was the rising gender-neutrality in education. Gender inequality in education is shared by many developing countries, and in Chinese history females had always been excluded from formal education. Not all women were illiterate, at least among those from gentry families. Girls could receive home education in literature, female ethics, and skills that would make them more competitive in the marriage market. However, even this type of training was not available for girls in the lower social classes in undeveloped areas. For example, around 1900 less than 1 percent of school-age girls in Yugan county (Jiangxi province) and Chenggong county (Yunnan province) had ever attended

---

[89] Wang Jie 王婕, 民國時期大學生就業研究 1912–1937 (Research on the Employment of Tertiary-Education Students in Republican China 1912–1937) (Zhengzhou, Zhengzhou University, 2012).
[90] Wang, 民國時期大學生就業研究.
[91] "太原通訊" (Taiyuan Communication), Takungpao, September 24, 1934.
[92] Zhu, 中國近代學制史料第三輯下.

sishu.[93] Allowing women the right to formal education after the turn of the twentieth century profoundly changed women's social position and the landscape of the labor market.

As noted, mission schools were the pioneers in educating women in China. In 1844, Miss Aldersey established the first mission schools specifically for girls in Ningbo, and a great number of mission schools exclusively for girls were opened in the following few decades.[94] In 1907, the Ministry of Education promulgated statutes which paved the way for the establishment of a great number of primary schools and teacher-training schools exclusively for girls;[95] and from 1912 fully functional mixed-gender schools were also allowed. The share of female students attending senior primary school in 1923 was 6.34 percent and by 1930 the figure had more than doubled, reaching 15 percent.[96] More systematic records are presented in Table 14.8, showing that the gender gap in secondary-school enrollment was pronouncedly narrowed. After 1916, the number of female students attending secondary school began to rise at an unanticipated pace, such that the female–male student ratio fell from one to seventy-nine in 1912 to one to seven in 1929 and continued to fall, finally reaching one to three in 1946. Looking at tertiary education, only 887 female students attended universities or colleges in 1922, accounting for 2.5 percent of all students, and this figure rose to 15.2 percent in 1936.[97]

Two patterns are worth highlighting. First, the private sector played an important role in promoting equal gender opportunities in education. By 1907, 428 schools exclusively for girls had been established, of which more than half were private. Second, another growth engine came from the teacher-training schools.[98] The tuition fee for teacher-training schools was substantially less than that for general education, while another attractive feature was that after graduation a job was guaranteed for every student,

---

[93] Yin and Tian, 民國人口資料彙編; Yugan county, Shangrao city, Jiangxi province, Fifth township, Fourth district, Household registration books, c. 1947.
[94] L.-D. Djung, *A History of Democratic Education in Modern China* (Shanghai, The Commercial Press, 1934).
[95] Wang Zhongtian 汪忠天, "國內大學及專門學校畢業生就業狀況的一個調查" (A Survey of the Employment Status of Graduates of Domestic Universities and Colleges), *Chinese Educational Circles* 22.6 (1934), 49–97.
[96] Li Huaxing 李華興, 民國教育史 (The History of Education through the Republic of China) (Shanghai, Shanghai Jiaoyu chubanshe 1997), p. 729.
[97] Yu Qingtang 俞慶棠, "三十五年來中國女子之教育" (Female Education in China during the Past Thirty-Five Years), in Zhuang Yu 莊俞 (ed.), 最近三十五年之中國教育 (Education in China during the Past Thirty-Five Years) (Shanghai, Shangwu Yinshuguan, 1931), pp. 175–214.
[98] The proportion of females in general secondary schools before 1930 did not exceed 4 percent, but girls accounted for about 18 percent of normal-school students (equivalent to secondary school). See Tao, 中國教育統計概覽, p. 4.

Table 14.8 *Gender composition in secondary schools (1912–1946)*

Year	Female students Number	Female students Proportion	Male students Number	Male students Proportion
1912	677	0.01	51,423	0.99
1913	470	0.01	57,510	0.99
1914	956	0.01	66,298	0.99
1915	948	0.01	68,822	0.99
1916	724	0.01	60,200	0.99
1922	3,249	0.03	100,136	0.97
1929	33,073	0.13	215,595	0.87
1930	59,939	0.15	337,009	0.85
1933	73,667	0.18	342,281	0.82
1946	379,087	0.26	1,106,060	0.75

Source: Education Committee 教育審委員會 (eds.), 第一次中國教育年鑑 (The First Chinese Education Yearbook) (n.l., Ministry of Education Press, 1934)

including females. Together with medical care and journalism, teaching was one of the most popular career choices for the "new women" throughout the first half of the twentieth century.[99]

The development of female education did not, however, suggest an equivalent increase in female participation in the labor market. Education could be considered a new fashion or accessory rather than a means to economic independence for women. Therefore many female students, especially those with high-level education, went back to family life after graduation. During the mid-1930s, a survey in urban Canton showed that only 16.4 percent of the female population was employed.[100]

The Rise of New Intellectual Elites

The upper tail of human capital has been found to be an essential driving force for modernization and industrialization in Europe.[101] From the late nineteenth century onwards, an emerging new intellectual elite group was

---

[99] To attract more students, those who enrolled in teacher-training schools were exempt from paying tuition fees, while their living expenses were also covered by public funding; in recompense, after graduation they had to serve at least three years in a local primary school. See Li, 民國教育史, pp. 512–13.
[100] Jin Zhonghua 金仲華, 婦女問題 (Women's Issues) (Shanghai, Shangwu chubanshe, 1936).
[101] M.P. Squicciarini and N. Voigtländer, "Human Capital and Industrialization: Evidence from the Age of Enlightenment," *Quarterly Journal of Economics* 130.4 (2015), 1825–83.

formed in China, including students returning from overseas together with graduates from major domestic universities. These knowledge elites exerted a profound impact on Chinese society over the course of the following decades.

Following the educational reform, there was an ever-growing number of Chinese who left home to study overseas. According to Wang, around 100,000 students went abroad during the first half of the twentieth century to study, and the majority of them chose to come back to China after graduation.[102] Among all destinations, Japan was the most popular because of its geographic proximity and cultural similarity, and also because it was much less expensive compared to the US and Europe. Between 1900 and 1911, 90 percent of the 20,000 Chinese studying overseas went to Japan.[103]

These foreign-educated scholars directly helped to professionalize this newly established education system in China, especially for tertiary education.[104] Over the period of study, a very large proportion of faculties and administrators working in major Chinese universities received their education abroad.[105] For example, in 1937, sixty-nine of a total of ninety-four professors in Tsinghua University had studied in the US.[106] These scholars brought back not only knowledge but also new ideas to reform existing educational institutions. One important case is that Peking

---

[102] Wang Qisheng 王奇生, "民國時期歸國留學生的出路" (The Employment of Foreign-Educated Students during the Republican Era in Chinese History), *Journal of Republican Era Studies* 3 (1994), 12–14.

[103] L. Yao, "The Chinese Overseas Students: An Overview of the Flows Change," 12th Biennial Conference of the Australian Population Association (2004), 15–17.

[104] Zhou Mian 周棉, "留學生群體與民國時期新式教育體制的建立" (The Group of Students from Overseas and the Establishment of a Modern Education System in the Period of Republican China), *Zhejiang Academic Journal* 5 (2012), 59–68.

[105] Using Beijing University as an example, Cai Yuanpei, the first chancellor, studied at the University of Leipzig for four years from 1907. His successors, Jiang Menglin and Hu Shi, were returnees from the USA. Jiang stayed in the USA for nearly ten yeas and got his doctoral degree at Columbia University. Hu went to Cornell University in 1910 and finally defended his Ph.D. thesis at Columbia University. Chancellor Mei Yiqi of Tsinghua University, who shouldered the position for seventeen years; President Zhu Kezhen of Zhejiang University; President He Lian of Nankai University; Presidents Liu Tingfang and Mei Yibao of Yenching University; President Yang Yongqing of Soochow University; President Li Zhaohuan of Shanghai Jiaotong University; Presidents Gu Yuxiu and Wu Youxun of National Central University; and others, were all outstanding students returned from overseas.

[106] Tsinghua University was funded by the "Gengzi Indemnity," also known as the "Boxer Indemnity." The same funding source also supported many outstanding students studying abroad. See Tsinghua University, 清華同學錄 (Schoolmate Records of Tsinghua University) (Beijing, Tsinghua University, 1937); Yi Chu Wang, *Chinese Intellectuals and the West, 1872–1949* (Chapel Hill, University of North Carolina Press, 1966).

University, led by Cai Yuanpei, who came back from Germany, quickly grew into an independent academic institute with a democratic management system and the spirit of "academic freedom and inclusiveness," and continues to be one of the best universities in China to this day.[107]

The influence of these new knowledge elites was not confined to classrooms. New ideologies, including democracy, nationalism, and communism, were introduced and spread to a much wider group of people outside the universities through public talks. Some of the auditors, including Mao Zedong, Hua Luogeng, and Shen Congwen, were strongly inspired and continued to shape the course of Chinese history. For instance, the New Culture Movement, which was a movement to lead a revolt against traditional Confucianism, has been considered to be an important watershed, marking a break between tradition and modernity in China; the leaders and followers of this movement also clustered in major universities, such as Peking, Tsinghua, and Fudan Universities.[108] Apart from educational institutions, these new knowledge elites also played an active role in other centers of literature and intellectual activity, such as publishing houses, journals, and literary societies throughout the first half of the twentieth century.

Lastly, this elite group with modern education also had a strong impact in the political arena, as many were recruited for government positions at all levels. For example, 22.5 percent of the staff working in the central government in 1916 had received education aboard.[109] In the Ministry of Agriculture, Industry, and

---

[107] Research association of studies on Cai Yuanpei, 蔡元培全集 (Collected Works of Cai Yuanpei), 4 vols. (Hangzhou, Zhejiang Jiaoyu chuban jituan, 1997). Founded in 1898, Peking University was originally known as the Imperial University of Peking. The admissions, the recruitment of teachers, and the designation of graduates were all controlled by the central government. It also served as the highest administration for education at its founding. As a result, it was unavoidably affected by bureaucratic ideology and practices. The main purpose of students who came here was a promising political career. When Cai took the position of president, he emphasized learning and research as the most important tasks of both teachers and students. Academic authority was highly esteemed and became dominant instead of administrative power. He invited many leading scholars full of enthusiasm to be teachers to join his team, while those teachers who did not aspire to academic work were gradually removed. In this way, Peking University became so attractive to those who were really interested in academia that many of the best scholars in that era chose to work there. See Feng Youlan 馮友蘭, "我所認識的蔡孑民先生" (My Thoughts on Mr. Cai Jiemin), *People's Daily Overseas Edition*, January 9, 1988.

[108] Zhou Mian 周棉, "論留學生群體作用於民國社會發展的諸種互動關係" (Impacts of the Group of Foreign-Educated Students on Social Development during the Republican Period of China), *Zhejiang Academic Journal* 5 (2015), 51–61.

[109] Tang Yueliang 唐悅良, "青年會與留學生之關係" (The Relationship between Qingnianhui and Returning Students from Overseas), *Eastern Miscellany* 14.9 (1917), 196–8.

Commerce, 49.8 percent of employees had foreign tertiary-education certificates, and this figure was about 40 percent in the Ministry of Transport and the Ministry of Justice.[110] Another long-term legacy of these new knowledge elites in the Chinese political arena was the creation of several political movements from the late nineteenth century. The earliest revolutionary organizations that tried to overthrow the Qing dynasty were founded outside China, and a majority of their early members were overseas students. About 90 percent of the earliest participants of the Tongmenghui (Alliance Society) were students who had returned from abroad. Similarly, after the foundation of Republican China, in the major political parties, Nationalist Party and the Communist Party, more than half of top leaders were foreign-educated students.[111]

Conclusion

A rich literature documents the important role of education and human capital for economic development in the modern world. China has a very long educational history, but the rapid expansion of mass education and modernization in the curriculum started relatively late, only after the early twentieth century. Over the period studied in this volume (from 1800), drastic changes occurred in the education system, and this chapter has attempted to survey several milestones.

The traditional Confucian teaching system had been operating in China for over a thousand years. Under this system, state bureaucrats and social elites were recruited using a merit-based examination. The provision of education was mainly taken on by private parties and the Confucian classics were used as teaching content. The major transformation in the education field during the period of study was the shift from this long-lasting traditional Confucian teaching system to a modern one that approximated a Western model. This change was a slow and difficult process that started in the 1860s, and generated the following three important improvements: public provision of mass education, curriculum reforms, and an increase in educational opportunities for girls. The new system educated millions of students, formed professional human capital, cultivated new intellectual elites, and encouraged modern economic growth in China.

---

[110] Tang, "青年會與留學生之關係," 196–8.
[111] C. Hsueh, *Huang Hsing and the Chinese Revolution* (Stanford, Stanford University Press, 1961). M. Zhou, "留学生与中国同盟会的创建" (Returned Students from Abroad and the Establishment of Tongmenghui), *Journal of Tsinghua University (Philosophy and Social Sciences)* 23.4 (2008), 46–54. Zhou Mian, "論留學生群體作用於民國社會發展的諸種互動關係"; Wang Xiaoting 王效挺 and Huang Wenyi 黃文一, 戰鬥在北大的中國共產黨人: 1920–1949 (CPC Members in Peking University 1920–1949) (Beijing, Peking University Press, 1991).

Even though the traditional education system discussed in this chapter ended more than a century ago, its legacy remains in China to this day. For example, the institutional heritage of the imperial examination system can still be found in national college entrance examinations, and admission for major universities still uses regional enrollment quotas just like the civil service examinations. Besides China, ninety-one out of 156 countries worldwide still recruited employees in the public sector via competitive examinations in 2015. Another important impact of the long history of education in China is the persistent culture of placing a high value on success in education. Chinese continue to emphasize human capital and education as an effective ladder for upward social mobility today. Despite the lack of public investment, Chinese parents are willing to invest heavily in their children's education.[112] Empirical evidence confirms that the historical regional patterns in educational achievement throughout history are associated with modern educational outcomes through the transmission of people's attitudes towards education by successive generations.[113] The persistence of this cultural transmission was partly interrupted during the Mao era (1949–1977), during which the merit of education was largely denounced and deadly attacks on scholars and intellectuals were prevalent.[114] The widespread educational breakdown indeed had a negative impact on later educational outcomes, but the culture of valuing education was only weakened shortly and continued to show strong persistence.[115]

[112] China's public investment in human capital has been small in comparison with nations at similar levels of economic development, and its geographical dispersion has been large. J.J. Heckman, "China's Human Capital Investment," *China Economic Review* 16.1 (2005), 50–70. This means that private investment plays an essential role in human capital formation even today. China, at all levels of government together, spent about 2.5 percent of GDP on schooling in the year 2000. In the US, this figure was 5.4 percent. In South Korea, it was 3.7 percent.

[113] T. Chen, J. Kung, and C. Ma, "Long live Keju! The Persistent Effects of China's Civil Examination System," *Economic Journal* 130.631 (2020), 2030–64.

[114] Chinese education has undergone major shifts between 1949 and 1977 in response to general swings in Chinese policy. The interruption was particularly catastrophic during the Cultural Revolution (1966–1976), when most schools in urban China were heavily disrupted. All the tertiary-level institutions ceased regular operation with no teaching carried out and no new students were admitted. Not only educational opportunities were disrupted; education quality was also compromised. Education became a Party device to cultivate political ideology rather than provide academic training. China's educational system only returned to normalcy after 1977 when the Cultural Revolution ended.

[115] X. Meng, and R.G. Gregory, "The Impact of Interrupted Education on Subsequent Educational Attainment: A Cost of the Chinese Cultural Revolution," *Economic Development and Cultural Change* 50.4 (2002), 935–59; J. Zhang, P.W. Liu, and L. Yung, "The Cultural Revolution and Returns to Schooling in China: Estimates Based on Twins," *Journal of Development Economics* 84.2 (2007), 631–9; Chen et al., "Long Live Keju!".

Further Reading

Baten, J., D. Ma, S. Morgan, and Q. Wang, "Evolution of Living Standards and Human Capital in China in the 18th–20th Centuries: Evidence from Real Wages, Age-Heaping, and Anthropometrics," *Explorations in Economic History* 47.3 (2010), 347–59.

Borthwick, S., *Education and Social Change in China: The Beginnings of the Modern Era* (Stanford, CA, Hoover Institution Press, 1983).

Chen, T., J.K.S. Kung, and C. Ma, "Long Live Keju! The Persistent Effects of China's Civil Examination System," *Economic Journal* 130.631 (2020), 2030–64.

Deng Hongbo 鄧洪波, 中國書院史 (History of Traditional Chinese Academia) (Shanghai, Dongfang chuban zhongxin, 2004).

Elman, B.A., *A Cultural History of Civil Examinations in Late Imperial China* (Berkeley, University of California Press, 2000).

Gao, P., "Risen from the Chaos: The Emergence of Modern Education in China," in D. Mitch and G. Cappelli (eds.), *Globalization and the Rise of Mass Education* (Cham, Palgrave Macmillan, 2019), pp. 279–309.

Ho, P., *The Ladder of Success in Imperial China: Aspects of Social Mobility, 1368–1911* (New York, Columbia University Press, 1962).

Jin Linxiang 金林祥, 中國教育制度通史 (A General History of Chinese Education), 6 vols. (Jinan, Shandong Education Press, 2000).

Ma Yong 馬鏞, 中國教育制度通史 (A General History of Chinese Education), 5 vols. (Jinan, Shandong Education Press, 2000).

Perkins, D.H., *China's Modern Economy in Historical Perspective* (Cambridge, MA, Harvard University Press, 1975).

Rawski, E., *Education and Popular Literacy in Ch'ing China* (Ann Arbor, University of Michigan Press, 1979).

Wang, M., B. van Leeuwen, and J. Li, *Education in China, ca. 1840–Present* (Leiden, Brill, 2020).

Wang, Y.C., *Chinese Intellectuals and the West, 1872–1949* (Chapel Hill, University of North Carolina Press, 1966).

Zhang Jie 张杰, 清代科舉家族 (Keju Hereditary Families in the Qing Dynasty) (Beijing, Social Sciences Academic Press, 2003).

PART II

★

1950 TO THE PRESENT

15

The Origin of China's Communist Institutions

CHENGGANG XU

Introduction

In the nineteenth century, the Chinese Empire – the longest-lasting empire in human history – was the largest economy on earth with a decent per capita GDP level. But it shrank rapidly after its collapse. Since the founding of the PRC in 1949, China had been one of the poorest economies in the world until the post-Mao reform, which has enjoyed high growth for three decades.[1] But a sustained slowing down since 2009 reminds us of the trend of the Soviet economy since the mid-1970s.[2]

Understanding the nature of the Chinese institutions and their drastic changes, particularly since the rise of the Chinese Communist Party (CCP), is critically important for making sense of the Chinese economy in the past seven decades. This is because China's institutions have been distinctive in the world both historically and contemporarily. After decades of unsuccessful Republican revolution efforts, in 1949 the CCP seized power by armed force, and transplanted Soviet-type totalitarian institutions into China. In this

---

I thank Patrick Bolton and Debin Ma for very helpful comments, and Nancy Hearst for copyediting. I have benefited greatly from comments in workshops at Utrecht, CKGSB, HUJI (Jerusalem), and the Coase Institute (Tel Aviv and Warsaw), and comments in my public lectures at Stanford, CUHK, Corvinus, FMSH-Paris, Sinica-Taiwan, WINIR-Hong Kong, and AEA-ACES. I acknowledge support from the CKGSB and the hospitality of Corvinus University of Budapest, Imperial College London, and the LSE.

[1] A. Maddison, *The World Economy: Historical Statistics* (Paris and Washington, DC, Organisation for Economic Co-operation and Development, 2003); C. Xu, "The Fundamental Institutions of China's Reform and Development," *Journal of Economic Literature* 49.4 (2011), 1076–1151.

[2] W. Chen, X. Chen, C.-T. Hsieh, and Z. Song, "A Forensic Examination of China's National Accounts," Brookings Institution paper on economic activity, conference draft, March 2019. The Soviet economy started to slow down steadily from the time when its per capita GDP reached one-third of the US level. Maddison, *The World Economy*. In comparison, Chinese per capita GDP (in purchasing-power parity) today is about one-quarter of that of the US. World Bank (2021), at https://data.worldbank.org/indicator/NY.GDP.PCAP.PP.KD.

chapter, totalitarianism is defined (or described) as a modern party-state institution, whereby in all respects the party totally controls (1) the state, (2) the armed forces, (3) the economy, (4) the media, and (5) the ideology.[3]

Importantly, the Chinese did not completely stick to a Soviet totalitarian model, like other Eastern Bloc nations. Instead, taking the totalitarian institutions as their root, the Chinese institutions have been further evolving, until today. Two waves of campaigns led by Mao – the Great Leap Forward (GLF) (1958–1960) and the Cultural Revolution (CR) (1966–1976) – changed Chinese institutions into what I call regionally decentralized totalitarianism (RDT), in which some of the features of Chinese imperial institutions reappeared prominently while fundamental features of totalitarianism were kept. Under China's RDT regime, the CCP, as the sole political party, monopolizes all political power and controls the most important personnel matters in the country, including the enormous party-state bureaucracy that penetrates every level of the entire society. It is because of this combination of an extremely high degree of political centralization and a high degree of administrative decentralization that Chinese institutions are unique in the world. Yet administrative and economic issues are highly decentralized to party-state agents at the regional levels.

The RDT institutions were the institutional basis for the post-Mao reforms.[4] From the 1980s, under its RDT regime, Chinese institutions created the powerful mechanisms, i.e. regional competition and local experimentation, that were responsible for the success of the early post-Mao reforms, particularly the creation and growth of the private sector within a totalitarian regime. With the changes during the early stages of the reform process, the Chinese RDT institutions gradually evolved towards what I called regionally decentralized authoritarian (RDA) institutions.[5] In comparison, authoritarianism is a less extreme type of autocracy in which limited pluralism is

---

[3] C.J. Friedrich and Z.K. Brzezinski, *Totalitarian Dictatorship and Autocracy* (Cambridge, MA, Harvard University Press, 1956). Regarding victims of the two major types of totalitarian regimes worldwide, "Communist regimes have victimized approximately 100 million people in contrast to the approximately 25 million victims of the Nazis." S. Courtois, "Introduction," in S. Courtois, N. Werth, J.-L. Panne, A. Paczkowski, K. Bartosek, and J.-L. Margolin, *The Black Book of Communism: Crimes, Terror, Repression* (Cambridge, MA, Harvard University Press, 2015), p. 15.

[4] In the media the post-Mao reform is often refered to as the Deng Xiaoping reform. But I will explain later in this chapter that this popular description is controversial, or errs in many important historical facts.

[5] C. Xu, "The Fundamental Institutions of China's Reform and Development."

allowed, economically and ideologically. But the hardcore CCP leaders would not tolerate the evolution from totalitarianism towards authoritarianism, so this trend was aborted, and we are observing a return to RDT since 2012. It is because of this combination of an extremely high degree of political centralization and a high degree of administrative decentralization that Chinese RDT/RDA institutions are unique in the world.

How and why have Chinese institutions evolved in the ways we observe? What are their impacts on the economy? What are their origins? This chapter will explain how Chinese RDT/RDA institutions originated from Chinese imperial institutions and Soviet totalitarian institutions. These explanations are a base for understanding later institutional changes which led to devastating disasters from the late 1950s to the mid-1970s, spectacular growth at earlier stages of the reform, and grave problems in recent years. Due to the space limitations of this chapter, my discussions will focus on key arguments and evidence, many of which are stylized facts abstracted from details, with some reference to my book in progress, *Institutional Genes: A Comparative Analysis of the Origin of Chinese Institutions*.

Institutional Genes: An Analytical Concept

Analyzing institutional evolution is a huge intellectual challenge. To facilitate our discussions, let me first briefly lay out my conceptual framework. When examining long historical processes of institutional change, one can observe some regularity whereby certain basic institutional elements appear repeatedly, even when there are important regime changes. More importantly, some of these repeatedly reproduced institutional elements have deep impacts on the long-term trajectories of further institutional changes. I call these repeatedly reproduced institutional elements "institutional genes."[6]

The institutional gene is defined as the basic institutional element that determines the players' incentives. They are repeatedly self-produced, reproduced, and evolved with the change of institutions over a long historical process. Institutional changes are endogenous processes in that, given the existing institutions and other constraints, they are created through strategic interactions among players (referring to all individuals in a society). The reproduction of institutional genes in a changing environment is caused by

---

[6] C. Xu, "Institutions and Institutional Genes," in Xu, *Institutional Genes: A Comparative Analysis of the Origin of Chinese Institutions* (forthcoming from Cambridge University Press).

players' selection of certain institutional elements from existing institutional genes out of self-interest. This sheds new light on the "path dependence" nature of institutional change, a popular concept in the literature of economic history.[7] We explain the processes of institutional evolution by identifying the reproduction and evolution of the institutional genes. This helps us understand the mechanisms of institutional evolution over and over again during historical processes, and their consequences.

For understanding institutional genes and their evolution, the following concepts are essential. Among institutions, those with rules that are followed regularly (including under threat and coercion) are stable.[8] An institution is regarded as an incentive-compatible institution if the incentives that the institution provides (including social norms) are compatible with the majority of players (including rulers and the ruled) in the institution: i.e. the players chose to follow the rules of the institution. Here, incentives consist of material and nonmaterial rewards and punishments, which can include imprisonment, torture, and killing. Thus coercive rules can also be incentive-compatible as long as individuals choose to follow under the threat of the rules.

Similarly, incentive-compatible (IC) transformation is defined as being when the incentives of the key players are consistent with the rules established by the transformation. Thus an IC transformation is more likely to be stable, whereas a non-IC transformation is more likely to be unstable, as the incentives of a majority of key participants are violated.

Institutional Genes in the Chinese Empire and the RDT/RDA Regime

To establish a foundation for later analysis of the origins of China's institutions in the remainder of this chapter, this section briefly illustrates how the institutional genes of the Chinese empire evolved and reproduced over the two millennia of the history of the Chinese empire, and outlines the institutional genes of contemporary Chinese RDT/RDA regimes. Figure 15.1 depicts the institutional genes of the Chinese empire.

In Figure 15.1 there are three basic institutional elements (blocks), reflecting the strong complementary relationship of these blocks. I call this gene

---

[7] D.C. North, *Institutions, Institutional Change, and Economic Performance* (Cambridge, Cambridge University Press, 1990).

[8] Here being stable is a neutral description which does not bear any normative meaning.

The Origin of China's Communist Institutions

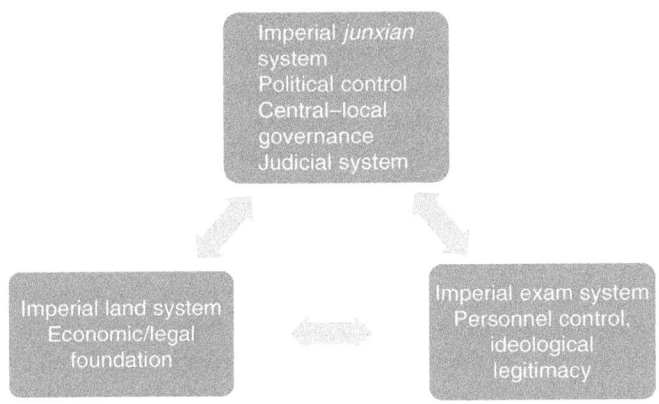

Figure 15.1 The institutional genes of the Chinese empire: an institutional trinity

map an institutional trinity.⁹ The central block is the bureaucracy, led by the emperor and the imperial court, the imperial *junxian* 郡县制 system. This system emerged during the Spring and Autumn period and became the dominant governance institution of the Chinese empire from 220 BC until the collapse of the Chinese empire in 1911.¹⁰ The *junxian* bureaucracy was composed of multiple levels, from the top – the imperial court and the central government – to the bottom – the county governments. The judicial system was completely integrated into the executive bureaucracy, and the emperor was the supreme judge of the empire.

The lower-left block of the institutional trinity is the imperial land system, featuring the ultimate imperial land property rights, which were the economic and legal foundation of the empire. This building block was established simultaneously with the creation of the *junxian* system. The emperor possessed ultimate rights to all the land in the entire empire.¹¹ Imperial land rights are indispensable for the survival and stability of the Chinese empire as they eliminated the economic and legal foundations for

---

⁹ C. Xu, "Institutional Genes of the Chinese Empire," in Xu, *Institutional Genes*.
¹⁰ Zhou Zhenhe 周振鹤 and Li Xiaojie 李晓杰, 中国行政区划通史 (The History of Chinese Administrative Divisions) (Shanghai, Fudan daxue chubanshe, 2009), p. 1.
¹¹ Beginning in the Song dynasty, landlords and peasants were allowed to trade their land rights on the market. But there were strict restrictions on the amount of land that could be purchased and accumulated. No one was allowed to possess an amount of land that would be sufficient to enable him to challenge the county government. Moreover, the emperor was entitled to repossess any land he needed or desired, or if the landlord was found to be disloyal or noncompliant with the throne.

the landed nobility; they also served to prevent anyone from accumulating landed power through the purchase of land.[12]

The lower-right block of the institutional trinity is personnel control and the imperial examination system. The emperor controlled all bureaucrats through selection, appointment, and promotion/demotion, among other things. By controlling the selection of candidates for the bureaucracy, the imperial examination system deprived everyone except the emperor of inherited powers. At the same time, by designing the content of the imperial examination, the emperor and the imperial court used it as an ideological control mechanism to maintain the legitimacy of their rule.

After the imperial examination system was created, many contradictions appeared between the aforementioned central and the lower-left blocks of the institutional trinity, as revealed by the unstable nature of the Qin–Han imperial institutions, when high officials in the bureaucracy could accumulate power by inheriting bureaucratic titles across generations. Despite the lack of *de jure* ownership of the land they managed, some high officials became de facto nobility, with their accumulated power. The creation and growing power of such de facto seigneurs gradually eroded and challenged the central authorities, eventually leading to the disintegration of the empire. The Chinese empire was not stabilized until the imperial examination system was established (during the Sui dynasty, 581 AD) and perfected (in the Tang dynasty, 618 AD, and the Song dynasty, 960 AD).[13] This stable and consolidated imperial examination institution lasted until the early twentieth century, making the Chinese empire distinctively different from other empires in the world.

To control the territory of what had been one of the largest empires in human history is an immense challenge. Figure 15.2 depicts the institutional genes of the administrative governance structure of the empire, i.e. the imperial *junxian* system, which was fully established during the Qin empire. After evolving for hundreds of years, this system was codified and institutionalized in the Sui Code, then essentially copied into the Tang Code, and then largely continued in the administrative laws of the later dynasties of the Chinese empire until the eventual dissolution of the system.[14]

---

[12] C. Xu, "Property Rights and Sovereignty under the Chinese Empire," in Xu, *Institutional Genes*.

[13] Zhang Xiqing 张希清, Mao Peiqi 毛佩琦, and Li Shiyu 李世愉, 中国科举制通史 (General History of the Chinese Imperial Exam System) (Shanghai, Shanghai renmin chubanshe).

[14] Zhou and Li, 中国行政区划通史.

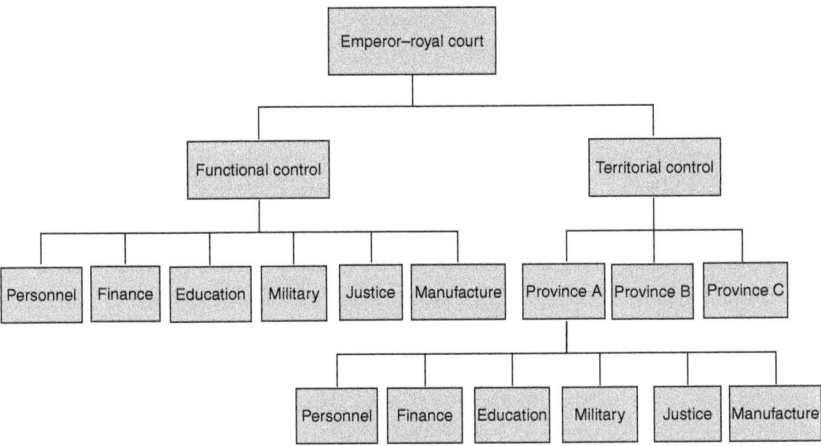

Figure 15.2 The institutional genes of the imperial *junxian* system

The top ruler of the *junxian* bureaucracy was the emperor, who governed all local governments via the imperial court. All bureaucrats in the subnational governments – at the provincial, prefectural, and county levels – were appointed and managed by the imperial court, and all of the appointed bureaucrats had to retire after completion of their tenures, i.e. by the rule that no one could pass power on to descendants. Another key feature of the *junxian* system was its decentralization of concrete administrative matters whereby subnational governments played central roles in local administrative matters. A good illustration of this feature is how administrative functions were co-ordinated at each level of government. At the national level, all administrative tasks were divided into six functions: personnel, finance, education, military, justice, and manufacturing/construction (*li* 吏, *hu* 户, *li* 礼, *bing* 兵, *xing* 刑, *gong* 工) and managed by six ministries (*liu bu* 六部).

Replicating this structure, at each subnational, provincial, prefectural, and county level, the local government controlled the six administrative functions, through six offices (*liufang* 六房), e.g. at the county level.[15] Importantly, it was the responsibility of the head of the local government to co-ordinate all the administrative functions within a jurisdiction. In

---

[15] For concrete information on stereotypical bureaucratic offices at the county level and the office layout in a typical county government, which impacted contemporary institutions, see Bai Hua 柏桦, 明代州縣政治體制研究 (Prefectural- and County-Level Political Systems during the Ming Dynasty) (Beijing, Zhongguo shehui kexue chubanshe, 2003); Miao Quanji 缪全吉, 明代胥吏 (Local Officials during the Ming Dynasty) (Taipei, Jiaxin shuini gongsi wenhua jijinhui, 1969).

contrast, although a minister had the same bureaucratic rank as a provincial governor, in general he would not make direct decisions regarding the functionalities of the subnational localities. This combination of political and personnel centralization and administrative decentralization represented a compromise between top-down control and implementation efficiency.[16]

As an illustration of the persistence of institutional genes, the institutional elements depicted above endured through dynasties and rebellions and have been replicated again and again not only in those dynasties established by rebellious elites or created by rebellious peasants who overthrew the preceding dynasty, but also in the dynasties established by the Mongols or the Manchus. Moreover, such institutional elements of the Chinese empire were reproduced even years after the collapse of the empire. When China's institutions were transformed from those of Soviet totalitarianism to those of RDT, one of the key institutional elements re-established was the *junxian* structure illustrated by Figure 15.2.

Before turning to explanations of why totalitarianism has prevailed in China, let us now compare the institutional genes of the past and present. Although the Chinese empire was dissolved more than a century ago and the CCP has always declared its ideology to be anti-feudal (which is the CCP's way of labeling the Chinese imperial system), similarities between the institutional genes of the Chinese empire and those of the Chinese RDT/RDA regime can be seen clearly. Parallel to Figure 15.1, Figure 15.3 depicts the governance structure of the Chinese RDT/RDA institutional trinity at an abstract level.[17] The seemingly superficial similarity between the institutional genes of the past and those of today provides deep insights, which will be explained below.

Similar to the structure of the institutional genes of the Chinese empire, the institutional trinity of the RDT/RDA regime comprises three basic institutional blocks: the party-state bureaucracy, party-state ownership of land/finance, and party-state control over personnel and ideology. Moreover, the judicial system is also fully integrated into the top-down party-state bureaucracy in the central block.

Akin to the Chinese empire, the lower-left institutional block is the economic, legal, and power foundation of the CCP and the RDT/RDA regime.[18] It consists of complete state ownership of

---

[16] Xu, "Institutional Genes of the Chinese Empire."
[17] C. Xu, "A Full-Fledged Totalitarian Regime in China," in Xu, *Institutional Genes*.
[18] The imperial land system of the Chinese empire is an essential part of its institutional genes, upon which totalitarianism based on state ownership is developed. C. Xu, "Property Rights as Institutional Genes," in Xu, *Institutional Genes*.

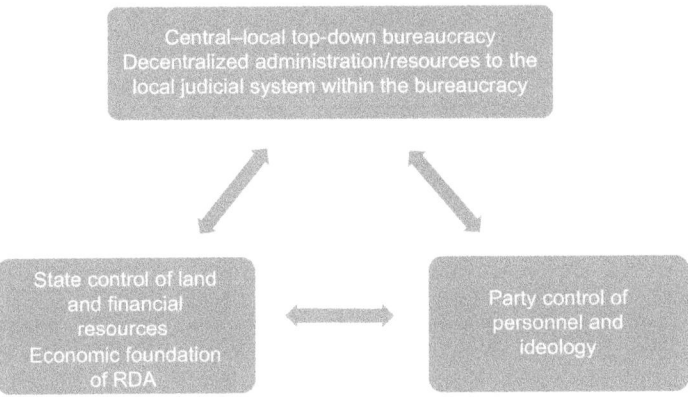

Figure 15.3 The institutional trinity of the RDT/RDA system

land;[19] overwhelming state ownership of financial resources and other assets, including most of the banks in China and the majority of companies listed on the Chinese stock markets; and monopolization of all strategic sectors in the Chinese economy. Similar to the imperial institution, the lower-right institutional block – control by the central party of national personnel and ideology – is the key element to guarantee ultimate control by the central authority over all government levels and all individuals.

Parallel to Figure 15.2, Figure 15.4 depicts a highly stylized governance structure of the central–local party-state bureaucracy of an RDT/RDA regime. This simplified figure shows only two levels in the hierarchy. In reality, the Chinese government consists of a multilevel hierarchy that, below the central level at the top, features three levels of subnational governments: the provincial level, the municipal level (or the prefectural level), and the county level. Most administrative, economic, and public-service functions are carried out by the subnational governments. Each region is self-contained, and each subnational government controls all major functions, such as personnel,[20] finance, industry, agriculture, and so forth within its respective

---

[19] The concept of ownership here is defined as the residual control rights of ultimate control rights. O. Hart, *Firms, Contracts and Financial Structure* (Oxford, Clarendon Press, 1995). According to the PRC State Constitution, the state has ultimate control rights over all land in the country, including "collectively owned" arable land, since the collectives must surrender their ownership to the state either when requested by the state or when their land is to be used for nonagricultural commercial purposes.

[20] Highly centralized control over nationwide personnel matters is implemented by a nested structure. The central authority directly controls personnel matters at the

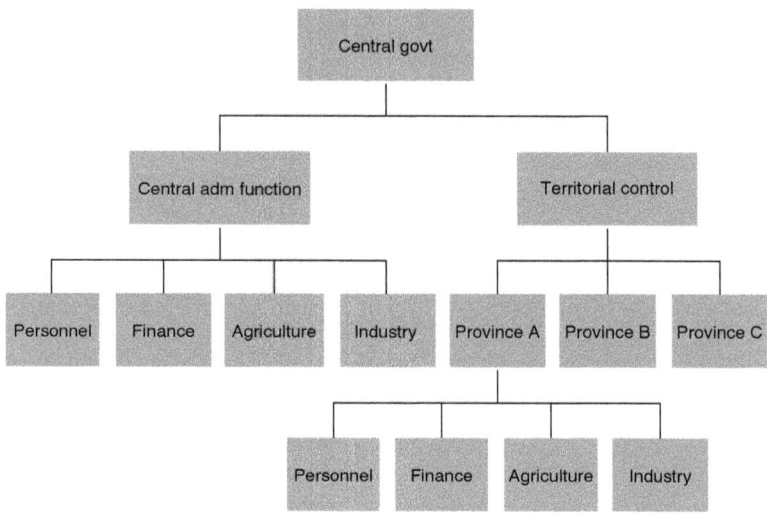

Figure 15.4 Stylized governance structure of China's RDT/RDA central–local regime

jurisdiction. The national government is relatively hands-off in most concrete operations of the national economy, whereas the subnational governments are deeply involved in the economies within their respective jurisdictions.[21] Comparing this structure with Figure 15.2, one can easily identify the related institutional genes in the imperial *junxian* system.

However, the Chinese empire and the RDT/RDA regime are categorically different in one crucial respect, the Leninist party, which was implanted from the Soviet Union to China and has ruled China totally for more than seven decades. The Party as a modern organization is ubiquitous, controlling the whole fabric of society from top to bottom. The next two sections explain briefly how totalitarian institutions were created in the world, and how they were introduced into China.

---

provincial level, whereas the provincial authorities directly control personnel matters at the city levels within their respective jurisdictions. Finally, the city-level authorities directly control county-level personnel matters within their respective jurisdictions. To guarantee that the central authority is able to control all important personnel matters, all key party-state positions are subject to rotation.

[21] Y. Qian and C. Xu, "Why China's Economic Reforms Differ: The M-Form Hierarchy and the Entry/Expansion of the Non-state Sector," *Economics of Transition* 1.2 (June 1993), 135–70; Xu, "The Fundamental Institutions of China's Reform."

The Origins of the Institutional Genes of Totalitarianism

It is well documented that the CCP was created by the Comintern, which was a Russian agency founded and led by Lenin almost immediately after the totalitarian regime was created in Russia. The CCP developed in China very rapidly. Only one decade after the creation of the CCP, the Chinese Soviet Republic was created (in 1931), when the Baltic states were not part of the Soviet Union yet. In less than two decades the CCP had taken over the entirety of China by military victory, and in 1949 established the People's Republic of China. However, the very foundations of the totalitarian regime – the ideology of Marxism–Leninism – and the organization of the Leninist party were completely foreign to the Chinese. For these foreign exogenous factors to play such a fundamental role in changing China so enormously, there must have been deep endogenous reasons. In the current section and the next, I look at shared critical institutional elements of China and Russia. Thus the creation of totalitarianism in Russia and its transplantation to China are not coincidental.

The first modern totalitarian regime in the world, Bolshevism, emerged from the following three institutional genes: (1) the Christian Orthodox church, which had almost completely penetrated Russian society and controlled Russian spiritual life; (2) the Russian imperial institutions, which almost completely controlled secular society, making the constitutional reforms more difficult; and (3) political terrorist organizations or secret and violent elite organizations, which completely controlled their members through discipline and terror.[22]

Both leaders of the Marxist movement and leading critics of Communism pointed out that Communism and violent Communist movements originate from Christianity,[23] and naturally the Christian church was essential for the creation of the first totalitarianism. For centuries nearly all Russians were members of the Russian Orthodox church. Russians' belief in and loyalty to

---

[22] See Xu, "Institutional Genes upon Which Totalitarianism Is Born," in Xu, *Institutional Genes*.

[23] F. Engels (1895), "A Contribution to the History of Primitive Christianity," published online by the Socialist Labor Party of America (www.slp.org), February 2007, at www.scribd.com/document/48277975/A-Contribution-to-the-History-Of-Primitive-Christianity-Frederick-Engels; K. Kautsky, *Communism in Central Europe in the Time of the Reformation* (Nabu Press, 7 January 2010); L. von Mises, *Socialism* (New Haven, Yale University Press, 1981; first published 1951). Kautsky and Mises discussed the bloody violence of the first communist city-state in Münster (Germany) created by radical Anabaptists in 1534.

the Orthodox church were deep and passionate. Moreover, the church was a pillar that supported the empire. Since Peter the Great, the czars had intertwined the religious order with the government to increase their power and to implement political reform, to use the church to rule the empire.

By borrowing some key elements from the church, the Bolsheviks transformed the revolutionary party into a political church, and Marxism–Leninism is the political religion of the church.[24] This political church incited and organized the masses to initiate and implement revolutionary actions. In addition to mobilizing the mass movement, the Bolshevik political church was essential to justify or legitimize the totalitarian regime.[25]

The second institutional gene of Bolshevism was the Russian imperial institutions. The power of the czars was much greater than that of Western European absolutists. The nobility, entrepreneurs, and merchants in Russia had been very weak since the emergence of the Russian empire, compared with their counterparts in Western Europe. The traditional Russian "parliament," the boyar Duma, which represented the nobility, was essentially a bureaucracy subordinate to the czar since Ivan IV. Even this was not allowed to last when Peter the Great abolished the boyar Duma completely.[26] The essential institutional elements of the czarist empire not only made the constitutional reforms difficult, but also prepared the institutional foundation for the forthcoming totalitarian regime.[27]

The third institutional gene of Bolshevism consisted of the terrorist organizations associated with the populist movement.[28] The first significant such organization was the Decembrists, a violent secretive organization composed of radical young military officials who, in the early nineteenth century, attempted to establish constitutionalism by launching terrorist campaigns.

A leading populist terrorist organization, Land and Liberty, directly influenced the birth and organization of Bolshevism. This party later split into several movements, among them are a proto-Marxist organization led by Georgi

---

[24] C. Xu, "Christianity as an Institutional Origin of Totalitarianism," in Xu, *Institutional Genes*. The similarities and differences among Christian denominations and their implications for totalitarianism are also discussed there.

[25] C. Xu, "The Creation of the First Full-Fledged Totalitarian Regime," in Xu, *Institutional Genes*.

[26] J.K. Sowards, *Makers of the Western Tradition*, 5th ed. (New York, St. Martin's Press, 1991), vol. 2, p. 29.

[27] Xu, "The Creation of the First Full-Fledged Totalitarian Regime."

[28] L.H. Haimson, *The Russian Marxists & the Origins of Bolshevism* (Cambridge, MA, Harvard University Press, 1955).

Plekhanov and a purely terrorist organization called People's Will.[29] Plekhanov was the first self-claimed Russian Marxist and was the founder of the social-democratic movement in Russia, the predecessor of the Bolshevik movement. Lenin, the founder of Bolshevism, was deeply influenced both by Plekhanov and by his own elder brother, who was a local leader of People's Will responsible for a failed attempt to assassinate the czar and was later executed.

Deeply rooted in Russian society, these three institutional genes were particularly appealing to radical revolutionaries, radical intellectuals or intelligentsia, and the masses at the bottom of society. The shared features of the czarist imperial institutions with totalitarianism rendered the transformation of Russia into a totalitarian state acceptable or even preferable among many radical revolutionaries, proletarians, and soldiers.

Introducing Totalitarianism into China

Totalitarianism is foreign to the Chinese. When the CCP was established in 1921, the number of Chinese who knew constitutionalism was far more than those who knew Marxism or Bolshevism. The CCP was only a small branch of the Comintern, which was quite unknown nationally and internationally at that time. But why did Bolshevism grow so fast in China and eventually become the dominant force there? Our explanation is in the roles of institutional genes. Indeed, China shares two of the three essential institutional genes of Bolshevism – an imperial institution and secretive organizations. The Chinese empire had established a more centralized and more sophisticated institution than its Russian counterpart. Arguably, popular support for imperial institutions among Chinese, for many of whom it might have been subconscious as it was the only known order, was even stronger than in Russia. Moreover, China had a long history of secretive rebellious organizations. One example is the triads that partnered with Sun Yat-sen's revolution. These were powerful mafia-type organizations established in the eighteenth century.[30]

But China would not have been able to create a native totalitarian regime on its own as a critical institutional gene was missing from Chinese soil: the Christian church,[31] the ideology, and ideology-centered institution. Without

---

[29] According to its leader, Lev Tikhomirov, the party's ambition was to organize a *coup d'état* to seize power. D. Offord, *The Russian Revolutionary Movement in the 1880s* (Cambridge, Cambridge University Press, 1986), pp. 26, 47–9.

[30] C. Xu, "China: From Constitutional Reform to Bolshevism," in Xu, *Institutional Genes*.

[31] Although Western missionaries had established hundreds of churches in many Chinese cities and towns beginning in the sixteenth century, the empire did not allow these churches to become influential in society.

the church and without many cultural connections with the West, not only did Chinese institutions and Chinese culture make it impossible to create a totalitarian ideology in China, but also no Chinese had ever even heard of Marxism until the early twentieth century. Marxism was only brought back to China with students who had been studying in Japan, and their knowledge of Marxism was extremely shallow.[32] Thus the mission of the Comintern was pivotal for the creation of the Marxist totalitarian regime in China.[33]

The Comintern was set up by Lenin in 1919 to wage a global Communist revolution, the success of which, according to Marxism–Leninism, was a necessary precondition for the survival of the Bolshevik Revolution. In 1920, Grigori Voitinsky, head of the Far Eastern Bureau of the Comintern, traveled to China to establish a Communist Party there. He contacted Li Dazhao, Chen Duxiu, and others, who later became the founders and first leaders of the CCP. Several months later, together they created the Comintern China Branch, the Chinese Communist Party. Then, in 1921, another Comintern representative, Maring (real name Henk Sneevliet) was sent to China directly by Lenin to chair the First Chinese Communist Party Congress.[34] The Constitution of the CCP (passed at the Second Chinese Communist Party Congress, in July 1922) declared that the CCP was a branch of the Comintern. The CCP's subordination to the Comintern remained until the dissolution of the Comintern in 1943.[35]

The reorganization of the Guomindang (KMT) and the creation of a KMT–CCP coalition sponsored by the Comintern was a vital step to foster the newborn CCP. In 1923 Adolf Joffe, a representative of Lenin, signed the Sun–Joffe Manifesto.[36] Thereafter, the Comintern provided large-scale military, financial, and personnel aid as well as training and advisers to the KMT, and created the Huangpu Military Academy in Guangzhou and Sun Yat-sen University in Moscow (officially called Sun Yat-sen Communist University of the Toilers of China) to train KMT and CCP officials.

At the 1924 First National Congress of the KMT, Sun announced that the KMT would be reorganized along the lines of the Bolshevik Party and

---

[32] Xu Liangying 许良英 and Wang Laidi 王来棣, 民主的历史 (History of Democracy) (Beijing, Law Press, 2015).
[33] T. Saich, *The Chinese Communist Party during the Era of the Comintern (1919–1943)* (n.l., CreateSpace Independent Publishing Platform, 2014).
[34] B. Lazitch with M.M. Drachkovitch (eds.), *Biographical Dictionary of the Comintern*, new, rvsd and exp. ed. (Stanford, CA, Hoover Institution Press, 1986), p. 436.
[35] Xu, "China: From Constitutional Reform to Bolshevism."
[36] W.L. Tung, *The Political Institutions of Modern China* (Dordrecht, Springer, 1968), p. 92.

China's revolution would "learn from Russia" (yi e weishi 以俄为师). But the long-run goal of the Comintern was to prepare the CCP to erode the power of the KMT in the near future.[37] Except for Sun Yat-sen, all the top KMT leaders, including Chiang Kai-shek, Liao Zhongkai, Chiang Ching-kuo, and so on, had trained in Russia or had spent lengthy visits in Russia. The Comintern's support for the KMT was maintained until 1927.

Under the leadership of the Comintern, in 1931 the CCP created the Chinese Soviet Republic, China's first totalitarian regime, with Mao Zedong elected as chairman, even though he was not yet a top CCP leader. To some extent, the Chinese Soviet Republic at that time was similar to the Ukrainian Soviet Socialist Republic that loosely became part of the USSR. In retrospect, the Chinese Soviet Republic was a prototype for the future PRC, with a constitution that was a simplified version of the 1924 Soviet Constitution.

In 1938, under the command of Comintern head Georgi Dimitrov, Mao Zedong became the top leader of the CCP at the Sixth Plenary Session of the Sixth Central Committee of the CCP, a position he would hold until his death in 1976.[38] Because Dimitrov's instructions were communicated orally to Wang Jiaxiang, the CCP envoy to the Comintern, without any witnesses, the credibility of this order is still contested by some Russian historians.

Inspired by Stalin and the Comintern, Mao consolidated his power by launching the Yan'an Rectification Campaign in 1942. From ideology to strategy, the Yan'an Rectification Campaign was essentially a Chinese version of the Stalinist Great Purge. The key reading of the Yan'an Rectification Campaign was Stalin's *History of the Communist Party of the Soviet Union (Bolsheviks): Short Course*; the primary strategy of the Yan'an Rectification Campaign was a Stalinist purge backed by terror, and the goal was to establish the absolute power of the leader by building a personality cult.

Following Stalin's steps after the 1936 Great Purge, "Mao Zedong Thought," coined by Wang Jiaxiang in 1943, was forcefully promoted in the CCP by Liu Shaoqi (a secretary of the Central Secretariat and vice chairman of the People's Revolutionary Military Council at that time, later the president of China, purged to death during the Cultural Revolution),[39] and

---

[37] Xu, "China: From Constitutional Reform to Bolshevism."
[38] He Fang, 党史笔记: 从遵义会议到延安整风 (Notes on the History of the CCP: From the Zunyi Meeting to the Yan'an Rectification Movement) (Hong Kong, Liwen chubanshe, 2005); Yang Kuisong, 毛泽东与莫斯科的恩恩怨怨 (Mao Zedong's Resentment of Moscow), 3rd ed. (Nanchang, Jiangxi renmin chubanshe, 2005).
[39] H. Gao, *1930–1945 How the Red Sun Rose: The Origins and Development of the Yan'an Rectification Movement* (Hong Kong, Chinese University Press, 2018).

became the core ideology of the CCP and entered the CCP Constitution at the Seventh CCP National Congress in 1945. Although the Yan'an Rectification Campaign was a duplication of Stalin's Great Purge and Wang's invention was an imitation of Kaganovich's creation of Stalinism in the mid-1930s, the ideology of the great leader created in the process took on a life and a soul of its own such that since then the CCP has become a fully fledged Bolshevik institution in its own right. Thenceforth, the Bolshevik institutional genes became part of China's institutional genes, dominating China's institutional evolution until today.

If Bolshevism, the first fully fledged totalitarian regime in human history, was so repressive, how was it possible for the Bolshevik Revolution to be incentive-compatible with its wide-ranging participants, from social elites to the vast masses of society?

Part of the answer is the Communist ideology, which has appealed to intellectual elites and the masses at the bottom of any highly unequal society. Yet, ironically, all totalitarian regimes are extremely unequal institutions. The other part of the answer is the conspiratory strategy common to secretive organizations. The Bolsheviks divided the grand revolutionary goal into stages, promising different goals at each stage. This strategy would make each stage incentive-compatible to the masses, and overall inconsistency between stages would be handled in other ways, often by violence. One example is Lenin's promise of a nationwide election to be held within three months immediately after the forced overthrow of the Russian Provisional Government, i.e. the October Revolution. He said the Bolsheviks would step down if they did not win a majority of the votes.[40] But after losing the election, the Bolsheviks declared that the election was invalid and arrested opposition-party leaders, thus triggering a multi-year civil war.

Learning from the Russian Bolsheviks, the CCP designed their ingenious strategy to change the incentive-incompatible grand revolution into a stagewise incentive-compatible revolution by making different and often contradictory promises over time. At each stage, the CCP issued appealing promises to participants, similar to what Lenin did in 1917–1918. The CCP has systematically breached its promises. To deal with the contradiction between assurances made at various stages of the revolution and reality, they use censorship, brainwashing, and suppression.

---

[40] V.I. Lenin, "Reply to Questions from Peasants," November 18, 1918, in Lenin, *Collected Works*, vol. 26 (Moscow, Progress Publishers, 1971), pp. 300–1.

For example, total nationalization, which was the goal of the Bolshevik Revolution, would not be incentive-compatible for the Chinese peasant masses.[41] To make the revolution incentive-compatible for the peasants, from the 1940s the CCP promised them ownership of private land and publicly announced that there would be no sovietization. However, after the CCP took and consolidated power, and penetrated every village and neighborhood and every corner of society, nationalization and collectivization began to be ruthlessly implemented. In the process, the social status of a handful of CCP village leaders was elevated. Most peasants hesitated to join the collectives, and after they did they later regretted it, but it was already too late for them to withdraw. Ultimately, almost all of them were forced to give up all their private assets. Only at that time did peasants find that to survive they had no choice but to join the collectives under the total control of the CCP.[42]

Similarly, for the seizure of power to be incentive-compatible, the CCP also promised democracy, freedom, and constitutionalism to the national capitalists and intellectuals. Consequently, a large number of liberal intellectuals joined the CCP.[43] To win the hearts of enlightened Chinese, in 1946 the CCP worked closely with the KMT and other parties to draft the Constitution of the Republic of China. In the process, the CCP delegates made numerous sensible motions to implement constitutional principles, including proactive protection of human rights measures, strengthening of checks and balances, and so forth. And most of those were incorporated into the final version of the Constitution (which, interestingly, remains the Constitution in Taiwan to this day).[44]

However, after taking power by military force in 1949, the CCP immediately withdrew its promises to implement constitutional principles in its provisional constitution – the Common Program of the Chinese People's Political Consultative Conference – promulgated in September 1949. The most important basic constitutional principles promised by the CCP, also written into the Republic of China Constitution that the CCP had supported,

---

[41] A Bolshevik revolution is a proletarian mass movement. With a weak urban proletarian force, the CCP was forced to organize and lead peasant rebellions, and seized power by peasant force. In many respects, the CCP revolution shared similarities with the peasant rebellions that had been an integral part of the repeated cyclical dynastic revolutions of the Chinese empire.

[42] Xu, "China: From Constitutional Reform to Bolshevism"; Xu, "A Full-Fledged Totalitarian Regime in China."

[43] Xu, "China: From Constitutional Reform to Bolshevism."

[44] Li Bingnan 李炳南, 政治协商会议与国共谈判 (The Political Consultative Conference and the KMT–CCP Negotiations) (Taipei, Yongye chuban gongsi, 1993).

such as a separation of powers, constitutional constraints on the power of the executive, a multiparty system, and so forth, all disappeared from the Common Program.[45] Article 1 of the Common Program declares that the People's Republic of China "carries out the people's democratic dictatorship." Article 15 states, "The organs of state power at all levels shall practice democratic centralism." It should be noted that the essence of the so-called "democratic centralism" is centralism alone and it is one of the basic Leninist principles established for the totalitarian Bolshevik party.

Creating a Fully Fledged Classic Totalitarian Regime

The Soviet Republic of China established in 1931 was a prototype totalitarian regime and the basis for later developments in the People's Republic of China. The creation of a fully fledged totalitarian regime began after the CCP took power. Stalinist institutions were fully transplanted into China. The first step, even before transplanting the Soviet model, was political centralization because previously all CCP-controlled territories had been governed as a kind of federation whereby each territory had its own banking system, legal system, and powerful leaders, such as Gao Gang in the northeast, Deng Xiaoping in the southwest, Xi Zhongxun in the northwest, and so forth. Beginning in 1950, all these powerful regional leaders were moved to the central government and "promoted" as national leaders.[46] Consequently, regional challenges and constraints on central authority were greatly weakened. Such centralization was well accepted by top CCP leaders as it was part of the institutional genes of the Chinese empire following the imperial pattern of enthroning the emperors.

The transplanting of the central planning institutions from the Soviet Union, including state ownership, bureaucratic resource allocation, and bureaucratic management, was one of the most critical elements in the creation of the Chinese totalitarian regime, perhaps second only to party building. A popular official slogan at that time was, "Today's Soviet Union is tomorrow's China."[47] In the early 1950s, the Soviets transferred to China 156 huge projects covering all sectors of manufacturing. Compared with the capital, equipment, technology, and management of modern state-owned

---

[45] Common Program of the Chinese People's Political Consultative Conference, at www .lawinfochina.com/display.aspx?id=abb13dba42840de7bdfb&lib=law (accessed April 28, 2020).
[46] Xu, "A Full-Fledged Totalitarian Regime in China."   [47] *People's Daily*, 15 October 1951.

firms associated with these projects, the far more important essence of these projects was the concrete implementation of central planning. Such large-scale and comprehensive aid gave China a chance to duplicate everything from the Soviet Union from the top to the bottom, from ideology to propaganda, from law to rule, from central planning to management, from technology to skills. The central planning apparatus was created as a duplicate of the Soviet system. In this system, almost all state assets, including the 156 Soviet-aided projects, were directly controlled by specialized central ministries, thus greatly strengthening the power of the central authority of the CCP. With this unprecedented Soviet aid and several campaigns which will be explained below, by the second half of the 1950s China had already established a fairly complete classic totalitarian regime.[48]

The PRC Constitution was even drafted under repeated pressure from Stalin. Advised by Soviet experts, the CCP drafted and passed the first PRC Constitution in 1954.[49] Unlike the Soviet Constitution, the Chinese Constitution recognized the peasants' rights to private land and the property rights of the owners of private firms. Again, this was part of the CCP's strategy of maintaining its united front, composed primarily of peasants, capitalists, and intellectuals, in the CCP's seizure of power.

However, immediately after passage of the Constitution, the CCP publicly announced that the Constitution would be transitional. Less than one year after the passing of the PRC Constitution, collectivization and nationalization began to sweep across the party-state, and the Constitution was de facto abandoned.[50]

Concerning the CCP's promises in the late 1940s that the PRC would be governed by a coalition of the CCP and democratic parties, the 1954 Constitution breached this promise by drastically decreasing the power of the democratic parties to participate in the governance of the PRC. The Chinese People's Political Consultative Conference degenerated from an acting congress to a rubber-stamp forum. Most national-level positions held by non-CCP members were abolished; all vice premiers were CCP members,

[48] R. MacFarquhar and J.K. Fairbank (eds.), *The People's Republic*, part 1, *Emergence of Revolutionary China, 1949–1965* (Cambridge, Cambridge University Press, 1987).
[49] Mao did not want to have any constitution in the PRC as it would be an unnecessary constraint on his dictatorial rule. But Stalin insisted that the CCP must implement a constitution for the PRC to be considered a "normal" nation. Zhang Ming 张鸣, "1954 年宪法是怎么来的: 从 '共同纲领' 到 1954 年宪法" (Where the 1954 Constitution Came From: From the "Common Program" to the 1954 Constitution) 炎黄春秋 (History of the Chinese People), 10 (2014), 28–33, at www.yhcqw.com/30/9628.html (accessed April 30, 2020).
[50] Xu, "A Full-Fledged Totalitarian Regime in China."

and only a very few ministers were members of the democratic parties. Over time, full-scale sovietization and the CCP's totalitarian control over firms, NGOs, and universities created strong discontent among intellectuals and democrats. Their grievances began to mount and spread rapidly.[51]

Triggered by Nikita Khrushchev's secret speech at the Twentieth Party Congress of the Communist Party of the Soviet Union (CPSU) and the Hungarian Revolution, both in 1956, the CCP launched a campaign to "let a hundred flowers bloom and let a hundred schools contend." Some years later, Mao described this campaign as a plot to lead the snake from out of his hole. Responding to this CCP initiative and unaware of the true intention of the Party, most democratic leaders, who only a few years earlier had been allies of the CCP, openly demanded that the CCP fulfill its promise to create a coalition government. Hundreds of thousands of intellectuals openly criticized the constitutional and administrative shortcomings of the totalitarian party-state. But within only several months, all of those who had dared to speak out were purged as "rightists," i.e. political enemies. Many of them were sent to labor camps or prisons; the luckier ones were placed under de facto house arrest.[52] In this "anti-rightist campaign," as it was officially called, 550,000 intellectuals, including more than 30,000 professors, were purged as rightists. These numbers should be placed in context. In 1956 China had a total of fewer than 240,000 engineers and there were even fewer intellectuals in business, finance, science, and the humanities.[53] Many of the so-called "rightists" were college students. Thereafter, constitutionalism was eliminated from Chinese college curricula and replaced by a so-called "politics course," which essentially was a course on Party doctrine.

The significance of the "anti-rightist campaign" is comparable to that of the "Yan'an Rectification." The Yan'an Rectification established a complete and independent totalitarian party, whereas after the anti-rightist campaign totalitarian rule was fully established over the entire country. Every person, regardless of whether or not she was a CCP member, had to strictly follow the Party line and the Party leader. The prohibition against dissident views cut off any channels of outside information and destroyed any possible checks and balances, thereby nurturing the conditions for future changes, such as the

---

[51] R. MacFarquhar, *The Origins of the Cultural Revolution: The Coming of the Cataclysm 1961–1966* (New York, Columbia University Press, 1997).
[52] Xu, "A Full-Fledged Totalitarian Regime in China."
[53] L. Orleans, *Professional Manpower and Education in Communist China* (Washington, DC: National Science Foundation, 1961), pp. 68–9, 74–5. See also the chapter by Perkins in this volume.

Great Leap Forward and the Cultural Revolution, and consequent catastrophes.

The widespread and punitively coercive suppression after the anti-rightist campaign established a foundation for a nationwide personality cult of the Party leader. Liu Shaoqi, the president of China, declared that Party members should become "tame tools (驯服工具)" or even "screws."[54] Students growing up in this environment were ready to follow any command whatsoever issued by the great and powerful leader. They had no clue about the basic rights of citizens, constitutions, laws, checks and balances, or even their own rights and interests. When a replica of the Soviet totalitarian regime was eventually established in China, totalitarian institutional genes also became part of Chinese institutional genes. Nevertheless, China soon deviated from the Soviet model. The classic totalitarian regime was transformed into a regionally decentralized totalitarian (RDT) state.

The Creation of Regionally Decentralized Totalitarianism (RDT): The Great Leap Forward and the Cultural Revolution

As noted above, before 1949 the CCP-controlled territories (i.e. the liberated areas) were governed by a quasi-federal structure. These regions enjoyed substantial autonomous power, and local forces were an essential part of the CCP power base. Political centralization after 1950 was more or less anticipated and tolerated by most CCP leaders as this had occurred whenever a new dynasty was established in Chinese history. However, full-scale implementation of the Soviet model would have allowed the central ministries to take over all the resources and powers from the regional governments. Sovietization would thus have caused resentment among regional officials.[55] In 1956, Mao addressed the issue of the central–local relationship in his speech entitled "On the Ten Major Relationships" (*lun shida guanxi* 论十大关系), revealing Mao's rethink of the institutional details of a totalitarian regime. Soon his thoughts were implemented through two waves of campaigns, the GLF and the CR, and totalitarianism with Chinese characteristics was born.[56]

---

[54] Liu Shaoqi, "同北京日报社编辑的谈话" (A Conversation with the Editor of the Beijing Daily) (June 8, 1958), at www.marxists.org/chinese/liushaoqi/1967/112.htm.
[55] C. Xu, "Regionally Decentralized Totalitarianism (RDT)," in Xu, *Institutional Genes*.
[56] Xu, "Regionally Decentralized Totalitarianism."

In 1958, after the anti-rightist campaign, which had further established Mao as the supreme and unchallenged leader, Mao launched the GLF, thus drastically moving China in a direction away from a classic totalitarian regime. The first step in this campaign was to further centralize Mao's political power by weakening the fragile remaining checks and balances within the Party and by suppressing other top leaders who held views that were slightly different from those of Mao. At the Second Session of the Eighth Congress of the CCP Central Committee in May 1958, Mao sharply condemned Zhou Enlai and forced him, as well as several vice premiers who were responsible for central planning, such as Chen Yun, Li Xiannian, Bo Yibo, and others, to make self-criticisms. All the party officials who supported Mao and criticized Zhou became more powerful or were promoted, such as Liu Shaoqi, Lin Biao, and Ke Qingshi (Party secretary of Shanghai).[57]

The series of institutional changes that began with the GLF and was completed during the CR (to be discussed below) created what I call a regionally decentralized totalitarian (RDT) regime, which featured the coexistence of, on the one hand, totally centralized control of society in ideology, politics, and even personal lives by the Party, and, on the other, decentralization in administration and management. The most important institutional change was the reintroduction of some of the institutional genes of the Chinese empire into the totalitarian institutional genes.[58] From an orthodox view of totalitarianism, the GLF and the RDT institutions created by the CCP were heretical to Marxism–Leninism. Thus the Soviet Union and other Eastern Bloc Communist countries criticized the GLF sharply and comprehensively.[59]

Although Mao had almost absolute power in the CCP, shaking up the established totalitarianism had to be revolutionary as the latter had strong backing from the whole international Communist movement led by Moscow and the nested interests of some top CCP leaders. Indeed, an important part of the efforts was officially called the Cultural Revolution, and the basic principle that Mao emphasized was a continuous revolution. The mechanisms of both the GLF and the CR were fanatic mass movements, and they featured fierce competition among regional forces, including regional governments.

---

[57] Xin Ziling 辛子陵, 紅太陽的隕落: 千秋功罪毛澤東 (The Fall of the Red Sun: The Sins of Mao Zedong) (Hong Kong, Shu zuo fang, 2007).
[58] Xu, "Regionally Decentralized Totalitarianism."
[59] Xu, "Regionally Decentralized Totalitarianism."

During the GLF, local governments competed over grain output per unit of land, over steel output, over promises of output, over the creation of novel Communist institutions (experimentation), and so forth. An essential part of the institutional foundation for regional competition was created at the beginning of the GLF campaign, a drastic decentralization to regional governments, with full-scale state ownership (or control) of all production assets.[60] It is important to point out that, since both were created from the same RDT institution, at an abstract level, the mechanism of the regional competition in the GLF is similar to that during the post-Mao reforms. Of course, as the party lines were different there were some key differences between the GLF and the post-Mao reforms. The GLF aimed to eliminate all markets, thus the competition was only over quantitative targets. Without independent channels to check the veracity of the claims made by local governments, these quantitative targets could be easily manipulated. In comparison, the post-Mao reforms attempted to re-establish markets, and the target of the competition was GDP growth or comprehensive market activities that could be verified independently, e.g. through random-sampling market surveys.

New institutions were created by trial and error through regional experimentation in both the GLF and the CR, which will be discussed below. Regional officials were incentivized to compete over the creation of institutions that would accelerate the transition to communism. The most prominent institution that was created during this campaign was the People's Commune (PC). The PC emerged in Chayashan town, Suiping county, Henan province, on April 20, 1958. The local party officials called this new institution the "Chayashan Satellite People's Commune" to commemorate the 1871 Paris Commune and the first Soviet satellite, sputnik 1, which had been launched some six months earlier. After revision by Mao, the charter of the PC was published in the party's theoretical journal, *Red Flag*, to promote the implementation of communes throughout the country. In late 1958, all rural communities were required to organize such communes and all peasants were required to join them. Under the leadership of the CCP, all Chinese peasants had "joined" a commune by the end of that year.[61]

Mao regarded the PC as the social foundation of the regime,[62] and he highlighted its features with two keywords, "large and public" (*yida ergong* 一大二公). "Large" refers to the scale of a commune, about 20,000 to 30,000 peasants in each commune, and the scope of a commune, which included

---

[60] Xu, "Regionally Decentralized Totalitarianism."
[61] Xu, "Regionally Decentralized Totalitarianism."
[62] At the peak of the GLF, many urban communities were also organized into PCs.

industry, agriculture, commerce, education, and the militia (*gong nong shang xue bing* 工农商学兵). "Public" refers to complete public ownership, i.e. elimination of all private property rights, and dominance by the CCP, which controlled all "publicly owned" assets in the nation. Every commune created tens or hundreds of commune–brigade industrial enterprises, the predecessors of the reform-era township and village enterprises (TVEs).[63] Thus each PC was a self-contained social unit.

A totalitarian society composed of tens of thousands of self-contained PCs made China distinctively different from the Soviet Union, which consisted of highly specialized large-scale enterprises. At the same time, the hard-core totalitarian institutions in the CCP were further consolidated, such as the cult of personality, the absolute power of the leader, the absolute control of the party, and so on. China's transformation from classic totalitarianism to an RDT regime is not coincidental as it involved essential institutional genes inherited from imperial China. Mao made this point clear at the Central Committee's Beidaihe meeting at the beginning of the 1958 GLF. He described himself as a combination of Karl Marx and Qin Shihuang. His so-called "Marx" referred to the imported totalitarianism, whereas his so-called "Qin Shihuang" referred to the imperial institutions.[64] A decade later during the CR Mao argued more explicitly that institutions of the Qin dynasty (*Qin youzai* 秦犹在) continued to exist in China to the present.[65]

Replacing central planning by regional competition and forcing peasants to work in communes during the GLF consequently not only destroyed information about cost, quantity, and quality in all sectors of the Chinese economy, but also forced the peasants to hide food as government procurements squeezed their rations and their seeds, such that their survival was threatened. The chaos and disincentives led to the largest man-made famine in human history, with the death of 30 million.[66]

Due to the great famine, the GLF was prematurely aborted and the newly created RDT institution was still primitive. The second wave of pushing towards the RDT, the CR, started in 1966 and lasted until 1976. On the one hand, the CR thrust the centralization of politics, ideology, and personnel

---

[63] Xu, "Regionally Decentralized Totalitarianism."
[64] Xu, "Regionally Decentralized Totalitarianism."
[65] Wang Nianyi 王年一, 大动乱的年代 (A Time of Great Upheaval) (Beijing, Henan People's Press, 1988), p. 470.
[66] This estimation is by Kung, in this volume. For narratives of the great famine, which occasioned 36 million deaths, see Yang Jisheng 杨继绳, 墓碑：中国六十年代大饥荒纪实 (Tombstone: A Record of China's Great Famine in the 1960s) (Hong Kong, Tiandi tushu youxian gongsi, 2008).

matters even further, to an unprecedented level. All power was concentrated in the hands of the top leader, Mao, and his lieutenants. On the other hand, as an essential part of the CR, most central ministries were entirely closed down and almost all centrally controlled assets were delegated to the regional governments.[67] The extreme centralization of politics and personnel matters and the frenzied decentralization of administrative powers were highly complementary to each other. The decentralized administrative powers weakened the de facto powers of the central administrators because they could challenge the top leader in technical respects as they were endowed with indispensable resources. In contrast, the regional officials had no chance to influence the central leaders as their powers were thinly distributed. Thus the weaker the central ministries were, the more powerful the supreme leader became.

At the peak of the CR, more than 98 percent of central government-controlled assets were handed over to the regional governments. Except the People's Liberation Army (PLA) and those making nuclear weapons and ballistic missiles, almost all state-owned enterprises (SOEs) were controlled by the regional governments. The number of centrally controlled SOEs dropped from 10,533 in 1965 to 142 in 1970. Most central commissions and ministries, including the Central Planning Commission, the Central Economic Commission, the State Statistical Bureau, and so forth, were left with no functions. Many ministries, such as the ministries of Metallurgy, Coal, Commerce, and others, were permanently abandoned.[68] Nevertheless, because an RDT structure was already in place and self-contained regional economies had already been operational since the GLF, and the RDT regime was consolidated and enhanced, during the CR there was no great famine and the economy did not completely collapse. Associated with the administrative decentralization, complementary to the frenzied cult of Mao's personality, the major driving incentive mechanism of the CR was regional competition at every stage: the Red Guard movements; the Seizing-Power campaigns; the agricultural Learn from Dazhai campaign; the Five Small Industries (FSI) campaign, and so on.

Similar to the GLF, which created tens of thousands self-contained PCs as a foundation for a primitive RDT regime, the CR created thousands of self-contained counties as a foundation for a consolidated and industrialized RDT regime. To make all counties autarkic in terms of metallurgy,

[67] MacFarquhar, *The Origins of the Cultural Revolution*.
[68] Xu, "Regionally Decentralized Totalitarianism."

energy, machinery, construction, construction materials, and chemistry, a nationwide FSI campaign was launched in 1970, whereby each county was required to establish its own SOEs in five sectors, namely steelmaking, coal mining, machinery, cement, and chemical fertilizers. By the end of the CR, a substantial proportion of Chinese counties had become self-sufficient.[69] At the cost of 30 million lives in the GLF, and arguably even higher human costs in the CR,[70] the RDT was fully consolidated and codified by the state Constitution in 1975. As will be explained in the next section, ironically the RDT is the institutional foundation of the once successful post-Mao reform.

The Evolution of Regionally Decentralized Authoritarianism during the Post-Mao Reforms

The CR era is one of the darkest periods in human history. The devastation of the CR awakened the majority of CCP elites as the legitimacy of the CCP was deeply shaken, thus paving the way for change in the CCP after Mao's death.

In its earlier stages, the post-Mao reforms induced an unintentional institutional change towards RDA.[71] The market replaced administrative planning in most areas of the economy; private property rights in production emerged and become the largest sector of the national economy; limited ideological pluralism and NGOs were somewhat allowed and accepted, although censorship still prevailed and tolerance was always contested, sometimes violently. The private and individualistic institutional elements grew fast, eroding RDT institutional genes. However, not surprisingly, limited liberalization and pluralism were not incentive-compatible with some powerful groups in the old regime, who regard the remaining RDT institutional genes as the foundation of their power and began to roll back the trend towards RDA from 2012. Sharing the same kind of institution with pre-1989 Soviet Eastern Europe, the CCP's negative reaction towards liberalism could be expected. The puzzling question is why China succeeded in creating

---

[69] Xu, "Regionally Decentralized Totalitarianism."
[70] According to a report by the Central Committee of the CCP published in the 1980s, more than a million people were killed and more than 10 million were injured or disabled, plus more than 113 million were politically persecuted during the CR. Cited in Yang Jisheng 杨继绳, "道路·理论·制度—我对文化大革命的思考" (The Course, Theory, and Institutions: My Reflection on the Cultural Revolution), Jiyi 记忆 (Memory), November 30, 2013, 2–23.
[71] C. Xu, "Institutional Evolution in the Post-Mao Era: Regionally Decentralized Authoritarianism (RDA)," in Xu, Institutional Genes.

a private sector in the early stages of reform. This question is addressed by examining the institutional genes inherited from the GLF and the CR.

Concerning both content and timing, the starting point of the post-Mao reforms was the ending point of the CR. The leaders of the *coup d'état* in 1976, which occurred several weeks after the death of Mao, arrested Mao's wife Jiang Qing and her lieutenants and removed those who insisted on continuing the CR from both the central leadership and the subnational levels. Consequently, a campaign was launched to transform the Party line from class struggle to economic development.[72] Changes in the Party line were associated with personnel changes at all levels of the party-state hierarchy. Those who had seized power during the CR were replaced by party-state officials who had been purged at the same time. Importantly, many of those who were purged during the CR were de facto political dissidents during the Mao era as they vehemently disagreed with the Party line and were keen to introduce change. Such a systematic political change paved the way for the coming decades of reform.

With changed leadership, CCP central leaders forged a new consensus on the following major issues: (1) the monopolistic political power of the CCP must not be challenged, i.e. maintaining the essence of the RDT regime unchanged;[73] (2) the Party line has changed and the essence of socialism should be interpreted as economic development, which is the least controversial objective among the competing powerful factions and infighting ideologies; and (3) the Mao type of personalistic leadership should be replaced by a consensus-based collective leadership.[74] These principles were documented in the communiqué of the Third Plenum of the Eleventh CCP Central Committee in December 1978,[75] which became the official manifesto for political, ideological, and economic change, whereas it emphasized maintaining socialism, particularly insisting that state and collective ownership

---

[72] Before Deng Xiaoping returned to power in late 1978, the major changes were led by Hu Yaobang, at the time general secretary of the CCP. J. Hu, "Hu Yaobang Selected the Breakpoint for the Reform," *Kaifang* 开放 (Kaifang magazine) 4 (2008), 66–8; Hu, "What Is 'Reform and Opening Up'? When Did It Occur?" *Zhengming* 争鸣 (Zhengming magazine) 4 (2009), pp. 66–70.

[73] The following argument by Deng depicts the goal of the CCP clearly: "to build socialism it is necessary to develop the productive forces ... Not until ... we have reached the level of the moderately developed countries shall we be able to say that we have really built socialism and to declare convincingly that it is superior to capitalism. We are advancing towards that goal." Deng Xiaoping, "To Uphold Socialism We Must Eliminate Poverty," April 26, 2987, in *Selected Works of Deng Xiaoping*, vol. 3, 1982–1992 (Beijing, Foreign Languages Press, 1994), p. 223.

[74] Xu, "Institutional Evolution in the Post-Mao Era."

[75] See http://cpc.people.com.cn/GB/64162/64168/64563/65371/4441902.html.

must not be touched. Consequently, "Four Modernizations" became the slogan of the Third Plenum, and "Reform and Opening Up" became the slogan after the 1987 Thirteenth Party Congress (when Zhao Ziyang was the CCP secretary general). Make no mistake, the change in the objective of the CCP from class struggle to economic development was always meant to be fully consistent with Communist ideology and to serve the survival of the CCP regime.[76]

As China was still suffering from the consequences of the CR in the late 1970s, the post-Mao reforms began by following the Eastern Bloc nations due to shared similar institutions and objectives. However, the reforms in all Eastern Bloc nations ran into deep problems caused by a totalitarian bureaucracy. China was no exception.

A totalitarian regime controls all power and resources in society through the Leninist party in a top-down manner with a long chain of command. The entire society and the national economy are ruled by millions of party-state bureaucrats, who enjoy great benefits from their powers. Moreover, superiors have to rely on their subordinates for information to evaluate their subordinates, but subordinates with better local information have no incentive to report truthfully. Their vested interests are major obstacles to any reform that challenges existing institutions. Not only will they not take any initiative to attempt such reforms, but also they will find excuses not to implement reforms in their respective jurisdictions, regardless of the Party line or the dictates of their superiors. However, implementing any reforms at least has to rely on subordinates. In reality, very often the reforms have to rely further on their initiatives as they are better informed regarding local information (à la Hayek). Thus a solution to the incentive problem in the party-state bureaucratic hierarchy is the key to determining what reforms are

---

[76] The survival of the CCP regime is exactly the reason Deng and his lieutenants argued in cracking down on the Tiananmen demonstration. Moreover, ideologically, according to Marx, one respect in which socialism is better than capitalism is in its higher capacity to advance "productive forces." Thus, in order to prove the validity of the Communist Party's doctrine, it is necessary to deliver a higher growth rate than the capitalist economies. For this reason, most Communist leaders in the Soviet Union and Eastern Europe, even including Mao in the 1950s, attempted to grow their economies, although such attempts all eventually ended in failure. After the collapse of the Soviet Union and the Eastern Bloc, the top CCP leaders believed that continued economic development was crucial for the survival of the regime. For example, Tian Jiyun, a vice premier in the 1990s, attributed the collapse of the Soviet Union and the Eastern Bloc to their decades of failure to improve productivity. Du Mingming and Qingquan Xu, "田纪云谈 1992 年中央党校讲话" (Tian Jiyun on his 1992 Speech at the Central Party School), *Yanhuang Chunqiu* 3 (2009), at www.yhcqw.com/11/4679.html (accessed May 22, 2020).

feasible, who will implement the reforms, and how the reforms will be carried out.

Given the failure to find such a solution, intrinsic resistance to institutional reforms by party-state bureaucrats in the Eastern Bloc countries led to the failure of two decades of reform attempts and ultimately to the total collapse of their totalitarian regimes. In contrast, in the early stages of Chinese reform, the private sector emerged and grew fast, which drove China's growth thereafter. A key observation for understanding why China differs is that all the reforms related to property rights in China were not designed by the central Party or state. Instead, these were experiments at local levels, and initially they were not even permitted. Under anticapitalist laws and rules, local governments initiated the experiments and assumed high risks, as recognition, formal rules, and/or the legalization of reforms related to property rights almost always occurred after the fact was established, and risks were taken.[77] What motivated local party-state bureaucrats to take such risks?

The mechanism which drove many local party-state bureaucrats to engage with experiments relating to property rights in the first two decades of the reforms was tournament-like regional competitions over the GDP growth rate launched by the central authority. Promotions of officials in subnational governments were linked to their relative performance vis-à-vis the performance of officials in other regions. This provided high-powered incentives to local bureaucrats.[78]

The central authority focuses on GDP growth as long as the Party is in power. But to fulfill this goal is not easy, as shown in the lessons from the Eastern Bloc. Thus regional governments were encouraged to find ways to develop faster than other regions. Under this mechanism, to succeed in the regional competition, many regional bureaucrats experimented with privatization, either partially or wholly, and indirectly or directly, even when private property rights were illegal. Only later were successful methods promoted or copied nationwide. The most prominent such examples include land reform (the "household responsibility system"), the special economic zones (SEZs) (protecting foreign private property rights for Chinese land), the TVEs and their later privatization,[79] the privatization of SOEs (starting in Zhucheng, Shandong province), and, most importantly, the

---

[77] Xu, "The Fundamental Institutions of China's Reform."
[78] Y. Qian and C. Xu, "Why China's Economic Reforms Differ: The M-Form Hierarchy and the Entry/Expansion of the Non-state Sector," *Economics of Transition* 1.2 (June 1993), 135–70.
[79] M.L. Weitzman and C. Xu, "Township–Village Enterprises as Vaguely Defined Cooperatives," *Journal of Comparative Economics* 18.2 (1994), 121–45.

rapid development of *de novo* private firms, among other things. The large-scale change in property rights was the foundation for the institutional change towards RDA. In 2004 the changed regime was codified in the PRC Constitution where private property rights are recognized.[80]

However, regional tournament-like competition requires strong conditions that do not always provide the desirable high-powered incentives in the long run. That is why Chinese practices during the post-Mao reforms appear unusual in comparison with the Eastern Bloc. The following is the set of conditions for tournament-like regional competition to be an effective incentive mechanism for national policies:

1. There must be a top-down hierarchical bureaucracy that effectively controls the appointment, supervision, evaluation, and execution of all subordinate-level bureaucrats.
2. All, or the majority of, subordinate bureaucracies must consist of self-contained structures.
3. The government focuses on only one well-defined and measurable objective.
4. The government's disregard for all other objectives does not result in serious consequences.

Here, 1 and 2 are institutional conditions; whereas 3 and 4 concern the nature of competition targets. All totalitarian and authoritarian regimes, including those in China and in the Eastern Bloc nations, satisfy condition 1. However, only Chinese RDT and RDA satisfy condition 2; whereas classic totalitarian institutions in the Eastern Bloc violate this condition.[81] These conditions are also helpful for understanding why regional competition was an essential part of the incentive mechanisms of the GLF and the CR after administrative powers and economic resources were systematically decentralized after 1958.

Indeed, at the beginning of the post-Mao era, when the party line focused on economic development, and China was so desperately poor that people were more willing to make sacrifices in other aspects in order to improve their income, conditions 3 and 4 are satisfied such that regional competition

---

[80] Xu, "The Fundamental Institutions of China's Reform."
[81] With the implicit assumptions 1 and 4, Maskin, Qian, and Xu provide a theory and preliminary evidence showing that the Chinese M-form (condition 2) can provide high-powered incentives for economic growth (i.e. condition 3); whereas by violating condition 2, the Soviet U-form will not be able to provide high-powered incentives for economic growth. E. Maskin, Y. Qian, and C. Xu, "Incentives, Information, and Organizational Forms," *Review of Economic Studies* 67.2 (2000), 359–78.

targeting GDP growth was effective during the early stages of the Chinese reforms.[82] Moreover, GDP as a comprehensive indicator of total market activities is well defined and well measured, and also it can be verified independently. Thus setting the GDP growth rate as the objective of local government competition categorically differentiates the consequence of the post-Mao reforms from that of regional competition during the GLF and the CR, although institutions were akin and strategies were also similar.

However, the role of any government regardless of the type of institution must always involve multiple dimensions. Associated with growth sustained over three decades and the authoritarian nature of governance, conditions 3 and 4 were violated substantially when China was no longer poor and when government-driven growth was associated with deep socioeconomic problems (e.g. land-grabbing local governments forced citizens in their jurisdictions to relocate by demolishing their homes, *qiang chaiqian* 强拆迁), such as social stability, inequality, degradation of the environment, corruption, and so forth. Even worse, tournament-type regional competition with multiple targets led to a race to the bottom for some targets. Thus regional competition as a solution for RDT/RDA bureaucrats, and associated growth performance, can only be transitional. The unprecedented fiscal stimuli of more than 1 trillion RMB spent during the global financial crisis pushed growth up temporarily, then it appeared to steadily slow down, with problems of overcapacity and overleveraging. Consequently, regional competition was abandoned.[83] But under the RDA institutions, there are no alternative effective solutions.[84]

Facing increasing troubles in the economy, calls for reforming the state sector, for better protections of property rights and human rights, and for further reform in general were strong and popular. Given that the private sector employed more than 90 percent of the labor force in China, these reform calls are incentive-compatible with the majority of Chinese.

---

[82] H. Li and L.-A. Zhou, "Political Turnover and Economic Performance: The Incentive Role of Personnel Control in China," *Journal of Public Economics* 89.9–10 (September 2005), 1743–62. After Maskin, Qian, and Xu, "Incentives, Information, and Organizational Forms," and Li and Zhou, "Political Turnover and Economic Performance," a sizable empirical literature in economics and political science provides systematic evidence that Chinese tournament-like regional competition is effective when the government's only objective is growth.

[83] C. Xu, "The Rise and Fall of the RDA," in Xu, *Institutional Genes*.

[84] There is no general optimum incentive solution for a bureaucracy when it has multiple objectives. B. Holmstrom and P. Milgrom, "Multi-task Principal–Agent Analyses: Incentive Contracts, Asset Ownership, and Job Design," *Journal of Law, Economics, and Organization* 7 (1991), 24–52.

However, events recently have gone in the opposite direction. This change is related to, but is more than, the change of the CCP leadership in 2012. These changes and policies against the popular demand and expectations need to be backed by strong coercive power.

This strong power consists of elements of the RDT institutional genes,[85] which have been eroded by privatization and by the transformation towards RDA. Indeed, from the beginning of the post-Mao reform, the ultimate purpose of the CCP is to sustain the totalitarian regime both politically and economically. This is manifested in Deng Xiaoping's Four Cardinal Principles of modernization announced in 1979 (upholding the socialist path, upholding the people's democratic dictatorship, upholding the leadership of the CCP, and upholding Mao Zedong Thought and Marxism–Leninism),[86] and is evident in his decision to crack down on the Tiananmen demonstrations in 1989 and to purge the reform-minded CCP secretary generals Hu Yaobang and Zhao Ziyang sequentially in 1986 and 1989.[87] The propaganda and ideological leading figures and agencies, state banks, large SOEs, and the State-Owned Assets Supervision and Administration Commission of the State Council (SASAC) have always been fighting against privatization and against amendments to the CCP Constitution in 2002 and the State Constitution in 2004. One argument which they have emphasized is that state assets are the foundation of Party rule.[88]

Since 2013 all private firms and NGOs, including foreign firms and organizations, are required to set up CCP branches within the firm and organization. "Everything must be led by the Party" is being enforced everywhere. Discussions of constitutionalism and judicial independence are prohibited. "Upholding and strengthening the Party's absolute leadership in political and legal affairs" becomes the rule above the law.[89] Criticism of or even dissent from top leaders is punished. Government media must follow the party

---

[85] The most important elements include: (1) the party/state which controls the society, the court, the legislature, and the armed forces; (2) the state sector of the economy, including the financial sector, land, and SOEs; and (3) the subnational level party/state bureaucracy (the RDT structure).
[86] "邓小平：坚持四项基本原则" (Deng Xiaoping: Upholding the Four Fundamental Principles), at https://baike.baidu.com/reference/280112/6b4atU-GeIeXMCJwbyQmCc4QXielLoTgnCZmNtYbbGoZ5sCwZZTYNwOhXn48UuE5NTm3yW7qXJ6Mw-q_hCSaPeHBr51NSIGlMJIpPP7HGOY5-verWOhtuw.
[87] Zhao Ziyang, *Prisoner of the State: The Secret Journal of Premier Zhao Ziyang* (New York, Simon & Schuster, 2009).
[88] Xu, "The Rise and Fall of the RDA."
[89] "中国共产党政法工作条例" (Regulations on the Political and Legal Work of the Communist Party of China), at www.gov.cn/zhengce/2019-01/18/content_5359135.htm.

(*dangmei xing dang* 党媒姓党). And the State Constitution has changed, allowing the state presidency to become for life. All bureaucrats, particularly subnational bureaucrats, are evaluated foremost on their loyalty to the top leader. Their morals have dropped drastically as their main goal now is not to make punishable mistakes.[90]

Conclusion

Enlightened Chinese elites have launched reforms and revolutions aimed to establish a constitutional republic since the late nineteenth century, and these endeavors are still unfulfilled to this very day. On the contrary, China has implanted Bolshevism and further created an RDT regime with deep local roots. The narrative of this chapter has explained how the institutional genes inherited from the Chinese empire impeded constitutional reforms, and instead nurtured Bolshevism in China with deep roots, and further localized it. After totalitarianism prevailed in China, the institutional genes were transformed into new forms. The institutional genes of today's RDT regime appear to be mutations of their counterparts in the Chinese empire, like grafting institutional genes of the Chinese empire onto the genes of totalitarianism. The persistence of the institutional genes implies the difficulties of changing China's fundamental institutions. Indeed, from Deng Xiaoping's "upholding the leadership of the CCP" in his Four Cardinal Principles to Xi Jinping's re-emphasizing Mao's words that "the Party is the leader of everything,"[91] from the cracking down in Tiananmen Square in 1989 to the suppression in Hong Kong in 2020, and from the continuous anti-peaceful-evolution efforts of the CCP from the 1950s to this day, the consistency in basic principles among the CCP leadership, and their tenacious resistance to constitutional reform, are evident.

Although institutional genes of the old regimes are persistent, institutional genes can mutate in diverging directions. Contrary to mainland China, sharing the same historical institutional genes, institutions in Taiwan have evolved into those of a full constitutional democracy. If in China the private sector, including NGOs and communal organizations (formal and informal), becomes the dominant sector in society and comes to enjoy full autonomy; if the judiciary becomes

---

[90] Xu, "The Rise and Fall of the RDA."
[91] "The Party is the leader of everything, from the Party, the government, the army, the people, the school, the East, the West, the North, the South, and the Center" (党政军民学、东西南北中，党是领导一切的), said Mao in 1962, as Xi repeated in 2018.

independent in protecting property rights and human rights; if a sufficient share of the population is enlightened about their basic rights and takes collective action to protect the their own rights and those of others, then new institutional genes will breed, and change. Under that situation, institutions in mainland China could eventually converge with what Taiwan has achieved.

Further Reading

Brandt, L., D. Ma, and T. Rawski, "From Divergence to Convergence: Re-evaluating the History behind China's Economic Boom," *Journal of Economic Literature* 52.1 (March 2014), 45–123.

Courtois, S., N. Werth, J.-L. Panne, A. Paczkowski, K. Bartosek, and J.-L. Margolin, *The Black Book of Communism: Crimes, Terror, Repression* (Cambridge, MA, Harvard University Press, 2015).

Friedrich, C.J., and Z.K. Brzezinski, *Totalitarian Dictatorship and Autocracy* (Cambridge, MA, Harvard University Press, 1956).

Gao, H., *1930–1945 How the Red Sun Rose: The Origins and Development of the Yan'an Rectification Movement* (Hong Kong, Chinese University Press, 2018).

Li, H., and L.-A. Zhou, "Political Turnover and Economic Performance: The Incentive Role of Personnel Control in China," *Journal of Public Economics* 89.9–10 (September 2005), 1743–62.

MacFarquhar, R., *The Origins of the Cultural Revolution: The Coming of the Cataclysm 1961–1966* (New York, Columbia University Press, 1997).

MacFarquhar, R., and J.K. Fairbank (eds.), *The People's Republic*, part 1, *Emergence of Revolutionary China, 1949–1965* (Cambridge, Cambridge University Press, 1987).

Maskin, E., Y. Qian, and C. Xu, "Incentives, Information, and Organizational Forms," *Review of Economic Studies* 67.2 (2000), 359–78.

Qian, Y., and C. Xu, "Why China's Economic Reforms Differ: The M-Form Hierarchy and the Entry/Expansion of the Non-state Sector," *Economics of Transition* 1.2 (June 1993), 135–70.

Wang Nianyi 王年一, 大动乱的年代 (A Time of Great Upheaval) (Beijing, Henan People's Press, 1988).

Xin Ziling 辛子陵, 紅太陽的隕落: 千秋功罪毛澤東 (The Fall of the Red Sun: The Sins of Mao Zedong) (Hong Kong, Shu zuo fang, 2007).

Xu C., "The Fundamental Institutions of China's Reform and Development," *Journal of Economic Literature* 49.4 (2011), 1076–1151.

Xu, C., *Institutional Genes: A Comparative Analysis of the Origin of Chinese Institutions* (forthcoming from Cambridge University Press).

Xu Liangying 许良英 and Wang Laidi 王来棣, 民主的历史 (History of Democracy) (Beijing, Law Press, 2015).

Yang Jisheng 杨继绳, 墓碑: 中国六十年代大饥荒纪实 (Tombstone: A Record of China's Great Famine in the 1960s) (Hong Kong, Tiandi tushu youxian gongsi, 2008).

Zhao, Ziyang, *Prisoner of the State: The Secret Journal of Premier Zhao Ziyang* (New York, Simon & Schuster, 2009).

16

China's Struggle with the Soviet Growth Model, 1949–1978

DWIGHT H. PERKINS

When the Communist Party of China announced a new government on October 1, 1949, the economy that government inherited was in shambles. China had been at war for over twelve years and much of the infrastructure of the country had been destroyed or badly damaged and prices were rising at 51 percent per month or 13,000 percent per year. The Guomindang government fleeing to Taiwan took much of the country's foreign-exchange and gold reserves with them, along with many of the managers of the banks and industrial firms. Inflation and war left many of the businesses that stayed barely able to function even when their managers and technicians did not flee.

The government that inherited this shambles had very little experience managing a modern urban economy. Their economic management experience was largely confined to overseeing some of the poorest regions of the rural economy, notably the area around Yan'an in the remote northwest. The one exception was in the northeast where the Soviet defeat of Japanese forces there in 1945 helped make it possible for the Communist forces to gain control of a major region with large cities and modern industry. Future economic leaders, notably Chen Yun, did gain experience there that was to help them later. For the most part, however, those charged with implementing economic policies in the region often had little formal education and their practical experience mainly involved military actions or farming. The Communist base areas, however, did have real economic problems that had to be dealt with.[1] To maintain the support of the people in their base areas, their efforts focused on the redistribution of land from richer landlords

---

This chapter has benefited greatly from the comments of its discussant, Xu Chenggang, at the Utrecht Conference.

[1] For an in-depth analysis of the economic policies of the Yan'an period, see P. Schran, "On the Yenan Origins of Current Economic Policies," in D.H. Perkins (ed.), *China's Modern Economy in Historical Perspective* (Stanford, Stanford University Press, 1975), pp. 279–302.

to poorer farmers, but the base areas also had to produce enough food and other necessities to maintain both an acceptable standard of living for the general population and a surplus to feed, clothe, and provide ammunition to the army. Furthermore, this had to be done in an area that was blockaded by both the Guomindang and Japanese armies, severely limiting the ability of the Communist-held regions to trade for necessities. The Communist armies could not survive for long in these circumstances using the tactics of the typical warlord army that met its needs mainly by pillaging the areas it controlled.

Given this background, it might have been expected that the new government would rely as much as possible on those remaining from the previous government who had experience managing the economic institutions of the modern urban sectors of the economy. To a limited degree that was the case, but it lasted for a comparatively brief period. The main tasks during 1949–1952 were to achieve as rapidly as possible a restoration of production in the enterprises that still existed and to end the hyperinflation. The latter was achieved by replacing the old currency with the new *renminbi* currency and then maintaining a government budget where revenue and expenditures were more or less in balance. Rapid recovery in production and hence taxation, together with the end of most fighting, also helped make a balanced budget feasible.

During these first years (1949–1952) the government completed the process of land reform that it had begun during wartime. Landlords were deprived of their land without compensation and the land was distributed to the peasants, as much as possible to the poorer peasants who were the mainstays of support for the revolution. Land to the tiller at this stage did not involve formation of co-operatives or collective farming except for a few experimental areas where it was done on a volunteer basis. The campaign did, however, involve considerable violence, with large numbers of former landlords killed or sent off to do hard labor. After 1952 experiments with co-operative forms accelerated, but there were debates within the government about how fast to push collectivization. Those debates were decisively ended when Mao Zedong ordered that virtually all of agriculture be formed into producer co-operatives on an involuntary basis where necessary in the winter of 1955–1956.

The government also early on began to establish direct control over key areas of the modern urban economy. Steps were taken almost immediately to nationalize the banking system and most of the transportation system. Under the Guomindang many key industries were run by the state and these simply changed management from one government to the next. The

Japanese-owned companies in the northeast and elsewhere were also transferred to Chinese government ownership. Even private Chinese-owned enterprises where management had stayed in China gradually lost most of their independence and were converted into joint state–private enterprises where the state was clearly dominant.

The transformation from private enterprise to joint state–private ownership began first in 1951 and 1952 during the war in Korea with the "Three Anti" and "Five Anti" political campaigns that were designed, among other purposes, to intimidate private-sector owners and managers into following the government's directives. These campaigns were followed by a variety of regulations designed to eliminate what the government perceived as undesirable private-sector practices, such as speculation. By 1955 it is unlikely that there was much, if any, resistance to the state effectively taking over these firms, converting former owners and managers into what in effect were employees. Foreign trade during this process was taken away from the producing enterprises and was put into the hands of state corporations. Only they could hold foreign exchange with which to purchase imports.

The Centrally Planned Command Economy

By 1955–1956 most of the institutions of what had become a Soviet-type economic system were in place. The first Soviet-style five-year plan theoretically covered the years from 1953 to 1957, although it was not actually published until July 1955. Annual plans, however, were made and implemented as early as 1953. Soviet advisers were stationed in key positions overseeing the economy to help China complete the process of creating a Soviet-type economic system. The regulations governing the various economic institutions were often little more than translations of the relevant Soviet regulations.

The Soviet-type system that China created had the following characteristics:

1 Except for a few state-managed farms, all agriculture was collectivized into what initially were called agricultural producer co-operatives that theoretically were managed by leaders elected by the members, but were in fact appointed by the Chinese Communist Party and were expected to follow orders from the Party and government. Land was held by the co-operative as a whole although individual farm families were allowed to have small private plots on which they could grow vegetables and raise pigs. Family

incomes within the co-operative were based on the number of "work points" earned by family members where the value of each point was determined by the total income of the co-operative minus certain collective expenses and investments.

2 Most commercial banks were abolished and the People's Bank of China became a monobank that performed the functions of both a central bank and a commercial bank. Enterprises were expected to deposit virtually all the money they received in this monobank.

3 Industrial decisions of what to produce and with what inputs were determined by a central plan that developed targets for all industrial products and inputs and then passed those targets down through the government bureaucracy that broke those national targets down into targets for each individual enterprise.

4 Commerce was in state enterprise hands for everything except small handicraft and subsidiary agricultural products that could be sold on small informal markets. Essential consumer products such as grain were rationed for urban residents and prices were set by the government. Farms received marketing quotas that they were expected to meet and farm purchase prices were set by the state. Industrial firms turned over their output to state commercial enterprises which then distributed them in accordance with plan targets at state-set prices – prices that had little relation to the supply and demand for the products.

That was the formal structure of state control of virtually the entire economy. The only areas by 1956 still mainly controlled by markets were small private plots and informal rural markets.

How this system was supposed to work and to a degree did work can best be understood by looking at its operation within the industrial sector. The planners drew up a detailed plan every five years giving a broad outline of what the economy was expected to produce, sector by sector. The real operational plan, however, was an annual plan that drew up what was intended to be a consistent set of output and input targets for each industry. That was then broken down into output and input targets for each industrial enterprise. Enterprises were legally required to implement these targets, but law in the Chinese (and Soviet) case was not an effective means for enforcing the plan targets.

Enforcement instead relied first on the fact that enterprises received the inputs required from state distribution enterprises that were supposed to make these allocations in accordance with the central plan. Supplementary inputs could not be obtained on the market because no such market existed. Enterprises could informally trade excess inputs for inputs they were short of, but only on a limited basis and prices played no role in these trades. Further backing up enforcement of the plan was the fact that the central bank, the People's Bank of China, was charged with checking to make sure that enterprise deposits and loan funds were only spent on items authorized by the plan.

Most profits of enterprises were turned over to the government, with small exceptions for research efforts and the like authorized in the plan. Investment in new plant capacity was funded out of the government budget and carried out according to the central plan by separate enterprises that on completion turned the investment over to the producing enterprise.

This centrally planned command system is capable in theory of producing a consistent set of targets that provide the individual enterprises with the inputs they need to meet the plan production targets for their enterprise. For this to happen in practice, however, the central planners have to collect enormous amounts of information about the specific conditions in each industry and each enterprise. Much of this information must be obtained from the enterprises themselves and those enterprises have an incentive to overstate the inputs needed to fulfill their output targets. Thus the system has a built-in tendency to use excessive inputs in production. To prevent this, the central planners typically adjust the information they get from the industries and enterprises, reducing the inputs requested or increasing the output targets for a given level of inputs. By this method they hope to pressure the enterprises to use the inputs more efficiently.

Even in an economic system where all enterprises have sophisticated means for collecting the required information, therefore, there are going to be input and output targets that will be inaccurate. One result in all systems of this type is that enterprises accumulate much larger inventories than would typically be the case when distribution and production are governed by market forces.

The Command System in Operation in 1956–1957

When the centrally planned command system was more or less fully implemented in 1955 and 1956, China's industrial economy was a far cry from the conditions ideally required for this system to operate efficiently. To begin with, the Chinese Communist Party leadership required that virtually all positions of authority be held either by members of the Party or by others with loyalty to the Party. The major sources of such people were institutions such as the Eighth Route Army that had won the revolution. But whatever their skill in warfare, few members of these core Party-supporting institutions had much experience with a modern industrial economy. Most were originally from the countryside and had little formal education.

A survey in 1955 found that only 5.73 percent of the top leadership in industrial enterprises had a university-level education or its equivalent. The situation was better with respect to the engineering and technical personnel in the enterprises, where 56.03 percent had a university education or its equivalent.[2] But China in 1955 had 125,000 industrial enterprises, of which perhaps 30,000 were classified as medium- or large-scale. Medium- or large-scale firms, however averaged less than 300 workers per enterprise. The other 90,000-plus firms averaged around fifteen workers each.[3] The engineers available in China by 1956 were drawn from roughly 170,000 who graduated after 1948 together with the roughly 70,000 graduates educated before 1949, many of whom did not remain in China.[4] One survey in 1955 indicated that there were only 32,000 engineers in China in that year, although one suspects that the definition of what constituted an engineer in this survey differed from the definition of an engineering graduate. The number of graduates before and after 1949 in "economics and finance" and in "science" was much smaller. Furthermore, the quality of many of these graduates was not particularly high. Many had fewer than four years of training and the training, at least after 1949, tended to be narrow and geared to immediate job requirements. Engineers, scientists, and economists, of course, also played an important role in many areas other than industry. It is not likely, therefore, that even the 30,000 large and medium firms averaged more than three or four university graduates each, and most of the small firms had none.

Given this situation, it is not surprising that the quality of the central planning effort was not very high. The relationship between plan targets and actual production for a limited number of high-priority industries is presented in Table 16.1.

---

[2] *Tongji gongzuo tongxun* 统计工作通讯 (Statistical Work Report), "The Breakdown and Organization of the Number of Workers and Employees in Our Country in 1955," 新华半月刊 (Xinhua Semi-monthly), January 25, 1957, 89.

[3] These figures were derived from various official Chinese sources in D.H. Perkins, *Market Control and Planning in Communist China* (Cambridge, MA, Harvard University Press, 1966), Table 9, p. 109.

[4] These data were derived from the graduation and enrollment rates for engineering and other graduates of universities and equivalent institutions before and after 1949 in L. Orleans, *Professional Manpower and Education in Communist China* (Washington, DC, National Science Foundation, 1961), pp. 68–9, 74–5.

Table 16.1 Annual plan completion record (% of plan target)

	1953	1954	1955	1956	1957
Steel	143.2	164.9		96.9	169.5
Electricity	112.9	134.2		161.4	121.1
Cement	210.8	208.7		105	112.7
Coal		197.8		108.1	284.2
Petroleum	103.9	163.7		83.8	87.5
Cotton yarn	148.1	193.5		113.3	97.6
Paper	785.7	185.7		135.3	
Sugar		38.8		32.3	
Cigarettes		30.1		36.2	

Source: the data on plan targets and their realization come mainly from the reports of ministers such as Bo Yibo and Li Fujun; see Dwight H. Perkins, "Industrial Planning and Management," in Alexander Eckstein, Walter Galenson, and Ta-chung Liu (eds.), *Economic Trends in Communist China* (Chicago, Aldine Publishing, 1968), Table 3, p. 611

That the government was able to implement central planning at this early stage of development was no doubt made easier by the fact that only certain key sectors followed through on the full plan process. The number of plan targets and input–output coefficients required was only a tiny fraction of what was required for Soviet Union plans. Many other sectors received some plan guidance but most of these small enterprises used simple machinery to produce farm tools or other household goods or processed raw materials such as oil seeds available locally. In these cases there was not much need to plan and co-ordinate their inputs and allocate them through the state distribution system. But where co-ordination of inputs and outputs with other industries was necessary, getting the input and output plan targets was made especially difficult by the fact that costs and the vintages of machinery in firms in many industries varied widely.

The Eighth Party Congress of the Chinese Communist Party in September 1956 was the occasion for the Party and government to modify this Soviet-type centrally planned command system to better fit the reality of the Chinese economy. The key speech was that by Chen Yun, who became minister of commerce in the fall of 1956 but more importantly was the leading economics figure in the Party.[5] In that speech Chen recognized the backward and small-scale nature of much of the industrial and commercial sectors. For

---

[5] This speech, "New Issues since the Basic Completion of the Socialist Transformation," is available in N. Lardy and K. Lieberthal, *Chen Yun's Strategy for China's Development: A Non-Maoist Alternative* (Armonk, NY, M.E. Sharpe, 1983), pp. 7–22.

the smaller-scale enterprises he recognized that many did not require co-ordination through a national plan or distribution through state distribution enterprises. Many probably did not even keep the kind of records that the central plan required, nor did they have the capacity to do so. Much of the statistical information collected from these smaller firms "turned out to be useless." By forcing all products to be purchased and sold by the state system, there was the real prospect that incentives would be generated that led to the neglect of many smaller products. Prices for these smaller items needed to reflect market conditions, and that was best accomplished by allowing producers to sell directly through local markets.

Large-scale enterprises and essential products, however, were to be strictly controlled by the plan and distributed through the state system. Chen, however, cautioned against the practice of some officials of simply combining a number of small enterprises in order to create larger enterprises. Artificial mergers of this sort where no economies of scale were present would undermine efficiency, not enhance it. Chen Yun was a supporter of planning but only for the most important and largest industrial sectors where he believed planning could be implemented efficiently. Given the primitive state of much of China's industry, it was far better to allow much of the rest of the economy to continue to be co-ordinated by markets. Establishing the centrally planned command system as the leading component of the economy but using market forces to supplement the plan, particularly in the distribution of many consumer products, was to remain Chen Yun's basic position throughout his career, including into the first decade of the post-1978 reform era. By the 1980s, however, the nature of China's industrial economy was very different from what it had been in the 1950s. In 1956 Chen's views placed him among the most "liberal" or pragmatic economic leaders who best understood the role that market forces could play, whereas by the 1980s Chen came to be seen as a "conservative" blocking moves toward a full market economy.

The state also took over internal management of the enterprises. A central issue in this area was the relationship between the plant manager, who in principle controlled daily production decisions and was more of a technocrat, and the enterprise Party secretary, who, also in principle, was supposed to ensure that the enterprise carried out the goals of the Party. The division of authority between these two figures would be a central issue throughout the pre-1978 period. During periods when major political campaigns dominated Chinese society, Party and political campaign goals typically dominated technocratic considerations, but 1956 and early 1957 were a period when pragmatic management considerations played a central role.

The state also replaced worker and manager wages set by market forces with wages set by the state. Urban worker wages were based on an eight-grade system where each grade in the mid-1950s was roughly a bit over 20 percent higher than the previous grade, with the top grade being roughly three times the lowest grade. There were other similar systems for management and technical personnel. This system, like central planning in other areas, was largely in place throughout the country by 1955 and 1956 and was patterned after similar wage structures in the Soviet Union. China also relied heavily on piece-work wages in 1955–1957. The main role of wages was to give workers incentive to work hard and develop their skills. In addition to wages, workers received a number of other benefits in kind. Housing and medical insurance, for example, were supplied by the enterprise. Higher-ranking personnel might receive larger apartments and other perquisites, such as access to an automobile for a limited few at the top of the enterprise.

Wages in China played little role in the allocation of labor. In this respect the situation in China was very different from that in the Soviet Union. Where the Soviet Union had a shortage of labor, China had a large surplus of unskilled labor based mainly in the countryside but ready to migrate to the cities when allowed. In the Soviet Union labor was largely free to move from one job to the next and migration from rural areas to the cities was actively encouraged in part through wage policies. In China, in contrast, skilled labor, particularly engineers and other highly skilled personnel, was directly allocated to jobs by the state. Changing employment from one enterprise to another was difficult and could mainly only be done with the permission of the enterprise one was leaving. An informal system developed that was still in place in the 1970s where a person wishing to transfer employment in one city to another city would attempt to trade his position with a worker in a similar position in the desired new location by posting a description of his position and his contact information on a local billboard or telephone pole.

The issue with unskilled workers was different. There the problem was that there were too many more than willing to migrate to jobs in the cities. As early as 1955 the government began taking steps to limit migration from the rural areas to the cities and to remove people from the cities who were not employed. The 1956 wage reform exacerbated the migration problem by raising the bottom wage as well as higher wages to levels that increased the incentive to migrate to the cities. In early 1958, in order to discourage migration, the government lowered the wage at the bottom end of the eight-grade system, making it roughly equal to the income of rural workers in each area plus a cost-of-living differential.

The situation in rural areas with respect to central planning was fundamentally different from that in the cities. The government did draw up plans for agriculture specifying such things as the sown area to be planted in a given crop and the level of production expected. There were also targets for the amount of the crop that was to be sold to the state purchasing enterprises. Planning for the 110 million farm families that existed in the 1950s was clearly impossible but the organization of these families into a million agricultural producer co-operatives made some degree of central direction seem feasible at least to some. However, there was enormous variation in the quality and quantity of land between co-operatives and the suitability of that land for particular crops. Adding to differences in land quality (and the many dimensions of quality that included location and topography) were variations in weather across regions and within regions from one day to the next. Then there was the fact that some farmers were more skilled or worked harder than others. To top things off there were even less reliable data on these conditions than was the case in small-scale industrial firms.

A centrally planned command system in agriculture, therefore, was never really implemented. There were efforts in the direction of such a system on the part of some cadres but again it was the voice of Chen Yun in 1956 and no doubt earlier that injected basic reason into the guidance given to agriculture. State direction with respect to crop production mainly took the form of efforts to establish quotas for the state purchase of a portion of the major crops produced. These quotas were backed up with price policies designed to ensure that co-operatives were sufficiently rewarded for their sales to make the sales at least to some degree voluntary. For large numbers of farm products such as vegetables and hogs, however, even that level of state guidance was impossible. Given the lack of refrigeration both in the countryside and in the cities, vegetables had to get from farm to market in a day or risk arriving spoiled. Hogs required personal care in the Chinese context that could only be appropriately managed by individuals or families, not even by the co-operative leadership and certainly not by a central planner. For these products families had their small private plots and local markets on which to sell their produce.

In China, unlike in the Soviet Union, the agricultural surplus available to the cities was not very large and the growing rural population (at 2 percent per year in the 1950s) meant that increasing production was essential. There was a genuine belief that the agricultural producer co-operatives would be a means for accelerating growth in agricultural output as well as the surplus available to the cities. The Chinese Communist Party may not have had many members with experience in modern urban industries, but it did have experience in the rural areas and with issues of agricultural production. Mao Zedong himself, unlike some of the other top leaders, grew up in a rural setting in Hunan province.

The logic behind the belief that co-operatives could be a vehicle for accelerating production growth rested on several basic ideas. One was the traditional practice of mobilizing rural labor to build rural infrastructure, notably to expand and improve irrigation systems. In the nineteenth century and much earlier, large-scale rural works could be built almost entirely by mobilizing rural labor to move large amounts of dirt and rock to form irrigation ponds, canals, and roads. Much of this mobilization in earlier times involved a degree of coercion because the largest beneficiaries of these efforts were the owners of land, but it was the tenants on this land, at least in the southern half of the country, that did most of the work. With the formation of co-operatives the increase in income resulting from construction by mobilized labor went to the whole co-operative rather than to landlords and rich peasants and that in turn raised the value of each work point earned. The incentive to participate in rural construction efforts was thus enhanced and the need for coercion by the co-operative leadership reduced.

The other main economic reason why the co-operative form was seen as a vehicle for increasing production started from the view that peasant farmers tended to be very conservative when it came to using new technology and new plant varieties. There was a good reason for this conservatism. Experimentation with a new technology that failed, leading the farmer's crop to fail, could mean that the farmer's family had nothing to eat until the next year's harvest. This is a problem throughout farming in low-income countries and it also limited the willingness of farmers in these countries to rely heavily on the market. Most farm families thus tried to raise enough grain to feed their families even if their land would normally produce more income by planting the fields with a crop such as cotton all of which would be sold on the market. With co-operatives, the leadership cadres could be ordered to carry out the use of new technologies that central planners and agricultural research labs believed would improve crop yields.

There were other barriers to increasing production that some in China believed co-operatives could help overcome. With family-based farming, plots of land tended to be small and often got even smaller when the death of the family head led the land to be further divided among the male heirs. Potentially offsetting all of these advantages, of course, was the fact that pooling of land and rewarding individuals and families with work points provided a weaker incentive to work hard and with skill than did family-owned farms where reward for effort and skill were directly related to the income the family received without any intermediate process such as the work point system. In addition, decision making, at least for major crops and collective construction activities, moved from the household head to the leadership of the co-operatives. This might have improved decision making over such things as labor allocation if the senior cadres had been more skilled managers and more knowledgeable about the land and the crops than most household heads. Selection of the senior cadres, however, was based on criteria that placed a heavy emphasis on loyalty to the Communist Party.

These were potential benefits, but were they actually realized in practice? The agricultural production growth rate, whether measured as gross value of output or as value added, was much the same in 1956–1957 (4.7 percent to 4.4 percent, 3.8 percent to 3.9 percent) and in the years immediately preceding the nationwide establishment of agricultural producer co-operatives. This in itself is a considerable achievement given the kind of disruption that often occurs with a fundamental restructuring of ownership and management of a rural economy. The number of hectares affected by natural disasters was also somewhat higher in 1957 than in earlier years.

Data published in the 1950s indicate that there was a large increase in the area under irrigation in 1956 and 1957, implying that labor mobilization had made effective use of rural surplus labor. From 1953 through 1955, irrigated acreage increased by an average of 1.25 million hectares per year. In 1956, according to these data, the irrigated acreage jumped by 7.9 million hectares, and in 1957 it rose by another 2.9 million hectares.[6] According to data published in the 1950s, the total area under irrigation was 34.7 million hectares in 1957, whereas data published in the early 1980s after the long statistical blackout estimated that total irrigated acreage in 1957 had been 27.3 million hectares, 7.4 million hectares lower than the earlier estimate.[7] The total area in the country irrigated by power (for pumps) in that year was only 1.2 million hectares. It is likely that the estimates of irrigated acreage in 1957 were from

---

[6] N.R. Chen, *Chinese Economic Statistics* (Chicago, Aldine, 1967), p. 289. The original data came from Guojia tongjiju 国家统计局 (National Statistical Office), *Ten Great Years*, p. 130.

[7] Guojia tongjiju 国家统计局 (National Statistical Office), *Statistical Yearbook of China 1981* (Hong Kong, Information and Agency, 1982), p. 185.

reports by local officials based on varying criteria. These optimistic reports may have had an influence on the senior leadership and on Mao Zedong in particular in their decisions with respect to agriculture in 1958.

The situation with respect to improvements in technology may also have been subject to local biases. The area planted to improved grain crop varieties, for example, rose from 20.6 percent of the total sown acreage in grain in 1955 to 36.4 percent in 1956 and 55.2 percent in 1957, an increase of 42.3 million hectares. Grain production in 1957, however, only rose by 6 percent over 1955, suggesting that a liberal definition was given to what constituted an improved grain variety. A more concrete example of technological change that failed to achieve expected gains is the country's experience with the double-wheeled double-bladed plow. These plows had worked well in a number of areas in 1954 and 1955 and the authorities concluded that every well-equipped co-operative should have a supply of these plows. At considerable cost to other priorities, they raised the plow production quota from 400,000 a year to at first 5 million plows, then cut that target back to 2 million plows. It turned out, however, that the plows were completely unsuitable for large areas of the country. By 1956, 1.2 million plows had actually been produced but only 800,000 of those had been sold and 40 to 50 percent of those sold were not being used.[8]

Finally there is the issue of how macroeconomic policies were managed in China once the Soviet-type economic system was in place. Under the centrally planned command system, achievement of price stability, balance-of-payments equilibrium, and employment growth was handled very differently from the methods used in a market economy.

The major macroeconomic issue in China in the 1950s was price stability. Employment growth, meaning urban employment growth, was largely governed by the level and type of investment, and that was the responsibility of the State Planning Commission. It was the State Planning Commission that determined the level and sectoral allocation of that investment using administrative (as contrasted to market) mechanisms. The level of investment outside the agricultural sector was largely determined by the excess of government revenue over its recurrent expenditures (household savings in the 1950s were small). That excess was in turn determined mostly by the profits and taxes paid by state enterprises (82 percent of revenue in 1956). Those state enterprise profits and taxes were determined by the prices from

---

[8] The account of the double-wheeled double-bladed plow appeared first in "Why There Is a Stopping of Production and an Obstruction of Sales of the Double-Wheeled Double-Bladed Plows," 计划经济 (Economic Planning), September 23, 1956, 1–4.

their sales minus the prices of their inputs (including wages). These industrial input and output prices were set by the state, with output prices deliberately set at a high level to generate more revenue.

Prices played no role in the allocation of inputs or in the State Planning Commission decisions concerning output targets.[9] Enterprise demand for inputs often exceeded supply but there was little pressure on input prices because enterprises could not use money to purchase additional inputs. There was no market on which to buy these inputs. If an enterprise desired more of a given input, it could lobby the State Planning Commission to give the enterprise a larger allocation or it could trade some of its excess inputs with another enterprise that had a surplus of the needed input. When an input was allocated to the enterprise, the enterprise did have to pay money for that input, but if the enterprise did not have the necessary funds, the central bank, the People's Bank of China, would lend the necessary funds without charging interest. The financial aspects of these transactions were mainly accounting devices having little role in determining what was produced. The central bank was thus a passive supplier of funds in support of the central plan. If the plan called for a particular allocation, the central bank had to finance it when needed. This passive role for the central bank would periodically become an issue in the pre-1978 period and was a source of inflation in the post-1978 reform period. It was also a major element in what has been called the "soft budget constraint."[10] State enterprises did not face hard budgets that forced financial discipline. That discipline was supposed to be provided by the state planners.

Maintaining balance-of-payments equilibria was controlled by the central planners in an even more straightforward way that eliminated most market forces. Enterprises were not allowed to deal directly with foreign customers. Enterprise output destined for foreign markets and purchase orders for foreign inputs were turned over to state trading companies that negotiated with the foreign suppliers. These negotiations could be with individual trading companies, as occurred at the annual Canton Trade Fairs, or could be part of country-to-country or country-to-trading-group

---

[9] The State Planning Commission did, to a limited degree, have to take the level of demand for consumer goods into account in setting prices. However, consumer prices could be and were made higher by limiting the amount of such goods available and the decision on the level of output of consumer goods was controlled directly by the State Planning Commission.

[10] The "soft budget constraint" term was originally used by János Kornai and refers to the fact that state enterprises in a centrally planned command system typically faced few pressures to use inputs efficiently.

negotiations. The state trading companies, when dealing with individual companies for the most part, would buy and sell at international prices. The state-set prices used to sell to or buy from the domestic producing enterprise typically had no relation to the international price.

There were also few capital movements into or out of China that the government had to deal with. There was no stock market in China and hence no portfolio investment. Foreign direct investment was prohibited except for a few projects supplied by the Soviet Union, and the trading enterprises and domestic enterprises could not borrow from abroad. Thus China had a modest level of foreign trade (in 1956 and 1957 exports plus imports equaled 10.4 percent of GDP as contrasted to 29.8 percent in 1990 after a decade or more of open trade and 40 percent in 2000). The domestic economy, however, was largely cut off from any influence on prices or production from the international economy. The exchange rate for *renminbi* could be set at any level the planners desired since it had no influence on trade. The central planners could plan the domestic economy without paying much attention to international economic forces except for when they set export and import targets for particular enterprises.

The restriction on foreign direct investment, together with the tight control of foreign trade that involved little effort to promote exports, meant that China had to follow one other characteristic of the Soviet-type economic system: the emphasis in the industrial sector needed to be focused on producer-goods industry if the country wanted to grow. Even in the First Five-Year Plan period (1953–1957), export earnings were only 5 percent of GDP and were an even lower 4 percent in the Fourth Five-Year Plan period (1971–1975). An investment rate of 30 percent would thus have to supply domestic investment goods for 25 of that 30 percent. A strategy of producing a large surplus of textiles and other consumer goods and then exporting them for the large share of the investment goods required was not possible. This relationship between industrial strategy and limited foreign trade was well recognized by Soviet theorists, notably Yevgeny Preobrazhensky, and was presumably understood by Chinese planners.

In this system achieving price stability became mainly a matter of ensuring that the incomes of the households did not exceed the availability of consumer goods in both rural and urban areas. In rural areas this meant ensuring that there were enough industrial goods produced to soak up income earned from the sale of grain and other crops and rural handicrafts. In urban areas the challenge was to keep wage growth more or less equal to the growth of industrial consumer goods plus the supply of food products from the countryside. The central bank had no real role in this process. Price stability was mainly in the hands of the central planners. As pointed out above, the task of the central planners was further simplified by the fact that China had a surplus of labor that eliminated pressure on unskilled wages and through that on prices. Enterprises did not compete for skilled labor through wage increases either, because skilled labor was not free to move to alternative employment.

The Transition from Pragmatic Planning to the Great Leap Forward

The first six or more years of Communist Party rule had transformed a rural peasant economy with a veneer of modern industry and services relying on market forces to an economy dominated by collective agriculture and a state-directed urban economy that rejected market forces in favor of state administrative directives. It was a radical change that involved considerable violence and economic disruption, but the Chinese economy continued to recover and grow throughout. The period from mid-1956 through the middle of 1957 was in sense a period of consolidation and adjustments to the new kind of economic system that had been created, represented by Chen Yun's modifications of central planning discussed above. Mao Zedong's speech on the "Ten Major Relationships" at the Eighth Party Congress also appears to have accepted a more pragmatic approach to the country's political and economic challenges.[11]

This period of roughly a year was also accompanied in mid-1956 by a similar movement in the political sphere, the "Hundred Flowers" movement ("let a hundred flowers bloom, let a hundred schools of thought contend"). This movement may in part have been motivated by a desire for constructive criticism, but Mao Zedong was disturbed by Khrushchev's secret speech in 1956 denouncing Stalin, and the Hundred Flowers campaign could also be used to "draw snakes out of their holes," as Mao later said. The Hundred Flowers campaign did elicit a torrent of criticism of the government and the Party in early 1957. By the middle of 1957 the Hundred Flowers movement had given way to the Party Anti-Rightist rectification campaign

---

[11] This speech would be republished during the reform period after 1978 as an effort to show that Mao's views were not necessarily opposed to reform efforts of the kind then underway. Mao Zedong, "On the Ten Major Relationships," April 25, 1956, in *Selected Works of Mao Zedong*, vol. 5 (Beijing, People's Publishing House, 1977), pp. 272–6.

that involved purging many of the critics, and that rectification campaign created the political environment that would lead to the Great Leap Forward.

There were elements of the earliest phases of the Great Leap that did not have the irrational political campaign aspects of a few months later. The economic reform measures introduced at the Third Plenum of the Eighth Party Congress, also introduced by Chen Yun, called among other things for the transfer of many industrial, commercial, and financial functions from the central government in Beijing to lower government levels. The idea was that this would give local units more flexibility to take into account local conditions and exercise their own creativity.[12] In a different political context, this transfer could be seen as a continuation of the adjustments to the centrally planned command system that began in 1956. Beijing was in no position to understand the great diversity of conditions that existed in different areas of China and it lacked the information needed to make suitable adjustments to local conditions. Many of the goods and services produced by industry also did not need to have their inputs and outputs co-ordinated at the national level.

In the actual context following the purges of the Anti-Rightist campaign, this decentralization transferred wide authority over the economy to cadres who, whatever their personal beliefs, were going to demonstrate that they were not "rightist." They would try their best to do whatever Mao wanted them to do. Mao himself, who had apparently been inspired by Khrushchev's goal of surpassing the United States in fifteen years, called for China to surpass the United Kingdom in fifteen years. That later became passing the United Kingdom in three years and the United States in ten years. The question then became one of how to implement this ambitious goal. Mao, whatever his other strengths and weaknesses, was a master at mobilizing large numbers of followers in enthusiastic political campaigns, and the Great Leap became a political campaign on an unprecedented scale.

Formally the leading economic group of the Party still headed by Chen Yun and including all of the senior economics ministers brought a semblance of planned decentralization to the process. Thus in April of 1958 the State Council directed all enterprises belonging to ministries, except for a handful of particularly important ones, to be transferred down, often far down, to the various levels of local government. In 1958 only 13.8 percent of industrial output was under central control, down from 39.7 percent in 1957. In

---

[12] This discussion of the early phases of the Great Leap Forward is based to a large degree on J. Wu, *Understanding and Interpreting Chinese Economic Reforms* (Mason, OH, Thomson/South-Western, 2005), p. 44–7.

September 1957 planning was to a large degree transferred to local governments and those local governments were given considerable leeway to make their own plan targets. The number of categories of materials and equipment planned by the State Planning Commission was reduced from 530 in 1957 to 132 by 1959. Of particular significance, local governments were authorized in July 1958 to make their own investment plans.[13]

In the campaign spirit of the time the leading economic group of the Party by the middle of 1958 had become a figurehead and the local governments and enterprises were implementing a massive expansion in investment and employing millions of new state enterprise workers. Total investment in the three years from 1958 to 1960 averaged over 33 billion *renminbi* (RMB) per year, as contrasted to RMB 14.3 billion in 1957. The number of state enterprise workers rose from 24.5 million at the end of 1957 to 45.3 million by the end of 1958 and 59.7 million by the end of 1960. The urban population by 1960 was 30 million above the 99.5 million people of 1957.[14]

This was what was happening in what had been the more organized and planned part of the industrial economy. Mao also got the idea that China's labor surplus in both rural and urban areas could be mobilized to accelerate the growth of the country's iron and steel industry. Tens of thousands of small-scale iron and steel furnaces suddenly, with Mao's blessing, appeared throughout the nation. These furnaces could not produce iron or steel from iron ore, but they could melt down scrap iron and steel and make simple tools using locally made molds. On a modest scale this might have been a useful addition to the making of farm tools, for example. There were a few such furnaces that later made their way to the New Territories in Hong Kong and made simple parts for such things as flush toilets, and they were able to make a profit in capitalist Hong Kong.[15] On the massive scale that actually occurred, it ended up diverting resources to highly unproductive uses. There was not enough scrap metal to feed these small furnaces so local cadres began taking perfectly good iron and steel instruments and melting them down in order to show their enthusiasm for meeting their inflated targets.

None of this massive expansion in investment and personnel was co-ordinated to make sure that what was being produced would be useable or that the necessary inputs would be available. By the latter half of 1958 there was no longer much, if any, co-ordination by the planners. The enthusiasm

---

[13] Wu, *Understanding and Interpreting Chinese Economic Reforms*, pp. 46–7.
[14] Wu, *Understanding and Interpreting Chinese Economic Reforms*, p. 50.
[15] This statement is based on personal visits to one of these small-scale furnaces by the author in 1961–1962.

and loyalty of the local cadres was supposed to offset the abandonment of planning, but political enthusiasm is not a mechanism for co-ordinating inputs and outputs. The result throughout industry was chaos. The statistical authorities and the local cadres reporting statistics on their achievements made the situation even worse. The statistics reported soon had no relation to reality.

The situation in rural areas was comparable. The underlying logic of what became the rural people's commune movement was not wholly irrational. The agricultural producer co-operatives of 1956–1957 solved the problem of relating local construction projects carried out by co-operative labor to who received the benefits from these efforts. But the problem still existed at a larger level. If a construction project required labor from five or ten co-operatives, but the project disproportionally benefited one or two of those co-operatives, then the incentive problem for the co-operatives that did not benefit remained. This problem could be solved by creating a much larger collective unit.

The rural people's commune was invented locally in Henan province. In August 1958 Mao Zedong visited the experimental Qiliying Rural People's Commune in northern Henan where a number of co-operatives had been formed into a single production unit and such vestiges of a market economy as private plots were abolished. Mao said that the experimental commune was "good" and that was apparently sufficient for the Party and government to launch a campaign to convert all of the co-operatives into communes. That started a competitive process among the country's rural cadres to form communes. The process of consolidation was completed before the year was over. Where the 700,000 agricultural producer co-operatives had averaged around 200 families each, the 26,000 communes averaged from 4,000 to 5,000 families each. In principle, management of crop production was to remain with a subunit of the commune, the brigade, which was roughly comparable to the previous co-operative. In practice rural cadres in general and the commune leadership in particular were under enormous pressure to produce dramatic results not only in crop production, but also in rural construction. By the winter of 1958–1959 rural China was engulfed in the largest movement to physically reconstruct the countryside in the history of the world. Hundreds of millions of farmers and their families moved massive amounts of dirt and rock to build dams and irrigation systems, to smooth uneven crop land, and much else.

The demands on the time of all rural adults for this construction work inevitably interfered with work on crops and other farm products. Vegetables and hogs were the first to decline sharply because these were produced on the private plots and sold on the market and both private plots and these markets had been abolished. The commune leadership, much like the national leadership, was focused on producing more grain and more cotton. In the words of Mao, grain was to be taken as the "key link" in agriculture (and steel was the key link in industry). There were adjustments as early as 1959 to restore limited private plots in an effort to support vegetable production. Decentralization of statistical reporting to the local level, combined with enormous political pressures on local cadres to show dramatic results, however, led to massive falsification of data. As a result, few in the leadership had any notion of the crisis that was building in the countryside (or in industry). The relatively good weather and resulting good harvest of 1958 further obscured the emerging crisis. Mao himself, for example, in mid-1958 was thinking about what to do with the large grain surplus.[16] China exported 41.6 million tons of grain in 1959, nearly 18 million tons above the annual average grain exports of 1955–1958,[17] despite the fact that grain production in 1959 was falling by 28 million tons (Table 16.2). Purchases of grain from farmers rose from an average of 44.6 million tons a year in 1955–1957 to 51.8 million tons in 1958 and 64.1 million tons in 1959.[18]

There was an attempt by Minister of Defense Peng Dehuai at the Eighth Plenum of the Eighth Party Congress in mid-1959 held on Lushan to recognize the magnitude of the disaster that was emerging. Mao purged him for his efforts and that ended any real resistance to Mao's desire to keep the Great Leap Forward going well into 1960 with only minor adjustments. Data reconstructed by the National Statistical Office many years later during the post-1978 reform period make clear that the 1959 grain harvest involved a sharp drop of 14 percent and the 1960 harvest was another 15 percent below that of 1959 for a two-year fall in output of 27 percent (Table 16.1). The fall in subsidiary farm products such as vegetables and pork was undoubtedly much larger but the data needed to estimate their decline probably do not exist.

The decline in industry lagged behind that in agriculture. Substantial parts of the initial increases in industrial output in 1958 and 1959 were real in that they reflected the fact that China had begun a number of large industrial investment projects in the mid-1950s, many with Soviet assistance, that were destined to go into production in those years. That said, there was enormous

---

[16] Wu, *Understanding and Interpreting Chinese Economic Reforms*, p. 50.
[17] National Statistical Office, *Statistical Yearbook of China 1981*, p. 372.
[18] Guojia tongjiju 国家统计局 (National Statistical Office), 历史统计资料汇编 (Compilation of Historical Statistics) *1949–1989* (Mason, OH, China Statistics Press, 2005), p. 26.

Table 16.2 *Impact of the Great Leap Forward on the economy*

	1956	1957	1958	1959	1960	1961	1962	1963
GDP (index 1952 = 100)	148.1	155.6	188.6	205.3	204.6	148.7	140.4	154.7
Primary value added (index 1952 = 100)	117	120.6	121.1	101.9	85.2	86.5	90.4	100.6
Gross value of agricultural output (index 1952 = 100))	121.9	128.7	131.9	113.9	99.5	97.1	103.2	115.2
Grain (million tons)	192.7	195	197.7	169.7	143.8	136.5	154.4	170
Cotton million tons)	1.445	1.64	1.969	1.709	1.063	0.803	0.75	1.2
Oil seeds (million tons)	5.086	4.196	4.77	4.104	1.941	1.814	2.003	2.458
Secondary value added (index 1952 = 100)	227.3	245.5	375.4	472.3	498.6	288.8	257.8	295.2
Steel (million tons)	4.47	5.35	8	13.87	18.66	8.7	6.67	7.62
Cement (million tons)	6.39	6.86	9.3	12.27	15.65	6.21	6	8.06
Electric power (billion kWh)	16.6	19.3	27.5	42.3	59.4	48	45.8	49
Cloth (billon meters)	5.77	5.05	6.46	7.57	5.45	3.11	2.53	3.34
Exports (billion US$)	1.65	1.6	1.98	2.26	1.86	1.49	1.49	1.65
Retail prices (index 1952 = 100)	119.5	121.3	121.6	122.7	126.5	147	152.6	143.6
Tax revenue (billion RMB)	14.09	15.49	18.74	20.47	20.37	15.89	16.21	16.43

Source: Guojia tongjiju 国家统计局 (National Statistical Office), 新中国六十年 (New China's Sixty Years) (Beijing, China Statistics Press, 2009), various years

waste of industrial resources in 1958 and chaotic construction of new and expanded enterprises. In 1960 the Soviet Union also abruptly withdrew the 1,400 specialists and technicians that it had in China, some of whom were probably supporting the new industrial projects. This removed one more influence on the side of rational planning and management and helped precipitate the sharp decline in industry that occurred in 1961.

The full nature of the crisis and the famine that resulted is the subject of a separate chapter in this volume and so will not be discussed further here. By 1960 the economy was in shambles, famine was beginning that was to lead to tens of millions of premature deaths, and rule by the Communist Party was threatened, or so it was widely perceived.

From Recovery to the Cultural Revolution, 1961–1964

The main task from late 1960 and for the next few years was to bring order to the economy and rapid recovery. Mao largely withdrew from direct involvement in this recovery effort and returned to his focus on "class struggle" – the struggle to inculcate values in the Chinese people that would prevent the restoration of bourgeois values. President and second in command Liu Shaoqi took overall charge of the recovery. Chen Yun was restored to a leading position in the design of economic matters. Mao would later claim that both Liu and Deng Xiaoping were ignoring him during this period. Mao's major concern was political but that concern did involve him in defending the Great Leap as having accomplished more good than bad. That view contrasted with that of many senior people in the party who had a much more negative view. Class struggle also meant making sure that the efforts at recovery did not go too far and undermine Mao's view of what constituted a true socialist society and economy. A true socialist economy, in his view, did not have much, if any, place for either markets or material incentives. In 1961 through early 1963, however, there was a brief interlude in which a more open debate was encouraged and in which the prominent economist Sun Yefang, for example, advocated for substantial enterprise autonomy that presumably would have required a reduced role for central planning and an increased role for market forces. That period of open debate ended in 1963 when the Socialist Education Movement got underway.[19]

The most urgent task in 1961 was to restore agricultural production and end the famine. To that end the massive rural construction effort was scaled back. The communes, with their three-tier structure (commune, brigade, and production team), continued to exist but the management of crop production was passed down and would eventually reside at the level of the production team until the late 1970s. In the early 1960s, however, there were also areas that applied what was labeled the "responsibility system" and that often involved turning production over to individual families. The "household responsibility system" was to reappear again in the first years of the reform period (1979–1983), at which time it led to the total elimination of the commune system, replacing it throughout the country with household-based production. It is unlikely that there was any such intent in the early 1960s, however, given Mao's opposition to anything that ended socialism in the countryside. It was probably mainly an attempt to let the poorest rural farmers do whatever they thought was necessary to survive. The responsibility system of the early 1960s, however, became one of the principal charges

[19] This brief discussion of the political background during the recovery years draws on the much more complete and nuanced discussion in A. Walder, *China under Mao: A Revolution Derailed* (Cambridge, MA, Harvard University Press, 2015); and R. MacFarquhar and M. Schoenhals, *Mao's Last Revolution* (Cambridge, MA, Harvard University Press, 2006).

brought against Liu Shaoqi and Deng Xiaoping in the first phases of the Cultural Revolution.

Private plots and limited free markets, as already indicated, had begun to be restored even earlier. To relieve pressure on farm families further, the government began to import substantial quantities of grain (mainly wheat) from abroad. Prior to 1961 China had exported over 20 million tons of grain a year and it still exported 10 million tons in the famine year of 1961. There were almost no imports of grain prior to 1961. In 1961, however, the government imported 5.8 million tons and kept importing grain on average at that level into the early 1970s (at which point grain imports rose even further).[20] These imports were mainly destined for consumption by urban residents, but they made it possible to reduce the purchase and tax quotas for farmers by roughly 10 percent.[21] In actuality, grain purchases averaged 35.3 million tons in 1961–1963, down 21 percent from the 1955–1957 average.[22] "Means of subsistence," which included grain but also other necessities for consumption, rose from a minuscule 5 to 8 percent of total imports in 1953 through 1960 to 38 percent in 1961 and an average of 44 percent in 1962–1964.[23]

Recovery in agriculture, however, was not rapid. Production of major crops was still well below the level of the pre-Great Leap period (1955–1957). The gross value of agricultural output has been estimated to have recovered to the level of 1955, although it is not clear how that figure was arrived at given the performance of major crops. Population, however, had also risen by 12.5 percent over that time so per capita output was still down from the pre-Leap level even if one accepts the gross-value estimate.

Serious malnutrition resulting in famine ended but that may have had as much to do with restoration of order in the transportation and statistical reporting systems. Famine in China throughout its history had more to do with the distribution of food, mainly grain, than it did with the level of production. Production failures in the past were often confined to small areas. When the imperial government was well run, the emperor regularly received reports on grain prices. Local grain price spikes were a good indication of a crop failure and the government could use its "ever-normal granaries" to supply the stricken area. China in 1959–1961 was an example of

---

[20] National Statistical Office, *Statistical Yearbook of China 1981*, p. 388.
[21] Grain purchase plus tax quotas in 1955–1956 and 1957–1958 averaged 62.5 million tons a year, although some of the agricultural tax quota was not paid in kind in grain. Perkins, *Market Control and Planning in Communist China*, p. 44.
[22] National Statistical Office, 历史统计资料汇编, p. 26.
[23] National Statistical Office, *Statistical Yearbook of China 1981*, p. 358.

a government where a modern version of this system had ceased to exist. The information reaching the top was falsified on a grand scale and the transportation system was busy with other priorities. The statistical system, along with a number of other government functions, however, was recentralized in 1962, including banking and finance, making it possible to gain an understanding of the food disaster and to use the transportation system to restore transport to the worst-affected areas.

Restoration of the industrial sector was somewhat more rapid than in agriculture. Basically the industrial planning and management system was restored to the system as it had existed in 1957 but with the decentralization started in 1958 still intact. A large share of industry was to be planned and inputs and outputs co-ordinated at provincial, county, and even lower levels, and that practice lasted until the first major industrial reform effort of the post-1978-reform period (which began in 1984). Only industrial sectors of critical importance were planned and co-ordinated at the national level. The official statistics for the early 1960s indicate that industry not only recovered to pre-Great Leap levels, but output by 1966 was more than double the level of 1957. This is not surprising because much new capacity was installed in Chinese industry both in the years just preceding the Great Leap and during the first phases of the Great Leap itself.

Employment in industry, however, did not recover to pre-Great Leap levels. Employment in urban areas in 1958–1960 nearly doubled from 32 million to 61 million workers and employees. The restrictions that had been designed prior to the Great Leap to ensure that rural-to-urban migration would be related to planned employment targets completely broke down and the urban population rose from 99.5 million in 1957 to 130.7 million in 1960. In the context of 1961–1965, this increase in employment was no longer needed as industry and urban services output fell sharply.

Rather than continue to support this inflated urban population, the government instead took steps to reduce that population as rapidly as possible. Employment in urban areas fell by 15 million by 1962 and 14 million were forced to return to the countryside by that year. The policies used to make this transfer back to the countryside remained in force until the early 1980s. They were draconian. To begin with, all households were registered as either urban or rural residents, the so-called *hukou* system. It was illegal to reside in urban areas unless one had an urban *hukou*. Enforcement of this restriction involved several elements. Enterprises wishing to hire additional workers were required to work through government employment agencies and the employment agencies were required to draw from the registered urban population for the most part.

Rural residents wanting to migrate had to first get the permission of their commune's leadership in order to leave legally. If they managed to get to an urban area, they had to apply to the local Public Security Bureau for a stay of over twenty-four hours. There were local residents throughout the cities charged with reporting any strangers appearing to be staying without permission. If the rural-to-urban migrant still managed to stay, that migrant faced the problem of how to get sufficient food and other necessities. Most necessities, including grain and edible oils, were rationed and could only be obtained with ration coupons no matter how much money one had.

This system in effect created a two-class system that persisted in China into the twenty-first century. Its impact in the 1960s through to 1978 was to hold China's urban population far below what it would likely have been if people had been free to migrate. The data in Figure 16.1 show that both urban population and urban employment peaked in 1960 and fell sharply in 1962. They both stayed low in 1963 and then began rising in 1964. The urban population had a particularly large increase in 1964 but this jump was probably an upward revision by the statistical authorities resulting from the 1964 population census (the first census since 1953). The population and many other statistics in 1958–1963 must have been educated guesses by the statistical authorities given the chaos of 1958–1961, not least in the statistical offices themselves.

From 1964 on, urban employment grew at a rate similar to the fairly rapid growth of 1953–1957 (5.0 percent 1965–1978 versus 5.2 percent 1953–1957), but annual urban population growth fell to 2.1 percent as compared to 6.8 percent during the more liberal rural-to-urban migration period of 1953–1957. Urban population growth in the 1960s and 1970s came almost entirely from the natural increase of urban residents. Migration from the countryside was negligible. The high growth in urban employment in the 1960s and 1970s was made possible mainly by the employment of urban women. In 1957 women made up only 13.5 percent of workers and employees (those employed and receiving wages mostly in urban areas) but in 1979–1980 they made up 48.4 percent of the industrial workforce and over half of most of the services workforce.[24]

---

[24] The figures presented here for 1979–1980 are not entirely comparable to those for 1957 but they do clearly support the view that the employment of urban women during the period of tight restrictions on migration from the countryside was very large. See N.-R. Chen, *Chinese Economic Statistics: A Handbook for Mainland China* (Chicago, Aldine, 1967), p. 473 (the original source was National Statistical Office, *Ten Great Years*); and National Statistical Office, *Statistical Yearbook of China 1981*, pp. 99–103. From 1965 through 1978 the number of women workers and staff in state enterprises (all enterprises were either state- or collective-owned) rose from 7.86 million to 21.26 million (Guojia tongjiju 国家统计局 (National Statistical Office), 中国劳动工资统计资料 1948–1945, (Statistics on Chinese Labour and Wages, 1948–1945), p. 32) and kept on rising

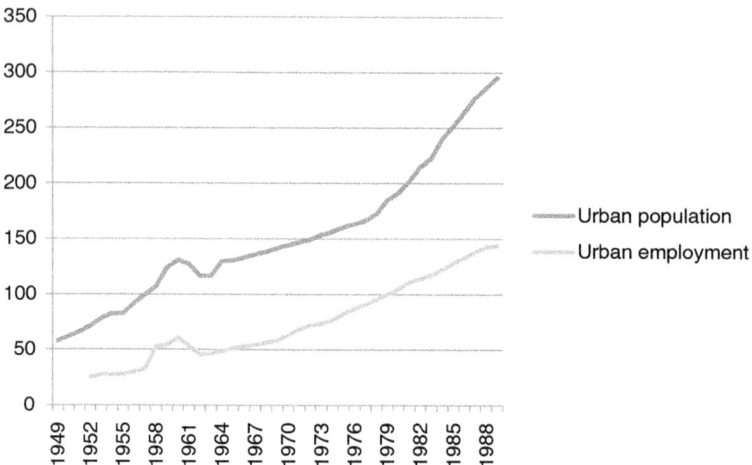

Figure 16.1 Urban population and employment growth 1952–1990 (millions)
Source: National Statistical Office, 新中国六十年, pp. 608–9

Another component of the Great Leap aftermath is that the government for a brief time lost control of prices. The official figures for the rise in retail prices in 1958 through 1964 are in Table 16.3. Again, given the collapse of the statistical systems, these are probably best-guess estimates of the statistical authorities. Because of the hyperinflation that helped bring the Communist Party to power in China, both the population and the Party have been very sensitive to increases in prices that most developing countries would consider to be quite modest. Even as late as 1988–1989 an annual average increase in consumer prices of 18 percent contributed to the political instability of those years. In 1961 an increase of 16 percent in the midst of the famine then underway must have contributed to the view that China was in a crisis and the actual rate may have been higher. As indicated earlier, China's main method for controlling inflation was to control the urban wage bill and the amount and prices of state-purchased agricultural crops. The crop failures sharply reduced the availability on the market of agricultural products and the chaos in industry reduced the availability of industrial consumer goods. Average wages had fallen as early as 1958 presumably because the large

---

in the 1980s and early 1990s (in all urban units), peaking at 58.9 million in 1995, but then began to decline after 1997 to only 41.6 million in 2002 (National Statistical Office, *China Statistical Yearbook*, 2003, p. 139).

Table 16.3 Wages and the urban cost of living (1957–1964)

	Urban cost of living index (previous year = 100)	Average urban money wage (yuan per year)
1957		571
1958	100.2	470
1959	100.9	430
1960	103.1	409
1961	116.2	380
1962	103.8	405
1963	94.1	371
1964	95.3	358

Source: National Statistical Office, 新中国六十年, pp. 610, 625

increase in the labor force occurred mostly at the low-skill end, but wages stayed down even after most of these unskilled migrants had been returned to the countryside. Wages stayed down through 1964 and then began to rise, but average nominal urban wages did not pass the level of 1957 until 1980, twenty-three years later. Consumer prices during 1965–1978, however, only rose at 0.2 percent per year, so the increase in urban wages of 2.5 percent a year over that same period was real even if it did not restore average wages to the 1957 level.

Clearly the government in 1962–1964 gave price stability a high priority and inflation was brought to an end quickly. Price stability, however, was bought at the cost of a decline in real average wages of 18 percent (from 1960 to 1962) and a far larger decline than that if one takes into account that the average wage in 1960 included 15 million low-skilled workers who had been returned to the countryside by 1962.

Economic Organization and Policies 1965–1978

With economic recovery achieved, China in 1965 drew up a Third Five-Year Plan (1966–1970). The regulations developed earlier to decentralize the planning and management of industry remained in place. The staff of the planning and implementation agencies, however, had lost most of their authority and so the plan was mostly on paper. Still, from that point on until well after the beginning of the reform period in 1978, the formal planning and management system for industry remained much the same. In 1971–1975 there was a Fourth Five-Year Plan. As in the 1950s there were annual plans that governed what was produced and distributed but did so within the broader guidelines of the five-year plans. That was the way the system was designed, but in reality the operation of this Soviet-type command system was modified in major ways by two other movements. The first of these was the Great Proletarian Cultural Revolution initiated by Mao in 1966 that among other things caused the collapse of the agencies responsible for planning. The second was the Third Front industrial development program created at much the same time to deal with the perceived growing military threat from both the United States and the Soviet Union.

The Cultural Revolution, unlike the Great Leap Forward, was initiated with political or "class struggle" ideological objectives. There was no specific economic content to these objectives and the movement did not make any major policy or organizational changes in the economic sphere. The movement, however, did have a major impact on the economy. To begin with, the first years, particularly 1967–1969, involved rising conflict between different factions of students and workers that at times resulted in pitched battles with military-style weapons. There was also the commandeering of passenger trains by students, "Red Guards," so that they could travel around the country fomenting "revolution." Those in positions of authority, including industrial plant managers, were attacked. Even high-priority military enterprises were not immune to Red Guard actions.[25] Anyone with a background that included international experience was particularly vulnerable. Unlike in the Great Leap Forward, however, the countryside, although not entirely immune, was less affected by the disruption.[26] Crops were planted and harvested and the production teams remained in charge of managing farm output. Private farm plots on which to raise vegetables continued to exist.

The disruption of the Red Guards was gradually brought to an end when the army was charged with the task of restoring order and ending the "civil war" between factions. The values inculcated during this first phase of the Cultural Revolution, however, did not disappear. There was a strong antiforeign element that had the effect until after 1976 of limiting efforts to promote foreign trade and import industrial complete plants and components. Powerful anti-intellectual currents continued and the role of experts was denigrated, inhibiting research. In propaganda, peasants were said to

---

[25] To give only one example, at the factory making jet engines for fighter planes in Xi'an, Red Guards locked up the senior management and the top engineers in a room in a factory for nearly a year (personal communication from one of the engineers held there).

[26] Macfarquhar and Schoenhals, *Mao's Last Revolution*, pp. 268–72.

have insight on technical matters superior to that of trained specialists. Perhaps most importantly, much of the leadership of government and industry was simply removed from position and sent to the countryside or to May 7 schools designed to re-educate leadership cadres. Many of these people were not restored to positions of influence until the early to late 1970s. Others died or committed suicide. There were still people in government who drew up plans and workers and foremen who carried out their daily duties, but there were few in charge who had the authority to make significant changes or develop new approaches.

The principal exception to this lack of leadership in the economic sphere was what was called the Third Front.[27] The Third Front was a major effort to relocate industry to the interior so that it would be less vulnerable to attack. It also involved an attempt to make the major economic regions self-sufficient so that if one was put out of commission the rest could still function. The decision to launch the Third Front was Mao's, but it reflected the very real possibility that China might be drawn into a major war with the United States or the Soviet Union or both.

The major American escalation in the Vietnam War began almost immediately after the November 1964 presidential election in the United States. The sustained aerial bombardment of Vietnam by the United States began in March of 1965. A US invasion of northern Vietnam was not seriously considered in part because of the fear that it would involve the United States in another war with China, as in Korea, but the Chinese could not be confident that that restraint would continue. China at the same time had broken its alliance with the Soviet Union and relations between the two countries steadily worsened, with China accusing the Soviet Union of restoring capitalism and the Soviet Union replying in kind. There was a major increase in Soviet military deployment along the border with China that in 1969 would break out into open conflict on an island in the Ussuri river.

Relocating the center of industry into the interior of the country was an enormously expensive undertaking. In 1963–1965, 38.2 percent of capital construction investment was allocated to the Third Front, with southwestern provinces receiving a particularly large share. Capital construction investment in Sichuan rose from 5 to 13 or 15 percent of national investment, and that in Guizhou rose from 1 or 2 percent to 5 percent.[28] The level of Third

---

[27] This discussion of the Third Front is based largely on B. Naughton, "The Third Front: Defense Industrialization in the Chinese Interior," *China Quarterly*, September 1988, 351–86.

[28] Naughton, "The Third Front," 362, 365.

Front investment nationwide in the Third Five-Year Plan (1966–1970) rose sharply to 52.7 percent of the national total and involved most of the interior provinces. In addition to this industrial investment, Mao called on the entire nation to "dig tunnels deep and store grain everywhere," and elaborate tunnel systems were dug under many and possibly nearly all cities.[29]

The Third Front effort was cut back sharply in 1972, although Third Front investment in the Fourth Five-Year Plan (1971–1975) was still 41.1 percent of the nationwide total. The reason for the change was almost certainly the opening up of relations with the United States. Following Henry Kissinger's visit to China in 1971 and the historic visit of President Nixon in February 1972 that established a working relationship between the two countries, there was no reason to defend against a possible American bombing campaign, although the perceived threat from the Soviet Union continued.

One further distortion brought about by the Cultural Revolution in its early phases belongs in any discussion of the impact of that movement on the economy. That was the chaos in the universities and secondary schools that concluded in 1968 with the universities being closed and most of the students, together with many high-school students, sent to the countryside. The universities were not reopened until 1972 and enrollment was still only a fraction of what it had been earlier.[30] In that year the total number of students officially enrolled in institutions of higher learning was 134,000, about half the level of 1956–1960. The number of such students enrolled each year did not pass a million until 1997.[31] Furthermore, selection of higher-education students when the schools did reopen was not based on examinations but mainly on the perceived ideological posture of the potential student. Entrance examinations were not reinstated until 1978.

The number of upper secondary-school students enrolled each year, in contrast, officially only dropped sharply in 1966 and 1967, although one doubts that much useful education was going on through 1968 and 1969. By 1970, the number of secondary-school students enrolled each year was four or more times the level of the late 1950s and that number kept climbing rapidly

---

[29] In 1979 when accompanying Senator Henry M. Jackson we were taken on a tour of Hohhot, the capital of Inner Mongolia. Somewhere in the middle of the city what looked like garage doors were opened and we drove down into the tunnel system and continued for about seven kilometers, passing side tunnels branching out in various directions. We ended up on the edge of hills outside the city. Hohhot was considered at the time to be on a likely invasion route of Soviet forces.

[30] For a further discussion see Walder, *China under Mao*, pp. 267–70.

[31] The enrollment figures are from Guojia tongjiju 国家统计局 (National Statistical Office), 新中国六十年 (New China's Sixty Years) (Beijing, China Statistics Press, 2009), pp. 674–5.

through 1977. Political interference, however, must have affected the quality of education negatively at the secondary level as well.

Any estimate of the impact on the economy of the school closings plus the chaos and highly politicized environment when they were open is not really possible. Many talented individuals were never able to reach their full potential. That was particularly true of those who reached the appropriate age for entrance when the schools were closed and many were not able to make up the loss later. According to the 1964 census, in that year there were 114 million people aged between seven and twelve and 70 million aged between thirteen and seventeen. Those were the age cohorts most impacted, but if enrollments had stayed at the levels of 1957–1960 (8.6 million total students in both lower and higher secondary schools on average in those years and 718,000 total students in institutions of higher learning), fewer than 15 percent would have gone on to secondary school and perhaps only 1 percent would have gone on to university. It would be decades of reform and rapid economic growth before most urban residents and a large but still minority share of rural residents would graduate from upper secondary school.

To complete the economic record of China prior to the Third Plenum of the Party Congress in December 1978 that marked the beginning of radical reform, the post-chaos period of 1973–1978 needs to be divided into two parts. Phase one involved Mao's acceptance of the need for order and the return of Deng Xiaoping as a principal manager of day-to-day affairs, first in foreign affairs, then the military, and finally in the economy. He was brought back to a position of power by Mao but he mainly worked closely with Zhou Enlai in this period. Zhou, however, was dying of cancer and not strong enough to actively play a day-to-day management role.[32]

The second phase was preceded in 1976 by, first, the death of Zhou, then the removal of Deng from office, and finally the death of Mao, followed by the arrest of the radical Cultural Revolution group, the "Gang of Four." In the background to this political drama was the Tangshan earthquake that killed hundreds of thousands and had much of the population of Beijing, among

---

[32] See, for example, the discussion of E. Vogel, *Deng Xiaoping and the Transformation of China* (Cambridge, MA, Harvard University Press, 2011), pp. 74–119. In July 1974 I accompanied Senator Henry M. Jackson to China on a visit that included a five-hour discussion with Deng. Zhou Enlai was said to be unavailable but the Chinese government people finally relented and allowed Jackson and his wife (but none of his aides) to spend a few minutes with Zhou in what was described to his aides by Helen Jackson, who had familiarity with such matters, as basically a hospital room in Zhongnanhai full of oxygen tanks, among other medical paraphernalia.

other places, living outdoors in fear of the aftershocks. With the end of the radical "leftists," there was a return to a more or less orderly centrally planned command system, but one unconstrained by attacks from the left on such issues as whether it was appropriate to import foreign technology.

The economy in 1973–1975 was run in a reasonably orderly centrally planned way, although political campaigns continued to have a prominent role. Exports began to grow from US$2.26 billion in 1970 (the same amount as in 1959) to US$5.82 billion in 1973 and US$7.26 billion in 1975. Imports that had shifted back toward producer goods in the Third Five-Year Plan continued at that level in the fourth plan. Because of the rise in exports, the shift back to imports of producer goods meant that their total rose 3.3 times from US$1.9 billion in 1970 to US$6.2 billion in 1975.[33] Particularly when this increase in foreign-made producer goods involved such things as complete chemical fertilizer plants, it was a source of political attacks from the Cultural Revolution radicals. However, while those attacks may have inhibited some trade deals, they did not stop many of them. Industrial growth accelerated to 9 percent per year in the fourth plan from 7 percent a year in the third plan, and conceivably the greater import of foreign producer goods played some role in this rise.

The year 1976 was mainly one of political upheaval, but the economy was affected and GDP fell by 1.6 percent as compared to a rise of 8.7 percent the year before. Of far greater importance for economic policy, as well as everything else, was the arrest of the Gang of Four and the end of radical criticism from the left. Deng Xiaoping was restored to a position of influence over the economy but he was not yet in overall charge as was to be the case by late 1978. Mao's designated successor, Hua Guofeng, still held the top leadership posts. The one policy change, and it was a major one, was to end the criticism of those wishing to import technology from abroad. Enterprises in 1977 were instead encouraged to go abroad for advanced technology and they reacted with enthusiasm. One international bank estimated that Chinese enterprises in 1977 and 1978 signed letters of intent to purchase goods from abroad worth around US$600 billion.[34] With exports in the two years of 1977–1978 of only US$17.3 billion, imports of such magnitude were out of the question and most of these letters of intent had to be torn up.

Offshore oil exploration was becoming an important possibility in the late 1970s as well and in the new atmosphere the government began negotiating

---

[33] These estimates were derived from data in National Statistical Office, *Statistical Yearbook of China 1981*, pp. 357–8.
[34] Verbal communication.

with foreign oil companies to participate in exploration and production – something that would have been impossible before 1976. GDP growth of 7.6 percent in 1977 involved an element of recovery from the disruptions of 1976, but the official 11.7 percent growth rate in 1978 was robust. At that point, the Third Plenum of the Eleventh Central Committee of the Communist Party late 1978, with Deng Xiaoping in charge, set China on a very different path.

An Evaluation of Economic Performance 1952–1978

An evaluation of China's overall economic performance during the pre-1978 period is best done taking the period as a whole. We have corrected the official GDP figures for this period for the distortion caused by the very high state-set industrial prices. The results of this calculation are presented in Table 16.4.

At 5 percent overall and 3.1 percent per capita, the published official GDP growth rates for 1958–1978, one would have cause to wonder why the Chinese government was concerned about the poor performance of the economy at all. Per capita GDP would have nearly doubled. In fact, even at market prices, per capita GDP increased by 50 percent, a lower but still nonnegligible figure. As the discussion that follows indicates, however, actual incomes and consumption of the population grew much more slowly than that.

Table 16.4 Price distortions in GDP growth estimates

	Official Chinese GDP growth rates (early-year state-set prices)	Chinese GDP growth rates (year 2000 market prices)
1953–1957	9.25	6.32
1958–1961	−1.13	−4.51
1962–1965	9.54	9.94
1966–1969	4.01	3.33
1970–1975	5.9	7.2
1958–1976	5	3.9

Note. The methodology used to recalculate GDP growth in year 2000 market prices is entirely based on official Chinese data. For more on the methodology see D.H. Perkins and T.G. Rawski, "Forecasting China's Economic Growth to 2025," in L. Brandt and T.G. Rawski (eds.), *China's Great Economic Transformation* (New York, Cambridge University Press, 2008), pp. 834–5.

Table 16.5 Sources of growth (1952–1990)

Period	GDP	Fixed capital	Raw labor	Education-enhanced	TFP growth
1952–1957	6.5	1.9	1.2	1.7	4.7
1958–1965	2.4	5.2	1.5	2.1	−1
1966–1978	4.9	7.7	2.4	3.1	−0.2
1979–1985	9.7	9.2	3.4	4.5	3.2
1986–1990	7.7	6.9	2.5	2.9	3.1

Source: this is a modified version of Perkins and Rawski, "Forecasting China's Economic Growth to 2025," Table 20.2, p. 839

An analysis of what was driving this GDP growth in the pre-1979 period can usefully start with an analysis of the sources of growth during these years. In 1952–1957 Chinese economic growth enjoyed a high-growth spurt. The investment rate had begun to rise but the growth rate of the capital stock was still very low. Growth was mostly (72 percent) explained not by the growth in labor and capital inputs, but by total factor productivity. It is not entirely clear why the growth rate of productivity in this period was so high given that the period included the potentially disruptive effects of the collectivization of agriculture and the state takeover of industry. The most likely explanation is that high growth was largely a result of the comparative stability of this period after years of civil war and hyperinflation. Growth was more a matter of bringing existing agricultural and industrial units up to full capacity than of an increase in new capacity.

The years 1958 through 1965 began with the massive mobilization of rural labor and the general chaos of the Great Leap Forward, followed by the famine and then recovery. Investment in modern plant and equipment also accelerated and that largely explains why GDP in 1965 was 21 percent higher than in 1957. The efficiency with which that plant and equipment were used, however, was undermined by the politics and chaos of the early part of that period and there is little doubt that that explains the decline in total factor productivity of capital and labor over the entire eight years.[35]

There was no total factor productivity growth in 1966–1978 either. GDP growth was mainly explained by the 7.7 percent annual average growth of capital throughout the period. The chaos of 1967–1968 is part of the reason for the slightly negative TFP estimate. The general inefficiency of Soviet-type centrally

---

[35] If the periodization was broken down further, it would show that there was a particularly sharp decline in TFP in the first years of the period followed by a rise that brought average TFP growth up to minus 1 percent.

planned economic systems, combined with the obvious inefficiency of Third Front investment, however, are probably the main reasons for the lack of productivity growth. The chaos of the early years of the Cultural Revolution was more like a series of worker strikes temporarily closing down or slowing production, with production quickly recovering when the strikes ended. Sorting out and quantitatively estimating the precise contributions of each of these components of inefficient growth, however, is far beyond what is possible in this chapter. Finally, what separated the performance of the first decade of reform after 1978 from what occurred before 1978 was not the slight acceleration in the growth rate of the capital stock. It was the large jump in total factor productivity.

The performance of GDP is one element of any appraisal of the pre-1979 period. What actually happened to the standard of living of the Chinese people in this period is arguably even more important and GDP growth does not necessarily translate into better living conditions for the majority of a country's population. We will begin with the rural population since that made up 87.5 percent of the total population, falling to 82 percent in the 1960s and staying at that level until 1978.

Several indicators related to rural incomes are presented in Table 16.6. The share of per capita agricultural value added (all wages and profits from farming, forestry, and fisheries) in GDP rose slightly during the First Five-Year Plan, fell sharply during the famine years, and then rose back to the level of 1957 but no further until the return to household agriculture after 1978. Essentially the same story holds true for the output of grain, the main source of calories in the Chinese diet.

The outlier index is the National Statistical Office's estimate of rural per capita consumption, which indicates that the decline in per capita consumption in the famine years was only 6.4 percent and the rise in per capita consumption by the 1970s was 50 or more percent above 1952 (or 35 percent above 1957). The estimated modest decline in the famine years does not appear to be plausibly related to the widespread malnutrition and death that occurred in those years. The growth in consumption after 1965 could be partly explained by the rise in income from rural industries that were actively promoted in the 1970s and mainly employed rural labor, but only partly. These industries only used 10 percent of the rural labor force in 1980, and probably fewer workers earlier, and their per capita incomes are not likely to have been much higher than the average wages from farming in the regions where they were located.[36] The most plausible conclusion is that the per

---

[36] This 10 percent share includes employees in commune, brigade, and team enterprises (roughly 30 million workers). In the 1970s, China included income from brigade and team enterprises in gross value of agricultural output and the contribution of brigade

Table 16.6 Per capita rural economic performance

	Primary value added	Grain output (per capita)	Rural consumption
1952	100	100	100
1957	110.9	109.6	116.8
1961	81.9	78.9	93.6
1965	105.4	100.4	125.2
1969	102.1	97.3	134.2
1975	112.1	114.4	150.4
1978	108.3	118.4	157.6
1984	162.6	155.6	272.2
1990	194	162.8	339.4

Source: National Statistical Office, 新中国六十年, pp. 608, 614, 637

capita consumption estimates are biased upward and give an overly favorable view of conditions in the countryside after 1958. This bias is not really surprising since reliable rural consumption figures require carefully managed sample surveys of rural areas and there is no evidence that surveys of that sort were carefully carried out in the 1958–1978 period as they have been in the post-1978 reform years.

Rural incomes, therefore, were nearly stagnant and did not grow by more than 10 percent or so (mainly due to rural small-scale enterprises) after 1957.[37] The situation in urban areas, in contrast, was different. Wages of workers and employees did not increase at all. The figures for nominal average wages for both state and urban collective enterprises are in Table 16.7. Wages in current prices peaked in 1957 and then fell, not recovering to the 1957 level until after 1978. Urban consumer prices rose significantly after 1957, peaking in 1962 and then falling, but not back to the level of 1957. From 1965 through 1976 consumer prices were unchanged, rising by a small amount in 1977 and 1978. Thus the nominal drop in wages in the early 1960s was reinforced by

and team enterprises to gross agricultural output in 1978 was 11.7 percent, up from around 2 or 3 percent in 1965. The total wage bill from commune, brigade, and team enterprise in 1980 was equivalent to only 8 percent of agricultural value added. The data on rural enterprises are from National Statistical Office, *Statistical Yearbook of China 1981*, pp. 137, 195.

[37] The National Statistical Office estimated the rise in nominal rural net income per capita to be seventy-three yuan in 1957, 107.2 yuan in 1965, and 117.1 yuan in 1977, but did not attempt to deflate these figures by the price increases in the early 1960s. Since prices rose hardly at all between 1965 and 1977, however, these nominal estimates are likely to be close to the real estimates. National Statistical Office, 新中国六十年, p. 627.

Table 16.7 Urban employment and consumption estimates

	Urban employees*	Urban population growth	Urban wages	Urban consumption per capita
1952	100	100	445	100
1957	128.9	138.9	624	131.7
1960	246.1	182.5	511	113.7
1962	182.5	162.8	551	101.9
1965	206.6	182.1	590	144.2
1970	253.9	201.4	561	158.3
1975	330.7	223.8	580	194.2
1978	382.7	240.8	615	217.6
1984	491.9	335.3	974	276.7
1990	685.5	421.5	2140	415.1

* Urban employees includes collective as well as state and private enterprises.
Source: National Statistical Office, 新中国六十年, pp. 608–10, 616

the price increase, but for the rest of the period real wages and nominal wages did not rise or fall.

What, then, explains rising urban household consumption per capita in 1965 through 1978? The primary answer, as discussed earlier, is that urban enterprises, blocked from bringing in migrants from the countryside, turned instead to women urban residents. The share of women in the urban labor force rose from under 15 percent of the total urban workforce to over 40 percent. In absolute numbers that was an increase of well over 30 million women, starting from a small base of 2 million urban employed women in 1955.[38] The average urban household in 1981 with 4.24 members included 2.39 employed persons. I have not found estimates for the 1950s but the number of employed persons per household must have risen by nearly one person. Still, from 1965 through 1978 urban consumption per capita increased at a rate of only 1.8 percent a year, far below the rates that would be achieved after 1978.

In addition, what urban areas were able to consume depended on what the government enterprises were willing to produce, and the centrally planned command economy did not often make decisions based on consumer preferences. In probably the most egregious example, the amount of urban living space per capita was allowed to decline to 4.4 square meters per capita in 1978.[39] Priority in construction and industry was not focused on consumer goods.

---

[38] Chen, Chinese Economic Statistics, p. 482.
[39] National Statistical Office, Statistical Yearbook of China 1981, p. 429.

Heavy industry (roughly similar to the producer goods industry) rose from 35.6 percent of industrial gross value output in 1952 to 57.3 percent in 1978. China's planners were following the closed-economy strategy of Preobrazhensky throughout the pre-reform era. Machines were produced in order to make more machines that someday in the future would make more consumer goods.

With respect to the distribution of income, China's image in this period was of a country that was one of the most egalitarian in the world. The land reform that began before 1949 and continued through the first years of Communist Party rule did significantly reduce income inequality. Land was given to the actual tillers, many of them former tenants paying rent to landlords.[40] The landlords were stripped of their land without compensation and often with the loss of their life. Urban private enterprises were in effect taken over by the state also without compensation to the private owners. Wealthy individuals who did not flee with their wealth lost most or all of it. Thus there is little doubt that inequality in income had fallen sharply by the mid-1950s.

The impression held by some visitors to China that this decline in inequality largely eliminated differences in income, however, was false. Within rural areas the work point system used to determine individual and hence family incomes in the co-operatives and communes was based on the amount of work each member did. That in turn led to some inequality between families with more than one adult worker. The major rural differences in income, however, were due to differences in the amount of co-operative or commune land per capita, the quality of that land, and its location (near a city meant much higher incomes for the members). For the most part the government did not attempt to reduce regional differences in inequality by moving farm families from poor regions to richer regions or vice versa. Such a move, if it had been tried, would probably have been politically explosive. Subsidies to the poorer communes were also limited until many years after the beginning of the reform period.

Urban inequality was driven mainly by government-set wage systems. The basic eight-grade system for most urban workers had a wage differential between each grade of about 20 percent, with the top grade roughly three times the bottom grade. There were also other systems for technical and management personnel and government officials, among others. The

---

[40] The one quantitative study I am aware of that estimated the impact of land reform on income distribution was by C. Robert Roll.

average monthly wage in 1957 was a bit over RMB 50 and wages of top professionals could be RMB 200 or more a month. The differential between the top and bottom wages in enterprises could be as much as sevenfold or more.[41] These wage systems came under attack during the Cultural Revolution but, however they may have been modified at that time, the system in the 1970s was much the same as had existed when it was set up in 1956–1957. Political attacks were not just against the wage structure but also against anything that appeared to the "leftists" to be emphasizing material incentives. Thus piece-rate wages were sometimes attacked and abolished, managerial bonuses were used sparingly or not at all, and individuals in the 1960s and 1970s could go for long periods without promotions.

There were in essence no property incomes in urban China from 1957 until well after 1978. The closest approximation to property incomes was the special privileges of the elite. The top government and enterprise officials had larger and better apartments and access to automobiles, and in some cases could command staff to provide them with services. At the very top, individuals such as Mao, Jiang Qing, and a few others could command airplanes and private automobiles. This top-level elite was a very narrow one, however. To give one a general idea of its size, the number of passenger automobiles in the country was 34,400 in 1957 and had only risen to 173,000 by 1975.

There were no surveys of inequality during 1958–1978, or at least none that have become publicly available, so it is not possible to measure in any precise way the Gini coefficient or some other measure of inequality for that period. There was, however, a major survey done in 1988 early in the reform period that has been analyzed in depth by a number of scholars.[42] This survey is not ideal for looking back at inequality before 1978. Still, 1988 was well before the rising role of private enterprises, the privatization of many of the township and village enterprises, the privatization of housing, and a level of rural-to-urban migration where most of those registered as being in rural areas between the ages of eighteen and forty were in fact working in the cities. Those changes would lead to an explosion in inequality, but in 1988 the level of inequality was probably only modestly above the level of the 1970s.

---

[41] See C. Howe, *Wage Patterns and Wage Policy in Modern China, 1919–1972* (Cambridge, Cambridge University Press, 1973).

[42] For analyses based on this survey, see K. Griffin and R. Zhao (eds.), *The Distribution of Income in China* (New York, St. Martin's Press, 1993). In addition to the chapter by the editors, see also the chapters by Carl Riskin, Li Shi, John Knight, Song Lina, Azizur Rahman Khan, and Terry McKinley.

The one element of inequality that can be measured for 1952 through 1978 is the difference between average urban and rural incomes. This difference is a major source of inequality in all countries and that was and is the case in China. Two alternative estimates of the urban–rural per capita consumption ratio and its changes over time are presented in Table 16.8. The "official" ratio is based on the National Statistical Office's estimates. The "estimate" ratio was obtained by dividing the official urban per capita income by rural per capita income, assuming that rural income in real terms was better represented by per capita agricultural value added than by the official estimates for rural per capita consumption in this period. This latter procedure may overstate the ratio in 1975 and 1978 because there was some commune industrial income that is not included in household income in those two years, but that income was not likely to have been much, if at all, more than 10 percent of total rural income.

If one accepts the "estimated ratio" as the more accurate, it is clear that the rural–urban consumption ratio rose rapidly from 1965 to 1978. The combination of slow agricultural growth with tight restriction on the migration of rural people out of the countryside was the main cause of this rise.

China's overall economic performance during 1958–1978 therefore involved modest GDP growth, little increase in per capita consumption in the rural areas, and 2 percent a year growth in urban areas. It is not surprising that China's leadership in 1978 saw this overall performance as inadequate, and that view was reinforced by the obvious superior economic performance of several of China's neighbors.

Table 16.8 Urban–rural per capita consumption ratio

	Official	Estimated
1952	2.37	2.37
1957	2.71	2.81
1961	2.85	3.6
1965	2.49	3.14
1969	2.41	3.44
1975	2.68	3.96
1978	2.93	4.59
1984	2.15	3.89
1990	2.85	4.66

Sources: see text

The post-1978 reform period is often described as a rejection of the Soviet-type centrally planned command system described in this chapter in favor of a market economy and capitalism – in effect a complete transformation of China's economic model. There is considerable truth in this characterization, but there were also elements of the pre-1978 economic system that persisted for some time after 1978 and in a few cases were still present during the second decade of the twenty-first century. That story, however, is covered in other chapters in this volume.

Further Reading

Donnithorne, A., *China's Economic System* (New York, Praeger, 1967).
Eckstein, A., W. Galenson, and T.-C. Liu (eds.), *Economic Trends in Communist China* (Chicago, Aldine, 1968).
Griffin, K., and R. Zhao (eds.), *The Distribution of Income in China* (New York, St. Martin's Press, 1993).
MacFarquhar, R., and M. Schoenhals, *Mao's Last Revolution* (Cambridge, MA, Harvard University Press, 2006).
Naughton, B., "The Third Front: Defense Industrialization in the Chinese Interior," *China Quarterly*, September 1988, 351–86.
Perkins, D.H., *Market Control and Planning in Communist China* (Cambridge, MA, Harvard University Press, 1966).
Walder, A., *China under Mao: A Revolution Derailed* (Cambridge, MA, Harvard University Press, 2015).
Wu, J., *Understanding and Interpreting Chinese Economic Reforms* (Mason, OH, Thomson/South-Western, 2005).

17

Living Standards in Maoist China

CHRIS BRAMALL

Introduction

Support for the Chinese Communist Party (CCP) in the late 1940s owed much to its willingness to "stand up" against external interference in Chinese affairs, whether by Japan, the USA, or any other colonial power. This nationalist agenda may have been the decisive factor in its victory during the civil war, and it continues to be a key driver of popular support for CCP rule.

Nevertheless, the CCP's social agenda – that, on assuming power, it would reduce poverty and inequality by promoting growth and by redistributing assets, particularly farm land – was also important in garnering support.[1] Precisely for that reason, much of the scholarship on the Maoist era has examined the degree to which this "promise of the revolution" had been fulfilled by the time of Mao's death. By the end of the 1980s, the settled conclusion was that this second CCP promise was largely unfulfilled. To be sure, the regime's achievements in terms of social indicators – especially life expectancy and morbidity – were recognized to be extraordinary, the mortality crisis of 1958–1962 notwithstanding. However, it was all but universally believed that the Party had failed to raise material living standards – and that this failure was both an indictment of Chinese socialism and a powerful explanation of the policy changes which occurred after 1976–1978. Little of significance has been published on these issues in recent years.[2] An

---

I am indebted to Tom Rawski, Debin Ma, and Xu Chenggang for their comments on an earlier version of this chapter.

[1] Xu Chenggang has suggested to me that the CCP never intended to keep these promises. However, even accepting this point, it seems reasonable to judge the CCP's record against generally accepted measures of "development" rather than in terms of whether it achieved its own self-defined objectives.

[2] Some of the more influential older pieces are N. Lardy, "Consumption and Living Standards in China, 1978–83," *China Quarterly* 100 (1984), 849–65; World Bank, *China: Socialist Economic Development*, vol. 1, *The Economy, Statistical System and Basic Data* (Washington, DC, World Bank, 1983); C. Riskin, *China's Political Economy* (Oxford, Oxford University Press, 1987); and C. Bramall, *In Praise of Maoist Economic Planning* (Oxford, Clarendon Press, 1993). A fine recent summary of China's development is

indication of the scholarly malaise is that, for something as pivotal as food consumption, we are reliant on the estimates made by Piazza in the early 1980s. His work was pioneering, but the sources available to him at that time were limited. A far richer range of Chinese materials is now available, and the time is therefore ripe for a re-evaluation of Maoist living standards.

This chapter takes up the challenge of re-evaluation. It begins by looking at estimates of per capita GDP and per capita income. However, our GDP estimates for Maoist China are based on fragile statistical foundations. In any case, per capita GDP is a poor guide to consumption. The same is true of data on per capita income. Accordingly, this chapter looks directly at trends in food consumption, the key component of material living standards. Then we consider broader measures of living standards, principally life expectancy. The sixth section expands the discussion to cover distributional questions.

The contribution made below is original in two respects. First, it offers new estimates of food consumption by using the abundant materials in Chinese which are now available. These allow us to construct more accurate food balance estimates of consumption (based on production data) than was previously possible. Second, it presents new estimates of rural income inequality, especially for the period immediately after land reform, based on more detailed information from the 1954 rural income survey.

Trends in Per Capita GDP

In thinking about the Maoist record on per capita GDP, it is logical to compare the late 1970s with the immediate prerevolutionary period. In practice, because of the distorting effects of both the war with Japan and all-out civil war between the CCP and the Guomindang in the late 1940s, the best comparison is with 1934–1936, when the Nanjing regime was relatively well established and before the Japanese invasion. The most consistent series on long-run per capita GDP is that estimated by Angus Maddison.[3] This shows average per capita GDP rising from US$570 in 1934–1936 to US$886 for the

---

offered in L. Brandt, D. Ma, and T. Rawski, "From Divergence to Convergence: Reevaluating the History behind China's Economic Boom," *Journal of Economic Literature* 52.1 (2014), 45–123. One recent paper is L.-L. Chen and J. Devereux, "The Iron Rice Bowl: Chinese Living Standards 1952–1978," *Comparative Economic Studies* 59 (2017), 261–310. However, this does little more than rehearse the findings of the older literature; it makes scant attempt to interrogate that literature's underlying assumptions or to engage with Chinese sources.

[3] A. Maddison, "World Population, GDP and Per Capita GDP, 1–2003 AD" (2010), at www.ggdc.net/Maddison (accessed March 25, 2016).

1974–1978 period, a long-run real-growth rate of around 1 percent per year (1990 prices). However, although the Maddison data are widely used, the limitations of his estimates for the 1930s are equally widely recognized.[4] The main problem is that the underlying yield and cultivated-area data are unreliable; because agriculture was the largest sector, this compromises the GDP estimates as a whole. The estimation of per capita GDP is rendered even harder by a lack of reliable population data; China's first modern and relatively reliable population census occurred only in 1953, and its results cannot easily be back-projected because of the impact of war.

We are on safer ground in comparing the early Maoist era with the 1970s because the establishment of the State Statistical Bureau (国家统计局, hereafter SSB) in the 1950s led to more systematic data collection. Even so, these estimates are still subject to considerable error. The data for the early 1950s were largely based on the old system of data collection used by the Guomindang's National Agricultural Research Bureau, which underreported cultivated area. Underreporting was also pervasive in the 1970s, both by collective farms (to avoid procurements) and by the private sector (widely viewed as a "capitalist remnant" during the Cultural Revolution). Putting these caveats aside, the SSB data suggest that per capita growth for 1952–1978 was 2 percent per year. A 2 percent per capita GDP growth rate is not a bad achievement and certainly better than China's record during the "Great Divergence" of the Qing era.[5] It would have been better still but for shocks inflicted by the Great Famine (1958–1962) and the early years of the Cultural Revolution (1966–1968).[6]

Trends in Per Capita Income

The real issue, however, is whether disposable income and consumption rose at the same rate as GDP. We know that the investment share was substantially higher by the late 1970s than it had been in the 1930s or the 1950s; a comparison of the estimates made by Liu and Yeh for the 1930s, and the

---

[4] K. Deng and P. O'Brien, "China's GDP Per Capita from the Han Dynasty to Communist Times," LSE Economic History Working Paper 229 (2016).

[5] The Qing data are sufficiently unreliable that we cannot be sure that growth accelerated; see Deng and O'Brien, "China's GDP."

[6] This is not the place for a discussion of the causes of slow growth. Most scholars would, of course, blame the system of Soviet-style central planning (systemic failures), but the impact of China's high level of military spending (especially on the program of Third Front industrialization, which focused mainly on inhospitable parts of western China) also played an important role. See Bramall, *In Praise of Maoist Economic Planning*.

World Bank for the 1970s, suggests that the share of gross capital formation rose from about 6 percent of GDP in the 1930s to 35 percent for 1974–1978. This rise in the investment share implies the possibility of a consumption squeeze. However, the outcome depends on whether the investment was productive. After all, the logic of the Maoist/Soviet approach to industrialization – set out in the classic Feldman model of the 1920s – was that raising the investment share in the short run, and using that higher rate of investment to expand the supply of producer goods, would lead to a dividend in terms of higher per capita consumption in the long run. We therefore need to measure consumption trends directly, and not just rely on GDP per capita as a proxy.

Rural Incomes

One way of evaluating consumption trends is to use the national surveys of rural income and expenditure. The surveys conducted during the 1950s were quite reliable. The first national survey by the SSB in 1954 covered 14,334 households.[7] The 1957 national survey sampled 17,378 households (Table 17.2), These surveys covered most provincial-level units. For example, the consumption part of the 1954 survey included households from twenty-one provinces; Yunnan, Jiangxi, and Tibet were the only provinces omitted. Later surveys were considerably smaller; the 1962 survey sampled 4,658 households and the 1965 one included 11,632 households. These SSB all-China surveys ceased after 1965, and resumed only in 1976 (though some provinces, such as Hubei, conducted their own surveys during the 1970s).

The surveys of the mid-1970s were smaller than those of the 1950s. That of 1976, covering 3,646 households, was but a shadow of the survey of 1954. The 1977 and 1978 national surveys of 6,089 and 6,095 households across twenty provincial-level units were little bigger. Only in 1979 was the 10,000-household mark breached, and the 1954 survey total was not exceeded until 1980. The small scale of the national surveys of the late 1970s meant that provincial subsamples were often very small indeed. Admittedly, some provinces were well represented in the national survey; 750 Hubei households were included in the 1979 survey.[8] But the overrepresentation of Hubei

---

[7] The number of households included in the national surveys is given in Table 17.2 below. For a useful English-language discussion, see Y. Matsuda, "Survey Systems and Sampling Designs of Chinese Household Surveys, 1952–1987," *Developing Economies* 28.3 (1990), 329–52.

[8] Hubei tongjiju 湖北统计局, 农民家庭经济调查资料 1974–1982 (Rural Household Economy Survey Materials 1974–1982) (Wuhan, Hubei tongjiju, 1983), p. 27.

meant the underrepresentation of other provinces. Even in the 15,914-household survey of 1980, provincial sampling was uneven. The Henan sample, for example, had increased from 270 households in 1978 to 1,296 in 1980, with thirty-six counties included instead of nine, and the Sichuan sample included 2,181 households. Moreover, the small samples for Ningxia and Shanghai (200 and 160 households respectively) reflected their small populations. However, some populous provinces were grossly underrepresented. For example, the Shaanxi survey included only 328 households, and the Hunan survey just 327 households in 1980.[9] There were other problems with the SSB surveys of the 1970s. Although the SSB used the comprehensive data collected by the Ministry of Agriculture for every collective in selecting production teams for inclusion, the production teams sampled during the mid-1970s were not randomly chosen but "typical examples" of rich, middling, and poor teams. By requiring the inclusion of a rich team in every three sampled from a population that was largely poor, the typical example methodology oversampled rich teams. *Within* teams, however, poor households were undersampled because they lacked the language and arithmetic skills needed to record annual income and expenditure. The overinclusion of rich teams, and the omission of many poor households, generated an upward bias to survey per capita income in 1977, and especially during 1978 when Deng Xiaoping assumed control. This suited the politics of the late 1970s; it was highly desirable that the surveys demonstrated the success of the post-Mao policy changes.

What the surveys did do was to reveal a national increase in per capita rural income from sixty-four yuan in 1954 to 133 yuan in 1978, marginally less than 3 percent per annum (Table 17.1). The rise occurred in poor provinces such as Guizhou, Sichuan, and Anhui; middle-ranking provinces like Jiangsu; and affluent provinces such as Liaoning. The real rate of increase was about 2 percent per year – smaller than the nominal rate but nevertheless significant enough.[10]

[9] The number of households surveyed by province in 1980 is listed in Henan tongjiju 河南统计局, 河南省农村经济调查统计资料 1982 (Statistical Materials from a Survey of Henan's Rural Economy, 1974–1982) (Zhengzhou, Henan tongji chubanshe, 1982), pp. 567–9.
[10] I use the implicit deflator from the State Statistical Bureau's real personal expenditure (*xiaofei* 消费) series to estimate real income growth here. Real rural incomes were affected by increases in the price of urban goods sold in rural areas. However, the trend in agricultural procurement prices also mattered. To be sure, rising procurement prices improved the internal terms of trade, which benefited surplus-producing collectives and is captured in the nominal income data. But a rising proportion of procured commodities was resold to the rural sector; by 1978, around 46 percent of expenditure

Table 17.1 Per capita net peasant income, 1954–1978 (current yuan)

	China	Guizhou	Anhui	Sichuan	Henan	Jiangsu	Liaoning
1954	64	51	61	56	66	71	105
1956	73	65	65	66	68	86	n/a
1957	73	64	75	68	65	86	109
1962	99	113	131	121	77*	107	n/a
1965	107	110	109	106	74	114	125
1975	113**	90	n/a	95**	n/a	n/a	128
1978	133	109	113	127	105	155	185

*1963, **1976

Note. These data show a significant increase in nominal income between 1957 and 1962 but the real increase was negligible because of inflation during the Great Leap Forward.
Sources: Nongyebu 农业部, 农业经济资料 1949–1983 (Materials on the Agricultural Economy) (Beijing, Nongmuyuye bu, 1983), p. 523; Zhonggong Sichuan sheng wei yanjiushi 中共四川省委研究室, 四川省情 (Conditions in Sichuan) (Chengdu, Sichuan renmin chubanshe, 1984), p. 226; Guojia tongjiju 国家统计局 (National Statistical Office), 各省自治区直辖市农民收入消费调查研究资料汇编 (Summary Research Materials from Rural Income and Expenditure Surveys in China's Provinces) (Beijing, Zhongguo tongji chubanshe, 1985), pp. 139, 223, 349, 434–6; Liaoning tongjiju 辽宁统计局, 辽宁省农村发展五十年 (Fifty Years of Rural Development in Liaoning) (Shenyang, Liaoning tongji chubanshe, 1999), p. 367; Jiangsu tongjiju 江苏统计局, 江苏农村经济五十年 (Fifty Years of Jiangsu's Rural Economy) (Beijing, Zhongguo tongji chubanshe, 2000), pp. 153–4; Anhui sheng renmin zhengfu 安徽省人民政府, 安徽五十年统计资料 (Statistical Materials on Fifty Years of Anhui) (Beijing, Zhongguo tongji chubanshe, 1999), p. 739

Alternative income data were collected by the Ministry of Agriculture (*nongye bu* 农业部, hereafter MOA) – see Table 17.2. The MOA had access to a comprehensive reporting system: every collective was required to report collective income and output data to the ministry. By estimating income generated in non-collective activities (notably household sidelines), the MOA was able to derive estimates of overall per capita income. However, the MOA grossly undersampled sideline activity and hence total income. In 1978, the MOA figures in Table 17.2 imply sideline income of just seventeen yuan,

was on commodities and (an imputed) 47 percent on own-produced goods, compared with 31 percent and 63 percent respectively in 1952. See Guojia tongjiju 国家统计局 (National Statistical Office), 中国国内生产直接核算历史资料 1952–1995 (Historical GDP Data on China, 1952–1995) (Beijing, Dongbei caijing daxue chubanshe, 1997), p. 44. The rise in agricultural procurement prices by 59 percent between 1954 and 1978 therefore had a significant impact on rural households, making them significant market purchasers of agricultural goods – most obviously, grain-deficit households.

Table 17.2 Alternative estimates of national per capita peasant income (yuan)

	Total net income per head		Of which: net collective distributed income per head		SSB sample size (households)
	SSB	MOA	SSB	MOA	
1954	64	n/a	2	n/a	14,334
1956	73	52	45	43	14,172
1957	73	52	43	41	17,378
1962	99	56	52	46	4,658
1963	101	57	55	46	9,724
1964	102	61	55	48	12,095
1965	107	66	63	52	11,632
1976	113	80	78	63	3,646
1977	117	81	76	65	6,089
1978	134	91	89	74	6,095
1979	160	103	102	83	10,282
1980	191	104	108	86	15,914
1981	223	117	116	101	18,529

Notes. (1) Net income here is gross income minus production costs. (2) Data are for nominal per capita income. (3) The first SSB survey was conducted in 1954 and the first reporting by collectives to the MOA was in 1956. Both surveys ceased during the late 1960s.
Sources: Nongyebu, 农业经济资料, pp. 516–17, 521, 523

whereas the SSB survey put the figure at forty-five yuan.[11] This SSB figure is more plausible; we know that decollectivization had begun in some areas by 1978, and that the restrictions on household activities imposed during the Cultural Revolution (on, for example, chicken and pig breeding) had been largely removed.

The key issue, however, is not the absolute level of income but the trend. The surveys may have been biased in the late 1970s, but it is not obvious that these biases changed much over time. Political imperatives during the 1950s – a wish to demonstrate the success of land reform and collectivization – led to a bias towards success. As for the 1970s, the political pressures were to exaggerate the damaging impact of the Cultural Revolution, when the SSB itself had been closed down, and its members rusticated, and to show that the Chinese economy had performed better after the arrest of the "Gang of Four" (October 1976). These pressures imparted some upward bias to the data for 1977–1978.

[11] These numbers are the difference between total and collective income in Table 17.2.

In short, therefore, the incentive to overstate success was present both in 1954–1957 and after 1976. The income trend therefore ought to be relatively unbiased. And this trend was clearly upwards. In fact, Table 17.2 shows that all five measures of per capita rural income rose significantly between the mid-1950s and the late 1970s.

Urban Income

Survey data for urban incomes are more scarce, probably because the collection of urban data was a lower priority for the CCP leadership: the urban population was comparatively small (18 percent of the total in 1978), and more affluent than the rural population because of higher urban wages and substantial subsidies.

Nevertheless, we do have large-scale survey results for 1956, 1957, and 1958, covering over 5,000 households.[12] There are also some surveys for individual cities. One such is that for Shanghai in the mid-1950s, which compares consumption in 1956 with 1929–1930.[13] Post-1957 urban data are more scarce, though we do have a national survey covering 3,537 households for 1964.[14] There are also some provincial data.[15] However, large-scale national sample surveys of consumption ceased between 1964 and 1980.

The urban survey results (Table 17.3) show a growth rate of around 3 percent per annum between 1952 and 1980, in line with rural income growth.[16] The urban retail price index rose by 0.5 percent per year, so real urban income growth was closer to 2.5 percent per year – about 0.5 percent

---

[12] These surveys necessarily included few households from any individual province. The 1957 Henan survey, for example, included 365 households drawn exclusively from the large cities of Zhengzhou, Luoyang, and Kaifeng. See Henan tongjiju 河南统计局, 河南省职工家庭生活调查资料汇编 (Summary Materials from a Survey of Living Standards in Worker Households in Henan) (Zhengzhou, Henan tongjij chubanshe, 1982).

[13] Guojia tongjiju 国家统计局 (National Statistical Office), "1927 年以来上海市工人生活水平的变化情况" (Changes in the Living Standards of Shanghai Workers since 1927), 经济研究资料 (Economic Research Materials) 16.7 (1957), 1–6. The data show, for example, that pork consumption was eight kilograms per person per annum, similar to the national estimate – therefore suggesting that the national survey was skewed towards more prosperous cities like Shanghai.

[14] National Statistical Office, 六五年计划, p. 15.

[15] Jiangxi tongjiju 江西统计局, 江西统计年鉴 1982 (Jiangxi Statistical Yearbook 1982) (Nanchang, Jiangxi tongji chubanshe, 1983), p. 249; Henan sheng renmin zhengfu diaocha yanjiushi 河南省人民政府调查研究室, 河南生情 (Conditions in Henan) (Zhengzhou, Henan renmin chubanshe, 1987), p. 623; Liaoning tongjiju 辽宁统计局, 辽宁城市人民生活史料 (Historical Materials on Urban Living Standards in Liaoning) (Shenyang, no publisher, 1986), pp. 145–6.

[16] These exclude subsidies and therefore understate true growth; see also the discussion of the urban–rural gap below.

Table 17.3 Selected per capita urban incomes, 1943–1980 (current yuan)

	China	Liaoning	Henan	Beijing	Guangdong	Wuhan
1952		191	137		126	
1956	242			220		
1957	254	236	216	251	151	210
1958	253			232		202
1962		231	229*	221		300
1965	243*	233	239	252	243	240
1978		494		365	402	402**
1980	514	508	444	501	462	538

* 1964, **1979.

Sources: Liaoning tongjiju 辽宁统计局, 辽宁城市人民生活史料 (Historical Materials on Urban Living Standards in Liaoning) (Shenyang, no publisher, 1986), pp. 145–6; Guojia tongjiju 国家统计局 (National Statistical Office), 六五年计划我国城镇居民家庭收支调查资料 (Survey Materials on the Income and Expenditure of Urban Households during the Sixth Five-Year Plan) (Beijing, Zhongguo tongji chubanshe, 1988), p. 15; Guojia tongjiju 国家统计局 (National Statistical Office), 全国职工家庭生活调查资料 1956, 1958, 1980 (National Survey Materials on Worker Living Standards 1956, 1958, 1980) (Beijing, Zhongguo tongji chubanshe, 1956, 1958, 1980); Henan sheng renmin zhengfu diaocha yanjiushi 河南省人民政府调查研究室, 河南生情 (Conditions in Henan) (Zhengzhou, Henan renmin chubanshe, 1987), pp. 621–2; Wuhan tongjiju 武汉统计局, 武汉统计史志资料 (Statistical Material Record for Wuhan) (Wuhan, Wuhan tongji chubanshe, 1988), p. 942; Beijing tongjiju 北京统计局, 北京五十年 (Beijing Fifty Years) (Beijing, Zhongguo tongji chubanshe, 1999), p. 373; Guangdong tongjiju 广东统计局, 广东统计年鉴 1990 (Guangdong Statistical Yearbook 1990) (Beijing, Zhongguo tongji chubanshe, 1990), pp. 436–7. These Guangdong figures are for living expenditure and therefore lower than for per capita income

above rural income growth. Much of the rise occurred after the mid-1960s and the main driver was rising participation rates, especially by women; the average wage increased very little. The regional pattern of increase shown is, at least in terms of absolute magnitudes, largely as one would expect. Wuhan, for example, developed rapidly in the heavy-industry-oriented late Maoist era and income growth reflects that industrialization. The same is true of Liaoning. By contrast, Henan's cities were smaller and not focal points for heavy industrialization. The same is broadly true of Guangdong. Urban incomes rose in Beijing at about the same rate as the national average, not perhaps surprisingly given that it was not a center of heavy industry.

Trends in Food Consumption

The data from surveys on per capita income and expenditure are broadly consistent, and tell a story of rising material living standards. Nevertheless, because of the sample biases discussed above, it is useful to have corroboration from other indicators. Perhaps the most useful alternative approach is to look at food consumption because it is a key metric for any poor country, and because it can be estimated from annual production – instead of sample surveys – using the food balance sheet method pioneered by the UN's Food and Agriculture Organization (FAO).[17] It therefore serves as an independent check on the income survey data.

Previous Estimates

Official output data suggest reasonable levels of food consumption in the 1930s and 1940s; one estimate by the FAO put daily food consumption at 2,226 kilocalories per day for 1931–1937.[18] However, this seemingly plausible figure is suspect. First, the population data used were gross underestimates in the order of 100 million (as China's first proper census, that of 1953, was to reveal). Second, the FAO estimate relied upon the *Crop Reports* compiled by the National Agricultural Research Bureau (NARB). These reports are problematic because they systematically underreported sown area and, for 1931–1937, excluded both Manchuria and ethnic minority regions in the west where the NARB was unable to collect data.[19] The exclusion of Manchuria was especially significant, both because it had a large population and because Manchurian calorie consumption was high: Shen, using Japanese-collected data, put Manchurian consumption at 2,557 kilocalories per day during 1935–1938.[20] Much scholarly effort has been expended on correcting these biases. Buck's large-scale *Land Utilization* survey of the early 1930s put food consumption levels at 2,537 kilocalories per day.[21] Liu and Yeh came up with a national estimate of 2,130 kilocalories for 1933, of which 1,936 kilocalories

---

[17] The food balance approach estimates consumption as the residual after the subtraction from crop production of net exports, stock increases, waste, processing losses, and that part of the crop used for seed, animal feed, and industrial inputs.
[18] T.H. Shen, *Agricultural Resources of China* (Ithaca, NY, Cornell University Press, 1951), p. 381.
[19] One of the most comprehensive compilations of the *Crop Report* data is that by Xu Daofu 许道夫, 中国近代农业生产与贸易统计资料 (Agricultural and Trade Statistical Materials for Modern China) (Shanghai, Shanghai renmin chubanshe, 1983).
[20] Shen, *Agricultural Resources of China*, p. 383.
[21] J.L. Buck, *Land Utilization in China* (Oxford, Oxford University Press, 1937); T.-C. Liu and K.-C. Yeh, *The Economy of the Chinese Mainland* (Princeton, Princeton University Press, 1965), p. 31.

came from grain crops.[22] However, Buck's estimate is too high because his team oversampled relatively prosperous villages and Liu and Yeh's otherwise careful estimates are flawed because of their partial reliance on Buck's work. I have therefore recalculated food consumption, and estimate that it averaged 2,191 kilocalories per day for 1931–1937.[23] It is purely coincidental that it is so similar to the FAO figure.

There are several series for post-1949 (Table 17.4).[24] The FAO series is most pessimistic: average consumption fell from 2,126 to 1,940 calories between 1946–1948 and 1975–1978. The MOA series is almost as pessimistic, and Piazza's series also shows little improvement, especially if the high figure for 1978 is disregarded.[25] Together, these estimates suggest that the Maoist record was poor.[26]

None of the estimates in Table 17.4 are reliable. The FAO series assumes very high feed grain use for pigs during the 1970s but Chinese pig feeding actually relied upon household scraps and scavenging, and made only modest use of grain. The Ministry of Agriculture data are available only for grain, pork, sugar, and vegetable oils (though these did account for over 90 percent of calories consumed), so we need to infer total consumption using additional data from other sources. And whilst Piazza's estimates are certainly superior to the others, he had only limited access to Chinese sources and therefore made questionable assumptions for grain used for seed and animal feed, as well as milling loss.[27]

---

[22] Liu and Yeh, *The Economy of the Chinese Mainland*, pp. 29–30. This post-1949 Chinese definition of grain includes potatoes, soybeans, and pulses.

[23] Details of my estimation methods are available on request.

[24] It makes sense to focus on four-year averages because of the impact of weather, an issue discussed further below. I have chosen to omit 1952 and 1953 because there are more questions about the data for these years – when the SSB had been barely established – than for the mid- to late 1950s. According to Liu and Yeh, *The Economy of the Chinese Mainland*, pp. 43–55, all the pre-1956 data are suspect. That may be true, but the change between the 1950s and 1970 is not sensitive to the inclusion of the data for 1954 and 1955.

[25] Piazza's early estimates were more optimistic; see A. Piazza, "Trends in Food and Nutrient Availability in China, 1958–1981," World Bank Staff Working Paper No. 607 (1983), 47–73. However, Piazza discarded his 1983 series when producing his 1986 book; see A. Piazza, *Food Consumption and Nutritional Status in the PRC* (Boulder, CO, Westview Press, 1986). This was because his 1983 series assumed implausibly high use of grain for animal feed in the 1950s – which lowers consumption for the 1950s and produces a marked upward trend. His 1986 series uses a more appropriate assumption about feed.

[26] Early World Bank estimates were also pessimistic. These put calorie consumption at 2,024 kilocalories in 1957 and 2,044 kilocalories in 1977, before surging to 2,441 kilocalories in 1979 as result of the early effects of reform. See World Bank, *China: Socialist Economic Development*, pp. 32, 118.

[27] For example, Piazza assumes that Chinese citizens consumed white rice; he therefore uses a milling/polishing loss rate of 33 percent in his calculations for both the 1950s and

Table 17.4 *Trends in food consumption during the Maoist era (calories per capita per day)*

	Piazza 1986	MOA	FAO
1952	2,083	2,280	2,126*
1953	2,048	2,266	n/a
1954	2,041	2,260	n/a
1955	2,232	2,273	n/a
1956	2,326	2,358	n/a
1957	2,217	2,336	n/a
1975	2,266	2,217	1,909
1976	2,235	2,210	1,875
1977	2,233	2,225	1,914
1978	2,413	2,280	2,062
1954–1957 average	2,204	2,307	2,126*
1975–1978 average	2,287	2,233	1,940
Change from 1954–1957 to 1975–1978	+83	−74	−186

* Average of 1946–1947 and 1947–1948; as with other countries, there are no FAO time series data for pre-1961. Data refer to the whole population.
Sources: FAO, *The State of Food and Agriculture 1948* (Washington, DC, FAO, 1948), p. 49; Nongyebu 农业部, 中国农村经济统计大全 (Statistics on the Chinese Rural Economy) (Beijing, Nongyebu, 1989), p. 58; A. Piazza, *Food Consumption and Nutritional Status in the PRC* (Boulder, CO, Westview Press, 1986), p. 77

However, the biggest problem is that previous estimates uncritically accepted official production data. These data are problematic because they underreport production (*manchan* 瞒产) on private plots during the 1970s. To be sure, grain was not the only crop grown on private land; Gao's villagers (in Jiangxi) focused upon green vegetables.[28] However, grain production usually featured prominently on private plots. The households studied by Potter and Potter in Guangdong, for example, grew sweet potatoes, soybeans, and rice

---

1970s. However, Hinton, relying upon his experience in the Chinese countryside, rejected Piazza's assumption, arguing that consumption of brown rice was commonplace, especially in lean years. W. Hinton, *Through a Glass Darkly* (New York, Monthly Review Press, 2006), p. 252. This critique is supported by the evidence provided by the big 1954 survey and in the *1959 Agricultural Handbook*; see Nongyebu 农业部, 农业经济资料手册 (Handbook of Materials on the Agricultural Economy) (Beijing, Nongye chubanshe, 1959). Both sources suggest that rice was lightly polished (these sources put the milling loss at between 24 and 29 percent of harvested weight). These are seemingly arcane technical issues, but the food balance methodology is such that overall consumption is sensitive to assumptions made about rice milling because it was the key grain crop.

[28] M. Gao, *Gao Village* (London, Hurst and Co., 1999).

as well as a range of vegetables, and Thaxton's villagers in Henan focused on sweet potatoes. And private-sector grain output was far from insignificant.[29] Soya and sweet potatoes were both classified as grain by China's State Statistical Bureau and, although private plots typically accounted for just 5 to 7 percent of cultivated area in the 1970s, their output share was considerably higher. This was because high procurement quotas at low prices for collectively produced grain induced a higher degree of labor intensity on private plots. Evasion of procurements was difficult.[30] However, private plots were not subject to procurement quotas and therefore substitution effects occurred between collective and private activity. Labor intensity fell on collectives, but the time and energy allocated to private plots rose significantly.

Private-sector activity *of itself* did not guarantee underreporting; private production could in principle still have been measured. The reporting problem arose because repeated Maoist attempts to outlaw private-sector activity caused widespread evasion. Take sweet potatoes. They were consumed directly in significant quantities but, more importantly, they were crucial pig fodder. Households were therefore determined to grow them, come what may. Moreover, sweet potato production was easy to hide. Potatoes were quite literally an underground crop; they were grown underground and stored in underground cellars. As a result, private-sector production remained significant during the 1960s and 1970s, just as it had during the famine years. Many local CCP officials even connived in this because *collective* pig breeding was generally a failure due to disease, lack of care, and the impossibility of collecting household food waste at a collective level. Allowing household pig rearing was therefore essential.

As to the scale of underreporting, official MOA national data put private-sector grain production at 6 million tonnes, around 2 percent of the 1978 total.[31] But other evidence suggests that it was higher. For one thing, the share of household income in total net rural income was no less than 27 percent in 1978 according to the SSB income survey. To be sure, some of this income came from pigs and poultry, but the production of sweet

---

[29] S. Potter and J. Potter, *China's Peasants* (Cambridge, Cambridge University Press, 1990); R. Thaxton, *Catastrophe and Contention in Rural China* (Cambridge, Cambridge University Press, 2008).
[30] It required collusion between collective farm workers and collective leaders, as well as inadequate higher-level monitoring, and appears to have occurred significantly only during the famine years.
[31] Nongyebu, 农业经济资料手册, pp. 143, 240, 519. I calculate this as a residual after subtracting collective and state farm production from the total.

potatoes was an especially important component of income. For another thing, the share of private plots in total cultivated area was around 6 percent in 1978. If the private share in grain output was equal to this area share, it would imply true private-plot grain production of 18 million tonnes. If productivity on private plots was double that on collective land – not implausible given very high labour inputs – true output would be close to 36 million tonnes. We also have direct SSB estimates of private-sector grain production. These put the private-sector total at 26 million tonnes for 1979, and 28 million tonnes in 1980.[32] Finally, some micro-studies (Thaxton's work in northern Henan, for example) suggest that privately produced grain contributed about 25 percent of grain consumption in the late Maoist era. If, as Thaxton discovered, private plots produced fifty kilograms per capita per annum in Henan – the official Henan data put the figure at only twenty-eight kilograms – that would imply a national total of nearly 40 million tonnes.[33] In short, multiple sources reveal significant underreporting of private grain production in the late 1970s. Understating output in the official publications served the political purpose of the 1980s of blackening the Maoist record and lauding the achievements of the Dengist regime.

Widespread underreporting during the 1970s also helps to explain the otherwise implausible increase in grain output reported in official Chinese sources between 1978 and 1984. If official sources are to be believed, grain output rose from 305 million tonnes to 407 million tonnes during 1978–1984, a rise of 4.7 percent per annum. By contrast, annual growth between 1965 and 1978, from a much lower base, was only 3.3 percent. The usual explanation is that there was indeed a one-off surge in production during 1978–1984 and that it occurred primarily because of agricultural decollectivization. But if the impact of decollectivization was so critical, it is hard to see why production grew at a very similar rate between 1977 and 1982 in counties which had decollectivized, and counties (the majority) which had not.[34] The best explanation of the apparent output surge is simply that a process of reintermediation occurred. This occurred because incentives for underreporting of output diminished due to rising procurement prices, and because controls on private-sector activity – both the type of production and the scale of private plots – were gradually lifted after 1976. By the mid-1980s, underreporting had largely ceased.

---

[32] *Renmin Ribao*, June 16, 1981. [33] Thaxton, *Catastrophe and Contention*, pp. 273–4.
[34] C. Bramall, "Origins of the Agricultural 'Miracle': Some Evidence from Sichuan," *China Quarterly* 143 (1995), 731–55.

Revised Estimates of Food Consumption

In the light of the underreporting and methodological problems that afflict existing food balance estimates, I have re-estimated consumption as follows.[35] For the 1950s, I accept the official production data but use the results of the SSB's 1954 income and expenditure survey for seed and animal feed.[36] I also assume that rice was lightly polished, in contrast to Piazza's assumption that white rice consumption was the norm. For the 1970s, a number of Chinese sources give estimates for seed and feed grain, which I use. I assume a milling figure of 70 percent for rice; the FAO/Piazza 67 percent milling rate implies that consumption of highly polished rice was normal in rural areas, which seems implausible.[37] My estimates for the 1950s and 1970s also accept official data on changes in the grain stock. However, I use revised estimates of grain production for the 1970s. Although there is no definitive answer to the extent of underreporting, the various sources mentioned above suggest that it was about 10 percent of official output, the equivalent of 30 million tonnes of grain. I therefore raise annual output for 1975–1978 by that amount.[38]

Putting these various assumptions together, and using the food balance approach to estimate consumption, generates the revised estimates shown in Table 17.5. I have included my estimates for 1931–1937 for comparative purposes but, because the figure is very similar to that for the 1950s, I focus on the change between 1954–1957 and 1975–1978.[39] As Table 17.5 shows, my estimates are virtually identical to those of Piazza for the 1950s; our assumptions are quite different but produce a similar result, mainly because my assumption of less rice polishing is offset by assuming higher use of grain for feed purposes. For the 1970s, however, my consumption estimate is around 4 percent higher. It reflects my assumption of output underreporting, which is only partly offset by my

---

[35] Full details of the methodology and sources are available from the author.
[36] Guojia tongjiju 国家统计局 (National Statistical Office), 1954 年全国农家收支调查资料 (Materials on the 1954 National Peasant Household Income and Expenditure Survey) (Beijing, Zhongguo tongji chubanshe, 1956).
[37] Most scholars are inconsistent in assuming a low milling rate. They argue that late Maoist living standards were low – yet simultaneously assume that the rural population consumed highly polished white rice. The evidence suggests that the rice milling rate fell from 71.5 percent in 1954 to 70 percent in 1978, implying a modest rise in rural consumption during the Maoist era – but that relatively coarse rice was still the rural consumption norm in the late 1970s.
[38] In other words, grain output on private plots was about 36 million tonnes, compared with the 6 million tonnes officially reported in 1978. This suggests that the yield was around double that on collectively farmed land, but it is somewhat below Thaxton's 40 million tonnes.
[39] I do not attempt to derive complete time series data because we lack reliable data on feed use, milling rates, and so on during the famine years.

Table 17.5 Contrasting estimates of food consumption, 1954–1978 (calories per head per day)

	Piazza 1986	My revised estimates
1954	2,041	2,084
1955	2,232	2,128
1956	2,326	2,352
1957	2,217	2,260
1975	2,266	2,367
1976	2,235	2,343
1977	2,233	2,342
1978	2,413	2,478
Average, 1931–1937	n/a	2,191
Average, 1954–1957	2,204	2,206
Average, 1975–1978	2,287	2,382
Change from 1954–1957 to 1975–1978	+83	+176

Sources: Table 17.4 above and text

assumption of higher livestock feed.[40] These revisions imply an overall rise in daily per capita consumption of about 180 kilocalories (8 percent) by the late 1970s.

My revised consumption series, showing a significant rise between the 1950s and 1970s, is more plausible than other estimates because the underlying assumptions are more solidly based on survey evidence that has become increasingly available. My series also accords with the urban and rural consumption surveys; the rural surveys, for example, show rice consumption rising from fifty-two kilograms per head in 1954–1957 to fifty-eight kilograms in 1977–1978, and meat consumption rising by 20 percent over the same period.[41] My estimates also fit with the data on rising heights and weights, which provide an alternative measure of nutritional intake. The best source here is the China Health and Nutrition Survey (CHNS), which covered both urban and rural areas. The survey has been repeated over a number of years and collected data by year of birth and height during survey years. The 2006

---

[40] I put grain use for animal feed at 33 million tonnes in 1978, about 9.5 percent of available grain. By contrast, Piazza's figure is 27 million tonnes. Piazza, *Food Consumption and Nutritional Status in the PRC*, p. 190. Both our estimates are far below the FAO figure of 70 million tonnes.

[41] Nongyebu, 农业经济资料手册, pp. 548–9. The production of fine grains (wheat and rice) rose from 56 percent of grain output in 1954–1957 to 61 percent in 1975–1978 – hardly the sign of an economy in crisis. Nongyebu 农业部, 中国农村经济统计大全 (Statistics on the Chinese Rural Economy) (Beijing, Nongyebu, 1989), pp. 146–53.

version of the survey shows a rise of around four centimeters of height between men and women born in the 1930s and those born in the mid-1970s. The data on average weight show a comparable upward trajectory.[42]

Evaluating China's Consumption Record

The increase in food consumption during the Maoist era is impressive enough at face value. It becomes even more so when properly contextualized. For one thing, the rise indicates that China had ended the chronic food insecurity which had been such a feature of the pre-1949 era, and which reappeared with devastating force during the Great Famine. And China had not only achieved basic food security: it had done so without any significant recourse to food imports. Second, food consumption levels in China by the 1970s were at least on a par with those of many other land-poor countries during the early days of their successful industrialization. For example, recent estimates by Broadberry et al. put British food consumption at only around 2,170 kilocalories between 1750 and 1800, and little better than 2,100 kilocalories even in the 1850s.[43] Consumption levels in fast-industrializing Meiji Japan were also rather low. Few question the notion of a British Industrial Revolution (or indeed a Japanese one) despite the stagnation of food consumption in the early decades of industrialization. China managed to industrialize *and* to raise consumption levels during the Maoist years. Third, Chinese food consumption levels would have been higher still in the late 1970s but for a run of unusually poor weather. I noted earlier that the apparent rise in output between 1978 and 1984 is exaggerated by underreporting in 1978, but equally serious is the distorted perception induced by weather fluctuations. One of the most interesting features of the period is that the weather – as proxied by rainfall – was considerably worse in the late 1970s than in 1982–1984, the years during which decollectivization was in full swing. If we look at patterns of rainfall in nine of China's key grain-producing provinces, a normal year saw a deviation from 1951–2000 average rainfall of 17 percent.[44] During 1976–1978, however, the actual deviation recorded by the sixty-two weather stations was five percentage points higher than normal (Table 17.6). By contrast, the deviation in 1982–1984

---

[42] CHNS, *China Health and Nutrition Survey* (2006), at www.cpc.unc.edu/projects/china/about/proj_desc (accessed July 4, 2012).

[43] S. Broadberry, B. Campbell, A. Klein, M. Overton, and B. van Leeuwen, *British Economic Growth 1270–1870* (Cambridge, Cambridge University Press, 2015), p. 289.

[44] In arithmetic terms, the deviation would be zero in a normal year, but I treat flooding and drought symmetrically by assuming that both were equally bad for output: flooding in one region only offsets drought in another region in arithmetic terms. This explains why a normal deviation was 17 percent; in any given year, some stations recorded drought and others recorded flooding.

Table 17.6 Rainfall deviations in 1976–1978 and 1982–1984 from the 1951–2000 norm (percentage points)

	Actual deviation	Normal deviation	Difference
1976	16	17	−1
1977	18	17	1
1978	22	17	5
Total deviation, 1976–1978	56	51	5
1982	13	17	−4
1983	19	17	2
1984	12	17	−5
Total deviation, 1982–1984	45	51	−6

Notes. (1) Data on rainfall are for sixty-two weather stations located in nine provinces – Anhui, Guangdong (including Hainan), Heilongjiang, Henan, Hubei, Hunan, Jiangsu, Sichuan (including Chongqing), and Shandong – which together supplied nearly 60 percent of grain output in the late 1970s. (2) The national deviation is calculated by averaging the deviation for each of the sixty-two weather stations.
Source: Data on the sixty-two stations are derived from the 160 weather station database at http://dss.ucar.edu/datasets/ds578.1/data/ (accessed May 9, 2009)

was six percentage points less than normal. In other words, the anecdotal accounts suggesting a string of excellent harvests during 1982–1984 are confirmed by the rainfall data, whereas the years between 1976 and 1978 saw more droughts and flooding than normal. In terms of single years, the twenty-five percentage point deviation recorded in 1954 (when there was extensive flooding along the Yangzi) was by some way the worst of the Maoist era.[45] Other bad years were 1956, 1963, and – of most interest for our purposes – 1978. By contrast, 1984 was the second-best year of the entire period, being second only to 1952 (when the deviation was just 11 points). It is therefore little wonder that output apparently shot up between 1978 and 1984; 1978 was a bad year and 1984 a very good year in terms of the weather.

To be sure, it is important not to exaggerate the improved level of food consumption. Even at close to 2,500 kilocalories per day, China's level of food consumption in the late 1970s was little more than adequate for a population

[45] Rainfall patterns during the Great Leap Forward were not particularly unusual. It is true that there was poor weather in the provinces of Sichuan, Henan, and Anhui, and that all three suffered severe famine. In principle, however, the central government could have reduced procurements in the three, and transferred grain to them from provinces where the weather remained good (especially in the northeast). Such transfers would not have offset the fall in production caused by policy failure, but they would have been enough to mitigate the impact of poor weather.

predominantly engaged in hard manual labour. Moreover, most kilocalories were provided by plant products (primarily grain and vegetables), and very few from meat or fish. And consumption levels in the 1970s were not so very much higher than they had been in the 1930s. Nevertheless, a positive appraisal of the Maoist record is in order on the basis of these new estimates. The old view that food consumption levels stagnated after the 1950s requires modification in the light of these new findings.

The Mortality Record

The Maoist record on life expectancy is even better than for material living standards (Table 17.7). The population censuses of 1953 and 1964 were impressively complete by the standards of poor countries. Nevertheless, they tended to underreport mortality (especially infant mortality) and therefore official estimates of life expectancy for the 1950s are too high; compare them with the Banister and World Bank estimates in Table 17.7. By the late 1970s, the underreporting problem was much less because of the careful 1973–1975 mortality survey, which collected data on the causes of over 15 million deaths during the three-year period but reached as far west as Tibet and Xinjiang.[46] The results of the 1982 census are therefore very reliable and, when combined with adjusted estimates for the 1950s, suggest a true life expectancy increase of around fifteen years at birth between 1957 and 1978, almost double the official increase. The infant mortality data exhibit very similar trends. This is hardly surprising because infant mortality was the main reason for low life expectancy in the 1950s. Nevertheless, the improvement is striking. Banister's reconstruction shows the infant mortality rate in 1978 as being about a quarter of what it was in the early 1950s, and the official data show that it was only around a third of its 1952 value.

China's remarkable mortality record contrasts sharply with that of India.[47] This is a useful comparison. The countries are of similar size, they broke free of colonial influences at approximately the same time, and they entered the postcolonial era with similar levels of development; China's life expectancy

---

[46] The survey covered twenty-four of China's provincial-level jurisdictions; it omitted Gansu, Hubei, Shandong, Guangxi, and Guangdong. See Rong Shoude 戎寿得, Li Junyao 黎均耀, Gao Runquan 高润泉, Dai Xudong 戴旭栋, Cao Dexian 曹德贤, Li Guangyi 李广义, and Zhou Youshang 周有尚, "我国 1973–1975 年居民平均期望寿命统计分析" (Statistical Analysis of Mortality and Life Expectancy in China in 1973–1975), in Beijing jingji xueyuan 北京经济学院, 中国人口科学理论 (A Symposium on Chinese Population Science) (Beijing, Zhongguo xueshu chubanshe, 1981), pp. 49–58.

[47] A. Sen, "Food and Freedom," *World Development* 17.6 (1989), 769–81.

Table 17.7 Life expectancy and infant mortality in China, 1952–1981

	Life expectancy (years at birth)			Infant mortality (per 1,000 live births)	
	Banister	World Bank	Official	Banister	Official
1952					133
1953	40			175	122
1954	42			164	112
1955	45			154	105
1956	47			143	106
1957	50		60	132	92
1958	46			146	119
1959	43			160	135
1960	25	43		284	121
1961	38	44		183	108
1962	53	44		89	73
1963	55	46	62	87	73
1964	57	47		86	79
1965	58	49		84	73
1966	59	51		83	64
1967	59	53		82	67
1968	60	55		81	55
1969	61	57		76	57
1970	61	59		70	51
1971	62	60		65	51
1972	63	61		60	52
1973	63	62		56	51
1974	63	63		52	50
1975	64	64	66	49	50
1976	64	64		45	45
1977	65	65		41	41
1978	65	66	68	37	41
1979	65	66		39	40
1980	65	67		42	43
1981	65	67	68	44	38

Notes. Official life expectancy data are given in life tables for the years shown. The 1957 and 1963 official estimates are based on very small rural samples, and therefore overstate the true level of life expectancy.

Sources: Judith Banister, *China's Changing Population* (Stanford, Stanford University Press, 1987), p. 116; World Bank, *World Development Indicators 2017*, at https://data.worldbank.org/data-catalog/world-development-indicators (accessed July 10, 2017); Zhongguo shehui kexueyuan renkou yanjiusuo 中国社会科学院人口研究所, 中国人口年鉴 1991 (Chinese Population Yearbook) (Beijing, Jingji guanli chubanshe, 1991), p. 537; Zhongguo renkou qingbao 中国人口情报中心, 中国人口资料手册 (Handbook on Chinese Population Materials) (Beijing, Jingji guanli chubanshe, 1986), pp. 475–516

was higher in the early 1950s (forty years at birth compared with thirty-seven years), but the difference was small. Despite these similarities, the life expectancy gap between China and India had grown to over ten years (sixty-six years compared with fifty-six years) by the early 1980s. In accounting terms, the "demographic gains" from this improvement more than offset the impact of the famine deaths that China experienced.

The reasons for China's success are relatively well known.[48] Part of it was down to public-health campaigns. Examples include a reduction in syphilis-related deaths (itself reflecting the campaign against prostitution and the increased use of penicillin), a ban on opium use, and the anti-schistosomiasis campaign implemented by draining and clearing waterways. More important for the mortality reduction, especially amongst infants, was the creation of a relatively simple but extensive system of rural health care which centered on immunization programs. At the center of the program were the "barefoot" doctors – paramedics perfectly capable of carrying out inoculation and giving health care advice. Although it has been fashionable in the last ten years to decry the achievements of this group – and their predecessors (strictly, barefoot doctors only existed after 1968) – their efforts were remarkably successful. Their key roles were in terms of the training of midwives, which was instrumental in the massive decline in the infant mortality rate, and inoculation against traditional diseases such as smallpox, diphtheria, and tuberculosis. By contrast, successive Indian governments provided high-quality health care for high-income earners in urban centers but neglected rural health care.[49]

Income Distribution

How can we square Maoist China's modest record on per capita GDP and food consumption with its outstanding achievements in terms of life expectancy? Part of the answer lies in the relatively low-cost but effective health care

---

[48] For a discussion of mortality and health care, see J. Banister, *China's Changing Population* (Stanford, Stanford University Press, 1987), pp. 78–120; J. Banister and S.H. Preston, "Mortality in China," *Population and Development Review* 7.1 (1981) 98–110; Gao, *Gao Village*, Chapter 6; J. Banister and K. Hill, "Mortality in China 1964–2000," *Population Studies* 58.1 (2004), 55–75; K.S. Babiarz, K. Eggleston, G. Miller, and Q. Zhang, "An Exploration of China's Mortality Decline under Mao: A Provincial Analysis, 1950–80," *Population Studies* 69.91 (2015), 39–56; R. Alvarez-Klee, "China: The Development of the Health System during the Maoist Period (1949–76)," *Business History* 61.3 (2019), 518–37.

[49] See J. Drèze and A. Sen, *An Uncertain Glory: India and Its Contradictions* (London, Allen Lane, 2013), Chapter 6.

system noted in the previous section. The rest probably lies in the more equal distribution of income and consumption that was the norm during the post-1949 era.[50]

Rural Inequality

Previous work on rural inequality has usually compared Roll's estimate of inequality for 1952 with the data published for the late 1970s when the SSB resumed data collection after the Cultural Revolution.[51] However, we now have data for other years, notably the results of the 1954 SSB income survey mentioned earlier. There are still many gaps – I have not, for example, seen any data for 1965, which was the year of a relatively large SSB income survey. Nevertheless, we can paint a more accurate picture of inequality than has hitherto been possible.

Inequality in rural China dropped sharply between the mid-1930s and 1949 as a result of land reform and CCP-led rent and interest rate reduction campaigns in regions "liberated" early (Figure 17.1). Inequality fell further once land reform was complete: the Gini for per capita income was just 0.18 in 1954. Further reductions occurred as a result of collectivization, which eliminated the rich-peasant economy and its associated sideline activities; by 1956–1957, the rural Gini was just 0.1, barely a quarter of what it had been in the mid-1930s.

The trajectory of rural inequality between 1957 and 1965 was probably upwards. Inequality *may* have declined further during the late 1950s as a result of the Great Leap Forward. However, the impact of the famine was to usher in a period of liberalization of the household economy, and even decollectivization in some provinces (notably Anhui). Evidence for Hebei, for example, shows that the share of sidelines rose from just 2.5 percent in 1957 to 30 percent in 1963, and it was still at 23 percent in 1965. In Anhui, the share rose from 29 percent in 1956 to 56 percent in 1962.[52] Of course, the extent of liberalization varied across provinces in the early 1960s and decollectivization was

---

[50] Considerations of space preclude a discussion of broader aspects of inequality, such as inequalities in power and human rights. The record of the Maoist regime was dismal in most of these areas. The central issue, as Sen, "Food and Freedom," rightly notes, is whether the lack of these freedoms was offset by the positive impact of food security (at least after 1962), and rising life expectancy, for the Chinese poor. The case can certainly be made that Maoist China's record, for all its failures, was far better than that of India precisely because of its achievements in terms of basic needs.

[51] C. Roll, *The Distribution of Rural Incomes in China* (London, Garland, 1980); I. Adelman and D. Sunding, "Economic Policy and Income Distribution in China," *Journal of Comparative Economics* 11.3 (1987), 444–61.

[52] Guojia tongjiju 国家统计局 (National Statistical Office), 各省自治区直辖市农民收入消费调查研究资料汇编 (Summary Research Materials from Rural Income and Expenditure Surveys in China's Provinces) (Beijing, Zhongguo tongji chubanshe, 1985), pp. 183, 237.

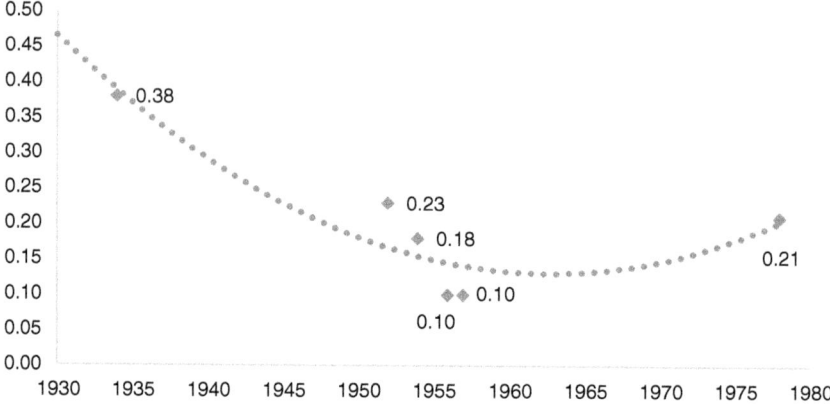

Figure 17.1 Gini coefficients for rural per capita income, 1934–1978
Note. The trend shown here is my interpretation of the data. I have used the Brandt–Sands estimate for per capita rural incomes for the 1930s.
Sources: L. Brandt and B. Sands, "Land Concentration and Income Distribution in Republican China," in T. Rawski and L. Li (eds.), *Chinese History in Economic Perspective* (Berkeley, University of California Press, 1992), p. 202; C. Roll, *The Distribution of Rural Incomes in China* (London, Garland, 1980); Guojia tongjiju 国家统计局 (National Statistical Office), *1954 年全国农家收支调查资料* (Materials on the 1954 National Peasant Household Income and Expenditure Survey) (Beijing, Zhongguo tongji chubanshe, 1956); Nongyebu 农业部, 农业经济资料手册 (Handbook of Materials on the Agricultural Economy) (Beijing, Nongye chubanshe, 1959), pp. 92–3; Guojia tongjiju 国家统计局 (National Statistical Office), 中国农村居民调查年鉴 2006 (Chinese Rural Household Survey Yearbook 2006) (Beijing, Zhongguo tongji chubanshe, 2006), p. 34

swiftly halted. Nevertheless, although the rise is difficult to quantify, rural inequality was higher by 1965 than it had been in 1957.

We know least about rural inequality between 1965 and 1978. It is likely that inequality fell back to its late 1950s levels during the late 1960s as collective farming was reimposed in renegade provinces, as sidelines were suppressed and because the relatively egalitarian need-based Dazhai work point allocation model was used. After the fall of Lin Biao in 1971, however, controls were relaxed and work point allocation was increasingly driven by work done. As a result, the share of household income in total income may have risen; Dikötter makes much of this, portraying the revival of the private sector as the engine of late Maoist growth.[53] There is some support for this: in Guangdong, the sideline share rose from 34 percent of total income in 1974 to

[53] F. Dikötter, *The Cultural Revolution* (London, Bloomsbury, 2016).

40 percent by 1980.⁵⁴ But Guangdong was probably exceptional. In Yunnan the sideline share barely changed between 1966 and 1976, hovering at around 34 percent. Even in Anhui, which decollectivized in the late 1970s, the sideline share was only 24 percent in 1978, well below the 37 percent recorded in 1966. Moreover, it is possible that, if we (controversially) assume that poor households focused more on sideline production than richer households because of desperation, rising household sideline income may have reduced inequalities. In the case of rural Hubei, for which we have data on 750 households, the rural Gini seemingly declined from 0.22 in 1974 to 0.19 in 1978.⁵⁵ But whatever the trend in the 1970s, there is little doubt that collective farming and restrictions on the private sector constrained inequality. The national survey results for 1978, for example, reveal a Gini for rural per capita income in that year of just 0.21, somewhat higher than twenty years earlier but nevertheless low by Chinese historical standards.

It is, of course, true that all these data on income inequality are suspect. The 1934 estimate probably understates inequality because the National Land Commission survey excluded much of southwestern China where landlordism was a particular problem. Second, many of the post-1949 surveys were colored by powerful ideological imperatives. For example, the 1954 survey covered over 72,000 peasants and disaggregated income and consumption by province and by class, which provides 115 data points. However, one of its purposes was to show the advantages of co-operation; for that reason, the usual class categories of poor peasant, middle peasant, rich peasant, and landlord were supplemented with that of co-operative members. Third, we know little about the surveys of 1956 and 1957. Fourth, the surveys of the late 1970s and early 1980s were small-scale and tended to undersample both rich and poor households.⁵⁶

For all that, we can be relatively confident about the trend: there was a sharp fall in inequality in the early 1950s, further falls in the mid-1950s, and

---

⁵⁴ Guangdong tongjiju 广东统计局, 广东省国民经济和社会发展统计资料 1949–88: 农业 (Statistical Materials on the Development of Guangdong's Economy and Society 1949–88: Agriculture Volume) (Beijing, Zhongguo tongji chubanshe, 1989), pp. 78–9.
⁵⁵ National Statistical Office, 各省自治区直辖市农民收入消费调查研究资料汇编, pp. 12–13, 152 and 183.
⁵⁶ C. Bramall, "The Quality of China's Household Income Surveys," *China Quarterly* 167 (2001), 689–705.

then a gradual rise from the early 1970s onwards. The catalysts for the long-run decline were undoubtedly land reform, collective ownership of land, and the suppression of private-sector production, moneylending, and commerce.

There is not much evidence that the decline in rural inequality was driven by a narrowing of income gaps between provinces. To be sure, the data for nominal per capita net peasant income do show a decline (Table 17.8). If we compare 1954 (the year of the first large-scale post-1949 income survey) with 1978 (the year in which large-scale income surveys resumed after the Cultural Revolution), the coefficient of variation for provincial-level jurisdictions declined significantly from 0.36 to 0.29. If we exclude the metropolitan centers of Beijing, Tianjin, and Shanghai, the decline is larger still (from 0.35 to 0.21).

However, this apparent decline in spatial inequality is misleading. For one thing, we need to adjust for differences in provincial inflation rates. If we proxy income by per capita personal expenditure, and employ the deflators used by the SSB, the apparent fall in the coefficient of variation (CV) is in fact reversed – the CV rises from 0.28 to 0.32 between 1952–1957 and 1973–1978. If we exclude Beijing, Shanghai, and Tianjin, the CV for real per capita personal

Table 17.8 Coefficients of variation (CVs) for provincial per capita net peasant income, 1954 and 1978 (current yuan)

	All provincial-level jurisdictions		Excluding metropolitan centers	
	1954	1978	1954	1978
Mean	79.1	143.7	73.8	134.2
SD	28.5	41.7	25.5	27.6
CV	0.36	0.29	0.35	0.21

Note. "Metropolitan" refers to Beijing, Tianjin, and Shanghai.
Sources: I estimate the 1954 data figures from the 1954 income and expenditure survey by subtracting production costs from gross income; see SSB, 1954 调查, pp. 155, 185, 218. Data for Yunnan, Ningxia, Beijing, and Shanghai are averages of the 1952 and 1957 values given in National Statistical Office, 各省自治区直辖市农民收入消费调查研究资料汇编. We lack data on Qinghai and Tibet, Guangdong includes Hainan, and Sichuan includes Chongqing. The 1978 data come from Guojia tongjiju (National Statistical Office), 各省自治区直辖市农民收入消费调查研究资料汇编 (Compilation of Survey Materials on Rural Income and Expenditure by Province) (Beijing, Zhongguo tongji chubanshe, 1985).

expenditure does decline, but rather modestly (from 0.28 to 0.24).[57] Second, the measure of inequality matters. If we calculate the Gini coefficients for per capita expenditure for 1954 and 1978 rather than the CV, the Gini rises from 0.126 to 0.137. Even if we exclude the metropolitan centers, the Gini coefficient barely declines (0.125 in 1954 and 0.121 in 1978). Third, the 1978 data are unreliable because the SSB samples were biased; as discussed earlier, the income estimates for 1978 are almost certainly too high. In fairness, however, the upward biases in the 1978 survey were *probably* also present in the 1954 survey, and therefore the reported trend in provincial incomes may still adequately capture the reality.

On balance, the safest conclusion is that spatial inequality at the provincial level changed little between the 1950s and the 1970s. It was the decline in intra-local inequality – due to land reform, collectivization, and the suppression of private-sector activity – which drove the decline in the overall rural Gini coefficient between 1952 and 1978.

Rural Poverty

Asset redistribution, income growth, and the partial allocation of work points on the basis of need did much to reduce poverty. A sign of China's success comes from the experience of provinces where food consumption levels were low in the 1950s. In Anhui, for example, calorie consumption rose from 1,967 kilocalories in 1957 to 2,333 kilocalories in 1978. For Sichuan, the rise was from 1,976 kilocalories in 1957 to 2,835 kilocalories in 1978. Jilin reported a rise from 1,970 in 1965 to 2,281 in 1978. The Fujian data show an increase from 1,800 kilocalories in 1954 and 1957 to 2,229 in 1978. And Hubei survey data record a rise from 1,855 kilocalories in 1954 to 2,222 kilocalories in 1978.[58]

A rare complete data series for the very poor province of Guizhou also shows a clear rise in grain and meat consumption between 1938 and 1978 (Figure 17.2). Meat consumption, for example, rose from around five kilograms per head to around 7.5 kilograms per head. Such survey estimates of consumption may well be more reliable than food balance estimates because they are not affected by the pervasive problem of output underreporting.

---

[57] I use the SSB deflators for per capita peasant expenditure because, flawed or not, it is better to use them than rely on current price data. As noted earlier, personal expenditure data are derived by the SSB from the national accounts.

[58] National Statistical Office, 各省自治区直辖市农民收入消费调查研究资料汇编, pp. 44, 174, 229, 340; Liu Hongkang 刘洪康, 中国人口—四川分册 (China's Population – Sichuan) (Beijing, Zhongguo caizheng jingji chubanshe, 1988), p. 369.

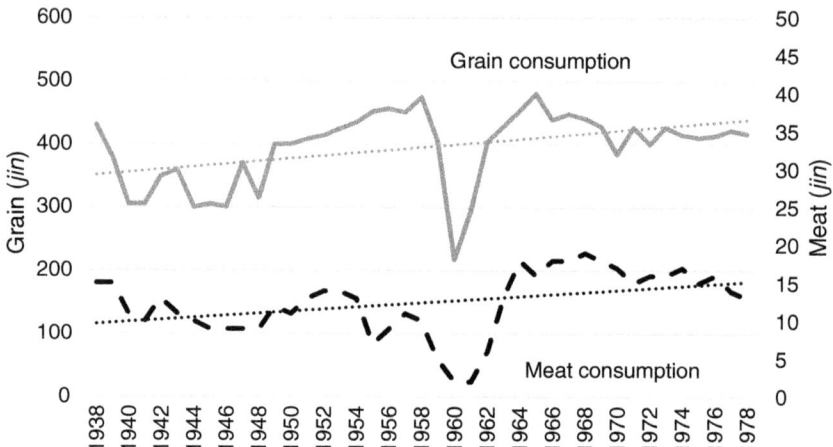

Figure 17.2 Per capita rural consumption of meat and grain in Guizhou, 1938–1978
Note. 1 *jin* = 0.5 kilograms.
Source: National Statistical Office, 各省自治区直辖市农民收入消费调查研究资料汇编, pp. 421–2

Moreover, the post-1949 trends look plausible enough, not least the dramatic decline in consumption during the Great Famine.

Nevertheless, and despite these long-run improvements in income and consumption, absolute poverty persisted in the Chinese countryside. In 1978, for example, there were 377 counties across China where distributed collective income was less than fifty yuan, well below the national average of eighty-nine yuan.[59] Of the 377 counties, many were located in geographically disadvantaged western China; there were fifty-eight in Guizhou, twenty-eight in Yunnan, twenty-four in Shaanxi, and twenty-seven in Gansu. Yet, as already observed for Henan, many poor counties were also located on the north China plain. There were forty-six very poor counties in Shandong, seventeen in Hebei, fifteen in Anhui, and, reflecting its low level of grain production, forty-five in Henan.[60] Moreover, the county data hide pools of poverty. Even within relatively rich provinces, income levels were low in many locations. Twenty-nine percent of Liaoning's 87,744 production teams had a per capita distributed income of less than fifty yuan in 1974, and that percentage rose to 31 percent in

[59] Nongyebu, 农业经济资料手册, p. 523. Total net per capita income, which includes sidelines and private-plot production, was 134 yuan.
[60] Nongyebu 农业部, 全国农村人民公社收银分配统计资料 1956–80 (Statistical Materials on Income Distribution in China's Communes, 1956–80) (Beijing, Nongyebu, 1981), pp. 142–3.

1976. Even in 1978, when the harvest was better, incomes in 19 percent of teams were still below the fifty-yuan mark.[61] This does not mean that there were poor *counties*; per capita income did not fall below fifty yuan in any Liaoning county in 1978. But there were pockets of poverty *within* otherwise well-off counties.

The main reason for persistent rural poverty was the low level of per capita grain production.[62] Grain was the key source of calories, providing around 85 percent in the late 1970s. Moreover, the lack of imports, the absence of private commerce, and fewer spatial transfers by the state than in the 1950s, meant that per capita production was a good guide to consumption.[63] At the top end, there were nine state-designated commodity grain bases which supplied most of the state-procured grain. In these nine, per capita grain output exceeded 800 *jin* in 1977. The Sanjiang plain base (northeastern Heilongjiang), for example, produced 885 *jin* per head, the Lake Taihu base (straddling the Jiangsu–Zhejiang border) produced 980 *jin*, and the highest figure was the 1,010 *jin* recorded in the Pearl river delta base in Guangdong.[64]

Elsewhere, however, grain output per head was lower (Table 17.9). Across great swathes of China, per capita production struggled to reach 700 *jin* per person. Much of this was a consequence of adverse physical geography, which militated against high grain yields in much of western China, on the loess plateau, and in the southeast. Conversely, growing conditions were more favourable on the (eastern) Yangzi river and in the "frontier" region of Manchuria. The real surprise is the low level of production in the Huai, Hai, and Huang river basins in eastern China, which encompass much of the north China plain. This vast area, covering the bulk of Hebei, Henan, Shandong, and Anhui provinces, was home to 23 percent of China's rural population, yet grain output per head in 1977 (306 kilograms) was well below the national average of 355 kilograms. Much Maoist energy went into improving irrigation in the region in order to expand multiple cropping, but per capita output

---

[61] Liaoning nongyeju 辽宁农业局, 辽宁农业历史资料 (Historical Materials on Liaoning's Agriculture) (Shenyang, Liaoning nongyeju, 1982), pp. 174–6.
[62] The suppression of sidelines in areas which had no comparative advantage in grain production (mountainous areas or coastal areas with saline soil) did not help, but most of the poor households in the 1970s were located in places where grain production did make sense.
[63] State grain procurements declined as a percentage of output between the 1950s and 1970s because excessive procurements were (rightly) blamed for exacerbating food shortages during the Great Leap Forward. In the absence of large-scale spatial transfers, the promotion of local grain self-sufficiency therefore became a key policy during the 1960s and 1970s.
[64] Nongye quhua weiyuanhui 农业区划委员会, 全国综合农业区划报告 (Comprehensive Report on China's Agricultural Regions) (Beijing, Nongyebu, 1980), p. 157.

Table 17.9 Per capita grain output by agricultural region, 1977

Region	Number of counties	Share of national rural population (%)	Per capita grain output (kilograms)
Manchuria	179	7	518
Inner Mongolia and along the Great Wall	129	3	342
Huang–Huai–Hai basin	383	23	306
Loess plateau	227	7	317
Middle and lower Yangzi valley	527	29	396
Southwest	418	19	318
Huanan	193	10	317
Northwest	127	2	386
Tibetan plateau	147	1	575
NATIONAL	2330	100	710

Note. Grain output in unhusked kilograms. These unhusked data exaggerate the true divide between the northern wheat region and the southern rice region because the milling rate for rice (67 percent) was much less than for grains such as wheat (around 98 percent).
Source: Nongye quhua weiyuanhui 农业区划委员会, 全国综合农业区划报告 (Comprehensive Report on China's Agricultural Regions) (Beijing, Nongyebu, 1980), p. 7

remained stubbornly low. The very persistence of low output testifies to the inability even of the mass mobilization of labor made possible by the Maoist model to overcome fundamental geographical constraints.

Urban Inequality

We can say less about inequality in the urban sector. Part of the problem is that the urban surveys for the 1950s made little attempt to measure inequality. This is especially true of the survey data collected by the SSB in the 1950s.[65] Some attempt to measure urban inequality was at least made in the 1960s. The 1964 survey, which covered 3,537 households, suggests a national urban Gini coefficient of around 0.2.[66] The available data for a handful of provinces are broadly

---

[65] For example, Guojia tongjiju 国家统计局 (National Statistical Office), 全国职工家庭生活调查资料 1956, 1958, 1980 (National Survey Materials on Worker Living Standards 1956, 1958, 1980) (Beijing, Zhongguo tongji chubanshe, 1956, 1958, 1980). There is some scattered information. For example, data on the size distribution for Shenyang suggest a Gini of 0.12 (Liaoning tongjiju, 辽宁城市人民生活史料, p. 215). However, these samples are too small and unrepresentative to tell us much.
[66] Guojia tongjiju 国家统计局 (National Statistical Office), 中国统计年鉴 1985 (Chinese Statistical Yearbook 1985) (Beijing, Zhongguo tongji chubanshe, 1985), p. 561.

consistent with this. For Liaoning province, for instance, we have data suggesting that the urban Gini declined to 0.22 in 1962, and to just 0.18 in 1965.[67] These Liaoning figures are comparable with the Henan urban Gini of 0.23 for 1964.[68]

The urban income surveys ceased during the Cultural Revolution and did not resume until 1977. For that year, Liaoning recorded an urban Gini coefficient of 0.16 in 1977.[69] We also have a figure for Hubei's urban population, which of course includes the major city of Wuhan, of 0.17. Both these estimates fit well with the reported national figure of 0.16 in 1978.[70] The same national figure was reported by the World Bank's mission to China for 1980.[71] It is worth recognizing, however, that the surveys were small in scale and not very representative of urban China. The national 1980 survey, for example, covered 8,715 households but 1,200 of these were from Beijing alone; oddly, Tianjin and Shanghai contributed only 500 households each, which was less than Shenyang's 600 households.[72]

These data suggest two conclusions. First, the data show that inequality declined; the urban Gini had fallen from 0.2 in 1964 to 0.16 by 1978. This is plausible given the impact of the Cultural Revolution on residual urban income differentials. There were strict controls on private-sector commerce and industry. There were limits to wage differentials within urban enterprises. And the virtual absence of rural-to-urban migration prevented the emergence of slums and an urban underclass. Second, the overall degree of urban inequality was low by world standards. Given controls on the private sector, the virtual absence of urban unemployment, narrow wage differentials, limits to rural–urban migration, and extensive income subsidies, it could hardly be otherwise.

Urban inequality did nevertheless persist, and as much by design as by accident. In part, this was because wage differentials were seen as an important way to motivate the urban workforce by rewarding those employed in testing jobs in heavy industries such as coal mining and steel manufacture. In

---

[67] Liaoning tongjiju, 辽宁城市人民生活史料, p. 81.
[68] Henan sheng difangshi zhi weiyuanhui 河南省地方市志委员会, 河南省志—人民生活志 (Henan Records – Living Standards) (Zhengzhou, Henan renmin chubanshe, 1995), p. 138.
[69] This is an interesting survey because it covered 6,935 urban households drawn from six Liaoning cities and seven counties (Liaoning tongjiju, 辽宁城市人民生活史料, p. 854). In size terms, this was similar to the 1980 national survey.
[70] Liaoning tongjiju, 辽宁城市人民生活史料, p. 81; Hubei tongjiju 湖北统计局, 湖北省国民经济统计资料 1949–1978 (Statistical Materials on the Hubei Economy 1949–1978) (Wuhan, Hubei tongji chubanshe, 1979), pp. 528–9.
[71] World Bank, *China: Socialist Economic Development*, p. 89.
[72] Liaoning tongjiju, 辽宁城市人民生活史料, p. 712.

1978, the average wage in state-owned coal mines was 810 yuan, compared with 605 yuan in food processing. Regional wage differentials also existed between the bigger cities. The average industrial wage in Shanghai was 881 yuan – it was higher still in "hardship" postings such as Tibet or Qinghai – but only 691 yuan in Fujian.[73] Within cities in the same provinces, there were also significant differences. In Sichuan, wages in state enterprises (of all types) were at their highest in Panzhihua at 711 yuan. They were lower in Chengdu (645 yuan) and significantly lower in some of the smaller cities; the Wanxian average was only 548 yuan.[74] By the standards of market economies, these were smaller differences, but they meant that significant urban income inequalities persisted even in Maoist China.

The Urban–Rural Income Gap

Despite the low levels of inequality within both urban and rural sectors, the overall degree of inequality in China in the late 1970s was still high by international standards. One influential estimate derived a rural Gini for 1978 of 0.22 and an urban Gini of 0.17 – but an overall Gini of 0.32.[75] This reflected the significant gap in average per capita income between China's urban and rural sectors.

Most of the literature uses official data on the urban–rural gap, which are themselves based upon the SSB's estimates of personal expenditure per head (Figure 17.3). In nominal terms, the gap rose from an average of 2.5:1 during 1952–1957 to 2.7:1 for 1974–1978. Adjusted for inflation, the gap averaged 2.6:1 during 1952–1957, rising to 3.1:1 during 1974–1978.[76] There was some provincial variation: in Liaoning, for example, the per capita income gap was about 1.7:1 in 1980.[77] Nevertheless, a significant urban–rural per capita expenditure gap was commonplace across China.

---

[73] Guojia tongjiju 国家统计局 (National Statistical Office), 中国劳动工资统计资料 1949–1985 (Statistical Materials on China's Labour Force and Wages, 1949–1985) (Beijing, Zhongguo tongji chubanshe, 1987) p. 159; Guojia tongjiju 国家统计局 (National Statistical Office), 中国劳动工资统计资料 1978–1987 (Statistical Materials on China's Labour Force and Wages 1978–1987) (Beijing, Zhongguo tongji chubanshe, 1989).

[74] Guojia tongjiju 国家统计局 (National Statistical Office), 1978 年城市国名经济基本情况统计 (Statistics on the State of the Urban Economy in 1978) (Beijing, Zhongguo tongji chubanshe, 1979), p. 143.

[75] Adelman and Sunding, "Economic Policy and Income Distribution in China," p. 453.

[76] Guojia tongjiju 国家统计局 (National Statistical Office), 中国统计年鉴 1991 (Chinese Statistical Yearbook 1991), p. 270.

[77] Based on a 1980 sample of 490 peasant households and 960 urban households. Liaoning tongjiju, 辽宁城市人民生活史料, pp. 840, 848.

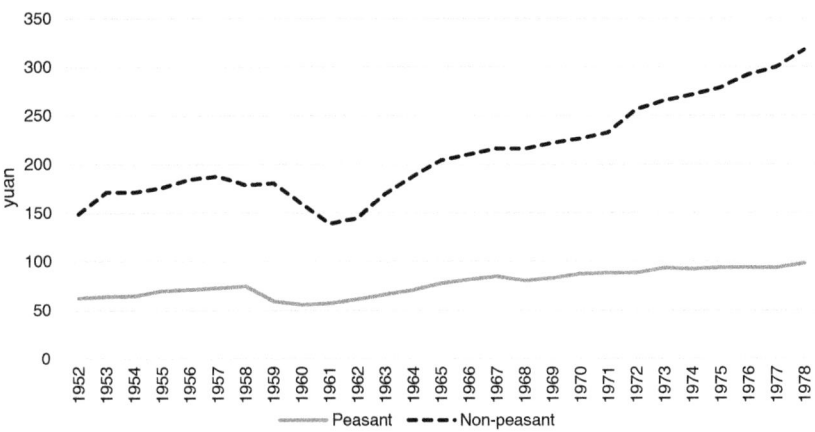

Figure 17.3 The urban–rural gap
Note. Data are for personal expenditure in real terms. The calculation uses the SSB's deflator.
Source: Guojia tongjiju 国家统计局 (National Statistical Office), 中国统计年鉴 1991 (Chinese Statistical Yearbook 1991) (Beijing, Zhongguo tongji chubanshe, 1991), p. 270

At first glance, the widening of the gap is surprising given that a range of explicitly pro-rural policies were pursued to prevent "urban bias." These included rural industrialization, the rapid expansion of rural education, and the "sending-down" of skilled labour and educated urban youth to the countryside. It appears, however, that these equalizing factors were offset by centripetal forces. On the one hand, urban incomes were pushed up by the growth of relatively highly paid urban jobs in higher-productivity heavy industry or the party-state bureaucracy (which was mainly based in urban centers). In addition, rises in urban participation rates offset relatively stagnant urban wages. On the other hand, rural incomes grew comparatively slowly because of state extraction of the rural surplus (via the manipulation of the internal terms of trade) to feed the urban state sector and to finance defense industrialization.

Most of the literature on the urban–rural gap is content to leave the discussion there. However, there are three important qualifications to this story. The first centers on the definition of "rural" and "urban." One of the features of Maoism was the program of Third Front construction initiated after 1964, whereby western China received high levels of defense-related investment. This investment created cities out of greenfield sites; one famous example is the steel-producing city of Panzhihua in southwestern Sichuan, which was classified as rural in the

1950s.⁷⁸ From an analytical point of view, this presents a problem: should Panzhihua be classified as urban or rural for the purpose of estimating the *change* in the urban–rural gap? It was manifestly rural in the 1950s, yet equally manifestly urban by 1978. This is important because treating places like Panzhihua as urban makes it almost impossible by definition for the urban–rural gap to close because any successful rural area ends up being reclassified as urban because of its prosperity. The difficulty here parallels the index number problem encountered in calculating growth rates: should one use the prices (read locational classification) of the first year (for which read rural) or the last year (urban)? In this particular case, it makes more analytical sense to classify Panzhihua as rural throughout the Maoist period because it is an example of successful development in an initially rural setting; it is an illustration of the countryside catching up.

A second difficulty in measuring the urban–rural gap is that the official gap estimates ignore the hefty subsidies paid only to the urban population. These subsidies covered foodstuffs, housing, heating, travel, and a range of welfare benefits. For state employees, they amounted to 80 percent of the wage by 1978.⁷⁹ Their impact was massive; they raise the urban–rural gap from around 3:1 to about 6:1 in the late 1970s.

The third problem relates to the prices used to measure non-marketed peasant production. If production is valued at 1952 retail prices (instead of state procurement prices), per capita peasant expenditure is raised by 26 percent in 1952, and by 20 percent in 1957. According to one set of estimates, this reduces the urban–rural gap from 2.4:1 to 1.9:1 in 1957.⁸⁰ The same sort of revision would be needed for the late 1970s. I do not attempt that here because it raises intractable questions about how to compute shadow retail prices in the context of the planned economy of the 1970s, but it is likely that using shadow prices would markedly reduce the urban–rural gap.

The net effect of all this is difficult to determine because the three factors discussed not only were significant but also operated in different directions: classifying "new" urban areas as rural and using notional retail prices to value non-marketed production would narrow the gap, whereas including urban

---

⁷⁸ The site chosen for Dukou city, later renamed Panzhihua, straddled two counties.
⁷⁹ Lardy, "Consumption and Living Standards in China," pp. 163–5; T. Rawski, "The Simple Arithmetic of Chinese Income Distribution," *Keizai Kenkyu* 33.1 (1982), 17.
⁸⁰ Guojia tongjiju 国家统计局 (National Statistical Office), 第一个五年计划全国国民收入生产和积累资料 (Materials on China's National Income, Production, Consumption and Accumulation during the First Five-Year Plan) (Beijing, Zhongguo tongji chubanshe, 1957), p. 16.

subsidies would widen it. It is probably safe to conclude that a significant urban–rural gap did exist in 1978; it is hard to see that urban reclassification and prices issues would eliminate a subsidy-adjusted income gap of around 6:1. However, we cannot go much further.

Conclusion

The revolutionary compact between the CCP and the Chinese peasantry in the 1930s and 1940s certainly rested in part upon the nationalist commitment to expel Japanese soldiers from Chinese territory and, more generally, for China to "stand up" against Western imperialism. But it also rested on a promise to deliver increases in living standards. This "promise of the Revolution" was not broken. Daily food consumption rose by well over 10 percent between the 1950s and 1970s. In this regard, Maoist China fared better than many other countries – Meiji Japan and Industrial Revolution Britain come to mind – during the early stages of their industrialization. China's intra-urban and intra-rural distributions of income and consumption were far more equal by the 1970s than during the 1930s. The proportion of the population acquiring a primary education increased dramatically. And, perhaps the greatest Maoist achievement, life expectancy at birth was twenty-five years higher than in the early 1950s.

Nevertheless, little more than basic food security had been achieved. Despite the rise in per capita real incomes and consumption, rural poverty was widespread in the 1970s even on the north China plain. Diets were heavy on grain and vegetables, but light on meat and vegetable oils. The great divide between countryside and city remained a chasm; the gilded literati of imperial China had been displaced by Party cadres and state employees, but the peasantry remained an underclass. Maoist China fared much less well than South Korea and Taiwan, despite starting from a rather similar point. In many respects, the level of material living standards achieved in China by the late 1970s was a meager return for the sacrifices that had been made. Moreover, no weighing of the Maoist record on the scales of history can ignore its appalling record on what Isaiah Berlin called "negative freedoms."[81] The Maoist regime certainly increased positive freedoms by expanding educational opportunity and basic health care. However, the Chinese population paid a terrible price. Mao himself admitted that the number of those killed during the land reform of the early 1950s exceeded 500,000. The death

[81] For a useful discussion of negative freedom, see Sen, "Food and Freedom," pp. 770–1.

toll during each of the purges of the late 1950s, during the Cultural Revolution, and in the early 1970s was equally high. China's penal colonies were full to overflowing. Its minority populations were repressed, and its intellectuals were continuously persecuted. Basic freedoms, notably the freedom to move locality and occupation and the right to speak free of constraint, were ruthlessly suppressed. The Maoist regime was a ghastly one in all these respects, and little has changed since 1976.

Whether any of this was an inevitable outcome of the Revolution is moot. I have argued elsewhere that the concomitant to Mao's commitment to ensuring that China "stood up" – in the sense of providing military security – was a squeeze on living standards; defense industrialization could not have been financed in any other way. Moreover, the suppression of human rights may have been necessary to extract the surplus to finance industrialization. And unflattering comparisons between China on the one hand, and Taiwan and South Korea on the other, are all very well, but China did not have access to US aid during the 1950s, or to US markets during the 1960s and 1970s. Nevertheless, China's defense industrialization, and everything that went with it, may not have been really necessary: the counterfactual proposition, that China could have established better relations with the USA (and the USSR) had Mao adopted a less hostile foreign policy before the rapprochement with Nixon of the 1970s, remains one of the great historical imponderables. But if one accepts the constraint imposed by the external threat, it may be that China came close to doing as well as it reasonably could have done – the disaster of the Great Famine aside – in terms of material living standards between 1949 and the time of Mao's death.

Further Reading

Babiarz, K.S., K. Eggleston, G. Miller, and Q. Zhang, "An Exploration of China's Mortality Decline under Mao: A Provincial Analysis, 1950–80," *Population Studies* 69.91 (2015), 39–56.

Banister, J., *China's Changing Population* (Stanford, Stanford University Press, 1987).

Bramall, C., *In Praise of Maoist Economic Planning* (Oxford, Clarendon Press, 1993).

Brandt, L., and B. Sands, "Land Concentration and Income Distribution in Republican China," in T. Rawski and L. Li (eds.), *Chinese History in Economic Perspective* (Berkeley, University of California Press, 1993), pp. 179–206.

Gao, M., *Gao Village* (London, Hurst and Co., 1999).

Guojia tongjiju 国家统计局 (National Statistical Office), 各省自治区直辖市农民收入消费调查研究资料汇编 (Compilation of Survey Materials on Rural Income and Expenditure by Province) (Beijing, Zhongguo tongji chubanshe, 1985).

Guojia tongjiju 国家统计局 (National Statistical Office), 中国国内生产直核算历史资料 1952–1995 (Historical Materials on Chinese GDP, 1952–1995) (Beijing, Dongbei caijing daxue chubanshe, 1997).
Liu, T.-C., and K.-C. Yeh, *The Economy of the Chinese Mainland* (Princeton, NJ, Princeton University Press, 1965).
Matsuda, Y., "Survey Systems and Sampling Designs of Chinese Household Surveys, 1952–1987," *Developing Economies* 28.3 (1990), 329–52.
Nongyebu 农业部, 农业经济资料 1949–1983 (Materials on the Agricultural Economy, 1949–1983) (Beijing, Nongmuyuye bu, 1983).
Piazza, A., *Food Consumption and Nutritional Status in the PRC* (Boulder, CO, Westview Press, 1986).
Potter, S., and J. Potter, *China's Peasants* (Cambridge, Cambridge University Press, 1990).
Riskin, C., *China's Political Economy* (Oxford, Oxford University Press, 1987).
Roll, C., *The Distribution of Rural Incomes in China* (London, Garland, 1980).
World Bank, *China: Socialist Economic Development*, vol. 1, *The Economy, Statistical System and Basic Data* (Washington, DC, World Bank, 1983).

18

The Political Economy of China's Great Leap Famine

JAMES KAI-SING KUNG

Introduction

Indisputably, the Great Leap Famine of 1958–1961 stands out in Chinese history as the most profound demographic catastrophe after six centuries of nearly uninterrupted population growth.[1] As some 30 million, or 5 percent of a population of 660 million, were wiped out within a short period of three years, it was by far the deadliest famine in human history.[2] However, until the demographic consequences of this catastrophe were fully revealed in the 1980s, the outside world assumed that China had solved its food problem

---

I would like to thank Cormac Ó Gráda for generously offering a number of insightful suggestions on an earlier draft, and Bingjing Li for useful comments. My greatest gratitude goes to Vicky Fangshu Jiang, whose enormously helpful assistance at an early stage greatly facilitated my writing, and to Wenbing Wu for excellent research assistance. I am also grateful for financial support provided by a GRF Grant (#17505519) and Sein and Isaac Souede. All remaining errors are, of course, mine.

[1] Unchecked population growth is the hallmark of a Malthusian regime. According to Malthus, excessive population growth in the absence of technical change would typically be corrected by wars, famines, and similar catastrophes. In the context of imperial China, population growth since the late fourteenth century was curbed only twice – once during the fall of Ming Dynasty in the seventeenth century, again during the Taiping Rebellion in the late nineteenth century. Unlike the Great Leap Famine, however, population loss during these episodes was caused by civil war. G. Clark, *A Farewell to Aims: A Brief Economic History of the World* (Princeton, Princeton University Press, 2007); T. Malthus, *An Essay on the Principle of Population* (London, Printed for J. Johnson, in St. Paul's Church-Yard, 1798).

[2] Thirty million represents the mid-point between the lowest and highest estimates (more below on this point). A death toll of this magnitude makes all other famines – including the North China Famine of 1876–1879 which wiped out between 9.5 million and 13 million people – pale in comparison. Going beyond China, the well-known Irish famine of 1845–1849 had a mortality of roughly a million people, while the 1973 Ethiopian Famine had a mortality estimated to be between 40,000 and 200,000. B. Ashton, K. Hill, A. Piazza, and R. Zeitz, "Famine in China, 1958–61," *Population and Development Review* 10 (1984), 613–45; C. Ó Gráda (2000). *Black '47 and Beyond: The Great Irish Famine in History, Economy, and Memory*, vol. 8 (Princeton, Princeton University Press); P. Gill, *Famine and Foreigners: Ethiopia since Live Aid* (New York, Oxford University Press, 2010).

following the founding of the People's Republic, when in fact the greatest famine in human history was just beginning to unfold.[3]

Until recently, the Great Chinese Famine had remained the "least understood event in human history."[4] The underlying causes of this human tragedy were unavoidably complex, as it occurred simultaneously with the Great Leap Forward (GLF) and all its attendant convoluted changes. The GLF was an unorthodox development strategy conceived by Mao to transform a predominantly agrarian China into a modern industrial state, chiefly by mobilizing a disproportionate pool of surplus rural labor to engage in economic activities outside agriculture, radically changing the ways by which agricultural production was organized.[5] Mao adopted a plethora of untried strategies to industrialize agrarian China at an incredibly rapid pace because he was constrained by a woeful lack of both capital and the advanced technology required to achieve this ambitious goal. These strategies resulted in his people bearing long-lasting, costly consequences. First, based on an optimistic but unfounded belief that China could increase its grain yields and output by leaps and bounds, Mao demanded more grain from the provinces to finance industrialization.[6] In addition, recent research has found that part of this "surplus" was also earmarked for export as China's relationship with the Soviet Union turned sour, obligating it to repay Soviet debt.[7] Regardless, excessive grain procurement has been found to have a discriminatory effect against the peasantry and correlates significantly and positively with excess deaths.[8] Were it not for the rigidity of central planning, the excessive consequences of planned procurement could have been corrected upon discovering that grain output actually fell short of the plan, which would have ameliorated

---

[3] The statement was made by Lord Boyd Orr in May of 1959, cited in Ashton et al., "Famine in China."

[4] G.H. Chang and G.J. Wen, "Communal Dining and the Chinese Famine of 1958–1961," *Economic Development and Cultural Change* 46 (1997), 1.

[5] The Great Leap Forward (*dayuejin* 大跃进) was part and parcel of the ideological slogan of the "Three Red Banners," which consisted also of "a general line for building socialism" (*shehui zhuyi jianshe zongluxian* 社会主义建设总路线) and "the people's commune" (*renmin gongshe* 人民公社), all of which were promulgated at the second plenary session of the Eighth National Congress on May 20, 1958.

[6] T.P. Bernstein, "Stalinism, Famine, and Chinese Peasants," *Theory and Society* 13.3 (1984), 339–77.

[7] H. Kasahara and B. Li, "Grain Exports and the Causes of China's Great Famine, 1959–1961: County-Level Evidence," *Journal of Development Economics* 146 (2020), 102513.

[8] J.K.S. Kung and J.Y. Lin, "The Causes of China's Great Leap Famine, 1959–1961," *Economic Development and Cultural Change* 52.1 (2003), 51–73; J.Y. Lin and D.T. Yang, "Food Availability, Entitlements and the Chinese Famine of 1959–61," *Economic Journal* 110.460 (2000), 136–58.

the death toll.⁹ Others, however, interpret excessive grain procurement as reflecting the extraordinarily strong incentives of provincial chiefs eager to rise through the political ranks from being lower alternate members to becoming full members of the Central Committee of the Chinese Communist Party during these politically tumultuous times, by remitting more grain to the center to signal their loyalty to Mao.¹⁰ Lower-level cadres had no alternatives but to comply.¹¹ Regardless of the cause, the excessive procurement of grain was a key feature of the GLF and strongly associated with the extra loss of life.

Second, to speed up industrial output, in particular of iron and steel, Mao allocated a substantial proportion of the rural labor force – some 30 to 50 percent – to manufacturing these items in the countryside using primitive "local methods" or *tufai* 土法, while confiscating farmers' private belongings such as cooking utensils and furniture as inputs to the "backyard furnaces" sprinkled all over the countryside – a "strategy" with allegedly similar catastrophic consequences.¹² Similarly, to stabilize yields Mao also sent many rural workers to work on irrigation projects during agricultural slack seasons, allegedly to the extent of leaving the crops unharvested in some places.¹³

Third, Mao also restructured the rural institutions as a cornerstone of his bold development strategy. Specifically, to facilitate large-scale irrigation works as well as to industrialize the countryside, Mao merged the agricultural

---

⁹ In addition, these authors find the corroborative evidence that famine severity was highest in provinces with greatest grain output. An implicit corollary of this thesis is that Mao would have been willing to cut back procurement should the circumstances warrant it – a highly questionable assumption. See, e.g., T.P. Bernstein, "Mao Zedong and the Famine of 1959–1960: A Study in Wilfulness," *China Quarterly* 186 (2006), 421–45. X. Meng, N. Qian, and P. Yared, "The Institutional Causes of China's Great Famine, 1959–1961," *Review of Economic Studies* 82.4 (2015), 1568–1611.

¹⁰ J.K.S. Kung and S. Chen, "The Tragedy of the Nomenklatura: Career Incentives and Political Radicalism during China's Great Leap Famine," *American Political Science Review* 105.1 (2011), 27–45; J.K.S. Kung, "The Emperor Strikes Back: Political Status, Career Incentives and Grain Procurement during China's Great Leap Famine," *Political Science Research and Methods* 2.2 (2014), 179–211.

¹¹ According to Oi, lower-level village (brigade and team) cadres typically had enormous incentives to negotiate with their leaders for a smaller grain quota. However, such bargaining was largely ineffective, as their leaders did not want to risk punishment for having delivered less grain than expected. J.C. Oi, *State and Peasant in Contemporary China: The Political Economy of Village Government* (Berkeley, University of California Press, 1989). Bernstein, "Stalinism, Famine, and Chinese Peasants."

¹² J. Becker, *Hungry Ghosts: Mao's Secret Famine* (London, John Murray, 1996); W. Li and D. T. Yang, "The Great Leap Forward: Anatomy of a Central Planning Disaster," *Journal of Political Economy* 113.4 (2005), 840–77.

¹³ Kung and Lin, "The Causes of China's Great Leap Famine."

collectives into gigantic people's communes (*renmin gongshe* 人民公社). Consisting of several thousands of farm households whose remuneration was narrowly differentiated, Mao emphasized "perfect socialist consciousness" while neglecting the importance of incentives for individual work in boosting agricultural productivity. While the damaging effect of the commune on work incentives is clearly recognized,[14] what remains disputable is whether the damage was because of the unwieldy size and narrow wage differentials of the commune, or possibly because it prevented diligent farmers from returning to individual household farming should they find their coworkers not delivering the minimum effort required for efficient team farming – a right they had had before they were forced into the commune and to remain in it ever since.[15] In any case, the consequences of the impaired work incentives are also well rehearsed.

In addition to its dampening effect on work incentives, and operating on the assumption that food would be provided free and unrestrictedly, the commune also allegedly destroyed the incentives for people to economize on food consumption by establishing a communal dining system, which arguably "triggered" the great famine.[16] The combination of a rigidly aggressive procurement policy, the misallocation of a sizeable part of the rural labor force, and the institution of a commune with negative repercussions on both work and consumption incentives all render a critical analysis of the underlying cause(s) of the Great Leap Famine an exceedingly daunting exercise.

And, if the simultaneous occurrence of these vastly intricate events were not complicated enough when unveiling the underlying causes of the great Chinese famine, we must still reconcile the possible causes described above with the Chinese government's claim that the catastrophe in question was largely an inadvertent consequence of "three consecutive years of bad weather" – a claim that, while in the minority, has nonetheless also received scholarly support.[17] Furthermore, presumably due to malnutrition resulting from the famine, many have examined a variety of long-term consequences

---

[14] D. Perkins and S. Yusuf, *Rural Development in China* (Baltimore, Johns Hopkins University Press, 1984).

[15] J.Y. Lin, "Collectivization and China's Agricultural Crisis in 1959–1961," *Journal of Political Economy* 98.6 (1990), 1228–52.

[16] Yang thus likens the incentives underlying communal dining to a "tragedy of the commons." D. Yang, *Calamity and Reform in China: State, Rural Society, and Institutional Change* (Stanford, Stanford University Press 1996). See also G. Hardin, "The Tragedy of the Commons," *Science* 162.3859 (1968), 1243–8. Chang and Wen, "Communal Dining and the Chinese Famine."

[17] Y.Y. Kueh, *Agricultural Instability in China, 1931–1990: Weather, Technology, and Institutions* (Oxford, Clarendon Press, 1995).

of the Great Leap Famine in respect of health, education, and socioeconomic status,[18] while others have attempted to link endurance of this catastrophe to the choice of farm institutions through the channel of "collective memory" and to economic development more generally.[19]

While the underlying *causes* of excess deaths during the GLF is certainly an issue of epic proportions, clearly it is not the only issue worthy of scholarly attention. For instance, the reaction of peasants to the myriad monumental changes imposed on them as a consequence of agricultural collectivization and the GLF in general, and more specifically the extraordinary pressure exerted upon them by officials to eke out the already meager amount of food on which their survival critically depended, are clearly topics deserving serious scholarly attention in the future.[20] As another example, our chapter is also reticent on the extent to which the famine in question was caused by starvation specifically or by infectious diseases such as typhus, dysentery, and malaria – a topic on which we have relatively scarce information.[21] As will become apparent, it is not easy to strike a balance in writing a review essay of this nature. While every effort was made to include as broad a coverage of everything related to the GLF as possible, it is inevitable that many important

---

[18] Y. Chen and L.-A. Zhou, "The Long-Term Health and Economic Consequences of the 1959–1961 Famine in China," *Journal of Health Economics* 26.4 (2007), 659–81; D. Almond, L. Edlund, H. Li, and J. Zhang, "Long-Term Effects of Early-Life Development: Evidence from the 1959 to 1961 China Famine," in T. Ito and A. Rose (eds.), *The Economic Consequences of Demographic Change in East Asia* (Chicago, The University of Chicago Press, 2010), pp. 321–45; X. Meng and N. Qian, "The Long-Term Consequences of Famine on Survivors: Evidence from a Unique Natural Experiment Using China's Great Famine" (No. w14917) (2009), National Bureau of Economic Research; T. Gørgens, X. Meng, and R. Vaithianathan, "Stunting and Selection Effects of Famine: A Case Study of the Great Chinese Famine," *Journal of Development Economics* 97.1 (2012), 99–111.

[19] Y. Bai and J.K.S. Kung, "The Shaping of an Institutional Choice: Weather Shocks, the Great Leap Famine, and Agricultural Decollectivization in China," *Explorations in Economic History* 54 (2014), 1–26; E. Gooch, "Estimating the Long-Term Impact of the Great Chinese Famine (1959–61) on Modern China," *World Development* 89 (2017), 140–51.

[20] Why, for instance, were Chinese peasants so docilely obedient even in the face of excessive grain procurement, when it became clear that it had proceeded to a point where it was a matter of life and death? Why did the resistance (or "counteraction," as it is called) that some peasants were observed to have put up fail to go beyond the concealment of production and private distribution of crops, as the late Chinese historian Gao Wangling discovered? What "survival strategies" other than, for example, migration, were involved? W. Gao, "A Study of Chinese Peasant 'Counter Action'," in K.E. Manning and F. Wemheuer (eds.), *Eating Bitterness: New Perspectives on China's Great Leap Forward and Famine* (Vancouver, UBC Press, 2011), pp. 272–94.

[21] Apart from the frequent mention of edema in several accounts, outright starvation appears to be an accepted cause of deaths in this great Chinese famine. C. Ó Gráda, *Eating People Is Wrong, and Other Essays on Famine, Its Past, and Its Future* (Princeton, Princeton University Press, 2015), pp. 145–7, contains a brief discussion of the subject matter.

topics such as those mentioned above had to be left out because either little is known about them or they go far beyond my limited expertise.

With this caveat in mind this chapter is thus intended to provide a thorough review of the relevant literature around which my own expertise revolves. We begin with a brief discussion of the various estimates of the demographic consequences of the Great Leap Forward, as well as outlining its salient features. We then provide a detailed review of the voluminous literature examining the underlying causes of the famine, by classifying the analyses into the categories of production, distribution, and consumption. This will be followed by a summary of the growing literature on the famine's long-term impact, both on the well-being of individual survivors and on institutional choice and economic development. A conclusion follows.

Excess Deaths and Salient Features

Estimates of Excess Deaths

With the demise of Mao and the downfall of the "Gang of Four" (*sirenban* 四人幫) China entered a new era. Under the new leadership of Deng, a pragmatic reformer, a population census was conducted in 1982 – an exercise that compiled and released useful data on the country's age distribution, fertility trends, birth and death registrations, and other vital statistics. Two striking features of the Great Leap Forward were revealed by these statistical data – a sharp rise in the death rate and a drastic decline in the birth rate. Taken together, the population declined by 13.5 million over the two years of 1960–1961.[22] A salient issue, in this context, is the number of excess deaths caused by this tragedy, where demographers define excess death rates as the difference between actual death rates and the rates predicted by the linear trend calculated using population data both before and after the Great Chinese Famine.[23] Estimates made by these

---

[22] A.J. Jowett, "The Demographic Responses to Famine: The Case of China 1958–61," *GeoJournal* 23.2 (1991), 135–46; *Statistical Yearbook of China*, 1983.

[23] J.S. Aird, "Population Studies and Population Policy in China," *Population and Development Review* 8 (1982), 267–97; Ashton et al., "Famine in China"; J. Banister, *China's Changing Population* (Stanford, Stanford University Press, 1987); A.J. Coale, "Population Trends, Population Policy, and Population Studies in China," *Population and Development Review* 7 (1981), 85–97; X. Peng, "Demographic Consequences of the Great Leap Forward in China's Provinces," *Population and Development Review* 13.4 (1987), 639–70.

demographers fall closely within the range of 23 to 30 million,[24] the upper end of which doubles the government's claim of 15 million.[25] Suspicious of its validity, Cao Shuji made a herculean effort to reconstruct excess deaths from county annals.[26] By totaling the population difference between 1958 and 1961 on a county-by-county basis, and by taking into account natural population growth and net migration, this demographic historian puts the tally at 32.5 million, which is strikingly close to the upper-bound estimates based on census data.[27]

Others have joined in the guessing game. For example, in a biography of Mao, Chang and Halliday increase the estimate of excess deaths – "close to 38 million people died of starvation and overwork"[28] – while Yang Jisheng, a journalist, concludes that a number of 36 million "approaches the reality but [it was] still too low."[29] More recently, historian Dikötter embraced the estimate proposed by Chen Yizi, a member of an investigation team in the 1980s famous for his anti-Mao stance who claimed to have firsthand access to "internal party documents,"[30] based on which he contended that the famine took 45 million lives "at a minimum."[31] While these revisions provide additional reference points, the analytic rigor of their estimates has been subjected to serious questioning.[32]

[24] For example, Aird, "Population Studies and Population Policy in China," and Coale, "Population Trends," put the death toll at 27 million; Ashton et al., "Famine in China" at 30 million; C. Ó Gráda, "Great Leap, Great Famine: A Review Essay," *Population and Development Review* 39.2 (2013), 333–46 at below 30 million; and Banister, *China's Changing Population*, at 30 million. By extrapolating data based on fourteen provinces to the remainder, Peng's ("Demographic Consequences of the Great Leap Forward") estimates put the excess death toll at 23 million.

[25] When estimating the death toll, most demographers make systematic adjustments for the underregistration of deaths that probably resulted from the breakdown of the registration system during the Leap, and from the ubiquitous omission of infant mortality in the census survey. Banister, *China's Changing Population*.

[26] Cao Shuji 曹树基, 大饑荒: 1959–1961 年代中國人口 (The Great Famine and China's Population in 1959–1961) (Hong Kong, Shidai guoji chuban youxian gongsi, 2005).

[27] A caveat is that Cao only managed to do so for seventeen provinces.

[28] J. Chang and J. Halliday, *Mao: The Unknown Story* (London, Jonathan Cape, 2005), p. 456.

[29] J. Yang, *Tombstone: The Great Chinese Famine, 1958–1962* (trans. E. Friedman, Guo Jian, and S. Mosher) (New York, Farrar, Strauss, and Giroux, 2012), p. 430.

[30] Cited in Becker, *Hungry Ghosts*, pp. 271–2. According to Chen, the famine cost between 43 and 46 million lives. However, Bramall is skeptical of the objectivity of Chen's estimate. C. Bramall, "Agency and Famine in China's Sichuan Province, 1958–1962," *China Quarterly* 208 (2011), 990–1008.

[31] Dikötter essentially arrives at his number simply by applying a 50 percent upward adjustment to Cao's estimate. F. Dikötter, *Mao's Great Famine: The History of China's Most Devastating Catastrophe, 1958–1962* (New York, Walker & Co., 2010); Cao, 大饑荒.

[32] The estimates by Yang and Dikötter are criticized as excessive as they relied heavily on an "implausibly low pre-famine death rate" for 1957, for which Western demographers such as Banister have proposed adjustments. However, Banister's estimate of 30 million

Salient Features

The Great Leap Famine has several salient features. The first is that the famine was disproportionately more severe in rural areas. While the death rate in the cities was 13.7 per thousand in 1960, it was in excess of twenty-eight per thousand in the countryside – an inequality that was allegedly rooted in China's grain procurement system having an inherent bias against the peasantry.[33] From this perspective, urban residents were guaranteed a minimum grain ration, but rural people were only entitled to what was left to them after grain was procured – the residuum. In normal times, when adequate food was available in rural areas, the peasants had enough to eat. However, during the famine, food ran short as a result of the exaggeration of grain output figures and consequent overprocurement, resulting in the difference in the availability of grain between urban and rural residents widening.[34] Crude evidence suggests that, while city dwellers were entitled to 303 kilograms per capita per annum during the famine period, their rural counterparts had only 223 kilograms, 26.4 percent less than urban consumption and 19 percent short of the recommended benchmark of 275 kilograms.[35]

A second salient feature is that excess deaths were highly unevenly distributed. In sharp contrast to the belief that mortality rates would be lower in large agricultural provinces, ironically these provinces seem to have suffered higher death tolls.[36] Indeed, using provincial-level data, Map 18.1a reveals that the famine was most severe in the southwestern province of Sichuan, a large and topographically diverse agricultural province; followed by Guizhou in the southwest and Anhui, another sizeable agricultural province in central China; Henan and Shandong in the north; and Gansu in the northwest.[37] A strikingly related feature is that excess deaths also

---

may still be on the high side. Drawing upon a demographic study using "much higher-quality data," Zhao and Reimondos arrived at an estimate of life expectancy for the famine population of 32.5 years, which is much higher than Banister's 24.6 years. Banister, *China's Changing Population*; Z. Zhao and A. Reimondos, "The Demography of China's 1958–61 Famine," *Population* 67.2 (2012), 281–308; Ó Gráda, "Great Leap, Great Famine."

[33] J.K.S. Kung and J.Y. Lin, "The Causes of China's Great Leap Famine, 1959–1961," *Economic Development and Cultural Change* 52.1 (2003), 51–73.
[34] Lin and Yang, "Food Availability, Entitlements and the Chinese Famine."
[35] K.R. Walker, "Food and Mortality in China during the Great Leap Forward, 1958–61," in R.F. Ash (ed.), *Agricultural Development in China, 1949–1989: The Collected Papers of Kenneth R. Walker* (New York, Oxford University Press, 1998), pp. 106–47.
[36] Meng, Qian, and Yared, "The Institutional Causes of China's Great Famine."
[37] Inspiringly, the demographic historian Cao Shuji found great disparity in the excess deaths (17 percent) between two adjacent provinces in central China, Anhui and Jiangxi. While Anhui was severely struck by the famine, Jiangxi came through unscathed. Chen provides an interesting comparative analysis between the two cases. Cao, 大饑荒;

vary substantially within the same province.³⁸ The prefectural-level data constructed by Cao allowed Kung and Zhou to compare variations in excess deaths both between and within provinces, which they did by computing two separate measures of standard deviation.³⁹ They find that the two measures are strikingly similar, suggesting that the severity of famine varied not merely between the provinces but also within them (see Map. 18.1b).⁴⁰ A more nuanced finding of their analysis is that the standard deviation of the severity of famine across prefectures in the famine-stricken provinces is much larger. Using Sichuan as an example, the within-province standard deviation of 4.2 is 40 percent higher than the between-province standard deviation of 2.99, suggesting that while for Sichuan as a whole the famine was indisputably severe, some prefectures within it came through unscathed. Bramall finds the same among the counties in Sichuan Province, in which the crude death rate ranged from eight per thousand to a high of 109 per thousand against the provincial average of thirty-nine and the national average of seventeen per thousand.⁴¹ Map 18.1c, which is drawn using county-level data, reveals this disparity vividly. The enormous variations that existed not just between provinces but also within them require new explanations that may include nuanced "local conditions" that may range from exogenous differences in terrain and cropping patterns to endogenous variations in, for instance, radicalism.⁴²

Y. Chen, "Under the Same Maoist Sky: Accounting for Death Rate Discrepancies in Anhui and Jiangxi," in Manning and Wemheuer (eds,), *Eating Bitterness*, pp. 197–225.

³⁸ In the light of the finding that the "three large(st) areas of severe famine" were "not confined within provincial borders," Garnaut makes the case that the Great Leap Famine should be analyzed in terms of regions rather than provinces. However, since a macro-region encompasses a spatial territory larger than that of a province, it would render the econometric analysis of the causes of death even more imprecise. A. Garnaut, "The Geography of the Great Leap Famine," *Modern China* 40.3 (2014), 323, Map 2.

³⁹ Cao, 大饑荒. J.K.S. Kung and T. Zhou, "Political Elites and Hometown Favoritism in Famine-Stricken China," *Journal of Comparative Economics*, 2020, at www.sciencedirect.com/science/article/pii/S0147596720300184?via%3Dihub.

⁴⁰ The within-province standard deviation is 2.58, whereas the between-province standard deviation is 2.99.

⁴¹ Bramall, "Agency and Famine in China's Sichuan Province."

⁴² As far as local radicalism is concerned, clearly some cadres (commune and above) were more eager than others to toe the Maoist line. However, systematic evidence of this is scarce. R. A. Thaxton Jr., *Catastrophe and Contention in Rural China: Mao's Great Leap Forward Famine and the Origins of Righteous Resistance in Da Fo Village* (New York, Cambridge University Press, 2008), presents an exception. To counter this limitation, Kung and Chen, "The Tragedy of the Nomenklatura," used the frequency with which high-yield "agricultural satellites" were reported by communes as a proxy for the variation in local radicalism.

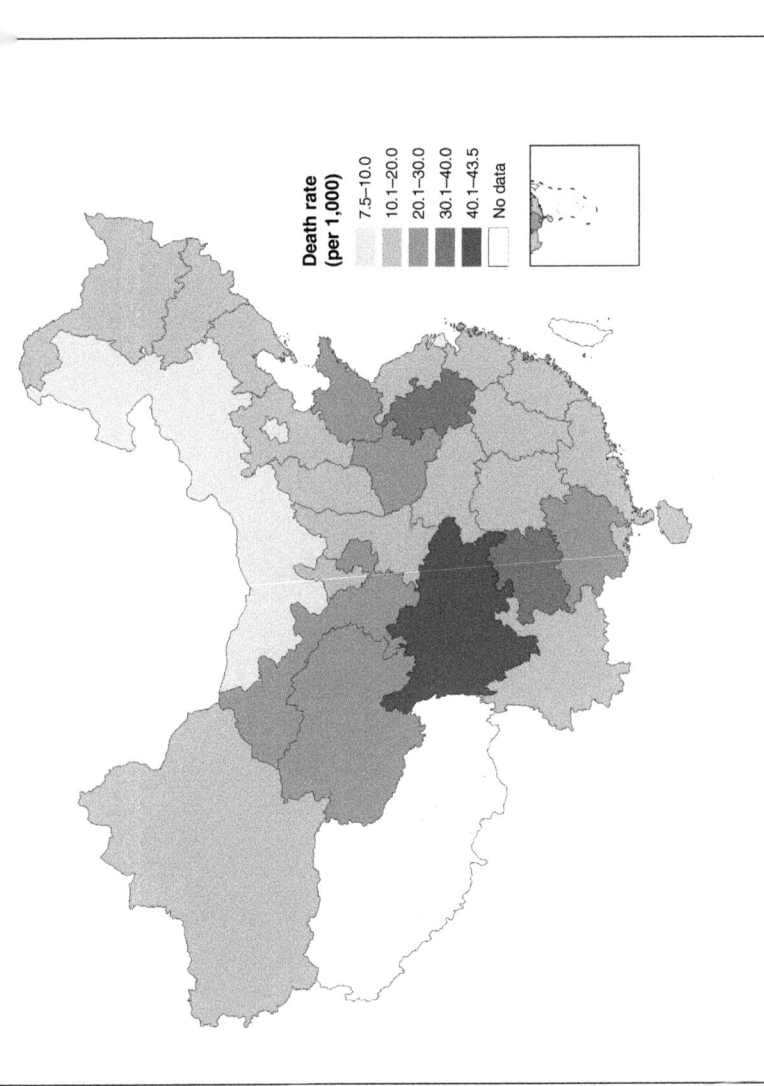

Map 18.1a Famine mortality by province, prefecture, and county, 1959–1961. (a) Average death rate (per thousand people) by province, 1959–1961. (b) Total excess deaths in 1958–1961 as a percentage of 1958 population by prefecture. (c) Average death rate (per thousand people) by county, 1959–1961 Source: (a) data reported by the National Bureau of Statistics (NBS); (b) adapted from Cao Shuji 曹树基, *1959–1961 年代中國人口* (The Great Famine and China's Population in 1959–1961) (Hong Kong, Shidai guoji chuban youxian gongsi, 2005); (c) adapted from H. Kasahara and B. Li, "Grain Exports and the Causes of China's Great Famine, 1959–1961: County-Level Evidence," *Journal of Development Economics* 146 (2020), 102513

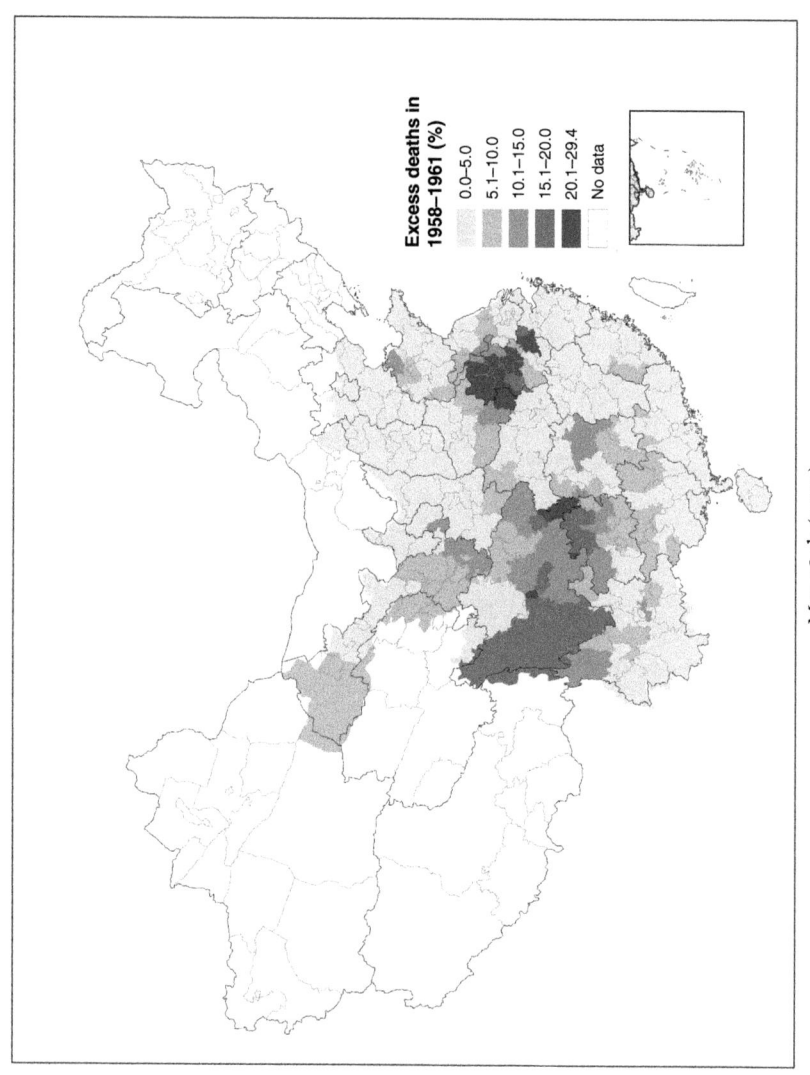

Map 18.1b (cont.)

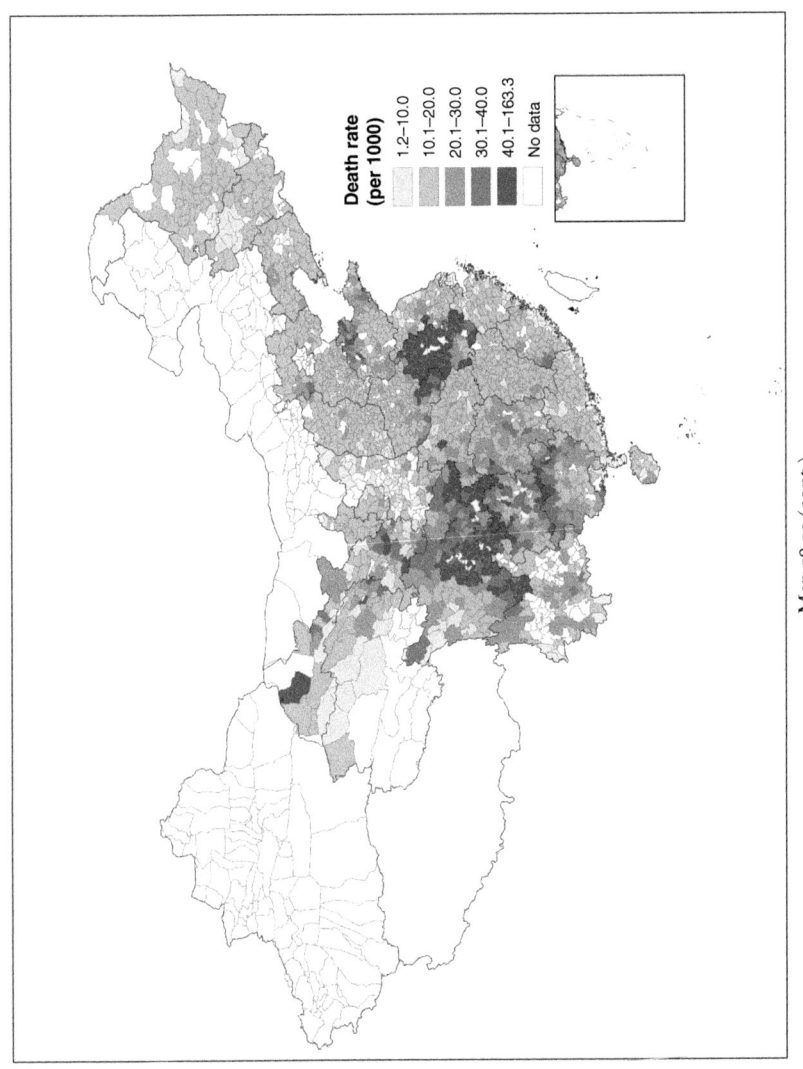

Map 18.1c (cont.)

Causes of Excess Deaths

Endeavors made by demographers to estimate the extent of population loss have inspired economists, political scientists, and historians alike to re-examine the underlying causes of the excess deaths experienced during this tumultuous period. On the basis of the extant literature we can divide the possible underlying causes into the three conceptual categories of (1) production, (2) distribution, and (3) consumption. First of all, the "production failure" hypothesis considers the famine to be the direct consequence of a shortfall in agricultural output and accordingly a decline in food availability – a failure primarily caused by exogenous weather shocks.[43] Conversely, analogous to Sen's famous "entitlement approach,"[44] the "distributional failure" thesis attributes the famine to a systemic failure to distribute the farm surplus effectively to those in need.[45] Finally, a third view attributes the Great Chinese Famine to irrational consumption behavior caused by the rules associated with the communal dining system – an "irrationality" that led to wasteful food consumption and rapid food depletion. As we shall see, the historical evidence and analytical rigor with which each of these perspectives is advanced to account for the famine varies enormously; hence they are not equally persuasive.

Before we analyze these perspectives in further detail, perhaps the reader should be reminded of the fundamental fact that China was in fact still a poor country by contemporary world standards in the mid-1950s, and as such it was vulnerable to the risks of a rash and overly ambitious policy such as the Great Leap Forward. Using the (admittedly crude) estimates of per capita GDP of the countries selected in the Maddison Project, we illustrate in Figure 18.1 that during the 1950s China not only trailed far behind the world's leading economies such as the United States and United Kingdom, but was also

---

[43] For example, see Kueh, *Agricultural Instability in China*.
[44] A. Sen, *Poverty and Famines: An Essay on Entitlement and Deprivation* (New York, Oxford University Press, 1981).
[45] For example, Lin and Yang, "Food Availability, Entitlements and the Chinese Famine," make the case that because the urban residents were guaranteed a minimum ration while their rural counterparts were subject to procurement that failed to consider their subsistence needs, the former were essentially protected in times of food shortages. To some extent this theory finds support in the argument that, even at the peak of the famine in 1960, the national grain output could provide up to 2,101 kilocalories per person on a daily basis – almost three times as much as the required calorie intake for survival, if the food was distributed equally among the people. Meng, Qian, and Yared, "The Institutional Causes of China's Great Famine."

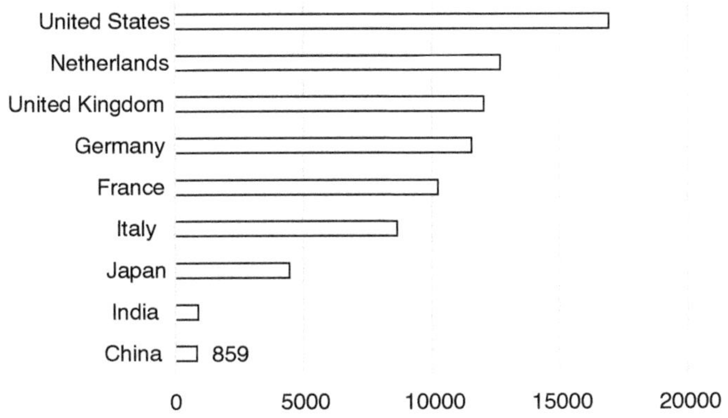

Figure 18.1 Average GDP per capita (in constant US$), 1950–1960
Source: J. Bolt, I. Robert, H. de Jong, and J.L. van Zanden, "Rebasing 'Maddison': New Income Comparisons and the Shape of Long-Run Economic Development," Maddison Project Working Paper 10 (2018)

well behind rising Japan and comparable only to similarly poverty-stricken India.[46]

Production Failure: Policy Blunder, Institutions, and Weather Adversity

Ambitious but Untried Policy

For Mao, the overriding goal of China's socialist economic development was to close the gap with major Western powers such as the United Kingdom and United States through the industrialization of a "capital-goods-producing" sector – a goal that required a vast increase in both agricultural and industrial output within a short period of time.[47] In the absence of the advanced technology required for industrialization and capital to finance importing it – China's comparative disadvantage – Mao looked to the peasants to foot

---

[46] Indeed, while not as famous as the Great Leap Famine, a large-scale famine, one that wiped out as much as 5 percent of China's population, occurred during the late 1920s and early 1930s. Bai and Kung, "The Shaping of an Institutional Choice." Writing in the 1920s, W.H. Mallory, *China: Land of Famine* (New York, American Geographical Society, 1926), aptly characterized China as a "land of famine." Further, even during the famine-free years of the 1950s, thousands were killed by hunger each year, with many more fleeing regions hit by harvest failures. F. Wemheuer, *Famine Politics in Maoist China and the Soviet Union* (New Haven, Yale University Press, 2014).

[47] Industrialization in that context required the agricultural sector to provide a surplus not only to generate export earnings but also to subsidize the "social wage" (cost of living) of urban industrial workers in state-owned enterprises.

the bill. Increasing the agricultural surplus sharply without injecting resources into it thus became an item at the top of the chairman's agenda. Emboldened by the peasants' display of "socialist enthusiasm" (*shehui zhuyi reqing* 社會主義熱情) in responding to his massive call to undertake irrigation projects in the slack winter months of 1957–1958, Mao decisively amalgamated the advanced agricultural co-operatives (*nongye gaojishe* 農業高級社) into people's communes (*renmin gongshe*), in part to facilitate the organization of large-scale public projects that required co-operation between townships, and in part to industrialize the countryside.[48] Under the "banner" of the Great Leap Forward, Mao put together a package of highly unorthodox development policies to achieve his unrealistic ambition of overtaking the United Kingdom in steel and iron production within the next twenty-five years and surpassing the United States within fifty to seventy years.[49] The core elements of this policy included the make-believe that it was scientifically feasible to increase crop output sharply and hence tax it in support of industrialization,[50] the massive mobilization of the rural labor force to engage in the production of steel and iron in the countryside, and not least an erroneous but determined decision by the chairman to slash the grain-sown acreage by close to 10 percent in order to grow oil-bearing and other economic crops[51] – all of which were conceived without considering

---

[48] In addition, the commune was intended to provide a comprehensive array of welfare including education (schools), health care (clinics), care services (daycare centers and old people's homes), weddings and funerals, and not the least the free supply of food in communal mess halls.

[49] Emboldened by the Soviet Union's success of launching its first satellite ("sputnik"), Mao ambitiously revised his targets of surpassing the United States in twenty to thirty years. By May 1958, these targets were further revised to seven years for the UK and eight to ten years for the US.

[50] Examples abound in the name of what Becker terms "false science." For instance, thousands of new colleges and universities were created at the commune or township level. Many scientists trained in the West were imprisoned or sent to perform manual labor during the "Anti-Rightist Campaign" that preceded the Great Leap. Other examples such as "close planting" and "deep ploughing," which were seen as key to increasing crop yields, instead respectively deprived plants of breathing space and destroyed soil structure, whereas increased "fertilization" by adding broken glass and bricks into the earth similarly stifled crop growth. See Becker, *Hungry Ghosts*.

[51] As reflected in a conversation the chairman had with a county party secretary in Hebei province in August of 1958. Mao's assessment of the agricultural sector in producing a huge surplus was clearly widely off the mark. The chairman asked, "How can you eat your way through so much grain? What are you going to do with your surplus?" The secretary replied, "We'll exchange the surplus for machinery." Mao then said, "And what will happen if you're not the only ones to have grain surplus and if every county has them? What if no one will want it?" The secretary answered, "We are going to make our sweet potatoes into alcohol." But Mao continued, "How can you use so much?" K. R. Walker, *Food Grain Procurement and Consumption in China* (Cambridge, Cambridge University Press, 1984), pp. 140–1.

the backwardness of Chinese agriculture in terms of mechanization, irrigation, and fertilizers.[52] However, evidence of the extent to which these false scientific practices had led to a reduction in crop output remains largely anecdotal, and hence unsubstantiated. We will therefore focus our review on more solid historical evidence.

Misallocation of the Rural Labor Force and Commune Organization

To increase iron and steel output beyond that produced by state-owned enterprises, Mao dispatched 90 million strong, young farmers – representing more than some 40 percent of the rural labor force – to undertake a variety of irrigation projects such as the construction of dams, water channels, and reservoirs, and to manufacture iron and steel at prospective iron ore deposits using "local methods" (*tufa*). By one estimate, the diversion of labor resources away from agriculture, which included a reduction in acreage sown with grain by nearly 10 percent, accounted for 33 percent of the overall decline in grain output between 1958 and 1961.[53]

Mao turned to the people's commune to boost farm output in the absence of technical change. After experimenting with gradualism for roughly half a decade, Mao eventually lost his patience when Deng Zihui, the then minister of agriculture, allowed 200,000 ill-managed elementary agricultural co-operatives (*chuji nongye she* 初級農業社) to dissolve. After this, Mao hastened the speed of agricultural collectivization by merging these smaller co-operatives into "advanced" ones, and completely abolished the peasants' private rights in land and other major farm implements.[54] By 1957 nearly all farm households belonged to an advanced agricultural co-operative. And in one fell swoop, the Chinese peasants were pushed one step further and became members of gigantic communes (*c.* 1958). It was following this particular transition that individual work incentives became severely

---

[52] In terms of mechanization, essential farm tasks were still performed by hand and with primitive tools, farm managers or cadres were mostly illiterate and lacked management skills, most land was yet to come under irrigation and was thus easily affected by natural calamities, and fertilizers were primarily organic and hence unable to increase yields sharply.

[53] Strictly speaking, the sharp reduction only applies to 1959. Regardless, the implied output elasticity is huge, a result that was probably confounded by other policy blunders. Li and Yang, "The Great Leap Forward."

[54] For instance, the target was to increase the agricultural collectives from 650,000 to 1.3 million co-operatives.

reduced, resulting in a low level of agricultural productivity for two decades, until agricultural decollectivization came about to revive it.

On the communal farm, not only was the level of work organization and income distribution raised from several hundred to thousands of households, but to alleviate the monitoring burden of team production Mao replaced the combined use of piece rates and time rates with an egalitarian wage system consisting of exceedingly narrow differentials between various labor grades.[55] Clearly, both of these changes reduced the peasants' incentive to put in their best effort[56] – a pitfall that Mao willfully neglected in his march towards Communism.

Lin, however, contends that *scale* alone cannot explain why China failed to recover its total productivity factor in agriculture to the level of the early 1950s, as all the anomalies that occurred at the onset of the Great Leap had already been corrected by the time the famine ended.[57] While acknowledging that the root cause of the supervisory problems lies in the sequential and nonstandardized nature of a labor-intensive agriculture,[58] Lin appeals to a key difference in the institutional arrangements before and after communalization as key to what he refers to as the "productivity paradox" in Chinese agriculture.[59] Specifically, Lin argues that, given the costliness of monitoring,

[55] The advanced agricultural co-operatives allegedly paid according to both piece rates on the basis of discrete farm tasks assigned to workers, and the amount of time spent each day working a myriad of tasks (the so-called "labor day" value), the latter determined on the basis of observable characteristics (age, gender, etc.). The difficulties that the agricultural collectives had experienced with these remuneration methods led Mao to criticize them as "trivially complicated philosophy" (*fansuo zhexue* 繁瑣哲學), and he dismissed them accordingly. Thus, on the communal farms, each worker was assigned one of six to eight labor grades based on skills, strengths, and attitude – an endeavor that completely eradicated the use of piece rates. While it was officially recommended that the highest grade should earn more than four times that of the lowest, the spread between them was so narrow that the difference between each successive grade was a mere 0.5 yuan per month. A. Donnithorne, *China's Economic System* (New York, Praeger, 1967); L. Deng, H. Ma, and H. Wu, 當代中國的農業 (Contemporary Chinese Agriculture) (Beijing, Dangdai zhongguo chubanshe, 1992), p. 156.

[56] D. Perkins and S. Yusuf, *Rural Development in China* (Baltimore, Johns Hopkins University Press, 1984).

[57] Lin, "Collectivization and China's Agricultural Crisis."

[58] Typically, a cropping cycle spans several months, involving as it does the nonspecialized farm worker shifting between myriad tasks dispersed over a large area at each stage. Together, the sequential nature and spatial dispersion of labor-intensive agricultural production renders monitoring an insurmountable task, leaving individual effort imperfectly measured and rewarded on the margin. M.E. Bradley and M.G. Clark, "Supervision and Efficiency in Socialized Agriculture," *Soviet Studies* 23.3 (1972), 465–73; P. Nolan, *The Political Economy of Collective Farms: An Analysis of China's Post-Mao Rural Reforms* (Cambridge, Polity Press, 1988).

[59] It is a paradox in the sense that Chinese agriculture achieved total factor productivity growth during both collectivization (bracketed 1952–1958) and de-collectivization (bracketed 1979–1984).

the only way to resolve the incentive problem inherent in team farming is to allow diligent farmers to "exit" team farming on discovering shirking by their lazy partners, which they can easily infer by observing both the level of total output and weather conditions – both of which are publicly available. But those lazy workers who treasure the series of small but long-term gains from co-operation might be willing to provide the minimum effort required to meet the demands of their diligent teammates, thereby (and this is the only means of) sustaining co-operative farming. Allegedly, this "exit right" was permitted before the people's commune was established in 1958, resembling an institutional setup analogous to that of a "repeated game," but vanished altogether as communalization forcibly changed the structure of incentives and payoffs to resemble those of a "one-shot" game, in the parlance of game theory. This nuanced but fundamental change thus destroyed the self-disciplining mechanism crucial to making collective farming feasible.

While novel, the hypothesis of the "exit right" has been criticized for its tenuous grasp on historical facts.[60] In particular, after becoming members of the advanced co-operatives, peasants were not entirely free to leave them, as local officials would be reluctant to let them go for fear of negative evaluation of their performance.[61] There is abundant evidence to show that, in order to stop those who wanted to quit collective farming, local cadres would resort to a combination of tactics ranging from moral persuasion to tortuous actions, so much so that returning to private household farming was unlikely to be a real option for many, despite what was stated in the Chinese Constitution.

As an alternative explanation of the productivity paradox, Kung and Putterman propose that the advanced agricultural collectives established in 1956–1957 might be nominal rather than real, in that the collectives, when besieged with problems of labor supervision, wittingly decentralized the organization of farm production all the way down to households via the equivalence in organization of the elementary co-operatives, which consisted of an average of some twenty-five households, while retaining

---

[60] It has also been considered faulty on the grounds of game-theoretic reasoning. When farmers are unable to leave a co-operative, as in the case of the commune, their interactions arguably assume the properties of a repeated nature. In contrast, when they are able to leave, they can choose to defect and leave after the first round of team farming. See, among others, X.Y. Dong and G.K. Dow, "Does Free Exit Reduce Shirking in Production Teams?", *Journal of Comparative Economics* 17.2 (1993), 472–84.

[61] J.K.S. Kung, "Transaction Costs and Peasants' Choice of Institutions: Did the Right to Exit Really Solve the Free Rider Problem in Chinese Collective Agriculture?", *Journal of Comparative Economics* 17.2 (1993), 485–503.

the work point system and unified income distribution practices at the higher (brigade) level – practices considered the cornerstone of collective agriculture.[62] Cleverly coined the "field responsibility system" (*tianjian guanli zeren zhi* 田間管理責任制), this decentralized institutional practice circumvented the ideological stranglehold of essentially using contracting (*bao* 包) to solve the incentive problem in collective farming. This alternative explanation remains inconclusive, however, as the archival survey conducted by Kung and Putterman covered only five (mostly) major grain-belt provinces.[63] Further research is thus required to ascertain the extent to which such nuanced flexibilities were indeed exercised in a highly politically charged context.

Three Consecutive Years of Bad Weather

Interestingly, with the exception of the Chinese government – who attributed the precipitous fall in grain output to "three consecutive years of natural disasters," few scholars have examined in detail the role played by weather conditions in 1959–1961 in causing the famine.[64] Kueh represents a notable exception.[65] On account of the statistics collected on farm acreage "physically struck" by natural disasters (*shouzai mianji* 受災面積) and on that "actually affected" by natural disasters (*chengzai mianji* 成災面積), Kueh admirably constructs a "weighted *shouzai* area index" as $\frac{1}{\sqrt{L_c L_n}}(A_c L_c - A_s L_n)$, in which he weighs *chengzai* area (A_c) and the balance of *shouzai* area $(A_s - A_c)$ by the assumed yield losses $((A_s - A_c)$ and $L_n)$. He then calculates the yearly percentage deviations of the "weighted *shouzai* area" from the mean of 1952–1984 and uses the series obtained as a proxy for weather instability for analyzing its impact on agricultural production.[66] Specifically, the weather instability index is constructed to predict the potential yield loss for each year, against which the actual yield loss is compared to ascertain the effect of

---

[62] J.K.S. Kung and L. Putterman, "China's Collectivisation Puzzle: A New Resolution," *Journal of Development Studies* 33.6 (1997), 741–63.
[63] Kung and Putterman, "China's Collectivisation Puzzle." The provinces were Hebei, Henan, and Shandong in the north; Anhui in the center; and Guangdong in the south.
[64] In that context, one cannot help but be reminded by Lin, "Collectivization and China's Agricultural Crisis," that it is unlikely that a country the size and diversity of China will be equally affected by bad weather for three years in a row, although Lin himself has not examined the effect of weather on the famine catastrophe.
[65] Kueh, *Agricultural Instability in China*.
[66] Given that farm acreage "actually affected" by natural disasters (*chengzai mianji*), if measured accurately, is a more direct measure of the effect of natural disasters, one may simply use this (albeit more endogenous) measure instead of the more complicated weighted index as Kueh does. Kueh, *Agricultural Instability in China*.

weather hazards on grain output.[67] Based on this formulation, Kueh finds that weather disturbance may have been the "single most important factor" in the decline in yield during the Great Leap, explaining 75 and 95 percent of the yield loss in 1960 and 1961 respectively.[68] In a way, Kueh's results may be taken as lending support to the Chinese government's claim that the famine was indeed to a large extent a consequence of "three consecutive years of bad weather."[69]

A key issue associated with Kueh's weather index is that *shouzai* and *chengzai* areas were enumerated based on *ex post* crop loss information, and are thus at best indirect measures of meteorological conditions.[70] Moreover, in the light of the various policy blunders alluded to earlier, these estimates are likely to confound the losses caused by human error, resulting in observational error and overestimation of the effect attributable to the weather.

To go beyond Kueh,[71] we turn to *disaggregated* meteorological data to examine the role of weather in production failure, by modeling the production variable, L_n, in province i and year t as

$$Y_{it} = \alpha_i + \beta_t + \gamma_1 Flood_{it} + \gamma_2 Drought_{it} + \gamma_3 Freeze_{it} + \epsilon_{it},$$

where α_i and β_t denote province and year fixed effects, and *Flood*, *Drought*, and *Freeze* stand for the three main specific weather hazards that presumably would bear upon output. Specifically, we measure the degree of weather hazards by the proportion to which output might be affected by flood, drought, and freeze, based on the deviation of monthly precipitation and

---

[67] Kueh's methodology involves comparing three types of per hectare grain yields: (1) the observed yield, (2) a trend yield variable derived from the application of fertilizer, and (3) a weather-predicted yield calculated from regression equations for the period 1952–1966 and 1970–1984, wherein the weather index is used as the key explanatory variable. Going by this framework, the disparity between the observed and trend yield is taken as the total actual yield loss, and the difference between weather-predicted yield and trend yield is interpreted as the weather-explained yield loss. A comparison of the two gives the proportion of yield loss caused by weather disturbances. Kueh, *Agricultural Instability in China*.

[68] Kueh, *Agricultural Instability in China*. Nevertheless, for 1959 Kueh considers the 9 percent sown-area curtailment to be more damaging to the total output collapse than the per hectare yield reduction caused by weather. Other estimates of the effect of the weather on output reduction are considerably smaller. For example, Bramall finds that drought explained 20, 11, and 9 percent of the output decline in each of the three famine years in Sichuan Province, whereas Li and Yang, based on a "retrospective survey" conducted in 1999, find that weather accounted for a 12.9 percent of the overall output collapse in 1958–61. Of course, both estimates have estimation issues of their own. Kueh, *Agricultural Instability in China*, pp. 216, 259; Bramall, "Agency and Famine in China's Sichuan Province"; Li and Yang, "The Great Leap Forward."

[69] Kueh, *Agricultural Instability in China*.   [70] Kueh, *Agricultural Instability in China*.

[71] Kueh, *Agricultural Instability in China*.

temperature from the norm for each province in each given year.[72] We report the two-way fixed effect estimates in Table 18.1.

To make our results comparable to those of Kueh,[73] we use the deviation of grain yield (interpreted as "yield loss") as the dependent variable in column 1. Specifically, we calculated yields by normalizing total grain output with the sown acreage, while yield loss is obtained by deducting the natural log of yield for each given year over the 1953–1966 period from the natural log of the mean yield for the entire pre-GLF period from 1953 to 1958.[74] As shown, adverse weather had a significant impact on yields: an additional month per year affected by flood, drought, or freeze damage is associated with an average reduction of yield of 0.029, 0.014, or 0.032 log points (or roughly 2.9, 1.4, or 3.2 percent).[75] Evaluated at the mean level of weather adversity in 1959–1961, the combined weather-predicted yield loss

---

[72] Data for monthly provincial temperatures for the 1954–1966 period are taken from C.J. Willmott and K. Matsuura, *Terrestrial Air Temperature: 1900–2010 Gridded Monthly Time Series v 3.01*, and *Terrestrial Precipitation: 1900–2010 Gridded Monthly Time Series v 3.02*. These data sets provide monthly mean temperature and precipitation data at 0.5 × 0.5 degree resolution (the size of a 0.5-degree grid square at the central latitude of China (43 degrees north) is fifty-six kilometers high by forty-one kilometers wide.) Grid-level values were interpolated from an average of twenty weather stations, corrected for elevation. Weather data were then aggregated to the province–year–month level. The same data set was used by Meng et al., "The Institutional Causes of China's Great Famine," and Kasahara and Li, "Grain Exports and the Causes of China's Great Famine." The computing formulas for the three weather shock variables are as follows:

$$flood_{it} = \frac{1}{12}\sum_{m=1}^{12} 1\{Z_{itm}^{rainfall} > 2\},$$

$$drought_{it} = \frac{1}{12}\sum_{m=1}^{12} 1\{Z_{itm}^{rainfall} < -0.5\},$$

$$freeze_{it} = \frac{1}{12}\sum_{m=1}^{12} 1\{Z_{itm}^{temperature} < -2\}.$$

To use *flood* as an illustrative example, we consider a province p to be affected by flood in month m of year t if the corresponding monthly rainfall has a Z-score above 2 (among a sample of provincial rainfall between 1990 and 2010), and code the corresponding province–year–month observation as 1, and 0 otherwise. Based on that, we add up the number of months m in a year t affected by flood, and then divide the sum by 12, which gives the proportion of year t affected by flood. We choose the rainfall Z-score benchmark for drought to be −0.5 as a crude means to adjust for the skewness of the data distribution.

[73] Kueh, *Agricultural Instability in China*.

[74] Expressed in the equation, $yield\ loss_{it} = log(average\ yield\ of\ 1953 - 58\ in\ province\ i) - log(yield_{it})$, $t = 1953, 1954, \ldots, 1966$.

[75] These numbers were obtained by dividing the coefficients in column 1 of Table 18.1 by 12 (months).

Table 18.1 Weather shocks and grain output, 1953–1966

	(1) Yield loss	(2) Output loss
Flood	0.342***	0.365***
	(0.101)	(0.093)
Drought	0.170***	0.109**
	(0.042)	(0.044)
Freeze	0.382**	0.048
	(0.142)	(0.147)
Year dummies	Yes	Yes
Province dummies	Yes	Yes
Observations	350	350
Number of provinces	25	25
R^2	0.639	0.622

Note. The dependent variable in column 1 is the logarithm value of grain yield loss per hectare. The dependent variable in column 2 is the logarithm value of the total grain loss. *Flood* is the proportion of a year affected by flood. *Drought* is the proportion of a year affected by drought. *Freeze* is the proportion of a year affected by freeze. Robust standard errors clustered at the province level are in parentheses. * significant at 10%; ** significant at 5%; *** significant at 1%.

is 0.071 log points (0.038 × 0.342(*flood*) + 0.316 × 0.170(*drought*) + 0.011 × 0.382 (*freeze*)).[76] Measured against the average yield loss of 0.184 log points across provinces in the Leap years, extreme weather conditions explain 38.4 percent (0.071/0.184) of the loss of yield. Evaluated separately for each of the three years, the weather-predicted yield loss is greater than the realized loss in 1959 – a finding that agrees with that of Kueh,[77] whereas weather contributes to 28 percent and 26.1 percent of total yield loss for 1960 and 1961 respectively, substantially lower than the 75 percent and 95 percent estimated by Kueh.[78]

In column 2, we estimate the effect of extreme weather on the deviation of total grain output. As expected, bad weather, or rainfall anomaly more specifically, lowers cropping prospects. Based on the average estimated effect, weather explains 27.6 percent of the loss of output over the three years.

[76] Respectively the average severity of flood/drought/cold across China in 1959–1961 is 0.038/0.316/0.011.
[77] Kueh, *Agricultural Instability in China*. [78] Kueh, *Agricultural Instability in China*.

Breaking down the average, again weather adversity more than accounts for the output loss in 1959 and explains 20.8 percent and 19 percent of the output loss in 1960 and 1961 respectively. Compared with the weather's estimated effect on grain yield per sown acreage, the magnitude in terms of output loss is smaller, due perhaps to the reduction in sown grain acreage. Summing up, the havoc wreaked by weather adversity with respect to both yield and output was most severe in 1959, but tapered off in the subsequent two years.

As we do not control for policy and institutional factors in the regressions, the effect attributed to weather is probably conflated and hence should be interpreted as an estimate of the upper bound. However, taking the omitted variable bias as given, our results based on provincial weather data refine the result of previous analyses on an aggregate level, and lend support to the claim made by Liu Shaoqi, China's vice president, that weather adversity was of secondary importance (accounting for roughly 30 percent) to policy and institutional factors in causing the production failure (which accounted for 70 percent).

Excessive Grain Procurement as a Key Determinant of Excess Death

There is now a growing consensus regarding the role played by (excessive) grain procurement in causing excess deaths. Euphemistically termed the Unified Purchase and Unified Sale System (*tonggou tongxiao* 統購統銷), the practice of compulsory grain procurement was implemented in 1953 to facilitate the transfer of surplus grain from the farm sector at below-market prices to fuel industrialization. Before 1959, the gross procurement rate stood at around 25 percent, but soared to 38 percent in 1959 and 1960, resulting in the peasants suffering from acute food shortages. It was only in 1961, on the heels of accumulating reports of starvation and related diseases, that the procurement rate was reduced to 25 percent and further scaled back in subsequent years.[79]

---

[79] A puzzle remains, nonetheless. Before 1949, tenant farmers had to pay their landlords a rent amounting to an average of 43 percent of the output value of their crops. While the magnitude of rents varied across regions and by crops (wet rice versus dryland farming) and depended on the "class status" of the farm households (upper, middle, and lower), the difference was small. It is possible that the 38 percent of grain procurement during the Great Leap represented only the average, and famine-stricken provinces or subunits (such as prefectures and counties) probably suffered disproportionately higher procurement ratios. The figure for provincial land rents in 1934 comes from Zhengmo Chen 陳正謨, 中國各省的地租 (Land Rents in Various Chinese Provinces) (Shanghai, Shangwu yinshuguan, 1936).

Against the sharp rise in grain procurement, Kung and Lin found, unsurprisingly, a positive correlation between grain procurement and excess deaths, after controlling for a host of factors including per capita grain output, ratio of rural population in a province's population (a proxy for urban bias), and several "political" variables such as communal dining – using mess hall participation rates as proxy.[80] While the level of grain procurement was exogenously set by upper-level government, the actual procurement that resulted was probably endogenously determined, depending on a gamut of factors to be discussed below, ranging from the alleged rigidity of the planning mechanism to the whims and ambitions of those who governed the local jurisdictions responsible for the procurement exercise.

Bureaucratic Rigidity and New Procurement Policy

For Meng, Qian, and Yared, the root cause of the famine lay in the rigidity of the central planning apparatus.[81] Inspired by the surprising positive relationship between agricultural productivity and the severity of famine, these researchers found that the grain procurement targets were set by the planners in Beijing in proportion to the projected grain output based upon historical production records (e.g. the past two to three years). These targets then trickled down to the provinces, prefectures, and ultimately counties.[82] Due to the enormous size of the country and the bureaucratic nature of the planning apparatus (as the amount of output procured from each level needed to be tallied and verified), it could take up to an entire year for Beijing to ascertain the actual amount of grain produced and procured in the previous year.[83] While this lag posed no problem when projected output growth did not deviate too much from actual output, it would impact negatively on the peasants when actual output turned out to be significantly

---

[80] Kung and Lin, "The Causes of China's Great Leap Famine." These other variables include Party membership density, which is defined as the ratio of Party members per 10,000 people in a province, and time of liberation, which is ranked according to the month and year in which a province was "liberated" by the Chinese Communist Party. Yang, *Calamity and Reform in China*; Kung and Lin, "The Causes of China's Great Leap Famine."

[81] Meng, Qian, and Yared, "The Long-Term Consequences of Famine."

[82] Ashton et al., "Famine in China"; Oi, *State and Peasant in Contemporary China*; Walker, "Food and Mortality in China during the Great Leap Forward."

[83] From a different perspective, political scientists tend to view the alleged "rigidity" as a result of lower-level (commune and brigade) cadres succumbing to the extraordinary political pressure generated by the process of grain procurement (Bernstein, "Stalinism, Famine, and Chinese Peasants"; Oi, *State and Peasant in Contemporary China*), which is clearly demonstrated by Da Fo village in Henan Province (Thaxton, *Catastrophe and Contention in Rural China*).

lower than expected against a procurement that had been ratcheted sharply upwards. This may explain why Meng et al. found a positive correlation between famine mortality and "production gaps," which is measured as the disparity between expected and realized grain production during the famine.[84] It was this bureaucratic rigidity in adjusting the procurement rate in response to realized grain output that led Meng et al. to conclude that the excess deaths that occurred during the Leap were essentially a "planning failure" – an allegation supported by their further proof that net procurement is positively correlated with historical productivity.[85]

While the center may have responded sluggishly (if at all) to an unanticipated decline in grain output during the famine years, whether or not this sluggishness was the product of the planning system remains debatable. For example, the fact that the Central Committee held two sets of planning accounts – an official "must-fulfill" account and a second "hoped-to-be-fulfilled" account – the "two-books syndrome," and used the latter as the de facto benchmark against which to evaluate the performance of provincial governments,[86] contained an inherent bias toward higher levels of grain procurement. When the unpublicized account became the effective target as it percolated down the administrative hierarchies, grain output had become grossly inflated by the time it reached the villages – a practice that was in striking accordance with the prevailing political atmosphere known as "winds of exaggeration" (*fugua feng* 浮誇風) – a tendency to boast of the possibility of sharp output growth.

But the alleged "rigidity" may have been due less to the cumbersome workings of the planning system than to the new procurement policy put in place in April of 1958 – a policy that inadvertently gave rise to higher procurement targets for the following reasons.[87] Perhaps the most fundamental change was that procurement quotas were no longer set on the basis of the average output of the past three years, but instead according to the

---

[84] Meng et al., "The Institutional Causes of China's Great Famine." Based on the documented planning mechanism, Meng et al. estimate "expected production" as a two-year lag of the production figure multiplied by the three-year moving average of the growth rates from two, three, and four years ago for each province. The "production gap" is hence constructed as the difference between the realized and expected output figures.
[85] Meng et al., "The Institutional Causes of China's Great Famine." Both regressions do not control for provincial fixed effects and contemporaneous production, however.
[86] According to the "Sixty Articles on Work Methods" penned by Mao.
[87] "國務院關於改進糧食管理體制的幾項規定" (Several Stipulations of the State Council on How to Improve the Grain Management System), April 1958.

government's *predicted* output over the subsequent year – a change that allowed, or perhaps even encouraged, the exaggeration of grain output.[88] The other change that may have given rise to inflexible grain procurement was that, while provincial governments were allowed to revise procurement quotas, they could only revise them upward. Of the two changes, the first would probably give rise to an inflated grain output, especially when 1958, a year of bumper harvest, was used as the base year for calculation,[89] whereas the latter tended to render the procurement policy "inflexible" to contemporaneous changes in output.

Excessive Grain Export as Another Culprit

More recently, by connecting grain procurement with exports, Kasahara and Li shed new light on the complexity of excessive grain procurement.[90] Due to the souring of the Sino-Soviet relationship, Beijing was forced to repay 1.5 billion yuan worth of Soviet loans. In patent disregard for the economic costs entailed,[91] Beijing exported up to 4.1 and 2.7 million metric tons of grain in 1959 and 1960 respectively – amounts that would have contributed to the caloric needs of 16.7 to 38.9 million peasants.[92] The blow was not spread evenly among the rural population, however, as the central government tended to export those crops that fetched higher prices on the international market – a strategy that subjected the regions specializing in relatively "valuable" crops to heavier extraction.[93] Using county-level data, and by interacting *historical* cropping patterns with grain-specific international price movements as a measure of "export shock," Kasahara and Li found that regions with higher exposure to exports retained less food and suffered from higher death rates.[94] This "pegging" relationship between procurement intensity and export exposure was

---

[88] Kung and Zhou, "Political Elites and Hometown Favoritism."
[89] The higher procurement rate set for 1959 was indeed premised on the bumper harvest of 1958.
[90] Kasahara and Li, "Grain Exports and the Causes of China's Great Famine."
[91] J.W. Garver, *China's Quest: The History of the Foreign Relations of the People's Republic* (New York, Oxford University Press, 2015).
[92] Kasahara and Li, "Grain Exports and the Causes of China's Great Famine."
[93] For example, given the price premium of rice and soybean, these two goods accounted for 81 to 95 percent of total grain exports in 1955–1961. More importantly, on the heels of their price hikes in 1957–1958, the exports of these two goods rose by 6.4 million tons and 2.0 million tons in 1958–1960, relative to the 0.06 million ton–0.99 million ton increase in wheat, maize, and other grains.
[94] Kasahara and Li, "Grain Exports and the Causes of China's Great Famine."

estimated to account for 15 percent of the excess deaths in 1960,[95] with the effect being greater in counties further from railroads, as the logistic costs of disaster verification and relief transportation were larger in areas not readily accessible by railroads.[96] The geography of mortality and its determinants – including the topography and transport network – are clearly an important issue, especially in the context of localized famine such as the case between adjacent counties and prefectures.

Taken together, the coexistence of procurement rigidity and excessive export inevitably raises the concern of how aware Mao was of the famine's severity, and his apparent lack of compassion and response to the grave situation that was unfolding in the countryside. One may take the innocuous view that the center was, perhaps, crippled by institutional barriers, ignorant of the meltdown on the ground during 1959–1961, hence the lag in adjustment to procurement. But this diagnosis is challenged by the radicalism rekindled in the wake of the Lushan Conference in July 1959,[97] when, after being challenged by Marshal Peng Dehuai, Mao single-handedly fired all the cylinders of the Leap, raising the targets of grain and steel production to realistically unattainable levels[98] – an act that Bernstein interprets

---

[95] This result may be overstated, however, given that their estimation fails to account for the effect of the resale of grain to rural areas (the data for which are lacking for most provinces), and the extent that resale of grain had a moderating effect on excess deaths, as Kung and Zhou, "Political Elites and Hometown Favoritism," found to be the case for Henan Province.

[96] Remoteness is a double-edged sword, however. If remoteness impedes the distribution of relief because of higher transportation costs, it should also have deterred procurement in the first place. Indeed, Garnaut, "The Geography of the Great Leap Famine," argues that the logistic difficulties of transporting large quantities of grain over vast distances limited the reach of the extractive regime, and as a result saved many lives from famine. Consistently, Gooch finds the same with terrain ruggedness and its associated transaction costs. However, using the case of Sichuan as an example, Bramall, "Agency and Famine in China's Sichuan Province," finds no apparent geography of mortality in terms of either access to transportation or topography, despite the fact that Sichuan exhibits enormous variations in the death rate across the counties. E. Gooch, "Terrain Ruggedness and Limits of Political Repression: Evidence from China's Great Leap Forward and Famine (1959–61)," *Journal of Comparative Economics* 47.4 (2019), 827–52.

[97] The Lushan Conference was originally designated to review and contain leftist extremism, but ended up seeing the purge of Marshal Peng Dehuai and the revival of the Leap campaign. The twist occurred after Peng handed the famous "Letter of Opinion" to Mao, in which he cautiously pointed out the Leap's problems such as "winds of exaggerations." Mao took offence at the criticism and publicly charged Peng with having "leaned towards the right for about 30 kilometers." It then followed that the rightist tendency was reinstated as the target of an ideological purge. Kung and Lin, "The Causes of China's Great Leap Famine."

[98] Kung and Lin, "The Causes of China's Great Leap Famine."

as willful neglect of the "expense on livelihood" in pursuance of political goals, rather than unwitting ignorance.[99]

The Role of Political Elites: Central versus Provincial Officials

The disproportionate importance of procurement in causing excess deaths and its highly endogenous origin inspired us to examine the possible exogenous determinants of variations in grain procurement across provinces. By taking the varying incentives of provincial leaders of different political ranks within China's centralized personnel system – the *nomenklatura* – as given, Kung and Chen saw the Great Leap as providing an exceptionally rare opportunity for those who were less senior in terms of political rank – the "alternative members" or AMs – to climb the career ladder of what essentially was a "closed" market with virtually no outside options, by procuring and remitting more grain to the center, signaling their unswerving loyalty to, and support for, Mao's fanatical campaign.

Given not only that their more senior counterparts – the "full members" or FMs – held more positions, but also that the positions held were more strategic and had distinctly more rights and privileges,[100] there was a powerful incentive for the AMs to get ahead. Further, unlike FMs, who faced a prohibitive barrier to reaching the highest echelon as Politburo members, AMs did not face similar barriers in their progress to becoming FMs.[101] Perhaps for this reason, AMs were found to have systematically procured roughly 3 percent more grain in provinces they governed than was procured in provinces governed by FMs.[102] Using this as a benchmark,

---

[99] Bernstein, "Mao Zedong and the Famine." However, it would be a stretch to go as far as to suggest that this willfulness was not accompanied by any personal struggle on Mao's part. Since the spring of 1960, a flush of reports of deaths and abuses came from provinces including Guizhou, Guangdong, Shandong, and Liaoning, which were treated by Mao with a flickering combination of lukewarm responses, doubt, "great anger," and self-deceptive negligence, reflecting his hesitancy and contradictory motivations. Only in October 1960 did Mao come to "grasp the dimensions" upon learning about the catastrophic situation in Henan, and supported abandoning the Leap, which, however, failed to put an immediate end to the deep-rooted leftism.

[100] For example, AMs were only allowed to express their opinions at plenary meetings; they were ineligible to vote on resolutions. See Kung and Chen, "The Tragedy of the Nomenklatura."

[101] At a notch above the FMs, Politburo members required the "prerevolutionary credential" of experience of the Long March, but a similar credential was not required of an FM. Kung and Chen, "The Causes of China's Great Leap Famine."

[102] However, Kung and Chen, "The Tragedy of the Nomenklatura," also find that the second in command in a province, the governor, did not exhibit the same career incentives. This may possibly be due to the fact that, unlike the first party secretary, the governor belonged to the government apparatus and was thus not predisposed to engage in radical actions.

political radicalism caused by "career concerns" can explain up to 16.83 percent of the overall excess death rate – exceeding even that of excessive exporting. On the basis of this finding, Kung employed a regression discontinuity approach to carry out a further comparison of the incentives of those AMs and FMs who were ranked near the cutoff threshold of ninety-seven (i.e. there were ninety-seven FMs at the time), and to identify the causal effect of membership status (i.e. AM versus FM) on excessive grain procurement based on the exogenous ballot ranking of the Eighth National Congress.[103] Doing so increases the magnitude from 3 percent for AMs as a group to 8 percent between those AMs on the verge of promotion and the lowest-ranked FMs who only saw a distant prospect of further career progression.

A question arising from this analysis is whether political elites could only do evil during the Great Leap. Inspired by the anecdote of Xi Zhongxun's appeal to arrange for "relief grain" to be shipped to his hometown of Fuping county in Shaanxi province, Kung and Zhou examined the possible role of members of the Central Committee (CC) in alleviating excess deaths during the Great Leap Famine.[104] In sharp contrast to the strong "career concerns" of regional officials, political elites who worked in the central government – specifically in the planning department and in charge of grain allocations – had alleviated excess deaths by redistributing grain to their hometowns, presumably on compassionate grounds. By regressing logged excess deaths during 1959–1961 against the birthplace (hometown) of the Eighth National Party Congress of 1958, Kung and Zhou found that having an additional native CC member in a prefecture helped to reduce the excess deaths in that prefecture by 46,500, accounting for 2.3 percentage points in the death rate when evaluated at the mean.[105] Moreover, while based on the evidence of just one province (Henan), these authors found that the channel of "relief grain" worked through the resale of grain or grain "sold back" to the countryside rather than through a reduction in grain procurement.

Taking advantage of this insight into what might underpin excessive grain procurement, perhaps we may reassess the *joint* significance of institutional rigidity and political radicalism within the same analytical framework using the following two-way fixed-effect model:

---

[103] Kung, "The Emperor Strikes Back."
[104] Kung and Zhou, "Political Elites and Hometown Favoritism." The father of Xi Jinping, Xi Zhongxun, was one of the "Eight Elders" of the Chinese Communist Party and a vice premier during 1959–1962.
[105] Kung and Zhou, "Political Elites and Hometown Favoritism."

$$P_{it} = \alpha_i + \beta_t + \delta_1 Q_{it} + \delta_2 Q_{it-2} + \theta Rank_{it} + \mu Y_{it} + \epsilon_{it},$$

where α_i, β_t, and ε_{it} are the same as previously defined, P stands for per capita net/gross/resale/extra grain procurement depending on the choice of dependent variable, and Q_{it} and Q_{it-2} stand respectively for the contemporary per capita grain output and per capita grain output lagging by two years. The panel covers the period from 1957 to 1965. Following Kung and Chen, *Rank* is a dummy variable indicating the provincial leader's political rank (i.e. FM, AM, or nonmember NM) in the Central Committee, while Y includes two control variables, per capita GDP and proportion of agricultural income.[106]

The results are reported in Table 18.2. In all the regressions we control for the fixed effects of province, year, and level of development (per capita GDP), as well as for the relative importance of agriculture. Using per capita net grain procurement as the dependent variable,[107] we first examine the "institutional-rigidity" hypothesis by assessing the relative importance of contemporaneous versus historical grain output in determining the dependent variable. On its own (columns 1 and 2), both variables exhibit a significant positive correlation with net grain procurement, but the two-year lagged variable has a much smaller estimated effect (0.154, column 2, versus 0.592, column 1). When put in pairs (column 3), however, the lagged output becomes insignificant, but contemporaneous output continues to be significant and has a similar magnitude. This result is further confirmed when we interact these two variables (separately) with the dummy variable of the Great Leap Forward (GLF) (column 4). Together, this evidence does not bode well with the "planning-rigidity" hypothesis, except that we must point out the caveat that this analysis is performed at the province (instead of the county) level. In column 5, we include political rank in the regression as a "horserace" with planning rigidity, and find that the variable AM is significant, reinforcing an earlier finding that AMs were more aggressive as a group in squeezing their people, even when controlling for current-year grain output. The two-year lag of grain output remains insignificant in this regression. In column 6 we add in the variable CC membership, which is defined as the number of Central Committee (CC) members in a given province for every million people, the purpose of which is to test whether political elites who served in the

---

[106] Kung and Chen, "The Tragedy of the Nomenklatura."
[107] Net procurement is obtained by subtracting resale of grain from gross procurement, whereas excessive net procurement is the difference between average net procurement during 1955–1957 and the amount procured during 1958–1961.

Table 18.2. The effects of grain output, political rank, and CC membership on grain procurement, resale, and excess procurement, 1957–1965

	(1)	(2)	(3)	(4)	(5)	(6)	(7)	(8)	(9)
Current-year grain output	0.592***		0.580***	0.393***	0.594***	0.595***	0.523***	−0.072***	0.201***
	(0.112)		(0.108)	(0.078)	(0.111)	(0.112)	(0.130)	(0.023)	(0.063)
Two-year lag of grain output		0.154**	0.068	0.116	0.088	0.080	0.146	0.066*	0.005
		(0.057)	(0.045)	(0.074)	(0.070)	(0.073)	(0.095)	(0.032)	(0.064)
GLF # current-year grain output				0.286**					
				(0.120)					
GLF # two-year lag of grain output				−0.114					
				(0.095)					
NM					0.042	0.074	−0.375	−0.450*	0.232
					(0.914)	(0.922)	(1.143)	(0.238)	(0.484)
AM					0.828***	0.821***	0.727**	−0.095	0.555***
					(0.276)	(0.279)	(0.326)	(0.066)	(0.184)
CC membership						−2.214**	−2.619*	−0.405	−2.779***
						(1.062)	(1.387)	(0.563)	(0.853)

Personal identity	No	No	No	No	Yes	Yes	Yes	Yes	Yes
Controls	Yes	Yes	Yes	Yes	Yes	Yes	Yes	Yes	Yes
Year dummies	Yes	Yes	Yes	Yes	Yes	Yes	Yes	Yes	Yes
Province dummies	Yes	Yes	Yes	Yes	Yes	Yes	Yes	Yes	Yes
Observations	225	225	225	225	225	225	225	225	225
Number of provinces	25	25	25	25	25	25	25	25	25
R^2	0.368	0.268	0.370	0.381	0.507	0.508	0.483	0.421	0.525

Notes. The dependent variable in columns 1–6 is the per capita net procurement. The dependent variables in columns 7–9 are per capita gross procurement, per capita resale, and per capita extra procurement. Current-year grain output is per capita grain output for the current year. Two-year lag of grain output is per capita two-year moving average of grain output. GLF is a dummy variable, which equals 1 if the year is from 1958 to 1961, otherwise 0. NM is nonmember. AM is alternate member. CC membership ratio is the number of Central Committee members per million population. Controls include lag of share of agricultural GDP and lag of GDP per capita. Robust standard errors clustered at the province level are in parentheses. * significant at 10%; ** significant at 5%; *** significant at 1%.

government might favor their "distant relatives" back in their "hometowns." Consistently with Kung and Zhou, the significantly negative coefficient suggests that provinces with greater representation by these political elites in the CC did suffer less in terms of net grain procurement.[108]

In the last three columns (7–9), we change our dependent variable to gross procurement, resale or sale-back grain (*fanxiao liang* 返銷糧), and excessive procurement respectively – all adjusted on a per capita basis, in order to examine the *channels* through which procurement intensity was affected. In column 7, we find that only contemporaneous but not historical grain output has a significantly positive effect on per capita gross procurement, which suggests flexibility. And while AM declines in significance (from 1 percent to 5 percent), it remains a significant determinant. We find the same with CC membership, which, while similarly declining in the level of significance (from 5 percent to 10 percent), remains significant.

In the case of resale grain (column 8), both contemporaneous and two-year lagged output are significant but operate in opposite directions. The negative effect of the current-year output on resale grain indicates, intuitively, that a larger grain output is negatively associated with the amount of grain sold back to the rural area. On the contrary, sale-back is positively (but only marginally) correlated with the two-year lagged grain output and with a comparable magnitude, suggesting that the resale amount in a given year was probably financed by the provincial government's stockpile from the average of the previous two years, which from 1958 onwards was assigned to deal with famines of an "average magnitude" (*yiban zaihuang* 一般災荒).[109] As they were eager to remit more grain to the center, AMs were unlikely to return more grain to the countryside, as revealed by the negative (albeit imprecisely estimated) coefficient. Finally, in column 9, contemporaneous production and AMs are jointly and positively significant in explaining the "excessive portion" of procurement in comparison with the level in 1955–1957 – a result that strikingly resonates with findings in the extant literature.[110]

---

[108] Kung and Zhou, "Political Elites and Hometown Favoritism."
[109] Before 1958, intra-provincial grain transfer was controlled directly by the central government, and provincial officials had to request permission for more grain sale-back. However, the new policy that came into effect in 1958 delegated full control over residual grain to provincial officials after delivery to the center was fulfilled. Z. Fan, W. Xiong, and L.-A. Zhou, "Information Distortion in Hierarchical Organizations: A Study of China's Great Famine," NBER working paper (2016); Kung and Zhou, "Political Elites and Hometown Favoritism."
[110] Kung and Chen, "The Tragedy of the Nomenklatura"; Kung, "The Emperor Strikes Back."

Consumption: Communal Dining

A third view seeks the most proximate cause of the famine in "irrational" consumption behavior as arguably manifested by the 2.65 million mess halls established in the autumn of 1958 as an integral part of people's communes. Depending on the extent to which the rural population were herded into the mess halls, which varied considerably from one province to another, the egalitarian distribution and free supply of food – vividly described in the slogan "Open up your stomach and eat as much as you can" – destroyed participants' incentive to economize on food, and hence resulted in wasteful consumption.[111] By early 1959, food shortages were reported to have occurred in many places, including where there were allegedly bumper harvests.[112]

In establishing the causal importance of communal dining, Chang and Wen developed a framework in which they eliminated many factors that could have caused the famine's onset;[113] these factors ranged from outright collapse of output and failure of distribution to demand shock and communal mess dining. For instance, they argued that the famine was unlikely to have been caused by a failure in food production, as 1958 was a year of bumper harvest. Likewise, while they see procurement as having aggravated the famine, it did not increase sharply until 1959, but the famine had already started in late 1958 rather than in early 1959. By the same token, the lack of a population explosion is also inconsistent with the famine being caused by a sudden demand for food.[114] By elimination, irrational consumption remains the only likely "triggering" factor of the famine. As mentioned earlier, participants in the mess halls were assumed to be driven by a mixture of fear of deprivation and perhaps euphoria over the free (and unlimited) supply of food, leading them to engage in self-destructive or what they call

---
[111] Chang and Wen, "Communal Dining and the Chinese Famine." As was documented by Potter and Potter and cited in Chang and Wen, "in 20 days peasants finished almost all the rice they had, rice which should have lasted six months." S.H. Potter and J. M. Potter, *China's Peasants: The Anthropology of a Revolution* (Cambridge, Cambridge University Press, 1990); Chang and Wen, "Communal Dining and the Chinese Famine."
[112] Bo Yibo 薄一波, 若干重大決策與事件的回顧 (Several Important Policy Decisions and Events in Retrospect) (Beijing, Zhonggong zhongyang dangxiao chubanshe, 1991).
[113] Chang and Wen, "Communal Dining and the Chinese Famine."
[114] While there was no sudden increase in population, the fact that Mao sharply increased the number of rural workers working in state-owned enterprises by 30 percent (from 99 million in 1957 to 130 million in 1961) to increase steel output put a greater burden on grain procurement, as it required an additional 6 million tons of requisitioned grain to be sent to Beijing, Tianjin, Shanghai, and Liaoning – cities and provinces where the lion's share of state-owned enterprises were located. To alleviate food shortages in cities during the aftermath of the famine, the Chinese government sent 20 million of these migrants back to the countryside and imported grain from abroad.

"irrational" consumption behavior – a behavior that would rapidly deplete the meagerly available food stocks.

One way of testing this hypothesis is to correlate the extent to which a province engaged its rural populace in communal dining practices and excess deaths, given the enormous variation that existed between provinces. Prima facie evidence suggests that provinces with severe casualties, such as Anhui, Guizhou, and Henan, all had participation rates of well over 90 percent. By contrast, the less-afflicted regions, such as those in the remote northeastern provinces, were far more moderate in implementing this policy.[115] In an attempt to expand on this claim, Liu, Wen, and Wei regressed a province's famine mortality against its mess hall participation rate at the end of 1959 – the only year for which data on communal dining are available, and found that communal dining can explain 8.7 to 16.8 percent of the variations in excess death rates during 1958–1961.[116] Their finding differs from that of Kung and Lin,[117] who found that the mess hall participation rate was an insignificant determinant of excess deaths when competing variables of political radicalism, such as Party membership density or time of liberation, are controlled for.[118] By contrast, grain procurement is consistently significant in their regressions. Between the two ends – procurement and consumption – the significance of (excessive) grain procurement implies that the countryside would probably have been left with insufficient grain for consumption, thereby rendering wasteful consumption a mere allegation.[119] This would seem to be the case especially after the Lushan Conference; Mao's rekindled effort to get the Leap firing on all cylinders notwithstanding, with the procurement of grain and steel escalated to unbelievably high levels, the possible role played by communal dining in causing excess deaths should not be exaggerated.[120]

[115] Kung and Lin, "The Causes of China's Great Leap Famine," 60.
[116] Y. Liu, J.G. Wen, and X. Wei, "Communal Dining System and the Puzzle of the Great Leap Famine," *China Agricultural Economic Review* 6.4 (2014), 698–716.
[117] Kung and Lin "The Causes of China's Great Leap Famine."
[118] While they have instrumented mess hall participation rates, their instruments with (1) the ratio of the participation rate in advanced agricultural co-operatives in 1956 to the participation rate of elementary agricultural co-operatives in 1954, and (2) population density in the rural areas, are both endogenous.
[119] In Da Fo village of Henan province, one of the famine-stricken provinces, substantial grain rationing – which allegedly amounted to 60 percent of the villagers' grain output – had long put an end to so-called "overconsumption." Thaxton, *Catastrophe and Contention in Rural China*, p. 127. As the author also remarks, overconsumption, if it ever existed, was "a practice of at least three harvests past" (p. 125).
[120] In fact, official evidence suggests that, perhaps in response to early signs of food shortages, by early 1959 communal dining had already lost its initial momentum and rigor. Not only were seasonal operations allowed, but also, in many instances,

There are other reasons why communal dining is an unlikely culprit. In an attempt to find out how communal dining was actually organized, I went through the press archive on mess hall organization. Of a total of 120 pertinent articles reporting on twenty-four provinces in the second half of 1958, I found that over 75 percent of these reports made no explicit reference to unrestricted food consumption in terms of how the commune dining kitchens were operated. Far from an "all-you-can-eat" scenario as conjured up by the political slogan, food was effectively allocated on the basis of age, sex, and labor grade, which is suggestive of a practice of differentiating food rationing on the basis of differential work contributions (labor grade) and needs (age and gender).[121] In other words, while food might have been provided free, the quantity was *rationed*, and hence the communal dining kitchen was not an unmanaged common that brings ruin to all – at least not for the entire country.

Long-Term Effects

In recent years, increasing attention has been paid to examining what may be considered the "long shadow" cast by the Great Leap Famine over the well-being of individual survivors, institutional choice, and comparative economic development. What emerges from these studies is that the shock imposed by the famine has exerted a persistent effect on these outcome variables of interest through biological inheritance, human capital accumulation, and even collective memory.

Individual-Level Outcomes

As individuals who were born or conceived during the famine (hereafter "famine cohort") enter midlife, it affords the researchers a unique opportunity to examine how malnutrition occurring at the fetal and/or infant stages might have led to adverse adulthood health outcomes,[122] and, as a consequence, disadvantages in a variety of educational and labor market

---

participation was reduced to a partial basis whereby only one meal a day was served and in-home preparation was allowed. Above all, only 20 to 30 percent of the mess halls remained nationally after this period of attrition. Bo, 若干重大決策與事件的回顧.

[121] Kung, unpublished research notes. Thaxton, *Catastrophe and Contention in Rural China*, similarly observes that unrestricted consumption in the mess hall of Da Fo village only lasted for a few months; thereafter food was rationed by coupons.

[122] The long-term effect of fetal and infant malnutrition on middle-age health is widely known as the "Barker hypothesis" in the medical literature. See D.J. Barker, "The Fetal and Infant Origins of Adult Disease," *British Medical Journal* 301.6761 (1990), 1111.

outcomes such as labor supply, educational attainment, and socioeconomic status.[123] In terms of health consequences, early-life exposure to the famine has been associated with stunting, obesity, schizophrenia, diabetes, and a higher likelihood of disability in adulthood. With its close link to nutrition, disease, and the economic environment, attained height is frequently used as an indicator of well-being. For example, in order to quantify the famine's long-term impact on human capital outcomes, Chen and Zhou drew upon the variations in famine exposure across both regions and birth cohorts, and found that, if not due to *in utero* nutritional deficiency, those who were born in 1959 and 1960 would have grown 3.03 and 3.0 centimeters taller respectively.[124] In turn, the height deficiency is apparently associated with a chain of unfavorable socioeconomic outcomes for the survivors. For the 1960 cohort, for instance, famine exposure as measured by an additional excess death per thousand in the population is associated with a 2.1 percent reduction in total labor supply and a 4.3 percent reduction in farm income.

A major issue associated with the difference-in-differences (DID) method typically employed in studies of this nature is self-selection, in that infants who survived the famine are likely to have (unobserved) stronger biological survivability than those who perished, or these children may have been born to physically and socioeconomically advantaged parents amid resource deficiency; in either case, the resulting selection bias would have attenuated the estimated effect of the famine. To overcome these challenges, Meng and Qian improved the DID estimator using quantile analysis based on the premise that attenuation would be less pronounced for individuals in the upper quantiles of the outcome distribution.[125] Adjusting the estimation this way leads to a 2.8-centimeter height reduction because of *in utero* exposure to famine. Yet another way to separate the selection effect from the stunting effect is to make use of the idea of heritability, according to which only the "tall genes" of the famine cohort (as opposed to environmentally induced stunting) would be passed down to their offspring.[126] On this assumption, children of the famine cohort would on average be taller than those unaffected by the famine, and their height could therefore be used to control for selection within a model that maps the relationship between the heights

---

[123] J. Currie and B.C. Madrian, "Health, Health Insurance and the Labor Market," *Handbook of Labor Economics* 3 (1999), 3309–3416, provide a comprehensive review of studies linking poor health conditions to lower education and labor market attainment.
[124] Chen and Zhou, "The Long-Term Health and Economic Consequences."
[125] Meng and Qian, "The Long-Term Consequences of Famine."
[126] Gørgens, Meng, and Vaithianathan, "Stunting and Selection Effects of Famine."

of parents and of children. This approach thus allows identification of the stunting effect separately from the selection effect. On the one hand, famine has the negative – stunting – effect of reducing the height of its cohort by one or two centimeters; on the other hand, this cohort is one or two centimeters taller than the average because of their superior genes (which allow them to survive) – the selection effect. The two effects cancel one another out.[127]

However, the assumption underlying Gørgens et al.'s methodology – that children of the famine survivors were able to transcend their parents' traumatic history and quickly rebound – is questionable in the light of studies focusing on the intergenerational effects of the famine.[128] For instance, Almond, Edlund, and Zhang found that the Chinese famine had not only altered the affected cohort's sex ratio towards a higher proportion of females, which was probably a result of higher male fetus susceptibility, but also famine-born mothers were in turn 1.2 percent less likely to give birth to boys, and 8 percent more likely to give birth to underweight babies.[129] However, these findings by economists are disputed by medical researchers. Using the Dutch Hunger Winter of 1944–1945 as context, Stein, Zybert, and Lumey find no evidence of an excess of female births among deliveries of human infants exposed to famine at any period of gestation.[130] The same disagreement applies to the claim of a higher risk of diabetes and its alleged transmission to future generations. The allegation that the Great Leap Famine was the origin of the prevalence of diabetes in China today is similarly disputed by Li and Lumey,[131] who argue that the observed prevalence of a wide range of chronic illnesses, including type 2 diabetes and

---

[127] That is, just because the survivors are of normal height (the observed outcome), it would be erroneous to suggest that the famine has done no harm to the survivors, as the "harm" is compensated for by self-selection.
[128] Gørgens, Meng, and Vaithianathan, "Stunting and Selection Effects of Famine."
[129] Almond et al., "Long-Term Effects of Early-Life Development." This result finds support from the Trivers–Willard hypothesis in evolutionary biology, which predicts that, by comparison with parents in "good conditions," those in "poor conditions" would "favor" the female offspring, as the survivability of male infants is lower than that of female infants; the chances are thus greater that daughters would survive during famine. See, e.g., C. Ó Gráda, *Famine: A Short History* (Princeton, Princeton University Press, 2009), pp. 107–8.
[130] A.D. Stein, P.A. Zybert, and L.H. Lumey, "Acute Undernutrition Is Not Associated with Excess of Females at Birth in Humans: The Dutch Hunger Winter," *Royal Society Biology Letters* 271 (2004), S138–41.
[131] P. Zimmet, Z. Shi, A. El-Osta, and L. Ji, "Epidemic T2DM, Early Development and Epigenetics: Implications of the Chinese Famine," *Nature Reviews Endocrinology* 14.12 (2018), 738–46. C. Li and L.H. Lumey, "Exposure to the Chinese Famine of 1959–61 in Early Life and Long-Term Health Conditions: A Systematic Review and Meta-analysis," *International Journal of Epidemiology*, 2017, 1157–70.

schizophrenia, among adults born during the famine is really due to uncontrolled age differences between the treated group and those who were born either before or after the famine. The health outcomes caused by stress *in utero* are thus at best inconclusive.

Another long-term consequence for individuals who suffered from the Great Leap Famine is educational attainment. However, the evidence is less conclusive in this regard. For example, Meng and Qian estimated that while prenatal famine exposure is responsible for 0.6 fewer years of schooling, the same impact cannot be found from exposure in infancy – the latter defined as individuals who were affected during their first year of life.[132] In contrast, Shi found that exposure to famine in infancy lowers the probability of completing high school by 0.5 percent.[133] In terms of marriage outcomes, Almond et al. concluded that the male famine cohort is more likely to stay spouseless, whereas Brandt, Siow, and Vogel found only negligible changes in the marriage rates of survivors, possibly because their reduced marital attractiveness was mitigated by the smaller size of the cohort.[134] Discrepancies between research results are even more pronounced in the case of the famine's impact on the labor supply, with available estimates ranging from no effect to a 13.9 percent reduction in total working hours.[135]

The lack of a consistent finding across studies is not unanticipated, in view of the difficulty of separating the famine's impact from that of later-life events. This is especially pronounced for the non-health aspects of long-term outcomes, as it remains unclear what and how subsequent environmental factors would interact with the initial health shock. Perhaps a particular topic that awaits illumination is the causal channels linking exposure to famine, health capital, and other socioeconomic outcomes.

---

[132] Meng and Qian, "The Long-Term Consequences of Famine."
[133] X. Shi, "Famine, Fertility, and Fortune in China," *China Economic Review* 22.2 (2011), 244–59.
[134] Almond et al., "Long-Term Effects of Early-Life Development." L. Brandt, A. Siow, and C. Vogel, "Large Demographic Shocks and Small Changes in the Marriage Market," *Journal of the European Economic Association* 14.6 (2016), 1437–68.
[135] While Meng and Qian, "The Long-Term Consequences of Famine," found that early-childhood exposure to the famine reduced the labor supply by an average of 13.9 percent, Shi, "Famine, Fertility, and Fortune in China," found no significant effect of infancy exposure. Between the sexes, Almond et al., "Long-Term Effects of Early-Life Development," found that exposure to famine increased the probability of not working by 3 percent for women and 5.9 percent for men.

Institutional Change and Development

In addition to affecting individuals, the Great Leap Famine also provides a rare opportunity to examine the possible role of history in shaping institutional choice. For example, is the bad, collective memory experienced during the Great Leap Famine associated with people's communes, so that when the opportunity to dismantle collective agriculture presented itself, as was the case during 1979–1984, those who suffered the most from the Leap would be the first to make the change?[136] The relative autonomy and long period over which provinces were allowed to switch to household farming presents a good quasi-natural experiment for the possible bearing of history on institutional choice.[137] In this experiment, Bai and Kung interpreted the variations in timing across the provinces as reflecting their perceived preferences for collective rather than family farm institutions, which in turn was determined by their relative preference for more efficacious provision of public goods such as irrigation or sharper incentives for individual work, on the assumption that collective agriculture enjoys a comparative advantage in the provision of public goods, but incentives for individual work are distinctly greater on family farms.[138] In short, this preference can be taken to represent a trade-off between the two types of farm institution with respect to their relative strengths and weaknesses.

Bai and Kung's remaining analysis thus hinges on the question of what determined the preference for one type of institution over the other across the Chinese provinces. To do so, they constructed a panel data set with which to examine the respective possible effects on institutional choice of the strengths of collective farms (using irrigation as proxy) and their weaknesses (using famine severity as proxy). For the dependent variable, the authors assumed that the earlier a province chose to decollectivize, the more it must have suffered from collective agriculture in general, and famine severity in

---

[136] For instance, whereas Anhui province, a poverty-stricken province in central China, jumped the gun and dismantled its collective farms before the Chinese Communist Party officially sanctioned it, the northeastern provinces were recalcitrant and dragged their feet even after the central government had explicitly recognized the virtues of household farming and endorsed it. Bai and Kung, "The Shaping of an Institutional Choice."

[137] In sharp contrast to the establishment of the people's communes, which was largely homogeneous and occurred over a narrow time window, it took nearly five years for the reverse process to occur, which reflects the fundamental difference in approach to implementing policy between Mao and Deng. Unlike Mao, Deng took his time to demonstrate the productivity advantages of household farming in order to conciliate conservative political opponents, many of whom still stood in the way of this institutional change.

[138] Bai and Kung, "The Shaping of an Institutional Choice."

particular. In sharp contrast to the conventional wisdom, which maintains that weather adversity – specifically drought – was an exogenous shock that predisposed villagers to switch over quickly to family farming,[139] Bai and Kung found that bad weather that occurred during decollectivization actually slowed down the switchover to family farming, presumably because collective agriculture was still considered to be more efficient at providing irrigation.[140] However, in provinces that suffered heavily from the Leap's famine in terms of mortality, weather shocks occurring during decollectivization effectively served as a painful reminder of the weaknesses of collective agriculture, thereby reversing the effect of bad weather on the choice of institutions, by predisposing these provinces to make the switchover sooner rather than later.[141] To further ensure that this analysis also holds at the village level, Bai and Kung employed the China General Social Survey (CGSS) of 2005 (which contains a question asking the village cadre the year in which they abandoned collective agriculture) to check robustness and confirm it.[142] Thus, through the channel of collective memory, the Great Leap Famine offers social scientists a rare opportunity to examine the role of history in institutional change.

Concerning its effect on development more generally, Gooch finds that an increase of one standard deviation in excess deaths during the famine is associated with a decrease in per capita GDP of 4,454 yuan half a century later, although she is reticent on the mechanism causing this result – a topic of future research.[143]

Conclusion

In this chapter we have reviewed several bodies of literature on China's Great Leap Famine – including its long-term consequences. Having killed an estimated 30 million people (if not more), it remains the deadliest famine in

---

[139] A production team by the name of Xiaogang in Anhui province became a household name as they secretly divided their collective holdings among the farm households after being struck by a severe drought, which made planting formidably difficult. The story of these highly motivated peasant households spending several days working extremely hard and eventually planting the wheat on the cracking dried earth speaks volumes for the paramount importance of individual work incentives.

[140] Bai and Kung, "The Shaping of an Institutional Choice."

[141] The same logic applies to irrigation. In provinces where irrigation had been built up during the period of collective agriculture, peasants would be more confident in dealing with weather risks even on their own, and this predisposed them to choose household farming sooner.

[142] Bai and Kung, "The Shaping of an Institutional Choice."

[143] Gooch, "Estimating the Long-Term Impact of the Great Chinese Famine."

human history. A unique feature of this great famine is that it occurred in the context of a bumper harvest, and under a regime whose leader was very ambitious and sanguine about the future of his country and the people. But a multitude of bold and untried policies, rooted in the fundamentally unrealistic goal of producing a substantially larger farm surplus to help fuel industrialization, made this grand scheme an utter failure.

For more than two decades, social scientists have been fascinated by this incident and tried to make sense of it. A variety of explanations have been offered. While some emphasize that it was excessive grain procurement that was primarily responsible for the observed excess deaths, other culprits included the thorough destruction of work incentives under the commune system, while still others put the blame on an irrational organization of communal kitchens. However, as we have seen, some arguments are more persuasive than others on the basis of logical reasoning, historical grounds, and not least analytical evidence. To a large extent, there is perhaps a "consensus" that grain procurement was a strong culprit. To this end, various attempts have thus been made to understand possible exogenous variations – both economic (institutional rigidity and excessive exporting, for instance) and political (career incentives) in the first place. In furthering the analysis of the role played by the human factor in this catastrophe, evidence has also been brought to bear on the suggestion that political elites were not all sinister during these tumultuous times; those who were not subject to the same strong incentives to climb the *nomenklatura*'s career ladder as their regional counterparts were found to have exerted themselves to ameliorate the food shortages faced by their "distant relatives." As with many other lesser known aspects of the Great Leap (and collective agriculture more generally), more research is required to confirm these suggestive claims and to reveal new findings.

As demonstrated by the works of Meng et al. and Kasahara and Li, research on the Great Leap Famine has clearly benefited from disaggregated data at the county level.[144] We can thus expect more works of this nature in the future. In the light of the still preliminary finding that the severity of famine varied as much within a single province as between them (or, for that matter, that there were variations involving subunits across provincial boundaries), future work on the extent to which the severity of famine might have been shaped by local variations in geography, history, economy, and politics would certainly benefit from the availability of these fine-grained data.

---

[144] Meng, Qian, and Yared, "The Institutional Causes of China's Great Famine." Kasahara and Li, "Grain Exports and the Causes of China's Great Famine."

Further Reading

Ashton, B., K. Hill, A. Piazza, and R. Zeitz, "Famine in China, 1958–61," *Population and Development Review* 10 (1984), 613–45.

Bai, Y., and J.K.S. Kung, "The Shaping of an Institutional Choice: Weather Shocks, the Great Leap Famine, and Agricultural Decollectivization in China," *Explorations in Economic History* 54 (2014), 1–26.

Bernstein, T.P., "Mao Zedong and the Famine of 1959–1960: A Study in Wilfulness," *China Quarterly* 186 (2006), 421–45.

Bramall, C., "Agency and Famine in China's Sichuan Province, 1958–1962," *China Quarterly* 208 (2011), 990–1008.

Cao Shuji 曹树基, 1959–1961 年中國的人口死亡及其成因 (The Death Rate of China's Population and Its Contributing Factors from 1959–1961), 中国人口学 (Chinese Population Science), 2005, 14–28.

Garnaut, A., "The Geography of the Great Leap Famine," *Modern China* 40.3 (2014), 315–48.

Kasahara, H., and B. Li, "Grain Exports and the Causes of China's Great Famine, 1959–1961: County-Level Evidence," *Journal of Development Economics* 146 (2020), 102513.

Kung, J.K.S., and S. Chen, "The Tragedy of the Nomenklatura: Career Incentives and Political Radicalism during China's Great Leap Famine," *American Political Science Review* 105.1 (2011), 27–45.

Kung, J.K.S., and J.Y. Lin, "The Causes of China's Great Leap Famine, 1959–1961," *Economic Development and Cultural Change* 52.1 (2003), 51–73.

Kung, J.K.S., and T. Zhou, "Political Elites and Hometown Favoritism in Famine-Stricken China," *Journal of Comparative Economics* (2020), at www.sciencedirect.com/science/article/pii/S0147596720300184?via%3Dihub.

Li, W., and D.T. Yang, "The Great Leap Forward: Anatomy of a Central Planning Disaster," *Journal of Political Economy* 113.4 (2005), 840–77.

Lin, J.Y., and D.T. Yang, "Food Availability, Entitlements and the Chinese Famine of 1959–61," *Economic Journal* 110.460 (2000), 136–58.

Meng, X., N. Qian, and P. Yared, "The Institutional Causes of China's Great Famine, 1959–1961," *Review of Economic Studies* 82.4 (2015), 1568–1611.

Ó Gráda, C., "Great Leap, Great Famine: A Review Essay," *Population and Development Review* 39.2 (2013), 333–46.

Walker, K.R., "Food and Mortality in China during the Great Leap Forward, 1958–61," in R.F. Ash (ed.), *Agricultural Development in China, 1949–1989: The Collected Papers of Kenneth R. Walker* (New York, Oxford University Press, 1998), pp. 106–47.

19

China's External Economic Relations during the Mao Era

AMY KING

When considering the question of China's external economic relations during the Mao era, the dominant narrative in the literature underscores the following view: Mao's China pursued a foreign economic policy that was autarkic, isolated from the global economy, and locked into a Soviet-inspired planned economy that provided limited incentives for economic interdependence with the outside world. For some, China's isolation from the global economy was the result of its position in the Soviet bloc, which was "heavily biased against foreign trade," and from its adoption of a centrally planned, socialist economic model that prohibited private interests from pursuing foreign investment or trade.[1] For others, Mao-era policies of autarky were inspired by a form of xenophobia that stemmed from the country's experience of Western predations during the nineteenth century, resulting in fear of economic dependence on foreign powers.[2] Finally, others emphasize the role of Mao's revolutionary ideology in explaining China's isolation from the global economy; Mao's tendency to view major international economic institutions and norms as counterrevolutionary and "hostile" to the Chinese state led him to disengage from international trade and other economic opportunities.[3]

The volume of China's external economic relations was undoubtedly limited during the Mao era when compared to both the Republican (1912–1949) and reform (1978–present) periods. During the Mao era, China did not participate in international capital markets, did not permit private foreign

---

[1] J.W. Garver, *China's Quest: The History of the Foreign Relations of the People's Republic of China* (New York, Oxford University Press, 2016), pp. 367–8.
[2] K. Reese, "Mainland China and Western Trade Credits," *Intereconomics* 2 (1976), 45.
[3] W. Hu, "China as a Listian Trading State: Interest, Power, and Economic Ideology," in G.J. Ikenberry, J. Wang, and F. Zhu (eds.), *America, China, and the Struggle for World Order: Ideas, Traditions, Historical Legacies, and Global Visions* (New York, Palgrave, 2015), p. 231.

direct investment in its economy, and pursued a government-led system of foreign-exchange control that severely restricted the development of external trade relations.[4] Consequently, China under Mao was ranked thirtieth in the list of the world's top exporting countries, and its trade accounted for just 0.8 to 1 percent of world trade between 1952 and 1978. By comparison, during the Republican era, Chinese trade accounted for approximately 2 percent of world trade until the 1930s, when the effects of the Great Depression and the War of Resistance against Japan took hold. Following Mao's death in 1976 and the introduction of reform and opening under Deng Xiaoping in 1978, China's trade levels then increased exponentially (see Figure 19.1). By 1990, China's share of world trade had recovered to levels not seen since the late 1920s. By 2003, China accounted for 5.8 percent of world trade (Table 19.1).[5]

Yet China was not as closed off to the outside world during the Mao era as these figures and dominant narratives suggest, particularly when viewed within the context of other developing countries, and within the context of its own tumultuous history of war. Within the first decade of the new People's Republic (1949–1959), Chinese foreign trade had grown faster than trade growth experienced among other developing countries and all other Asian countries. And while China's membership of the Soviet bloc did shape the country's patterns of trade, particularly during the CCP's first decade in power, by the late 1960s more than two-thirds of China's trade was taking place with non-Communist countries, stretching across Asia, Africa, Europe, the Americas, and Oceania.[6] Characterizing China as "autarkic" or "isolated" during the Mao era therefore obscures the ways in which the Chinese economy was connected to the external world between 1949 and 1978. China's patterns of trade, its receipt of foreign investment and loans, and its own distributions of foreign aid were shaped by a combination of five key factors: its place in the Soviet bloc and its adoption of the Soviet economic model, the Cold War geopolitical and economic order, the legacy of Japanese empire and war with Japan, the impact of imperialism, and the CCP's own domestic political campaigns. Perhaps most importantly, though, the impact of these factors was felt not only on the size and direction of China's external

---

[4] N.R. Lardy, *China in the World Economy* (Washington, DC, Institute for International Economics, 1994), pp. 1–2.

[5] W. Keller, B. Li, and C.H. Shiue, "China's Foreign Trade: Perspectives from the Past 150 Years," *World Economy* 34 (2011), 884; A. Maddison, *Chinese Economic Performance in the Long Run: 960–2030 AD* (Paris, Development Centre of the Organisation for Economic Co-operation and Development, 2007), pp. 55–60.

[6] Y. Zhang, *China in International Society since 1949: Alienation and Beyond* (Basingstoke, MacMillan Press in association with St. Antony's College, Oxford, 1998), pp. 28–9.

Table 19.1 Chinese export levels, 1913–2003

	Exports in 1990 prices US$ million	Exports as % of GDP in 1990 international US$ million	Exports in current prices US$ million	Chinese exports as % of world exports in current US$
1913	4,197	1.2	299	1.6
1929	6,262	2.3	660	2.0
1952	8,063	2.6	820	1.0
1978	15,639	1.7	9,750	0.8
1990	62,090	2.9	62,090	1.9
2003	453,734	7.1	438,230	5.8

Source: A. Maddison, *Chinese Economic Performance in the Long Run: 960–2030 AD* (Paris, Development Centre of the Organisation for Economic Co-operation and Development, 2007), p. 88

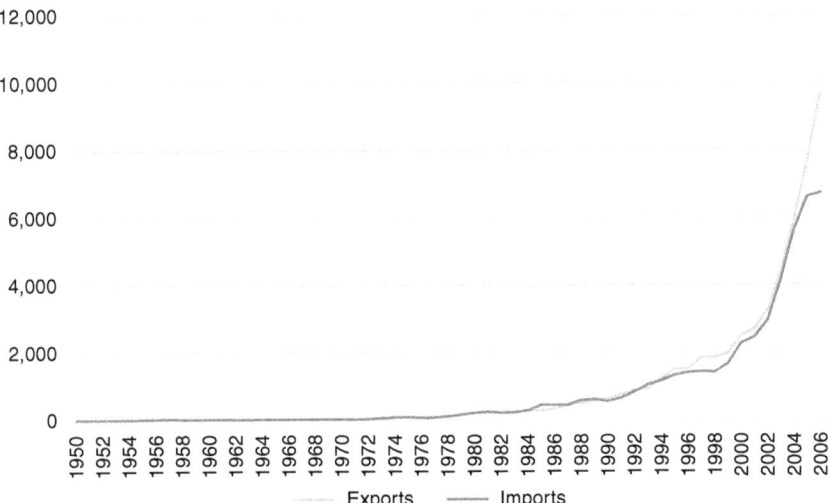

Figure 19.1 Chinese total trade, 1950–2006 (in US$ million at current prices)
Source: State Statistical Bureau of the People's Republic of China, *Statistical Yearbook of China* (New York, Praeger, various years). All *Statistical Yearbook of China* current prices used throughout this chapter are based on exchange rates issued by the People's Bank of China (1950–1978) and the Bank of China (1979–2006)

trade, loan, foreign aid, and investment ties, but also in CCP thinking about China's place in the global economy, and the role of foreign economic policy in the country's wider relations with the outside world. Chief among CCP foreign economic policy ideas was the notion that economic development – through rapid industrialization and access to advanced technology – was of critical import for "backward" countries who were attempting to catch up, re-establish economic and political sovereignty, secure themselves in an era of industrialized military power, and obtain greater power and influence on the world stage. Despite sweeping changes in the nature of China's engagement with the global economy since Mao's death, these core ideas have ongoing resonance in China today.

The Soviet Bloc and Adoption of the Planned Economy

The Soviet Union was China's most important economic partner during the first decade of the new People's Republic. Moreover, the Soviet economic model's influence shaped the Chinese economy long after the relationship had been disrupted by the Sino-Soviet split. In the winter of 1949, senior CCP leaders began discussing in earnest with their Soviet counterparts China's economic development goals. China's economy had been ravaged by the preceding years of war against Japan, by civil war between the Communists and Nationalists, and by the Republican government's adoption of Bretton Woods trade and financial policies in the late 1940s. As a result, the country's industrial base had been badly eroded, agricultural production remained lower than pre-1937 levels, and overly ambitious economic policies had upended China's trade balance with the United States and depleted the country's foreign-exchange reserves.[7] Given these dire economic conditions, Mao informed Anastas Mikoyan, the Soviet minister for foreign trade, in February 1949 that "after the ending of the Civil War the *main task* of the party will amount to economic construction."[8] However, Mao admitted that the CCP had little experience in governing urban areas of China, and thus would be heavily dependent on the Soviet Union for help in reconstructing

---

[7] W.C. Kirby, "The Chinese War Economy," in S.I. Levine and J.C. Hsiung (eds.), *China's Bitter Victory: The War with Japan, 1937–1945* (New York, M.E. Sharpe, 1992), pp. 185–6; N. R. Lardy, "Economic Recovery and the 1st Five-Year Plan," in R. Macfarquhar and J. K. Fairbank (eds.), *Cambridge History of China*, vol. 14, *The People's Republic*, part 1, *The Emergence of Revolutionary China, 1949–1965* (Cambridge, Cambridge University Press, 1987), p. 144; for more on the impact of the KMT's postwar trade and financial policies, see the chapter by Grove and Kubo in this volume.

[8] "Memorandum of Conversation between Anastas Mikoyan and Mao Zedong," February 5, 1949, History and Public Policy Program Digital Archive, APRF: F. 39, op. 1, D. 39, ll. 74–7. Reprinted in A. Ledovskii, R. Mirovitskaia, and V. Miasnikov, *Sovetsko-kitaiskie otnosheniia*, vol. 5, book 2, *1946–fevral' 1950* (Moscow, Pamiatniki Istoricheskoi Mysli, 2005), pp. 78–80, trans. Sergey Radchenko (emphasis in original). See http://digitalarchive.wilsoncenter.org/document/113323.

and developing large cities like Changchun, Anshan, Beijing, Tianjin, and Shanghai.[9] The Soviet Union, Mao reasoned, had long-standing economic interests in northeast China, and in cities like Dalian "there is a whole array of enterprises that we are in no position to exploit without Soviet assistance."[10] Even more fundamentally, the Soviet Union's economic model – and its own transformation from an economically "backward" country into a modern, industrialized one – represented a powerful blueprint for the CCP. Soviet economic ideology encapsulated a "scientific" approach to managing the economy, and a central role for the state in both economic planning and ownership of industry.[11]

Nevertheless, we should not overstate the influence of Soviet economic ideology on Mao-era China; approaches to state-led industrial development adopted by both the Guomindang and the Japanese in China during the 1930s and 1940s laid the groundwork for the CCP to graft on Soviet plans for rapid industrialization after 1949. As Morris Bian, Linda Grove, and Tōru Kubo argue elsewhere in this volume, ideas about the necessity of state-led industrial development took particular hold in China in the 1930s and 1940s as war with Japan accelerated the need for Chinese military preparedness. In Free China, the KMT government introduced a series of national plans for the development of iron, steel, energy, chemicals, and heavy machinery to underpin China's military industries. In Japanese-controlled occupied China and Manchuria, Japanese forces had similarly maintained strong state-led approaches towards the development of heavy industry as a means of fueling Japan's war machine. The CCP was relatively late to understand the relationship between heavy industry and national defense because the Party had spent the years of war with Japan as a force fighting a guerrilla war based in rural areas with little in the way of industry. But as the CCP took control of China's cities, and then confronted a new Cold War environment shaped by war against the United States in Korea, Mao and his cadres quickly came to understand the connection between economic – and particularly industrial – development and the country's ability to defend itself in

---

[9] "Memorandum of Conversation between Anastas Mikoyan and Mao Zedong."
[10] "Record of Talks between I.V. Stalin and Chairman of the Central People's Government of the People's Republic of China Mao Zedong," January 22, 1950, History and Public Policy Program Digital Archive, Archive of the President, Russian Federation (APRF), f. 45, op. 1, d.329, ll. 29–38. Translated by D. Rozas. See http://digitalarchive.wilsoncenter.org/document/111245.
[11] W.C. Kirby, "China's Internationalization in the Early People's Republic: Dreams of a Socialist World Economy," *China Quarterly* 188 (2006), 876; for more on China's experience with the Soviet economic model, see Perkins's chapter in this volume.

wartime.[12] In his conversations with Mikoyan in early 1949, Mao reflected, "In order to finally destroy the enemy, one should grow strong economically." Moreover, acknowledging the legacy of Japanese and KMT-led economic planning in the heavy industrial sector, Mao admitted that the prospects for China's industrial development were relatively favorable, particularly in northeast China, because nearly half of the industrial capital in that region was already controlled by the state rather than by private interests.[13] Subsequently, throughout 1949 and early 1950, Mao, Zhou Enlai, Liu Shaoqi, and other senior CCP officials held countless conversations with Stalin and other Soviet counterparts to discuss the Soviet Union's model of industrial development, and the precise goods and technical assistance that the CCP hoped to obtain from Moscow in order to roll out that model. By the end of his otherwise difficult visit to Moscow in the winter of 1949–1950, Mao had succeeded in negotiating an agreement for the Soviet Union to extend a loan of US$300 million to China, which would help to finance China's import of industrial plants and equipment from the Soviet Union. The two sides also reached agreement on the creation of a series of Sino-Soviet joint-stock companies, which would manage railways, shipyards, mining, and petroleum extraction across northeast China and Xinjiang, and agreed to dispatch a large number of Soviet engineers and other technical experts to assist with designing the construction of new industrial sites across China.[14]

Yet China's signing of these trade and co-operation agreements with the Soviet Union was never designed to preclude the development of Chinese economic ties with countries outside the Soviet bloc. As part of their negotiations with Moscow, CCP leaders explained their desire to take a relatively relaxed approach towards foreign and private capital in China, particularly during the Party's first years of governing. Although the CCP had adopted a policy at its Sixth Party Congress to confiscate foreign capital and nationalize all private capital in China, Mao explained to Mikoyan that the CCP needed to be "flexible" in implementing this policy. This was in part because of the difficulty of disentangling foreign capital from Chinese capital, and in part because the CCP was eager not to unnecessarily antagonize China's "bourgeoisie" immediately upon coming to power. Mao stressed to his

[12] A. King, "'Reconstructing China': Japanese Technicians and Industrialization in the Early People's Republic of China," *Modern Asian Studies* 50.1 (2016), 141–74.
[13] "Memorandum of Conversation between Anastas Mikoyan and Mao Zedong," February 5, 1949.
[14] A. Eckstein, *Communist China's Economic Growth and Foreign Trade* (New York, McGraw-Hill, 1966), pp. 138–9; Z. Shen and D. Li, *After Leaning to One Side: China and Its Allies in the Cold War* (Washington, DC, Woodrow Wilson Center Press, 2011), p. 120.

Soviet counterparts that the Chinese economy would be socialist in character, but that "we are not shouting about this so as not to scare someone away."[15] This approach reflected the principles underpinning the CCP's postwar economic reconstruction policy of New Democracy, first adopted in 1941 and maintained until the end of the Korean War in 1953. New Democracy enabled the CCP to focus on rapidly rebuilding the Chinese economy, and improving the country's industrial base, while staving off political opposition from rural landowners and other members of the "bourgeoisie" by permitting a range of capitalist economic practices.[16]

At the same time, Moscow also counseled the CCP towards greater openness to the non-Communist world. In January 1949, Mao explained to the Soviet leadership that China's foreign trade would take place primarily with the Soviet Union and other members of the Soviet bloc, and that "only those things, which [the USSR and the socialist bloc] do not need, will be exported to capitalist countries."[17] However, over the spring and winter of 1949, Stalin and Mikoyan continually encouraged Mao to be willing to engage in trade with capitalist countries under certain conditions. Stalin recognized that such trade would likely be important for China's economic development, and could assist in reducing China's economic dependence on the Soviet Union.[18] Just as importantly, such trade could also offer China a source of political leverage in its dealings with the capitalist bloc, particularly on the question of diplomatic recognition of the PRC. As Stalin explained to a visiting CCP delegation in July 1949,

---

[15] "Memorandum of Conversation between Anastas Mikoyan and Mao Zedong," February 6, 1949, History and Public Policy Program Digital Archive, APRF: F. 39, op. 1, D. 39, ll. 78–88, reprinted in Ledovskii, Mirovitskaia, and Miasnikov, *Sovetsko-kitaiskie otnosheniia*, vol. 5, book 2, pp. 81–7. See http://digitalarchive.wilsoncenter.org/document/113352.

[16] "Turning China into a Powerful, Modernized, Socialist, Industrialized Country," September 23, 1954, in *Selected Works of Zhou Enlai*, vol. 2 (Beijing, Foreign Languages Press, 1989), p. 142.

[17] "Memorandum of Conversation between Anastas Mikoyan and Mao Zedong," January 31, 1949, History and Public Policy Program Digital Archive, APRF: F. 39, op. 1, D. 39, ll. 7–16, reprinted in Ledovskii, Mirovitskaia, and Miasnikov, *Sovetsko-kitaiskie otnosheniia*, vol. 5, book 2, pp. 37–43. See http://digitalarchive.wilsoncenter.org/document/112436.

[18] "Cable, Filippov [Stalin] to Mao [via Kovalev]," April 19, 1949, History and Public Policy Program Digital Archive, APRF: F. 45, op. 1, D. 331, ll. 24–5, reprinted in Ledovskii, Mirovitskaia, and Miasnikov, *Sovetsko-kitaiskie otnosheniia*, vol. 5, book 2, pp. 120–1. See http://digitalarchive.wilsoncenter.org/document/113356. "Cable, Stalin to Kovalev," April 26, 1949, History and Public Policy Program Digital Archive, APRF: F. 45, op. 1, D. 3331 [sic, probably 331], L. 3, reprinted in Ledovskii, Mirovitskaia, and Miasnikov, *Sovetsko-kitaiskie otnosheniia*, vol. 5, book 2, p. 126. See http://digitalarchive.wilsoncenter.org/document/113357.

You have a really good magic weapon [*fabao* 法宝], which is that imperialism wants to do business [*maimai* 买卖] with you. The imperialist countries' economic crisis has already begun. I think the powers could quickly decide to try and recognize you. You can first do good business with them and then discuss the recognition issue.[19]

Stalin's advice to Mao would significantly influence how the CCP approached foreign trade during the 1950s and 1960s, although Stalin did not foresee in 1949 that the onset of the Cold War would soon inhibit China's ability to trade with the "imperialist" world. Instead, over the course of the 1950s, the Soviet Union, and the Soviet bloc more generally, came to occupy an increasingly important position in the Chinese economy. Unlike the rest of the Soviet bloc economies, China never became a formal member of the Council for Mutual Economic Assistance (COMECON).[20] Rather, its trade with the Soviet bloc was organized via a series of bilateral trade agreements, modeled upon other trade agreements used by the COMECON members, which it signed with the Soviet Union, Czechoslovakia, North Korea, East Germany, Poland, Hungary, Bulgaria, Romania, Mongolia, Albania, and North Vietnam between 1950 and 1954.[21] The most important of these trade partners was easily the Soviet Union, which became critically important in aiding China's postwar rebuilding and in giving China access to the industrial goods it needed to make the leap from an agrarian to an industrialized economy. China imported from the Soviet Union industrial plants and equipment, machinery, petroleum and petroleum products, and metals and metal ores. In return, China exported to the Soviet Union raw materials, soybeans, foodstuffs, metals, textiles, and clothing. The latter two categories of goods became increasingly important in China's export profile as the country rehabilitated its textile industry, and, by 1963, two-thirds of Chinese exports to the Soviet Union comprised fabrics, clothing, and footwear. This pattern of trade reflected China's development strategy of rapid industrialization, which underpinned the country's First Five-Year Plan (1953–1957). China was utterly dependent on access to Soviet capital goods to achieve this rapid industrialization, particularly in the first decade of the Mao years. In 1950, machinery and other capital goods represented around 10 percent of

---

[19] "Cable, Liu Shaoqi to Mao Zedong," July 18, 1949, History and Public Policy Program Digital Archive, 建国以来刘少奇文稿 (Liu Shaoqi's Manuscripts since the Founding of the PRC), vol. 1 (Beijing, Zhongyang wenxian chubanshe, 2005), pp. 30–7. Translated for CWIHP by D. Wolff. See http://digitalarchive.wilsoncenter.org/document/113439.
[20] Kirby, "China's Internationalization in the Early People's Republic," 884.
[21] Eckstein, *Communist China's Economic Growth and Foreign Trade*, pp. 139–40.

China's imports from the Soviet Union, but by the end of that decade capital goods had swelled to more than 60 percent of Chinese imports from the Soviet Union. Indeed, Alexander Eckstein notes that within the Communist bloc, China absorbed more than half of the Soviet Union's worldwide exports of industrial goods and more than two-thirds of complete industrial plant.[22]

Pursuing the Soviet-inspired path of rapid industrialization required much more than just access to Soviet imports, however. The Soviet Union's provision of industrial *expertise* to China, in the form of technicians, economic advisers, engineers, and scientists, was an equally significant dimension of China's economic relationship with the Soviet bloc during the PRC's first decade. As Dwight Perkins argues elsewhere in this volume, China faced a severe shortage of skilled engineers, scientists, and economists in its early years. The country thus became highly dependent on the estimated 10,000 to 12,284 Soviet, and 1,500 Eastern European, technical experts who were sent to China between 1949 and 1960.[23] A further 10,000 Soviet military experts also spent time in China in the 1950s, and many thousands of Chinese students studied at Soviet universities and other training centers.[24] Soviet bloc technicians became a vital source of the specialist advice that China needed to transform industrial goods into working plants, factories, and other industrial sites. In May 1953, at the start of the First Five-Year Plan, for example, Li Fuchun, then vice chairman of the PRC's Central Economic and Financial Commission, negotiated an agreement with Moscow to receive technology and equipment to develop ninety-eight new Chinese industrial projects, including coal mines, metal-processing factories, power plants, and oil refineries.[25] Yet without the simultaneous provision of Soviet technicians – whose numbers peaked in 1956 – these industrial projects would never have been realized. Together, Soviet industrial goods and expertise transformed the Chinese economy and gave the Soviet Union a powerful means of influencing China's economic direction.[26]

Nevertheless, China's economic relationship with the Soviet bloc posed a range of challenges for CCP economic planners. The first was that Chinese imports from the Soviet Union were relatively more important to China's

---

[22] Eckstein, *Communist China's Economic Growth and Foreign Trade*, pp. 149–53.
[23] Eckstein, *Communist China's Economic Growth and Foreign Trade*, p. 169, Shen and Li, *After Leaning to One Side*, p. 118.
[24] Shen and Li, *After Leaning to One Side*, pp. 118, 127.
[25] S.G. Zhang, *Beijing's Economic Statecraft during the Cold War, 1949–1991* (Washington, DC and Baltimore, Woodrow Wilson Center Press and Johns Hopkins University Press, 2014), p. 61.
[26] Shen and Li, *After Leaning to One Side*, pp. 117, 127.

economic planners than were the goods that China exported to the Soviet Union. Between 1950 and 1955, as China was preparing for and carrying out its First Five-Year Plan, Chinese imports from the Soviet Union increased more rapidly than did the size of her exports to the Soviet Union (see Figure 19.2). The structure of the Sino-Soviet trade agreement was such that it required that trade be balanced on an annual basis, and China was simply unable to export sufficient goods to the Soviet Union to meet its demands for Soviet industrial imports. The result was a trade imbalance, which had to be financed through a combination of increased Chinese exports and Soviet loans.[27] The trade imbalance was particularly acute during the Korean War years (1950–1953), when China began importing both industrial goods *and* military equipment from the Soviet Union. Paying for these imports required China to expand dramatically its export of agricultural and raw-material products, and to direct Soviet loans towards Korean War spending, which occupied nearly 60 percent of China's total budget.[28] The Soviet Union was generous in its provision of loans to China, which existed in the form of both formal Sino-Soviet loan agreements – one of 1.2 billion yuan agreed to in 1950, and another of 520 million rubles agreed to in 1954 – and a series of other ad hoc loan arrangements. According to Feng-hwa Mah, Moscow provided a total of 5.2 billion yuan in credits to China between 1950 and 1957.[29] However, the generosity of these loans was somewhat undermined by the fact that more than half of Moscow's total 1950s loan package was diverted towards financing China's involvement in the Korean War.[30] Moreover, the terms of the Soviet loan agreements placed China in a highly precarious position. The Soviet Union charged a low interest rate of just 1 percent on the loans it extended to China, yet required that these loans be amortized over a period of just ten years. This was a much shorter time frame than comparable international loans, and placed a very large debt-servicing burden on the Chinese economy. Alexander Eckstein estimates that, over the course of the 1950s and 1960s, between 10 and 40 percent of China's total export earnings in

---

[27] Eckstein, *Communist China's Economic Growth and Foreign Trade*, pp. 135, 154–5.
[28] "From the Diary of N.V. Roshchin: Memorandum of Conversation with Chinese Premier Zhou Enlai on 24 July 1951," July 27, 1951, History and Public Policy Program Digital Archive, AVPRF, f. 0100, op. 44, por. 13, pap. 322, ll. 44–57, translated by D. Wolff. See http://digitalarchive.wilsoncenter.org/document/118735.
[29] F.H. Mah, "Foreign Trade," in A. Eckstein, W. Galenson, and T.C. Liu (eds.), *Economic Trends in Communist China* (Chicago, Aldine, 1968), pp. 703, 728–9.
[30] M. Nakajima, "Foreign Relations: From the Korean War to the Bandung Line," in Macfarquhar and Fairbank, *Cambridge History of China*, vol. 14, pp. 277–8.

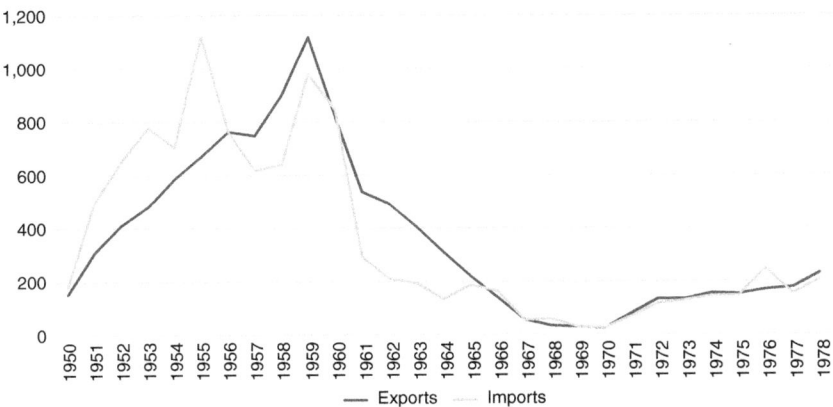

Figure 19.2 Chinese exports to and imports from the Soviet Union, 1950–1978 (in US$ million at current prices)
Source: *Statistical Yearbook of China* (1981), p. 363

the Sino-Soviet trade relationship went towards its repayments of loans to the Soviet Union.[31]

Second, as William Kirby has argued, the Soviet economic bloc displayed inherent structural weaknesses that inevitably limited the development of trade ties between Soviet bloc members. As planned economies, which did not use freely floating prices or convertible currencies, Soviet bloc economies had to engage in the painstaking process of continuous renegotiation of trade agreements that met the requirements of both their foreign trade counterparts and their own national economic plans. In addition, many of the countries within the bloc were developing, war-torn countries, who sought to use the Soviet model of rapid industrialization as a way to rebuild and transform their economies. The result, however, was a considerable lack of diversity within the bloc; member economies each focused on the development of heavy industry and thus found it difficult to pursue trade on the principle of comparative advantage.[32]

Finally, though the Soviet economic model and Soviet industrial goods and expertise provided significant economic benefits to China, membership of the Soviet bloc separated China from economic partners that were more naturally suited to China in terms of geography and historical familiarity. Located at some distance from the Soviet Union and Eastern Europe, China's exports and imports to and from the Soviet bloc had to travel overland via the Trans-Siberian Railway, which considerably added to the cost and duration of transport. One

[31] Eckstein, *Communist China's Economic Growth and Foreign Trade*, p. 161.
[32] Kirby, "China's Internationalization in the Early People's Republic," 882–7.

estimate suggests that geographical distance added an additional 30 percent to the cost of China's imports from the Soviet Union, when compared to the prices paid by its Eastern European counterparts.[33] At the same time, Soviet and Eastern European goods and industrial advice were often deemed less suitable to Chinese conditions than those from other historical economic partners, such as Japan. In 1949 and 1950, Chinese workers living in northeastern Chinese cities complained that Soviet railway expertise paled in comparison to that possessed by the highly proficient Japanese engineers who had been based in northeast China as part of Japan's colonial project since the 1930s.[34] By comparison, Soviet experts were provided with little or no understanding of or training in China's history, culture, or economic conditions, and typically had little in the way of Chinese language skills. Rather, it seems that the primary factor shaping their selection to travel to China was that they had the correct political background and displayed loyalty to the Communist Party of the Soviet Union.[35] Unsurprisingly, their resulting experiences in China were rarely positive ones. The lack of language skills and familiarity with the local Chinese context, coupled with China's own lack of technical expertise, led to poor communication between Soviet and Chinese workers, and delays in applying the Soviet Union's technical experience to the Chinese context. As the 1950s progressed, Chinese officials began to complain that Soviet and European imports were costly and that their economic planning advice was not always well suited to Chinese conditions. In 1957, the CCP elected to reduce its overall expenditure on technical advice from the Soviet Union, and instead to draw on "fewer but better" Soviet experts.[36] The following year, as the number of Soviet bloc experts in China began to decline, Chinese foreign minister Chen Yi began looking elsewhere for expertise, and in particular to Japan. As Chen explained in a meeting with the Japanese president of the Japan–China Import–Export Association,

> China has a saying: "neighbours are dearer than distant relatives." We have built a relationship with Europe, but the road is far and it costs a lot in time and money to reach, so it is not worthwhile. Japan is only separated by a strip of water, and so it is relatively convenient ... With respect to planning, European experts' plans are not compatible with, and do not suit, China's situation. Japanese experts' plans would be relatively more suitable to us.[37]

---

[33] Eckstein, *Communist China's Economic Growth and Foreign Trade*, p. 172.
[34] King, "Reconstructing China," 142–3. [35] Shen and Li, *After Leaning to One Side*, p. 123.
[36] Shen and Li, *After Leaning to One Side*, pp. 129–31.
[37] PRC Foreign Ministry Archive, File 105-00595-03, February 7, 1958, "陈毅副总理接见日本中日输出入组合理事长南乡三郎谈话记录" (Records of the Meeting between Foreign Minister Chen Yi and Japan's China–Japan Export–Import Association President, Nangō Saburō), pp. 2, 11–12.

It is difficult to overestimate the role that the Soviet Union played in aiding China's economic reconstruction, and facilitating China's external economic ties to the Soviet bloc, during the PRC's first, crucial, decade in power. Nevertheless, there were problems baked into the Sino-Soviet economic relationship from the start, not the least of which was the significant development gap that existed between China and her Soviet "elder brother."[38] This gap made the economic relationship a complementary one, but also an unbalanced one, and by the end of the 1950s CCP leaders were increasingly resentful of China's structural dependence upon the Soviet Union. That resentment would play an important role in catalyzing the Sino-Soviet split and China's eventual turn to the non-Communist world, as we shall see in more detail in the sections that follow, although economic factors alone are certainly not sufficient to explain the breakdown of the Sino-Soviet relationship.[39] Ultimately, the Soviet Union was the PRC's first and most important economic partner, and the positive and negative aspects of this relationship would have a profound effect both on the pattern of China's external economic relations and on the ideas underpinning the CCP's foreign economic policy.

Cold War Geopolitical and Economic Blocs

The second critical factor shaping the pattern of China's external economic relations, particularly during the first decade of the PRC's existence, was Cold War competition between the United States and Soviet Union, and their creation of rival economic blocs. If the Soviet Union was to define one half of the geopolitical and economic blocs that shaped the global economy during the Cold War, the United States was equally important in defining the other half. However, the impact that the unfolding Cold War would have on China's patterns of trade was not immediately apparent. The United States and key allies in Europe established a set of trade controls on Soviet bloc countries in the winter of 1949–1950, which limited the export of goods that could aid the development of their military and industrial capabilities. Although China was initially included within this set of trade restrictions, the United States remained China's second most important trade partner, behind the Soviet Union, until the end of 1950. As Rosemary Foot makes clear, the US Truman administration elected not to cut completely its trade

---

[38] R. Terrill, "China and the World: Self-Reliance or Interdependence?", *Foreign Affairs* 55.2 (1977), 300–1.
[39] Eckstein, *Communist China's Economic Growth and Foreign Trade*, pp. 136–7.

with the new Communist nation because it knew that such a policy would enjoy little support from among US allies, and because it recognized that maintaining US trade with China might have the effect of limiting Soviet influence on China.[40]

However, all this was to change in October 1950 when the CCP made the decision to send forces across the Yalu river into Korea to aid North Korean forces who had invaded the southern half of the Korean peninsula in July that year. China's involvement in the Korean War, and the failed efforts by both the US and China to deter one another's involvement in that war, fundamentally transformed the political, military and economic relationship between China, the United States, and US allies. The United States introduced trade controls on China that were far stricter than those applied to the rest of the Soviet bloc. The general Soviet bloc controls entailed a complete embargo on a first category of goods that could contribute directly to a country's military capabilities, but permitted limited trade in a second category of industrial goods, and free trade in a third category of goods, provided that those goods were reported to a central organizing body known as COCOM.[41] By comparison, the export controls applied to China were far more restrictive. The United States not only completely banned all American trade and shipping with China, but also demanded that its allies block exports to China of goods in all three categories, and created a further list of 200 goods that US allies should also embargo. Ultimately, the US-led trade embargo on China was designed to limit access to the goods and industrial technology that China needed to aid its Korean war effort and its own economic development. As such, the US economic sanctions became an integral part of the US containment strategy in Asia.[42]

The result of the trade embargo was an abrupt and distinct shift in the pattern of China's external economic relations. As depicted in Table 19.2, in 1950 the PRC's leading trade partners included countries in the Western bloc such as the United States and Great Britain, while others such as West Germany and Canada enjoyed smaller but still significant trade ties with the PRC. However, by 1952, the United States and its allies had experienced a major drop in their trade with the PRC. The Cold War geopolitical order had a clear impact upon the direction and composition of China's trade.[43] Throughout the 1950s, China's

---

[40] R. Foot, *The Practice of Power: US Relations with China since 1949* (Oxford, Oxford University Press, 1995), pp. 52–4.
[41] Foot, *The Practice of Power*, 52.
[42] S.G. Zhang, *Economic Cold War: America's Embargo against China and the Sino-Soviet Alliance, 1949–1963* (Washington, DC, Woodrow Wilson Center Press, 2001), p. 20.
[43] Eckstein, *Communist China's Economic Growth and Foreign Trade*, pp. 186–8.

trade with the Soviet bloc would occupy around two-thirds of China's total trade, while trade with the non-Communist world comprised the remaining one-third (Figure 19.3). Moreover, because of strict controls on the export of "strategic" military and industrial goods to China, the composition of goods traveling between China and the non-Communist world was also quite different to that between China and the Soviet bloc. Most non-Communist countries could only export to China light manufactured consumer goods, foodstuffs, paper, rubber, and chemical fertilizers, and what little machinery and equipment was permitted under the US-led embargo. In exchange, China exported agricultural goods, textiles, and iron and steel products to non-Communist countries.[44] Outside the Soviet bloc, Hong Kong represented the most important market for Chinese exports in the non-Communist world, particularly in the early years of the PRC. China was a crucial source of food for Hong Kong, while a large proportion of Chinese exports were rerouted from Hong Kong on to third countries. The combination of Hong Kong's extensive expertise in banking, insurance, and shipping, and the fact that dozens of non-Communist countries could more easily house trade officials and consulate staff in Hong Kong than on the mainland, allowed Hong Kong to facilitate China's trade with the rest of the world.[45]

Table 19.2 China's five largest trading partners, 1950–1952 (as % of China's total trade)

Ranking	1950 Country	%	1951 Country	%	1952 Country	%
1	USSR	30.0	USSR	41.3	USSR	54.9
2	United States	21.1	Hong Kong and Macau	31.8	Hong Kong and Macau	15.7
3	Hong Kong and Macau	14.5	Czechoslovakia	3.6	German Democratic Republic	5.5
4	United Kingdom	6.5	German Democratic Republic	3.0	Czechoslovakia	5.0
5	Malaysia	5.4	Poland	2.6	Pakistan	4.2

Source: Statistical Yearbook of China (1981), pp. 359–71

[44] Eckstein, Communist China's Economic Growth and Foreign Trade, pp. 184–9.
[45] Eckstein, Communist China's Economic Growth and Foreign Trade, pp. 193–7.

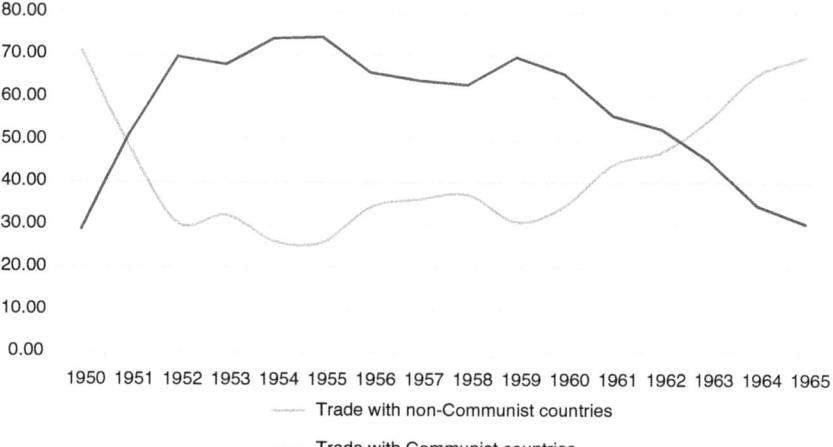

Figure 19.3 China's trade with Communist and non-Communist countries, 1950–1965 (percentage of China's total trade)
Source: R.L. Price, "International Trade of Communist China, 1950–65," in Joint Economic Committee of the U.S. Congress (ed.), *An Economic Profile of Mainland China* (New York, Frederick A. Praeger, 1968), p. 584

Beyond the makeup of China's trading partners, the US-led embargo also impacted CCP thinking about economic statecraft in two key ways. First, their experience of economic sanctions helped the CCP to develop a greater understanding about the vulnerability of China's economy to Cold War geopolitical "shocks."[46] CCP leaders had not anticipated the US-led trade embargo and, when it came, were surprised by how quickly the embargo disrupted the Chinese economy. Indeed, the CCP had hoped that war in Korea might actually benefit the Chinese economy by creating new opportunities to export strategic materials such as tung oil, silk, and animal hides. The CCP was quickly disavowed of this belief with the introduction of sanctions that made it almost impossible for US or European firms and trading companies to ship to China, sign new trade deals with China, or obtain letters of credit in US currency. Furthermore, without access to new inflows of foreign currency, the CCP had to scramble to protect the existing foreign currency reserves it possessed, and to resort to barter trade.[47] The introduction of controls on the export of strategic goods also jeopardized China's ability to develop light and heavy industry. The CCP needed access to machinery, construction supplies, and replacement parts to repair and rebuild industrial sites around the country. Chinese officials had previously relied heavily

---

[46] Zhang, *Economic Cold War*, pp. 83–93. [47] Zhang, *Economic Cold War*, pp. 83–4, 90–1.

on the US, Japan, and Great Britain for access to these industrial goods. However, given the strategic nature of most of China's desired imports, the US embargo prohibited American, Japanese, and British companies from signing contracts for the export of these goods to the PRC, and pushed China even more firmly in the direction of the Soviet camp to source strategic goods.

The second lesson Beijing learned through this experience was the instrumental value of economic statecraft. Beginning in the early 1950s, China quickly responded to the US-led trade embargo by promoting trade with US allies. In a way, China was mimicking the United States' approach of using economic policy as a tool to achieve its wider foreign policy and national security objectives. However, unlike the US approach, which emphasized denying trade with adversaries, China instead sought to use economic *inducements* to achieve its foreign policy and security goals. In response to the US-led embargo, the CCP deployed a strategy of economic inducement and political persuasion to try to "drive a wedge" between the United States and its allies, and ultimately disrupt the multilateral system of economic sanctions against China.[48] In September 1952, the Chinese Foreign Ministry agreed to allow the newly established Chinese Committee for the Promotion of International Trade (CCPIT) to provide Chinese industrial data to certain imperialist countries, such as Britain and Japan, in order to boost bilateral trade and obtain badly needed goods.[49] Similarly, in April 1952, CCP officials – under the leadership of Nan Hanchen, governor of the People's Bank of China – participated in an International Economic Conference in Moscow that was designed to build trade between the socialist and capitalist blocs. Nan lobbied delegations from non-Communist countries in Asia and Europe to attend the conference, and in Moscow signed contracts with a host of Western European companies to begin exporting goods to China.[50]

By the mid-1950s, China was carrying out a centralized campaign to promote trade with US allies, many of whom were equally enthusiastic about reinstating the lucrative China trade relationship. In 1954, during an address to a delegation of British Labour Party members visiting China, Zhou Enlai noted that countries such as Britain and France were desperate for economic development and saw China's population of 600 million as a vast,

---

[48] Zhang, *Economic Cold War*, p. 46.
[49] A. King, *China–Japan Relations after World War Two: Empire, Industry and War, 1949–1971* (Cambridge, Cambridge University Press, 2016), pp. 84–5.
[50] King, *China–Japan Relations after World War Two*; V. Zanier, "'Energizing' Relations: Western European Industrialists and China's Dream of Self-Reliance. The Case of Ente Nazionale Idrocarburi (1956–1965)," *Modern Asian Studies* 51.1 (2017), 136–7.

untapped export market. For Zhou, trade ties were a vital "battle line" that China could use to "improve its relations with Western countries."[51] Indeed, the issue of economic sanctions became a source of great friction in the United States' relationships with key allies such as Britain and Japan. The British Labour Party and other British business groups lobbied hard for the relaxation of trade controls against China which, they argued, were hurting British business interests.[52] Similarly, in Japan, a coalition of business, the left-wing opposition, and politicians from the ruling conservative Liberal Democratic Party joined forces to put pressure on the Japanese government and the United States to allow Japan to import from China low-cost raw materials and foodstuffs such as soybean, iron ore, and coal.[53] This pressure continued to mount throughout the mid-1950s, and in 1957, unable to persuade its allies to maintain the tough line on China, the United States watched as Britain, Japan, and a host of its other European allies took the unilateral decision to relax partially their sanctions on China. Although the United States would maintain strict sanctions against China until the 1970s, the reintroduction of trade with US allies transformed China's trade patterns. As Figure 19.3 indicates, the proportion of China's trade with the non-Communist world increased steadily from 1959, and by 1963 the majority of China's trade was taking place with non-Communist countries. That year and thereafter, Western European countries and Japan became regular exporters to China of industrial equipment, machinery, and whole plants, and began eagerly hosting trade exhibitions in China to encourage yet further trade.[54]

The Legacy of Japanese Empire and War with Japan

Thus far we have seen how China's external economic relations during the Mao era were shaped in large part by the CCP's relationship with the Soviet Union, and by the Cold War geopolitics that characterized China's external environment after 1949. Yet, throughout the Mao era, China pursued an economic relationship with one country, Japan, that does not fit neatly the ideological or geopolitical categories that we typically use to analyze the CCP's foreign economic policies. China's economic relationship with Japan between 1949 and 1978 was the legacy of a half-century of trade, investment,

---

[51] "推进中英关系,争取和平合作" (Driving Forward Sino-British Relations, Striving for Peaceful Co-operation), August 12, 1954, in 周恩来外交文选 (Selected Works on the Diplomacy of Zhou Enlai) (Beijing, Zhongyangwenxian chubanshe, 1990), p. 81.

[52] Zhang, *Beijing's Economic Statecraft*, pp. 53–4.   [53] King, *China–Japan Relations*, p. 102.

[54] C. MacDougall, "Eight Plants for Peking," *Far Eastern Economic Review* 23 (January 1964), 155–8; Zanier, "'Energizing' Relations," pp. 165–8.

and people-to-people ties that had developed between the two countries on the back of Japan's colonial presence in China during the first half of the twentieth century. That these economic ties not only endured but flourished after 1949 – despite Japan's brutal eight-year war with China, in the face of the CCP's deeply entrenched anti-imperialist ideology, and in the absence of a diplomatic relationship between the two countries – is testament not only to the deep economic complementarity between China and Japan, but more importantly to the way in which Japan's leap from agrarian to industrialized nation shaped CCP thinking about its own development path.[55]

The large-scale, modern economic relationship between China and Japan originated in the early 1900s, following Japan's surprise victory over the Qing Chinese government in the first Sino-Japanese War (1894–1895). Japan's defeat of China enabled the imperial Japanese government to compel China to sign the Treaty of Shimonoseki, which granted most-favoured-nation status to Japanese firms, citizens, vessels, and property in their dealings with China.[56] Within a decade of the war's end, the trade relationship with Japan had grown to 15 percent of China's total trade; Japan imported from China raw materials such as coal and soybean, and exported to China textiles, metals, and machinery.[57] Not only did war between China and Japan help to facilitate this flourishing trade relationship, but the war – and China's shock defeat by its smaller neighbour – actually encouraged reformers within the Qing government to look to Japan as a source of ideas about how to modernize their country's military, government, education system, and industry. In the first decade of the twentieth century, China sent some 25,000 students to study in Japan. Over the next three decades, these students would bring home Japanese-inspired models for trade exhibitions, industrial schools, and manufacturing centers.[58] Yet a much

---

[55] King, *China–Japan Relations*.
[56] The granting of "most-favoured-nation (MFN) status" to foreign countries engaged in trade with China first took place via the 1843 Treaty of Nanking, as a concession obtained following Britain's defeat of Qing China in the First Opium War (1839–1842), and was later extended to the United States via the 1844 Treaty of Wangxia. Japan had sought MFN status with China since 1870, but was not able to obtain such rights until its victory over China in 1895. See S. Murase, "The Most-Favored-Nation Treatment in Japan's Treaty Practice during the Period 1854–1905," *American Journal of International Law* 70 (1976), 284–8.
[57] Y.K. Cheng, *Foreign Trade and Industrial Development of China: An Historical and Integrated Analysis through 1948* (Washington, DC, Washington University Press, 1956), p. 18.
[58] J. Lee, "Where Imperialism Could Not Reach: Chinese Industrial Policy and Japan, 1900–1940," *Enterprise and Society* 15.4 (2014), 655–71; D. Reynolds, *China, 1898–1912: The Xinzheng Revolution and Japan* (Cambridge, MA, Harvard University Press, 1993), p. 42; M. Jansen, "Japan and the Chinese Revolution of 1911," in J.K. Fairbank and K.C. Liu (eds.), *The Cambridge History of China*, vol. 11, *Late Ch'ing, 1800–1911*, part 2 (Cambridge, Cambridge University Press, 1980), p. 348.

darker strain of thinking also traveled from Japan to China during the first half of the twentieth century. Inspired by the lessons of Germany's defeat in World War I, the imperial Japanese government grew increasingly concerned about their country's lack of natural resources and late push for industralization, and thus sought to expand Japan's colonial footprint in Northeast Asia. Manchuria, where Japan had enjoyed rights to the Guandong peninsula since its victory in the Russo-Japanese War (1904–1905), was now viewed by Japan as a rich source of industrial and agricultural raw materials and as a future base for Japan's heavy industrial production. In 1932 the imperial Japanese government formally established the Japanese-controlled state of "Manchukuo," and over the next decade would implement a strategy of state-controlled heavy industrialization and agricultural development, and the creation of a market for Japanese exports.

Japan's colonial presence in Manchuria bestowed important legacies for China, which would influence CCP thinking and economic ties with Japan throughout the Mao era.[59] As discussed above, Manchuria served as an important testing ground for Japan's experiments with an economic planning model that linked heavy industrialization with military modernization. The heavy industries Japan left behind in Manchuria would become a valuable foundation for the CCP as it pursued its own industrialization drive in northeast China after 1949. Manchuria also became a critical meeting point for Japanese and Chinese individuals who would play a role in helping to build the China–Japan economic relationship during the Mao era. Throughout the 1930s and early 1940s, Japanese technicians, engineers, bureaucrats, and captains of industry helped to develop Manchuria's economic plans, industrial sites, and trade ties with Japan. After 1949, Japanese such as Takasaki Tatsunosuke, who had served as vice president of Manchurian Heavy Industries and the Anshan Iron and Steel Works, became an important advocate for reviving Japan's trade relationship with the PRC. In 1949–1950, Takasaki provided the Chinese Foreign Ministry with the names of Japanese industrial firms and price lists for goods that could be used to help reconstruct northeast China, and in 1955 Takasaki – who had become the director of Japan's postwar Economic Planning Agency – served as an important voice in the Japanese domestic debate pushing for the relaxation of Japan's Cold War-era economic sanctions on China.[60] Similarly, Chinese such as Sun Pinghua, who served in Manchuria's Ministry of Economics during the 1940s, would go on to play an influential role in developing the postwar economic

[59] This paragraph draws on King, *China–Japan Relations*, Chapter 2.
[60] C.W. Braddick, *Japan and the Sino-Soviet Alliance, 1950–1964: In the Shadow of the Monolith* (Oxford, Palgrave Macmillan, 2004), p. 116.

relationship between the PRC and Japan. In 1955, Sun became the deputy head of the PRC's first trade delegation to Japan, which was instructed by the Chinese Foreign Ministry and Foreign Trade Ministry to lobby Japanese companies, politicians, and industrial experts to find ways to expand the bilateral economic relationship. Finally, the CCP made good use of the approximately 20,000 Japanese technicians and other skilled workers who were left behind in northeast China at the end of World War II. Between 1949 and 1953 these technicians were put to work across mines, research laboratories, factories, and industrial sites in the northeast, and called on to train less-skilled Chinese workers as the CCP endeavored to rebuild key industrial sites in northeast cities such as Anshan and Dalian.[61]

Throughout the 1950s, the size of the China–Japan economic relationship remained modest and was significantly outranked by China's trade with the Soviet bloc (Figure 19.4). This was due in large part to the Cold War economic embargo, which severely restricted Japanese exports of "strategic goods" to China. Nevertheless, between 1952 and 1962 the two countries worked creatively to negotiate four rounds of "unofficial" trade agreements, which were organized around different classes of goods that Japan was permitted to export to China. The trade agreements were "unofficial" because the two countries did not enjoy a diplomatic relationship – Japan recognized the Republic of China as the legitimate government of China – and thus trade was negotiated between committees, politicians, and business representatives on the Japanese side who could plausibly describe themselves as one step removed from the ruling government.[62] No longer able to export heavy industrial goods or machinery, Japan's chief exports to China became agricultural machinery, textile machinery, and light manufactured products such as radios and typewriters, and increasingly chemical fertilizer, as the CCP pursued increasingly ambitious agricultural targets in the lead-up to the Great Leap Forward. While the bilateral trade relationship became a short-term casualty of the Great Leap Forward, as we shall see below, by 1965 Japan had replaced the Soviet Union as China's largest trade partner.

Of course, the effects of Japanese colonialism and its aggressive war with China also bestowed a powerful legacy on foreign economic policy thinking

---

[61] King, "Reconstructing China."
[62] The major Japanese committees included the Japan Association for the Promotion of International Trade and the China–Japan Trade Promotion Diet Members' League. On the Chinese side, the agreements were negotiated via the CCPIT or by representatives from the Chinese Foreign Ministry.

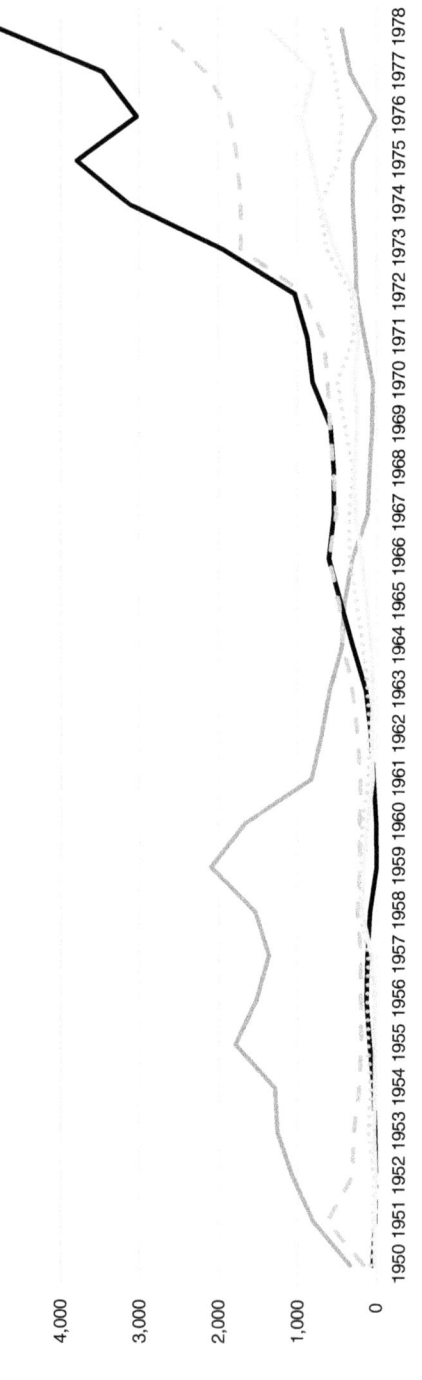

Figure 19.4 China's bilateral trade with leading trade partners, 1950–1978 (in US$ million at current prices)
Source: *Statistical Yearbook of China* (1981), pp. 359–71

in Mao's China. China's defeat by a more industrially developed Japan in the First and Second Sino-Japanese Wars underscored for successive generations of Chinese leaders and reformers the importance of industrialization as a way to stave off colonial predation by more powerful countries. As the Cold War unfolded and the PRC faced new wars in Korea and Indochina, CCP leaders began reflecting on the history of Japan's industrialization process. Though the CCP was determined not to follow Japan's path in becoming a colonial power, Mao frequently reflected on the "great benefits" that industrialization had brought to Japan, and the valuable connections Japan had fostered between the military and industrial halves of its economy.[63] Moreover, as the only Asian country to have made the leap from agrarian to industrialized country, Japan served as a powerful exemplar for the CCP. The Soviet Union's economic model provided the blueprint for China's centrally planned economic system, but as Mao and other CCP officials so often stated, Japan represented what it was possible for an "Eastern country" (*dongfang guojia* 东方国家) to achieve. As Sino-Soviet relations soured in the late 1950s and early 1960s, it was Japan's development path, Japanese industrial goods and technology, and Japanese industrial advisers that increasingly provided the CCP with a useful basis for comparison.[64] Finally, the CCP's pursuit of an economic relationship with Japan, in which Japan served as the more advanced, technologically developed partner, shaped CCP thinking about questions of "self-reliance" (*zili gengsheng* 自力更生) in its external economic relations. Over the course of the 1960s and early 1970s, Japan became an increasingly important industrial partner for China, such that, by 1971, Japan supplied more than 60 percent of China's total industrial plants and advanced technologies.[65] Nevertheless, this dependence on Japanese plants and technology met the CCP's definition of "self-reliance" for two reasons. First, as Zhou explained in 1962, "China is emphasizing the approach of self-reliance, but this certainly does not mean that we have to produce everything ourselves to achieve self-reliance. In order to increase the speed [of development] we

---

[63] "在关于日本经济政策和国防工业发展问题的一份材料上的批语" (Written Comments on Materials Concerning Japan's Economic Policies and Military Industrial Development), July 16, 1961, in 建国以来毛泽东文稿 (Selected Manuscripts of Mao Zedong since the Founding of the Republic), vol. 9 (Beijing, Central Documents Press, 1996), pp. 530–1.
[64] King, *China–Japan Relations*, Chapter 6.
[65] Y. Yokoi, "Plant and Technology Contracts and the Changing Pattern of Economic Interdependence between China and Japan to 1989," in C. Howe (ed.), *China and Japan: History, Trends, and Prospects* (Oxford, Oxford University Press, 1996), p. 130.

ought to buy what we need."⁶⁶ Second, in pursuing the contracts for these plants, the CCP cleverly negotiated deals that ensured that the technology behind the plant equipment would be transferred to China, thereby helping to pave the way for China's eventual indigenous production of industrial technology. So determined were Chinese negotiators in this strategy, one observer argues, that "the level of technology and the quality of the plant are usually of greater concern to the Chinese than the final price."⁶⁷

The Legacy of Imperialism

The fourth factor to shape the pattern of China's external economic relations during the Mao era was China's experience of semicolonialism during the late nineteenth and early twentieth centuries. China's experience of imperialism impacted upon Mao-era thinking about economics, dependence, and national security. CCP discourse on the exploitative nature of the international economic order became particularly prominent in the mid-1950s, as China began to associate much more closely with the experiences of other newly independent countries, and influenced Beijing's efforts to build trade and aid relationships with them. In April 1955, the PRC attended the Asia–Africa Conference, in Bandung, Indonesia, along with a group of twenty-nine other newly independent countries from Asia and Africa. The "Bandung conference," as it came to be known, represented the first time that a group of Asian and African countries had met in an international forum, independent of the Western and colonial powers. At the Bandung conference and in its aftermath, the CCP began to articulate new ideas about decolonization as a key driver of world revolution, and that the imperialist international economic order had jeopardized the security of "backward" states like China.⁶⁸ In its place, CCP leaders called for a new international economic order founded upon "equality and mutual benefit" (pingdenghuhui 平等互惠). This concept had developed through conversations between Chinese premier Zhou Enlai, Indian prime minister Jawaharlal Nehru, and Burmese president U Nu in 1954 and 1955, and became a key plank in the "Five

---

⁶⁶ Quoted in Morizumi Kazuhiro 盛純和弘, 五十年の変遷—孫平化氏に聞く (Fifty Years of Change: Interviews with Mr Sun Pinghua) (Beijing, Jinri zhongguo chubanshe, 1995), p. 157.
⁶⁷ Reese, "Mainland China and Western Trade Credits," 49.
⁶⁸ On the former point, see J. Chen, "Bridging Revolution and Decolonization: The 'Bandung Discourse' in China's Early Cold War Experience," *Chinese Historical Review* 15.2 (2008), 238.

Principles of Peaceful Co-existence" adopted at the Bandung conference. In his speech to fellow countries at Bandung, Zhou Enlai, who led the Chinese delegation, argued that "countries whether big or small, strong or weak, should all enjoy equal rights in international relations," including in the realm of foreign trade.[69] Yet Zhou continued with a warning: the "backward" countries of Asia and Africa would not be able to enjoy equal or mutually beneficial trade relations with the Western powers until they had escaped from the "shackles of colonialism."[70]

Zhou Enlai's speeches at Bandung and his reports back to Mao Zedong following the conference demonstrate that the CCP saw a clear link between a country's overall level of economic development and its ability to withstand imperialist exploitation by more advanced foreign powers. But extolling the virtues of economic development and mutually beneficial trading relations at Bandung also represented the first step in a long-term strategy by the PRC to "win over" countries in Asia and Africa, "dilute their relationships" with the "American imperialists," and obtain diplomatic recognition from those countries that did not yet recognize the PRC as the legitimate government of China.[71] In their preparations for Bandung, officials in the Ministry of Foreign Affairs and Ministry of Foreign Trade argued that China could achieve these goals by expanding "equal and co-operative" economic ties with Asian and African countries, by warning them of US attempts to "manipulate and monopolize" their markets and depress global prices for raw materials, and by using the economic successes of China's first five years of development as a positive exemplar for other newly independent countries.[72] Thus, at Bandung, Zhou and his fellow delegates advocated a host of new measures designed to help Asian and African countries move up the value chain and become more than just agrarian exporters of raw materials.[73] They called on participating countries to diversify trade markets rather than relying on former colonial masters to buy up raw material exports, break down old colonial patterns of trade by sending representatives to each other's countries, and create a permanent regional trade institution to help build and

---

[69] "Zhou's Speech to the Plenary Session of the Asian–African Conference," April 19, 1955, in *China and the Asian–African Conference (Documents)* (Beijing, Foreign Languages Press, 1955), p. 14.
[70] "Zhou's Speech to the Plenary Session of the Asian–African Conference," p. 10.
[71] "我参加亚非会议贸易活动方案(草案)" (Draft of China's Plan for Its Participation in the Trade Activities of the Asia–Africa Conference), March 8, 1955, PRC Foreign Ministry Archive, File No. 207-00070-01.
[72] "我参加亚非会议贸易活动方案(草案)."
[73] "我参加亚非会议贸易活动方案(草案)," p. 17; "Final Communique of the Asian–African Conference," in *China and the Asian–African Conference*, pp. 68–71.

organize Asian–African trade ties.⁷⁴ The Chinese delegation also endorsed the idea of creating a long-term buy-and-sell agreement, or some other regional price stabilization method, that would both stabilize and raise global prices for raw materials.⁷⁵

In advocating these measures, PRC officials made clear their view that foreign trade and international economic ties were an essential characteristic of the modern international system. It is therefore notable that their call for "mutually beneficial" and "equal" trade relations between countries did not equate to autarky or cutting oneself off from the global trading system.⁷⁶ Instead, as Zhou argued in 1956, no country – not even the "large developed countries" such as the United States and the Soviet Union – could be self-reliant; instead, all were required to import certain "essential things."⁷⁷ Yet despite their efforts to use the Bandung conference to catalyze a transformation in regional trade practices, the PRC delegation had little success in achieving many practical outcomes. A combination of countries' ongoing economic dependence on their former colonial powers and new Cold War geopolitical alignments made it very difficult to overcome existing patterns of trade and foreign aid. Countries such as the Philippines, Thailand, and Turkey, all of whom were US or NATO allies, believed that they "must rely" on the United States for access to capital and technology, and were hesitant to create a new permanent economic institution that might stand in opposition to existing groupings such as the United Nations. Similarly, Zhou believed that the nonaligned states such as India and Indonesia had opposed China's proposal to create an intra-regional bank or regional trade bloc because they continued to feel "mostly reliant" on countries outside the region for foreign aid, capital, and technology. Thus Zhou concluded that even if fellow Asian and African nations had succeeded in achieving formal political independence, they had yet to achieve real economic independence.⁷⁸

---

⁷⁴ "周恩来关于经济合作问题致中共中央并毛泽东的报告" (Zhou Enlai's Report to Mao Zedong and the CCP Central Committee on the Problem of Economic Co-operation), April 30, 1955, in 中华人民共和国外交档案选编(第二集)中国代表团出席 1955 年亚非会议 (Selected Works from the Foreign Ministry Archive of the People's Republic of China (vol. 2): China's Delegation to the 1955 Asia–Africa Conference) (Beijing, Zhongguo tongji chubanshe, 2007), pp. 90–3.
⁷⁵ "周恩来关于经济合作问题致中共中央并毛泽东的报告," pp. 90–1.
⁷⁶ "Zhou Enlai's Report on the Asian–African Conference, Made at the Meeting of the Standing Committee of the National People's Congress," May 13, 1955, in *China and the Asian–African Conference*, pp. 44–5.
⁷⁷ *Selected Works of Zhou Enlai*, p. 237.
⁷⁸ "周恩来关于经济合作问题致中共中央并毛泽东的报告," p. 92.

Despite these failures, the PRC took a number of unilateral steps at Bandung and throughout the late 1950s and 1960s that were simultaneously designed to meet its goals of transforming the international economic order into a more equitable one for developing countries, and "winning over" countries with ties to the United States and, later, the Soviet Union. At Bandung, the Chinese delegation pledged that China would contribute industrial equipment and technology to countries in Asia and Africa.[79] Over the next decade, despite its own low levels of economic development, China provided nearly US$2 billion in grants, low-interest loans, technicians, and industrial construction assistance to other developing countries. The majority of China's aid was dispatched to Communist countries also experiencing political or military turmoil, such as North Korea – which was the recipient of China's first foreign aid grant in 1953 – North Vietnam, Hungary, and Albania.[80] Nevertheless, China was also a generous provider of foreign aid to non-Communist and nonaligned countries in South and Southeast Asia. Alexander Eckstein finds that between 1949 and 1964, China provided around US$800 million in loans to non-Communist countries, almost half of which was dispatched to neighboring countries such as Burma, Indonesia, Cambodia, Laos, Sri Lanka, Nepal, and Pakistan.[81] Moreover, China matched its Bandung rhetoric by establishing trade missions in India, Nepal, Egypt, Lebanon, and Syria, and demonstrated a willingness to trade with a host of Asian and African countries on terms that were frequently unfavorable to China.[82] As the PRC's relations with the Soviet Union began to decline in the late 1950s and early 1960s, the PRC then used its competitive foreign aid strategy to persuade countries like Albania, North Korea, and North Vietnam to transfer their allegiance from Moscow to Beijing.[83] China's strategic use of foreign aid also extended to Africa. In 1963, Zhou Enlai embarked on a two-month, ten-country visit across Africa, where he outlined an economic assistance strategy rooted in principles of self-reliance, independence, equality, and mutual benefit. Though China's aid levels to Africa would not match those provided by the Soviet Union, Zhou's emphasis of these foreign-aid principles during the Africa tour was designed to differentiate China's

---

[79] "周恩来关于经济合作问题致中共中央并毛泽东的报告," pp. 90–1.
[80] C. Garratt, "China as a Foreign Aid Donor," *Far Eastern Economic Review* 31.3 (1961), 83.
[81] Eckstein, *Communist China's Economic Growth and Foreign Trade*, pp. 161–2, 214.
[82] "我参加亚非会议贸易活动方案(草案)"; Zhang, *Beijing's Economic Statecraft*, pp. 110–15, 154–5; G.T. Hsiao, "Communist China's Trade Treaties and Agreements," *Vanderbilt Law Review* 21.5 (1968), 637–43.
[83] Eckstein, *Communist China's Economic Growth and Foreign Trade*, pp. 167–8. Zhang, *Beijing's Economic Statecraft*, Chapter 5.

approach from that of Moscow, which, the CCP believed, had the effect of cultivating dependency upon the Soviet Union.[84]

Finally, China's experience of imperialism had a profound impact on how China conceived of its own economic dependence upon the Soviet Union. Throughout the late 1950s and the 1960s, the themes of "self-reliance" and "independence" became increasingly important in Chinese foreign economic policy thinking. At Bandung, Zhou Enlai exhorted his counterparts to resist accepting foreign aid that came with "disadvantageous" political or economic conditions.[85] It is perhaps no coincidence that the same year as the Bandung conference, China became increasingly unwilling to accept foreign aid from the Soviet Union. In 1955, Soviet aid to China began to slow, and by 1957 it had almost completely ceased.[86] Part of the explanation for declining levels of Soviet aid to China lies with Moscow's own decision making and political crises within the Soviet bloc, such as the 1956 Polish and Hungarian crises, which drew Moscow's attention and resources elsewhere.[87] Nevertheless, Shu Guang Zhang argues that throughout the late 1950s, Beijing became increasingly wary of the fact that China's economic dependence on Soviet foreign aid, loans, and industrial goods and expertise made China susceptible to potential Soviet efforts to influence China. As a result, CCP leaders adopted a range of measures to try and limit China's dependence upon the Soviet Union, despite the reality that China was still very poor and in need of goods and expertise from Moscow. For instance, the CCP worked hard to establish a "mutually beneficial" or more "symmetric" trade relationship with Moscow by expanding Chinese exports to the Soviet Union as a way to compensate for Soviet credits to China, and by supplying the Soviet Union with agricultural products and "strategic" raw materials, such as rubber, which Moscow was unable to import from elsewhere. In addition, Beijing took great care to pay back Soviet loans on time or even early, despite the cost this imposed on the Chinese economy.[88]

The Impact of Domestic Political Campaigns

The last factor to have shaped China's external economic relations during the Mao era was the domestic political campaigns and crises initiated by the CCP

---

[84] R. Scalapino, "Sino-Soviet Competition in Africa," *Foreign Affairs* 42.4 (1964), 641–2, 649. See also Zhang, *Beijing's Economic Statecraft*, pp. 116–17.
[85] "周恩来关于经济合作问题致中共中央并毛泽东的报告," pp. 90–1.
[86] Eckstein, *Communist China's Economic Growth and Foreign Trade*, p. 182.
[87] Zhang, *Beijing's Economic Statecraft*, p. 70.
[88] Zhang, *Beijing's Economic Statecraft*, pp. 65–6.

throughout the 1950s and 1960s. These campaigns and crises were numerous, but two interconnected events in particular – the Great Leap Forward and the Sino-Soviet split – had the greatest impact upon China's external economic relations. To understand the events of the Great Leap Forward and the Sino-Soviet split requires us to cast our eyes back to the mid-1950s, when China's economy, domestic political environment, and international relations were rocked by Mao's politicization of economic decision making, tensions with the Soviet leadership, and growing awareness that the Soviet economic model was not entirely well suited to China's domestic conditions.[89] In 1955, Mao ignored the advice coming from Moscow and from his own Party's more moderate economic planners, such as Zhou Enlai and Chen Yun, and adopted a particularly radical form of Stalinist economic planning designed to accelerate rural collectivization and to achieve wildly ambitious targets in cotton, grain, and steel production. This "Little Leap Forward," as it came to be known, was a precursor for the eventual Great Leap Forward launched in the late 1950s. Despite their attractiveness in theory, the Little Leap and later Great Leap Forward were impossible to achieve in practice; the policies adopted resulted in disastrous shortages of industrial raw materials and agricultural products, production bottlenecks, and widespread famine in China's rural areas.[90] In order to achieve the demanded increases in agriculture and steel outputs, in 1958 and 1959 the CCP's State Planning Commission stepped up China's imports of rolled steel and chemical fertilizer from the Soviet Union, Japan, and Western Europe (as depicted in Figure 19.5).[91] Indeed, China became a highly unpredictable trade partner for these countries as its economic planners requested faster delivery schedules and demanded higher and higher levels of trade.[92]

It was not long before the economic policies of the Great Leap Forward, and the highly charged domestic political environment in China, began to have a dramatic impact on China's two most important economic relationships: those with the Soviet Union and Japan. The Soviet Union was itself embarking on a set of corrections to Stalin's earlier economic policies under the new leadership of Nikita Khrushchev, leading to discord between Mao's own

---

[89] For more on the Soviet model, see Perkins's chapter in this volume.
[90] A.L. Chan, *Mao's Crusade: Politics and Policy Implementation in China's Great Leap Forward* (Oxford, Oxford University Press, 2001), pp. 17–24; F.C. Teiwes and W. Sun (eds.), *The Politics of Agricultural Cooperativization in China: Mao, Deng Zihui, and the "High Tide" of 1955* (Armonk, NY, M.E. Sharpe, 1993).
[91] C.J. Mitcham, *China's Economic Relations with the West and Japan, 1949–1979: Grain, Trade and Diplomacy* (London, Routledge, 2005), pp. 19–20, 42–3; Zanier, "'Energizing' Relations," pp. 159–63.
[92] Eckstein, *Communist China's Economic Growth and Foreign Trade*, pp. 140–1.

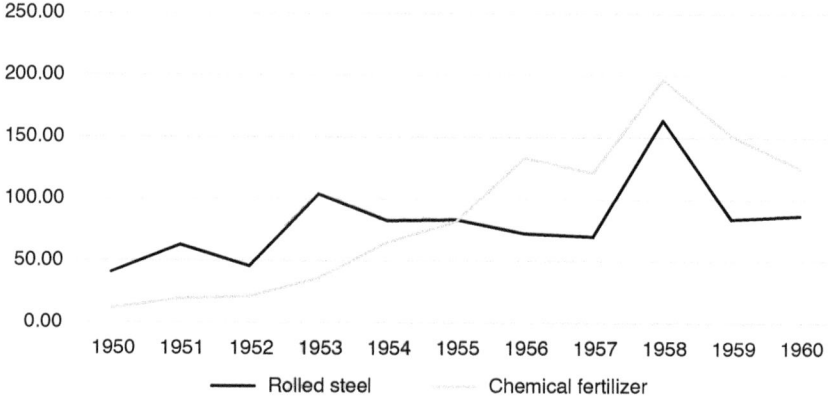

Figure 19.5 China's imports of rolled steel and chemical fertilizer, 1950–1960 (in tens of thousands of tons)
Source: *Statistical Yearbook of China* (1981), pp. 385–9

economic vision and that being pursued by China's Soviet "elder brother." Mao now sought to achieve a socialist revolution in China that would be "fuller, quicker, and more effective" than that of the Soviet Union.[93] At the same time, the Soviet leadership grew increasingly concerned about China's domestic and international behavior when Mao launched the second Taiwan straits crisis in 1958, in a bid to mobilize the domestic Chinese population around the economic goals of the Leap.[94] Sino-Soviet antagonism had a direct impact on the Soviet technicians working in China, upon whom China remained highly reliant. On July 16, 1960, Khrushchev announced that all remaining Soviet technicians in China were to be immediately recalled back to the Soviet Union. Within a month of this announcement, more than 1,300 Soviet technicians had left China, taking with them both the blueprints and the expertise for around 250 ongoing or planned construction projects, the effect of which was made even more severe when Khrushchev announced the abrogation of a dozen economic and technical aid agreements with China.[95] In response to Khrushchev's move, the CCP tried to punish Moscow by suspending or postponing unsigned trade contracts, canceling orders of plant equipment,

---

[93] Shen and Li, *After Leaning to One Side*, pp. 156–7; Z. Shen and Y. Xia, "The Great Leap Forward, the People's Commune and the Sino-Soviet Split," *Journal of Contemporary China* 20.72 (2011), 861–8.
[94] T.J. Christensen, *Useful Adversaries: Grand Strategy, Domestic Mobilization, and Sino-American Conflict, 1947–1958* (Princeton, NJ, Princeton University Press, 1996), pp. 204–5.
[95] Eckstein, *Communist China's Economic Growth and Foreign Trade*, p. 153; Zhang, "Sino-Soviet Economic Cooperation."

and refusing to supply basic consumer goods to the Soviet Union.[96] Bilateral trade between the two countries peaked in 1959, but declined sharply the following year (Figure 19.1), and would never again reach the heights that the two countries had enjoyed in the first decade of their alliance. The China–Japan economic relationship faced a similar fallout from the politics of the Great Leap Forward, but one that was far more temporary than that experienced between China and the Soviet Union.[97] As noted above, China and Japan had built small but significant trade ties since the early 1950s, through three rounds of "unofficial" trade agreements. In 1958, the two sides were in the midst of negotiating a fourth agreement that, if passed, would shift the relationship in a more official direction by allowing the two countries to exchange trade representatives and establish permanent trade offices in either country. However, when the Republic of China (ROC) learned of these negotiations, Chiang Kai-shek protested the agreement and threatened to launch an economic boycott of Japan in retaliation. In its haste to respond to Chiang's threats, Japan's Kishi government reiterated that it did not recognize Communist China, would not pursue any kind of official relationship with the PRC, and would not allow the PRC flag to be flown in Japan. In the midst of the back-and-forth between Japan, the PRC, and the ROC, two Japanese youths tore down a PRC flag that had been flying at a trade exhibition in the city of Nagasaki. The combination of Kishi's statement and the "Nagasaki flag incident," as it came to be known, inflamed an already tense domestic political environment in Beijing. In the middle of 1958, the Chinese Foreign Ministry announced that it would not permit trade with Japan unless Japan agreed to "three political principles": "That Japan should not (1) adopt policies hostile to China; (2) participate in any plot aimed at creating two Chinas; and (3) obstruct the normalisation of relations with China."[98] Over the next two years, trade between China and Japan almost completely ceased, falling from US$80 million in 1958 to less than US$200,000 in 1960, before beginning to slowly increase again in 1961 and 1962. Yet even in the midst of the complete breakdown in Sino-Japanese trade between 1958 and 1960, the CCP worked behind the scenes to find ways to reopen the bilateral economic relationship. To do so, Zhou Enlai and other senior CCP officials met not only with traditional "friends" of the CCP, such as representatives from Japan's Socialist and Communist parties, but also with leading politicians and officials from Japan's ruling conservative Liberal Democratic Party. Through speeches, *People's Daily* editorials and conversations

---

[96] Zhang, *Beijing's Economic Statecraft*, p. 88.
[97] The following paragraph draws on King, *China–Japan Relations*, pp. 135–57.
[98] R.K. Jain, *China and Japan, 1949–1980*, 2nd ed. (Oxford, Martin Robertson, 1981), p. 44.

with Japanese counterparts, CCP leaders from Mao downwards made it clear that they were eager to work with Japan to find a way to reopen the economic relationship once Prime Minister Kishi was no longer in power. By late 1959, Mao, Zhou, and Liao Chengzhi – the Chinese Foreign Ministry's leading Japan hand – had each explained to visiting groups of Japanese their views about the importance of the China–Japan trade relationship, not only because of its role in restoring friendship and co-operation between the two countries, but also because of the role that Japanese technology and industrial goods and expertise could play in assisting China's reconstruction.

Finally, the Great Leap Forward had unintended consequences on China's import and export of grain and other agricultural products. In 1958, China had been required to expand dramatically its exports of grain and other agricultural products in order to pay for the imports of steel and chemical fertilizer needed to pursue the Great Leap Forward. This was a perverse outcome, which exacerbated growing domestic grain shortages within China.[99] Yet within two years the situation had reversed. In 1960 and 1961, the Chinese leadership acted to alleviate domestic famine by stepping up imports of foreign grain. The two key beneficiaries of this shift in policy were Canada and Australia, countries which had developed limited trade ties with China in the mid-1950s, and which were blessed with record grain surpluses at the very moment at which Beijing was looking to expand its grain imports. In 1960 and 1961, Beijing signed multiple agreements with the Canadian Wheat Board, the Australian Wheat Board, and a host of other Canadian and Australian agricultural exporting firms for the export of wheat, flour, barley, and oats to China. As Figure 19.6 indicates, China's imports from Australia increased ninefold between 1960 and 1961, and twelvefold with Canada over the same period. Because China could not afford to correspondingly increase its exports to these countries, the Canadian and Australian governments – spurred on by domestic agricultural lobby groups eager to expand the China trade relationship – agreed to fund this increased grain trade through six-, nine-, and twelve-month credit agreements with China.[100]

Conclusion

China's external economic relations underwent a dramatic shift after the Mao era. The reform era saw the relaxation of central control over prices, foreign exchange, and trade; the restoration of normal relations with the United

---

[99] Mitcham, *China's Economic Relations with the West and Japan*, p. 40.
[100] Mitcham, *China's Economic Relations with the West and Japan*, Chapter 3.

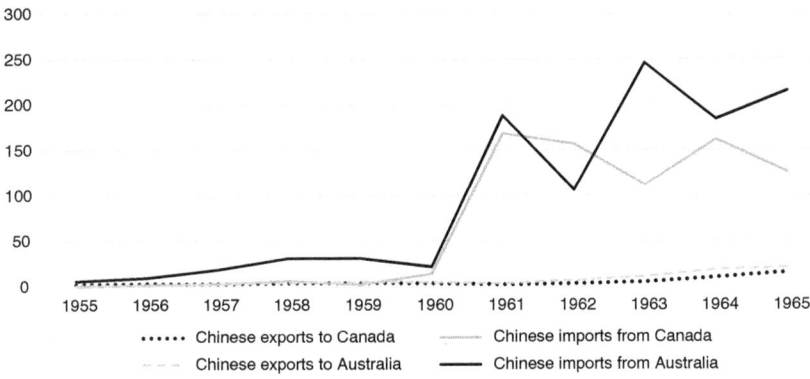

Figure 19.6 China's trade with Canada and Australia, 1955–1965 (in US$ million at current prices)
Source: *Statistical Yearbook of China* (1981), pp. 359–71

States; and China's eventual entry into major international organizations such as the International Monetary Fund, World Bank, and World Trade Organization. Each of these moves helped to bring an end to the depressed levels of trade that China had experienced under Mao, such that, by 1994, China's share of world trade had finally reached levels not seen since the 1920s.[101] Yet the significance of the Mao era extends beyond the mere fact of China's relatively low levels of trade, its prohibition of foreign direct investment, and its absence from international capital markets and economic organizations during this period. Rather, the significance of the Mao era lies in how China's economic interactions with the outside world during these three decades shaped a range of CCP ideas about foreign economic policy and China's place in the global economy. First, the CCP viewed the international economic order as one in which a state's relative level of development determined its vulnerability to exploitation at the hands of more economically advanced, and thus powerful, states. This was an economically deterministic view of the international system, in which the CCP perceived the world as divided into camps of "backward" countries – agrarian, nonindustrialized producers of raw materials – and "advanced" countries – those who had made the leap to industrialization and who subsequently exploited "backward" countries for their raw materials and

---

[101] Keller, Li, and Shiue, "China's Foreign Trade," 886; Maddison, *Chinese Economic Performance in the Long Run*, pp. 85–6.

export markets. These ideas had their origins in Qing and Republican China as the country encountered Japan's highly coercive industrial development path, and were reinforced in the Communist era as China confronted the severe trade controls that formed a key plank in the United States' Cold War containment strategy. During the Mao years, the pursuit of rapid industrialization to achieve "catch-up" growth was the core organizing idea behind China's economic relationships with the Soviet Union and, later, Japan. It was also the idea that motivated the CCP in its failed attempts to create a new international economic order, premised on the notion of "mutual equality and benefit," that would allow developing countries in Asia and Africa to make the transition from "backward" to "advanced" economies.

Second, China's external economic relations during the Mao years were shaped by ideas about "self-reliance," which became an increasingly important – though frequently misunderstood – slogan in Chinese political and economic discourse in the late 1950s and early 1960s. Like the idea of "backwardness," self-reliance also had its origins in China's historical experiences of war and semi-colonization; Mao introduced the idea of "self-reliance" (zili gengsheng) during China's War of Resistance against Japan as a way to strengthen the CCP in the face of food scarcity and economic isolation.[102] Yet self-reliance was never simply translated into policies of autarky or import substitution in Mao's China. Rather, the CCP viewed foreign economic assistance and access to overseas advanced technology as entirely consistent with a policy of self-reliance.[103] Indeed, one author has suggested that self-reliance more accurately represented a spectrum of thinking within the CCP. At times, such as during the politically charged atmosphere of the Great Leap Forward or the Cultural Revolution, Mao and others derided foreign influence in the Chinese economy, and China's trade with countries such as Japan and the Soviet Union suffered as a result. Frequently, though, self-reliance was conceived in more expansive ways: while China should avoid foreign control over its economy, CCP leaders acknowledged that in order to become truly self-reliant, China would need to adopt technology from more advanced countries and learn from the industrial development paths of others.[104]

---

[102] L. Yang, "Self-Reliance," in C. Sorace, I. Franceschini, and N. Loubere (eds.), *Afterlives of Chinese Communism: Political Concepts from Mao to Xi* (Canberra, Australian National University Press, 2019), pp. 231–3.
[103] Zhang, *China in International Society since 1949*, pp. 39–40.
[104] Terrill, "China and the World," 297–9. For a related argument that Chinese foreign economic policy during the Mao era was animated by CCP debates over the correct path to self-reliance, see L. Reardon, *The Reluctant Dragon: Crisis Cycles in Chinese Foreign Economic Policy* (Seattle, University of Washington Press, 2014), pp. 5–8.

Third, China was both a target and a practitioner of economic statecraft during the Mao era. From their very earliest months in power, CCP leaders learned how economic instruments could be used as a tool of foreign and security policy. In 1949, the Soviet leadership advised Zhou Enlai of the potential for China to use its economic power as a form of positive inducement in its relations with the West. Just as quickly, China was subjected to US-led trade sanctions that not only transformed China's trade partners and restricted its access to a wide range of "strategic materials," but also demonstrated to the CCP how economic sanctions could be used as a weapon of war. Absorbing these lessons over the next three decades, the CCP's foreign economic policy was frequently shaped by two, sometimes competing, goals. The first goal was a desire to overturn what the CCP saw as an unjust economic order used by imperialist countries to their advantage, and to create instead an order that was more equitable for developing countries. Yet paired with this ideal was a second, more tactical, understanding of foreign economic policy as a form of statecraft. Throughout the Mao era, the CCP sought to use methods such as access to its lucrative market, barter trade, and unconditional foreign aid as a way to undercut the US-led trade embargo, to persuade countries to extend China diplomatic recognition, to make China more attractive to developing countries, and to draw an explicit contrast between itself and the United States and the Soviet Union.

Ideas about industrialization as a way to overcome "backwardness," about self-reliance, and about economic statecraft have exerted an influence on Chinese economic thinking beyond the Mao era. As a more powerful, market-oriented, and economically open China embarks on new domestic and foreign economic policy initiatives, traces of Mao-era ideas and experiences resonate. The "Made in China 2025" plan, for example, is designed to reduce China's reliance on foreign technology by increasing the share of indigenously produced materials and technology to 70 percent by 2025, and to place Chinese manufacturing at the forefront of the world's most advanced industries, including aerospace, robotics, and shipping. Similarly, the "Belt and Road initiative," introduced by the Xi government in 2013, is an ambitious plan to open up trade, finance, investment, and infrastructure links between China and a network of countries stretching from North Africa to the South Pacific. These initiatives draw on Mao-era ideals about using advanced technology and industrialization to make China a more modern and powerful country by 2049 – the centenary of the founding of the PRC – and about reforming the global economy to increase the participation and economic development – on "equitable" and "mutually beneficial terms" – of developing countries.[105] And yet, as in the Mao era, the ideals underpinning these initiatives are also tempered by a darker vision of the global economic order and the strategies needed to survive in it. This darker vision reflects the views of a country whose experiences of colonialism, military–industrial warfare, an unreliable Soviet ally, and Cold War economic statecraft have taught its leaders that China can never truly escape dependency unless it masters indigenous production of advanced technologies, and who believe that China remains an unequal power in an international economic order led by the United States and Europe. These twin commitments are at once designed to reshape the global economy for the benefit of all, and to make China a far more powerful state within it.

Further Reading

Cheng, Y.-K., *Foreign Trade and Industrial Development of China: An Historical and Integrated Analysis through 1948* (Washington, DC, Washington University Press, 1956).

Eckstein, A., *Communist China's Economic Growth and Foreign Trade* (New York, McGraw-Hill, 1966).

King, A., *China–Japan Relations after World War Two: Empire, Industry and War, 1949–1971* (Cambridge, Cambridge University Press, 2016).

Kirby, W.C., "China's Internationalization in the Early People's Republic: Dreams of a Socialist World Economy," *China Quarterly* 188 (2006), 870–90.

Lardy, N.R., "Economic Recovery and the 1st Five-Year Plan," in R. Macfarquhar and J. K. Fairbank (eds.), *Cambridge History of China*, vol. 14, *The People's Republic*, part 1, *The Emergence of Revolutionary China, 1949–1965* (Cambridge, Cambridge University Press, 1987), pp. 144–83.

Liu, T.-C., and K.-C. Yeh, *The Economy of the Chinese Mainland: National Income and Economic Development, 1933–1959*, vols. 1, 2 (Santa Monica, CA, RAND Corporation, 1963).

Mah, F.-H., "Foreign Trade," in A. Eckstein, W. Galenson, and T.-C. Liu (eds.), *Economic Trends in Communist China* (Chicago, Aldine, 1968), pp. 671–738.

Mitcham, C.J., *China's Economic Relations with the West and Japan, 1949–1979: Grain, Trade and Diplomacy* (London, Routledge, 2005).

Price, R.L., "International Trade of Communist China, 1950–65," in Joint Economic Committee of the US Congress (ed.), *An Economic Profile of Mainland China* (New York, Frederick A. Praeger, 1968), pp. 579–608.

Reardon, L, *The Reluctant Dragon: Crisis Cycles in Chinese Foreign Economic Policy* (Seattle, University of Washington Press, 2014).

---

[105] State Council of the People's Republic of China, *Action Plan on the Belt and Road Initiative*, March 30, 2015; State Council of the People's Republic of China, *Made in China 2025*, July 7, 2015.

Zanier, V., "'Energizing' Relations: Western European Industrialists and China's Dream of Self-Reliance. The Case of Ente Nazionale Idrocarburi (1956–1965)," *Modern Asian Studies* 51.1 (2017), pp. 133–69.

Zhang, S.G., *Beijing's Economic Statecraft during the Cold War, 1949–1991* (Washington, DC and Baltimore, Woodrow Wilson Center Press and Johns Hopkins University Press, 2014).

Zhang, S.G., *Economic Cold War: America's Embargo against China and the Sino-Soviet Alliance, 1949–1963* (Washington, DC, Woodrow Wilson Center Press, 2001).

Zhang, Y., *China in International Society since 1949: Alienation and Beyond* (Basingstoke, MacMillan Press in association with St. Antony's College, Oxford, 1998).

20

The Chinese Economy in the Reform Era

BARRY NAUGHTON

Introduction

December 1978 was a political, economic, and social turning point for China. As the balance of power within the top leadership shifted, a search for new policies began that deepened into what came to be called "reform and opening" and culminated decades later in a multistranded transition to a market-based economy. This new policy orientation was accompanied by a shift in development strategy that permitted China to take advantage of its factor endowments and structural conditions and dramatically accelerate economic growth. Thus 1978 marks not only the beginning of "reform," but also the start of the Chinese "economic miracle," a remarkable thirty-two-year period, through 2010, during which GDP grew at an annual rate of 10 percent. Chinese economic structure and Chinese society were utterly transformed. An extraordinary distance separates the vibrant upper-middle-income, predominantly market-based, economy that is China today from the troubled, isolated low-income country that was China at the end of the Cultural Revolution. This chapter builds its narrative around the systemic and structural changes that transformed China, especially in the thirty years between 1978 and 2008.

It is important not to oversimplify the 1978 pivot. China was not a blank slate, nor did policy makers flip a switch to turn China from a command into a market economy. Extreme institutional distortions and poor policies held back the Chinese economy, and although they were serious and deep, they also provided the opportunity for a quick growth acceleration when they were ameliorated. Economic policy is multidimensional, made up of many "bundles" of policies, with each bundle having its own political and economic logic. This chapter focuses selectively on a few key policy arenas: rural reforms and economic opening in the early 1978–1982 period, and then, after 1984, overall reform strategy and industrial and financial reforms.

Nearly every aspect of policy was contested, fought over through nearly the entire transition period. Policy contention and uncertainty dogged the Chinese leadership especially in the early years of reform, and it took many years for policy initiatives to coalesce into a coherent approach to economic reform. Gradually, though, successful reforms took hold, increasing the growth and resilience of the economy. In turn, this created the conditions that drove massive economic structural change and enabled the ensuing "growth miracle." There was always a great deal of contingency: the composition of political power was a key short-run determinant of policy at each juncture, and policy approaches changed abruptly and dramatically. Policy making was driven forward by crisis, but market reforms succeeded in pulling the economy out of crisis by uncovering new sources of demand, improving incentives and productivity, and fostering greater factor mobility and flexibility. In the early 1990s, an especially thorough and abrupt shift in political conditions led to dramatic new departures in market reform policy.

This historical epoch come to an end during the first decade of the twenty-first century. As the economy moved out of crisis, market-oriented reforms lost momentum, and the underlying conditions for miracle growth were naturally exhausted. This chapter seeks to give the transition process a degree of coherence, while remaining true to its complexity. It is important to note that the coherence sought here is *not* the economic coherence that emerged *ex post*: economists have already shown persuasively *how* reform worked in China.[1] Rather, the intention is to show the coherence in the way Chinese decision makers faced and reacted to challenges, perceived their choices and options, and the way these choices shaped actual outcomes. It is a coherence, in other words, that includes mistakes, retreats, and opportunities missed, even in the context of a broad advance.

The Baseline

GDP and Well-Being

Where did China stand economically in 1978? By the seemingly straightforward measure of GDP per capita (on which subsequent growth rates are based), the picture was stark. China was a low-income country, among the poorest in the world. Even after converting to purchasing-power parities (PPPs), in an effort to

---

[1] Y. Qian, *How Reform Worked in China: The Transition from Plan to Market* (Cambridge, MA, MIT Press, 2017). See also John McMillan and Barry Naughton, "How to Reform a Planned Economy: Lessons from China," *Oxford Review of Economic Policy* 8.1 (Spring 1992), 130–43.

Table 20.1 Development indicators, 1978

	China	Upper middle
Overachiever		
Life expectancy at birth	66	65
Literacy	65.5%	68.8%
Energy consumption per capita (kilograms of oil equivalent)	617	781
R & D share of GDP	1.5%	N/A
GDP data		
GDP per capita, constant 2010 US$	307	2,674
GDP per capita, PPP 2011 US$	1,536	c. 5,000
Underachiever		
Urbanization	17.9%	34.8%
Caloric consumption	2,080	2,477*

* World average

correct for China's highly distorted price system, China's GDP per capita of $1,500 was comparable to – but lower than – large sub-Saharan African countries, such as Sudan or Congo. Yet, as the top panel (Overachiever) of Table 20.1 shows, many of China's other indicators were far above what one would expect from a low-income economy.[2] Indeed, in life expectancy, literacy, and perhaps most strikingly energy use per capita, China looked just like upper-middle-income economies of the day. Life expectancy and literacy measure human capital, while energy use is a good proxy for physical capital: China's endowment of both human and physical capital was much greater than we would expect of a low-income economy. Moreover, by any measure of institutional capacity, or social capital, China would again look completely different from any other low-income economy. Rural society was organized into a three-level institutional hierarchy consisting of communes, production brigades, and production teams. The communes, corresponding to traditional market centers, tied the countryside into a national economic network. Almost every commune had a rural credit co-operative and a supply and marketing co-operative, as well as schools and a rudimentary clinic. China was completely different from any other low-income economy.

[2] GDP per capita comparisons based on purchasing-power parity, 2011 price basis. This and other indicators in Table 20.1 from World Bank, World Development Indicators, accessed November 15, 2019. Life expectancy and literacy from China's 1982 census; R & D share from National Bureau of Statistics, *40 Years of China's Science and Technology* (1990). Caloric consumption from Food and Agriculture Organization, http://faostat3.fao.org/download/FB/FBS/.

One might look at these indicators and conclude that China was "really" more developed than it seemed, and by extension that the Cultural Revolution "wasn't so bad." Such arguments are mistaken. What the data show most clearly is an economy grievously underperforming its potential. Given the stock of physical, human, and social capital – accumulated at enormous cost – the production of useful goods and services was appallingly low. Other physical indicators help explain why (Table 20.1 lower panel, "Underachiever"). China was sharply under-urbanized, well below middle-income countries, and was even below the low-income average of 19.2 percent. Labor power was bottled up in the countryside, kept there by China's household registration system, which permitted almost no migration to the city. Despite the compulsory retention of labor, China's collective farms weren't producing enough to bring the population above subsistence level. According to the Food and Agriculture Organization's food balances, China's average caloric availability had hovered below 2,000 calories per person for more than a decade. The 2,000-calorie threshold – which reflects reasonably well the level at which population can avoid widespread malnutrition – was breached for the first time only in 1978.[3] Finally, the calculations of real income are based on the assumption that money income can buy goods, whose scarcity is captured through price indices, but rationing was pervasive in China, not only for grain and cotton cloth, but for mundane goods such as soap and tofu.

Economic Challenges and Institutional Structure

Two existential challenges overshadowed everything else: agriculture and population. First, could China feed itself? China had been importing modest amounts of food grain annually since the collapse of the Great Leap Forward. Could agricultural output be increased as population and consumption demand increased? Nobody was sure. China's extraordinary and distinctive institutions reached into even small villages, and contributed to some aspects of development, such as basic health and education. But these same institutions tightly constrained many types of economic activity and clearly held back food production and overall economic performance. The Cultural Revolution variant of collective agriculture was especially restrictive.

---

[3] Bramall (this volume) argues that FAO data understate actual caloric availability, due to undercount of private plots and overcount of nonfood uses of grain, and estimates 2,566 kilocalories per day. Taking FAO as the lowest and Bramall as the highest estimates, estimated consumption is still very close to subsistence levels, considering low diversification of diet and prevalence of demanding physical labor.

Farmers were forbidden to sell grain in rural markets, and draconian limits were put on private plots, household handicrafts, and even barnyard animals. For fifteen years, Dazhai, a poor village in Shanxi province, had been promoted as a Maoist model. Dazhai provided an indigenously developed model of mobilizing labor to expand agriculture by hacking fields out of steep slopes and building new irrigation systems. Dazhai abolished private plots and local markets altogether, and also delinked farmer income from farmer productivity by assigning work points in a public evaluation process of an individual's attitude and effort (rather than output). Dazhai also aggressively pushed for larger-sized collectives, which further diluted the monitoring and surveillance capacity of smaller teams. Post-Mao leaders had picked up and promoted the Dazhai model to assert Maoist legitimacy, and well into 1978 they were insisting that one-third of all counties should become "Dazhai-style" counties by 1980.[4]

Could this institutional system produce enough food to feed China? Even those initially committed to the Dazhai model gradually conceded that agriculture needed much more help, which meant reducing compulsory grain procurements, raising prices, and increasing access to credit. This would allow farm collectives to purchase more modern inputs, especially tractors, fertilizer, and improved seeds.[5] But would that be enough?

The second existential challenge was population. Between the census years of 1964 and 1990, the population of working age (fifteen to sixty-four) doubled, growing at 2.6 percent per year. In 1978, China was smack dab in the middle of this population surge. Could all these people be fed? Could jobs be found for them? In urban and rural areas alike, services and small-scale manufacturing – huge sectors in most developing economies – were highly restricted and woefully underdeveloped. Throwing open all these restricted activities had the potential to unleash a quick output response and also rapid growth of employment. All the restricted sectors – farming and farm sideline activities, urban services and small-scale manufacturing – are among the most labor-intensive sectors in a developing economy.

Today, when population growth rates have declined dramatically in China and worldwide, it is easy to recognize that population growth brings

---

[4] Fan Yinhuai 范银怀, 从大寨到大邱庄 (From Dazhai to Daqiuzhuang) (Beijing, Zhongguo fazhan, 2013). Li Jingping 李静萍, 农业学大寨运动史 (History of the Movement to study Dazhai) (Beijing, Zhongyang Wenxian, 2011).
[5] F.C. Teiwes and W. Sun, *Paradoxes of Post-Mao Rural Reform: Initial Steps toward a New Chinese Countryside, 1976–1981* (Abingdon, Routledge, 2015), pp. 51–4.

economic opportunity as well as challenges. But at the time, China's leaders anxiously surveyed the population growth they saw around them, and worried that they would be overwhelmed by the impending demographic tidal wave. Birth control policies were tightened in 1977–1978, and the draconian "one-child policy" was adopted in September 1980.[6] The simple fact is that China was following an inappropriately capital-intensive development strategy: a country with abundant labor resources was giving priority to development of the most capital-intensive industries, including steel, machinery, and armaments.[7] This inefficient development strategy held back growth, of course, but more critically meant that China was unable to respond to the profound challenge of feeding a rapidly growing population.

China was mired in a vicious cycle of shortage, poverty, and inefficiency. Institutional fixes to short-run crises ended up creating long-term economic distortions. Rural–urban migration had been halted in the 1960s after the collapse of the Great Leap Forward, in order to guarantee grain to urban residents. As a result, surplus rural workers were penned up in the countryside. Even so, urban labor also seemed to be in surplus: low-productivity make-work jobs were created to disguise unemployment, 17 million high school graduates were sent to the countryside during the Cultural Revolution, and urban labor markets disappeared as scarce jobs were rationed. The "Soviet growth model" (see the chapter by Perkins in this volume) was held in place by strict enforcement of twin state monopolies, over grain purchases and over industry. Individuals who pursued their own interests, selling household products, or moving to the city, faced severe penalties. Distortion built on distortion. If the institutional obstacles could be removed, there could be a quick economic rebound. However, policy makers faced paralysis because of their ideological commitment to socialist institutions, and because of the complex interdependencies among different institutions. The potential benefits were enormous if China could escape from this straitjacket.

---

[6] Liang Zhongtang 梁中堂, 中国计划生育政策史论 (A History of China's Planned-Birth Policies) (Beijing, Zhongguo fashan, 2014). F. Wang, Y. Cai, and B. Gu, "Population, Policy, and Politics: How Will History Judge China's One-Child Policy?", *Population and Development Review* 38 (2012) (supplement), 115–29.

[7] J.Y. Lin, F. Cai, and Z. Li, *The China Miracle: Development Strategy and Economic Reform* (Hong Kong, Chinese University of Hong Kong Press, 2003).

Development Strategy and the 10-Year Plan

Chinese leaders, including Mao Zedong, had long dreamed of a strong, industrialized China. During the Cultural Revolution, from 1966 to 1976, industrialization was subordinated to political struggles and ideological purity, and long-run objectives for the economy lay dormant, but they were not forgotten. In the mid-1960s, Zhou Enlai and Mao Zedong had laid out two interrelated objectives for the year 1980. The first was to realize a "basically self-sufficient national industrial system,"[8] and the second was to "basically realize agricultural mechanization."[9] Both objectives were strategic responses to the massive setback of the Great Leap Forward (1958–1960): with China now forced to import grain and relations with the Soviet Union irreparably damaged, self-reliance was the only option. Zhou Enlai in 1964 embraced spending fifteen years building an independent industrial system, until 1980, when it would launch a broader growth process with the "Four Modernizations." Mao Zedong took the same date as the target for agricultural mechanization, which would replace the failed utopian experiment of Great Leap-era communes.

These slogans and objectives had been in the background when Chinese policy makers resumed coherent economic planning in 1972–1974, after the most chaotic period of the Cultural Revolution. But planners also had a new opportunity: China's oil production had increased steadily through the 1960s and 1970s, and after global oil prices spiked in 1973, China faced a lucrative opportunity to export oil. A multiyear, US$4.3 billion technology import program was put together, signaling that agricultural mechanization would now include chemicalization, based on imported fertilizer factories (see the chapter by King in this volume). Planners began work on a Ten-Year Plan to cover 1975–1985, intentionally straddling the fast-approaching 1980 target year. Imported industrial plant, embodying the latest foreign technology, would enable China to break the agricultural bottleneck. China's development strategy would consist of high investment, technological borrowing, and massive provision of industrial inputs to agriculture. China would try to outrun its problems of low systemic efficiency and an inappropriate

---

[8] Zhou Enlai, "Report on the Work of Government," December 21 and 22, 1964, partial report in *Peking Review*, 1965.1. In January 1975 Zhou specified that the long-term target had been 1980 (three five-year plans).
[9] Zheng Yougui 郑有贵, "中国农业机械化改革的背景分析与理论反思" (Background Analysis and Theoretical Reflection on the Reform of Chinese Agricultural Mechanization)," January 6, 2015, at http://ww2.usc.cuhk.edu.hk/PaperCollection/Details.aspx?id=1630.

development strategy, rather than resolve them, starting a new "big push" in order to resume the industrial march to great-power status.

Political dysfunction prevented policy makers from following through on this strategy. In 1975, Deng Xiaoping had been put in charge of policy and seemingly designated Mao's successor, but the very next year Mao fired Deng and he was subjected to months of vitriolic criticism. These enormous political swings meant that the Ten-Year Plan was never issued during Mao's lifetime, nor were the annual plans for 1975, 1976, or 1977 ever officially promulgated.[10] The economy was on autopilot as the succession struggle intensified. This is one of the paradoxes of the Chinese experience: it was a "planned economy" with a development strategy, but without an actual plan.

Poor planning was evident throughout the economy. Chinese planners had never achieved the detailed control of specific materials and enterprises that Soviet planners routinely exercised. In 1977, a huge backlog of unfinished construction, poorly located and poorly designed, sometimes outfitted with indigenous technology solutions that didn't work, presented painful choices: throw good money after bad, or abandon projects on which billions had been spent? These were the economic legacies of the Cultural Revolution: an impressive endowment of human, physical, and institutional capital that was being squandered; a crisis in agriculture and employment that was about to become much worse; and a supposedly "planned" economy the institutions of which had rotted from the inside out. When a new leadership took over after the death of Mao Zedong in 1976, they had unprecedented leeway to adjust policy, but also faced extraordinary challenges.

The Beginning of Economic Reform and the Strategy of Economic Opening

Hua Guofeng emerged as China's leader at the end of 1976, and Deng Xiaoping rejoined the top leadership in the middle of 1977. Although there was inevitably tension between Hua and Deng, they initially agreed to work together. Co-operation was facilitated by the fact that Hua, Deng, and other top leaders agreed on a simple economic strategy: rehabilitate the entire economic mechanism, from top to bottom; return to the framework of the aborted Ten-Year Plan; and achieve agricultural mechanization and prepare for the "Four Modernizations" by 1980. Deng Xiaoping, who hated delays and

[10] Liu Guoguang 刘国光 (ed.), 中国十个五年计划研究报告 (A Research Report on China's Ten Five-Year Plans) (Beijing, Renmin chubanshe, 2006), pp. 378–90, esp. 379–80.

consistently supported rapid growth, strongly supported this program. However, Deng was not in charge of economic policy, which was instead managed by three veteran vice premiers who all served continuously from (at least) 1975 through 1982: Li Xiannian, Yu Qiuli, and Gu Mu.

As the economy recovered, Chinese policy makers had to address two basic concrete issues. The first related to China's biggest problem and the second to China's biggest opportunity. The biggest problem, as discussed earlier, was agriculture: policy makers had already agreed to put more resources into agriculture – in order to get more out – but they were uncertain and divided about how far to go (as discussed below). Hit by bad weather and the adverse impact of the Dazhai movement, agricultural output shrank in 1977. The biggest opportunity was technology import. Largely cut off from most sources of global technology for over a decade, Chinese leaders saw the enormous potential benefit from expanded technology import. China's industry recovered faster in 1977 than expected, growing 14 percent. With this uneven performance, policy makers became entranced by a vision of bigger and faster import of industrial technology, which, in the spirit of the Ten-Year Plan, would fuel faster growth and eventually break the agricultural bottleneck once and for all.

Technology Import

During 1977 and 1978, all the top policy makers gave strong support to policies intended to increase exports (of oil) and imports (of industrial machinery embodying advanced technology). Working groups spread out from China to learn basic things about their capitalist neighbors.[11] In 1978, twenty top-level missions visited fifty-one countries. What they saw astonished them: Japan, in particular, after thirty years of sustained growth near 10 percent per year, was prosperous, modern, and highly productive. Chinese visitors, including Deng Xiaoping and Hua Guofeng, realized the extent to which China had fallen behind Japan and the capitalist West. Moreover, the shibboleths of Marxist economics could be seen to be patently false: capitalist workers were not impoverished, society was well ordered, and workers were well educated. Vice premier Gu Mu led a team to five countries in Western Europe and briefed top leaders in June 1978 for over seven hours, galvanizing opinion to support reform and further opening.[12] The capitalists were eager

---

[11] Chen Jinhua 陈锦华, 国事忆述 (The Eventful Years) (Beijing, Zhonggong Dangshi, 2005); C.-J. Lee, *China and Japan: New Economic Diplomacy* (Stanford: Hoover Institution Press, 1984), pp. 36–75.
[12] Gu Mu, 谷牧回忆录 (Memoirs of Gu Mu) (Beijing, Zhongyang Wenxian, 2014), pp. 319–26.

to do business with China, Gu Mu reported, and were willing to provide cheap credit. China's most important partner was to be Japan, and Nippon Steel's Yoshihiro Inayama led the Japanese business elite in advocating rapprochement with China. China and Japan signed a long-term trade agreement in February 1978, providing a framework for the export of Chinese coal, coking coal, and oil in return for advanced Japanese machinery. These visits thus confirmed for top leaders like Deng Xiaoping the necessity of reform, the possibility of rapid growth, and the virtue of rapidly expanding business with the capitalist powers.[13]

Enthusiasm for the technology import program grew, and its scope doubled, and then doubled again. A July 1977 draft had called for $6.5 billion worth of industrial plant imports (through 1985), but by the summer of 1978 a two-month-long State Council meeting approved a program to import a total of $80 billion through 1985.[14] In this giddy period, projected imports increased more than tenfold in a single year. The Baoshan Steel Mill project emerged as the flagship and proof of concept, located in Shanghai because Shanghai had the highest skills and the best project management capabilities in the country. An existing proposal for a large blast furnace in Shanghai was repurposed, and morphed through several rounds of negotiation into a gigantic integrated steel mill imported from Nippon Steel, Japan.[15] It was a huge project, with initial payments of 400 billion yen (about $2 billion), more than 1 percent of China's GDP, for the largest and most complex project China had ever built.

However, as the technology import program gathered momentum, it spiraled out of control, and ultimately fell apart. Bureaucrats scrambled to get their projects included, and projects were approved without serious economic analysis. Site selection, technology choice, and careful analysis of financing options were all neglected. Even Baoshan Steel, the best of the best, ran into substantial problems with site preparation and co-ordination of the many project components. In fact, there was no room for error, for China had almost no foreign-exchange reserves. Reserve data were secret at the time, but subsequent release revealed that China had only $167 million in

---

[13] Xiao Donglian 萧冬连, "The Systematic Investigation and Use for Reference of Foreign Experience in the Early Days of Reform," 中共党史研究 (Research in Chinese Communist Party History) 4 (2006), 22–32. E. Vogel, *Deng Xiaoping and the Transformation of China* (Cambridge, MA, Harvard University Press, 2011), pp. 85–7, 118–19, 217–27, is especially good on the impact of foreign experience on Deng Xiaoping.

[14] Li Zhenghua 李正华, "1978 年国务院务虚会研究" (A Study of the 1978 State Council Theory-Oriented Meeting), *Dangdai Zhongguoshi Yanjiu* 17.2 (March 2010), 4–13.

[15] C.-J. Lee, *China and Japan: New Economic Diplomacy* (Stanford, Hoover Institution Press, 1984), pp. 36–75. Chen, 国事忆述.

reserves at the end of 1978, enough for only five and a half *days* of import coverage, while the standard "rule of thumb" for reserve adequacy is three *months'* worth of imports.[16] Then oil output stopped increasing: after two decades of steady growth, China drilled 7 million meters of wells in 1978 without discovering a single new field. Top-level commitment to the import program began to waver, and support for the Baoshan project, which had been solid through 1978, just barely held together for approval at the end of December. This was the economic background for the Third Plenum turning point.

The Party Work Conference and Third Plenum, November–December 1978

Given its historical importance, it is remarkable that no thorough or reliable account of the 1978 policy turning point exists. However, from existing accounts, we can deduce a few significant economic policy events that occurred during two consecutive meetings, a thirty-four-day Party Work Conference, followed by the five-day Third Plenum, that extended through most of November and December 1978. Such meetings are usually completely predictable. Work conferences permit discussion, but participants are divided into closely monitored small groups, and the plenum is then convened to rubber-stamp policies finalized behind closed doors. The year 1978 was completely different. The Work Conference was called to discuss agricultural policy and the plans for 1979 and 1980. However, on the third day, Party elder Chen Yun stood up in his small group and declared that economic policy couldn't be fixed until deep political issues from the Cultural Revolution were addressed. Chen then proceeded to name names, putting on the table literally scores of top leaders who had been purged by Mao and imprisoned, and still not fully exonerated. The effect was electric. Support for Chen's speech spread rapidly to other groups, and boiled over into anger and recriminations against Cultural Revolution beneficiaries, still in power, and the demand that they be dismissed.[17] In the wake of this unprecedented open debate, the discussion of economic policy was completely derailed, but three major outcomes were ultimately extremely consequential to the economy.

---

[16] Revised data given in *China Statistical Abstract*, 2019, p. 164.

[17] Yu Guangyuan 于光远, 1978:我亲历的内次历史大转折 (1978: The Historic Turning Point That I Experienced), reprint (Hong Kong, Tiandi, 2008), pp. 56–67. Zhu Jiamu 朱佳木, 我所知道的十一届三中全会 (The Third Plenum That I Knew) (Beijing, Dangdai Zhongguo, 2008), pp. 98–102.

First, Chen Yun returned to the top Party leadership, joining the Standing Committee of the Politburo, which was thus dominated by Party elders. Chen Yun is universally characterized as an economic policy "conservative," but his conservatism was rooted first and foremost in macroeconomic policy. For Chen Yun, an out-of-control, heavy-industry-based "Leap" was the worst nightmare in Chinese policy making, a thing he had repeatedly warned against. If this "Leap" were to be funded by risky debt to the capitalists – a group for whom Chen Yun never entirely lost his antipathy – it would be even more dangerous. Thus, when, on December 10, Chen Yun gave a talk to his small group about economic policy, it signaled the death knell for the grandiose technology import program and, ultimately, the whole Ten-Year Plan. Chen Yun was not initially given formal economic responsibilities, but only three months later, in March 1979, he was put in charge of economic policy, and immediately pushed through a three-year "Readjustment" (*tiao-zheng* 调整). Readjustment meant reducing investment and growth, and shifting resources to consumption.[18] It implied that everything, including reform, would be subordinated to the need to reduce stress on the economy. It was to be the beginning of a multiyear program of macroeconomic restraint.[19]

Second, Deng Xiaoping, who had skipped the first half of the Work Conference in order to visit Singapore and Thailand, returned to find the conference out of control. Deng immediately stepped in, assumed de facto control, and, to close the conference, delivered one of the best speeches of his life. Deng stepped up the reform rhetoric, stressing "thought liberation" and "looking to the future." Deng also insisted that the rancor against Cultural Revolution beneficiaries be controlled, and that nobody be openly fired. Deng thus succeeded in assuming leadership, moving the Party toward reform, and maintaining the appearance of unity to the outside world.

Third, the Work Conference failed to resolve the questions about agricultural policy. Debate about agricultural policy had been building for a year. A key role was played by Wan Li, who in June 1977 had been appointed head of Anhui, a major agricultural province with arguably more problems than any other place. Wan Li had absolutely no experience with agricultural policy,

---

[18] "Readjustment" is capitalized throughout this chapter to emphasize that it is a major policy package, not a modest "adjustment" of policy. The earlier Readjustment of 1961–1962, which the 1979 Readjustment echoed, was a complete reversal of policy in the wake of the Great Leap Forward collapse.

[19] Although Li Xiannian had arguably been the strongest proponent of the overambitious technology import plan, Chen Yun was able to bring him along in supporting Readjustment in 1979.

but had a reputation as an unusually bold, plain-spoken, and sometimes abrasive leader, and was extremely close to Deng Xiaoping. Anhui had suffered more than any other province in the Great Leap Forward famine, with excess deaths accounting for a cumulative 10 percent of the population over 1959–1961. Agricultural production and farmer confidence in the collective system had never really recovered. Wan Li quickly signaled his openness to a series of bold experiments with "responsibility systems" in agriculture, in which farm households or small groups took responsibility for production on specific plots, turning over a procurement quota but keeping any additional output. Wan Li publicized these actions and reported them to the central government, which considered them legitimate, since they were controlled local government "experiments." However, they remained highly controversial.

Wan Li had been scheduled to make a speech about Anhui policy at the Work Conference, but it was canceled amidst the turmoil. In an acrimonious exchange, Chen Yonggui, the chief proponent and beneficiary of the Dazhai model, claimed that "everything [Wan Li] is doing is capitalism." The draft agricultural-policy documents were full of formulaic rhetoric and explicitly prohibited distributing land to individual farm households. Amidst broad dissatisfaction, the original drafts were discarded and party stalwart Hu Qiaomu was put in charge of assembling a new document out of suggestions put forward by the small groups. However, Hu's draft pleased almost no one and it maintained explicit prohibitions against giving households responsibility for land, tightly constraining experiments like those in Anhui. By one account, Hu Qiaomu was asked to add a phrase allowing experimental implementation in remote mountainous and poor areas, and replied, "No way! No way! Put that in the document and it will spread around the country . . . the dam will burst."[20] A provisional document was issued, with the Dazhai model stripped out and the language toned down, but none of the contradictions resolved. Despite the enthusiasm and sense of a breakthrough fostered by Deng's speech, little progress was actually made on core economic issues.

---

[20] Chen Guanren 陈冠任, 17 个省,自治区和直辖市改革启动纪实 (A Record of How Reform Was Launched in 17 Provinces) (Beijing, Zhonggong Dangshi, 2009), p. 21. Wan Li 万里, "农村改革是怎么搞起来的?" (How Were Rural Reforms Kicked Off?), in Xu Qingquan 徐庆全 (ed.), 中国经验: 改革开放30年高层决策回忆 (The Chinese Experience: 30 Years of Reform and Opening, Recollection of High-Level Policy Makers) (Jinan, Shandong renmin chubanshe, 2008), pp. 135–6. Li, *Movement to study Dazhai*, pp. 369–75; Zhang Guangyou 张广友, 改革风云中的万里 (Wan Li amongst the Storms of Reform) (Beijing, Renmin chubanshe, 1995).

What Changed after the Third Plenum?

The Third Plenum effectively terminated two mistaken policy initiatives – the Dazhai model and the technology-import-based Ten-Year Plan – but made no decisions on what would replace them. Politically, the landscape had changed fundamentally, but the main economic issues were still unresolved. A broad commitment to undefined reforms – to which Deng Xiaoping had given great impetus – opened up political space, permitting proliferating experiments with decentralization, expanded autonomy, and improved incentives. Economically, Chen Yun's Readjustment opened up space, by delaying and reducing big government commitments, and freeing up resources for consumption and experimentation. New economic and political options were on the table.

Readjustment allowed Chinese policy makers to sidestep one of the most difficult problems that faces all reform programs. Reform policy makers relax controls and decentralize decision making, only to be met with an explosion of social demands. Citizens are emboldened to demand things they have long wanted and finally have hope of achieving. Firms owned by an ill-defined "public," facing uncertain rules and budget constraints, jump at new opportunities. The resulting explosion of demand destabilizes the reform process, leading to economic imbalances and inflation, and unnerving policy makers who may not be able to satisfy surging expectations. In the wake of the 1979 Readjustment, this dynamic was damped down, because resources were made available to meet emerging demands. For example, the 17 million urban youth sent to the countryside during the Cultural Revolution, emboldened, demanded the right to return home. In December 1978, Deng Xiaoping asked them to be patient, promising that policy would change sometime later. This position was untenable: three weeks after the Third Plenum, the central government capitulated, and within months 10 million sent-down youth had returned home.[21] Policy shifted to finding work for these returned youth, by opening up new shops and workshops in the cities. It took two years, but gradually the excess unemployment created was worked down.

Readjustment made it possible for China to move away from a deeply flawed development strategy. The technology import drive had collapsed under the weight of its own short-term problems, but the long-term defects

---

[21] Gu Hongzhang 顾洪章 (ed.), 中国知识青年上山下乡大事记 (Chronology of China's Educated Youth Sent to the Countryside) (Beijing, Zhongguo jiancha, 1997). Chen, 17 个省, pp. 421–5. T. Gold, "Back to the City: The Return of Shanghai's Educated Youth," *China Quarterly* 84 (December 1980), 755–70.

of the program's strategic approach were even more important. The technology import program was premised on the idea that advanced technology could provide a "quick fix" to the economy, without making more fundamental – and difficult – changes in the economic system and strategy. When the import program was abandoned, it enabled China to move away from the strategy it had been following for thirty years, of extracting resources from the countryside and pumping them into capital-intensive heavy industry. This had meant continuously suppressing domestic consumption, and, crucially, keeping up the economic pressure on the countryside. When the technology import program collapsed, at the end of 1978, the way was open to shift development strategy comprehensively to consumption (on the demand side) and labor-intensive sectors (on the supply side), bringing the entire economy in line with its underlying factor endowment.[22]

Finally, Readjustment enabled economic problem solving and policy experimentation that contributed to the long-run success of market transition. For example, as farmers were allowed into nonfarm activities, a November 1979 document allowed "township and village enterprises" to enter almost all sectors, abandoning previous policies to focus on "aid-to-agriculture" enterprises, like fertilizer, agricultural equipment, and cement. A radical new approach had been enabled that became a key component of market transition. The top leaders, collectively speaking, were not yet committed to radical reforms, but they had abandoned their commitment to the old economic system.

Opening Up: One Step Ahead and One Step Behind

By pulling the plug on the overinflated technology import program, China averted a short-run foreign-exchange crisis, but the fundamental economic challenges were still severe. With oil output growth in doubt, China's ability to earn foreign exchange was even more limited than before, while her appetite for foreign technology was greater than ever. The search for innovative ways to earn foreign exchange, underway since 1977, now became more urgent than ever. Inevitably, the search focused on Hong Kong.

---

[22] D. Solinger, *From Lathes to Looms: China's Industrial Policy in Comparative Perspective, 1979–1982* (Stanford, Stanford University Press, 1991). B. Naughton, *Growing Out of the Plan: Chinese Economic Reform, 1978–1993* (New York, Cambridge University Press, 1995), pp. 59–96.

The Hong Kong Connection

Hong Kong had been experiencing explosive growth since the late 1950s, driven by manufactured exports. Tiny Hong Kong, with half a percent of China's population, exported twice as much as the entire Chinese mainland in 1978. Both Chinese policy makers and Hong Kong entrepreneurs were sensitive to the enormous opportunities presented by Hong Kong's rise: Hong Kong skills and trading networks together with cheap Chinese labor and land could create a powerful economic combine that would earn abundant profit and foreign exchange. Hong Kong was also an implicit rebuke to Maoist economic policy. Local Chinese farmers had been slipping across the supposedly sealed Hong Kong border for decades and now a new wave of immigrants took advantage of China's social relaxation. Almost 20 percent of Shenzhen's population lived in Hong Kong, and in Zhuhai population had actually declined over twenty-five years due to emigration to adjacent Macau. Deng Xiaoping identified the refuge flow as an international political problem that could only be resolved by domestic economic policy changes.[23]

Already in 1977 an initiative began that was destined to transform China's export economy. A few "export-processing" contracts were signed, under which Hong Kong businessmen sent raw materials to their home villages in the Pearl river delta. The village would earn a processing fee for, e.g., sewing a zipper into a pair of blue jeans, and return the product to the owner. Starting from nothing, this "export processing trade" generated US$1 billion in exports by 1981. Processing trade sidestepped China's cumbersome customs procedures and high tariffs, allowing exports to drive growth long before comprehensive reforms were ready. Thirty years later, processing trade would grow from blue jeans to laptop computers and earn an astonishing half a trillion US dollars per year. Moreover, processing trade was not restricted to a zone, and Hong Kong's export-driven economy spilled out into the Pearl river delta and, eventually, across the country.

"Export production bases," mainly producing food for Hong Kong, already existed, and in March 1978 Guangdong bureaucrats proposed diversification into manufacturing and tourist centers. Shortly thereafter, a more innovative initiative emerged from the China Merchants Steam Navigation (CMSN) company, a state-controlled company which dates back to China's 1872 "Self-Strengthening" efforts. CMSN had been converted into a Hong Kong

---

[23] Tao Yitao 陶一桃 and Lu Zhiguo 鲁志国 (eds.), 中国经济特区史论 (A Historical Treatise on China's Special Economic Zones) (Beijing, Shehui Kexue Wenxian, 2008), pp. 11, 15, 223–4.

corporation owned by the Chinese Ministry of Transportation after 1949. Shenzhen native Yuan Geng, an aggressive, straight-talking, and visionary manager, took over CMSN in mid-1978, and proposed moving CMSN's existing shipbreaking business from Hong Kong to Shenzhen.[24] Crucially, Yuan proposed that CMSN would own the land and host other land-constrained Hong Kong businesses. In January 1979, after careful preparation, Yuan Geng visited Beijing and proposed a two-square-kilometer development zone to Vice Premier Li Xiannian, who was still in charge of economic policy. Li looked at the map Yuan had thoughtfully provided and replied, "Land? Sure, you can have some; what if I give you this peninsula?" circling the entire (fifty-square-kilometer) Shekou peninsula.[25] Yuan Geng prudently declined the generous offer, but broke ground only six months later on his two-square-kilometer patch.

Special Economic Zones

Shekou hurtled forward in the second half of 1979, but there was profound uncertainty about the definition and scope of special economic zones (SEZs). The core idea – an export-processing zone – was easily accepted, since these provisions were already incorporated in the proliferating export-processing contracts. Provincial leaders in Guangdong had big ideas, and in mid-1979 they received permission from the central government, including endorsement from Deng Xiaoping, to move ahead with a bold interpretation of a special economic zone. Crucially, the province was put in charge of drafting the regulations. Deep disagreements ensured prolonged controversy and revision, but the thirteenth draft was ultimately adopted as law in August 1980.

Four special economic zones were created, each oriented to a Chinese business community outside the People's Republic. Priority was given to Shenzhen, adjacent to Hong Kong, which was given expansive borders, in fact enveloping Shekou, which retained its autonomy. Provisions to allow and attract foreign investment were multisided: foreign-invested firms would have access to long-term land use rights at concessionary rates, income tax holidays, and duty-free import of capital equipment. Beyond these concrete provisions, the zones were granted a broad mandate that included "systems and policies that are different from the rest of China, and which primarily

---

[24] Yuan Geng 袁庚, "The Ten-Year Brilliance of Shekou," in Xu, *The Chinese Experience*, pp. 260–72. W. Huang, "The Tripartite Origins of Shenzhen," in M. O'Donnell (ed.), *Learning from Shenzhen: China's Post-Mao Experiment from Special Zone to Model City* (Chicago, The University of Chicago Press, 2017), pp. 65–85.
[25] Tao and Lu, 中国经济特区史论, pp. 25–6. L. Li, *Breaking Through: The Birth of China's Opening-Up Policy* (Oxford, Oxford University Press, 2009), pp. 73–6.

employ market adjustment."[26] The zones would be allowed to grow outside the scope of China's command economy.

In essence, SEZ policy created a series of concentric circles. Shekou became a curious zone within a zone. As a subsidiary of Hong Kong corporation CMSN, Shekou was a state-owned enterprise but exempt from the normal bureaucratic hierarchy. It had the ability to borrow money and invest in infrastructure, and it became a pioneer of a vast range of economic reform experiments, including flexible land and labor policies that were impossible in the rest of China at the time. Shekou was thus a uniquely dynamic actor inside the zone. Shenzhen SEZ itself launched a much broader program of urban development, commercial housing, and tourism, in addition to export-oriented manufacturing. Outside the zone, the two provinces of Guangdong and Fujian were given special powers, including almost complete budgetary autonomy. Fujian's inclusion demonstrated that Guangdong was not to be a unique case, even though it took years for the Xiamen SEZ there (oriented to Taiwan) to reach critical mass. Both provinces aggressively exploited the broad grant of undefined policy autonomy to expand provisions for export processing and favorable treatment for foreign investment over broad regions.[27] The SEZs thus became the symbolic center of a broad program of economic opening. After a few years, Deng Xiaoping decided that the SEZs had been his idea, and he became their advocate. This enhanced the symbolism of the SEZs, and made them a signal of China's commitment to openness and acceptance of foreign businesses. Yet the idea remained controversial, and the leadership commitment in fact subsequently wavered. Nevertheless, the broad definition of SEZ policy, integrated into national legislation in August 1980, endured.

The Shanghai Exception

Shanghai was a sharp contrast to Guangdong. The national government was highly dependent on Shanghai for budgetary revenues, Shanghai's industrial skills made it a primary actor in industrial upgrading, and Shanghai's high incomes and tight organization were a point of political pride. Conservatives, led by Chen Yun, wished to keep Shanghai under tight control. Chen Yun – himself a Shanghai native – had a lifelong suspicion of the entrepreneurial

---

[26] Communist Party Center, "Summary of the Meetings of Guangdong and Fujian Provinces," May 1980, cited in Tao and Lü, 中国经济特区史论, p. 30.
[27] Tao and Lü, 中国经济特区史论, pp. 14–32, 218–46. Y.C. Jao and C.K. Leung (eds.), *China's Special Economic Zones: Policies, Problems and Prospects* (Hong Kong, Oxford University Press, 1986).

instincts of Shanghai businessmen.[28] While experimentation could be acceptable in peripheral provinces like Guangdong, it could not be countenanced in the core of the planned economy. Private firms were springing up across China, but Shanghai remained dominated by state-owned firms. When foreign investment did begin trickling into Shanghai, it was primarily channeled into joint ventures with state-owned enterprises, such as Shanghai Auto, which dominated the Shanghai industrial and export economy.[29]

Chen Yun's attitude toward Shanghai helps explain a surprising outcome. When Chen Yun took control of economic policy in April 1979, he was determined to cut back the overgrown technology import program, and the Baoshan steel mill was obviously on the chopping block. Chen Yun agonized, visited Baoshan, and convened four successive Beijing meetings. Many were surprised when Chen gave Baoshan his blessing (though he instructed managers to stretch out the timing and substitute domestic equipment when possible). Chen felt that Baoshan had the right mix of government control, local technological expertise, and proper sequencing, and that it could serve as a model for future technology import.

The differential treatment of Shanghai and Guangdong led to an enduring feature of the Chinese economy. Different provinces competed both economically and to secure favorable treatment from reform policy makers. Reforms worked: while the share of Guangdong and Fujian in China's exports soared from 16 percent to 46 percent between 1978 and 1995, the lower Yangzi – with Shanghai at its core – dropped back from 35 percent to 21 percent, losing its traditional primacy. Not surprisingly, Shanghai and other regions began to agitate for more autonomy and reform provisions. Domestically, almost every province and central ministry set up subsidiary firms in Shenzhen to take advantage of reform provisions, a total of 3,900 by the end of the 1980s.[30] Competition for access to reform privileges became an important policy driver.

Rural Reform after the Third Plenum

Rural policy had been gradually relaxing from the Dazhai promotion of 1977. Now, the state was putting more resources into agriculture, lowering

---

[28] Chen Yun 陈云, "Several Important Orientations to Economic Construction," December 22, 1981, in 陈六文选 (Selected Works of Chen Yun), vol. 3 (Beijing, Renmin chubanshe, 1995), pp. 306–7.
[29] Y. Huang, *Capitalism with Chinese Characteristics: Entrepreneurship and the State* (New York, Cambridge University Press, 2008), Chapter 4.
[30] Tao and Lu, 中国经济特区史论, p. 32.

procurement quotas, paying higher prices, and providing more credit. Moreover, a growing emphasis on autonomy for the collectives meant more freedom to raise the crops and animals that farmers wanted as well. Despite these changes, the core rural institutions and property rights remained largely unchanged through 1979. As farmers gained more political and economic decision-making authority, they began to demand greater institutional flexibility. Farmers began to argue that, since government policy acknowledged their rights to decision-making autonomy, they should also be allowed to change the way land use and farmer compensation were determined.[31]

This demand set off a complex interactive process of bottom-up demands and top-down policy change, as both farmers and policy makers probed to see what they could achieve and what they should accept.[32] Initially, the agricultural collectives themselves were sacrosanct, a core tenet of PRC policy. Rural land policy had been a critical component of Communist victory in the civil war and thus of Communist Party legitimacy. Mao Zedong had personally insisted on rapid collectivization (in 1955) and communes (in 1958), and criticized proponents of "dividing up the land" and "going it alone" (in 1962). To call for the dissolution of agricultural collectives was to directly repudiate Mao Zedong. It is impossible to know what farmers thought, because for twenty years government coercion had foreclosed their options. Farmers who tried to leave collectives could easily find themselves in prison. In 1978, farmers of Xiaogangcun in Anhui leased land to households, but signed – in blood – a contract promising to raise each other's children in case they were arrested. Although these farmers were later celebrated as models of reform (and courage), their fears at the time were not unreasonable.

As farmers in many regions tried out a huge variety of incentive arrangements, different views among top leaders gradually coalesced into two camps. The more reformist leaders, especially Wan Li in Anhui and Zhao Ziyang in Sichuan, argued that farmers must be allowed to modify their own institutions, without having to worry about constant official intervention (or punishment). The more conservative leaders, such as Hua Guofeng, Li Xiannian, and Li's associate, Wang Renzhong, were not against institutional experimentation, but for them this permission was premised on the continuing predominance of the

---

[31] D. Kelliher, *Peasant Power in China: The Era of Rural Reform, 1979–1989* (New Haven, Yale University Press, 1992). K.X. Zhou, *How the Farmers Changed China* (Boulder, Westview Press, 1996).
[32] Lu Mai 卢迈, "The Policy Process of China's Rural Reform," 二十一世纪 (Twenty-First Century) (Hong Kong) 50 (December 1998), 14–23. Du Runsheng 杜润生 (ed.), 中国农村改革决策纪实 (A Virtual Record of China's Rural Reform Policy) (Beijing, Zhongyang Wenxian, 1998), pp. 80–97. Wan, "农村改革是怎么搞起来的?".

collectives, which they hoped would be *strengthened* by improved incentives and higher incomes. The reformists had no desire to mount a frontal assault on collectives, which would be self-defeating and create enormous uncertainty; the conservatives had no desire to strangle experimentation, which would hobble the rural economy. As a result, for about three years after the Third Plenum, argument raged back and forth.

The institutional form at the center of this debate was "contracting output to households" (*baogandaohu* 包干到户), which gave a household control over a plot of land in return for the delivery of an agreed quantity of grain after the harvest. Contracting output was the tipping point between two competing conceptions of the collectives. Contracts initially for one season could be (and were) easily extended for three years and longer, and the households quickly gained control of land, "renting" from the collectives. For conservatives, this was not only ideologically unacceptable, but also undermined their broader economic strategy of extracting surpluses from the farmers to support industrialization. They wanted to be able to instruct collectives to purchase tractors, machinery, and fertilizer coming from the new factories they envisioned, and they wanted to go on mobilizing millions of farmers every winter for construction of irrigation networks and roads.

Farmers were not enthusiastic about buying big tractors or being pressed into annual labor gangs, reformers pointed out, but worked harder under institutional arrangements they had a hand in creating.[33] Thus, early on, reformers emphasized the importance of staying receptive to a range of "production responsibility systems" (PRSs) and not tabooing household contracting. Whether reformers understood from the beginning that household contracting would ultimately lead to the dissolution of collectives and emerge as the dominant rural system is unclear. In March 1979, a meeting of provincial agricultural cadres addressed the question left open at the Third Plenum. All acknowledged that varieties of PRS were spreading, but the more conservative central leaders, still in charge of policy, came and stressed the importance of collective agriculture. Household contracting could be permitted only in very special circumstances of isolated households in the mountains.[34] Still, no rollback was contemplated, and the door to acceptance of household contracting was cracked open.

---

[33] In economists' terms, the strategy of equipping farmers with machinery was "labor-augmenting," which was not China's greatest need. By contrast, both fertilizer and incentive reforms were "land-augmenting."

[34] Liu Kan 刘堪, "回顾 1979 年7省农口干部座谈会" (Looking Back on the 1979 Conference of Agriculture Cadres from Seven Provinces), in Du, 中国农村改革决策纪实, pp. 80–97.

In early 1980, Zhao Ziyang became acting premier and took over the economics portfolio from Chen Yun, while Wan Li was promoted to head agricultural policy in Beijing. These personnel changes must have sent a strong message to local officials, who in many respects were caught in the middle. The collective system made their job much easier, since it gave them direct authority over rural resources, yet many saw that collectives held back local growth. Local officials were charged with interpreting and implementing changing central policies, so they were very sensitive to upper-level signals. Local officials sometimes flip-flopped, as the example of Guizhou, one of the poorest provinces, shows. The province was one of the few whose backward, dispersed farmers were legitimately permitted to experiment with household contracting, and various flavors of PRS spread in 1978–1979. However, provincial officials worried that they were too far ahead of central policy, and in December 1979 shifted gears and sent out teams to "rectify" the PRS (and village officials). The result was a fiasco, with some farmers refusing to plant if their contracted plots were not returned. After a couple of months, provincial officials ended their "rectification," and later swung to the other extreme, adopting permissive policies province-wide. By the beginning of 1981, the province was sending work teams to the village again, but this time to assist farmers signing written contracts with the collectives, clarifying property rights for the land they had received.[35]

Not every place went to extremes like Guizhou, but everywhere local officials made the most important practical decisions: counties typically adopted new policies all at once.[36] As farmers saw that the amount of coercion in the system was being reduced, they were emboldened to push. The policy issues were resolved through a gradual back-and-forth between top policy makers and farmers. By mid-1980, Zhao Ziyang was in a position to demonstrate something we might call "active compromise" – the ability to find a formulation for market reform that soothed the fears of conservatives while opening up further policy change. In his "Letter on Current Rural Policy," Zhao expressed concern that constant change in rural policy would disrupt the busy summer season underway. He suggested that household contracting should be permitted in poor and backward areas. While household contracting was not appropriate in prosperous areas with healthy collectives, if these areas were experimenting then they

---

[35] Chi Biqing 池必卿 and Gao Chunsheng 高春生, "Circumstances of Guizhou Implementing Household Contracting in the Whole Province," in Du, 中国农村改革决策纪实, pp. 268–98.

[36] J. Unger, "The Decollectivization of the Chinese Countryside: A Survey of Twenty-Eight Villages," Pacific Affairs 58.4 (Winter 1985–1986), 585–606.

should continue without interruption.[37] This created a presumption of permissiveness, which in fact supported the spread of PRSs. Ultimately, in January 1982, the PRS, including household contracting, was officially affirmed. In 1983, in most parts of the country, communes were abolished, with their governmental functions transferred to the new townships, and income-earning activities spun off as "township and village enterprises" (TVEs).

Despite its inconsistency, the interactive policy process through which the state retreated provided a number of benefits. First, it prevented the process from getting out of control, becoming a frantic division of assets, and it allowed policy makers and the Communist Party to save face and protect the position of its agents in the countryside. The change in rural society and property was enormous, a genuine "second revolution" in the Chinese countryside, but it was a controlled revolution. Second, it enabled an apparently fair and egalitarian distribution of land. In part, this is because the initial distribution of land was seen as provisional and was carried out locally, in a group process within the collective. Third, it allowed a negotiation about the bundle of private property rights that farmers were achieving. Farmers "gradually enlarged the range of their contracts, accumulated more and more private rights, and entered into a network of market contractual relationships of a greater and greater variety."[38] The end result was acceptable both to the farmers, who were allowed to return to household farming, and to the policy makers, who until then had seen collectives as an indispensable part of socialism. The collectives survived in name as the ultimate owner of the land, but, given the opportunity to invest in their own farms, farmers defected en masse from the collectives.

Achievement, Hesitation, and Renewed Reform

In 600 days, between the December 1978 Third Plenum and late summer 1980, policy makers achieved astonishing results and locked in important economic reforms. Despite this, toward the end of 1980, policy changed abruptly and a much more conservative policy line emerged. Ironically, during this conservative period, policies already enacted unleashed a new economic dynamism that propelled China into a new reform phase.

---

[37] Zhao Ziyang 赵紫阳, "A Letter on Current Rural Policy," June 19, 1980, in 赵紫阳文集 (Collected Works of Zhao Ziyang), vol. 1 (Hong Kong, Chinese University of Hong Kong Press), pp. 44–5.

[38] Q. Zhou, "How Deng's Drama Unfolded (Part 1)," *Caixin*, August 27, 2019, 04:22 p.m., at www.caixinglobal.com/2019-08-27/how-dengs-drama-unfolded-part-1-101455513.html.

Renewed Readjustment and Policy Vacillation

At the end of 1980, the emergence of inflation and renewed imbalances triggered a new Readjustment.[39] Officially, consumer price inflation in 1980 was 7.5 percent, and prices were certainly rising faster toward year's end. Chen Yun called for a do-over of the three-year Readjustment of 1979, which he insisted had not been implemented thoroughly enough, and should be restarted. The leadership fell in line behind Chen Yun: investment was cut back sharply, effective in January 1981; many reforms were paused; and GDP growth dropped to 5.1 percent, the lowest in the first decade of reform.

Macroeconomics drove policy change, but the shift was broad and long-lasting, sustained through 1983. Austerity policies were adopted regardless of their effect on market-oriented reforms: for example, cash balances of enterprises and local governments were frozen and borrowed by the central government. Economic reforms came under sustained criticism and assault. Until this time, despite disagreement about specific policies, the policy environment had been buoyed by broad enthusiasm for vaguely defined reform and the need to repudiate Cultural Revolution legacies. Now, a systematic antireform view began to be articulated that linked reform to corruption, crime, and a loss of national sovereignty. The SEZs, in particular, came under sustained attack. Conservatives, including Chen Yun, criticized the SEZs for breeding corruption and undermining national sovereignty. In 1982, central documents repeatedly declared that SEZs were premised on maintaining the dominant position of public ownership and implementing the same laws and basic economic system as the rest of China. This policy principle threatened to cripple the SEZs' role as a test bed for broader reforms. Deng Xiaoping quietly acquiesced and personally signed off on a 1983 crackdown on "spiritual pollution" that linked urban crime with liberalization and foreign influence. Market reforms skidded to a halt.

A New Economic Dynamics

While politicians marked time, at the grass roots the economy was accelerating as the effects of the 1979–1980 reforms worked their way through the system. After mid-1980, the agricultural PRS spread rapidly, and increasingly took the more radical form of contracting land to households. From

---

[39] This murky policy shift clearly had political as well as economic drivers. Chinese policy makers were concerned about international issues such as the emergence of the Polish Solidarity labor movement and the election of Ronald Reagan in the US. Domestically, long-term personnel decisions after the removal of Hua Guofeng as Party head may have touched off complex bargains among the most powerful elders, Deng and Chen.

14 percent at year's end 1980, adoption jumped to 45 percent, then 80 percent by the end of 1982, and it was finally nearly universal by 1983, at 98 percent of all villages. With the spread of the production responsibility system from 1981 through 1984, agricultural growth accelerated. Economists have shown that change in rural property rights accounted for the largest share of the productivity increase.[40] Agricultural output quickly responded. The vital grain harvest surged from barely 300 million metric tons in 1978 to 387 million metric tons in 1983, dispelling worries about China's ability to feed itself. Simultaneously, output of economic crops such as cotton and oilseed doubled.

Equally significant, as farm households gained control of their cropping and labor allocation decisions, they decided they could produce more crops with fewer hours of (more intense) work. Farm households began releasing family members for nonagricultural pursuits, notably to the TVEs which had been thrown open during the course of 1979. Agriculture achieved the remarkable result of rapidly expanding output while decreasing direct labor inputs. Between 1978 and 1984, China created 80 million new jobs, almost entirely by dramatically expanding labor-intensive subsectors. Roughly a third were in newly diversified agriculture, a third in rural manufacturing or construction, and a third in urban manufacturing or services. Urban unemployment, which had surged in 1978–1979, now fell again, and availability of consumer goods expanded dramatically. China could feed itself and employ its massive population: rural reforms turned out to be a prerequisite for China to sidestep the demographic tidal wave and reap the benefits of its "demographic dividend."

Growth of foreign trade was also rapid, although labor-intensive exports took longer to begin their takeoff. Exports doubled between 1978 and 1982, and while oil was still the largest item and mainstay of exports, labor-intensive exports grew and slightly expanded their share. As these structural changes fell into place, and the most drastic of the 1981 Readjustment policies were relaxed, the economy accelerated. From 1983 through 1988, the economy roared ahead at over 10 percent per year, the first period of "miracle growth" that China enjoyed.

---

[40] J.Y. Lin, "Rural Reform and Agricultural Growth in China," *American Economic Review* 82 (1992), 34–51, which also provides national PRS percentages. J. McMillan, J. Whalley, and L. Zhu, "The Impact of China's Economic Reforms on Agricultural Productivity Growth," *Journal of Political Economy* 97.4 (August 1989), 781–807. A. de Brauw, J. Huang, and S. Rozelle, "The Sequencing of Reform Policies in China's Agricultural Transition," *Economics of Transition* 12.3 (2004), 427–65.

China was enjoying quick economic returns from the abandonment of its former, capital-intensive development strategy. Rural households pivoted quickly to diversified household production and participating in nearby township and village enterprises. In cities, young people were absorbed into hastily created service and manufacturing jobs. New lower-cost combinations of production factors that had previously been outlawed now experienced explosive growth. In the TVE sector, growth was driven by labor-intensive manufactures such as textiles and garments, furniture, and plastic and metal products. These are the typical "early industrialization" sectors that power the initial stages of economic development everywhere: having skipped these sectors in its early command-economy growth, China was now well placed to rapidly catch up. Vast labor-intensive sectors were quickly created and opened up a powerful, sustainable growth path, which used China's underlying comparative advantage, and which China followed for the next two decades and more.

These outcomes vindicated reformers and created a powerful argument for further market-oriented reforms. Has there ever been a more unambiguous demonstration of the power of incentives and markets than the adoption of the PRS by Chinese farmers? Farmers worked harder and smarter with control over their own land, and produced more with less. Chinese farmers gave reform-oriented policy makers far more room for maneuver. In addition to the demonstration effect, reforms unleashed new market forces that created a demand for further reform. TVEs produced industrial goods and services that competed with existing urban state-owned enterprises (SOEs). TVEs were the opening wedge of an army of new entrants who broke down the monopoly that SOEs had previously enjoyed over most industrial products. This created unprecedented pressure on SOEs and ultimately on the government budget, which was dependent on profit remitted from SOEs. Policy makers had to devise policies that would allow SOEs to respond to this new competitive challenge. As economic conditions eased, the fact-based argument in favor of reform strengthened, opening the way for a running start to renewed market-oriented reforms.

Reform Renewal in 1984

In January 1984, Deng Xiaoping kicked off renewed reforms by visiting the Shenzhen and Zhuhai SEZs. Having been a lightning rod for criticism, the SEZs now served as a bellwether, symbolizing the fate of the entire economic reform program. Emboldened by the success of rural reforms, Deng declared the SEZs an unqualified success, and SEZ-like provisions were extended to fourteen coastal cities in May. To drive the point home, the October 1 National Day parade in Beijing included a float from Shekou flouting its most controversial slogan: "Time is money; efficiency is life."

The job of translating enthusiasm into realistic policy making now fell to the premier, Zhao Ziyang. Inevitably, his first step was to get buy-in from the elders, especially Chen Yun. With pressure from Deng Xiaoping in the background, and Zhao's talent for active compromise very much in evidence, all Standing Committee members signed off on a letter Zhao wrote on September 9, 1984.[41] At the subsequent Third Plenum in October, a broad (but vague) new reform program was endorsed. China's economy was rechristened a "commodity economy" (a half-hearted version of a market economy) and the scope of compulsory planning was to shrink, in favor of an ill-defined "guidance planning" and increased market transactions. Enterprise incentives and autonomy were to expand, and prices to be reformed.[42] These powerful ideas legitimated widespread reform experimentation, but didn't provide much concrete guidance: this was no reform blueprint. Instead, an intense period of policy creativity and reform experimentation was launched that lasted through the fall of 1988.

The 1980s

The five years from 1984 through 1988 were one of the most creative periods of the entire reform era. Confronted with a treacherous political and economic environment, Zhao Ziyang moved market-oriented reforms decisively forward. Although the period was ended by the traumatic events at Tiananmen Square in June 1989, the overall record was one of positive achievement.

The Reform Challenge and the Political-Economy Matrix

Zhao Ziyang was in charge of day-to-day economic policy making, but above him were the three powerful elders on the five-man Politburo Standing Committee. Deng Xiaoping was generally an ally on economic reform issues, but the support of Chen Yun and Li Xiannian was far from unconditional.

---

[41] Zhao Ziyang 赵紫阳, "A Letter to the Standing Committee on Three Questions about Economic System Reform," September 9, 1984, in 赵紫阳文集 (Collected Works of Zhao Ziyang), vol. 2, pp. 484–9, which includes the 批示 pishi (approval and commentary) of the elders.

[42] "Party Center Resolution on Economic System Reform," October 20, 1984, in 赵紫阳文集 (Collected Works of Zhao Ziyang), vol. 2, pp. 490–508.

Each of the elders had strong views on certain topics and substantial interest groups arrayed behind them. Zhao had to achieve "buy-in" from many powerful players, and many senior leaders could veto specific policies. With many "veto-gates," it was difficult to move policy decisively in any given direction.[43]

At the same time, the economic policy choices had now become far more complex than before. Reform could now "move into the city" from the countryside, but the core of the planned economy was still intact. In this system, state-owned factories dominated the industrial sector and responded to plans and administrative commands from the government, and the government was still dependent on traditional institutions to steer the economy. The state-owned factories made large profits, buying inputs at low state–state prices and selling at high controlled prices. In turn, they turned the bulk of those profits over to the government, which used them to fund its own operations and invest in industrialization. The system was now fraying at the edges, as firms had been given more autonomy and better incentives, but it had not been fundamentally changed. Zhao Ziyang confronted the problem of how to transform the core of the system.

It is customary to divide the elders into a reform camp under Deng Xiaoping and a conservative camp under Chen Yun. There is much truth in this, but it is important not to oversimplify the situation. Chen Yun was conservative in important respects: he believed in cautious macroeconomic policy, balanced budgets, low inflation, and government steerage of the economy. Moreover, he was extremely sensitive to corruption and speculation, and suspicious of capitalists and foreign businesses. Yet Chen was also appreciative of the power of markets, and sensitive to the use of market prices as signals of relative scarcities. He had long advocated for markets on a small scale, for example for farm products. Chen famously likened the Chinese economy to a "bird in a cage," in which the job of planners like himself was to make the cage as commodious as possible, but never to allow the bird to fly away.

Chen Yun never systematically laid out his mature views on the socialist economy, but we can extrapolate from his earlier views to sketch a version of "conservative reform." The breakthrough reforms of 1978–1982 had resolved the immediate crises of food shortage, underemployment, and scarcity of foreign exchange. The feeble institutional capacity and huge ideological

---

[43] Zhao Ziyang, *Prisoner of the State: The Secret Journal of Premier Zhao Ziyang* (New York, Simon & Schuster, 2009).

hurdles inherited from the Maoist era had been ameliorated, and the small-scale markets Chen Yun had long advocated had been resuscitated. In this environment, conservative reformers would have focused on improving management in state firms and shoring up the state monopoly of select critical sectors, while gradually stepping up planning. Such an approach could have sustained rapid growth for a while, and left China with a dualistic economy in which a modern state-dominated industrial sector coexisted with a sprawling small-scale private rural, handicraft, and service sector. Such a system is common in many developing countries, and would have been a completely plausible outcome in China. However, such an approach never really materialized in China. It would have required that planning and state ownership be strengthened at a time when the driving economic force was coming from dispersed, generally small-scale, labor-intensive manufacturing and services that didn't benefit at all from planning or public ownership. It would have required somebody with remarkable vision and determination to drive the economic system in this coherent, but counterintuitive, direction. As Chen Yun aged and stepped back, and as younger thinkers were increasingly taken with comprehensive marketization and the promise of really dramatic productivity improvement, no such leader emerged in China. As a result, the conservative camp became a brake on reform, but never developed its own independent program.

The core industrial system confronted policy makers with an enormous mass of entangled issues: how to reform industry (especially state-owned industry), the fiscal and financial systems, and the price system. Policy makers had to come up with a coherent package of policies, and they also had to mobilize the political will to make difficult and disruptive changes. In the USSR and Eastern Europe, especially Poland, an influential body of opinion held that the only way to carry off such a difficult policy exercise was to do everything at once, moving quickly so the economy could recover from the shock and adapt to new economic and property relations. Typically, this "big-bang" approach involved rapid price decontrol, with price liberalization and macroeconomic stabilization combined, followed by rapid privatization.[44] Rapid big-bang transition never had much appeal in China. The immense pressure to find jobs for the rapidly growing labor force plus the intuitive understanding that China had strong growth potential limited the economic

---

[44] For example, O. Blanchard, R. Dornbusch, P. Krugman, R. Layard, and L. Summers, *Reform in Eastern Europe* (Cambridge, MA, MIT Press, 1991); J. Sachs and W.T. Woo, "Structural Factors in the Economic Reforms of China, Eastern Europe, and the Former Soviet Union," *Economic Policy* 4.1 (1991), 101–45.

appeal of the big bang. Politically, the desire to maintain Party control and social stability meant that big bangs could not be countenanced. What was Zhao Ziyang to do?

Looking for Room to Maneuver

Seeking to find a path between systemic stagnation and big-bang destabilization, Zhao Ziyang was receptive to extraordinarily diverse influences. Zhao listened to foreign economists, seeking institutional advice from the World Bank, and from individuals as diverse as Milton Friedman and Alvin Toffler.[45] Domestically, Zhao reached outside the economic bureaucracy to groups not burdened by institutional interests, essentially empowering competing brain trusts to suggest new policies. One group of senior economists, which evolved into the Development Research Center, was informally led by Xue Muqiao, who had long practical experience dating back to the 1940s. These veterans, given their familiarity with socialist economic categories, suggested key transitional concepts, such as the "commodity economy," which legitimated initial steps toward marketization even when conservatives vetoed the idea of a market-led economy.[46] Another group of young economists, predominantly in their thirties and with no link to the traditional bureaucracy, provided many bold new ideas that Zhao eagerly absorbed. Organized into the System Reform Institute and the Rural Development Research Institute, these iconoclastic and activist economists dreamed up new initiatives, and communicated intensively outside official channels.[47] Zhao presided over what sometimes seemed like a perpetual brainstorming session. This reflected the excitement, idealism, and diversity that characterized the 1980s more broadly in China, but also the extraordinarily complex political and economic landscape through which Zhao had to navigate.

The Emergent Strategy of 1980s Economic Reform

Zhao Ziyang was able to cobble together a coherent approach to reform. At its core, Zhao's approach was to infuse the entire Chinese system with incentives for economic growth. During the Cultural Revolution, virtually

---

[45] A. Wood, "China: Long-Term Development Issues and Options, Past and Present," University of Oxford, TMCD working paper series No. 079 (January 2019). J. Gewirtz, *Unlikely Partners: Chinese Reformers, Western Economists, and the Making of Global China* (Cambridge, MA, Harvard University Press, 2017).

[46] B. Naughton, *Wu Jinglian: Voice of Reform in China* (Cambridge, MA, MIT Press, 2013).

[47] I.M. Weber, *How China Escaped Shock Therapy: The Market Reform Debate* (New York, Routledge, 2020). The September 1984 Moganshan meeting was a pivotal moment for this group. Liu Hong 柳红 (ed.), 莫干山会议 (The Moganshan Meeting) (Beijing, Dongfang, 2019), contains memoirs and documents.

all individual incentives had been sublimated to collective political objectives. Early reforms had restored basic incentives to industry – things like hourly and piece rates for workers and bonuses for managers – but now Zhao went much further. Indeed, Zhao sometimes pushed it to extremes, supporting a vast range of incentive mechanisms, tailored to specific situations, that provided rewards for those who worked harder or smarter.

Industrial enterprise reform – pioneered in the late 1970s by Zhao when he was still Party boss in Sichuan province – had at its core a system of profit retention. In the mid-1980s, these reforms spread to almost all state firms, providing firms with retained funds that they could use for bonuses, worker housing or services, and investment.[48] Within the firm, the "factory manager responsibility system" gave managers top authority, displacing the Party secretary. Within government, provinces signed up for a variety of budgetary deals with the center that allowed them to retain revenues above a stipulated control figure. Universities and research institutes were encouraged to set up subordinate profit-making companies to supplement their budgets at a time when the government couldn't contribute much. Every sector had its own incentive mechanisms.[49] Incentives went beyond the purely financial: local government officials began to have economic growth and fiscal revenue targets written into their performance contracts. Promotion, it was made clear, would depend on successful local economies.

Stronger incentives heightened tensions within the highly distorted bureaucratic economy. Prices were fixed and diverged widely from costs, and economic opportunities were very unequally distributed. As incentives were strengthened in general, individuals also had stronger incentives to chase rent-seeking opportunities, bend rules, and become corrupt. Two mechanisms were introduced to contain these defects: "particularistic contracting" and the dual-track system. Particularistic contracting occurred when enterprises (and organizations and local governments) agreed to turn over to their superiors a specific amount of profit or revenue, typically based on the previous year's performance.[50] This equalized opportunity to some extent, and also allowed marginal retention rates to be higher, further reinforcing incentives. The inspiration obviously came from the rural reforms, and it was easy to implement. Profit contracting, however, enmeshes firms in complex bargaining relations with their superiors – what will

---

[48] Naughton, *Growing Out of the Plan*, pp. 97–135, 200–243.
[49] Tian Jiyun 田纪云, "Ten Major Economic Reform Measures of the 1980s," in Xu, *The Chinese Experience*, pp. 56–78. Tian was vice premier during this period.
[50] S. Shirk, *The Political Logic of Economic Reform in China* (Berkeley, University of California Press, 1995).

next year's contract be? – and it inevitably has a short half-life in a dynamic economy.

Firms were allowed to operate on a "dual track." They were required to meet their legacy obligations – producing planned output with planned inputs and selling at plan prices – but could also sell outside the plan at market prices (conditional on fulfilling their plan). Thus every commodity had two tracks and two prices (plan and market). Chinese planning had always been weak, so firms generally had some surplus capacity to produce outside the plan. In the extreme case, with a fixed plan, all of the action takes place on the market track, and the firm faces market prices on the margin. With particularistic contracting and the dual track, everyone is as well off as they were before (because of the contract), but has been given a new opportunity to expand in a market direction. With economic growth, the market track will expand and the economy will "grow out of the plan."[51] The dual-track system also allowed state-owned enterprises to trade at market prices with TVEs, which had never really been planned. Thus it contributed to market integration, tearing down the barriers that protected the monopoly industry system.

However, this system had two major defects. First, it made corruption much easier, since simply reselling a low-price plan good on the high-price market could be very lucrative and was hard to monitor. Second, particularistic contracting made it harder to reform the economic parameters that govern the overall economic system, such as the tax system. In essence, every enterprise had a different tax rate. The dual track could drive prices to their market levels, but it could never drive taxes, for example, to levels that were either uniform or appropriate.

Facing these problems, Zhao Ziyang heard conflicting advice from proponents of two very different approaches. The young economists around the System Reform Institute proposed using the dual-track system as a full-blown transition strategy. Recognizing its defects, they nonetheless argued that this would incentivize managers to push for more autonomy and market-friendly strategies. They argued that the economy was capable of rapid growth and could withstand short-run disruptions and inflation, and urged quick movement through to a market economy.[52] A competing group of more established, usually older,

---

[51] Naughton, *Growing Out of the Plan*. W. Byrd, "The Impact of the Two-Tier Plan and Market System in Chinese Industry," *Journal of Comparative Economics* 11.3 (September 1987), 295–308.
[52] Both sides were reformers committed to a transition toward a market economy, and neither side had sympathy for a "big-bang"-type reform. The young economists preferred to lead with incentive and ownership reforms, delaying price reform; the

economists argued strongly that the priority was to first establish a "relaxed" low-inflation macroeconomic environment. Once that was achieved, a two-step price and tax reform should follow: an immediate, ambitious adjustment of some of the most distorted prices – such as low energy prices – followed promptly by full price liberalization. The debate was formulated in terms of underlying principles and institutions, and often styled as "ownership reform" versus "price reform." In fact, differences over short-term macroeconomic policy were often the focus of heated debate. As is so often the case, the policy outcomes were not decided by the quality of the competing arguments but rather by fluctuating macroeconomic conditions and by treacherous political circumstances.

Economic Policy Cycles

Through the 1980s, there had been a clear pattern of macroeconomic cycles, visible in Figure 20.1 below.[53] Inflation peaked in 1980, 1985, and 1988, and later in 1995. Each of these inflation peaks also marks a phase of a policy cycle, coming after a wave of reforms. Four clear combined policy and macroeconomic cycles mark the first twenty years of reform. These cyclical processes reflect the intrinsic reform problems discussed earlier. Reforms lead to a surge in social and economic demands. This is particularly true when firms have "soft budget constraints," meaning that they might avoid repaying their debts. Enterprise managers with soft budget constraints will exploit their increased freedom of action to increase their investments (which provide higher profit and status).[54] Reform and decentralization thus lead to rapid expansion of aggregate demand, outrunning supply, and ultimately to inflation and/or shortages. Policy makers react to these imbalances with top-down re-control, suppressing investment and aggregate demand, and reversing or scaling back decentralization and reform. After de-control succeeds, the stage is set for a new phase of decentralization, reform, and expansion.

The distinctive feature of Chinese cycles is that phases of the cycles correspond with regular shifts in the influence of top policy makers. Given the dispersal of elder power between reformers (led by Deng) and conservatives (led by Chen Yun), policy-making authority oscillated among these

older group preferred to lead with price reform (including parameters like taxes), deferring incentive and ownership reforms.

[53] National Bureau of Statistics, derived from monthly data at www.stats.gov.cn/tjsj. Only annual data are available for 1978 through 1982.
[54] J. Kornai, *The Shortage Economy* (Amsterdam, North-Holland, 1980).

policy makers along with the economic cycle. When conditions were favorable, reformers (Zhao Ziyang first among them) would seize the initiative, often with Deng Xiaoping creating a protective umbrella of pro-reform rhetoric. Reforms would generate an explosion of activity, optimism, and accelerated growth, but would also lead to increased inflation and imbalances. At this point, Chen Yun would find his voice, speaking out for economic stability and against speculation. Conservatives would demand macroeconomic adjustment, seek to restrict credit and investment, and attack reforms which they had never fully accepted. It is striking that as one side stepped forward, the other side would step back, avoiding an irreconcilable split among the elders. Conservatives stepped in to damp down the irrational exuberance of the high-reform phase, but without ever really articulating an alternative vision of "conservative reform."

The policy episodes described earlier fit easily into this cyclical framework, which has long been noted by China analysts.[55] In the first cycle, vigorous reforms in 1980 led to imbalances and inflation that triggered a major intervention by Chen Yun and a multiyear backlash against reforms. In the second cycle, Deng's visit to Shenzhen in 1984 presaged major reforms in 1984–1985, followed by a surge of inflation and an unprecedented trade deficit. Under pressure, Zhao Ziyang maintained day-to-day authority and carried out partial re-control in 1985–1986. This second cycle was not quite complete when Zhao contemplated adopting a "comprehensive reform package," tabled by the price reform group in late 1986. To have accepted the price reform package, Zhao would have had to strictly carry through the macroeconomic control policies associated with the conservative group. Under great political and economic pressure, Zhao declined to maintain tough macro-control or adopt the comprehensive price reform program. His default acceptance of profit contracting pleased many of his supporters, but contributed to the acceleration of inflation that became evident within months. Zhao was finding it difficult to thread a path between these conflicting forces, and building pressures were soon to overwhelm him.

The Mid-term Crisis of Reform, 1989–1991

China had moved onto a high-growth track in the mid-1980s, which Zhao Ziyang was understandably hesitant to disrupt. Inflation gradually accelerated through 1987 and 1988 (Figure 20.1), and the gap between market and

---

[55] J. Fewsmith, *Dilemmas of Reform in China: Political Conflict and Economic Debate* (Armonk, NY: M.E. Sharpe, 1994).

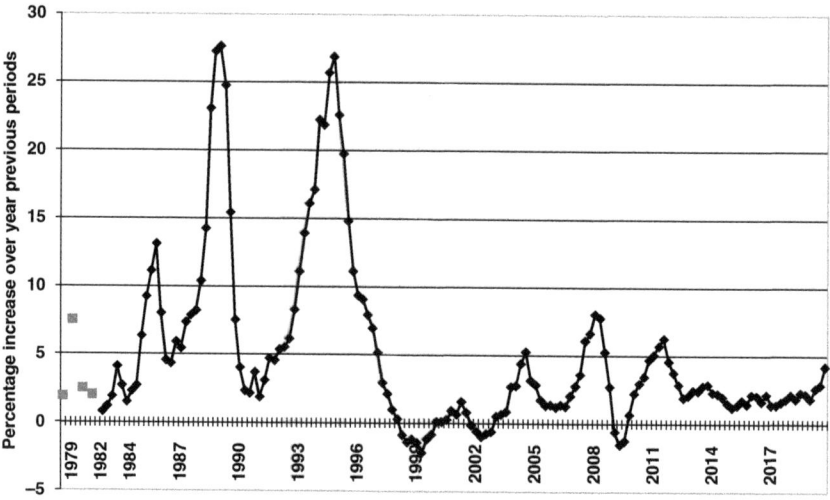

Figure 20.1 Consumer inflation (1979–2019)
Note: quarterly data begin in 1982; annual data for 1979–1981 shown as gray squares.

plan prices also widened, creating unprecedented opportunities for corruption through arbitrage between the two prices. Public discontent increased, and the more conservative elders, headed by Chen Yun, became disaffected. This complex economic situation interacted with some sensitive political events.

A cascade of political events began in December 1986 when Deng Xiaoping deposed Hu Yaobang, the Party head and nominal top leader. Deng had grown dissatisfied with Hu Yaobang's performance in handling student protests and other issues. Despite some differences over economic policy, Hu Yaobang and Zhao Ziyang overall had formed a powerful team that strongly favored reform. Zhao Ziyang was now "promoted" to take Hu's position as general secretary. At first, Zhao thought he could control the situation, and the Thirteenth Party Congress in October 1987 announced an unprecedented theoretical program for further reform. China was declared to be in a "primary" stage of socialism, in which production forces were underdeveloped and institutional diversity could be embraced. Led by Deng Xiaoping and Chen Yun, all of the elders retired from the Standing Committee, the apex of formal power.

However, Zhao's promotion turned out to be a poisoned chalice. Zhao gained in nominal authority, but the elders maintained their influence behind the scenes and Zhao lost a key ally in Hu Yaobang. Moreover, when promoted to Party general secretary, Zhao had to turn over direct control of economic policy to his successor as premier, Li Peng. When surging inflation led to a new re-control policy in September 1988, Zhao Ziyang was caught in a power squeeze. Chen Yun was peering unhappily over his shoulder; Deng Xiaoping was urging bold reforms; and the policy of re-control was actually in the hands of two conservatives, Li Peng and Yao Yilin. Top-down controls damped investment and growth, and quickly pushed the economy to its maximum pain point, with growth slowing before inflation had begun to come down.

It was in this fraught economic and political environment that, on April 8, 1989, Hu Yaobang had a heart attack in a Politburo meeting, and died in the hospital a week later. Scattered student demonstrations exploded into massive nationwide memorials and protests, as demonstrators called for the social and political liberalization advocated by Hu Yaobang, and an end to corruption and inflation. The situation spiraled out of control: Zhao Ziyang's unwillingness to use military force against protesters in Tiananmen Square on June 4, 1989, led to his deposition, the violent suppression of the demonstrations, and the loss of power of an entire cohort of pro-reform policy makers.

From June 4, 1989, through the end of 1991, conservatives dominated economic policy. They blamed economic reform for a dazzling range of negative outcomes: inflation, shortages of energy and key producer goods, liberalism, and student unrest. Conservatives interpreted inflation and sporadic shortages as symptoms of deep structural imbalances and, to a surprising extent, sought to roll back economic reforms. To control inflation, they advocated stronger planning and increased supply of energy and key heavy industrial products. Price controls were imposed on outside-plan markets, and financial balances of both enterprises and local governments were frozen. Conservatives were openly hostile to private business, and the small emergent urban private sector shrank by half between 1988 and 1990 under combined political and economic pressure. In rural areas, collective institutions were re-emphasized and farmers pushed to join so-called "new cooperatives." The economy slowed to a standstill in the second half of 1989 and the first half of 1990, as it worked through these drastic policy changes.

Conservatives were hobbled by their lack of a real program. The acute issues they were most concerned with quickly disappeared: the inflation rate dropped and even turned briefly negative in mid-1990, while shortages of producer goods and electricity evaporated. Struggling to put together a plan, a newly re-empowered Planning Commission drafted a Five-Year Plan for

1991–1995 that prioritized recentralization and a new program of investment in "basic industries." It estimated that GDP could grow at 6 percent annually, and worker wages should grow only 2 percent annually.[56] In fact, planners grievously underestimated the potential of their own economy, which would grow twice as fast in the next five years. It wasn't the same economy as in 1978–1979 any more. It was three times as big, with a huge and vibrant small-scale sector, and with much more resilience and flexibility, the direct result of a decade of successful economic reform.

The Reform Breakthroughs of the 1990s

The years of conservative dominance after June 4, 1989, disappeared with remarkable speed, and were then conveniently forgotten. The conventional turning point is the "Southern Tour" (*nanxun* 南巡) that Deng Xiaoping took in January–February 1992, in which he rebuked ideological opposition to economic reforms and declared that "development is the only hard truth." Deng proclaimed that markets existed under both socialism and capitalism, and therefore should not be subject to ideological litmus tests. These pronouncements touched off a new round of reform. Clearly this was a catalytic event, and Deng seemed to effortlessly overturn the entire policy orientation. For an eighty-eight-year-old man, it was a remarkable display of political theater.

But of course, the change ran much deeper. Through 1991, the ground had been shifting underneath Chinese decision makers. The new Party leader, Jiang Zemin, was trying to establish his own authority and gradually understood that this would require a more pro-market position. Growth was accelerating as conservative controls on the economy fell away. However, Deng Xiaoping worried about his legacy as he saw that changes were being blocked by conservative leaders who operated under Chen Yun's patronage, or at least believed that they did. Increasing frustration and anger on Deng's part led him to make his historic journey.[57] Thereafter, everything changed with breathtaking speed. The 1992 Party Congress forthrightly declared that the reform objective was a "socialist market economy," and in October 1993

---

[56] Liu Guoguang, 中国十个五年计划研究报告, pp. 547–602, esp. 552, 557.
[57] Zhou Ruijin 周瑞金, "改革开放 30 年的思考" (Reflection on 30 Years of Reform and Opening), Reuters China, October 8, 2008, at www.reuters.com/article/idCNChina-2508 820081009; S. Zhao, "Deng Xiaoping's Southern Tour: Elite Politics in Post-Tiananmen China," *Asian Survey* 33.8 (1993), pp. 739–56; Ma Licheng 马立诚, 交锋三十年 (Thirty Years of Confrontation) (Nanjing, Jiangsu renmin chubanshe, 2008), esp. pp. 150–1.

a new Third Plenum adopted a comprehensive program to be implemented by century's end. Policy had swung 180 degrees in less than two years. Most remarkable, almost all the proposed measures were actually implemented.

A Dizzying Shift in Political and Economic Conditions

What led to this remarkable change? First, the sense of crisis, already palpable after the Tiananmen events, was intensified by internal and external events. Internally, the erosion of state capacity continued unabated. To a certain extent, the reform strategy followed under Zhao Ziyang was responsible for an inevitable erosion of budgetary revenues as a share of GDP and a weakening of the instruments of the command economy. Reforms had relaxed the state monopoly over industry and allowed new entrants to compete away monopoly profits on which government revenues depended. Conservatives had pledged to reverse this trend but failed, and budgetary revenues were again declining as a share of GDP (Figure 20.2).[58] Externally, the gradual unraveling of the Soviet system accelerated and culminated in the shocking dissolution of the Soviet Union in December 1991. Socialist self-confidence was profoundly undermined. Simultaneously, the ease with which the US military pushed Iraq out of Kuwait (in February 1991) showed that the US had mastered a "revolution in military affairs" that other countries, including China, hadn't even begun. The conservative response to this internal and external turmoil was to hunker down and reassert the purity of socialist ideals, but Deng Xiaoping and many others understood that only accelerated reform could address the challenges. Worldwide, it was obvious that market economies had outperformed command economies, and the prestige of the US model was at an all-time high. Since the conservatives had no viable economic program, their exposed position collapsed when Deng pushed on it, and the policy spectrum narrowed substantially.

Second, within China, the makeup of power was changing. From the Third Plenum through the end of the 1980s, a group of revolutionary elders had held ultimate authority in a variety of fields, including the economic. Now, the inevitable passage of time was bringing this dispersion of ultimate authority among elders to an end. Several influential elders passed away in 1992–1993, including Li Xiannian, Hu Qiaomu, and Wang Zhen, and the Central Advisory Commission, which had served as an instrument of elder power, was abolished. Finally, Deng used this situation to push back at Chen Yun in unmistakable fashion, using special economic zones as a symbolic

---

[58] National Bureau of Statistics, 中国统计摘要 2019 (China Statistical Abstract 2019) (Beijing, Zhongguo Tongji), pp. 68, 22.

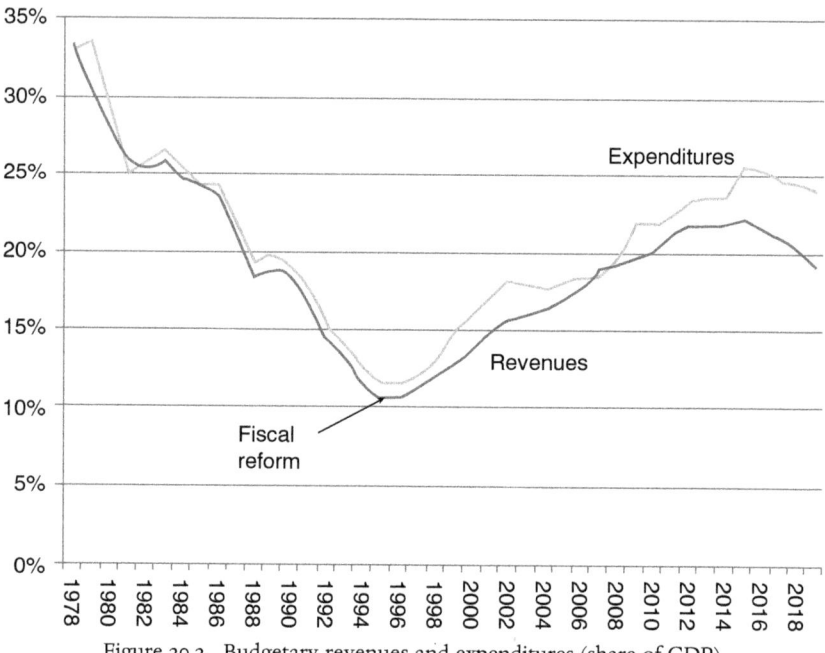

Figure 20.2 Budgetary revenues and expenditures (share of GDP)

issue. Deng said, "when we set up the four SEZs ... we didn't think about Shanghai's superiority in human capital ... if we had made Shanghai an SEZ back then, it wouldn't look [as backward] as it does today."[59] In fact, it was Chen Yun who had insisted on the exclusion of Shanghai from the ranks of SEZs. Now, Deng used the death of Li Xiannian to suggest to Chen Yun that he make a gesture of support for the new policies. Chen Yun did so in his "Memorializing Li Xiannian," which was printed on the front page of the *People's Daily*. "We didn't recognize the full importance of SEZs," said Chen.[60] It signaled Chen's capitulation and marked the end of an era of elder dominance of policy.

---

[59] "Key Points of Talks in Wuchang, Shenzhen, Zhuhai, and Shanghai," January–February 1991, in 邓小平文选 (Selected Works of Deng Xiaoping), vol. 3 (Beijing, Renmin chubanshe, 1994), p. 366.
[60] Chen Yun, "悼念李先念同志" (Mourning Comrade Li Xiannian), *People's Daily*, July 23, 1992, 1. Reprinted in 陈云文选 (Selected Works of Chen Yun), vol. 3, pp. 378–9. Chen's personal secretary, Zhu Jiamu 朱佳木, tells of Deng's suggestion to Chen, "Chen Yun and Deng Xiaoping in the Early Reform Period," *Dangdai Zhongguoshi Yanjiu* 17.3 (May 2010), 14.

Finally, as the economy recovered from the post-Tiananmen crackdown, it became clear that the structural conditions of the economy were changing. The demographic tidal wave that had so worried policy makers had begun to ebb, and the extraordinary growth of the labor force from 1964–1990 was finally beginning to ratchet down. Jobs had been found in new labor-intensive sectors, which made the economy stronger and more productive. The urgency and difficulty of finding jobs for urban dwellers had declined. Labor market reforms that might increase short-term unemployment didn't seem as inconceivable as they once had. Even more consequentially, it might become possible to lower the barriers keeping rural workers from migrating to the city (the *hukou* system). New economic opportunities were opening up at the grass roots.

A New Turning Point

These rapid but profound shifts in political and economic conditions initially outpaced the ability of policy makers to design appropriate responses. As the policy environment liberalized, in the wake of Deng's Southern Tour, there was a nationwide scramble to take advantage of new opportunities. Local government officials had already been incentivized to support economic growth, and they had seen national GDP growth surge to over 10 percent during the 1980s. Now, in 1992, growth was surging again – ultimately to 14 percent for the year – and there was a wild scramble to be part of this growth. "Zone mania" spread, as local officials set up literally thousands of "special zones" in every Chinese province, which gave them a flexible tool to attract investment from outside, and generate lucrative development contracts for friends and relatives.

Economic growth was accommodated with rapid credit growth, and inevitably led to a new wave of inflation. As Figure 20.1 shows, inflation began to creep up during 1992, and then took off, finally peaking in the fourth quarter of 1994 at 27 percent. Inflation caused other problems: policy makers had lowered the official nominal value of the *renminbi* (RMB) between 1989 and 1991, but inflation subsequently caused the real exchange rate to appreciate, leading to a current-account deficit, and a modest drawdown of reserves. Increased disequilibria led to a bigger role for the existing "swap market" for foreign exchange, where transactions took place at a relatively uncontrolled market rate. The swap market RMB plummeted to more than ten to the US dollar for a period in 1993, opening up a huge difference with the official rate and pulling almost all transactions into the swap market.

In some respects, economic control collapsed. It was during this period that an image of "Wild West" Chinese capitalism was created, the sense that anything was possible for those with money and influence. Early movers, in a position to take advantage of unprecedented opportunities and lax supervision, established new private fortunes. In Shenzhen, a curious incident occurred when officials pushed out ahead of national policy by establishing a local stock market. Stock prices were soaring along with inflation, and there was huge demand for shares. Local officials decided on a lottery, selling 10 million tickets for 100 RMB each, with each ticket giving a 10 percent chance of buying a share. The gambling aspect only added to the appeal, and a million people lined up the morning of August 10, 1992, but tickets sold out within hours. For forty-eight hours, angry crowds roamed the city, denouncing insider trading and corruption. The following day an additional tranche of 10 million tickets was released, a corruption investigation was announced, and the city gradually calmed down.[61]

Anxiety and uncertainty mounted as inflation rose to a peak in 1994. Coincidentally, the inflation peak was almost identical to that in the fourth quarter of 1988, but this time there were no surviving elders in a position to demand a reform rollback. Zhu Rongji had been brought to Beijing from Shanghai in 1991 as vice premier to manage the economy, and in July 1993 he concurrently became head of the People's Bank of China, the central bank, to strengthen its authority and ability to stand up to local interest groups. Jiang Zemin was able to consolidate his position at the top, with Zhu serving as top economic policy maker, while Premier Li Peng stayed on as a (weakened) counterweight. This created a much more decisive political system, a big change from the dispersed, elder-dominated system of the 1980s, and Zhu was able to take bold economic measures. Even so, inflation remained a serious problem in the background for the next five years, finally dropping below 5 percent in 1997. Steady restraint in credit and monetary policy was indispensable, and relatively tight monetary policy became an essential feature of the market reform measures of the late 1990s. Overall, then, the political outcome of inflation was the opposite of that in 1989: it contributed to the consolidation of a group of market-oriented leaders and to the policy-making breakthrough at the 1993 Third Plenum.

---

[61] Tao and Lu, 中国经济特区史论, pp. 77–8.

Another Third Plenum: A Reform Blueprint for Systematic Reforms

At the Third Plenum of that Central Committee in the fall of 1993 policy makers adopted a resolution that was a blueprint for the next stage of market-oriented reforms.[62] This contrasted sharply with earlier policy making, in which measures had almost always been incremental, and grand reform plans had repeatedly failed to gain traction. Remarkably, no authoritative agency within the government was capable of producing the building blocks of this further stage of reform. Instead, a loose grouping of outside economists produced policy papers for the Party's Economics and Finance Leadership Small Group, which drafted the resolution.[63]

The reform policy debates that had previously divided the economic community now receded: two inflationary episodes, combined with the collapse of most planning instruments, made many previous contentious issues obsolete. Economists now divided their policy recommendations into several functional areas which could be tackled separately, sidestepping the sequencing problems and need for prior macroeconomic stabilization that had dogged the earlier comprehensive reform programs. The year 2000, only seven years distant, was put forward as the target date for the creation of a "nationwide integrated and open market system." The resolution contained fifty articles, the majority of which included a concrete, operational objective. Remarkably, most of these operational goals were achieved. Table 20.2 shows twelve key provisions with an assessment of the extent to which implementation was ultimately achieved. Key milestones are shown. In most cases, implementation was carried out through specific measures that are recognizably those envisioned by the drafting groups.

As Table 20.2 shows, the document contained both broad goals and immediate actions. For the first time, implementation included a substantial role for legislation, including foundational laws on corporations and banks. While immediate legislation was needed to create a market regulatory system, it was recognized that actually building a credible system was a long-term and incremental process. The document was thus a realistic mix of immediate, incremental, and long-term objectives. While earlier programs

---

[62] Communist Party Central Committee, 关于建立社会主义市场经济体制若干问题的决定 (Resolution on Several Issues of Establishing a Socialist Market Economic System) (November 14, 1993) (Beijing, Renmin chubanshe, 1993).

[63] In addition, the independent think tanks patronized by Zhao Ziyang were disbanded after June 1989, while the official think tanks were paralyzed by ideological rectification. Ironically, financial support from the Ford Foundation allowed one cluster of economists to remain active. Chen, 国事忆述; Naughton, *Wu Jinglian*, pp. 251–60.

Table 20.2 Twelve key provisions of the 1993 Resolution on Creating a Market System

Article	Content	Implementation	Milestone
6	Corporatization of large firms, especially state-owned enterprises	Yes, mostly	1994 Company Law
8	New ownership agency for state-owned enterprises	Yes, late and partial	2003 State Asset Commission
9	Diverse ownership economy; public ownership as "mainstay"	Yes	Incremental
11	Prices: market prices, handful of government-set prices	Yes	Immediate
12	Creation of wholesale, retail, and futures market institutions	Yes	Incremental
15	New regulatory agencies for fair market competition	Yes, mostly	Incremental
16	Government functions shift to indirect and regulatory control	Yes, mostly	1998 government re-organization
18	Fiscal: increase revenues; unify and lower tax rates	Yes	1994 fiscal reform
19	Accelerate financial system reform; separate central bank and commercial banks; new development banks	Yes	1995 laws for central, commercial and development banks
22	Macroeconomic control centralized	Yes	1994 fiscal reform and 1998 financial reorganization
23–4	Wages: more flexible wage-setting; greater differentiation	Yes	Incremental
26–8	Create a multilayer system of social security	No, mostly	–

had been broad, vague, and sometimes overly ambitious, this one initiated a multiyear program of market creation and market building.

The other fundamental difference between this reform program and 1980s reform is that this program went forward under the presumption that the central government would be strengthened. The pressure of inflation meant that control over financial institutions should be tightened and centralized, and credit and monetary policy exercised more authoritatively by an empowered central bank. The fiscal power of the state needed to be strengthened since revenue had plummeted as a share of GDP (Figure 20.2). Thus, while in the 1980s the most urgent need had been to begin dismantling an omnipresent command-economy system, by the 1990s the command economy was largely gone, and the challenge to policy makers was to devise more effective instruments, to strengthen the state without reverting to direct controls. Fiscal reform was perhaps the most urgent. The proposed solution was a mixture of tax reform and recentralization. Tax reform involved shifting to lower and more uniform rates. The centerpiece was the value-added tax (VAT), imposed in principle on all forms of economic activity. Income tax rates for enterprises were unified across different ownership types, and a personal income tax introduced.

The most contentious part of fiscal reform was the allocation of new taxes to different levels of government, since this involved recentralizing taxation authority (especially that over the VAT). In fact, the reform was designed so that the central government would take a much larger share than its own expenditure needs, and then redistribute the surplus to local governments. This would obviously give the central government more control, and a much stronger position vis-à-vis the local governments. Having just recently been freed from the shackles imposed during the conservative ascendancy, local officials were understandably reluctant to surrender fiscal resources. Zhu Rongji spent over a month flying to most provincial capitals, jawboning governors and Party secretaries, pressuring them to give up control over their revenues in the national interest. Evoking national crisis, Zhu was ultimately able to prevail.

To be sure, representing the national government, Zhu Rongji had abundant resources with which to achieve the acquiescence of local government officials in this recentralization. The center would guarantee a minimum level of resources for each province, so they would not be worse off in absolute terms. More fundamentally, Zhu was able to offer local officials unprecedented freedom of action to operate more entrepreneurially, especially with respect to land development and investment. A new urban economic system gradually grew from this, in which local governments parlayed their control of urban land into a developmental resource. In the long run, fiscal reform and recentralization achieved a dramatic turning point in the trend of fiscal revenues to GDP (Figure 20.2). Moreover, by putting the national budget on a sustainable foundation, Zhu was able to shift the battle against inflation onto the monetary realm, enabling the gradual control of inflation.

By the late 1990s, China had established the basic infrastructure necessary to run a modern market economy. Some parts of the new system were embryonic. Capital markets in general were underdeveloped, as the Shanghai and Shenzhen stock markets made a modest and wobbly start, and the issuance of corporate bonds was tightly restricted. Overall, though, the pace of institutional construction was extraordinary. The panoply of new institutions established a roughly level playing field, creating conditions under which firms of different ownership forms could compete and co-operate under common rules. China had emerged from the post-Tiananmen chaos with a workable government commitment to market-oriented economic reform, and followed through on this commitment.[64]

The High Tide of Reform

A final stage of heightened reform activity came in 1998–2000. Zhu Rongji took over as premier in 1998 and increasingly put his personal stamp on policy. Real GDP growth had been extraordinary during the 1990s, well over 10 percent annually from 1993 through 1996. However, inflation had also remained high, and, with a sustained effort to control inflation, growth began to slow in 1996 and 1997. Almost as soon as the banking system had been restructured, an effort was made to tighten access to credit by commercial banks, which in turn had no choice but to restrict the flow of credit to enterprises. In essence, a hard budget constraint was being imposed on banks, which passed on that hard budget constraint to the enterprises. Market conditions shifted from chronic excess demand to a relative buyer's market, and firms were put under pressure to reorient their business strategy and become more market-responsive (the shift in inflationary dynamics is

---

[64] From this time, the English-language economic literature expands dramatically and many good overviews are available. A. Kroeber, *China's Economy: What Everyone Needs to Know*, 2nd ed. (Oxford, Oxford University Press, 2020). B. Naughton, *The Chinese Economy: Adaptation and Growth*, 2nd ed. (Cambridge, MA, MIT Press, 2018). L. Brandt and T. Rawski (eds.), *China's Great Economic Transformation* (Cambridge, Cambridge University Press, 2008). J. Wu, *Understanding and Interpreting Chinese Economic Reform*, 2nd ed. (Singapore: Cengage Learning Asia, 2015).

clearly visible in Figure 20.1). Just as market conditions were softening, the unexpected arrival of the Asian financial crisis in the second half of 1997 brought an additional shock. Growth slowed to below 8 percent in 1998 and 1999, and firms were under unprecedented market pressure.

In the event, Zhu decided to allow market forces to push many of the least profitable state-owned enterprises out of business. China never embraced a process of formal privatization, instead adopting a policy to "safeguard the large firms, and let the small firms go" (*zhuada fangxiao* 抓大放小) (officially in 1999). Under the conditions of that time, the most radical part of this policy was certainly "let the small go," since this implied that many small state factories would be allowed to go bankrupt, and others would be quietly acquired by their managers or by emerging entrepreneurs. In essence, small publicly owned firms were left to fend for themselves, put on the same basis as the now legitimated private businesses. "Safeguarding the large," particularly in retrospect, is equally significant: rather than tackling the difficult task of large-firm privatization, policy makers decided to maintain but reorganize the largest state firms, often setting up two or three large state firms in a sector with controlled competition. Total employment in state-controlled industry declined from 45 million in 1992 to 18 million by 2006, with the largest reductions occurring in 1998 through 2003 (Figure 20.3). The pace of "downsizing" was slower in nonindustrial enterprises, but even faster in collective firms, which were predominantly industrial. Overall, urban public-enterprise workers declined from 112.6 million to 52.3 million between 1992 and 2006. The workforce declined by 60.3 million workers, more than half. Industry was transformed: state-owned enterprises (SOEs) accounted for 60 percent of above-scale employment as late as 1998, but only 20 percent by the mid-2000s.[65] This was a profound social shock and there was widespread dissatisfaction. In the industrial northeast, layoffs were the largest, unemployment benefits ran out, and there were large protests. Nationwide, large-scale unrest was avoided and most laid-off workers received some transitional support.

Zhu Rongji also pushed for entry into the World Trade Organization (WTO). The arduous negotiation was finally completed in 1999, and China entered the WTO in December 2001, beginning a three-year phase-in period. WTO membership was seen as being complementary to state-sector reforms. Linking up with global norms and regulations (*jiegui* 接轨) would lock in the

---

[65] National Bureau of Statistics, *China Statistical Yearbook* 2019, Tables 4-3, 13-3, 13-5, combined with earlier years. Figure 20.3 shows employment in large ("above-scale") industrial enterprises. Data adjusted to include state-controlled corporations, as well as traditional SOEs.

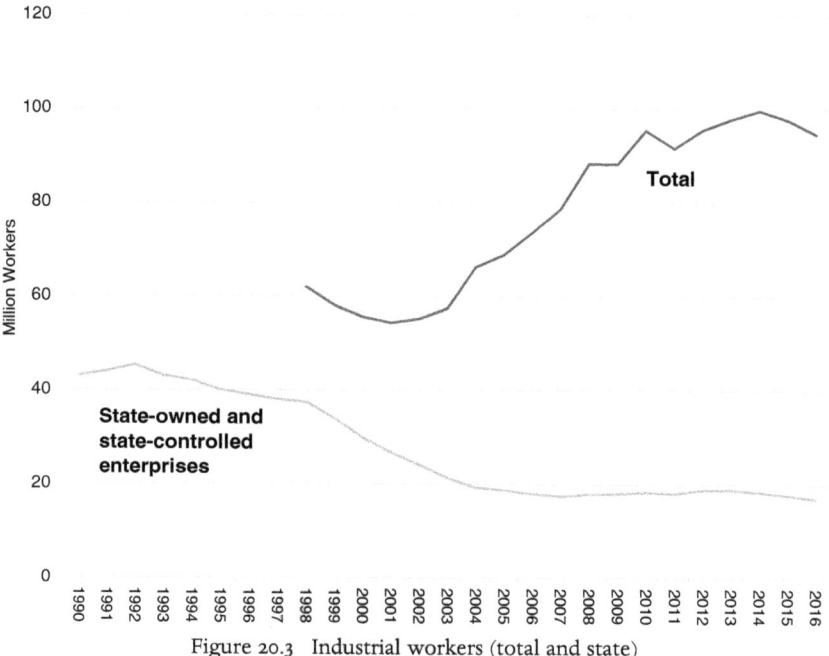

Figure 20.3 Industrial workers (total and state)

reform achievements, strengthen the government's commitment to a new regulatory regime, and, eventually, provide a new source of demand that would speed the economic recovery. Thus, by the time Zhu Rongji reached the end of his term as premier in spring of 2003, a fundamental transformation had been completed. The institutional framework for a market economy had been created, and market forces had shifted the balance of the economy decisively away from the state sector and towards a new, mixed, corporate economy founded on substantial private ownership. The most difficult years of the transformation were over, and China was poised for a new growth acceleration, with the international market playing an enhanced role.

The End of Reform and Post-transition China

As China entered the twenty-first century, demographic conditions began to change rapidly, and it was clear that the end of miracle growth was on the horizon. More surprisingly, after the Hu Jintao–Wen Jiabao leadership succeeded to power in 2002–2003, market-oriented reforms gradually lost momentum. There was no dramatic policy turning point, and most outside observers at the time believed that market-oriented reforms were moving ahead. In retrospect, however, it is clear that the era of reform and opening was winding down.

Broadening of the Policy Agenda

After 2003, the policy agenda steadily expanded. With the fiscal crisis overcome (Figure 20.2), resources were available to finance a more activist approach to government. To start with, that meant finally tackling overdue social issues. Premier Wen Jiabao took a particular interest in rural areas, where the collapse of the collectives had left institutional needs unfilled for twenty years. Increased investment in basic rural education and health care was overdue. However, farmers were already subject to direct taxes and a burdensome system of improvised fees, so the resources could not be raised locally. Wen addressed these problems with urgency: rural taxes and fees were cut, increased fiscal redistribution from higher to local-level governments was introduced, and a program to support universal primary education (through sixth grade) was adopted.[66] Beginning in 2005, a system of rudimentary rural health insurance was rolled out which provided publicly supported access to health care for the overwhelming majority of rural residents. China had exhausted its demographic dividend, and stood on the threshold of an aging society, so efforts to patch up the national social security system took on increasing urgency.

Policy makers now began a search for new drivers of economic growth in the post-"growth miracle" era. High-technology industry moved to the top of the policy agenda, and government-steered industrial policies returned, at first modestly, and then expanded rapidly.[67] When the global financial crisis (GFC) hit, in 2008–2009, these policies were absorbed into a bold stimulus program, which pumped the equivalent of 18 percent of GDP into the economy through both fiscal and credit-based instruments. The perceived success of this program led Premier Wen Jiabao to declare in the aftermath that the "superiority of the socialist system consists in … the ability to concentrate resources to accomplish big things."[68] This emphasis has marked

---

[66] C. Wong, "Rebuilding Government for the 21st Century: Can China Incrementally Reform the Public Sector?", *China Quarterly* 200 (December 2009), 929–52.

[67] L. Chen and B. Naughton, "An Institutionalized Policy-Making Mechanism: China's Return to Techno-industrial Policy," *Research Policy* 45 (2016), 2138–52.

[68] Wen Jiabao, "Report on the Work of the Government (2010)," Third Session of the 11th National People's Congress, March 5, 2010, at www.scio.gov.cn/xwfbh/xwbfbh/wqfbh/2015/20150305/xgbd32605/Document/1395827/1395827.htm.

Chinese policy proclamations ever since. China is far from the fiscal crisis of the early 1990s. In short, China shifted from a political economy in which market-oriented reforms were the focus of policy makers and the prerequisite for solving other problems, to a more "normal" political economy in which competing demands jostled for the attention of policy makers.

Reform Stalls Out

The policies adopted by the Hu–Wen administration were potentially complementary to continued market-oriented reforms, and were generally supported by reform-oriented economists and outside observers like the World Bank. A repaired social safety net and support for domestic innovation would clearly strengthen China's market economy. Nevertheless, gradually the impetus behind market-oriented reform weakened. The year 2005 saw the last unambiguous case of centrally designed market-oriented reforms. In that year, policy makers moved boldly to recapitalize and restructure state commercial banks. Banks were relieved of 1.4 trillion RMB in bad loans (8 percent of 2005 GDP), and then reorganized into corporations. Strategic investors were brought in, and the banks were listed on international stock markets. Designed under the previous administration, this was perhaps the last manifestation of the Zhu Rongji era. By contrast, other apparently ambitious reforms were announced with some fanfare, but then faded away without much effect. A "Program for Capital Market Development" and a "Charter of Private Enterprise Rights" met this common fate.

Indeed, if anything, state firms gained status relative to private firms. A number of prominent private entrepreneurs came under attack, and some were jailed on corruption charges.[69] Following a series of disastrous mine accidents in 2005 and 2006, private coal mines in Shanxi province were renationalized. To be sure, there was no massive rollback of privatization, but the shrinkage of the state sector ground to a halt (Figure 20.3). Overall, the economy continued to grow and diversify, so robust growth of the private sector still took place. Despite widely acknowledged needs for domestic capital market reforms, liberalization of the household registration system, and further fiscal reforms designed to accommodate new social expenditures, no major efforts were mounted. It was not until 2013 – well after this time period – that a new "Third Plenum" made a significant effort to renew reform momentum.

[69] Ma, 交锋三十年.

Why Did Market-Oriented Reform Lose Momentum?

The reasons for the post-2005 slowdown of reform are, strictly speaking, outside the scope of this chapter. Yet three observations may shed light on the dynamics that were in play throughout the reform era. First, reforms have up-front costs, while the benefits appear only after a lag. Reforms of the 1990s ultimately led to an acceleration of growth, as GDP growth rose above 10 percent from 2003 through 2010, notwithstanding the GFC in 2008–2009. This was the final phase of China's miracle growth era. Powering the economy was the explosive post-WTO-entry growth of China's exports, which *tripled* between 2002 and 2006 to almost $1 trillion. Yet, in the lag between policy and benefit, policy makers crafted a response in their own interest, and that response was exactly the opposite of that of the early 1980s. Successful rural reforms then emboldened reformers to push ahead, but equally successful reforms simply induced complacency in the mid-2000s. In the absence of crisis, Chinese policy makers found it difficult to keep the reform process moving ahead. Leaders did not have sufficient motivation to tackle a range of entrenched interests.

Second, a stronger and better-resourced state provided new policy levers that allowed policy makers to achieve a diverse range of objectives as well as more effective direct control. National leaders looked for instruments to implement a range of social, economic, and strategic objectives that no longer depended on market-oriented reform. In the state sector, the recovery of profitability and growth of revenues made control of state firms an attractive proposition, and gave policy makers incentives to block further growth of competition in order to maintain rents. It also became much more attractive to use financially stable state firms to contribute to industrial policy objectives.

Finally, external events matter and the GFC of 2008–2009 had a profound effect. Chinese policy makers interpreted the GFC as severely tarnishing the free-market model exemplified by the US, while their massive stimulus program was welcomed around the world, thus confirming the wisdom of their own state-led policies. Although the reform slowdown clearly pre-dated the GFC, the shock of the GFC thus sealed in the big change in policy orientation and signaled the definitive end to the reform era. By coincidence, the growth rate dropped below 10 percent after 2010, and has continued to decline since. Thus both the reform era and the miracle growth era, born together thirty-two years earlier, came to an end at about the same time.

Conclusion

By the year 2010, the Chinese economy was utterly different from the economy on the eve of reform. It was, of course, much bigger and with higher incomes, and it was also far more diverse and flexible, with much higher skill levels and capabilities. Due to the extraordinary speed of growth, the economy faced new structural challenges that were the inverse of those of 1978. Then the largest challenge had been to quickly develop labor-intensive sectors; by 2010, the need was to accommodate the looming reduction in the size of the labor force, and move into higher-skill goods and services. The one-child policy seemed urgent in 1978, but by 2005 it was widely understood to be hobbling economic development, and it was finally abolished in 2015. As growth inevitably slowed, an entirely new set of policy choices emerged.

For thirty years, reform, opening, and market transition dominated the concerns of policy makers. However, as this chapter has demonstrated, the definition and objective of "reform" were constantly contested, and some groups questioned the need for it altogether. Policy battles over specific reforms were sustained and, at times, fierce. The narrative in which Deng Xiaoping and pragmatic reformers came to power at the Third Plenum and then instituted reforms is hopelessly oversimplified. Indeed, were it not for the extraordinary success of rural reforms, the reform infant might well have been smothered in its crib. Consensus was transitory and rare.

Rather, improvised solutions, remarkable policy entrepreneurs, and hybrid organizations played a critical role throughout. Innovators like Yuan Geng, who put together a peculiar corporate–governmental hybrid early on in the Shekou zone, were essential in driving the process forward. The township and village enterprises were primarily publicly owned, nominally collective enterprises, yet they played a crucial role in introducing market forces and competition. Even the PRS is best seen as an institutional innovation, the outcome of a prolonged negotiation between the powerful state and the farmers, with their long-standing demand for "land to the tillers." These processes of institutional innovation and policy entrepreneurship required support from the top levels as well, leaders who had to provide a protective umbrella and occasional decisive policy interventions. That top-level support came most importantly from Deng Xiaoping, Zhao Ziyang, and Zhu Rongji, three leaders whose role was indispensable.

Yet that fertile symbiosis was surprisingly delicate. It broke down twice in the 1980s, at the end of 1980 and again after June 4, 1989, but was patched up again both times. The precarious nature of the pro-reform ecosystem meant that changes in the distribution of power among the leadership could drive dramatic changes in policy. This was most obvious in 1992–1993, when apparently modest shifts in power led to an unprecedented decisiveness and focus on a broad complex of market-oriented reforms. Thus, while the Chinese political system was broadly continuous during this period, modest changes could drive really big changes in policy making. Most surprisingly, the reform symbiosis fell apart altogether after 2005, when top policy makers became distracted by competing objectives, and local policy entrepreneurs found themselves with much less protection and much less space for experimentation. Despite the astonishing, world-altering success of market-oriented reform, the leadership nonetheless stepped back from further reform policy making. Perhaps this reflects the truism that only in the face of crisis will difficult reforms be enacted that create risk and threaten the benefits of entrenched power holders. After 2005, as China's exports accelerated, the sense of crisis evaporated, and so did the urgency of reform.

Yet until this time, market-oriented reforms were sustained over multiple decades, and, broadly speaking, reforms achieved their main objectives in the end. It is not accidental that this period of sustained reform-oriented policy coincided with China's miracle growth phase. The dynamism and growth potential inherent in the miracle growth phase acted like wind beneath the wings of China's economic reforms. Measures that were taken to liberalize labor-intensive sectors in the early phase – household sidelines, small-scale manufacturing, and urban services, to say nothing of agriculture itself – unlocked productivity at the micro level. Just as important, they enabled the economy to move onto a much more efficient and promising growth path, bringing China's prodigious human resources to bear. This broad truth gave coherence to the inchoate process of reform policy making. Policy makers got quick confirmation that reforms were succeeding, and they were quickly reminded of the imminence of crisis if they did not get the economy onto the right path.

The quick economic response to reforms helped dampen the inevitable fluctuations and dilemmas in the reform process. Reforms face a deep-seated dilemma: reform unleashes new demands immediately, while economic gains are only manifest after many months, or even years. As we have seen in the narrative of China's reforms, these broad forces often played out in a cyclical manner, as new demands disrupted economic equilibrium, causing economic and social tension, and some reform backtracking. Yet with rapid economic responsiveness, and throughout the miracle growth era, policy makers managed to get the reform agenda back on track. This outcome can be ascribed to the challenges that policy makers faced, the sense of crisis, and the ultimate conclusion that only market-oriented reform provided viable answers to the developmental challenges that China faced.

Further Reading

Brandt, L., and T. Rawski (eds.), *China's Great Economic Transformation* (New York, Cambridge University Press, 2008).

Byrd, W.A., *China's Rural Industry: Structure, Development, and Reform* (Washington, DC, World Bank, with Oxford University Press, 1990).

Chen Jinhua 陈锦华, 国事忆述 (The Eventful Years) (Beijing, Zhonggong Dangshi, 2005).

Du Runsheng 杜润生 (ed.), 中国农村改革决策纪实 (A Virtual Record of China's Rural Reform Policy) (Beijing, Zhongyang Wenxian, 1998), pp. 80–97.

Enright, M.J., *Developing China: The Remarkable Impact of Foreign Direct Investment* (Abingdon, Routledge, 2016).

Li Langqing, *Breaking Through: The Birth of China's Opening-up Policy* (Hong Kong, Oxford University Press, 2010).

Naughton, B., *Growing Out of the Plan: Chinese Economic Reform, 1978–1993* (New York, Cambridge University Press, 1995).

Naughton, B., *The Chinese Economy: Adaptation and Growth*, 2nd ed. (Cambridge, MA, MIT Press, 2018).

Qian Y., *How Reform Worked in China: The Transition from Plan to Market* (Cambridge, MA, MIT Press, 2017).

Tao Yitao 陶一桃 and Lü Zhiguo 鲁志国 (eds.), 中国经济特区史论 (A Historical Treatise on China's Special Economic Zones) (Beijing, Shehui Kexue Wenxian, 2008).

Vogel, E., *Deng Xiaoping and the Transformation of China* (Cambridge, MA, Harvard University Press, 2011).

Walter, C., and F.J.T. Howie. *Red Capitalism: The fragile Financial Foundation of China's Extraordinary Rise* (Singapore: Wiley & Sons (Asia), 2011).

Wu Jinglian, *Wu Jinglian: Voice of Reform in China* (ed. Barry Naughton) (Cambridge, MA, MIT Press, 2013).

Yu Guangyuan 于光远, 1978: 我亲历的那次历史大转折 (1978: The Historic Turning Point That I Experienced), reprint ed. (Hong Kong, Tiandi, 2008).

Zhao Ziyang, *Prisoner of the State: The Secret Journal of Premier Zhao Ziyang* (New York, Simon & Schuster, 2009).

21

China's Great Boom as a Historical Process

LOREN BRANDT AND THOMAS G. RAWSKI

Overview

Beginning in the late 1970s, China's economy produced the largest growth spurt in recorded history. This striking departure from the economic experience of the previous 200 years encourages onlookers to view recent economic success as a "miracle" that requires neither economic nor historical explanation. Such thinking ignores common elements that have shaped China's long-term economic trajectory: forces propelling spurts of innovation and growth, restrictions that often impede these dynamic forces, and enduring features of China's polity that generate tensions between centralized authoritarian power and economic growth. Neglect of these historical legacies invites misconceptions about the current boom's origin and the economy's likely future path. History and economics figure prominently in our analysis of both.

China has experienced repeated bursts of innovation and accelerated growth. More than a century before China's recent growth explosion, the opening of coastal treaty ports, largely outside Qing jurisdiction, expanded international and domestic commerce that served as conduits for new technology and ideas. Extension of foreign privilege to include the operation of treaty port factories curtailed domestic opposition to modern manufacturing, opening the door to long-term industrial expansion. During the early decades of the twentieth century, these developments propelled structural change and modern economic growth in two regions – the lower Yangzi area adjacent to Shanghai and the northeast.

The authors, who are entirely responsible for what follows, gratefully acknowledge advice from Debin Ma, Evelyn Rawski, Andrew Batson, Philipp Boeing, Chris Bramall, Jeffrey Guarneri, Lyric Hale, Charles Hayford, Carsten Holz, Ruixue Jia, Wolfgang Keller, Nicholas Lardy, Lillian Li, Stephen Morgan, Andrew Nathan, Kevin O'Rourke, Dorothy Solinger, Jeffrey Williamson, Tim Wright, and Haihui Zhang.

Despite differences in timing, scale, and geographic scope, these episodes share important commonalities. Innovation and growth arise primarily from decentralized initiative rather than state direction. External opening – forced or voluntary – and relaxation of domestic constraints encourage bottom-up development. The opening of nineteenth-century treaty ports and late twentieth-century special economic zones, the post-Mao shift from collective to household farming, and the subsequent expansion of rural industry demonstrate the potential of localized or sectoral innovation to unleash unexpected and momentous consequences.

Episodes of growth acceleration coincide with interludes of state weakness and retreat. The nineteenth-century opening of treaty ports, the imposition of a free-trade regime, and, in 1895, ceding foreigners the right to establish factories on Chinese soil all reflect Qing inability to resist foreign pressure. Official weakness also facilitated financial innovation: "modern banking gathered momentum, particularly through the 1920s, when central authority was at low ebb."[1]

China's current boom began amid extreme state incapacity after the Cultural Revolution had "effectively destroyed" China's "apparatus of civilian rule," left "the legitimacy of the CCP [Chinese Communist Party] ... deeply shaken" and "severely damaged the national bureaucracy, leaving it weak and divided" and rendering Beijing unable to "monitor compliance with many kinds of orders."[2] Temporary withdrawal of central oversight permitted local leaders and groups of households to defy official mandates by reviving and extending short-lived rural reforms begun after the 1959–1960 famine.

Premier Zhu Rongji extended domestic-market liberalization by agreeing to constraints on state economic actions as part of China's 2001 accession to the World Trade Organization (WTO).

The link between political frailty and economic dynamism is no accident. The enduring features of Chinese political regimes – imperial, Republican, and Communist – give rise to powerful tensions between authoritarian control and the bottom-up institutional change, experimentation, and entrepreneurship that foster productivity growth, the core component of long-term economic advance. While Chinese states have become powerful

---

[1] N. Horesh, *Shanghai's Bund and Beyond: British Banks, Banknote Issuance, and Monetary Policy in China, 1842–1937* (New Haven and London, Yale University Press, 2009), p. 41.

[2] A.G. Walder, "Bending the Arc of Chinese History: The Cultural Revolution's Paradoxical Legacy," *China Quarterly* 227 (2016), 617–18; L.T. White III, *Unstately Power: Local Causes of China's Economic Reforms* (Armonk, NY, M.E. Sharpe, 1998).

champions of development, repeated episodes during the past 200 years highlight consistent elite preference for systems that allow rulers to concentrate decision making and appropriate resources in ways that enhance their control but ultimately limit economic advance.

Enduring Features of Chinese Political Regimes

What are these enduring features of the Chinese polity, which John Fairbank described as resting on "ancient structures of social order and political values that are too deep for rapid change?"[3]

The closely intertwined objectives of today's Chinese rulers hardly differ from the goals of Qing emperors. Both seek to maintain stability and regime control, to harness domestic prosperity and advanced technology for military and security purposes, and to match or overtake neighbors and potential rivals.

State structure is equally consistent over time. Power resides in self-perpetuating authoritarian hierarchies. Interlocking sets of economic, social, and political ties that align interests within national elites and between rulers and citizens enhance regime longevity. Checks and balances limiting state action are notably absent. Custom and law promote order and harmony; they legitimate and strengthen, rather than constrain, the state. There is little tolerance for dissent. Official surveillance, nowadays reinforced by electronic technology, identifies violators. Harsh penalties silence all but the most determined critics.

The state promotes ideologies – Confucianism, Chinese variants of Marxism, and, currently, elements of both – that portray the incumbent polity and its leaders as founts of moral authority and bulwarks of stability. Ideological commitment is an important criterion for official appointment. Shared ideology offers a partial substitute for bureaucratic supervision, allowing officials to enjoy wide discretion in governing as long as outcomes satisfy their superiors' expectations.

While severely limiting ordinary citizens' voice in governance, Chinese regimes strive, often successfully, to secure popular support. Meritocratic systems of educational advancement and official recruitment – including the former imperial examinations, the more recent civil service examinations (*guokao* 国考), and the current system of competitive school and college admissions – offer mobility paths that expand regime capability while

---

[3] J.K. Fairbank, "The Unification of China," in R. MacFarquhar and J.K. Fairbank (eds.), *The Cambridge History of China*, vol. 14, *The People's Republic*, part 1, *The Emergence of Revolutionary China, 1949–1965* (Cambridge, Cambridge University Press, 1987), p. 26.

legitimating elite privilege. Censorship, information control, and state monopoly over educational curricula steer public opinion in directions that benefit the incumbent regime.

This system invites widespread investment in scaling finely variegated hierarchies of rank and distinction that bind individuals and groups to the incumbent regime. The People's Republic of China (PRC) has expanded the traditional complex of individual recognition, which now embraces even schoolchildren, and established new award ladders for firms and localities. Today, as under the Qing, these distinctions, as well as promotion through the state's *nomenklatura* system, bring substantial accretions of wealth, prestige, and security.

At every level, power and authority rest on personal patronage networks in which long-term exchanges of money, favors, and loyalty build support for leaders, while offering subordinates a combination of opportunity and protection. Leaders mobilize network supporters – local gentry and merchant guilds under the Qing, multilevel coalitions of like-minded officials under the PRC – to advance their policy agendas. Ambitious leaders need a constant flow of resources to support adherents, enlist new clients, and compete with rivals.

This financial imperative reinforces long-standing elite preference for administrative structures that concentrate decisions in the hands of officials who enjoy wide discretion. Leaders seek personal control over important decisions, in part to facilitate access to continuing resource flows. Personal and network interests figure prominently in official and private choices regarding appointments, promotions, contracts, and institutional arrangements.[4]

Despite episodic enforcement efforts, the culture of gift exchange that permeates these personal networks infuses government systems and elite culture with a comfortable tolerance for bribery. As prime beneficiaries of irregular transactions, Communist elites, like their Qing and Republican predecessors, ignore readily available disciplinary mechanisms: updating land registers in the Qing era or publicizing officials' personal and family assets in today's China. A popular ditty attributed to both Guomindang and Communist leaders cynically portrays corruption as the lifeblood of Party operations: "Fight corruption and destroy the Party, neglect corruption and

---

[4] J. Osburg, *Anxious Wealth: Money and Morality among China's New Rich* (Stanford, Stanford University Press, 2013), offers a granular account of local networking.

destroy the country" (*fanfu wangdang, bufan ze wangguo* 反腐亡党, 不反则亡国).

Injecting network interests into policy formation and public administration imposes costs that extend far beyond informal side payments. Networks stifle competition. Reserving opportunities for insiders excludes interlopers. When external competition does exist, insiders can leverage connections (*guanxi* 关系) to sidestep inconvenient legal or regulatory requirements that rivals cannot avoid. As a result, network involvement transforms apparent market exchanges into landscapes pockmarked with efficiency-sapping barriers and distortions. During the nineteenth century, Shannon Brown finds, a "symbiotic coalition of Chinese merchants, organized in guilds, and government officials – was quite effective in preventing innovation ... [so that] market forces alone could not overcome vested-interest opposition ... even in the transfer of a demonstrably superior technology."[5] Between 2004 and 2012, firms linked to members of China's Politburo obtained land "for less than half the price paid by their unconnected counterparts to obtain land of comparable quality."[6]

These foundations, which have survived the transition from empire to People's Republic, weave authoritarian hierarchy, individual ambition, and personalist networking into a fabric that binds citizens to the state, motivates widespread support for official priorities, and enhances security for both rulers and subjects. Unfortunately, the same structures and mechanisms impose costs that diminish economic performance. Openness to Western technology and ideas, and rebuilding efforts following episodes of state weakness, illustrate the structural tensions between authoritarian control and economic growth.

The Promise and Danger of Openness

While recognizing the need to embrace technological advance as a vehicle for building national strength, elite thinking harbors deep suspicion of the institutional penumbra surrounding Western technology. Wei Yuan 魏源, an early nineteenth-century reformer, supported "the adoption of Western naval hardware and technology" while embracing "ideals, inspiration, and

---

[5] S.R. Brown, "The Ewo Filature: A Study in the Transfer of Technology to China in the 19th Century," *Technology and Culture* 30.3 (1979), 550–68; Brown, "Cakes and Oil: Technology Transfer and Chinese Soybean Processing, 1860–1895," *Comparative Studies in Society and History* 23.3 (1981), 449–63.

[6] T. Chen and J.K.S. Kung, "Busting the 'Princelings': The Campaign against Corruption in China's Primary Land Market," *Quarterly Journal of Economics* 134.1 (2019), 223.

historical traditions [that were] wholly shaped by Yuan and Ming precedents."⁷

Several decades later, Zhang Zhidong 张之洞, a prominent official, popularized this perspective in the epigram 中学为体, 西学为用, meaning that China would *utilize* (*yong* 用) Western technology and devices while retaining its own cultural *essence* (*ti* 体). This formulation reverberates across the centuries, echoing earlier discussion surrounding the importation of Buddhism and prefiguring the embrace of "self-reliance" by both Mao Zedong and Xi Jinping.⁸

Twentieth-century nationalists viewed China's treaty ports "not as spark plugs or vital centers but as malignant tumors."⁹ Such attitudes prompted PRC planners to limit investment in coastal cities and sparked Cultural Revolution attacks on individuals with overseas ties.

Xi Jinping has revived fears that the ideas, attitudes, and institutional arrangements associated with Western technology and thinking threaten the foundations of China's polity. Limiting foreign travel by academics and researchers, removing foreign textbooks from college curricula, and forbidding classroom discussion of specific topics all follow this agenda. His signature "Made in China 2025" initiative, an inward-looking, Soviet-style plan to pursue advanced technology with minimal international involvement, reflects long-standing distrust of the "software" associated with imported technology.

A contrary perspective welcomes the absorption of Western institutions along with advanced technology. As early as 1859, Hong Ren'gan 洪仁玕, a Taiping leader who studied and worked with Christian missionaries before joining the rebels, produced a document that Stephen Platt describes as offering "for the very first time in a Chinese context ... a litany of proposals that ... would become catch-phrases for later Chinese reformers."¹⁰ Hong's admiration for private business, democratic government, impartial news reporting, rule of law, and open trade "entitle him to a place in the front

---

⁷ J.K. Leonard, *Wei Yuan and China's Rediscovery of the Maritime World* (Cambridge, MA, Harvard University Council on East Asian Studies, 1984), pp. 198–9.
⁸ W.T. DeBary, W.T. Chan, and C. Tan (eds.), *Sources of Chinese Tradition*, vol. 2 (New York, Columbia University Press, 1964), p. 82; The Encyclopedia of Buddhism, at https://encyclopediaofbuddhism.org/wiki/Essence-Function.
⁹ R. Murphey, *The Outsiders: The Western Experience in India and China* (Ann Arbor, University of Michigan Press, 1977), p. 228.
¹⁰ S.R. Platt, *Autumn in the Heavenly Kingdom: China, the West, and the Epic Story of the Taiping Civil War* (New York, Knopf, 2012), pp. 59–61. F. Michael, *The Taiping Rebellion: History and Documents*, vol. 3 (Seattle, University of Washington Press, 1966–1971), pp. 751 ff. provides a translation of Hong's proposal.

rank of Chinese who tried ... to commend Western ideas to the attention of their countrymen."[11]

The post-1978 reform era revived support for reduced state control, greater market orientation and increased international openness in opposition to the Mao-era tendency to repress dissent, suffocate private business, suppress market allocation, and minimize global involvement. Strong resistance to liberalizing initiatives obliged reformist Premier Zhao Ziyang to portray policies that gave "full play" to market forces, embraced "the renewed centrality" of foreign economic and technical exchange, and favored the coast as steps toward "the initial stage of socialism" and the achievement of "self-reliance."[12]

In 2013, the CCP Central Committee, seemingly accepting recommendations from a team of Chinese and World Bank researchers,[13] called for an economy "centering on the decisive role of the market in allocating resources ... [and] greatly reducing the government's role in the direct allocation of resources."[14] At the same time, persistent concern over foreign influence triggered fierce pushback.

A 2013 circular, widely cited as "Document 9," cites a litany of "false ideological trends," including democracy, the rule of law, unfettered journalism, and market opening. It excoriates proponents of these heresies for aiming to "gouge an opening through which to infiltrate our ideology" and even "denying the legitimacy of the CCP's long-term political dominance." The authors conclude that allowing "any of these ideas to spread ... will disturb people's existing consensus on important issues."[15]

The Conflicting Objectives of State Rebuilding Efforts

Rebuilding efforts following episodes of governmental weakness reveal the pull of traditional patterns of centralized authoritarian control. While fortifying political power, these initiatives reinforce tensions between political and

---

[11] K.W. So, E.P. Boardman, and C. P'ing, "Hung Jen-Kan, Taiping Prime Minister, 1859–1864," *Harvard Journal of Asiatic Studies* 20.1–2 (1957), 294.

[12] J. Gewirtz, *Unlikely Partners* (Cambridge, MA, Harvard University Press, 2017), pp. 116, 191, 196.

[13] World Bank and Development Research Center of the State Council, PRC, *China 2030* (Washington, DC, World Bank, 2013).

[14] "Decision of the Central Committee of the Communist Party of China on Some Major Issues Concerning Comprehensively Deepening the Reform," January 16, 2014, at china.org.cn/china/third_plenary_session/2014-01/16/content_31212602.htm, accessed October 10, 2017.

[15] "Communique on the Current State of the Ideological Sphere," translation at chinafile.com/document-9-chinafile-translation, accessed March 3, 2021.

economic goals inherent in the structure and operating mechanisms of Chinese political systems. Consider the initial decade of Guomindang leadership and then the PRC rebuilding efforts during the 1990s.

The Guomindang established its Nanjing government in 1927 following a fifteen-year interregnum during which regional military leaders jousted with a succession of weak administrations in Beijing. The Guomindang focused on two objectives: control and development.

Control involved external and internal dimensions. While working to regain tariff autonomy and to abolish foreign concessions, extraterritoriality, and other trappings of the nineteenth-century treaty regime, Nanjing sought to forge a military that could overcome domestic and foreign threats.

The Guomindang also set out to assemble a developmental state. While shortages of time and money, along with military exigencies, hindered implementation, detailed plans and initial achievements in multiple sectors "became available to the Communists, and many planners and technicians joined them ... providing the nucleus for much that the Communists later accomplished."[16]

Conflict between political and economic objectives quickly emerged. Guomindang leaders sought to weaken the bankers and industrialists whose businesses had led the lower Yangzi region's considerable growth achievements. Top officials organized and invested in new companies, which often "did little more than shift commerce from ... private merchants" to politically connected newcomers. The same officials steered official procurement toward these new firms, which they endowed with "special privileges or monopoly powers." To compete, private operators sought partnerships with officials or their relatives.[17] In the mid-1930s, monetary changes and the introduction of a fiat currency relaxed the discipline that China's private banking system had imposed on government spending and borrowing.

Sixty years later, the PRC launched its own rebuilding effort following the near-anarchy of the Cultural Revolution and a decade of decentralized development that further weakened the center. Although PRC leaders, unlike their Guomindang predecessors, faced no external military threat, the shadow of Soviet collapse hovered menacingly in the background.

During the spring of 1989, nationwide urban protests attracted support among government and Party personnel. After the Tiananmen massacre,

---

[16] A.N. Young, *China's Nation-Building Effort 1927–1937: The Financial and Economic Record* (Stanford, Hoover Institution Press, 1971), p. 388.

[17] P.M. Coble Jr., *The Shanghai Capitalists and the Nationalist Government, 1927–1937* (Cambridge, MA, Harvard Council on East Asian Studies, 1980), pp. 221, 232–5, 243–8.

China's leaders struggled to solidify Party cohesion and central authority. Success rested in part on resolving the frustrating imbalance between their ambitious plans and the meager funds at their disposal following "a rapid and dramatic erosion in the traditional tax base" that lowered both the GDP share of government revenues and the center's share of fiscal resources.[18]

To navigate this complex and risk-laden environment, state and Party leaders advanced a policy agenda that combined recentralization and market opening, features that appealed to multiple interest groups and therefore promoted a broad policy consensus. Deng Xiaoping's ringing endorsement of growth electrified the nation. Fiscal and banking reforms reversed the decline in resources available to the center. A succession of policies, including relaxation of controls over labor mobility, state-sector restructuring, tariff reduction, and exchange rate depreciation enlarged the scope of market forces in both domestic and international transactions. Restoration of incentives and expansion of market activity narrowed major gaps that had accumulated within China's sclerotic planned economy: domestic production rose toward potential levels, while rising technology imports extended the economy's production frontier.

As high-speed growth continued, bold measures – privatizing urban housing and many state enterprises and township and village enterprises (TVEs), pushing whole sectors into market competition, dismissing millions of state-sector workers, and ending material allocations – relieved the center of vast fiscal burdens. Rapid growth of exports and of both domestic and foreign investment further enlarged the array of resources subject to central influence.

The center, having enlarged its revenues and shed costly obligations, now possessed ample financial resources to support both domestic and international objectives. The streamlined agenda for the domestic economy focused on expanding infrastructure networks, strengthening a slimmed-down state sector, nurturing "national champions" within the ranks of centrally managed state firms, and absorbing strategic technologies. Growing fiscal capacity, foreign-exchange earnings, and financial resources enabled Beijing to expand overseas aid, outbound investment, Olympic sponsorship, and other efforts to strengthen China's international standing and, by doing so, enhance the regime's domestic legitimacy.

These measures delivered superlative results. Living standards rose. High-speed growth vaulted China into global prominence as an industrial and trade

---

[18] C.P.W. Wong and R. Bird, "China's Fiscal System: A Work in Progress," in L. Brandt and T.G. Rawski (eds.), *China's Great Economic Transformation* (Cambridge, Cambridge University Press, 2008), pp. 431–3.

powerhouse. Success bred confidence, encouraging the Party to relax its grip on daily life.

Beneath the surface, however, these advances rest on structures and mechanisms that recall Guomindang administration during the 1930s and nineteenth-century Self-Strengthening efforts involving official–merchant collaboration (*guandu shangban* 官督商办). Officials direct resources toward firms they can influence – often at the expense of more dynamic alternatives. Loyalty to leaders and responsiveness to official requests determine the selection of managers. Individuals shuttle between corporate and government positions.[19] Webs of personal influence muddle the interests of leaders and firms at every administrative level. Officials routinely commandeer corporate resources to support personal or policy agendas. Their relatives and cronies colonize important businesses. The need to shore up Party structures battered by Cultural Revolution turmoil and frayed by the lure of "plunging into the sea" (*xiahai* 下海) of private business dictated a relaxation of financial discipline to satisfy the expectations of modestly compensated officials and Party functionaries in a society that increasingly measures status in monetary terms.[20]

Under the PRC, the vast reach of state economic influence magnifies the impact of political intervention. After falling through the mid- to late 1990s, the state's share of GDP has remained remarkably constant at 45 percent, with nonfinancial state-owned enterprises (SOEs) consistently accounting for over 20 percent.[21] A succession of SOE mergers has consolidated central control within strategic industry and service sectors. Between 2003 and 2019, central-level enterprise groups under the State-Owned Assets Supervisory Commission (SASAC) fell from 186 to 97, while the number of subsidiaries under these groups nearly doubled and their registered capital increased more than fivefold.[22] The state continues to dominate China's financial system, which has grown rapidly relative to GDP. Much of China's rapidly

---

[19] F. Liu and L.L. Zhang, "Executive Turnover in China's State-Owned Enterprises: Government-Oriented or Market-Oriented?", *China Journal of Accounting Research* 11 (2018), 132–3, give examples of executives shifting between managerial and official posts and note that "most SOE executives" hold administrative ranks that allow them to occupy government positions.

[20] Wage compilations show average 1993 salaries in government and Party organizations lagging behind earnings of workers in high schools, physical education, hotels, warehouses, and construction. See 中国劳动统计年鉴 1994 (China Labor Statistics Yearbook 1994) (Beijing, China Statistics Press, 1994), pp. 109–10.

[21] A. Batson, "The State Never Retreats," *Gavekal Dragonomics*, 1 October 2020, 6–7.

[22] L. Brandt, R. Dai, and X. Zhang, "The Anatomy of China's State-Owned Enterprises," unpublished MS, 2021.

growing overseas foreign direct investment comes from state or state-connected firms.

Following two decades of transition from plan to market, liberalizing reform slowed dramatically after China's 2001 entry into the World Trade Organization. While committing enormous resources to economic development, the Hu Jintao and Xi Jinping administrations have retreated from the market opening, global co-operation, and private initiative largely responsible for China's recent prosperity. Instead, they have promoted state enterprises, top-down decision making, self-reliance, and Party involvement in business management, arrangements that past Chinese experience identifies as potent sources of inefficiency. Pursuing breakthrough innovations rather than more predictable efforts to narrow the gap separating domestic and global production frontiers heightens the risk of disappointing outcomes.

Amid continuing expansion of China's scientific, technological, and organizational capabilities, multiple studies find a steep falloff in productivity growth in the wake of the 2008 financial crisis. Deterioration in this core component of China's economic prospects underlines the continuing tension between the demands of state building and the requirements of economic growth, which we see as an inevitable consequence of the tradition of authoritarian rule to which Chinese elites remain committed.

Nineteenth-Century Developments

Internal and external shocks diminished the power and authority of the nineteenth-century Qing state. Domestic uprisings, most notably the mid-century Taiping Rebellion, drained the imperial treasury and forced the center to rely on provincial gentry to organize and finance regional armies. At the same time, growing foreign pressure, initially from the European powers and subsequently from Japan, undermined Qing sovereignty, resulting in the treaty port system described in James Kung's Chapter 11 of this volume.

Domestic rebellion in which incumbent Han elites supported imperial Manchu rulers in defense of the status quo destroyed cities, turned fertile agrarian regions into wastelands, and created waves of refugees. Foreign incursions, by contrast, injected new technologies and breached trade restrictions, thus encouraging economic growth. Telegraphic communication and steam transport lowered transaction costs and linked domestic and overseas markets. Treaties eliminating trade barriers and limiting taxation of overseas trade created new opportunities for Chinese farmers and consumers. Transit passes intended to exempt foreign goods from internal taxes intensified domestic competition by permitting Chinese merchants to avoid transit taxes and other restrictions on internal trade.[23] High domestic interest rates encouraged foreign banks and mercantile houses to inject new funds into China's capital-scarce economy, lowering the cost of financing business within the treaty ports and along major commercial routes linked to overseas trade.[24]

The creation of semi-autonomous treaty ports unleashed a flood of innovation, especially in Shanghai, which anticipated Shenzhen's contemporary role as a magnet for ambitious and entrepreneurial migrants, an entry port for new ideas, and a hotbed of institutional innovation.[25] The relative obscurity of both locales – Shanghai as a county seat, Shenzhen as a sleepy village – limited the capacity of conservative elites – degree-holding gentry in nineteenth-century Shanghai, advocates of state-owned enterprise in late twentieth-century Shenzhen – to obstruct innovation. In both instances, local economic dynamism prompted competitive reactions elsewhere: self-initiated open ports under the Qing,[26] multiplication of special economic zones in the PRC, and relaxation of restrictions on entry and competition in both systems.

Despite their differing economic consequences, internal and external challenges to Qing rule were mutually reinforcing. Domestic turbulence limited the capacity of the Qing state to resist foreign incursions. Foreign-controlled schools, newspapers, and publishers quickly transformed Shanghai and other foreign-controlled locales into transmission belts for new ideas, technologies, and institutional arrangements.[27] The Taiping leadership, for example, included men who had lived, worked, and studied in Hong Kong, ceded to Great Britain in 1842.

This double-barreled assault on the Qing imperium opened new channels of mobility entirely separate from the long-standing paths of academic examination and mercantile degree purchase.[28] The desperate struggle to subdue the Taipings established military success as an alternate route to high

---

[23] E. Motono, *Conflict and Cooperation in Sino-British Business, 1860–1911: The Impact of the Pro-British Commercial Network in Shanghai* (New York, St. Martin's Press, 2000).

[24] Y.P. Hao, *The Commercial Revolution in Nineteenth-Century China: The Rise of Sino-Western Mercantile Capitalism* (Berkeley, University of California Press, 1986), pp. 106–10, 345.

[25] R.X. Jia, "The Legacies of Forced Freedom: China's Treaty Ports," *Review of Economics and Statistics* 96.4 (2014), 596–608.

[26] Kung, Chapter 11 in this volume.   [27] Kung, Chapter 11 in this volume.

[28] E. Kaske, "Fund-Raising Wars: Office Selling and Interprovincial Finance in Nineteenth-Century China," *Harvard Journal of Asiatic Studies* 71.1 (2011), 69–141, documents the growing sale of both degrees and offices.

office for men with little academic distinction.[29] "Modern" schools in Hong Kong and various treaty ports produced cosmopolitan graduates whose technical knowledge, language skills, and business acumen marked them as indispensable allies of the provincial magnates whose defeat of the Taipings thrust them into national prominence.

These developments initiated a gradual rise in the economic payoff to "modern" relative to Confucian education.[30] As change spread beyond the treaty ports to encompass new activities like railways, elite families began to withdraw their sons from traditional schooling. The resulting erosion in a key bulwark of the imperial system accelerated when China's crushing defeat in the 1894–1895 Sino-Japanese War, followed in 1900 by the rout of antiforeign Boxer militias at the hands of a Western military expedition, forced traditional elites to recognize the inevitability of sweeping change.

Notwithstanding the dynasty's ignominious collapse following decades of directionless economic fluctuation, the century's closing decades substantially enhanced China's longer-term potential for economic advance. Telegraphic communication, along with steam and rail transport, rested on solid beachheads.[31] Expanded access to modern education, along with the multiplication of information flows, produced a considerable group of prosperous, cosmopolitan, often Western-educated elites.[32] Domestic opposition to Chinese-owned factories crumbled after the Treaty of Shimonoseki allowed Japanese nationals and, thanks to most-favored-nation treaty provisions, other foreigners to enter manufacturing. As with international trade and domestic commerce, privileges won through foreign military pressure encouraged domestic economic growth.

Beginning around 1900, a "wave of scientific translations [most] from Japanese sources" broadcast new knowledge.[33] Conservative resistance to

---

[29] J.W. Esherick, *Ancestral Leaves: A Family Journey through Chinese History* (Berkeley, University of California Press, 2011), pp. 67–8; D.R. Reynolds with C.T. Reynolds, *East Meets East: Chinese Discover the Modern World in Japan, 1854–1898* (Ann Arbor, Association for Asian Studies, 2014), pp. 8, 229.

[30] N. Yuchtman, "Teaching to the Tests: An Economic Analysis of Traditional and Modern Education in Late Imperial and Republican China," *Explorations in Economic History* 63 (2017), 70–90.

[31] R. Thompson, "The Wire: Progress, Paradox, and Disaster in the Strategic Networking of China, 1881–1901," *Frontiers of History in China* 10.3 (2015), 395–427.

[32] Y.P. Hao, *The Comprador in Nineteenth Century China: Bridge between East and West* (Cambridge, MA, Harvard University Press, 1970), p. 102, for example, places the number of current and former compradors at 20,000 by 1900.

[33] D. Wright, "Yan Fu and the Tasks of the Translator," in M. Lackner, I. Amelung, and J. Kurz (eds.), *New Terms for New Ideas: Western Knowledge and Lexical Change in Late Imperial China* (Leiden: Brill, 2001), p. 235.

imported technologies, factory industry, and modern education diminished. By 1911, China's economy and society were far more open to competition and change than in 1800 or 1850. The Guangxu Emperor's 1893 edicts ordering officials to halt the prior practice of seizing assets from returning overseas migrants illustrates this growing openness.[34] The farm sector, although far from dynamic, comfortably supported growing urban and nonagricultural populations in the lower Yangzi and Lingnan regions.

Despite these gains, substantial obstacles continued to restrict China's growth prospects. Modernizing advances remained local rather than regional or national. The state, a key link in all latecomers to modernization, remained weak and unfocused. In the late 1880s, "the Japanese government's published annual budget was a matter of amazement to many Chinese."[35] Writing in 1897, William Mayers described the operation of China's central government as "registering and checking the actions of various provincial administrations [rather] than ... assuming a direct initiative in the conduct of affairs."[36] Even for the management of currency, "the Board of Revenue couldn't be the source of a coherent monetary policy. It had no power to inspect the quality of provincial coins ... [and] could comment on provincial memorials [to the throne] only if they were referred to the Board."[37]

The Republican Period

A tumultuous interregnum that began and ended with regime change, China's Republican era (1912–1949) witnessed extremes of political instability, cultural ferment, and openness to international exchange, along with modest economic growth, considerable expansion of state capability, and the emergence of trends that foreshadowed future developments.

Following the Qing collapse, a succession of republicans, monarchists, and military leaders failed to restore political unity. The Nanjing-based Nationalist administration under Chiang Kai-shek (Jiang Jieshi) won international recognition following the successful Northern Expedition (1927). Its sphere of actual control, however, was less than complete even before

---

[34] M.R. Godley, *The Mandarin-Capitalists from Nanyang: Overseas Chinese Enterprise in the Modernisation of China 1893–1911* (Cambridge, Cambridge University Press, 1981), pp. 240–1.
[35] Reynolds and Reynolds, *East Meets East*, p. 341.
[36] Quoted in F.H.H. King, *A Concise Economic History of Modern China (1840–1961)* (New York, Praeger, 1969), pp. 21–2.
[37] King, *A Concise Economic History of Modern China*, p. 34.

Japanese armies forced the shift of its capital to Wuhan and later to Chongqing.

Chinese elites, shaken by humiliating military setbacks and the Qing collapse, plunged into an intense and disputatious search for cultural renewal. Elite gentrymen who had formerly met modern innovations with visceral hostility now invested in railways and joined newly established chambers of commerce. Radical ideas, fostered in treaty port schools and championed by students returning from overseas studies, leapt to the fore. As Chapter 14 in this volume by Gao, Van Leeuwen, and Wang shows, new subjects, textbooks, and ideas spread far beyond coastal enclaves. Newspapers and radio broadcasts amplified the circulation of novelty.[38] In distant Shanxi, a school principal reprimanded a traditionally educated teacher who encouraged students to celebrate the lunar New Year.[39] Hu Shi (1891–1962), a Cornell University graduate and future Chinese ambassador to the United States, cruelly mocked the ignorance of ordinary folk.[40]

Elite preference for authoritarian politics survived this intellectual turmoil. Early English–Chinese dictionaries rendered "democracy" as "disorderly administration by the many" and "abuse of power by the mean."[41] A 1903 visit to North America convinced the influential reformer Liang Qichao that "resort to rule by ... majority ... would be the same as committing national suicide ... the Chinese people must for now accept authoritarian rule."[42] Nearly a century later, Andrew Nathan observes that most Chinese intellectuals, including opponents of the Communist Party's political monopoly, continue to "fear the disorder they believe would flow from any weakening of party control ... [and] accept the party's claim that political order ... requires leaders with strong authority."[43]

The inflow of new ideas reflected a general climate of openness. China's share of global trade rose from 1.3 percent in 1913 to 2.1–2.3 percent during 1927–1929 and 3.7 percent in 1936; comparable PRC figures languished below 1 percent

---

[38] W.H. Yeh, *Shanghai Splendor: Economic Sentiments and the Making of Modern China, 1843–1949* (Berkeley, University of California Press, 2007), p. 34.

[39] H. Harrison, *The Man Awakened from Dreams: One Man's Life in a North China Village 1857–1942* (Stanford, Stanford University Press, 2005), p. 97.

[40] *Chabuduo xiansheng* 差不多先生 (Mr. Close-Enough), available at https://zh.m.wikisource.org/zh-hans/%E5%B7%AE%E4%B8%8D%E5%A4%9A%E5%85%88%E7%94%9F%E5%82%B3.

[41] G.T. Jin and Q.F. Liu, "From 'Republicanism' to 'Democracy': China's Selective Adoption and Reconstruction of Modern Western Political Concepts (1840–1924)," *History of Political Thought* 26.3 (2005), 479–80.

[42] A.J. Nathan, *Chinese Democracy* (Berkeley, University of California Press, 1986), p. 60.

[43] Nathan, *Chinese Democracy*, p. 231.

throughout 1968–1980, regaining the 1936 level only after the year 2000.[44] Throughout the early twentieth century, China was also a major beneficiary of foreign direct investment, much of it from advanced countries. By the 1930s, China held more than 10 percent of the global stock of inbound foreign direct investment and over 15 percent of the stock located in developing nations, with the largest portion directed toward (mostly rail) transportation.[45]

Openness strengthened the economy, particularly in coastal regions where modern education, returned overseas students and migrants, and frequent interaction with foreign business stoked the transfer of technologies and the spread of commercial knowledge among would-be Chinese entrepreneurs. The history of numerous industries, among them mining, railways, banking, department stores, textiles, and matches, reflects this beneficial mélange.[46]

While limited growth of fiscal revenue, much of it immediately needed for the military, signaled the continuing restriction on governmental development efforts,[47] comparing the Nanjing decade (1927–1937) with circumstances in 1880 or 1910 highlights major expansion of the state's capacity to formulate and implement effective development programs.

Unlike its imperial and Republican predecessors, the Nanjing-based Guomindang administration pursued a well-defined economic agenda centered on revenue expansion; extending control over banking, finance, and the monetary system; developing military-linked production; deepening regional and national economic integration; and building an officially directed education system.

Public administration no longer resembled the Qing Board of Revenue, which acted as a "transmission center of documents and repository for ledgers ... [that] rarely initiated policy."[48] Central government agencies, ranging from the National Resources Commission and the Ministry of Finance to the Cotton Control Commission, their staffs now bolstered by highly trained professionals, many with advanced overseas degrees, designed and began to implement a wide array of economic-policy endeavors.[49]

---

[44] See the online appendix at www.cambridge.org/EconomicHistoryChina.
[45] See the online appendix at www.cambridge.org/EconomicHistoryChina.
[46] Among many others, see S. Cochran, *Big Business in China: Sino-Foreign Rivalry in the Cigarette Industry, 1890–1930* (Cambridge, MA, Harvard University Press, 1980); and E. Köll, *Railroads and the Transformation of China* (Cambridge, MA, Harvard University Press, 2019).
[47] T.G. Rawski, *Economic Growth in Prewar China* (Berkeley, University of California Press, 1989), pp. 12–32.
[48] M.B. Kwan, *The Salt Merchants of Tianjin* (Honolulu, University of Hawaii Press, 2001), p. 32.
[49] W.C. Kirby, "Engineering China: Birth of the Developmental State, 1928–1937," in W. H. Yeh (ed.), *Becoming Chinese: Passages to Modernity and Beyond* (Berkeley, University of

Although the absence of political unification, rifts within the central administration, budgetary weakness, and growing military pressure limited progress, even critics chronicle advances such as the "successful work of the National Economic Council ... in improving the production of silk, cotton, and tea."[50] Beyond Nanjing, provincial governments and educational institutions initiated a variety of projects intended to distribute superior wheat seeds, control silkworm egg disease, improve tea garden management, upgrade equipment for handloom weavers, and so on.[51]

Political disunity did not preclude long-term policy co-ordination, in which "different levels of government, regardless of ... political fragmentation, closely interacted" to advance shared objectives. Remarkably, by "1926, prison reform across the country was impressive enough" to merit "a positive assessment by a traveling committee of the [thirteen-country] Commission on Extraterritoriality in China," which advised that "extraterritoriality might be abolished by foreign powers."[52]

Political fragmentation and Japanese military pressure notwithstanding, domestic and international openness, expansion of new skills and capabilities, declining resistance to new technologies and ideas, and growing public sector support contributed to modest but significant economic expansion and structural change during the decades preceding the outbreak of full-scale war in 1937. Two regions experienced the full array of developments associated with modern economic growth. Chinese entrepreneurship powered growth in the Shanghai-centered lower Yangzi area, with a population of 60 million, matching Japan's. In the northeastern region of Manchuria, populated by over 30 million, foreign investment, much of it from semiofficial Japanese companies, led a broad-based expansion. In both areas, growth of aggregate and per capita output during the prewar decades approached or exceeded Japan's.[53]

California Press, 2000), pp. 137–60; M. Zanasi, *Saving the Nation: Economic Modernity in Republican China* (Chicago, The University of Chicago Press, 2006).

[50] L.E. Eastman, *The Abortive Revolution: China under Nationalist Rule, 1927–1937* (Cambridge, MA, Harvard University Press, 1974), p. 219.

[51] T.H. Shen, "First Attempts to Transform Chinese Agriculture, 1927–1937," in P.K.T. Sih (ed.), *The Strenuous Decade: China's Nation-Building Efforts, 1927–1937* (New York, St. John's University Press, 1979), p. 220; L.M. Li, *China's Silk Trade: Traditional Industry in the Modern World, 1842–1937* (Cambridge, MA, Harvard University Council on East Asian Studies, 1981), pp. 188–96; R. Gardella, *Harvesting Mountains: Fujian and the China Tea Trade, 1757–1937* (Berkeley, University of California Press, 1994), pp. 146–69.

[52] F. Dikötter, *The Age of Openness: China before Mao* (Hong Kong, Hong Kong University Press, 2008), p. 15.

[53] D.B. Ma, "Economic Growth in the Lower Yangzi Region of China, 1911–1937: A Quantitative and Historical Analysis," *Journal of Economic History* 68.2 (2008), 355–92; K. Chao, *The Economic Development of Manchuria: The Rise of a Frontier Economy* (Ann

A small but dynamic modern sector led the way in both regions, with the pace of industrial growth exceeding comparable figures for Japan, India, and Russia/the USSR during the prewar decades.[54] Although foreign firms benefited from a head start, favorable treaty provisions, and superior access to capital, Chinese-owned firms offered powerful competition: by 1933, they contributed 73 percent of nationwide manufacturing output and 78 percent in China proper.[55]

The expansion of manufacturing, with textiles and food processing in the forefront, enlarged demand for cotton and wheat. Factory interests complemented official efforts to improve rural storage facilities, promote standardized crops, and expand rural credit.[56] Transport improvements, along with a monetary revolution that substituted paper notes issued by private banks that were freely convertible to silver for unwieldy silver coins and bullion, reduced transaction costs, magnifying the spread effects of urban-based growth.[57] Rising per capita incomes may have extended beyond the coastal cities and their rural hinterlands to encompass the entire economy.[58]

While the quantitative dimensions of nationwide growth remain uncertain, two decades of Guomindang rule introduced distinctive changes that prefigured important elements of PRC economic structure, institutions, and policy. State management displaced private control in banking and in important segments of manufacturing. Industrial expansion began to shift toward military-linked producer industries even before 1937. Wartime pressures intensified these trends and widened the geographic dispersion of industrial activity.[59]

Arbor, Michigan Papers in Chinese Studies, 1983), pp. 14–15; R. Minami and F. Makino, *Asian Historical Statistics 3: China* (Tokyo: Tōyō Keizai Shinpōsha, 2014), pp. 515–16.

[54] L. Brandt, D.B. Ma, and T.G. Rawski, "Industrialization in China," in K.H. O'Rourke and J.G. Williamson (eds.), *The Spread of Modern Industry to the Global Periphery since 1871* (Oxford, Oxford University Press, 2017), p. 199.

[55] Brandt, Ma, and Rawski, "Industrialization in China," p. 208; and Rawski, *Economic Growth*, p. 74.

[56] Zanasi, *Saving the Nation*, focuses on cotton improvement.

[57] Rawski, *Economic Growth*, Chapters 3, 4; D.B. Ma, "Financial Revolution in Republican China during 1900–37: A Survey and a New Interpretation," *Australian Economic History Review* 59.3 (2019), 242–62.

[58] Rawski, *Economic Growth*, p. 342, concludes that nationwide per capita output rose by 22 to 24 percent between 1914–1918 and 1931–1936. This conclusion, however, rests on estimates of agricultural output trends, which require considerable error margins.

[59] Brandt, Ma, and Rawski, "Industrialization in China," pp. 209–12. P. Schran, *Guerrilla Economy: The Development of the Shensi–Kansu–Ninghsia Border Region, 1937–1945* (Albany, State University of New York Press, 1976), p. 153, cites contemporary accounts indicating that armaments production in the Communists' Shaanxi base area represented "crude work" that turned out limited quantities of "inferior arms."

While government operations reflected the efforts of "the Guomindang elite ... to reform China's administrative bureaucracy by adopting and adapting American theories of public administration,"[60] policy objectives and industrial organization converged toward the preferences of the post-1949 PRC administration. The organization and even the terminology (*danwei* 单位) developed around state-owned industrial firms in wartime China remain in daily use eighty years later.[61] William Kirby describes the Guomindang's prewar efforts as the "birth of the developmental state," and notes that, following the emergence of the PRC, the Nanjing regime's "main industrial planning committee did not disband ... [but] simply reported to a new government."[62] Guomindang determination to subordinate banking to the financial requirements of the ruling government and party and to limit the scope of independent action on the part of leading enterprises, business owners, and corporate managers foreshadows government–business relations in today's China.[63]

The Guomindang years also witnessed a dramatic change in economic ideology. Although many prominent officials and researchers – among them T.V. Soong, H.H. Kung, Franklin Lien Ho, and H.D. Fong – boasted economics degrees from prominent US universities, expert opinion turned against market outcomes. A 1941 account noted that "the urgent need for creating a planned economic system has almost become a consensus both within and outside the government." A review of 574 essays published between 1938 and 1944 in "a leading economic journal" found "'unanimous agreement' on the desirability of creating a planned economic system in China."[64]

The Era of the Planned Economy

The establishment of the People's Republic in 1949 ended a century marked by multiple episodes of warfare, regime change, and monetary chaos that severely limited economic growth. The new government installed a Soviet-

---

[60] M.L. Bian, "Building State Structure: Guomindang Institutional Rationalization during the Sino-Japanese War, 1937–1945," *Modern China* 31.1 (2005), 38.
[61] Bian, "Building State Structure," 66.
[62] Kirby, "Engineering China," 137; W.C. Kirby, "Continuity and Change in Modern China: Economic Planning on the Mainland and on Taiwan, 1943–1958," *Australian Journal of Chinese Affairs* 24 (1990), 135. After severing China's northeast region and establishing Manchukuo as a separate state, the Japanese authorities developed a Soviet-style five-year plan for 1937–42; see Minami Manshū tetsudō kabushiki kaisha chōsakai 南滿洲鐵道株式會社調查課 (ed.), 滿州五カ年計画概要 (Summary of Manchukuo's Five-Year Plan) (Dairen, 1937).
[63] Coble, *Shanghai Capitalists*. [64] Bian, "Building State Structure," 60.

inspired plan system that governed China's economy for three turbulent decades.

Rapid Removal of Long-Standing Constraints on Growth

Firm nationwide political control, reinforced by universal presence of Communist Party branches, provided the new government with an unprecedented capacity to implement policy even at the village level with minimal reliance on unofficial intermediaries. Sweeping and often violent campaigns stifled potential resistance from landed and mercantile interests.

Fiscal expansion demonstrated the new regime's control. The ratio of government revenue to GDP, which had languished below 10 percent for centuries, exceeded 20 percent throughout the planned-economy period.[65] Growth initiatives benefited from political unity, the cessation of internal warfare, and the return of monetary stability following destructive wartime hyperinflation.

Beginning in 1953, a succession of five-year plans pushed investment to new heights. Focusing on upstream sectors linked to industrial expansion and military hardware, new developments extended trends established during the Guomindang regime's final decade.[66] Support from the Soviet bloc, which provided the largest ever transfer of technology along with technical advice and short-term loans, facilitated the emergence of new industries. Soviet support clustered around 150 major projects, which absorbed nearly one-fifth of overall investment spending under the First Five-Year Plan (1953–7).[67]

These plans combined the expansion and upgrading of production capabilities with major investments in human resources. Local governments worked to universalize primary-school enrollment. Literacy and vocational programs improved adult skills. Publishing houses distributed cheap technical manuals. Despite limited food supplies during and after the 1959–1961 Great Leap Famine, improvements in sanitation, nationwide immunization programs, and campaigns to improve maternal and infant health reduced mortality rates and increased life expectancy.[68]

---

[65] *China Compendium of Statistics 1949–2008* (Beijing, China Statistics Press, 2010), pp. 9, 18.
[66] Brandt, Ma, and Rawski, "Industrialization in China," 199–200, 209–12.
[67] Z.K. Dong 董志凯 and J. Wu 吴江, 新中国工业的奠基石 156项建设研究 (1950–2000) (Foundations of New China's Industry: A Study of 156 Projects (1950–2000)) (Guangzhou: Guangdong jingji chubanshe, 2004), p. 333; and Guojia tongjiju gudingzichan touzi tongjisi 国家统计局固定资产投资统计司 (ed.), 1950–1985 中国固定资产投资统计资料 (Statistical Materials on China's Fixed Asset Investment, 1950–1985) (Beijing, China Statistics Press, 1987), p. 50.
[68] R. Hayhoe (ed.), *Contemporary Chinese Education* (Armonk, NY, M.E. Sharpe, 1984); D. M. Lampton, *Health, Conflict and the Chinese Political System* (Ann Arbor, Michigan Papers in Chinese Studies, 1974); K.S. Babiarz, K. Eggleston, G. Miller, and Q. Zhang,

Economic Outcomes: Growth, Incomes, and Productivity

Notwithstanding setbacks from the 1959–1961 famine and, on a lesser scale, from the Cultural Revolution, GDP expanded briskly, with industry occupying a growing share of total output. China's growth exceeded results in other large, low-income nations, with real per capita output growing at an estimated annual rate of 1.8–2.3 percent, which cumulates to a rise of 60 to 82 percent between 1952 and 1978.[69]

This growth, however, occurred primarily at the extensive margin, with expansion powered by rising investment. Three decades of planning failed to deliver productivity growth – the central ingredient in sustained economic modernization. At the aggregate level, Perkins and Rawski find positive annual growth of total factor productivity (TFP) during 1952–1957,[70] after which the trend turns negative, with an average annual decline of 0.5 percent during 1957–1978.[71] Sectoral studies show consistently poor productivity results. For industry, authors whose work produces the most favorable outcomes find the small increases during 1957–1978 "disappointing both in comparative terms and in relation to the massive injections of technology and human capital characteristic of Chinese industrial development."[72] Two careful studies of plan-era agriculture arrive at similar outcomes: decline or small gain during 1952–1957, long-term decline thereafter.[73]

In the absence of productivity growth, the rising share of investment in overall expenditure restricted consumption opportunities, especially for the

---

"An Exploration of China's Mortality Decline under Mao: A Provincial Analysis, 1950–80," *Population Studies* 69.1 (2015), 39–56; A.L. Piazza, *Food Consumption and Nutritional Status in the PRC* (Boulder, Westview Press, 1986).

[69] D. Morawetz, *Twenty-Five Years of Economic Development, 1950 to 1975* (Baltimore, Johns Hopkins University Press, 1977), p. 5; per capita income estimates, both in international dollars, from Penn World Tables, v. 9.1, accessed June 23, 2020, and from A. Maddison, *Chinese Economic Performance in the Long Run* (Paris, OECD, 1998), p. 40.

[70] TFP is the quotient of separate indexes of output (usually GDP or value-added) and a combined input measure. Rising (falling) TFP reflects increases (reductions) in average output per unit of combined capital, labor, and materials.

[71] D.H. Perkins and T.G. Rawski, "Forecasting China's Economic Growth over the Next Two Decades," in Brandt and Rawski (eds.), *China's Great Economic Transformation*, p. 839.

[72] K. Chen, G.H. Jefferson, T.G. Rawski, H.C. Wang, and Y.X. Zheng, "Productivity Change in Chinese Industry, 1953–1985," *Journal of Comparative Economics* 12 (1988), 587; see also R.M. Field, "Slow Growth of Labour Productivity in Chinese Industry, 1952–81," *China Quarterly* 96 (1983), 641–64.

[73] S.G. Fan and X.B. Zhang, "Production and Productivity Growth in Chinese Agriculture: New National and Regional Measures," *Economic Development and Cultural Change* 50.4 (2002), 833; A.M. Tang, "Food and Agriculture in China: Trends and Projections, 1952–77 and 2000," in A.M. Tang and B. Stone, *Food Production in the People's Republic of China* (Washington, DC, International Food Policy Research Institute, 1980), p. 28, using his adjusted TFP measure.

80 to 85 percent living in the countryside. Nicholas Lardy finds, "Except for a few years ... average per capita food consumption [between 1949 and the late 1970s] ... does not appear to have reached the prewar level."[74] Urbanites, most employed in the state sector, received benefits denied to villagers: employment security, pensions, and subsidized food, health care, housing, education, and transport. The historically modest gap between urban and rural living standards – Charles Roll places per capita rural consumption at "about 81–88" percent of the urban average during the 1930s and "approximately the same" in 1955 – subsequently widened dramatically.[75] Yang and Zhou cite a National Bureau of Statistics working paper showing that urban per capita incomes in 1980 were more than triple the rural average.[76] Mobility restrictions and food rationing protected higher urban living standards by limiting migration into the cities.

Explaining Productivity Stagnation

The PRC's plan system ramped up investment outlays, but the new regime created distortions and inefficiencies that completely offset anticipated productivity benefits arising from national unity, monetary stability, strong government, growth-oriented policies, new technology, and improved human capabilities. Why did three decades of economic planning fail to deliver the anticipated material benefits?

The new system severely curtailed the engines of prewar growth: private entrepreneurship, commercial competition, and market integration that allowed growing circulation of commodities, information, capital, technology, and individuals within and across China's national boundaries. The planned economy's crude instruments – state-owned enterprises, inflexible prices, and government-mandated production quotas, supply links, investment projects, and job assignments – sufficed for fulfillment of official targets, but only at the cost of creating large pools of underutilized resources.

The planned economy's corrosive effect on individual incentives was particularly damaging to the rural economy. The collectivization of agriculture frayed the connection between personal effort and reward for three-quarters of China's workforce. This encouraged widespread shirking, as

---

[74] Nicholas Lardy, "Food Consumption in the People's Republic of China," in R. Barker and R. Sinha (eds.), *The Chinese Agricultural Economy* (Boulder, Westview Press, 1982), p. 159.
[75] C.R. Roll Jr., *The Distribution of Rural Incomes in China: A Comparison of the 1930s and 1950s* (New York, Garland, 1980), p. 124.
[76] D.T. Yang and H. Zhou, "Rural–Urban Disparity and Sectoral Labour Allocation in China," *Journal of Development Studies* 35.3 (1999), 112.

individuals and households diverted resources toward private plots, which, beginning in 1958, occupied less than 10 percent of cultivated acreage. A Guangdong team leader explained, "People aren't lazy all the time, just when they do collective labor. When they work on their private plots, they work hard," adding that a task that formerly required six man-days of household labor might consume sixteen man-days of collective effort.[77]

Incentive problems also limited industrial advance. Socialist planning, discussed at length in Chapter 16 in this volume by Dwight Perkins, imposed a framework of rigid prices, mandated production quotas, and state control over the distribution of materials as well as intermediate and final products. This system generates a panoply of dysfunctional responses observed in all centrally planned economies. Neither firms nor individual workers benefit from exceeding minimum requirements. Improvements in cost, product quality, or customer service become uncompensated gifts to buyers or to the state, which absorbs all profits. Factory managers prioritize physical output targets at the expense of quality, cost, and customer service.

Unprecedented Gap between Actual and Potential Output

Divergence between rising capabilities and stagnant productivity signaled an unprecedented gap between actual production and the level of output that existing resources, technologies, and skills could deliver. The unexpected growth explosion following the onset of reform in the late 1970s illuminates the enormous scale of this latent potential. We focus on three areas: trade, agriculture, and industry.

Latent Potential in International and Domestic Exchange

Except for the transfer of Soviet technology during the 1950s, China's plan-era economic strategy promoted self-reliance at the expense of participation in domestic and international commerce. While a US-led boycott limited China's global trade options, all restrictions on domestic commerce and much of China's international isolation reflected the commitment of China's leaders to self-reliance and local self-sufficiency. Hostility to foreign involvement terminated China's prewar standing as a substantial recipient of overseas investment. Curtailment of fruitful opportunities for domestic and international exchange imposed major economic costs.

---

[77] S.W. Mosher, *Broken Earth: The Rural Chinese* (New York, The Free Press, 1983), pp. 39–40.

During China's absence from active engagement with global trade and investment, which extended for nearly fifty years from 1937, rising post-World War II direct investment from advanced nations, steep reduction in transaction costs, and major increases in trade flows, including exports of labor-intensive manufactures from low-income countries, offered opportunities that China ignored. China's long withdrawal from international exchange deprived the economy of benefits from imported technology and from efficient utilization of available resources. Shifting to domestic suppliers of capital equipment following the 1960 break with the Soviet Union had a "catastrophic effect on the quality of equipment."[78] Clinging to self-reliance also ignored a potential export bonanza in labor-intensive manufactures arising from the availability of vast numbers of literate, underemployed rural youths at wages far lower than in overseas rivals.[79]

Restricting domestic trade unraveled long-standing patterns of regional specialization. Costs were particularly high in the farm sector, as limited availability of outside grain supplies necessitated the conversion of fields best suited to growing sugar, peanuts, rape, soybeans, and other commercial crops to grain cultivation. These shifts reduced incomes for former producers of cash crops and for their former customers, who mounted inefficient efforts to replace cash crop purchases with local production.[80]

Latent Potential in Agriculture

Historically, Chinese agriculture operated close to the production frontier determined by available land, labor, water, fertilizer, and technology. With no "artificial barriers" to the diffusion of "new seeds, new crops, and better cropping patterns ... there was no great back-log of advanced but essentially 'traditional' technique ... that could be exploited readily."[81] From the start of the PRC, investment and new technology rather than land reform or collectivization held the key to future agricultural growth. Collectivization initially

---

[78] P. Zeitz, "Trade in Equipment and Technological Development: Evidence from the Sino-Soviet Split" (unpublished, 2010).

[79] Even though average Chinese industrial wages in 1991 reached 3.8 times the 1978 level, a multinational comparison found 1991 hourly labor costs in China's increasingly export-oriented textile and garment sectors to be less than one-tenth of comparable costs in Japan, Hong Kong, and Taiwan. See 中国统计年鉴 (China Statistics Yearbook) (hereafter *Yearbook*) 1992, Table 4-33; and L. Moore, "The Competitive Position of Asian Producers of Textiles and Clothing in the US Market," *World Economy* 18.5 (1995), 589.

[80] N.R. Lardy, *Agriculture in China's Modern Economic Development* (Cambridge, Cambridge University Press, 1983), pp. 48–82.

[81] D.H. Perkins, *Agricultural Development in China, 1368–1968* (Chicago, Aldine, 1969), p. 53.

sought to increase farm output and resource transfers out of agriculture without diverting investment from industry to agriculture. But its adverse side effects – erosion of incentives and "technological commandism" – delayed effective implementation of major advances in new high-yielding seed varieties and promoted uneconomic expansion of triple-cropping and agricultural mechanization prior to the revival of household farming in the late 1970s.[82]

The immediate post-reform surge in rural output and TFP beginning in the late 1970s demonstrates the "gigantic waste of labor and resources" resulting from plan-era rural policy.[83] Extraction of resources from the agricultural economy to support industrial production and investment occupied the core of China's plan-era growth mechanism. Sluggish farm performance tied the bulk of China's workforce to the land, slowing the transfer of labor to higher-productivity occupations. Slow growth of food output limited the farm sector's capacity to feed China's cities, necessitating the diversion of scarce foreign exchange to support grain imports. Undernutrition further slowed the growth of farm output.

As China entered the 1970s, deteriorating agricultural conditions threatened to upend the delicate balance among food production, grain procurement, and rural nutrition. The procurement system, essential to feeding China's cities, showed increasing disarray. Sichuan, China's most populous province and a major victim of the 1959–1961 famine, lurched from grain surplus to deficit amid the threat of renewed food shortages.[84] Net procurement, the grain available for transfer from rural to urban areas, declined in most years, as did grain stockpiles, forcing a discomfiting choice between higher grain imports and further reduction of reserves.[85]

Beyond its economic implications, the deteriorating extraction mechanism reflected a severe erosion of central authority. Lax controls enabled rural officials to divert grain to local advantage: Politburo member Li Xiannian 李先念 complained that collectives reported rising grain requirements for seed and feed despite the absence of increases in cultivated acreage or meat production.

---

[82] T.B. Wiens, "Technological Change," in Barker and Sinha, *Agricultural Economy*, pp. 110–20; and Wiens, "The Limits to Agricultural Intensification: The Suzhou Experience," in US Congress, Joint Economic Committee, *China under the Four Modernizations* (Washington, DC, US Government Printing Office, 1982), pp. 462–74.

[83] W.J. Shan, *Out of the Gobi: My Story of China and America* (Hoboken, NJ, Wiley, 2019), p. 240.

[84] F.S. Zhao 赵发生 et al. (eds.), 当代中国的粮食工作 (Grain Work in Contemporary China) (Beijing, Zhongguo shehui kexue chubanshe, 1988), p. 145. Provincial Party secretary Li Jinquan's 李井泉 September 1975 submission to the State Council demanded prompt attention to Sichuan's request for procurement relief to avoid "repeating the mistake of 1959."

[85] Zhao et al., 当代中国的粮食工作, pp. 166–7.

Latent Potential in Industry

In addition to the weak incentives mentioned earlier, the chief source of latent industrial production potential stems from the plan system's rigidity. Even without considering planners' limited access to timely and reliable information, the primitive calculators available to Mao-era planners limited the feasible number of product categories.[86] Fine-tuning production quotas to include, for example, assortment requirements for metal fasteners or shoes, was impractical. The difficulty of modifying complex production arrays meant that successive annual plans rarely incorporated major adjustments. Frequent supply lapses encouraged firms to accumulate inventories. In the late 1970s, "China ... carried a much larger volume of inventories and incomplete construction than ... the Soviet Union," where stockpiles were far greater than in market economies.[87]

Both during the plan era and today, widely varying capabilities across firms in specific industries amplify inefficiencies arising from weak exit mechanisms for poor performers, a problem that persists today.

Industrial policies generated additional sources of latent capacity. During 1953–1978, "heavy" industry absorbed 43 percent of overall state-sector basic construction expenditure and 90 percent of outlays for industry.[88] This approach lavished resources on capital-intensive operations that often churned out low-quality products. Although coastal producers generally delivered superior performance in terms of quality, cost, and productivity, planners directed the bulk of investment toward interior regions. This reached a peak under the "Third Front" program, which channeled over 40 percent of national investment during 1963–1975 to a massive and largely uneconomic heavy industry complex in China's central and western regions intended to guard against possible invasion.[89] Emphasis on local self-sufficiency encouraged the proliferation of inefficient local production.[90]

---

[86] China's material allocation system, which included fewer than 600 items, was "much less extensive than the Soviet" system, which spanned "as many as 65,000" items. C.P. W. Wong, "Ownership and Control in Chinese Industry: The Maoist Legacy and Prospects for the 1980s," in U.S. Congress, Joint Economic Committee, *China's Economy Looks toward the Year 2000*, vol. 1, pp. 577, 603.

[87] B. Naughton, *Growing Out of the Plan: Chinese Economic Reform 1978–1993* (Cambridge, Cambridge University Press, 1995), p. 49.

[88] Guojia tongjiju gudingzichan touzi tongjisi, 1950–1985 中国固定资产投资统计资料 (Statistical Materials on Chinese Fixed Capital Invesment in 1950–1985), pp. 43, 44, 97.

[89] B. Naughton, "The Third Front: Defence Industrialization in the Chinese Interior," *China Quarterly* 115 (1988), 351–86.

[90] A. Donnithorne, "China's Cellular Economy: Some Economic Trends since the Cultural Revolution," *China Quarterly* 52 (1972), 605–19.

Even as food supply issues stalled China's economic growth, the widening gap between actual and potential output both within and beyond the farm sector offered the possibility that suitable reforms could rapidly generate large increases in output. In addition to directly raising agricultural production, rural reform promised to promote economy-wide growth by accelerating the reallocation of labor into nonagricultural activities in which returns were even higher. This is exactly what happened.

The Reform Era

China's economy entered the reform era in difficult straits. Three decades of socialist planning had expanded the scale and scope of industry and upgraded its technical capabilities; the new system also delivered notable advances in education, public health, and life expectancy. Despite these gains, massive inefficiency kept the economy far below its potential. Lagging food production left hundreds of millions underfed and threatened to destabilize key flows underpinning the economy's advance.

In sharp contrast, four decades of reform have brought a remarkable transformation. Some metrics now identify China's economy as the world's largest. Rapid structural change has steeply reduced the importance of agriculture, with the primary sector's share of aggregate output falling from 27.7 percent in 1978 to less than 10 percent beginning in 2009. Official estimates show that primary-sector employment has fallen even faster, from 83.5 percent in 1978 to half or less beginning in 1997 and 26.1 percent in 2018. Industry and services have moved to the forefront, with services gradually taking the lead, surpassing industry's share of employment in 1994 and output in 2012. Massive population shifts have raised the urban share of China's population to 60 percent.[91] China has emerged as a great trading nation, a global science and innovation powerhouse,[92] and both a leading recipient and a major source of overseas investment.

Our analysis emphasizes the twin processes of economic transition – the shift from plan to market in the allocation of resources, and structural transformation, most notably the movement of people and resources out of agriculture and into industry and services. Along with productivity

---

[91] *Yearbook* 2019, Tables 2-7, 3-2, 4-2. Official sources overestimate employment in the primary sector, which includes forestry and fisheries as well as agriculture.

[92] R.B. Freeman and W. Huang, "China's 'Great Leap Forward' in Science and Engineering," in A. Geuna (ed.), *Global Mobility of Research Scientists: The Economics of Who Goes Where and Why* (London, Academic Press, 2015), pp. 155–75.

improvements within individual sectors, the transfer of resources along productivity-enhancing paths toward nonagricultural activity, non-state enterprises, and coastal locations delivered more than three-fourths of the increase in per capita incomes during the first three decades of the reform era, with the rest coming from capital deepening and rising education levels.[93]

The central role of productivity growth and resource reallocation during China's long boom conceals deep-rooted tensions between economic advance and the state's noneconomic objectives. Rapid productivity growth in non-state industry and services has elevated returns to investment and thus sustained the incentives for high rates of capital formation. By the start of the global financial crisis in 2008, the non-state sector's share of investment had increased from slightly more than 10 percent in 1978 to nearly half.[94] The rest went to the state sector, where returns to capital were often negative and productivity growth was only a third or a quarter of what the non-state sector delivered. Despite these dismal economic returns, China's leaders continue to promote state-sector investment, which over the last decade has averaged roughly 20 percent of GDP, to advance multiple noneconomic objectives – patronage and network building, national security, and demonstrations of national might. In the wake of the 2008 crisis, policies that steer resources toward the state sector and extend official intervention in private-sector management threaten to curtail China's economic growth.

We divide the reform era into three phases: reform from below, extending into the early 1990s; the following decade and a half of more organized, centrally directed reform initiatives; and the current period, beginning with the global crash, dominated by top-down innovation plans.

Stage 1: Reform from Below – Decentralized Initiative and Central Reaction

Reform commenced in the villages. While scholars dispute the relative importance of spontaneous grassroots action and local government decisions in the rapid shift from collective to household cultivation, the impotence of central leadership is indisputable. Major documents issued by central CCP bodies in 1979 and 1980 bristle with calls for restoring rural workers'

---

[93] X.D. Zhu, "Understanding China's Growth: Past, Present, and Future," *Journal of Economic Perspectives* 26.4 (2012), 108.

[94] L. Brandt and X.D. Zhu, "Accounting for China's Growth," University of Toronto Department of Economics Working Paper 394 (2010), Figure 2.

production enthusiasm (*shengchan jijixing* 生产积极性), while prohibiting household cultivation, lauding collectives as the "unshakable foundation" of agrarian progress and denying that household activity could support "the establishment of modern agriculture."⁹⁵

Subsequent developments highlight the center's irrelevance. Noting that contracting to households had aroused "great enthusiasm among the masses," the summary of a 1981 agricultural reform conference notes that "since reality has already outrun the [1980] directive ... delegates suggested that the Center promptly formulate new documents reflecting the new circumstances."⁹⁶

Restoration of household farming, along with partial decontrol of rural marketing and individual entrepreneurship, propelled swift increases in both agricultural output and productivity,⁹⁷ even as millions abandoned farming for newly emerging opportunities in industry and services. Sichuan and Anhui, provinces that had suffered the most during the Great Leap Famine, led these rural reforms.⁹⁸ The suddenness of the ensuing shift from near-stagnation to rapid growth, which generated nationwide improvements in rural incomes and food availability, reveals the centrality of institutional changes that simultaneously restored incentives, encouraged greater work effort, and allowed agriculture to exploit the untapped potential of new seeds, chemical fertilizer, and expanded irrigation accumulated under the collective regime.⁹⁹

Alongside these rural developments, growing awareness that prolonged isolation had stranded Chinese industry and technology far behind its East Asian neighbors, as well as North America and Western Europe, inspired plans for a big push to upgrade domestic technology and equipment.¹⁰⁰ The

---

⁹⁵ 中国农业年鉴 1980 (Beijing, Nongye chubanshe, 1981), pp. 57–8; 中国农业年鉴 1981 (Beijing, Nongye chubanshe, 1982), pp. 409–10.
⁹⁶ "全国农业经济问题讨论会纪要" (Summary of the National Symposium on Agricultural Issues), 农业经济问题 (Agricultural Economic Issues) 10 (1981), 2. Also A. Watson, "Agriculture Looks for 'Shoes That Fit': The Production Responsibility System and Its Implications," *World Development* 11.8 (1983), 713.
⁹⁷ J.Y. Lin, "Rural Reforms and Agricultural Growth in China," *American Economic Review* 82.1 (1982), 46, attributes 48.69 percent of the output growth during 1978–1988 to decollectivization. Fan and Zhang, "Production and Productivity Growth," Table 5, find that, with 1952 = 100, TFP in agriculture (based on constant 1980 prices) jumped from 67 in 1978 to 82 in 1982 and 129 in 1992.
⁹⁸ D.L. Yang, *Calamity and Reform in China: State, Rural Society, and Institutional Change since the Great Leap Forward* (Stanford, Stanford University Press, 1996).
⁹⁹ J.K. Huang and S. Rozelle, "Technological Change: Rediscovering the Engine of Productivity Growth in China's Rural Economy," *Journal of Development Economics* 49.2 (1996), 337–69.
¹⁰⁰ D.H. Perkins, "Reforming China's Economic System," *Journal of Economic Literature* 26.2 (1988), 618.

collapse of this effort, which quickly outran China's puny export earnings, prompted hesitant urban reforms aimed at "enlivening" operations within the plan system by modestly extending state enterprise managers' decision-making authority and expanding opportunities to buy and sell industrial materials and products.

The dual-track system, which preserved administered prices for plan-related distributions while allowing market sales of above-plan output, broadened market opportunities and sharpened incentives within the state sector.[101] It also encouraged the growth of more efficient producers, particularly benefiting TVEs clustered in coastal provinces. Dual pricing created market-based price signals in nearly every sector, a critical step in expanding market-oriented reform, and modestly sharpened incentives within the state sector. At the same time, the arrangement preserved rents accruing to plan participants. This reduced opposition to market reform, but created lucrative opportunities to resell underpriced goods acquired through plan allocations at higher market prices.

Expansion of overseas trade and investment, led by the creation of special economic zones, added an international dimension to China's boom. China's opening coincided with efforts by Taiwan and Hong Kong entrepreneurs, responding to rising wages in their home markets, to find low-cost venues for labor-intensive export production. The combination of local land and labor along China's coast with the market knowledge, manufacturing experience, and financial resources of these operators shifted growing numbers of rural workers into manufacturing jobs and brought rapid growth of factory exports.

Although the initial reforms affected the entire economy, the largest impact occurred outside the cities and beyond the state sector. Unlike rural reform, which often involved little more than lifting restrictions that had suppressed long-standing patterns of production and marketing, urban reform required the construction of new and unfamiliar institutions, to which state enterprises, managers, and workers, many with no experience of market discipline,[102] would have to adapt. Such changes inevitably encountered opposition from entrenched interests.

Not surprisingly, individuals and firms on the fringes of the plan system took the lead. Rural incomes jumped upward, narrowing the gap with city

---

[101] W. Li, "The Impact of Economic Reform on the Performance of Chinese State Enterprises, 1980–1989," *Journal of Political Economy* 105 (1997), 1080–1106.

[102] State-owned industrial firms numbered 15,190 in 1955 and 83,400 in 1980; see N.R. Chen, *Chinese Economic Statistics* (Chicago, Aldine, 1967), p. 182; and *Yearbook 1981*, 204.

folk.[103] Rural firms soon penetrated urban markets, slashing the profits of state-owned rivals.[104] Collective and privately owned firms gained a foothold in the new export sector. Relaxation of mobility restrictions sparked the initial phase of what later developed into a tidal wave of migration into China's cities; the late 1970s and early 1980s saw the return of many urbanites "sent down" to rural villages, while villagers sought opportunities to fill gaps created by the plan system's repression of retail and service businesses.[105]

With increases in output, productivity, profits, and revenues clustered in rural areas and in non-state enterprises under the supervision of local governments, the center found itself scrambling to fund its priorities. Both the ratio of government revenue to GDP and the center's share of overall revenue, much of it derived from SOE profits, declined.[106] The center's unwillingness to reduce urban real incomes by imposing higher grain prices saddled the state budget with growing outlays to bridge the gap between rising grain costs and lower fixed retail prices. A further obstacle arose when state-owned commercial banks, responding to reform-enhanced profit motives, steered resources to emerging non-bank financial institutions (NBFIs) that extended credit to fast-growing collectives and private firms.

The state now lacked sufficient budgetary and banking support to implement plans for expanding employment, wages, and investment in the lagging state sector. Urban SOE employment increased more than 50 percent during 1978–1994. The center turned to the People's Bank of China (PBOC), China's central bank, to extend lending to the commercial banks, which used these additional resources to implement the credit plan's provisions for "state sector working-capital and fixed investment needs."[107] This short-term response proved costly, as PBOC intervention caused increases in money supply and prices, rekindling memories of wartime hyperinflation – a key

---

[103] D.Y. Yang and F. Cai, "The Political Economy of China's Rural–Urban Divide," Stanford Center for International Development, Working Paper No. 62, 2000, p. 32, find that in real terms the urban–rural ratio for consumption (not income) dropped from 2.9 in 1978 to 1.9 in 1985, then rebounded to 2.5 in 1992.
[104] B. Naughton, "Implications of the State Monopoly over Industry and Its Relaxation," *Modern China* 18.1 (1992), 14–41.
[105] D.J. Solinger, *Chinese Business under Socialism: The Politics of Domestic Commerce, 1949–1980* (Berkeley, University of California Press, 1984), p. 325, notes that the number of shops, restaurants, and commercial centers "under commercial departments, in urban and industrial and mining areas," dropped from 1 million to 180,000 between 1957 and 1978.
[106] Wong and Bird, "China's Fiscal System," 433.
[107] L. Brandt and X.D. Zhu, "China's Banking Sector and Economic Growth," in C. W. Calomiris (ed.), *China's Financial Transition at a Crossroads* (New York, Columbia University Press, 2007), p. 97.

ingredient in the CCP's victory over the Guomindang.[108] Official intervention to limit monetary growth by constricting the supply of credit to the dynamic non-state sector restrained inflation, but also lowered the overall growth rate. The result was a series of stop–go cycles in which periods of accelerated growth led by non-state firms alternated with intervals of reduced credit and output growth.[109]

Despite these tensions, which helped to spark the unrest that culminated in top-level purges and violent suppression of mass protests in 1989, this initial stage of reform delivered an astonishing turnaround that accelerated the growth of overall output. In stark contrast to the plan era, the initial reforms increased personal incomes and released several hundred million villagers from the scourge of absolute poverty.[110]

For the first time, China experienced widespread productivity growth, reflecting the joint impact of transition and development. Transition partially restored market exchange, market prices,[111] personal mobility, and openness to entry and competition from both domestic and overseas firms and products. This enabled China's first ever large-scale shift out of agriculture, as non-primary employment more than doubled, adding over 150 million workers between 1978 and 1992.[112]

Deng Xiaoping's endorsement of growth and rejection of long-standing egalitarian emphasis highlighted an unprecedented alignment of incentives,[113] as a widely shared preference for growth now united villagers seeking to escape collective control, workers hungry for bonuses, managers and bankers pursuing profits, and officials whose career prospects and informal incomes now rested increasingly on raising output.[114]

---

[108] K.N. Chang, *The Inflationary Spiral: The Experience in China, 1939–1950* (Cambridge, MA, MIT Press, 1958).

[109] L. Brandt and X.D. Zhu, "Redistribution in a Decentralized Economy: Growth and Inflation in China under Reform," *Journal of Political Economy* 108.2 (2000), 422–39.

[110] M. Ravallion and S.H. Chen, "China's (Uneven) Progress against Poverty," *Journal of Development Economics* 82.1 (2006), 1–42.

[111] By 1990, market prices governed just over half of retail transactions and exchange of agricultural products; for production materials, the share of market pricing was 36.4 percent. H. Dinh, T.G. Rawski, A. Zafar, L.H. Wang, and E. Mavroeidi, with X. Tong and P.F. Li, *Tales from the Development Frontier: How China and Other Countries Harness Light Manufacturing to Create Jobs and Prosperity* (Washington, DC, World Bank, 2013), p. 77.

[112] *Yearbook* 2019, Table 4–2.

[113] E.F. Vogel, *Deng Xiaoping and the Transformation of China* (Cambridge, MA, Harvard University Press, 2011), 242, dates this from 1978, when "allowing some regions and enterprises to get rich first" was a major theme of Deng's December 13 speech to the Central Party Work Conference.

[114] H.B. Li and L.A. Zhou, "Political Turnover and Economic Performance: The Incentive Role of Personnel Control in China," *Journal of Public Economics* 89 (2005), 1743–62.

Along with remarkable economic advance, China's initial reforms exposed a fundamental duality between the economy's dynamic segments, which clustered outside the cities and beyond the state sector,[115] and the lagging, resource-hungry state sector. A stark performance gap separated the two: between 1980 and 1992, growth of output, labor productivity, and TFP in state-owned industries was only a half to a third of that in collective and private firms.[116] Even so, Beijing continued to see the state sector as central to its pursuit of multiple objectives, many extending beyond narrowly economic outcomes, and as a portfolio of resources available to supplement state appropriations and to reinforce loyalty within the ruling coalition.

Heavy reliance on the state sector explains why, despite its evident economic weakness, the annual "flow of resources through the financial system making its way to the state sector" during 1978–1994 amounted to 15 to 20 percent of GDP.[117] As China gradually recovered from the tempestuous events of 1989, further reform seemed essential to resolve a fundamental conflict between the desire for continued rapid growth and the drain from large-scale transfers to underperforming segments of the economy.

Stage 2: Major Reform Initiatives Extend Market Forces and Restore Central Control

Suppression of the June 1989 Beijing protests left China's central leadership badly shaken. Ousting CCP general secretary and former premier Zhao Ziyang and his allies while mobilizing the army to terminate public protests fractured the top echelons of power and blurred lines of control over routine economic administration.

The economy stumbled: employment growth during 1988–1989 dropped to less than one-third of the average over the preceding decade, while nominal investment outlays declined for the first time since 1980–1981.[118] The GDP share of government revenue and expenditure, which had stabilized at the end of the 1980s following a decade of decline, resumed its downward march.

---

[115] Y.S. Huang, "How Did China Take Off?", *Journal of Economic Perspectives* 26.4 (2012).
[116] G.H. Jefferson and T.G. Rawski, "Enterprise Reform in Chinese Industry," *Journal of Economic Perspectives* 8.2 (1994), 48, 56.
[117] Brandt and Zhu, "China's Banking Sector and Economic Growth," 96–9. Over this period, more than 60 percent of capital formation, and two-thirds of all new banking loans, went to the state sector.
[118] Employment data from *Yearbook* 1991, Table 4-8; investment data from *Yearbook* 1991, Tables 5-20, 5-35; and from 1950–1985 中国固定资产投资统计资料, pp. 49, 216.

Despite this unlikely start, Deng Xiaoping's 1992 "Southern Tour" ignited an avalanche of growth that outstripped the impressive early reform achievements. This renewed growth rested, in turn, on constructive actions that swept aside multiple constraints and further expanded the influence of market forces, while restoring the power and authority of the CCP and the central state. Major reforms affected public finance, banking, state enterprises, and market opening.

Fiscal Restructuring

Tax reform implemented in 1994 reversed the long decline in the GDP share of fiscal revenue, increased the central government's claim on overall revenue, and, perhaps most important for re-establishing central authority, ensured that province-level units, "including Shanghai and Beijing," became "dependent on central transfers to finance expenditures."[119]

Bank Reform

During the 1980s, the main source of investment funding shifted from budgetary grants to bank loans. State enterprises, the main recipients, "turned increasingly to bank credit without much concern about their future ability to repay."[120] This led to an epidemic of payment arrears: estimates show that, by 1998, half or more of bank loans were "non-performing."[121]

During the late 1990s, the central government took major steps to rectify this dangerous situation. Newly created asset management companies purchased vast tranches of bad loans, thereby recapitalizing the floundering state-owned commercial banks. The center increased its control over the financial system: shuttering weak financial firms, closing down most NBFIs, reorganizing the central bank's subnational branches to reduce the influence of provincial and local leaders, and increasing the influence of high-level officials in the appointment and promotion of bank executives.

The removal of bad loans, coupled with the establishment of policy banks to shoulder the burden of noncommercial finance, greatly strengthened the lending capacity of China's four giant commercial banks. Although politically directed lending continued, the commercial element in bank operations deepened.[122]

---

[119] Wong and Bird, "China's Fiscal System," 437.
[120] B. Naughton, *The Chinese Economy: Transitions and Growth* (Cambridge, MIT Press, 2007), p. 306.
[121] Brandt and Zhu, "China's Banking Sector and Economic Growth," 128.
[122] J. Stent, *China's Banking Transformation* (New York, Oxford University Press, 2017). A textile executive commented, "Banks are not the same as before. Now if you have no money and can't repay, they won't lend to you" (May 1996 interview).

State Enterprises

The focus of reform shifted from flows (of new workers, new investments, and above-plan output) toward more complex realignments affecting embedded resource stocks, including workers and entire firms. Beijing's vision of the state sector's role narrowed, with textiles, food processing, and other industries now classed as "competitive," implying that preservation of state-sector dominance, and even the survival of individual firms, were no longer essential.

Privatization, often via management buyouts, multiplied, as did bankruptcies and closures. The overall number of state-owned enterprises plunged from 262,000 to 112,000 between 1997 and 2007; for industry, the total declined from 103,300 in 1992 to 20,680 in 2007.[123] Severe culling eliminated over one-third of state-sector personnel, formerly endowed with (often heritable) lifetime tenure; between 1996 and 2000 alone, the state-sector headcount plunged from 113 million to 67 million.[124]

Bottom-up initiatives originating with provincial and local authorities, which had gained control over large segments of state-owned industry following decentralization programs in 1957 and 1970,[125] dominated these downsizing efforts. Subnational governments welcomed opportunities to shed the burden of maintaining weak enterprises, including TVEs and other collective enterprises as well as state-owned firms, that could not withstand intensifying market pressures.

The center, by contrast, acted to strengthen enterprises under its direct control. Following the 2003 creation of the State-Owned Assets Supervisory Commission (SASAC), policy effort focused on the complex and rapidly expanding operations of roughly 100 giant state-owned enterprise groups in key commodity (petroleum, grain), manufacturing (steel, aluminum, aircraft), infrastructure (railroads, electricity, telecoms), and financial (banking, insurance) sectors. These efforts helped to maintain the state's share in GDP while increasing the share of the state sector under central government control.

---

[123] K.J. Lin, X.Y. Lu, J.S. Zhang, and Y. Zheng, "State-Owned Enterprises in China: A Review of 40 Years of Research and Practice," *China Journal of Accounting Research* 13 (2020), 34; *Yearbook* 1995, Table 12-1; *Yearbook* 2008, Table 13-8 (including state-controlled industrial units).
[124] *Yearbook* 2005, Table 5-4.   [125] Wong, "Ownership and Control."

Market Opening

The scope of market-based transactions continued to expand. Rapid growth of highway and water transport, much of it in the hands of unregulated private operators, contributed to the erosion of local protectionism and interprovincial trade barriers.[126] Analysis based on monthly data for ninety-three products in thirty-six major cities found that "prices did converge" during 1990–2003, and that "the patterns of convergence ... were highly comparable" to observations from "the United States, Canada, and European countries" – all indicating the powerful influence of market forces.[127]

Employment became increasingly market-based. The former system of job assignments faded, as graduating students and employers sought mutually advantageous matches. Market expansion unleashed a torrent of internal migration – a familiar phenomenon in China's modern history.[128] In 2001, Premier Zhu Rongji bluntly advised "laid-off workers ... to find jobs on the private labor market."[129]

SOE reform and sweeping privatization of collective enterprises, together with modest improvements in the legal protections surrounding private ownership and Jiang Zemin's 2001 decision to admit entrepreneurs to Communist Party membership, improved the position of private business. These changes, along with widespread privatization of collective firms, spurred explosive growth in the private sector's share of output and especially employment. Between 1992 and 2007, urban private employment rose from 10.6 million to 78.9 million; in the countryside, 2007 private-enterprise employment surpassed 110 million.[130] These trends benefited from

---

[126] *Yearbook 2010*, Tables 16-4, 16-8, 16-24, shows that between 1990 and 2007, China's truck fleet increased from 3.7 to 10.5 million vehicles; during the same period, the length of highways as well as the annual volume of freight carriage along inland waterways more than tripled.

[127] C.S. Fan and X.D. Wei, "The Law of One Price: Evidence from the Transitional Economy of China," *Review of Economics and Statistics* 88.4 (2006), 694.

[128] In addition to overseas migrations, major domestic population movements include Qing-era migration into Sichuan, the resettlement of lands devastated by the Taiping wars, and large-scale population movement into Manchuria during the late nineteenth and early twentieth centuries. See M. Bastid-Bruguiere, "Currents of Social Change," in J.K. Fairbank and K.C. Liu (eds.), *The Cambridge History of China*, vol. 11, *Late Ch'ing, 1800–1911*, part 2 (Cambridge, Cambridge University Press, 1980), pp. 582–6; T. R. Gottschang and D. Lary, *Swallows and Settlers: The Great Migration from North China to Manchuria* (Ann Arbor, University of Michigan Center for Chinese Studies, 2000).

[129] Q.W. Zhu, "Domestic Market Fuels Growth," *China Daily*, August 6, 2001, 4.

[130] *Yearbook 2011*, Table 4-2; 中国乡镇企业及农产品加工业年鉴 2008 (electronic edition, no page or table numbers, accessed June 29, 2020). Both urban and rural employment include individual proprietorships.

"extremely rapid growth of credit to private and individual businesses" following the 1994 implementation of China's Company Law.[131]

In the late 1990s, sweeping privatization of urban housing created a property market that hugely increased the wealth of urban households, creating opportunities for new owners to finance private businesses and overseas education for their children.[132]

Along with domestic opening, China moved to rejoin the global economy. Hesitant initial steps, notably the opening of tiny special economic zones, developed into a powerful push to regain and then surpass China's prewar footprint in global trade and investment. Tariff reductions and other measures implemented ahead of China's 2001 accession to the World Trade Organization created "one of the developing world's most open trade and FDI regimes," highlighting China's growing involvement in cross-border flows of commodities, investment, technology, information, and individuals.[133]

Rapid expansion of international trade and investment added momentum to domestic growth. China's share of global merchandise trade grew from 0.9 to 2.2 percent between 1980 and 1992 – neither exceeding the prewar figures noted above – to 2.7, 3.6, and 7.7 percent in 1995, 2000, and 2007. China's trade share overtook Japan's in 2004.[134] Rising foreign direct investment (FDI), much of it from Taiwan and Hong Kong, and often directed toward export-oriented manufacturing, along with authorization of growing numbers of domestic firms to conduct international trade,[135] brought considerations of cost and profit to the fore, shifting trade patterns toward the underlying structure of comparative advantage. Chinese firms began to join international supply chains, accelerating the spread of management skills.

Beginning in the 1990s, large FDI inflows enabled China to recover its prewar standing as a major destination for overseas investment. China's share of the global FDI stock housed in developing nations, which exceeded

---

[131] Lardy, *Markets over Mao*, p. 102.
[132] H.M. Fan, G.L. Gu, W. Xiong, and L.A. Zhou, "Demystifying the Chinese Housing Boom," in M. Eichenbaum and J.A. Parker (eds.), *NBER Macroeconomics Annual 2015* (Chicago, University of Chicago Press, 2016), pp. 105–66.
[133] L. Branstetter and N.R. Lardy, "China's Embrace of Globalization," in Brandt and Rawski, *China's Great Economic Transformation*, p. 676.
[134] Post-1949 figures from https://data.wto.org, accessed July 14, 2020.
[135] Branstetter and Lardy, "China's Embrace of Globalization," p. 635, note the number of companies authorized to conduct international trade: twelve in 1978, 800 in 1985, and 35,000 in 2001.

15 percent during the 1930s, achieved similar levels again by the late 1990s.[136] While China has consistently been among the top three recipients of FDI since the early 1990s, its share of the worldwide FDI stock in 2019 remains below half of the 1930s figure of 11 percent.[137]

Outcomes

Market opening encouraged accelerated structural change that moved resources toward more productive uses. The primary sector's GDP share dropped from one-fifth to one-tenth between 1992 and 2007, while the tertiary (service) sector's share jumped from 36 to 43 percent. The official measure of China's primary-sector labor force peaked in 1991; by 2007, it had declined by 83.7 million. Employment growth clustered in the service sector, which added 113 million workers during the same years.[138]

The growing influence of market forces pulled resources into coastal regions, which increased their weight in overall production and investment while dominating export production and absorption of incoming foreign investment.[139] The share of China's eastern region in overall fixed investment jumped from about one-third prior to 1975 to over 60 percent during the mid-1990s.[140] A 2008 survey clearly demarcated the geographic locus of economic dynamism: of 140 million internal migrants who had left their home counties, 70 percent originated in China's central or western regions, and 62 percent had moved to eastern provinces, which housed 43 percent of the national population.[141]

Growing internationalization intensified the impact of domestic-market opening on competition, cost reduction, and quality improvement. Tariff reductions and other liberalization measures implemented ahead of China's

---

[136] The Asian financial crisis temporarily lowered China's FDI inflows and its share of the global FDI stock.

[137] Calculated from UNCTAD, *World Investment Report 2020*, Annex Table 1; these data exclude FDI flows into Hong Kong.

[138] *Yearbook 2019*, Tables 3-2, 4-2.

[139] X.J. Jiang, *FDI in China: Contributions to Growth, Restructuring and Competitiveness* (New York, Nova Science Publishers, 2004), p. 82, notes that, as of late 2001, 86 percent of FDI had located in China's eastern region.

[140] NBS, "固定资产投资水平不断提升对发展的关键性作用持续发挥" (The Ongoing Rise in the Level of Fixed Asset Investment Continues to Play a Key Role in Development), at 70prc.cn/2019-09/19/c_138404706.htm, posted September 19, 2019, accessed June 29, 2020.

[141] *Yearbook 2009*, Table 3-4; 2008 年末全国农民工总量为 22542 万人 (At the End of 2008, the Total Number of Migrant Workers Nationwide Was 225.42 Million), at stats.gov.cn/ztjc/ztfx/fxbg/200903/t20090325_16116.html, accessed July 13, 2020. The data on regional origins and destinations are limited to migrants with fixed employment.

WTO accession represented "a watershed" that forced widespread cost reductions.[142] Growing competition from imports and from an expanding array of domestic producers created pressures that increased productivity and reduced both the level and the dispersion of sales markups.[143]

Foreign-invested firms occupied a "vital role ... [in] transfers of technology, production and organizational skills, managerial know-how, and marketing expertise" that powered "robust progress" in China's "capacity to manufacture a growing array of internationally competitive products."[144] Overseas firms, eager to capitalize on low Chinese costs, promoted domestic supply chains to feed their Chinese assembly plants. Along with the arrival of overseas component manufacturers, these supply networks absorbed thousands of local firms: by the year 2000, "of Motorola's 700-odd suppliers in China ... more than 400 are domestic."[145]

These changes generated striking economic results. Following a brief slowdown in the wake of the 1989 disturbances, rapid growth resumed: measured at international prices, per capita income rose at an annual rate of 6.4 percent during 1992–2007.[146] As in the initial reform phase, productivity growth, dormant prior to 1978, continued as the primary driver of expansion for the entire economy and for industry, the largest sector.[147]

The period between 1992 and the 2008 global financial crisis represents an interlude of relative political calm in which contentious debate about the long-term objective of economic policy continued even as major reforms delivered large and tangible benefits to advocates of both market transformation and state-led development.

Liberalizing reformers rejoiced as openness, entry and competition swept across large swathes of China's economic landscape. Jiang Zemin's dual 2001 initiatives, first opening the CCP to private entrepreneurs, and then proposing a "socialist market economy with Chinese characteristics," fanned expectations of gradual convergence to market outcomes. Beyond economics, the broad liberalizing agenda of disgraced former CCP general secretary Zhao Ziyang "happened by evolution," with growing "separation of

---

[142] Branstetter and Lardy, "China's Embrace of Globalization," p. 656.
[143] L. Brandt, J. van Biesebroeck, L.H. Wang, and Y.F. Zhang, "WTO Accession and Performance of Chinese Manufacturing Firms," *American Economic Review* 107.9 (2017), 2784–820; Y. Lu and L.H. Yu, "Trade Liberalization and Markup Dispersion: Evidence from China's WTO Accession," *American Economic Journal: Applied Economics* 7.2 (2015), 221–53.
[144] L. Brandt, T.G. Rawski, and J. Sutton, "China's Industrial Development," in Brandt and Rawski, *China's Great Economic Transformation*, pp. 622–3.
[145] Jiang, *FDI in China*, 29.   [146] Calculated from Penn World Tables v. 9.1.
[147] Perkins and Rawski, "Forecasting," 839; Brandt et al., "WTO Accession."

responsibilities and spheres of authority," leaders chosen "for their policy relevant expertise ... economic policy-makers at all levels suffer less and less frequently from intervention by the ideology-and-mobilization specialists," while "neither the top leader nor the central Party organs interfere as much in the work of other agencies" as in the past, and "ideological considerations have only marginal, if any, influence on most policy decisions."[148]

Developments between 1992 and 2007 equally reinforced the position and prospects for state-led development. The collapse of the Soviet Union alarmed Chinese elites. Fears that China might experience similar centrifugal pressures reinforced CCP claims that it alone could ensure national unity and guide China to a position of global prominence. Patriotic education campaigns promoted "national greatness," echoing early twentieth-century political discourse. A string of diplomatic triumphs – the 1997 return of Hong Kong, 2001 entry into the World Trade Organization, and the selection of Beijing to host the 2008 summer Olympics – highlighted the CCP regime's capacity to deliver benefits extending far beyond economic growth.

In tandem with growing market influence, developments between 1992 and 2007 multiplied the power of the central state. Beijing maintained strong control over large segments of the economy, including major upstream industries (petroleum, electricity), railroads, and large segments of the service sector (finance, telecoms). Fiscal and banking reforms massively enlarged the central state's command over resources, while state-sector downsizing, urban housing privatization, and the termination of urban food subsidies eliminated large fiscal burdens. Economic success created vast pools of discretionary funds: between 1992–1993 and 2007, central government revenue, state enterprise assets and profits, nationwide financial deposits, and foreign-exchange reserves each rose far more rapidly than China's GDP.[149] Giant centrally supervised enterprise groups, some with thousands of subsidiaries, amassed 2007 profits equivalent to 4 percent of GDP.[150] Their opaque corporate structures, along with booming infrastructure spending, multiplied opportunities to distribute rents, a key link in maintaining elite support, on a grand scale. One account describes state-directed investment as "the prime enabler of corruption."[151]

---

[148] A.J. Nathan, "China's Changing of the Guard: Authoritarian Resilience," *Journal of Democracy* 14.1 (2003), 11–13.
[149] All measured at current prices. See the online appendix referenced in note 44 above.
[150] B. Naughton, "SASAC and Rising Corporate Power in China," *China Leadership Monitor* 24 (2008), 2.
[151] J. Du, Y. Lu, and Z.G. Tao, "Government Expropriation and Chinese-Style Firm Diversification," *Journal of Comparative Economics* 43 (2015), esp. 166–8; J. Osburg,

Deep resource pools enabled the implementation of large, top-down development projects, notably a major initiative to develop China's western region, begun in the year 2000, and the initial phase of building national networks of expressways and high-speed rail lines. Beyond these specific programs, the incoming leadership group headed by Hu Jintao and Wen Jiabao abandoned former premier Zhu Rongji's downsizing of central government scale and functions in favor of a more activist approach. Beginning in 2003, the new leaders shifted technology upgrading "expenditure ... towards domestic research and development ... and away from technology import," raised "direct government expenditure on techno-industrial projects," and instituted a steep rise in "the number of industrial policies" that supported "specific sectors, firms, or technologies."[152]

The fifteen years prior to the 2008 financial crisis witnessed rapid evolution of China's economy. Growth flourished, largely driven by rising productivity. Domestic and international opening enlarged the influence of market signals and pressures. Reforms also expanded the state's command over resources, encouraging a turn toward governmental activism. With movement toward marketization "stalled out" following the 2003–2004 turn toward governmental activism, the overall weight of market elements in China's economy began to recede in advance of the 2008 global crash.[153]

Stage 3: Toward State Capitalism

The 2008 global financial crisis enhanced state influence in China, as in all major economies. Beijing responded to the steep downturn with a blizzard of new credit, most channeled through state-controlled entities and directed toward urban infrastructure. Following a rapid recovery, growth continued, although at considerably reduced rates that some analysts view as exaggerated.[154]

"Global Capitalisms in Asia: Beyond State and Market in China," *Journal of Asian Studies* 72.4 (2013), 824.

[152] L. Chen and B. Naughton, "An Institutionalized Policy-Making Mechanism: China's Return to Techno-industrial Policy," *Research Policy* 45 (2016), 2141.

[153] B. Naughton, "The Return of Planning in China: Comment on Heilmann–Melton and Hu Angang," *Modern China* 39.6 (2013), 651.

[154] Y.Y. Hu and J.X. Yao, "Illuminating Economic Growth," IMF Working Paper 19/77 (2019); W. Chen, X.L. Chen, C.T. Hsieh, and Z.M. Song, "A Forensic Examination of China's National Accounts," *Brookings Papers on Economic Activity* 1 (2019), 77–141.

State Control to the Fore

Economic policy redoubled the emphasis on state leadership and adopted a new trajectory in which cutting-edge innovation supplants technological catch-up as the key driver of expansion. President Xi's "China Dream" sees domestic prosperity and technical advance as twin springboards for a nationalist agenda targeting regional and global leadership across multiple arenas: innovation, trade, investment, diplomacy, science, and the military. Two signature policies, "Made in China 2025" and "One Belt, One Road" illuminate current economic priorities. Both contrast sharply with the recommendation of greater openness, entry, competition, and market allocation in *China 2030*, a major 2013 study by the Development Research Center under China's State Council and the World Bank.

Made in China 2025, a long-term program developed by the Chinese Academy of Engineering, a bastion of top-down planning, establishes timetables for attaining an array of advanced manufacturing milestones, often including specific figures for output volume and domestic or even global market share.[155] With its focus on quantitative targets and neglect of competition, prices, and costs, this program, while dealing with a new set of industries and technologies, embodies a top-down, nonmarket strategy that echoes China's plans of the 1950s. Its nonmarket approach resembles subsequent initiatives, especially the 2006 "National Medium- to Long-Term Plan for the Development of Science and Technology" and the 2010 "Decision of the State Council on Accelerating the Fostering and Development of Strategic Emerging Industries."

The Belt and Road program proposes a vast network of energy and infrastructure facilities spanning the entire Eurasian land mass, with extensions to Africa and Latin America. This initiative, which combines aid, lending, trade, and diplomacy, seeks to deepen China's ties with low- and middle-income nations, in part to offset weakening demand growth for Chinese products in advanced markets.[156] This agenda showcases Chinese capabilities in design, finance, management, construction, and hardware manufacture linked to an array of upstream industries, many awash in excess production capacity. While China continues as a leading global destination

---

[155] J. Wübbeke, M. Meissner, M.J. Zenglein, J. Ives, and B. Conrad, "Made in China 2025: The Making of a High-Tech Superpower and Consequences for Industrial Countries," MERICS Papers on China No. 2, 2016.
[156] The share of China's exports to advanced nations declined from 54.6 to 47.7 percent between 2007 and 2018. *Yearbook* 2008, Table 17-8; *Yearbook* 2019, Table 11-5.

for foreign investment, Belt and Road projects spearhead its emergence as a major source of outbound international investment.

These huge programs represent the leading edge of official economic intervention, which has achieved a scale without historical precedent. China's government spending exceeds its US counterpart.[157] Beijing's control over financial resources extends far beyond official budgets. China's state-dominated financial system remains responsive to official directives, as do managers of China's world-leading foreign-exchange reserves and the leaders of nonfinancial state enterprises, whose combined assets eclipse those of the 500 largest US companies.[158]

This multiplex arsenal supports outlays of astonishing breadth and scale. Some 90 percent of companies with A-shares listed on the Shanghai exchange received government subsidies in 2016. The China Integrated Circuit Industry Investment Fund, established in 2014, "invested in more than 70 projects and companies" following initial fund-raising. Subsequent contributions lifted funding to US$51 billion. China's shipbuilding industry, which reported 2005 output of RMB 125.7 billion, received "policy support" valued at RMB 550 billion between 2006 and 2013.[159]

Government intervention extends beyond China's national borders. UNCTAD data show that China's stock of outbound FDI, much of it in the hands of state enterprises, now exceeds the stock of inward FDI. Overseas lending, partly in support of Belt and Road projects, represents a further extension of official activity: year-end 2018 debts of "73 of the world's poorest countries" held by the Chinese state and state-owned financial institutions amounted to US$104 billion, matching the total ($106 billion) owed to the World Bank.[160]

Chinese advances in multiple segments of technology-intensive activity – Internet software, supercomputers, electric vehicles, high-speed rail, green energy, high-voltage power transmission, artificial intelligence, and genetics,

---

[157] See the online appendix referred to in note 44.
[158] See the online appendix referred to in note 44.
[159] D.H. Xu 徐东华 (ed.), 中国装备制造业发展报告 2017 (Report on the Development of Equipment Manufacturing Industry in China 2017) (Beijing, Shehui kexue wenxian chubanshe, 2017), p. 87; B. van Hezewijk, "Big Fund = Big Impact? 'Winning the Future' of the Semiconductor Industry," August 24, 2019, at www.linkedin.com/pulse/big-fund-impact-winning-future-semiconductor-industry-van-hezewijk; TX Investment Consulting Co., Ltd., "全求船舶制造业特续景气,国内造船企业加速整合" (Accelerate the Consolidation of Domestic Shipbuilding for the Continued Prosperity of the Shipbuilding Industry) (February 28, 2007), 7; P.J. Barwick, M. Kalouptsidi, and N.B. Zahur, "China's Industrial Policy: An Empirical Evaluation," NBER Working Paper 26075, 2019, 2.
[160] "The Debt Toll," The Economist, July 4, 2020, 63.

among others – demonstrate the new strategy's capacity to promote innovation. At the same time, multiple constraints limit the effectiveness of the vast resources deployed in pursuit of innovation.

Constraints: Ongoing, New, and Resurrected

China's economic system channels vast resource flows into unproductive activities. Top-down selection of priorities steers investment in directions that often clash with domestic capabilities and with China's international comparative advantage. Politics pervades the allocation process, delivering resources and opportunities into the wrong hands, while bypassing worthwhile industries, projects, and proprietors.

SOE priority status has survived decades of underperformance. From 1978 to 2007, the state sector "contributed essentially zero to aggregate growth in total factor productivity."[161] Additional evidence confirms the deleterious impact of state ownership on growth, profitability, and structural change. Entry barriers and subsidies allow plodding, overstaffed state firms to remain profitable;[162] at the same time, soft budget constraints exempt long-time money losers from financial discipline, dragging returns downward.[163] The growing complexity of SOE structures conceals payoffs to allies, wealth extraction, and waste. Negative consequences of state ownership extend beyond the SOEs themselves to encompass the sectors and regions they inhabit: "in almost every dimension – the rate of start-up of new firms, size of firms, TFP, and wages ... new firms are weaker where the SOEs are more dominant."[164]

Announcement of official priorities sparks rampaging investment as officials, agencies, companies, and organizations pursue the anticipated cornucopia of financial and reputational bounty. In 2016, a "robot craze" prompted local governments to announce 2020 output targets that amounted to a considerable multiple of overall demand projections.[165] Inflated R & D

---

[161] Zhu, "Understanding China's Growth," 119.
[162] Insiders at one of China's largest energy firms regard two-thirds of the company's workforce as superfluous (personal communication).
[163] N.R. Lardy, *The State Strikes Back: The End of Economic Reform in China?* (Washington, DC, Peterson Institute for International Economics, 2019), pp. 52, 55, 89, shows declining return on assets for state firms after 2007, with the share of loss makers regularly exceeding 40 percent.
[164] L. Brandt, G. Kambourov, and K. Storesletten, "Barriers to Entry and Regional Economic Growth in China," University of Toronto, Department of Economics, Working Paper 652, January 5, 2020.
[165] Wübbeke et al., "Made in China," 25.

spending,[166] low-quality patents,[167] phantom companies,[168] unaudited venture funds,[169] and dubious projects burden Chinese industrial policy with long tails of excess.

The ubiquity of procedures that allow "particularistic bargains" rather than "universal rules" enables officials to distort seemingly market-based transactions to benefit favored participants.[170] Officials can readily manipulate government-managed auctions and supplier certification processes to steer business opportunities toward preferred clients.[171] In return for access to urban real estate at discounted prices, companies associated with relatives of top leaders accelerate the promotion of provincial officials.[172] Similarly privileged "princelings" orchestrate lesser rivulets of efficiency-sapping resource diversion in every locality and sector.

Xi Jinping's emphasis on top-down strategizing and enthusiasm for the "dominance" (*zhuti diwei* 主体地位) and "leading role" (*zhudao diwei* 主导地位) of public ownership and state-controlled enterprises enlarges these costs. Casting state-owned enterprises as lead actors in national economic strategy diminishes prospects for favorable outcomes. The growing sway of official mandates over financial resources, investment opportunities, and approval mechanisms stifles decentralized experimentation and limits private-sector options.[173] New constraints, beginning with the installation of frontier innovation as the centerpiece of China's policy agenda, expand the burden of system costs.

---

[166] "中国科研经费水分大:'节省'经费发'福利' 经济参考报," June 3, 2007, at techweb.com.cn/news/2007-03-06/162748.shtml; Y.T. Sun and C. Cao, "China's Research Is Work in Progress," *China Daily*, May 11, 2015.

[167] A.G.Z. Hu, P. Zhang, and L.J. Zhao, "China as Number One? Evidence from China's Most Recent Patenting Surge," *Journal of Development Economics* 124 (2017), 107–19; P. Boeing and E. Mueller, "Measuring Patent Quality: Development and Validation of ISR Indices," *China Economic Review* 57 (2019), available at https://browzine.com/articles/332678339.

[168] R.C. Dai, X.Y. Liu, and X.B. Zhang, "Detecting Shell Companies in China," presentation at ASSA annual meeting, January 4, 2020.

[169] N. Xiang, "Rise of Trillion-RMB Government Funds Reshapes China's Investment Landscape," January 13, 2017, at chinamoneynetwork.com/2017/01/13/rise-of-trillion-rmb-government-funds-reshapes-chinas-investment-landscape, accessed September 11, 2017.

[170] S.L. Shirk, *The Political Logic of Economic Reform in China* (Berkeley, University of California Press, 1993), p. 336.

[171] H.B. Cai, J.V. Henderson, and Q.H. Zhang, "China's Land Market Auctions: Evidence of Corruption?", *RAND Journal of Economics* 44.3 (2013), 488–521.

[172] Chen and Kung, "Busting the 'Princelings'." The authors note that recent anticorruption efforts appear to have reduced these discounts by 40–50 percent.

[173] S. Heilmann, *Red Swan: How Unorthodox Policy Making Facilitated China's Rise* (New York, Columbia University Press, 2018).

Current policy replacing market-propelled catch-up with officially mandated innovation targets adds both cost and risk. Investing in activities that enjoy a comparative cost advantage is widely seen as a key contributor to China's recent boom. This has meant that Chinese firms, often working within the anonymity of global supply chains, have pursued incremental advances rather than "'moonshot innovations' – not for them 'iPhone envy'."[174] With "Made in China 2025" in the forefront, current policy stands this approach on its head, focusing precisely on "moonshot innovations" spanning a vast spectrum from large-scale passenger aircraft and space exploration to genetics and nanotechnology.

Attempting frontier innovation in a middle-income economy with a limited command of the human, industrial, and organizational resources that underpin innovation systems in advanced nations multiplies the risks associated with any such effort. Surveys of China's engineering industries highlight weaknesses in precision, durability, quality control, software development, and commercialization of research results – all critical to innovative success.[175] Growing hostility to foreign involvement, especially in strategic and advanced sectors, invites premature import substitution, further compounding the dangers surrounding the main thrust of China's current economic agenda.

Structural change has added constraints in two areas: services and urbanization. The tertiary or service sector, now the largest contributor to both output and employment, includes retail, hospitality, and other low-skill, labor-intensive industries. The technology-intensive service segment includes entrepreneurial and innovative operators such as Baidu, DRI, and Huawei, along with state-owned financial and telecom giants whose main asset is the official umbrella that protects them from competition.

Despite the achievements of a few globally competitive firms, weak performance predominates. Exclusion of private operators limits competition and raises costs in air and rail transport, finance, insurance, and telecommunications, among others. The protectionist nature of China's innovation policy is evident in digital services, where China ranks as the global leader in restricting cross-border trade.[176]

---

[174] G.S. Yip and B. McKern, *China's Next Strategic Advantage: From Imitation to Innovation* (Cambridge, MA, MIT Press, 2016), pp. 82–3.
[175] Annual issues of D.H. Xu 徐东华 (ed.), 中国装备制造业发展报告, address these issues in considerable detail.
[176] *OECD Services Trade Restrictiveness Index: Policy Trends up to 2020* (Paris, OECD, 2020), pp. 12–13.

Massive internal migration reflects both the attraction of vibrant urban economies and the distortions associated with decades of policy discrimination against rural areas. National policy often appears to conflate cause and effect, anticipating that enlarging city boundaries, reassigning farmland to nonagricultural pursuits, and relocating villagers into high-density housing clusters will somehow elevate productivity. Municipal governments, reflecting concern over the cost of providing health and education benefits as well as urban contempt for migrants' low cultural level, hesitate to absorb these newcomers, and sometimes seek to drive them away.

Revival of pre-reform obstacles to growth completes the roster of constraints that limit China's growth prospects.

China's current leader has resurrected the pre-reform personality cult. As under Mao, many actions must once again await the leader's personal decision. Deng Xiaoping's pragmatism fades as specialized bureaucracies give way to party loyalists. China's constitution now decrees that "east, west, south, north, the party leads on everything."[177]

These changes add fresh burdens to the economy. Party review of business decisions in state and even private firms will complicate already labyrinthine decision mechanisms. Growing pressure on private firms "to set up party committees with an increasing say over strategy" steers activities in directions that deliver political rather than commercial returns. Not surprisingly, available data show declining profitability for non-state industrial and service firms.[178] Educational quality must suffer as teachers shelter behind rote learning and academics give way to "Xi Jinping thought." As in the past, increased emphasis on orthodoxy and suppression of dissent, the bedfellows of politics in command, will attenuate the critical thinking essential to innovation.

Strident emphasis on "autonomous" (*zizhu* 自主) innovation built upon "independent Chinese intellectual property" illustrates how growing nationalist preoccupation has curtailed involvement with foreign firms, technologies, and components. Enhanced focus on security and on civil–military

---

[177] N. Grünberg and K. Drinhausen, "The Party Leads on Everything," *Merics China Monitor*, September 24, 2019, 10.

[178] "The New State Capitalism: Xi Jinping Is Trying to Remake the Chinese Economy," *The Economist*, August 15, 2020. NBS data show the return on assets for above-scale private industry falling from 12 to 14 percent during 2010–2012 to just over 7 percent in 2018–2019. For services, see L. Brandt, "Policy Perspectives from the Bottom Up: What Do Firm-Level Data Tell Us China Needs to Do?", in R. Glick and M.M. Spiegel (eds.), *Policy Challenges in a Diverging Global Economy* (San Francisco, Federal Reserve Bank of San Francisco, 2015), p. 297.

integration sharpens this nationalist policy edge. With foreign businesses complaining that "strong-arm tactics ... marked difficulty in getting licenses" and deportation of foreign managers make them "feel unwelcome in China," it is hardly surprising that the number of foreign-invested enterprises and their share in both output and exports began to decline well in advance of the abrupt deterioration of US–China relations in 2020.[179] Rising barriers led the European Commission to identify China as "the EU's most restrictive trading partner."[180]

Trade disruptions involving rare earths, cars, beef, barley, medical supplies, sports, and tourism, among others, have become a routine instrument of China's foreign policy, encouraging foreign partners to diversify away from China. Domestic activities suffer as well: even in scientific fields, researchers face restrictions on participation in international projects and conferences. Foreign textbooks now arouse suspicion: in an apparent exception, business schools are "mostly spared from curbs on the use of imported textbooks."[181]

Strong conflict between the vast resources mobilized to support China's innovation ambitions and the daunting obstacles hindering China's economic progress invites a review of recent productivity trends, which combine multiple factors into a single measure of economic advance.

Productivity

Ongoing decline in the size of the labor force and in the share of GDP going to investment dictates the dependence of future growth on increases in TFP, which measures the level of output per unit of combined inputs. Socialist planning raised output amidst stagnant productivity. Reform abruptly reversed this failure. Multiple studies track China's transition to "intensive" growth – with the majority of output expansion attributable to higher productivity rather than increased quantities of labor and capital inputs – for three decades from 1978.

---

[179] R. Legaspi, "More U.S., Foreign Businesses Feel Unwelcome in China," *China Topix*, January 9, 2015 at chinatopix.com/articles/31659/20150109/more-us-foreign-businesses-feel-unwelcome-in-china.htm, accessed July 25, 2020. *Yearbook 2019*, Tables 13-3, 13-9, show sharp reduction in foreign-invested industrial firms along with employment and share of overall industrial output after 2007. L. Brandt and K. Lim, "Accounting for Export Growth in China," MS, 2020, use China's trade transactions Customs data to show a decline in the share of exports by foreign firms.

[180] "Report from the Commission to the Parliament and the Council on Trade and Investment Barriers 1 January 2018–31 December 2018," Brussels, n.d., 28.

[181] "MBAs with Chinese Characteristics," *The Economist*, February 15, 2020, 57.

Beginning in 2008, however, we see a return to "extensive" growth powered by larger inputs. A succession of studies using national, provincial, and enterprise-level data point to a marked decline in productivity growth since the eve of the global financial crisis.[182] The size of the private sector and the scale of productivity deterioration suggest that declining performance encompasses both private and state enterprise, with areas of stagnant or declining productivity dwarfing pockets of dynamism.

China enters the reform era's fifth decade with its economy far larger and more sophisticated, its people more prosperous and better educated, its command of modern technology far greater, and the expertise of its policy makers far deeper than in 1978. Despite these astonishing advances, the revival of plan-era policy approaches and political strategies now confronts China's economy with the same challenge it faced in the 1970s: how to overcome self-imposed obstacles that prevent improvements in knowledge and capabilities from generating intensive growth that outruns the accumulation of resources.

Conclusion

China's boom, a major event in global economic history, has transformed a poor, backward, isolated economy into a prosperous and dynamic global giant. This stunning departure is no miracle, but rather the consequence of readily understandable changes in core elements of China's economy. The restoration of economic incentives, reflecting Deng Xiaoping's call to "let some people get rich first," invited every individual, enterprise, and official to pursue income-enhancing opportunities. Gradual opening of domestic and international markets, along with partial relaxation of long-standing restrictions on entry, competition, and mobility, expanded the universe of available choices.

Modest institutional opening prompted a rush to exploit the untapped potential accumulated under socialist planning. Initial opportunities clustered in the countryside, where thousands of enterprises and millions of villagers, freed from the shackles of collective farming and enforced self-sufficiency,

---

[182] D. Dollar, "China's New Macroeconomic Normal," unpublished, 2016; C.E. Bai and Q. Zhang, "Is the People's Republic of China's Current Slowdown a Cyclical Downturn or a Long-Term Trend? A Productivity-Based Analysis," Manila, Asian Development Bank Institute Working Paper No. 635, 2017; S.J. Wei, Z. Xie, and X. B. Zhang, "From 'Made in China' to 'Innovated in China': Necessity, Prospect, and Challenges," *Journal of Economic Perspectives* 31.1 (2017), 549–70; Brandt and Lim, "Accounting for Export Growth in China."

streamed into long-forbidden markets and occupations. Decentralized movement of labor, materials, and capital toward financially rewarding activities brought massive change: hundreds of millions left farming, millions of new firms emerged, and vast resources poured into China's coastal provinces.

Long before the recent boom, Qing-era Chinese society harbored elements favorable to economic growth. Wide dispersion of entrepreneurship, commercial acumen and sophistication, universal regard for education, informal contract enforcement mechanisms, and competent local administration all contributed to the initial reform response and its subsequent extension. These growth-enhancing features supported Qing-era prosperity and commercialization, but, enmeshed in tightly interlinked economic, political, and social institutions, lacked the capacity to generate an economy-wide response to the appearance of new markets and new technologies in the nineteenth and early twentieth centuries.

During the twentieth century, growing state strength and the gradual buildup of physical and human capital eroded long-standing obstacles to growth. Wartime disruption and then the deficiencies of the PRC plan system delayed the realization of these gains. Beginning in the late 1970s, the combination of reforms that broke both old and new barriers to growth and Deng Xiaoping's effort to harmonize the incentives of government and citizens unleashed a boom that revealed the full power of China's economic system.

Remarkable economic gains have not eliminated the tension between the demands of political stability and economic development that pervades China's governance arrangements. Systematic misallocation via networking cements elite loyalty and promotes critical support for regime survival, but the long-term economic cost is staggering. The rent seeking that honeycombs policy implementation propels high levels of income inequality and causes massive waste[183] – as when large shares of funds awarded for constructing public projects vanish into private pockets before work commences.[184]

---

[183] Analyses of contemporary inequality find that the top 1 percent of households receive roughly 15 percent of overall income. See https://wid.world/country/china, focused on 2005–2015; and T. Piketty, L. Yang, and G. Zucman, "Income Inequality Is Growing Fast in China and Making It Look More Like the US," at https://blogs.lse.ac.uk/businessreview/2019/04/01/income-inequality-is-growing-fast-in-china-and-making-it-look-more-like-the-us. These estimates resemble those for the late Qing: C.L. Chang, *The Income of the Chinese Gentry* (Seattle, University of Washington Press, 1962), pp. 327–8, finds that gentry families comprised 2 percent of China's population and received 24 percent of overall income during the 1880s.

[184] Participants indicate that skimming may absorb 30 percent of costs for airports or stadiums and mention higher figures for road building (personal communication).

Long before China's post-1978 growth explosion, Qing territorial expansion, suppression of mid-nineteenth-century rebellions, and the PRC's recovery from both self-inflicted and external shocks demonstrated the durability and resilience of Chinese authoritarian systems. The most dynamic episodes of change and growth, however, cluster around interludes of state weakness, when ruptures in the carapace of restrictions surrounding elite interests enable China's populace to deploy its remarkable commercial talents.

Shanghai's pre-1937 development into Asia's premier financial complex, as well as a commercial hub and manufacturing center, illustrates this potential. Several decades later, post-Cultural Revolution erosion of central authority enabled nationwide rural reforms. The astonishing boom that followed demonstrated the capacity of unheralded "peasants" to lift China's vast countryside onto an elevated growth trajectory that liberated hundreds of millions from absolute poverty even as crumbling commune finances reduced funding for social welfare. The subsequent surge in private entrepreneurship extended "development from below" into the urban economy, where private firms garnered large shares of output and employment wherever they managed to gain a foothold.

The 1990s spawned a unique concatenation of expanded market opening with massive growth and centralization of state-controlled fiscal and financial resources. SOE reforms decanted tens of thousands of enterprises and tens of millions of workers into the grip of market discipline, while sweeping reductions in barriers to international trade and investment intensified domestic competition, elevated quality standards and forced widespread reductions in profit margins. While the multiplication of state-controlled resources stabilized a regime shaken by Tiananmen, the economic benefits of market opening extended robust productivity growth until the 2008 global financial crash.

Long-standing tension between market- and state-led economic strategies resurfaced following China's 2001 WTO entry. Unlike the 1990s, there is little sign of mutually acceptable initiatives. The market economy vision, most clearly articulated in the 2013 document *China 2030*, anticipates a retreat of the state, and especially of state-owned enterprises, from the "commanding heights" of an open economy led by private business – changes that would sharply reduce the resources available to state and Party leaders.

Aside from a brief flurry in 2013, when a Central Committee decision endorsed the notion of building an economy in which "market forces dominate," the rival vision of state economic leadership has captured the imagination of China's ruling elites. Support for state direction over market dominance came from many sources. The economic success of Japan, Taiwan, and South Korea has built a global constituency promoting government entrepreneurship as the wellspring of technological development. Many Chinese viewed the absence of globally prominent Chinese firms, brands, and technologies as signaling the failure of openness to end China's economic subordination to former colonial powers. Concern about China's need to develop its own military technology bolstered nationalist objections to economic opening. Unavoidable reliance on state intervention to alleviate the 2008 financial crisis reinforced this view of market frailty and deepened support for increased government management of the economy.

The administration of Xi Jinping has moved decisively toward state control. Core elements extend practices familiar from seventy years of Chinese economic planning. Policy directives, notably Made in China 2025, set overall strategy and lay out investment priorities. State-owned enterprises take the lead in implementing top-down initiatives. The current policy constellation incorporates new dimensions and revives former practices.

Reflecting China's recent economic advance, the current array of strategic industries and technologies includes many new entrants. Recent plans for both well-established and novel sectors revolve around bold plans to reach and then extend global technological frontiers.

China's effort to redirect development from widespread, decentralized incremental efforts that add value through improvements in cost, quality, and design to more concentrated pursuit of targeted innovations in a narrow range of products and technologies faces formidable challenges. Extending technological frontiers is always a high-risk proposition. Launching a "breakthrough" strategy from a middle-income platform beset by weaknesses in key domestic supply chains and limited downstream demand adds fresh layers of risk.

Assigning vast resources to a talented and highly motivated corps of domestic researchers will surely deliver successes – already visible in State Grid's technical advances in high-voltage electricity transmission and in the commercial achievements of firms like Alibaba, Pinduoduo, and Tencent.[185] When measured against the enormity of the world's largest economy, however, even considerable numbers of isolated breakthroughs may fail to

---

[185] Y.C. Xu, "The Search for High Power in China: State Grid Corporation of China," in L. Brandt and T.G. Rawski (eds.), *Policy, Regulation and Innovation in China's Electricity and Telecom Industries* (Cambridge, Cambridge University Press, 2019), pp. 221–61.

deliver economy-wide productivity increases, leading to a Soviet-style outcome in which the occasional sputnik illuminates galaxies of mediocrity.

Looking beyond efforts to scale the heights of advanced technology, the absence of major reforms during the two decades following China's 2001 entry into the WTO has burdened the economy with an immense backlog of costs. Excess capacity in steel, electricity, and many other industries; state-sector firms often bulging with surplus employees; and zombie companies held together with patchworks of subsidies, loans, and tax concessions exemplify the distortions that permeate every corner of China's vast economic landscape. Past outcomes invite expectations that strengthening Party control and promoting self-reliance will accelerate the pace of cost accretion.

The decade following the global financial crisis has seen a return to the plan-era pattern in which growth arises almost entirely from the accumulation of labor and capital. Mounting signs of a steep fall-off in productivity growth warn that the current state-led economic strategy may prematurely terminate China's remarkable growth explosion.

Some will see this skepticism as "misleadingly wrong" and "encouraging a complacent and dangerous underestimate of China's potential trajectory."[186] China's growth potential is indeed large. With its remarkable human resources, competent public administration, and per capita income roughly one-fourth the US level, China faces an unmistakable opportunity to navigate a lengthy runway of intensive growth.

For the moment, however, China's leaders have turned away from openness and competition, the conventional tools for traversing the path from middling to high levels of productivity and income. China's current policy constellation ignores abundant evidence, much of it from China itself, highlighting the benefit of shifting from plan to market, redistributing resources from state to private firms, and allowing increased access to foreign firms, imported products, and external technologies. Unless China's leaders once again demonstrate that they are "imaginative and flexible" and can "shift policy decisively, comprehensively, and without regard to procedural or legal niceties,"[187] disappointment seems more likely than triumph.

Whatever the outcome and whatever its future course, China will continue to grapple with dilemmas that have bedeviled two centuries of modernization efforts. How can China embed a creative, freewheeling culture of

---

[186] "The New State Capitalism."
[187] T. Orlik, *China: The Bubble That Never Pops* (New York, Oxford University Press, 2020), pp. 198–9.

economic and technical innovation within an authoritarian system whose leaders feel threatened by unorthodox thinking? How can China resolve the concern arising from fears that indiscriminate opening to Western technology and ideas endangers the edifice that Confucian and Communist thinkers have long seen as the foundation of authoritarian rule and social stability?

Further Reading

Breznitz, D., and M. Murphree, *Run of the Red Queen: Government, Innovation, Globalization and Economic Growth in China* (New Haven, Yale University Press, 2011).

Elvin, M., and G.W. Skinner (eds.), *The Chinese City between Two Worlds* (Stanford, Stanford University Press, 1974).

Huang, Y.S., *Capitalism with Chinese Characteristics* (Cambridge, Cambridge University Press, 2008).

Mülhahn, K., *Making China Modern: From the Great Qing to Xi Jinping* (Cambridge, MA, Harvard University Press, 2019).

Rozelle, S., and N. Hell, *Invisible China: How the Urban–Rural Divide Threatens China's Rise* (Chicago, The University of Chicago Press, 2020).

Schell, O., and J. Delury, *Wealth and Power: China's Long March to the Twenty-First Century* (New York, Random House, 2013).

Skinner, G.W. (ed.), *The City in Late Imperial China* (Stanford, Stanford University Press, 1977).

So, B.K.L., and R.H. Myers (eds.), *The Treaty Port Economy in Modern China: Empirical Studies of Institutional Change and Economic Performance* (Berkeley, University of California Institute of East Asian Studies, 2011).

Walder, A.G., *China under Mao: A Revolution Derailed* (Cambridge, MA, Harvard University Press, 2015).

Walter, C., and F. Howie, *Red Capitalism: The Fragile Financial Foundation of China's Extraordinary Rise* (Hoboken, John Wiley, 2011).

Whiting, S.H., *Power and Wealth in Rural China* (Cambridge, Cambridge University Press, 2009).

Zelin, M., J.K. Ocko, and R. Gardella (eds.), *Contract and Property in Early Modern China* (Stanford, Stanford University Press, 2004).

Index

Page numbers in **bold** refer to content in tables; page numbers in *italics* refer to content in figures and maps.

absolutism, 45
accounting systems, 202
Africa, 711
Aglen, Francis, 263
agriculture, 87–8. *See also* Great Famine (1958–1961)
    collectivization, 566, 567, 574–7, 583–4, 586–8, 681–2, 798–9
    farm size and productivities, **103**
    freight transportation, 475–6
    land institutions, distribution, and credit, 115–20, **118**, **121**
    long-term output trends, 88–99, *89*, *91*, *92*, **93**, *94*
    models of, 99–107, *105*, *106*
    new elements (Qing era to 1949), 107–15, *110*, *116*
    pre-1979 living standards, 599–601, **600**, 633–4, **634**
    Qing-era land reclamation, 51–4
    Reform Era, 725–6, 740–4, 745–6, 803
    rural finance (1930s–1940s), 298–307, **301**, **302**, **303**, **305**, **306**
    sideline production, 104–7, *106*
Almond, Douglas, 679
American Silver Purchase Act (1934), 238, 298
Anhua, Hunan, 69, 70
Anhui province, 629, 631, 803
annual budget appropriations, 190
anti-Japanese base areas, 159, 163
Anti-Rightist campaign, 550–1, 580
apprenticeship, 503–4, 513
arsenal industry, 127, 171–3
Asian Financial Crisis (1997), 767
Australia, 716, *717*

authoritarian control, 775, 776, 779, 781
authoritarian hierarchy, 777, 779
authoritarian politics, 49, 274, 789
authoritarian rule, 43, 228, 264, 785, 789, 828
authoritarian system, 44, 532, 825, 828. *See also* regionally decentralized authoritarianism (RDA)
aviation, 487–8

Bai, Ying, 393, 519, 681–2
Balazs, Étienne, 5
Bandung Conference (1955), 708–11
Bank of China (BoC), 220–2, 223, 226–8, 272, 292, 297–8, 312
Bank of Communications (BoCom), 215, 220–1, 222, 223, 226–8, 297–8, 312
Bank of the Great Qing, 215
banks, 281, **282**, **283**, *283*, 284–6, **285**. *See also* native banks (cash shops)
    apprenticeships, 504
    banker networks, 317–19, **318**
    commerce and industry finance, 311–12
    competition with the nationalist state, 226–8, 296–8
    co-operation with the nationalist state, 228–32
    depositing money, 235, 320, 568
    evolution of the money system, 216–20, *217*, *218*
    geography of, 287–9, *289*, *290*, 292–4, *358*, *378*
    government bonds, 277
    issuing of banknotes, 44, 210, 215, 219, 220–4, *221*, 226–7
    Reform Era, 766, 770, 805, 808

banks (cont.)
  relation with university development, 396, **397**
  rise of Chinese institutions, 40–1
  social status of, 317–19, **318**
  state's takeover of, 222–4, 568
  statistical data, 21–2, 22, 24
  treaty ports system, 373–8, 374, 375, 377, **379**, 380
Bao Shichen 包世臣, 59, 75, 84
Baodi, Hebei, 145
Baoshan Steel, 731, 740
barefoot doctors, 626
Bastid, Marianne, 251
Baxian, Sichuan, 336
Beijing, 41, 43, 47, 85, 86, 88, 91, 96, 110, 122, 166, 182, 183, 207, 224, 226, 227, 232, 233, 234, **239**, 242, 243, 248, 251, 252, 253, 254, 255, 256, 258, 260, 261, 262, 263, 264, 265, 266, 270, 271, 272, 273, 275, 277, 280, 281, 284, 286, 292, 294, 295, 297, 298, 299, 307, 309, 312, 313, 316, 317, 320, 322, 323, 328, 333, 336, 341, 356, 361, 371, 401, 426, 460, 468, 469, 471, 489, 490, 492, 495, 500, 501, 504, 506, 509, 513, **517**, 524, 526, 528, 537, 544, 557, 564, 580, 581, **585**, **611**, **614**, **617**, 620, 624, 628, 629, **630**, 630, 631, 632, **634**, 636, 637, 638, 641, 658, 665, 667, 675, 689, 691, 692, 693, 701, 702, 707, 708, 709, 710, 711, 712, 715, 716, 721, 726, 727, 729, 730, 732, 734, 735, 737, 738, 740, 741, 743, 751, 759, 760, 762, 763, 774, 776, 783, 784, 794, 799, 800, 803, 807, 808, 809, 814, 815, 817
  banks, 292–4
  currency use, 225, 226–7
  education, 514, 518
  family firms, 327
  infrastructure, 180, 476, 485, 487
  living standards, 64, 95, 96, 614
  Olympic Games (2008), 814
  Tangshan earthquake (1976), 595
  warlord era finance, 261–6, **262**
Beijing Stock Exchange, 313
Beijing–Hankou railroad, 474, 476, 481, 483
Beiyang Xuetang, 130
Belt and Road initiative, 719, 816, 817
Bergère, Marie-Claire, 144
Berlin, Isaiah, 639
Bernstein, Thomas P., 668
bimetallism, 208–9
birth control, 65, 727
birth rates, 63, 65
body shares, 337–8

Bolshevism, 541–3, 546–7
bondholders, 41, 230
bonds, 44, 229–32, 255, 263, 264, 272
  stock markets, 313–16, **314**, **315**
  wartime, 277
Boserupian framework, 100–3, 101
bottom-up development, 46, 240, 741, 776, 809
Boxer Rebellion (1899–1901), 130, 244, 255, 259–60
Boyd Company, 128
Brandt, Loren, 119, 680
Bretton Woods Agreement (1944), 160, 688
Britain
  business organization, 345
  consumption, 622
  industrialization, 16, 354
  infrastructure, 467
  investment, 439, 440
  loans, 275
  trade, 20, 72–3, 422–5, 435, 701
  treaty ports system, 360–1, 367
British American Tobacco Company, 112, 131, 477
British East India Company, 423
Broadberry, Stephen, 622
Brown, Shannon, 779
Buck, John, 88, 102, 120, 615
Burgess, John, 514
bus transportation, 486
business organization, 324–5
  early twentieth-century developments, 348–51
  family firms, 325–32
  private ordering, 332–42
  Western influence, 342–8

Cai Yuanpei 蔡元培, 525
California School, 27, 28, 87, 100
Campbell, Cameron, 65
Canada, 716, 717
Canton System, 422, 427
Cao Shuji 曹树基, 648, 650
Cao Yu 曹禺, 317
capital flow, 235, 236, 439, **440**
capital markets, 448, 450
capitalism, 7, 27–8
censorship, 778
central account offices, 350–1
Central Air Transport Corporation (CATC), 487
Central Bank (PBoC), 220, 222, 223–4, 231, 272, 297, 568, 569, 578, 580, 762, 805
Central China Cocoon and Silk Company, 158

Index

Central China Promotion Company, 158
central control, 32, 258, 259, 274, 581, 784, 807–15
centralization of state-controlled fiscal and financial resources, 825
centralized authoritarian control, 781
central-level enterprise groups, 784
centrally supervised enterprise groups, 814
centrally planned command system. *See* planned (command) economy
ceramics, 132
Ch'en Huan-chang 陈焕章, 1
Ch'ien, Tuan-Sheng, 514
Chairman Mao. *See* Mao Zedong 毛泽东
Chan, Wellington, 344, 348
Chang Chung-li 张仲礼, 499, 507
Chang, Gene Hsin, 675
Chang Jung, 648
Chang Yu-fa 张玉法, 357, 367–9, 385
Changchun, Jilin, 294
Changshu, Jiangsu, 146
Changzhou, Jiangsu, 59
Chao Kang 赵冈, 92, 100, 101, 119
Chartered Bank, 40
Chefoo Convention (1876), 258
Chen Duxiu 陈独秀, 544
Chen Hansheng, 5
Chen Hongmou 陈宏谋, 52, 54
Chen Jitang 陈济棠, 193
Chen Qiyuan 陈启源, 134, 149, 341
Chen Shuo, 669
Chen Yi 陈毅, 696
Chen Yizi, 648
Chen Yonggui 陈永贵, 734
Chen Yun 陈云, 565, 571–2, 574, 581, 586, 732–3, 739–40, 745, 748, 749–50, 755, 756, 759
Chen Yuyu, 678
Cheng Linsun, 286
Chenggong, Yunnan, 521
Cheong Weng Eang, 341
Cheung Sui Wai, 68
Chiang Ching-kuo 蒋经国, 545
Chiang Kai-shek 蒋介石, 188, 196, 267, 272, 274, 463, 466, 485, 545, 715, 788. *See also* Jiang Jieshi
China Dream, 816
China Economic Statistics Institute, 203
China Health and Nutrition Survey (CHNS), 621
China Integrated Circuit Industry Investment Fund (CICIF), 817
China Merchants Steam Navigation Company (CMSNC), 169, 174–6, 307, **308**, 344, 465, 492, 737

China National Aviation Corporation (CNAC), 487
Chinese Economic Yearbook, 306
Chinese Monetary History, 8
Chinese Revolutionary Alliance, 406
Chinese Textile Construction Company, 163
Chong, Ja Ian, 255, 266
Chongqing, 159, 189, 487
Christianity, 391
Chuan, Han-sheng 全汉升, 67, 68
Chuxing Company, 351
civil service exams, 28, 405, 500, *501*, 502, 519, 777
Cixi, Empress Dowager of Qing, 38, 171
class struggle, 585–6, 592
climate change, 50
Cohen, Myron, 333
Cohen, Paul, 26–7, 34
Cold War, 692, 697–702
collectivization, 657–60, 725, 741–4, 798
Comintern, 541, 543, 544
commerce. *See also* business organization; international trade
    apprenticeships, 504
    domestic trading, 66–9, 370–3, *372*
    economic effects from new technology, 444–7, *445*, **446**
    financial capital, 307–12
    Maoist era, 568, 797–8
    money market integration, 232–4
commercial law, 37
Common Program (1949), 548
communal dining, 675–7
communes, 553–4, 583, 645, 657–9, 675–7, 724
communication infrastructure, 457–64
Communist institutional origins, 531–3
    analyzing institutional evolution, 533–4
    creation of a totalitarian regime, 548–51
    empire comparisons, 534–40, *535*, *538*, *539*
    origins of totalitarianism, 541–3
    regionally decentralized authoritarianism (RDA), 556–63
    regionally decentralized totalitarianism (RDT), 551–6
    totalitarianism's introduction to China, 543–8
company founders, 148–52
company law, 181, 182, 200, 345, 347–8, 469, 811
competition, 29, 740, 779, 786, 788, 812, 816, 820, 825, 827
conflict between political and economic objectives, 782
Confucian Classics, 28, 42, 43, 170, 359, 499, 501, 510

Confucianism, 2, 29, 34, 42, 169, 390, 496, 510
consolidated tax, 274
Constitutionalists, 405–11, 407, **408**
constraints, 776, 794, 818–22
consumption
  communal dining, 645, 675–7
  Maoist era trends, 599–601, **601**, **604**, 604, 615–24, **617**, **621**, **623**, 631–2, 632
  Qing era, 62, 64–5, 94–6
  Republican era, 109
contracts, business, 334–6
copper, 74–5, 208, 211–13
  debasement of, 224–6
corruption, 778
cotton
  modern industries, 23, 23, 111, 131–2, 141–6, **143**, 155
  postwar era, 163
  Qing-era industry, 70–1, 73, 104, 113, 426
  wartime production, 159
Council for Mutual Economic Assistance (COMECON), 692
counterfeiting, 212, 214, 225
Crop Reports, 615
crop yields. *See* agriculture
cross investment, 340
Cuba, 488
Cultural Revolution (CR), 532, 554–6, 557, 592–3, 594–5, 728, 732, 751
currency, 208–11
  Daoguang depression, **74**, 74–7
  government–private sector relationship, 224–32
  major currencies overview, 211–16
  Maoist era, 566
  money market integration, 232–5, 238
  Nanjing era, 44
  postwar era, 162
  pre-1950 period, 24, 25
  role of banks, 219–20, 221
  role of the state, 220–4
  tax collection, 250

Da Long, 130
Da Sheng, 149, 150
Dai Yi 戴逸, 48
Dalian, Liaoning, 234
Dane, Richard Morris, 262
Daoguang depression, 73–7
Daoguang, emperor of Qing 道光皇帝, 49, 51, 54, 56, 73, 85, 97, 426
Dazhai, Shanxi, 726, 734

decentralization, 39, 537, 555, 581, 584, 588, 754
  See also regionally decentralized authoritarianism (RDA)
decentralization programs (1957 and 1970), 805
decentralized development, 782
decolonization, 708
defense industries, 127–8, 154, 155, 171–3, 186–7
deflation, 73
demographics. *See* population changes
Deng Xiaoping 邓小平, 548, 562, 586, 587, 595, 596, 647, 729, 731, 733, 735, 737, 739, 745, 747, 748, 755, 756, 758–60, 783, 808
Deng Zihui 邓子恢, 657
depositing money, 234–5, 320, 341, 568
Dernberger, Robert, 355–6
developmental state
  central state enterprises, 188–91
  Guangdong enterprises, 192–6
  Guizhou enterprises, 198–202
  ideology and policy of, 184–8
  public versus private enterprise, 202–6
  Shanxi enterprises, 196–8
Dexin, 483
Dikötter, Frank, 628, 648
Dimitrov, Georgi, 545
Ding Richang 丁日昌, 171
Ding-wu Disaster, 98
Discovering History in China, 26
Doctrine of Nationalism, 187
Doctrine of People's Livelihood, 187
domestic public debt, 41, 44
Dongting lake, 52
double-cropping, 60, 102
Dream of the Red Chamber, 316
droughts, 51, 98, 623
Du Xuncheng 杜询诚, 21, 292, 373, 374
dual-track system, 753–4, 804
Duan Qirui 段祺瑞, 265, 266
Dundas, Henry, 423
Dutch East India Company, 423

East India Company, 72, 423
Eastern Bloc nations, 558–9, 560, 692, 695–6
Eckstein, Alexander, 693, 711
ecological decay, 50–7
Economic Growth in Prewar China, 164
Economic Principles of Confucius and His School, The (1911), 1
education, 496–7, 777. *See also* overseas study
  Cultural Revolution era, 594–5
  modern universities, 394–9, **395**, **396**, **397**, 400, 404

Index

new system, post-1905, 509–18, *510*, **511**, **516**, **517**, **518**
role of missionaries, *392*, 392–4, **393**
socioeconomic changes, 519–26, **520**, **523**
traditional system, pre-1905, 359, 497–508, *499*, *501*, **506**, **508**
egg products, 138
Eighth Party Congress (1956–1958), 571, 580, 581, 584, 670
Eighth Route Army, 570
electricity supply, 358, 382, *385*, *386*, 489
Elvin, Mark, 9, 87, 100
employment levels, 588–9, *590*, **601**, 601, 746, 767, 801
energy industry, 191
Eng, Robert, 339
engineers, 396–9, **397**, *400*, **520**, 570
England. See Britain
entrepreneurs, 127, 132, 148–52, 350–1, 810
Essay on the Principle of Population, 58
Europe
  living standards comparison, 62–3
  market prices, 67
  trade, 70, 425–6
European Union (EU), 822
exchange rates, 74–5, 160–1, 250, 352, 761
exchange reserves, 814
exploitation, 119–20
export-oriented industrialization, 132–40

Fairbank, John, 26, 419, 777
family firms, 325–32, 348–9
family management, 150
famine, 51, 485, 554, 587. *See also* Great Famine (1958–1961)
Fan Xudong, 342, 350
Fang Xing 方行, 62–3, 64
farm size, 88, 102–3, **103**
Farmers Bank of China, 299
Faure, David, 181, 343
Fei Xiaotong 费孝通, 5, 136
feudalism, 3, 6, 7
Feuerwerker, Albert, 8, 9, 461
fiat money system, 44, 238
financial institutions, 280–7, **282**, **283**, **285**. *See also* banks; native financial institutions
  business and commerce, 307–12, **308**, **310**
  geography of, 287–94, *288*, *289*, *290*, *291*, *293*
  rural finance, 298–307, **301**, **302**, **303**, **305**, **306**
  social status of, 316–21, **318**
  state's role, 294–8
  stock markets, 312–16, **314**, **315**
financial trade associations, 319

First Five-Year Plan (1953–1957), 489, 490, 567, 579, 692, 694, 794
First National Finance Conference (1928), 270
First World War (1914–1918), 144, 311
Five Small Industries (FSI) campaign, 555
floods, 50–1, 52, 54, 98, 623
Foochow Naval Shipyard, 172
Food and Agriculture Organization (FAO), 615, 616, 725
Food and Money Semi-Monthly (Shihuo banyuekan 食货半月刊), 4
Foot, Rosemary, 697
foreign-aid strategy, 711–12
foreign debt (FD), 356, 365–70, *367*, *368*
foreign direct investment (FDI), 22, 356–7, *370*, 414–17, **439**, 439–42, **440**, *442*, 790
  impact of treaty ports, 365–70, *367*, *368*, *369*, *371*
  railroad lines, 472
  Reform Era, 738, 740, 811–12, 817
foreign firms, 373–6, *374*, *375*, **379**, 440–2
  railroad construction, 466–7
  Reform Era, 813
  relation with university development, 396–9, **397**
foreign influence, 442–8, *445*, **446**, *449*, *450*
foreign trade. *See* international trade
Four Cardinal Principles, 562
Fourth Five-Year Plan (1971–1975), 579, 591, 594, 596
France, 701
freight transportation, 473–80, **491**, 491–2
Friedman, Milton, 751
frontier innovation, 819–20
Fu Yiling 傅衣凌, 7
Fujian province, 631, 739, 740
Fukang (native bank), **310**
Furong, Sichuan, 83
Fuzhou, Fujian, 172

Gamble, Sidney, 514
Gang of Four, 596
Gansu corridor, 287
Gansu province, 289
Gao Gang 高岗, 548
Gao, Mobo, 617
Gao Wangling 高王凌, 49, 61
Gaojia yan dike, Qingjiang, 56
Gaoyang, Hebei, 145, 151
Gaozong, emperor of Qing, 78. *See also* Qianlong Emperor
gap between actual and potential output, 797–801

Index

gap between urban and rural living standards, 796
Ge Zhaoguang 葛兆光, 30, 38
gender inequality, 521–3, **523**
gentry degrees, 82
Germany, 187, 467, 524
Gesellschaft (impersonal social relations), 6
Global Financial Crisis (2008), 561, 769, 771, 815
Gooch, Elizabeth, 682
grain procurement, excessive, 664–74, **672**
grain tribute, 55–6
Grand Canal, 55–6, 246, 248
Great Depression, 111, 136, 238, 267, 271
Great Divergence debate, 10, 87
Great Famine (1958–1961), 642–7
  communal dining's impact, 675–7
  excess death estimates and salient features, 647–50, 651
  excessive grain procurement, 664–74, **672**
  long-term effects, 677–82
  production failures, 655–64, **663**
Great Leap Forward (GLF), 532, 552–4, 580–5, **585**, 643–7, 656, 712–16, 728
Great Northern Telegraph Company, 460
gross domestic product (GDP), 18–20, **19**, 23, 238, **239**, 245, 446, 531, 723–9, **724**
  Maoist era, 596, **597**, 597–600, **598**, 607–8, 655
  Reform Era, 559, 561, 760, 766, 807, 812
  treaty ports, 358, 388, **389**
Gu Mu 谷牧, 730
Gu Yanwu 顾炎武, 30
guandu shangban enterprises, 344–5
Guangdong Enterprise Corporation (GDEC), 193–6
Guangdong province, 38, 72, 136, 138, 192–6, 212, 614, 628, 738, 740
Guangxi province, 320
Guangxu, emperor of Qing, 38, 171, 364, 788
Guangzhou (Canton), 57, 70, 192, 316, 360, 422, 514, 523
guilds, 66, 342
Guiyang, Guizhou, 202
Guizhou Enterprise Corporation (GZEC), 198–202
Guizhou province, 198–202, 631, 743
Guo Family Shop, 326–7
Guo Le, 149
Guo Moruo 郭沫若, 3
Guo Songtao 郭嵩焘, 41, 173
Guo Songyi 郭松义, 90

Hai river basin, 50–1
Halliday, Jon, 648

Halsey, Stephen, 254, 492
Han dynasty, 417
Han river, 52, 53
handicrafts, 124–7, *126*
  and agriculture, 104–7
  Communist era, 568
  new export-oriented industries, 138–40
  socialization of, 163
  textiles industry, 131, 133, 138, *139*, 140, 144–6
Hangzhou Electric Light Company, 346–7
Hangzhou, Zhejiang, 483
Hankou, Hubei, 69, 70, 217, *218*, 309, 444
Hanyang Iron Works, 179
Hanyeping Company, 178–80, 307
Hao Yen-p'ing, 343
Hart, Robert, 252, 254, 259, 459
He Changling 贺长龄, 56
He Liping 贺力平, 76
He Ziquan 何兹全, 4
health care, 626, 769
Henan province, 485, 583, 614
Hengjialou dike, Henan, 55
Hengzhou, Hunan, 65
Heshen 和珅 (Qing official), 49, 50
high-level equilibrium trap, 100, 106
highlands settlement, 52–4
Hino Kaisaburō, 4
Ho, Chun-Yu, 228
Ho, Hon-wai, 251
Ho, Ping-ti 何炳棣, 9, 58, 97
hoarding, 234
Hong Kong, 286, 294, 345, 422, 434, 582, 699, 737–8, 811, 814
Hong Kong and Shanghai Banking Corporation (HSBC), 40, 296
Hong Liangji 洪亮吉, 58, 84
Hong Ren'gan 洪仁玕, 780
honorary titles, 295
Hou Yangfang 候杨方, 99
household contracting, 743
household division. *See* family firms
household subsidiary activities, 104–7
Housheng Cotton Mill, 311
Hu Jintao 胡锦涛, 785
Hu Qiaomu 胡乔木, 734
Hu Shi 胡适, 789
Hu Yaobang 胡耀邦, 562, 756–7
Hu Yuanhe lineage trust, 331
Hua Guofeng 华国锋, 596, 729, 741
Huaibei district, 81
Huainan district, 81
Huang Jingbin 黄敬斌, 63, 64
Huang, Philip, 87, 100, 102, 105

834

Huang Zongxi 黃宗羲, 30
Huang Zongxian, 134
Huang Zunxian 黃遵憲, 38
Hubei Coal Mining Company, 176
Hubei province, 52, 71, 80, 629, 631
Hubei Textile Bureau, 351
Huguang Loan (1911), 261, 264
Huizhou, Guangdong, 93, 98
hukou system, 588
Hunan province, 38
Hundred Days Reform (1898), 38
Hundred Flowers movement, 580
Hupei Cotton Cloth Mill, 178, 179
hyperinflation, 45, 566

ideological change (1850–1950), 15–18
    age of culture, 41–3
    age of institutions, 38–41
    age of machines, 34–7
    economic statistics, 18–26, *19, 21, 22, 23, 25*
    end of the financial revolution, 44–5
    Qing political regime, 28–31
    Western impact and Chinese response framework, 26–8, 32–4
Imperial Academy, 500
imperial examination system, 536, 777
imperial land system, 535
Imperial Post Office, 459
Imperial Telegraph Administration, 176, 461–3
import-substitution industries, 140–8, **141**, **143**
incentive problems, 116, 117, 558, 583
incentive-compatible (IC) transformation, 534, 546–7
incentives, 231, 234, 533–4, 555, 560, 752–3, 796–7
income inequality, 627–31, *628*, **630**, 634–9, *637*
income trends (Communist era), 602–4, 608–14, **611**, **612**, **614**
India, 439, 517, 624
industrialization. *See* handicrafts; modern industries
inefficiency, 598, 727, 785, 796, 800, 801
inflation, 61, 63, 73, 162, 277, 590, **591**, 754, 755, *756, 757*, 761–2, 766
infrastructure, 152, 182, 357, 457–8
    and agriculture, 112, 475–6
    freight transportation, 473–80, **491**, 491–2
    interruptions to railroad development, 471–3
    motor roads and aviation, 484–8
    passenger transportation, 480–4, *481*
    postal and telegraph communication, 459–64
    postwar rail expansion, 488–92, **491**

    steamships and railroads, 464–71, *468*
innovation, 101, 439, 772, 776, 786, 818, 819–20, 821, 826
insurance companies, 292, *293*
intellectual elites, 523–6
interest rates, 119–20, **121**, 210, 236–8, *237*, 448
    rural finance, 299, 302, **305**
International Development of China, 185
international relations (Maoist era), 685–8
    Cold War geopolitical and economic blocs, 697–702, **699**, *700*
    impact of domestic campaigns, 712–16
    legacy of imperialism, 708–12
    legacy of Japanese empire, 702–8
    Soviet Union and the planned economy, 688–97
International Settlement, Shanghai, 32
international trade, 414–17, 434, 687, **687**
    commodity-level trade, 448–55, **451**, *454*
    country composition, 433–5, **435**, *436*
    export-oriented production, 132–40
    integrated statistics, 442–4, *443*
    Maoist era, 596, 686, 691–6, *695*, 697–702, **699**, *700*, 704–5, *706*, 709–10, 713, *714*, 715–16, *717*
    Maritime Customs records, *129*, 429–33, *431*
    opium, 75–7
    postwar era, 160–2
    pre-1839 era, 417–28
    pre-1950 period, 20–1, *21*, 35–7
    Qing maritime trade, 71–3
    Qing trade networks, 57
    Reform Era, 730–2, 737, 811
    steamships, 464–5
    tea export, 69–70
    volume of, 436–8, *438*
interregional trade. *See* commerce
involution, 99–107
Irish potatoes, 109
iron industry, 582, 656
Iwai Shigeki, 279
Iyigun, Murat, 31

Jamieson, George, 248, 340
Japan
    consumption, 622
    cotton industry, 142–3
    education, 515, 517
    gross domestic product (GDP), *19*, 19
    industrialization, 126, 131–2, 146–7, 707–8, 730
    industry in occupied areas, 156–9, 704
    infrastructure, 463, 464, 471, 479–80, 493

Japan (cont.)
  investment, 439
  legacy of empire, 702–8
  Meiji influence on China, 38–9
  overseas study, 401, 404–11, **408**, 524
  scholarship, 2, 4, 6
  silk production, 114, 116, 136–8
  technical expertise, 696, 705
  trade, 72, 434, 702, 704–5, 715–16
  treaty ports system, 367
  Western impact on, 31
Jardine, Matheson & Co., 134, 142, 426, 441, 466
Jian family, 349
Jian Yujie, 149
Jian Zhaonan, 149
Jiang Jieshi 蒋介石, 43. See also Chiang Kai-shek
Jiang Qin, 503
Jiang Qing 江青, 557
Jiang Rongzhuang, 338
Jiang Zemin 江泽民, 758, 762, 810, 813
Jianghan Plain, 54
Jiangnan Arsenal, 127, 172
Jiangnan region, 57, 59
  commerce and industry, 68, 136, 144
  consumption, 62
  living standards, 64
  population change, 63
Jiangsu province, 56, 272, 317
  infrastructure, 468
  population change, 59
  taxation, 264
  textiles industry, 115, 135, 144
Jiaqing, emperor of Qing 嘉庆皇帝, 49–50, 54, 55, 78, 79, 82
Jiaxing, Zhejiang, 60
Jicheng bao, 346
Jilin City, Jilin, 57
Jilin province, 631
Jin Guantao 金观涛, 29
Jinan Puyi sugar factory, 114
Jingdezhen, Jiangxi, 66
Jingzhou, Hubei, 54
Jin-Pu Railway, 180
Jiuda Salt Refinery, 350
Joffe, Adolf, 544
joint household economies. *See* family firms; private ordering
joint-stock companies, 175, 344, 345, 690
Joint-Stock Companies Act (1856), 345
Ju Qingyuan 鞠清远, 4
junxian system, 535, 537, *538*

Kaiping Coal Mines, 176–7
Kaixian Gong Village, 106
Kang Youwei 康有为, 38, 42
Kangxi, emperor of Qing 康熙皇帝, 51, 69, 71, 73, 391, 420
Kasahara, Hiroyuki, 667
Kaske, Elisabeth, 82, 470
Katō Shigeshi, 4
Keller, Wolfgang, 448
Keynesian economics, 6
Khrushchev, Nikita, 713–15
Kiakhta, Russia, 69
Kincheng (Jincheng) Banking Corporation, 311
Kirby, William, 695, 793
Kitamura Hironao, 67
Koito Seisakujo, 157
Köll, Elisabeth, 180
Kong Xiangxi 孔祥熙, 267
Korean War (1950–1953), 694, 698
Kraus, Richard, 67, 68
Kueh, Yak Yeow, 660–1
Kuhn, Philip A., 49
Kung, James Kai-sing, 393, 503, 650, 659, 665, 669–70, 676, 681–2
Kuran, Timur, 31
Kuznets, Simon, 20, 390

labor allocation, 573–4
laissez-faire principle, 170
land acreage, 97–8
land distribution, 119–20, 566, 602
land institutions, 115–19, **118**
land tax, 246, 248, 261, 267–70, 273
Lardy, Nicholas, 796
Late Qing Reform (New Policies, 1903–1911), 112, 130, 244, 256
latent capacity, 800
latent potential
  in agriculture, 798–9
  in industry, 800–1
  in international and domestic exchange, 797–8
League of Nations, 448
Lee, James, 60–1, 65
Legalism, 170
Lenin, 541, 543, 544, 546
Leninist party, 540, 541, 558
Levine, Ross, 232
Lewis, W. Arthur, 355
Li Bingjing, 667
Li Bozhong 李伯重, 59–60, 68
Li Chihua, 679
Li, Dan, 228

Li Dazhao 李大钊, 544
Li Fusun, 230, 232
Li Hongzhang 李鸿章, 35, 38, 141, 171, 174–5, 180, 307, 343, 466
Li, Lillian, 51
Li lineage, 333
Li Peng 李鹏, 757, 762
Li Quanshi 李权时, 268
Li Siyou lineage trust, 332
Li Xiannian 李先念, 738, 741, 748, 799
Li Yingzhou, 338
Li Yuanhong 黎元洪, 351
Liang, Ernest, 473
Liang Fangzhong 梁方仲, 5
Liang Qichao 梁启超, 33–4, 38, 41–2, 43, 350, 789
Liang-Huai salt district, 81, 84
Liao dynasty, 51
Liao Zhongkai 廖仲恺, 545
Liaoning province, 65, 614, 635
life expectancy. *See* mortality rates
lijin duties, 248–51, *251*, 252, 258–60, 264, 265, 267, 270, 478
Lin, Justin Yifu, 658, 665, 676
Lin Man-houng, 77
Lin Zexu 林则徐, 427
lineage trusts, 328–32, 349
Lingnan region, 50
Linxiang, Hunan, 69
literacy rates, 505
Liu family, 333
Liu Hongsheng 刘鸿生, 149, 351
Liu Mingchuan 刘铭传, 180
Liu Qingfeng 刘少奇, 29
Liu Shaoqi, 545, 586, 587, 664
Liu Ta-Chung, 608, 615
Liu Yan 刘晏, 168
Liu Yuan, 676
living standards (Maoist era), 606–7
  agricultural output, 633–4, **634**
  food consumption trends, 615–24, **617**, **621**, **623**, 632
  income inequality, 627–31, *628*, **630**, 634–9, *637*
  income trends, 608–14, **611**, **612**, **614**
  mortality record, 624–6, **625**
  per capita GDP trends, 607–8, 723–5
  rural poverty, 631–4
living standards (Qing era), 62–6
loans, 237. *See also* rural credit
  Maoist era, 690, 694
  Nanjing Decade, 272
  Qing era, 259, 261, 296

warlord era (1912–1927), 261–3, 266, 472
wartime, 275
Lü Xuehai, 138
Lumey, L.H., 679
Lushan Conference (1959), 668, 676
luxury goods, 57, 73, 426

Ma, Debin 马德斌, 64, 137
Ma Jianzhong 马建忠, 173
Ma Jinhua, 266
Ma Junya, 144
Macartney, George, 1st Earl Macartney, 15, 423–4
Macau, 422, 737
machinery, adoption of, 385–8, **388**
Mackay Treaty (1902), 260, 264
macroeconomics. *See* money markets
Maddison, Angus, 607
Made in China 2025, 719, 780, 816, 820
Mah, Feng-hwa, 694
maize, 108
Makino Fumio, 125
Malthus, Thomas, 58, 60
Malthusian framework, 100–3, *101*
management styles, 148–52
Manchuria, 23, 127, 156–7, 160, 471, 479–80, 488, 615, 704–5, 791
Manifesto of the First Nationalist Party Congress, 185
Mann Jones, Susan, 49
Mao Zedong 毛泽东, 27, 45, 545, 550
  agricultural decisions, 566, 577, 728
  Communist institutional origins, 551–5
  death of, 595
  Great Famine (1958–1961), 668
  Great Leap Forward, 643–5, 713–14
  Soviet relations, 688–92
  transition to the Great Leap Forward, 580–4
Maritime Customs Service (MCS), 33, 40, 252–4, *253*, 271, 273
  government bonds, 227, 229, 231, 263, 264
  postal system, 459–60
  tax collection, 36, 71–3, 248, 258–9
  trade records, 20, 128, 415, 429–33, *431*, 442–4, 451–2, 454
maritime trade, 71–3, 85
market
  forces, 569, 572–3, 578, 580, 747, 767, 783, 807–15, 825
  integration, 232–40, *236*, *237*
  opening, 810–12, 825
  outcomes, 812–15

Index

market's role in allocating resources, 781, 801, 812
Marks, Robert, 50
marriage, 66
Marxism, 3, 6–7, 27, 45, 544
Marxism–Leninism, 541, 544, 552
match production, 147
Mawei Shipbuilding Yard, 128
May Fourth Movement (1919), 266
Mayers, William, 788
Meiji era, Japan, 16, 17, 31, 38–9, 42, 130, 167, 405, 493
Meng family, 327, 348
Meng Zhang, 57, 337
Meng Xin, 665, 678
Mentougou coal mines, 336
merchants
 as business managers, 344–5
 business organization, 334, 337–8, 340, 342–3
 currency use, 214
 industrial entrepreneurship, 148–9
 pre-1839 trade, 420, 422
 state–enterprises relationship, 168, 170, 173–81, 784
 steamship companies, 465
metalworks, 178, 582, 656
Mexico, 215
migration, 108, 573, 589, 821
Mikoyan, Anastas, 688, 690
military institutions, 248
Minami Ryoshin, 125
Ming dynasty, 7, 69, 208, 244, 419, 421
Minimum List of Commodities (MLC), 448
mining industry, 23, 311, 336–7, 635, 770
Minong, Taiwan, 333
minting bureaus, 211
missionaries, 359, 390–4, *391*, *392*, **393**, 402, 514
Miyazaki Ichisada, 4
modern industries, 124–7, *126*
 company founders and management, 148–52
 education's role, 519–21, **520**
 export-oriented production, 132–40, *135*, *139*
 financial capital, 307–12, **308**, **310**
 import substitution, 140–8, **141**, **143**
 industrialization from abroad, 127–8, *129*
 Maoist era, 568–80, **571**, 584, 800–1
 postwar reorganization, 160–4, *161*, *165*
 role of treaty ports, 357–8
 technology transfer, 128–32, 146
 wartime, 152–60, *154*, *155*, *165*
Mokyr, Joel, 31, 390

money market, 208–11
 centrally planned command system, 577–8
 government–private sector relationship, 224–32
 integration of, 232–40, *236*, *237*, **239**
 major currencies overview, 211–16
 role of financial institutions, 216–20, *217*, *218*, *221*
 role of the state, 220–4, 294–8
moonshot innovations, 820
Morck, Randal, 338
Mori Tokihiko, 143
mortality rates, 63, 624–6, **625**
 Great Famine (1958–1961), 647–50, *651*
Motono, Eiichi, 36–7
motor vehicles, 486
Mukden Incident (1931), 471
munitions industry, 154, 379, 382, **383**
Murphey, Rhodes, 25
Muslim Rebellion (1862–1873), 98
Myers, Ramon, 9, 82

Naitō Konan, 2, 4
Nakai Hideki, 142
Nakamura Jihei, 67
Nan Hanchen, 701
Nanhai, Guangdong, 134, 341
Nanjing University, 112, 120
Nanjing, Jiangsu, 43, 66, 114, 371
Nanyang Brothers Tobacco Company, 113, 131, 149, 349
Nanyang Gongxue, 130
Nathan, Andrew, 789
National Agricultural Research Bureau (NARB), 615
National Capitalism and the Old Chinese Government, 373
National Commercial Bank, 312
National Defense Planning Commission, 203
National Federation of Education, 521
National Resources Commission, 153, 154, 189–91, 203, 205
native banks (cash shops), 214, 235, 281, **282**, **283**, 284–6, **285**, 291, *291*, 295, 297, 298
 commerce and industry finance, 307–12, **308**, **310**
 rural finance, 299, 300
 social status of, 317
Native Customs, 248, 253, 259, 273
native financial institutions, 213, 216, *217*. *See also* native banks (cash shops)
native-place affiliations, 340–1
natural disasters, 98–9, *99*, 576, 595, 660–4, **663**

838

Index

navigation transport, 174–6
Needham, Joseph, 390
network interests, 778–9, 802, 824
networks, of bankers, 317–19, **318**
New Culture Movement, 525
New Democracy, 691
New World crops, 53, 93, 108–9
newspapers, 344, 346
Ni Yuping, 85
Niida Noboru, 6
Ningbo, Zhejiang, 294, 317, 364, 446, 522
Ningjin, Hebei, 75
Nippon Railway, 493
Nippon Steel, 731
Nishijima Sadao, 7
North China Development Company, 157
Northern Expedition (1927), 788
Northwestern Industrial Corporation (NIC), 196–8

oil production, 596, 728
on-the-job training (OJT), 131
one-child policy, 727
openness, 17, 455, 691, 739, 779–81, 788, 789, 813
opium, 73, 75–7, 111, 249, 250, 259, 423, 426–7
Opium War (1839–1842), 15, 31, 35, 48, 73, 124, 213, 247, 342, 360, 391, 414, 427
Opium War (1856–1860), 254, 361, 428
Oriental culture, 2, 3
overseas study, 400–11, 402, **403**, 408, 524–5

Panzhihua, Sichuan, 636, 638
paper money, 210, 215–16, 219, 226–7
    role of the state, 220–4
Paris Peace Conference (1919), 265
partnerships, 150, 151. *See also* family firms
    private ordering, 332–42
Party Work Conference (1978), 732–4
passive investors, 340
patronage, 36, 59, 458, 778
pawnshops, 280, 281, **282**, **283**, 284, **285**, 295
    rural finance, 299, 300, 306
    social status of, 316, 320
Pearl river delta, 737
Peking University, 525
Peng Dehuai 彭德怀, 584
Peng Nansheng 彭南生, 146
Peng Shihong, 197
Peng Xinwei 彭信威, 8
Peng Yuxin 彭雨新, 69
Peng Zeyi 彭泽益, 66–7, 76
pengmin (shed people), 53

People's Bank of China. *See* Central Bank (PBoC)
People's Commune, 553–4, 583, 645, 657–9, 675–7, 724
Perkins, Dwight, 9, 59, 68, 90, 96, 232, 505, 795
personal networks, 778–9
petroleum industry, 191
Piazza, Alan, 607, 616
Ping County coal mine, 307
planned (command) economy, 45, 567–80, 749
    productivity stagnation, 796–7
Platt, Stephen, 780
Plekhanov, Georgi, 543
Pomeranz, Kenneth, 16, 62–3, 70, 83
population changes
    diffusion of New World crops, 108
    Maoist era, 588–9, *590*, 726–7
    Qing era, 57–66, 98–9, *99*
    Reform Era, 801
porcelain, 66
postal system, 459–60
postwar industrial reorganization, 160–4, *161*
Potter, Sulamith, 617
Pottinger, Henry, 428
poverty, 631–4
price increases. *See* inflation
primary school enrollment, 794
primary sector. *See* agriculture
Prince Gong (Yixin), 171
prison reform, 791
private ordering, 332–42
private plots, 567, 574, 584, 587, 617–18, 619, 726, 797
privately owned firms, 155, 373, 493. *See also* foreign firms
privatization, 559, 562, 603, 750, 767, 809, 810–11
producer co-operatives, 566, 567, 574–6, 583, 657, 724
productivity growth, 233, 598–9, 801–2, 806, 813, 815, 822–3, 825
    fall in, 658, 785, 795, 796–7, 823, 827
property rights, 83, 115, 117, 535, 554, 559–60
provincial finances, 245, 251–5
    Qing centralization, 255–61, **256**, **257**
public finance, 244–6
    Nanjing Decade, 267–72, **269**
    Qing centralization, 255–61, **256**, **257**
    Qing fiscal governance, 77–82, **80**, 246–55, *251*, *253*
    warlord era (1912–1927), 261–6, **262**
    wartime, 272–7, **276**
public-health campaigns, 626

Puqi, Hubei, 69
purchase shares, 300
Putterman, Louis, 659

Qi Xin Cement Co., 181
Qian Changzhao, 187, 189, 191
Qian, Nancy, 665, 678
Qianlong, emperor of Qing 乾隆皇帝, 15, 48–9, 77, 79, 82, 421, 423–4. *See also* Gaozong, emperor of Qing
Qianmen, Beijing, 327
Qimen, Anhui, 333
Qin Shihuang 秦始皇, emperor of Qin, 45, 55
Qing political regime, overview, 28–31, 48–50
Qingdao–Ji'nan railroad, 474
Qiyang, Hunan, 67
qiying baotai formula, 48
Qu Fulu, 338
Quan Hansheng 全汉升, 4, 5, 178

railroad army corps, 489
Railroad Bureau, 472–3
railroad development, 180, 260, 466–71, 468
 freight transportation, 473–80
 interruptions to, 471–3
 passenger transportation, 480–4, 481
 postwar expansion, 488–92
Rawski, Thomas, 20, 22, 164, 233, 465, 473, 475, 499, 505, 795
Readjustment Program (1979–1981), 733, 735–6, 745
Red Flag, 553
Red Guards, 592
Reform Era, 722–3, 801–2
 baseline, 723–9, **724**
 beginning of economic reform, 729–36
 breakthroughs of the 1990s, 758–68, **764**, 768, 807–15
 creativity of the 1980s, 748–58, 756, 802–7
 culmination and post-transition, 768–71
 opening up foreign exchange, 736–40
 post-Global Financial Crisis (2008), 815–23
 renewed reform and dynamics, 744–8
 rural reform, 740–4
regional competitions, 559–61
regional currencies, 209, 213
regional merchant groupings, 340
regionally decentralized authoritarianism (RDA), 532, 556–63
regionally decentralized totalitarianism (RDT), 532–3, 551–6
Reinhardt, Anne, 465, 492
Remer, C.F., 439

remittance houses, 281, **282**, **283**, 283–6, **285**, 287, 288, 295–6, 297
Reorganization Loan (1913), 261, 264, 266
Report on Conditions of Chinese Industry, 203–4
responsibility system, 586, 660, 744, 745
Restoration Society, 406
revenue figures, **262**, 760
 Nanjing Decade, **269**
 Qing era, 78–82, **80**, **256**, **257**
 wartime, **276**
Revive China Society, 406
revolutionists, 406–11, 407, **408**
rice prices, 63, 67
rice trade, 52, 67–9, 72
Rishengchang, 338
road development, 484–7
Roll, Charles, 796
Rong family, 149, 311, 321, 349
rotating credit societies, 280, 281, **282**, **283**, 285
Rubin, Jared, 31
Ruifuxiang, 327, 348
rural construction, 583, 586
rural co-operative treasuries, 287, 292, 293, 299–300, **301**, **302**, **303**, 306
rural credit, 119–20, **121**, 298–307, **301**, **302**, **303**, **305**, **306**
rural reforms, 740–4, 746, 771
Russell & Co., 134
Russia, 69, 439, 471. *See also* Soviet Union (USSR)
 origins of totalitarianism, 541–3
 totalitarian influence on China, 544–6

S.C. Farnham and Co., 128
salt industry, 80–1, 337
 family firms, 328, 329–30, 331–2
 Sichuan province, 66, 83–4
 taxation, 247, 249, 250, 260, 262–3, 264, 271, 273
Sands, Barbara, 119
Santiaoshi district, Tianjin, 130
seagoing junk business, 170
seasonal labor, 104–5, *105*
Second National Finance Conference (1934), 270
self-initiated ports (SIPs), 357, 358, 362, 363–5, *365*, **366**, 371
 long-term effects of, 388, **389**
 modernization, 376–8, **388**, 388
 overseas study, **403**
 universities, 394–9, *396*, **397**, 400
self-reliance, 707, 711, 718, 781, 797
Self-Strengthening Movement, 35, 38, 167

Index

arsenal industry, 171–3
  business organization, 345
  modern industries, 343–4, 357, 379
  officials and business enterprise, 173–81
  origins of, 577–8
semi-industrial firms, 151–2, 163, 164
sericulture, 114–15, *116*, 135, 136
sex ratios, 65
Shaanxi province, 52, 75
Shandong province, 468, 485
Shang Yue 尚鉞, 7
Shanghai
  banks, 40, 217–19, *218*, 223, 227, 229, *237*, 272, 292–4, 296, 311
  cotton industry, 23, 142, 143, 145, 159
  education system, 518
  infrastructure, 461, 466, 483, 487
  Reform Era, 739–40, 760
  silk industry, 133–4, 136
  trade, 70, 436–8, *438*, 442–4, *443*, 446, 731
  treaty ports system, 371, 786
  Western impact and investment, 27, 32, 363, 441
Shanghai Commercial and Savings Bank, 217, 311, 320
Shanghai–Hangzhou railroad, 484
Shanghai Merchant Steamship Company, 150
Shanghai–Nanjing railroad, 475, 481
Shanghai Native Bankers' Association, 40
Shanghai Stock Exchange, 313, 315, 817
Shanghai xinbao, 346
Shangyu, Zhejiang, 326
Shanxi province, 196–8, 284, 288, 339, 521
Shaoxing, Zhejiang, 317
sharecropping, 116
shareholder partnerships, 332–42
shares market, 346–7
shed people (*pengmin*), 53
Shekou, Guangdong, 739
Shen Baozhen 沈葆楨, 172
Shen Xin company, 149, 150
Shenbao, 346, 347
Sheng Xuanhuai 盛宣怀, 130, 174, 177, 179–80, 296, 461
Shenyang, Liaoning, 234
Shenyi tang, 331
Shenzhen, Guangdong, 737, 738, 747, 762, 786
Shi Zhihong 史志宏, 90, 93, 97
Shiba Yoshinobu, 9
shipbuilding, 127–8, 493, 817
Shiue, Carol H., 448
Shunde, Guangdong, 135
Siam, 72

Sichuan province, 470, 803
  ecological changes, 52
  financial institutions, 288, 300
  Great Famine (1958–1961), 650
  living standards, 631, 636
  modern industries, 153, 593
  salt industry, 66, 250
  silk industry, 135, 158
silk industry, 111, 131–2
  business organization, 339
  export-oriented, 133–8, *135*, 139
  freight transportation, 475
  sericultural improvements, 114–15, *116*
  wartime production, 158–9
Silk Road trade, 417
silver, 208–10, 213–15
  Daoguang depression, **74**, 74–7
  money market integration, 232–5, 238
  role of banks, 219–20
  role of the state, 220
Sinking Fund Commission, 44, 229–32
Sino-American Trade Commercial Treaty (1946), 162
Sino-Foreign Salt Inspectorate, 262, 271, 273
Sino-Japanese War (1894–1895), 31, 33, 37, 38, 130, 179, 244, 255, 259, 401, 463, 467, 703
Sino-Japanese War (1937–1945), 185, 189, 197, 198, 205
  modern industries, 152, *154*, *155*
  public finance, 272–7, **276**
Skinner, G. William, 9, 71
small-scale firms, 151–2, 164, 571, 767
Smithian growth, 102
smuggling, 80, 430, 478
soap production, 147–8
Social History Debate, 3
Soda Saburo, 135
SOEs. *See* state-owned enterprises (SOEs)
Sogabe Shizuo, 4
soil fertility, 53
Sommer, Matthew, 66
Song dynasty, 215, 328, 342
Song family, 43
Song Ziwen 宋子文, 44, 267, 271, 272
Songjiang–Taicang region, 145
South China Sea, 418, 420
South Manchurian Railway, 156, 287, 471, 479–80
Southeast Asian trade, 72
Southern Huai salt industry, 250
Southern Tour (1992), 758, 808
Soviet Growth Model (1949–1978)
  centrally planned command economy, 567–9

Soviet Growth Model (1949–1978) (cont.)
  command system in 1956–1957 period, 569–80, **571**
  early years, 565–7
  economic recovery 1961–1964, 585–91, *590*, **591**
  evaluation of economic perfomance, **597**, 597–605, **598**, **600**, **601**, **604**
  organization and policies 1965–1978, 591–7
  transition to the Great Leap Forward, 580–5, **585**
Soviet Union (USSR), 187, 479, 593, 688–97, 713–15
  Cold War geopolitical and economic blocs, 697–702
  loans and aid, 275, 712
  railway development, 488
  technical expertise, 490
  trade, *695*
Spanish pesos, 209, 214
special economic zones (SEZs), 738–9, 745, 747, 759, 804
Spence, Jonathan, 390
sprouts of capitalism, 7, 27
Stalin, 545, 549, 691–2
Standard International Trade Classification (SITC), 448
state capitalism, 153, 815–23
state incapacity, 759, 776
State Planning Commission, 577–8, 582, 713
State Statistical Bureau (SSB), 608, 609, 618, 619, 634
state trading companies, 578
state weakness, 776, 779, 825
state's non-economic objectives, 802
state–enterprises relationship, 167, 344. *See also* planned (command) economy
  arsenal industry, 171–3
  developing central state enterprises, 188–91
  Guangdong enterprises, 192–6
  Guizhou enterprises, 198–202
  ideology of the developmental state, 184–8
  officials and business enterprise, 173–81, 784
  origin of self-strengthening, 577–8
  public versus private enterprise, 202–6
  Reform Era, 809, 818
  Shanxi enterprises, 196–8
state-led development, 152, 813
State-owned Assets Supervisory Commission (SASAC), 562, 784
state-owned enterprises (SOEs), 66, 127, 152, 184–6, 189, 555–6, 740, 747, 753, 767, 784, 809, 826

state-sector downsizing, 809, 814
Stauffer, Milton, 391
steam engines, 385–8, *387*, **388**
steamships, 464–6
steel industry, 156, 582, 656
stock markets, 312–16, **314**, **315**, 762
Study of China's Ancient Society (1930), 3
Sudō Yoshiyuki, 6
sugar, 62, 114
Sugihara, Kaoru, 132
Suiping, Henan, 553
Sun Lanzhi, 76
Sun Pinghua, 704
Sun Yat-sen 孙逸仙, 185, 188, 261, 263, 266, 406, 493, 543
Sun Yefang 孙冶方, 586
Sun Yingde, 341
Sun–Joffe Manifesto, 544
Sunrise (Cao Yu), 317
surveillance, 777
Suzhou, Jiangsu, 466
Suzuki Chusei, 53
sweet potatoes, 108, 618
symbolic capital, 170
System Reform Institute, 753

Taiping Rebellion (1851–1864), 33, 35, 60, 63, 85, 98, 124, 127, 171, 224, 244, 343, 429, 466, 786
Taiwan, 339, 811
Taiyuan, Shanxi, 197
Takasaki Tatsunosuke, 704
Tanaka Issei, 63
Tanaka Masatoshi, 7
Tangshan earthquake (1976), 176, 595
Tang–Song transition, 2, 4, 6, 417
Tao Xisheng 陶希圣, 4
Tao Zhu, 56, 81
Tawney, R.H., 25
tax collectors, 250, 254
taxation. *See also lijin* duties
  Nanjing Decade, 267–72
  Qing era, 79–80, 244, 247, 248–51, *251*, 252–5, *253*, 258–60, 429–30
  Reform Era, 765, 808, 812
  remittance houses, 295–6
  silver payments, 213, 214
  trade, 36–7, 248–51, *251*, 429–30
  warlord era (1912–1927), 261, 262–6
  wartime, 272–7
tea, 62, 69–70, 72, 110, 426
teacher-training schools, **518**, 518, 522
technical education, 128, 130–1, 132, 173, 359
technological changes

842

economic effects from, 444–7, 445, **446**
pre-1950 period, 34–7
technology transfer, 128–32, 146, 730–2
telegraph communication, 460–4
Telford, Ted, 65
Temple Destruction Movement, 512
tenancy system, 116–17, **118**
Teng, Ssu-yu, 26, 419
textiles. *See* cotton industry; silk industry
TFP (total factor productivity), **598**, 795, 799, 807, 822
Thaxton, Ralph A., 619
Third Five-Year Plan (1966–1970), 591, 594, 596
Third Front, 593–4, 637, 800
Third National Finance Conference (1941), 273
Third Plenum (1978), 732, 735–6
Third Plenum (1993), 763–6, **764**
Three Doctrines of the People, 185, 186, 192, 511
Three Gorges, 98
Tiananmen Square Protests (1989), 562, 757
Tianjin, 130, 147, 217, 218, 294, 317, 444, 461, 467, 476
Tianjin Arsenal, 128
Tianjin Soap Company, 147
Tianjin Technology and Business University, 520
Tianjin–Pukou railroad, 467–70, 474, 478, 483
timber industry, 337
Ting Zhili, 515
tobacco, 112–13, 274, 477
Toffler, Alvin, 751
Tokugawa era, Japan, 31, 42, 72, 505
Tong Kingsing 唐景星, 174, 177
Tongcheng, Anhui, 65
Tongmenghui (Alliance Society), 526
Tongrentang, 327, 335
Tongzhi Restoration (1861–1875), 35
Tongzhi, emperor of Qing, 171
total factor productivity. *See* TFP (total factor productivity)
Township and Village Enterprises (TVEs), 746, 747, 753, 783, 804
Toyota company, 157
transfer of technology. *See* technology transfer
translated works, 38
transportation infrastructure, 457–8
  freight transportation, 473–80, **491**, 491–2
  interruptions to railroad development, 471–3
  motor roads and aviation, 484–8
  passenger transportation, 480–4, *481*

postwar rail expansion, 488–92, **491**
steamships and railroads, 464–71, *468*
Treaty of Nanking (1842), 21, 252, 360, 371, 379, 391, 427–8, 464
Treaty of Shimonoseki (1895), 37, 142, 259, 362, 364, 376, 441, 703
Treaty of Tientsin (1858), 391, 428, 464
treaty ports system, 15, 40, 44, 354, 356, 358–9
  early industrialization, 124, 128
  foreign investment and debt, 365–70, *367*, *368*, *369*, *370*, *371*, **439**, 439–42, **440**, 442
  geography of, *365*, *369*
  hinterland economic zones, 427–8
  human capital development, 390–9, *391*, *392*, **393**, *395*, *396*, **397**, 400
  long-term effects of, 388, **389**
  Maritime Customs records, 429–33, *431*
  market integration, 370–3, *372*
  modernization, 373–88, *374*, *375*, *377*, *378*, **379**, *380*, *382*, **383**, *385*, *387*, **388**
  origins of, 360–3, *361*, *362*
  overseas study, 402–4, **403**
  spillover benefits, 447–8
  taxation, 36, 252
  trade, 414, 427
Triads, 543
tributary system, 29, 246, 418–20
Tsinghua University, 524
Twitchett, Denis, 9

underutilized resources, 796
United States of America (USA)
  Cold War trade embargo, 697–702
  gross domestic product (GDP), **239**, 246
  infrastructure, 488
  loans, 275
  overseas study, 524
  trade, 136, 161–2, 435
  Vietnam War, 593
universities, 394–9, *395*, *396*, **397**, 400, 404, 524, 594

van de Ven, Hans, 252, 259
Vietnam, 593
Viraphol, Sarasin, 72
Vogel, Hans Ulrich, 75
Voitinsky, Grigori, 544
von Glahn, Richard, 61, 68, 74, 77, 82

wage levels
  Maoist era, 573–4, 590–1, **591**, 600, 602, 614, 636
  Qing era, 61, 64, 95, 96, *105*
Wan Li 万里, 733–4, 741, 743

843

Wancheng dike, Hubei, 54
Wang Fansen 王汎森, 17, 30
Wang Jiaxiang 王稼祥, 545
Wang lineage trust, 329–30
Wang Luman, 296
Wang Qisheng 王奇生, 524
Wang Renzhong 王任重, 741
Wang Yangming 王阳明, 43
Wang Yaosheng 王耀生, 502
Wang Yeh-chien 王业健, 63, 73, 75, 79, 82, 245
Wang, Yejian 王业健, 237
Wang Zhiyi, 54
Wangquantang, 327
Warnings to a Prosperous Age, 130
Washington Naval Conference (1921), 265
water control, 54–6
Weber, Max, 3, 393
Wei Xian, Shandong, 145
Wei Yuan 魏源, 56, 79, 170, 779
Wei Xiahai, 676
Weifang, Shandong, 152
well-field system, 169
Wen Jiabao 温家宝, 769
Wen lineage, 331
Wen Xiang 文祥, 171
Wen, Guanzhong James, 675, 676
Weng Wenhao 翁文灏, 186, 187, 188, 189, 191
Wen-hsin Yeh, 317
Western culture, 2, 41–3
Western impact, 354–60, 779–81
    business organization, 342–8
    firms and banks data, 21–2, 22
    foreign investment and debt, 365–70, *367*, *368*, *369*, *370*, *371*
    human capital development, 390–9, *391*, *392*, **393**, *395*, *396*, **397**, *400*
    impact–response framework, 26–8, 32–4, 40
    long-term effects of treaty ports, **388**, **389**
    overseas study and political change, 400–11, *402*, **403**, *408*
    self-initiated ports (SIPs), 363–5, *365*, **366**
    treaty ports and market integration, 370–3, *372*
    treaty ports and modernization, 373–88, *374*, *375*, *377*, *378*, **379**, *380*, *382*, **383**, *385*, *387*, **388**
    treaty ports system, 36–7, 360–3, *361*, *362*
Western scholarship, 8–11
White Lotus Rebellion (1796–1804), 54, 79, 246
Will, Pierre-Étienne, 52
Wittfogel, Karl, 3
working capital, 338–40
World Bank, 609, 624, 635, 751, 770, 781
World Trade Organization (WTO), 767, 776, 785, 811, 814
Wright, Mary, 35
Wright, Tim, 144
Wu Chengming 吴承明, 10, 69, 73, 109, 275
Wu Dingchang, 198–9, 200
Wu Hui 吴慧, 90, 92, 94
Wu Songdi, 233
Wu Xiaozhen, 65
Wuchang Uprising (1911), 406
Wuchang, Hubei, 63
Wuhan, Hubei, 614, 635
Wuxi, Jiangsu, 114, 115, 135, 137
Xi Jinping 习近平, 780, 785, 816, 819
Xi Zhongxun 习仲勋, 548, 670
Xianfeng, emperor of Qing 咸丰皇帝, 224
Xiang river, 52
Xiangyin county, Hunan, 54
Xianning, Hubei, 71
Xiaogangcun, Anhui, 741
Xiaoshan, Zhejiang, 63
Xicun, Guangdong, 192
Xie Nanming, 149
Xin Deyong, 98
Xinhai Revolution (1911), 359, 400, 401, 406
Xinjiang region, 49, 77, 289
Xiuning, Anhui, 333
Xu Dixin 许涤新, 109
Xu Rongting, 351
Xu Run, 307
Xu Xinwu 徐新吾, 145
Xue Muqiao 薛暮桥, 751

Yan Xishan 阎锡山, 196–7, 288
Yan Yutang, 149
Yan Hongzhong, 236
Yan'an Rectification Campaign (1942), 545, 550
Yan'an, Shaanxi, 565
Yang, Dennis Tao, 796
Yang Fan, 338
Yang Jisheng 杨继绳, 648
Yang Lien-sheng, 8
Yang Nianqun 杨念群, 34
Yang Xifu, 52
Yanglinzhai, Hunan, 54
Yangzhou, Jiangsu, 81, 84
Yangzi river, 52, 362, 464–5, 467
Yao Yilin 姚依林, 757
Yared, Pierre, 665
Yeh, Kung-chia, 608, 615
Yellow River, 55, 246, 247
Yinghe (Qing official), 56

Yong An company, 150
Yongtai Company, 114, 137
Yongzheng, emperor of Qing 雍正皇帝, 51, 82
Yongzhou, Hunan, 67
Yoon, Wook, 462
Yu Jieqiong, 74
Yu Zhiqing, 149
Yuan Geng 袁庚, 738
Yuan Shikai 袁世凯, 130, 173, 181, 226, 261–4, 266
Yuchtman, Noam, 520
Yue Fengyi, 327
Yue Xianyang, 327
Yuezhou, Hunan, 364
Yugan, Jiangxi, 521
Yunnan province, 153, 629

Zeng Guofan 曾国藩, 35, 38, 43, 171
Zhang Fangzuo, 131
Zhang Jian 张謇, 132, 149, 178–9, 185, 342, 467
Zhang Naiqi, 316
Zhang Zhidong 张之洞, 113, 173, 178–9, 351, 364, 401, 780
Zhangjiakou, Hebei, 69
Zhangqiu, Shandong, 55
Zhao Erxun, 114
Zhao Ziyang 赵紫阳, 562, 741, 743, 748–9, 751–2, 755–7, 781
zhaoshang system, 168, 170
Zhejiang province, 60, 82, 115, 272, 317
Zheng empire, 419
Zheng Guanying 郑观应, 130, 141, 149, 173, 461
Zhili Gongyiju, 131, 148
Zhili province, 50, 130, 174, 468, 485, 502
Zhou Enlai 周恩来, 552, 595, 707, 709–12, 715, 728
Zhou Heng Shun factory, 130
Zhou Xuexi 周学熙, 149, 181, 185
Zhou Yumin, 252
Zhou Ziqi, 264
Zhou Hao, 796
Zhou Li-An, 678
Zhou, Titi, 650, 670
Zhu Jiaye, 521
Zhu Rongji 朱镕基, 762, 765–8, 776, 810
Zhu Xianfang, 131
Zigong, Sichuan, 329, 331, 337, 339
Zongli Yamen (Foreign Office), 254
Zuo Zongtang 左宗棠, 171, 172, 254

For EU product safety concerns, contact us at Calle de José Abascal, 56–1°, 28003 Madrid, Spain or eugpsr@cambridge.org.

www.ingramcontent.com/pod-product-compliance
Ingram Content Group UK Ltd.
Pitfield, Milton Keynes, MK11 3LW, UK
UKHW022239220326
469255UK00018B/258